THE WORKS OF JONATHAN EDWARDS

VOLUME 23

Harry S. Stout, General Editor

Plate from Frances Quarles, *Emblemes* (1635). Courtesy of Beinecke Rare Book and Manuscript Library, Yale University.

JONATHAN EDWARDS

The "Miscellanies"

(Entry Nos. 1153–1360)

EDITED BY
DOUGLAS A. SWEENEY

CHAIR, DEPARTMENT OF CHURCH HISTORY AND THE
HISTORY OF CHRISTIAN THOUGHT
TRINITY EVANGELICAL DIVINITY SCHOOL

New Haven and London

YALE UNIVERSITY PRESS, 2004

Funds for editing The Works of Jonathan Edwards
have been provided by The Pew Charitable Trusts, Lilly
Endowment, Inc., and The Henry Luce Foundation, Inc.

Set in New Baskerville type by The Composing Room of Michigan,
Inc., Grand Rapids, Michigan. Printed in the United States
of America by Vail-Ballou Press, Binghamton, New York.

Library of Congress Cataloging-in-Publication Data

Edwards, Jonathan, 1703–1758.
 The miscellanies : entry nos. 1153–1320 / edited by
Douglas A. Sweeney.
  p. cm. — (The works of Jonathan Edwards ; v. 23)
Includes bibliographical references and index.
 ISBN 0-300-10102-3 (alk. paper)
 1. Congregationalism. 2. Congregational churches—
United States—Doctrines. 3. Theology, Doctrinal.
I. Sweeney, Douglas A. II. Title.
 BX7117 .E3 1957 vol. 23
 [BX7232]
 285.8 s—dc22
 [230/.

                                    2003020330

A catalogue record for this book is available from the
British Library.

The paper in this book meets the guidelines for permanence
and durability of the Committee on Production Guideline's for
Book Longevity of the Council on Library Resources

10 9 8 7 6 5 4 3 2 1

PREVIOUSLY PUBLISHED

PAUL RAMSEY, ed., *Freedom of the Will*
JOHN E. SMITH, ed., *Religious Affections*
CLYDE A. HOLBROOK, ed., *Original Sin*
C. C. GOEN, ed., *The Great Awakening*
STEPHEN J. STEIN, ed., *Apocalyptic Writings*
WALLACE E. ANDERSON, ed., *Scientific and Philosophical Writings*
NORMAN PETTIT, ed., *The Life of David Brainerd*
PAUL RAMSEY, ed., *Ethical Writings*
JOHN F. WILSON, ed., *A History of the Work of Redemption*
WILSON H. KIMNACH, ed., *Sermons and Discourses, 1720–1723*
WALLACE E. ANDERSON AND MASON I. LOWANCE, eds.,
    Typological Writings
DAVID D. HALL, ed., *Ecclesiastical Writings*
THOMAS A. SCHAFER, ed., *The "Miscellanies," a–500*
KENNETH P. MINKEMA, ed., *Sermons and Discourses, 1723–1729*
STEPHEN J. STEIN, ed., *Notes on Scripture*
GEORGE S. CLAGHORN, ed., *Letters and Personal Writings*
MARK VALERI, ed., *Sermons and Discourses, 1730–1733*
AVA CHAMBERLAIN, ed., *The "Miscellanies," 501–832*
M. X. LESSER, ed., *Sermons and Discourses, 1734–1738*
AMY PLANTINGA PAUW, ed., *The "Miscellanies," 833–1152*
SANG HYUN LEE, ed., *Writings on the Trinity, Grace and Faith*
HARRY S. STOUT AND NATHAN O. HATCH, eds., *Sermons and*
    Discourses, 1739–1742

CONTENTS

EDITORIAL COMMITTEE   v
LIST OF ILLUSTRATIONS   viii
NOTE TO THE READER   ix
EDITOR'S INTRODUCTION   1

The "Miscellanies," Entry Nos. 1153–1360   37

GENERAL INDEX   717
INDEX OF BIBLICAL PASSAGES   745

ILLUSTRATIONS

Frontispiece   Plate from Frances Quarles, *Emblemes* (1635).

Page
96   "Miscellanies," Bk. 8, No. 1181.
241   "Miscellanies," Bk. 9, No. 1297.
462   "Miscellanies," Bk. 9, No. 1351.
641   "Miscellanies," Bk. 9, No. 1359.

NOTE TO THE READER

Preparation of the Text

The text of Jonathan Edwards is reproduced in this Edition as he wrote it in manuscript, or, if he published it himself, as it was printed in the first edition. In order to present this text to modern readers as practically readable, several technical adjustments have been made. Those which can be addressed categorically are as follows:

1. All spelling is regularized and conformed to that of *Webster's Third New International Dictionary,* a step that does not involve much more than removing the "u" from "colour" or "k" from "publick" since Edwards was a good speller, used relatively modern spelling, and generally avoided "y" contractions. His orthographic contractions and abbreviations, such as ampersands, "call'd," and "thems." are spelled out, though pronounced contractions, such as "han't" and "ben't," are retained.

2. There is no regular punctuation in most of Edwards' manuscripts and where it does exist, as in the earliest sermons, it tends to be highly erratic. Editors take into account Edwards' example in punctuation and related matters, but all punctuation is necessarily that of the editor, including paragraph divisions (especially in some notebooks such as the "Miscellanies") and the emphasizing devices of italics and capitalization. In reference to capitalization, it should be noted that pronouns referring to the deity are lower case except in passages where Edwards confusingly mixes "he's" referring to God and man: here capitalization of pronouns referring to the deity sorts out the references for the reader.

3. Numbered heads designate important structures of argument in Edwards' sermons, notebooks, and treatises. Numbering, including spelled-out numbers, has been regularized and corrected where necessary. Particularly in the manuscript sermon texts, numbering has been clarified by the use of systematic schemes of heads and subheads in accordance with eighteenth-century homiletical form, a practice similar to modern analytical outline form. Thus the series of subordinated head number forms, 1, (1), *1*, a, (a), in the textual exegesis, and the series, I,

First, 1, (1), *1*, a, (a), in Doctrine and Application divisions, make it possible to determine sermon head relationships at a glance.

4. Textual intervention to regularize Edwards' citation of Scripture includes the correction of erroneous citation, the regularizing of citation form (including the standardization of book abbreviations), and the completion of quotations which Edwards' textual markings indicate should be completed (as in preaching).

5. Omissions and lacunae in the manuscript text are filled by insertions in square brackets ([ ]); repeated phrases sometimes represented by Edwards with a long dash are inserted in curly brackets ({ }). In all cases of uncertain readings, annotation gives notice of the problem. Markings in the text designate whole word units even when only a few letters are at issue.

6. Minor slips of the pen or obvious typographical errors are corrected without annotation. Likewise, Edwards' corrections, deletions, and internal shifts of material are observed but not noted unless of substantive interest.

7. Quotations made by the editor from the Bible (KJV) and other secondary sources are printed *verbatim ac literatim.* Edwards' quotations from such sources are often rather free but are not corrected and are not annotated as such unless significant omissions or distortions are involved.

In this group of notebook entries, Edwards cited and quoted from various sources. Some of these excerpts are verbatim, in which case the wording and punctuation have been checked against the originals. Bracketed ellipses indicate significant omissions not marked by Edwards. Other excerpts he paraphrased. In either case, Edwards was not merely a passive copier; he re-organized materials, interjected his own comments, and added references to his own and others' works.

Within these entries, a wide array of authors and works, classical, early church, and otherwise, are mentioned and quoted. Edwards replicated virtually all of these quotations (and, consequently, their inaccuracies) from seventeenth- and eighteenth-century works upon which he relied. An effort has been made to fill out these references; to identify, where necessary, lesser known figures; to provide the more familiar titles of some works; to explain vague references or allusions, and to supply the source references given by the seventeenth- and eighteenth-century compilers when Edwards himself did not do so.

Another characteristic of these entries is that they include a number of instances of Latin, Greek, and Hebrew passages. Translations are pro-

vided in the footnotes, except where Edwards' own text gives the meaning of the word or passage. In the case of repeated phrases, only the first
occurrence is translated.

Acknowledgments

A volume of manuscripts like these could not have been published—
at least not well—without the help of many scholars on both sides of the
Atlantic Ocean. Though founded by Perry Miller, the Yale Edition rests
more squarely on the textual labors of Thomas Schafer, Wilson Kimnach
and Kenneth Minkema, all of whom have devoted their lives to editing
Edwards' massive corpus, and each of whom trained me in the art of de-
ciphering Edwards' cryptic hand. Ken Minkema, especially, served as my
mentor at the Edition, becoming a cherished friend and colleague in the
process. Kyle Farley, our assistant, made life at the office much more interesting than it would have been without his intellectual verve and love
of life. And Harry Stout, our General Editor, taught us all how to persevere with fortitude and a passion for the Edition's public significance.

At the Beinecke Library, Ellen Cordes and her circulation staff have
supported my work on Edwards for years. Paul Stuehrenberg and his staff
have helped at Yale's Divinity Library; Rob Krapohl and his staff have
helped at Trinity's Rolfing Library. Various other scholarly colleagues
have also contributed to this volume. I am most grateful to my successor
at the Edition, Peter Thuesen, for his help with Edwards' manuscripts after I moved away to Chicago; to David Trobisch for his help with early
modern Greek ligatures; to Robert Yarbrough for his help with Edwards'
work on the Septuagint; to Keith Beebe and Lee Bond for bibliographical help in Scotland; to Stephen Stein for answering editorial queries of
various kinds; and to David Kling for ready and able scholarly wisdom.
Several research assistants at Trinity also improved this volume markedly:
especially Brandon Withrow and Matthew Harmon, who logged many
hours on this project, but also Robert Caldwell, David Michelson, Jonathan Loopstra, Joe Thomas and John Mark Yeats. Latin passages were
translated by Robert Huitt of Yale University's Classics Department. Excerpts from the early nineteenth-century copy of the "Miscellanies" by
Sereno Dwight have been published courtesy of Andover-Newton Theological School, Newton Centre, Massachusetts.

Ken Minkema, Wilson Kimnach, Ava Chamberlain, and Robert Brown
pored over my "Editor's Introduction" and offered beneficial criticism.
Susan Laity has worked her usual magic at Yale University Press. And last

but not least, several administrators at Trinity Evangelical Divinity School have pitched in with generous institutional support, including Greg Way-bright, Tite Tiénou, Harold Netland, and Jim Moore.

Wilma and David Sweeney have fueled this project with a steady stream of divine love, increasing my "experimental knowledge" that true "charity suffereth long," indeed that "charity never faileth." So has the one to whom our family would like to dedicate this volume: the best teacher I have ever had, Jack Fitzmier, without whose aid I would not be writing these words today.

Funding for this volume and for the Edition as a whole has been provided by the Pew Charitable Trusts, Lilly Endowment, Inc., the Henry Luce Foundation, Inc., and Yale University.

EDITOR'S INTRODUCTION

WITH the publication of this volume readers have access for the first time to the most comprehensive printed edition of Edwards' "Miscellanies."[1] The most controversial and commonly cited of Edwards' sets of private notebooks, the "Miscellanies" represent his most sustained and serious efforts to rough out his theological reflections. Edwards began this nine-book series while still in his late teens (in 1722), adding to it throughout his last thirty-five prolific years. As one who thought "with his pen in his hand,"[2] he used these intellectual workbooks to extend and clarify his ideas about an exceptionally wide range of issues and themes.[3]

"Miscellanies," Nos. 1153–1360 constitutes the twenty-third volume of *The Works of Jonathan Edwards,* as well as the last of the four volumes in the Yale Edition of Edwards' "Miscellanies." The earlier "Miscellanies" are found in volumes 13, 18, and 20, edited respectively by Thomas A. Schafer, Ava Chamberlain, and Amy Plantinga Pauw. Each of these volumes owes its textual origins to the painstaking manuscript labors of

1. Yale's letterpress edition of JE's "Miscellanies" lacks only entry Nos. 891, 922, 1067 and 1068, all of which treat what JE termed either "Prophecies of the Messiah" or "Fulfillment of the Prophecies of the Messiah." No. 1069, "Types of the Messiah," is located in *The Works of Jonathan Edwards, 11, Typological Writings,* ed. Wallace E. Anderson and Mason I. Lowance (New Haven, Yale Univ. Press, 1993), 191–328. Unless otherwise indicated, all manuscripts referred to in this volume are located at The Beinecke Rare Book and Manuscript Library, Yale University. After the initial citation, individual volumes in the Yale Edition are referred to as *Works,* followed by the volume number.

2. This phrase comes from JE's student and first biographer, Samuel Hopkins, in his *Life of the Late Reverend, Learned and Pious Mr. Jonathan Edwards . . .* (Boston, 1765), 41. Hopkins' depiction is worth quoting at length: "Every thought on any subject, which appear'd to him worth pursuing and preserving, he pursued, as far as he then could, with his pen in his hand. Thus he was all his days, like the busy bee, collecting from every opening flower, and storing up a stock of knowledge, which was indeed sweet to him, as the honey & the honey-comb. And as he advanced in years and in knowledge, his pen was more and more employed, and his manuscripts grew much faster on his hands."

3. An excellent introduction to this notebook series may be found in Thomas A. Schafer's "Editor's Introduction" to *The Works of Jonathan Edwards, 13, The "Miscellanies," a–500* (New Haven, Yale Univ. Press, 1994), 1–160.

Schafer, a veritable patriarch of the tribe of scholars working most closely with Edwards' papers. But each also covers a different period of Edwards' thirty-five-year career. Despite the many continuities tying the "Miscellanies" together, then, the differences between the volumes reward attention.

Volume 13, *The "Miscellanies," a–500,* covers the period of Edwards' early intellectual development (1722–31). Its entries reflect the concerns of a sober young Congregational clergyman, as well as the reveries of a recent convert newly enthralled by life in the Spirit. Volume 18, Nos. 501–832, covers the period when Edwards came of age as a pastor-theologian (1731–40). It corresponds to the time of his greatest success as a local parish minister, a time when this success garnered for him an international reputation, especially through the publication overseas of his *Faithful Narrative* (1737). Volume 20, Nos. 833–1152, covers the tumultuous period of New England's Great Awakening, a period when Edwards' reputation for clerical wisdom spread even further but which ended with his dismissal from his world-famous pulpit in Northampton (1740–51).

The present volume, by contrast, covers the final years of Edwards' life (1751–58), the period of his work at the Stockbridge mission and short-lived presidency of Princeton (then referred to as the College of New Jersey). Indeed, the bulk of the material presented here dates from the end of his sojourn in Stockbridge,[4] a fact that sheds new light on our understanding of his regular routine at the Indian mission. In the pages that follow, I offer a summary of Edwards' life in this period, outlining the ways in which these "Miscellanies" fit into Edwards' vocational agenda.

A "Multitude of Affairs": Edwards' Life in the 1750s

Many attempts have been made to account for Edwards' time at the Stockbridge mission. But despite a spate of recent efforts to portray his work with the Indians more accurately, a myth persists that Stockbridge proved to be for him a sylvan retreat—a place removed from the usual grind of weekly ministry in Northampton where Edwards could finally concentrate on living the blissful life of the mind.[5] As we shall see, Ed-

---

4. A word count of the "Miscellanies" that follow reveals that JE drafted a full 71 percent of this material during or after 1756, penning less than 30 percent in the period 1750–55. Thanks go to research assistant Matthew S. Harmon for this (and all other such) quantitative information.

5. For a useful summary of the new, more accurate view of JE in Stockbridge, see *The Works*

wards did manage to produce a tremendous amount of writing there. But he did so in the midst of a remarkably busy schedule, one full of the same pastoral priorities that had always governed his life.

In fact, almost as soon as Edwards moved in, he entered into a dispiriting series of struggles for control of the mission's programs. This is not the place to rehearse the dreary details of those struggles;[6] but it should be said that they drained Edwards of the lion's share of his time and energy. Coming as they did while he was still smarting from blows in Northampton, moreover, they kept him yet again from a life of leisurely contemplation.

While Edwards had visited Stockbridge from January to March 1751 (six months after his dismissal from Northampton), he did not assume his pastoral duties until that summer. By then, a full two years had elapsed since the sudden death of the Rev. John Sergeant, Edwards' clerical predecessor, and local residents had grown uncertain about their future. The town's twelve or so English families—led by Edwards' own relatives, the Williams clan—had tried to settle two younger, more malleable men in their pulpit before turning to Edwards. They had also continued their lucrative practice of dirty dealing with the Indians, exploiting the mission for personal gain and staffing its teaching posts with incompetents.[7] The Stockbridge Indians, for their part, had begun to grow weary of this ill treatment and suspicious of the intentions of their English partners in faith and commerce. Scores remained at the Stockbridge mission, attending the church and English schools.[8] But enthusiasm was clearly dwindling for this mixed bag of God and Mammon.

To make a long and depressing story short, Edwards devoted the first two-and-a-half years of his ministry in Stockbridge to curtailing corruption at the mission, training the locals in "true religion," and gaining control of the mission schools. These efforts culminated in February 1754 when the mission's leading patron, the English philanthropist (and Bap-

---

of Jonathan Edwards, 16, Letters and Personal Writings, ed. George S. Claghorn (New Haven, Yale Univ. Press, 1998), 17–25. See also Rachel M. Wheeler, "Living Upon Hope: Mahicans and Missionaries, 1730–1760" (Ph.D. diss., Yale Univ., 1998); and George M. Marsden's *Jonathan Edwards: A Life* (New Haven, Yale Univ. Press, 2003), 375–431.

6. On these, see *Works, 16*, 17–25.

7. See Lion G. Miles, "The Red Man Dispossessed: The Williams Family and the Alienation of Indian Land in Stockbridge, Massachusetts, 1736–1818," *New England Quarterly* LXVII (March 1994), 45-76; Patrick Frazier, *The Mohicans of Stockbridge* (Lincoln, Univ. of Nebraska Press, 1992).

8. At the time of Sergeant's death in 1749, 218 Indians (mainly Mahicans) lived in Stockbridge—42 of them were full members of the local church, 55 of them were enrolled in the local school (taught by Timothy Woodbridge), and 12 of them took part in a special boarding program.

tist minister) Isaac Hollis, awarded Edwards exclusive control of the Stockbridge schools. But coming as it did nearly five years after Sergeant's death, Hollis' decision arrived too late to secure the vitality of the mission. Morale was low, and for good reason. The previous year a mysterious fire had razed the schoolhouse used by the boys, and a strategic group of Mohawks had left the mission once and for all. Thus Edwards and Hollis had finally achieved a lasting peace for the Stockbridge ministry. But it was a peace that came at a price. The mission had clearly deteriorated, and so had Edwards' health.

Indeed, part of the price that Edwards paid for this resolution to conflicts in Stockbridge was an ebb in his writing schedule and a marked decline in his health. To be sure, in the early 1750s he published two substantial treatises, *Misrepresentations Corrected* (1752) and *Freedom of the Will* (1754), and by most standards this represents a major achievement. But he wrote the first of these—little more than an extension of arguments made in his *Humble Inquiry* of 1749—before his Stockbridge troubles began to intensify. And he had been working on the second since the middle of the 1740s. Compared to the literary pace he had established in the 1740s, then, the early 1750s were lean years for Edwards' scholarship.

The "Miscellanies" bear this out. As can be seen in the table of "Selected Dates for the Composition of 'Miscellanies,' Nos. 1153–1360," Edwards drafted an unusually small amount of this material in the early 1750s.[9] Understandably, he found little time to work in these notebooks in 1750. During the first half of that fateful year, he was still in the throes of controversy in Northampton; during the second, he probably finished his unpublished "Narrative of the Communion Controversy."[1] The following year he drafted entries on the will and related topics. And by August 1752 he had started his final draft of *Freedom of the Will.* But by then he had begun complaining of "the multitude of affairs which have continually pressed my mind." Moreover, as he explained to the Rev. John Erskine in November, his work on *Freedom of the Will* "was soon broke off; and such have been my extraordinary avocations and hindrances, that I have not had time to set pen to paper about this matter since." The Stockbridge struggle had come to a head. He had been traveling in September. And there was precious little time for serious writing.[2]

9. For more on dating, see below, "Note on the Text," pp. 33–36.

1. See *The Works of Jonathan Edwards, 12, Ecclesiastical Writings,* ed. David D. Hall (New Haven, Yale Univ. Press, 1994), 507–619.

2. See *Works, 16,* 477, 539–41. In September of 1752 JE traveled to New York City and northern New Jersey, where he met with the correspondents of the Society for Propagating Christian

**Selected Dates for the Composition
of "Miscellanies," Nos. 1153–1360**

Entry	Date
1180	no earlier than March 1751
1181	no earlier than April 1751
1184	no earlier than the second half of 1752
1200	no earlier than August 1752
1227	no earlier than 1753
1277b	no earlier than March 1754
1281	no earlier than 1756
1358	no earlier than 1757

Not until 1753 did Edwards resume his former level of prolific literary production. During the first half of that year, he finished *Freedom of the Will*. As he exulted to Erskine in April, "[A]fter many hindrances, delays, and interruptions, divine providence has so far favored me . . . that I have almost finished the first draft."[3] He also worked at length in his manuscript notebook entitled "Controversies," first on "Efficacious Grace" (a theme that Edwards had written about for years in a series of notebooks on "Moral Agency," whose title he changed to "Efficacious Grace" after using their contents in *Freedom of the Will*), and then on "The Nature of True Virtue" (an interest fueled, perhaps, by his feud with the morally challenged Williams clan).[4] Meanwhile, he picked up his pace a bit in the "Miscellanies" as well.

But no sooner had Edwards returned to his earlier scholarly routine than he succumbed to "the longest and most tedious sickness that ever I had in my life." On April 15, 1755, he related the following in a letter to Erskine:

> I [have been] followed with fits of the ague, which came upon me about the middle of last July, and were for a long time very severe and exceedingly wasted my flesh and strength, so that I became like a

---

Knowledge, preached to the Presbyterian Synod of New York, met with trustees of the College of New Jersey, and stayed in Newark with daughter Esther and her new husband, Aaron Burr. His sermon to the Presbyterians was published as *True Grace, Distinguished from the Experience of Devils: in a sermon, preached before the Synod of New-York, convened at New-Ark, in New Jersey, on September 28, n.s. 1752* (New York, 1753). JE's friend John Erskine was the leading evangelical in the Church of Scotland.

3. *Works, 16*, 594.

4. On these manuscripts and their history, see *The Works of Jonathan Edwards, 21, Writings on the Trinity, Grace and Faith*, ed. Sang Hyun Lee (New Haven, Yale Univ. Press, 2002), 198–327.

skeleton. I had several intermissions of the fits by the use of the Pe-
ruvian bark; but they never wholly left me till about the middle of last
January. In the meantime, I several times attempted to write letters
to some of my friends about affairs of importance; but found that I
could bear but little of such writing. Once, in attempting to write a
letter to Mr. [Aaron] Burr, a fit of the ague came upon me while I was
writing; so that I was obliged to lay by my pen. When my fits left me,
they left me in a poor, weak state, all over bloated; so that I feared
whether I was not going into a dropsy. I am still something swelled,
and much overrun with scorbutic maladies. Nevertheless, I have of
late gradually gained strength.[5]

Despite his lingering "scorbutic maladies" (symptoms caused by scurvy),
Edwards was on the mend by spring, and able once again to do some
writing. His trials continued, however, when just as he was recovering
from this illness another disaster struck that nearly took his life. In April
1755, on a trip to Windsor to visit his family, Edwards received a "great
hurt" by what he described as "a dangerous fall from my horse, the horse
pitching heels over head with his whole weight upon me."[6] Clearly, his
patience was being tested. He was a wreck, physically speaking, and increasingly frustrated by all the time that was wasting away.

To make matters worse, the citizens of Stockbridge faced a military
threat from the awkward alliance of Frenchmen and Indians conspiring
against them just beyond the New England frontier. The town had suffered attack the previous year when a band of Schagticokes descended
from Canada, killing four residents and inciting "a great alarm."[7]
Though Stockbridge would not be harmed again, its people would live
in chronic fear, Edwards himself remaining distracted by the threat of
further invasion. His own home served as a garrison throughout the remainder of the French and Indian War. "What will become of us, God
only knows," Edwards told his colleague Gideon Hawley. His fears abated
slightly when English troops were stationed nearby. But Edwards continued to worry, viewing the risk of further violence as a trial sent from
above. As he had written a few years earlier while still exasperated with
the Williamses, so he would repeat throughout the rest of his time at the
mission: "I think God by these things calls me to expect no other than

5. *Works, 16,* 662–63. On this illness, see also JE's letter to Thomas Foxcroft, December 20,
1754, in *ibid., 16,* 654–55.
6. *Works, 16,* 668.
7. The attack took place on September 1, 1754, while JE was ill.

to meet with difficulties and trials while in this world. And what am I better than my fathers, that I should expect to fare better in the world than the generality of Christ's followers in all past generations?"[8]

But despite his numerous tribulations, and with marked determination, Edwards produced a prodigious amount of scholarship during the final years of his life. In the spring of 1755, he got back up on his literary horse and rode so hard that during the remainder of his tenure at the mission (a period of two-and-a-half years) he generated well over a thousand pages of scholarly prose. In addition to most of the material printed below, he extended his "Controversies" notebook, completed his manuscript book on "Faith," and finished three published treatises as well—*Original Sin* (1758) and the posthumously printed *Two Dissertations* (*The End for Which God Created the World* and *The Nature of True Virtue*, published together in 1765). Edwards also laid plans at this time for his unpublished "Harmony of the Old and New Testament."[9] And he designed his unfinished magnum opus on the "History of the Work of Redemption."[1] In fact, many of his later "Miscellanies" functioned as drafts of parts of these works.[2]

It is no wonder, then, that when Richard Stockton wrote to Edwards in September 1757, reporting on Edwards' recent election by the Princeton trustees to their vacant presidency, Edwards demurred on grounds of poor health, protesting further that "my engaging in this business, will not well consist, with those views, and that course of employ in my study, which have long engaged, and swallowed up my mind, and been the chief entertainment and delight of my life." This was not, as is often suggested, simply a customary display of false modesty in the face of great honor. Edwards' health, which had never been good, had suffered terribly in Stockbridge. Consequently, Edwards related,

8. *Works, 16,* 687, 691, 548.

9. On this project, see especially Kenneth P. Minkema, "The Other Unfinished 'Great Work': Jonathan Edwards, Messianic Prophecy, and 'The Harmony of the Old and New Testament,'" in Stephen J. Stein, ed., *Jonathan Edwards's Writings: Text, Context, Interpretation* (Bloomington, Indiana Univ. Press, 1996), 52–65.

1. For information on JE's plans for a major treatise on the history of redemption (which he was building on his famous sermon series of 1739), see especially the three manuscript notebooks he kept on this project held in the Edwards Papers, Beinecke Rare Book and Manuscript Library, Yale University; and John F. Wilson, "Jonathan Edwards' Notebooks for A History of the Work of Redemption," in *The Works of Jonathan Edwards, 9, A History of the Work of Redemption,* ed. John F. Wilson (New Haven, Yale Univ. Press, 1989), 543–56.

2. For a sampling of these, see entry Nos. 1254 and 1325 (on original sin); 1168, 1182, 1184, 1208, 1218, 1225, 1266[a], 1275, 1277[a], and 1355a (on themes in the *Two Dissertations*); 1176 and 1260b (on the history of redemption); and 1172, 1192, 1193, 1194, 1283, 1290, 1327, and 1347, 1353a (on the harmony of Old and New Testament).

> I have a constitution in many respects peculiar unhappy, attended with flaccid solids, vapid, sizy and scarce fluids, and a low tide of spirits; often occasioning a kind of childish weakness and contemptibleness of speech, presence, and demeanor; with a disagreeable dullness and stiffness, much unfitting me for conversation, but more especially for the government of a college. This poorness of constitution makes me shrink at the thoughts of taking upon me, in the decline of life, such a new and great business, attended with such a multiplicity of cares, and requiring such a degree of activity, alertness and spirit of government.

He confessed, in all honesty, that his poor health was of grave concern, and would no doubt prove a major detriment to his leadership of a college. It was only a matter of time before these concerns of his were realized, and Edwards died as a result of assuming the college's presidency in such a condition.[3]

Moreover, Edwards had finally found himself able to focus closely on his writing, to pursue the theological projects that had so long required attention. They had never taken precedence over the daily demands of pastoral ministry, but they had always been for Edwards "the chief entertainment and delight of my life." Now that the mission's crisis had subsided, he could take more delight at home in his study and, truth be told, the burdens of college administration did not appeal. He would do what the Lord willed—even move his family to Princeton. But he had to admit that his desire was to stay in Stockbridge. "My heart is so much in these studies," he wrote to Stockton and the other trustees, "that I cannot find it in my heart to be willing to put myself into an incapacity to pursue them any more, in the future part of my life, to such a degree as I must, if I undertake . . . the office of a president." Besides his projected "History of the Work of Redemption" and "Harmony of the Old and New Testament," he noted that he had "also many other things in hand, in some of which I have made great progress." He continued, "[S]ome of these things, if divine providence favor, I should be willing to attempt a publication of." Further, "[S]o far as I myself am able to judge of what talents I have, for benefiting my fellow creatures by word, I think I can write better than I can speak." The presidency was very important. But Edwards was right about his gifts. And so "on the whole" he was "much at a loss, with respect to the way of my duty in this important affair: I am

---

3. *Works, 16,* 726.

in doubt, whether if I should engage in it, I should not do what both you and I should be sorry for afterwards."[4]

In the tradition of New England's Congregationalists, Edwards convened a council of regional pastors to seek God's will in this affair. Originally scheduled for December 21, their meeting was delayed by inclement weather, taking place despite "yet more difficult" conditions on January 4, 1758. As Edwards related to Gideon Hawley, the council "proceeded to hear and judge of the matter and unanimously determined that my call was clear to go, etc. I am therefore by the will of God about to set out on my journey in a few days, being greatly pressed to go speedily by letters after letters from the Trustees, and by two of their number, viz. Messrs. [Caleb] Smith and [John] Brainerd, whom they sent to Stockbridge."[5]

God had spoken. Edwards obeyed, despite his genuine reluctance.[6] Soon after arriving in Princeton, he received an inoculation for smallpox. An epidemic had broken out, and before the rise of modern medicine clergy were often called upon to show support for their local physicians—who were often clergymen themselves—by setting examples of early therapeutic courage.[7] Edwards never contracted a full-blown case of the smallpox, but in his weakened physical condition he developed a fatal "secondary fever."[8] His untimely death occurred on March 22, 1758, at the age of fifty-four, just two months after he had assumed the presidency at Princeton.

Scholars have speculated for years about what Edwards might have accomplished had he survived his final illness. As often as not, such speculation has proven unhelpful and even misleading.[9] But when compared

4. *Works, 16,* 726, 729.

5. *Works, 16,* 737.

6. As reported in Hopkins' *Life,* 79, "When they [the council] published their judgment and advice to Mr. Edwards and his people, he appear'd uncommonly mov'd and affected with it, and fell into tears on the occasion; . . . and soon after said to the gentlemen, who had given their advice, that it was a matter of wonder to him, that they could so easily . . . get over the objections he had made against his removal, to be the head of a college; which appear'd great and weighty to him."

7. See Patricia A. Watson, *The Angelical Conjunction: The Preacher-Physicians of Colonial New England* (Knoxville, Univ. of Tennessee Press, 1991).

8. Hopkins, *Life,* 80: "a secondary fever set in; and by reason of a number of pustles in his throat, the obstruction was such, that the medicines necessary to stanch the fever, could not be administer'd. It therefore raged till it put an end to his life."

9. In the tradition of Perry Miller, many scholars continue to suggest that JE intended at the end of his life to publish a "Rational Account of the Main Doctrines of the Christian Religion." As the story usually goes, this crowning achievement of JE's career was to be a systematic presentation of his previously "hidden" religious views. That this was not JE's intention has been

with the other materials Edwards produced in his final years, the later "Miscellanies" offer some clues as to what was coming. The "Miscellanies" open a window onto Edwards' larger intellectual concerns during the last years of his life.

"Notions That Prevail in Our Nation": A Guide to Edwards' Interlocutors

As Edwards wrote to Erskine in the summer of 1752, "I am fond of knowing how things are going on in the learned world." And as he added three years later, referring to a recent book by David Hume, "I am glad of an opportunity to read such corrupt books; especially when written by men of considerable genius; that I may have an idea of the notions that prevail in our nation."[1] Glad, indeed. Edwards' appetite for such notions proved nothing short of voracious, as attested by all who have perused his celebrated "Catalogue" of reading. Comprising 720 entries on titles that Edwards wanted to read—many of which he did acquire—the "Catalogue" reveals the vast horizons of his mind. When viewed in conjunction with his "Account Book," which lists another 120 titles, it becomes clear that this man who never left the northeastern American colonies circumnavigated the globe with his mind's eye.[2]

Edwards did so by participating in the transatlantic "republic of letters," the storied literary network of leading Enlightenment intellectuals.[3] He labored deliberately on the outskirts of this controversial re-

---

clear to specialists for some time. But the force of Miller's interpretation of JE's mind continues to be felt. On this problem, see especially *Works, 13,* 6–8, and *Works, 18,* 18, 24–34.

1. *Works, 16,* 493, 679. JE did not identify the title of the "corrupt" book he had read by Hume. Three possibilities are mentioned in JE's "Catalogue" of reading: *A Treatise of Human Nature* (London, 1739–40); *Philosophical Essays Concerning Human Nature* (London, 1748); and *An Enquiry Concerning the Principles of Morals* (London, 1751). See *The Works of Jonathan Edwards, 27, Catalogues of Reading,* ed. Peter J. Thuesen (New Haven, Yale Univ. Press, forthcoming).

2. On the "Catalogue" as an indicator of JE's intellectual horizons, see the classic but now dated essay of Thomas H. Johnson, "Jonathan Edwards' Background of Reading," *Publications of the Colonial Society of Massachusetts* 28 (1931), 193–222 (significantly, Johnson concluded that JE always remained something of a provincial intellectually). A more accurate and up-to-date assessment of JE's mental world may be found in Peter J. Thuesen, "Editor's Introduction," in *Works, 27.*

3. Though the term "republic of letters" dates back at least to the early years of the Italian Renaissance, it is used most often to refer to the literary network of European scholars whose candid and often subversive (and not always legal) exchange of ideas continues to characterize for many the age of Enlightenment. The best book-length treatment of this republic's informal structures of communication and collaboration is Anne Goldgar's *Impolite Learning: Conduct and Community in the Republic of Letters, 1680–1750* (New Haven, Yale Univ. Press, 1995), though her focus on Huguenot refugees in Holland keeps her from devoting much attention to the Anglo-American world. See also Peter N. Miller's recent book on the world of Nicolas-

public, engaging it mainly through the portal of British Dissent. Moreover, he opposed what he considered its promotion of infidelity, combating the "Arminian" and deistic tendencies of its more radical devotees. But he engaged it nonetheless, remaining fully apprised of Enlightenment thought. He shared his opponents' guarded optimism regarding the progress of world history (though for very different reasons), their emphasis on the importance of rational inquiry and investigation, even their concern to promote a more ethical way of life in the modern West. He was certainly not the only conservative cleric to participate in the Enlightenment. And the shopworn depictions of him as medieval have proven deficient.[4]

Claude Fabri de Peiresc (1580–1637), *Peiresc's Europe: Learning and Virtue in the Seventeenth Century* (New Haven, Yale Univ. Press, 2000), which offers an extraordinary treatment of the early seventeenth-century republic of letters. On the historiography of the republic of letters, see especially Françoise Waquet, "Qu'est-ce que la République des lettres?: Essai de sémantique historique," *Bibliothèque de l'école des chartes* 147 (1989), 473–502. On American participation in this network, see Norman S. Fiering, "The Transatlantic Republic of Letters: A Note on the Circulation of Learned Periodicals to Early Eighteenth-Century America," *William and Mary Quarterly* 33 (1976), 642–60; Ned C. Landsman, *From Colonials to Provincials: American Thought and Culture, 1680–1760* (New York, Twayne Publishers, 1997), 31–56; and, most recently, David D. Hall, "Learned Culture in the Eighteenth Century," in *A History of the Book in America*, vol. 1, *The Colonial Book in the Atlantic World*, ed. Hugh Amory and David D. Hall (Cambridge, Cambridge Univ. Press, 2000), 411–33. On JE and the republic of letters, see especially Thuesen, "Editor's Introduction," in *Works*, 27; and Robert E. Brown, *Jonathan Edwards and the Bible* (Bloomington, Indiana Univ. Press, 2002), 1–26. Significantly, JE developed his "Catalogue" (in part) on the basis of his reading in the eighteen volumes of the English periodical, *Republick of Letters* (begun in 1728), owned by a local ministerial association.

4. Peter Gay, *A Loss of Mastery: Puritan Historians in Colonial America* (Berkeley, Univ. of California Press, 1966), 88–117, is only the most notorious interpretation of JE as a medieval thinker. The historiography of the age of Enlightenment is immense, and beyond the scope of this introduction. Useful benchmarks may be found in James Schmidt, ed., *What Is Enlightenment?: Eighteenth-Century Answers and Twentieth-Century Questions*, Philosophical Traditions (Berkeley, Univ. of California Press, 1996). On the most radical Enlightenment thought, Jonathan I. Israel, *Radical Enlightenment: Philosophy and the Making of Modernity, 1650–1750* (Oxford, Oxford Univ. Press, 2001), offers a helpful, up-to-date summary, though one that exaggerates the significance of the radicals he studies and overdramatizes their role in undermining traditional orthodoxies. On the "Arminian" roots and ramifications of several important strains of Enlightenment thought, see especially the following works of Hugh Trevor-Roper: "The Religious Origins of the Enlightenment," in Trevor-Roper, *The Crisis of the Seventeenth Century: Religion, the Reformation, and Social Change* (Indianapolis, Liberty Fund, 1967), 179–218; *Catholics, Anglicans and Puritans: Seventeenth Century Essays* (1987; Chicago, Univ. of Chicago Press, 1988); and *From Counter-Reformation to Glorious Revolution* (Chicago, Univ. of Chicago Press, 1992). On the "uniquely clerical nature of England's experience of Enlightenment and Counter-Enlightenment," see esp. B. W. Young, *Religion and Enlightenment in Eighteenth-Century England: Theological Debate from Locke to Burke* (Oxford, Clarendon Press, 1998), 15 and passim (a book that includes insightful discussions of some of JE's largely-forgotten interlocutors, such as William Warburton and Daniel Waterland). On England's anti-clerical Enlightenment, see also J. A. I.

Edwards' later "Miscellanies" attest most powerfully to his cosmopolitan frame of mind and his eagerness for intelligence on European intellectual trends. Approximately 38 percent of the material printed below consists of extracts copied by Edwards out of the works of other authors—a telling statistic that highlights the uniqueness of this material in Edwards' corpus, as well as the challenges it has presented from an editorial point of view.[5] The later "Miscellanies" comprise nothing less than a vast repository of learning on early modern Anglo-American history and culture. They serve to underscore Edwards' devotion—raised to an unprecedented level during the final years of his life—to engage the Enlightenment from the point of view of his Calvinist faith. And they reflect his early efforts to make good on this devotion, selecting and organizing material from among his leading sources in preparation for the treatises he left sadly incomplete.

Nearly a third of the material below (32.8 percent) comes from the pens of just five scholars, all of whom were Europeans and important intellectual influences: Andrew Michael Ramsay (10.3 percent), Ralph Cudworth (9 percent), Philip Skelton (6.6 percent), Johann Friedrich Stapfer (4.6 percent), and Thomas Goodwin (2.3 percent).[6] As will be seen in the extracts themselves and in the brief vignettes of these men

Champion, *The Pillars of Priestcraft Shaken: The Church of England and its Enemies, 1660–1730*, Cambridge Studies in Early Modern British History (Cambridge, Cambridge Univ. Press, 1992). For an impressive synthesis of the "Arminian," clerical, and anti-clerical elements of Enlightenment thought in Britain, see J. G. A. Pocock, *Barbarism and Religion, Volume One, The Enlightenments of Edward Gibbon, 1737–1764* (Cambridge, Cambridge Univ. Press, 1999). And for a forceful argument regarding the relationship between the Enlightenment and British Dissent, see Donald Davie, "Enlightenment and Dissent," in Davie, *Dissentient Voice: The Ward-Phillips Lectures for 1980 with Some Related Pieces* (Notre Dame, Univ. of Notre Dame Press, 1982), 22 ff.

5. Due to the amount of copied material in the "Miscellanies" that follow, as well as to the fact that this is an edition of JE (and not of his sources), I have had to restrict my editing to JE's work itself and so have resisted the frequent temptation to annotate his sources (not to mention his sources' sources). Whenever possible, I have obtained the editions that JE used himself, employing them as a guide in the punctuation of the extracts (and in the insertion of ellipses wherever JE passed over material in his sources without notice). Frequently, however, JE reverts to rough paraphrases and summaries of these works, in which cases I have had to punctuate the extracts on my own.

6. In addition to the material extracted from these five authors, JE copied approximately 5 percent of the material that follows from a variety of other sources, taking the most from John Reynolds, *The Religion of Jesus Delineated* (3,510 words, or 1.2 percent of the total); Thomas Sherlock, *Several Discourses Preached at the Temple Church*, 2 vols. (2,145 words, or 0.7%); George Turnbull, *The Principles of Moral and Christian Philosophy* (1,477 words, or 0.5%); and John Brine, *A Treatise on Various Subjects* (1,092 words, or 0.4%). See the relevant annotations below for complete bibliographical citations.

that follow, their writings put Edwards in touch with the pulse of modern European culture, both on the vein of the Enlightenment as well as that of Reformed theology. As Gerald McDermott has recently written, roughly a quarter of the "Miscellanies" (including much of the material gleaned from these five authors) deals with the deist threat alone, a fact that discloses a "strange, new Edwards," one unfamiliar to nonspecialists.[7] This volume reveals a concern for more than the views of a handful of English deists, however. These entries reflect Edwards' conversance with a wide range of modern thought. In fact, they reveal that the later Edwards devoted his most arduous scholarly labors to rearticulating his faith within the idioms of the Enlightenment.

ANDREW MICHAEL RAMSAY (1686–1743)

The most extensively quoted author in the "Miscellanies" that follow is Sir Andrew Michael Ramsay, known in France as Chevalier de Ramsay. As a Roman Catholic convert and an ardent anti-Calvinist, Ramsay represents an unlikely source of influence on Edwards' thought. But as a student of world religions and an apologist for Trinitarian Christianity, he provided Edwards with abundant ammunition for his battles against the forces of heterodoxy.

Tradition has it that Ramsay was born in the port town of Ayr in southwestern Scotland. The son of a Presbyterian baker and an Episcopalian mother, he was reared in the Church of Scotland and sent to the University of Edinburgh. Though trained for ministry in the Kirk, his distaste for predestination precluded his ordination and by 1708 he had joined a fellowship of Scottish mystics led by George Garden, a former clergyman from Aberdeen deposed for Episcopal and Jacobite views. Ramsay left Scotland in 1710, never to return. He migrated first to Holland to consult with the exiled Frenchman Pierre Poiret, a Protestant mystic and frequent adviser to Garden's circle back in Scotland. Later that year he moved to France to meet with the famed Archbishop Fénelon, under whose guidance in Cambrai he soon converted to Roman Catholicism. The two grew close, Ramsay remaining with his new mentor until his death in 1715, after which Ramsay devoted the rest of his life to scholarship and teaching. Writing on a wide array of topics—religion, history, literature, politics, and education, among others—he also tutored royal families in France as well as England, in-

---

7. Gerald R. McDermott, *Jonathan Edwards Confronts the Gods: Christian Theology, Enlightenment Religion, and Non-Christian Faiths* (New York, Oxford Univ. Press, 2000), 3, 39.

cluding the children of the would-be James III, Pretender to the British throne.[8]

Edwards copied the most from Ramsay's posthumous magnum opus, *Philosophical Principles of Natural and Revealed Religion* (1748–49), a work he had noticed first in excerpted form in the London *Monthly Review*. In this "Great Work," as its author called it, Ramsay had mounted an apologetic for the reasonableness of religion, arguing for an analogy between the reliability of reason and revelation, between the religion of nature and that of supernatural belief. Ramsay contended in this work for views that Edwards would deem heretical, such as the preexistence and restoration of every soul to divine favor. As we shall see, however, his opposition to modern unbelief (in forms as various as materialism, Socinianism, and especially deism) funded Edwards' own uniquely Reformed apologetic. And Ramsay's tendency to see vestiges of Christian truth in the world religions informed Edwards' appropriation of the "traditions of the heathen . . . concerning the Trinity, the nature of the Deity, the paradisaic state, the fall, the redemption of the Messiah, the fall of angels, [and] the nature of true religion."[9]

Edwards also copied from Ramsay's best-selling work, the *Travels of Cyrus* (1728),[1] a fictive adaptation of the biblical account of Cyrus the Great, king of Persia and ruler of most of the ancient Near East by the time of his death in 530 B.C.E.[2] The speculative story of Cyrus' moral and mental training to govern the ancient world, the *Travels* narrates his spiritual odyssey through the schools of Zoroaster, Egypt, Greece, Crete, Tyre, and eventually Babylon. Ramsay affirms throughout this work a universal sense of divinity that ties the human race together across its cultural divides. Most interesting to Edwards, though, was Ramsay's lengthy appendix to this work, entitled "Discourse upon the Theology and Mythology of the Pagans." Finding confirmation there that "the first religion of mankind" proved, in Edwards' summary, "agreeable to the

8. On Ramsay's life and work, see especially G. D. Henderson, *Chevalier Ramsay* (London, Thomas Nelson and Sons, 1952); and G. D. Henderson, *Mystics of the North-East* (Aberdeen, The Third Spalding Club, 1934), 51–55 and passim. Ramsay's life and conversion to Catholicism are also narrated in *Catholic Doctrines and Catholic Principles Explained; with a Brief Account of the Conversion of the Dutchess of York . . . as Written by Herself. Also, a Sketch of the Life, and an Account of the Conversion of Sir Michael Ramsay, to the Catholic Church, by Arch-Bishop Fenelon, as Given by Ramsay Himself* (New York, William Higgins, 1817), 62–86.

9. Taken from the heading of entry No. 1181.

1. First published in French as *Les Voyages de Cyrus, avec un Discours sur la Mythologie des Payens* (Paris, 1727), an English edition of Ramsay's *Travels* was published in London the following year. JE used the 8th edition, which was published in London in 1752.

2. See especially the biblical book of Ezra.

religion of the Holy Scriptures," Edwards went on to exploit this material in his typology of the religions, discerning Christian imagery in the teachings and practices of a host of non-Christian faiths.[3]

RALPH CUDWORTH (1617–88)

After Ramsay, Edwards copied the most from the Cambridge Platonist Ralph Cudworth, an Anglican cleric and the leading Hebraist at Cambridge for half of the seventeenth century. Nondogmatic in his theology and uncommitted to Calvinist principles, Cudworth was yet another improbable influence on Edwards' response to modern thought. But as a learned opponent of materialism and a defender of classical theism, Cudworth lent Edwards a lot of support in his defense of Christianity.

Cudworth was born at Aller in the county of Somerset, the son of an Anglican clergyman, a Cambridge scholar, and a one-time chaplain to James I and his wife, who had worked for a while as a nurse to Henry, Prince of Wales. Enrolling at Emmanuel College, Cambridge, in May 1632, Cudworth proceeded to take both bachelor's (1635) and master's (1639) degrees. Like his father before him, he became a Fellow at Emmanuel soon after completing this course of study and, recognized widely for his achievements in both linguistics and religious philosophy, he went on to serve as Master of Clare Hall, Regius Professor of Hebrew, and Master of Christ's College in Cambridge as well. Averse to religious sectarianism, Cudworth got along fairly well with both the Puritans of the Interregnum and the Anglicans of the Restoration. His circle of Cambridge Platonists—which included, among others, his eminent colleagues Benjamin Whichcote, John Smith, and Henry More—was known for its broad-minded, anti-Calvinist version of Protestantism. But as apologists for "true religion" against all forms of modern skepticism, these men appealed in various ways to a wide range of traditional Christians, not least to conservative Calvinists like Edwards.[4]

3. Quotations taken from the heading of entry No. 1351. I will further discuss JE's typological interpretation of the religions below.

4. Interestingly, Cudworth's brother James lived in Scituate, Massachusetts. On Cudworth's life and thought, see especially J. A. Passmore, *Ralph Cudworth: An Interpretation* (Cambridge, Cambridge Univ. Press, 1951); and Lydia Gysi (Mother Maria), *Platonism and Cartesianism in the Philosophy of Ralph Cudworth* (Bern, Herbert Lang, 1962). On the Cambridge Platonists and their writings, see especially C. A. Patrides, "'The High and Aiery Hills of Platonisme': An Introduction to the Cambridge Platonists," in Patrides, ed., *The Cambridge Platonists* (London, Edward Arnold, 1969), 1–41; Ernst Cassirer, *The Platonic Renaissance in England*, trans. James P. Pettegrove (1953; New York, Gordian Press, 1970); J. Deotis Roberts, *From Puritanism to Platonism in Seventeenth Century England* (The Hague, Martinus Nijhoff, 1968); and, most recently, G. A. J. Rogers, J. M. Vienne, and Y. C. Zarka, eds., *The Cambridge Platonists in Philosophical Con-*

The only one of Cudworth's writings we know Edwards read and sought to appropriate was *The True Intellectual System of the Universe* (1678). The culmination and synthesis of a lifetime of reflection, Cudworth's *System* offered a strong defense of the reality of a divine intelligence that grants order to the universe and its eternal moral ideas. According to Cudworth, this intelligence has been recognized for millennia, leading to monotheism among the best of the ancient philosophers. Indeed, though witnessed to most clearly among the ancients by the Jews, pagans had always been able to read the very "signatures" of God in human consciousness, religious symbolism, and the natural world as well.[5] Edwards would echo Cudworth's insistence that unbelief was nothing new, and that it had always been contradicted by transcendental argumentation. Edwards was eager, furthermore, to garner support for his own typology of non-Christian religious thought. Thus after making brief use of the *System* in entry Nos. 1343 and 1358 (where Cudworth is used to show "that the heathens generally worshipped but one supreme, eternal, universal, uncreated Deity"), Edwards let Cudworth steal the show in No. 1359—entitled "Extracts from Dr. Cudworth Concerning the Opinions and Traditions of Heathen Philosophers Agreeable to Truth Concerning Matters of Religion." A massive entry in which Edwards lifted well over 25,000 words from Cudworth, it comprises nearly one tenth of the material printed below. Clearly, Edwards found in Cudworth a worthy ally in the struggle against the "pagan" religious naturalism of the Enlightenment.

PHILIP SKELTON (1707–87)

Of English ancestry on his father's side, Philip Skelton was born at Derriaghy (near Lisburn) in county Antrim, northern Ireland, the son of Richard Skelton, a local farmer, as well as a gunsmith and a tanner, and

---

text: *Politics, Metaphysics, and Religion* (Dordrecht, Kluwer Academic Publishers, 1997). Emily Stipes Watts, "Jonathan Edwards and the Cambridge Platonists" (Ph.D. diss., Univ. of Illinois, 1963), though now rather dated, remains the most comprehensive treatment of JE's interest in this group. But see also Daniel Walker Howe's discussion of Edwards in "The Cambridge Platonists of Old England and the Cambridge Platonists of New England," in Conrad Edick Wright, ed., *American Unitarianism, 1805–1865* (Boston, Massachusetts Historical Society and Northeastern Univ. Press, 1989), 87–119. On Cambridge Platonism among JE's Puritan predecessors, see Norman Fiering, *Moral Philosophy at Seventeenth-Century Harvard: A Discipline in Transition* (Chapel Hill, Univ. of North Carolina Press, 1981).

5. Lenore Thomas Ealy, "Reading the Signatures of the Divine Author: Providence, Nature, and History in Ralph Cudworth's Anglican Apologetic" (Ph.D. diss., Johns Hopkins Univ., 1997).

Arabella (Cathcart) Skelton, a farmer's daughter from Derriaghy. He trained at a Latin school in Lisburn beginning in 1717 before entering Trinity College, Dublin, seven years later. He received a bachelor's degree from Trinity in 1728 and ordination in the Church of Ireland the following year. Skelton spent the bulk of his life in the service of various minor Anglican parishes—Drummully (adjacent to Newtown-Butler), Monaghan, Pettigo (or Templecarn), Devenish and, most famously, Fintona (or Donacavey) in county Tyrone—engaging all the while in teaching and scholarship. Perhaps best known for his charity (he sold his substantial personal libraries on two separate occasions, using the proceeds to feed the poor), he was also a devoted Anglican and able defender of revelation. He lived in retirement in Dublin from 1780 to 1787.[6]

Edwards quotes from Skelton in a dozen different entries, but quotes by far the most in entry No. 1350, entitled "The Necessity of Revelation. Extracts from *Deism Revealed*." The only one of Skelton's works we know that Edwards actually read, *Ophiomaches, or Deism Revealed* (1749) was a series of dialogues between two deists, named Dechaine and Cunningham, a Christian minister named Shepherd, and a doubtful layman, Templeton. Recommended for publication by none other than David Hume, it offered a refutation of the deists' standard objections to Christian orthodoxy, providing Edwards with both information on the teachings of the deists and assistance in his attempt to counteract their religion of nature. Both Skelton and Edwards spent much of their lives combating human self-sufficiency, championing the Bible as essential for reliable knowledge of God's will.

JOHANN FRIEDRICH STAPFER (1708–75)

Though Edwards quotes fewer words from Johann Friedrich Stapfer than from Ramsay, Cudworth, or Skelton, Stapfer appears in far more entries than any of Edwards' other sources. Indeed, his *Institutiones Theologicæ Polemicæ Universæ* (5 vols., 1743–47) functioned for Edwards as a current reference book on Continental Reformed thought. Born in Brugg, near Zurich, Stapfer studied in Bern and Marburg and traveled in the Netherlands before settling down back home in Switzerland north of the Alps. He worked as a military chaplain from 1738 to 1740, as a tu-

---

6. On the life and work of Philip Skelton, see especially Samuel Burdy, *The Life of Philip Skelton* (1792; Oxford, Clarendon Press, 1914). Cf. Robert Lynam, ed., *The Complete Works of the Late Rev. Philip Skelton, Rector of Fintona, . . . to Which Is Prefixed, Burdy's Life of the Author* (1770; London, R. Baynes, 1824).

tor in Diessbach (near Bern) from 1740 to 1750, and as a pastor in Diessbach from 1750 until his death twenty-five years later.[7]

Scholars usually mention Stapfer only in reference to "Stapfer's scheme" regarding the doctrine of imputation, a scheme that Edwards employed in *Original Sin* (1758).[8] But as revealed throughout the "Miscellanies," Edwards actually consulted Stapfer on a broad range of doctrinal issues, citing him frequently as an authority on the state of Reformed theology. Though Stapfer published two other great works, his *Grundlegung zur wahren Religion* (12 vols., 1746–53) and *Sittenlehre* (6 vols., 1757–66), Edwards appears not to have known them (understandably, since the latter work was largely published after his death). What Edwards did know of Stapfer's work, however, he assimilated assiduously. On topics ranging from biblical prophecy to bodily resurrection, from "natural fitness" (discussed below) to justification by grace through faith, Stapfer aided Edwards' attempts to contemporize his own teaching, bringing the traditions of Reformed Protestantism to bear on the discourse of the Enlightenment.

THOMAS GOODWIN (1600–1680)

Despite the fact that Thomas Goodwin ranks only fifth among Edwards' sources, in the Anglo-American world he remains by far the best known. Born in Rollesby (near Yarmouth), England, the son of Richard and Catherine (Collingwood) Goodwin, he studied at Christ's College, Cambridge (B.A. 1616), and then at Catherine Hall, Cambridge (M.A. 1620), where he won a fellowship. Beginning in 1628 he lectured at Trinity Church in Cambridge, becoming vicar there in 1632. Just two years later, though, he resigned this post at the prodding of John Cotton, leaving the Church of England and founding an independent church in London, where he became the leading Independent clergyman in England. In 1639 he fled to Holland and led the English church in Arnheim. But toward the end of 1640, upon the commencement of the Long Parliament, he returned to London and started another church at St. Dunstan's-in-the-East. By 1643 he had joined the Assembly in Westminster, eventually serving on the committee that drafted its *Directory for Public Worship* (1645). Though invited to New England by Cotton (1647), various friends and colleagues persuaded him not to go. He received a

7. There is precious little scholarship on the life and work of Stapfer, especially in English. For basic biographical information, consult *The New Schaff-Herzog Encyclopedia of Religious Knowledge*, vol. 11 (New York, Funk and Wagnalls Company, 1911), 64–65; and *The Works of Jonathan Edwards, 3, Original Sin*, ed. Clyde A. Holbrook (New Haven, Yale Univ. Press, 1970), 83.

8. For JE's use of "Stapfer's scheme," see especially *Works, 3*, 391–93.

government chaplaincy in 1649. He became president of Magdalen College, Oxford, the following year. As a chief adviser to Oliver Cromwell, he served on various civil commissions. And he and John Owen led the committee of Independent congregationalists who drafted the Savoy Declaration in 1658. With the Restoration of the Stuarts, Goodwin's star began to fade and he spent the rest of his life away from England's corridors of power. Deprived immediately of Magdalen's presidency, he soon resumed his pastoral ministry and served a Dissenting church in London until his retirement.[9]

As with Stapfer, Edwards quotes Goodwin in a diversity of contexts, largely agreeing with his perspective on the Bible and theology. Edwards read closely in Goodwin's *Works,* making the most of his *Exposition on the Epistle to the Ephesians,* which is featured prominently in Edwards' entry No. 1274: "The Saints in Heaven Shall Partake of Christ's Own Happiness and Glory." Like Goodwin before him, Edwards revered this Pauline notion of union with Christ, shared by the saints both past and present, here on earth as well as in heaven. A central feature of Paul's epistle "to the saints which are at Ephesus" (Eph. 1:1), it lay at the root of Goodwin's and Edwards' view of salvation. As Goodwin explained in a note that Edwards copied on Eph. 2:5, "the Godhead dwells in the human nature of Christ, and is a quickening Spirit to him, and by virtue of our relation to him, having union with him, he quickens us, and never rests till he hath brought us to that union with God, in our measure and proportion that Christ hath." Joyous words to the likes of Edwards—and crucial, too, to his view of his opponents' religious teachings. For if it is true that Christians share a mystical union with their Maker, that they are animated and motivated by *super*natural grace, then the religion of nature and reason promoted by Europe's modern liberals was largely bereft of that without which there is no "true religion" at all.[1]

"A Remarkable Time in the Christian World": Major Themes in the Later "Miscellanies"

If there was one concern that Edwards' major interlocutors shared in common, it was that modern thought promoted the neglect of revela-

9. Though much has been written on Goodwin, he still has no modern, critical biographer. The early memoirs by Robert Halley and Goodwin's son, Thomas Goodwin the Younger, remain the most comprehensive sources of biographical information. See *The Works of Thomas Goodwin, D.D., Sometime President of Magdalene College, Oxford* (Edinburgh, James Nichol, 1861–66), 2, vii–lxxv.

1. Cf. R. Tudur Jones, "Union with Christ: The Existential Nerve of Puritan Piety," *Tyndale Bulletin* 41 (November 1990), 186–208.

tion. And if there is one concern that integrates the "Miscellanies" that follow, it is Edwards' determination to defend a supernatural view of the world, one in which "true religion" and "true virtue" take their rise from revelation and take shape by means of supernatural grace. To be sure, this is a collection of miscellaneous reflections, not a monographic treatise written to promote a single theme. Moreover, much of this material reflects an extension of Edwards' interest in issues and doctrines that had preoccupied him for years. Nevertheless, a careful study of the entries printed below reveals an Edwards acutely concerned—indeed, more deeply than ever before—with the lack of faith among the ranks of European intellectuals. It reveals an Edwards who devoted the latter years of his scholarly life to renewing confidence in and dependence on God's providential care within an intellectual culture increasingly saturated with naturalism.

A MODERN SUPERNATURALISM

As Edwards noted in entry No. 1263, tellingly titled "God's Immediate and Arbitrary Operation,"

> There are many who allow a present, continuing, immediate operation of God on the creation . . . but yet, because so many of the constant changes and events in their continued series in the external world come to pass in a certain, exact method, according to certain, fixed, invariable laws, are averse to allow that God acts any otherwise than as limiting himself by such invariable laws, fixed from the beginning of the creation, when he precisely marked out and determined the rules and paths of all his future operations, and that he never departs from those paths—so that, though they allow an immediate divine operation now, in these days, yet they sup[pose] it [is] what is limited by what we call LAWS OF NATURE, and seem averse to allow an ARBITRARY OPERATION to be continued, or ever to be expected, in these days.

Edwards responded by arguing forcefully that "of the two kinds of divine operation, viz. that which is arbitrary and that which is limited by fixed laws, the former, viz. arbitrary, is the first and foundation of the other, and that which all divine operation must finally be resolved into, and which all events and divine effects whatsoever primarily depend upon." Further, "even the fixing of the method and rules of the other kind of operation is an instance of arbitrary operation." Clearly, then, Edwards was not what many today would term a typically "modern" religious scholar. He did not adhere strictly to "critical" scientific methods. But his engagement with these methods from a supernaturalistic perspective pervades the writings in this volume, as well as the rest of his later writings.[2]

In a helpful recent book on Edwards' theology and its significance, Michael McClymond describes entry No. 1263 as "programmatic" for Edwards' labors on the relationship between the natural and the supernatural orders. Put more specifically for our purposes, this entry points to Edwards' effort throughout the bulk of the later "Miscellanies" to undermine the religious effects of modern naturalism—to shore up faith in a world interpreted more reliably with revelation than by the latest canons of natural reason alone. It could be argued, moreover, that this effort became his passion in the later 1750s, that during his final years of life Edwards sought above all else to illuminate what he took to be God's "arbitrary operation," God's supernatural activity or, in the favored words of his Puritan forebears, God's "special providence" in the world.[3]

2. On the religious ramifications of science in the early modern period, see especially John Hedley Brooke, *Science and Religion: Some Historical Perspectives,* Cambridge History of Science (Cambridge, Cambridge Univ. Press, 1991), 52–81, and 357–61 (for a slightly dated though still helpful bibliography on this topic).

3. Michael J. McClymond, *Encounters with God: An Approach to the Theology of Jonathan Edwards* (New York, Oxford Univ. Press, 1998), 110. In the words of Avihu Zakai ("Jonathan Edwards and the Language of Nature: The Re-Enchantment of the World in the Age of Scientific Reasoning," *The Journal of Religious History* 26 [Feb. 2002], 15–41), JE resisted "the mechanization of the natural world," constructing "a teleological and theological alternative . . . whose ultimate goal was the re-enchantment of the world by reconstituting the glory of God's majestic sovereignty, power, and will within the order of creation" (15, 32). Important commentary on entry No. 1263 may also be found in Sang Hyun Lee, *The Philosophical Theology of Jonathan Edwards* (Princeton, Princeton Univ. Press, 1988), 68–75, who clarifies that JE's supernaturalism was conditioned by his appreciation for God's use of the laws of nature and so-called "secondary" causes. Indeed in JE's view, ever since the creation God has acted in the world in relation to—though not in a way that is limited or restricted by—things already created. Thus, as he explained later on in No. 1263, creation *ex nihilo* is "the only divine operation that [is] absolutely arbitrary, without any kind of use made of any such antecedently fixed method of proceeding as is called a law of nature." For JE, there are levels or grades of God's arbitrary activity in the world. And "the higher we ascend in the scale or series of created existences, and the nearer in thus ascending we come to the Creator, the more the manner of divine operation with respect to the creature approaches to arbitrary in these respects." But even God's most spiritual work among us is commonly "mixed with" (or performed in relation to) God's natural activity, or accomplished in part by means of natural laws. Helpful treatments of the Puritans' supernatural worldview include David D. Hall, *Worlds of Wonder, Days of Judgment: Popular Religious Belief in Early New England* (New York, Alfred A. Knopf, 1989), and Michael P. Winship, *Seers of God: Puritan Providentialism in the Restoration and Early Enlightenment* (Baltimore, Johns Hopkins Univ. Press, 1996).

Taken together, then, the entries in this volume of Edwards' "Miscellanies" present an aspect of his thought often neglected by early leaders of the post–World War II revival of Edwards studies. In the hands of Perry Miller, H. Richard Niebuhr, and Joseph Haroutunian, Edwards appeared more often than not as a "radical theocentrist" (or a "radical monotheist"), one whose God was supremely transcendent, hard to pin down in the world below, and inaccessible by the trail of evidentialist analysis. Edwards himself, in this view, proved undeterred by the temptation to social and cultural relevance. He proved uninterested (in the main) in moral or rational apologetics. And he felt no need to defend his God against the critics of his Calvinism, or to accommodate his thought to their concerns.[4] Indeed, in the views of the neo-orthodox (such as Niebuhr and Haroutunian) as well as their atheistic sympathizers (such as Miller and his band of "atheists for [Reinhold] Niebuhr"), Edwards ran so far ahead of his "enlightened" counterparts that he rarely bothered to bog himself down in their chief concerns. To be sure, he made good use of Locke's empirical psychology, Berkeley's immaterialism, and the Cambridge Platonists as well. But he picked and chose from their works selectively, never engaging them head on. And he proved entirely uninterested in apologetics or natural theology.[5]

But if the "Miscellanies" that follow tell us anything about Edwards, it is that he took the leading concerns of Enlightenment thinkers very seriously. Indeed, Sydney Ahlstrom was not far off when in 1961 he referred to Edwards as this country's "Dordtian philosophe."[6] As nearly all specialists will attest, Edwards was theocentric. And he rejected what he

4. In the words of Haroutunian, JE "revitalized" the "theocentric piety of Calvinism" on the basis of his recognition that "religion was *independent* of the problems of social morality and civil government. . . . Calvinistic theology was thus *separated* from its temporary social and political aspects, and restated as a religion of permanent human significance" (ed. italics). Further, the universal greatness of JE's thought was largely lost on his epigones "because its theocentric character, its supreme regard for the glory of God and His sovereignty over man, made it ill-fitted to give expression to the ideals of the eighteenth century New England and to meet its immediate social needs. The social and political forces of the time gave rise to principles which were either inimical or irrelevant to the spirit of Edwardsean theology." Joseph Haroutunian, *Piety Versus Moralism: The Passing of the New England Theology* (New York, Harper & Row, 1932), xxix–xxx.

5. For more on JE's reputation among historians such as Miller, Niebuhr, and Haroutunian, see Douglas A. Sweeney, "Edwards and His Mantle: The Historiography of the New England Theology," *New England Quarterly* 71 (March 1998), 97–119.

6. Sydney Ahlstrom, "Theology in America: A Historical Survey," in *The Shaping of American Religion,* ed. James Ward Smith and A. Leland Jamison (Princeton, Princeton Univ. Press, 1961), 243–51.

believed to be the worst of modern liberalism. But he also showed himself to be a uniquely *modern* supernaturalist—a label that was not in Edwards' view an oxymoron. He never became a *rational* supernaturalist as such people are usually depicted, for he refused to defend his Calvinism on strictly secular grounds. But he was a culturally responsive, intellectually responsible supernaturalist, an Enlightenment Calvinist if you will, a Reformed apologist who was even something of a modern evidentialist. In Edwards' view, God's Word and Spirit reveal God's truth and create faith. But God's works prepare the way for their reception in our souls. So rational analysis of the evidence of divinity in our world is crucial to human flourishing, as well as to salvation. As Edwards phrased this in entry No. 1358,

> [W]e can have no other proper manifestations of the divine nature but by some effects of it: for we can't immediately look upon and behold God, and see what he is intuitively. The invisible things of God are seen by the things that are made. The word of God itself is no demonstration of the superior, distinguishing glory of the supreme God, any otherwise than by the works of God, and that two ways: 1. as we must have the perfections of God first proved by his works, in order to know that his word is to be depended on; 2. as the works of God, appealed [to] and declared in the word of God, declare and make evident that divine greatness and glory which the word of God declares. There is a difference between declaration and evidence. The word declares, but the works are the proper evidence of what is declared.[7]

EDWARDS' CRITIQUE OF THE "GENEROUS DOCTRINES"

Edwards analyzed the evidence of the divine within the world primarily in reaction to Enlightenment "infidelity," especially as he found it

---

7. Insofar as JE was an evidentialist, he fit in well with what E. Brooks Holifield terms "the evidential temper" of early American theology. See Holifield's *Theology in America: Christian Thought From the Age of the Puritans to the Civil War* (New Haven, Yale Univ. Press, 2003), 108–9. On this aspect of JE's thought, see also McDermott, *Jonathan Edwards Confronts the Gods*, McClymond, *Encounters with God* (esp. chapters one and six), and Brown, *Jonathan Edwards and the Bible*, three books that, taken together, represent a greater scholarly interest in JE's apologetic strategy than has existed since the early nineteenth century (by which time the first two collections of JE's "Miscellanies" had been published in Great Britain and the United States). Note also the more narrowly Old School Presbyterian studies of JE's apologetics by John Gerstner, "An Outline of the Apologetics of Jonathan Edwards," *Bibliotheca Sacra* 133 (1976), 3–10, 99–107, 195–201, 291–98; and Scott Oliphint, "Jonathan Edwards: Reformed Apologist," *Westminster Theological Journal* 57 (Spring 1995), 165–86.

among the deists and Arians of England.[8] Such unbelief was nothing new. Indeed, New Englanders had been fighting it since the early eighteenth century in treatises like Cotton Mather's *Reasonable Religion* (1700).[9] But by the early 1750s Edwards complained that "it now appears to be a remarkable time in the Christian world; perhaps such an one as never has been before. Things are going downhill so fast; truth and religion, both of heart and practice, are departing by such swift steps that I think it must needs be, that a crisis is not very far off." He worried about what he referred to as "those lax principles of the new divinity," promoted by those who "have imbibed the generous doctrines (as they are accounted) which are so much in vogue at the present day, and so contrary to the strict, mysterious, spiritual, soul-humbling principles of our forefathers." As alluded to above, these "generous doctrines" had mainly to do with the prevalence of virtue and salvation beyond the bounds of the Christian faith—and with the extent to which these depended upon God's supernatural aid. The proponents of natural religion were making deep inroads into British culture with their suggestion that the religious life most pleasing to the Creator could be practiced without any reference to an alleged revelation, that salvation can be achieved by means of consistent moral effort and is accessible to all who live by the (universal) laws of nature.

Edwards knew that such "generous doctrines" undermined people's

8. JE employs the term "infidelity" most visibly below in No. 1312, "CHRISTIAN RELIGION. THE UNREASONABLENESS OF INFIDELITY." JE's followers, moreover, employed the term more often than he, most famously in Timothy Dwight's poem, *The Triumph of Infidelity* (1788). On the rise of deism (a notoriously slippery term) in modern England, see especially Champion, *The Pillars of Priestcraft Shaken;* Peter Byrne, *Natural Religion and the Nature of Religion: The Legacy of Deism* (London, Routledge, 1989); Robert Sullivan, *John Toland and the Deist Controversy* (Cambridge, Mass., Harvard Univ. Press, 1982); Henning Graf Reventlow, *The Authority of the Bible and the Rise of the Modern World,* trans. John Bowden (Philadelphia, Fortress Press, 1985; 1980), esp. "Part III: The Climax of Biblical Criticism in English Deism," 287–410; Frank E. Manuel, *The Eighteenth Century Confronts the Gods* (1959; New York, Atheneum, 1967), esp. 57–84; and, for a useful rhetorical analysis, James A. Herrick, *The Radical Rhetoric of the English Deists: The Discourse of Skepticism, 1680–1750* (Columbia, Univ. of South Carolina Press, 1997). On English Arianism, see also Maurice Wiles, *Archetypal Heresy: Arianism through the Centuries* (Oxford, Clarendon Press, 1996). Cf. W. R. Ward, *Christianity under the Ancien Régime, 1648–1789* (Cambridge, Cambridge Univ. Press, 1999); Knud Haakonssen, ed., *Enlightenment and Religion: Rational Dissent in Eighteenth-Century Britain* (Cambridge, Cambridge Univ. Press, 1996); Young, *Religion and Enlightenment in Eighteenth-Century England;* and Gordon Rupp, *Religion in England, 1688–1791* (Oxford, Clarendon Press, 1986).

9. Other early American works opposed to enlightened unbelief included Cotton Mather's *Reason Satisfied and Faith Established* (1712), and Increase Mather's *Discourse Proving That the Christian Religion Is the Only True Religion* (1702). The best short summary of the rise of deism in America is found in Holifield, *Theology in America,* ch. 7.

faith in the Bible, thus promoting what he referred to as infidelity. And he despised the growing tendency among his nation's most "generous" thinkers to dismiss with disdain those who defended his own particularistic faith—a faith in which "[e]very good gift and every perfect gift is from above, and cometh down from the Father of lights" (Jas. 1:17), a faith in which sinners were saved "without the deeds of the law" (Rom. 3:28). As he fretted to Thomas Gillespie in November 1752, "[T]hese modern, fashionable opinions, however called noble and generous, are commonly attended, not only with a haughty contempt, but an inward, malignant bitterness of heart towards all the zealous professors and defenders of the contrary spiritual principles, that do so nearly concern the vitals of religion, and the power of experimental godliness." By the end of his life, moreover, Edwards feared that even the press itself had begun to apostatize, an omen that portended further contempt for divine truth. As he complained to his literary agent, the Boston clergyman Thomas Foxcroft, "I wish that at this day, when every evangelical doctrine is run down, and such bold attempts are made to drive all out of doors, the press mayn't labor only with performances that are leveled against Christ, and the religion he taught."[1]

Edwards confronted such performances in places other than the "Miscellanies." In fact, almost everything he wrote after his ejection from Northampton deals in one way or another with this trend.[2] But the entries printed below provide the most comprehensive picture of Edwards' engagement with his sources of information on the "generous doctrines," from the Cambridge master Daniel Waterland (1683–1740) to the Anglican Bishop William Warburton (1698–1779), major figures in Edwards' day but largely neglected by even the best of Edwards scholars ever since.[3] They also provide the most comprehensive indication of the

1. *Works, 16*, 491, 546, 695.
2. Aside from his published treatises and the later "Miscellanies," JE's most significant engagement with the problem of unbelief occurs in a major entry in the book of "Controversies" (a notebook devoted in large measure to this and related problems). Entitled "IMPORTANCE OF DOCTRINES AND OF MYSTERIES IN RELIGION," this entry attempts to "show how this way of rejecting everything but what we can first see agreeable to our reason, tends by degrees to bring everything relating not only to revealed religion but even natural religion into doubt, to make all appear with dim evidence like a shadow or the ideas of a dream till they are all neglected as worthy of no regard."
3. Significantly, and to cite just one example of this sort of scholarly neglect, Warburton's robustly providentialist *Divine Legation of Moses* (along with the typological exegesis and use of language it represents), though largely ignored by Edwards scholars and other historians of religion, attracted an enormous amount of attention during much of the eighteenth century and continues to incite the interest of various students of language theory. Indeed, Warburton was

state of Edwards' agenda for responding to unbelief—an agenda that, if not for Edwards' premature death, would surely have shaped his writing schedule for years to come.

These entries demonstrate, for example, that in his final years of life Edwards compiled a mountain of data on the "traditions of the heathen" (19.3 percent of the material printed below) in preparation for a show-down with the proponents of natural religion. Europe's age of explo-ration had yielded a surge in its body of knowledge on the religions and moral practices of many non-Western nations. In response to those who used this knowledge to relativize the religions, suggesting that the "hea-then" had all they needed in nature and reason for moral living, Edwards argued that his opponents often romanticized foreign cultures and failed to see that their most noble beliefs depended on revelation, and reflected—imperfectly, but powerfully nonetheless—Christian truth as found in the Bible. In making this argument, Edwards appropriated the *prisca theologia,* a tradition developed initially by early Christian Platon-ists but fine-tuned by neo-Platonists during and after the Renaissance. It taught an "ancient" (*prisca*) knowledge of God revealed supernaturally to the Jews (including forebears like Adam and Noah) and spread pri-mordially through them to most of the nations of the world. Though cor-rupted to various degrees through its transmission by fallen sinners, this ancient theology explained why the best of pagan philosophers—such as Plato—proved so compelling to many Christians and seemed to res-onate with Scripture.[4] For Edwards, it also explained why many of the

---

so well known, and so often caricatured, in his time that Laurence Sterne made use (and fun) of his reputation in *Tristram Shandy* (where Warburton was represented as John della Casa, the prude and polemical Archbishop of Benevento). And his quirky linguistic views have received attention in recent years from the likes of Jacques Derrida and John Milbank. See, for exam-ple, Derrida's *Of Grammatology,* trans. Gayatri Chakravorty Spivak, corrected ed. (1967; Balti-more, The Johns Hopkins Univ. Press, 1997), 98, 272–73, 284–87, 335n., 347n.; Paul J. Kor-shin, "The Development of Abstracted Typology in England, 1650–1820," in Earl Miner, ed., *Literary Uses of Typology, from the Late Middle Ages to the Present* (Princeton, Princeton Univ. Press, 1977), 147–203; Paolo Rossi, *The Dark Abyss of Time: The History of the Earth & the History of Na-tions from Hooke to Vico,* trans. Lydia G. Cochrane (1979; Chicago, Univ. of Chicago Press, 1984), 236–45; and John Milbank, "William Warburton: An Eighteenth Century Bishop Fallen among Post-Structuralists," *New Blackfriars* 64 (July/August 1983), 315–24, and (September 1983), 374–83. On Warburton's life and thought, see also J. S. Watson, *The Life of William Warburton, D.D., Lord Bishop of Gloucester . . .* (London, 1863); A. W. Evans, *Warburton and the Warburtoni-ans: A Study in Some Eighteenth-Century Controversies* (Oxford, Oxford Univ. Press, 1932); and Robert M. Ryley, *William Warburton* (Boston, Twayne Publishers, 1984). On Waterland's life and thought, see the memorial in Jeremiah Seed, *The Happiness of the Good in a Future State Set Forth: In a Sermon Occasion'd by the Death of Dr. Waterland* (London, 1741); and Robert T. Holtby, *Daniel Waterland, 1683–1740: A Story in Eighteenth-Century Orthodoxy* (Carlisle, C. Thurnam, 1966).

4. JE went so far as to speculate in No. 1162 that some philosophers may have enjoyed a su-

world's religious traditions appeared so full of types and vestiges of Christian revelation. As Edwards summarized this theory in entry No. 1338,

> [M]ostly the greater part of the heathen world, have not been left merely to the light of nature. They have had many things, especially in times of the old testament, that were delivered to mankind in the primitive ages of the world by revelation, handed down from ancestors by tradition, and many things borrowed from the Jews—and, during those ages, by many wonderful dispensations and displays towards the Jews—wherein God did in a most public and striking manner display himself and show his hand: [so] that the world had, from time to time, notices sufficient to convince them that there was a divine revelation extant, sufficient to induce 'em to seek after it. And things to make revelation public and spread it abroad, to extend the fame of it and its effects to the utmost ends of the earth, and to draw men's attention to it, have been vastly more and greater than before.[5]

Edwards tapped into this tradition, as we have seen, through Ramsay and Cudworth, but also through many others, from Theophilus Gale (1628–78) to William Dawes (1671–1724). His preoccupation with it points yet again to his concern to counter naturalism with what he labeled the "necessity of revelation" (a theme that, by itself, constitutes another 13.8 percent of the material printed below). In more than one entry by that title, Edwards confronted Matthew Tindal, the well-known deist whose major work, *Christianity as Old as the Creation* (1730), had repudiated the need for supernatural religion. "Tindal's main argument," Edwards noted in No. 1337, "is that the LAW OF NATURE IS ABSOLUTELY PERFECT. But how weak and impertinent is this arguing," he continued,

---

pernatural inspiration: "It may be worthy of consideration whether or no some of the HEATHEN PHILOSOPHERS had not, with regard to some things, some degree of INSPIRATION of the Spirit of God, which led 'em to say such wonderful things concerning the Trinity, the Messiah, etc. Inspiration is not so high an honor and privilege as some are ready to think. It is no peculiar privilege of God's special favorites."

5. For a useful review of the numerous travelogues and other reports of "heathen" cultures in seventeenth- and eighteenth-century England, see Donald F. Lach and Edwin J. Van Kley, *Asia in the Making of Europe*, vol. 3, *A Century of Advance, Book One: Trade, Missions, Literature* (Chicago, Univ. of Chicago Press, 1993), 547–97. Cf. David A. Pailin, *Attitudes to Other Religions: Comparative Religion in Seventeenth and Eighteenth Century Britain* (Manchester, Manchester Univ. Press, 1984); and Manuel, *The Eighteenth Century Confronts the Gods*. On the *prisca theologia*, see also D. P. Walker, *The Ancient Theology: Studies in Christian Platonism from the Fifteenth to the Eighteenth Century* (Ithaca, Cornell Univ. Press, 1972); Peter Harrison, *"Religion" and the Religions in the English Enlightenment* (Cambridge, Cambridge Univ. Press, 1990), 131–38; and Champion, *The Pillars of Priestcraft Shaken*, 133–69. On JE's appropriation of the *prisca theologia*, see McDermott, *Jonathan Edwards Confronts the Gods*.

"that because the *law of nature* (which is no other than natural rectitude and obligation) is perfect, that therefore the *light of nature* is sufficient." In a manner first made famous in his *Freedom of the Will*,[6] Edwards lambasted Tindal's theory as an "empty, insipid kind of doctrine. It is an idle way of spending time and ink and paper, to spend them in proving that what is in its own nature perfectly true is perfectly true, and what is in its nature perfectly good is perfectly good; or that which is, is, and is as it is."

Edwards had argued earlier in No. 1297 that "mankind need means of certainty, clearness and satisfaction in things that concern their welfare, in proportion to the importance of those things." And while natural reason can put us in touch with the truths of natural law, it has no access to the most essential information for moral living: "whether there be a future state of happiness and misery, what that state is, what the will of God is, what are things which please him, what are those things which will displease him and make us the objects of his anger and hatred, whether there be any reconciliation after we have offended, and how it may be obtained." Indeed, for Edwards, "[I]t is exceeding apparent that, without a revelation, mankind must be forever in the most woeful doubt with respect to these things." And "this appears not only by the state of the heathen world, wise and unwise, learned and unlearned, polite nations and barbarous, ages after ages, before the light of Christianity came abroad in the world, but also by what appears in these late ages among those that renounced divine revelation, even the wisest and greatest of 'em, and such as are of the strongest and most acute abilities." Those such as Tindal, he meant to say.

In the end, Edwards opposed the "generous doctrines" of his opponents because he believed that human beings depend on God for all their good, whether natural or supernatural. Affirming a radical doctrine of providence, he went so far as to turn the religion of nature and reason on its head. In a classic passage in *Original Sin,* a treatise he penned along with these entries, Edwards claimed not only that God designed the laws of nature at first, but that "God's *upholding* created substance, or causing its existence in each successive moment, is altogether equivalent to an *immediate production out of nothing,* at each moment, because its existence at this moment is not merely in part from God, but wholly from him; and not in any part, or degree, from its antecedent ex-

6. On JE's use of this kind of logical argumentation to deconstruct the views of his opponents, and especially on his employment of the so-called method of the *reductio* (in which the arguments of one's opponents are broken down until proven internally inconsistent), consult Leon Chai, *Jonathan Edwards and the Limits of Enlightenment Philosophy* (New York, Oxford Univ. Press, 1998).

istence."[7] If God were to cease creating and sustaining the world to-morrow, in other words, the laws of nature—and nature itself—would cease to exist. Such was Edwards' view of the importance of God's "arbitrary operation," and thus of the extent to which the deists and other naturalists had erred. Not only did God create the world originally, but God continues to create it now, from moment to moment, day to day, and year to year. Returning again to Edwards' text in No. 1263, then, we find the following rhetorical questions aimed at the deists and their ilk: "If there be a God who is truly an intelligent, voluntary, active being, what is there in reason to incline us to think that he should not act, and that he should not act upon his creatures, which, being his creatures, must have their very being from his action and must be perfectly and most absolutely subject to and dependent on his action?" Further, if God "acted once," as even the deists will admit, "why must he needs be still forever after and act no more?"[8]

Edwards refuted the "generous doctrines" in several other notable ways. In addition to his arguments for revelation and special providence, he affirms in the entries below a traditional view of the Bible itself, as well as the supernatural worldview that the biblical texts assume. In response to the early rise of the higher criticism of the Bible, he defends its divine inspiration, the historicity of its contents, and traditional views of the provenance of its books. He affirms the veracity of the Bible's own account of the miraculous. He spends a great amount of time on the reality of heaven and hell (13.9 percent of this volume). Indeed, in entry Nos. 1348 and 1356, he seems to have drafted part of a treatise on the doctrine of reprobation (this theme alone comprises 8.3 percent of this volume). And in response to the resurgence of Arian views across the Atlantic, Edwards devotes two major entries to the divinity of Christ, Nos. 1349 and 1358 (which together comprise another 8.3 percent), working again toward a treatise while suggesting to various colleagues that they defend this doctrine as well.[9]

---

7. *Works, 3,* 402. Essential interpretations of this passage that address the question of JE's occasionalism may be found in Douglas J. Elwood, *The Philosophical Theology of Jonathan Edwards* (New York, Columbia Univ. Press, 1960), 33–64; Norman Fiering, "The Rationalist Foundations of Jonathan Edwards's Metaphysics," in Nathan O. Hatch and Harry S. Stout, eds., *Jonathan Edwards and the American Experience* (New York, Oxford Univ. Press, 1988), 73–101; and Lee, *The Philosophical Theology of Jonathan Edwards,* 47–75, 107.

8. On JE's providentialism, particularly as it informed his uniquely Christian historiography, see also C. A. Patrides, *The Grand Design of God: The Literary Form of the Christian View of History* (London, Routledge & Kegan Paul, 1972).

9. See JE's correspondence on Feb. 11, 1757, with both Thomas Foxcroft and Edward Wigglesworth, in *Works, 16,* 695, 699. And note that JE's own son-in-law, the Rev. Aaron Burr, wrote

REFORMED ORTHODOXY REVISITED

Like most apologists then and since, Edwards infused the doctrines he championed with a modicum of new meaning, most famously in the realm of soteriology. If space permitted, it would be useful to assess the theological significance of Edwards' frequent appeal below to the "reasonableness" of these doctrines. As Edwards mediated his Calvinism to the world of the eighteenth century on topics as contested as election and the atonement, he clearly expanded the semantic range of his inherited vocabulary, thus giving rise to the first indigenous theological movement in American history.[1]

He did this mainly in published works such as *Freedom of the Will* and *Original Sin,* both of which he finished in Stockbridge, and each of which presents a novel and controversial—though not sui generis—view of its subject.[2] But as others have pointed out, Edwards had also begun to do this in his notebooks with other doctrines, most significantly with the doctrine of justification. In volume 21 of Edwards' *Works,* Sang Hyun Lee

---

on this topic in a book that JE quotes in No. 1358, *The Supreme Deity of Our Lord Jesus Christ . . .* (Boston, 1757). On biblical study and biblical criticism in the Britain of JE's day, see especially Reventlow, *The Authority of the Bible and the Rise of the Modern World;* Klaus Scholder, *The Birth of Modern Critical Theology: Origins and Problems of Biblical Criticism in the Seventeenth Century,* trans. John Bowden (1966; London, SCM Press, 1990); Gerard Reedy, S. J., *The Bible and Reason: Anglicans and Scripture in Late Seventeenth-Century England* (Philadelphia, Univ. of Pennsylvania Press, 1985); and John Drury, ed., *Critics of the Bible, 1724–1873,* Cambridge English Prose Texts (Cambridge, Cambridge Univ. Press, 1989). On JE's engagement with this criticism, see especially Brown, *Jonathan Edwards and the Bible.* On views of the afterlife and future punishment in JE's day, see also Philip C. Almond, *Heaven and Hell in Enlightenment England* (Cambridge, Cambridge Univ. Press, 1994); Piero Camporesi, *The Fear of Hell: Images of Damnation and Salvation in Early Modern Europe,* trans. Lucinda Byatt (1990; University Park, The Pennsylvania State Univ. Press, 1991); D. P. Walker, *The Decline of Hell: Seventeenth-Century Discussions of Eternal Torment* (Chicago, Univ. of Chicago Press, 1964); and Carl R. Trueman, "Heaven and Hell in Puritan Theology," *Epworth Review* 22 (Sept. 1995), 75–85. On JE's doctrine of hell (which is also developed in "Controversies"), the recent summary by Stephen R. Holmes, *God of Grace and God of Glory: An Account of the Theology of Jonathan Edwards* (Grand Rapids, Eerdmans, 2001), 199–240, is a useful place to begin.

1. For more on this movement, referred to most frequently as the "New Divinity" or "the New England Theology," see Joseph A. Conforti, *Jonathan Edwards, Religious Tradition, and American Culture* (Chapel Hill, Univ. of North Carolina Press, 1995); Allen C. Guelzo, *Edwards on the Will: A Century of American Theological Debate* (Middletown, Conn., Wesleyan Univ. Press, 1989); Douglas A. Sweeney, *Nathaniel Taylor, New Haven Theology and the Legacy of Jonathan Edwards* (New York, Oxford Univ. Press, 2003); and David W. Kling and Douglas A. Sweeney, eds., *Jonathan Edwards at Home and Abroad: Historical Memories, Cultural Movements, Global Horizons* (Columbia, Univ. of South Carolina Press, 2003).

2. On the historical significance of these books, see especially the introductions by Paul Ramsey and Clyde Holbrook to *Works, 1* and *3.*

has offered a systematic analysis of justification as Edwards defended it in response to modern criticisms. It is worth adding here, however, that Edwards' work on the doctrine of justification also comprises 6.4 percent of this volume. When viewed together with his labors on justification at Yale College, his published sermon on the topic, and other manuscript materials, these "Miscellanies" expand our knowledge of Edwards' effort to recontextualize this doctrine in relation to the leading concerns of his day.[3]

They reveal, for example, his enduring commitment to the language of federal theology[4] and the notion, as Edwards states it in No. 1161, that "God has no consideration of any goodness in [the creature] when he justifies by faith." However, they also reveal his reliance on the likes of Daniel Williams (c. 1643–1716), the English Presbyterian best known for opposing antinomianism, for defending the views of the controversial Puritan pastor Richard Baxter (1615–91), and for arguing, in Edwards' words, that "perseverance in faith [is] a necessary means of continuing in a state of justification" (No. 1186). Finally, they showcase Edwards' development of his doctrine of "natural fitness" and its role in his explanation of justification.[5] He had inherited the concept of "fitness" from his Reformed scholastic forebears.[6] He had used it for years, moreover, in his attempt to account for the relation of faith and works

3. JE's work on justification at Yale culminated in the writing of his master's thesis, or *Quæstio*, which may be found in *The Works of Jonathan Edwards, 14, Sermons and Discourses, 1723–1729*, ed. Kenneth P. Minkema (New Haven, Yale Univ. Press, 1997), 55–66. JE's published sermon entitled *Justification by Faith Alone* may be found in *The Works of Jonathan Edwards, 19, Sermons and Discourses, 1734–1738*, ed. M. X. Lesser (New Haven, Yale Univ. Press, 2001), 147–242. Cf. *Works, 18*, 12–18, 37–39. For JE's material on justification in the "Controversies" notebook, see *Works, 21*. Others who have written on the historical significance of JE's doctrine of justification include Thomas A. Schafer, "Jonathan Edwards and Justification by Faith," *Church History* 20 (December 1951), 55–67; and Anri Morimoto, *Jonathan Edwards and the Catholic Vision of Salvation* (University Park, The Pennsylvania State Univ. Press, 1995).

4. Contra Perry Miller, *Jonathan Edwards* (New York, William Sloane Associates, 1949), 30–32, 76–78, a commitment to federal theology and its forensic language of justification is found throughout JE's writings. For examples in the entries that follow, see Nos. 1177, 1215, 1220, and 1353.

5. See especially Nos. 1260a, 1279, and 1346.

6. Adrian Heerebord (1613–1661) of Leiden, for example, had made good use of the concept of "fittingness" in his *Meletemata philosophica* (1654). And as Peter A. Lillback emphasizes in *The Binding of God: Calvin's Role in the Development of Covenant Theology* (Grand Rapids, Baker Book House, 2001), 206–9, there is a strong connection between justification and good works dating back to the very beginning of the Reformed tradition, and found quite clearly in the writings of Hieronymus Zanchius, Johannes Piscator and Francis Turretin (one of JE's favorite polemical theologians).

in the affair of human salvation.[7] He never defined it succinctly. But he extends it further here, explaining in No. 1346,

> If God had not regarded fitness and propriety in the affair of man's salvation, the whole mediatorial scheme might have been set aside, or never have taken place. If free grace exercised in a way of mere sovereignty, without regard to propriety, was all that was requisite, there would have been no need of the means and methods provided for man's salvation in the admirable scheme which infinite wisdom hath contrived. Therein appears the wisdom of this method of salvation, viz. in the perfect propriety that is observed throughout the whole of the complicated scheme and the fit connection of one part with another, or of one thing with another, in everything belonging to this great salvation.

Justification comes by grace alone, but not solely by divine fiat. In God's providence, it is fitting that it should depend on the plan of salvation, require faith, and lead to good works.

It might be argued that, for Edwards, all of these themes fit together in his Trinitarian, typological view of reality. And while this theme is covered in part in the previous volume of Edwards' "Miscellanies,"[8] it bears repeating in conclusion here as well. Edwards devoted less than 1.5 percent of the matter printed below to a discussion of the Trinity per se. But throughout his notes for the *Two Dissertations* and magnum opus on redemption, not to mention his reflections on revelation and its types, Edwards suggests that all that is receives its existence from the eternal, Trinitarian fountain of Being. It becomes more real, good, true, and even beautiful, moreover, the further it returns to this glorious fountain and takes part in God's own life.

Because for Edwards God creates the world ex nihilo, "out of nothing," or out of nothing (Edwards would say) but God's own Trinitarian life, all that is reflects that life (to one degree or another), from the traditions of the "heathen" to the justification of the redeemed. Much of the race, Edwards lamented, will be cut off from the glory of God, suffering endless, horrid punishment for its sins. But while the damned will

7. See his use of this concept, for example, in his published sermon on justification. *Works, 19,* 147–242.

8. See the "Editor's Introduction" to *The Works of Jonathan Edwards, 20, The "Miscellanies," 833–1152,* ed. Amy Plantinga Pauw (New Haven, Yale Univ. Press, 2002); Amy Plantinga Pauw, *The Supreme Harmony of All: The Trinitarian Theology of Jonathan Edwards* (Grand Rapids, Eerdmans, 2002); and *Works, 11.*

languish forever in a diminished, discordant state, God will translate the people of faith—to use the idiom of Edwards' Bible—"from glory to glory."[9] Indeed, their union with the Trinity will intensify forever. Even heaven will be a place of eternal increase and expanding joy, a place where God will be "all in all" (that is, the ultimate antitype), and thus a place where earthly images and shadows of the divine will pale forever in the light and love of God. For Edwards, heaven stands as the utter fulfillment of all our earthly longings, a place where our spiritual senses will finally become satiated with God.[1] For as he portrayed it rather poignantly in No. 1296, it is the "garden of the universe," and a proper "palace of its infinitely glorious king." What is more, "[T]he alteration that was made in heaven at [Christ's] ascension, after his passion, though it was exceeding great and glorious, yet was but, as it were, the blossoming of the tree. But that which will be at Christ's second ascension, after the day of judgment, will be, as it were, the tree's bringing forth in ripeness and perfection, in all its branches, its lovely, sweet and abundant fruit."

Note on the Text

The entries in this volume take up the very end of Book 7 and the entirety of Books 8 and 9 of the "Miscellanies" manuscripts. Book 7 opens with No. 1069 and concludes with No. 1155. Its cover is constructed from a smooth brown ream wrapper that is not inscribed by Edwards, but notations in later hands read "Types of the O[ld] T[estament]" (a variation of the title of No. 1069, "Types of the Messiah") and "A Manuscript of the late Rev. Jonathan Edwards, President of Nassau Hall College, Princeton, New Jersey." There are also several notations in pencil: one is "X," indicating an inventory number assigned to the manuscript; another is "#1069 to 1155"; and still another is a comment beginning "Arguably . . . ," the rest having been rubbed away to the point that it is indecipherable. The paper is one infolded folio quire of 142 pages. Nos. 1153–55 are written on the last seven extant leaves of the notebook. No. 1153, separately paginated by Edwards, starts on L. 65. Two-thirds of L. 67, or the fifth and sixth pages of the entry, have been cut out, and the entirety of L. 71, which contained the conclusion of No. 1153 and the beginning of No. 1154, is missing (the text has been supplied from the nineteenth-

---

9. See JE's MS sermon on II Cor. 3:18 (72).
1. Cf. Paul Ramsey, "Heaven Is a Progressive State," in *Works, 8,* 706–38.

century copy of the "Miscellanies" at Andover Newton Theological School). The ink that Edwards used throughout Book 7 varies from dark to medium brown, with the exception of the first paragraph of No. 1155, which is gray.

Book 8 contains Nos. 1156–1253. It has a cover made from a coarse brown ream wrapper, which was inscribed "VIII" by Edwards twice on the front and back. Other inscriptions on the cover in other hands include, on the bottom front, "For Dr. Edwards, New Haven," and on the top front, upside down, "Reverend Jonathan Edwards, New Haven." Beside this address, Jonathan Edwards, Jr., wrote the following entry numbers: "1194, 1241, 1243, 1249." The pages are made of a single infolded quire of forty-six folio leaves. Edwards paginated the first entry, No. 1156, 1–10, and a later owner of the manuscript paginated the remaining pages 11–92. The inks in the book alternate between dark brown and black. The handwriting is generally good, especially for those entries consisting of excerpts from various sources. One characteristic of the orthography that stands out in this notebook is Edwards' use of capitalized words and phrases within the entries to signal content, a device he uses with increasing frequency in the "Miscellanies" and other late notebooks, perhaps as a visual cue and to help index their contents.

Book 9 is the final book of the "Miscellanies." It has several unique qualities. In contrast to the previous books in the series, mostly folios with covers, it is quarto in size and lacks a cover. In its present state, the volume consists of a series of stacked, infolded quires of twelve leaves each. The paper that became Book 9 was originally one large quarto volume, bound and ruled in double columns. Edwards obtained the volume from an unidentified owner, whose entries appear at the bottom of some pages. To compose his own entries, Edwards turned the pages upside down. He numbered the pages up through p. 1140. Some blocks of pages are missing, though they do not affect the continuity of the extant entries. The current pagination runs 1–184, 687–708, 785–92, 801–1140, with a single blank, unnumbered leaf at the end. Following many entries are one or more blank leaves, indicating that Edwards intended to add to them. The last entry he numbered was No. 1346, on p. 182 of the notebook; the remaining materials were later supplied with entry numbers by Edwards, Jr., which is why in this edition entry numbers after No. 1346 appear in square brackets. The inks in Book 9 vary between dark brown and black. The writing is angular and spiky—characteristics of Edwards' late hand. Here, too, we see another device Edwards used late in life: writing the chapter numbers of books of the Bible in capital roman numerals (perhaps a way to distinguish more easily between chapter and verse numbers).

The materials that make up entry Nos. [1347] through [1360] have several distinctive aspects. First, they all have running heads that not only identify the general topic of the entry but also vary according to the specific information on the pages—no doubt something Edwards did to help himself find his way around the often considerable amount of information. In this vein, Edwards also composed tables or indexes to several large entries, such as those on the divinity of Christ and extracts from *The Travels of Cyrus*. Finally, these late materials contain some of the lengthiest extracts that Edwards ever made from writings by other authors. Both the length of the passages that Edwards laboriously copied and the neatness with which he did it indicate that the books from which he copied were borrowed. Instances of extracted materials include No. [1350], from Skelton's *Deism Revealed;* No. [1351], from *The Travels of Cyrus;* No. [1355], from Ramsay's *Philosophical Principles;* and the longest, weighing in at fifty-five manuscript pages, No. [1359], from Cudworth's *True Intellectual System of the Universe.*

Edwards' wide-ranging textual engagement with various periodicals, pamphlets, and books provides a series of chronological benchmarks for the dating of these entries. The first benchmark is located in Nos. 1180 and 1181, comprised of quotes from Andrew Michael Ramsay's *The Philosophical Principles of Natural and Revealed Religion* (2 vols. Glasgow, 1748–49), as excerpted, respectively, in the March and April 1751 issues of *The Monthly Review.* No. 1184 contains a quote from Gilbert Tennent's *The Divine Government over All Considered . . . Preach'd June the 7th, 1752 . . .* (Philadelphia, 1752). A dating of no earlier than the latter half of 1752 for entry Nos. 1184 ff. is confirmed by the quote in No. 1200 from John Jackson's *Chronological Antiquities,* in *The Monthly Review,* for August 1752. Not many entries on, in No. 1227, Edwards quotes from Samuel Davies, *A Sermon, Preached before the Reverend Presbytery of New-Castle, October 11, 1752* (Philadelphia, 1753). This means that in more than two years' time, Edwards had written only about forty entries. Nor was his rate of production to improve over the next several years. No. 1277b briefly quotes from an extract of Voltaire's *History of Europe,* published in *The Monthly Review* of March 1754, and No. 1281 cites Richard Baxter on Rev. 14:13, as quoted in last volume of Philip Doddridge's *Family Expositor,* published in 1756. So, over the period of almost three years, Edwards wrote only about sixty entries.

Beginning in 1756, however, his activity soars. Between then and the end of his life (even though his final months were taken up with his new duties as college president), he adds approximately eighty entries—some of them the longest he had yet written—nearly the entire contents of Book 9. Toward the end of this furious spate of composition, Edwards quoted in No. 1358 from son-in-law Aaron Burr's *The Supreme Deity of Our Lord Jesus Christ, Maintained,* published in Boston in 1757. Roughly tallied, then, from 1751 to 1755 Edwards wrote about 100 entries totaling approximately 145 (mostly) folio pages, but in the 80 entries composed in 1756 and 1757 added some 560 octavo pages—double the output in less than half the time. Quantified in this manner, we can see that Edwards was not exaggerating when he described to the trustees of Nassau Hall the amount of work he had recently completed.

THE "MISCELLANIES,"
ENTRY NOS. 1153–1360

1153.[1] MORAL INABILITY. FREE WILL. SELF-DETERMINING POWER. The following positions may be laid down as most clear and evident relating to voluntary agents as subject to moral government:

There is no command given by God or men, or that ever is given by one intelligent being to another, that does directly and properly respect anything further than the disposition and acts of the will of that intelligent being that is commanded; i.e. nothing else by any command given to an intelligent, voluntary substance is directly and properly the thing commanded and required of that substance but such acts of its will. It is the soul, that is an intelligent substance, only that is properly commanded; that only is a capable subject of commands, for that being only is properly a capable subject of commands that is capable of perceiving commands given. But when in commands that are given to the soul nothing else is required by those commands but its own acts (for a command is to do something, i.e. to do something itself), a command is not given to one thing that another thing should do something. And though the actions of one thing may have respect to the actions or motions of another and have influence upon them, yet the [object of the command][2] directly and properly is the action of the thing commanded itself, and not the effects of its actions. Though the effects may be connected with the actions, all that a command given to an intelligent thing properly re-

---

1. One large quarto leaf (pp. 3–14 of the entry) and two thirds of another (pp. 5–6 of the entry), both of which contain parts of this entry as well as important cues to the order in which JE wanted the text arranged, have been cut out of the original MS. Fortunately, however, the Andover copy was made before this MS was mutilated. Further, much of the text is reproduced in *Freedom of the Will*, Pt. II, Sec. 5. What follows relies on the order of the Andover copy, but reproduces the text of the original MS wherever possible. Notice is given where the text follows that of the Andover copy.

There is a note in the margin of the original MS, written in JE's hand opposite the heading of No. 1152, that reads "see moral agency, p. 71." The reference is to JE's third (of three extant) MS notebooks on "Efficacious Grace." (JE's three-volume notebook series on "Efficacious Grace" was initially entitled "Moral Agency"; he changed the title to "Efficacious Grace" after publishing *Freedom of the Will*.) On p. 71, JE began a new section entitled "Natural Notions. Common Sense." See *Works, 21*, 265–66.

2. These words are supplied from the Andover copy.

spects as a command to a thing is what that thing should do or act. And therefore the commands that are given to the soul of man do properly respect or reach nothing further than the acts of the soul, and therefore respect nothing directly or properly beyond such and such acts of the will: for the soul itself has no other acts that are its own whereby to fulfill any command. And although the motions of the body follow the acts of the will by the law of nature, which the Creator has established, yet that don't make the motions of the body the acts of the soul. The acts of the will, therefore, only are properly the acts that are required by any command God gives us, for our actions and all our duties and performances that are required or commanded, so far as they are properly ours, are no other than such and such acts of the will.

Other things beside the habit and acts of the will are respected by the commands of God only indirectly, viz. as connected with the will. So far, therefore, as any good thing is connected with the will and its acts, so far, and so far only, is it the subject of a command, obligation or duty. And so far, and so far only, as any good exercise of the faculties of the soul or members of the body is not implied in or connected with the will and its acts, is it not the proper subject of a command or matter of our duty, but is what we are justly excused and free from; and that for that reason, and that only, because it is not implied in or connected with the good will, and so is not what we can be properly voluntary in.

Hence it follows that no other sort of inability to any action or performance, consisting in the exercise of the faculties of the soul or members of [the] body, renders that performance not properly the matter of a command or duty, but such an one as implies want of a connection between that action or performance and the disposition and act of the will. If there be any sort of inability to that good thing that does in no wise interfere with, hinder or stand in the way of a close, proper and immediate connection with or implication in the act of the will, then that sort of inability does in no wise hinder any good thing from being the proper subject matter of a command. And with respect to any command supposed to require any such performance, 'tis in vain for any to plead their inability and to say they can't do it unless they would if they could; for willing, as has just now been shown, is all the thing directly required of 'em. Let 'em perform this, let 'em exhibit the compliance of the will, and they have done their duty, and that which is all that is directly required of the soul in all commands whatsoever. And if there be anything else desirable that don't attend this compliance of the will and inclination, that don't prove to [be] implied in it or connected with it, from that they are excused. (See this position more particularly handled, p. 46).[3]

If there be any act or determination of the soul, or any exertion or alteration whatsoever prior to the act of the will, or any voluntary act in the case as it were directing and determining what the will shall be, that exertion or determination is not what any command does properly respect, because it is no voluntary act: because by the supposition it is prior to any voluntary act or act of the will, being that which determines the will in its acts and directs it how to act.[4]

If the soul is self-determined [in] its own acts of will (as some suppose), that determination is an act of the soul. For certainly it is an active determination that is supposed. And therefore if the act of the will be determined by the soul itself, it is determined by some antecedent act, or act prior to the particular volition directed and determined (see No. 1155).

If any say "No, there is no necessity of supposing that the soul's determination of the act of will is anything prior to the act of will itself, but the soul determines the act of will in willing, or directs its own volition in the very act of volition so that, in willing as it does, it determines its own will"—they that say thus can mean no more [than] that the soul's determination of its act of will is in the very time of the act of will itself, and not before it in order of time. But that does not make it the less before it in the order of nature, so that the particular act of volition should really be consequent upon it, as an effect is on the cause that it depends on. Thus that act on which determines the direction of the motion of a body may not be prior to the motion itself in order of time, but it may direct the motion of the body in moving it; but yet the action that determines the motion is not the less before the motion directed and determined in the order of nature, as that by which the determined motion is caused and on which it depends.

Nothing else can be meant but this by such an objection against the priority of the determination of the act of will to the act of will itself, unless any will say that the soul's determining its own act of will (and that the determination of the act of the will) is the very same with the act of will itself that is determined. But this is to talk nonsense. If the particu-

---

3. MS: "handled in the last paragraph, the next page," or the paragraph beginning, "From the things that have been already laid down and proved . . ."

4. JE directs himself to "next p[age] but three p. 6," but the top two-thirds of pp. 5–6 of this entry are missing; the next two and a half paragraphs are transcribed from the Andover copy.

lar act of will that[5] appears or comes into existence be something properly directed or determined at all, then it has some cause of its being in such a particular, determined manner and not another. And that determination or deciding what shall be the particular manner of its existence is not the very same with the thing determined, but something prior to it and on which it depends.

If there be any meaning at all in any talk about determining the will as to its acts, the meaning must be determining which way it shall act, or what the particular acts shall be, whether thus or thus. And this plainly supposes that there is some cause of the particular acts of the will, or some cause, ground or reason that the will is exerted this way and not the other, something that causally determines and decides which way the act shall be.

If the particular determined or precise act of will that exists is not consequent or dependent on something preceding determination and direction, or the determination of the act be nothing at all either preceding or diverse from the very act of will itself, then that particular act of will is an existence that has no cause, and so is no effect at all, but is absolutely something that has started up into existence without any cause, determination, reason or foundation of its existence; which is as great an absurdity as to suppose the world that had from eternity been nonexistent to start into existence all at once at a particular moment, absolutely without any cause. And besides, to insist and contend earnestly [for] the soul's determining its own acts of will, and then to say that its determination of its acts of will is the very same with the acts of will themselves, is to dispute and contend about nothing. For thus the dispute is not at all about the reason or ground of the acts of will, or any of the souls acts; but what is contended for it seems come to no more than this: that the soul wills what it wills and determines what it determines, or that the mind acts what it acts and that it has those acts that it has, and is the subject of what it is the subject of; or what is, is.

But no command does properly, directly and immediately respect any action or exertion whatsoever but that which is voluntary: for what a command requires is that the will of the being commanded should be conformed to the will of him that gives the command. What a command has respect to and seeks is compliance and submission. But there is no compliance, submission or yielding in that which is not voluntary. Hence 'tis plain that if there be any sort of act or exertion of the soul prior to its

---

5. The original MS resumes here.

acts of will, or voluntary acts directing and determining those acts of the will, they cannot be subject to any command. If they are properly subject to commands and prescriptions at all, it must be only remotely, as those prior acts and determinations are connected with and dependent on some acts of the will in the soul prior to them. But this is contrary to the supposition: for it is supposed that these acts of the soul are prior to all acts of the will, all acts of the will being directed and determined thereby.[6]

But if any shall insist that the act of the soul—that is, in determining its own acts of will—is subject to the command of God, that that determining exertion or directing act that directs the consequent volition is either obedience or disobedience to the command of God, I desire such persons to consider that, if there be any obedience [in] that determining act, it is, to be sure, obedience wherein the will has no share; because, by the supposition, it precedes each act of the will, because each act depends on it as its determining cause and, therefore, it is wholly an involuntary act; so that if, in these acts, the soul either obeys or disobeys, it obeys and disobeys wholly involuntarily—it is no willing obedience or rebellion, no compliance or opposition of the will. And what sort of obedience and rebellion is this?[7]

It will prove according to all schemes that the necessity, negative or positive (i.e. the necessity or impossibility), of such acts of the will as are fit and proper to be in such a nature as man's, and not beyond the capacity of his faculties, don't render them improperly the subject matter of prescription and command—if by necessity be meant only a prior certainty, determination or fixedness. For even according to the scheme of those that hold what they call[8] a sovereignty of the will, and hold that the soul determines its own volitions or acts of will, if this be true in any proper sense, then there is some act of the soul prior to those volitions that it determines: for the soul's volitions, by this supposition, are effects of something that passes in the soul—some act or exertion of the soul prior to the volitions themselves—directing, determining and fixing the consequent volition. For, according to them, the volition is a determined effect; and if it be, it is determined by some act, for a cause lying perfectly dormant and inactive does or determines nothing any more than that which has no being.

---

6. JE here has a cue to "p. 13" of the entry, which is part of a missing leaf. The passage that follows has been transcribed from the Andover copy.

7. The original MS resumes here.

8. MS: "called."

Whatever determines the acts of the will, yet the acts of the will themselves, being determined effects or effects decisively fixed by some prior determining cause, the acts themselves must be necessary. And whatever that be that determines or decides what these acts shall be, whether the soul itself or something else, it alters not the case, as to the acts themselves being fixed and necessary events. The determination of the act of will must be prior to the act determined, as has been demonstrated. And by the supposition of the act of the will being determined by it, it is dependent on it and necessarily consequent upon it. If it be wholly determined by it, as it is by the supposition, then it is wholly dependent on it and altogether necessarily consequent upon it. If the acts of the will are determined by any cause whatsoever deciding what they shall be, and ben't events absolutely without any cause, then there is a fixed connection between these effects and their cause. As when we [see] a body in a motion in a particular direction: if that direction of motion ben't absolutely without a cause, something has determined the motion to such a course, and the direction of motion depends and is necessarily connected with the preceding action of something that gave the moving body that direction. And whether we suppose the moving body to determine the direction of its own motion or to be determined by something else, it alters not the case as to the dependence of the effect itself on its cause, or of the direction of motion on the determination or determining act by which it is decided.

So that, according to the scheme even of those that hold a sovereignty of the will in this sense, the volitions and acts of the will themselves are all determined effects, fixed by something preceding; and so, in the sense that has been spoken of, are either necessary or impossible. See book on the Freedom of the Will, p. 53, § 2.[9] See Chubb, p. 389, a little past the middle ("self-determining power becomes a necessary cause," etc.).[1] And again, if any are in that scheme that[2] the acts of the will don't come to pass by any determining or directing cause at all, but arise purely accidentally, yet still they are necessary as to the soul that is the subject. For if the soul be subjected to chance after this manner—that its voli-

---

9. Not a reference to the published treatise but to a MS notebook, no longer extant. JE often kept a series of temporary notebooks in which he roughed out the material in his major treatises. In this as in other cases, JE discarded the notebook material after publishing *Freedom of the Will*.

1. "Treatise XXVIII. Eight Discourses, viz. I. Some Farther Reflections on Natural Liberty . . . ," in Thomas Chubb, *A Collection of Tracts, on Various Subjects* (London, 1730), p. 389.

2. Read "wherein."

tions arise by pure accident, without any determining cause whatsoever—then to be sure the soul has no hand in them, and neither causes nor prevents them, but is necessarily subjected to what chance brings to pass from time to time; as much as the earth that is inactive is subject to what falls upon it and necessarily without what falls not upon it. That which is by chance, without dependence on any determining cause, is by the supposition not caused nor hindered by any determination of the subject of it, nor can be so far as it is by chance, without dependence on a determining cause (see Paper of Minutes, No. 4, pp. 8–9).[3] So that it is evident to a demonstration on all suppositions that, if the volitions or acts of the will of any creature are ever properly the subject matter of duty, prescription or command, merely the necessity or impossibility of these volitions in that sense, that their being or not being is determined by a prior certainty and fixation, does not hinder any of those volitions— that are proper to be in a thing of such a nature as man's soul—from being properly the matter of divine prescription and command.

Hence it follows that no inability to any good act of will that don't consist in any incapacity of the human nature and faculties to be the subject of such an act, but amounts to no more than such a kind of negative necessity, certainty and fixation as has been spoken of, either through an unsuitable and hateful aversion already fixed and settled, or any other cause that don't bring such a necessity by making the volition impossible, by rendering the thing required such as the faculties of human nature are not capable to be made the subjects of, but only by determin-

---

3. Probably a reference to the notebook entitled "The Doctrines [of] the Word of God, Especially [the . . .] Justice [and] Grace of God, Explained and Defended, and the Contrary Errors That Have of Late Prevailed Confuted," otherwise known as the "Gazeteer Notebook" because it was made from pages of *The Gazeteer* weekly newspaper. The pertinent entries on pp. 8–9 read:

FREE WILL. SELF-DETERMINING POWER.

Corol. Seeing it is so, that this necessity or certainty of the acts of will not being at all inconsistent with our freedom and moral agency, and our being properly the subject of commands and rewards and punishments with respect to these acts of [the will], hence it follows that our freedom, moral agency, etc., are not inconsistent with the absolute decrees of God determining these acts of will, and with absolute election, etc.

Another *Corollary*, showing that as it is not inconsistent with commands {and rewards and punishments with respect to these acts of the will}, so not with offers, calls and invitations. And that therefore that the absolute decrees of God are not inconsistent with such offers, calls, etc. [. . .]

According to the usual meaning of the word POWER, if persons have a thing in their choice, they have it in their power.

ing the will against it—I say, it follows from what has been said that no such sort of inability to any good act of the will does in any wise render it improperly the matter of divine prescription and command. For that is what I have just now shown: that an act of the will's being either necessary or impossible in that sense, merely that the act of the will or the absence of the act is certain by some determination and fixation, don't make it the less the matter of divine prescription.[4]

Hence, that the absolute decrees of God's foreordaining or predetermining the volitions of men are in no wise inconsistent with God's moral government—as exercised with respect to those volitions, as commanding or forbidding, rewarding or punishing them—I say, absolute decrees are not inconsistent with those merely because they infer such fixation and certainty of those volitions. If they are inconsistent with such a divine moral government with regard to those volitions, it must not be on account of such a certainty or necessity, but on some other account. For it has been now proved that such a necessity of particular volitions does not render such volitions or acts of the will not properly the matter of duty, and so of prescription and command, and consequently of the proper enforcements of commands and sanctions of law.[5]

From the things that have been already laid down and proved, it also follows that, as to those things that are not the subject matter of duty and commands directly (as the dispositions and acts of the will themselves), but only indirectly (as other good actions and performances of the human nature, consisting either in any exercise of the faculties of the soul or motions of the body), no other sort of inability to them renders them improperly the subject matter of prescription and command, but only that inability that consists in the want of connection between them and those good acts of the will that are proper to be in such a nature as man's, and are fit exercises of his faculties. For it has been already shown that those good acts of the [will] that are proper to be in such a nature as man's, and not beyond the capacity of his faculties, are[6] the proper matter of command. And it has also been already shown that all such things as are connected with such acts of the will, are also properly the subject matter of command. Therefore certainly it follows that those things only that are not connected with such acts of the will are not the proper matter of command; and this implies that no other sort of inability to them

4. The original MS stops here. The passage that follows has been transcribed from the Andover copy.
5. The original MS resumes here.
6. MS: "or."

but such as implies a want of such connection, makes 'em to be not the proper subjects of command. So that, if there be anything that man is supposed to be required to do—any exercise, affection or exertion of mind that he is required to have, or any outward deed that he is required to perform—that he may in any sense be said to [be] unable to [do], that don't excuse him or render the thing not properly the matter of his duty and prescription to him, unless the inability be such as implies a want of connection between that thing and the good act of will that is properly required of him. So that he may properly have that good act of will fully exerted and yet can't do the thing required, there being no connection between his will and the performance. If there be the good act of will that is properly required and fully exerted, and the performance ben't connected and don't follow, then the man is excused, but otherwise not.

Again[7] it is further evident that, if there be some act of will about the performance required that the performance don't prove to be connected with—so that, in some kind of sense, the person may be said to be willing to do it or to desire to do it, and can't—yet is he not excused unless his act of will be a properly good act, and that act relating to this thing that is properly required of him. If there be some sort of act of will about it that the performance is not connected with, that don't at all excuse the man for want of the performance, as long as the good act properly required is absent which, if it were present, the performance would be found to be connected with it. For if this other act of will don't excuse for the want of the proper act required, no more can it excuse for the want of the performance that is connected with the proper act required. For it is the connection of the performance with this proper act, and that only, that causes our duty to be concerned in it, and not its connection with some other act of the will that is diverse from the proper act required. And therefore 'tis the want of a connection with this proper act of the will, and not its want of connection with some other act diverse from [this proper act], that causes our duty not to be concerned in it.

Thus, for instance, if an old, notorious drunkard, that is under the power of a violent and invincible appetite after strong [drink], be supposed to be commanded entirely to forsake his drunkenness and required so to do under pain of eternal damnation, and has some kind of willingness to forsake this vice (i.e. his reason tells him that the pain of eternal damnation will be so great an evil that it will far more than coun-

---

7. There is a note here in the margin of the original MS, written in JE's hand, that reads "see moral agency, p. 71." See above, p. 39, n. 1.

tervail all the pleasure or good that he shall have from this vice, and therefore [he] wishes he could forsake it), but his actually forsaking it don't prove to be connected with such a sort of act of will, this don't excuse him unless this be the proper act of will that is required of him relating to this matter. But the act of will required of him be not such an indirect willingness, which is not so properly a willingness to do the thing commanded to be done as a willingness to escape the punishment threatened; but the act of will required of him be a proper, direct and full willingness actually to forsake this vice and all those deeds that belong to it. If this be the volition required, and he has this, and the performance don't prove to be connected with it, then is the man excused, but not otherwise. Or we will suppose the violent lust the man is under the invincible power of, is not any sensitive appetite, but some unreasonable malice and an insatiable, devilish malignity of spirit against some excellent and most worthy person, and very highly deserving of him; and the thing required of him under pain[8] of damnation is to leave off injuring that person; and he finds the same sort of willingness to it that in the forementioned instance the drunkard has to[9] forsake his cups; because the first performance does not prove to be connected, it does not at all excuse him, because his willingness is no proper, direct and full willingness actually to comply with the command.

The case is the same and equally evident, and the evidence more direct and plain, if the thing required be not any external performance that is connected with some act of the will, but only the act of the will itself, or some good compliance of the heart, that is properly required of him. According to the foregoing positions, if[1] this act of the will required be wanting, but yet there is some other indirect act of the will which[2] the person, to escape punishment, or on some foreign considerations, is willing to will or wishes he was willing, but yet remains without the proper act of will required, his indirect willingness in such a case cannot excuse the want of the proper willingness that is required.

As for instance, suppose a man has a most amiable and agreeable and every way deserving woman for his wife, and be required to love her and

---

8. The original MS stops here. The passage that follows has been transcribed from the Andover copy.

9. Andover copy reads: "so."

1. The Andover copy originally read "and" here. An editor, probably Sereno Dwight himself, changed "and" to "if."

2. The Andover copy originally read "about by" here. An editor changed the words to "which."

choose her above all other women, or to love her in the choice and ac-
quiescences of his will, as relinquishing all other women; but he instead
of this is overpowered by a violent lust towards some vile and notorious
strumpet, whereby he has his heart alienated from his wife, and has no
delight in her, but an aversion to her; but yet he is sensible that its being
with him as it is in this respect is like to prove the utter ruin of himself
and his family, and therefore wishes it was otherwise—he wishes that he
loved his wife as well as he does his whore, and that his heart cleaved to
her with so full a choice and entire compliance that he could have as
much pleasure and delight in her as in the other. His indirect willingness to cleave in his love and choice to his wife does not[3] at all excuse
him for the want of actual love and choice.

Or if a child has an excellent father, that has ever been kind to him
and has every way in the highest degree merited the respect, honor and
love of his child, and this child be commanded by God to love and honor
his father, but he is of so vile a disposition that he, notwithstanding, in-
veterately hates him; but notwithstanding, being sensible that his hatred
of his father will prove his ruin by his father's disinheriting him or otherwise, wishes it was otherwise, but remains still under the invincible
power of his cursed dispositions and so in a settled hatred of his father:
his indirect willingness to love and honor his father don't excuse for the
want of the actual compliance of his heart with the duty required of him
towards his father.

And further, we will suppose [the] thing required be that a man make
choice of God as his highest portion and chief good, or that his heart
should cleave to Christ Jesus and acquiesce in him as his Savior, his guide,
his Lord and best friend. And, through fear of damnation as the consequence of the want of such an act of will or choice of heart, he wishes he
could find it in himself, but yet remains destitute of it. That indirect willingness he has don't at all excuse him for the want of the proper act of
will required.

It is further evident that such an indirect willingness as has been spoken of can't at all excuse for the want of that good act of will that is required, provided that good act of will be properly and fitly required
(which is a thing supposed), for this reason: that this other indirect willingness don't answer the command fitly given, or (which is the same
thing) it don't answer the man's duty. If the man's duty is not answered
by what he does, then what he does don't excuse or acquit him. For 'tis

---

3. The original MS resumes here.

his doing something that answers the obligation only that acquits him with respect to that obligation, and not his doing something else that does not answer it. But now this other indirect willingness don't answer the man's duty or satisfy the command that requires of him another willingness quite diverse from that.

And as to such good acts of the will or exercises of the heart as have been mentioned, viz. a man's making choice of God as his portion and highest, his heart's cleaving to Christ as a most excellent Savior, or any other holy exercises of the will, inclination or affection that are proper to be in the heart of man: it will further appear that such an indirect willingness to these things as has been spoken [of], or their wishing through fear of punishment they could exercise such a will and disposition, but find themselves unable—i.e. they don't find such exercises to be connected with such wishings and wouldings—I say, it will further appear that such a willingness or desire for these things cannot excuse for the want of them, or at all acquit the person that remains destitute of them, let his willingness and desires through such fear be never so true and real, and so in that respect sincere. Because if they excuse and acquit the person, it must be on one of these two accounts: either, 1. because these desires are in effect the thing required; or, 2. that there is that virtue or goodness in them that balances the goodness and virtue of the thing required, and so countervails the want of it.

As to the first of these, that these indirect desires from foreign considerations are not in effect, the same thing that is required has been observed already as contrary to the supposition. And therefore if such a willingness excuses persons, it must be on the other account, viz. that there is some virtue or goodness in such an indirect willingness to balance the goodness of the exercise required, or countervail the want of it. A willingness to do a good thing required of us can't countervail the want of that good thing unless it be a good willingness. If there be no true goodness or virtue in it, then certainly it has nothing to countervail the want of true goodness and virtue. A kind of willingness that is not truly a good willingness can't excuse for the want of a good willingness.

Supposing a son is possessed by a most inveterate enmity against a wealthy and excellent father that is so great as hinders his behaving towards him as a dutiful child, which provokes his father to shut up his hand towards [him] who otherwise might have his pockets full of money; supposing also the son to be a person of violent and impetuous lust, but is not under advantage to gratify his lust, not having money to spend upon his whores by reason of the penury which his undutifulness brings upon him, which causes him to wish that his heart was otherwise towards his father; but yet so rooted and vehement is his devilish malignity of spirit towards his honorable father that he still remains under the power and government of it: I suppose that that desire or willingness that he has to love and honor his father (though he sincerely, i.e. really and truly, desires it for that end, that he may gratify his violent lust) don't at all excuse the want of that love or countervail his remaining enmity. And the plain reason is that there is no virtue or goodness in it to make up for the want of the virtue required, or countervail the badness of his enmity. This is the proper reason. And, therefore, if he had the same indirect willingness, [or] some other from a principle not so heinous as this, yet if it was from no good principle and so it was a willingness that had no goodness in it, still it would not at [all] excuse or countervail for the want of the goodness required, and that because the reason holds good, viz. that there is no goodness at all in the willingness and, consequently, nothing at all to countervail the defect of goodness, and so no excuse at all.

Sincerity[4] and reality in this willingness don't make it the better. That which is real and hearty is sincere, whether it be in virtue or vice. Some persons are sincerely bad and others are sincerely good. Others may be sincere and hearty in things in their own nature indifferent; but being sincere and hearty and in good earnest is no virtue, unless it be in a thing that is virtuous. A man may be sincere and hearty in subscribing to a covenant offered him by a crew of pirates or gang of robbers, obliging himself to join with them, and yet there be no virtue in his sincerity. The devils are sincerely and heartily willing and desirous to be freed from the torments of hell, but this don't make their will or desires virtuous.

And as an having a real, sincere and hearty willingness to one's duty don't make his willingness to be virtuous, or such as can excuse him in a defect of compliance with any supposed duty unless that willingness be from a good principle, so it is with endeavors arising from such a will. The endeavors have no more goodness in them than the will that the endeavors arise from. If a young man that hates his father (as was represented before) from the violence of lust, and that he may be under advantage to gratify that, is willing to love his father, his willingness has no goodness in it, nor can excuse for the want of the required love. And if from such a willingness he endeavors to love his father, neither have his endeavors—though as sincere as his willingness—any virtue in them, or

---

4. Compare the following section on sincerity to *Freedom of the Will*, Pt. III, Sec. 5, in *Works*, *I*, 312–19.

excuse for the want of the required love, any more than his willingness. The endeavor, considered as the act of the willing agent, can't be any better than the will it proceeds from. For his endeavor is no further his act than as it is an expression of his will. But certainly there is no more goodness or virtue in the exercises and expressions of a will than there is in the will itself that is exercised and expressed. And therefore the sincerity of endeavors, or a person's truly endeavoring a thing and doing what they can from a real willingness to obtain the thing they endeavor for, don't render those endeavors at all virtuous unless that will itself that the endeavors proceed from (the reality of which denominates the endeavors sincere) be virtuous, and can't excuse a person in the defect of the thing endeavored for any more than the will itself.

The devils that possessed the Gadarene were doubtless really afraid Christ was going to torment 'em, and were sincerely willing to avoid it. And if we also suppose they were sincere in their endeavors to avoid it when they cried, "Thou Son of God most high, we beseech thee, torment us not" [Luke 8:28], these endeavors, however sincere, had no more virtue in them than the will they proceeded from. And if we suppose they did whatever they could in their endeavors, still it alters not the case.

That such indirect desires and wishing from mere fear and self-love—and from no other principles than are as much in the hearts of devils and angels—han't any virtue or goodness in them to be a balance[5] for the goodness of those holy exercises of heart required, though never so real and sincere, is easily proved. (Here largely show the evidence of this, if ever I should write anything on this subject to be published.) Their being sincere alters not the case, unless a being sincerely afraid of hell is[6] a virtue. The sincerity of the act don't make it virtuous unless the sincerity of the principle makes it virtuous.

SINCERITY.

From what has been said, it is evident that persons' endeavors, however sincere and real, and however great, and though they do their utmost, unless the will that those endeavors proceed from be truly good and virtuous, can avail to no purposes whatsoever with any moral validity, or as anything in the sight of God morally valuable (and so of weight through any moral value to merit, recommend, satisfy or excuse, or make

5. MS: "to ~~Balance be a Ba~~ that ~~that~~ be a Balance."
6. MS: "being."

up for any moral defect), or anything that should abate resentment or render it any way unjust or hard to execute punishment for any moral evil or want of any moral good. Because, if such endeavors have any such value, weight or validity in the sight of God, it must be through something in them that is good and virtuous in his sight. For surely that which in his sight is good for nothing, is in his sight wholly and entirely vain and without any positive moral value, weight or validity, and can have no weight at all in a moral sense, positively and properly; though there may be something negative in it, as through those endeavors persons may avoid some positive evils that otherwise would be committed, and so may in some respects avoid incurring further guilt. As he that saves his neighbor from drowning, not from love to him, but merely from covetousness and because his own interest is concerned: though what he does is nothing good in the sight of [God], yet hereby he avoids the greater guilt that would arise in the sight of God through such a degree of murder as he would actually be guilty of, if he should stand by and see him drown when he could easily help him. Here see No. 5, p. 54.[7]

There is an exceeding great and unknown deceit arises from the use of language, from the great ambiguity of the word *sincere*. Indeed, there is a vast indistinctness, unfixedness and ambiguity in most (or at least very many) of the terms that are used to express those mixed modes (as Mr. Locke calls them)[8] that appertain to moral and spiritual matters, whence arise innumerable mistakes, strong prejudices, and endless controversy and inextricable confusion.

The word *sincere* is commonly used to signify something good and virtuous. Men are habituated to such an understanding of it, so that the expression, whenever it is used, excites that notion, and naturally suggests something to the mind that is indeed very excellent; much the same with the words *honest* and *upright*. Yea, something more we conceive by it: not only something that is honestly and truly good, and good in the sight of him that sees not only the outward appearance but the heart, but also good with all the heart and from the bottom of the heart. And therefore men think that if a person be sincere in his endeavors to do his duty or

7. The reference is unclear. It may well be to a MS series of notes that no longer survives, or to a fifth notebook in the series on "Moral Agency," of which only the first three are extant (published in *Works*, 21).

8. John Locke's notion of "mixed modes" was developed beginning in the first edition of his *Essay Concerning Human Understanding* (London, 1690), II, xxiii. Much has been written concerning JE's use of Locke, but see especially *Works, 6*, 15–18, 24–26 and, on mixed modes, 359–60.

to obtain any moral qualification that is supposed to be requisite, he is altogether to be justified, and it would be hard and unreasonable to blame him, much more to punish him, for being unsuccessful. For to say he is thus sincere suggests to the mind as much as that his heart and will is good. There is no defect of duty as to his virtuous inclination. He honestly and uprightly desires and endeavors to do as he is required. His will and heart fully comply with his duty, but only the thing supposed to be required don't prove to be connected.

Whereas it ought to [be] observed that the word sincere has these different significations:

First. Sincerity, as the word is often used, signifies no more than reality of will and endeavor with respect to anything that is professed or pretended, without any consideration of the nature of the principle or aim whence this real will and true endeavor arises. If the man has some real will or desire to obtain a thing, either direct or indirect, or does really endeavor after a thing, he is said sincerely to desire it and endeavor it, without any consideration of the goodness and virtuousness of the principle he acts from and the excellency of the end he acts for. What is meant by the man's being sincere in his desire or endeavor is no more than that the appearance and show there is of a desire or endeavor is not a mere pretense and dissimulation, when indeed he don't at all desire or endeavor the thing that he pretends to. Thus a man that is kind to his neighbor's wife that is sick and languishing, is very helpful in her case and makes a show of desiring and endeavoring her restoration to health and vigor, and not only makes such a show, but there is a reality in his pretense—he does heartily and earnestly desire her restoration and uses his true and utmost endeavors for it—he is said sincerely to desire and endeavor it because he does so truly, though perhaps the principle he acts from is no other than a vile and scandalous lust, he having secretly maintained a criminal intercourse and lived in adultery with her, and earnestly wishes for her restored health and vigor, that he may return to his criminal pleasures. So a man may be said sincerely to hate his neighbor that don't merely pretend to it. Or,

Secondly, by sincerity is meant not merely a reality of will and endeavor of some sort or other, and from some consideration or other, but a virtuous sincerity. That is, that a man, in performing those particular acts that are the matter of virtue or duty, there is not only the reality of the matter or thing to be done, but also the reality of the form and essence of the virtue [that] appertains to it, consisting in the aim that governs the act and the principle that is exercised in it. There is not only the reality of the act that is, as it were, the body of the duty, but also the soul that should properly belong to such a body, or those inward principles wherein consists the real virtue that properly should belong to the act. In this sense a man is said to be sincere when he acts with a pure intention, not from sinister views or for by-ends. He not only in reality desires and endeavors after the thing to be done or the qualification to be obtained, but he wills the thing directly and properly, as neither forced nor bribed. His choice is free in the matter. He seeks it as virtue and chooses it for its own [sake], as delighting in virtue, so that not only the thing itself in the matter of it, upon some account or other, is the object of the willing, but the virtue of the thing is properly the object of the will.

In the former sense, a man is said to be sincere in opposition to a mere pretense and show of the particular thing to be done or exhibited, without any real desire or endeavor at all. In the latter sense, a man is said to be sincere in opposition to that show of virtue there is in merely doing the matter of duty, without the reality of the virtue itself in the soul and essence of it that there [is] a show of. A man may be sincere in the former sense, and yet in the latter be (in the sight of God, who searches the heart) a vile hypocrite; and his deeds and endeavors, though in some sort sincere, may before God [be] good for nothing and of no significancy or avail.

In the latter kind of sincerity only is there any true virtue, and this is the thing that in the Scriptures is called sincerity, uprightness, integrity, truth in the inward parts, and being of a perfect heart. If a man be sincere in his will, desires and endeavors in this respect, this is of some value in the sight of God. And if there [be] such a sincerity, and such a degree of it as there ought to be, and it be found that anything that might be supposed to be required is not connected with it, the man indeed [is] wholly excused and acquitted in the sight of [God]. His will shall surely be accepted for the deed, for such a will is all that is in strictness required of him by any command of [God], as we showed before. The commands of God given to any spiritual, voluntary being respect nothing else directly and properly but the habits and acts of the will. But as to the other kind of sincerity, of desires and endeavors: as was observed before, it being good for nothing in God's sight, is not accepted with him as[9] of any

---

9. The original MS breaks off here. The remainder of this entry has been transcribed from the Andover copy.

weight or value to recommend, satisfy, excuse, or counterbalance any good thing that is mentioned. See Bk. 1 on Free Will, p. 54.[1]

ABSOLUTE PROMISE TO NATURAL MEN.

Corol. 1. Hence we learn that there is nothing appears in the reason and nature of things—from the consideration of any moral weight or validity of that former kind of sincerity that has been spoken of—at all obliging us to believe, or leading us to suppose, that God has made any positive promises of salvation or grace, or any saving assistance, or any spiritual benefit whatsoever, to any endeavors, strivings, prayers, or obedience of those that hitherto have no true virtue or holiness in their hearts; though we should suppose all the sincerity and the utmost degree of endeavor that it is possible should be in a person without holiness.

SALVATION OF THE HEATHEN.

Corol. 2. Hence we learn that there is nothing appears in the reason and nature of things, as considering the things forementioned, that can justly lead us to determine that God will certainly reveal Christ and give the necessary means of grace, or some way or other bestow true holiness and saving grace, and so eternal salvation, to those heathen that are sincere (in the manner that has been explained above) in their endeavors to find out the will of the Deity and please him according to that light, that they may escape his future displeasure and wrath and obtain happiness in their future state through his favor.

1154.[2] FREE WILL. CONTINGENCY. SELF-DETERMINING POWER. If the volitions of the mind or its acts of will have any cause, then they are connected with their cause. For an event not to be dependent of a cause, or not to be connected with a cause, and to be without a cause, are all the same thing: for the very notion of causality consists in that dependence or connection that there is between cause and effect. If there be no such relation between one thing [and another], consisting in such a dependence of one thing on another and connection of one thing with the

---

1. Apparently a reference to "Efficacious Grace," Bk. 1. The passage on p. 54[–55] begins "Whitby's EXPOSITION OF TEXTS RELATING TO EFFECTUAL GRACE." See *Works, 21*, 213–14.

2. The leaf on which the first part of this entry was written has been cut from the original MS. The following transcription is based on the Andover copy.

other, that one thing is dependent on and connected with the virtue and influence of the other, then it is certain there is no such sort of relation between them as is signified by the terms cause and effect. So far as an effect is connected with its cause, so far it is the effect of that cause; so much causality is there in the case, and no more. The cause properly does bring to pass no more of any effect than is connected with it. If we say the connection be not total but partial, that the effect, though it has some connection with the cause, yet is not entirely connected with it, that is as much as to say that it is not all that is in the effect that is the effect of that cause, but part of it arises from thence and part some other way. To say that there are some effects which are not fully and certainly connected with those things that are actually their causes, is the same thing as to say that there are some causes that have actually an efficient power, and exertion of their powers, and yet that this power and exertion are not an effectual power and exertion. For by effectual we mean that which is actually sufficient, without any further[3] causality in the case, to produce the effect. And this surely supposes that,[4] on such a power and exertion of that power, the effect will certainly follow. Because if it does not follow, it proves in fact that there is not a sufficiency of power or exertion in the cause to produce the effect, which is contrary to the supposition.

Again, if there be nothing comes to pass that is not absolutely without any cause, then it will follow that there is a certain connection between cause and effect. Or (in other terms) it will follow that, if there be a cause that produces any effect, then that cause being put [in exercise], and precisely with the same power and the same exertion of power, and every way under same circumstances, will certainly evermore produce the same effect. For otherwise something[5] does or may come to pass that is absolutely without cause (which is contrary to the supposition); or particularly, this will or may come to pass absolutely without any cause or reason, viz. this difference that appears, viz. that this effect sometimes proves in fact[6] to allow the cause, and sometimes not, though the cause be the same, the power and exertion and circumstances of exertion all precisely and universally the same. See book on the Freedom of the Will, p. 51, last paragraph.[7]

---

3. Andover copy: "farther."
4. Andover copy: "that the effect."
5. Andover copy: "there will something."
6. Andover copy: "in fact sometimes."
7. Not a reference to the published treatise but to a MS notebook no longer extant. See above, p. 44, n. 9.

If[8] anything could come to pass at a particular time without a cause, I scruple not to affirm that it could not be foreseen. As for instance, we will suppose that till 5750 years ago there was no other being excepting the Divine Being; and then this world, or some particular body or spirit, all at once started out of nothing, without any concern of God in the matter, but absolutely without cause or any reason at all why it started into being then rather than sooner or later, or why such a thing came into being and not something else, why of such dimensions rather than less or greater, etc., or why anything should come into being at all. I say, if this be supposed, it will follow that such an event could not be fore-known. It could not be foreseen that such a thing would at that time come into being. It could not be foreseen that that thing would come into being rather than another, when there was absolutely no more reason why that should rather than another. It could not be foreseen that it should come into being at such a time rather than another, when there was absolutely nothing to give any superior weight or value to that moment to cause that to preponderate rather than any other with respect to that event.

Such a future event as has been supposed could not be known, because it would be absolutely in its own nature unknowable by the supposition, as some things can't be done because they are absolutely and in their own nature impossible. I call that absolutely and in its own nature impossible, which the greatest degree of strength supposable has no tendency to, and which no increase of strength makes any approach to. So I call that absolutely unknowable, to the knowledge of which the greatest capacity of discerning supposable has no tendency, and which no increase of discerning makes any approach to. But if something thus comes into existence absolutely, without any cause or anything prior as the reason why it should come into existence, its futurity is such a thing that no increase of discerning causes any approach or tendency to the knowledge of it. And that appears because a great degree of discerning has a greater tendency to the knowledge of things, or enables better to know things, no otherwise than [as] it enables better to discern the evidence of things. But an increase of discerning has no tendency to a discerning evidence where there is none. But in the case of the supposition before us, of a future existence that is absolutely without any reason why it should be, there is, even by the supposition, absolutely no preceding ev-

---

8. Original MS resumes.

idence of it. If there be no reason why such an existence should be rather than another, then all things at present are exactly equal and the same with respect to that and other supposed existences, and therefore there is at present no more evidence that that will be than something else that never will be. If there be at present no reason why that existence should be rather than another, then no reason can be seen why it should be rather than another. If there be at present some more evidence that that will be than another, that prevailing evidence consists in something. But this is contrary to the supposition: for by the supposition, at present all things are equal with respect to each, and there is nothing whatsoever preponderating with respect to either. If there be evidence at present of this futurity (as I said), the evidence consists in something, and therefore either consists in the thing itself or something else. If it be self-evident, then the evidence that now is of the future existence consists in the thing itself, is foreseen by the evidence there is in the thing itself. But this is contrary to the supposition, for it is supposed that the thing itself at present is not. There is no such thing at present in any respect for the evidence of it to be seen in it. And there is no evidence of it in anything else; for by the supposition, there is at present nothing else. For by the supposition there is nothing at all at present in existence that is in any respect whatsoever connected with it or related to it. And therefore there can be no evidence or proof or argument of it, for the very notion of proof or argument implies relation and connection with the truth proved or argued.

God, therefore, on this supposition, by his infinite capacity of discerning, can't discern any proof or evidence of this futurity, because there is none to be discerned. He can't discern it in himself, for by the supposition he is not the author of it, nor is any way concerned, nor is there anything in himself connected with it. He can't discern it in anything else, for there is by the supposition nothing else.

If anyone shall say that God by his omniscience can know things without evidence, I desire that he would consider again what he says. For to say that God knows things without evidence, is the same thing as to say that things are known to him without being evident to him, i.e. they are very clear, evident and certain when they are not at all evident. If things are evident to God, then he sees evidence of 'em; there is something that is evidence in his eyes, though it may be not in the eyes of others. But we may be sure that that which is evidence in his eyes is good and real evidence in its own nature. See Book concerning Free Will, at the beginning, but especially pp. 6 ff.[9] See Stebbing, p. 236, and Dr. Clark's *Demonstration,* Prop. 10.[1]

1155. FREE WILL. SELF-DETERMINING POWER. They that hold a self-determining power in the will, would be understood that the will is active in determining itself, or that it determines its own volitions by its own act. For they are strenuous in it that the soul is not merely passive [in] conversion and turning of the will to good, etc. They cry out of the Calvinists for making the man passive. They insist upon it that men are active in it, so that there is another act preceding the act of the will according to them.

Again, if the will determines the will, then the will in so determining itself does something; to determine the will is to do something. And therefore this determination is a doing or act of the will. So that here we have plainly an act of the will determining an act of the will, and the will determining all its own acts by some preceding act of its own, which is a contradiction; because this supposes an act of the will before the first act determining that. If the will determines its own acts by its own acts, then it determines its own volitions by its volitions. For if the will be determined by an act of the will, 'tis determined by a volition. That which [is] an act of the will, and not an act of the understanding or any other faculty, is a vo[lition].[2] Surely, every act of the will is a volition. See back, No. 1075[b].[3] See also [No. 1153,] p. 41.[4]

---

9. See above, p. 44, n. 9.

1. The reference is to Henry Stebbing's *A Treatise Concerning the Operations of the Holy Spirit Being the Substance of the late Reverend and Learned Dr. William Claggett's Discourse Upon That Subject, with Large Additions* (London, 1719), ch. XIV, which is a continuation of ch. XIII, "Of the evil Consequences which are supposed to follow from maintaining the Grace of God to be resistible." Stebbing writes, p. 236: "Now as to God, if it be the Principle of those Men [who support resistible grace], that he cannot foresee contingent Events, it is not ours; 'on the contrary, we believe (induced thereto by Reason and Scripture) that all Events are known to God, even those what depend upon the free Will of Man; and therefore that he knew that some would be converted, and who those were, altho' at the same time it was in the nature of the thing possible for them not to be converted.'" Stebbing, like JE, goes on to cite Samuel Clarke, *A Demonstration of the Being and Attributes of God: More Particularly in Answer to Mr. Hobbs, Spinoza, and their Followers* (London, 1705), Prop. X (pp. 150–221), where Clarke argues "That the Self-Existent Being, the Supreme Cause of all Things, must of Necessity have Infinite Power."

2. MS damage; part of the word has been rubbed away at the lower right-hand corner of the page.

3. *Works, 20,* 460.

4. MS: "see also the 11 page back &c.," i.e. the sixth and seventh paragraphs of No. 1153, beginning, "If the soul is self-determined [in] its own acts of will . . ."

1156. OBSERVATIONS ON THE AGREEABLENESS OF THE CHRISTIAN RE-
LIGION TO REASON.

It has elsewhere been observed how agreeable to reason the doctrines
of God's MORAL GOVERNMENT, A FUTURE STATE, THE END OF THE WORLD,
A FUTURE CONFLAGRATION, A DAY OF JUDGMENT, and A DIVINE REVELA-
TION are.[5]

'Tis most agreeable to reason that there is a future state of rewards and
punishment, wherein God will reward and make happy good men and
make wicked men miserable. And if there be a future state of happiness
to God's favorites, 'tis rational to suppose that this FUTURE STATE should
be ETERNAL, because otherwise God's greatest favorites, and those to
whom God gives the greatest rewards in another world, would in one respect have most to torment them, viz. the fear of death, the dreadful and
eternal end of that sweet happiness. The sweeter and more happy life is,
the more terrible death and the thoughts and expectations of it. 'Tis not
likely that God would add such a sting to the sweetest enjoyments and
rewards of his greatest favorites. 'Tis rational, therefore, to suppose that
the life he gives them after death is life eternal, life that is not to have an
end by another, worse death, consisting not only in the destruction of
the body but the abolition of the soul. God has not made man like the
brutes, who can't contemplate futurity and therefore have no alloy to
present enjoyments by the prospect of an end by death. And if it be so
that there be an eternal state of happiness in another world set before
us for us to seek after, then how rational are the Christian doctrines and
precepts of heavenly mindedness; weanedness from the world; behaving
as pilgrims and strangers on the earth; not laying up treasure on the
earth, but in heaven; selling all for the kingdom of heaven; not looking
at the things which are seen, which are temporal, but at the things which
are not seen, which are eternal. Hence also the reasonableness of Christian precepts of PATIENCE under SUFFERINGS, seeing these afflictions are
but for a moment in comparison of the duration of a future weight of
glory. See further, pp. 65–67.[6]

Since the doctrine of ORIGINAL SIN and the exceeding depravity and
CORRUPTION OF [HUMAN] NATURE is so agreeable to experience, and also
men's obstinacy in sin and folly under all manner of means, this makes
the doctrines of REGENERATION, and the SOVEREIGN GRACE OF GOD in it,

5. For previous "Miscellanies" entries on these topics, see "Table" in *Works, 13.*
6. MS: "p. 5." This reference is to the long passage beginning, "The doctrine of the gospel
concerning another and an invisible world," and ending "heirs of this inheritance."

exceeding rational. And seeing the extreme stupidity of mankind is so evident in a senseless[ness] of the amiableness of the Divine Being, the unreasonableness and hatefulness of vice, the reasonableness and excellency of virtue, the reality and importance of future and eternal things; and their sottishness and madness in their expectations of happiness here; and in the value that [they] set upon the vain things of this world: hence how rational is the doctrine of divine ILLUMINATION and the TEACHINGS of God's Spirit opening the blind eyes, turning from darkness to light, taking away the heart of stone and giving an heart of flesh, etc.

Since reason teaches that a divine revelation is peculiarly necessary to teach us a way of reconciliation with God after we have offended him by sin, this being a thing depending on God's sovereign pleasure, and so what strength and clearness of reason don't at all help to the discovery of; therefore 'tis the more reasonable to suppose that when a divine revelation is given, it should be very much taken upon about this, viz. about THE WAY OF A SINNER'S RECONCILIATION TO GOD AND THE JUSTIFICATION OF A SINNER, and that this should be very much THE SUBJECT OF THAT BIBLE that contains the divine revelation to mankind.

Since experience teaches that mankind in general is in a fallen and exceedingly depraved state, and there are many things also whence it may be argued that God has not utterly cast off mankind, but that he is reconcilable to sinful man, and that therefore there must be a revelation of the way of reconciliation; since 'tis also evident that all mankind are not actually reconciled, and comparatively but few, inasmuch as there [are] but few good men and most remain wicked; and since reason teaches that there must be a future, eternal state of rewards for the good, and that there must be some revelation to ascertain and declare this, that this reward may properly be set before men as God's promise and an enforcement of God's commands and an certain encouragement to the good under the difficulties and sufferings they meet with in the ways of virtue: 'tis also very rational to suppose that God in this revelation would appoint that those who are gathered out of this corrupt, polluted world and brought to true virtue, are reconciled to God and are interested in the eternal happiness of another world, should be UNITED in one HOLY SOCIETY or CHURCH; for in their moral state they are greatly distinguished and separated from the rest of the world, seeing they are united in so great and infinitely important an interest, wherein the rest of the world have no concern with them, seeing they must needs by their virtue and piety be greatly united in affection, and disposed to withdraw from the rest of the world and unite themselves one to another in a society by themselves for mutual intercourse and assistance in their common concern, their great business of the service of God and their great interest, since they are all as pilgrims and strangers on earth and since they all belong to one country, are of one kindred, as it were, being of one heavenly Father, and are engaged as soldiers to oppose the same enemies, the vices that prevail in the world, and to promote the same kingdom, viz. the reign of virtue.

If the Most High, by his gracious dispensation, brings a number of virtuous holy ones out of this corrupt, miserable world by a revelation of his will, so that virtue and goodness shall have an interest established and maintained in the world, 'tis fit it should have a visible interest and, to that end, that the virtuous and good should be gathered into a visible society.

How reasonable is the Scripture doctrine of ONE GOD and the other invisible heavenly beings that are concerned in the affairs of the government of the world, though beings of very great power and exalted dignity and different degrees and orders, having a diverse superintendency over the various parts of God's creation and over the affairs of mankind in particular, and over different countries and kingdoms, and so may be called thrones, dominions, principalities and powers; yet all his ANGELS, his mere servants, in perfect dependence on him and subjection to him, employed as ministers of his kingdom, servants employed by him in the administration of the affairs of his dominion, and those that are to fulfill and execute his will, and so that all divine adoration belongs to him alone. How much more rational is this than the old heathen notions of a multiplicity of gods or heavenly beings to be the joint objects of trust, dependence and divine adoration.

'Tis evident to reason that there is but one eternal, self-existent, independent, infinite Being, and that all other beings are his creatures, wholly receive their being from him and are upheld in being by him, and so are infinitely below him and are universally and perfectly dependent on him. 'Tis evident to reason that the whole creation is all the fruit of one single power, and of one wisdom, the contrivance of one design; and that the same design that contrived the whole for certain ends, governs it to those ends and continually orders and manages all the affairs of it to fulfill the purposes for which he contrived things in his creation. And therefore none of the inferior beings, who are all God's creatures, can properly in any respect be looked upon or respected as fellow governors of the world with the Supreme Being. They are not his assistants in governing the world; their power don't at all help him. They are not his counselors; he is not assisted by their wisdom; their contrivance and design is not joined with his. And therefore 'tis reasonable that they should not be sharers with him in our adorations, trust, and devotion of mind, and dedication of ourselves.

What we are to have respect to in our adoration, reliance and supplications is to that Will that governs and disposes, and not to others whose design, wisdom and will is not joined with him, whose wisdom and will is as dependent on the Supreme Being as ours, and who need the divine favor and the help of the divine wisdom and will as much as we, and [are] as much in his hands and at his disposal; are fellow creatures, at an equal distance, as entirely and absolutely dependent as fellow subjects and fellow servants, as much under authority and command; are fellow worshippers that should worship with as much humility, and who can do us no good but as servants and instruments of the Supreme Being, so that all the benefit we have by them is his kindness. If we are to adore these fellow creatures, and pray to them, and make humble supplication to them, and offer praises to them, etc., as well as the Supreme [Being], how is there any proportionable or suitable distinction maintained in the respect we show to them and him?

And besides, 'tis not reasonable that we should make these inferior beings the objects of adoration, invocation and praise, for we don't know them. We don't [know] who they be, if any of them have the special care or charge of us, of our families, cities or nation. We don't know who they are, nor what care they have of us, what power they have with respect to us, what subordinate dependence we have on them, what benefits we have received from them, or what they can do for us. Nor can we know how far their knowledge extends, whether they know our wants and desires, or whether they hear us when we pray to them or praise 'em.

As the Supreme Being has made the world, so he has made us. As he is the author of the whole system of the visible universe, so [he] is our author, who are the head and the end of the system to which the other creatures are subjected, and for which they are evidently made, contrived and ordered. He is the author of the frame of our bodies and the father of our souls, the author of their faculties. And he is our preserver and governor, and we live, move and have our being in him. And he is evidently our moral governor, as reason plainly teaches. And we are absolutely dependent on him, his power and wisdom, alone; are subject to his design and will. And 'tis he that orders all events concerning us. If he governs the rest of the system, in a more special manner does he govern us, and dispose all things that concern us, that are the head and end of the system. Therefore none of our fellow creatures should share with him in our adoration, self-dedication, dependence, prayer and praise.

The doctrine of the gospel concerning ANOTHER and an INVISIBLE WORLD, to which good men are to be transferred and where they are to have their inheritance and fixed abode, is most rational on this account: 'tis manifest that this visible world is corruptible in its own nature. Such is the nature and constitution of it, that it must come to an end. And 'tis unreasonable to suppose that the Creator would have it gradually to perish, languishing in a decayed, broken, miserable state through thousands of ages, gradually growing more and more wretched, before it is quite destroyed. Therefore 'tis reasonable to suppose that there will be a time wherein its Creator will immediately interpose to put the world to an end[7] and destroy it suddenly. And at that time, all the living inhabitants of the world that are not taken from it and translated to some other abode must perish and be destroyed in a very awful manner by the immediate hand of God, with most inexpressible manifestations of his mighty power and great majesty, which will have infinitely more dreadful appearances of divine wrath and fury than is in the most terrible thunderstorms or earthquakes.

And who can believe that at that time, when God in this manner immediately interposes, he will make no distinction between the good and virtuous, that are his favorites, and his enemies, that this awful destruction and great wrath shall come upon all alike. There will be no necessity of it from the course of nature, for at that time, by the supposition, God will put an end to the course of nature. God will immediately and miraculously interpose. The whole affair shall be miraculous, and by God's immediate hand. And therefore a miraculous deliverance of the good will not be at all beside God's manner of operation at that time. He can as easily and, without departing any more from the stated course of things, miraculously deliver the virtuous as he can miraculously destroy the wicked. Therefore we may well suppose that at that time when God is about to put an end to the frame of this visible universe, the virtuous will be translated into some other world, now invisible and beyond the limits of the visible world.

And if God designs thus to deal with all the good that shall be found

7. MS: "and."

alive on the earth at that time, how rational is it to suppose that he intends to deal in like manner with the good in all generations, that they all are translated into that distant, invisible world. Without doubt the world into which God will receive his saints when this corruptible world shall perish, shall be incorruptible. He won't translate 'em from one corruptible world to another, do so great a thing [as] to save 'em from one world that is to perish to carry 'em to another world that is to perish. Therefore they shall be immortal and have eternal life. And doubtless that world will be unspeakably better than this and free from all that destruction, [that] fleeting, fading, perishing, empty nature that attends all the things of this world; and their bodies shall be immortal and as secure from perishing as the world is to which they are translated.

This makes it most reasonable to suppose that good men in all ages are translated to that world: for why should so vast a difference be made between the virtuous that be of the last generation and the virtuous of all preceding generations, that they should be so distinguished from the wicked and so preserved when they perish, and should be received to a state of such pure, glorious and eternal happiness, and the virtuous of all preceding generations perish with the rest of the world, having no distinction in their death, but be equally exposed to the fearful ravages death makes in all its terrible forms from generation to generation, and equally exposed to the calamities of life while they live? Seeing there is a far distant and invisible world provided for some of the virtuous inhabitants of this world, 'tis reasonable to suppose that all the good shall have their habitation and inheritance together there as one society partaking of the same reward, as they were of the same race of mankind, and loved and served God and followed him in the same state here below, in the performance of the same duties, the same work, and under like trials and difficulties.

'Tis also hence rational to suppose that there should be a RESURRECTION of the bodies of the saints of all past generations. For from what has been observed before, 'tis the bodies of the saints of the last generation will be preserved from perishing with the world, and will be translated. And doubtless, if all the good of all generations are to have a like reward and are to dwell together in the same world in one society, they shall be in a like state partaking of a like reward.

Corol. Hence there must be some notice given of this invisible world of rewards to mankind on earth, and what way so rational as by DIVINE REVELATION, God's testimony and promise? And how reasonably is full credit to God's testimony and dependence on his promise required, and so LIVING BY FAITH and not by sight required of all the heirs of this inheritance. See back, p. 61.[8]

The reasonableness of the Scripture doctrine of a GENERAL PUBLIC JUDGMENT at the end of the world: "'Tis meet this judgment should be conspicuous, public and solemn. As men have been openly good or bad, so it is proper, they should meet with a public retribution. Men have sinned in privacy; have covered their lusts, their murders, their rapines, injustice and cruelties with secrecy; and have been instigated to their villanies, by hope of impunity. It is meet they should be disappointed, and have their enormities brought to light. The religious have been clandestinely so. Their prayers and alms, their penitence, humility, faith and patience, have been chiefly known to the Father of spirits. Hypocrites have been[9] passed for saints, and faithful worshippers have been stigmatized as hypocrites and villains. 'Tis meet there be a day of detection. That persons and hearts and actions should be laid open; and a public discrimination made betwixt him that served God, and him that served him not." *Religion of Jesus Delineated*, p. 118.[1] See also my sermons on this subject on Ps. 94:6–10.[2]

The reasonableness of that doctrine that JESUS CHRIST is appointed JUDGE of the world: "The Son of God has come and dwelt in this world of ours; [he] has come upon the high errand and office of an eternal redemption, in order to an eternal salvation. Here he was egregiously vilified and slighted; his person and ministry and works, reproached and rejected. Here he was ranked with notorious criminals, sceptered and crowned in scorn. Barbarously nailed and hanged on the cross, and ignominiously dispatched out of the world. And yet at the same time, he was Lord of life and glory: he purchased the world into his own hand; has died and rose, and lives again to be Lord of the dead and of the living. He is capable of judging the world in righteousness. He knows all persons, all hearts and minds, and all transactions of the world, from the beginning to the end. Reason then and equity will dictate, that he should be the judge. It is meet, that he should be publicly seen, that was so little known, while he was here. It is fit the world should see, who they have despised and disregarded: who it was, that came to redeem the world and be sacrificed for the life of it. It is meet, he should come to acknowledge his friends and give them leave to rejoice in him; to call his

8. MS: "p. 1," referring to the first two paragraphs of this entry.
9. Reynolds reads: "here."
1. [John Reynolds], *The Religion of Jesus Delineated* (London, 1726), 118.
2. JE's sermons on Ps. 94:6–10 are no longer extant.

implacable adversaries to an account, and render vengeance to those that would not obey him. 'Tis meet, that every eye should see him; even they that pierced him, and trampled upon his blood, and would not be saved thereby. Accordingly, this judgment has the Father committed to the Son, that he may right himself, and vindicate his cause, and teach men to honor the Son as they honor the Father. All hearts, and wills, and knees, will be ready to bow to him, in that day." *Religion of Jesus Delineated,* pp. 118–19.[3]

'Tis reasonable to suppose that if God should[4] give to mankind a revelation to teach him what virtue was suitable for such a creature as man in his exceeding corrupt, broken and miserable state, and such virtue and religion as would be the way for such to be acceptable to God, and the way to the happiness of such creatures—I say, 'tis reasonable to suppose that he should teach a different kind of virtue, consisting in a different sort of frame and exercise of heart, from the virtue which philosophers teach from their own reason. NATURE OF TRUE SAVING VIRTUE.

[The] reasonableness of the DOCTRINE OF THE RESURRECTION will appear, if we suppose that an union with the body is the most natural state of perfection of the human soul (which may be argued from that, [that] this was the condition in which the human soul was created at first), and that its separation from the body is no improvement of its condition, being an alteration brought on by "sin, and was inflicted on the transgressors, under the notion of evil, even expressly, as punishment, upon the forfeiture of a privilege; from whence we must conclude that the former state of union to the body was a better state than the disunion which was threatened. Sin introduced" that death that consists in "the separation of body and soul. [. . .] The state of innocency was embodied, the state of guilt was disembodied." Winder's *History of Knowledge,* pp. 59–60.[5] Therefore as Christ comes to restore from all the calamities which came from sin, 'tis most reasonable to suppose that he will restore the union of soul and body.

How reasonable to suppose that the salvation of the Messiah, which was to be a general salvation of mankind, should not be from particular evils or enemies, or the redemption of one particular nation, from Egypt or Babylon, but the general enemies and evils of all mankind and the

---

3. [Reynolds], *The Religion of Jesus Delineated,* 118–19.

4. MS: "should not."

5. Henry Winder, *A Critical and Chronological History of the Rise, Progress, Declension, and Revival of Knowledge, Chiefly Religious . . .* (2 vols. London, 1745–46), *1,* 60. On JE's ownership of Winder, see *Works, 15,* 45, n. 3.

general foundations and authors of all their evil, as sin and Satan. See papers on History of the Work of Redemption, vol. 1, pp. 1–2.[6]

The reason and fitness of CHRIST'S APPEARING IN THE WORLD IN SO LOW AND MEAN A CONDITION: "'Ut status Christi talis esset, qualis conspectus est' (verba sunt judiciosissimi Turretini, vol. II, Dissert. XII, § xii), 'id optime quadrabat cum scopo ipsius adventus, et religionis ab ipso instituendæ. Sane, si venisset, ut esset monarcha terrenus, alio longe cum adparatu prodire debuisset. Sed regnum ejus non fuit de hoc mundo (John 18:36). Venit, ut regnaret in animos non in corpora. Venit, ut homines avocaret à rebus terrenis et ad cœlestia exigeret. Venit, ut doceret virtutes difficillimas, patientiam, mansuetudinem, injuriarum tolerantiam, etc. Venit denique, ut nos Deo conciliaret, peccatumque aboleret sacrificio sui ipsius (Heb. 9:26). Quæ omnia non aliter melius quam per statum ejus humilem, mortemque probrosam, obtinere potuere.'" Alphonsus Turretinus, as cited by Stapferus, *Theolog. Polem.*, vol. 2, p. 1172.[7]

That if God intended to be gracious to mankind, who are apparently become corrupt and miserable; if he designed any such thing as a restoration, 'tis analogous to what is apparently God's manner in his providence that he appoint some PARTICULAR PERSON to be the SAVIOR and the instrument of so great good. 'Tis evident that it has ever been God's manner in other cases to bestow the greatest public benefits by particular persons. These have been the instruments of deliverance from great public calamities, from the oppression of enemies, and of raising nations and great communities to great worldly wisdom, honor and prosperity: for instance, from sacred history, in Noah, Joseph, Moses, the

---

6. This reference is to the first of three MS notebooks JE kept in preparation for his major, uncompleted work on the history of God's work of redemption. On pp. 1–2, JE argues that "The redemption out of Egypt, the most celebrated of all their [i.e. ancient Israel's] salvations, was remarkably attended with such circumstances as to show their need of a greater salvation, even a being saved from their sins, and to show that their great deliverance, and all other temporal salvations, are in vain without it."

7. "'That the status of Christ was such as it was perceived' (the words are those of the most judicious Turrentinus, vol. II, Dissert. XII, § xii), 'it fit best with the scope of his coming and of the religion to be instituted by him. Indeed, if he had come as an earthly monarch, he ought to have come from afar to another place with splendor. But his kingdom was not of this world (John 18:36). He came to reign over spirits, not bodies. He came to call men from earthly matters and to drive them to heavenly ones. He came to teach the most difficult virtues—patience, gentleness, tolerance of being injured, and the rest. He came, finally, to reconcile us to God and to destroy sin by his own sacrifice (Heb. 9:26). There were able to obtain all these things in no better way than through his humble status and disgraceful death.'" Johann Friedrich Stapfer, *Institutiones Theologiæ Polemicæ Universæ*, (5 vols. Tiguri, 1743–47), 2, 1172.

judges in Israel, David, Solomon, Hezekiah, Josiah, Cyrus, Mordecai; and from profane history, Cyrus, Alexander, the Roman conquerors, Czar Peter the Great, men that were deified among the heathen, and many others.

(See at the end of No. 1190.) How often are the miracles wrought in Egypt spoken of as clear evidences that he that wrought them was the supreme God and the only true God. Ex. 7:3–5; ch. 8:10, 19, 22; ch. 9:14, 29; ch. 10:2; ch. 11:7; ch. 12:12; ch. 14:18.

The reasonableness of the doctrine of FAITH as the main condition of salvation. Though true virtue be essentially the same in all—the same in mankind before and after the fall, the same in all intelligent creatures, both men and angels—yet the leading exercise of true virtue may differ according to the different nature, state and circumstances of the creature, the different relation it stands in to God, and its different leading concern with its Creator, and the diverse principal means and manner of God's manifesting himself to the creature, and the different intercourse he maintains with it. And if these things are considered, it will appear reasonable every way that FAITH should be the leading virtue of fallen man, a subject of the salvation of Jesus Christ, or candidate for it, to whom God principally makes himself known by the gospel of Jesus Christ.

Virtue is essentially the same in men and women, in parents and children. Yet the leading exercises of relative virtue may differ in these by reason of difference of nature, state, circumstances and relation. Thus, considering the weakness and dependence of the woman, and her relation to her husband as her head, her guide, defense, provider and husband, those exercises peculiarly proper for her and amiable in her, in her circumstances, and peculiarly endearing to her husband, are chaste reservation of herself for him, meek submission and resignation of herself to him, and affiance in him. On the other hand, the proper leading exercises of virtue in him, and most endearing of him to her, are fortitude, generosity, tenderness, compassion, etc. So the leading relative virtues of a child in minority are submission and dependence; but of the father, parental tenderness, watchful care, etc.

And nothing is more plain than that the most proper and suitable leading exercises of every kind, rank, and state of beings is to be determined from the particular nature, state, circumstances, connections and relations they stand in with respect to the chief objects of duty. For 'tis state and relation that bring duty, and is the ground of particular obligations and determinations of virtues. And therefore, according as state and relation is different, so will the determinations of the leading exercises of virtue be diverse.

Now whatever is considered in the nature and circumstances of fallen man under the gospel of salvation by the Son of God, everything will show that faith, as I have elsewhere described true faith,[8] is certainly the most proper leading exercise of virtue for us. This will appear if we consider what is most affecting and most to be attended to in our present fallen circumstances, being sinful, miserable, weak, poor, helpless, unworthy and lost. This will also appear if we consider the leading character and relation under which God now reveals himself to us thus sinful, miserable, helpless creatures, even that of our Savior. And the grand affair, in regard to which is our chief concern with God, is salvation. And that notion under which chiefly all those benefits wherein our happiness consists is exhibited, is salvation, and benefits that are spiritual and chiefly unseen and future. This will also further appear if we consider [that] the way, manner, and principal means by which God makes himself known to us in our fallen state, and the only means by which he manifests himself to us in the forementioned character and relation, and makes known those mentioned benefits wherein our happiness consists, and directs in answerable conduct and behavior, is divine revelation, or the Word of God.[9]

1157. MEANS OF GRACE. "How the word concurreth to salvation."

1. "There is a twofold operation upon the soul, physical and moral. The physical operation is the infusion of life; the moral operation is in a way of reason and persuasion: both these ways are necessary, not of any need in God, but mere love to us. God worketh strongly like himself, and sweetly, that he may attemper his work to our nature, and suit the key to the wards of the lock. . . . The soul of man is determined [. . .] by an object without, and a quality within: the object is propounded with all its qualifications, that the understanding may be informed and convinced, and the will and affections persuaded in a potent and high way of reasoning: but this is not enough to determine a man's heart without an internal quality or grace infused, which is his physical work upon the soul. There is not only a propounding of reasons and arguments, but a pow-

8. Possibly a reference to "Faith," no. 136. See *Works, 21,* 463.

9. The remaining two-thirds of the page on which JE finished No. 1156 are blank, indicating that he probably intended to add to this entry later. He started No. 1157 at the top of a new page.

erful inclination of heart . . . . as to the physical [. . .] operation, the Word is not the instrumental cause, but God worketh immediately: for the Word written and preached, voice, letters, syllables, are not subjects capable of receiving spiritual life to convey it to us: I say, there is not any such virtue in the sound of syllables and sentences of the Word, but the Spirit doth this work immediately. But as to the moral operation in a way of argument and persuasion: so the Word is the instrument.

"2. Though the infusion of life be God's immediate work, yet because 'tis done in concomitancy and association with the Word, therefore the effect is ascribed to the Word, as well as to the Spirit: so the law of God is said to 'convert the soul,' Ps. 19:7. And the gospel is said to be the 'power of God to salvation,' Rom. 1:16, that is, God doth not ordinarily work any other way: and hath tied us to depend upon him in the use of this means for such an effect. . . . [God doth] convey his power in concomitancy with the Word, though not by the Word; i.e., there is not any natural force put into it to produce such an effect.

"3. In the moral way the Word hath a double operation; first it prepareth to receive the gracious principle. Secondly, it exciteth the gracious principle newly infused, to actual believing and turning to God."

This is taken out of Dr. Manton's fifth volume of sermons, pp. 886–87.[1]

1158. CHRISTIAN RELIGION. 'Tis of itself a great proof of revealed religion that the Jews should for so many ages retain the knowledge of the true God, and the notions of him (his nature, attributes, works and worship) agreeable to the most refined reason, when all the nations about 'em, and all the rest of the world, were enveloped in the grossest idolatry. It was not owing to anything peculiar in the genius of that people, any distinguishing taste they had for learning beyond other nations. They were unacquainted with the sciences that were in vogue in Greece and Rome, and seemed to have been as prone to idolatry in themselves as other nations.

1159. That CHRIST PURCHASED SAVING FAITH and CONVERTING GRACE for such as shall be saved, appears in that he purchased the Spirit. But faith and conversion are the effects and fruits of the Spirit.

1. Thomas Manton, *A Fifth Volume of Sermons Preached by the Late Reverend and Learned Thomas Manton, D.D.* (London, 1701), 886–87. See also roughly contemporaneous excerpts from this volume in "Faith," nos. 122 and 125 (*Works, 21*, 458–60).

Christ's seeing his seed and his justifying many by his knowledge is spoken of as the consequence and reward of his death, and what he purchased. That Christ's people should be willing in the day of his power seems to be spoken of, as Ps. 110, as in like manner the fruit of God's well-pleasedness in his labors and sufferings, as his being set on God's right hand till his enemies should be made his footstool.

They are by the purchase of the Redeemer redeemed from amongst men, which implies that he has purchased that they should be actually taken out from amongst men and separated from them. But this is done in their effectual calling. They are redeemed from the earth, but they are separated from the earth in their conversion or effectual calling: for 'tis in their conversion that they go and sell all that they have, turn from earth to heaven, become pilgrims and strangers in the earth and fellow citizens with the saints in heaven. See also Gal. 1:4, he gave him for us "that he might redeem us from this present evil world."

The Spirit poured out at and after Pentecost to propagate the kingdom of God and convert Jews and Gentiles, was evidently the fruit of Christ's purchase by his preceding sufferings and part of the reward of his labors he received at his ascension. He ascended on high and entered into the holiest of all by his own blood and, by that, obtained this gift for men, yea, for the rebellious.

Drawing men to Christ is the fruit of his being lifted up on the cross. Christ buys or redeems men that they may be his. He redeems 'em from their sins, from all iniquity, that he may purify them to himself, a peculiar people zealous of good works. They are redeemed from their vain conversation by the precious blood of Christ. And 'tis by conversion, by faith, that men become actually his, come to him, and are brought into his possession. God, in giving them faith, brings them to him and gives 'em to him, and they give themselves to him. He purchases his spouse that he may present her to himself. This is first done in conversion, when the soul is first brought to Christ to give up itself to him in the marriage covenant. Christ's portion is his people, and Jacob is the lot of his inheritance. But Christ's portion is a purchased possession. But he is brought to his possession by conversion.

Of old, the deliverance of the people out of Egypt from their taskmasters and the gods of Egypt was by a typical redemption. And in the antitype, men are redeemed from their sins that they are servants to, and are redeemed from the bondage of Satan.

The portion which the Father had given the Son was to be obtained by purchase. But Christ obtains this portion by the faith by which men come to him. They that the Father hath given me shall come to me, says Christ.[2]

Christ was exalted in order to bring to effect the things obtained by his suffering. But Christ was exalted to give repentance. Baptism is a representation of conversion or regeneration. The giving the Spirit in conversion is spiritual baptism, by which we are baptized into Christ or into his mystical body. And in that work it is that the Spirit becomes our spirit; we are then made to drink into one Spirit. See I Cor. 12:13. But we come by this spiritual drink no other way than by Christ's sufferings, as of old the children of Israel partook of that spiritual or mystical drink that typified the Spirit of Christ no other way than by the rock's being smitten with a rod. Compare John 4:14 with ch. 7:38–39.

1160. EVIDENCES OF A FUTURE STATE FROM THE OLD TESTAMENT.[3] Besides those texts in the Old Testament that do directly speak of a future state, the Old Testament affords the following evidences and confirmations of a future state: especially Solomon's writings and, above all, the book of Ecclesiastes.

1. 'Tis often declared in the Old Testament that God will bring every work into judgment; that there [is] verily a God that judgeth in the earth; that his eyes are on the ways of men; that he considers all his goings; that sins of the wicked and the good deeds of the righteous are exactly observed and written in a book of remembrance, and none of them forgotten; that they are sealed up in a bag and laid up among God's treasures, and that he will render to every man according to his works; that the Judge of all the earth will do right and that, therefore, God will not destroy the righteous with the wicked; that, as to the righteous, it shall be well with him, for he should eat the fruit of his doings; that, as to the wicked, it shall be ill with him, for the reward of his hands shall be given him; that it is impossible it should be otherwise; that there is no darkness nor shadow of death where the workers of iniquity can hide themselves from God the Judge; that God cannot forget his people—a woman may sooner forget her sucking child; that God has graven them on the palms of his hands; that God beholds and takes notice of all their afflictions and pities them as a father pities his children, but that he is the enemy of wicked men; that their sins shall find them out; that though hand

2. Possibly an allusion to John 6:39.

3. See also JE's small MS, "Places of the Old Testament Which Intimate a Future State, or Naturally and Directly Lead to Expect One," Trask Library, Andover Newton Theological School, Edwards Collection, f. ND5.4–5.

join in hand, the wicked shall not go unpunished; that the way of righteousness is a certain way to happiness and the way of sin a sure way to misery. Solomon himself is above all other penmen of the Old Testament in observing the great difference between the righteous and the wicked in this respect, the greatness and the certainty of it, etc. See Prov. 1:31–32; and 2:11, 21–22; and 3:2, 4, 8, 13–18, 21–26, 32, 35; 4:5–13, 22; 8:17–21, 35–36; 9:5–6, 11–12; 10:16–17, 27–29; 11:7–8, 18–19, 21, 30–31; 12:2–3, 14, 21, 28; 13:9, 13–15, 21; 14:19, 26–27; 15:3, 6, 24; 16:3–7; 19:23; 21:15–16, 18, 21; 22:4, 8; 23:17–18; 24:1–5, 12, 15–16, 19–22; 28:10, 13–14, 18; 29:6; and many other places in that book of Proverbs. And in Eccles. 12:13–14 Solomon declares that to "fear God, and keep his commandments" is "the whole [duty] of man," because "God will bring every work into judgment, with every secret thing, whether it be good, or whether it be evil." And [in] ch. 2:26 he says, "God giveth to a man that is good in his sight wisdom, and knowledge, and joy: but to the sinner he giveth travail, to gather and to heap up, that he may give to him that is good before God." And ch. 3:17, "I said in my heart, God shall judge the righteous and the wicked." And ch. 5:8, "If thou seest the oppression of the poor, and violent perverting of judgment and justice in a province, marvel not at the matter: for he that is higher than the highest regardeth; and there be higher than they."

And yet the same Wise Man in this book of Ecclesiastes says, ch. 6:8, "What hath the wise more than the fool? what hath the poor, that knoweth to walk before the living?" And elsewhere in this book [he] particularly observes that "all things come alike to all," and "there is one event to the righteous, and to the wicked" [Eccles. 9:2]; and as dieth the wise man, so the fool [Eccles. 2:16], etc. These things are most palpably and notoriously inconsistent unless there be a future state.

In Eccles. 8:14 the Wise Man says, "There is a vanity which is done upon the earth; that there be just men, unto whom it happeneth according to the work of the wicked; again, there be wicked men, to whom it happeneth according to the work of the righteous." And yet in the same breath, in the two foregoing verses, he speaks with the utmost peremptoriness that God will surely make a vast difference between the righteous and the wicked, so that he will make one happy and the other miserable, and that it never can in any instance be otherwise; yea, it will not finally prove otherwise in these instances wherein it seems most to be otherwise, and God seems to be most unmindful of the provocations of the wicked and of the righteousness, of them that fear God. "Though a sinner do evil an hundred times, and his days be prolonged, yet SURELY

I KNOW that it shall be well with them that fear God, which fear before him: But it shall not be well with the wicked, neither shall he prolong his days, which are as a shadow; because he feareth not before God" [vv. 12–13]. And in the beginning of the next chapter, "that the righteous, and the wise, and their works, are in the hand of God: no man knoweth either love or hatred by all that is before them. All things come alike to all: there is one event to the righteous, and the wicked" [Eccles. 9:1–2].

Now if both these seemingly opposite assertions are true, then it is true that there is a future state. The Wise [Man] observes that the righteous sentence of the Judge, who will surely make so great a difference between the righteous and the wicked, is not executed in this world; on which account wicked men are greatly emboldened in sin, as he observes in the same place, ch. 8:11. "Because sentence against an evil is not executed speedily, therefore the heart of the sons of men is fully set in them to do evil." And therefore there is some other time besides the time of this life for the executing the sentence, which he observes will so surely be executed. In vv. 12–13 it is said: though a sinner's days be prolonged, yet he shall not prolong his days, that are as a shadow. How can both these be true, but only in this sense: that though his life be prolonged in this world, yet the longest life here is short and is but a shadow; and when he dies he perishes—his life and happiness shall not be prolonged beyond this momentary state, as the life of the righteous will be.

So he says, ch. 7:15, "there is a just man that perisheth in his righteousness, and there is a wicked man that PROLONGETH his life in his wickedness." And yet in two or three verses before, v. 12, he observes that 'tis a peculiar excellency of wisdom, wherein it differs from riches and all other things that are an uncertain defense to a man, that wisdom gives life to them that have it. And also, in two or three verses after, he advises to hold this fast as an unfailing truth (v. 18): that he that fears God shall come forth out of all destruction and calamity; and [in] ch. 8:5, "Whoso keepeth the commandment shall feel no evil thing." And therefore it must be some other life that is meant besides this temporal life, which he observes is sometimes prolonged in wicked men, and with regard to which righteous men sometimes perish in their righteousness, and with regard to which life there is one event to wise men and fools, as in ch. 2:14–16, "The wise man's eyes are in his head; but the fool walketh in darkness: and I myself perceived also that one event happeneth to them all. Then said I in my heart, As it happeneth to the fool, so it happeneth even to me; and why was I then more wise? Then I said in my heart, that this also is vanity. For there is no remembrance of the wise more than of the fool for ever; seeing that which now is in the days to come shall all be forgotten. And how dieth the wise man? as the fool."

Compare these things with Prov. 12:28, "In the way of righteousness is life; and in the pathway thereof is no death." And ch. 13:14, "The law of the wise is a fountain of life, to depart from the snares of death." Ch. 3:18, "She is a tree of life to them that lay hold upon her: and happy is every one that retaineth her." V. 22, "So shall they be life to thy soul." Ch. 4:22, "They are life to those that find them." And ch. 10:17, "He is in the way of life that keepeth instruction." And 11:30, "The fruit of righteous is a tree of life." [Ch.] 14:27, "The fear of the Lord is a fountain of life, to depart from the snares of death." [Ch.] 16:22, "Understanding is a wellspring of life unto him that hath it." Ch. 21:21, "He that followeth after righteousness and mercy findeth life, and righteousness, and honor." So ch. 22:4, "By humility and the fear of the Lord are riches, and honor, and life." Ch. 4:4, "keep my commandments, and live"; so ch. 7:2. And ch. 9:2, "forsake the foolish, and live."

In [Ecclesiastes,] ch. 5:5[–6], it is said, "Better is it that thou shouldst not vow, than that thou shouldst vow and not pay. Suffer not thy mouth to cause thy flesh to sin; neither say thou before the angel, that it was an error: wherefore should God be angry at thy voice, and destroy the work of thy hands?," signifying the dreadful danger of false swearing and breach of vows. And yet as to what happens in this life, it is said that "All things come alike to all," and that "there is one event to the righteous, and to the wicked," and that "as is the good, so is the sinner; and he that sweareth, as he that feareth an oath" [Eccles. 9:2].

In ch. 5:8 'tis signified that there is a remedy from the wrong, injustice and oppression of men in power by the judgment of the supreme Judge. The same is implied in ch. 3:16–17. And yet what is said, ch. 4:1–2, implies that oftentimes in this case there is no remedy in this life. "So I returned, and considered all the oppressions that are done under the sun: and behold the tears of such as were oppressed, and they had no comforter; and on the side of their oppressors there was power; but they had no comforter. Wherefore I praised the dead which are already dead more than the living which are yet alive."

In Prov. 10:7 Solomon says, "The memory of the just is blessed: but the name of the wicked shall rot." And of this memory or good name of the just he says, Eccles. 7:1, that it "is better than precious ointment" (meaning the precious ointment they were wont to anoint the children of great and rich men with when first born) and that upon this account the day of a godly man's death (followed with a good name and so blessed a memory) is better than the day of one's birth. And yet the same Wise Man says, Eccles. 2:16, "there is no remembrance of the wise man more than of the fool; seeing that which now is in the days to come shall be forgotten. And how dieth the wise man? as the fool." By which it is evident that 'tis with regard to something that follows death in another world, and not in this, that the death of the righteous is much preferred to the death of the wicked, on the account of the blessed memory and good name of the righteous and the rotten, stinking name of the other.

Again, in ch. 6:3–4, an untimely birth is said to be better than one that lives in this world in great prosperity, if he have no burial and his name be covered with darkness, implying that he is far worse off after death for having no burial, and his name covered with darkness. And yet [it] will follow that he is neither the worse nor the better for anything done in this world to his corpse or his name, after he is dead. I say it will follow from what is observed, ch. 9:5–6, "The dead know not anything, neither have they any more a reward; for the memory of them is forgotten. Also their love, and their hatred, and their envy, is now perished; neither have they any more a portion for ever in any thing that is done under the sun." "There is nothing better, than that a man should rejoice in his works; for who shall bring him to see what shall be after him?" [Eccles. 3:22]. So ch. 6:12. By which it is evident that by burial and the name of the deceased person are meant something diverse from anything that remains or is brought to pass in this world.

Balaam says, "Let me die the death of the righteous, let my last end be like his" [Num. 23:10], implying that there is something in their death vastly preferable to the death of the wicked. And the Psalmist, Ps. 37:37–38, says, "Mark the perfect man, and behold the upright: for the end of that man is peace. But the transgressors shall be destroyed together: the end of the wicked shall be cut off." And Ps. 26:9, "Gather not my soul with sinners, nor my life with bloody men." And Prov. 10:25, "As the whirlwind passeth, so is the wicked no more: but the righteous is an everlasting foundation." And Prov. 11:7, "When a wicked man dieth, his expectation shall perish: and the hope of unjust men perisheth." And ch. 14:32, "The wicked is driven away in his wickedness: but the righteous hath hope in his death." Thus 'tis abundantly represented as if there were a vast difference between the righteous and the wicked. And yet 'tis declared that, as to anything pertaining to this world, there is no difference. Eccles. 2:16, "How dieth the wise man? as the fool." Compare Ps. 49:10.

And although Solomon says in Prov. 11:7 that "When a wicked man dieth, his expectation and hope perishes," as if this were peculiar to wicked men—yea, he says expressly, ch. 14:32, "The wicked is driven away in his wickedness: but the righteous hath hope in his death"—yet the same Wise Man, after observing that there [is] one event to the righteous and wicked, both in life and in death, Eccles. 9:3, he in the next verses proceeds to say that to him that is joined to all the living there is HOPE, intimating that there is no more hope for him, whether he be righteous or wicked, after [he is] dead, i.e. as to any good in this world, which is plainly his meaning; for he in the following words proceeds to observe that they have no more "a portion for ever in any thing that is done under the sun."

And though it be so often observed to be the peculiar excellency of wisdom and righteousness that it delivers from death, and gives life and length of days, and makes the years of life many, and though he does abundantly set forth the great peace, comfort, pleasure, profit and satisfaction, and exceeding gain, excellent advantage and good reward of wisdom and virtue, so 'tis worth the while to get it by all means, with all our gettings, to buy it and sell it not, and that they that obtain [it] are happy, yea, exceeding happy; yet this same Wise Man does in effect tell us that by LIFE he don't mean this present life, and that the profit, gain and happiness he speaks of is no good of a temporal nature. For as to this life and all the good that belongs to it at best, he says, "All is vanity and vexation of spirit, and that there is no profit under the sun" (Eccles. 2:11, with the preceding part of the book). And he there plainly shows that he means that 'tis thus both with respect to wise men and fools, righteous and wicked (vv. 14–16), and then tells us that he esteemed life in this sense, even the present life with the best it had, worse than nothing—v. 17, "Therefore I hated life"—and declares that he judges that, for any good in this life, death is better than life, and that they are best off who never yet received life. Eccles. 4:2–3, "Wherefore I praised the dead which are already dead more than the living which are yet alive. Yea, better is he than both they, which hath not yet been, who hath not seen the evil work that is done under the sun."

In ch. 2:20–22, he speaks expressly of the life of a righteous man whose labor is in wisdom and in knowledge and in equity, and says of it, "what hath he of all his labor?" and that all his days are sorrows, and his travail grief, and that a man may well despair as to any happiness or real profit in this life. He declares that long life in this world is so far from being so exceeding a felicity that, if a man should live a thousand years twice told, yet there is no good or benefit in it all; and that the wise in this respect has no more than the fool (Eccles. 6:6–8); and that if a man have both long life and continual prosperity through the whole of it, 'tis all worth nothing. Eccles. 11:8, "But if a man live many years, and rejoice in them all; yet let him remember the days of darkness; for they shall be many. All that cometh is vanity." And in ch. 6:12 this whole life is called "vain life."

The Wise Man in this book of Ecclesiastes does greatly recommend it to his readers to fear God (Eccles. 3:14, ch. 8:12, ch. 12:13), and to fear him as a Judge that will bring every work into judgment (ch. 12:13–14, ch. 11:9–10). And yet if there be no other life but this, he in effect tells us all over this book, we have nothing to fear, no punishment from the Judge, no calamity in a way of displeasing him any more than in a way of doing what is well pleasing in his sight.

'Tis an argument that the scriptures of the Old Testament afford for a future state, that 'tis so often observed in those sacred writings as a thing very remarkable that man should be mortal, that he should in this respect be like the beasts that perish and like the flowers and grass of the field. Ps. 49:10–12, "For he seeth that wise men die, likewise the fool and the brutish person perish, and leaveth their wealth to others. Their inward thought is, that their houses shall continue forever, and their dwelling places to all generations; they call their lands after their own names. Nevertheless man being in honor abideth not: he is like the beasts that perish." And vv. 19–20, "He shall go to the generation of his fathers; they shall never see light. Man that is in honor, and understandeth not, is like the beasts that perish." Why should it be taken notice of as something remarkable, that man should be mortal and die as the beasts do, if there be nothing in the nature and circumstances of mankind by which he is distinguished from the beasts that would naturally lead one to expect an answerable distinction in this respect? If it be no more than is to be expected considering man's nature, capacity, state in the world, business, end of his creation, views and natural desires—I say, if considering these things, there is nothing in man that should lead us any more to expect that man should be immortal than the beasts, or that should make it[4] any more wonderful or remarkable that man should die than the inferior creatures, then why is such a remark put upon it?

And besides, 'tis plainly signified that man's superior nature and circumstances to the beasts, or his being in honor, does require or naturally lead us to expect that man should be distinguished in this respect

4. MS: "making."

from the beasts. For that is mentioned as the thing that renders it remarkable, that man should die as the beasts that he is [superior to] in honor.

The words of Solomon are very emphatical, Eccles. 3:18–20, "I said in my heart concerning the estate of the sons of men, that God might manifest them, that they might see that they themselves are beasts. For that which befalleth the sons of men befalleth beasts; even one thing befalleth them: as the one dieth, so dieth the other; yea, they have all one breath; so that a man hath no preeminence above a beast; for all is vanity. All go to one place; all are of the dust, and all turn to dust again." This would not be spoken with so much emphasis, as a thing very remarkable and difficult to conceive of, as a vanity and evil and confusion, if there was nothing in it indeed wonderful, nothing pertaining to the nature which God had given mankind or the state he had set him in, leading one to expect that man should differ from the beasts in this, nothing that should make it appear congruous and fit that God should make man (unless under his remarkable displeasure) to be distinguished from the inferior creatures by immunity from death, and that he should enjoy eternal life.

And if it be so, then we may determine that there is great reason to suppose that there is some way that good men shall be delivered from death, and that they shall enjoy eternal life in some invisible world after death. For good men are spoken of abundantly in the Old Testament as fully in favor with God, having all their sins perfectly done away as if they never had been, and as being very dear and precious in God's sight, that God greatly delighted in. And the bestowment of life is abundantly spoken of as the excellent fruit of this, his distinguishing love and favor. And the durableness of the benefits of his favor is often spoken [of] as a proper testimony of the greatness of it, their being more durable even than the everlasting mountains, yea, than heaven and earth (Ps. 102, latter end; Is. 51:6, ch. 54:10). And it can't answer the design of these great declarations of God's favor that, although particular saints shall die, yet a succession of them shall be continued and their prosperity shall last. For if there be no future state, then they are ever the better for what happens to their posterity or successors after their death, as is often observed in the Old Testament, and especially in the book of Ecclesiastes.

If God has perfectly forgiven all the sins of the righteous, and they are so high in his favor, and the great evidence of this favor be the durableness of the benefits that are the fruits of it, and the chief fruit is life, then 'tis at least to be expected that they will escape that mortality which is such a remarkable disgrace to those that have the human nature, and wonderful to behold in those whom the Most High has made to differ so much from the beasts in capacity, dignity, end and desires. We may surely expect that these high favors shall, with regard to life and durableness of happiness, not be mere beasts and have no preeminence above 'em, that[5] he should be like the grass and the flowers of the field, which in the morning flourisheth and groweth up [but] in the evening is cut down and withered; that all his happiness and benefit of God's favor should be like a shadow, like a dream, like a tale that is told; that it should be as a span and should pass away as the swift ships, as the eagle that hasteth to the prey; that it should be swifter than a weaver's shuttle, to which things the life of man is compared in Scripture.

The things of this world are spoken [of] as having no profit or value, because they are not lasting, but must be left at death, and therefore [are] mere vanity (i.e. wholly worthless) and not worthy that any man should set his heart on it (Ps. 49:6 to the end; Prov. 23:4–5; Prov. 11:7; Eccles. 2:15–17, ch. 3, ten first verses, v. 19, ch. 5:14–16). But the rewards of righteousness are abundantly represented as exceeding valuable and worthy that men should set their hearts upon them, because they are lasting (Prov. 3:16, 8:18, 10:25, 27; Is. 55:3; Ps. 1:3 to the end; Jer. 17:7–8; and innumerable other places). How can these things consist one with another unless there be a future state?

'Tis spoken as a remarkable thing, and what one would not expect, that good men should die as wicked men do, as it seems to be by good men's dying a temporal death as wicked men do (Eccles. 2:16; ch. 9:3–5). And therefore it may be argued that it does but seem to be so, but that in reality it shall not be so, inasmuch as, though good men die a temporal [death] as wicked men do, yet as to their happiness they die not, but live forever in a future state.

It is an evidence of a future state that in the Old Testament so many promises are made to the godly of things that shall be after they are dead, which shall be testimonies of God's great favor to them and blessed rewards of his favor: so many promises concerning their name, and concerning their posterity and the future church of God in the world; and yet that we are so much taught in the Old Testament that men are never the better for what comes to pass after they are dead concerning these things, i.e. if we look only at the present life without taking any other state of existence into consideration (Job 14:21; Eccles. 1:11, 3:22 and

5. MS: "and that."

9:5–6). Yea, the Wise Man says expressly that the dead have no more a reward, Eccles. 9:5, i.e. in anything in this world.

That man shall die as a beast seems to be spoken of, Eccles. 3:16 to the end, as a vanity, an evil, a kind of mischief and confusion that appears in the world. Therefore this is an argument that God, the wise orderer of all things who brings order out of confusion, will rectify this disorder by appointing a future state.

Those representations of the Old Testament, wherein the life of man is set forth as being so exceeding short, as a flower, as a shadow, as a dream, a tale that is told, as a span, a moment, etc., have no propriety at all [in] them any other way than as man's life is short in a comparative view, compared with things pertaining to men, that would naturally lead us to expect that it should be incomparably longer, such as the dignity of man's nature above all other creatures, his being made in the image of God, his being of a capacity so much superior, his being made for such an end and business, and capable of such an happiness, made capable of looking forward and having some apprehension of an endless life, his necessary desires of such a life, etc.; otherwise, why is not the shortness of the duration of other things in like manner set forth and insisted on, which do not last longer than the life of man? But if it be so, indeed, that man's life is exceeding short considering his nature, end, capacity and desires, then doubtless the righteous, who are represented as high favorites of God, who shall be the subjects of his blessing every way, and particularly shall have life as the great fruit of his favor and blessing, will have a life or duration that shall be long, answerably to their nature, desires, etc.

'Tis an argument that the Old Testament affords for the proof of a future life and immortality that we are there taught that mortality is brought in by sin, and comes as a punishment of sin. Therefore 'tis natural to suppose that, when complete forgiveness is promised, and perfect restoration to favor, and deliverance from death, and the bestowment of life as the fruit of this favor, that eternal life and immortality is intended.

1161. JUSTIFICATION. See p. 23 of my printed *Discourse on Justification.*[6] God, in justifying a sinner by faith, looks on him as the sinner by that act of faith looks on himself, for doubtless there is an agreement between

---

6. *Discourses on Various Important Subjects, Nearly Concerning the Great Affair of the Soul's Salvation* (Boston, 1738), 23; see also *Works, 19,* 163–64.

the act of God in justifying and the act of the person which God requires in order to his justification. But in the act of that faith which God requires in order to a sinner's justification, he looks on himself wholly as a sinner, or ungodly. He has no consideration of any goodness or holiness of his own in that affair, but merely and only the righteousness of Christ. And thus he seeks justification of himself, as in himself ungodly and unrighteous, by the righteousness of another. And so it is that God looks on him in justifying him. God has no consideration of any goodness in him when he justifies by faith, as that faith by which he has justified has no consideration of any goodness in him. And as justifying faith has respect only to the righteousness of another, so has he that justifies by faith.

1162. It may be worthy of consideration whether or no some of the HEATHEN PHILOSOPHERS had not, with regard to some things, some degree of INSPIRATION of the Spirit of God, which led 'em to say such wonderful things concerning the Trinity, the Messiah, etc. Inspiration is not so high an honor and privilege as some are ready to think. It is no peculiar privilege of God's special favorites. Many very bad men have been the subjects of it, yea, some that were idolaters. Balaam was an idolater and a great sorcerer or wizard, and yet he was the subject of inspiration, and that even when in the practice of his witchcraft, when he went to seek by enchantment. Yea, the devils themselves seem sometimes to have been immediately actuated by God and forced to speak the truth in honor to Christ and his religion. So the devil at the oracle of Delphos was probably actuated by God, and compelled to confess Christ, and own that the Hebrew child had to be above him, and had sent him to hell and forbidden him to give forth any more oracles.[7]

Why might not Socrates and Plato and some others of the wise men of Greece have some degree of inspiration, as well as the wise men from the East who came to see Christ when an infant? Those wise men dwelt among the heathen as much as the wise men of Greece, and were in like manner Gentiles born of heathen and brought up among them, and we have no reason to think that they were themselves less of heathen than several of the Grecian philosophers, at least before they were the subjects of that inspiration that moved them to follow the star that led them to Christ.

Pharaoh and his chief butler and baker were the subjects of a sort of

7. On the source of this reference, see *Works, 18,* 508, n. 3.

inspiration in the dreams they had, for 'tis evident those dreams were divine revelations. And [so] were Nebuchadnezzar's dreams. He, though a heathen and very wicked man and great idolater, yet had a revelation concerning Messiah and his future kingdom in his dream of the great image and the stone cut out of the mountains without hands.

If it be objected that, if we suppose some of the heathen philosophers to have truths suggested to 'em by the inspiration of the Spirit of God, we must suppose that God gave these revelations without giving with them any certain evidences by which others to whom they declared them might determine them to be such, or by which they might be obliged to regard and receive them as such: allowing this to be the case, yet a good end might be answered in giving these revelations nevertheless. Though they could be no rule to the heathen among whom they lived, yet they might be of use these three ways: (1) they might dispose the heathen nations, as they had occasion to converse with the Jews and to be informed of the revelations and prophecies that they had among them, to attend the more to them and to inquire into them and their evidences; (2) they might prepare the Gentile nations, that had among them the records of these sayings of their most noted and famous wise men, to receive the gospel when God's time came for its promulgation among these nations, by disposing them the more diligently and impartially to attend to it; (3) they may be of great benefit to the Christian church ages after they were delivered, as they serve as a confirmation of the great truths of Christianity; (4) we know not what evidence God might give to the men themselves that were the subjects of these inspirations that they were divine and were true (as we know not what evidence was given to the wise men of the East of the divinity of their revelations). And so we know not of how great benefit the truths suggested might be to their own souls.

1163. It may be worthy to be considered what has been so much insisted against all AUTHORITY OF COUNCILS and all POWER OF THE CIVIL MAGISTRATE in matters of religion, viz. that if this power be everywhere claimed and used, much more hurt will be done by it than good, and that more hurt has actually been than good in the exercise of such power. I say, it may be worthy of consideration whether this argument has not been overstrained, and too much concluded from it; whether from the same kind of arguing it would not follow that parents should never have liberty to instruct their children at all in any principles of religion, because such an abuse is commonly made of this liberty that ten times as much hurt has come of it as good; and whether we mayn't as well argue that it would be best that mankind should be without a power of reason, because commonly this power has been improved to do more hurt than good; and so of all other powers and abilities God has given to mankind. God has given a faculty of understanding and will to rule over the inferior principles of the human nature and the members of the body. But can we justly argue, because men have made such an ill use of these powers in directing the members and exertive powers, that they have done more hurt than good thereby, that therefore 'tis best that all mankind should be deprived of the power of using their members as their minds shall direct? It may be with regard to councils and rulers in societies as 'tis with ruling faculties in particular persons.

1164. TRUSTING IN OUR OWN RIGHTEOUSNESS. The words of Peter to Simon Magus, Acts 8[:20], "Thy money perish with thee, because thou hast thought that the gift of God may be purchased with money": I say these words seem to argue the very fatal consequence of men's trusting in anything of theirs, any price they have to offer for salvation. The Holy Sprit is by way of eminency the gift of God, and is the sum of salvation and of those saving benefits that are purchased by Christ. And the Holy Spirit in his ordinary saving influences, in[8] conferring grace and glory, is a much higher benefit than the extraordinary gifts of the Spirit. And there is a greater disproportion between the worth of the former and our best righteousness than between the extraordinary gifts of the Spirit and silver and gold.

1165. CONVICTION, HUMILIATION, CONVERSION. There is great reason, from the account the Scripture gives us of the manner and circumstances of Paul's conversion, to think that grace is sometimes given with the first awakenings of conscience, before comfort in a sense of the pardon of sin, and that the work of humiliation to fit for this comfort is afterwards, after grace is truly infused.

1. Because when Paul, when first awakened and convinced of sin, before his terrors of conscience were fully removed by Christ's gracious word by Ananias, Christ comforts him, in some measure declaring his favor and love to him, and his gracious purpose of making him an apostle and a glorious instrument of multitudes of both Jews and Gentiles, and of his gracious assistance and protection in the performance of this, so great a work. See Acts 26:16–18. Now it cannot reasonably be supposed

---

8. MS: "is."

that Christ would thus declare his love [to] him, and the great purposes of his grace concerning him, while he yet continued fully an enemy in his heart, without any mortification of that enmity, and while God held him under the guilt of sin and condemnation for it, and the wrath of God abode upon him.

2. When Christ appeared to Ananias to send him to Paul, before that which most properly may be called Paul's comfort, Christ encourages him with that, "behold, he PRAYETH" (Acts 9:11). Not that he had never prayed before externally. That strict sect of the Pharisees, of which Paul was, abounded in prayer, constantly attended it every day at the stated hours of prayer, besides extraordinary prayer at their fasts (which often were twice a week) and at other times. But these were not counted worthy of the name of prayers, because they were not the prayers of faith (see Hos. 7:14, Ps. 78:34–36). Calling on the name of the Lord is often in the New Testament mentioned as the terms of salvation.

1166. TRINITY. CHRIST THE LOGOS, the Wisdom or Idea of God. See Lardner's *Credibility*, vol. 6, p. 602.[9]

1167. FUTURE STATE. IMMORTALITY OF THE SOUL. That the state of divine judgment and retribution is hereafter, in another life and not in this, is manifest from that, that some of the highest acts of virtue consist in dying well, in denying ourselves of life in a good cause, for God and for a good conscience, or rather than commit what is in itself vicious and vile, for our country, for the church of good men and the interest of that holy society. See Lactantius as quoted by Lardner, vol. 9, p. 109.[1]

1168. TITLE TO A TREATISE: *The Nature of True Virtue, and the Way in Which It Is Obtained.*

1169. MYSTERIES. Supposing that mankind in general were a species of far less capacities than they are, so much less that when men are come to full ripeness of judgment and capacity they arrived no higher than to that degree that children generally arrive to at seven years of age; and supposing a revelation to be made to mankind, in such a state and degree of capacity, of many such propositions in philosophy as are now

---

9. Nathaniel Lardner, *The Credibility of the Gospel History . . .* (17 vols. London, 1727–57), *6*, 602. Concerning Lardner and his significance to JE, see *Works, 5*, 66–67.

1. Lardner, *The Credibility of the Gospel History, 9*, 109.

looked upon as undoubted truths; and let us suppose at the same time the same degree of pride and self-confidence as there is now: what caviling and objecting, etc., would there be. Or supposing a revelation of these philosophical truths had been made to mankind in their present degree of natural capacity in some ancient generation, suppose that which was Joshua's time, in that degree of acquired knowledge and learning which the world had arrived at then.

1170. CHRISTIAN RELIGION. NECESSITY OF A REVELATION. The slow progress the world makes in the investigation of truth in things that seem pretty obvious, as in that instance of the roundness of the earth, may evince the necessity of a revelation to guide men into the knowledge of truth in divine things, that are needful to be known in order to our being happy in the knowledge and favor and enjoyment of God.

1171. MYSTERIES. If things which fact and experience make certain, such as the miseries infants sometimes are the subjects of in this world, etc., had been exhibited only in a revelation of things in an unseen state, they would be as much disputed as the Trinity and other mysteries revealed in the Bible.

1172. DOUBLE SENSES OF SCRIPTURE. See Warburton's *Divine Legation*, vol. 3, pp. 631–78.[2] The prophecies of the seventy years' captivity had a twofold accomplishment.

1173. "Now those expressions of the Apostle" concerning CHRIST'S SATISFACTION AND RIGHTEOUSNESS, AND THE OPERATIONS OF THE SPIRIT, "are to be understood in the common sense and meaning of the words, and not as far-fetched metaphors; for it is evident, that in all this he does not affect the arts of oratory, nor assume a magnificent air of writing, nor does he raise himself into sublimities of style, nor rove in an enthusiastic way, when he treats of these subjects; but while he is ex-

---

2. William Warburton, *The Divine Legation of Moses Demonstrated, on the Principles of a Religious Deist, from the Omission of the Doctrine of a Future State of Reward and Punishment in the Jewish Dispensation* (2 vols. London, 1741), 2, 631–78, where Warburton defends the "secondary or double sense" (p. 631) of Old Testament Jewish prophecy against the claim of the deist Anthony Collins in *A Discourse of the Grounds and Reasons of the Christian Religion* (London, 1724) that the Old Testament contains no prophecies of Christ. Warburton divided vol. 2 of the *Divine Legation* into two parts—perhaps the reason for JE's reference to vol. 3 of this lengthy work, as the passage he refers to is found in Pt. 2 (Bk. 6, sec. 6). The following sentence is a later addition by JE.

plaining to us these great things of the gospel, he avoids the wisdom of words and oratory, and he talks in a plain, rational, and argumentative method to inform the minds of men, and give them the clearest knowledge of the truth." Watts' "Orthodoxy and Charity," p. 12.[3]

1174. Reasons against Dr. Watts' notion of the PRE-EXISTENCE OF CHRIST'S HUMAN SOUL.[4]

1. God's manner with all creatures is to appoint them a trial before he admits them to glory and confirmed happiness. And especially may this be expected before such honor and glory as the creating [of] the world and other things which Dr. Watts ascribes to this human soul.

2. If the pre-existing soul of Christ created the world, then doubtless it upholds and governs it. The same Son of God that did one, does the other. He created all things, and by him all things consist. And, if so, how was his dominion confined to the Jewish nation before his Incarnation, but extends to all nations since? Besides, there are many things ascribed in the Old Testament to the Son of God, in those very places which Dr. Watts himself supposes to speak of him, that imply his government of the whole world, all nations—the same person that is spoken of as King of Israel.

3. According to this scheme, the greatest of the works of the Son in his created nature, implying the greatest exaltation, [was] his first work of all, viz. his creating all things, all worlds, all things visible and invisi-

---

3. "Orthodoxy and Charity" is the title of one of the discourses in Isaac Watts, *The Glory of Christ as God-Man Display'd, in Three Discourses* (London, 1746).

4. In *The Glory of Christ as God-Man Display'd*, Isaac Watts argued that "the human soul of our Lord Jesus Christ had an existence, and was personally united to the divine nature, long before it came to dwell in flesh and blood; and that by this glorious person, God the Father managed the affairs of his ancient church as his own supreme minister and as the great mediator and king of his people, and that at a certain appointed period of time God sent down this blessed soul, willingly divested of primitive joys and glories, to take flesh in the womb of the virgin, to dwell in the body of an infant, and grow up by degrees to the perfection of a man, and in this body to suffer a thousand indignities and injuries from men and devils, and to sustain intense pains or agonies from some unknown manifestations of the wrath of God against sin, and at last submit to death and the grave." See "Discourse III. The Glories of Christ as God-Man displayed, by Tracing Out the Early Existence of His Human Nature . . . " The quotation is from pp. 147–48. For an interpretation of this view in its historical context, see especially J. Van Den Berg, "The Idea of the Pre-Existence of the Soul in Christ: An Argument in the Controversy Between Arian and Orthodox in the Eighteenth Century," in J. W. Van Henten et al., *Tradition and Re-Interpretation in Jewish and Early Christian Literature: Essays in Honour of Jurgen C. H. Lebram*, Studia Post-Biblia 36 (Leiden, Brill, 1986). Cf. Donald Macleod, "God or god? Arianism, Ancient and Modern," *The Evangelical Quarterly* 46 (1996), 121–38, who compares Watts's view to that of Philip Doddridge, another of JE's sources.

ble, whether they be thrones and dominions, principalities or powers— or at least before ever he had any trial at all of his obedience, etc. At least this work seems much greater than judging the world at the last day, which the Scripture often speaks of as one of the highest parts of his exaltation, which he has in reward for his obedience and sufferings. And Dr. Watts himself supposes his honors since his humiliation to be much greater than before.

4. The Scripture represents the visible dominion of Christ over the world as a complex person, or sitting at the right hand of God and governing the world as the Father's vicegerent, as a new thing after his ascension. But by Dr. Watts' scheme it cannot be so.

5. Satan or Lucifer, before his fall, was the morning star, the covering cherub, the highest and brightest of all creatures.

6. On this scheme it will follow that the covenant of redemption was made with a person that was not *sui juris,* and not at liberty to act his own mere good pleasure with respect to undertaking to die for sinners, but was obliged to comply on the first intimation that it would be well-pleasing to God and what he chose.

7. According to that scheme, the man Christ Jesus was not properly the son of the virgin and so the Son of Man. To be the son of a woman is to receive being in both soul and body in a consequence of a conception in her womb. The soul is the principal part of the man, and sonship implies derivation of the soul as well as the body by conception. Not that the soul is a part of the mother as the body is. Though the soul is no part of the mother and be immediately given by God, yet that hinders not its being derived by conception, it being consequent on it according to a law of nature. 'Tis agreeable to a law of nature that, where a perfect human body is conceived in the womb of a woman and properly nourished and increased, a human soul should come into being. And conception may as properly be the cause whence it is derived as many other natural effects are derived from natural causes or antecedents. For 'tis the power of God [that] produces these effects, though it be according to an established law. The soul being so much the principal part of man, a derivation of the soul by conception is the chief thing implied in a man's being the son of a woman.

8. According to what seems to be Dr. Watts' scheme, the Son of God is no distinct divine person from the Father. So far as he is a divine person, he is the same person with the Father. So that in the covenant of redemption the Father covenants with himself, and he takes satisfaction of himself, etc., unless you will say that one nature covenanted with another,

the two natures in the same person covenanted together, and one nature in the same person took satisfaction of the other nature in the same person. But how does this confound our minds instead of helping our ideas and make them more easy and intelligible.

9. The Son of God, as a distinct person, was from eternity. 'Tis said, Mic. 5:2, "his goings forth were of old, from everlasting." So Prov. 8:23, "I was set up from everlasting, from the beginning, or ever the earth was." So he is called, Is. 9:6, "The everlasting Father." I know of no expressions used in Scripture more strong to signify the eternity of the Father himself.

10. Dr. Watts supposes the world to be made by this pre-existent soul of Christ, and thinks it may properly be so said, though the knowledge and power of this pre-existent soul could not extend to the most minute parts, every atom, etc. But 'tis evidently the design of the Scriptures to assure us that Christ made all things whatever in the absolute universality. John 1:3, "All things were made by him; and without him was not any thing made that was made." Col. 1:16–17, "For by him were all things created, that are in heaven, and that are in earth, visible and invisible, whether they be thrones, or dominions, or principalities, or powers: all things were created by him, and for him: and he is before all things, and by him all things consist." Now if we suppose matter to be infinitely divisible, it will follow that, let his wisdom and power be as great as they will, if finite, but a few of those individual things that are made were the effects of his power and wisdom; yea, that the number of the things that were made by him are so few that they bear no proportion to others that did not immediately fall under his notice; or that of the things that are made, there are ten thousands times, yea, infinitely more not made by him than are made by himself, and so but infinitely few of their circumstances are ordered by his wisdom.

11. 'Tis said, Heb. 2:8, "Thou hast put all things in subjection under his feet. For in that he put all in subjection under him, he left nothing that is not put under him." Here 'tis represented that God the Father has put every individual thing under the power and government of another person distinct from himself. But this can't be true of the human soul of Christ, as it must be, according to Dr. Watts' scheme, let the powers of that be never so great, if they are not infinite. For things and circumstances and dependencies and consequences of things in the world are infinite in number and, therefore, a finite understanding and power cannot extend to them. Yea, it can extend to but an infinitely small part of the whole number of individuals and their circumstances and conse-

quences. Indeed, in order to the disposing of a few things, in their motions and successive changes, to a certain precise issue, there is need of infinite exactness, and so need of infinite power and wisdom.

12. The work of creation, and so the work of upholding all things in being, can in no sense be properly said to be the work of any created nature. If the created nature gives forth the word, as Joshua did when he said "Sun, stand thou still" [Josh. 10:12], still is not that created nature that does it. That being that depends himself on creating power don't properly do anything towards creation, as Joshua did nothing towards stopping the sun in his course. So that it cannot be true in Dr. Watts' scheme that that Son of God, who is a distinct person from God the Father, did at all, in any manner of propriety, create the world, nor does he uphold it or govern it. Nor can those things that Christ often says of himself be true, as, "The Father worketh hitherto, and I work"; "Whatsoever the Father doeth, those doeth the Son likewise" (John 5:17, 19). 'Tis very evident that the works of creating and upholding and governing the world are ascribed to the Son, as a distinct person from the Father.

13. 'Tis one benefit or privilege of the person of Christ, when spoken of as distinct from the Father, to have the Spirit of God under him, to be at his disposal and to be his messenger, which is infinitely too much for any creature. John 15:26 and 16:7, 13–14; Acts 2:33.

1175. HUMILIATION. Lev. 26:40–42, "If they shall confess their iniquity, and the iniquity of their fathers, with their trespass which they have trespassed against me, and that they also have walked contrary unto me; and that I also have walked contrary unto them, and have brought them into the land of their enemies; if then their uncircumcised hearts be humbled, and they accept the punishment of their iniquity: then will I remember my covenant with Jacob," etc. Here the condition of their deliverance from that punishment of sin here spoken of, even their captivity and banishment from God's presence and the privileges of his people, is: 1. conviction of their sinfulness, or confessing their iniquity; 2. their conviction of their sin as it is against God, a trespassing against him and walking contrary to him; 3. a conviction of God's displeasure and anger for sin, or God's walking contrary unto them; 4. the humiliation of their hearts for sin, consisting in their accepting the punishment of their iniquity, which implies two things: (1) a conviction of conscience of their deserving the punishment, or of the justice of God in inflicting it, from a sense of the heinousness of sin; (2) an approbation of heart of this justice of God, or such a manifestation of his great hatred of sin, implying a sense of the hatefulness of sin and a disapprobation of [a] heart of sin, or a hatred of it.

As such an humiliation as this, implying such an accepting this punishment [of] sin, was required in order to a deliverance from that punishment, so undoubtedly with equal reason the like humiliation and the like acceptance of the threatened eternal punishment of sin is required in order to a deliverance from it.

1176. PROGRESS OF THE WORK OF REDEMPTION. DAY OF JUDGMENT. See Mr. Robe's description of Christ's last coming in the second volume of his sermons, Ser. 11.[5]

1177. CHRIST'S RIGHTEOUSNESS. OBEDIENCE. A probable reason why Christ's righteousness, as imputed to us, is so often in Scripture called by the name of the *righteousness of God,* is that the Holy Spirit saw fit that the name given to the righteousness by which we are justified under the new covenant, should be such as should denote the principal and most proper distinction between the righteousness by which men are justified under this covenant from that by which mankind would have been justified by the first covenant if Adam had stood in his integrity. The distinction don't consist in that, that we are not justified by our own righteousness but the righteousness of another, for no more should we have been justified by our own righteousness if Adam had stood, but as much by the righteousness of another, the righteousness of a surety or representative, as now.

But here lies the great distinction: If Adam had maintained his integrity and finished his work, we should have been justified by the righteousness of man, of mere man; it would have been properly an human righteousness. But it was the will of God to bring mankind into a greater dependence on himself for happiness, and so that his righteousness, by which he should have a title to happiness, should not be the righteousness of an human but a divine person; so that the creature should be abased and annihilated, and all should be of God and in God; that the righteousness should not be the righteousness performed by man, as an human person by himself, but by a divine person; and that the value of

5. James Robe, *A Second Volume of Sermons, In Three Parts, For the Most Part Preached at the Celebration of the Lord's Supper, by James Robe, A.M., Minister of the Gospel at Kilsyth* (Edinburgh, 1750), Pt. I, Sermon 11, "On the Glorious Appearing of Jesus Christ" (on Matt. 24:30, originally preached 1731), pp. 153–67. Thanks to Robert Yarbrough, Lee Bond, and especially Keith Beebe for tracking down this reference at New College Library, Edinburgh.

it that should render it prevalent to recommend us should not be the value of any human virtue or beauty in itself considered, but should arise from the infinite dignity of the divinity to which the man Christ Jesus was personally united.

Another great distinction between the way of justification by the new covenant and that by the old, is that an interest in the righteousness of the new covenant is obtained by faith, and therefore 'tis called the righteousness which [is] by faith and the righteousness which is of God through faith. 'Tis [not] by nature, by any natural union, dependence, or derivation from the person who wrought out righteousness, but a spiritual, active union.

The union of the soul to God, or to the divine person who wrought our righteousness, by that act of the soul by which it acknowledges God as the author of this righteousness, looks to him for it, and ascribes to him all the glory of it, by which God is much more exalted and his glory more advanced than if men came by this righteousness through a natural union and derivation, without any knowledge or act of theirs. The glory of God in our justification is greatly secured and advanced by these two things: 1. that our justifying righteousness is the righteousness of God, the righteousness not of an human but a divine person, so that a divine person is the author of it and the value of it arises from the dignity of the divine nature; and 2. as the very bond of union, by which we are united to this divine person so as to be interested in his righteousness, is that principle and act of the soul by which we know that the righteousness is thus the righteousness, and by which we cordially and with all our hearts ascribe it wholly to him and give him all the glory of it.

1178. IMPUTATION OF ADAM'S SIN. See Mr. Davies of Virginia, his sermon on the primitive state of man.[6]

1179.[7] ETERNITY OF HELL TORMENTS. Those words of Christ in the sixth chapter of Luke, v. 24, "Wo unto you rich! for ye have received your consolation," are inconsistent with the notions of those who suppose the wicked are to suffer a long while in hell but finally are to be made happy in the favor and enjoyment of God.

6. Samuel Davies, *A Sermon on Man's Primitive State: and the First Covenant. Delivered before the Reverend Presbytery of New Castle, April 13th, 1748* (Philadelphia, 1748). In the MS, JE drew a vertical line through the entry.

7. An aborted entry No. 1179, located just before this one in the MS, was crossed out entirely by JE. It reads as follows: "1179. HOLY GHOST, HIS DIVINITY. See Glas' Notes, No. 5, p. 7, etc."

And those words of Christ concerning Judas, "good had it been for that man that he had never been born" [Mark 14:21; Matt. 26:24], are a clear evidence that the damned are not finally to be received to a state of happiness.

1180. TRINITY. The following is taken from *The Philosophical Principles of Natural and Revealed Religion,* by the Chevalier Ramsay,[8] in the *Monthly Review, for March 1751,* p. 341. "The eternal, self-existent, infinite Being presents himself to the mind under the notion of a simple, uncompounded, indivisible essence, without distinction of parts, without succession of thoughts, and without division of substance: yet he contains necessarily the three real distinctions of *spirit conceiving, idea conceived,* and *love proceeding from both;* which in the supreme infinite are not three simple attributes, or modes; but three distinct persons, or self-conscious, intellectual agents. The infinite spirit, by a necessary, immanent, eternal activity, produces in himself his consubstantial image equal to him in all his perfections, self-origination only excepted; and from both proceed a distinct, self-conscious, intelligent, active principle of love co-equal to the Father and the Son, called the Holy Ghost. This is the true definition of God in his eternal solitude, or according to his absolute essence distinct from created nature."

1181. TRADITIONS OF THE HEATHEN, PARTICULARLY THE CHINESE, CONCERNING THE TRINITY, THE NATURE OF THE DEITY, THE PARADISAIC STATE, THE FALL, THE REDEMPTION OF THE MESSIAH, THE FALL OF ANGELS, THE NATURE OF TRUE RELIGION. Taken from *The Philosophical Principles of Natural and Revealed Religion,* by Chevalier Ramsay. See *Monthly Review, for April 1751,* pp. 437–38; Ramsay, vol. 2, pp. 39–42.[9] "The Chinese, whose origin goes back, very near to the times of the Deluge, have five original or canonical books called *King.* [. . .] The names of these books are *Y-King, Chu-King, Chi-King, Tchunsion,* and *Liki.* These books were looked upon as of very remote antiquity, in the time of Confucius, who lived about 600 years before our Savior. All the other books of any note in China, are commentaries upon these five; and these five canonical books are honored in that country with the same veneration we pay

8. Andrew Michael Ramsay, *The Philosophical Principles of Natural and Revealed Religion* (2 vols. Glasgow, 1748–49), as excerpted in *The Monthly Review, for March 1751,* a London periodical.

9. JE later inserted the concluding reference, presumably when he acquired a copy of Ramsay's *Philosophical Principles.* Throughout this entry, Ramsay's and JE's spelling of the names of Chinese gods and authors is preserved.

1181

"Miscellanies," Bk. 8, showing the beginning of No. 1181, "Traditions of the Heathen, Particularly the Chinese. . . ." Courtesy of Beinecke Rare Book and Manuscript Library, Yale University.

to the holy Scriptures. I shall not found any of my reasonings upon the explication of the hieroglyphical Chinese characters, in which some Europeans pretend to find the sublimest mysteries; I shall quote only these passages of the original books, about which the Chinese interpreters agree; confine myself as much as possible to the commentaries made upon these sacred books before the coming of our Savior, by Confucius, or his most ancient disciples, and mention no authors later than the twelfth century, ere Europeans or Christians had any communication with China. As the Chinese books I mention are already brought into Europe, and lodged in several great libraries, those who understand the language may ascertain the truth of the following quotations.

"In the books called *King,* God is called Chang-Ti, or the sovereign emperor, and Tien, the supreme heaven, the intelligent heaven, the self-existent unity, who is present everywhere, and who produced all things by his power. Tehu-hi, in commenting upon these expressions, says, 'The supreme unity is most simple, and without composition. He lasts from all eternity, without interruption. He is ancient and new; he is the source of all motion, and the root of all action. If you ask what he does, he is eternally active. If you would know where he is, he exists everywhere, and nourishes all things.' Kouan-y-antsee, a very ancient philosopher, in commenting upon the same sacred books, says, 'Heaven and earth, though they be of an immense extent, have figure, color, number and quantity. I conceive something that has neither color, figure, number, nor quantity; and therefore I say, that he who made the heavens and the earth is intelligent and eternal. He who produced all things, was not produced himself; he who destroys all things, is indestructible: therefore he who made the heavens is not the heavens, and he who made the earth is not the earth; the heavens are not self-existent, but were produced by another, as an house cannot exist by itself, unless it be made.' Yntchin adds, 'If there were nothing in nature but matter and motion, this would not be the sovereign lord and intelligent governor of all things.' Hoian-nantsee says, 'If you ask me, whence all things come, I will answer, that all things were made by the great unity, which is the origin of all things, and the sovereign power that none can resist. He who knows this great unity, knows all; he who does not know him, knows nothing.' Liou-pouci says, 'that the supreme unity comprehends all perfections in a sovereign degree; we cannot discover his beginning, nor his end; his origin, nor his bounds; and all things flow from him.'

"The same books of *King* call God Tao, which signifies reason, law, eternal code; Yen, word or speech; Tching-Che, sovereign truth. The philosopher Laotsee, in commenting on these passages, says, 'that reason which can be expressed, is not the eternal reason. What is eternal cannot be changed. He was before the heavens and the earth, without beginning. He will last after the world, without end. He cannot be comprehended by thought, nor seen by the eye, nor expressed by words.' Hoian-nantsee adds, 'this eternal reason feeds the heavens, and supports the earth. He is most high, and cannot be reached to; he is most profound, and cannot be fathomed; immense, and cannot be measured; yet he exists entirely everywhere in the least thing.'" See No. 1355.[1]

Ibid., pp. 441[-42]. Our author proceeds to examine the hints and shadows of this doctrine[2] preserved among the pagans, beginning with the Chinese, in whose canonical books he says the following surprising passages are to be found. "In the book *Tonchu,* we read these words: 'The source and root of all is one. This self-existent unity produces necessarily a second; the first and second by their union produce a third; in fine, these three produce all. Lopi, in commenting on these passages, says, 'that this unity is triple, and this triplicity one.' Laotsee, in his fourteenth chapter called 'Tsanshuen,' or the Elogium of Hidden Wisdom, says, 'He that produced all, and is himself unprejudiced, is what we call Hi. He that gives light and knowledge to all things, and is himself invisible, is what we call Yi. He that is present everywhere, and animates all things, though we don't feel him, is called Ouei. Thou wilt in vain interrogate sense and imagination about these three, for they can make thee no answer. Contemplate by the pure spirit alone, and thou wilt comprehend, that these three united are but one.' Li-yong, in commenting upon this passage of Laotsee, says, 'Hi Yi, Ouei have no name, color, nor figure. They are united in the same spiritual abyss, and by a borrowed name they are called unity; [. . .] but an unity that is triple, and a triplicity that is one. To speak thus, is to understand what is most excellent in the law of wisdom.' The book *Sleeki* says, 'The ancient emperors sacrificed every three years solemnly to him that is one and three.' Choueuen, in commenting upon the hieroglyphic that expresses unity, says, 'that in the beginning the supreme reason subsisted in a triple unity, and that this unity created the heavens and the earth, separated them from each other, and will at last convert and perfect all things.'"

Ibid., pp. 444[-46]. "Besides the supreme God (says our author),

1. MS: "B. 9. p. 939 &c." MS p. 939 coincides with the very beginning of the entry, so JE intends the entirety of it.
2. I.e. of the Trinity.

called Changti, Tien and Yao, the ancient books of China talk of a minister of the supreme God, whom they call the Holy or the Saint by excellence. His different names in the Chinese language are Wen-wang, or the prince of peace; Chin-gin, the divine man; Chang-gin, God-man; Tient-see, son of the sovereign lord; Kiunt-see, son of the king; Kigen, son of heaven. The original books talk of him, as reuniting in one person all divine attributes and human qualities. In the book *Y-King,* we read these expressions: 'The Saint, or the Great Man, unites all the virtues of heaven and earth,' 'The Saint made the heavens,' and 'the Great Man created the universe.' Tching-ming-hian, in commenting upon these places, says, 'Before the Saint made the heavens, Tien was Lord; when the Great Man made the heavens, he himself became Lord.' The book *Chu-King* says, 'Heaven helps the people of the inferior regions; he gives them a guide and a teacher, and therefore he is the faithful minister of the supreme Lord, who gave him out of love the whole universe to govern; the instructions of the Saint are those of the supreme God himself. Tien is the Saint without a voice; the Saint is Tien speaking with a human voice.' The book *Lunghong* adds, 'The heart of the sovereign Lord is in the breast of the Saint; the counsels and rebukes of heaven are in the mouth of the Saint.' Tchouantsee says, 'that the Saint contains in himself the heaven and the earth. He has the form of a man, but the heaven and the earth are reunited in him.' The commentator adds, 'Since he has the form of a man without the passions of men, he is heaven-man.' The book *Siang-Sangasko:* 'What has the Great Man done?' He answers, 'He made the heavens, the earth, and all things.' Kouci-rout-see says, 'We know in consulting the ancient traditions, that though the Saint is to be born upon earth, yet he existed before anything was produced.' [. . .]

"The same books talk of his suffering state, and of his incarnation here below. The book *Chi-king* says, 'The Saint is the beautiful man of the west.' Laot-see says, Confucius maintained that the Saint was to come from the west; and that upon this proverb, the Emperor Hanmingti sent to the Indies to carry away the idol Fse. The book *Tchon-yong,* wrote by the nephew of Confucius, says, 'that the Saint is the middle between the heaven and the earth, that he alone can convert the hearts, and that he is the beginning and the Lord of all things. How sublime are the ways of the Saint! How extensive is his doctrine! If you consider his immensity, he nourishes and supports all things. If you regard his sublimity, he touches the heavens. We expect this Great Man, and he is to come after three thousand years.' The book *Y-King* contains these wonderful expressions: 'By the justice of the Saint, the world shall be reestablished in the ways of righteousness. He will labor and suffer much. He must pass the great torrent, whose waves shall enter into his soul; but he alone can offer up to the Lord a sacrifice worthy of him.' Laotsee says that the Saint pronounced these words: 'He that takes upon him the filth and dust of the kingdom shall be king of the universe.'[3] Tchouantsee says, 'The common people sacrifice their life to gain bread, the philosopher to acquire reputation, the nobility to perpetuate their family. The Saint dies to save the world. He does not seek himself, but the good of others. He enriches others and impoverishes himself, that is, according to Isemakouang, he loses himself to save others.'

"The same books talk of the triumphant state of the Messiah, who is to banish sin and sufferings; and to restore all things to their primitive perfection and felicity. In the book *Chi-king*, we find these words: 'We expect our King, when he comes, he will deliver us from all our miseries. We expect our King, when he comes, he will restore us to a new life.' Mengtsee, a disciple of Confucius, in speaking of the Saint, says, 'that the people expected him, as the dry grass expects the clouds and the rainbow.' In the third ode of the book of *Chi-king*, we read these words: 'He that is the only King and sovereign Lord sees two sorts of creatures, or nations that have abandoned him; but the Most High will not forever abandon them. He seeks for a man after his own heart, who can extend his empire. In this view he turns his eyes towards the west. It is there that he shall dwell, and reign with this new King. The Lord will restore men to their primitive virtue. Heaven has given itself an equal. Wen-wang, or the prince of peace, alone knows how to love his brethren. He makes all their happiness and all their glory. The Lord has enriched him with all his riches, and given him the universe for a recompense. The Lord said unto Wen-wang, Mount up first to the sacred mountain, in order to draw all the world after thee. See these rebels that do not obey their sovereign, arm thyself with my wrath, display thy standards, range thy troops, restore peace everywhere, fix the happiness of thy empire. Suddenly Wen-wang gains the top of the mountain. Rebellious spirits enter into your caverns. This is the mountain of the Lord, where you cannot be admitted. These living fountains are the pure waters wherein the subjects of Wen-wang are to quench their thirst. Wen-wang himself has chosen this mountain, he himself has opened the clear streams. It is hither that all

3. JE inserted this statement, which does not appear in *The Monthly Review* excerpt, after he had acquired Ramsay's *Philosophical Principles*.

the faithful nations must come. It is here that all the kings will meet.'"
See forward, No. 1200.

[Ibid., p. 451.] Concerning PARADISE. "We find these admirable expressions in an ancient book called *Chan-Hai-King*, in describing the
mountain Kouenlun, which was the middle of the world: 'All that could
be desired, wondrous trees, marvelous fountains, and flowery shades,
were found upon that sacred hill, or hidden garden. This mountain is
the inferior place of the sovereign lord, and the animal Kaiming guards
the entry of it.' Another author, called Hoi-ai-nang-wang, in speaking of
the first earth, says, 'This delicious garden, refreshed with zephyrs, and
planted with odoriferous trees, was situated in the middle of the mountain, which was the avenue of heaven. The waters that bedewed it, flowed
from a source called the fountain of immortality. He that drinks of it,
never dies. From thence flowed four rivers, a golden river, betwixt the
south and the east; a red river, betwixt the north and the east; a peace-
ful stream, betwixt the south and the west; and the river of the lamb, betwixt the north and the west. These magnificent floods are the spiritual
fountains of the sovereign Lord, by which he heals the nations and fruc-
tifies all things.' Tchou-angtre, in speaking of this primitive state, says,
'that it was the age of perfect virtue, . . . that man, entirely ignorant of
all evil, never abandoned virtue, and lived in perfect innocence, with simplicity, exempt from all cupidity.' Hoainantsee says, 'that in the first age
of perfect purity, all was in great concord, and the passions did not occasion the least murmur. Man united from within to sovereign reason,
all his actions from without were conformed to sovereign justice. His
soul, far from all dissimulation and falsehood, received a marvelous felicity from heaven, and the purest delights from earth. The seasons observed immutable laws; the winds and rains did not disturb the earth;
the sun and moon filled all with their benign influences, and the five
other planets never turned out of their courses.' The book *Sleeki* adds,
'that in this first antiquity and beginning of the world, the heavens and
the earth corresponded to the desires of men; the seasons were always
temperate, without any extremes, and man was endued with true virtue.
Then there were no calamities, sickness, nor death; and this was called
the great time of nature."

[Ibid., pp. 452–53.] "We find in the same books several vestiges of the
FALL OF MAN. In the book *Chi-king* it is said, 'Heaven placed mankind
upon a high mountain, but Taiwang made it fruitless by his fault. Wen-
wang, or the king of peace, endeavored to render to the mountain its
primitive beauty, but Taiwang contradicted, and opposed his will.' The

same book adds, 'Our misery has lasted these many ages; the world is lost; vice overflows all, as a mortal poison. We possessed happy, fruitful fields, a woman robbed us of them; all was subjected to us, a woman threw us into slavery. She hates innocence, and loves vice. The wise husband raised up a bulwark of walls. The woman, by an ambitious desire of knowledge, demolished them. Our misery did not come from heaven, but from a woman. She lost humankind; she erred first, and then sinned. She kindled the conflagration, that augments every day. Ah! unhappy Paossee, it was thou that kindled the fire that consumes us. The interpreter Lopi says, that after nature was spoiled and degraded, the birds of the air, the beasts of the field, the reptiles and the serpents conspired to hurt man; after that man had acquired the false science, all the creatures became his enemies.'

"These books talk of the renovation of the earth by the Saint. We have quoted already, many admirable passages on this head. . . . We shall content ourselves with adding one passage more, on this glorious restitution of the earth to its primitive paradisiacal form: 'The Lord looks with pleasure upon the sacred mountain. It is the abode of peace; there grow none of the trees employed to make warlike instruments. It is an eternal kingdom; it is the work of the Most High.' In other places of these sacred books it is said, 'that the kingdom of the middle, is a kingdom where the holy Son of heaven is to reign. He allows no wicked men to enter there; but he banishes them into the dark abodes of beasts and monsters. The subjects of that kingdom are called Tien-min, or heavenly people; Leang-min, upright people; Tsee-min, people of the sun, because they were governed by the holy Son of heaven, who perfects them from within, and from without; and nourishes them by his supreme virtue and celestial doctrine, so that they cry out with joy, The Son of heaven is truly the father of his people, and the Lord of the universe.'"

[Ibid., p. 454.] Concerning the FALL OF THE ANGELS. "The ancient books of the Chinese talk thus concerning the angelical spirits. In the book *Y-King* we read these words: 'The rebellious and perverse dragon suffers by his pride. His ambition blinded him, he would mount up to heaven, and he was thrown down to the earth. At first, his abode was in the high places, but he forgot himself, he hurt himself, and he lost eternal life.' The book *Chi-king* says, 'It is evident by the ancient traditions of our fathers, that Tchi-y-cou, or the beautiful, became deformed. The son of heaven was the first author of all revolt; but his rebellion extended at length to all nations, and deluged the world with crimes.' Chan-kai-king says, 'that Hoangti, or the sovereign Lord, ordered a celestial spirit to precipitate Tchi-y-cou into the black valleys of miseries.' Hoi-ai-nantsee says that Chong-chong disputed empire with the sovereign Lord of the universe, and raging with fury, he struck his head against a mountain. Then the pillars of heaven were broken, the earth subsided, and its position became oblique; Yao precipitated Chong-chong into the lower places, and the regions of darkness.'"

[Ibid., pp. 455–57.] "The original books of the Chinese (says our author) speak very oft of three necessary means of reuniting the soul to God: by contemplation or prayer; by the sacrifice of the passions, or mortification; by humility, or self-denial. . . . Meng-tsee, in commenting on the book *Chu-king,* says 'truth, justice and charity are the titles which make us approach to heaven, and which heaven alone confers. To watch over our heart, and to nourish our minds, is the true worship that heaven demands.' We find in the same book *Chu-king,* these admirable maxims: 'Sovereign perfection consists in being reunited to the supreme unity. The soul was at first all luminous, but it was obscured at last. We must labor to restore it to its primitive light. Now it is only by destroying all false desires and self-love, that we can discover the celestial reason. To fancy that we have virtue, is to have very little of it. The study of wisdom consists in being very humble, as if we were incapable of anything; and yet be ardent, as if we could do all.' In the book *Chi-king* we read these words: 'The sovereign Lord said to Wen-wang, or the prince of peace, I love a pure and simple virtue like thine. It makes no noise. It does not dazzle from without. It is not froward and proud. In seeing thee, one would say, that thou hast no light nor knowledge, but to conform thyself to my orders. The supreme Tien hates the proud, and loves the humble. There is not one instant, wherein I cannot offend Tien; how then can we have one moment's joy in this miserable life? The august heaven loves only those who declare themselves lovers of justice and virtue. Watch continually over the least things. When thou art in the secret of thine house, don't say, None see me, for there is an intelligent spirit that sees all. Tien pierces into the bottom of hearts, as light into a dark room. We must endeavor to correspond to his lights, as a musical instrument perfectly tuned. We must unite ourselves to him, as two marbles, that seem but one. We must receive from his hand, so soon as he opens it. He enlightens us continually; but by our disorderly passions we shut up the entry of our souls.' Telluchi, in commenting upon these passages, says 'that it is not sufficient to regulate the outward man, but that we must watch over the least motion of the inward man.' A commentator upon Tchuchi, and one of his disciples, defines thus the perfect sage: 'He is full of sweetness and condescension. He is humble, and always ready to yield to others. One would say, in hearing him, that he knows nothing and is capable of nothing. The sublimest virtues are founded on humility; and there is no man so enlightened, as he that believes his lights are bounded. The book *Tu-his,* wrote by Confucius, and commented on by his disciple Tsengt-see, speaks continually of restoring in us that primitive light and purity, which the soul received from heaven, upon its first creation, which it has lost by sin, and which heaven alone can render to it, by its internal irradiations and influences. The canonical books of China, and the most ancient commentators upon them, who lived long before the Christian era, are full of such passages, in commendation of internal prayer, purity and humility, inward recollection, and continual vigilance and true self-denial."

1182. END OF CREATION. GLORY OF GOD.[4] Many argue that it must be that all men should make their own happiness their highest end in all things because, in whatever end men pursue, they seek to gratify some inclination. They pursue it because they are inclined to it. They seek it as what pleases them, and what they conceive would be well pleasing to 'em if obtained. Thus when a man from benevolence seeks the prosperity of another, he seeks the other's happiness because it is agreeable to him and would, if obtained, be pleasing to him or, which is the same thing, would contribute to his pleasure or happiness. Therefore, still he seeks his own happiness and seeks nothing any otherwise than as something that would be pleasing and happifying to him. And so they suppose that 'tis evident from the very nature of benevolence that, when a man acts from it, he therein seeks his own happiness and makes it his ultimate end.

And yet some of those that are in this scheme strongly insist that God cannot make his own glory his ultimate end, for that reason, because he can't make his own happiness his end, being already infinitely happy, and does not need any manifestation of his glory to make him more happy; and therefore he must act only from benevolence, seeking the happiness of his creatures and making that his ultimate end, and not his own happiness, and so run into a great inconsistence. For[5] they suppose

---

4. The line drawn through the left side of this entry, as well as the entry's unusual number of crossed-out words and emendations, suggest that JE intended this material for reuse in his *Dissertation Concerning the End for Which God Created the World*—an intention fulfilled primarily in ch. 1, sec. 4 of that work. See especially *Works, 8,* 452–53, n. 8.

5. MS: "For. 1."

it may be argued from the very nature of benevolence, [or] that which is to have pleasure or happiness in the happiness of another, that he that acts from benevolence makes his own happiness his ultimate end. And yet they insist that God can't make his own happiness his ultimate [end], but must act only from benevolence, speaking these two in opposition one to another. Speaking of acting from benevolence was opposite to his making his own happiness his ultimate end, and excluded and disproved it, which yet in the other case they suppose necessarily infers and implies it.

God's making his own glory his end no more implies his seeking his own happiness than his making the creatures' good his end. 'Tis true that his seeking his own glory implies that he is well-pleased and gratified in glorifying himself, as herein he does what appears in his eyes beautiful and fit to be accomplished, as doubtless 'tis fit in itself that infinite glory should be manifested. So in making the creatures' happiness [his end] he, by the supposition, does as really please and gratify himself as in the other, inasmuch as by his benevolence he delights in the happiness of the creatures.

1183. CONSCIENCE IN NATURAL MEN, SPIRITUAL SENSE. Conscience in natural men concerning the moral good and evil of their own actions may be summed up in the dictate of their minds concerning their treatment of others, in this respect, viz. the acceptance they should give such treatment in case they were in the place and circumstances of their treatment or behavior, and he in theirs, how they should approve or resent, or what they should expect and think the case required.

1184. Add this to No. 864.[6] PROVIDENCE. GOD'S MORAL GOVERNMENT OF THE WORLD. GLORY OF GOD THE END OF THE CREATION. "The blessed God [. . .] never acts without design, and his designs are ever worthy of himself, and bear the characters of his attributes. Whatever honor might be reflected on the divine wisdom and power by the first production of things, it would be soon eclipsed by their consequent irregularities, without the interposure of his providence. As it is absurd to suppose, that an infinitely wise being should make creatures for no end at all; so it is equally absurd to imagine, that he does not conduct them to the end de-

6. JE's reference concludes, "B. 3, p. 2 of that number, at this mark," followed by a cue sign. The corresponding cue mark is found at the end of the third paragraph of No. 864 (*Works*, 20, 95).

signed by his providence. Now it is only creating wisdom that perfectly understands universal nature, that perfectly spies every spring of motion, and therefore can correct the errors of the universe. 'Tis only an infinite mind, in concurrence with almightiness, that can take thorough cognizance and proper care of that grand system of beings, the spacious theater of nature contains; that can allot to every creature its portion, [. . .] and forasmuch as no mere creature possesses these perfections of infinite wisdom and power, the world must needs be governed by him that made it.

"And indeed if we consider his nature and attributes, we may soon perceive that he is not only qualified for, but in some measure necessitated to, take upon him the government of the universe: for does not the end and perfection of his attributes consist in their exercise? Certainly the end of wisdom is design, the end of power is action, and the end of goodness doing good: to say that these perfections are not exercised upon proper objects and occasions, is to represent them as insignificant. Of what use would the wisdom of Jehovah be, if he had nothing to design or direct; to what purpose his almightiness, if all things were done without him, and of what avail his goodness, if he ever left the innocent a prey to misfortunes; there must therefore be a providence that governs all.

"The Almighty has implanted in most creatures, a natural care of their offspring, and represents it as an argument of the want of understanding in the ostrich, that she 'leaveth her eggs in the earth, [. . .] forgetteth that the foot may crush them, [. . .] and is hardened against her young ones as though they were not hers' [Job 39:14–16]. Now can we, without inconsistency and blasphemy, impute such a careless character to God, respecting the offspring of his power?" Mr. Gilbert Tennent's two sermons at the opening of the Presbyterian Church in Philadelphia, pp. 12–13.[7]

1185. Concerning the reasonableness of the doctrine of the IMPUTA-TION OF CHRIST'S RIGHTEOUSNESS, see Dr. Williams' fourth volume of sermons, pp. 88–94.[8]

---

7. Gilbert Tennent, *The Divine Government over All Considered, and The Necessity of Gratitude, for Benefits Conferred (by It,) Represented, in Two Sermons, Preach'd June the 7th, 1752, in the Presbyterian Church Lately Erected in Arch-Street, in the City of Philadelphia* (Philadelphia, 1752), 12–13.

8. The reference is to a passage in Daniel Williams' "Justification by Imputed Righteousness," the second of his *Discourses on Several Important Subjects*, vol. 4 (London, 1750), pp. 88–94, in which the Presbyterian divine (best known for his Baxterian opposition to antinomianism) de-

1186. Concerning PERSEVERANCE IN FAITH as a necessary means of continuing in a state of JUSTIFICATION, see Dr. Williams' fourth volume, pp. 187–92, [and] fifth volume, pp. 119–20, 136–38.[9] See next No. but one.[1]

1187. ETERNITY OF HELL TORMENTS. See Dr. Williams' fifth volume, pp. 383–91.[2]

1188. See No. 1186. See [No.] 729.[3] PERSEVERANCE. JUSTIFICATION. It seems to be because continuance in faith is necessary to continuance in justification, at least in part, that the Apostle expresses himself as he does, Rom. 1:17, "For therein the righteousness of God is revealed from faith unto faith: as it is written, The just shall live by faith." Or the righteousness of God is revealed, as we receive it and have the benefit of it, from faith, or by faith, unto faith. For 'tis by faith that we first perceive and know this righteousness, and do at first receive and embrace it, and do at first become interested in it. And being once interested in it, we have the continuance of faith in the future persevering exercises of it made sure to us, which is necessary in order to a suitable continuance [in a] justified state. And, faith continuing, our interest in God's righteousness continues, and we are continued in a justified state, and shall certainly have the future eternal reward of righteousness.

And thus that is fulfilled, "the just shall live by faith" [Rom. 1:17], agreeable to that, I Pet. 1:5, "We are kept by the power of God through faith unto salvation"; and agreeable to that, Heb. 10:35–39, "Cast not away therefore your confidence, which hath great recompense of reward. For ye have need of patience, that, after ye have done the will of

---

fends a Calvinistic understanding of forensic imputation. On the publishing history of Williams' *Discourses,* see *Works, 13,* 500, n. 8.

9. The references are to passages in Williams' "Mr. [Nathaniel] M[ather]'s False Charge Confuted," in *Discourses on Several Important Subjects, 4,* 187–92, and "Peace with Truth; or An End to Discord," in ibid., *5,* 119–20, where Williams argues that "God doth require believers to persevere in faith and holiness, as a means of their continuance in a state of salvation"; that "it is not blameable legal fear, for believers to be solicitously cautious in resisting temptations, and striving in Christ's strength to persevere, and this lest they eternally perish"; and that "a man that hath once believed, if he should fall under the reigning power of sin and corruption, ought to suspect that he is not in a state of salvation" (*4,* 187–91). See also No. 856, *Works, 20,* 83.

1. I.e. No. 1188, where JE continues with this theme.

2. The reference is to a passage in Williams' "A Letter on the Discourse of Free-Thinking," *Discourses, 5,* 383–91, in which Williams defends the eternity of hell torments against the incredulity of more liberal ministers.

3. *Works, 18,* 353–57.

God, ye might receive the promise. For yet a little while, and he that shall come will come, and will not tarry. Now the just shall live by faith: but if any man draw back, my soul shall have no pleasure in him. But we are not of them who draw back unto perdition; but of them that believe to the saving of the soul"; and ch. 3:6, 14, 18, 19, and 4:1, 11; Heb. 6:4, 11, 12; and the former part of the fifteenth chapter of John, "Abide in me, and I in you. . . . If a man abide not in me, he is cast forth as a branch . . . ; continue ye in my love. If ye keep my commandments, ye shall abide in my love; even as I have kept my Father's commandments, and abide in his love" [vv. 4–10]. It was impossible that Christ should not continue in his Father's love. He was entitled to such help and support from him as should be effectual to uphold him in obedience to his Father. And yet it was true that, if Christ had not kept the Father's commandments, he could not have continued in his love. He would have been cast out of favor.

See Rom. 11:22, Col. 1:21–23, I Tim. 2:15, II Tim. 4:7–8, Rom. 4:3 compared with Gen. 15:6, I John 2:24–28.

1189. INVITATIONS OF THE GOSPEL are directed to reprobates. See Matt. 22:1–5 ff.; Luke 14:16 ff.; Matt. 20:16 and 22:14; Acts 13:38; Hos. 11:7; Prov. 4:24 ff.; Rev. 3:18, 20; Proverbs, chs. 8 and 9; Matt. 9:13; John 6:29.

1190. CHRISTIAN RELIGION. SUCCESS OF THE GOSPEL IN THE OVER-THROW OF HEATHENISM. CHRIST'S MIRACLES. God, in Ex. 4, at the beginning, when Moses objected that perhaps the people would not believe that he had sent him, directed him to work two miracles to convince them, viz. the transmutation of his rod to and from a serpent and, secondly, the making his [hand] leprous and healing the leprosy. And 'tis to be noted that the preference is given to the last miracle, as being especially what might well be regarded as a good evidence of Moses' divine mission. V. 8, "And it shall come to pass, if they will not believe thee, neither hearken to the voice of the first sign, that they will believe the voice of the latter sign." By which it is manifest that such a sort of miracles as Christ wrought, and which he most abounded in, viz. his healing the bodies of men when diseased, were a proper and good evidence of a divine mission. See here Kidder's *Demonstration*, Pt. II, p. 5c, d.[4] Moses turned

---

4. At this point in his *Demonstration of the Messias* (2nd ed., corr., London, 1726), Richard Kidder infers from God's giving Moses miraculous powers that "the power of working miracles,

water into blood (Ex. 4:9 and 7:19); Christ turned water into wine. The former is spoken of as a sure evidence of divine power (Ex. 7:17).

Moses tells Pharaoh, Ex. 8:10, that the frogs should be removed, "that thou mayest know that there is none like the Lord our God." The magicians could bring up frogs, but not remove 'em. They brought plagues, but took away none. But if the driving out the frogs was such an evidence of[5] the distinguishing power of the Almighty, how much more the driving out devils from the bodies and souls of men, silencing his oracles, turning them out of their temples, and out of those who used curious arts, as at Ephesus, and afterwards abolishing their worship through the Roman Empire.

For the gods that were worshipped in the heathen world were devils, by the testimony of the Old Testament (Ps. 106:37) and even by the testimony of the writings of Moses (Deut. 32:17 and Lev. 17:7), which last place calls the idols of Egypt devils. Christ, by the prevailing of the Christian religion, cast out those devils out of that very land of Egypt. And which was the greatest work: to drive the frogs out of Egypt, or to drive the impure spirits that were the gods of Egypt? 'Tis spoken of (Is. 19:1) as a glorious manifestation of the majesty of God that he should ride on a swift cloud and should come into Egypt, and the idols of Egypt should be moved at his presence (see also Jer. 43:12). But when Christ came into Egypt in the preaching of his gospel, it moved, dispossessed and banished the idols of Egypt and abolished them out of the world. And not only did Christ thus drive away the devils, the false gods, out of Egypt, but out of all the nations round about Canaan that were known by the Israelites, or that we read of in the Old Testament, even to the utmost extent of the then-known heathen world, and far beyond it. These gods were by Christ dispossessed of their ancient tenements, which they had held age after age, time out of mind; utterly abolished, so that they have had no worshippers now for a great many ages—no temples, no sacrifices, no honors done 'em. They are old, obsolete things now, utterly disregarded in the world.

And 'tis abundantly spoken of in the Old Testament as a future, glorious work of God, greatly manifesting his power and majesty, that [he]

---

tended to gain, a belief, that God had sent him" and that "the greater number of miracles, which he should do, would have the greater force to this purpose. And if this be true, then the miracles, that Jesus did, are a good evidence of his mission from God: And that he wrought more than Moses did, gives us still a greater ground to receive him, than Moses gave the men of Israel."

5. MS: "that."

should prevail against and destroy the gods of the heathen, and abolish their worship. (See the "Fulfillment of the Prophecies of the Messiah," §§ 139, 153.)[6] But our Jesus has the honor of this glorious work. See No. 1194.

Again, when Korah and his company charged Moses and Aaron with taking too much upon them, Moses says, Num. 16:5, "tomorrow the Lord will show who are his, and who is holy; and will cause him to come near unto him: even him whom he hath chosen will he cause to come near unto him." And again, vv. 28–30, "Hereby ye shall know that the Lord hath sent me to do all these works; for I have not done them of my own mind. If these men die the common death of all men," etc. If the miraculous taking away [of] men's lives be so great an evidence of Moses' and Aaron's divine mission, and of their being holy and chosen and appointed of God, how much is raising men from the dead an evidence of thence. Which is the greatest work: to take away men's lives, or to restore them to life after they are dead, or indeed miraculously to save them from death when they are sick with mortal diseases? Again, God's causing the earth to open and swallow up those wicked men is no more an evidence of a divine hand than Christ's preventing the sea from swallowing up those that were in the ship by immediately quieting the winds and sea by a word's speaking, when the ship was even covered with waves through the violence of the tempest; and at another time upholding Peter from sinking and being swallowed up by the tempestuous sea when walking on the water. Elisha's causing iron to swim is mentioned in the Old Testament as a great miracle. But this was not greater than His[7] own walking on the water, and causing Peter to walk upon it.

When Elijah had restored to life the widow's son, she says upon it, I Kgs. 17:24, "by this I know that thou art a man of God, and that the word of the Lord in thy mouth is truth." But this sort of miracles Christ wrought, besides rising from the dead himself.

Let Christ's feeding the multitude with a few loaves and fishes be compared with Elisha's miracle in II Kgs. 4:42–44, and also that, vv. 1–7. Cur-

---

6. In the MS, JE refers to an entry on "p. 121" of "Fulfillment," later numbered sec. 139, which begins, "It was foretold that in the times of the Messiah's kingdom, the true God would very visibly and remarkably show himself above the gods of the heathen, triumphing over them to the confounding of them and their worshipers." Sec. 153 begins, "It was foretold that in the days of the Messiah's kingdom, instead of worship so much consisting in sacrifices of birds and beasts and carnal ordinances and external performances, that worship should be appointed and maintained in the church of God that should be more simple and spiritual, consisting in prayer, praise, humility, brokenness of heart, obedience, almsgiving, etc."

7. I.e. Christ's.

ing the leprosy of Naaman is one of the most celebrated of Elisha's miracles. The king of Israel speaks of healing the leprosy as a peculiar work of God (II Kgs. 5:7). Naaman himself was convinced by it that the God of Israel was the only true God.

Moses speaks of God's stilling the tempest in Egypt, and causing the thunder and hail to cease, as that which will convince Pharaoh that the earth was the Lord's (Ex. 9:29). Then, by parity of reason, Christ's stilling the tempest and causing the winds and seas to obey him, was an evidence that the earth and seas were his.

Moses turned water into blood, and that was one of the signs by which he was to convince the people of his divine mission. He was to take some of the water of the river and pour it out on the dry land, and it was to be turned to blood. But this was not a greater work, nor so glorious, as Christ's turning water into wine.

Abraham's conquering the four kings and their armies with his armed servants and confederates, of perhaps five or six hundred in all, is celebrated in Scripture as a glorious work of God and a remarkable evidence of the sovereignty and absolute supremacy of Jehovah, his being the first and the last (Is. 41:1–7). And in a peculiar manner the victory of Jehovah therein over the false gods of the conquered nations is celebrated. It greatly affected Melchizedek, King of Salem, and convinced [him] that he[8] was God's chosen friend, chosen that he and his posterity might be blessed as God's people. But what is this to Jesus' conquering the world in its greatest strength, and when united under that which by the prophet Daniel is represented as the greatest and by far the strongest monarch, by his handful of poor, weak, illiterate disciples?

Christ's victory over the false gods of the nations in this conquest was far more conspicuous than[9] the opposition was to them. Strife was more directly with them; the thing professedly sought and aimed by Christ in the conflict was the utter destruction of these false gods, the entire rooting them out and abolishing their worship out of the world. And such a victory as this was obtained: these false gods were forsaken, their oracles silenced, their temples destroyed, their images everywhere burnt, and their remembrance made to cease; so that now, for many ages, they have not been remembered any otherwise but as instances of the great blindness and folly of their votaries.

And 'tis further to be observed that, in that forty-first chapter of Isa-

---

8. I.e. Abraham.
9. MS: "as."

iah, this very victory of Abraham is spoken of as a representation of this great victory of the Messiah over the idols of the nations.

The work of Gideon in conquering the Midianites and the multitudes that were joined with them, by 300 men, with the light of lamps and sound of trumpets, is celebrated as a great work of God's power (Judg. 6:14 and 7:2, 7). But this is but a mere type of Christ's conquering the world by the preaching of the gospel. This victory over Midian is spoken of in Scripture as representing the conquests of the Messiah (Is. 9:4).

Elisha's smiting the army of the Syrians with blindness is mentioned as a great miracle (II Kgs. 6:18 ff.). But opening the eyes of the blind, as Christ did, is a much greater miracle.

Moses and other prophets wrought many miracles, whereby they brought great judgments on men. But miracles of the beneficent kind were ever noted in the church of God as greater, and more distinguishing of a divine hand, than of the contrary kind. See *Synopsis* on Ex. 7:12.[1]

See back, [No. 1156,] p. 70.[2]

1191. TRINITY, intimations of it in the Old Testament. See Bp. Kidder's *Demonstration*, Pt. 3, pp. 81–92, 113–16. The opinion of the Jewish doctors concerning it, ibid., pp. 82–87, 90–114.[3]

1192. CHRISTIAN RELIGION.

1. 'Tis a great argument that JESUS is the TRUE MESSIAH, that he is the person that has actually brought life, and immortality to life, which is so agreeable to reason and so agreeable to the innumerable dark hints given in the Old Testament; that he hath declared with great plainness of speech a future state of rewards and punishments, as is most rational and agreeable to the nature of true religion and virtue, and tending most properly to promote these things, according to what is taught by the reason of mankind in its best improvement, and as it appeared in the wisest philosophers, and by the word of God delivered in the Old Testament, which show how essential to true virtue and religion are weanedness from the riches, pleasures and honors of this world, and a readiness

---

1. Matthew Poole, *Synopsis Criticorum aliorumque Sacrae Scripturae Interpretum* (4 pts. in 5 vols., London, 1669–76), *I*, Pt. I, cols. 342–43.

2. MS: "p. 9." The passage here referred to is the fifth paragraph from the end of No. 1156. This reference and the preceding paragraph are a later insertion in different ink.

3. For these passages in Kidder, see JE's essay entitled, "Question: In What Sense Did the Saints Under the Old Testament Believe in Christ to Justification?" in the section on "Justification" in the "Controversies" notebook (*Works*, *21*, 372–408).

to lay down our lives for God, and to place our happiness in God, in the knowledge of him, in union and communion with him, conformity to him and dwelling with him.

'Tis exceeding manifest from reason and the Old Testament that such a state of future rewards and punishments is appointed by the great moral governor of the world, and that these rewards and punishments are the grand sanction of the divine law and all God's commands, and consequently that it must be in God's design some time or other plainly to reveal [them] to the world and not always to keep hid as it were behind a veil. But Jesus is in fact the person that has brought to light such a future state as reason says there is; and as we now, being taught by Jesus, can see to have been hinted often in the Old Testament; and has actually brought it to be the received doctrine among mankind, received by all the chief nations of the world as one of the most fundamental articles of their faith and religion, and as that which is plainly exhibited without a veil[4] and made evident beyond controversy, and fully established among his followers.

Seeing this was to be done, and that God had a design to bring these things thus to light at last, and forborne for so many ages, there is the greatest reason to suppose that it was to be done by the Messiah, who is prophesied of as God's greatest prophet and teacher, and light of the world, who should bring good tidings, who should most clearly reveal the divine law and covenant and publish good tidings and salvation. See "Fulfillment of Prophecies of the Messiah." It was foretold that eternal life should be a benefit of the Messiah's kingdom (ibid.).[5]

Our Jesus is the person that has most plainly and rationally taught the doctrines of the resurrection and general judgment, and fully introduced and established these doctrines, agreeable to the hints and prophecies of the Old Testament (ibid.).[6]

2. 'Tis a great evidence that Jesus is the Messiah, that he hath abol-

---

4. MS: "vain."

5. JE probably means § 18 of No. 1068, "Fulfillment," which begins, "It was foretold that in the days of the Messiah that God would accomplish some very eminently great work of goodness for his people, that was called *that good thing that God had promised them.*" JE goes on to observe that this "good thing" was salvation, and that "God should bring to pass this great SALVATION and peace for his people by the Messiah." "Fulfillment," § 180, begins, "Eternal life is often spoken of in the prophecies of the Old Testament as the fruit of the Messiah's salvation."

6. No. 1068, "Fulfillment," § 173, "By the prophecies of the Old Testament, one fruit or attendant of the Messiah's coming and kingdom should be the resurrection of the dead"; and § 175, "It was foretold in the ancient prophecies that the Messiah should be the judge of the world."

ished the ceremonial law and introduced a spiritual, rational service fit for all nations, which reason, with the Old Testament, show plainly was a thing to be done by the Messiah.

3. 'Tis a great argument that Jesus is the Messiah, that there is such a correspondence between him and what he did, suffered, and the doctrine he taught and administration he introduced, and the types of the Old Testament. 'Tis plain these types did mainly point to the Messiah and were to be fulfilled in him, and 'tis evident that they are remarkably fulfilled in Jesus.

1193. CHRISTIAN RELIGION. JESUS THE TRUE MESSIAH. HIS SPIRIT OF PROPHECY. See [No.] 1044. Great changes in kingdoms and nations coming to pass according to God's prediction is often spoken of by God himself in the Old Testament as a great evidence of his being the only true God, vastly distinguished from all other gods and infinitely above 'em; particularly his foretelling the great changes brought to pass in the world relating to his church and people, such as great deliverances and salvations to his own people and great judgments and destruction to those nations that injure them and are their enemies, which things Christ foretold and were accomplished exactly according to his prediction. And the foretelling these very things, which Christ foretold, is spoken of expressly as an evidence of true divinity, yea, and a distinguishing characteristic of the Messiah.

Thus in Is. 41:21 to ch. 42:21, concerning which passage of Scripture the following things are worthy of note:

1. That the foretelling the revolutions of nations and monarchies, and particularly the destruction of Babylon by Cyrus, is greatly insisted on by God as a great evidence of his being the true God, and as most clearly and greatly distinguishing him from all pretenders to divinity. See ch. 41:21–27. See also ch. 44:25 to the end, and 46:10. But Jesus was one that professed divinity and foretold revolutions of nations as great and strange as this, yea, far more wonderful. He foretold the destruction of Jerusalem (and the nation of the Jews, and the deliverance of Christians that were in it), that had been the Holy City; and the nation of the Jews, that had been God's own people, and whose protector he had in a special manner been, and towards whom he exercised a more peculiar providence. It was a greater thing for such a city and such a nation to be destroyed than for Babylon to be destroyed. And it was a greater evidence of divine foreknowledge to foretell how he would dispose of those who had for many ages been his peculiar people and peculiar treasure, which

he took a special care of above all nations, than to foretell what should happen to a nation of aliens.

2. In this very place such a spirit of prophecy, or ability to foretell such future events, is spoken of as that wherein the Messiah himself should be distinguished from the gods of the heathen (ch. 41:27 to 42:4). Here when it is said, v. 28, "there was no counselor," special respect is had to their magicians and false prophets. See ch. 47:12–13 and Dan. 2:2.

3. Here the foretelling the conversion of the Gentiles from their heathenism, from idolatry, is spoken of as the prerogative of the true God, a glory that should not be given to another. Ch. 42:8–9, with the foregoing part of the chapter and what follows to v. 17.

Again, the foretelling the gathering of God's people from all nations and enlightening of the blind and opening the ears of the deaf is spoken of as greatly and evidently distinguishing the true God and his servant, the Messiah (ch. 43:6–13). But thus did Jesus.

So in ch. 44:3–8, foretelling the conversion of multitudes to profess themselves the people of the true God is spoken, and the exact accomplishment is spoken of and insisted in, as a certain and very distinguishing note of the true God. But thus did Jesus.

And in the twenty-fifth and twenty-sixth verses of the same chapter, God declares that he frustrates the predictions of false pretenders but will confirm the word of true prophets, and particularly of his servant, i.e. the Messiah, called God's servant often in the preceding chapters. Here see Is. 19:12.

In ch. 45:21 to the end, a foretelling the conversion of the Gentiles from idolatry to worship the true God is spoken of in like manner as an high prerogative and certain evidence of the true God.

In ch. 48, a person's foretelling such great salvations, as speaking in his own name, is spoken of as a great evidence that the person which foretells is the same that does the work. (Here see the passage in No. 1194.)[7]

1194. See No. 1190.[8] CHRISTIAN RELIGION. SUCCESS OF THE GOSPEL. The turning the wilderness into a fruitful field is spoken of [9] by God as a peculiar work of God, a certain sign of a divine hand. Is. 41:18–20, "I

---

7. MS: "the next p. b." The passage here referred to, the third paragraph of No. 1194, is on p. 116.

8. MS: "p. 3. b." JE refers to the fourth paragraph of No. 1190, pp. 109–10, where there is a cross-reference to No. 1194.

9. MS: "as."

will open rivers in high places, and fountains in the midst of the valleys: I will make the wilderness a pool of water, and the dry land springs of water. I will plant in the wilderness the cedar, the shittah tree, and the myrtle, and the oil tree; I will set in the desert the fir tree, and the pine, and the box tree together: that they may see, and know, and consider, and understand together, that the hand of the Lord hath done this." 'Tis evident this is not intended in a literal sense, but signifies a happy change in the state of mankind, from a state wherein men are represented as barren, and as briers and thorns, and like wild beasts, to a morally excellent and happy state.

This might be proved by the frequent use of such figures in Scripture prophecy. But 'tis manifest this was effected in a remarkable manner by Jesus Christ and his apostles and followers, according to Christ's word and his prediction, in the turning of the world from heathenism to the knowledge and worship of the true God, to becoming apprehensions of his moral government, and from all manner of vice to virtue.

(Here see No. 1193.)[1] And this circumstance may be observed, that it being done at Christ's word, according to his prediction, when he foretold it, as a thing that he would effect, and being done afterwards by his messengers in his name, pretending only to act as his servants: I say, its being done with these circumstances, this did as much show that he was the doer of it as that he healed the sick and cast out devils when those things were so done at his word, that when he spake and commanded the effect to be, it immediately was. It makes the relation between the effect and his word, and the dependence of the latter on the power of him that speaks the word, as evident.

This effect of turning the wilderness into a fruitful field, or an effect described in like figures of speech, is spoken of by God as one of the greatest of the works of God, far greater than those that were wrought for Israel in bringing them out of Egypt. Is. 43:15–21.

And if we consider the particular circumstances of the fulfillment of the predictions of Jesus in the success of his gospel, and compare them with what is spoken of in the Old Testament as the peculiar and distinguishing work of God, the evidences of the authority and divinity of Jesus will appear yet greater. Disappointing and baffling the power and subtlety of the potent, the crafty and the cruel, in their attempts for the destruction of the poor, the helpless and the meek, and, finally, in a remarkable manner giving them the ascendant and victory over them and

1. MS: "in the last p. d." The cross-reference is at the very end of No. 1193.

terribly destroying their oppressors and persecutors, is often spoken of as a peculiar work of the Most High, as remarkably manifesting a divine hand and gloriously displaying God's supreme power and wisdom and divine mercy. So Job 5:11–16; the song of Hannah in I Sam. 2; Job 12:17–19; particularly God's thus baffling the attempts of the heathen against those that fear him and that hope in his mercy, Ps. 33:10 to the end; so Ps. 46, throughout.

We find these things often spoken of as the peculiar and glorious work of the most high, in prophecies of the days of the Messiah, with a particular application to what he will do for his people that are weak and helpless, in the times of his kingdom. So Is. 25:1–8; Is. 40:22–24, with [v.] 27 to the end; Is. 41:11–12 ff., ch. 54:15–17, ch. 49:24–26; Ps. 68, throughout; Ps. 118:5–23. Yea, this is spoken of as the work and glory of the Messiah himself. Ps. 72:4; Is. 11:4; and Ps. 45:3–5.

These things are fulfilled in the most remarkable manner than ever they were by far in disappointing and baffling of the policy, power and rage of the greatest, wisest, most potent empire of the heathen that ever was in the world, in their greatest rage and violence, to the bringing of the church of Christ to a complete victory, so as to overthrow the ancient, long-established heathenism of the world in all the nations anywhere taken notice of in Scripture, so that it never has revived anymore.

And 'tis remarkable that it is foretold, particularly in Is. 42, that the Messiah should set judgment in the earth, and his law or religion among the nations, particularly the isles of Europe, against strong opposition and through great sufferings, under which his church should seem ready to be extinguished like a bruised reed and smoking flax, but that finally judgment should be brought forth to victory.

1195. CONFLAGRATION. That the fire with which Christ will appear at the day of judgment will be the fire in which Christ's enemies will suffer their proper punishment, even that great vengeance and consummate misery which he will come to execute upon them, that everlasting destruction which they shall suffer from his presence and from the glory of his power, is very manifest by II Thess. 1:8–9. But when it is said Christ will appear in flaming fire, how unreasonable would it be to doubt whether this fire be the same with that flaming, vehement fire which is elsewhere spoken as what shall attend his [coming] and shall be for the perdition of ungodly men, II Pet. 3.

Again, when it is said that the heavens and earth that are now are kept in store reserved unto fire against the judgment and perdition of ungodly men, certainly the words imply that they are kept in store for that perdition of which ungodly men shall be condemned to at the day of judgment. And we know that is everlasting perdition, and that they are reserved for that fire which they shall then be adjudged to, and that is everlasting fire, Matt. 25.

In the second chapter of this epistle [II Pet.], v. 4, the fallen angels are said to be "reserved unto judgment." And in v. 9 the unjust are said to be reserved "unto the day of judgment to be punished." And here in this third chapter, v. 7, the heavens and the earth are said to be reserved unto the day of judgment and their perdition. The word "reserved" is the same in the original in each place. Now it would be as reasonable to suppose that the Apostle, when he speaks of the devil's and wicked men's being reserved unto the day of judgment to be punished in the second chapter, he has respect to a temporary punishment, as to suppose that when in the third chapter he speaks of fuel kept in store unto fire against the day of their judgment and perdition, he has respect to a temporal perdition.

Again, the word "judgment," as well as "perdition," has respect to wicked men according to the most natural construction of the words, so that 'tis as much as to say: "reserved unto fire against the day of condemnation and destruction of ungodly men." If it had been so expressed, it would have been most evident that the destruction spoken of was that which they are to be condemned to at the day most eminently called the day of the judgment or condemnation of wicked men. The word κρισις is commonly put in the New Testament for condemnation or damnation. See John 5:29. The ἀνάστασιν[2] κρίσεως is the resurrection of damnation.

1196. GOD'S MORAL GOVERNMENT. So much evidence of the most perfect exactness of proportion, harmony, equity and beauty in the mechanical laws of nature, and other methods of providence which belong to the course of nature, by which God shows his regard to harmony, fitness, and beauty in what he does as the governor of the natural world, may strongly argue that he will maintain the most strict and perfect justice in proportion and fitness in what he does as the governor of the moral world.

1197. TRINITY, intimations of it in the Old Testament. In Ex. 20:2–3, when it is said in the third verse, "Thou shalt have no other gods before

2. MS: "ανασυοις."

me," the word is the same as in the foregoing verse, where it is said, "I am the Lord thy God, which brought thee out of the land of Egypt"— *Elohim* in both verses. I am the Jehovah, thy *Elohim*. Thou shalt have no other *Elohim*. Yet the latter *Elohim* is joined with an adjective of the plural number, which seems naturally to lead the children of Israel, to whom God spake these words, to suppose a plurality in the *Elohim* which brought them out of Egypt, implied in the name Jehovah. See further, [No.] 1241.

1198. CHRIST'S COMING BEING SPOKEN OF AS NIGH AT HAND. See [No.] 842, and note on Matt. 16:28.[3] What Christ says to his [disciples], Luke 17:22, is a confirmation that Christ's second coming would be long delayed. "And he said unto the disciples, The days will come, when ye shall desire to see one of the days of the Son of man, and ye shall not see it." By the days of the Son of man is meant the days of Christ's personal appearance in this lower world, perhaps including both his first and second appearing, but with a special reference to his second appearing, as is manifest from the context (see from v. 20 to the end, especially v. 26). It further appears by what is said in the former part of the next chapter, which is a continuation of the same discourse, and still with reference to the same thing, viz. his coming (especially by v. 1, and 7–8). See *Synopsis* on v. 22.[4]

1199. CHRIST'S COMING being spoken of as nigh at hand. See the next preceding No., and also [No.] 842. Having particularly considered the sayings of the apostles that have an appearance as though they expected Christ's last coming in their day, I would now consider the sayings of Christ which have such an aspect. And to clear this matter the following things may be observed:

1. Christ often speaks of his last coming as that which would be long delayed. Matt. 25:5, "While the bridegroom tarried, they all slumbered and slept." Luke 20:9, "A certain man planted a vineyard." [Matt. 25,] v. 19, "After a long time the lord of those servants cometh, and reckoneth with them." Matt. 24:48, "My lord delayeth his coming." So Luke 17:22 (see on this text in the preceding No., above).

2. 'Tis evident that when Christ speaks of his coming, his being re-

---

3. "Miscellanies" No. 842, in *Works*, 20, 57–64, and *Notes on Scripture*, nos. 197, 414, and 464, in *Works*, 15, 115–19, 421–22, 554. In the "Blank Bible" at this text, JE referred to "Scripture" nos. 484, 197, and 414, and to "Miscellanies" Nos. 1199, 842, and 1198.
4. Poole, *Synopsis Criticorum*, IV, Pt. I, cols. 1066–1067.

vealed, his coming in his kingdom, or his kingdom's coming, he has respect to his appearing in those great works of his power, justice and grace which should be in the destruction of Jerusalem, and other extraordinary providences which should attend it. So in Luke 17:26 to the end, with ch. 18:1–8, Christ speaks of *the kingdom of God's coming, of the coming of the days of the Son of man, of the Son of man's being revealed,* and *of the Son of man's coming.* But yet 'tis evident he has respect to the destruction of Jerusalem by ch. 17:37, "And they answered and said unto him, Where, Lord? And he said unto them, Wheresoever the body is, thither will the eagles be gathered together." See also ch. 19:13–15.

So when the disciples had been observing the magnificence of the temple and Christ had said to 'em, "Verily I say unto you, There shall not be left here one stone upon another, that shall not be thrown down" [Matt. 24:2], having respect to the destruction of Jerusalem, [and] the disciples ask him when these things should be and what should be the signs of his coming and of the end of the world by Christ's coming, they have plainly a respect to that time of the destruction of the temple which Christ had spoken of. And therefore their question is thus expressed by St. Mark, Mark 13:3–4, "Tell us, when shall THESE THINGS be? and what shall be the sign when all THESE THINGS shall be fulfilled?"; and in like manner by St. Luke, ch. 21:7. And Christ has many things in his answer agreeable to this sense of his question. In his answer he proceeds to speak of his coming and of the destruction of Jerusalem both in one. He warns 'em to beware of others that should COME in his stead (Matt. 24:4–5). Then he proceeds to tell 'em what will precede the END, i.e. the end of the world, which the disciples inquired after; and tells 'em what shall be signs of its approach (Matt. 24:6–16); and then speaks of the desolation of Jerusalem and of the land as that END, and that coming of his which they inquired after (Matt 24:15–21, 28 and, more plainly, Luke 21:20–24).

3. 'Tis manifest that the event [to] which Christ sometimes has respect by his coming, by his coming in his kingdom, by the end of the world, etc., he did not suppose would be at the time of the destruction of Jerusalem. He speaks of that event as attended with the general judgment and all nations being gathered before his judgment seat to receive an eternal sentence (Matt. 25, latter part); and that this judgment shall be attended with the general resurrection of the dead (John 5:21–22, 25–30); and that after this resurrection, and at the end of this world, the saints shall neither marry nor be given in marriage, but shall be as the angels of God in heaven (Matt. 22:30, especially Luke 20:34–36); and that at this last coming and end of the world all the wicked of all na-

tions shall be cast into a furnace of fire, into everlasting fire (Matt. 13:39–42. Ch. 25:40, 46); and the righteous shall then be as wheat gathered into God's barn, shall enter into the kingdom prepared for 'em before the foundation of the world, shall be received to Christ to live with him where he is, in his Father's house, in heaven, and shall shine forth as the sun in the kingdom of their Father in the possession of immortal life (Matt. 13:30, vv. 39, 43; ch. 25:34, 46; John 14:1–3; ch. 17:24).

But 'tis evident that when Christ spake of the destruction of Jerusalem, he did not expect that these things would be accomplished at that time. For he speaks of that destruction that should be of his enemies as, not of all nations or the whole wicked world, but as principally confined to Judea, and therefore directs his people that are at Judea, when they see signs of its approaching desolation, to flee out of Judea to the mountains, and warns others in other countries not to go into it (Luke 21:20–22; Matt. 24:15–17; Mark 13:14–15). He speaks of the great disadvantages they should be under who should be with child or give suck, and directs 'em to pray that their flight may not be in the winter, nor on the sabbath day (Matt. 24:19–20; Mark 13:17–18; Luke 21:23). But how do those things agree to the time when they should be as the angels of God in heaven, should be received with Christ to heaven and there shine forth as the sun? He speaks of destruction as being by war, by the sword of men and by the Roman armies (Luke 21:23–24). There shall be great distress in the land and wrath upon this people, and they shall fall by the edge of the sword and shall be led away captive into all nations. Matt. 24:28, "wheresoever the carcass is, there will the eagles be gathered together" (so Luke 17:37). Matt. 22:7, "But when the king heard thereof, he was wroth: and sent forth his armies, and destroyed those murderers, and burnt up their city."

Luke 19:43–44, "For the days shall come upon thee, that thine enemies shall cast a trench about thee, and compass thee round, and keep thee in on every side, And shall lay thee even with the ground, and thy children within thee; and they shall not leave in thee one stone upon another."

'Tis said, Luke 21:24, that after the destruction of Jerusalem the Jews should "be led away captive into all nations: and Jerusalem should be trodden down of the Gentiles." By this it appears that Christ had no thought that then the world should be destroyed, all mankind disposed in their eternal state, the righteous in heaven and the wicked all cast into a furnace of fire.

Christ supposes that the nations should remain after the destruction of Jerusalem, and the kingdom of God taken from them[5] and given [to] another nation. Matt. 21:41, 43, "They say unto him, He will miserably destroy those wicked men, and will let out his vineyard unto other husbandmen, which shall render him the fruits in their seasons. . . . Therefore I say unto you, The kingdom of God shall be taken from you, and given to a nation bringing forth the fruits thereof." Luke 20:15–16, "What therefore shall the lord of the vineyard do unto them? He shall come and destroy these husbandmen, and shall give the vineyard to others." And it appears by the parable of the marriage supper that the gospel should be preached to the Gentiles and be gloriously successful among them after Jerusalem's destruction. Matt. 22:7–10, "But when the king heard thereof, he was wroth: and he sent forth his armies, and destroyed those murderers, and burnt up their city. Then saith he to his servants, The wedding is ready, but they that were bidden were not worthy. Go ye therefore into the highways, and as many as ye find, bid to the marriage. So those servants went out into the highways, and gathered together all as many as they found, both good and bad: and the wedding was furnished with guests." From these things it follows:

4. That when Christ speaks of his coming, and his coming in his kingdom, etc., as being in that generation, and before some that were then alive should taste of death, there is no need of understanding him of his coming to the last judgment. But he may well be understood of his coming at the destruction of Jerusalem, which, as has been shown, he calls by these names and which he also distinguishes from his coming to the last judgment and consummation of all things. Yea,

5. 'Tis evident that he did not suppose that his coming to the last judgment and consummation of all things would be 'til a long time after the destruction of Jerusalem. The calling of the Gentiles instead of the Jews is spoken as what should be principally after the destruction of Jerusalem (Matt. 21:41, 43; Luke 20:15–16; Matt. 22:7–10). But this Christ himself speaks of as a gradual work in the parables of the grain of mustard seed and of the leaven hid in three measures of meal (Matt. 13:31–33; Luke 13:19–21; see Mark 4:26–32). And 'tis very manifest that Christ did not suppose that he should come to the consummation of all things till long after the destruction of Jerusalem, by Luke 21:24, where 'tis said the[6] Jews, after the destruction of Jerusalem, should "be trodden down of the Gentiles, till the times of the Gentiles should be fulfilled." 'Tis con-

5. I.e. the Jews.
6. MS: "of the."

siderably manifest that Christ, in these words as in some other things he says in the same discourse, has his respect to what is said in the last chapter of Daniel, in the great tribulation he speaks of (Matt. 24:21–22). He has manifestly in his eye what is said in Dan. 12:1. And in what he says here of the times of the Gentiles, he has respect to the times spoken of, Dan. 12:6–7, as will be manifest by comparing and observing the agreement. But these times are there spoken of as very long.

1200. See [No.] 1181.[7] TRADITIONS OF THE CHINESE concerning the MESSIAH. "Confucius' notion of God was, that he was the supreme truth and reason, or the fountain from whence truth and reason are communicated unto men. . . . That he was the original and ultimate end of all things, eternal, infinite, immovable, who produced and sustains all things. That he is one, supremely holy, supremely intelligent and invisible. And having discoursed of the perfection of reason and virtue, he used these remarkable words: 'We must wait for the coming of this perfectly holy man; and then we may hope, that, having such a guide and teacher, virtue, which is of such an excellent nature, will be brought into practice and be performed by men.'

"A little after, Confucius is related to say of the emperor, who ruled according to the law of reason, and example of the God of heaven, 'that such a one need not doubt but his virtue will be approved by that holy person who is expected to come upon earth; even though an hundred ages should pass before his coming.'

"And according to tradition universally received amongst the Chinese, Confucius was often heard to say 'that in the west the holy one will appear.'" Jackson's *Chronological Antiquities,* in *The Monthly Review, for August 1752,* pp. 97–98.[8]

1201. CEREMONIAL LAW was not immutable. See notes on I Chron. 11:39 and II Chron. 29:34.[9] God often appointed altars to be built for

7. The reference to No. 1200 in No. 1181 is on p. 101, above.
8. Excerpt from John Jackson, *Chronological Antiquities: or the Antiquities and chronology of the most Antient Kingdoms, from the creation of the world* (3 vols. London, 1752).
9. In the "Blank Bible" note on I Chron. 11:39, JE observes that some of David's "worthies" were Ammonites and Moabites, and that Ruth was a Moabitess, though Deut. 23:3 forbids any of these people from "entering into the congregation," which demonstrates that "eminent piety prevailed" over the law and that "evangelical qualifications" were more important than "legal" ones. And in the note on II Chron. 29:34, JE writes that, among other instances, the Levites' helping to slay the sacrifice, though contrary to the law (Lev. 1:5–6), "shows that the ceremonial law is not immutable."

the offering [of] sacrifices, besides the altar before the sanctuary, as in the command to Gideon (Judg. 6:26), the command to Elijah [I Kgs. 18:31–32], etc.

1202. The TEN TRIBES, how that many of these were incorporated with those that were of the kingdom of the house of David and with the Jews that returned from the captivity.

1. Part of the tribes of Dan and Simeon were within the tribe of Judah, and there continued and seemed to be, as it were, lost in that tribe (Josh. 19:1–9). And though some of these, it seems, after the reigns of David and Solomon, withdrew, left their original habitation and went over to the kingdom of Jeroboam (see I Chron. 4:31), yet some still remained in the inheritance of Judah, and were there in the reign of Hezekiah and were not carried captive with the rest of the Ten Tribes (see I Chron. 4:31). See Henry's notes on I Chron. 4:24–43.[1]

2. While David was in Ziklag, there joined themselves to him a considerable number of the Ten Tribes, as of Gad and of Manasseh (I Chron. 12:8–15, and 19–22), which we must suppose continued with him during the seven years that he reigned in Hebron, while the rest of the tribes they belonged to submitted themselves to Ishbosheth. And probably many of them living so long in Judah with David took up their settled abode there and returned no more to their old habitations.

3. The tribe of Levi generally left the country of the Ten Tribes and resorted to the kingdom of Judah, and remained there (II Chron. 11:13–14).

4. In Rehoboam's time, soon after the division of Israel into two kingdoms, great numbers out of all the tribes of Israel left their old habitation and dwelt in the territories of the king of Judah (II Chron. 11:16).

5. A great number of the Ten Tribes joined themselves to the kingdom of Judah in Asa's time (see II Chron. 15:9).

6. Again, a number fell to the kingdom of Judah in Hezekiah's time (II Chron. 30:11).

7. And again, a number of the remnant of the Ten Tribes in Josiah's time (II Chron. 34:6, 9).

8. It is very probable then, when the Jews were carried captive by Neb-

1. The reference is to Matthew Henry's *Commentary on the Whole Bible: Wherein Each Chapter Is Summed up in Its Contents, the Sacred Text Inserted at Large in Distinct Paragraphs, Each Paragraph Reduced to Its Proper Heads, the Sense given, and Largely Illustrated with Practical Remarks and Observations*, Vol. 2, *Joshua to Esther* (London, 1710; New York, 1800), 847–48, where Henry covers the same ground as JE does here.

uchadnezzar and afterwards were set at liberty by the kings of Persia to return to their own land, that many of the Ten Tribes returned with them. For they were doubtless most of them within the Persian dominion, and were included in the grants that these kings made to such as had been carried captive out of that land to return to it again. Thus we have an account of some that were originally of Bethel, Ai and Jericho, cities of the Ten Tribes that returned with Zerubbabel and Joshua (Ezra 2:28, 34). And the children of Ephraim and Manasseh are spoken of as dwelling at Jerusalem after the captivity (I Chron. 9:3).

9. 'Tis probable many of the Ten Tribes mixed with their brethren of Judah and Benjamin that stayed behind, and were dispersed abroad in other countries and never returned to their own land.

10. 'Tis observable that, after the return from the captivity, the people that united in the worship of God at Jerusalem are looked upon as consisting of twelve tribes, as usual. And, therefore, at the dedication of the temple they offered twelve he goats for a sin offering, according to the number of the tribes of the children of Israel (Ezra 6:17). See also ch. 8:35.

1203. See [No.] 1201. THE CEREMONIAL LAW was not so invariable but that from time to time it gave place when the moral reason of things required it. Thus in Ruth's admission, who was a Moabitess; so in the admission of an Ammonite and Moabite among David's worthies (I Chron. 11:39, 46); David's eating the showbread; Solomon's hallowing the middle court to offer sacrifice, though the law forbid the offering sacrifice anywhere but upon the altar (II Chron. 7:7); in the uncleans' eating the Passover in Hezekiah's time (see II Chron. 30:17–20); and the Levites' helping to slay the sacrifices (see notes on II Chron. 29:34).[2] Gideon, who was of the tribe of Manasseh, executed the office of a priest, offered sacrifice on another altar besides that before the tabernacle, by divine appointment (Judg. 6:24 ff.).[3]

These[4] things show the ceremonial law not to be immutable, and are intimations that it one day was to be wholly abolished, to give place to the moral reason of things on the great change to be made in the days of the gospel, when all nations should be God's people.

2. For the "Blank Bible" note on II Chron. 29:34, see p. 123, n. 9.

3. In the MS, the final sentence of this paragraph is appended at the end of the following paragraph but was apparently meant for insertion here.

4. MS: "This."

1204. We may judge what the Scripture means when it speaks of KNOW-ING GOD AND JESUS CHRIST as a thing peculiar to the saints by compar-ing the following texts: John 17:3; John 10:14–15; Matt. 25:12; Deut. 33:9; Job 9:21; Ps. 31:7.

1205. FUTURE STATE. We see that God provides some proper good for the satisfaction of the appetites and desires of every living thing. There is no appetite of any beast, bird, fish, insect, or animalcule but God has made provision of an answerable good, something suitable, proportion-able and adequate to it. And will he not make provision for the best, most rational, noble appetites in the world, the desires of virtue and love to God? Would he so order things that, the higher these appetites are, the more disappointment men must suffer, the more must they must be crossed, which is the case if there be no future state?

1206. CHRISTIAN RELIGION concerning the FALL, the need of a REV-ELATION in order to know whether there be any FORGIVENESS of sin to obtain, and how far and upon what terms, and whether REPENTANCE will be accepted, and what and how far, and to discover an ATONEMENT. SAT-ISFACTION. The substance of what follows is taken from the preface to *The Religion of Jesus Delineated,* pp. xi–xxv.[5]

All having sinned "and incurred the divine [. . .] displeasure; it was needful, the philosopher should say and show what hope or expectation he has, of the divine favor and forgiveness. For, if there be no forgive-ness with God, I am afraid, there will be no religion. The philosopher's light will be but small if he can not descry the iniquity and rebellion of human nature, against God. And it will [be] (I fear) [but] a false light, if it does not descry, that iniquity and rebellion against the infinite God, Creator and preserver of all things, is an unmeasurable evil and indig-nity. He must not be an infinite God (as he is confessed to be) whose dis-pleasure and punitive power is not dreaded; and whose pardon and fa-vor is not most highly valued. If there is no prospect of pardon and reconciliation, despair sure, will prevent repentance, and consequently, religion. As also the wrath of the Almighty will blast the soul, and deny the means, or a blessing on the means that are to lead us to repentance.

"We should have been pleased now to hear, what such a rational philosopher has to say in the discovery and assurance of divine forgive-ness. . . . The pardon, that is indulged by a mortal prince, is an act of

---

5. "Preface," in [Reynolds], *The Religion of Jesus Delineated,* pp. xi–xxv.

grace, much more must the forgiveness of the supreme governor of the world be so. How then the light of nature, or law of reason will assure us of a free, gracious act of the eternal God, let the rationalist judge.

"If the light of nature proclaims to the world, forgiveness of sin, we should suppose, that it is either a total or [a] partial forgiveness. If it is only a partial forgiveness, then, though we sit under the patience and forbearance of God, at present; though we enjoy sun and rain, and fruit-ful seasons, in this world, we may be sent to fearful punishment in the next; may be remitted to a flaming purgatory, or, at best, to those low spirited pleasures the poets fancied in their Elysian fields. The territo-ries of the dead will be hung all in darkness. If a total remission be, by the philosopher's light, opened to us, it will show us a discharge in due time, from the penalty, that is inflicted on the body. And a discharge from that will show us a dismission from the grave. And that dismission will be a resurrection from the dead. Which neither old nor new philosophers say anything of.[6] Strange, there should be so deep a silence, in so im-portant a matter, and so necessary (as remission of sins is), in the reli-gion of nature.

"And here we should have been glad to have had the philosopher con-sider the dismal phenomenon of death; and to have heard what he would argue concerning it. As, whether it were the attendant of innocent na-ture, or of the guilty only. If of the innocent nature, would the good Cre-ator make pure and honorable vessels, so soon to be broke to pieces? If of the guilty only, how long has nature been thus guilty? Is there any his-tory of the world, that makes mention of an immortal people? And then how comes it to reign over those that have not actually sinned, and thereby contracted guilt? How great a part of mankind dies in infancy? And therefore how can they be supposed to have been set in a state of probation? . . . if primitive ancestors sinned, how comes it, that penalty must be produced down to latest posterity? Does natural light show [us], that posterity may be punished for the transgression of remote ances-tors? And if it may, and such a visible penalty (with all the forerunners and consequences of it) continually lies upon mankind, how shall we be delivered from it? Or must we never be delivered from death and the grave? Does not the philosopher's light here leave him; and the darkness call for some supernal revelation? But what religion of nature shall we now have without REMISSION OF SINS?

6. Reynolds reads: "Which yet neither the old philosophers, nor this modern one (with all his reason) says any thing of."

"It will doubtless be said, that it is man's duty to repent; and that, upon REPENTANCE, we may be assured, God will pardon the sin, and be reconciled. But this important case should be a little further considered [. . . .] It may seem rational indeed to conceive, that an offending creature is obliged to repent of his offense against his great and good Creator. Repentance may seem his first duty, or the first part of his return to his duty to his God. What can be accepted from an impenitent spirit?

"But [. . .] how does it appear, that REPENTANCE must needs obtain a PARDON, or that all the penitent must needs be forgiven? For,

"I. It will not be said that all temporal governors are obliged (in reason and equity) to pardon all the penitent criminals in all their dominions. Just execution may be due to the community. The honor and dignity of the government must be supported. It is supposed, that the divine legislator himself has forestalled his vicegerents (the secular princes) from the pardon of willful murder, much less will he be obliged (by any of our regret and repentance) to pardon that and all other sins of such despicable subjects as we.

"II. A wise governor would scarce publish a law, beforehand, in which he promised pardon and impunity to the most flagrant transgressors of all his laws, in case they should repent. Let us suppose, there was once a state of innocency (and there must have been so, as long as we are sure, that God made man good) we cannot rationally suppose, that man, in that state, had a law (in reason and nature) assuring him, that in case he transgressed any of the laws, or all the laws, he was then under, he should, upon his repentance, be immediately pardoned. Such a pardoning law would be the ready way to supplant precedent laws, to make man negligent of his obedience to them, and to enervate the force of any penal sanction added to them. And if the light and law of reason did not, in the state of innocence, promise pardon to future, penitent transgressors, how does it do it since? Reason was as clear then, as it is now, and as much God's law then, as it is now. And the nature and perfections of God would be as much known then, as now. It is true, reason does not say, that the penitent shall be equally punished with the impenitent. So much duty as is performed in and by repentance, so much guilt will be prevented which would be contracted, by and for the omission of such duty. And thereupon so far as the goodness of God leads us to repentance, it would lead us to a proportional impunity. But it does not follow, that the performance of a small part of duty must procure the pardon of a great deal of sin. But,

"III. What is this repentance that is supposed to be such an infallible security of the divine forgiveness? Is it a perfect abhorrence of all sin; and a perfect return to God, and to full obedience to him, for the future? Were it so (though it would not compensate or atone for, past impiety) yet more might be said on the behalf of it. But since it is an imperfect repentance (proceeding from an imperfect knowledge, both of the evil of sin that has been committed, and of God, against whom it has been committed) it is but an imperfect duty; and raises us but to an imperfect obedience. And so the repentance itself, and the obedience it leads us to, will both stand in need of forgiveness. Now that which, itself, stands in need of forgiveness, will scarce procure forgiveness for a deal of sin and impiety: may sin and repentance go on forever in a perpetual round? To allow [of] this (says the learned Dean of Chichester) differs nothing from allowing a liberty and impunity to sin without repentance (*Discourse of Prophecy,* [*3,*] p. 58).[7] At least, to admit that repentance, that must consist with future sin [. . .] and to forgive the sins, that are intermixed with repentance must be the act of sovereign unobliged clemency and grace.

"IV. At what time must this repentance begin and commence? If early and in youth; how shall I be assured, that the sins and impenitence of thirty or forty years will be forgiven? Or will a long adjourned, late repentance be accepted with God, in order to a full forgiveness? How will the religion of nature assure me of that? Or has it nothing to say in this case? O how defective will it be! If I have sinned fifty years, and have but one month to live; will reason assure me, that the repentance of one month (suppose it to be true) will obtain the forgiveness of all the sins of fifty years? What evidence of that? Sure I am, it is hard to persuade the sensible conscience, that one notorious sin (such as murder, adultery, blasphemy) will, upon any repentance, be forgiven. *Prima est hæc ultio, quod se judice, nemo nocens absolvitur.*[8] And I have some reason to suspect, that some gentlemen and persons of distinction, that have lived long in impiety, are driven from due thought of repentance and reformation, by a terrified mind, that tells them, their sins, are too many and too flagrant to be forgiven. And so there is no more to do (think they) but drink on, and revel on, and despair and die. [. . .] But if the light of nature does[9] not assure us, that a late repentance, will be accepted to forgiveness, it does not assure us, that repentance, as such, will be favored with such a blessing.

7. Thomas Sherlock, *The Use and Intent of Prophecy, in the Several Ages of the World: in Six Discourses* (2nd corr. ed., London, 1728).
8. "This is the first vengeance, that no criminal is absolved when he himself is the judge."
9. Reynolds reads: "will."

"V. But if we are[1] assured, that forgiveness may, upon repentance, be some how or other obtained, it should be considered, whether that forgiveness must be an absolute, gratuitous one, or must be procured by some sufficient atonement made to the offended majesty.

"I. If forgiveness must be absolute and gratuitous (i.e. unobtained by propitiation; gratuitous to us it will be whether so obtained or no), then,

"1. What meant the numerous expiations and expiatory sacrifices, that were so generally made by mankind? Were they all contradictions to the law of truth? Did they implicitly confess, that God had been offended? That there was some excellency or dignity, pertaining to God, that must be atoned! That by some bloody propitiation he is really atoned! And did the law of truth deny all this? Or did the God of truth never give any attestation to the acceptableness of propitiatory sacrifice? And,

"2. Is there no perfection in the divine nature, that, in case of sin and designed forgiveness of sin, would require an honorary propitiation made thereto? . . . it might be[2] proper to consider what the necessary purity and rectitude of that nature is, what the holiness and the justice is, and its contrariety to all moral evil and turpitude. . . . it would be useful to inquire, whether there be such a perfection as justice, belonging to the divine nature . . . . the philosopher must sure[3] acknowledge, that there is some divine attribute or perfection, that we know not how to call better, than by the name of vindictive or punitive justice. Plutarch has his tract, *De sera Numinis vindicta.* The poet can say, '*Raro antecedentem scelestum deseruit pede pœna claudo.*'[4] The earth is full of divine judgments, or the awful demonstrations of divine justice. Many are cut off in their sins, as if they were not to be forgiven. Many are so punished, as if it were designed, that their sin should be read in their punishment. Upon commission of notorious sin, conscience is so terrified, that many choose strangling and death, rather than the horrors of their own mind; *occultum quatiente intus tortore flagellum.*[5] And our author," the author of *The Religion of Nature Delineated,* "says, [. . .] 'that if it be reasonable, that the transgressors of reason should be punished, they will, most certainly, one time or other be punished.'

"3. Consideration should be had, whether there may not be pertaining to the divine being, something analogous to what, in superiors and

1. Reynolds reads: "were."
2. Reynolds reads: "have been."
3. Reynolds reads: "sure must."
4. "Rarely did punishment, with limping foot, abandon a preceding crime."
5. " . . . with the executioner within shaking a hidden whip."

persons of eminence, is called, sense of honor; which, in its regulation, is but a due care to act according to a person's proper sphere and dignity. The divine being cannot but be conscious of his own incomparable perfection and essential glory, of his transcendent dominion and authority, and of the vast obligation he has laid upon all intelligent beings (whose essence and powers he upholds) to regard his law and will. And if, in this view of his own incomparable glory, he sees it unmeet and unsuitable to his matchless highness and grandeur, to forgive a world of impiety (idolatry, enmity, blasphemy, and all manner of abomination) committed against himself, without a suitable, vast propitiation, what has the world to say against it! Surely, reason [. . .] or the nature of things has something to say, that the religion of guilty nature [. . .] should be founded on some great and glorious propitiation, presented to the majesty of heaven."

1207. LORD'S DAY. The Israelites in all their solemn feasts were to remember and praise God for their redemption out of Egypt, as seems by Ps. 81:1–7. How much more should Christians commemorate that infinitely greater redemption of Jesus Christ, of which the other was but a shadow, by keeping a holy day.

That the main design of the sabbath is to commemorate and celebrate God's works of mercy and salvation from enemies is manifest by the 92nd Psalm.

1208. END of the CREATION. GLORY OF GOD. Nature of REDEMPTION. SATISFACTION OF CHRIST. Nature of TRUE VIRTUE AND RELIGION.[6] When we are considering with ourselves what it would have been fit and proper for God to have a chief respect to and make his highest end in creating a world (if he did create one) and in establishing a system of intelligent creatures, and what he should have the greatest regard to in his governing the world and regulating things in this created system of intelligence, and what they should make their highest end, and whom they and what they should have chief regard to, and what regard, or regard to what being or beings, should reign in their hearts and have the chief rule and dominion in their behavior, it may help us to judge of this matter with the greater satisfaction and ease to consider what would be determined

6. Use marks throughout this entry indicate JE's use of the material elsewhere, most likely in his *Two Dissertations*. Indeed, as Paul Ramsey notes, JE reworked almost all of it into his *End for Which God Created the World* and *Nature of True Virtue*. See *Works*, *8*, 8, 8–9n, 46n, 425n, 426n, 445–46nn, 447n, 448n, and 451n.

by some third being of perfect wisdom (if such an one were possible), different both from the Creator and the created system, not interested in or concerned with either, but only occasionally stepping in to decide this matter.

Or if we make the supposition thus: that perfect and infinite wisdom, justice and rectitude were a distinct person or being, not interested either in the Creator or his created system any otherwise than only that it was his office to decide or order these matters between both most properly and suitably and to be a kind of umpire between them, to determine and settle what is most proper and agreeable to natural reason and rectitude with respect to one another, without partiality, without favor or affection to either side: would not such a being or person, in such an office, in judging of the forementioned matters, that he might determine what is most fit and worthy, equally view the whole that is then before him, i.e. the sum of all being, the universality of existence, as together making one whole, consisting of created and creating existence, which all together is the whole of what is to be the object of regard?

And now, in order to determine what sort and what measure of regard each part of this whole is to be the object of, or how every individual belonging to this universality or sum total is to share regard or respect of those intelligences that are concerned with this whole, that each part may have its proper portion, and the portion that it is worthy of, and that in the nature of things it is most fit and suitable that it should have, and that all things may be most properly adjusted in the most proportionable, reasonable and beautiful manner, everything must be weighed in an even balance. And in adjusting the proper measures and kinds of regard that every part of the sum of existence is to have, care must be taken that greater existence, or more existence, should have a greater share than the less, that a greater part of the whole is worthy more to be looked [upon] and respected than a lesser part, and that in proportion (other things being equal), and that the more excellent is more worthy to be regarded than the less excellent. And, in adjusting the degree of regard, these two things are to be considered conjunctly, viz. greatness and goodness, or the degree of existence and the degree of excellence.

Such an arbiter, in considering the system of created beings by itself, would determine that the general system, consisting of many millions, was of greater importance, and was to have a greater share of regard, than only one individual. For however considerable some of the individuals might be, so that they might be much greater and, as it were, have a greater share of the sum total of existence than another, yet one don't exceed another so much as to be in any measure worthy to be put in the balance with all the rest of the system. And in adjusting the degrees of regard proper for the individuals, the degree of the importance and excellence of each must be considered, so that the greater and more excellent should have a greater share than the less worthy. And in adjusting the measures of regard due to every part of the sum total of universal existence, including the infinite and eternal Creator and Lord of all, then this Supreme Being, with all in him that is great and considerable and excellent, and in any respect worthy, is to be as it were put into the balance against the creature, against individuals, and against the whole system. And according as he is found to outweigh, in such proportion is he to have a greater share of regard.

And as it would be found in such a case that the whole system of created beings in comparison of him is as the light dust of the balance (which is taken no notice of by him that weighs with the balance, and is as nothing and vanity), so must the arbiter determine with regard to the regard he must have. And as he is infinite and has all possible existence, perfection and excellence, so he must have all possible regard. As he is every way the first and Supreme Being, and his excellence is in all respects the original excellence, the fountain of all good, and the supreme beauty and glory, so he must in all respects have the supreme regard. As he is God over all, at the head of all, reigning with most absolute dominion over all, on whom all are dependent and all perfectly subordinate and subject, so it is fit that he should be the object of regard in such a manner that respect to him [must] reign over all our respect to other things, and that regard to creatures should be universally and perfectly subordinate and subject to our regard to him.

When I speak of the regard proper in this manner to be shared and directed towards different parts of the sum total of intelligent existence, I mean regard in general, or the regard of the whole, not only the regard of individual creatures, or of all creatures, but the regard of all intelligent existence, created and increated. 'Tis fit it should be thus with respect to the regard of the Creator as well as the creature. For 'tis as fit that his regard should be proportionable to the worthiness of objects as that the regard of creatures should. And thus such an arbiter as I supposed must be supposed to decide the matter, as he would decide most properly, beautiful and agreeable to truth. Such a judge would determine. And therefore he must determine that all things should proceed accordingly, that all that is done and acted by this universality of existence, all proceedings, managements and conduct through the whole, ought to be according to such a rule, that all intelligent creatures should thus make the Supreme Being the object of their supreme regard and perfectly subordinate to it their regard to everything and, consequently, that they should make him their supreme end in all things, and also that the Creator himself should supremely regard himself, and act in all things supremely with regard to himself, making himself his supreme end in creating and governing the world and all that he does with respect to the created system.

Such an arbiter as I have supposed, as he would decide how things should proceed most fitly, according to the nature of things, would determine that the whole created system, the whole universe, including all creatures, animate and inanimate, should in all its proceedings or revolutions and changes, great and small, that come to pass in it, as it were act with and from such an absolutely supreme regard to God as its last end that every wheel, both great and small, of the vast machine should, in all their motions, move with a constant, immutable regard to God as the ultimate end, as much as if the whole system were animated and actuated by one, common soul that were possessed of such perfect wisdom and rectitude, or as if such an arbiter as was before supposed, being possessed of such perfect wisdom and rectitude, became the common soul of the universe and animated and actuated it in all its proceedings. Thus such a supreme arbiter and director as I have supposed must determine that things should proceed, as he would determine that things should proceed most beautifully. See papers on the End of the Creation, pp. 22–24.[7] SATISFACTION FOR SIN.

Now let us consider how such an arbiter, whose office it should be to regulate all things within the whole compass of existence according to the most perfect propriety, would determine in case the creature should injure the most high, cast contempt on the majesty and trample on the authority of the infinite Lord of the universe: whether he would not determine that, in such a case, that the injury should be repaired, his majesty vindicated and the sacredness of the authority thoroughly supported, and that it was very requisite, in order to things being regulated and disposed most fitly and beautifully, that such injuries should not be forgiven in the neglect of this, or without due care taken of this matter. If it be fit that the[8] honor of God's majesty should be maintained at all, in any degree (which I suppose none will deny), then why is it not most

---

7. These papers are no longer extant.
8. MS: "Gods."

fit that it should be maintained fully? If it would be quite improper and unsuitable that the dignity of the Supreme Being, the sacredness of the authority of the infinitely great governor of the world, should be entirely neglected, should be suffered at all times and to the greatest degree to be trampled on, without any care to defend or support it, and that the majesty of this great king, as to the manifestation of it, should be obscured by his enemies to the greatest degree, and that continually and forever, without any vindication or reparation at all, then why is it not most suitable and most becoming that the vindication should be thorough, and the reparation complete and perfect?

Hitherto I have gone on a supposition of there being a third person besides the Creator and the creature, a person of perfect discerning, and comprehension of understanding, and rectitude of disposition, not interested or concerned with either the Creator or the created system, only as having it for his office to state the highest propriety, fitness and beauty with regard to their concerns one with another and acts one towards another. The thing which has been supposed is impossible. But the case is nevertheless just the same as to what is most fit and suitable in itself, as if there were such an arbiter to state and determine it. And therefore 'tis as proper for God to act according to this greatness, fitness, and accordingly to give rules to his creatures, and make establishments for them, and regulate all things in the system of created intelligencies and with relation to the intercourse between him and them, as much as if he were dictated and directed in everything by such a third person, and as much as if such an arbiter were not only the soul of the world, but were a common spirit animating the sum total of existence consisting of God and the creature.

There is no such third person to be umpire in the affair. Nor is it possible it should. Therefore it is fit that God himself [should be the arbiter]. There is no third being differing from both God and the world, possessed of perfect discerning and rectitude, to give rules of propriety to both. Nor can there be any. Nor is there need of any, seeing God himself is possessed of that perfect discerning and rectitude and, on this account, it belongs to him to be supreme arbiter, supreme lawgiver, and that his own infinite wisdom and rectitude should state all rules, and all methods of proceeding and mutual intercourse between him and the creature. There must be some supreme arbiter of right fitness and propriety or else these things will be liable to fail and not take place in some instances. And if there must be such an one, it must be God. It belongs to him and 'tis proper for him to state all things according to the highest propriety, rectitude, reason and beauty of things, without partiality to either[9] side. And if he should fail, he would as it were fail of the business of his proper office.

Though he is not animated by the spirit of a third person of infinite wisdom and rectitude, yet he is animated and directed by a spirit of infinite wisdom and rectitude, though it be his own Spirit. And seeing it is a Spirit of infinite wisdom and rectitude, [it] does not the less infallibly direct him according to wisdom and rectitude than if it were not his own.

'Tis not the less belonging to God to act in all these things just as an indifferent, perfectly wise arbiter between God and creatures would do because he is, as it were, interested, and is one party concerned. Because a being interested unfits one to be a determiner or judge no otherwise than as interest tends either to blind a person and mislead him to think that is most reasonable and suitable which is not, or to incline him to act contrary to his judgment. But that God should be in danger of either of these is contrary to the supposition. For it is supposed that he is possessed of the most absolutely perfect discerning. And that supposes that he can't be blinded or misled in his judgment. And 'tis also supposed that he is possessed of the most perfect rectitude of heart. And that supposes that he can't be inclined to go contrary to his judgment.

Objection I. Some may be ready to say that, seeing God himself is the supreme determiner of all things, who is one party in transactions between him and his creatures, it may be proper for him not to determine in every respect as it would be proper for an indifferent being no way interested to do, because that would too much limit his generosity. An indifferent, third being might fitly determine that 'tis proper that God should be the supreme object of respect, that all creatures should make him their supreme end, and that he should be the supreme end of all things, to whom all the[1] course of nature and the whole frame of the universe in all its motions should have respect and tendency as its last end, that this would [be] no other than equal and just in itself, but yet that it might show a noble generosity in God, when he himself orders and regulates all things, to deny himself, forego his own right, and make the good of his creatures his last end. Seeing it is so that God himself is the supreme determiner in his own cause, it would look like selfishness in him in his actions to prefer himself to all other being.

Ans. I answer, such an objection must arise from a very inconsiderate,

9. MS: "other."
1. MS: "the all."

ignorant notion of the vice of selfishness and the virtue of generosity. If by selfishness be meant a being's disposition to regard to himself, this is no otherwise vicious or unsuitable than as the public weal exceeds the value or importance of self compared with others—as to created beings one single person must be looked upon as vastly less, and so his interest of less importance, than the interest of the whole system. And therefore a contracted, confined spirit, a disposition to prefer self as if that was more than all, is exceeding vicious. And a foregoing one's own interest for the sake of others is no further excellent, no further worthy of the name of generosity, than it is treating things according to reason, and a prosecuting what is worthy to be prosecuted, and an expression of a disposition to prefer something to self-interest that is more worthy to be valued. If God be so great and so excellent that all other beings are as nothing to him, and all other excellency be as nothing, and less than nothing, and vanity in comparison of his excellency, and God be omniscient and infallible, then he knows that he is infinitely the most valuable being. And therefore if it is fit that his heart should be agreeable to this infallible, all-comprehensive understanding, this clear and perfect and infinitely bright light, then 'tis suitable that he should value himself infinitely more than his creatures, and act accordingly in all his proceedings with respect to his creatures, and that he should require an answerable disposition and conduct in his intelligent creatures.

Obj. II. Some may object and say, if the case were so that God needed anything, or his happiness could be advanced by the world that he hath made, or the goodness of his intelligent creatures extended to him, or they could be profitable to him, it might be fit that God should make himself or his own interest his highest end in creating and governing the world. And it might be proper for his creatures to make him their highest end in what they do. But seeing it is not so, but God is above all need and all capacity of being added to, or advances as to his welfare or interest, therefore it cannot be suitable that God or his creatures should make this their supreme end. For it would be improper and foolish in either to seek that which can't possibly be obtained and which don't need to be obtained. The highest good that can be brought to pass by anything that can be done by either God or created beings is the happiness of the creature. Therefore this is properly made the highest end by both.

Ans. 1. Though it be true God's happiness is infinite, eternal, unchangeable and independent, and so can't properly be added to, nor[2]

2. MS: "not nor."

can he be dependent on the creature for it, yet something seems to be supposed in the objection that is not true. And that is that God is not happy in anything that he sees in the creature, in what he sees of the creature's qualifications, dispositions, state and action, or that no part of God's happiness (to speak of God according to our manner of conception) consists in what he sees of those things in the creature.

God may have a true, proper and real delight, and so a part of his happiness, in seeing the state of the creature, in seeing its happy state, as he may delight in the exercise of his own goodness, and so in gratifying the inclination of his own heart, and yet all his happiness be eternal and immutable. For he eternally has this disposition, and eternally sees and enjoys this future gratification of it as though it were present. And, indeed, all things are present to him; with him is no succession, no past and future. And he is independent in this delight. He brings the thing to pass by which he is gratified by his own, independent power. And as it is with the creature's happiness, so it is with his holiness. God really delights in it in the same manner. So it is in God's being glorified, his glories shining forth, being expressed, exhibited and communicated. This is in itself fit and excellent, and therefore God delights in it. But as he accomplishes it himself by his independent power, so God is independent in this delight; and that, although the dispositions and voluntary actions of his creatures are made the means of it, yet these are perfectly in God's hands and disposed of by God's independent power, so that still God is independent on it and, as if he sees it perfectly from eternity, so his delight in it is eternal and immutable.

And if it should here be said that it seems reasonable to suppose that God's infinite happiness should be in himself, that he should be his own infinite and all-sufficient, complete, objective good, and that the creature, or any [of] its beauty, or anything it does, should not be any part of it, or be requisite to make the objective happiness full and complete: I answer that, although God has truly delight in the creature's happiness and holiness, yet still his happiness is in himself. For these are but communications of himself. They are wholly beams from this fountain. God's delight in these things is only a delight in his own brightness communicated and reflected, and in his own action of communicating, which is still to be resolved into a delight in himself. (See what I have formerly written on this subject.)[3]

[Ans.] 2. Let it be considered whether our not being able to profit God

3. See No. 1182, above, pp. 104–5.

is any good evidence that God ought not to be supremely loved, and our love to God ought not to be as much as may be answerable to his infinite superiority to all other beings in greatness, excellency and the subordination of all things on him, the dependence of all on him, i.e. whether love and benevolence to him ought not absolutely to reign in our hearts, and all our regard to creatures and all our affections and actions be subordinate to that. If it be so, then our not being able to profit God is no argument that we should not make those things that love and benevolence to God most naturally and directly tends to and seeks our supreme end, or what we have a supreme respect to in what we do from this love. Indeed, 'tis an inconsistence to suppose otherwise. For, doubtless, love ought to seek that which love tends to. Love should seek to gratify itself. Love is not fit to be had and cherished any further than it is fit to be gratified. The nature of love is a disposition or tendency. But that tendency is not to be sought and cherished as excellent which, when we have it, must be opposed and not allowed of.

Therefore, if we ought to love God, we ought to make what love to God tends to our end (under that ratio, or in that manner, that therein we have respect to God and gratify our regard), which is the same thing as to make him our end. Love seeks to please and honor the beloved. It is averse to his displeasure and dishonor, and therein seeks God; and that, whatever we think about God's being added to by anything we can do, love, in seeking to please and honor God, seeks God. And if we ought to have supreme love to God, then we ought supremely to seek what love to God tends to. And that is supremely to seek God. And that is to make God our [end] supremely; and that, in whatever way we do this, if it be chiefly in showing kindness to our neighbors, yet if this be done chiefly from love to God, then herein we make God our highest end. There is no other way. If our regard to God ought to be supreme, we must make him our highest end.

Corol. 1. The things which have been observed show plainly that a supreme regard to the Deity is essential to true virtue, and that those schemes of religion or moral philosophy, however well in some respects they may treat of benevolence to mankind and other virtues depending on it, yet if a supreme respect to God and love to him ben't laid in the foundation, and all other virtues handled in a connection with this and subordination to it and dependence on it, are not true schemes of philosophy but are fundamentally wrong. And whatever other benevolence or generosity towards mankind (and other virtues or qualifications which go by that name) any are possessed of that are not attended with a love to God, which is altogether above them and to which they are subordinate and on which they [are] dependent, there is nothing of the nature of TRUE VIRTUE and RELIGION therein. And it may be asserted in general that nothing is of the nature of true virtue or religion in which God is not the first and the last, or which, with regard to its exercises in general, have not their first foundation and source in apprehensions of God's supreme glory and worthiness, and an answerable supreme esteem of and love to him, and which has not respect to God as the supreme end.

Corol. 2. What has been observed may serve to show the reasonableness of the doctrine of the SATISFACTION OF CHRIST (see back, p. 134),[4] that it is most rational to suppose that God did determine to forgive such as had cast contempt on his infinite [glory and worthiness], and his authority as the infinitely high Lord over all, and to take such into favor. Infinite wisdom would some way or other so contrive the matter that the injury done to the appearance or exhibition of the dignity and sacred authority of this great king should be fully repaired, and his majesty entirely vindicated and set forth in all awfulness, inviolable sacredness and worthiness of regard and reverence.

It can't here be reasonably objected that God is not capable of properly receiving any satisfaction for an injury because he is not capable of receiving any benefit. A price offered to men satisfies for an injury because it may truly be a price to them, or a thing valuable and beneficial. But God is not capable of receiving a benefit. For God is as capable of receiving satisfaction as he is an injury. 'Tis true, he can't properly be[5] profited; so neither can he be properly hurt. But as rebelling against him may properly be looked upon as of the nature of an injury or wrong done to God, and so God is capable in some proper sense of being the object of injuriousness, so he is as capable of being the object of that which is the opposite of injuriousness, or of the repairing of an injury.

If you say: "What need God have any care for the repairing the honor of his majesty when it can do him no good? No addition can be made to his happiness by it." You might as well say: "What need God care when he is despised, dishonored, and his authority and glory trampled on, when it does him no hurt?" 'Tis a vain thing here to pretend that God cares only because it hurts the creatures' own happiness for 'em to cast contempt of God. Is that agreeable to the natural light of all men's minds, the natural sense of their hearts and the dictates of conscience

---

4. MS: "see the fourth page back. a. b. c." The paragraph referred to begins, "Now let us consider how such an arbiter . . ."

5. MS: "to."

(which unavoidably and necessarily arise after some very direct, most profane and daring opposition to and reproach of the most high), that God is now angry and much provoked only because the audacious sinner has now greatly hurt himself, and hurt his neighbors that happen to see him? No. This is entirely diverse and alien from the voice of natural sense in such a case, which inevitably suggests that God is provoked, as one will regard himself for himself, as having a direct respect to his dignity and majesty. And this is agreeable to the strictest reason.

'Tis impossible, if God infinitely loves and honors himself as one infinitely worthy to be loved and esteemed, that he should from the same principle proportionably abhor and oppose opposition to himself and contempt of himself. And if it [is] in its own nature decent and becoming of him thus to love himself, then it is in its own nature fit and becoming in him to hate opposition to himself. And for the same reason, and from the same principle, God, when he is contemned and injured and his authority and glory trampled in the dust, he will be disposed to repair the injury done to his honor and raise his injured majesty out of the dust again.

As I observed before, 'tis requisite that there should be some supreme arbiter of absolute rectitude and fitness with regard to the sum total of existence that should determine and fix what is most proper to take place in all that is acted, or comes to pass, with relation to God and the creature. Otherwise supreme fitness and rectitude might be liable to fail, and give place to something else, and to be justled out of the universality of things, and have no place. And 'tis fit that the Supreme Being, who is first, independent, and self-existent, and infinitely wise, and infinitely and immutably holy and just, should be this supreme arbiter. But it is not necessary that this office should belong to each person of the Trinity. 'Tis most proper that he that is the first person, from whom the other two are, that he should be the person that should have this office, to determine rectitude and propriety for the three persons and for all creatures. And, consequently, nothing is in the way but that one of the other persons should act under him in affairs relating to rectitude between God and the creature, as in repairing the honor done to God by the sin and rebellions of the creature, making satisfaction, etc.

1209. FUTURE STATE. "There must be a future state; otherwise indeed are moral powers and their acquisitions by labor and industry made to very little purpose; nay, willfully destroyed in a manner to which we see nothing that bears any likeness or analogy in the whole course of nature.

To suppose no future state succeeding to this, is to suppose God to do what no man could do without being limited in power, or extremely capricious, to lay a noble foundation, and not carry on the building; or sow, manure, and cultivate, merely to have the pleasure of destroying things in their blossom, and when they are near to maturity, or when the harvest is at hand. God will, must perfect every good work he hath begun. He must therefore complete the moral building that may be raised upon so goodly a foundation, and which, as far as it is advanced, promises a very perfect superstructure. Shall there be spring in the moral world, and no harvest? Surely the work is not finished when moral powers are brought, by due culture, and variety of discipline and probation, to be fit for higher exercises than they could be qualified for before they were come to this maturity and vigor. If it stops here, it is a very imperfect work; nay, it is a cruel work; it is a cruel end to such an excellent beginning; and an end it in no respect looks like or threatens.

"The same excellent disposition which alone disposed [God] to create moral beings capable of high improvements to all eternity, and to place them in a first state where their powers might have the properest means and materials of exercise for their improvement, must excite him to place them afterwards in a situation suited to their improvements made in this state. We know that a state designed merely for probation and discipline cannot always last; [. . .] so neither can it in the nature of things; for all material things must wax old, and wear out. But moral powers are of a different kind: they do not wear out; they must be willfully destroyed, if they cease to be. And can he who is infinite goodness take pleasure in destroying moral powers, and in disappointing all their natural hopes and desires . . . and [in] knocking down at once all the acquisitions made by them with much patience and suffering, with earnest labor and struggling? . . . here the effects of virtue and vice are not fully complete. They cannot be so till after a state of trial. For in it the effects of trial only can appear, and not the full harvest. But effects appear which do indeed promise an excellent harvest; effects which are themselves the first fruits, or at least the beautiful pleasant blossoms that betoken a joyful harvest to come in its due season. Effects which show us how happy the virtuous mind may, must be, if after its state of formation and trial it is placed in circumstances for which it is become fit." Turnbull's *Christian Philosophy,* pp. 118–21.[6]

See further, [No.] 1211.

---

6. George Turnbull, *The Principles of Moral and Christian Philosophy* (2 vols. London, 1740), 2, 118–21.

1210. LORD'S DAY. THE PERPETUITY of the FOURTH COMMANDMENT.[7]
Mr. Turnbull, in his *Christian Philosophy*, having cited a passage from Mr.
Locke on education concerning the great importance of the improvement of the understandings of children,[8] after having mentioned some
reasons why he had quoted it, proceeds, pp. 231–34:

"And in the next place, to give me an opportunity of remarking, how
much the improvement of our understanding depends upon education,
and consequently upon the care, [. . .] of society about education. The
many beneficial advantages of that close social dependence among
mankind, of which this is an essential, or necessary part, are very evident,
and have been already treated upon. All therefore I would now observe
on this head is, that a state which does not take proper care to put and
keep the education of the youth of the higher ranks in life upon a good
foot, neglects the most essential thing to the well-being of every private
person, and of society in general; the most essential thing to the end of
government, if that be public happiness; and when this is not the end,
and the proper means to it are not carefully pursued, a state of government is indeed much worse than a state of nature. This needs no proof;
for it is indeed with the consent of all thinking men, in education, that
the foundation stones of private and public happiness, private and public virtue, things in their nature absolutely inseparable, must be laid; according to it will the superstructure be. As for those that have time and
the means to attain to knowledge in a well-governed state, it is indeed a
shame for them to want any helps or assistances for the improvement of
their understanding, that are to be got. Those who by the industry and
parts of their ancestors have been set free from the constant drudgery
to their backs and bellies others lie under, should bestow some of that
time, which commonly is either very foolishly, if not wickedly spent, or
lies very heavy on their hands, on the improvement of their heads, and
to enlarge their minds with pleasant and useful knowledge.

"But the public care of education ought to extend yet further, and
comprehend in it the whole body of the people, in such a manner, as
that not only all useful arts and crafts may be understood and brought
to perfection; but that all, even the meanest may have opportunities of
being instructed in the principles of virtue and true religion. Now, here
I cannot but observe, that the one day of seven, besides other days of
rest, allows in the Christian world time enough for this (had they no
other idle hours) if they would but make due use of these vacances from

7. Cf. JE's sermon on "The Perpetuity and Change of the Sabbath," in *Works, 17*, 217–50
8. John Locke, *Some Thoughts Concerning Education* (London, 1690).

their daily labor, and apply themselves with as much diligence to the study of religion, as they often do to a great many things that are useless, and yet more difficult. This is certainly true, provided any care were taken of the common people in their infancy; or those whose sacred business it is to instruct them, would take due pains to enter them according to their several capacities into a right way to this knowledge, and to assist and encourage them in their endeavors to improve in it. And this shows us what an excellent institution it is, by which a convenient portion of time is thus set apart from labor, to be dedicated to the improvement of the mind; and teachers are appointed for that beneficial end. None can choose but approve such an institution, if they have any just sense of the dignity of human nature, and of the common unalienable rights and privileges of mankind, and of the chief end of society and government; or unless they inhumanly and barbarously, as well as impiously think, that the bulk of mankind are made to be mere beasts of burden, whose understandings ought to be put out, as certain Scythians are said to have done the eyes of their slaves, or kept in darkness that they may be more tame drudges; less apt to rebel, because less sensible of bad usage; and that if they are allowed so much as any diversion, or respite from labor, it should be for the same reason as bells are hung about the necks of pack-horses or mules. Experience shows, that the original make of their minds is like that of other men; and they would be found not to want understanding fit to receive very useful instruction, if they were but a little encouraged and helped in it, as they should be by those who in Christian countries are employed and maintained for that most beneficial, noble end."[9]

1211. FUTURE STATE. "It becomes the Father of rational beings, it is agreeable to his wisdom and goodness to pursue the best methods of promoting virtue: for of all his works rational beings are the most excellent: and the highest excellency of rational beings is [. . .] a virtuous temper and right action. It therefore highly becomes the universal Father and governor, to make everything contribute to the increase, the promotion, the honor and advantage of virtue. It must be the noblest exercise of his wisdom and goodness, and the greatest benefit to the universe, to execute a scheme for forming, exercising, exhibiting, illustrating and rewarding the virtue of all beings, according to their several ranks and degrees; and if that be the scheme God intends and pursues, he will cer-

9. Turnbull, *The Principles of Moral and Christian Philosophy*, 2, 231–34.

tainly make the promotion of virtue the measure and rule by which he acts, in conferring benefits and favors, in distributing happiness and misery; and consequently virtue must be sufficiently taken care of in all its stages; and vice cannot in the ultimate result of things be the gainer, the triumpher; but must, on the contrary, be made fully to feel its odiousness to God, on account of its intrinsic deformity and guilt, its contrariety to the rational nature, and its repugnancy to all the noblest exercises of moral powers." Turnbull's *Christian Philosophy*, p. 432.[1]

1212. SATISFACTION OF CHRIST. Texts taken from Rawlin on *Justification*[2] which show that the holiness and justice of God insist on sins being punished: Lev. 10:3; Ps. 11:6–7; Ex. 34:7; Job 34:10–11; Job 10:14, ch. 7:20; Josh. 24:19.

1213. SATISFACTION OF CHRIST. Some things which Chubb says, about pp. 125–26.[3] Though we should allow that "the holiness of God disposes him to hate sin, and punish the sinner," yet "those dispositions [...] don't take from the freedom of God's will." As to what is said of God's being obliged in justice to punish sin, "every being is left free, by the laws of common equity and justice, to dispose of his own peculiar property as he will, and is not accountable to any for the use or non-use, the enjoying or not enjoying, or disposing of the same. . . . if God is pleased to punish the sinner [...], nothing which the sinner can do for himself, or any other do or suffer for him, [...] can properly merit his exemption from punishment, or give a right to claim his discharge at God's hand."

In pp. 130–31, "as it is unreasonable to suppose that God punishes the sinner for punishment's sake, to gratify an angry passion; so if he should punish the innocent in the guilty's stead, this would be so far from retrieving his honor, so as to repair the damage done by sin, that on the contrary it would add to his dishonor, by representing him as unjust and unholy, in punishing the innocent, and letting the guilty go free. And though the person suffering should voluntarily offer himself to suffer in

---

1. Ibid., 2, 432.

2. Richard Rawlin, *Christ the Righteousness of His People; or, The Doctrine of Justification by Faith in Him: Represented in Several Sermons, Preached at the Merchants Lecture at Pinners Hall* (London, 1741; Edinburgh, 1797).

3. Actually, the quotations in this paragraph are from pp. 127–28 of Chubb, *A Collection of Tracts, on Various Subjects*. These and all subsequent Chubb extracts in this entry are found in his "Treatise VIII. An Enquiry concerning Sinners' Deliverance from Condemnation . . ."

the sinner's behalf, it makes no alteration in the case, because such a voluntary offer makes no alteration in the sinner; he is as guilty after it as before, and consequently is as much the proper object of punishment as before. And the innocent person, as he doth not contract the guilt of the other, by that voluntary offer, he being as innocent as before, so that offer cannot make him the proper object of punishment, and consequently the suffering of the innocent cannot make satisfaction for the guilty."

P. 131, "whoever doth that which God is so well pleased with as to pardon the sinner for its sake, such a one may fitly be esteemed a savior or redeemer to the sinner." This "in a secondary and less proper sense, may be called the price of a sinner's redemption." P. 132, and so "that which [God] is thus pleased to accept, [. . .] may, in a secondary and less proper sense, [. . .] be said to merit" a sinner's redemption.

In pp. 135–36, he insists that a sinner's pardon is of "free grace and bounty," and therefore can't properly be merited by the death of Christ; and that Christ did not properly pay our debt, because it was his duty to die. He did it in obedience to God, and so [it] was a debt he himself owed to God.

P. 139, he supposes that Christ redeems sinners from "thralldom" to sin and Satan by his death, as Tit. 2:14, I Pet. 1:18, as his death is a "prevailing argument with the sinner" to forsake sin, as it was an evidence of his divine mission.

And in p. 140, that "the suffering and death of Christ are instrumental towards delivering sinners from condemnation, as they were an acceptable act of obedience, and recommended him so to the Father's love, that he exalted him to his right hand, to be an intercessor . . . and are an argument with God, to pardon believing penitent sinners, for Christ's sake." Ibid., he says the Scriptures that speak of Christ as a price, a ransom, etc., are "figurative," as when it is said, Is. 43:3, "I gave Egypt for thy ransom."

1214. SATISFACTION OF CHRIST. 'Tis said that God is not obliged to fulfill his threatenings of punishment of sin. Not to dispute about the import of the word "obliged," let [it] be considered whether it is not fit that God should fulfill his threatenings. If any answer no, then I would inquire further whether fitness of things don't require that God should pay some regard to his threatenings that belong to his law as its sanctions; whether the law with its sanctions ben't published and exhibited that they may view it as a rule of proceeding between the Lawgiver and subjects; and whether it can [have] the influence intended, or indeed any significancy, if it ben't understood as such in some measure.

Therefore, if it ben't fit that God should act impertinently and insignificantly, it surely [is] fit that some regard should be paid to it, not only in the actions of the subject, but also in the proceedings of the Judge. And if it be fit that some regard should be paid to it, how great a regard. If the rule may be set aside and departed upon in one instance, why not in two? And why not in four? Where are the limits? The threatenings are no further sanctions than they are supposed to be declarations of truth. Therefore is it not fit that truth is a thing that should always attend them in an inviolable manner? If God has reserved to himself the liberty to depart from the rule at his pleasure, without any signification beforehand or any reason given to determine what his pleasure will be, then how can the subject know but that he will always depart from it?

1215. Concerning the declaration or manifestation which God made of his mind to Adam concerning the rule of his duty to God, and what [God] expected of him, enforced with threatenings of his displeasure in case of a violation of that rule and promises of his favor in case of a compliance, especially Adam's consent being supposed—I say, as to this being called a COVENANT, we have this to warrant us in it: that it is agreeable to the sense in which the Scripture uses the word covenant everywhere. That there was a promise of favor in case of compliance as well as a threatening of wrath in case of disobedience we have all manner of reason to suppose from the nature of the thing, and from what we read about the tree of life, and from what the Apostle says, Rom. 7:10 (see also Rom. 10:5 and Rev. 22:14), of the commandment's being "ordained to life" (see [No.] 1074).[4] The consent of mankind is no more express to the covenant of grace under the gospel than Adam's consent before the fall. Adam's consent before he fell must be supposed, for his dissent would have been sin, which, to suppose before he sinned, is a contradiction.

1216. INCARNATION, SATISFACTION AND RIGHTEOUSNESS OF CHRIST. "Sponsori nostro id incumbebat præstandum quod lex à nobis exigit, ut δικαιωμα illius impleatur. Rom. 8:4. Nosque juxta antiquam conventionem servemur. Legi autem hominibus latæ nisi per hominem satis-

4. See *Works*, 20, 458–59.

fieri non potest: neque quoad præcepta, quæ Spiritum et animam et corpus sancta servari ac Deo impendi postulant, neque quoad commina-
tiones, quibus et corpori et animæ sua mors indicitur. Unde necesse est,
sponsorem nostrum vere hominem esse, ut corpore atque anima omnem justitiam impleat, Matt. 3:15. Et utriusque morte subita, suos à
morte vindicet, Heb. 2:14. Hinc est quod Apostolus individuo nexu hæc
duo copulet, Factus ex muliere, et factus sub lege, Gal. 4:4. Indicans
proximum incarnationis Christi finem esse, ut in natura sua humana illi
subjiciatur legi, quæ homini primum lata est. Witsius in *Symbolum Exercitationes,* XIV, xxx–xxxi." Quoted by Rawlin on *Justification,* pp. 84–
85.[5]

1217. SATISFACTION OF CHRIST. Rom 3:25–26, "whom God hath set
forth to be a propitiation through faith in his blood, to declare his righteousness for the remission of sins that are past, [. . .] that he might be
just, and the justifier of him that believeth in Jesus."

"To declare his righteousness, the rectitude of his nature, or his punitive justice. . . . So the word δικαιοσυνης properly signifies, and in this
sense is frequently used. See II Thess. 1:5–6; II Tim. 4:8; Rev. 15:5–7,
and 19:2. Grotius,[6] to evade the force of this text, in favor of the doctrine of Christ's satisfaction, would have it translated 'goodness,' or
'bounty': and in support of this, refers to several passages, where the
word צדק or צדקה is so rendered by the LXX; 'which as we deny not,' says
Dr. Owen, 'that in some places, in the Old Testament, where it is used
by the LXX, it doth, or may do so, so we say here, that sense can have no
place, which nowhere is direct and proper: for the thing intended by it

5. "This requirement which the law demands from us weighs upon our bondsman, i.e. that
its righteousness be fulfilled (Rom. 8:4). And let us be kept near the old covenant. However, it
is not possible to satisfy the law pertaining to human beings except through a human being.
Nor is it possible, as far as the precepts which demand that the spirit, soul, and body be kept
holy and open before God, nor as far as the threats with which its death is shown both to body
and soul. Whence it is necessary that our bondsman truly was a human being, in order that he
might fulfill all justice in body and in spirit (Matt. 3:15). And by the sudden death of whom,
he liberates his own from death (Heb. 2:14). For this reason the Apostle joins these two in an
inseparable yoke, 'Made from a woman, and made under the law' (Gal. 4:4), showing the final
end of the incarnation of Christ, that he might be subjected in his human nature to that law
which first pertains to human beings." JE is quoting from Rawlin, *Christ the Righteousness of His
People,* who in turn is quoting from Hermann Witsius, *Exercitationes Sacræ in Symbolum Quod Apostolorum Dicitur,* 4th ed. (Herbornae Nassaviorum, 1712), pp. 213–14.

6. Hugo Grotius' *Defensio fidei catholicae de satisfactione Christi* (Oxford, 1636), published in
English as *A Defence of the Catholick Faith Concerning the Satisfaction of Christ* (London, 1692), 36–
40.

in that sense is expressed before'" (in the foregoing verse), "'in those words, "freely by his grace," and is not consistent with that that follows, "that he may be just," which represents God as he is, "a just Judge."' [7]

"Mr. Locke[8] has offered another exposition of these words, and by the 'righteousness' here spoken of, understands the righteousness of God, in keeping his word with the nation of the Jews, notwithstanding their provocations; or, as he explains it more fully in his notes on v. 5 to which he refers, God's 'faithfulness' in keeping his promise of saving believers, Gentiles as well as Jews, by righteousness through faith in Jesus Christ. But this seems to be as ill supported as that of Grotius. For I cannot find one single passage in the whole New Testament, where δικαιοσυνης θεο is used in that sense. Most certainly it is used in a very different sense in this context, vv. 21, 23, and throughout this epistle, where it always signifies, either the righteousness by which we are justified, or that perfection of God which makes such righteousness necessary to our justification. In the former sense it is used, ch. 9:30–31, and ch. 10:4. And both these senses seem to have place, ch. 10:3, where the word is used twice in one verse. And as to the sense which it bears in the fifth verse of the third chapter, which is the only passage Mr. Locke refers to in support of his opinion, 'tis evidently to be understood there of the justice of God, that perfection which is manifested and displayed in punishing the sin and unrighteousness of men; the sense it likewise bears in the text under consideration. Not to add, that the Apostle speaks here of the 'remission' of the sins of particular persons, even of all that died in faith under the dispensation of the Old Testament, and not of the remission of the sins of the Jews nationally considered, as Mr. Locke is obliged to understand it consistently with the sense of the text. Compare Heb. 9:15." Rawlin on *Justification*, pp. 94–95.

Again, ibid., pp. 104–105, "'It were,' as an excellent writer has expressed it,[9] 'manifestly more honorable, and worthy of God, not to have exacted any recompense at all, than to have accepted, in the name of a sacrifice, such as were unproportionable, and beneath the value of what was to be remitted, and conferred. What had been lower, must have been infinitely lower; let anything be supposed less than God, and it falls im-

---

7. Rawlin is quoting John Owen, *Vindiciæ Evangelicæ: or The Mystery of the Gospell Vindicated* (Oxford, 1655).

8. John Locke, *A Paraphrase and Notes on the Epistle of St. Paul to the Romans* (London, 1707), 27, 31–32.

9. Rawlin is quoting from John Howe, "The Living Temple," ch. VIII, § 2, in *Works* (2 vols. London, 1724), *1*, 195.

mensely short of him. Such is the distance between created being, and uncreated, that the former is as nothing to the latter; and therefore, bring the honor and majesty of the Deity to anything less than an equal value, and you bring it to nothing. And this had been quite to lose the design of insistence upon a recompense; it had been to make the majesty of heaven cheap, and depreciate the dignity of the divine government, instead of rendering it august and great.'"

1218. END OF THE CREATION, GLORY OF GOD, etc.[1] It can't be properly said that the end of God's creating of the world is twofold, or that there are two parallel, coordinate ends of God's creating the world, one to exercise his perfections *ad extra,* another to make his creatures happy. But all is included in one, viz. God's exhibiting his perfections, or causing his essential glory to be exercised, expressed and communicated *ad extra.* 'Tis true that we must suppose that, prior to the creatures' existence, God seeks occasion to exercise his goodness, and opportunity to communicate happiness, and that this is one end why he gives being to creatures. And so we must conceive that, prior to the creatures' existence, he seeks occasion to exercise other attributes of his nature that can have none but creatures for their objects, as his justice, his faithfulness, his wisdom, etc. But a disposition to seek opportunity and occasion for the exercise of goodness towards those that now have no being, and so a being disposed to give being to creatures that there may be such an opportunity, is not the same attribute that we commonly call goodness, any more than a disposition to seek opportunity or occasion to exercise justice, and so to give being to creatures that there may be such occasion, is not the same attribute that we call justice.

God seeks occasion for the exercise of one and the other of these attributes, by giving existence to beings that may be capable objects of their exercise, in the same manner and for one common reason, viz. because it is in itself fit and suitable that these attributes of God should be exerted and should not be eternally dormant. 'Tis true, 'tis from an excellent disposition of the heart of God that God seeks occasion to exercise his goodness and bounty, and also his wisdom, justice, truth. And this, in one word, is a disposition to glorify himself according to the Scripture sense of such an expression, or a disposition to express and communicate himself *ad extra.*

---

1. In the MS, there are use marks throughout this entry, indicating JE's appropriation of this material in the *Dissertation Concerning the End for Which God Created the World.* See *Works, 8,* 429*n.*

I know there is an inconsistence in supposing that God inclines to exercise goodness and do good to others merely for the sake of the honor of his goodness. For the very notion of goodness is an inclination of heart to do good to others and, therefore, the existence of such an inclination must be conceived of as prior to an inclination to honor it. There must first be an inclination of heart to do good before God desires to honor that inclination. So, in like manner, it is an inconsistence to suppose that God is inclined to exercise justice and do justly only for the sake of the honor of his justice: for justice itself is an inclination to do justly, which must exist before God is inclined to honor it. Therefore God's glorifying himself, that glorifying himself which is the end of the creation, is a different thing from properly seeking his honor.

They that suppose God's inclination to make occasions for the doing good or communicating happiness, by giving being to capable subjects of it, to be what is properly called God's goodness, seem to have a notion of a bountiful disposition in the heart of God disposed to increase the sum of happiness which is to be found in the universality of existence. But there is no such thing. Man's benevolence and bounty, taking his own good and the good of the person benefited by him together, increases the sum of good. And therefore 'tis more easy to conceive of a benevolent disposition in a creature wishing for the being of new subjects of kindness, because the goodness of his nature causes him to love to see a great deal of happiness. But God sees no more by making creatures that they may be happy. He hath in his Son an adequate object for all the desires of this kind that are in his heart. And in his infinite happiness he sees as much happiness as can be. When new beings are made that are infinitely less, and there is opportunity to do them good, God sees not the sum of happiness increased.

The more proper notion signified by all such words as goodness, kindness, bounty, favor, grace, etc., includes love, benevolence or good will. But that is not properly love or good will that has the existence of the object loved first supposed. A disposition to make an object, that it may be loved and that we may have good will towards, must be prior to another, and properly distinct from love and goodwill itself. It may be an excellent quality. But it must be [a] quality of some other denomination. If it be called goodness and grace, it must be in a less proper sense.

To desire new beings to communicate happiness to 'em, especially without increasing the sum of happiness, don't agree with the notion mankind have of goodness, benevolence, grace, etc. Men may call this disposition in the heart of God by the name of goodness if they please.

But 'tis properly referred to another perfection, of which it is one sort of exercise, viz. the disposition that is in the infinite fountain of good, and of glory and excellency, to shine forth or to flow out, which shining forth or flowing out of God's infinite fullness is called God's glory in Scripture.[2]

Indeed God, in making the creature happy, seems as it were to express or exhibit himself *ad extra* two ways: not only does one of his perfections exercise itself in it, viz. his goodness; but there is something of God actually communicated, some of that good that is in God, that the creature hereby has communion in, viz. God's happiness. The creature partakes of the happiness of God, at least an image of it. And we must therefore conceive that there is a disposition in God, not only to exercise his attributes and perfections in this, but also to communicate of his divine good.

But then it is to be considered that God don't only communicate of happiness, but also his holiness and his understanding and power, or an image of these. And we must conceive that there is truly a disposition in God to communicate of these as well as his happiness, which general disposition, though in itself excellent, seems to be a disposition besides the goodness of God, or at least is called so in a less proper sense and in a more extensive sense than that which is more frequently called God's goodness. But although there are several kinds of good in God that are communicated, and though, according to our manner of conceiving things, there are two ways of God's exhibiting himself *ad extra*—1. his perfections that we conceive to be an active nature are exercised *ad extra,* as his power, wisdom, justice, goodness, holiness; 2. the good that is in him is communicated *ad extra*—and though this good be of various kinds, according to our manner of conceiving; yet as all that good that is in God, of whatever kind, belongs to his essential glory and brightness, and there is the same fitness that each part of this brightness or glory should shine forth in every possible way, and be both exercised and communicated, and that all this good should flow out, and that God is disposed that each part should do so, may well be referred to one general disposition, and the effect may well be called by one name, viz. God's glory, Δοξα, כָּבוֹד.

---

2. Here JE deletes the following passage: "Men may be ready to think it may properly be distinguished from that disposition which there is in God to exercise the attributes of justice, faithfulness, etc., as quite of a different nature. But this probably must arise from the like imperfection in our manner of conceiving of God, from whence we are ready to conceive of God's happiness not as a part of the excellency of his nature, but entirely a different sort of good from excellency. But."

Both these dispositions, of exerting himself and communicating himself, may be reduced to one, viz. a disposition effectually to exert himself, or to exert himself in order to an effect. That effect is the communication of himself, or himself *ad extra,* which is what is called his glory. This communication is of two sorts: the communication that consists in understanding or idea, which is summed up in the knowledge of God; and the other is in the will, consisting in love and joy, which may be summed up in the love and enjoyment of God. Thus that which proceeds from God *ad extra* is agreeable to the twofold subsistences which proceed from him *ad intra,* which is the Son and the Holy Spirit, the Son being the idea of God or the knowledge of God, and the Holy Ghost which is the love of God and joy in God.

Although the things which God inclines to and aims at are in some respect two—viz. exercising or exerting the perfections of his nature; and the effect of that, viz. communicating himself—yet these may be reduced to one: viz. God's exerting himself in order to the effect. The exertion and the effect ought not to be separated as though they were two ends. One is so related to the other, and they are so united, that they are most properly taken together as one end and the object of one inclination in God. For 'tis not an ineffectual exertion that God aims at or inclines to. And God, in aiming at these, makes himself his end. 'Tis himself exerted and himself communicated, and both together are what is called God's glory. The end, or the thing which God attains, is himself, in two respects: he himself flows forth; and he himself is pleased and gratified. For God's pleasure all things are and were created.

God had made intelligent creatures capable of being concerned in these effects, as being the willing, active subjects or means, and so they are capable of actively promoting God's glory. And this is what they ought to make their ultimate end in all things. See No. 1225.

1219. COMMUNICATION OF PROPERTIES with respect to the divine and human nature of Christ. Such a communication of properties and characters with respect to Christ in the language of Scripture, which divines suppose to have its foundation in the union of the divine and human natures of Jesus, is not absurd. 'Tis no way disagreeable to the way of speaking common among all mankind, that is, supposing such an union of two natures in one person. Something like this, in some respects, is the union of soul and body in one human person. These natures are very diverse one from another. And yet "by virtue of the union of soul and body in man, the properties of soul and body, which are so very different, are affirmed of the person, though agreeing only to one of the principles of which he is constituted. Thus, for instance, we say [. . .] 'He is fair, well-proportioned,' etc., though only so with respect to his body; and that 'He is learned, wise, thoughtful,' etc., though only so with respect to his soul: that is, we affirm that of the person, which only agrees to one of the constituent principles of his nature considered by itself. In other instances we affirm that of the person, which agrees to neither of the constituent principles of his nature considered alone, and is only true of the man as constituted of both; as when we say of Peter, that he served his country with honor, purchased such an estate, etc., here we attribute that to Peter, which belongs neither to soul nor body considered alone, but only to the man as compounded of both. And thus it is with respect to Christ, by virtue of the wonderful union of two such distinct natures in his person. When we say of him, that he suffered and died, we mean it of his human nature only; when we say of him, that he 'thought it no robbery to be equal with God,' that he is omniscient, omnipresent, etc., we mean it only with respect to his divine nature; and when we say of him, that he is the Mediator, the Redeemer and Savior of sinners, we mean it of his person constituted of both natures." See Rawlin on *Justification,* p. 240.

1220. CHRIST'S RIGHTEOUSNESS, how did it consist with the wisdom of God to give mankind a law at first, and place him in a state of trial, insisting on it that, before he should have confirmed happiness, he should first honor the law, and honor him the Lawgiver, by performing the most exact and perfect obedience under temptations, and through a certain time of trial, if after all he was willing, after man had sinned, e'en to forego all this and to bestow confirmed happiness upon him only for his being by a mediator freed from guilt. Man was so perfectly free from guilt when he first came out of God's hands at the creation of the world. And if, finally, that was all that God intended to insist on it, why did he not then immediately give man eternal life (he having that qualification) without a constitution appointing such a thing as obedience through a state of trial, which was attended with so much uncertainty, and such a dreadful risk as all mankind's being exposed to everlasting ruin, besides those extensive and dreadful consequences that have actually come on mankind in general through all ages in the dreadful havoc temporal death makes, and its universal reign, and other dismal calamities, which overspread the nations of the earth through all generations?

1221. CHRIST'S RIGHTEOUSNESS, how Christ has the first and chief benefit of it. He has so not only as he is a vessel of largest capacity, but also as there are some things peculiarly belonging to Christ, some circumstances exceedingly heightening the merit of it, not imputed to believers. For as Mr. Rawlin observes in his discourses on *Justification*, p. 268, "though by the imputation of Adam's sin our state is affected, and we really become guilty; yet there are many circumstances and aggravations in Adam's sin, which are peculiarly his: and it can be no more argued from our being justified by the imputation of Christ's righteousness, that we are as righteous as he, than it can be argued from the imputation of Adam's sin, that every one of his posterity are, in every respect, as guilty and criminal in the sight of God as Adam himself was."

Remember: if I have opportunity, more fully to consider this matter, and carefully consider what is mentioned of aggravating circumstances of Adam's sin not imputed to his posterity in my sermon on Gen. 3:11;[3] and consider what circumstances in Christ's obedience answering them are not imputable to believers.

1222. HEAVEN, the paradise of God, ITS PLACE. That the place of the heaven of the blessed is not in the upper regions of the air may be argued from Solomon's so very often calling earthly things, enjoyments and affairs, things "under the sun," when speaking of their vanity, etc.— the trouble, fatigue, vexation, the changeableness, instability, vicissitudes, unsatisfactoriness, wickedness, folly, confusion, mysteriousness and darkness of the methods of God's providence, injustice, unprofitableness, uncertainty, and the unexpected changes that attend these things—evidently calling these things by this name as a distinguishing appellation. Therefore we may well argue that heaven, that state of the blessed, which it is evident is so far from being attended with this vanity, vexation, vicissitude, short continuance, uncertainty, sin, folly, unsatisfactoriness, darkness, confusion, etc., and so much the reverse of all these things, is not a world under the sun.

See Eccles. 1:3, 9, 14; 2:11, 17–20, 22; 3:16; 4:1, 3, 7; 5:13, 18; 6:12; 8:9, 15, 17; 9:3, 6, 9, 11, 13; 10:5.

In ch. 9:6, it is said of them that are dead that they have no more "a portion forever in anything that is done under the sun," which would be

---

3. A series of four sermons preached in Feb. 1739 on the doctrine, "The act of our first father in eating the forbidden fruit was a very heinous act."

far from being true if the heaven of glorified saints was in our atmosphere. See note on Job 22:12.[4]

1223. It is an argument that INSPIRATION AND MIRACLES are not to be restored in order to the healing of the nations of their idolatry, superstitions and other corruptions and prejudices against Christianity, that it is said, Rev. 22:2, the nations shall be healed by the "leaves of the tree" of life that bears "twelve manner [of] fruits," signifying the gospel as delivered in the doctrine of the twelve apostles. The leaves of that tree which bears these twelve manner of fruits are the leaves of our Bibles, especially of the New [Testament] delivered to the church of God by the apostles, or under their direction, and confirmed by them. 'Tis under this same tree the church is to be raised up and have that spiritual resurrection which she shall have after the fall of Antichrist, which we read of, Rev. 20. Here see note on Cant. 8:5.[5] See forward, No. 1230.

1224. MILLENNIUM, or sabbatism of the world, will not be much more than a thousand years.

1. Mankind would forget the corruption of nature, would be insensible of the dreadful ruin sin has brought on the nature of man, would not be so sensible of the great benefit of the redemption of Christ.

2. The curse of God on this world, consisting in the calamities of it, would not be very sensible. The world would scarcely appear as a great wilderness in the way to a land of rest. God's people would be under great temptation not to behave themselves as pilgrims and strangers on earth, forget to live as not of the world and to lay up treasure in heaven.

3. 'Tis not probable that so much of the Scripture would have been calculated for the church in a suffering state, and both for the church and the world in a state of so great pollution, temptation and danger.

4. The distinguishing grace of God in election would grow much out of sight. See No. 836.[6]

---

4. In the "Blank Bible," JE maintains that this text shows that "the heaven of the blessed" is "the highest of the heavens."

5. In the "Blank Bible," JE states that the things mentioned in Cant. 8:5 are of a "mystical significance." The apple tree "probably signifies that tree of life (Rev. 22:2)," and "under this tree the church shall have a spiritual resurrection from its low state."

6. *Works*, 20, 50–52.

1225. END OF THE CREATION, GLORY OF GOD.[7] It is a thing in itself infinitely valuable and worthy of regard that God's glory should be known by elect creatures to all eternity. The increasing knowledge of God in all elect creatures to all eternity is an existence, a reality infinitely worthy to be, in itself worthy to be regarded by him to whom it belongs, to order that to be which of all possible things is fittest and best and most valuable (see back, [No.] 1218). If existence is more worthy than defect and nonentity, and if any created existence is in itself worthy to be, then this knowledge of God and his glory is worthy to be. The existence of the created universe consists as much in it as in anything. Yea, it is one of the highest, most real and substantial parts of all created existence, most remote from nonentity and defect.

1226. Need of REVELATION to reveal PARDON. Reason of SATISFACTION. CHRISTIAN RELIGION. See back, [No.] 1206. "If pardon and salvation are designed for the world, it is altogether meet, that they should be proclaimed and promised. If they are not proclaimed and promised, there will be no sufficient assurance of 'em. Patience is not pardon; forbearance is not forgiveness. And if the divine patience administer some hope; yet the judgments of God upon the world will suggest as much anxiety and dread. And so through fear of death and destruction, the self-conscious mind must be, all its time, subject to terror and bondage. . . . If it be so hard for a sensible mind now, upon a public proclamation and promise, to believe the forgiveness of sins, it would be much more difficult to believe it without any such security.

"If pardon and salvation must be publicly proclaimed and promised to the guilty world, there will be an impediment or bar laid against it by the divine purity and justice. . . . What sort of a Deity must that be [. . .] that has an equal respect to good and evil? . . . Universal rectitude requires, that equity and equitable law should be maintained and executed in the territories, that are to be governed.

"That there is vindictive justice in God, seems evident. 1. From the excellency and perfection of his nature; by which he must hate all moral turpitude, and all the workers of iniquity. 2. From his jealousy and concern for his own glory; by which he will be displeased with all that is contrary thereto. 3. By the judgments which are continually executed in and

7. JE drew a vertical line down left side of this entire entry, indicating again his appropriation of this material in the *Dissertation Concerning the End for Which God Created the World.* See *Works, 8,* 22, 712–13.

upon the world for transgression; and sometimes by such special judgments, that have been an evident retaliation; or have marked out the sin in the punishment. 4. By the dictate of natural conscience, that often trembles upon the commission of great enormities, and expects, that great transgressors should meet with some signal token of divine vengeance; when the Barbarians saw the venomous animal hanging on Paul's hand, they concluded him some great criminal, whom, though [he had] escaped from the rage of the sea, yet vengeance [. . .] would not suffer to live. 5. By the offense which men usually take at divine providence, when it permits men to proceed and prosper in their notorious villanies. [. . .] 6. By the early and universal practice of propitiatory sacrifices in the world. If they were at first instituted by God, then God would have an acknowledgment of our sin, and his righteous displeasure, in the atonement, that was made him. If they were voluntarily taken up and practiced by men, there is an indication of mind and conscience, that some deference must be paid to divine justice; and that, to such a degree, that they were sometimes ready (in their ungoverned imaginations) to sacrifice the fruit of their body, for the sin of their soul.

"The righteousness of God being thus evident in itself, and acknowledged by the world, that if man was to be pardoned by public edict and covenant, it was altogether congruous thereto, that there should be some great, valuable sacrifice slain and offered to God, for the sin of the world. It was meet, that there should be a public demonstration of the holiness and purity of God; and of his hatred of sin; that the world may not be tempted to abuse his goodness and presume upon his mercy. It is meet, that his dominion and authority should be supported, that had been so rejected by the world. That his law (the rule of his government) should be asserted and maintained. That his honor and glory (after so much contempt and disgrace, as the impious world had cast upon him) should be raised up and illustrated. That the pardoning edict (being founded in sacred blood) should be established and ratified. That by a joint demonstration of justice and love, the world may be driven from sin and drawn to repentance and God. And here divine wisdom shines in reconciling righteousness and grace together, and accomplishing our salvation in the way and method of an eternal redemption.

"This sacrifice should be valuable above all created excellence and power. There is a world of most aggravated heinous offenses to be atoned for. It is an infinite majesty, that has been offended. It is an infinite justice that is to be propitiated. It is an infinite impunity (an exemption from an endless punishment, an advancement to an endless felicity) that is to be procured. All that intelligent creation can do for the Creator, is due to him on its own account. Let all the intelligent creatures take heed to themselves, that they do not, by their own fault [. . .], fall under the displeasure of God. His majesty and justice may despise their interposure on the behalf of an apostatized, sinful world." [Reynolds,] *Religion of Jesus Delineated,* pp. 135–38.

1227. OF PROPHECIES being fulfilled in several events. "It is the glorious characteristic of the revelations of that God, who comprehends the most distant futurities in one view, to foretell some intermediate event of lesser importance, in such majestic language as will naturally carry the reader's mind forward to some more important event at a greater distance, similar to it, in which these august predictions have a more complete accomplishment. Thus the reign of Solomon is celebrated in such exalted language, as can fully agree to none but a greater than Solomon, who now reigns over his spiritual Israel (Ps. 72). Thus the coming of Christ in the flesh, and the destruction of Jerusalem by the Romans, is described both by the prophets, and by Christ himself, in such majestic strains, and under such dreadful images, as unavoidably suggest to us the most lively ideas of his final advent, and the conflagration of the world. And thus the prophet Isaiah, while he has the happy restoration of the Jews in view more immediately, is transported far beyond that period, to those more glorious seasons, when living religion shall have a more extensive propagation through the world; when Jerusalem, in a spiritual sense, shall be made the praise of the whole earth, and all nations her denizens." Mr. Davies' *Sermon before the Presbytery of New Castle,* pp. 3–4.[8]

1228. CHRISTIAN RELIGION. CREDIBILITY OF CHRIST'S MIRACLES. "If sin, universally spread, brought universal death into the world; if it was worthy of a compassionate God to send some one into the world to take away sin; if miracles were the best proof of his mission; if his own resurrection was the most convincing miracle that could be wrought, and at the same time carried with it the most experimental assurance of an happy victory over all the effects of sin, and a comfortable renovation of the moral world; and if it was as easy with God to raise up his Son from death, as it is for one man to awake another out of sleep; I think the res-

8. Samuel Davies, *A Sermon, Preached before the Reverend Presbytery of New-Castle, October 11, 1752* (Philadelphia, 1753), 3–4.

urrection of Christ very far removed from improbability." *Deism Revealed,* vol. 1, p. 24.[9] See further, No. 1231.

1229. FUTURE STATE. REVEALED RELIGION. As we see that in this world the greatest prosperity don't always attend virtue, nor the greatest adversity always attend vice, but that it very often happens contrariwise, so the inward perturbation and remorse which arises from vice, and the pleasure of reflection and self-approval, are by no means of them proper and sufficient sanctions of the law of nature. "Punishments annexed to this law ought to be proportionable to the violations of the law. Remorse of conscience is not always in proportion to the heinousness of crimes, for an old habitual sinner [. . .] feels less remorse after the committal of the most enormous crimes, than the raw unpracticed sinner does after transgressions of a much more venial nature; so that [. . .] the punishment grows less, as the crime, to which it is applied, grows greater [. . .]. Nature, left to itself, runs almost unavoidably into habits of wickedness; and, as fast as it does, rids itself of its remorses, which ought still be growing stronger and keener, as habit tempts it to greater enormities. From hence it appears, that some greater punishment, not diminishable by the decay of the moral sense, [. . .] ought to be expected, in order to prevent our falling into the grossest crimes, or to make examples of us, if we do." *Deism Revealed,* vol. 1, p. 124.

"The happiness of particular nations and earthly societies bears a most minute proportion to that of God's universal kingdom; and yet 'tis confessed that the peace and pleasure which naturally attends the practice of virtue, and the remorse which attends vice, are not sanctions of the law of nature sufficient for the defense and preservation of earthly societies and kingdoms, but human laws enforced with the sanctions of civil punishments must be added. If the laws of nature were sufficiently clear," as the Deists say they are, "those of society need never, in cases purely moral, tell us our duty; and if they were sufficiently enforced, society would have no occasion to institute other enforcements of much greater cogency, in order to their being observed. Nay, if the law of nature were, in the several respects of clearness, authority, and obligation, perfect and sufficient, society itself would be altogether needless. Men would observe justice, and practice beneficence towards one another, without adventi-

9. Here and below, JE is quoting from Philip Skelton, *Deism Revealed. Or, The Attack on Christianity Candidly Reviewed in its Real Merits, as They stand in the Celebrated Writings of Lord Herbert, Lord Shaftesbury, Hobbes, Toland, Tindal, Collins, Mandeville, Dodwell, Woolston, Morgan, Chubb, and Others.* He indicates several times that he is using the 2nd ed. (2 vols. London, 1751).

tious obligations. A lover of liberty would not care to enter into society to become subject to magistrates, to support expensive contributions, to tie himself up to burdensome forms, and stoop to the will of others, if he found he could live independent, and converse and traffic safely with mankind, in a state of nature. The arguments, drawn from the supposed sufficiency of reason and nature, to invalidate the NECESSITY OF REVE-LATION, prove with the same force, be it greater or less, that society is un-necessary. If the laws of nature be able to effect their own end, and that end is moral instruction and obligation; then, indeed, there can be no sort of occasion for other laws, neither divine, nor human: however, it will be worthwhile to consider, whether the evil dispositions and vices of men do not force them into society; and, again, whether civil society, con-sidered in itself, is at all able to remedy the evils they seek to shelter them-selves from [. . .]. If a law should come forth, although from a known authority, and conceived in the plainest terms, forbidding murder un-der the penalty of all that severity which men are by nature disposed to exercise upon themselves, after doing such an action; and enjoining beneficence by a promise of all those rewards which men, after doing good offices, are enabled by nature to confer on themselves; it would be looked upon as a burlesque upon laws." *Deism Revealed,* [vol. 1,] pp. 128–29.[1] See further in the beginning of the next number.

1230. CHRISTIAN RELIGION. THE NECESSITY OF A REVELATION TO RE-VEAL PARDON AND AN ATONEMENT. See back, Nos. 1206 and 1226. "'Tis very clear that natural religion hath a necessary dependence on revela-tion, and on that part of Christianity which may be called supernatural: for religion, in any sense, is but a name, without a well-grounded hope of immortality, which no man ever had, or, for ought we can tell, ever could have had, if some superior Being had not revealed it to him. That man who does not believe in his own immortality, can never conceive himself to be anything else, than a better kind of brute, concerned only in present and sensible things, given up to appetite and passion, and, af-ter a few years existence in vanity and vexation, perishing forever in the dreadful gulf of annihilation. Yet, to believe in the immortality of the soul, and to be convinced we shall account hereafter for our actions to almighty God by any law, is to all men, for all have sinned, a most shock-ing article of faith, if an atonement for sin is not also to be believed in; because it affords us no other prospect, but that of judgment, wherein

1. Actually, JE begins quoting (rather loosely) from pp. 125–29.

as we must plead guilty, and stand self-convicted, so there is nothing to prevent our being condemned by Almighty God to a punishment, of which we know not the limits, either in point of severity or duration. Now [. . .] the doctrine of an atonement carries us directly to that of Christ's incarnation, and a personal distinction in God [. . . .] so that the mere light of nature, in our present circumstances, can afford us either no religion, or such an one as can serve no other purpose, but that of driving a rational and thinking mind to despair." *Deism Revealed*, vol. 1, pp. 172–73.

"Lucretius had good reason to object to the pagan, that is, as [. . .] Lord Herbert calls it, the natural theology, that it afforded no hope of forgiveness after sinning.

> . . . At mens sibi conscia facti,
> Præmetuens adhibet stimulos, terretque flagellis;
> Nec videt interea, qui terminus esse malorum
> Possit, nec qui sit pœnarum denique finis;
> Atque eadem metuit magis hæc ne in morte gravescant.[2]

"[. . .] God must be considered not only as merciful, but as just also, and capable of inflicting punishments, as well as dispensing rewards. If the subjects know they are to be forgiven, the penalties of the law are of no effect.

"[. . .] Mercy, shown publicly to all, can hardly fail of encouraging all to transgress, should they be tempted to it.

"[. . .] And if there are any degrees of wickedness so great that the light of nature gives us no ground to expect pardon, how shall we know what those degrees are? Does the light of nature plainly point out the limits?

"God is the supreme monarch of the whole universe, it belongs to him to see justice done, to render to every man according to his deeds, in order to support the dignity of his laws, on which the happiness of all the free and intelligent creation depends; and which if anyone might transgress with impunity, on merely repenting, I cannot see how his kingdom [. . .] can be preserved. Everyone will repent some time or other, if he thinks he is to be pardoned, and thereby exempted from intolerable

---

2. " . . . But the mind, conscious in itself of the deed, / turns, fearing, toward the stings and is fearful of the whips; / It does not see, meanwhile, what conclusion there can be of evils / nor, finally, what end of punishments there is; / And it fears the same things more lest these grow worse in death." Lucretius, *De Rerum Natura*.

punishments; by which means it will come to pass, that no one shall suffer, and so the penal laws of God will be in vain, although the world shall be filled with wickedness, and by no temptation so much, as by this very expectation of impunity on repentance deferred as long as the delinquent pleases.

"Let us know whether the law of nature promises pardon for sin; whether for all sins, or only for some; and, if some only, what those sins are, and whether absolutely, or on certain conditions; and, if the latter, what those conditions are. These [. . .] are points well worth inquiring after.

"Besides, God's assistance is necessary to true repentance. Before a sinner can begin to be the object of God's favor, he must cease to be what he was before, and commence a new man. Now no man can make a new man. None but the Creator can make a new man, or a new creature. There is a degree of strength necessary to a true repentance, such as no man is master of." *Deism Revealed,* [vol. 1,] pp. 239–44.

"Mere repentance can make no satisfaction to justice for injuries and offenses past; it can only put a man in the way of his duty for time to come, which he owes to God, and which, therefore, can clear no scores with him. As to the reformation of a transgressor, together with his disposition to lead a new life for the time to come, it may be rendered very precarious by the supposed easiness of obtaining pardon. [. . .] Man [. . .] is frail, and, in hopes of being pardoned again, may again transgress, unless his reason tells him he cannot be forgiven a second or third offense.

"[. . .] Although he, who murders a man, repents, and, for the time to come, carefully avoids the least approach to such an action; yet, in his latter behavior, he only does what it was always his duty to do, and no more; but makes not atonement to his poor neighbor, whom he hath deprived of life; nor to the community, from which he hath cut away a member; nor to God, whose creature and image he hath defaced. The Deists can never show, on their principles, that the murderer, or any other criminal, can make the least atonement or reparation for either the offenses he commits against God, or the wrongs he does to man, in cases where restitution is out of the question. They say the observation of the natural law alone can render men acceptable in the sight of God; and propose it as the only rule by which they are to act, and, consequently, to be judged. It is by this that, according to the deistical hypothesis, all men must stand issue before Almighty God, and be acquitted for the observation, or condemned for the transgression, of it. Now I [. . .] appeal to experience, and to the heart and conscience of every man, whether he does not live in the daily transgression, be it in higher or lower instances, of those laws, which he believes God requires the observation of at his hands; and whether, after the most sincere repentance, and the most thorough reformation he can make of his life and conduct, he finds not enough of evil dispositions and lapses to lament in himself, and put him in mind, that he is one of those debtors, who, having nothing to pay in towards former accounts, is still adding to, and inflaming, the debt. Thus, I think, it appears pretty plainly, that, if all men have sufficient means of knowing their duty, as the Deists insist they have; and if every man transgresses the rules of his duty, as his conscience cannot but inform him he does; the whole race of mankind are lost forever.

"[. . .] It is certainly for the good of men in general, and of all intelligent beings, that the laws of God, on which all order and happiness necessarily depend, should be duly enforced; and this can never be, [. . .] if the punishment, annexed to the transgression of them, [. . .] may be evaded by repeated repentances, after repeated sins; which is but trifling with the laws, and the majesty of their author. The Deists themselves own that he who transgresses the law of nature is without excuse, since that law is sufficiently made known to him, and placed even within his own heart. This makes willful offenders of all mankind, and justifies their judge in laying on them all those severities, whatever they are, which he hath annexed to the transgression of his law, and made fully known to men, as a main and necessary enforcement of that law. There is no reason to think that sinful men will ever cease to sin, if they do not stand in awe of such severities, or that they will ever give up their sinful, but long-indulged delights, if they be not encouraged so to do by better-grounded hopes of pardon, than the mere light of nature can give them. We may be confident they will not in this life, and to repent in the next may, for ought nature can tell us, be too late." *Deism Revealed,* vol. 1, [pp.] 239–49.[3]

"I appeal to the hearts of all men whether to suppose, as many do of late, that God will only punish the vilest delinquents so far, as to make those of them to amend their behavior in another world, who die in their sins: would not be wholly to defeat the good ends proposed by the law; and whether such a medicine, substituted in the place of a punishment, would not unchain the outrageous appetites and passions of mankind, and turn the world into an hell of confusion and misery. What a sight

3. Actually, JE quotes from pp. 246–49.

would this be, for all the other intelligent beings of the creation! To see the evil let loose upon the good, and wretched men, already too prone to wickedness, tempted to become devils, by a promise of pardon beforehand! [...] a law, without a penalty equal to the strong tendency to evil in many or most of the subjects, instead of being a defense to good men, would most miserably oppress them. Their respect for the law, and its author, would effectually tie up their hands, while the worst of men, with a license prompted by hopes of impunity and reconciliation with God, would oppress and plunder, and cut their throats at discretion." *Deism Revealed,* vol. 2, p. 64.

"A religion, that does not tell us what will please or displease God, tells us nothing; and a religion, that can neither bind us firmly to our duty, nor afford us rational hopes of pardon from God, after we have acted against the rules of our duty, is an hideous religion, that serves only for condemnation." *Deism Revealed,* vol. 2, p. 84.

1231. See [No.] 1228. CHRISTIAN RELIGION. CREDIBILITY OF CHRIST'S MIRACLES. "If the fact of Christ's RESURRECTION, on account of its unusualness, appears improbable, it will, on account of its expediency, appear, in an higher degree, probable, if duly considered. [...] Seeing philosophy, and other ordinary means, had proved insufficient to retrieve mankind from ignorance, wickedness, and misery, if God has mercy on mankind, and has not utterly forsaken the world and cast it off, recourse must be had to extraordinary and supernatural means, that is, to revelation; for we cannot possibly conceive any other effectual expedient for such a purpose; nor can we conceive, how the person, by whom the revelation should be made, could prove himself to be a messenger sent from God, without working miracles. Were he vested with no higher signs of power than other men, his plainer dictates would appear to be no more, than the obvious suggestions of common sense, or, at most, of philosophy; and if he delivered any doctrines undiscoverable by the force of reason, they would appear to be less; in either respect he could only teach in his own name, not in that of God, and consequently without authority or effect. That it is highly probable God would send us an instructor, thus qualified and empowered, and that this is not a probability, only invented by divines to serve the purposes of Christianity, appears evidently from hence, that Plato fell into the same way of thinking, long before our Savior came into the world. He was strongly of opinion, that God would send some person, or being, into the world, who should teach mankind how they ought to serve the Supreme Being." (See "Miscellanies," No. 1350.)[4] "But, had such a person appeared in Plato's time, that philosopher would, no doubt, have expected from him the signs and credentials of a divine commission, which could have been nothing else, but miracles; for without miracles the pretended messenger could have had no right to dictate to Plato, nor to assume any higher character, than that of a philosopher." *Deism Revealed*, vol. 2, pp. 16–17.

1232. INFINITE EVIL OF SIN. SATISFACTION OF CHRIST. EQUIVALENCE OF HIS SUFFERINGS to sinners' eternal punishment. Besides the dignity of Christ's sufferings directly arising from the dignity of his person, "there is another consideration, by which the value of our Savior's sufferings ought to be estimated. As an indignity is always rated by the presumption, and as the presumption bears an exact proportion to the meanness of the person insulting, and to the greatness of the party insulted; so, in like manner, all acts of condescension being estimated by the humility, and that, again, by the dignity, of the condescending person, and by the lowness and demerit of the party condescended to." *Deism Revealed*, vol. 1, pp. 252–53.

1233. There is nothing impossible or absurd in the doctrine of the INCARNATION of Christ. "If God can join a body and a rational soul together, which [are] of natures so heterogene and opposite, that they cannot of themselves act one upon another, may he not be able to join two spirits together, which are of natures more similar? [. . .] And if so, He may, for ought we know to the contrary, join the soul or spirit of a man to Himself. . . . Had reason been so clear in it, that a God cannot be incarnate, as many pretend, it could never have suffered such a notion to gain ground, and possess the minds of so many nations, nay, and of Julian himself, who says, that Jupiter begot Æsculapius out of his own proper substance, and sent him down to Epidaurus to heal the distempers of mankind. Reason did not hinder Spinoza, Blount, and many other modern philosophers, from asserting, that God may have a body; or rather, that the universe, or the matter of the universe, is God. . . . Many nations believed the incarnation of Jupiter himself. . . . Reason, instead of being utterly averse to the notion of a divine incarnation, hath easily enough admitted that notion, and suffered it to pass, almost without contradic-

4. MS: "B. 9. p. 855. [col. 1] c. and 859. [col. 2]." The paragraphs in No. 1350 referred to begin, respectively, "'Tis no wonder that many heathen nations believed a future state . . ." and "If a few persons of superior talents and applications should discover . . . " (Pp. 450, 456.)

tion, upon the most philosophical nations of the world." [*Deism Revealed,* vol. 2, pp. 82–84.] MYSTERIES.

1234. MYSTERIES. The MYSTERY of the TRINITY not absurd and [a] contradiction. "The point seems to be beyond the grasp of human understanding. However, it may be observed, that, in thinking of the eternity and immensity of God; of his remaining from eternity to the production of the first creature, without a world to govern, [...] of the motives that determined him to call his creatures into being; why they operated when they did, and not before; of his raising up intelligent beings, whose wickedness and misery he foresaw; of the state in which his relative attributes, justice, bounty, and mercy, remained, through an immense space of duration, before he had produced any creatures to exercise them towards; in thinking, I say, of these unfathomable matters, and of his raising so many myriads of spirits, and such prodigious masses of matter, out of nothing, we are lost and astonished, as much as in the contemplation of the Trinity. [...] We can follow God but one or two steps in his lowest and plainest works, till all becomes mystery, and matter of amazement, to us. How, then, shall we comprehend himself? how shall we understand his nature, or account for his actions? [...] in that he contains what is infinitely more inconceivable than all the wonders of his creation put together." *Deism Revealed,* vol. 2, pp. 93–94.

Those that deny the Trinity because of the mysteriousness of it, and its seeming inconsistence, yet generally own God's certain prescience of man's free actions, which they suppose to be free in such a sense as not to be necessary, so that we may do or may not do that which God certainly foresees. They also hold that such a freedom without necessity "is necessary to morality," and that "virtue and goodness consist in doing good, when we might do evil." And yet they suppose that "God acts by the eternal law of nature and reason," and that it is impossible that he should "transgress that law, and do evil," because "that would be a contradiction to his own nature," and yet that he is infinitely virtuous, which "seems a flat contradiction. To say, that the infinite goodness of God's nature makes it utterly impossible for God to do evil, is the same exactly as to say, he is under a natural necessity not to do evil. And to say he is morally free, is to say he may do evil. Now the necessity and freedom in this case being both moral, the contradiction is flat and plain, and amounts to this, that God, in respect to good and evil actions, is both a necessary and free agent. Dr. Clarke, in his treatise on the attributes, labors to get clear of this contradiction upon these principles of liberty, but without success; and leaves it just where [. . .] all men, who hold the same principles, must be forced to leave it.[5]

"Therefore, they hold such mysteries in respect to Deity that are even harder to be conceived of, and properly expressed and explained, than the doctrine of the Trinity.

"When we talk of God, who is infinite and incomprehensible, it is natural to run into notions and terms, which it is impossible for us to reconcile. And in lower matters, that are more within our knowledge and comprehension, we shall not be able to keep ourselves clear of 'em. To say, that a curved line, setting out from a point within an hair's-breadth of a right line, shall run towards that right line as swift as thought, and yet never be able to touch it, seems contradictory to common sense; and, were it not clearly demonstrated in the conchoid of Nechomedes, could never be believed." Matter is "infinitely divisible" and, therefore, "a cubical inch of gold may be divided into an infinity of parts. [. . .] And there can be no number greater than that which contains an infinity." Yet "another cubical inch of gold may be infinitely divided also" and, therefore, "the parts of both cubes must be more numerous, than the parts of one only. [. . .] Here [. . .] is a palpable contrariety of ideas, and a flat contradiction of terms. We are confounded and lost in the consideration of infinites. [. . .] and surely most of all, in the consideration of that infinite of infinites. [. . .] We justly admire that saying of the philosopher, that 'God is a Being whose center is everywhere, and circumference nowhere,' as one of the noblest and most exalted flights of human understanding, and yet not only the terms are absurd and contradictory, but the very ideas that constitute it, when considered attentively, are repugnant to one another. Space and duration are mysterious abysses, in which our thoughts are confounded with demonstrable propositions, to all sense and reason, flatly contradictory to one another. Any two points of time, though never so distant, are exactly in the middle of eternity. The remotest points of space, that can be imagined or supposed, are, each of them, precisely in the center of infinite space." *Deism Revealed*, vol. 2, pp. 109–11.

Here might have been added the mysteries of God's eternal duration, it being without succession, without before and after, all at once, "*vitæ interminabilis tota simul et perfecta possessio.*" See *The Nature of the Human Soul*[6] on this head, and particularly consider the many contradictions which seem here implied.

5. Samuel Clarke, *A Demonstration of the Being and Attributes of God* (London, 1705).
6. The Latin ending the previous sentence translates, " . . . at once a total and complete pos-

1235. THE FULLNESS OF TIME when Christ came. "Had Christ been sent, and his religion fully and finally revealed, in the first age of the world, both the memory of the first, and the effect of the last, must have been entirely lost, or so distorted and corrupted in a few ages, that posterity would have been little the better for such a mission or revelation; or else God must have made an infinity of other revelations, in order to ascertain or perpetuate the Christian to future times. Arts, sciences, languages, commerce, must have been all taken out of the natural course of invention and improvement, and all at once revealed; or else it would have been impossible to transmit our religion to very distant times or countries, with any tolerable degree of purity; or, admitting it had been possible, yet what opinion must posterity have entertained of a religion handed down to them from nobody knew whom, from times, and by means, utterly unknown, which no mortal could account for, as being previous to all memory, all records, and all history? How would our Libertines, so nice and scrupulous about authorities, have liked such a religion as this? *Deism Revealed,* vol. 2, p. 142.

"Alexander the Great [. . .] went over to Asia, and conquered all the countries from the Mediterranean, and the Hellespont, to the Ganges; and he and his followers established the Grecian arts and language throughout that extended empire, which comprehended Egypt also, and the adjacent countries. The language of this empire, which exceeded those of other countries in beauty, regularity, and preciseness of expression, was also the learned and fashionable language of the Romans, who, after making themselves masters of the Western world, added the Greek empire to their conquests; by which means the Greek tongue, being understood both in the East and West, became an admirable vehicle for the religious knowledge that was to be conveyed by it to the world. Such were the preparatives to that fullness of time, spoken of in Scripture for the introduction of a true and universal religion. After the nations had thus been united by conquest, by commerce, and by a general language, the Jews, who saw by the prophecies of Jacob and of Daniel, that the time for their deliverance was approaching, vainly be-

---

session of an unending life," and is a quote from Andrew Baxter (1686–1750), *An Enquiry into the Nature of the Human Soul, wherein the Immateriality of the Soul is evinced from Principles of Reason and Philosophy* (London, 1730), p. 375, where Baxter goes on to state (pp. 375–76): "There is certainly no succession of *idea, desires, will in the Infinite or Necessary Mind,* and therefore no *change or mutability* in it. This follows when it is shewn that the manner of existence of a necessarily existing mind must be itself necessary and immutable . . . Thus there is really no actual succession in the *manner* of *God's* existence, that is, in his eternity, nay, not after the existence of a material world. The changes and successions that then happen, happen to something else not to HIM. . . . Time or eternity are only affections of Being, and nothing existing by themselves."

lieving, that their Messiah was to be a temporal prince, and to advance them to an empire over all the world, published certain verses, under the name of Sibylline Oracles, to give 'em the greater credit with the Romans. In one of these, which were all founded on the prophecy of Daniel, it was foretold, that at the time when Pompey took Jerusalem, nature was about to bring forth a king for the Roman people; at which, says Suetonius, the Senate being frightened, made a decree, that no child born that year should be brought up. In another they foretold the rise of an heavenly kingdom, which should prevail, as soon as the Romans should conquer the Egyptians. In a third they predicted the same, upon the extinction of the Lagean line, which happened at the death of Cleopatra. These pretended oracles, which the Jews spread about everywhere, received no small addition of credit from a very old prophecy, which, according to Suetonius and Tacitus, was taken from the sacred writings of the priests, and foretold that a mighty king should be born among the Jews, who should govern the whole world. By these, and such like means, [. . .] the expectation of some very extraordinary person was raised, and that expectation universally spread, and directed to one and the same place and time. In that place, and at that time, was Christ born.

"From the transgression of our first parents, the means of redemption and salvation commenced in a revelation. A promise was given to our first parents, that 'the seed of the woman should bruise the head of the serpent.' The celebration of the sabbath, an abhorrence of incest, the practice of sacrificial atonements, and of sacerdotal mediation, with many other notices of the like nature, were divinely revealed, and handed down to posterity. The propagation of these, with the improvement of arts, sciences, and languages, the planting of colonies, the rise and growth of empires, the extensive intercourse occasioned by trade, the warlike expeditions both by land and sea, the general course of conquests, captivities, and political alliances, were all so disposed and directed by almighty God, as to prepare the world for his Son's arrival. Curiosity and vanity may raise disputes among philosophers, and these disputes create infinite doubts and uncertainties. Ambition and revenge may breed quarrels among kings, and those quarrels make hideous havoc and distraction in the world; yet out of all this confusion shall God bring order. The short-sightedness of human science shall prove the necessity of divine revelation. The pride, and tyranny, and wars of princes, shall pave the way to true liberty and peace. The philosopher shall dispute, and the commander, though he thinks nothing less, shall conquer, for Christ; who, though 'he was brought as a lamb to the slaughter, yet shall now have his portion with the great, and divide the spoils with the strong.' He gathers where prophets and philosophers have strewed; he reaps where kings have sown. That prodigious empire, which it cost so much worldly wisdom, and labor, and blood, to raise; which was extended from Scythia to Numidia, from India to the British Isles; after it had ten times made war upon him, and persecuted him with fire and sword, Christ conquers with the celestial armor of truth, righteousness, peace, and the word of God. We cannot sufficiently admire the wisdom of God in such a wonderful disposition of events, in sending the necessary religion into the world in the most knowing age, when its credentials could be best examined, and its vouchers best recorded; nor his power in supporting it against the united policy and strength of the whole world. But such are the effects, when God works. Occurrences and transactions at an infinite distance shall, by the extensive schemes of providence, be brought together, and united in his designs." *Deism Revealed,* vol. 2, pp. 148–51.

1236. TRADITIONS OF THE CHINESE concerning THE MESSIAH and THE TRINITY. "It is probable that some of the Israelites that had been carried into captivity penetrated as far as China, long before the Christian era; because in that country notices are yet to be found, to which we cannot rationally assign any other original, than some acquaintance with the Jews. If we may believe the traditions of the Chinese, Confucius, their great philosopher, who lived above five hundred years before Christ, had this remarkable saying often in his mouth, 'It is in the West that the true saint is to be found.' And Laokun, who lived before Confucius, was as remarkable for another saying, which seems to point at the Trinity: 'Eternal Reason produced one, one produced two, two produced three, and three produced all things.' They tell us further, that Mimti, one of their emperors, who reigned about sixty years after Christ, sent ambassadors, at the instigation of an apparition, to look for the saint that heaven had informed him was in the West." *Deism Revealed,* vol. 2, p. 148.

1237. IMPUTATION OF SIN AND RIGHTEOUSNESS. These are by many supposed to be contrary to common sense. But, if so, "that is contrary to common sense, which is confirmed by universal experience. The son everywhere suffers for the sins of his father, in hereditary poverty and sickness. [. . .] To say it is inconsistent with the justice of God, is to run into atheism and blasphemy. Estates are often, and justly, settled on the posterity of a person, who died in the service of his country, and they enjoy the benefit of their patent, without any merit of their own, while un-attainted of high treason, merely for the merit of their ancestor. This le-gal imputation of merit, or application of the fruits arising from the merit of another, is never deemed unjust among men. Even when the reward is pecuniary, and arises out of the public funds, those who are taxed for these funds, never grudge the bounty, paid out of their own pockets, to the descendants of such as have sacrificed their lives for the good of the community. In this channel, estates, annuities, and honors, descend to many generations; and I question much, whether any other tenure gives, in the eye of reason, so equitable a title. Thus, [. . .] the entail both of merit and demerit goes down, from a good or bad man, to his posterity, by a necessity of nature, or a constitution of state, independent of the will, and previous to the behavior, of him who inherits. Now, [. . .] it will be impossible [. . .] to show, that God may not do that by grace, which he hath done by nature, and which the head of every community hath a right to do by legal and civil appointment. . . . The son is often par-doned even the crime of high treason, on account of his father's services, and fidelity. And nothing can be more consistent with justice, than a par-don so obtained, provided sufficient security can be produced for the fu-ture loyalty of the son. [. . .] And surely we must own that God is vested with an higher plenitude of power to prescribe terms, on which imputed and vicarious merits may be accepted, than any earthly legislature, or king.

"And as to the objection against laying on one person the punishment due to the sins of another, that God tells us by the mouth of the prophet Ezekiel—that 'the father shall not suffer for the iniquity of the son, nor the son for the iniquity of the father; but that the soul that sinneth, it shall die'—that passage hath no reference to the case in question. The Israelites complained, that they had been punished for the sins of their forefathers; and nothing can be plainer, from a variety of passages, than they had actually suffered severely by means of the idolatry, and other sins, of their ancestors and kings, which brought on them a long train of calamities; such as drought, famine, pestilence, the sword, and captivity. But God, in this passage, declares, that it shall be no longer so; and that, for the future, every man shall suffer only for the sins of his own com-mittal. This, now, is only a particular dispensation, and contrary to an-other, that had continued till that time, and therefore cannot, but by implication, be applied to the supposed substitution of our Savior's suf-ferings, in the room of our own: nor can it, even by implication, show, that this substitution is unjust." *Deism Revealed,* vol. 1, pp. 250–51.

1238. HUMILIATION. The spirit of self-sufficiency "is older than the world. [. . .] It was self-sufficiency made the devil aspire to independency: he thought himself too wise, too great, and glorious a being, to be anything less than God. He said, 'I will exalt my throne above the stars of God: I will be like the Most High.'" The sin of Eve implied the same spirit. "The devil insinuated to her, that the prohibition laid on her, [. . .] was the effect of mere will and arbitrariness; that to eat the forbidden fruit, [. . .] would open her eyes, she being, as yet, kept in the dark by her fear of God, [. . .] it would make her wise, like God, [. . .] knowing good and evil. [. . .] The devil [. . .] infused his own pride, and love of independency: thence it was that conceit, affectation of knowledge, and inordinate love of pleasure, became the source of all sin; and it is worth observing, that, in proportion as those dispositions render anyone self-sufficient, they, to this day, also render him corrupt and wicked. The mother of mankind, having eat the forbidden fruit, became self-sufficient, and was qualified to be a teacher of Libertinism to her husband [. . .]. The sacrifices of Abel were better received than those of Cain: the pride of Cain could not brook this preference, although the effect of infinite wisdom; but, swelling him with self-sufficiency, put him upon arraigning God of partiality, and murdering his brother. Were not Korah, and his company, very self-sufficient, when they said to Moses and Aaron, 'Ye take too much upon you, seeing all the congregation is holy, every one of them? Will ye put out the eyes of these men?' [. . .] Saul, being made king, was lifted up with self-sufficiency, and invaded the priestly office, thinking there was no necessity, that a meaner man should come between God and him. An independent spirit was the sin of Jeroboam, who, rather than suffer his subjects to worship the true God at Jerusalem, which might have brought them again under the dominion of David's posterity, set up the golden calves at Dan and Bethel, and gave the Israelites a religion of their own. . . . In later times the Jews, forsaking the simplicity of that religion God had given them, followed the various and contradictory traditions of their rabbis, by which the commandments of God were explained away, and rendered ineffectual. Those must certainly be very self-sufficient instructors, who had the boldness to make the word of God speak a language contrary to its own end and intention, because more agreeable to theirs. It was self-sufficiency that dictated all the idolatry of the Gentiles: what an high opinion must they have of themselves, who choose or make their own gods! All their philosophy, excepting that of Socrates and Plato, who acknowledged the blindness of human nature, and the necessity of a divine instructor, was evidently derived from the same source: for not one, but those two, founded his morality on any sense of religion, or ever dreamt of an inability in man to render himself perfect and happy. . . . Had all men, Jew as well as Gentile, in the times of our Savior and his apostles, been sensible of their own ignorance; would not this [. . .] have procured Christianity an easier admission, in every country where it was preached? [. . .] Men must feel their own wants, before they will either look for, or accept a supply. A man who thinks himself hail and sound, will laugh at the physician, who pretends to prescribe to him. It was nothing else but self-sufficiency that made our religion appear foolishness to the Greeks, and, indeed, to all whoever, in any age, pretended to a reason for rejecting it: of those who received it, there were not a few disgusted at its simplicity, and confident enough of their own abilities, to imagine they could improve it by alterations or additions of their own. The foremost of these were those heretics, conceitedly styled, by themselves, Gnostics. [. . .] The rejecting the doctrine of the Trinity was only a compliment made to their own reason by the Sabellians, the Photinians, the Samosatenians, the Arians, and, after them, by the Mahometans, who disbelieved that doctrine on no one argument in the world, but because it was not to be accounted for by their all-sufficient understandings. . . . Popery borrows a great deal from the belief of human sufficiency; for on what else is the doctrine of merits, and supererogation, founded? To what end is such an abundance of human inventions, of ceremonies unknown to the primitive ages, and of pious frauds; if that church allows Christianity, as its author left it, to be sufficient, and does not think herself able to new-model and alter it for the better? [. . .] And since the Reformation the Pope no sooner ceased to be the sufficiency of some men, than they set up a sufficiency of their own, and became popes to themselves: hence arose a crop of wild extravagant fancies, as monstrous as it was various. [. . .] I shall only take notice of the Socinians, who of all men, the Deists only excepted, pay the highest respect to their own understandings." *Deism Revealed,* vol. 2, pp. 206–11.

"How wise, how perfect, how independent a creature is man, in human speculation! but how weak and purblind, how corrupt, and prone to wickedness, when weighed in the balance of experience! When the necessity of revelation is to be invalidated, man is, by nature, a gloriously enlightened, a well-disposed, a just, and benevolent being: yet, when he is to be taught and trained to either religious or social duties, he is, for the most part, found either very stupid, or perverse; and when he is to be dealt with in a way of business, all manner of precautions and securities are found necessary to guard against the effects of his disingenuity. This being, who, by the strength of his unassisted reason, can know so little, and who, by the corrupt disposition of his will, can practice less, stands in no need of God's instructions, nor of stronger motives to the performance of his duty, than what arise within himself; is, in a word, perfect and self-sufficient. The experiments of five thousand years, all ending in the grossest folly and wickedness, are not enough to convince him, that he can neither be good, nor happy, without the divine assistance." *Deism Revealed,* vol. 2, p. 215.

1239. NECESSITY OF REVELATION. One thing wherein the deficiency of natural light appears is this: that if men without revelation should suppose that they should be forgiven on repentance and reformation, and also that there is a future state, yet the light of nature alone never could be sufficient to ascertain the limits of their day of probation, and satisfy 'em on sure grounds that repentance shall never be accepted in some future state, or whether ever the time would come when the case of sinners would be hopeless or past remedy by repentance.

1240. The CERTAINTY and SENSIBILITY of that future DAMNATION which God hath threatened may be argued strongly from these words, Ezek. 6:10, "And they shall know that I am the Lord, and that I have not said in vain that I would do this evil unto them," though the punishment there spoken is not the punishment of sinners in a future world.

1241. See back, [No.] 1197. TRINITY, intimations of it in the Old Testament. Ps. 58:11, "Verily there is a [. . .] God that judgeth in the earth" (*Elohim Shophetim,* which literally is *"Elohim,* Judges," in the plural number). See the evident distinction made between Jehovah sending and Jehovah sent to the people and dwelling in the midst of them in Zech. 2:8–9, 11; and 4:9. See [No.] 1243.

1242. THREATENINGS, ABSOLUTE, the certainty of their fulfillment. In Josh. 23:14–16, Joshua makes use of the exact fulfillment of all God's promises to the people of Israel as an argument with them to assure them of the certain fulfillment of his threatening.

1243. TRINITY. See No. 1241. Josh. 24[:19], "And Joshua said unto the people, Ye cannot serve Jehovah: for he is an holy God" (*Elohim Ked'hoshim,* "He is the holy Gods"). Not only is the word *Elohim* properly plural, the very same that is used, v. 15, but the adjective "holy" is plural. A plural substantive and adjective are used here concerning the true God, just in the same manner as in I Sam. 4:8, "who shall deliver us out of the hands of these mighty Gods?," and in Dan. 4:8, "in whom is the spirit of the holy gods" (so vv. 9, 18, and ch. 5:11). That the plural number should thus be used with the epithet "holy" agrees well with the doxology of the angels, "Holy, holy, holy, Lord God of hosts," etc. (Is. 6 and Rev. 4). See [No.] 1249. See many instances of this kind in *Synopsis* on Deut. 4:7.[7]

1244. TRADITIONS of the heathen concerning ORIGINAL SIN. The author of *The Strength and Weakness of Human Reason,* etc., as cited by Mr. Moncrieff against Dr. Campbell, pp. 55–56,[8] says that the opinion of the degenerate and corrupt state of man "is not peculiar to the Jews and Christians; for several of the heathen philosophers acknowledged and maintained it by the mere influence of the light of nature and reason. Antoninus, the philosophic emperor, confesses that 'we are born mere slaves' (i.e. in the sense of the Stoics, slaves to our vicious inclinations and passions) 'destitute of all true knowledge and sound reason.' The Platonists are well known to believe a pre-existent state wherein all souls sinned. [. . .] Their own daily experience in themselves, and their wise observations of the world, convinced them that all mankind come into the world with propensity to vice rather than virtue, and that man is not such a creature now as he came from his Maker's hand." Thus far the author of the *Inquiry,* etc. Mr. Moncrieff adds, p. 56: "Plato speaks of the human nature as greatly degenerate and depraved, and infested with all manner of disorders. And Democritus is said to affirm the diseases of the soul to be so great, that if it were opened it would appear to be a sepulcher of all manner of evils. Mr. Gale, in his *Court of the Gentiles,*[9] who takes notice in his book of the manner in which these philosophers have expressed themselves, having likewise cited some expressions of Seneca's,

---

7. Poole, *Synopsis Criticorum, 1,* Pt. I, cols. 763–764.

8. Isaac Watts, *The Strength and Weakness of Human Reason; or, the important question about the sufficiency of reason to conduct mankind to religion and future happiness, argued between an inquiring Deist and a Christian divine* (London, 1731; 2nd corr. ed., London 1737), p. 31, cited in Alexander Moncrieff, *An enquiry into the principle, rule, and end of moral actions, wherein, the scheme of selfish-love, laid down by Mr. Archibald Campbell, . . . in his Enquiry into the original of moral virtue, is examined, and the received doctrine is vindicated* (Edinburgh, 1735).

9. Theophilus Gale, *The Court of the Gentiles: Or a Discourse touching the Original of Human Literature, both Philologie and Philosophie, From the Scripture & Jewish Church* (2 vols. London, vol. 1, 1672, vol. 2, 1677).

he tells us that Jansenius breaks forth into a rapture upon observing these philosophers speak more truly about the corruption of man's nature than Pelagius and others of late."

1245. See [No.] 769, at the end of that number.[1] ELECTION. Eph. 1:4, "According as he hath chosen us in him before the foundation of the world, that we might be holy and without blame before him in love." The question is: In what sense are we said to be chosen *in Christ?* The meaning, as Dr. Goodwin (in his *Works,* vol. 1, pp. 54 ff.) shows,[2] cannot be a being chosen because it is foreseen we shall believe in Christ. Nor yet is it choosing us from a foresight of his satisfactions and merits as our surety. Christ purchased our salvation, but not our election. But God first loved us and then gave his Son for us. Christ loved us and then gave himself for us. God first gave us to his Son that, in eternal election,[3] he might take care that we might be redeemed and not lost.

Nor, in the third place, is the meaning that God hath chosen us that we might be in Christ. 'Tis not said, God hath chosen us that we might be in Christ and that we might be holy, but "he hath chosen us in him [. . .] that we might be holy." We are chosen in him before the foundation of the world that we might be holy. 'Tis not likely that those words, "before the foundation of the world," would have been placed where they are, between being chosen in Christ and "that we might be holy," if the meaning had been that we were chosen before the foundation of the world to be in Christ and to be holy. And that this is not the sense is confirmed by the connection with what is said in the foregoing verse, where it is said, he "hath blessed us with all spiritual blessings [. . .] in Christ," and then for example's sake or explanation's sake, adds, "According as he hath chosen us in him," which argues that the meaning is not merely that we are chosen to be in him, but our being looked upon in him is some way the ground of our being chosen from eternity to be holy and happy, as it is the ground of being blessed with spiritual blessings in time. And besides that it is thus, is confirmed by[4] Eph. 3:11, "According to the eternal purpose which he purposed in Christ."

1. *Works, 18,* 418.

2. The reference is to Thomas Goodwin's sermon on (primarily) Eph. 1:4–5, which is "Sermon V" of his *Exposition on the First, and Part of the Second Chapter, of the Epistle to the Ephesians,* in *The Works of Thomas Goodwin, D.D.* (London, 1681).

3. MS: "election that."

4. JE deletes: "other scripture. So God is said to give us grace *in Christ* before the world was, II Tim. 1:9, which implies that our being beheld in Christ is the ground of our having a title to grace by an act of divine donation before the world was. See also Eph."

Nor, in the fourth place, is the meaning only that we are elected with Christ, that Christ and we were elected together at the same time. For so one saint is elected together with another saint, but yet he is not said to [be] chosen in him. But we must suppose that Christ, in some respect, is first in this affair, and some way or other the ground of our being chosen, and God's election of him some way or other including and inferring the election of particular saints.

Therefore, for the explaining of the matter, what follows may be observed:

1. All things that God ever decreed he decreed for the sake of his beloved. And all was decreed to be brought to pass by his Son. He being the end of all God's works *ad extra,* therefore the accomplishment of all was committed to him. It was left with him to bring all to effect. Col. 1:15–19, "Who is the image of the invisible God, the first born of every creature: for by him were all things created, that are in heaven," etc., "all things were created by him, and for him: and he is before all things, and by him all things consist. And he is the head of the body, the church: who is the beginning, the firstborn from the dead; that in all things he might have the preeminence. For it pleased the Father that in him should all fullness dwell." Therefore probably it is that the sum of God's decrees is called the purpose which he purposed in Christ Jesus, Eph. 3:11, by the particle ἐν, signifying that what God purposed, he purposed for Christ and purposed to accomplish by Christ.

2. That which more especially was God's end in his eternal purpose of creating the world, and of the sum of his purposes with respect to creatures, was to procure a spouse, or a mystical body, for his Son. Therefore, if God's purpose of the creation of all things, and purpose of the whole series of events, may be called a purpose which he purposed in Christ Jesus (because the end of all was to procure a spouse, or body, for his [Son]), and all was decreed to be effected by him, more especially may his purpose with respect to those very individual parts of the creation[5] that in the decree were chosen to be the very spouse herself. His decree in appointing the individual creatures that were chosen to be members of his body, the accomplishment of God's purposes with respect to which were more especially committed to Christ—I say this purpose may well, in a more peculiar manner, be called a purpose which God purposed in Christ Jesus. And the determination or election of these individual created beings might be called an election in Christ, and they said to be chosen in Christ.

5. MS: "creature."

3. As God determined in his eternal decrees to create a world, to communicate himself, and his Son might have an object for the object of his
infinite grace and love, so God determined that this object should be
one. His special aim in all was to procure one created child, one spouse
and body of his Son for the adequate displays of his unspeakable and
transcendent goodness and grace. Therefore, though many individual
persons were chosen, yet they were chosen to receive God's infinite good
and Christ's peculiar love in union, as one body, one spouse, all united
in one head. Therefore they were all chosen to receive those divine communications no otherwise than in that head. Here are very worthy to be
noted the Apostle's words in the ninth and tenth verses following [Eph.
1:9–10], which is a continuation of the same discourse and where still
the Apostle has reference to that election in Christ spoken of here in this
fourth verse: "Having made known to us the mystery of his will, according to his good pleasure which he purposed in himself: that in the dispensation of the fullness of times he might gather together in one all
things in Christ, both which are in heaven, and which are on earth; even
in him."

As God chose every particle of inanimate matter that should be animated and receive life in the body of a man when man should be created, that should be animated either at the first creation of that body or
afterwards by nourishment, every individual particle was chosen singly
to receive life. But it was not chosen to receive life as a single, separate
particle, but no otherwise than in that living body, and as partaking of
the life of the body, and as united to the head, and partaking of the vital influence of the head and vitals of that body, and of the soul that
should animate it. Thus are particular elect persons chosen to spiritual
life, to holiness and happiness in Christ. They are chosen singly. But in
their very first election there is respect to their union in the body of
Christ. They are first chosen to be in the intended body of Christ, to be
members of his spouse. And this is a ground of their being chosen: to be
conformed to the head, and their partaking of the life, the holiness and
happiness of the head. And after this is the consideration of the circumstances of the individual chosen members, as sinful and miserable,
etc., and the appointment of the particular way how they should come
to conformity and participation with the head, how way should be made
for it by Christ's satisfaction, righteousness, etc.

4. God, in thus determining to communicate his peculiar love and
goodness to many individual creatures, as all united into one body of his
Son, he chose the race of mankind to be that species of creatures out of
which he would take a number to constitute one created, dear child and

one body of his Son. And, therefore, he chose one of that species to be
the head of the body, who should be also the head of the whole creation,
the first born of every creature, who should have the most transcendent
union with the eternal *Logos,* even so as to be one person, and the rest
to be strictly united to him. Therefore Christ, with respect to his human
nature, more especially is called the elect of God. God's love to the eternal *Logos* itself is not by sovereign election, but by merit and natural necessity in the highest degree. But that that individual creature should be
so exalted was the fruit of sovereign election. Therefore he was, as it were,
the first elect and the head of election. All are elected only as his members, that in all things he might have the preeminence. When God had
determined that the elect object of his love should be one, all the members one body, united in one head, the first thing was to choose a head,
even as when a man goes about to choose materials for a building the
first thing is to choose a stone for the foundation.

Now upon these things, I would observe:

(1) That as in that grand decree of predestination, or that sum of
God's decrees, called the purpose which God purposed in Christ Jesus,
the appointment of Christ, or the decree respecting his person (in the
order wherein we must consider these things), must be considered first;
as Christ was appointed as the author and foundation of what was appointed with respect to the rest, and that both as accomplishment of the
decrees was wholly committed to him and left with him to bring all to effect, and also as the man Christ Jesus is to be considered as the first of
the elect, the head of the elect body, the foundation of the whole building. And,

(2) The election of all Christ's elect people is for the sake of Christ in
two respects: first, it was for the sake of Christ that God determined there
should be a created body for the special communications of his goodness. It was that his Son might have a spouse provided. But this is not a
reason of the distinction in election, or why one was elected and not another, which was of God's sovereign pleasure. Secondly, it was [for] the
sake of Christ that God set his love on the elect and determined to make
'em holy and happy. Because he had chosen 'em to be members of
Christ's body, and gave 'em to Christ to that end, and so, looking upon
them as now his, he loved them for his sake. It must needs be so, the nature of things shows. For as after the Father had given the particular persons to Christ, Christ himself thenceforward looked upon them and
loved them as his own, and had their names written on his heart, so it
must be that God the Father, after he had given them to Christ, must love

'em as his Son's on account of their belonging to him. And this is a quite different thing from his justifying them and accepting them as the objects of complacence and favor for the sake of Christ's righteousness. The former is loving them for Christ's infinite, divine, eternal dignity and glory. The latter is accepting them on the account of the righteousness Christ performed as their mediator in their stead, the price he paid after he was incarnate to purchase favor and rewards for them.

Concerning this, it must be noted that this is not distinguishing them from others first of all, choosing 'em from amongst others to be some of Christ's for his sake. That is of God's mere good pleasure. But 'tis loving them and appointing them to holiness and happiness for Christ's sake after thus selected and distinguished.

3. The appointment of the elect to holiness and happiness, or to conformity to the Son of God, was consequent on their being, in the decree, instated into the body of Christ and united to such a head, in this respect: that one ground or reason why God appointed them to this conformity was the fitness and requisiteness of a conformity between head and members in the same body. God would have the members holy and happy because it was altogether suitable that the members should be as the head. But this requisiteness is a result of the decreed union of those members with this head.

1246. The Saints Higher in Glory Than the Angels. 'Tis evident that the four and twenty elders in the Revelation do represent the church, or company of glorified saints, by their song, ch. 5:9–10, "Thou art worthy to take the book, and to open the seals thereof: for thou wast slain, and hast redeemed us to God by thy blood out of every kindred, and tongue, and people, and nation; and hast made us unto our God kings and priests: and we shall reign on earth." But these are represented from time to time as sitting in a state of honor, with white raiment and crowns of gold, and in seats of dignity, thrones of glory, next to the throne of God and the Lamb, being nextly the most observable and conspicuous sight to God and Christ and the four animals. Ch. 4:4, "And round about the throne were four and twenty seats: and upon the seats I saw four and twenty elders sitting, clothed in white raiment; and they had on their heads crowns of gold." So ch. 5:6, "And I beheld, and, lo, in the midst of the throne and of the four beasts, and in the midst of the elders, stood a Lamb as it had been slain." And the angels are represented as further off from the throne than they, being round about them as they are round about the throne. Ch. 5:11, "And I beheld, and I heard the voice of many angels round about the throne and the beasts and the elders: and the number of them was ten thousand times ten thousand, and thousands of thousands." So ch. 7:11, "And all the angels stood round about the throne, and about the elders [. . .], and fell down before the throne on their faces, and worshipped God." These things make the matter of the superiority of the privilege of the saints in heaven very plain.

1247. ANGELS. That they are as the nobles and barons of the court of heaven, as dignified servants in the palace of the King of kings, is manifest by Matt. 18:10 (see my notes);[6] so in their being called thrones, dominions, principalities and powers.

1248. [That] the INFLUENCES AND FRUITS OF THE SPIRIT that are mainly insisted on in the New Testament are not the extraordinary gifts of the Spirit is manifest by this: the Apostle speaks of the Corinthians as remarkably abounding in miraculous gifts of the Spirit. The Apostle says, I Cor. 1:5–7, that in everything they were enriched by Christ, in all utterance and in all knowledge, so that they came behind in no gift. And it appears by many other passages in his epistles to that church that they excelled in miraculous gifts of prophecy, knowledge, tongues, miracles, etc. But yet the Apostle charges 'em with not being spiritual, but carnal and babes in that which is spiritual. I Cor. 3:1–4, "And I, brethren, could not speak unto you as unto spiritual, but as to carnal, even as unto babes in Christ. I have fed you with milk, and not with meat: for hitherto ye were not able to bear it, neither yet now are ye able. For ye are yet carnal: for whereas there is among you envying, and strife, and divisions, are ye not carnal, and walk as men? For while one saith, I am of Paul; and another, I of Apollos; are ye not carnal?"

1249. See [No.] 1243. TRINITY. 'Tis an argument that the Jews of old understand that there were several persons in the Godhead; and particularly that when the cherubim, in the sixth [chapter] of Isaiah, cried "Holy, holy, holy, Lord of hosts," that they had respect to three persons; that the seventy interpreters, in several places, where the Holy One of Israel is spoken [of], use the plural number: as in Is. 41:16, "thou [. . .] shalt glory in the Holy One of Israel" (in the LXX it is εὐφρανδήσῃ ἐν τοῖς ἁγίοις Ἰσραηλ); Is. 60:14, "the Zion of the Holy One of Israel" ('tis

---

6. This verse, according to JE's "Blank Bible," "denotes the honor and dignity of the angels in heaven as being as it were barons and nobles of the court of heaven."

οιων ἁγίου Ισραηλ); so Jer. 51:5, "filled with sin against the Holy One of Israel" (ἀπὸ των αγιων Ισραηλ).[7] See No. [1256].[8]

1250. JUSTIFICATION, how it is BY FAITH, that it is by uniting us to Christ, so that we should properly be looked upon as *in him,* by the following places, as the words are in the Greek: Gal. 2:17, "justified in Christ;"[9] Eph. 4:32, "in Christ hath forgiven you;"[1] Gal. 3:11–14, "But that no man is justified by the law in the sight of God, it is evident: for, The just shall live by faith. And the law is not of faith: but, The man that doth them shall live in them. Christ hath redeemed us from the curse of the law, being made a curse for us: for it is written, Cursed is every one that hangeth on a tree: that the blessing of Abraham might come on the Gentiles in Christ Jesus;[2] that they might receive the promise of the Spirit through faith"; Is. 56:6–7, "the sons of the stranger, that join themselves to the Lord" (which is the same with actively uniting themselves to him), " . . . and taketh hold of my covenant; even them will I bring to my holy mountain," etc.

1251. The ETERNAL DEATH of the wicked NOT ANNIHILATION. Death, under the notion of annihilation, is spoken of as an end to suffering. Thus death, which is an annihilation as to any concern in the enjoyments or calamities of this world, and all temporal actions and sensation, is frequently spoken as a refuge from the miseries of the world, and is often wished for as such (Rev. 9:6, Job 3:20–21). So Moses, though the meekest man on earth, desired rather to die than to have the burden which lay upon him continued, that he might not see his wretchedness (Num. 11:15). So Elijah. But future punishment is spoken of often as sensible misery which the wicked shall see and know, and which shall convince 'em, etc., and therefore is not of that kind that implies a most effectual and absolute and everlasting abolishing all sensibility of wretchedness or misery, and all capacity of any sensibility. And as the Scripture represents the matter, the wicked, on the approach of the last judgment, will desire eternal death in this sense, as a refuge from the punishment approach-

7. Jer. 51:5 in the KJV (which is based on the Masoretic text of the Old Testament, produced in the early Middle Ages) actually corresponds to Jer. 28:5 in the LXX, where this Greek phrase is found, and which is ordered differently than the Masoretic text throughout the book of Jeremiah.

8. MS: "Bk. 9. p. 7 [col. 2]."

9. KJV: "justified by Christ."

1. KJV: "for Christ's sake hath forgiven you."

2. KJV: "through Jesus Christ."

ing, crying to the mountains and rocks to fall on them (see Rev. 6:16, Hos. 10:8, Luke 23:30). But how inconsistent is this with the punishment feared and which they seek refuge from being nothing else but eternal annihilation.

1252. UNITY OF THE GODHEAD. "Absolute infinite excludes all negation, privation, and defect" (Ramsay's *Philosophical Principles of Religion,* vol. 1, p. 42). "Absolute infinite excludes all duality and plurality of substance. [. . .] If there were two or more absolute infinites, their perfections, powers, and forces united in one sum, would be greater than those of one singular absolute infinite. [. . .] Therefore there cannot be in nature a duality, nor plurality of distinct, self-existent, independent and absolutely infinite substances. [. . .] That which exhausts the whole plenitude of perfection in all senses, can admit of no others of its kind." Ibid., p. 48.

1253. TRINITY. Ramsay's *Principles,* vol. 1, pp. 74–85. "The absolutely infinite mind must be infinitely, eternally and essentially active and productive of an absolutely infinite effect.

"Absolute infinite contains all possible perfections: infinite activity, as the production of an infinite effect, is a supreme perfection: therefore the absolutely infinite mind must be infinitely, eternally and essentially active, and consequently productive of an absolutely infinite effect; since an absolutely infinite cause, acting according to all the extent of its nature, must necessarily produce an absolutely infinite effect.

"Men generally imagine that God is infinitely active, only because he can produce innumerable beings from without, or distinct from himself; but unless the faculty be forever reduced into act, it is not infinite activity, but infinite power. It is a real inaction, though it supposes an infinite capacity of acting. Now such inactive powers as lie dormant during a whole eternity in God, are absolutely incompatible with the perfection of the divine nature which must be infinitely, eternally, and essentially active." And since God "cannot be eternally active from without, or upon anything external; he must be eternally active from within; and since his essence is indivisible, and cannot act by parcels, he must be necessarily, and immanently active, according to the whole extent of his infinite nature. Now an absolutely infinite agent that acts according to all the extent of its absolutely infinite nature, must necessarily produce in itself an absolutely infinite effect; otherwise the effect would not be proportionate to the cause; and so the cause would not act according to all the extent of its absolutely infinite nature, which is contrary to the supposition. Moreover, the production of an absolutely infinite effect is a far greater perfection than the creation of any number of finite effects how great soever; and therefore this immanent fecundity must be an essential, co-eternal, consubstantial perfection of the divine nature.

"Hence absolutely infinite in his pure and solitary essence, antecedent to all creation must have produced within himself, an eternal, necessary, absolutely infinite effect.

"Hence an absolutely infinite mind or intelligent subject supposes an absolutely infinite object or idea known, otherwise it would be only an infinite capacity of knowledge, and not an infinite understanding that knows and possesses its object. Let us now examine what this infinite effect and object of the divine mind must be.

"The absolutely infinite effect and object of the absolutely infinite mind can be no other than its own IDEA, IMAGE, or REPRESENTATION.

"An absolutely infinite and infinitely active mind supposes an absolutely infinite effect produced, and an absolutely infinite object or idea known. God cannot produce any absolutely infinite effect from without, and consequently can have no other absolutely infinite object of his thought but himself or his own idea, image, or representation: therefore God's own idea, image, or representation of himself must be an absolutely infinite effect, and object of the absolutely infinite mind.

"The Deists, Unitarians, and Socinians deny this eternal generation of the Word, because they do not fully enter into their own spiritual natures, to examine what passes in themselves. When we think, it is clear that the object of our thought is distinct from our thinking faculty; otherwise we would think equally at all times, and have always the same idea; since we have always the same powers. Our ideas are changeable and imperfect modes of the mind; whereas God's idea of himself is a permanent, necessary and essential image, and not a free, accidental mode. All our simple ideas are produced in us by other objects that act upon us, while we are altogether passive. Whereas this consubstantial idea of the divine mind, is not produced by any other object distinct from itself. It is conceived from within, not received from without; it is produced, not perceived. We may therefore in comparing absolute infinite with finite spirits (which, as we shall show, are his living images), distinguish in him the thinking subject or MIND CONCEIVING; from the object of this thinking essence or the IDEA CONCEIVED.

"Some moderns will say that intelligence is not action, and that to know is not to produce. I answer that perception is not an action; but conception is the highest act of the understanding. To receive ideas, sensations, or modifications from objects that act upon us is, purely passive. But to form or create in the mind new ideas, is a real production. We do not form our simple ideas; we receive them from external objects that act upon us. God is impassable and eternal, and so cannot be acted upon by other objects. He does not perceive, but he CONCEIVES his essential, consubstantial idea, image, or representation; he does not receive this idea from others, he produces it in himself. We form our complex ideas by a successive combining of our simple perceptions. God forms his consubstantial idea by one unsuccessive act. Now this is the highest and most exalted of all activities and perfections.

"Hence absolute infinite, in his pure, and solitary essence, antecedent to the production of any finite ideas, is infinitely intelligent, self-knowing, and self-conscious; as well as infinitely active and productive of an eternal, immanent and absolutely infinite effect, object, or idea.

"Hence this generation of the LOGOS, or of God's consubstantial idea, is sufficient to complete the perfection of the divine understanding; for an infinite mind can desire nothing more to fill, enlighten, and satiate it, than an infinite object.

"The eternal, permanent, consubstantial idea God has of himself, produces necessarily in him an infinite, eternal, and immutable LOVE.

"Thus it is certain that antecedent to all communicative goodness towards anything external, God is good in himself and just to himself, as he is infinitely, eternally, and essentially active and intelligent; because as he produces within himself an absolutely infinite effect and idea, so he is infinitely, eternally, and essentially good and just. Infinitely good, because from the knowledge and enjoyment of his consubstantial idea flows an infinite sensation of joy, an unbounded love, an unspeakable pleasure, and an eternal self-complacency, which constitute his uninterrupted happiness. Infinitely just, because it is this permanent love that constitutes his essential justice; for by this love he renders to himself all that is due to his supreme perfection. He does not therefore want to create innumerable myriads [of]³ finite objects to exert his essential beneficence and equity; since he produces within himself from all eternity one infinite object that exhausts, so to speak, all his capacity of loving, beatifying, and doing justice.

"The Deists, Unitarians, and Socinians, who deny the doctrine of the Trinity, cannot explain how God is essentially good and just, anteced-

3. MS damage.

ently to, and independent of the creation of finite; for God cannot be eminently good and just, where there is no object of his beneficence and equity. If then he be essentially, eternally and necessarily good and just, he must be so immanently; he must be so in himself; he must therefore find an infinite object within himself, to whom he displays all his essential love, beneficence and equity.

"Hence God's consubstantial love of himself is sufficient to complete the felicity of his infinite will. Here all its motions, tendencies and desires fix, concenter and reunite. Wherefore all other acts and productions, that do not necessarily flow from and enter into this consubstantial love, are not essential to the perfection of the divine will.

"To complete the idea of perfect felicity, there must be an object loving as well as an object loved. [. . .] Such is the nature of love, that it must be communicative. Infinite love therefore must be infinitely and necessarily communicative. It must have an object on which it exerts itself, and to which it displays itself; into which it flows, and that flows back to it again. There is a far greater felicity in loving and being loved than in loving simply. It is the mutual harmony and correspondence of two distinct beings or persons, that makes the completion of love and felicity. [. . .] Hence God could not have been infinitely and eternally loved, if there had not been from all eternity, some being distinct from himself, and equal to himself, that loves him infinitely; since, as we have shown, creation could not be coeternal.

"The eternal, infinite, and immutable love, which proceeds from the idea God has of himself, is not a simple attribute, mode, or perfection of the divine mind; but a living, active, consubstantial, intelligent being or agent." These things from Ramsay's *Principles,* vol. 1, pp. 74–85.

Therefore, "we may represent the divine essence, under these three notions, as an infinitely ACTIVE MIND that conceives; or as an infinite IDEA that is the object of this conception; or as an infinite LOVE that proceeds from this idea. . . . There are three, there can be but three; and all that we can conceive of in the infinite mind may be reduced to these three; infinite LIFE, LIGHT, AND LOVE. Ibid., p. 88.

"They are not three simple attributes or modalities, because they are distinct intelligent principles, and self-conscious agents. They must therefore be three distinct beings, realities, somethings, or persons; because the idea of personality includes that of an intelligent self-conscious agent. Ibid., p. 91.

"Hence we may conceive in the divine nature three real distinctions, and we can conceive of no more; since all we can comprehend of absolute infinite, is either MIND conceiving, IDEA conceived, or LOVE proceeding from both. GOD self-existent; GOD OF GOD; and GOD THE HOLY GHOST. These three distinctions in the Deity are neither three distinct independent minds, as the tritheists alleged; nor three attributes of the same substance represented as persons, as the Sabellians affirmed: nor one supreme, and two subordinate intellectual agents, as some refined Arians maintain: but three co-eternal, consubstantial, coordinate persons co-equal in all things, self-origination only excepted." Ibid., p. 97.

"This eternal commerce of the co-eternal three is the secret fund of the Deity. [. . .] All those who are ignorant of the doctrine of the Trinity, of the generation of the Logos, of the procession of the eternal Spirit, and of the everlasting commerce among the sacred three, look upon God's still eternity, and solitude, as a state of inaction and indolence." Ibid., p. 100.[4]

1254. SUPERNATURAL PRINCIPLES. "In a state of pure and exalted nature, no finite intelligence can obey the law of eternal order by its own natural and inherent force; without supernatural grace and assistance.

"Finite intelligences by their own natural and inherent force, can have nothing but themselves, and their own happiness; the natural tendency of the will towards God as beatifying and as relative good is not the love of God according to the laws of eternal order: therefore in a state even of pure and exalted nature, no finite intelligence can obey the law of eternal order by its own natural and inherent force; without divine supernatural grace and assistance.

"The natural love of God as beatifying to us, as relative good, as the source of eternal pleasure, is not loving God for himself. This is not loving him according to the laws of eternal order. It is only loving him for our own sakes, a desire to satisfy our insatiable thirst for happiness; and, as I have said, this desire is common to us with the devils and the damned. It is nothing beyond the reach and power of finite minds; or rather it is a necessary and natural consequence of the invincible love we have for self. To love God for himself, to love him as he loves himself, to love him for his infinite perfections, as sovereign justice and eternal order, to rise above ourselves, and lose our selves in him by a total preterition of self, we must be enlightened, inspired and animated by a superior force continually descending upon us and investing us. As 'tis God alone that can enlighten us, so 'tis he alone that can love himself in us. As no man can

---

4. "Miscellanies," Bk. 8 ends here.

know the Father but by the Son, so no man can love the Father but by the Holy Ghost. As the supernatural light by which we know God is the emanation of the eternal Logos, and a participation of that light by which he knows himself, so the supernatural love by which we can love God, is an emanation of the Holy Ghost, and a participation of that love by which he loves himself.

"By this great principle we come to understand the true distinction between nature and grace. . . . The natural properties of finite beings are those which they have by creation, as inseparable adjuncts of their essence. The supernatural graces of God, are perfections which the creature receives immediately from the divine action. . . . Thus in spiritual agents, or the intelligent images, the powers of perceiving, comparing, and willing, of knowing their being, and of desiring their well-being are essential properties, inseparable from their nature, and communicated to them by God the Father, in giving them existence: but supernatural light and love, their seeing God as he is, and their loving him as he deserves, are impressions that come from the immediate operation of the eternal Word and the Holy Ghost.

"Hence 'tis absolutely false, that there ever was, or can be a state of pure nature, wherein souls by their own inherent force could love God as he deserves, without any supernatural grace or immediate influence of the Holy Ghost: as it is impossible that there can be any state of pure nature wherein the soul can know God as he is, without any supernatural illumination or irradiation of the eternal Word. Men indeed may acquire by a successive comparison of their ideas a natural knowledge and love of God, but not the supernatural knowledge and love we are speaking of. If this were otherwise, the soul might beget within itself the eternal Logos, and the Holy Ghost; be its own light, and its own love; its own perfection, and its own happiness.

"Hence the will may have two motives of action, natural self-love, and the supernatural love of God.

"Hence there is an essential difference betwixt the natural activities of the understanding concerning God, and the supernatural illuminations of the eternal Logos; so there is an essential difference betwixt the natural tendency of the will towards God as beatifying, as relative good, as the source of infinite pleasure; and the supernatural action of the Holy Ghost, which makes us love God for himself, according to the law of eternal order. The one is common to us with the devils and the damned; the other makes us resemble angelical and beatified spirits.

"Since we never can love the creatures in an irregular manner but for our own interest, or the pleasure they procure us, hence it follows that false self-love is the primitive source of all moral evil, and a self-idolatry that erects the creature into the place of God, that usurps upon all his rights, that renders itself the center of all the creation, and the end of all its actions, and thereby engenders all passions, sins, and crimes." These things from Ramsay's *Principles*, vol. 1, pp. 309–15.

1255. ORIGINAL OF IDOLATRY. CORRUPTION OF ANCIENT TRADITIONS CONCERNING THE MESSIAH, etc. "The first sages of the most remote antiquity made use of sensible signs and images to represent intellectual and spiritual truths. All the different parts of nature were employed in this sacred language; the sun, the moon, the planets, and fixed stars.

"Hieroglyphics and symbols" were "incontestibly the most ancient manner of writing, according to the sentiment of all learned men. [...] If this be so, then it is certain that according as the world increased and was peopled after the deluge, the sons and grandchildren of Noah who had heard the pious instructions of their common father, and seen the terrible judgments of God upon the world, ought to have been very careful and solicitous to preserve those sacred monuments and hieroglyphical records of religion.... Every head of a family might have had them copied, and carried to the country he went to inhabit with his family. Thus the symbolical characters, images and representations of [...] truth, were much the same in all nations. Of this we have uncontestible proofs, since the symbols of the Chinese are very often the same with those wrote upon the Egyptian obelisks yet preserved: for all the Chinese characters are hieroglyphics. We find also, that the Gauls, Germans and Britains long before they were conquered by Julius Caesar, had much the same symbolical representations of their sacred mysteries and deities, as the Egyptians, Greeks and Romans. Moreover, it is certain, that very oft there is a great resemblance betwixt the Hebraic symbols and the pagan hieroglyphics. [...] Wherefore, we may reasonably conclude, that wherever this similitude is found, the same truths are indicated by both; since the original source of tradition was the same to all nations. The most part of the primitive fathers of the church taught expressly that many of the pagan symbols, fables, and sentiments were relative to, and representative of the divine mysteries of our holy religion, which the first heathens had learned from the ancient tradition of the Noevian patriarchs.

"By succession of time, the true original sense of the sacred symbols and hieroglyphics was forgot, men attached themselves to the letter, and the signs, without understanding the spirit and the thing signified. Thus, the pagans fell by degrees into gross idolatry and wild superstition. They mistook the original for the picture; the images of the sun, moon, and stars, of men and women, of animals, plants, and reptiles, for sacred and divine powers residing in these visible creatures. Thus, according to the expression of the divine doctor of the Gentiles, 'they changed the glory of the uncorruptible God, into an image made like unto corruptible man, and to birds, and four-footed beasts and creeping things.' . . . The poets invented fables, obscured all anew by their wild fictions. . . . But all the wiser nations and philosophers complain of the abuse they made of the sacred hieroglyphics, and the corruptions they introduced into religion.

"As in the hieroglyphical language there are no conjugations, tenses, nor moods, the future was often taken for the past; thus, all the ancient traditions and symbols that expressed our SAVIOR's pre-existent, suffering and triumphant state were confounded in one, and interpreted of imaginary heroes, or conquerors who had signalized themselves in different countries and corners of the earth." Ramsay's *Principles,* vol. 2, pp. 11–16.

1256. TRINITY. See [Nos.] 1249 and 1243, concerning INTIMATIONS of the TRINITY in the OLD TESTAMENT, and the opinion of the ancient Jews. Where it is said in our translation, "Remember thy Creator in the days of thy youth" (Eccles. 12[:1]), in the Hebrew it [is] "thy *Creators,*" in the plural number, which agrees with the manner of speaking, Gen. 1[:26], "Let us make man in our image."

Ramsay, in his *Principles,* vol. 2, p. 116, says, from Dr. Alix,[5] "'Philo acknowledges a generation in God from all eternity. He says in many different places, that God begets the Word in himself; that this Word is wisdom; and that this wisdom is the eternal Son of God; that God is called the God of gods, not with relation to created intelligences, whether human, angelical, or seraphical, but in relation to his own[6] consubstantial powers, which are not simple attributes, but eternal, uncreated, infinite principles of action, represented by the two wings of the cherubim that covered the tabernacle.' Moreover," says Chevalier Ramsay, "Dr. Alix has shown, that the Chaldee Paraphrasts, or Targumists, speak in the same manner as Philo. 'They ascribe to the Word the creation of the world, the pardon of sin, the mediating between God the Father and the crea-

5. Ramsay is quoting from "Dr. Alix against the Unitarians."
6. Ramsay: "two."

tures. Yea, they attribute all the other personal characters of acting, speaking, answering, commanding, giving laws, and receiving supreme worship and adoration, to the Son and Holy Ghost, whom they call very oft "the two hands of God." In fine, the cabbalistical Jews that are of later date, than the Targumists, speak in the same manner. They fix the number of three persons in the divine essence; they speak of the emanation of the two last from the first, and say, that the third proceeds from the first by the second. They call the first person Ensoph, the second Memra, and the third Binah.' The cabbalistical Jews were called so from the Hebrew word *cabal*, which signifies tradition, because they pretended to have collected into one body, all the ancient traditions of the Jewish church." Thus far Chevalier Ramsay. See "Controversies" papers.[7]

1257. OPINIONS AND TRADITIONS OF THE PERSIANS concerning the necessity of HUMILIATION and self-denial, disinterested love, in order to future happiness. "No company is more closely attached to us than self-love; it almost never forsakes us, though none more blind and ignorant. It is easier to root out, and carry off a mountain with the point of a needle, than to tear away pride, and vain-glory from the heart of a man. . . . humility is the source of love to God and benevolence to men. . . . Fly and make thy retreat into the kingdom of self-annihilation, and there thou shalt find rest. . . . A religious poverty is the privation of everything, and that glorious surrender to God, with which he favors the most perfect. We must be robbed of all our goods, and must annihilate the soul, before we can arrive at him who alone possesses all things. Those who regard themselves, and live for themselves, are always in danger of losing themselves by a multiplicity of objects; but those who entirely forget themselves, are found in unity with God. Boldly destroy whatever is ascribed to your own powers; and enter the royal path of self-denial. By treading in this, where we see nothing, we at last reach that sacred retreat, where we behold God alone. The saints are those who are most united to God, and consequently enjoy his intimate presence. They are

7. MS: "p. 215," a reference to the section on Justification in the "Controversies" notebook, in this case to the essay entitled "Question: In What Sense Did the Saints Under the Old Testament Believe in Christ to Justification?" The passage JE intends reads: "'Tis evident also by the Targums, and other ancient writings of the Jews, that the Jews of old had a notion of a distinction of persons in the Godhead. However, the modern Jews, out of opposition and enmity to Christianity, do strenuously deny it. Here see Bp. Kidder, *Demonstration*, Pt. III, pp. 81–83, and 94–97, and so on to p. 116. See concerning the authors of the Targums, ibid., p. 107." For the source of the passage and a description of the references to Kidder, see *Works*, 21, p. 375, n. 5.

enemies to themselves in this life, and become the friends of God in the next. . . . They have wiped out of their heart and mind, all the traces of pride and hypocrisy. . . . The true marks of a good man in this state, are tenderness of heart, hatred of the world, and a distrust of one's self [. . .]: on the contrary, the marks of the bad man, are hardness of heart, a love of the world, a great confidence of himself and in the creatures, and impudence. . . . We must absolutely renounce an attachment to our own light, which is a manifest impiety, and self-idolatry: since after we have gone the round of all other beings, we shall find, that there is properly no other true light, but God alone. I serve God by love, and I cannot but serve him. We must serve him independent of all fear and hope, with the love of a friend: for he regards us with a pure love of benevolence. . . . Humility must lead us to an annihilation in the unity of God. Then we know perfectly that we are nothing; and by this knowledge, we confess that God is all. The most sublime knowledge of God can never arise in our souls, till all the ideas we have of ourselves and our powers, are annihilated in our eyes. The rays of divine light can only arise from self-denial and annihilation; and by these rays alone is the heart renewed, and the affections changed. . . . When I retire into myself, I see nothing in the universe more vile and miserable. . . . Thy friend, O God, has no view to any other advantage in this world, than to praise thee; and pretends to nothing in heaven, but the enjoyment of thee. One man will demand of thee, the enjoyment of paradise, and its delights; another, a deliverance from hell and its pains: for me, I ask, neither the one, nor the other. My sole desire is, that thy will may be accomplished in me. If thou shalt be pleased with me, both in this world and the next, I have my desire, and resign all the rest into thine hands. Thou menacest me with a separation, that will forever deprive me of thy presence. Do with me what thou pleasest, provided I am not forever deprived of thee. There is no prison more bitter, none more mortal: for what can the soul do that is separated from God, but languish in disquiet, and be tormented with a perpetual agitation? A hundred thousand deaths though most cruel may be borne: they can have nothing so terrible, as the privation of thy divine countenance. The acutest maladies, nay all the evils of a whole age together, are nothing to me, and appear incomparably more easy, to be borne, than the least distance from thee. The smallest separation from thee renders our land barren, infects and dries up our waters; what then would it be, were it eternal? without it, the fire of hell could not burn; and by it only is it made so ardent. In fine, it is thy presence alone that supports us, and loads us with every good thing; and thy absence is the cause of all our ills. The man never dies, O God, who lives but for thee: a thousand times happy he then, whom thou animatest by thy spirit."

These things are taken from Ramsay's *Principles of Religion,* vol. 2, pp. 422[–28], who introduces them thus: "The modern Persians and Turks, have the grandest and noblest ideas about internal piety, true self-denial, and self-annihilation before God; as appears from the following extracts out of some of their principal writers, as translated by Herbelot in his *Bibliothèque Orientale.*"[8]

1258. IMMORTALITY OF THE SOUL. FUTURE STATE. Nothing is more manifest than that it is absolutely necessary in order to a man's being thoroughly, universally and steadfastly virtuous that his mind and heart should be thoroughly weaned from this world, which is a great evidence that God intends another world for[9] virtuous men. He surely would not require 'em in their thoughts, affections and expectations wholly to relinquish this world if it were all the world they were to expect, if he had m[ade][1] 'em for this world wholly and only, and had created the world for them to [be] their only country and home, all the resting place he ever designed 'em for.

1259. CHRIST'S RESIGNING UP THE KINGDOM TO THE FATHER. The "mediator's kingdom [. . .] receives a double consideration. First, consider him as [. . .] mediator of his church considered under imperfection, either of sin or misery or any other want, till his church shall be complete. Or secondly, consider him as he is head of his church made complete and fully perfected in all parts and all degrees.

"Jesus Christ has a double relation to his church, the one as a head simply considered [. . .]; and he hath the relation of a Redeemer and [a] mediator for us as we are sinners, and under misery [. . .], distress and [. . .] imperfection. Now, [. . .] while the church remaineth thus imperfect, [. . .] while there is any such thing as guilt or the appearance of it, or any imperfection (as till the final sentence there is), so long is Jesus Christ a mediator for us to God, as under some misery, some want, some danger, he standeth between God and us, and God hath given him all power in heaven and in earth, that he may give eternal life to them that believe, [. . .] that he should be able to free us. And so long Jesus Christ ruleth in a way of conquest, destroying sin and death and all en-

8. Ramsay's reference is to Barthelemy d'Herbelot, *Bibliothèque Orientale: ou Dictionnaire universel, contenant généralement tout ce qui regarde la connoissance des peuples de l'Orient* (Paris, 1697).
9. MS: "from."
1. MS damage affects this word and the bracketed word in the next line of the entry.

emies and redeeming the body and bringing body and soul together, and lastly pronouncing a final sentence; and in this sense it is that the Scripture usually speaks of his sitting at God's right hand to intercede for us (as it is Rom. 8:34, and by sitting there he meaneth reigning), to destroy enemies, to put us out of danger of death and condemnation. But when once this final sentence is past, then this work of a mediator, his reigning thus as a Redeemer of us considered under sin and misery ceaseth, for when once that final sentence is past then all sins are forever and ever forgiven, never to be remembered more, God then looks upon us as in his first project without spot or wrinkle forever; then Christ presenteth us to the Father, 'Lo, here I am, and the children thou hast given me, here they are just as thou didst look upon them in thy primitive choice.' And so now considered, I say his kingdom ceaseth, for there will be no need of it; and this indeed is an answer which learned Cameron[2] delivereth upon that place, I Cor. 15.

"But yet then take Jesus Christ as our head," (which is indeed "a distinct thing from his sitting at God's right hand), so he is forever a head. We were chosen in him at first, [. . .] so we are considered in him forever, and exalted in him, our persons in his person, and God then (having forgiven all sin and misery, and the mediator's office for intercession, etc., being laid aside), he is all in all both to Christ and us, and so now he delivereth up the kingdom unto God the Father.

"When he hath delivered up this kingdom of his redeemership unto God the Father, yet he sitteth down with this honor forever, that it was he that did execute this office of a mediator, so that not a soul is lost, not a sin left unsatisfied for, not an enemy unsubdued, he sitteth down like a mighty and glorious conqueror. He is not a general in war longer, that kind of kingdom and rule ceaseth, yet he hath this honor [. . .], that he it is that did these and those exploits, brought in all those rebels, subdued all enemies, and remaineth a glorious dictator. So that indeed and in truth Jesus Christ shall then reign more gloriously with his Father (though it is more especially appropriated to him till the day of judgment), than ever he did before; for then he reigneth triumphantly, whereas before he reigned as one that was conquering to conquer. And as David said, when all his enemies were subdued, 'Am I a king this day?' So will Jesus Christ say, he never was kinged so much as now." Dr. Goodwin's *Works*, vol. 1, pp. 440–41.[3]

2. Possibly Dr. Archibald Cameron (1707–53).

3. The quotations are from "Sermon XXXIII" of *The Works of Thomas Goodwin*, vol. 1, Pt. I, pp. 440–41.

1260a. JUSTIFICATION, NATURAL FITNESS. They that object against explaining the manner in which faith is that, in a peculiar manner, BY
which we are interested in Christ and justified by him, by its being that
qualification by which, peculiarly, it becomes naturally fit that a person
should be looked upon as in Christ, as though the supposition of such a
fitness were inconsistent with the freedom of grace in this method of justification, insisting that the gospel doctrine of justification by grace
through faith supposes no fitness in such a condition of justification in
itself at all more than in anything else, but that its being appointed the
condition of an interest in Christ depends solely and absolutely on God's
mere good pleasure and sovereign and arbitrary will: such as these might
as well object against union to Christ's person being requisite to communion in his benefits.

All will allow that union with Christ, a real union, is, according to the
gospel constitution, the condition of partaking of his benefits, and, I
trust what none will deny, that there is a natural fitness in it that persons
should be united to Christ, or be in Christ, in order to their being looked
upon as his, belonging to him, interested in him, and so partaking with
him; and that it would be naturally unfit that they should be looked upon
as relatively in him or belonging to him if not really united to him, as if
their souls or minds were not united to him; and that this is a requisite
condition on account of the natural fitness of it; and that divine wisdom
appoints it on that account. And yet I suppose no one will imagine[4] that
this in the least detracts from the freedom and sovereignty of divine grace
in appointing[5] the way of obtaining an interest in Christ and his benefits.

1260b. PROGRESS OF THE WORK OF REDEMPTION. CREATION OF NEW
HEAVENS AND NEW EARTH. "The other world was six days a-making," and
"went on by degrees; so it will be in that which is called the world to come.
'The kingdom of heaven is like [. . .] a grain of mustard-seed, which is
the least of all seeds, and yet the greatest in the end.' The Apostle speaking of conversion, Gal. 4, calls it a delivering us from this present evil
world; 'Old things are past away' (says he), 'and all things are become
new.' Here is a creation, a beginning, here is the first day's work, and
God never will leave till he hath perfected this world; and because the
perfection of it is not yet, therefore it is said to be a world to come."

4. MS: "image."
5. MS: "appointed."

It "begun when Christ began to preach . . . ; therefore it is, that as the first world hath a seventh day for the celebrating the creation of it, so hath this new world now a LORD'S DAY; and of that LORD'S DAY doth the Apostle speak, Heb. 4, as here he doth of this new world, [in] Heb. 2. And the Holy Ghost, when Christ was set in heaven, fell then upon the feast of Pentecost, which was upon the first day of the week, our LORD'S DAY, as Lev. 23:15–16.

"'Repent,' says John the Baptist [Matt. 3:2], 'for the kingdom of heaven is at hand.' The world to come is coming upon you. [. . .] And says Christ himself, Mark 1:14, 'Repent, for the kingdom of heaven is at hand'; and Matt. 16:28, 'There are some that stand here that shall not taste of death till they see the Son of Man come in his kingdom.'

"The foundation of this world to come was thus laid by our Savior Christ in bringing in the gospel, and was prophesied in Dan. 2:44. He saith expressly there, 'That in the days of these kings' (which principalities and powers stand for[6] those monarchies; for he came stealing into the world when the Roman monarchy first began [. . .]) 'shall the God of heaven set up a kingdom which shall never be destroyed; but it shall break in pieces and consume all these kingdoms, and it shall stand forever.' This same new world, you see, it began in the flourishing and height of the Roman monarchy. Now, what did Jesus Christ do when he came into the world and went up into heaven, when he began his new world? Consider what the world was before.

"The devil was worshipped in all parts of the world [. . .]. Our Lord and Savior Christ flingeth him down; 'I saw Satan' (saith he) 'fall down like lightning.' Where heathenism did not prevail, there did Judaism, all the ceremonial law [. . .]. He throweth them all down; the Apostle Paul calleth it 'shaking of the earth,' Heb. 12:26. Here is a great deal of this world gone presently, and falling down like Dagon before the new world. He converteth by his apostles, millions of souls all over the world; and how is conversion expressed [in] I Cor. 5:17? 'Old things are past away, all things are become new.'

"And this is but the first day's work of this world to come; the world is yet to come. . . .[7] After this first day's work, then cometh the night of popery. But Christ will have a second day's work. He will not cease till he hath thrown out every rag, the least dross and defilement, that popery brought in or continued in the world. And we are under the second day's

---

6. MS: "of."

7. From this point forward JE is loosely paraphrasing Goodwin.

work (if I may so express it), we are but working up still to a purer world; working to the perfection of the new world. And Jesus Christ will never rest till he hath thrown out all the dross of this world, both in doctrine and worship (which conforming to the world hath brought in), but for a second degree of this world, he will never rest till he hath brought all the world (i.e. the generality of men) to be subject to him; which is another degree of this world to come.

"This new world will have a further perfection that it yet hath; it shall grow up to a world, that the generality of mankind, both Jew and Gentile, shall come into Jesus Christ. He hath had but little takings of the world yet, but he will have before he hath done; the world was made for him, and he will have it before he hath done. [. . .]

"Another degree of this world to come is after the general resurrection of both the just and unjust."

These things are taken from Dr. Goodwin's *Works,* vol. 1, Pt. I, pp. 446, 453−55.[8]

1261. OCCASION OF THE FALL OF THE ANGELS. "It is supposed by some, and that rationally and probably, by Zanchi,[9] whom I account the best of Protestant writers in his judgment, and likewise by Suarez,[1] the best of the Schoolmen, that upon the very setting up, or at leastwise upon the notice that the angels had of the setting up of a kingdom, for the man Christ Jesus, predestinated for to come (which whether it was without the fall predestinated, as some, or upon supposition of the fall, as others, yet so much might be revealed to them), and that the human nature was to be assumed up into the second person, and he to be the head of all principality and power, and that angels and men should have their grace from him; this they say being declared to be the will of God, their very refusing of this kingdom, and to be subject unto Christ, as man thus assumed, was their first sin: and that now in opposition hereunto they did set up another kingdom against him. Thus I say, these writers, that I have mentioned, do think, and they allege that place in the epistle of Jude, v. 6, where the sin of the angels being described, it is said, 'they kept not their first estate, but left their own habitation' (which say they is not there brought in as their punishment), they left the station God

---

8. The quotations themselves are taken from Sermons XXXIII–XXXIV in Goodwin's *Works,* vol. 1, Pt. I, pp. 446, 454–55, 459.

9. Girolamo Zanchi (1516–90), author of *The Doctrine of Absolute Predestination Stated and Asserted.*

1. Francis Suarez (1548–1617), whose most influential work was *Metaphysical Disputations.*

had set them in, and they left their dwelling in heaven, to set up a kingdom here below, in opposition to Christ, and so to have an independent
kingdom of themselves, for which God hath condemned them into eternal torment, and to hell, 'and delivered them into chains of darkness, to
be reserved unto judgment,' II Pet. 2:4. And to set up this great kingdom is their business, and therefore they do now associate themselves
together, not out of love, but as becometh rational creatures that would
drive on a project and design."

These writers not only go upon this place in Jude, but that, "John 8:44,
where Christ lays open both the devil's sin, and the sin of the Jews. The
sin of the Jews was, that they would not receive that truth which Christ
had delivered to them, as he tells them, v. 45. 'Because I tell you the truth,
ye believe me not,' and not receiving it, they sought to kill him. Now if
you ask what that truth was, which Christ had so much inculcated upon
them, you shall see [at] v. 25 what it is. They asked him there, 'Who he
was? Even the same,' saith he, 'that I have told you from the beginning,'
the 'Messiah,' the Son of God [. . .]. 'If the Son make you free, you shall
be free indeed,' v. 36. This was the great truth that these Jews would not
receive. Now he tells them likewise, v. 44, that Satan, 'their father the
devil, abode not in the truth; he was the first,' saith he, that opposed and
contradicted this great truth, and would not be subject to God, who revealed this, nor would he accept, or embrace, or continue, or stand, he
would quit heaven first; and so from hence came to be a murderer, a
hater of this man Christ Jesus, and of this kingdom, and of mankind; for
he that hateth God, or he that hateth Christ, he is, in what in him lieth,
a murderer of him, and he showed it in falling upon man.

"And they back it with this reason why it should be so meant, because
otherwise the devil's sin, which he compares theirs unto, had not been
so great as theirs. There had not been a likeness between the sin of the
one and the other. His sin would have been only telling a lie, a lie merely
in speech; and theirs had been a refusing that great truth Jesus Christ as
the Messiah and head. And so the devil's sin would have been less than
theirs, whereas he is made the great father of this great lie, of this great
stubbornness to receive Christ, and to contradict this truth; and 'this,'
saith he, 'he hath opposed from the beginning,' with all his might, and
he setteth your hearts a-work to kill me.

"But I say, I will not stand upon this, because I only deliver it, as that
which is the opinion of some, and hath some probability. However this
is certain, whatsoever his sin was, he hath now, being fallen, set up his
kingdom in a special manner against Christ: and so Christ hath been the

great stumbling stone; and angels fell upon it, and men fall upon it. So that indeed the first quarrel was laid in this, God himself proclaimed it at the very beginning. And a little would make one think, that there was something before, when God denounced the sentence against the serpent, 'The seed of the woman shall break the serpent's head,' which though spoken to the serpent, comes in by way of curse, as striking at the very spirit of the devil's sin; 'he shall break thy head,' saith he, thou wouldest have lifted up thyself, 'he shall crush thee.'

"God, I say, proclaimed the war, and the quarrel hath continued from the beginning of the world to this day, and will do, until Satan be put out of the air; for so long he is to have his kingdom, though Christ beateth him out of it every day in the world, and so will continue to do, till he hath won the world from him, and then he will chain him up in the bottomless pit." This from Dr. Goodwin, vol. 1 of his *Works*, Pt. II, pp. 32–33.[2] See forward, No. 1266b.

1262. CONFLAGRATION. 'Tis an argument that the fire of the conflagration shall be that fire in which the wicked shall have their eternal punishment, that the great deluge that destroyed the wicked world in Noah's time was a type of it.

There are many things that make it manifest that that deluge was designed as a great and very signal type and representation of the eternal destruction of the wicked, and that the ark that saved Noah's family and the elect creatures of all sorts, was a type of Christ, or of the provision made by him for the salvation of the church and of an elect number of all kinds and all nations under heaven, in whom is neither Greek nor Jew, circumcision nor uncircumcision, barbarian, Scythian, bond or free [Col. 3:11], and in whom the wolf shall dwell with the lamb, the leopard lie down with the kid, etc. [Is. 11:6] (see sermons on the subject).[3] God's wrath is often compared to overwhelming waters.

The apostle Peter evidently speaks of this deluge as a type of the final conflagration. II Pet. 3:5–7, "For this they are willingly ignorant of, that by the word of God the heavens were of old, and the earth standing out

2. Goodwin's *Works*, vol. 1, pt. II, pp. 32–33.

3. JE's reference is uncertain; there are no extant sermons by him that treat the deluge and ark as types of the conflagration and Christ. JE could mean sermons on the types, including that on Gen. 24:58 (July 1742), in which he shows how Rebekah "is a type of the church and the believing soul in its mystical marriage with Christ"; and on Gen. 43:3 (Feb. 1742) with the doctrine, "Joseph was a remarkable type of Christ." Alternatively, he may intend sermons on the scriptures alluded to, such as the one on Col. 3:11 (1736), "Christ is the Christian's all." Or, he could be referring to a series of sermons no longer extant.

of the water and in the water: whereby the world that then was, being overflowed with water, perished: but the heavens and the earth, which are now, by the same word are kept in store, reserved unto fire against the day of judgment and perdition of ungodly men." Here these two great events, these grand destructions of the world, are evidently compared one with [the other], as represented one by the other. The Apostle plainly speaks of that deluge as containing the instruction, argument and evidence of a type that, if properly attended with an unbiased judgment and right disposition of heart, would convince those scoffers of the truth of the antitype, or thing signified, viz. the final conflagration.

1263.[4] GOD'S IMMEDIATE AND ARBITRARY OPERATION, in all instances of it, at least in this lower world, whether through all ages on men's minds by his Spirit, or at some particular season extraordinarily requiring it in what is called miracles, is that which there is a strong and strange disposition in many to object against and disbelieve; but for what reason, unless it be something in the disposition of the heart, is hard to imagine. See concerning such prejudices, MacLaurin's *Discourses,* pp. 314–15 ff.[5]

If there be a God who is truly an intelligent, voluntary, active being, what is there in reason to incline us to think that he should not act, and that he should not act upon his creatures, which, being his creatures, must have their very being from his action and must be perfectly and most absolutely subject to and dependent on his action? And if he acted once, why must he needs be still forever after and act no more? What is there in nature to disincline [us] to suppose he mayn't continue to act towards the world he made, and is under his government? And if he continues to act at all towards his creatures, then there must be some of his creatures t[hat][6] he continues to act upon immediately. 'Tis nonsense to say he a[cts] upon all mediately, because in so doing w[e] go back *in infinitum* from one thing acting on another without ever coming to a prime, present agent, and yet at the same time suppose God to be such a present agent.

There are many who allow a present, continuing, immediate operation of God on the creation (and indeed such are the late discoveries

4. For a discussion of this entry, see "Editor's Introduction," pp. 20–21.

5. This reference, a later insertion, is to Sec. IV, "Of divine supernatural operations and mistakes concerning them," in John MacLaurin's "An Essay on the Scripture-Doctrine of Divine Grace," in his *Sermons and Essays,* pp. 314–31.

6. A tattered margin affects this and some other words in the remainder of this paragraph and throughout the next two.

and advances which have been made in natural philosophy that all men of sense, who are also men of learning, are comp[elled] to allow it), but yet, because so many of the constant changes and events in their continued series in the external world come to pass in a certain, exact method, according to certain, fixed, invariable laws, are averse to allow that God acts any otherwise than as limiting himself by such invariable laws, fixed from the beginning of the creation, when he precisely marked out and determined the rules and paths of all his future operations, and that he never departs from those paths[7]—so that, though they allow an immediate divine operation now, in these days, yet they sup[pose] it [is] what is limited by what we call LAWS OF NATURE, and seem averse to allow an ARBITRARY OPERATION to be continued, or ever to be expected, in these days.

But I desire it may be well considered whether there be any [rea]son for this.

Of the two kinds of divine operation, viz. that which is arbitrary and that which is limited by fixed laws, the former, viz. arbitrary, is the first and foundation of the other, and that which all divine operation must finally be resolved into, and which all events and divine effects whatsoever primarily depend upon. Even the fixing of the method and rules of the other kind of operation is an instance of arbitrary operation.

When I speak of arbitrary operation, I don't mean arbitrary in opposition to an operation directed by wisdom, but in opposition to an operation confined to and limited by those fixed establishments and laws commonly called the laws of nature. The one of these I shall therefore, for want of better phrases, call *a natural operation;* the other, *an arbitrary operation.*

The latter of these, as I observed, is first and supreme, and to which the other is wholly subject and absolutely dependent, and without which there could be no divine operation at all and no effect ever produced and nothing besides God could ever exist. Arbitrary operation is that to which is owing the existence of the subject of natural operation, the manner, measure and all the circumstances of their existence. 'Tis arbitrary operation that fixes, determines and limits the laws of natural operation.

Therefore arbitrary operation, being every way the highest, it is that wherein God is most glorified. 'Tis the glory of God that he is an arbitrary being, that originally he, in all things, acts as being limited and directed in nothing but his own wisdom, tied to no other rules and laws

7. MS: "and that he never departs since that departs from those path."

but the directions of his own infinite understanding. So in those that are the highest order of God's creatures, viz. intelligent creatures, that are distinguished from other creatures in their being made in God's image, 'tis one thing wherein consists their highest natural dignity, that they have an image of this. They have a secondary and dependent arbitrariness. They are not limited in their operations to the laws of matter and motion, so but that they can do what they please. The members of men's bodies obey the act of their wills without being directed merely by the impulse and attraction of other bodies in all their motions.

These things being observed, I would now take notice that the higher we ascend in the scale of created existence, and the nearer we come to the Creator, the more and more and more arbitrary we shall find the divine operations on the creature, or those communications and influences by which he maintains an intercourse with the creature. And it appears beautiful and every way fit and suitable that it should be so. See [No.] tt.[8]

But before I proceed particularly to show this, I would observe how any divine operation may be said [to] be more or less arbitrary, or to come nearer to that which is absolutely arbitrary in the sense I have spoken of, viz. in opposition to a being limited by those general rules called laws of nature. An operation is absolutely arbitrary when no use [is][9] made of any law of nature [and] no respect had to any one [su]ch fixed rule or method.

There are three ways that those operations which are not absolutely and perfectly arbitrary may approach near to it:

1. One is by arbitrary operations being mixed with those that are natural, i.e. when there is something in the operation that is arbitrary and tied to no fixed rule or law, and something else in the operation wherein the laws of nature are made use, and without which the designed effect could not take place. Instances will be given of this afterwards.

2. Another way is when, though some law or rule is observed, the rule is not general or very extensive, but some particular, exempt rule, being an exception to general laws of nature, and a law that extends to comparatively few instances. This approaches to an arbitrary operation, for the less extensive the limitation of the operation, or the smaller the number of instances or cases by which it is limited, 'tis manifest the nearer the operation is to [being] unlimited, or limited to no number of cases

---

8. *Works, 13*, 189–91.
9. A damaged margin affects this and other words in the remainder of the paragraph.

at all. Thus supposing there were an exception to the general law of gravitation towards the center of the earth, and there were one kind of bodies that, on the contrary, had an inclination to fly from the center, and that in proportion to the quantity of matter, but that [that] sort of bodies [was] nowhere to be found but in some one, certain island, and very rarely to be found there. This kind of operation would be nearer to arbitrary and miraculous than other divine operations, than those that are limited by the general laws of nature that obtain everywhere through the world.

3. Another way wherein a manner of operation approaches to arbitrary is when the limitation to a method is not absolute, even in the continued course of that sort of operations, so that the law fails of the nature of a fixed law, as all that are called laws of nature are. God generally keeps to that method, but ties not himself to it, sometimes departs from it according to his sovereign pleasure.

Having mentioned these things, I now proceed particularly to observe how, the higher we ascend in the scale or series of created existences, and the nearer in thus ascending we come to the Creator, the more the manner of divine operation with respect to the creature approaches to arbitrary in these respects, or in one or other of them.

Thus, in the first place, if we ascend with respect to time and go back in the series of existences or events in the order of their succession to the beginning of the creation, and so till we come to the Creator: that we, after we have ascended beyond the limits and rise of the laws of nature, we shall come to arbitrary operation. The creation of the matter of the material world out of nothing, the creation even of every individual atom or primary particle, was by an operation perfectly arbitrary. And here, by the way, I would observe that creation out of nothing seems to be the only divine operation that [is] absolutely arbitrary, without any kind of use made of any such antecedently fixed method of proceeding as is called a law of nature.

After the creation of the matter of the world out of nothing, the gradual bringing of the matter of the world into order was by an arbitrary operation. It was by arbitrary divine [operation] that the primary particles of matter were put in motion, and had the direction and degree of their motion determined, and were brought into so beautiful and useful a situation one with respect to another. But yet the operation by which these things was done was not so absolutely, purely and unmixedly arbitrary as the first creation out of nothing. For in these secondary operations, or the works of what may be called a secondary [creation], some use was made of laws of nature before established; such, at least, as the laws of resistance and attraction, or adhesion and *vis inertiæ*, that are essential to the very being of matter, for the very solidity of the particles of matter itself consists in them. But the putting these particles into motion supposes 'em to exist. In the moving inert, resisting and adhering matter, there is use made of the laws of resistance and adhesion. They are presupposed as the basis of this secondary operation of God in causing this resistance, *vis inertiæ,* and adhesion to change place, and in causing the consequent impulses and mutual influences which is the end of those motions and dispositions of the situation of particles. So that the creation of particular natural bodies, as the creation of light, the creation of the sun, moon and stars, of earth, air and seas, stones, rocks and minerals, the bodies of plants and animals, was by a mixed operation, partly arbitrary and partly by stated laws, and thus as we descend from the first creation out of nothing through the rest of the operations of the six days.

But it may be proper here to remark these following things:

(1) Immediate creation seems not entirely to have ceased with that first work by which the world in general was brought out of nothing. But after that, there was an immediate creation in making of the souls of Adam and Eve, and also with respect to the greater part of the body of Eve.

(2) The mixing of arbitrary with natural operations was not only in arbitrarily making use of laws already established, as in setting material things in motion, variously compounding them, and the like, but also in establishing new, more particular laws of nature with respect to particular creatures as they were made, as the laws of magnetism,[1] many laws observable in plants, the laws of instinct in animals and the laws of the operation of the minds of men.

(3) Most things in the visible world were brought into their perfect state, so as to [be] of such a particular kind or to [be] complete as to their species, and species of creatures, by a secondary creation, which is a mixed operation, excepting the creation of the highest orders of creatures, viz. intelligent minds, which were wholly created complete in their kind by an absolutely arbitrary operation. What may be said hereafter may lead us to the reason of this.

And if we proceed in the succession of existences till we come to the Supreme Being the other way, viz. to the end of the world—for though proceeding thus from preceding to future be according to a more com-

---

1. MS: "~~electricity~~ magnetism."

mon way of speaking descending, yet 'tis as truly ascending towards God as proceeding the other way, for God is the first and the last, the beginning and the end—now, I say, if we ascend up to God this way, proceeding in the succession of events till we come to the end of time, this way of proceeding will again bring us to a disposition of the world by a divine, arbitrary operation through the universe. For God will not leave the world to a gradual decay, languishing through millions of ages under a miserable decay till it be quite perished and utterly ruined according to a course of things, according to the laws of nature, but will himself destroy the world, will roll the heavens together as a scroll, will change it as a man puts off an old garment and wears it not till it gradually drops to pieces, and will take it down as a machine is taken down when it has answered the workman's end. And this he will do by an arrest on the laws of nature everywhere, in all parts of the visible universe, and by a new disposition and mighty change of all things at once. For though all the laws of nature will not be abolished, those laws before mentioned, on which the being of the primary particles of matter [depends], will be continued. Yet the arbitrary interposition, entirely beside and above those laws and in some respects contrary to 'em and interrupting their influence, may be said to be universal, as it will be in all parts of the material creation. And very many of the laws of nature will be utterly abolished, particularly many of the laws peculiarly respecting plants and animals, and human bodies, and man's animal life.

If we ascend towards God in the scale of existence according to the degrees of excellency and perfection, the nearer we come to God the nearer we shall come to arbitrary influence of the Most High on the creature, till at length, when we come to the highest rank, we shall come [to] an intercourse as is in many respects quite above those rules which we call the laws of nature. The lowest rank of material things are almost wholly under the government of the general laws of matter and motion. If we ascend from them to plants, which in many things are governed by more particular laws, distinct from the laws common to all material things, the laws of vegetation are doubtless many of them distinct from the general laws of matter and motion and, therefore (by what was observed before), nearer akin to an arbitrary influence. If we ascend from the most imperfect to the most perfect kind of plants, we shall come to more particular laws still. And if from thence we rise to animals, we shall come to laws still more singular. And when we rise to the most perfect of them, we shall find particular laws or instincts yet nearer akin to an arbitrary influence.

If we rise to mankind, and particularly the mind of man, by which especially he is above the inferior creatures, and consider[2] the laws of the common operations of the mind, they are so high above such a kind of general laws of matter, and are so singular, that they are altogether untraceable. The more particular laws are the harder to be investigated and traced. And if we go from the common operations of the faculties of the mind and rise up to those that are spiritual, which are infinitely of the highest kind, and are those by which the minds are most conversant with the Creator and have their very next union with him, though these are not altogether without use made of means and some connection with antecedents and what we call (though improperly in this case) second causes, yet the operation may properly be said to be arbitrary and sovereign, the connection after the manner of the invariable laws of nature never erring from the degree and exact measure, time and precise state, of the antecedent.

And if we ascend from saints on earth to angels in heaven, who always behold the face of the Father which is in heaven and constantly receive his commands on every occasion, the will of God not being made known to them by any such methods as the laws of nature but immediately given on all emergences, we shall come to greater degrees of an arbitrary intercourse.

And if [we] rise to the highest step of all next to the Supreme Being himself, even the mind of the man Christ Jesus, who is united personally to the Godhead, doubtless there is a constant intercourse, as it were infinitely above the laws of nature. N.B.: When we come to the highest ranks of creatures, we come to them who themselves have the greatest image of God's arbitrary operation, who 'tis therefore most fit should be the subjects of such operations.

And if we ascend towards God, conjunctly proceeding in our ascent both according to the order of degrees and the order [of intercourse],[3] we shall find the rule hold. Still the more arbitrary shall we find the divine influence and intercourse, and to a higher degree, than by ascending in one way singly.

Thus if we ascend up to intelligent creatures, men and angels, who are next to the Creator, and then go back to the beginning of the world, even to their creation, we shall find more of an arbitrary operation in their creation and being brought to perfection in their kind than in the cre-

---

2. MS: "consider to."
3. There is an important lacuna here in the MS. The Andover copy supplies "of events."

ation of any other particular species of creatures. Thus it was not in the creation of angels as it was in the formation of sun, moon and stars, minerals, plants and animals, who were formed out of pre-existent principles by a secondary creation, as it is called, presupposing, making use of, and operating upon these principles, as subsisting by certain general laws of nature already established. But the angels were immediately created, and made perfect in their kind at once, by a primary creation, [an] operation absolutely arbitrary, as perfectly so as the creation of the primary particles of matter themselves. And so with respect to the creation of the soul of man.

And after these intelligent beings were created, at first the divine intercourse with them must be much more arbitrary than it is now. They could not be left to themselves and to the laws of nature to acquire that knowledge and exercise of their faculties by contracted habits and gradual association of ideas, as we do now, gradually rising from our first infancy. If man had been thus left, he must needs have soon perished. But we must suppose that there was an extraordinary influence and intercourse God had with man, far above the law of nature, immediately instructing, enlightening and conducting him, and arbitrarily fixing those habits in his mind which now are gradually established through a great length of time. So afterwards, for some time, God continued a miraculous intercourse with our first parents. And we see that for many of the first ages of the world. And arbitrary intercourse of God with mankind, not only some particular prophets of one nation or posterity, but with eminent saints of all families—I say, such an arbitrary intercourse was much more common in those first ages than afterwards.

And if we proceed in the order of time the other way, to the end of the world, and till we come to him who is the End as well as the Beginning, 'tis true we shall find that an arbitrary influence will then be exerted everywhere throughout the creation, but more especially and many more ways towards intelligent beings: for instance, towards mankind, in bringing souls departed from the other world, in raising the dead to life, in miraculously changing the living, in taking up the saints to meet the Lord, in gathering all, both good and bad, before the judgment seat, and in all the process of that day. The laws of nature must be innumerable ways departed from and an extraordinary operation succeed in the manifestation of the Judge, in the manifestation of the judged one to another, in manifesting and declaring the actions of particular persons, and the secrets of their hearts, and the grounds of the sentence, and in all the process of that day. If the laws of nature were not in numberless ways to be departed from in these things, the day of judgment would take up more time by far than the world has stood. And in the execution of the sentence on both the righteous and the wicked, the glorious power of God will be wonderfully and most extraordinarily manifested in many respects, above all that ever was before, in the arbitrary exertions of it.

And if we look to the beginning and end, the birth and death, of each individual person of mankind, we shall find the same rule hold as concerning the beginning and end of the race of mankind in general. The soul of every man, in his generation or birth, must be immediately created and infused. Or if we say that it is according to a fixed law of nature that the Creator forms and introduces the soul, it being determined by a law of nature what the precise state of the prepared body shall be when the soul shall begin to exist in it, yet it must be a law of nature that is most peculiar and widely differing from all other laws of nature, and independent of them.

And so again, the Creator immediately and arbitrarily interposes when a man comes to die, in disposing of that soul that he infused in his birth.

And if we consider the church, or that part of mankind, that society of intelligent beings, which God hath chosen for his part and portion, his peculiar treasure, that part that is united to God, conformed to him, and truly, actively answers the end of the creation, and are God's own family, which are truly the head of the creation, and the end of all the rest, and next of all to God—I say, if we consider this society, and go back to its beginning till we come to God the Father of, and to Christ the foundation of, it, at the times when the church had its foundation laid and when it was as it were formed and established, we shall come to arbitrary operations.

Now thus to ascend to the laying of the foundations of the church is a different thing from going back to the beginning of the creation, because the church is established and built up by a quite different work of God, called the new creation, or creation of new heavens and new earth, which is a work carried on from the beginning to the end of the world. And the foundation of the church was laid by several remarkable degrees, periods at each of which God appears in an extraordinary manner and operates by an arbitrary influence.

One period wherein the foundation of the church was laid was immediately after the fall, when God appeared in arbitrary manifestations and operations to his church, and continued for ages so to do.

Another period was after the flood, where again we shall find [God] extraordinarily manifesting himself to Noah and maintaining an arbitrary intercourse with him and his family.

Another and yet far more remarkable season of laying the foundation of the church was the time of the calling of Abraham, which was attended and followed with many great and extraordinary revelations and arbitrary influences.

Another time which may in an especial manner and above all others be called the time of laying the foundation of the Jewish [church] was in Moses and Joshua's time. And how many and great were the miraculous and extraordinary operations and influences of God towards his people at that time.

Another season was the time of calling David, the great ancestor of Christ, to the throne, and setting up his kingdom, and the building the temple, and establishing the temple worship, which was attended with the beginning of a succession of prophets which lasted to the captivity, and a very extraordinary intercourse with David and innumerable revelations made to him.

But far above all was the time when Christ came, was incarnated, lived on earth, died, rose again, ascended into heaven and sent the Holy Spirit from thence, the time of laying the foundation of the church of God. All the preceding were but the forerunners and preparatives for this. This especially was the time of laying the foundation of the new creation, or the new heavens and the new earth. And that time, even that age wherein Christ and his apostles lived, being about 100 years, was above [every other age] that ever was, an age of supernatural, extraordinary and arbitrary operations and communications from heaven, on several accounts:

1. Then the greatest things were done by arbitrary power, and most out of and beyond the course of nature: as the incarnation of Christ, the conception of a child in the womb of a woman without intercourse with a man, the union of the soul of the child conceived in such a manner with[4] the divine *Logos*, the rising of Christ from the dead to everlasting life, the alteration made in the human nature of Christ at his ascension into heaven, and the alteration made in his state from such meanness, abasement, suffering and subjection to his enemies (see note on Eph. 1:19–20)[5]—these are infinitely greater effects than the creation of the

---

4. MS: "of."

5. "Scripture," no. 502, on Eph. 1:19–22, in *Works, 15,* 599–601. In the "Blank Bible," JE simply refers to "Scripture" no. 502.

world—the great degrees in which the miraculous influences of the Spirit of [God] was given to Christ and to his apostles, and the great degrees in which a spirit of saving grace was given, which is properly supernatural and in many respects arbitrary in its operation.

2. In the multitude of the instances of arbitrary operation on the minds of so great a number of persons, and the number of extraordinary, arbitrary revelations given and effects wrought.

3. In the greatness, importance and vast extent of the influence of these extraordinary operations and effects in the system and series of things.

Such wonderful effects of God's arbitrary operations were there in laying the foundation of the church, and so at the finishing of the superstructure, the completing of the church, and its full consummation in perfection, glory and happiness at the day. The effects of God's arbitrary operation towards his church will be unspeakably greater than towards the wicked (though they will be exceeding great); as the Apostle says [Eph. 1:19–20], according to the exceeding greatness of God's power, which [he] wrought in Christ in his resurrection, exaltation and glorification. Then will all the work of sanctification and glorification of all the saints, begun in their conversion, be completed in its highest conformity to Christ's glory by a work far greater than the creation of heaven and earth.

So if we consider the beginning or creation and end of each individual saint or member. Thus in their beginning or creation—I mean their beginning as saints or their conversion—commonly at the time of that, God's sovereign, arbitrary interposition and influence on their hearts is much more visible and remarkable than ordinarily they are the subjects of in the course of their lives. And when they come to die, the positive effects of God's arbitrary influence are immensely greater in the souls of the saints in their glorification than in the souls of the wicked in their damnation.

Thus, let us proceed which way we will in the series of things in the creation, still the higher we ascend, and the nearer we come to God in the gradation or succession of created things, the nearer it comes to that: that there is no other law than only the law of the infinite wisdom of the omniscient first cause and supreme disposer of all things who, in one, simple, unchangeable, perpetual view, comprehends all existence in its[6] utmost compass and extent and infinite series.

6. MS: "it is."

'Tis fit that it should be so, as we proceed and go from step to step among the several parts and distinct existences and events of the universe, that which way soever we go, the nearer we come to God, the less and less we should find that things are governed by general laws, and that the arbitrariness of the supreme cause and governor should be more and more seen. For he is not seen to be the sovereign ruler of the universe, or God over all, any otherwise than he is seen to be arbitrary. He is not seen to be active in the government of the world any other way than it is seen he is arbitrary. It is not seen but that he himself, in common with his creature, is subject in his acting to the same laws with inferior beings any other way than as it is seen that his arbitrary operation is every way and everywhere at the head of the universe, and is the foundation and first spring of all.

1264. THE DEVIL BEFORE THE FALL THE HIGHEST OF ALL CREATURES. The devil, having respect to what he was before his fall, is called Lucifer, or the morning star. A star is very often in Scripture used as the symbol of a prince or ruler. This is very evident particularly in Matt. 2:2, "Where is he that is born King of the Jews? for we have seen his STAR in the east, and are come to worship." See also Num. 24:17, Rev. 8:10–11. The moon and the stars are said to rule by night. So we read of the DOMINION which the stars have in the earth (Job 38:31–33). And as the angels in general are called stars, signifying in part that dominion which they have whereby they are called in the New Testament thrones, dominions, principalities and powers, so as Satan was Lucifer or the morning star, the brightest of all the stars, this naturally leads us to suppose that he was that creature that was set at the head of the universe, in greatest authority, as God's prime minister of state. Christ, being of the highest authority as well as greatest glory of all, is represented in the Revelation by his being called "the bright and morning star" [Rev. 22:16]. So Satan's being called the morning star represents his excelling all other creatures in authority.

1265. TRINITY, intimations of in the OLD TESTAMENT. Zech. 2:8, "For thus saith the Lord [. . .]; after the glory hath he sent me to the nations that spoiled you." Here is a plain distinction between the Lord of Hosts that was sent and God sending. Is. 54:5, "Thy makers are thy husband"; Ps. 149:2, "in his makers"; Is. 44:2, "The Lord thy makers";[7] and as Dr. Goodwin says in multitudes of places.

---

7. Compare with the KJV, in which the last three phrases are translated, respectively, "For thy Maker is thine husband," "in him that made him," and "the Lord that made thee."

1266[a]. GLORY OF GOD, THE END OF THE CREATION. God's glory, as it is spoken of in Scripture as the end of all God's works, is, in one word, the EMANATION of that fullness of God that is from eternity in God *ad extra,* and towards those creatures that are capable of being sensible and active objects of such an emanation. It consists in communicating himself to those two faculties of the understanding and will, by which faculties it is that creatures are sensible and active objects or subjects of divine emanations and communications.

God communicates himself to the understanding in the manifestation that is made of the divine excellency and the understanding, idea or view which intelligent creatures have of it. He communicates his glory and fullness to the wills of sensible, willing, active beings in their rejoicing in the manifested glory of God, in their admiring it, in their loving God for it, and being in all respects affected and disposed suitably to such glory, and their exercising and expressing those affections and dispositions wherein consists their praising and glorifying God; and in their being themselves holy, and having the image of this glory in their hearts, and as it were reflecting it as a jewel does the light of the sun, and as it were partaking[8] of God's brightness, and in their being happy in God, whereby they partake of God's fullness of happiness.

This twofold emanation or communication of the divine fullness *ad extra* is answerable to the twofold emanation or going forth of the Godhead *ad intra,* wherein the internal and essential glory and fullness of the Godhead consists, viz. the proceeding of the eternal Son of God, God's eternal idea and infinite understanding and wisdom and the brightness of his glory, whereby his beauty and excellency appears to him; and the proceeding of the Holy Spirit, or the eternal will, temper, disposition of the Deity, the infinite fullness of God's holiness, joy and delight.

1266b. Add this to No. 1261. OCCASION OF THE FALL OF THE ANGELS. The same Dr. Goodwin, in the second volume of his *Works,* in his discourse on *The Knowledge of God the Father, and of His Son Jesus Christ,* speaking of the pride of some, has these words: "A lower degree of accursed pride [. . .] fell into the heart of the devil himself, whose sin in his first apostatizing from God, [. . .] is conceived to be [. . .] a stomaching that man should be one day advanced unto the hypostatical union, and be one [. . .] person with the Son of God, which his[9] proud angelical

8. MS: "partake."
9. MS: "whose."

nature (then in actual existence THE HIGHEST OF CREATURES) could not brook."[1]

1267. OPINIONS OF THE ANCIENT JEWS CONCERNING A FUTURE PUN-ISHMENT. We have an account in the books of Maccabees that "Eleazar, one of the principal scribes of the Jews, an aged man, and discreet, when he was advised by his friends to make as if he did eat of the flesh, taken from the sacrifice commanded by the king, that in so doing he might be delivered from death, with great scorn rejected their advice upon this consideration; that, though for the present time he should be delivered from the punishment of men, yet should he not escape the hand of the Almighty, either alive or dead. And the son of Sirach tells us, that sinners are kept against the mighty day of their punishment. [. . .] And the seven brothers, mentioned in the Maccabees, were plainly full of the belief of a state of future retribution." Abp. Dawes' *Works*, vol. 2, pp. 38–39.[2]

1268. NATURAL CONSCIENCE, ITS FOREBODINGS OF PUNISHMENT. TRA-DITIONS OF THE HEATHEN CONCERNING THIS. "'So great is the power of conscience, that those, who have committed any fault, live in perpetual fear of punishment' (Tullius [Cicero's] oratio, *Pro Milone*). 'Many sorrows and perturbations of mind, repentance and continual tumults and disorders, diffidence concerning even their present state, and black and melancholy suspicions of their future ones, are the natural consequences of men's evil actions' (Plutarch, ed. Paris, p. 556). 'In proportion to men's sins, their fears will grow upon them, and never let them be quiet; for these, they will be scourged and mightily tormented' (Seneca, *Epistulæ Morales*, 97–98, 105). Wicked men 'night and day carry about in their own breasts a witness against themselves, which doth secretly terrify, lash and torture them, and fill them with dreadful apprehensions of punishments to come' (Juvenal, *Satire* 13). 'Nay, even Lucretius himself doth, more than once, acknowledge this to be the common case of mankind.'" These things from Abp. Dawes' *Works*, vol. 2, pp. 5–6.[3]

1269. TRADITIONS AND OPINIONS OF THE HEATHEN CONCERNING A FUTURE JUDGMENT. "Diodorus Siculus expressly tells us of the Egyptians,

---

1. Goodwin, *Of the Knowledge of God the Father, and His Son Jesus Christ*, in *Works*, 2, 4.

2. William Dawes, "The Certainty of Hell-Torments, from Principles of Nature and Reason," in *The Works of the Most Reverend Father in God, Sir William Dawes, Bar., Late Lord Archbishop of York*, vol. 2 (London, 1733), 38–39.

3. JE gleaned these classical citations from Dawes' sermon, "The Pains and Terrors of a Wounded Conscience Insupportable," in ibid., pp. 5–6.

that 'the Greeks imitated their funeral rites, in relation to the punishment of the wicked in hell, and the pleasant meadows provided for the good.' And the Greeks [. . .] were indeed so fully persuaded of the certainty of future punishments, that many of their learned men are said to have written books professedly concerning them. And their wisest and gravest philosophers, as well as their poets [. . .] have given us very particular descriptions of the torments of the wicked in hell. And therefore Justin Martyr tells them that, 'in what we Christians say, as to the punishments of wicked men after death, and the rewards of good men, we say the very same things with their poets and philosophers.' And much to the same purpose, Eusebius and Theodoret. Nor do the Latins [. . .] fall a whit short of the Greeks as to their opinions in this point [. . .]. And accordingly Tertullian, and other apologists for the Christian faith to the Latins, frequently tell them, that their 'learned men agree so exactly with the Christians, in what they hold as to future punishments, that it is hardly to be doubted, but that they first received their knowledge of these things, from the Christians' ancestors, or their books.' To the Greeks and Romans we may add several other nations, which were contemporary with them, as the ancient Indians and Gauls, the Britons, the Getæ, the Hyperborei, etc., who are all upon record in history, for agreeing, either directly or by natural consequence, in the belief of future punishments for the wicked. [. . .] We shall find the same amongst our new discoveries in the West, and the remotest parts of the East Indies." These things from Abp. Dawes' *Works,* vol. 2, pp. 41–43.[4]

1270. GREATNESS OF HELL TORMENTS. "The very heathen themselves, by the mere light of nature, seem to have been perfectly well assured of" the inconceivable greatness of hell torments. "For not only their poets [. . .] but also their best and gravest philosophers, do both expressly assert the extremity and intolerableness of hell-torments, and likewise give us such terrifying and amazing descriptions of them, as may abundantly convince us, that they did really believe them to be infinitely great [. . .]. A small taste of which you may be pleased to take in Plato only, who, under the person of one who is supposed to have seen hell, and afterwards to have returned to this world again, tells us what dreadful spectacles he there saw: how he beheld men tortured, with numberless tortures of all sorts; some burning in rivers of fire, others shivering and freezing in streams of excessive coldness, some tossed about and torn by wild beasts,

4. Dawes, "The Certainty of Hell-Torments, from Principles of Nature and Reason," in *Works,* 2, 41–43.

others incessantly burnt with the lamps of the furies, and more particularly some [...] bound hand and foot, then fleed,[5] and thrown upon thorns and prickles, to be tortured." This from Abp. Dawes' *Works,* vol. 2, pp. 100–01.[6]

1271. THE RIGHTEOUSNESS by which believers are justified is called GOD'S RIGHTEOUSNESS, not merely because 'tis a righteousness of God's providing, nor is thereby meant only that 'tis a fruit of God's wonderful contrivance and extraordinary dispensation, but because 'tis a righteousness of God's working and inherent in God, i.e. in a divine person. This is agreeable to the style of the gospel. Thus the rest that remains for the people of God, the rest which God has provided for them and which they enter into, is called God's rest, in that sense, that 'tis Christ's own rest, the rest which he himself enters into (compare Heb. 3:11, 14, and ch. 4:5, 9–10). So it is said in God's light we shall see light [Ps. 36:9], and that the saints shall drink of the river of God's pleasures [Ps. 36:8], and shall enter into the joy of their Lord [Matt. 25:21, 23], and the glory of the saints, which is the fruit of righteousness, is [the] glory of God [Phil. 1:11]. Rom. 3[:23], we "have sinned, and come short of the glory." So the kingdom of God is promised to them, and the inheritance which is reserved for the saints in heaven (or in the holy places) is called Christ's inheritance (Eph. 1:18).

See "Notes on Scripture," no. 318.[7]

1272. DEVILS, their present state in hell. Dr. Goodwin, in his *Exposition on Ephesians,* Pt. II, pp. 39–40:[8] If the devil were full of torment, "it is certain [...] he could not be busy to tempt; and the reason is clear, for the fullness of God's wrath, which men shall have in hell, takes up all the intention; [...] the wrath of God would distract the creature, when it cometh in the fullness of it. Now the devil hath all his wits about him, all his wiles, all his methods; therefore certainly they are not full of torment. And likewise, if they had not ease, yea, a pleasure in wickedness in some respect, they would not be so busy; for they have lusts and desires, 'The lusts of your father, the devil,' says Christ, 'ye will do' [John 8:44]. Now then, when they have put men upon what they do desire, there is a satisfaction of their lusts, and there [is] in some respects some pleasure

---

5. Archaic variant of "flayed," or skinned alive.
6. Dawes, "The Greatness of Hell-Torments," in *Works,* 2, 100–01.
7. "Scripture" no. 318, on Rom. 1:16–18, in *Works, 15,* 294–96.
8. Goodwin, *Exposition on Ephesians,* in *Works,* vol. 1, Pt. II, pp. 39–40.

arising, that sets them on work. And this may seem to be one difference between the place of men's souls departed, that go to hell, that are in a place of torment, as it is called, Luke 16, and the devil's place; God having not appointed them a ministry, to work in the children of disobedience, as he hath done the devils."

1273. How the Pope Is Antichrist. Dr. Goodwin, ibid. (see foregoing No.), pp. 40–41:[9] The devil "was worshipped in the world [. . .] as [a] god. And therefore, it is said, Rev. 12, that he and his angels were in heaven; why? because they were worshipped as gods: 'And he was cast out into the earth, and his angels were cast out with him' [Rev. 12:9]. When Constantine turned Christian, all the world turned Christian too; then all his devils were thrown down, from having that worship as they always had before. But [. . .] when he ceased to be a god, [. . .] that he might imitate God, who hath set up his Son Jesus Christ, he likewise hath set up his son, Antichrist, [. . .] whose kingdom and the devil's are in many things just alike." 'Tis said, Rev. 14:2, "'the dragon did give the beast his power, and seat, and great authority.'" [. . .] Antichrist "is the eldest son of Satan, as Christ is the eldest Son of God."

1274. The Saints in Heaven Shall Partake of Christ's Own Happiness and Glory, and of the enjoyment of that love of God by which God loves his own dear Son. Thus Dr. Goodwin (ibid., p. 158)[1] on that text, Eph. 2:4, "for his great love wherewith he hath loved us," says: "It is the same love wherewith he loveth his Son. For that you have a known place in John 17:23, 26. At the twenty-fourth verse, saith Christ, '*thou hast loved me before the foundation of the world*, [. . .] and thou hast united me to thyself'; '*thou art in me, and I in thee*' (so v. 21), and 'thou hast united a company of thine [. . .] unto me,' '*I in them, and thou in me*' (so saith v. 23); and then what follows? '*that the world may know that thou hast loved them, as thou hast loved me.*' As he is united to God, and we to him, so God loveth us with the same love wherewith he loved him. And then again, you have the like expression, v. 26. 'That the love wherewith thou hast loved me may be in them.' God loved all his creatures: he loved Adam, but not with that kind of love wherewith he loved Christ; but he loveth his elect with the same kind of love wherewith he loved him [. . .]. He loveth [him] as his Son, and he loveth them as daughters married to him:

9. Ibid., vol. 1, Pt. II, pp. 40–41.
1. Ibid., vol. 1, Pt. II, p. 158.

as a father loveth a son, and a daughter married unto him with the same kind of love, and differing from his love to the servants, or to any else that are about him. And therefore you shall find that still this love comes in with a distinction, Rom. 8[:39]. 'Nor height, nor depth, nor any other creature, shall be able to separate us from the love of God, which is in Christ Jesus.'"

Pt. II, pp. 187–88,[2] on those words, we are quickened 'together with Christ' [Eph. 2:5]: "You must know, brethren, God the Father, who is the great quickener, he is the author, the great fountain of life; and Jesus Christ, as God-man, hath life given from the Father to him, that he might raise us. You have two places, John 5:24–25. At the twentieth-sixth verse, 'as the Father hath life in himself, so he hath given to the Son to have life in himself.' [. . .] And John 6:57, 'As the living Father hath sent me, and I live by the Father: so he that eats my flesh, shall live by me.' So that now it is plain, that God having infinite life and happiness [. . .] (for what is the life of God, but his own holiness and happiness, and the entireness of his own nature, for his own blessedness, for his own pleasure?), God hath ordained, and laid up eternal life in his decree; but Jesus Christ is to be eternal life, to communicate that life that is in himself to us, I John 1:1. [. . .] God purposed, that man should live in union and communion with him, and partake of that life that he himself lives and communicates it as far as the creature is capable: 'He hath given us eternal life' [I John 5:11]. Well! where hath he put it for us to have it? 'And' (saith he), 'this life is in his Son' [I John 5:11]. . . . So he gives it unto them, he living by the Father, [. . .] they live by him. So that to express it more fully, the Godhead dwells in the human nature of Christ, and is a quickening Spirit to him, and by virtue of our relation to him, having union with him, he quickens us, and never rests till he hath brought us to that union with God, in our measure and proportion that Christ hath. . . . We are said to be quickened with Christ, because the same life that Jesus Christ is quickened with, we are; it is called the 'life of Jesus,' I Cor. 4. [. . .] It is the same life; the same Spirit that quickened him, quickeneth us, Rom. 8:10. [. . .] If we be quickened truly, we live with the same life that Christ did."

Pt. III, p. 76.[3] "Christ is worth all God is worth . . . ; he is heir, and shall have all. And the gospel makes him yours with all his riches [. . .]. Thus the Apostle argues and pleads the evidence of the right a Chris-

2. Ibid., vol. 1, Pt. II, pp. 187–88.
3. Ibid., vol. 1, Pt. III, p. 76.

tian hath to all things, I Cor 3[:22–23], 'all things are yours, and ye are Christ's, and Christ is God's.' God himself can be worth but all things, Christ is worth what God is . . . . And you have as much as Christ hath. [. . .] All things are given to be inherited, Rev. 21:7, by the same; and as sure a title as Christ, Rom. 8:7, we are put into God's will, 'joint heirs with Christ,' . . . . Rom 8:30, 'If he hath given us Christ, shall he not with him give us all things freely.' . . . 'You know,' says the Apostle, II Cor. 8:9, 'the grace of Christ; how when he was rich, he became poor [. . .] for your sakes,' to enrich you. Now what must these riches come to think you, which are laid up for you, whereas Christ was as rich as God himself; [. . .] had as good an estate every whit. Now of all these [. . .] he emptied himself [. . .], left himself not worth one farthing, [. . .] had not a hole to hide himself in, 'made himself of no reputation' [Phil. 2:7], of no account or reckoning, making over all to you; and what must this come to? The riches of God put out to use, to be received with advantage again."

Ibid., Pt. III, p. 114.[4] "In him we are beloved with the same love Christ himself is, John 17:23. 'Thou hast loved them as thou hast loved me'; and therefore v. 27 adds and makes this a further favor granted at his request, 'that they might be where he is.'"

Ibid., p. 190,[5] speaking of our being quickened together with Christ: "do but consider the excellency of this life: it is a greater life than when we were in Adam, infinitely greater; we are quickened with Christ, with the same life that Christ is quickened with. [. . .] John 10:10, 'I am come that ye might have life, and that ye might have it more abundantly.'"

Ibid., pp. 226–28,[6] speaking on those words in Eph. 2[:6], "hath made us sit together in heavenly places in Christ Jesus," says: "The Apostle had used the word 'sit' of Christ, ch. 1:19–20. 'He hath set him at his own right hand in heavenly places.' It noted out there, the advancement of Jesus Christ to that glory and happiness which he hath in heaven, at God's right hand; and it must needs imply as much done for us, only here he leaves out 'at God's right hand,' and the reason you shall see anon. It is as much as to make us partakers of the same kingly state, of all the same pleasures and honors, and power, and glory of this kingdom, which Jesus Christ himself possesseth. The raising up, is but fitting the body with those heavenly properties, such as Jesus Christ had, that he

---

4. Ibid., vol. 1, Pt. III, p. 114.
5. Ibid., vol. 1, Pt. II, p. 190,
6. Ibid., vol. 1, Pt. II, pp. 226–28.

might be fit for the glory and pleasure of heaven [. . .]. Now when he hath put such endowments upon the body at the resurrection, then he placeth them in the midst of that glory, and those pleasures which Christ is in; and look what seats of glory he runs through, they shall run through too, and be partakers of. In a word it is thus: Jesus Christ is King of the other world, and you all shall be nobles of that world, of that kingdom, and sit together with him; even as it is said of Joshua the high priest, in Zech. 3:8. 'Thou, and thy fellows that sit before thee': for so indeed in the great Sanhedrin, in the meetings of the high priest, and the other priests, they sat in a ring, and so they sat all before him, but yet they sat all with him. This is a type, and was a type of Jesus Christ and his fellows, as they are called, Ps. 45, and that in respect of glory, they being partakers of the same kingdom with him. And in that place of Zechary [Zech. 3:8], he saith, that these men that sat before Joshua the high priest, were '*men of wonder*,' or 'men of signs' [. . .]; the word is taken for being types and signs [. . .]; for Joshua, and all those priests that sat before him, were but types of our great high priest that sits in heaven, and of all that sit there with him. . . . So in Luke 22:29, 'I appoint unto you a kingdom, as my Father hath appointed unto me'; and what follows? 'You shall sit on thrones, judging the twelve tribes of Israel.' And [. . .] Rev. 3:21, 'To him that overcometh will I grant to sit with me in my throne, even as I also overcame, and am set down with my Father in his throne.' So as indeed, [. . .] it is all one to be partakers of that kingdom Jesus Christ is advanced unto, to be heirs, and to be co-heirs with him."

Sitting together in heavenly places in Christ "implies first the pleasures of that kingdom. . . . Now it is familiar in the Old Testament, and in the New, [. . .] to express the pleasures of heaven by sitting at a table, to banquet it with the great king that maketh that feast. So in that Luke 22:29, 'That you may eat and drink at my table, in my kingdom.' . . . The poets set forth the pleasures of heaven by nectar and ambrosia, which was but an imitation of the Jewish and Scripture language. The same our Savior [. . .] useth in the New Testament, Matt. 26:29 [. . .], 'I will not henceforth drink of this fruit of the vine, till I drink it new with you in my Father's kingdom.' . . . We need not have recourse for the interpreting of that place, to his drinking with his disciples after his resurrection; for it is clearly meant of his drinking with them in heaven, after he hath delivered up the KINGDOM TO GOD THE FATHER; for we shall sit in heaven then, and enjoy this new wine, which is the Holy Ghost filling us with the Godhead, that is, filling us with the pleasures and blessedness that is in God himself. Here then is one thing that sitting in heavenly places doth imply, it is enjoying the same pleasure and happiness that our Lord and Savior Jesus Christ himself doth.

"Secondly, it implies not sitting only, as at a table, but it imports also the honor and power of that kingdom; that we are all fellow nobles with Jesus Christ [...]. Luke 22:30, 'You shall sit on thrones, judging the twelve tribes of Israel'; Rev. 3[:21], 'I will grant them to sit with me on my throne.'"

Ibid., p. 247.[7] "All that God will bestow upon us in heaven, it shall be out of the same kindness which he beareth to Jesus Christ himself. He will use you kindly when you come thither. Do but think how kindly he used his Son [...] when he said, 'Sit here, till I make thine enemies thy footstool': why, the same kindness he bears to Christ, he bears to us, and out of that kindness he bears to Christ he will entertain us there forevermore, and heartily and freely spend his utmost riches upon us [...]. Here he shows that it is the same kindness; the same kindness wherewith he embraced Jesus Christ as the head, he embraceth the whole body also, and out of that kindness will entertain them everlastingly, as he hath done Jesus Christ. As we and Christ make but one body, so God's love to Christ and us is but one love: there is one Father, one Spirit, and one love, and indeed one Christ; for both body and head make but one Christ. I need not stand upon this, you have it in John 17:23. 'Thou hast loved them, as thou hast loved me'; [and] v. 22, 'The glory which thou gavest me, have I given them.' And what can be said more to show us what great glory that in heaven will be, whenas Jesus Christ is not only an example and pattern of it, but when it proceeds out of the same kindness, that God's heart is set upon towards Jesus Christ himself?"

Ibid., Pt. III, p. 56,[8] "When Adam was alone, before God made the woman, he blessed Adam, and in him blessed her afterwards to be made. This you may find, [in] Gen. 2:26–27. He gave all the world to Adam, and in giving it to him he gave it to his wife, and to his seed that should come of her. So was it here, when Jesus Christ and God were alone in heaven, before the world was, he undertaking to be an husband, God considering the church in him, 'He did bless us with all spiritual blessings in heavenly places in him'; he gave all to Christ, and in Christ gave all to her, and to all her seed, and to all that should come of her. 'All is yours,' saith the Apostle, 'because ye are Christ's, and Christ is God's,' I Cor. 3[:23]."

---

7. Ibid., vol. 1, Pt. II, p. 247.

8. Goodwin, *Thirteen Sermons Preached on Diverse Texts of Scripture, upon Several Occasions,* in *Works,* vol. 1, Pt. III, p. 56. The quotation that follows is taken from a sermon Goodwin preached on Eph. 5:30–32.

1275. That GLORY OF GOD that is the END OF GOD'S WORKS is not only [a] MANIFESTATION OF HIS EXCELLENCY but [a] COMMUNICATION OF HIS HAPPINESS. Goodwin's *Works*, vol. 1, Pt. II, p. 246,[9] on those words, Eph. 2:7, "That . . . he might show the exceeding riches of his grace in his kindness towards [us] in Christ Jesus": "It implies, that God [. . .] will rejoice over you in glorifying of you: it imports that he will not do it merely to show his riches, as Ahasuerus made a feast, and invited all his nobles, to show the riches of his glorious kingdom; God indeed will bring us to heaven, and show the exceeding riches of his grace, and that is the chiefest end he aims at: but now Ahasuerus, he did not do this in kindness, [. . .] but God, as he will there show forth the exceeding riches of his grace, for the glorifying of it, so he will do it in all the sweetness and kindness that your souls can desire or expect."

Ibid., p. 250.[1] "It hath been questioned by some, whether [. . .] the first moving cause to move God to go forth to save men, was the manifesting his own glory, or his kindness and love to men which he was pleased to take up towards them? I have heard it argued with much appearance of strength, that however God indeed in the way of saving men, carries it as becomes God, so as his own glory and grace shall have the preeminence; yet that which first moved him, that which did give the occasion to him, to go forth in the manifestation of himself, which else he needed not, was rather kindness to us, than his own glory: yet so, as if he resolved out of kindness and love to us to manifest himself at all, he would do it like God, and he would show forth the exceeding riches of his grace, as that that alone should be magnified. Now the truth is, this text (Eph. 2:7) compounds the business, and doth tell us plainly and truly, that the chief end is that God should glorify his own grace, [. . .] it puts the chief and original end upon the showing forth the exceeding riches of his grace; yet so, as he hath attempered and conjoined therewith the greatest kindness, the greatest loving affection, for the way of manifesting of it, so as in the way of carrying it, it shall appear it is not simply to glorify himself, but out of kindness towards us: he puts that in, as that which shall run along with all the manifestation of his own glory. And therefore now he makes in the fourth verse, mercy and great love to us, to be as well the fountain and foundation of our salvations, as the manifestation of the riches of his grace here."

9. In what follows, JE is actually quoting again from Goodwin's *Exposition on Ephesians*, in Goodwin's *Works*, vol. 1, Pt. II, p. 246.
1. JE took the following quotation from ibid., vol. 1, Pt. II, pp. 250–51.

Ibid., p. 253.[2] Because "the chief and utmost thing" that God desireth "is the manifestation of the riches of his grace, it argues [. . .], that his end of manifesting himself, was not wholly for himself, but to commu-nicate unto others; why? Because grace is wholly communicative; there can be no other interpretation of 'showing riches of grace,' but to do good unto others. If he had said, that the supreme end had been the manifestation of his power and wisdom, it might have imported some-thing he would have gotten from the creature, not by communicating anything unto them, but manifesting these upon them: he could have shown his power and wisdom upon them, as he hath done upon men he hath cast into hell, and yet communicated no blessedness to them. No, saith God, my highest and chiefest end is not so much to get anything from you, but to show forth the riches of my grace towards you. That look as faith, which is the highest grace in us, it is merely a receiving grace from God: so take grace, which is the chief thing God would exalt, what is it from God? A mere bestowing, communicating property and at-tribute; it imports nothing else but a communication unto us. It is well therefore for us, that God hath made that to be the highest end of our salvation in himself, when he will aim at himself too, to be that which shall communicate all to us; it is (saith the text) to 'show forth the riches of his grace.'"

Ibid., Pt. III, p. 63.[3] "Our all-wise and infinitely blessed Lord who had from everlasting riches of glorious perfections [. . .], which though he himself knew and was infinitely blessed in the knowledge of them, though no saint or angel had ever been, or ever knew them, yet all these his glorious perfections being crowned with goodness, hath made him willing to make known what riches of glory were in him unto some crea-tures which yet were in Christ, his goodness moved him to it, for *bonum est sui communicativum*, and it is the nature of perfection also to be *man-ifestativum sui*,[4] and that not because any perfection is added to it when made known, [. . .] but that they might perfect others: this set him upon some ways to make known his riches, and his glory, to some that should be made happy by it, and to that end he would have saints, his saints as being beloved of him, unto whom he might as it were unbosom himself and display all the riches of glory that are in him, into whose laps he

---

2. JE took the following quotation from ibid., vol. 1, Pt. II, pp. 253–54.

3. JE took the following quotation from Goodwin's "The Glory of the Gospel. A Sermon on Col. 1: 26–27," in *Thirteen Sermons, Works,* vol. 1, Pt. III, p. 63.

4. The first Latin phrase in this sentence translates, "the sharing of oneself is good," and the second, "making oneself known."

might, withal, pour out all his riches, that they might see his glory, and be glorified in seeing of it, John 17:3, 24." See [No.] 1277[a].

1276. ANGELS IGNORANT OF THE MYSTERY OF THE GOSPEL TILL CHRIST'S COMING. Dr. Goodwin's *Works,* vol. 1, Pt. III, p. 64.[5] On Col. 1:26–27, "Even the mystery which hath been hid from ages and generations, but now is made manifest to his saints. To whom God would make known what is the riches of the glory of this mystery, among the Gentiles, which is Christ in you the hope of glory," the Doctor says: "this doctrine of the gospel [. . .] he kept hid and close in his own breast; not a creature knew it, no not the angels who were his nearest courtiers, and dearest favorites; it lay hid in God, Eph. 3:9, even hid from them, v. 10. A mystery which when it should be revealed should amaze the world, put the angels to school again, as if they had known nothing in comparison of this, wherein they should know over again all those glorious riches which are in God, and that more perfectly and fully than ever yet. And so after they had a little studied the catechism and compendium, there should [. . .] come out a large volume, a new system of the riches of the glory of God, the mystery of Christ in the text, which is the last edition also, [. . .] now set out, enlarged, perfected, wherein the large inventory of God's glorious perfections is more fully set down, [. . .] with additions."

1277[a]. See 1275. GLORY OF GOD THE END OF HIS WORKS. Dr. Goodwin observes (vol. 1 of his *Works,* Pt. II, p. 166)[6] that riches of grace are called RICHES OF GLORY in Scripture. "The Scripture speaks of riches of glory, Eph. 3:16. 'That he would grant you according to the riches of his glory.' Yet eminently mercy is there intended; for it is that which God bestows, and which the Apostle there prayeth for. And he calls his mercy there his glory, as elsewhere he doth, as being the most eminent excellency in God. . . . That in Rom. 9:22, and v. 23 compared, is observable; in v. 22, where the Apostle speaks of God's making known the power of his wrath, saith he, 'God willing to show his wrath, and make his power known.' But in v. 23, when he comes to speak of mercy, he saith, 'that he might make known the riches of his glory . . . upon the vessels of mercy.'" There are many other passages in that volume to the like purpose.

5. Goodwin, "The Glory of the Gospel," in *Works,* vol. 1, Pt. III, p. 64.
6. Goodwin's *Exposition on Ephesians,* in *Works,* vol. 1, Pt. 2, p. 166.

1277[b]. LORD'S DAY. This that follows is taken from an extract of M. de Voltaire's *History of Europe, with a Preliminary View of the Oriental Empires,*[7] in the *Monthly Review* of March 1754, Article 23, p. 201, speaking of the Chinese: "And what is most worthy of observation is, that [from] time immemorial they have divided their months into weeks of seven days."

1278. INCARNATION. THE ADVANTAGE WITH THE GLORY OF GOD APPEARING TO US IN THE PERSON OF CHRIST, GOD-MAN. Dr. Goodwin's *Works,* vol. 1, Pt. III, p. 66.[8] Christ "is the Son of God, [. . .] and therefore the express image and brightness of his Father's glory. . . . But this image, you will say is too bright for us to behold it shining in his strength, we being as unable to behold it in him, as we were to see his Father himself, who dwells in light inaccessible. . . . Therefore that yet we may see it as nigh and as fully and to the utmost that creatures could; this Godhead dwells bodily in the human nature, and so shining through the lanthorn of his flesh we might behold it: his human nature and divine make up but one person, and being so, are united together in the nighest[9] kind of union that God can be to a creature, and the nearest and fullest communications always follow upon the nearest union. To him therefore as man are communicated these riches of glory that are in the Godhead as nearly and fully as was possible unto a creature; and being thus communicated, must needs shine forth in him to us to the utmost that they ever could unto creatures. And therefore more clearly than if millions of [. . .] worlds had been created every day on purpose to reveal God to us. God having stamped upon his Son all his glory, that we might see the glory of God in the face of Jesus Christ, II Cor. 4:6."

1279. JUSTIFICATION. NATURAL FITNESS OF FAITH. Dr. Goodwin, vol. 1 of his *Works,* Pt. II, p. 298.[1] "Now if [. . .] the right to salvation, be an entire gift that is given at a lump, then there was no grace that was so fit in the heart of man to answer this gift, as faith. For faith is a mere receiver."

---

7. Possibly Voltaire's *General History and State of Europe* or *Memnon: Histoire Orientale* (Paris, 1747)

8. Goodwin's "The Glory of the Gospel," in *Thirteen Sermons, Works,* vol. 1, pt. III, p. 66.

9. The remainder of this sentence is obscured by MS damage; reading taken from Andover copy.

1. JE took the following quotation from Goodwin's *Exposition on Ephesians,* in *Works,* vol. 1, pt. II, p. 298.

1280. JUSTIFICATION.[2] The peculiar concern of FAITH is not that of being the CONDITION of salvation in the promises, for [it] is the Christian's "work and labor of love." These things are "things that accompany salvation" as the condition of the promises of it, so that by God's righteousness and faithfulness [. . .] obtained to bestowment [. . .]. See Heb. [6:9].

1281. HADES. SOULS OF SAINTS rewarded before the RESURRECTION. SAINTS IN HEAVEN have communion in the prosperity of the CHURCH ON EARTH. There are three things very manifest from Heb. 6:12, "That ye be not slothful, but followers of them who through faith and patience inherit the promises."

1. That the souls of the saints do go to a state of rewards and glorious happiness before the RESURRECTION; that although the resurrection be indeed the proper time of their reward, and their happiness before be small in comparison of what it will be afterwards, yet that they are received to such a degree of happiness before that they may be said to be in possession of the promises of the covenant of grace.

Those whom the Apostle has reference to when he speaks of them that now inherit the promises are the Old Testament saints, and particularly the patriarchs, as appears by the next words, where the Apostle [instances][3] in Abraham and [the . . .][4] promise made to him, and of his patiently enduring and then obtaining the promise. Again, 'tis manifest the things promised to Abraham which the Apostle speaks of were things which were not fulfilled till after his death. And 'tis manifest by what the Apostle expressly declares in this epistle that he supposed that Abraham and the other patriarchs did not obtain the promises while in this life (ch. 11:13). Speaking there of these patriarchs in particular, he says "These all died in faith, not having received the promises."

But here he speaks of them as now inheriting the promises. The word, as 'tis used everywhere in the New Testament, implies actual possession of the inheritance. And so, as 'tis used in the Septuagint, it generally sig-

2. Worn out margins have rendered much of this entry undecipherable, and there is no copy in the Andover transcript; the following is a conservative estimate of the contents of the entry, which appears to have been written in reference to Heb. 6:9 ff. Fortunately, No. 1281 is a continuation of JE's commentary on this pericope.

3. In the MS, this word is virtually illegible. Dwight (*8*, 600) transcribed the word "instances," a plausible rendering.

4. At this point, the text in the MS (at the bottom of a frayed MS page) is virtually illegible. Dwight (*8*, 600) reads "in Abraham and the promises made to him," but the phrase in the original was clearly longer.

nifies the actual possessing of an inheritance, lot, estate or portion. And that a being now in actual possession of the promised happiness is what the Apostle means in this place is beyond dispute, by what he says, as further explaining himself, in the words immediately following, where he says that Abraham, "after he had patiently endured, obtained the promise." He not only has the right of an heir to promise, which he had while he lived, but he actually obtained it, though he died not having received the promise.

And that we should suppose this to be the meaning of the Apostle is agreeable to what he says, ch. 10:36, "For ye have need of patience, that, after ye have done the will of God, ye might receive the promise"; and that, when he speaks here of Abraham's having obtained the promise after patiently enduring, [he] don't mean only in a figurative sense, viz. that the promise of multiplying his natural posterity was fulfilled after his death, though he was dead and his soul asleep, knowing nothing of the matter. For the word is in the present tense: "inherit the promises." Not only did obtain them, but continue still to possess and enjoy them, though Abraham's natural seed had been greatly diminished, and the promised land at that time under the dominion of the heathen, and the greater part of the people at that time broken off by unbelief and rejected from being God's people, and their city and land and bulk of the nation on the borders of the most dreadful destruction and desolation that ever befell any people.

2. If we compare this with what the Apostle says elsewhere in this epistle, 'tis manifest that the saints he speaks of inherit the promises in heaven, and not in any other place, in the bowels of the earth or elsewhere, called HADES. For 'tis evident that the promised inheritance, which they looked for and sought after—and the promises of which they by faith were persuaded of and embraced, and the promises of which drew their hearts off from this world—was in heaven. This is manifest by ch. 11:13–16, "These all died in faith, not having received the promises, but having seen them afar off, were persuaded of them, and embraced them, and confessed that they were strangers and pilgrims on the earth. For they that say such things declare plainly that they seek a country. And truly, if they had been mindful of that country from whence they came out, they might have had opportunity to have returned. But now they desire a better country, that is, an heavenly: wherefore God is not ashamed to be called their God: for he hath prepared for them a city." And the heavenly inheritance in the heavenly Canaan, or land of rest, which Christ has entered into, is that which the Apostle all along in this epistle

speaks of as the great subject matter of God's promises, which the saints obtain through faith and patience (ch. 3:11, 14; and ch. 4:1, 3, 9–11; ch. 8:6; and 9:15; and 10:34; and 12:1–2, 16 to the end).

3. Another thing which may be strongly argued from this is that the happiness of the SEPARATE SOULS of saints in heaven consists very much in beholding the works of God relating to man's redemption wrought here below, and the steps of infinite grace, wisdom, holiness and power in establishing and building up the CHURCH OF GOD ON EARTH. For what was that promise which the Apostle here has special reference to and expressly speaks of? That Abraham obtained after he had patiently endured, which promise God confirmed with an oath, and that we Christians and all the heirs of the promise partake with Abraham in, and in the promises of which to [be] greatly confirmed we have strong consolation and good hope. The Apostle tells us, vv. 13–14, "For when God made promise to Abraham, because he could swear by no greater, he sware by himself, saying, Surely blessing I will bless thee, and multiplying I will multiply thee." This promise is chiefly fulfilled in the great increase of the church of God by the Messiah, and particularly in the calling of the Gentiles, pursuant to the promise made to Abraham that in his seed all the families of the earth should be blessed (Rom. 4:11, 13, 16–17; Heb. 11:12).

When the Apostle speaks of their inheriting the promises, he seems to have a special respect to the glorious accomplishment of the great promises made to the patriarchs concerning their seed now in these days of the gospel; as is greatly confirmed by ch. 11:39–40, "And these all, having obtained a good report through faith, received not the promise: God having provided some better thing for us, that they without us should not be made perfect," plainly signifying that they received not the promise in their lifetime, the promise having respect to that better thing that was to be accomplished in that age in which the Apostle and those he wrote to lived, and that the promise they relied upon was not completed, and their faith and hope in the promise not crowned till they saw this better thing accomplished. Rev. 14:13, "they rest from their labors; and their works do follow them" ("Follow with them," μετ'αὐτῶν, not to come many thousand years after them, as Mr. Baxter observes). Doddridge on Rev. 14:13.[5]

---

5. JE is citing Richard Baxter as quoted in Philip Doddridge, *Family Expositor: Or a Paraphrase and Version of the New Testament* (6 vols. London, 1739–56), 6, 541, n. h.

1282. The glory of heaven advanced at CHRIST'S ASCENSION. "Although I have no apprehension of the *Limbus Patrum* fancied by the Papists, yet I think the fathers that died under the old testament had a nearer admission into the presence of God, upon the ascension of Christ, than what they enjoyed before. They were in heaven before, the sanctuary of God; but were not admitted within the veil, into the most holy place, where all the counsels of God in Christ are displayed and represented. There was no entrance before either as to grace or glory within the veil, Heb. 9:8. For as I said, within the veil are all the counsels of God in Christ laid open, as they were typed in the holy place. This none could or were to behold, before his own entrance thither. Wherefore he was their forerunner also." Dr. Owen on Heb. 6:20, p. 178.[6]

1283. OLD TESTAMENT SAINTS SAVED BY CHRIST. It is manifest that all that ever obtained the pardon of their sins, from the foundation of the world till Christ came (if any at all were pardoned), obtained forgiveness through the sacrifice of Christ, by Heb. 9:26, "For then must he often have suffered since the foundation of the world: but now once in the end of the world hath he appeared to put away sin by the sacrifice of himself" (see Owen on the place, p. 459d, c.).[7] V. 28, "Christ was once offered to bear the sin of many." And the next verses, ch. 10:1–4, "For the law having a shadow of good things to come, and not the very image of the things, can never with those sacrifices which they offered [. . .] make the comers thereunto perfect. For then would they not have ceased to be offered? because that the worshippers once purged should have had no more conscience of sins. But in these sacrifices there is a remembrance again made of sins every year. For it is not possible that the blood of bulls and of goats should take away sins." And vv. 10–11, "By the which will we are sanctified through the offering of the body of Jesus Christ once and for all. And every priest standeth daily ministering and offering often times the same sacrifices, which can never take away sins." And many other places there are in this epistle to the like purpose. Add to

6. The quotation is from John Owen, *A Continuation of the Exposition of the Epistle of Paul the Apostle to the Hebrews* (London, 1680), p. 178, which is part of Owen's four-volume commentary entitled *Exercitations on the Epistle to the Hebrews* (London, 1668–84).

7. The reference is to Owen, *A Continuation of the Exposition of the Epistle of Paul the Apostle to the Hebrews*, p. 459, where Owen argues that those who "had their sins expiated, pardoned, and were eternally saved" before the time of Jesus were redeemed "by virtue of the sacrifice or one offering of Christ."

this that the Apostle says, "without the shedding of blood there is no remission" [Heb. 9:22]).[8]

'Tis manifest that some were pardoned through Christ before he was offered, as he to whom Christ said, "Son, be of good cheer; thy sins are forgiven thee" [Matt. 9:2], and others. And Christ's disciples evidently were in a state of pardon and acceptance with God before Christ's death, and yet Christ, when he institutes the Lord's Supper, speaks of his blood as that which was shed for the remission of their sins (compare Luke 22:19–20 and Matt. 26:28). Christ tells his disciples that, if he washed them not, they had no part with him, and tells them that they were clean, excepting Judas (John 13:8, 10–11). Christ declares himself their friend, and teaches 'em to call his Father their Father, and declares that the Father had received him already to favor, and was ready to answer their prayers because they had loved him and believed in him, and tells 'em that he gives 'em his peace, etc. Christ says, John 5:24, that he that believed on him should not come into condemnation, but had eternal life, and was passed from death to life; and, ch. 3:18, that he that believed on him was not condemned. See John 6:4 to the end.

1284. DEATH ETERNAL, NOT ETERNAL ANNIHILATION. 'Tis manifest that God's design in punishing his enemies is in part to convince them of his greatness, majesty, and to make 'em know their folly in despising him, as well as to make his glory and majesty visible to others, even to the whole universe. Ex. 9:14–17. See Ps. 50:21.

1285. CHRIST'S MIRACLES. The curing of the leprosy was a special manifestation of the power. For, as is observed in *Synopsis*,[9] the leprosy which was among the Jews seems to be no disease that came by any natural means, but to [be] a special plague sent by God, as was the leprosy of a garment and of an house, and, therefore, was not to be removed but by the same hand that sent it.

1286. CHRIST'S MIRACLES. God was very jealous for his own honor with respect to the miracles that were wrought by the prophets in his name, that his power should be acknowledged in the miracle, and all the glory ascribed to him and none assumed by the instrument. Therefore,

8. The last sentence is a later addition.
9. See, for example, Poole's notes on the leprosy of Moses (Ex. 4: 6–8), Miriam (Num. 12: 10–15), Naaman the Syrian (II Kgs. 5), and Uzziah (II Chron. 26:16–21), in *Synopsis Criticorum, I*, Pt. I, cols. 331, 659–60, and *I*, Pt. II, cols. 614–21, 857–58.

God was so provoked with Moses and Aaron, because they sanctified him not as they ought to have done in bringing water out of the rock, that he refused on this account to suffer them to enter into the promised land (Num. 20:11–12). And, therefore, if Jesus had been an impostor, it is altogether incredible that he would have so countenanced and in such a degree winked at Jesus, his working miracles in his own name, and as by his own power, claiming the power to work the same works that the Father wrought, and so making himself equal to God, as the Jews charge him, John 5:17–23.

1287. PROPHECIES respecting diverse events. The Spirit of Christ, which was in the prophets, spake in the same manner with Christ himself when he was on earth. Christ often, when he was speaking of something that was a type of some spiritual thing, or when some typical thing was spoken of to him, in his speech would[1] pass directly and immediately from the type to the antitype, so that, while [he] seemed to be speaking of the image, he indeed meant the thing represented by it.

Thus when Christ was in the temple at Jerusalem, and had been speaking of that temple, he said, "Destroy this temple, and in three days I will raise it up," speaking of the temple of his body, of which the temple at Jerusalem was a type (John 2:19 ff.). So when Christ was washing the disciples' feet, and Peter says unto him, Lord, "Thou shalt never wash my feet," Christ replies, "If I wash thee not, thou hast no part with me." What was spoken of at first was that external washing which Christ intended as a sign of a spiritual washing. Peter speaks of this. And Christ in his reply seems to speak from this, but indeed in his real intention passes from that, and leaves that which was the sign, and speaks of that spiritual washing, which was the thing signified (John 13:8). So when he delivers the cup to the disciples the night wherein he was betrayed, he tells his disciples that he would no more drink of that fruit of the vine until he should drink it new with them in his heavenly Father's kingdom. He had been speaking of that fruit, of that wine, that was in that cup, and seemed to be speaking of it still, but indeed passes immediately from that and means the spiritual and glorious blessings signified by it [Matt. 26:29, Mark 14:25, Luke 22:18].

'Tis often the manner of inspired persons, in prophecies and divine songs uttered more immediately on occasion of, or with respect to, some lesser mercy and benefit, of a more private nature, as it [were] to leave

---

1. MS: "to."

that and insist chiefly on some infinitely greater and more extensive work of God's power and grace that the other is but a shadow of. We have a very clear instance of this in the song of Hannah (I Sam. 2).

1288. CHRIST'S MIRACLES. What was wrought with respect to Nebuchadnezzar when he was driven from men, became like a wild beast so that no man could confine or tame him, and afterwards restoring him to his right mind, is represented as a very great miracle, a divine work, remarkably demonstrating the infinite and uncontrollable power of God, and his supreme and most absolute dominion of him whose work this was, and was wrought for that end; as manifest by Dan. 4:2–3, "I thought fit to show the signs and wonders that the Most High hath wrought towards me. How great are his signs! and how mighty are his wonders! his kingdom is an everlasting kingdom, and his dominion is from generation to generation." V. 17, "This matter is by the decree of the watchers, and the demand by the word of the holy ones: to the intent that the living might know that the Most High ruleth in the kingdom of men, and giveth it to whomsoever he will." To the like purpose, vv. 25–26. Vv. 34–35, "And at the end of the days I Nebuchadnezzar lift up mine eyes unto heaven, and mine understanding returned unto me, and I blessed the Most High, and I praised and honored him that liveth forever and ever, whose dominion is an everlasting dominion, and his kingdom is from generation to generation: and all the inhabitants of the earth are reputed as nothing: and he doth according to his will in the army of heaven, and among the inhabitants of the earth: and none can stay his hand, or say unto him, What dost thou." V. 37, "Now I Nebuchadnezzar praise and extol and honor the king of heaven, all whose works are truth, and his ways judgment: and those that walk in pride he is able to abase."

But if this work wrought on Nebuchadnezzar was so great a miracle, so evidently divine, and so clearly demonstrating the divinity of the Author of it, and his infinite power, supreme dominion, then this is a clear proof that the miracle that Christ wrought on the poor Gadarene was a divine work, and a sufficient evidence of the divinity and the infinite power and supreme and most absolute power of Jesus who wrought it. He was no less wild and untamable than Nebuchadnezzar. Matt. 8[:28], he "was exceeding fierce, so that no man might pass by that way." Mark 5:3–5, "no man could bind him, no, not with chains: because that he had been often bound with fetters and chains, and the chains had been plucked asunder by him, and the fetters broken in pieces: neither could any man tame him. And always, night and day, he was in the mountains, and in the tombs, crying, and cutting himself with stones." Luke 8:27, he "ware no clothes, neither abode in any house." This man Christ restored perfectly, as of his own power and authority. The devils, the possessed, behave as sensible that they are under his power. They speak to him as one that has power to expel them, to confine, punish and torment them. They fall down before him as before the Son of God most high, beseeching him not to torment them and not to command them to go out into the deep, but to suffer them to enter into the herd of swine. And Christ commanded the devil, saying, "Come out of the man, thou unclean spirit" (Mark 5:8, Luke 8:29). But the man who had been possessed of the devils was perfectly delivered and sat at Jesus' feet, "clothed, and in his right mind" (Luke 8:35).

1289. FUTURE STATE. "Never could the boldest Epicurean bring the lightest appearance of argument against the possibility of such a state, nor was there ever anything tolerable advanced against its probability. We have no records of any nation which did not entertain this opinion. Men of reflection in all ages, have found at least probable arguments for it; and the vulgar have been prone to believe it, without any other argument than their natural notions of justice in the administration of the world. [. . .] This opinion is interwoven with all religions." Hutcheson on the *Passions*, 3rd ed., p. 190.[2]

1290. CHRISTIAN RELIGION. It strongly argues that, when God gave the OLD TESTAMENT, he intended some further and far more glorious revelation of his mind and will that, in the Old Testament, are so many hints of an another world and a future eternal state of rewards and punishments, and yet that these things are nowhere spoken more plainly and insisted upon more fully, particularly and didactically. For if there be such a state, doubtless the things of it are infinitely greater than the things of the present state, and the things that concern it infinitely more important than the things of this world. The things of that future, eternal state must be the grand things of all, to which the religious concerns of this life must all be subordinate, and in comparison of which temporal things are nothing. This argues that a then-future revelation was reserved of, far more plain and clear of the chief things of religion and of the greatest concern between God and man.

2. Francis Hutcheson, *An Essay on the Nature and Conduct of the Passions and Affections, with Illustrations on the Moral Sense* (London, 1728; 3rd ed., 1742), p. 190.

234

1291. LORD'S DAY, SCRIPTURE CONSEQUENCES. I know of no Christian that denies it to be contrary to the revealed will of God, that a man should at once have many wives. Polygamy is universally esteemed gross and most scandalous impiety among Christians. And yet the prohibition is not very plain and express, but is inferred by consequence.

1292. IMMORTALITY OF THE SOUL. See [No.] gg.[3] If all the creatures God has made are to come to an end, and the world itself is to come to an end and so to be as though it had never been, then it will be with all God's glorious, magnificent works, agreeable [to] what is said of the temporal prosperity of the wicked, Job. 20:6–8: though its excellency be never so great, yet it shall perish forever. It shall all fly away as a dream. It shall be chased away as a vision of the night. It shall vanish totally and absolutely, be as though it had not been.

1293a. PROPHECY respecting various events. Concerning that prophecy of Elijah concerning Ahab, I Kgs. 21:19, "Thus saith the Lord, In the place where dogs licked the blood of Naboth shall dogs lick thy blood, even thine," 'tis evident that it looked to two distinct events in which it was accomplished, one of them, that which we have an account of in the next chapter, concerning Ahab himself, after he was shot with an arrow at Ramoth Gilead: "So the king died, and was brought to Samaria; [. . .] and the dogs licked up his blood; and they washed his armor; according to the word of the Lord which he spake" [I Kgs. 22:37–38]. In these last words, "according to the word of the Lord which he spake," is a plain and express reference to the foregoing prophecy. And yet the prophecy had not its principal accomplishment in that event, but in another, which happened in his son's days, agreeable to what God himself said to Elijah, ch. 21:28–29, "And the word of the Lord came to Elijah the Tishbite, saying, Seest thou how Ahab humbleth himself before me? because he humbleth himself before me, I will not bring the evil in his days: but in his son's days I will bring the evil upon his house." And we find the event agreeing hereto in what happened to Jehoram, his son. He met Jehu in the portion of Naboth, and there was slain by him. And when Jehu had shot him through the heart, he said to Bidkar, his captain, "Take up, and cast him in the portion of the field of Naboth the Jezreelite: for remember that, when I and thou rode together after Ahab his father, the Lord laid this burden upon him; Surely I have seen yesterday the blood

3. *Works, 13,* 185.

of Naboth, and the blood of his sons, said the Lord; and I will requite thee in this plat, saith the Lord. Now therefore take and cast him into the plat of ground, according to the word of the Lord" [II Kgs. 9:25–26].

Concerning this prophecy, I would observe the following things:

1. Here is a plain and most undeniable instance of one prophecy respecting two distinct events, and being accomplished (at least in part in each).

2. The prophecy was fulfilled but in part in the first event. Though the dogs licked up the blood of Ahab, yet it don't appear that it was in the portion of Naboth. They licked the blood that was washed out of the chariot in the pool of Samaria.

3. There are some things in the prophecy that seem most suited to one event, and others to the other. The prophecy was that the dogs should lick Ahab's blood. That was most exactly fulfilled in the first event. In the latter it was not the blood of Ahab himself that was shed, but of his son. But there are other things in the prophecy most suited to the last event, as that they should lick Ahab's blood in the portion of Naboth and, what seems to be implied, that his dead body shall be cast out without burial and left to the dogs.

1293b. LORD'S DAY. When God appeared in any place, that place was holy. It was sanctified by God's presence. So Christ sanctified the first day of the week by appearing from time to time on that day. Ps. 111:4, "He hath made his wonderful work to be remembered." Doubtless he has made his most wonderful work of all to be remembered.

1294. HELL TORMENTS, THEIR EXTREMITY: THE JUSTICE OF IT. Hutcheson's *Inquiry Concerning Moral Good and Evil,* Sec. 2, pp. 140–41, 4th ed.: "'Tis true, indeed, all the passions and affections justify themselves; while they continue (as Malebranche expresses it), we generally approve our being thus affected on their occasion, as an innocent disposition, or a just one, and condemn a person who would be otherwise affected on the like occasion. So the sorrowful, the angry, the jealous, the compassionate, approve their several passions on the apprehended occasion." These things may lead us to see the reason why men don't see that sin deserves so great a punishment.[4]

---

4. Francis Hutcheson, *An Inquiry into the Original of Our Ideas of Beauty and Virtue* (4th ed., London, 1738), pp. 140–41.

1295. SATISFACTION OF CHRIST, the need of it. Late philosophers seem ready enough to own the great importance of God's maintaining steady and inviolable the laws of the natural world. It may be worthy to be considered whether it is not of as great or greater importance that the law of God, that great rule of righteousness between the supreme moral governor and his subjects, should be maintained inviolate. See on this subject, MacLaurin's *Discourses,* pp. 324 ff.[5]

1296. NEW HEAVENS AND NEW EARTH, concerning the external part of HEAVEN's being made NEW and far more glorious after the day of judgment. We see a pleasant and most agreeable change in these lower heavens and earth on the coming of the natural sun in the spring. "It is turned," as God says, Job 38:14, "as clay to the seal." The face of the heavens and the earth put on new beauty, are clothed in new garments, appear in raiment of new life, glory and joy. The sun does as it were impart, if I may so say, some of its own life and pleasantness and glory to it, and makes as it were a new heaven and new earth. This probably is a faint resemblance of the alteration made, not only in the spiritual inhabitants of heaven but in the external parts, the material habitation, at Christ's first and second ascension, and solemn entrance into it, especially the second, which shall be after the day of general judgment.

The most perfect and beautiful material parts of this lower creation are, in a sort, animated, having a vegetative life, and these parts we see receive a great alteration and are made unspeakably more excellent and beautiful on the presence of the sun. 'Tis probable that the material parts of that most perfect part of all the creation, the heaven of heavens, the paradise of God, are most resembled by the most perfect parts of this world.

Indeed, in some respects the animated parts of this lower, material world are less perfect than some of those that are not animated, particularly in that they are not so durable. Hence, perhaps some may be ready to imagine that all susceptibleness of change in material things is an imperfection of them, as arguing corruptibleness and a being easily destroyed, as we see grass, leaves, flowers, and plants in general, that so easily put on a new form, are easily destroyed and sooner decay and come

5. John MacLaurin, "An Essay on the Scripture-Doctrine of Divine Grace," in John Gillies, ed., *Sermons and Essays by the Late Reverend Mr. John M'Laurin, One of the Ministers of Glasgow, Published from the Author's Manuscripts* (Glasgow, 1755), pp. 324–26.

to a dissolution than other things that are hardest, most fixed and fur-
thest from any such mutability, as gold, diamonds, etc.

But because we see it to be so here, this is no argument that it is so in
all other worlds. 'Tis no evidence that hardness and fixedness of substance is necessary to durableness.[6] It will certainly be otherwise in
heaven. The glorified bodies of the saints will be exceeding far from this
fixedness. They, as we must suppose, will be most flexible, movable and
agile, most easily susceptive of mutation, both from the acts of the indwelling soul and also from the influence of Christ, who will be as it were
the animating soul of that whole world, the common fountain of all life,
and animating influence, and yet will be immortal and incorruptible.
The fixedness of these inanimate parts of this lower world is really an imperfection, wherein appears most of that chief imperfection of material
things, as below the things which are spiritual, even their inert quality,
or what philosophers call *vis inertiæ*.

This is one way wherein the glorified bodies of the saints will be spiritual bodies. They will in the respects mentioned, viz. their agility and sus-
ceptiveness of the influence of spiritual beings, and particularly the Being of beings, be more like spirits. And 'tis probable that, in some analogy
to this, all the material parts of the heavenly world will be spiritual in being, as it were animated, and susceptible of impressions and happy alterations, and as it were resemblances of the glory and joy of Christ, the
sun of that world.

Though I suppose that the material parts of the highest heavens will
be as animated, yet I intend not that they shall truly [have] what we call
a vegetative life, appearing in a tendency to increase and be productive
of new parts and other things of the same kind in a succession of generations. There may be in the material parts of heaven that which shall
have as great a resemblance of life and spirituality, and much greater,
without this, by its great susceptibleness of influence from the fountain
of life,[7] by its receiving a new form and a new perfection of nature, on
new manifestations of the glory of Christ, and by putting on appearances
of new joy and gladness, to us now inconceivable, of[8] the new joy and
happiness of Christ in his human nature and mystical body.

The appearances of life in the vegetative world here below are in anal-

6. MS: "durable."
7. MS: "fountain of life and influence there."
8. MS: "on."

ogy to the life of the bodies of men, which is by nutrition and appears in increase and generation. But in heaven, the material parts of that paradise of God probably will be in analogy to the more perfect life of the bodies of saints above, which is not in this manner, but by being quickened, exhilarated, beautified and glorified by the presence and influence of Christ, and receiving communications of his beauty and happiness.

Probably the parts even of that material habitation will be susceptible of mutations from the presence of Christ and exhibition of his joy and glory, analogous to these in some most excellent manner, according to laws to us unknown, and above all invention of our wisdom, and quite beyond our present conception. We don't know wherein the beauty of the external parts of the heavenly world [will consist]. We can conceive of nothing more beautiful of an external kind than the beauties of nature here, especially the beauty of the more animated parts of this world. We never could have conceived of these if we had not seen them, and now we can think of nothing beyond them. And, therefore, the highest beauties of art consist in imitation of them. But doubtless there are other kinds of external beauty possible to infinite wisdom, transcendently above these.

We can't conceive of the beauty of the bodies, of the glorified bodies, of the saints, what kind of beauty it will be and how it will differ from the beauty of our bodies of flesh and blood. But as the Apostle intimates in the fifteenth chapter of First Corinthians, it will be something analogous to the difference there is between a seed put into the ground and the flourishing plant that springs from it. The seed appears like an inert, lifeless thing with but little beauty. But the beautiful plant appears like a living thing. Therein is much of its superior excellency: that it appears to have more life, and so [to be] more like a spiritual thing.

The animated parts of this lower world have the greatest beauty because they have most of a resemblance of spiritual beauty, or of beauties of minds. This world that we live in would be a dull place in comparison of what it is if it had nothing growing on it that had life, if it had not, as it were, [been] clothed, as it were with a living garment, though the ground were gold and the hills solid diamonds, sapphires, emeralds, etc. And, as we may conclude, the beauties of the material parts of heaven, that garden of the universe and palace of its infinitely glorious king, will have the highest sort of beauty that material things can have, and therefore will have the greatest resemblance of beauties of mind, and so will be most like animated things.

Therefore, I think it exceeding probable that, as on the ascent of the sun in the spring the face of the earth, being clothed with an animated garment, is changed and made new by the influence and impression the sun makes upon it, and in some respect every morning when the sun rises the sun gives all a new form by its impression, as a seal on the clay—Job 38:12–14, "Hast thou commanded the morning . . . that it might take hold on the ends of the earth . . . ? It is turned as the clay to the seal; and they stand as a garment"—so I think much more may we well suppose the heavenly world is changed on the ascension of that spiritual Sun, whose beams are omnipotent and on whose influence the nature, form and qualities, and the very being of all things, absolutely depends, and of whose power and glory the sun, with all extensive and powerful influence, is but a weak and faint shadow.

The Scriptures from time to time represent as though a most happy and glorious alteration should be made in the face of the world when Christ should reign in his glory, or shall have accomplished the redemption and happiness of his people, as though the heavens and earth should rejoice, the mountains and hills break forth into singing, the fields be joyful and all the trees clapping their hands, the deserts being glad and blossoming as the rose and having the excellency of Carmel and Sharon given to it, because they shall see the glory of the Lord and the excellency of God (Ps. 96:12–13 and 98:8–9; Is. 44:23, and 49:13, and 55:12 and 35:1–2). Doubtless there shall be something that will answer these representations in the highest perfection of all when Christ shall ascend to reign in his greatest glory in heaven, having accomplished the most complete redemption and happiness of all his elect people.

The description given of the New Jerusalem in Rev. 21 leads us to suppose that, after the end of the world, not only the inhabitants of heaven but the place of habitation itself shall, as it were, put on new and beautiful garments, that on that joyful occasion that shall be then it may be prepared as a bride adorned for her husband.

There is in this world no inanimate, durable substance that has so great a resemblance of that susceptibleness of a new form and glory on the approach and appearance of the Sun of righteousness as those bodies that are transparent, such as glass, crystal and various kinds of precious stones, which, when brought into the sun's light, are all as it were transformed, and put on immediately the image of that beauty which is presented, and reflect that glory that shines upon them. We find, in that forementioned description of the New Jerusalem, the various parts of that glorious city compared to such things as these. We are told that the city had the glory of God, and her light was like to a stone most precious, even like a jasper stone, clear as crystal. And the foundations and the gates and the walls are represented as all made of precious stone, and the street of the city as pure gold, and yet like clear glass.

The alteration that was made in heaven at his ascension, after his passion, though it was exceeding great and glorious, yet was but, as it were, the blossoming of the tree. But that which will be at Christ's second ascension, after the day of judgment, will be, as it were, the tree's bringing forth in ripeness and perfection, in all its branches, its lovely, sweet and abundant fruit.

1297. The Necessity of REVEALED RELIGION. Mankind need means of certainty, clearness and satisfaction in things that concern their welfare, in proportion to the importance of those things: whether[9] there be a future state of happiness and misery, what that state is, what the will of God is, what are things which please him, what are those things which will displease him and make us the objects of his anger and hatred, whether there be any reconciliation after we have offended, and how it may be obtained.

We see that God takes care of mankind and all other creatures, that usually they may not be without necessary means, by foresight or something equivalent, of their own preservation and comfortable existence, and that in things of infinitely less importance.

But it is exceeding apparent that, without a revelation, mankind must be forever in the most woeful doubt with respect to these things, and not only these things, but if they are not led by revelation and divine teaching into a right way of using their reason, in arguing from effects to causes, etc., they would forever remain in the most woeful doubt and uncertainty concerning the nature and the very being of God.

This appears not only by the state of the heathen world, wise and unwise, learned and unlearned, polite nations and barbarous, ages after ages, before the light of Christianity came abroad in the world, but also by what appears in these late ages among those that renounced divine revelation, even the wisest and greatest of 'em, and such as are of the strongest and most acute abilities, by the account which Dr. Leland gives of the deistical writers of the last and present age:[1]

---

9. MS: "But whether."

1. John Leland, *An Answer to a Late Book Intituled Christianity as Old as the Creation* (2 vols. London, 1733).

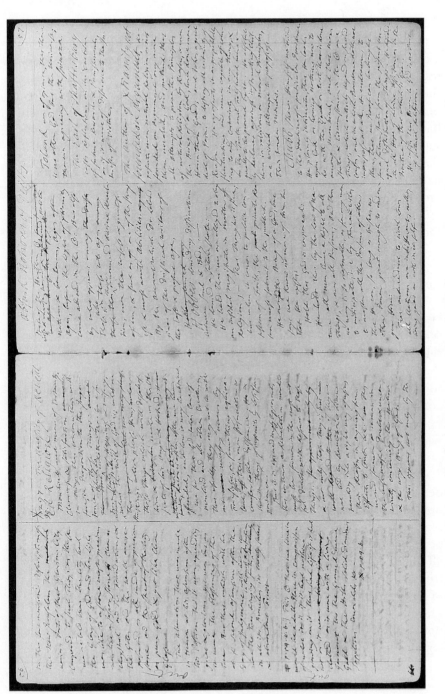

"Miscellanies," Bk. 9, showing the beginning of No. 1297, "The Necessity of Revealed Religion." Courtesy of Beinecke Rare Book and Manuscript Library, Yale University.

HOBBES denied any distinction between soul and body. He denied a future state. He held that we are obliged to obey an infidel magistrate in matters of religion; that thought is free, but when it comes to public confession of faith, the private reason must submit to the public. He owns the being of a God, but says we know no more of him but that he exists; holds that God is corporeal. He held that by the law of nature all men have a right to all things, and over all persons; and that no way is so reasonable as for any man to anticipate, i.e. by force and wiles, to master all the persons of others that he can, so long as he sees no other power great enough to endanger him; that antecedent to civil laws all actions are indifferent, nothing being good or evil in itself.

TOLAND was of opinion that there is no other God but the universe, therein agreeing with Spinoza.

THE EARL OF SHAFTESBURY casts reflections on the doctrine of future rewards and punishments, as if it were of disservice to the interests of virtue.

The AUTHOR OF *CHRISTIANITY NOT FOUNDED ON ARGUMENT*[2] represents even natural religion as not founded on argument any more than revealed, and pretends that all attempts to prove the principles of natural religion by reason, and even the being of a God, have done more harm than good, and takes a great deal of pains to destroy all certainty of reason. He represents it as perpetually fluctuating and never capable of coming to any certainty in anything, and as though truth and falsehood were equally to be proved by it. He absolutely declares against instructing children on religious or moral principles, as a wicked attempt to prepossess their tender minds.

CHUBB shows himself no friend to the doctrine of a particular providence. He plainly intimates that he looks upon God as having nothing now to do with the good or evil that is done among mankind, and that man's state and circumstances in the world are things which entirely depend on second causes, and in which providence doth not interpose at all. He endeavors to show that no proof can be brought for a future state from the present unequal distribution of things. He discardeth all hope of divine assistances in the practice of that which is good. He insists that prayer to God is no part of natural religion. He represents it as absolutely doubtful whether the soul be material or immaterial, or whether it be equally perishable with the body and, if it be, whether it be equally per-

---

2. Henry Dodwell, *Christianity not founded on argument: and the true principle of Gospel-evidence assigned* (London, 1741).

ishable with the body and shall die with it, or shall subsist after the dissolution of the body. These are points, he says, which he cannot possibly determine, because he has nothing to ground such determination upon, and at the same time declares that, if the soul be perishable with the body, there can surely be no place for argument with regard to a future state of existence to men, or a future retribution. It is easy to see that he inclines most to think the soul is material.

He absolutely discards the proof of a future state from the present, unequal distributions of divine providence. He signifies that, if there be a future retribution, 'tis most probable that only those shall be called to an account who have been greatly subservient to the public good or hurt of mankind. And as he supposes but few will be called to an account, so 'tis only for some particular actions, and that they will not be called to an account for foolishly using the names and terms by which the Deity is characterized. The only offense against God is, he thinks, the want of a just sense of his kindness, and the not making a public profession of gratitude to him. And whether this will make a part of the grand inquest he declares himself unable certainly to judge. But he plainly insinuates that he thinks it will not, since among men it has been looked upon to be a mark of greatness of soul to despise and overlook such ingratitude rather than to show any resentment at it. The only thing, therefore, for which he supposes men will be accountable is their injuries and benefits one to another, and these only when done to the public. He afterwards sets himself to show that things would be as well ordered in the world without the expectation of a future judgment as with it, and that the belief of it is no great advantage to society.

MR. HUME declares that the knowledge of the relation of cause and effect is of the highest importance and necessity, and that all our reasonings concerning matter of fact and experience, and concerning the existence of any being, are founded upon it. Yet he sets himself to show that there is no real connection between cause and effect, and that there can be no certain, nor even probable, reasoning from the one to the other. He endeavors to subvert all proofs of a particular providence, of a future state, and of an intelligent cause of the universe. He speaks of the doctrine of the being of God as uncertain and useless. He opposes the arguments from God's distributive justice to a future state, and denies that we have any evidence of any further degrees of justice on God than we see exercised on this present state.

LORD BOLINGBROKE insists that we must not ascribe to God any moral perfections distinct from his physical, especially holiness, justice and goodness; that he has not these attributes according to the idea we conceive of them, nor anything equivalent to those qualities as they are in us; and that to pretend to deduce moral obligations from these attributes, or to talk of imitating God in his moral attributes, is enthusiasm and blasphemy; that God made the world and established the laws of this system at the beginning, but that he doth not now concern himself in the affairs of men or, if he doth, that his providence only extends to collective bodies, but hath no regard to individuals, to their actions or events that befall them; that the soul is not a distinct substance from the body; that the whole man is dissolved at death; that the doctrine of future rewards and punishments is a fiction that hath no real foundation in nature and reason, and that to pretend to argue for future retributions from the apprehended unequal distribution of this present state is absurd and blasphemous; that the sanctions of the law of nature and reason relate not to men individually, but collectively considered; that self-love is the only original spring from which our moral duties and affections flow; that polygamy is founded on the law of nature; that there is no such thing as natural shame or modesty.

He intimates adultery not to be contrary to the law of nature if it can be acted secretly. He seems to think that the law of nature forbids no incest but that of the highest kind, viz. the conjunction between fathers and daughters, sons and mothers. He insists that the ground of the obligation of the law of nature is not its being the will and appointment of God, but its being conducive to human happiness. He holds that the laws of nature in general, and the particulars of moral duty derived from them, are very uncertain, and in which men have always been very apt to mistake and make wrong conclusions.

These things from Dr. Leland's *View of Deistical Writers.*

I think a little sober reflection on these things which appear among the Deists, weighing them together with the nature of things, may convince that a general renunciation of divine revelation, after the nations have enjoyed [it], would soon bring these nations to be more absurd, brutish and monstrous in their notions and practices than the heathens were before the gospel came among them. For,

[1.] Those nations had many things among them derived originally from revelation, by tradition from their ancestors, the ancient founders of nations, or from the Jews, which led 'em to embrace many truths contained in the Scripture. And they valued such tradition. It was not in general their humor to despise such an original of doctrines as to contemn it, as supposing it had its first foundation in divine revelation; but, rather, valued any doctrines highly on this account, and had no notion of setting them aside in order to the drawing everything from the foundation of their own reason. By this means they had a great deal more of truth in matters of religion and morality than ever human reason would have discovered without those helps.[3]

But now the humor of the Deists is to reject everything that they have had from supposed revelation, or any tradition whatsoever, and to receive nothing but what they can clearly see, and draw out the demonstrable evidence of, from the fountain of their own, unassisted reason. And then,

[2.] The heathen by tradition received and believed many great truths of vast importance that were incomprehensible. And it thus was no objection with them against receiving them that they were above their comprehension.

But now 'tis a maxim with the free thinkers that nothing is to [be] believed but what can be comprehended. And this leads 'em to reject all the principles of natural religion (as it is called) as well as revealed. For there is nothing pertaining to any doctrine of natural religion, not any perfection of God, no, nor his very existence as from eternity, but what has many things incomprehensible. And,

3. The heathen of old, in their reasonings, did not proceed in that exceeding haughtiness and dependence on their own, mere, singular understanding, disdaining all dependence on teaching, as our Deists do, which tends to lead 'em to reject almost all important truth out of an affectation of thinking freely and independently and singularly. The heathen, some of them, professed their great need of teaching, and of divine teaching. And,

4. The heathen did not proceed with that enmity against moral and divine truth, having not been so irritated by it. They were willing to pick up some scraps of this truth which came from revelation, which our Deists reject all in the lump.

See a further reason under the next number, viz. No. 1298.

1298. NECESSITY OF REVELATION. If we suppose that God never speaks to or converses at all with mankind, never from the beginning of the world ever said anything to 'em, but has perfectly let 'em alone as to any voluntary, immediate and direct signification of his mind to them, in any respect teaching, commanding, promising, threatening, counseling, or

---

3. On the *prisca theologica*, see "Editor's Introduction," pp. 26–27.

answering: such a notion, if established, would tend exceedingly to atheism. It would naturally tend to suppose that there is no Being that made and governs the world. And if it should nevertheless be supposed that there is some Being that is in some respect the original of all other beings, yet this notion would naturally lead to doubt of his being properly an intelligent, volitive Being, and to doubt of all duties to him implying intercourse, such as prayer, praise, or any address to him, external or internal, or any respect to him at all analogous to that which we exercise towards rulers or friends or any intelligent beings we here see and know. And so it would tend to overthrow every doctrine and duty of natural religion.

Now in this respect Deism has a tendency to a vastly greater degree of error and brutishness with regard to matters of religion and morality than the ancient heathenism. For they had no such notion that the Deity never at all conversed with mankind in these ways mentioned, but received many traditions, rules and laws as supposing they came from God, or the gods, by revelation.

See the preceding number, viz. No. 1297.

1299. CHRISTIAN RELIGION. The outward provision which God makes, through the ages of the world, for the temporal benefit and comfort of mankind, in causing his sun to shine upon them, his rain to descend upon them, and in innumerable other things, is a great argument that God is not an implacable enemy of mankind, in a settled and full determination finally to cast 'em off and never again to admit 'em to favor. For these kind dispensations of heaven have an abundant show and appearance of goodness, kindness and favorableness. They are as so many smiles of heaven on mankind, from which they might justly conceive hope that God was placable and was not averse, and [not] determined[4] to be their everlasting, irreconcilable enemy.

For if this be the case, they are no tokens of goodness, kindness or favor at all. For if their Creator has wholly rejected them and cast them [off], determining never to receive them to favor anymore, these things can do 'em no good. They can be of no significancy to 'em. They are not what they seem. The supposition would imply this horrid blasphemy in it: that these are all as so many delusive and deceitful smiles. They have a show of fatherly care and tenderness, and of a disposition in God to favor to mankind, but imply no such thing, men being indeed reserved for

4. MS: "placable & was ~~in~~ averse not & determined."

nothing but wrath and ruin, without mercy, there being nothing but irreconcilable hatred hid under the disguise of those smiles.

And if God be reconcilable, it will follow that he must make a revelation to mankind, to make known to 'em the terms and method of reconciliation. For God, who is offended, alone can tell us on what terms he is willing to be reconciled, and how he will be at peace with us and receive us to favor.

And there surely is nothing which can be pretended to be any revelation of this kind if the holy Scripture is not.

Obj. That the Scriptures are communicated to but few of mankind, so that, if a revelation of the method of reconciliation be necessary, then a very great part of those that enjoy these external benefits and bounties of divine providence still have no opportunity to obtain reconciliation with God, not having the benefit of that reconciliation. So that, notwithstanding these seeming testimonies of favor and placableness, it is all one to them as if God was irreconcilable. For still, for want of the knowledge of the method of reconciliation, 'tis all one to them as though there were no such method, and as though no reconciliation were possible.

To this I answer:

1. The case of mankind is not just the same as if there were no such thing as reconciliation for the greater part of the world, or as though reconciliation were utterly impossible. For although the circumstances of a great part of the world be such that their reconciliation be very improbable, yet 'tis not utterly impossible. There is a way of reconciliation, and it is publicly known in the world. And God ever ordered things so in the world of mankind, so fixing the bounds[5] of their habitation, together with the circumstances of the revelation that has existed in the world, as have afforded opportunities to the generality of the habitable world that, if their mind has been as much engaged in the search of divine truth as they ought to be, they might have felt after God and found him, and might probably come to an acquaintance with divine revelation.

2. If there have been some parts of mankind, in some ages, for whom it was next to impossible that they should ever come to know that revelation which God has made, yet that hinders not the force of the argument for God's placableness to sinners, and so that there must be in being a revelation of a method of reconciliation.

They[6] may be a proof that [God] intends favor to some of mankind,

---

5. MS: "bonds."
6. I.e. external benefits and bounties of divine providence.

but yet be no proof that he intends that all shall actually have the benefit of his favor. None will deny but that those outward blessings of God's goodness were intended for the temporal benefit of mankind, and yet there are many of mankind that never actually receive any temporal benefit by many of them. None will doubt but that God aims at man's outward good in providing wheat, and other kinds of grain, and grapes, and many other fruits, which the earth produces for men's subsistence and comfort in the world, as also the most useful animals, horses, neat cattle and the like. But yet a very great part of the world were wholly destitute of the most useful of these. All the innumerable nations that dwelt on this American side of the globe were, from age to age till the Americans came hither, wholly destitute of wheat, rye, barley, peas, wine, horses, neat, cattle, sheep, goats, swine, poultry and many other useful animals and fruits, which abounded in the other continent.

And 'tis probable that some of those gifts of nature and providence which are most useful to mankind were what all men were without the benefit of for many ages, as metals, wine, and many things used for food, clothing and habitations. The lodestone, with regard to its polar direction, was doubtless intended for the use of mankind, but yet 'tis but lately that any of 'em have had any benefit of it. Glass is a great gift of providence, and yet but lately bestowed, and so some of the most useful medicines.

And with regard to those things which are most universally useful, some have the benefit of them[7] in vastly lesser degrees than others, as the heat of the sun.

If it should be further OBJECTED that, if it be so that God's true aim in those outward benefits of providence that have the appearances of favor be real favor to mankind, and so that the true happiness of mankind should be the consequence, one would think it should be the effect in all places where those blessings are bestowed: I answer that it will not follow. God may grant those things in all parts of the world which in their main design may evidently be the benefit of mankind, and yet not have that effect in all places where they are given. As the rain is a thing in which the main design of him who orders the being of such a thing as rain in the world is making the earth fruitful, yet it don't follow that he designed this should actually be the effect in all parts of the globe where the rain falls. For it falls on the sea—as well as the dry land—which is more than one half of the globe, but yet there it cannot answer this intention.

7. MS: "it."

1300. CHRISTIAN RELIGION. THE DIVINE LEGATION OF MOSES. "It is an argument that Moses spake and acted not of himself, but as being divinely led and instructed, that the doctrine that he taught so far excelled the doctrine even of the wisest of the heathen. It is not credible that a [man] born and educated in the midst of Egyptian superstition should know and teach those things of himself.

"He clearly taught those things which to the Gentiles appeared as things attended with the greatest uncertainty and perplexity, and which were most remote from their hypotheses. For he shows that the origin of the world was from one God, the creator of heaven and earth, concerning which the Gentiles inquired with great anxiety, but could find where to set their foot.

"The things which he taught concerning God were perfectly agreeable to reason, yet exceeding remote from the notions even of the most learned and polite of other peoples, who taught things concerning God so mean and vile that they were altogether unworthy of the supreme being.

"This is the singular nature of the Jewish doctrine, and a truly divine character: that it wholly tends to God; it everywhere savors of God; it magnifies and exalts God; and in one word, it wholly, in everything that appertains to it, is fitted for and tends to the glory of God. And by this note this doctrine is evidently distinguished from all human doctrines. For in all the doctrines of men you may see them seeking their own glory. You may see that they accommodate the doctrines they deliver to the dispositions and manners of great men, and men in power. But this has entirely respect unto God. God is the scope and end of all things. God is concerned in all things, sees all things, directs all things, works all. All things are directed to his glory alone.

"Who is there that would assert him to be an impostor, who refers everything not to himself, but to God alone?

"And if Moses did not receive his doctrine from God, which way in the world should it come to pass that a people noted for their rude and uncultivated [ways], and despised very much by other nations as remarkably inferior for ingenious arts, politeness of manners, and ignorant of philosophy and sciences, should nevertheless so vastly excel all nations in their notions of divine [things], and alone should have right sentiments in questions of the most sublime and exalted nature?

"And with respect to the laws of Moses, they were by no means formed in such a manner as was to be expected if what Moses aimed at was to found a republic by fraud, and thereby thoroughly to subject the Jewish people to himself. For they that make use of imposture are wont to accommodate themselves to the dispositions of the people, or at least not to militate against those dispositions of theirs that are strongest of all, and which have possessed their minds from their youth by long custom. So Mahomet, when he founded a new religion, he patched it with such precepts as were agreeable to the genius of most people in his time, and was careful to indulge even the carnal affections and passions of men, that the effeminate Asiatics might find such things in the religion he established as might satisfy their lusts.

"But the people of Israel were so propense to idolatry, as abundantly appears from the whole Mosaic history and their other ancient monuments, that it appears to have been next to impossible for him to restrain them from it by the strictest laws and most severe punishments.

"Yet Moses alone, though he himself was educated in idolatry, undertakes so great a work as entirely to banish idolatry from a people so exceedingly given to it, and encompassed round on every side with idolaters. But who can persuade himself that he ever had power to do this of himself, of his own head and by his own power, without any divine direction, command or assistance? If he was an impostor, why did not he indulge the people in that matter, that he might get their favor? Or why did he not at least content himself with changing the idolatry into another form, that he might in some degree gratify the disposition of the Hebrews?

"The other moral precepts of the law of Moses are so formed that they everywhere inculcate the most sincere love and fear of God, and most strictly require every duty towards our neighbor. And not only are fornication and other sins of that kind (which were looked upon as mere trifles among the nations) proscribed by the most severe threatenings, but also all internal concupiscence, which don't so much attempt to break forth into act, is condemned by the most sacred precepts.

"And this law requires even the circumcision of the heart, or an entire extirpation of evil affections, and don't so much as allow any gratification of evil desires, even in the least thing.

"And Moses' laws from the beginning were so perfect that they never needed to be changed for the better, but [were] continued with such wisdom from the beginning, although it was [in] times of the greatest rudeness that they were brought at once to the utmost height of their perfection, which never happens in human laws. And for this reason these laws were never changed, which yet is very frequently wont to happen to all laws merely human.

"All these things do abundantly show that Moses had the character not of an impostor, but of a divine messenger."

These things from Alphonsus Turretinus, as cited by Stapferus in his Polemic Divinity, 2, 696–700.[8] See further, No. 1305.

1301. CHRISTIAN RELIGION. NECESSITY OF REVELATION. "Id [vero] observandum, quod sapientissimi etiam Gentilium nil nisi conjecturas et dubia de Deo rebusque divinis protulerint; ut in re certissima incerti semper feurint; ignorabant quæ scire maxime intererat, dubitabant de rebus summi momenti.

"Ita Cicero doctrinam de divina Existentia ejusque Natura dubiam proponit, dum Lib. I. de Nat. Deorum dicit: 'Cum multaæ res in Philosophia nequaquam satis adhuc explicatæ sunt, tum per dificilis, Brute, quod tu minime ignoras, et perobscura quæstio est, de natura deorum.' Deorum etiam [Existentiam] nonnisi verisimilem statuit; an mundus ab æterno extiterit, an vero creatus fuerit; an detur Providentia, summa semper Philosophorum dissensione certatum esse [. . .]. In doctrina etiam de [Animæ] immortalitate, sine qua tamen vix officiorum Religionis vera dantur incitamenta, anxii hærebant. Unde Socrates, Ethnicorum sapientiorum princeps, in Apologia sua dubium se hærere [haud obscure] innuit, [. . .] Apologiam [suam] hisce [tandem] verbis concludit: Tempus est jam hinc abire; me, ut moriar; vos, ut vitam agatis: Utrum autem sit melius, Dii immortales sciunt, hominum quidem scire arbitror neminem. [. . .] Seneca permulta egregia de hac materia, præcipue in Epistolis suis differit, veritatis tamen convictus minime erat"; where several passages are cited showing his doubt. Stapferus, *Theol. Dogmat.*, pp. 828–29.

"Quoad dependentiam hujus mundi à Deo, ratione Existentiæ, paucissimi ex Gentilibus fuerunt, qui eam agnoscerent . . . vel statuebant, materiam ab æterno extitisse et ex illa à Principio aliquo bono mundum hunc formatum fuisse; aut etiam quoad formam, perpetua rerum revolutione systema hoc universi esse æternum, vel fortuito atomorum concursu hanc rerum Ordinem et nexum ortum esse." Ibid., p. 836.[9]

8. Stapfer, *Institutiones Theologiæ Polemicæ*, 2, 696–700; John Alphonse Turretin was the author of *Dissertatio theologica de excellentia œconomicæ Novi Testamenti supra veterem* (Geneva, 1730). Though JE's usual practice was to copy the Latin of Stapfer's *Institutiones* into his notebooks, in this instance he went to the trouble of translating the material into English.

9. "This should be noted, that even the wisest of the Gentiles produced nothing except conjectures and doubtful musings about God and divine matters, so that in the most sure matter they were always unsure. They were ignorant about what things were the most important to know, they hesitated about matters of utmost concern.

1302. CHRISTIAN RELIGION. NECESSITY OF REVELATION. "Patet, nullam homini, nisi in Dei Bonitate, spem, nullam post naufragium [illud] præter Dei misericordiam superfuisse tabulam. Ut autem secure illi inniteretur, et trepidantem ad quævis minitantis cœli murmura tranquillaret conscientiam, opus fuit, ut non dubiis de ea certior fieret argumentis. Ex insitis menti Ideis illud tantum cognoscere poterat, Deum qua est sapientia et Potentia, gratiam si velit facere posse. At velle, nonnisi ex singulari Dei Revelatione constare poterat. Hærere ergo illum inter spem metumque anxium, necesse erat. Donec Deus, benignæ voluntatis suæ solus idoneus interpres, certum illi ad felicitatem iter patefaceret et fluctibus è tautis hominem, tantisque tenebris, in tam tranquilla, ac tam clara luce locaret." Herm. Alex. Roell. cited by Stapferus in *Theolog. Polem.*, p. 259.[1]

"Thus Cicero puts forth a hesitant doctrine about the existence of the divine and about its nature when he says in the first book of *Concerning the Nature of the Gods:* 'How exceedingly have the objects of philosophy been in no wise satisfactorily explicated heretofore, through difficulty and dullness; accordingly thou art least of all knowledgeable, and very obscure is inquiry of the nature of the gods.' Whether the world existed from eternity, whether it had been created, whether there was providence, had always been debated with great dissension of the philosophers [. . .]. Even in the doctrine about the immortality of the soul, without which nevertheless true incitements of the duties of religion are scarcely given, they were anxiously stuck. Whence Socrates, the prince of the pagan wise men, in his *Apology* admits (by no means obscurely) that he stands doubtful [. . .]. He finishes his defense with these words: 'It is time now to depart. For me to die, for you to live life. But which is better, the immortal gods know; indeed, I think that no human knows.' [. . .] Seneca promulgated very many distinguished remarks about this material, chiefly in his Epistles, but he had by no means been convinced of its truth; where several passages are cited showing his doubt." [. . .]

"As far as the dependency of this world on God, by reason of existence, there were very few Gentiles who were ignorant about it or they . . . decided that matter had existed from eternity and from that matter this world had been formed by some good principle; or even as far as its form, that this system of the universe is eternal by a continuous turning of things or that by a chance concurrence of atoms this order and binding of things arose." Stapfer, *Institutiones Theologiæ Polemicæ*, 2, 828–29, 836.

1. "It is clear, that no hope remained for humankind, unless in the goodness of God, no revelation after that shipwreck beyond the mercy of God. However, in order that man should rest securely on the revelation and quiet his consciousness which was agitated at vague murmurs of the threatening heavens, that revelation needs to be made more certain with unassailable arguments. From the ideas innate to the mind the great fact could be known, that God, wherein is wisdom and power, is able to do graciously if he wishes. But that he wishes could be established only from the unique revelation of God. Therefore, it was necessary that man remained anxiously between hope and fear until God, the sole appropriate interpreter of his good will, should open up for man a sure road to happiness and should place him in such a peace and so clear a light out of such great waves and such great darkness." Herman Alexander Roell (1653–1718), whose "Dissert. de Rel. Rat." Stapfer cites in *Institutiones Theologiæ Polemicæ, 1*, 258–59.

1303. PLANETS, the uncertainty of their being inhabited. That some of the planets are such huge things, so vastly bigger than the globe of the earth, is no certain sign of their being inhabited. This planet we dwell upon may, nevertheless, be as it were elected to infinitely greater and more important purposes. Such an election there is with regard to the seed of plants and animals. Where there is one that is used for the purposes for which they are fitted, to produce a future plant or animal, vast multitudes are, as it were, thrown away in divine providence. Those seeds are as great a work of God, perhaps, as the bodies of Saturn or Jupiter, notwithstanding their vast bulk. The greatness of the bulk is but a shadow of greatness or importance. Nevertheless, they may [be], as it were, rejected and neglected of God, when a far lesser body may be chosen before them, as 'tis with divine election as exercised among mankind. A poor child may be infinitely more made of by God than some mighty potentate that rules over a large empire, though such a prince is like a vast, huge body in comparison with the other. But truly his greatness is but the shadow of greatness.

1304. NECESSITY OF REVELATION. CHRISTIAN RELIGION. The religion that is required of us consists in the disposition and affections of mind we ought to have towards God, and our behavior with respect to him. Therefore, in order to know what is that religion that becomes us, we must know that God is, and what manner of being he is, what perfections he has, and what concern we have with him, or what notice he takes of us, what relation we stand in to him, and what dependence we have upon him.

Not only is it necessary that we should know that God is, and what he is, in order to know what that religion which is our duty is, but also 'tis requisite that we should know those other things mentioned, viz. what concern we have with him, etc. If we have no concern with him, nor he with us, if he has no relation to us and we have no dependence upon him, and he takes no notice of us and concerns himself nothing at all with us, then surely all will allow that the foundation of religion, consisting in the regard of our minds and exercise of our hearts and acts of respect or service towards him, do (at least in a very [great] measure) cease.

Whatever we hear of the excellencies of a person in China, or India, or some distant age, yet if we have no concern with him, nor he with us, no service from us to him is properly our duty. There can be no intercourse, nothing to excite the exercises and services of friendship according to the human nature. There can be no application of mind to the person. Excellencies in such circumstances do but little to draw forth respect and engage the heart. According to the human [nature], such distance and exclusion from all concern is, as to influence on the heart, much like exclusion from reality of existence. As 'tis in the natural and material world, magnitude and quantity of matter attract but little at an immense distance.

The duties proper in creatures one towards another arise from their mutual concern, relations and connections. So it is with respect to our duty to God. Supposing it could be (and were indeed) so that [a] superior being of great excellency were the creator of some other world, at an immense distance from this, and we knew of it and had notice of his being and excellency, but knew he had no manner of concern with this our creation and took no notice of us: in how great a degree should we be without the foundation of religion towards such a being.

And therefore, doubtless, in order to our knowing what that religion is that is our duty towards God, we must know not only that he exists, and what manner of being he is, but also must know the mutual concern he has with us, etc. And therefore it be a matter of great necessity or importance that we should have and exercise that religion that becomes us. 'Tis necessary and of great importance that we should have clear notice of God's being and perfections and our concern with him, or such manifestations and evidences of his being and perfections, and the notice he takes of us, and our relation to him and dependence on him, as is so clear and full as to be sufficient to determine and satisfy our minds. And if God looks upon it a thing of great importance that we should exercise that religion that becomes us, and much insists upon it we should, we may determine that he also looks upon as a thing of great importance that we should have such clear notice of these things.

But we have sufficient evidence that it is of great importance that we should exercise that religion that becomes us, and that our Creator looks upon it to be so, and does greatly insist upon it. It is self-evident that our duty, or that which becomes us, is of importance, for that is what is meant by being of importance, viz. being a thing worthy to be regarded, and the opposite of which is worthy to be avoided. But that which is amiable and the contrary of which is hateful, that is worthy to be regarded and the contrary avoided. But the very notion of a thing becoming of us implies fitness or amiableness, and that the contrary is hateful. And if duty or becoming temper and behavior in general be of importance, then the greatest duties, or those that we are most obliged to, are proportionably of greatest importance.

But that we should have respect to God, who is infinitely the greatest and best of beings, and [whom we] have infinitely the greatest concern with and dependence upon, is the greatest duty, and that which we are under infinitely the greatest obligation to. And as it [is] of so great importance that we should exercise that religion that is our duty, so we must suppose that our Creator looks upon it so, and that 'tis proportionably agreeable to his will; or in other words, it is a thing proportionable, fit and amiable in his eyes that we should do so.

That God has regard to men's doing their duty, and not [being] careless about it, is evident from these considerations:

'Tis evident that God is not negligent of the world that he has made. He has made it for his use and, therefore, doubtless he uses it, which implies that he takes care of it and orders and governs it, that it may be directed to the ends for which he has made it.

If God regards the state of the world, he will especially regard the state of the intelligent part of the world, which is transcendently the most important, and that for which all the rest is evidently made, and without which all the rest is nothing.

God regards the moral state of the intelligent world, as its well-being and preservation depends upon it. Wickedness tends above all things to ruin it, if let alone. It tends to its greatest confusion and disorder, and utter destruction, as a fire that will wholly consume it. And its beauty and excellency above all things, and indeed summarily, consists in [virtue].

We see that God takes care of the well-being, good state, regularity and beauty of those parts of the world that are infinitely of less importance. Therefore, surely he is not careless about these things in the intelligent world, the highest part of the creation, the head of all, that is next to himself. And from what has been said, it is evident that he will not be careless about man's duty to him, or respect to him or to their religion, which is infinitely the most considerable and important part of his duty.

God cannot be indifferent about reasonable creatures' respect to him—whether they love or hate him, whether they are his friends or enemies, whether they bless or curse him, whether they fall in with his design [or] end in creating them and the world or set themselves against it and live in opposition to it—not only as he loves what is beautiful and hates what is hateful, but as he loves himself, loves his own end, seeks what he seeks, and is inclined to what he is inclined to.

'Tis evident that, as God has made man an intelligent creature, capable of knowing his Creator and discerning God's aims in creation (and particularly in creating himself) by seeing the nature and tendency of things, and has made him a volitive and active creature, capable of willingly[2] and actively falling in with his aims and promoting them, so it must be that he has made him to serve him and, consequently, to have respect to him and love him.

See, further, sermon on God's moral government from Ps. 90:6–10.[3]

From these things it must needs be, according to what was before laid down, that God looks upon it as of great importance that men have and exercise that religion that becomes them—and greatly insists upon it. Therefore, it follows from things before observed that he greatly insists upon it that men should exercise that respect to him that is agreeable to his nature and perfections, and his concern with us, the relation he stands in to us, and the dependence we have on him.

Having established these things, I would now proceed further and say that, seeing God so much insists upon it that we should have and exercise that religion towards him that becomes his perfections, and that concern we have with him and dependence we have upon him, we may well conclude that he will not deny mankind the means necessary to render them capable of this, and therefore will not deny them the necessary means of some clear, evident and distinct knowledge, not only of his existence and perfection, but also of the relations he stands in to us, and of the things wherein we are dependent on him, and in general [depend] on him, seeing that (as has been proved) the religion that becomes us towards God depends on these things as their necessary ground, as well as on his existence and perfections.

In order to a proper and necessary foundation and support of the religion founded on God's being, perfections, and on our particular relation to God and dependence on his perfections, 'tis not sufficient that we only have some uncertain conjecture concerning these things, but that we should have clear notice of 'em, and determining, satisfying evidence. Such is the nature of man, that entire friendship and respect does not [obtain] towards an object of an uncertainly conjectured existence and excellency, and that we in a doubtful manner conjecture takes notice of us and has such and such concern with us. And, therefore, 'tis doubtless agreeable to the will of God that mankind should have clear

2. MS: "willings."
3. No sermon on this text is extant.

and full notice of the things forementioned, as it must be his will to afford necessary means for the being of that religion in his creatures towards which becomes them.

If God did not afford necessary means for the exercise and support of that religion which becomes us towards God, then it would follow that he did not take care for the existence and support of that which in his own eyes is most important in the regularity, beauty and order of the world. But from what has been already proved, God does take care of this, and therefore doubtless will give mankind necessary means for the clear, evident and distinct knowledge of the concern he has with them, and their dependence on him, at least in its more important articles. As for instance, we may conclude that he will not deny mankind sufficiently clear and evident knowledge of his concern with them as their Creator and preserver, and the Author of all their outward good things, and as their Judge to recompense their behavior. Or, if there [are] any other relations that God stands in to them of like importance, then doubtless it is the will of God to give like, clear and full evidence of them also.

But now, from these things, I infer that, if there be any such thing as forgiveness of sin, and salvation from sin and its evil consequences, then God has certainly given a revelation to mankind to make this clearly and distinctly known, with the terms, method and means of it. Because if so, these things will follow:

1. That then God sustains a relation entirely new, and distinct from the natural relation of a Creator, preserver, etc., viz. that of a Savior. And we have a new concern of God, and a new dependence on him, entirely distinct from that which is by nature, no less important than that, and which renders a new kind of regard to God, and so a new sort of religion, proper and becoming to be in man, suitable to this new religion and those our new concerns with God, and corresponding therewith.

2. That we cannot have any clear, certain and distinct knowledge of this new relation, etc., any other way than by divine revelation.

I shall show each of these in their order:

1. If there be any forgiveness of the sin we are guilty of, and deliverance from sin and its consequences, then God stands in a new relation to us, even that of a Savior, and we have new concerns with him founded upon it. Which new relation is no less important than that of the Author and preserver of our nature, and the bestower of natural enjoyments; and consequent new regards to God, and new duties founded on this new relation, become us, which are no less important than the duties of natural religion.

That the relation of a Savior from our sin and its consequences is no less important than the other, will appear from the following considerations:

'Tis evident that mankind in general have forsaken and renounced the Author and preserver of their beings, and the fountain of all that pertains to their well-being—i.e. their hearts have forsaken him—in that they don't love God so much as they do other things. Therefore, they have taken away their hearts from God, have dethroned God in their hearts, and have given their hearts to other things, that belong to God, have set up other things in the throne of God. They subject God in their hearts to things that are infinitely mean and worthless, and vile in comparison of God. This is attended unavoidably with enmity to God, as rebelling against a lawful prince and setting up another in his stead is turning enemy to the lawful prince. So men naturally disregard God's glory and supreme dominion. They have truly no sincere consent of heart to it or delight in any such thing, but rather are against it, and have naturally no relish for the infinite, supreme beauty of the divine nature, nor any proper gratitude to him, as the fountain of all the good that belongs to our being. And this certainly is rebellion and revolt, and a renouncing and casting off the Supreme Being as to his infinite excellency and dignity, and as to that supreme dominion of his, founded on that dignity, and the relation of a Creator, preserver and fountain of all good.

Now 'tis pretty manifest that such a forsaking and renouncing the Author of our being and of all good, and thus turning enemy to him, forfeit his favor, and friendship, and the benefit we have from this fountain of good. And that implies that it deserves that we should be totally undone. A casting off the Author of our being deserves plainly that he should cast us off, that he should cause that our being should not be for our good. And that, our being his enemies, deserves that he should be and act as our enemy, and so that he should cause our being to be only for our misery. And if we have deserved these things, then unless we are forgiven, at least in part, these things will come upon us.

From these things it appears that, if we are ever forgiven and restored from this utterly ruined and undone state, it will be as great a thing as our creation, and equivalent to a new creation from nothing, in order to a new preservation and new enjoyment of the benefit of being. So that, hereby, God stands in a new relation to us, even that of a Savior, and we have a new concern with him and dependence upon him, of equal importance with that of our Creator, preserver, etc. And if our misery, that we deserve, be worse than a state of non-existence, as it would be easy to prove that it must be infinitely worse, then this new relation of a Savior is infinitely more important than the other. From whence it follows that new duties arise, new regards towards God, and a new religion becomes us which is [of] no less importance,[4] and which it is of.

And it will further follow from things before shown that it must be agreeable to the word of God that men should have means of clear, full and distinct notice of this new relation that God stands in to us as our Savior, and his concern with us in that matter, and the manner of our dependence on him in that matter—and, consequently, that we have sufficient means for a certain knowledge that God is willing to forgive us, and of the terms on which, and what salvation we may obtain, how far we may be restored to favor, what happiness such sinful creatures may obtain, the way and means of salvation, and the way in which we may obtain an interest in it—in order to know the duties which arise from these things, the regards which become us towards God as our Savior, and the dispositions and affectations and exercises answerable to the concern we have with God in that affair. As in order to the subsistence and support of natural religion, we need clear manifestations of the perfections of God, and clear evidences of our dependence on God in the course of nature and common providence, so in order to the subsisting of the new religion proper to be exercised towards God as our Savior, we need clear manifestation of the work of salvation, and of the manner of the exercise and displays of God's perfections in that work, and our particular dependence on him in that affair.

And therefore, from what has been before observed, 'tis doubtless agreeable to the will of God that we should have such clear manifestations and evidences. And if this can't be without a revelation, then 'tis doubtless the will of God that we should have a revelation, i.e. if there be any such thing as forgiveness and salvation for us. And this is what I would now proceed to show,

2. That we cannot have any certain, clear and distinct knowledge of these things concerning our restoration and salvation without a revelation. 'Tis said by some that the light of nature and reason is sufficient to teach us that a good God stands ready to forgive sinners on their hearty repentance. But I think it plain that our reason only never, never would give us a clear and evident notice of this.

A wise governor, in governing, will not be influenced wholly and only

---

4. MS: "importance & which it is of." The Andover copyist emended it to read "no less importance than natural religion," crossing out the remainder of the sentence.

by goodness and pity. Wisdom, on many accounts and in many cases, may prevent his forgiving offenders. And who could tell in what manner wisdom might influence and determine the Supreme Ruler of the world in this matter? Who could tell what ends he might have in view to induce him not to forgive men that, in the manner before mentioned, [had] forsaken and renounced him, and turned enemies to him, and [not] show mercy to such (p. 262)?[5] We see by fact and experience that it don't necessarily follow from God's goodness that he will prevent all misery of his creatures, but that, nevertheless, his wisdom induces him to order innumerable and extreme calamities. So that his wisdom causes him not to do everything that, in itself considered, would be an act of goodness and mercy. If so, not only would he prevent all misery, but make all his creatures ten thousand times happier than they are, and make ten thousand times more creatures to be happy than he does.

'Tis natural to suppose that other things become the supreme Governor of the world besides pity and goodness, and particularly that justice and hatred of sin become him. It is not natural to suppose that he cannot be provoked or offended by injuriousness, and an unreasonable spirit and treatment, and particularly by an injurious disposition and behavior towards himself, in ingratitude, enmity and contempt. At least we can't be certain from the light of nature that he can't be provoked by these things. If we may judge by what seems to be dictated by the hearts of the generality of mankind through the face of the earth and in all ages, 'tis natural for the mind of man to suppose that the Deity is greatly provoked by these things. And if he is provoked by sin, and does greatly abhor and resent it, 'tis natural to suppose that he is disposed to punish it, and with severity. This also agrees with the notions of mankind in all ages and nations.

And if other perfections besides goodness, such as justice, holiness, hatred of sin, and wisdom, as it regards the most perfect state of the universal system, in the whole series of events—I say, if such other perfections must have their ends regarded, and so have a hand in determining, with respect to offenders, rebels and enemies, whether they shall be forgiven and received to favor, and, if any such, how many, and who, and when, and to what degree, and what benefits they shall receive, and in what way they shall be saved, and by what means, on what terms, etc.,

5. JE later inserted this reference to the ninth page of the MS entry, the paragraph beginning "Reason alone cannot certainly determine, that God will not insist on some satisfaction for injuries he received."

how[6] shall it be clearly determined without a revelation how great a hand other perfections besides goodness may have in this affair? And how great a regard will be paid to other ends besides the ends of mere pity and goodness? How many and various the ends may be which God in his wisdom may see fit to provide for, and how important they may be in his eyes? Who can tell how far he may think fit to proceed in punishing to vindicate his own majesty, to maintain his own authority and the dignity of his government, and to maintain inviolate the grand rule of government? And who can tell what may be best for the system of universal existence, taken in its utmost extent and with regard to the whole of its duration and the eternal series of events? Will not reason say that, if God be perfectly wise, he will order the methods of his proceeding in the moral government of the world so as to make provision for the obtaining the best ends in the best manner, meaning by best that which is so in an universal and perfect view of all things in their utmost extent and utmost duration? And how can reason alone fully and clearly determine and satisfy those, who are so infinitely far from being capable of such a view, what is best in this sense?

So if we suppose that determined, that 'tis God's will there should be some way of salvation, reason will determine that the method and means, terms and degrees, etc., shall be such as are wisest and best in the foregoing sense, viz. with regard to the influence of each part of the scheme or method of salvation on the whole extent and duration of existence, comprehending that infinite variety of particular beings, circumstances and events. But who will say that man's reason alone is sufficient to determine what method of salvation is wisest in this sense: what degree of mercy, what deliverance and happiness, what means of salvation, what terms of enjoying the benefit of it, will have the best and most perfect influence in such a sense?

Will any say that man's understanding and reason alone make it certain that the infinitely wise, holy and righteous Governor of the world stands ready to forgive all offenders, how great soever their offense, and how far soever they go in their opposition, rebellion, enmity, and ingratitude, and contempt, and how long soever they continue in these things, and how far soever they proceed in acting upon their enmity and contempt? If not, then who shall set the bounds? Can man's reason fix the limits and say that men may go so far in offending and yet find mercy, and no further?

6. MS: "And how."

Reason alone cannot certainly determine that God will not insist on some satisfaction for injuries he receives. If we consider what have in fact been the general notions of mankind, we shall see cause to think that the dictates of men's minds who have been without revelation have been contrariwise, viz. that the Deity will insist on some satisfaction. Repentance makes some satisfaction for many injuries that men are guilty of one towards another, because it bears some proportion to the degree of injury. But reason will not certainly determine that 'tis proper for God to accept of repentance as some satisfaction for an offense when that repentance is infinitely disproportionate to the heinousness of the offense, or the degree of injuriousness that is offered. And reason will not certainly determine that the offense of forsaking and renouncing God in heart, and treating him with such indignity and contempt as to set him below the meanest and vilest things, is not immensely greater and more heinous than any injury offered to man, and that, therefore, all our repentance and sorrow fall infinitely short of proportion in measure and degree.

If it be said that we may reasonably conclude and be fully satisfied in it that a good God will forgive our sin on repentance, I ask what can be meant by repentance in the case of them that have no love nor true gratitude to God in their hearts, and that have such an habitual disregard and contempt of God in their hearts as to treat created things of the least value with greater respect than him? If it be said that thereby is meant being sorry for the offense, I ask whether that sorrow is worthy to be accepted as true repentance that don't arise from any change of heart, or from a better mind, a mind more disposed to love God and honor him, being now so changed as to have less disregard and contempt—whether or no sorrow only from fear and self-love, with a heart still in the same state as to disregard of God, be such as we can be certain will be accepted. If not, how shall a man who, at present, has no better heart, but yet is greatly concerned for himself through fear, know how to obtain a better heart? How does it appear that he, if he tries only from fear and self-love, can make his heart better, and make himself love God? What proper tendency can there be in the heart to make itself better till it sincerely repents of its present badness? And how can the heart have sincerity of repentance of its present badness till it begins to be better, and so begins to forsake its badness by truly disapproving it from a good disposition, or better tendency, arising in it? If the disposition remains just the same, then no sincere disapprobation arises, but the reigning disposition approves itself. And that tends nothing to destroy itself but, on the contrary, to confirm itself. The heart can have no tendency to make itself better till it begins to have a better tendency. For therein consists its badness, viz. having no good tendency or inclination. And to begin to have a good tendency or, which is the same thing, to begin to have a sincere tendency or inclination to be better, is the same thing as to begin already to be better.

So then, it seems that they that are now under the reigning power of an evil heart can have no ability to help themselves, how sensible soever they may be of their misery, and concerned through fear and self-love to be delivered. But they need this from God as part of their salvation, viz. that God should give 'em sincere repentance, as well as pardon and deliverance from the evil consequences of sin. And how shall they know without revelation that God will give sinners a better heart, to enable 'em truly to repent, or in what ways they can have any hope to obtain it of him?

And if it were so that men could obtain some sincere repentance of their being wholly without that love of God that they ought to have, yet how can reason determine that God will forgive their sin till they wholly forsake it, or till their repentance is perfect, till they relinquish all their sinful contempt, ingratitude, regardlessness[7] of God, or, which is the same thing, till they fully return to their duty, i.e. to that degree of love, honor, and gratitude, and devotedness to God that is their duty? If they have robbed God, who can certainly say that God will forgive them till they restore all that they have robbed him of, and give him the whole that he claims by the most absolute right? But where is any man that repents with such a perfect repentance? And if there be ever any instances of it in this world, who will say that 'tis in every man's power to obtain it, or that there certainly are no lower terms of forgiveness? And, if there are, who can tell certainly where to set the bounds, and say precisely to what degree a man must repent, how great must his sorrow be in proportion to his offenses, etc., etc.?

Or who can say how long a man's day of probation shall last? Will reason alone certainly determine that, if a man goes on for a long time presumptuously in his contempt, rebellion and affronts, presuming on God's goodness, depending [on it] that, though he does thus abuse his grace as long as he pleases, yet if he repents at any time God will forgive him and receive him to favor, forgiving all his presumptuous, aggravated rebellion, ingratitude and provocation, and will receive him into the

---

7. MS: "regardless."

arms of his love? Will reason only fully satisfy the mind, that God stands ready to pardon and receive to favor such a sinner after long continuance in such horrid presumption and most vile ingratitude? Or will reason fully determine as a certain thing that God will do it if men thus presumptuously spend their youth, the best part of their lives, in obstinate and ungrateful wickedness, depending that God will stand ready to pardon afterwards? And, in short, how can reason alone be sufficient to set the bounds and say how long God will bear with and wait upon presumptuous sinners, how many acts of such ingratitude and presumption will he be ready to forgive, and on what terms, etc.—I say, how can reason fix these limits with any clear evidence that shall give the mind a fixed establishment and satisfaction?

Since, therefore, if there be anything as the forgiveness and salvation of sinful men, new relations of God to men (and concerns of God with men, and a new dependence of men on God) will arise, no less important and probably much more important[8] than these, those which are between God and man, as God is his Creator and the Author of his natural good. And God must manifest his perfections in new displays of them, in a new work of redemption or salvation, contrived or ordered by his infinite wisdom, and executed by his power, in a perfect consistence with his justice and holiness, and a greater manifestation of his goodness than are made in God's works as the Author of nature. So these things must be the foundation of new regards to God, new duties, and a new religion, founded on these displays of God's perfections in the work of salvation, and on the new relations God sustains towards men, and the new dependence of men on God, and new obligations laid on men in that work; which may be called revealed religion, different from that natural religion which is founded on the works of God as Creator and the Author of nature (and our concerns with God in that work), though not at all contrary to it or subversive of it, but in addition to it and perfect agreement with it.

The light of nature teaches that religion that is necessary to continue in the favor of God that made us. But it cannot teach us that religion that is necessary to our being restored to the favor of God after we have forfeited it.

1305. See at the end of No. 1300. CHRISTIAN RELIGION. "Ex Dictis colligere licet, 'Religionem et Gentem Judaicam mirum quoddam Phœ-

---

8. MS: "of important."

nomenon esse, cui explanando increduli omnino impares sunt; sed quod, posito Religionis Judaicæ (qualis olim fuit) Veritate et divinitate, optime resolvitur.' Sunt verba Celeb. Turret. [. . .] 'Quis [contra] unquam illorum in Egypto Commorationem (Populus enim fuit ab Egyptiis plane diversus)? Quis illorum ex terra illa exitum mirabilem, populi numerosissimi in Desertis Arabiæ Annorum quadraginta commorationem? Quis singularem eorum ab omnium reliquorum placitis diversam, sed maxime excellentem doctrinam? Quis omnia Religionis eorum Instituta explicabit? Quis porro mira post tempus possessionis Palaestinæ illorum fata exponet, Assyriacam Babilonicamque captivationem, et in terram patriam reductionem? Quis fatalis illorum per Romanos Vastationis, non vastationis et subjectionis totalis, sed exterminationis, ex terra Cananæa, plenariæ ejectionis, absque ulla reditus spe, rationem reddet? Quis ænigma illud evolvet, quod nobis Populus hic ab omnibus aliis plane diversus et singularis præbet, Populus cui maledictio fronti inscripta est, omnibus exosus, plane mirabilis, ubique extorris. Quis, inquam, Historiam sacram non admittens, omnia hæc solvere poterit; Mosen vero et Prophetas si audiamus, via plana ac facilis est.'"[9] Stapferus, *Theol. Polem.*, Tom. II, [pp.] 1074–75. To these things should have been added their being kept an entirely distinct nation for this 1700 years, scattered all over the world, mixed with all other nations.

1306. CHRISTIAN RELIGION. It adds to the evidence which is given to the truth of Christianity, by the multitudes of miracles wrought by Christ and his apostles and followers in the first century, that there were no pre-

---

9. "From the law it is permitted to gather that 'the Jewish religion and race is some amazing thing, which unbelievers are totally unequal in explaining, but which is best resolved by positing the truth and divinity—such it once was—of the Jewish religion.' The words of the celebrated Turretin are [. . .] 'Who, contrarily, will ever explain the sojourn of the Jews in Egypt (for they were clearly a different people from the Egyptians)? Who their marvelous exodus from that land and a wandering of that very numerous people in the Arabian desert for forty years? Who their unique, different from all other opinions, but most excellent teaching? Who will explain all the institutes of their religion? Further, who will set forth their astounding fate after the time of the possession of Palestine, the Assyrian and Babylonian captivity and the return to their native land? Who would give the reason of their fatal devastation through the Romans, not of devastation and total subjection, but of extermination, of their total ejection from the land of Canaan from any hope of return? Who would solve that riddle which this people—unique and clearly different from all others, a people whose forehead has been inscribed with reviling, utterly hated by all, clearly astonishing, exiled everywhere—offers us? Who, I say, not admitting the sacred history, would be able to solve all these things? But if we hear Moses and the prophets, the way is clear and easy.'"

tenses of inspiration or miracles among the Jews—at least not worth the taking notice of—in Judea or any other part of the world.

If all this multitude, that long-continued series of miracles pretended to be wrought in confirmation of Christianity, were fictions, vain pretenses, or enthusiastic whims and imaginations, why were there no pretenses or imaginations of the same sort on the other side, among the Jews, in opposition to these? Those of the Jews that were opposite were vastly the greater part. And they had as high an opinion of the honorableness of those gifts of prophecy and miracles, had as much in their notions and temper to lead 'em to a fondness for the claim of such an honor to their party. They were exceeding proud and haughty, proud of their special relation to God and their high privilege as the peculiar favorites of heaven, and in that respect exalted far above Christians, and all the world; which [was] a temper of mind (as we see abundantly) above all others leading men to pretenses of that nature, and leading them to the height of enthusiasm.

There could be nothing peculiar in the constitution of the first Christians arising from a different blood, peculiarly tending in them to enthusiasm beyond the rest of the Jews. For they were of the same blood, the same race and nation. Nor could it be because they wanted for zeal against Christianity, and desire to oppose and destroy, or wanted for envy, and great and virulent opposition of mind to any pretenses in the Christians to excel them in the favor of God, or excellency of any gifts or privileges whatsoever. They had such zeal and such envy even to madness and fury.

The true reason, therefore, why so vast a multitude of miracles were said and believed to be openly wrought among Christians for so long a time, even for a whole age, and none among the Jews, must be that such was the nature and state of things in the world of mankind, especially in that age, that it was not possible to palm false pretenses of such a kind upon the world; and that those who were most elated, most ambitious of such an honor, could see no hope of succeeding in any such pretenses; and because the Christians indeed were inspired, and were enabled to work miracles, and did them, as was pretended and believed, in great multitudes, and that continually for so long a time. But God never favored their adversaries with such a privilege.

1307. Of Prophecies Respecting Different Events. "Hoc attendendum, quod talia extant Vaticinia, quæ non solum ad specialem aliquem eventum, sed ad generalem aliquem respiciunt Ecclesiæ statum, qui vero uno tempore felicior altero est. Inde fit ut haud raro interpretes divinorum Oraculorum hoc modo inter se dissentiant, ut unus Vaticinium aliquod præcise huic casui, alter alteri applicet; et licet dissentiant, facile tamen conciliari queat, utrumque enim verum esse potest.

"Nec hoc omittendum quod mundus spiritualis, sive Civitas Dei, res omnium operum divinorum pulcherrima, duas habeat partes; mundus enim hic est vel Typicus vel Antitypicus; et qualis inter Mundum *Physicum* et *Mysticum* summa est harmonia ac consensus, ita in mundo Spirituali typico et antitypico per summi Opificis Sapientiam admirabilis est conformitas; ut quæ in mundo typico eveniunt, etiam in antitypico contingant, ut magna eventuum celeberrimorum sit similitudo. Hinc in plurimis Prophetiis implementum historicum in mundo typico quærendum, ita ut historia illa typum rerum in Mundo antitypico eveniendarum gerat. Factum hinc ut multi interpretes sensum litteralem in eventu Mundi typici quæsiverint, alii implementum ejusdem Vaticinii in mundo antitypico invenisse sibi videantur, et hoc modo dissentiunt, proprie tamen consentiunt." Stapferus, *Theol. Polem.*, vol. II, pp. 1087–88.[1]

1308. PROPHECIES OF SCRIPTURE, why it is not proper their meaning should be perfectly plain. "Varia sunt propter quæ Vaticinia summum Claritatis gradum habere non debent; neque enim necessum est, ut anre eventum ea plane intelligantur; neque opus ut humana industria atque sapientia ad eorum implementum aliquid contribuat, quod omnino fieret, si homines omnem [. . .], qua aliquid fieri debet, clarissime præs-

---

1. "This should be noticed, that so many prophecies exist, which not only reflect special events but also the general state of the church, which indeed is more blessed in one time than another. Thence it follows that by no means rarely do interpreters of the divine oracles differ in this way among themselves, that one applies a certain prophecy precisely to this situation and another interpreter applies it to another situation. It is allowed that they dissent; nevertheless it is easy for them to be reconciled, for each can be true.

"It should not be forgotten that the spiritual world, or the City of God, the most beautiful of all divine works, has two parts. For this world is either a type or an antitype. And such is the height of harmony and consensus between the *physical* and *mystical* world; thus in the spiritual world there is admirable conformity through the wisdom of the most high Creator for typical and antitypical, that whatever happens in the typical world also occurs in the antitypical, so that there is a great similarity of renown events. Hence in some prophets the historical fulfillment should be sought in the typical world, so that that history bears a type of things which should happen in the antitypical world. It happens hence that many interpreters seek a literal sense in an event of the typical world, others seem to have found for themselves the fulfillment of that prophecy in the antitypical world, and in this way they dissent, but properly agree." Stapfer, *Institutiones Theologiæ Polemicæ*, 2, 1087–88.

cirent. Neque denique divina consilia ab hominibus eventum præscientibus irrita reddi debent." Stapferus, *Theol. Polem.*, vol. II, p. 1088.[2]

1309. CHRISTIAN RELIGION. DIVINE AUTHORITY OF THE BOOK OF DANIEL. Porphyry would have it that the book of Daniel was forged after the times of Antiochus Epiphanes.[3] Against this the following things do argue:

1. As Alphonsus Turretinus, quoted by Stapferus, observes, "That among the whole nation of the Jews, there never was any controversy concerning this matter."[4]

This would be exceeding strange if the book had been written so late as the time of Antiochus Epiphanes, which was[5] about 400 years after the captivity, especially when this book has been received among them not only as a book truly written by Daniel, but also as a genuine writing of his universally received into the Jewish canon as part of the holy Scripture and, as such, read in their synagogues, as their canon has been delivered down from generation to generation.

It does not appear that, after Malachi's death, ever any pretended to have the spirit of prophecy among them, or to palm any writing of his own on the people as of divine inspiration. There seems to have been prevailing among them no humor of forgery of any such kind. And if there had been any such fictitious pretense, started after several hundred years' entire cessation, 'tis in the highest degree incredible that it should be received by all the people, and that, too, at once, without any great controversy about the matter, and allowed to be a divine writing. People are apt to be startled and alarmed at new things that they have been very much unused [to], and that are above all that any of them have long pretended, claiming an honor far above all that any have pretended for some ages.

And especially is it unlikely that they would, without much controversy, all agree to give this new book a place in the canon of their Scripture so long after their canon had been settled, and had remained unaltered

2. "There are various reasons why prophecies ought not have the highest degree of clarity. For it is not necessary that they are understood before the event; nor is it needed that human industry and wisdom contribute anything to their fulfillment. The latter would certainly occur if human beings knew clearly beforehand everything by which something ought to happen. Nor, finally, ought divine counsels be returned void from the foreknowledge of human beings." Ibid., 2, 1088.

3. Porphyry made this argument in Bk. XII of his famous tome against Christianity, Κατα Χριστιανων.

4. See below, p. 271, n. 7.

and without addition, as being supposed to be finished and sealed up. The canon of holy and divine writings among them was a very sacred thing, that to which they paid a vast regard. And so great an addition, so new made, so long after all the rest, must needs have made a great noise.

It is to be observed that, so late as this, were among them [men] who made it their business to study and teach word of God, contained in the canon of their Scripture, containing what they called their Law and the Prophets; and they had synagogues everywhere, all over the land and in all parts of the world; and everywhere it was the established custom to read the Law and the Prophets in their synagogues. Now who can think that a book forged after the times of Antiochus Epiphanes could have been introduced into this sacred canon as a divine book, one of the books of their holy prophets, to be kept and read in their synagogues by the whole people through the land of Canaan, and through the whole world, without any remarkable controversy or any memorable noise or ado?

It is further to be considered that this book appears with a pretense of its being written by the prophet Daniel in the time of the captivity. In it, Daniel speaks of himself as the writer (Dan. 8:1 ff., and 9:2, and 10:11–12). We are told expressly that he wrote his visions (Dan. 7:12) and that he was commanded to write his prophecies in a book (ch. 12:4). (See Witsius, *Miscellaneorum,* p. 254.)[6] And the book is received and put into the Jewish canon under his name. But if this book appeared first under this pretense after the times of Antiochus Epiphanes, the whole Jewish nation must know that it was a new book to them, and that they had never heard of any such book before. Therefore, great doubts would most naturally immediately arise in their minds how it should come to pass, if this book were written in the time of the captivity by so great a prophet, of such exceeding fame, how it should now first appear, and never be heard of till now. It would be strange indeed if, under these circumstances, it should be received universally, all over the world, with such high credit as to be added to the sacred canon by all, without any remarkable controversy.

Surely many strange things must be supposed in the people to make this credible. And, among others, this must be supposed, viz. that there was a strange, credulous humor in the people as to things of this kind, a

5. MS: "were."

6. Hermann Witsius, *Miscellaneorum Sacrorum Libri Quatuor* (3rd ed., Herbornæ Nassaviorum, 1712–35), *1,* 254.

fondness for adding to their canon and an aptitude to receive any new writing as of sacred authority. But nothing of this appears from any other instance. No other new writing was thus received among them. 'Tis true, fabulous writings were forged among them, as many strange stories in their Apocrypha; but never received among them, or any part of them, as part of the canon of their Scriptures.

'Tis further to be considered that the Jews were divided into opposite, contending sects, who differed greatly among themselves and had great controversy one with another—and, among other things, about their canon. The Saducees differed greatly from the Pharisees. And the former admitted only the five books of Moses into their canon, though they did not deny the other writings to be really written by those whose names they bore. Surely these would have made a great noise if the rest of the Jews had so easily received and made so much of a writing so lately forged, especially seeing Dan. 12:2 is so especially against their most favorite tenet as to a resurrection. This sect at least would have kept alive the remembrance of this folly of the rest of the Jews.

The Samaritans also, who lived in the midst of the country, and were such bitter enemies of the Jews, and disliked the writings of the prophets, would have been forward to expose such folly of the Jews.

The matter of the first finding and receiving this remarkable book and adding it to the canon must have been a famous event among [the Jews], and have made a noise on several accounts, not only by the controversy raised thereby, but as a great and remarkable event in the series [of] events attending the state of things amongst them. But that all should be without the least trace or footstep in history, or any remaining account of any such event, but that it, the whole affair, should presently sink into oblivion and so universally pass among the people as though this book had always been part of their canon and universally received as such, even from the time of the captivity, is quite incredible.

But thus it is: no trace of any such event remains, no hint of any time that this book first appeared after the captivity, or of any controversy about its being truly the writing of Daniel, or about its being received as a part of the canon among any that received more than the Pentateuch, either in any records or writings of the Jews, or histories or monuments of any other nation or sect, though the book be spoken of particularly in very ancient writings, as in Josephus, who expressly speaks of this book as received and read among the Jews as of the most certain and undoubted authority (see Witsius, *Miscellaneorum,* [vol. 1], p. 254).

This book is spoken of in the Evangelists as cited by Christ as a part of the Jewish Scripture, and [by] the apostle Paul (Heb. 11). And there [was] no appearance of any controversy about the book in his time. And, before that, the book of Daniel is plainly referred to in the first book of the Maccabees, second chapter, vv. 59–60, where the glorious fruit of faith in Ananias, Mishael and Azarius is spoken, and of Daniel in his preservation from the mouths of the lions.

2. The Book of Daniel is extant in the translation of the Seventy, which was made into Greek before the times of Antiochus Epiphanes. See Poole's *Synopsis, Prolegomena in hunc librum,* col. 1391.[7]

3. Josephus gives an account of this book being shown to Alexander the Great by Jaddua the high priest. So Stapferus,[8] Prideaux,[9] and Witsius in *Miscellaneorum,* [vol. 1], p. 255.

4. Stapferus, Tom. 2, p. 1081, as follows: "hoc [. . .] addimus, quod maximum pondus nobis habere videtur, quod si liber hic post Antiochi Epiphanis demum ætatem fuisset exaratus, fraus subreptionis hujus libri in canonem sacrum latere nequaquam potuisset, propter nimiam temporis differentiam, quæ inter Danielis vitam et prophetiæ vel libri hujus editionem et in canonem receptionem intercessisset; quadringentorum enim circiter annorum spatium tempus hoc complectitur. Quis igitur fingere sibi poterit, seris demum hisce temporibus librum hunc et quidem propheticum præfixo Danielis nomine, rebus maximis in eo contentis jamjam gestis, fraude subrepsisse et communi populi Judaici consensu, aliter enim fieri non poterat, in canonem fuisse receptum."[1]

7. The reference is to Poole's *Synopsis Criticorum, III,* Pt. 2, col. 1391. "The translation of the Seventy" is a reference to the Septuagint, which most scholars believe was translated beginning in the early third century B.C.E. Antiochus Epiphanes was the anti-Semitic king of Syria who reigned from 175–163 B.C.E., and whose attack on Jerusalem in 169 B.C.E., plundering of the Jewish Temple, and general imposition of Greek culture on the Jews led to the Maccabean revolt.

8. Stapfer, *Institutiones Theologiæ Polemicæ,* 2, 1080–81, translated in *Miscellaneous Observations on Important Theological Subjects* (Edinburgh, 1793), p. 335: "I add this, which seems to me to have the greatest weight, that if this book had been written after the time of Antiochus Epiphanes, its surreptitious insertion into the sacred canon, could not have been concealed, on account of the great length of time which intervened between the life of Daniel, and the publishing of this prophecy or book, and the reception of it into the canon: for this time comprehends the space of about 400 years. Who therefore can persuade himself, that, at such a late period, this book, containing prophecies, having the name of Daniel prefixed to it, and relating most important facts which had already taken place, crept in by fraud, and was by the common consent of the Jewish people (for otherwise it could not have come to pass), received into the canon of Scripture?"

9. Humphrey Prideaux, *The Old and New Testament Connected in the History of the Jews and Neighboring Nations . . .* (London, 1725), 2, 695–97.

1. "We add this, which seems to us to have great weight, the fact that if this book had been finally produced after the age of Antiochus Epiphanes, the stolen fraud of this book would by

5. The greater part of the book is written in genuine Hebrew (see Witsius, *Miscellaneorum*, [vol. 1], p. 255). And it is not likely that a book forged 400 years after the Hebrew had ceased to be spoken among the people would have been so. Other fabulous books that were written among them after the captivity were not written in that language.

6. Other things are foretold in this book besides those which came to pass in Antiochus' times, no less wonderful and no less plainly and exactly agreeing with the events which came to pass in later times, as the prophecies concerning the Roman Empire. And some of them have come to pass many ages since that time, yea, many ages since Christ's time.

7. The prophet Ezekiel makes mention of Daniel as one of the most holy men, and also one of the greatest and most familiar friends of God, one of the wisest men that ever were in the world (Ezek. 14:14, 20, and 28:3). These things may well lead us to suppose that he was a great prophet. If he was a great prophet, it would be strange that none of his prophecies were written in that age when the prophets, especially all that were of great note, wrote their prophecies.

1310. CHRIST'S MIRACLES. "Ea quæ APPOLLONIO TYANEO, referuntur miracula, à Hierocle et Porphyres Christianæ fidei opposita facile evanescunt, si ad sequentia adtendimus. 1. Quod juxta Historiam celebris hic Philosophus, pessimæ indolis homo fuerit, Reipublicæ perturbator, ad Idolatriam alios seducens; unde liquet, illum ratione vitæ et doctrinæ suæ sanctissimo Domino nostro è diametro fuisse oppositum.

"2. Adeo absurda sunt, adeo ridicula, quæ ipsi adscribuntur miracula plurima, ut non modo lectori præjudiciis non occupato fabulosa statim appareant, sed et semetipsa refellant.

"3. Nullo porro illorum narratio nititur fundamento fide digno, scriptor enim Apollonii vitæ Philostratus centum post Philosophum hunc annis vixit; Juliæ piæ Imperatricis jussu chartis, quæ de Philosopho hoc nobis constant, mandavit. Subsidium, quod hæc Septimii Severi uxor ad

---

no means have been able to hide in the sacred canon, because of the great difference of time which came between, on the one hand, the life of Daniel and the edition of this book or prophecy and, on the other, reception into the canon. For the space of around four hundred years comprises this time. Therefore, who could conceive in his mind that this book in so late a time—indeed a prophetic book with the name of Daniel affixed, with the greatest things contained in it already done—crept in by fraud and was received into the canon by the common consensus of the Jewish people, for it otherwise could not have been received." Stapfer, *Institutiones Theologiæ Polemicæ*, 2, 1081.

vitam Apollonii describendam Philostrato suppeditavit, fuere chartæ nonnullæ, quæ ipsi ab ignoto quodam fuere traditæ, quas à damidæ quodam Apollonii discipulo provenire asserebat[-] ex quibus deinde Philostratus historiam quam habemus compilavit, quam incerta ergo hæc omnia sint, quivis perspicere facile poterit; ut in meram tandem resolvantur traditionem et Fabulam." Stapferus, *Theol. Polem.*, Tom. II, pp. 1115–16.[2]

1311. MIRACLES wrought in Christ's and the apostles' days. "Concedimus in nonnullis distinctu difficillimum esse, num aliquid per ipsas Naturæ fieri potuerit vires, an vero illas excedat? Neque à quoquam petimus, ut id pro miraculo habeat, de quo dubium superest, utrum Naturæ vires ad effectum illum producendum suffecerint?

"Sed ut homimum incredulitati, hac in re Deus succurreret, non uno tantum tempore, aut loco, non unius generis tantum miracula, non ab unica tantum persona, non præsentibus paucissimis tantum hominibus, non talia solum patrari curavit, sive potius ipsemet patravit miracula, quæ essent ambigua et de quibus constare non posset, num ex naturali proveniant effectu nec ne?

"Ingens nimirum inter ea quæ in sacris Litteris recensentur miracula, occurrit numerus; de quibus per circumstantias omnes liquet, caussas omnes naturales abesse, et ubi evidentissimum est, eventus illos ad id operum divinorum genus pertinere, per quæ vocatur id, quod non est, ut sit, et ubi aliquid ex nihilo creatur, dum ex statu mundi antecedente sequi minime potest. Si ergo in uno aut altero facto dubium aliquod oriri posset, annon ex caussis physicis id productum fuerit, vel an non fraus aliqua adsit, innumera alia adsunt, quæ ut ita explicentur, impossibile

2. "Those miracles which are attributed to Apollonius of Tyre by Hierocles and Porphyres against the Christian faith easily vanish, if we attend to the following:

"1. The fact that this celebrated philosopher, according to the history, was a man of the worst laziness, a disturber of the state, seducing others to idolatry. Whence it is evident that he, by his way of life and doctrine, had been diametrically opposed to our most holy Lord.

"2. The several miracles which they themselves ascribe are so absurd, so ridiculous, that not only do they immediately appear so to the reader not taken by prejudices, but they also refute themselves.

"3. Further, their narrative relies on no trustworthy basis, for the writer of the life of Apollonius, Philostratus, lived a hundred years after this philosopher. By order of the pious Empress Julia, he entrusted to paper what exists for us about this philosopher. The help which this wife of Septimius Severus supplied to Philostratos to describe the life of Apollonius was not some papers; these had been given to him by some unknown person. Philostratus used to assert that they came from some disciple of Apollonius. From these, he compiled the history we have. Therefore, how uncertain all these things are, anyone could easily see; that they finally melt into pure tradition and fable." Ibid., 2, 1115–16.

plane est, neque id unquam ab ullo Adversariorum præstitum fuit." Stapferus, *Theol. Polem.*, Tom. II, pp. 1103–04.[3]

1312. CHRISTIAN RELIGION. THE UNREASONABLENESS OF INFIDELITY.
"'Quid homine indignius esse potest, quam nescire, et nescire velle,
quænam hujus Mundi caussa, quis ordo, quis finis sit, cujus Numine
moveatur? Quid turpius quam ignorare, quis eum miserit in mundum,
unde venerit, quo abeat, quid vel miserum vel beatum faciat, quæque
miseriæ ac felicitatis caussæ, quæ malorum remedia, quid vel sperandum
vel metuendum sit: atque ea ratione in perpetua vivere dubitatione atque
alternantium spei et metus agitatione, et animum nunc huc celerem,
nunc dividere illuc, neque loco stare posse? Quæ vero insania, obfirmare
contra hæc animum, seipsum fugere, ac voluntarium eligere exilium, et
notum nimis omnibus, ignotum sibi mori velle? Imo Gloriæ ducere, de
Deo, de animæ immortalitate, de proemio et poena post hanc vitam, du-
bitare, et nec spe, nec metu, cum credula scilicet Plebe tangi? Miseros
revera, et pessimos simul ac perditos homines, qui invita et reclamante
conscientia agnoscere nolunt, quod experiundo, nolentes volentes,
debent, se alterius stare ac cadere arbitrio!'" Roellius, as cited by Stapferus, *Theol. Polem.*, Tom. I, p. 512.[4]

---

3. "We concede that it is most difficult in distinction to some, whether any could be done
through the very powers of nature or whether it truly exceeded them. Nor do we seek from
anyone that he holds that for a miracle, about which there is still doubt whether the powers of
nature would suffice to produce such an effect.

"But in order that God in this matter might help the unbelief of men, did he take care to
produce not only such things, not only in one time or place, not only miracles of one kind, not
only by one person, not only with a few people present, or did he rather himself produce miracles which were ambiguous and about which it could not be certain whether they came from
natural causes or not?

"Truly a vast number occurred among those miracles which are rehearsed in the sacred letters. It is evident that all natural causes were absent from these. Most evident is the fact that
those outcomes pertain to that type of divine work through which that which is not is called,
as if it is, and where something is created out of nothing, while it can by no means follow from
the pre-existing state of the world. If then, in one deed or another some doubt could arise about
whether it had been produced from physical causes or whether some fraud was present, there
are uncounted others where it is plainly impossible to explain them thus. Further, no adversary ever did explain them thus." Ibid., 2, 1103–04.

4. Ibid., *1*, 512, quoting from Herman Alexander Roell, "Dissert. de Religione rationali, §
clxxviii," translated in *Miscellaneous Observations*, p. 378: "'What can be more unworthy of a man,
than to be ignorant, and to be willing to be ignorant, of what is the cause, what the order, and
what the end of this world, and by whose power it is moved? What can be more base than for
a man willingly not to know who sent him into the world; whence he came; whither he is going; what conduct of his shall be followed with misery or with happiness; what are the wages of
misery and of happiness; what are the remedies of evils; what is to be hoped, and what is to be

1313. CHRISTIAN RELIGION. NECESSITY OF REVELATION. THE KNOWL-
EDGE OF DEISTS FROM REVELATION. "Aiunt quidem, qui Revelationis tum
Necessitatem tum veritatem agnoscere nolunt, ex Ratione colligi posse,
quiquid magni de Attributis atque Providentia divina tradat Revelatio.
Sed non attendunt, hoc quidem facile fieri posse ab illis, qui semel Revelationis lumine illustrati sunt: qui hac luce utuntur, illi nullo negotio ostendere possunt, quomodo infinita Dei Attributa cum Rationis principiis
conformia sint: ast perpendant, an in omnibus idem præstare possent,
si hoc lumine carerent. Unde judiosissime Theologus acutissimus Sam.
Werenfelsius *De Præstan. Relig. Revel.*,[5] de hisce disserit, dicens: Videant
ne nimium Rationi suæ tribuant Rationales nostri. Dicunt, solo Rationis
ductu inveniri posse totam illam Religionem, quæ in sacris Litteris traditur, aut saltem quod in ea præcipuum est. Nihil dictu facilius est, illis
qui jam cognoscunt Religionem istam. Tunc illum dicendum fuisset, si
per totam vitam, de Religione hac nihil audivissent. Nunc vero similes
mihi videntur iis, qui, postquam [à] præceptoribus, quidquid sciunt,
didicerunt, videri tamen volunt αυτοδιδακτοι: aut, cum de præclaris in-
ventis audiunt, putant, se hæc omnia, nisi jam inventa essent, ipsos fuisse
inventuros. Quod si cognoscere velimus, quid possit Ratio hominis in in-
venienda Religione, non nostram Rationem consulere debemus, quos
verbum Dei in viam deduxit, quos in eadem dirigit, sed Rationem illorum, quibus hoc verbum est ignotum. Hic vero quæ monstra pariat sibi
relicta Ratio, testantur omnium Gentilium exempla, inter quos fuere
plurimi, qui non minus Ratione valuerunt, ac Rationales nostri. Dicam
verbo, Religio mere rationalis, qualis in Mundo reperitur, est Religio
Gentilium: Religio deistarum est Religio illorum, qui, postquam ex sacris Litteris omnia depromserunt quæ placent, dicunt se ea ratiocinando
invenisse."[6] Stapferus, *Theol. Polem.*, Tom. I, pp. 503–04.

---

feared; and in that manner to live in perpetual doubt, and perpetual agitation, by hope and
fear alternately succeeding each other, so that the mind sometimes is precipitately inclined this
way, sometimes that way, and is incapable of rest? Is it not the greatest madness for a man to
endeavor to strengthen his mind against those things, to flee from himself, to choose a voluntary banishment, and, being ignorant of his own character, which is too well known to others,
to choose death? nay, to glory in doubting concerning the immortality of the soul, and future
rewards and punishments, on the pretense that he is not touched with either hope or fear, like
the credulous multitude? He is certainly miserable, and, at the same time, the worst and most
abandoned of men, who, against the remonstrances of his conscience, is unwilling to acknowledge what, whether willing or unwilling, he ought from experience to acknowledge, that
he stands or falls at the will of another.'"

5. Stapfer cites "Diss. III. p. 131, 132."
6. "Indeed they say, who do not want to know both the necessity and truth of revelation, that

1314. CHRISTIAN RELIGION, how it excels the heathen morality. Religio Christiana "ad observationem Religionis Naturalis fortiter hominem obstringit et vult, ut motiva omnium suarum actionum ab Attributis divinis desumat et per consequens omnia propter Deum creatorem, conservatorem atque communem Benefactorem suscipiat, ut omnia tendant in illius Gloriam: Præcepta huc facientia omnia ex ipsa Dei natura fluunt, dum Deum ut perfectissimum, amabilem et venerabilem proponunt, ut Ens potentissimum, simul Justissimum et æquissimum, in omnibus quas suscipimus actionibus metuendum: ut Ens optimum amandum, quærendum et in eo omen fiduciam ponendum præcipiunt. [. . .]

"Quantum [etiam] hic antecellit Christianae Religio omnes illas, quas Ratio Revelationis lumine non illustrata protulit. Non dicam de crassioribus atque barbaris Populis, sed de iis, quos sapientissimos humana Ratio habuit, qui inter illos, qui divinem Revelationem plane ignorarunt, maxime egregia præcepta moralia hominibus præscriptserunt: sed quot quæso Ethica inveniuntur defectus! qui virtutibus omne pretium adimunt, easque mancas faciunt.

"Primo enim præcepta sua non firmo superstruebant fundamento, nec vera obligatione firmabant et justis motivis faciebant, dum illa non derivabant ex hominis à Deo Creatore et Conservatore dependentia, neque ab Attributis divinis motiva desumebant, aut veræ ac solidæ et perennis felicitatis promissione incitamenta virtuti addebant, sed potius

---

they are able to gather by reason whatever great thing revelation gives about attributes and divine providence. But they do not attend to the fact that this is very easily done by those who have once been illuminated by the light of revelation. Those who use this light are able to show effortlessly how the infinite attributes of God conform with the principles of reason. But let those who lack this light carefully examine whether they are able to show the same truth in everything. Whence the most brilliant theologian, Samuel Werenfelsius, very wisely discussed these things in *De Præstan. Relig. Revel.*, saying: 'Let them see whether our reasonings contribute much to their reason. They say that by reason alone they are able to find all that religion which is given in the sacred scriptures, or at least what is excellent in that religion. Nothing is easier to say for those who already know that religion. That could have been said, if through all of life they heard nothing about this religion. But now to me they seem like those who, after learning from teachers whatever they know, wish to seem self-taught. Or, when they hear about illustrious findings, they think, that they themselves were about to discover all these things, unless they have already been discovered. But if we wish to know what the reason of humans can do in discovering religion, we ought not consult our reason, we whom the word of God has led into and directs in the way, but the reason of those to whom this word is unknown. Here the examples of all the Gentiles is witness to what our reason bears when left to itself. Among the Gentiles were many who were no less strong in reason than our thinkers. I will say in a word: wholly rational religion, such as is found in the world, is the religion of the nations. The religion of the Deists is the religion of those who, after they have drawn out of the holy Scriptures everything they please, say that they found them by rationality.'" Stapfer cites "Diss. III. p. 131, 132" of Samuel Werenfels (1657–1740).

omnia virtutis fundamenta evertebant, dum omnia incerta putabant nullo certissimæ spei fulcro nixa.

"Secundo id, [quod] veram actionis moralis essentiam constituit, in ipsorum Philosophia morali non docebatur, quis nempe omnium nostrarum actionum finis generalis atque verus esse debeat; non enim Dei, sed propriam Gloriam quærebant.

"Ipsa, tertio, officia, quæ præscribebant, [. . .] erant imperfecta multisque pravis intermixta, plurimaque et maxime momemtosa, præcipue quæ Deum respiciunt, omissa, ut integrum Theologiæ Naturalis systema, si omnia simul sumantur, quæ omnes omnium temporum sapientes dixerunt, vix ac ne vix quidem confici possit. Religio illorum discenda erat à Philosophis et sacerdotibus, ea quæ priores docebant [. . .] Ritus, qui non mente sed Corpore fiebant et ex quibus vera sapientia addisci non poterat. Unde Lactantius, Lib. IV. Cap. 3. *De Vera Sapientia.* Quoniam igitur, inquit, Philosophia et Deorum Religio disjuncta sunt, siquidem alii sunt professores sapientiæ, per quos ad Deos non aditur, alii Religionis Antistites, per quos sapere non discitur, apparet, nec illam esse veram sapientiam, nec hanc Religionem.

"Nulla tandem præter Christianam solam existit Religion, quæ hominem in ipsa etiam morte non deserit, et non tantum spe certissima et solidissima Immortalitatis mactat, sed talia etiam ipsi post mortem præmia expectanda confirmat, quæ ipsius felicitatem ad summum culmen perducunt et in eum statum collocant, in quo intelligendo et volendo ad ultimum Creaturæ rationalis finem, propter quem condita est, nempe Dei Creatoris, Benefactoris et salvatoris munificentissimi Gloriam et Laudes vivere potest; Præmium certe summa Dei sapientia et Bonitate, nec non creaturæ rationalis conditione dignissimum.

"Reliquæ Religiones omnes aut in triste et lamentabile nihilum tandem definunt, aut quæ de futuro hominis statu docent, Fabulæ crassissimæ sunt, [. . .] nullo enim ipsorum opinio nitebatur fundamento, sed meræ conjecturæ in conscientiæ reliquiis residuæ erant."[7] Stapferus, *Theol. Polem.,* p. 508–11.

7. "The Christian religion strongly binds a human to the observation of natural religion and wants to get the motives of all its actions from the divine attributes. It wants, through following all things on account of God the Creator, to take him up as the conservor and common benefactor so that all things tend to his glory. From here, all the precepts flow out of the nature of God itself, while they propose God as the most perfect, lovable and venerable, as a being most powerful, at the same time most just and fair, who should be feared in all actions we undertake, as the best being who should be loved and sought, and in that way the sign of appointed confidence.

"How much also here does the religion of Christianity excel all those which reason, unen-

1315. CHRISTIAN RELIGION. THE HISTORY OF THE NEW TESTAMENT EARLY WRITTEN. CHRIST'S PROPHECIES OF THE DESTRUCTION OF JERUSALEM, ETC., WRITTEN BEFORE THE ACCOMPLISHMENT. "Acta Apostolorum ante Hierosolymitanum Excidium exarata fuisse, non unum est quod suadet. [. . .] Tempore Captivitatis Paulinæ exaratam fuisse hanc Historiam inde patet, quod cum omnia Pauli gesta exactissime narrentur, nulla tamen ejus e vinculis liberationis fiat mentio; sed Historiagraphus in medio illius Historiæ definit. Lucas vero antequam Acta Apostolorum scripsit, jam Evangelium suum litteris consignaverat, ad id enim statim ab Actorum initio provocat, antiquius vero adhuc Matthæi Evan-

---

lightened by the light of revelation, brings forth. I do not speak about the rather crass and the barbaric peoples, but about those, which human reason holds as the most wise, who among those, who clearly do not know divine revelation, wrote the most outstanding moral precepts for human beings. But how many defects, I ask, are found in their ethics! They deprive all cost from virtues, and maim them.

"For first they did not build their precepts on a sure foundation, nor did they strengthen them with true obligation and make them with just motives, as long as they did not derive them out of dependency on the Creator and Conservor of man. They did not take up motives from the divine attributes, nor did they add incitements to virtue by the promise of true, solid, and continual blessedness. Rather, they overturned all the foundations of virtue as long as they thought that everything was uncertain and had no leg of the surest hope on which to lean.

"Second, that which they decided was the true essence of moral action was not taught to a moral man in their philosophy. (Indeed, that ought to be the general and true end of all our actions.) For they sought their own glory, not that of God.

"Third, the duties themselves which they prescribe, [. . .] were incomplete and mixed with many depraved ones. Many more of great importance, chiefly those which reflect upon God, are omitted, with the result that the whole system of natural theology—if all things which all the wise men of all times have spoken are taken up together at once—scarcely and not even scarcely can be accomplished. Their religion was what had to be learned from the philosophers and priests, that which earlier [men] used to teach as rites which were done by the body not the mind and from which true wisdom could not be learned. Whence Lactantius, Bk. IV, ch. 3, *On True Wisdom.* Therefore, he says, seeing that philosophy and the religion of the gods have been separated, if indeed there are some professors of wisdom through whom nothing is added to the gods and there are some priests of religion through whom it is not taught to be wise, it would appear that the former is not true wisdom nor the latter true religion.

"Finally, no religion exists except Christianity alone which does not desert a human being even in death itself. Not only does it honor [the person] with a most sure and firm hope of immortality, but it also confirms for him such rewards as should be expected after death. These rewards lead his blessedness to the highest summit and settles [him] into that state in which, by understanding and willing toward the final end of the rational creature, on account of which it was created, he is most certainly able to live for the praises and glory of God the Creator, Benefactor, and most generous Savior. Surely this reward is most worthy of the highest wisdom and goodness of God and of the condition of the rational creature.

"All the remaining religions either end finally in a sad and lamentable nothingness, or what they teach about the state of man to come are the crassest fables, [. . .] for their opinion rested on no foundation, but were pure conjectures in the remnants of left-over knowledge."

gelium est; unde hæc omnia jam ante urbis eversionem scripta fuerint oportet.

"Nec omittendum, ipsa hæc Christi vaticinia ita comparata esse, ut ea neutiquam post Politiæ illius sacræ abrogationem litteris consignata esse ex illorum modo quom clarissime appareat; in illis enim, stylo prophetico, mundi Finis immediate cum veteris Mundi typici abrogatione conjungitur, ac si unum alterum statim exciperet; quod factum non fuisset, si post urbis demum vastationem vaticinia hæc ab hominibus impostoribus fuissent edita, hoc enim in casu stylum Prophetis maxime consuetum evitassent.

"Nec obscurum etiam ex Epistolis Paulinis pro Evangeliorum justo tempore desumi potest argumentum. Maxima enim illarum pars jam ante priora Pauli vincula exarata fuit, quod certissime, ex accuratissimis Chronologis constat; Historiam vero Evangelicam ubique in scriptis suis præsupponit." Stapferus, *Theol. Polem.*, Tom. II, pp. 1127–28.[8]

1316. CHRISTIAN RELIGION. CHRIST HAD THE SPIRIT OF PROPHECY. THE DESTRUCTION OF JERUSALEM WAS MANY WAYS A REMARKABLE TESTIMONY.

1. He often foretold it, with its time and circumstances and consequences. And that great and extraordinary event, in all its dreadful circumstances and great consequences, exactly answered his predictions. And that it did so abundantly proved that he was a true prophet, and the word in his mouth that he spake in the name of God was the truth, and

8. "That the Acts of the Apostles had been written before the fall of Jerusalem, there is not only one argument which is persuasive. [. . .] It is clear that this history had been written at the time of Paul's captivity, because, although all Paul's deeds are told with utmost detail, nevertheless, there is no mention of his liberation from chains. Instead, the historian ends in the middle of Paul's history. Certainly Luke wrote before the Acts and had already committed his own Gospel to letters, for he immediately refers to it at the beginning of Acts. Moreover, Matthew's Gospel is surely earlier. Whence it is necessary that all these things would have been written already before the overthrow of the city.

"Nor should it be omitted, that these very same prophecies of Christ were compared thus, so that it very clearly appears from them that they by no means were committed to writing after the destruction of the sacred commonwealth. For in them, in prophetic style, the end of the world is joined intimately with the abrogation of the type of the old world. So if you accept one you immediately accept the other. It would not have been done, if these prophecies had been edited after the ruin of the city by impostors, for in this case they would have avoided the style so fitted to the Prophets.

"It is possible to take up a clear argument also from the Pauline epistles on behalf of a proper time of the Gospels. It is most certain from the most accurate chronologies that the bulk of the Gospels had already been written prior to Paul's imprisonment; indeed, he presupposes the gospel history everywhere in his own writings."

indeed the word of God, and consequently that his doctrine concerning himself was the word of God, or was divine doctrine.

And here this is to be observed, that in the other desolations and captivities that had been in Israel, God sent prophets to foretell them and forewarn the people of them, especially the prophets Hosea and Amos. And what abundant predictions and forewarnings were given of the destruction of Jerusalem by the Chaldeans, and their captivity into Babylon, by many prophets, particularly Isaiah, Micah, Huldah, Habakkuk, Zephaniah, Jeremiah and Ezekiel, though that destruction was but a little thing in comparison of the second destruction by the Romans, and the captivity that followed but a little thing and of short continuance in comparison with that which has followed the latter. And, therefore, 'tis altogether unlikely that God should send no prophet at all to predict or forewarn the people of this, but that there should be a perfect silence about it for more than 500 years before it happened. But it was not so. The people had a far greater, more remarkable and affecting warning and predictions of this than the others, not by a prophet that spake on earth, but by the Prophet of prophets, the great prophet of God, the only begotten Son of God, that is, the Lord from heaven.

In other respects, God made his hand in this last destruction far more visible—both by an extraordinary interposition in the strange and unusual incidents and circumstances of it, and also in extraordinary signs, forerunners and presages of it—than in former destructions (see No. 972),[9] which is another thing that makes it the more incredible that God should not interpose and manifest himself in this respect also, viz. in forewarning of and giving the reasons of it by the Spirit of prophecy. It appears it was the mind of God to give previous notice of it in extraordinary presages in abundance. Why then should there be a total silence in God's more usual manner of presignification by prophecy?

2. Christ, who thus exactly foretold this great event, declared at the same time the reason why God [would] bring such a judgment. And he declared it should be for their rejection of him, and the contempt and malignity towards him, his gospel and his church, as the prophets who foretold the destruction of Israel and Jerusalem of old withal declared the reasons of it. And it would be a strange thing if that which has been far above all others the greatest judgment that ever God brought on his

9. JE refers to "p. 11. 12. p. 9. e. 10. a" of No. 972, "Christian Religion. That Jesus Truly Had the Spirit of Prophecy," which largely consists of excerpts from Tillotson's *Works*. JE specifically intends the first and third points of the section containing "*Reflections* on the foregoing prophecies of Christ, and their exact fulfillment." *Works*, 20, 265–66, 267–69.

people Israel, which in its duration has continued much longer than the whole time of their dwelling in the land of Canaan, should be brought on them without anyone to tell them the reason of it, and leave 'em all this while in the dark about it.

And 'tis reasonable to suppose that he that was let so particularly and exactly into the secret of the divine will with respect to the event also was able truly to declare for what reason and end it was brought to pass. But as there was no other forewarning of the event since Daniel's time (who intimated that it should be for rejecting the Messiah) but Christ's prediction, so no other reason was given but that which he gave, which therefore should be received as the true reason. But if God brought that destruction for not receiving Christ, how great a testimony of God is this to Christ's divine authority?

3. Christ foretold this great event as that which he himself would bring to pass (Luke 19:27); that it should come by his forsaking them and not protecting them (Matt. 23:34–39, Luke 13:34–35); that it should be his curse, represented by his cursing the barren fig tree [Matt. 21:19; Mark 11:13–14]; that it should be by his coming (Luke 17:30 with context, and Matt. 24:3 ff.). See how the fulfillment of such a prediction with such a circumstance is often spoken of in the Old Testament as an evidence of the divinity of the prediction, and also of the divinity of the prophet, No. 1044.[1]

4. The circumstances and incidents of this great event were such as remarkably showed it to be the mind of God that the Mosaic dispensation should be abolished, and to show that God thenceforward [would] have no more regard to the peculiar institutions or promises of it (see No. 972);[2] besides the consequence in the blotting out the family of Aaron and tribe of Levi by the confusion of their tribes, and their temple and land being so long in desolation, and the people in dispersion, by which means God has now made it impossible for the rites of that dispensation to be upheld for a much longer time than ever they were attended, which is a great testimony from heaven that that dispensation is at an end and, consequently, that the Messiah before that had appeared, and that the doctrine of Christ—in which he taught that the time was come that men should no more worship in that mountain, nor Jerusalem, but should worship God in spirit and in truth—was the word of God, and that he was the Messiah.

---

1. MS: "pp. 4–5," the conclusion of the entry, including points 2 and 3. *Works*, 20, 387–88.
2. MS: "p. 13," i.e. point 6 under the section of No. 972 containing "*Reflections* on the foregoing prophecies of Christ, and their exact fulfillment." *Works*, 20, 270–71.

5. That the punishment of the Jews had so many shrewd marks and signatures of the displeasure of God for their despising, evil treating, and crucifying Jesus, is another thing that makes this awful event a seal of his divine mission and authority. See No. 972.[3]

6. That Christ's followers, the Christians that were in the city, were by a wonderful providence generally delivered, being guided by Christ's prophetic directions. See No. 972.[4]

1317. CHRISTIAN RELIGION. CHRIST NO IMPOSTOR. "Quid salvator benignissimus hac ratione lucratus esset, nisi ærumnas, supplicium, crucem? Omnia enim mundana commoda procul abfuerunt; neque enim Regnum terrestre, uti Muhammedes stabilire volebat [. . .].

"Neque [porro] illius doctrina ita erat comparata ut hominum ingenio attemperata fuerit. Neque tales placitorum illius ratio, ut per ea hominum favorem expectare potuerit. Solent Impostores se suamque doctrinam loci temporisque circumstantiis accommodare: [. . .] hominum moribus ac temperamento indulgent; cedunt ubi nimiam resistentiam sentiunt; alte radicatis et præconceptis hominum opinionibus non è diametro sese oponunt; sed iis sese attemperant; mutant quædam et nova addunt, ita tamen ut antiqua retineant.

"Plane aliter Christus egit, talem nimirum protulit doctrinam, quæ præjudiciis Judæorum è diametro erat opposita, totum illorum Cultum externum à Mose ipsius Dei jussu institutum abrogatum voluit; cultum, quem maxima Judæorum pars ad mundi usque finem perduraturum existimabat, et in cujus observatione omnem suam salutem quærebant; Cultum à reliquis Populis diversum, in quo Judæi [tantopere] gloriabantur; Cultum, inquam, rei magnatum inter Judæos maxime inservientem, dum Populum ab ipsis dependentem faciebat: hunc cultum, inquam, antiquatum voluit. Si Impostor fuit, qui sectæ studio tenebatur; qui multos quærebat asseclas; quare non opinionibus Judæorum altissime radicatis hac in re melius favit? Quare id quod maxime amabant, in quo summan quærebant gloriam, plane remotum volebat? Quare non potius Politiæ Judaicæ ac Cultus publici Restauratorem se dixit? Nosce-

3. MS: "p. 13, and p. 8 e," respectively, point 5 of "*Reflections*," and a paragraph towards the end of the first subpoint under head (3), beginning, "And so obstinate were they, that neither those calamities that they suffered . . . " *Works, 20,* 270, 264.

4. MS: "p. 7 d., p. 11 d." Respectively, subpoint 1 under point (3) beginning, "The unparalleled greatness of their calamity and destruction"; and the paragraph under point 3 of "*Reflections*" beginning, "And indeed all along the hand of God was very visible against them; for when in the beginning of their rebellion, Cestius Gallus, the Roman commander . . . " *Works, 20,* 262, 268.

bat, quam Judæi de messiæ Persona atque negotio opinionem habebant; quare, cum ab iis Messias haberi volebat, si Impostor fuit, non illorum opinioni hac in re quantum potuit se accommodavit? Quare in omnibus contrarium exhibuit?

"Qui fit, ut primatum vitia tam acriter reprehenderit, et per hoc in illorum odium incurrerit? Quare hoc in media illa Republica fecit? Cur non potius illorum auram captare studuit?

"Sed nec Ethnicorum sapientiæ illius doctrina respondit, unde non solum Judæis offensio, sed Græcis stultitia fuit. Novam ergo doctrinam attulit; sive ut melius loquar, quæ omnibus Populis nova plane visa fuit, nihil aut ex Judæorum aut Gentilium placitis retinuit.

"Sed nec hominum vitiis, lubidini Carnis, Ambitioni, aut aliis sceleribus homini quam maxime familiaribus indulsit, quod tamen omnes illius et sequentium temporum Impostores et Pseudo-doctores fecere. Sed contra severissimas contra omnes mundi illecebras tulit Leges; quidquid, inquit, ad peccandum pellicit, aut impellit, vitandum et abjiciendum est, etiamsi sit oculo reliquisque membris carius. Non solum actiones, sed libidinosas etiam cogitationes prohibet. Omnem vindictæ cupidinem à quovis Christianæ Civitatis consorte sepositam vult. Amorem universalem, inimicorum etiam, requirit. Omnem in Cultu divino hypocrisin damnat. Imo introitum in Regnum Cœlorum sive Ecclesiæ suæ communionem difficillimum facit. Omnibus mimirum Impostoribus, ne unico quidem excepto, et Pseudo-prophetis sufficit, ut homines sectæ et Doctrinæ suæ nomen dent; at Dominus noster meram professionem inutilem plane asserit, neque contentus est mero doctrinæ suæ assensu, sed exactissimam Legis divinæ observationem postulat. 'Non,' inquit, 'quisquis ad me dicit: Domine, Domine, intrabit in cœleste Regnum; sed qui fecerit; quod vult meus Pater, qui est in Cœlis' [Matt. 7:12]. Imo Perfectiones divinas, ceu perfectissimum vitæ nostræ exemplar proponit, et plenariam suimetipsius abnegationem à discipulis suis postulat. Nullum terrestre commodum Apostolis suis promittit; verbera, Persecutiones, mortem, odium, Excommunicationem ex Ecclesia Judaica, ipsis Evangelium prædicantibus expectanda esse asserit. Matt. 10. 'Eritis omnibus invisi propter nomen meum. Tempus erit, quum omnes deum à se coli putabunt, qui vos interfecerint' [John 16:2]. Omnem ambitionem ab asseclis suis procul abesse vult, 'Nisi mutati fueritis, et pueris similes redditi, non intrabitis in cœleste Regnum' [Matt. 18:3].

"Omnia hæc ab Impostoris et Pseudo-prophetæ Characteribus non solum longissime remota, sed è diametro opposita sunt; quod quivis præconceptis opinionibus non occupatus Lector facile agnoscet.

"Testimonii sui veritatem cruciatibus gravissimis, inter ludibria pro-
brosissima, usque ad mortem dirissiman confirmavit. Hinc magistrum
suum hac in re discipuli etiam imitati sunt.

"Inquiunt Adversarii, Omnes Religiones, [à Veritate] etiam maxime
abhorrentes suis gloriari Martyribus, mirum propterea non esse, si et
Apostoli cum suo magistro ad tuendam Religionem suam martyrium
subierint.

"Ingens vero hic deprehendimus discrimen. Alii mortem subeunt,
quia mendacium quod profitentur verum esse credunt; si vero Christus
et Apostoli Impostores et seductores extitissent, mortem pro eo perpessi
fuissent, quod ipsimet falsissimum esse persuasi fuissent, id quod omni
probabilitatis specie plane destitutum est." Stapferus, *Theol. Polem.*, Tom
II, pp. 1132–36.[5]

---

5. Translated in *Miscellaneous Observations*, pp. 378–82: "What could the most merciful Savior have gained in this way, but misery, punishment, and crucifixion? For all worldly conveniences were far from him: nor did he wish, like Mahomet, to establish an earthly kingdom.
Neither was his doctrine adapted to the disposition of mankind; nor were his precepts and institutions such, that he could expect to win by them the favor of men. Impostors are wont to
accommodate themselves and their doctrine to the circumstances of time and place; to indulge
the manners and constitutions of men: they give way where they perceive too great opposition;
they do not directly oppose preconceived and deeply rooted opinions; but they adapt themselves to them, they change some things, and add some things new, yet so that they retain the
old ideas.

"Christ plainly acted a very different part. His doctrine was directly opposite to the prejudices of the Jews. He insisted upon it, that all their external form of worship, instituted by Moses,
according to the command of God, was abolished; a form of worship, which the greatest part
of the Jews thought would continue to the end of the world, and on the observance of which
they entirely depended for their salvation; a form of worship different from that of other nations, and in which the Jews gloried; a form of worship in the highest degree subserving the interest of the chief men among the Jews, as it made the people dependent on them. This form
of worship, Christ insisted, was become obsolete, and as such to be laid aside. If he was an impostor, attached to a sect, and sought many followers; why did he not, in this instance, favor the
opinions of the Jews, which were most deeply rooted? Why did he insist on the abolition and
removal of that, of which they were most fond, and in which they sought the highest glory? Why
did he not rather profess himself to be a restorer of the Jewish government and public worship? He well knew what opinion the Jews entertained concerning the person and work of the
Messiah. Why, then, since he wished to be received by them as the Messiah, did he not, if he
were an impostor, accommodate himself, to the utmost of his ability, to their opinion in this
particular? Why did he, in all respects, exhibit himself directly the contrary to their opinion
and expectation?

"Whence came it to pass that he so sharply reprehended the vices of their chief men, and
thereby incurred their hatred? Why did he do it so publicly? Why did he not rather court their
favor?

"Nor did his doctrine coincide with the wisdom of the Gentiles. Therefore, it was not only a
stumbling-block to the Jews, but foolishness to the Greeks. Thus, he introduced a new doctrine,
or, to speak more properly, a doctrine which plainly appeared to all people new. He retained
nothing of the favorite principles of either Jews or Gentiles.

1318. CHRISTIAN RELIGION. THE APOSTLES NOT ENTHUSIASTS. "Quis quæso persuadere sibi poterit, homines quammaxime rudes, cerebri non omnino sani et fanaticos, talem, summa cum harmonia protullisse et ubique, tam voce quam litteris inculcasse doctrinam, quæ sapientissimas, imo longe sapientiores de Deo tradat notiones, quam omnium qui hactenus vixerunt Philosophorum. Qui porro cultum plane rationalem pra;escripsurunt; qui, contra communes hominum opiniones, Deum non cæremoniis externis, sed cultu plane spirituali prosequendum dixerunt; ut animus non minus quam corpus ad summi Numinis reverentiam componatur; qui porro præscripserunt vivendi regulas, quas infensissimi etiam revelatæ Religionis hostes approbare coguntur, sive ad assensum quasi rapiuntur. Si homines hi fanatici et insani animi fuissent,

---

"He gave not the least indulgence to the vices, to the carnal lust, to the ambition or other wickednesses most familiar to man in his present state of depravity: yet this indulgence was granted by all the impostors and false teachers of our Lord's time, and the times following. On the other hand, he enacted and published the most pure laws against all the allurements of the world. Whatever, says he, entices and incites to sin, is to be avoided and rejected, though it be more dear than an eye, and the other bodily members or organs. He not only forbids the overt actions of lust, but also lustful thoughts. He requires every member of the Christian church to lay aside every desire of revenge, and to exercise an universal love of even enemies. He condemns all hypocrisy in divine worship: nay, he makes the entrance into the kingdom of heaven, or the communion of his church, most difficult. Without doubt, it satisfies all impostors and false prophets, without one exception, that they have given to men the name of their sect and doctrine: but our Lord in the plainest terms asserts, that a mere profession of Christianity is useless. Nor is he contented with the mere assent to his doctrine; but demands the most exact observance of his law. 'Not every one,' says he, 'who saith unto me, Lord, Lord, shall enter into the kingdom of heaven, but he that doth the will of my Father who is in heaven.' Nay, he proposes the divine perfections as the most perfect pattern of our life, and demands of his disciples the most entire denial of themselves. He promised even to this apostles no worldly advantage; but declared, that hatred, stripes, persecutions, excommunication from the Jewish church, and death, were to be expected by the preachers of the gospel. Matt. 10, 'Ye shall be hated of all men for my name's sake: the time will come, when all that kill you shall think that they do God service.' So far from encouraging ambition in his followers, he declared, that unless they should be so changed as to become like little children, they should not enter into the kingdom of heaven.

"All these are not only most remote from the characters of an impostor and false prophet, but are diametrically opposite to them, as will be acknowledged by every reader who is uninfluenced by preconceived opinion.

"Our Lord confirmed the truth of his testimony, by patiently enduring the most reproachful mockery, and the most grievous tortures unto death. Hence his disciples have imitated their Master in this particular.

"The opposers of Christianity say, that all religions, even those which are most consistent with each other, agree in this, that they boast of their martyrs; and that, therefore, it is not wonderful that the apostles and their master underwent martyrdom to support their religion. But here we find a great difference. Others undergo death, because the falsehood which they profess is believed by them to be a real truth. But if Christ and his apostles were impostors and seducers, they suffered death for that which they themselves knew to be most false: which is plainly without any appearance of probability."

certe hujus rei vel in illorum vita vel scriptis aliquod deprehenderetur vestigium: sed percurrat quis omnia Evangelia, Epistolas omnes, nihil plane ibi invenitur, ex quo vel minima hujus rei probabilitas erui posset.

"Minime etiam credibile est, maximam hominum partem ab hominibus stultis atque mente captis sibi imponi atque decipi se passam fuisse, in re quæ opinionibus suis plane adversa, et in doctrina, quæ nec sæculi hujus commodis nec carnis voluptatibus favebat, sed omnibus carnis illecibris plane contraria erat. . . . Altissimas tamen longe lateque radices egit; neque ad breve admodum tempus, sed per multorum sæculorum imo mox duorum milleniorum cursum semper propagata, omni tempore à varii generis hominibus recepta, non à credula plebe solum, sed à Principibus etiam ac magnatibus; non à stultis modo ac simplicibus, sed à sapientibus, acutissimisque etiam Philosophis, ab eruditis æque ac idiotis. An quæso probabile est, placita nova ab insanis ac fanaticis hominibus inventa ac disseminata tantam omni tempore fidem invenisse. Mox pereunt fanaticorum somnia; apud ignaros forsan applausum inveniunt, Philosophi ea rident; sed oportet ipsam doctrinam Christianam ita comparatam esse, ut sapientissimus etiam sese commendet et virtuti quammaxime deditis, quis eam merum fanaticismum dixerit? Non armorum vi, non subdolis artibus illa diffusa ac propagata fuit; nulla humano auxilio munita, neque ibi præcipue Apostoli Evangelium prædicarunt, ubi Populi rudes ac ignari nullis disciplinis exculti erant; sed Hierosolymis, in Græciæ urbibus, ubi Philosophi existebant acutissimi, Romæ denique omnium scientiarum sede; mundo scientiis exculto novam illam doctrinam annuntiarunt, 'ne quis imposturam simplicitati factam esse, posset suspicari,' inquit Lud. *Vives de Veritate Fid.* Lib II. Non tenebras quæsiverunt primi Evangelistæ, sed in lucem prodierunt, neque ab aliis postulabant, ut absque exploratione verbis suis fidem adhiberent, sed dicta sua examinari volebant. [. . .] I Thess. 5:21–22.[6] [. . .] I John 4:1. 'Quin turpi occultatione repudiata, non nos callide gerimus, neque divinam doctrinam fallaciter tractamus, sed Veritatis declaratione nos ipsos apud omnem hominum conscientiam in Dei conspectu commendamus'" [II Cor. 4:2].[7] Stapferus, Tom. II, pp. 1136–40.

---

6. MS: "19, 20." In the MS, a copyist interlineated "21, 22" to indicate the verses that Stapfer actually quotes.

7. "Who, I ask, could persuade himself that men so unlearned, of utterly unsound mind and fanatics, produced such a teaching with complete harmony and that they inculcated it everywhere with both voice and writing? Their teaching passes on the wisest notions about God, indeed far wiser than those of all the philosophers who have thus lived. Those men prescribed a worship clearly rational. They—against the common beliefs of human beings—said that God

1319. CHRIST'S MIRACLES not performed by human art and sleight of hand. "Si unum aut alterum tantum patratum fuisset Miraculum, idque in objectis parum notis, atque præscentibus paucissimis testibus, qui facile decipi potuissent; si miracula illa unius tantum generis fuissent; si aliquot vicibus tantum reiterata essent, objectio hæc speciem aliquam habet. Sed 1. tanta Christi inter Judæos fuit fama, ut si non omnes et singuli eum cognoverint, quoad nomen saltem omnibus notus fuerit; ut non obscurus aliquis Propheta fuerit in deserto commorans, inter homines plebejos solum; fama, inquam, ejus tanta fuit, ut omnium attentionem excitaverit. 2. Eos, qui inter Judæos acutissimi erant, habuit Adversarios, Pharisæos et Sadducæos, homines litteratos ac Legis doctores, hi ubique homines habebant subornatos, qui ad dicta ac[8] facta ejus attentissimi erant. Anne credibile, nullam unquam fraudem ipsos dete-

---

should be followed not in external ritual but in a spiritual worship; that the mind no less than the body is appointed to the reverence of the highest divinity. Furthermore, they prescribed rules of living which even the most hostile enemies of revealed religion are forced to approve or are compelled as if to assent. If these men were of a fanatical and unsound mind, certainly some vestige of this would be apprehended either in their lives or their writings. However, if someone goes through all the Gospels, all the Epistles, surely nothing is found there from which even the least probability of this could be dug up.

"It is not at all credible that the greater part of humankind had allowed itself to deceived by foolish men and imposed upon as captives in mind in a situation which was clearly adverse to their own opinions and in a doctrine which favored neither the conveniences of this age or the desires of the flesh, but was evidently contrary to the allurements of the flesh. . . . Nevertheless, it sent out very deep roots wide and far. Nor was that for a brief spate of time, but through many ages—rather almost two thousand years—it has continually propagated its course, received in every time by different classes of people, not only by credulous common folk, but also by princes and magnates; not only by fools and simpletons, but by the wise, even the most astute philosophers; by the erudite as well as by the unschooled. Or, I ask, is it probable that pleasing news, invented and disseminated by unsound and fanatic men had found such a great faith at this time? The dreams of fanatics soon perish; perhaps they find applause with ignorant men, philosophers laugh at them. But it is fitting that Christian doctrine itself be judged thus, that even the wisest commend themselves both to its virtue and especially to those given over to it. Who would call it pure fanaticism? It was spread and propagated not by force of arms, not by crafty artifice, nor was it fortified by human aid. The apostles did not chiefly preach the gospel where unlearned and ignorant people uncultivated by any teachings were, but in Jerusalem, in the Greek cities where the most astute philosophers were, and finally in Rome, the seat of all knowledge. They announced this new doctrine to a world cultivated by knowledge, 'in order that no one would be able to suspect that a deceit for the simple was made,' says Ludolf [of Saxony], *Vives de Veritate Fid.*, Bk. II. The first Evangelists did not seek darkness, but they went out into the light. They did not ask of others that they adhere to the faith without an exploration of their words, but they wanted what they said to be examined. [. . .] I Thess. 5:19–20. [. . .] I John 4:1. 'Hardly in repudiated and base secrecy, we do not bear ourselves craftily, nor do we handle the divine teaching falsely, but by the declaration of truth, we commend ourselves to the whole conscience of men in the sight of God'" [II Cor. 4:2].

8. MS: "&."

gere potuisse, si mera impostura fuisset? 3. Christus non in locis obscuris atque à hominum colluvie remotis patravit miracula, sed in urbibus, in maxima omnis conditionis hominum frequentia. 4. Non una vice id præstitit, sed per tres integros annos sæpissime ea repetiit. 5. Opera hæc ita erant comparata, ut per caussas naturales fieri minime potuerint; morbos longo tempore inveteratos sanavit, non unius sed varii generis; idque præstitit in Personis, quæ multis annis omnium conspectui erant expositæ, ut illarum status nemini non notus esset. Mortuos resuscitavit, non tales de quibus dubium essa potest num revera mortui fuerint, sed tales, qui jam à pluribus diebus mortui et qui in conceptu omnium mortui erant; anne credibile illum tot vicibus, tot casibus et tamdiu, tanto hominum numero fucum facere potuisse?" Stapferus, Tom. II, p. 1141 [−42].[9]

1320. LORD'S DAY. That saying of our Savior to his disciples, "But pray ye that your flight be not in the winter, nor on the sabbath day" (Matt. 24:20), is a very great evidence of the Christian sabbath. For 'tis quite incredible that Christ here meant that they should pray that they might not be hindered from the usual observation of the Jewish sabbath at that very time when he would utterly put an end to the Jewish dispensation, and entirely abolish all remains of it in so remarkable and extraordinary a manner, and should so greatly testify his displeasure to the Jews for their adhering so strongly to it and making so much of it. Not only was

---

9. "If one or two great miracles had been produced, and that in little known objects and with very few witnesses present who could be easily deceived; if those miracles had been so many of one kind; if they were not repeated in so many places; then this objection has some appearance. But 1. The fame of Christ was so great among the Jews that if not all individually knew him, at least as far as his name he was known to all. They knew that he was not some obscure prophet lingering in the desert only among the common people; his fame, I say, was so great that he stirred up the attention of all. 2. He had those who were the most astute among the Jews as enemies: Pharisees and Saducees, educated men and teachers of the law. These had men everywhere ready who were most attentive to Christ's words and deeds. Or is it believable that they were never able to uncover any fraud if he had been a mere impostor? 3. Christ did not produce his miracles in obscure places and removed from the dregs of humanity, but in cities, in the greatest gathering of every condition of men. 4. He did not perform it at one time, but through three whole years he very often repeated them. 5. These works have been so judged that they are by no means able to be accomplished through natural causes. He healed those who had been sick for a long time and not of one but of various kinds; he produced them in people who had been exposed to the sight of all within a span of many years, with the result that their state was not unknown to anyone. He revived the dead, not such as about whom it could be doubted whether they really were dead, but such as who were dead for many days in everyone's opinion. Or is it believable that he was able to foist deceit in so many times, in so many situations, for so long, and on such a great number of people?"

the destruction of Jerusalem a dispensation by which God put a final end to that dispensation, but such were the particular circumstances of that awful judgment as to show remarkably that God poured contempt upon the festivals of that dispensation, and its weekly sabbaths in particular (see "Miscellanies," No. 972).[1]

Now is it credible that Christ should direct Christians as to have so great a regard to the Jewish sabbath at that very time which was appointed for the entire abolishing of it and the pouring of contempt of it? And is it credible that he should give such a direction—with such circumstances as would tend to lead Christians to suppose that Christ had so great a regard to the strict observation of the Jewish sabbath at that time as particularly to direct 'em so long beforehand to pray that they might not be interrupted in their observation of it—when that was the very time appointed for his utterly abolishing of it, and for an extraordinary, most visible and public testimony of his utter disregard of it?

But 'tis evident it was the will of Christ that there should be some sabbath that it was his will his church should have the most sacred regard to, even at that time of his abolishing and most visibly disregarding the Jewish sabbath. And what sabbath can this be but the Christian sabbath?

1321. CHRISTIAN RELIGION, the Apostles no impostors who knew that the miracles of Christ and his resurrection that they gave account of were mere figments of their own, but told such lies as seeking their own glory, as the heads of a party, etc.

"Si dicipere voluerunt Apostoli, si gloriam propriam quæsiverunt, quare [. . .] proprios nævos tam ingenue referunt? Quare nec propriam tarditatem, nec continuas altercationes, nec Petri abnegationem, nec [. . .] omnium Apostolorum desertionem reticent? Si merum figmentum narrant, quare non ex composito scripserunt? [. . .] Neque[2] ab unico scripti sunt novi Fœderis Libri, sed à pluribus, qui sibi non contradicunt, ita tamen scribunt, ut facile appareat, ipsos non ex compacto egisse. Qui vero fieri potest, si res hæc merum figmentum fuit, ut mire in omnibus inter se consentiant?

"Facta, quæ apostoli memorant, non in terris longinquis, non tempore remoto, non inter homines ignotos gesta fuere; sed eo in loco, ubi Apostoli ea narrant ac scribunt; ea ætate, qua omnia litteris fuerant consignata; inter eos homines, inter quos, Apostoli prædicant et scribunt,

---

1. MS: "p. 13," or points 5 and 6 under "*Reflections*." *Works, 20,* 270–71.
2. MS: "non."

quique num res vera an falsa fit optime scire poterant. Facta hæc proponunt non ceu ignota, sed generalem illorum cognitionem quasi supponunt, et quæ summam rei faciunt Judæorum Principibus, inimicissimis Adversariis suis, in os dicunt. Non ita agere solent Impostores ac fabularum inventores, sed figmenta sua tegere solent, ne fraus detegatur.

"Si ea quæ narrabant oppido falsa fuere, qui fit ut propter impudentissiman atque audacissimam fraudem non reprehensi fuerint? Quare disciplinæ Christianæ inimici juratissimi putidissimas hasce fabulas non in commodum suum verterunt, atque monstrarunt, omnia ab Apostolis prolata merum figmentum esse, certutadinem operum illorum nullo niti fundamento? Nulla re citius Christiana Religio in ipso ortu suo extingui potuisset, quam si eo ipso tempore historiæ, qua nititur, falsitas demonstrata fuisset. Nihil fuisset quo hominum animi ab hac doctrina avocari potuissent, quam si à Judæorum Magistris ac magnatibus fabula hæc ac impostura detecta fuisset, si Apostolos fraudis convicissent. Tanta fuit magistratus Judæorum erga Paulum reliquosque Apostolos acerbitas, ut nullam prætermiserint occasionem eos vituperandi, omniaque arripuerint, quæ in Apostolorum ac disciplinæ Christianæ detrimentum cedere videbantur. At de miraculorum ac Resurrectionis Jesu Christi veritate altum ubique est silentium; cum tamen sola hujus fictionis demonstratio ad totam Christianam Religionem subvertendam suffecisset. Quare non magistratus Judaicus et alii Christianorum hostes tam voce quam scriptis fraudem in aperta luce collecant, aliosque hac ratione ne decipiantur præmuniunt?

"Dignissima sunt, quæ hic probe perpendantur, verba Theologi acutissimi Joh. Allp. Turretini diss. de miraculis quæ ita habent. 'Sic se gerunt Apostoli, ut pateat eos nihil simile metuere, deque veritate suae narrationis plene ac perfecte securos esse. Etenim, aperte agunt; nihil dissimulant; circumstantias omnes recensent; notant loca; notant tempora singulorum eventuum; notant nomina personarum; notant sacerdotes, magistratus, privatos homines, eos omnes denique, quorum aliquæ his in factis partes fuerant; provocant ad testes illo tempore superstites; et Paulus quidem quingentos Resurrectionis dominicæ testes adpellat: coram omnibus, Judæis, Gentilibus, Philosophis, Regibus, Magnatibus, Facta illa audacter promulgant, Ea memorant, inculcant, repellunt, nulla non occasione, nullis non in locis. Non metuunt, non sunt solliciti, ne sibi non credatur; Res maxime miras ac stupendas ita nude ac secure tradunt, quasi ea nemo in controversiam vocare possit. Nullum artificium, nulla cautio, nullæ latebræ, nullæ offuciæ, in omnibus deprehenduntur. Sic dicunt, sic agunt apostoli. Quis vero capiat, impostores ea sese ratione gerere? Quis capiat, homines rudissimos, artifices imperitissimos, fraudem omnem ita celare, externam speciem virorum proborum ita mentiri, ut ne minimum quidem deceptionis indicium adpareat. *Simplex est veritat sermo.* Ubi vero major simplicitas, major ingenuitas, apertiora sinceritatis ac veritatis indicia, quam in modo quo facta illa ab Apostolis commemorantur.'

"Nulla inquam Religio, nulla secta plures, Christiana disciplina habuit Adversarios; nulla potentiores, nulla doctiores; si figmenta atque fabulæ in Apostolorum scriptis fuissent contentæ, dubium nullum est quin eas detexissent, si hi rei Christianæ accerrimi hostes solidi quidquam atque certi contra narrationes Apostolicas scivissent, certe non siluissent. Qui fit ut in omnibus Judæorum scriptis discipulorum Christi fraudas nullibi detegantur et probentur? Quod altum silentium, ac meræ quas proferunt criminationes rei veritatem maximopere stabilit." Stapferus, *Theol. Polem.*, Tom. II, pp. 1143–47.[3]

3. Translated in *Miscellaneous Observations*, pp. 384–86: "If the apostles meant to deceive; if they sought their own glory, why did they so ingenuously relate their own faults? Why did they secrete neither their own slowness to believe, nor their continual altercations, nor Peter's denial of his Lord, nor the desertion of him by all the apostles? If they related a mere fiction, why did they not write by agreement? The books of the New Testament were not written by one man, but by many. These do not contradict themselves, or each other: yet they so write, that it easily appears, that they did not act from agreement. But how could it come to pass, if the whole affair was a mere fiction, that in all things they so wonderfully agree among themselves?

"The facts which the apostles relate, are not said to have taken place in distant countries, in remote times, among unknown men, but in the very place in which the apostles related and wrote them; at that time in which all events were recorded in books; among those men, among whom the apostles preached and wrote, and who were under the best advantages to know whether those facts did really take place or not. They exhibit these facts not as unknown, but do, as it were, take for granted, the general knowledge of them, and declare those things which make the sum of the affair, in the face of the rulers of the Jews, their chief enemies. Impostors and inventors of fables are not wont to act thus, but carefully to conceal their fictions from detection.

"If those things which they related to the town were false, whence did it come to pass, that they were not blamed on account of their most impudent and most audacious fraud. Why did not the sworn enemies of Christian institution turn those state fables to their own advantage, and show, that all things pretended by the apostles, were mere fictions, and that the certainty of those works had no foundation? The Christian religion could, in its beginning, have been extinguished by nothing more easily, than by demonstrating, at that very time, that the history on which it depended, was a falsehood. There was nothing by which the minds of men could more effectually have been called off from this religion, than clear proof given by the magistrates and chief men of the Jews, that the apostles were guilty of fraud, and that the story which they told, was a fable and an imposture. So great was the bitterness of these magistrate toward Paul and the other apostles, that they let slip no opportunity of reproaching them; and they eagerly laid hold of every thing which could be turned to the disadvantage of the apostles, and of Christianity. But concerning the truth of the miracles and of the resurrection of Jesus Christ, there is every where a deep silence; though the mere demonstration that these things were fic-

1322. CHRISTIAN RELIGION. THE TRUTH OF THE HISTORY OF THE NEW TESTAMENT. "Ex vagis hominum rumoribus historiam evangelicam confectam fuisse, non modo omni plane probabilitate caret, sed plane absurdum est; neque enim in fabulis omnia adsunt certitudinis criteria, uti hic, dum notantur, omnes temporis, loci, personarumque circumstantiæ, omnia quæ narrantur inter se consentiunt, non unus modo, sed multi scriptores, de quorum fide ut dubitemus caussa nulla adest, idem dicunt, summus inter eos ubique deprehenditur consensus; quod in figmentis ac fabulis Romanensibus contingere minime potest.

"Sed qui fieri potuit, quæsumus, ut tot hominum myriades tam cito ac tam facile et quidem constantissime figmento fidem adhiberent, quod nonnisi vago aliquo rumore nitebatur? Et quidem, ex Adversariorum nostrorum mente, tali assentiebantur fabulæ, cui superstructa erat talis Doctrina, quæ nec hominum præjudiciis consentanea erat, nec sapientiæ Judæorum aut Græcorum Philosophorum favebat, cupiditatibus

---

titious, would have been sufficient for the total subversion of the Christian religion. Why then did not the Jewish magistrates and other enemies of the Christians, exhibit, both in their declarations and writings, clear and public proof of the cheat, and thereby guard others from the delusion?

"The words of that most acute divine, Joannes Alphonse Turretin, in his *Discourse Concerning Miracles*" (Stapfer cites "§ xxxiv") "are well worthy to be considered in this place. They are as follows: 'The apostles conducted themselves in such a manner, that it is manifest that they feared nothing of the kind, and that they were fully and perfectly secure concerning the truth of their story. For they acted openly; they disguised nothing; they mentioned all circumstances, marked the places and times of all events; they named the persons, the priests, the magistrates, the private men, and all those who bore any part in the facts: they appealed to the witnesses then alive; and Paul appealed to five hundred witnesses of the resurrection of our Lord. They boldly published those facts before all, Jews, Gentiles, philosophers, kings and magistrates; they related them, they inculcated them, they defended them, on all occasions, and in all places. They were not afraid, they were not anxious, lest they should not be believed. They told the most wonderful and stupendous events as simply and securely, as if no body could call them in question. No art, no caution, no reservation, no coloring is to be found in any of them. In this manner did the apostles speak and act. But who can imagine, that impostors would act in this manner? Who can imagine, that unlearned men, ignorant mechanics, could so conceal all fraud, and so mimic the outward appearance of honest men, that not even the least sign of deception appears? *The word of truth is simple.* But where is there greater simplicity, greater candor, and more manifest signs of sincerity and truth, than in the manner in which the apostles relate the facts of the gospel?

"'No religion, no sect, had more enemies than Christianity; none had enemies more powerful or more learned. If there had been fictions and fables in the writings of the apostles, no doubt they would have detected them. If those most inveterate enemies of Christianity had known anything solid or certain against the accounts given by the apostles, most certainly they would not have kept it in silence. How does it come to pass, that in all the writings of the Jews, the frauds of Christ's disciples are nowhere pointed out, and proved? Which profound silence, and the mere criminations, without support, they threw out against the apostles, are a strong confirmation of the apostolical narrations.'"

vero carnis è diametro adversa. Unde nonnisi veritatis certitudine hominibus sese commendare poterat. [. . .]

"Tolle miracula (inquit[4] judiciosissimus Alp. Turretinus) an concipi potest, viles piscatores, quales erant Apostoli, tale consilium, qualis fuit Gentilium omnium à receptis sacris abductio, et ad Christianam fidem conversio, animo finxisse atque suscipisse? Fac miracula meram fraudem esse: an concipi potest fraudem illam, à tot Adversariis, adeo potentibus, adeo perspicacibus, demonstratam modo irrefragabili atque eversam non esse? Aufer miracula; an concipi potest, universum terrarum orbem, absque armis, absque opibus, absque ullis humanis auxilliis, ad Christiam fidem adductum esse?"

"Et hoc denique notandum, quod infensissimi illi primorum sæculorum Doctrinæ Christianæ hostes miraculorum Evangelicorum veritatem non negent. Sed ad illorum vim eludendam alia effugia quærant; unde Judæi dicunt, illum magica artes in Egypto didicisse; ut alia ejusmodi nullius ponderis subterfugia, quæ ex iis quæ antea diximus corruunt, taceamus." Stapferus, *Theol. Polem.*, Tom II, pp. 1148–51.[5]

4. MS: "ait."
5. "The idea that the evangelical history was made out of the aimless rumors of men certainly not only lacks all probability, but is clearly ridiculous. For there are not all the requisites of certitude in fables as there are here; while there are noted, all times, places, people and circumstances, all things which are told agree among themselves, not only one, but many writings (about the truth of which there is no cause for use to doubt), writings which say the same thing, the highest agreement among themselves being everywhere detected. [None of this] can be attained in figments and Roman tales.

"But how can it happen, we ask, that so many myriads of people so quickly, so easily and so constantly fix their faith to a figment which only rests on aimless rumor? And indeed, as our adversaries suppose, they agreed with such a fable, upon which such a teaching had been built, which did not agree with the prejudices of men, nor was favorable to the wisdom of the Jews or of Greek philosophers, but was diametrically adverse to the desires of the flesh. Whence, without the certainty of truth, it was not able to commend itself to men. [. . .]

"Remove the miracles (says the most discerning [Joannes] Alphonse Turretin)." (Stapfer cites "Dissert. de Miraculis § pen. ult.") "Can it then be conceived that lowly fishermen, such as were the apostles, made and undertook such a plan as leading away all the Gentiles from their traditional religion and converting them to the Christian faith? Make the miracles a pure fraud. Can it then be conceived that that fraud was shown irrefutably and was not overturned by so many adversaries, so strong, so perceptive? Take away the miracles. Can it then be conceived that the whole earth has been led to Christian faith without arms, without force, and without any human aids?

"And finally, this should be noted, the fact that those aggressive enemies of Christian doctrine in the early ages do not deny the truth of evangelical miracles. But they seek other ways of evading their power; whence the Jews say that He learned magic arts in Egypt. As others of this kind are subterfuges of no importance (which fail because of those things we said earlier), let us keep silence." For the last paragraph of this excerpt, JE goes back in Stapfer, *Institutiones*, 2, from p. 1151 to p. 1150.

1323. CHRISTIAN RELIGION. EVIDENCES OF CHRIST'S RESURRECTION. "Hanc [vero] difficultatem non minimi ponderis arbitrantur, quod Jesus Christus post suam ex mortuis resurrectionem nemini ex inimicis suis aparuerit [. . .]. Putant [. . .] ad homines [. . .] convincendos, omni modo utile ac necessarium fuisse, ut Christus summis sacerdotibus, reliquisque ex Judaicis senatoribus, nec non Præfecto Romano Pontio Pilato, ut et omnibus Hierosolymorum incolis, [. . .] ut in templo quam in plateis publice doceret, uti id ante mortem suam sæpissime fecarat; quo factum ut omnium oculis veritas exposita esset, neque ullum in hominum animis remaneret dubium.

"Iniquum omnino hoc petitum est, cujusque effectus Adversariorum opinioni minime respondisset. Nam 1. hostes disciplinæ Christianæ per Christi resuscitati Aparitionem vel conversi fuissent, vel non conversi: si prius, nec hoc in casu illorum testimonium in incredulorum animis plus valeret, quam Apostolorum; nam Paulo infensissimo suo inimoco apparuit, qui propterea semper et ubique veritatem professus est, attamen illius testimonium [. . .] non plus valet, quam Matthæi aut Johannis; quam primum enim se Doctrinæ Evangelicæ convictum aliquis dicit, illius verba incredulis jam suspecta videntur. Si vero apud plurimos posterius evenisset, ut conversi non essent, mille iterum invenissent fictiones ac effugia, et nonnisi præstigias ac phantasma à Cacodaemone productum dicerent.

"2. Si testis aliquis fide dignissimus asseveraret, Christum omnibus hisce apparuisse, ipsi non magis fidem adhiberent ac Paulo Apostolo testanti, Christum è mortuis suscitatum apparuisse plusquam quingentis una vice, qui eo, quo hæc scribebat, tempore adhuc plurimam partem in vita superstites erant.

"3. Hinc fieret ut, si Christus omnibus Hierosolymæ incolis apparuisset, plus adhuc Increduli poscerent, ut scilicet Tiberio etiam Romano, [. . .] ut toti etiam Populo Romano apparuerit; sed nec hoc ipsis sufficeret, licet factum esset, vellent ut hanc usque diem Christus in Terra mansisset atque universo Mundo sese monstraret; nec etiam continua hæc Christi ad mundi finem usque apparitio incredulis sufficeret, neutiquam enim fidem adhiberent, hunc qui nostris temporibus Jesum se profiteretur, eundem illum esse, qui à Judæis ad supplicium tractus fuit; nova miracula poscerent, et si fierent, eundem apud scepticos ac Incredulos habitura essent effectum, quem olim apud incredulos Judæos habebant, qui per Cacodæmonem atquae præstigias sive magicas artes ea fieri dicebant. Et ita scepticismus Theologicus ac Incredulitas res miserrima est, ubi omnia externa media insufficientia sunt.

"4. Plusquam duodecim et quingenti testes, ut in re momentosissima requirantur, iniquum est; qui his fide dignissimis, et contra quos ne infensissimi quidem hostes quidquam habuerunt quod proferant, qui his, inquam, assensum denegat, is etiam nec pluribus eum præbebit."[6]

(I would here add that it did consist with the state that Christ rose to—as a state of eternal life and felicity, having finished all his humiliation and suffering—that Christ should manifest himself to his enemies after his resurrection, freely conversant with them as before. For if many had remained still his enemies, and continued to reject [him]—as there is the greatest probability they would—he would still be exposed to suffer from them as the object of their hatred, reproach and contempt and, in many respects, to be ill treated by them.

And then, if he had only appeared sometimes, or at a distance, with-

6. "But they think this difficulty to be very weighty, the fact that Jesus Christ, after his resurrection from the dead, appeared to none of his enemies [. . .]. They think [. . .] that it was in every way useful and necessary for convincing men that Christ (appear) to the high priests, to the rest of the Jewish elders, to the Roman prefect Pontius Pilate, also to all the inhabitants of Jerusalem, [. . .], in both the temple and streets where he used to teach, just as he had very often done before his death. If this were done, the truth would be exposed to the eyes of all, nor would any doubt remain in the minds of men.

"This request is completely unfair and its accomplishment would by no means answer our adversaries' feelings. For 1. The enemies of Christian teaching either would have or would have not be converted through the appearance of the risen Christ. If the former, the testimony in their case in the minds of the incredulous would not be stronger than in the case of the Apostles. For He appeared to Paul, his most aggressive enemy, who then always and everywhere proclaimed the truth, but his testimony [. . .] was no stronger than that of Matthew or John; for as soon as anyone says that they are convinced of the evangelical doctrine, his words already seem suspect to the incredulous. But if the latter, that they were not converted, they would find again a thousand feignings and evasions, and they would say that they were delusions and a phantom produced by an evil spirit.

"2. If any witness most worthy of trust should affirm that Christ had appeared to all these, they would apply no more trust than to the witness of Paul the apostle that Christ appeared raised from the dead to more than 500 in one place, most of whom, at the time he was writing those things, were still living.

"3. From this it would happen that, if Christ had appeared to all the inhabitants of Jerusalem, the incredulous would ask even more, that of course he should appear also to the Roman Tiberius, [. . .] and to the entire people of Rome. However, this would not satisfy them, though it be done, for they would want Christ to remain on the earth to this very day and show himself to all the world. Even this continuing appearance of Christ to the end of the world would not satisfy the incredulous, for they would by no means trust that this Jesus who shows himself in our time, is that same one who had been led to death by the Jews. They would ask for new miracles, and if they were done, they would have the same effect with the skeptics and unbelievers which they once had with unbelieving Jews, who said they were done through an evil spirit and either illusion or magic arts accomplished them. And thus theological skepticism and unbelief are the most wretched things, when all external media are not enough.

"4. It is unfair that they require more than twelve and 500 witnesses; the one who denies to these most worthy of trust and against whom not even the most aggressive enemies had anything which they brought forth; the one, I say, who denies assent to these, is one who will not offer assent to even more witnesses."

out freely conversing with them or admitting them near to him, and they had nevertheless still continued his enemies after Christ had exposed himself to their view and trusted the credit of his resurrection and of his religion to their testimony, they, if they had been wicked enough—as, in all probability, many of 'em were—would have acted the part of false witnesses to the world and to future generations, and have made such a lying representation of the affair as should tend to disparage him and his doctrine, and might have contradicted the testimony of the apostles and more impartial witnesses with respect to the manner and circumstances of his appearance. It was not safe nor proper to entrust so important a truth as the resurrection of Christ to be delivered to the world and to future generations through the hands of such prejudiced, malicious and wicked, crafty witnesses.

But, on the other hand, if most of [the] rulers of the nations had been convinced and converted, so as to become the friends of Christ, and had used their influence to promote Christianity in the world, it would rather have turned to the discredit of Christianity with those who are deistically inclined. They would have said then that Christianity had worldly power and wisdom and wealth on its side, and would have ascribed the propagation of it to that, would have suspected that it was only a contrivance of the Jewish nation to aggrandize themselves in the eye of the world as a people dignified above all others, on whom the whole world must depend for their highest honor and happiness, and must look on them as the fountain of all true religion, true wisdom, and virtue, and eternal salvation, and must receive all their doctrines and precepts, by which they must guide themselves through the whole course of their lives.[7] The whole story, if written by some of their great men, would have been suspected as the effect of a crafty conspiracy of theirs to aggrandize themselves.)

"Quæstio omnis huc tandem redit: an divinæ sapientiæ magis convenisset, ut Christus omnibus [. . .] sese redivivum exhibuisset, an vero si paucioribus tantum apparuerit? At eadem difficultas de Religione naturali formari potest: quare scilicet Deus non ita clare sese hominibus cognoscendem præbeat, ut ne minimum quidem dubium in ullo Articulo supersit, qua ratione fieret, ut scepticismus Philosophicus omnis plane tolleretur. [. . .]

"Veritatum tam Naturalium quam revelatarum tanta est certitudo, [. . .] ut quivis [. . .] veritatis amore ductus, unique inveniat, ubi pe-

7. MS: "lives from them."

dem figere possit. Si vero tales reperiantur homines, qui de omnibus etiam clarissimis ac certissimis rebus dubitant, [...] iis convincendis nec etiam miracula maxima ac præsentissima sufficerent, sed in ipsa illorum mente miraculum fiat oportet [...]. Unde liquet nonnullorum incredulitatem non incertitudine vel obscuritati Revelationis, sed mentis corruptioni plenariæ adscribendam esse. [...]

"Deus salva sua sapientia ergo Judæos plura facere non potuisset; nam Christus plus quam tres integros annos inter ipsos versatus, publice in templo, in plateis et ubique Doctrinam suam inculcabat; cuivis eum audire licitum fuit; illius Doctrinam Judæorum Doctores explorare potuissent, num ex Deo sit nec ne? [...] Tot et tam stupenda in omnibus Israëlitarum urbibus paravit opera, ut si illius doctrinæ fidem habere noluissent, miraculis tamen credere debuissent. Futuram Resurrectionem suam Judæis prædixit, idque non clam sed publice; unde etiam nota fuit prædictio illa ipsi senatui Judaico, quæ caussa fuit cur sepulcrum custodiri curarunt; ipsorum ergo fuit omni studio indagare, num res sese revera ita habitura sit, dum præmoniti erant. Imo post Resurrectionem factam, ipsis de momentosissima hac veritate [statim] à militibus nuntius ferebatur. ... Ut vera Christus ostiatim eos visitaret, illisque sese monstraret, prorsus indigni erant."[8] Stapferus Theol. Polem. Tom. II, pp. 1157[-63].

---

8. "The whole question finally returns to this: whether it would be more fitting to divine wisdom that Christ should exhibit himself alive to all [...], or that he should show himself so great to a few? But the same difficulty can be asked about natural religion: why does God not present himself to be known so clearly to human beings that there would be no doubt at all remaining in any discourse, by any reason made, and that all philosophical skepticism would be clearly removed?

"There is so great a certainty of natural as of revealed truths, [...] that anyone [...] led by the love of truth would find it everywhere he is able to fix his foot. But if such men are discovered who hesitate about everything, even the most clear and certain matters, [...] not even the greatest and most immediate miracles would be sufficient to convince them. But it is fitting that the miracle be made in their very mind. [...] Whence it remains that the unbelief of some should be ascribed not to the uncertainty or obscurity of revelation but to the corruption of their flabby mind. [...]

"Therefore, God by his wisdom would not be able to make more things with respect to the Jews; for Christ, having lived more than three whole years among them, used to propagate his teaching in the temple, in the streets, and everywhere. Anyone could hear him. The Jewish teachers could have examined whether or not his doctrine was from God. [...] He performed so many and such astounding works in all the cities of the Israelites, that if they were unwilling to have faith in his teaching, nevertheless they ought to have believed the miracles. He predicted his own resurrection to the Jews, and that not privately but publicly. Whence that prediction was also known to the Jewish senate itself, which was why they took care to guard the tomb. Therefore, it was theirs to search out with all zeal whether the matter truly would happen, seeing that they were forewarned. On the contrary, after the resurrection, a message was

1324. CHRISTIAN RELIGION. One evidence of the truth of the facts that were the ground of the Christian faith is that Christianity was propagated so far, in all parts so early, when there [was] so great and manifold opportunity to inquire into the truth of these facts without possibility of failing of a discovery of the falsehood of them, if they had been false.

"Plinius Secundus [. . .] sub Imperatoris Trajani Imperio Præfectus in Bythinia erat, cujus Epistola ad Imperatorem extat Lib. X, Epist. 97, in qua scribit: Christianorum numerum incredibilem esse, ut fana ac altaria fere deserta sint, neque instituto examine se ullius criminis reos ipsos judicare potuisse. Illos Jesum divino honore atque cultu prosequi, idque tanta cum pertinacia, ut mallent mortem etiam quam maxime ignominiosam perpeti, quam Christi abnegatione Diis sacrificare, tantum esse periclitantium numerum, ut nulla ætas sit, nullus ordo, qui non in periculum vocetur; infectas esse peste hac non urbes modo, sed & vicos & agros. Ex quibus omnibus clarissime patet, religionem Christianam post Christi mortem sæculo primo ad finem currente jam longe lateque disseminatam fuisse."[9] Stapferus, *Theol. Polem.*, Tom. 2, 1168–69.

1325. ORIGINAL SIN agreeable to the doctrine anciently maintained by the Jews. "Ita Menasse *De Fragil. Hum.*, p. 129. 'Gen. 8:20. Non maledicam ultra Terræ propter hominem, nam appetitus hominis malus est à juventute ejus; hoc est, ab eo tempore, quo prodit é ventræ suæ matris. Nam simul ac ubera sugit, concupiscentiam suam sequitur, et adhuc infans, occupatur ab ira, invidia, odio, ac ceteris vitiis, quibus tenera illa ætas est obnoxia. Prov. 22:15. Salomon dicit: "Stultitiam alligatam esse animo pueri."' Ad quem locum ita observat R. Levi Ben Gersom: in principio jam ipsi stultitia quasi adnata est. De peccato hoc omnibus hominibus communi et originali David dixit, Ps. 51:7. '"Ecce, in iniquitate

---

carried immediately from the soldiers to them concerning this most momentous truth. . . . Indeed, they were utterly unworthy that Christ would visit them from door to door and show himself to them."

9. Translated in *Miscellaneous Observations*, p. 387: "'Pliny the younger, in the reign of the emperor Trajan, was governor of Bithynia, and his epistle to the emperor is extant, Lib. X, Epist. 97; in which he writes, "That the number of the Christians was incredible, so that the temples and altars were forsaken; that he, upon examination, could not assert that they were guilty of any crime; that they rendered divine worship to Jesus, and that with so great perseverance, that they would rather suffer even the most ignominious death, than, in the denial of Christ, to sacrifice to the gods. That the number of those who were exposed to the laws by a profession of the Christian religion was so great, that it included those of every age and rank; that not only the cities, but the villages and country were infected with this plague"' (as he was pleased to call Christianity). 'From all which it most clearly appears, that the Christian religion, toward the close of the first century, was spread far and wide.'"

genitus sum, et in peccata fovit me mater mea." In quem locum ita habet Aben Ezra, "Ecce propter concupiscentiam innatam cordi humano dicitur, in iniquitate genitus sum, atque sensus est, quod à nativitate implantatum sit cordi humano 'jetzer harang,' figmentum malum. Quod vero dicit, et in peccato fovit me mater mea, est modus loquendi peregrinus, quasi calefacta est ex me.' Et Menasse Ben Israel *de Fragilit*. p. 2. 'En, in iniquitate formatus sum, et in peccato fovit me mater mea. Sive aut hoc intelligatur de matre communi, quæ fuit Eva; sive de sua solum David dixerit; significare voluit, esse peccatum quast naturale, et inseparabile in hac vita. Ideo et post commissum delictum Eva concepit, et quotquot postea geniti sunt, non juxta regulam, recte rationi conformem, sed affectus perturbatos, et libidinosos producti sunt.' Addit: recte aliquem ex sapientibus Judæorum, nempe R. Aha, observasse: 'Davidem significare, voluisse, etiam piis, et virtute excellentibus, impossible esse, nunquam in aliquod peccatum incurrisse.' Idem quod David, Jobus etiam asserit Cap. 14. 4. dicens: 'Quis dabit mundum de immundo? Ne unus quidem.' De quibus verbis ita Aben-Ezra: 'Sensus est sicuti ejus, in iniquitate genitus sum, quia homo fit ex re immunda.' Omnes vero homines universaliter corruptos esse confitetur R. Josephus Jahias apud Menassem *de fragilit. hom*. pag. 5. ubi verba ejus allegat dicentis: 'Potuit ne hoc fieri, Domine, quod in judicium, et ad rationes tecum conferandas vocaveris, ideo quod tibi non serviverim semper promto animo, et debita perfectione? Hoc impossibile est homini terreno; quoniam non est justus in terra, qui non peccet. Qui posset dare, aut facere aliquid, quod esset ab omni parte purum, velut Angeli, cum sit impurus per se et materialis?' [. . .] Menasse Lib. III. *de Resurrect*. pag. 343. 'Itaque si illo sæculo nemo peccaverit, nemo etiam morietur. Nam juxta VETERUM sententiam, non est mors absque peccato, neque pœna absque delicto.' Ex quibus Menassis verbis ita argumentari licet: ubi est pœna, ibi etiam præsupponitur culpa. Atqui pœna peccati sive mors est universalis, dum non adulti solum sed et infantes recens nati, moriuntur; e[rgo] et culpa universalis est."[1] Stapferus, *Theol. Polem.*, Tom. III, pp. 36–38.

---

1. "Thus Menasse [ben Israel] in *De Fragil. Hum.*, p. 129: 'Gen. 8:20, "I will not curse the earth further on account of man, for the appetite of man is evil from his youth"; this is, from that time he comes forth from his mother's womb. For as soon as he goes under the breast, he follows his own desire, and even while still an infant he is seized by anger, envy, hatred and other vices, to which that tender age is liable. Prov. 22:15, Solomon says that "foolishness has been bound to a boy's mind."' At which place, Rabbi Levi ben Gersom observes thus: 'In the beginning already foolishness is his as if inborn.' Concerning this sin common and original to all human beings, David said, Ps. 51:7, 'Behold, I was born in wickedness, and into sins my mother

Ibid., pp. 132–33. "Ita Sal. Jarchi ad Gemaram Cod. Schabbath fol. 142. pag. 2. 'Et hæc non tantum ad peccatores referenda est: quia in omnibus maledictionibus primi hominis omnes ejus generationes conveniunt.' Et Josephus Gorionides Lib. 1. Cap 14. 'Adamum denique (inquit) omnium habitatorum terræ partem seduxit uxor ejus, ut transgrederetur præceptum Dei sui, quare ipsi et posteris ejus post eum mors incumbit.' Et Menasse Ben Israel, in Præstat. de Fragil. hum. dicit: 'Ostendere erat animus, quo pacto primus omnium parens, amissa, quam ante habuerat, justitia, posteritatem in sui generaret consortium supplicis.' Et Munsterus ad Evang. Matthæi ex Libris Fascic. Myrrhæ sequentia verba assert, Pag. 126. 'Dixit Dominus ben. homini primo cum malediceret ei: spinam et tribulum germinabit tibi, et comedes herbam agri: vult id, quod propter peccatum ejus omnes nati ab eo fiunt impii et dura fronte, similes spinis et tribulis, juxta verbum illud Domini, loquentis ad Prophetam, spinæ et irritatores tecum sunt, et cum scorpionibus habitas. Et totum islud est à serpente, qui fuit Diabolus Sammaël, qui emisit venenum mortiferum et corruptivum in Evam, causamque præstitit mortis ipsi Adam, dum comederet fructum.' Egregius etiam est locus quem habet Josephus de Voisin, in Martinum Raymundum, pag.

---

fostered me.' In which place Aben Ezra holds thus: 'Behold, because of desire inborn in the human heart it is said, in wickedness I was born, and it was realized that from birth was planted in the human heart "jetzer harang," an evil image. What he says truly, "and in sins my mother fostered me," is a strange way of saying, "as if she was troubled by me."' And Menasse Ben Israel, in *De Fragilit.*, p. 2: 'Look, I was formed in wickedness, and in sin my mother fostered me. Whether this should be understood as from our common mother, that is, Eve, or whether David spoke only about his own, he wished to show that sin is what is natural and inseparable in this life. So even after the crime was committed, Eve conceived and as many as were born later, were produced not according to the pattern rightly conformed to reason, but according to stirred up emotions and lusts.' He adds that one of the Jewish wise men, certainly Rabbi Aha, had observed that David wanted to signify both to the pious and to those excelling in virtue, that it is impossible that they had never run into some sin. Job asserts the same thing as David, ch. 14:4, saying: 'Who will make the clean from the unclean? Not even one.' Concerning these words Aben-Ezra says thus: 'The sense is just the same as: I was born in wickedness, because a man is made from an unclean thing.' Rabbi Joseph Jahias, in Menasse's *De Fragilit. Hom.*, p. 5, confesses that truly all men have been corrupted. There he says: 'Is it possible not to happen, Lord, that you call me into judgment and to the ways that should be brought to you; therefore that I should not serve you always with a ready spirit and an owed perfection? This is impossible for earthly men, since there is no just man on earth who does not sin. Who could give or make anything which would be pure in every part, just as the angels, when he is impure himself and material?' [. . .] Menasse, Bk. III, *De Resurrectione* [*Mortuorum*], p. 343: 'Thus if no one should sin in that age, no one would die. For according to the opinion of the ANCIENTS, there is no death without sin, and there is no punishment without transgression.' From Menasse's words, it may be argued thus: where there is punishment, there also is blame assumed. And punishment of sin, that is, death, is universal, seeing that not only adults but also newborn infants die. Therefore also blame is universal."

471. magistri Menachem Rakanatensis, Sect. Bereschit, ex Midrasch
Tehillim, citante Hoornebeckio contra Judæos Lib. 4. Cap. 2. p. 354. qui
ita habet: 'Non est mirum cur peccatum [Adami et Evæ exaratum sit, et
sit signatum annulo regis, ad generationes sequentes prapagandum:
quia quo die creatus est Adam, absoluta sunt omnia; ita ut ipse extiterit
perfectio et complementum totius mundani opificii; sic quando ille peccavit, totus mundus peccavit, cujus peccatum nos portamus et patimur.
Quod non ita se habet in peccatis posteritatis ejus.'"[2]

There is the greatest reason to suppose that those ancient rabbis of
the Jewish nation would never have received this doctrine of original sin
unless it had been delivered down to them from their forefathers which
were before Christ; that it is a doctrine that is very disagreeable to those
notions wherein the religion of the unbelieving Jews does most fundamentally differ from the religion maintained among Christians, particularly their notion of justification by their own righteousness and privileges as the children of Abraham and the like, without standing in need
of any satisfaction by any sufferings of the Messiah, on which account the
modern Jews do now universally reject the doctrine of original sin and
corruption of nature: [as] that divine from whence I have cited these
things observes. And 'tis not at all likely that the ancient Jews, if no such
doctrine had been delivered down to 'em from their forefathers, would

2. "Thus Solomon Jarchi, *Ad Gemaram Cod. Schabbath,* fol. 142. p. 2: 'And this should not be
referred so much to sinners, because in all the curses of the first man all his generations gather.'
And Josephus Gorionides, Bk. 1, ch. 14: 'Finally,' he says, 'his wife seduced Adam as part of all
the inhabitants of the earth, that he should transgress the command of his God, for which reason death follows him and his descendants after him.' And Menasse Ben Israel, in *Præstat. de
Fragil. Hum.,* says, 'This was to show by what agreement the first parent, when the righteousness
which he had had earlier was lost, should give birth to a posterity of those sharing in his punishment.' And Munster, *Ad Evang. Matthæi* in the books *Fascic. Myrrhæ,* asserts the following
words, p. 126: 'The Lord spoke well to the first man when he cursed him: "It will bring forth
thorns and thistles for you, and you will eat the grass of the field." He wants that which on account of his sin all born from him will be made impious and from a hard face, like thorns and
thistles, according to that word of the Lord, speaking to the Prophet, "thorns and irritations
are with you, and you will live with scorpions" [Ez. 2:6]. And all that is from the serpent, who
was Sammael the Devil, who sent out death-bearing and corrupted poison against Eve, and
Adam presented the cause of death to her when he ate the fruit.' Admirable also is the place
which Josephus of Voisin has in Martin Raymund, p: 471, master Menachem Rakanatensis, sec.
Bereschit, from *Midrasch Tehillim,* cited in [Anthony] Hornbeck, *Contra Judæos,* Bk. 4, ch. 2,
p. 354, who holds thus: 'It is not to be wondered why the sin of Adam and Eve was written down,
and why it was signified by the ring of the king to be propagated for following generations: because on the day that Adam was created, all things were finished; thus that he should stand out
as the perfection and the complement of the whole of world's creator. So when Adam sinned,
all the world sinned, whose sin we bear and suffer. Because he does not hold himself thus in
the sins of his posterity.' "

have received from the Christians, with whom they were at so great enmity, a doctrine which men in general are so apt to be prejudiced against,
and which was a doctrine peculiarly agreeable to the Christian notions
of the spiritual salvation of Jesus, and contrary to their carnal notions of
the Messiah and his salvation and kingdom.

1326. CHRISTIAN RELIGION, the greatest means of knowledge. "Omnium oculi hac disciplina collustrantur; nullibi enim terrarum, cujus rei
ipsa experientia optimus testis est, omnis generis scientiæ, tam divinæ
quam humanæ, ita sunt excultæ, quam ubi christiana [floret] religio; ut
quæ alias ignota essent & humanæ rationi inaccessa atque abscondita ibi
pandantur. Neque certiora vel sublimiora de cœli terræque creatione
atque gubernatione, de homine ejusque miseria atque redemptionis
modo alibi traduntur, quam ibi ubi christiana viget disciplina." Stapferus,
Theol. Polem., Tom. 3, [p.] 67.[3]

1327. CHRISTIAN RELIGION. FULFILLMENT OF THE PROPHECIES OF THE
MESSIAH in the Conversion of the GENTILES from Heathenism by the
Means of JESUS. "In eo [autem porro] magnum illum Prophetam sese
exhibuit, quod non solum unius alicujus Populi, sed omnium etiam Gentium doctor extiterit. Gentes ad ipsum convertendas esse toties tamque
auguste in Prophetarum oraculis prædictum est, ut impossibile sit, tam
varia dicta, totiesque repetita, à Judæis aliter quam de gentium ad Deum
atque Messiam conversione explicari posse. . . .

"Jesum vero Nazarenum esse Gentium doctorem, adeoque hoc etiam
ipsi Messiæ competere criterium, non inde solum patet, quod Discipu-
los suos jussit, ut vadant doctum omnes gentes [Matt. 28:19]. Sed ipse
effectus rem testatur. Si pristinum nimirum Gentilismi statum confer-
imus cum eo, qui Jesu Nazareni ejusque Apostolorum tempora sequu-
tus est, ingentem ratione doctrinæ atque Religionis Ethnicorum factam
fuisse mutationem, nemo est quo ignoret aut negare possit. Eundem
nimirum nunc Deum Jehovam colunt, quem Abrahamus olim Isaacus et
Jacobus professi sunt. Neque unus tantum et alter homo ad veri Dei cognitionem et ad fidem in Messiam, quem Jesum Nazarenum esse confite-

3. "The eyes of all are illuminated by this teaching. No place on earth has knowledge of every
kind, both divine and human, not been so refined as where the Christian religion flourishes.
Of this fact experience itself is the best witness. Those things which otherwise would be unknown and inaccessible and hidden from human reason is there opened. For nothing more
certain and sublime is given about the creation and governance of heaven and earth, about
man and his wretchedness and of redemption any place than where Christian teaching thrives."

mur, adductus est, sed Populi integri, ac nationes integræ; ut alia plane Theologia, Religio alia introducta fuerit à Jesu Nazareni Discipulis, toto cœlo ab ea distans quæ olim inter Gentiles obtinuit.

"Observationes sequentes hisce addimus, quæ omnes certissima nituntur Experientia, historiarumque Fide. 1. Nihil unquam ejusmodi ante Jesu Nazareni illiusque discipulorum tempora contigisse; rarissimi enim fuere Proselyti Judæorum doctrinam amplexi; nunc autem, dici vix potest quantus Gentilium numerus brevissimo temporis spatio ad Doctrinam in veteris ac[4] novi Testamenti Libris contentam profitendam persuasus fuit. 2. Id non factum [est] vi aut[5] armis, sed simplici doctrinæ hujus, per homines nullis externis prærogativis instructos, prædicatione ac commendatione. 3. Doctrinæ hæc pravis hominum affectibus ac perversis studiis minime favebat, aut carnalibus lenociniis sese commendabat; sed carnis concupiscentiis è diametro est adversa. 4. Ipsimet Judæi non diffitentur, totam illam doctrinam in Libris N. T. contentam Jesu Nazarena ejusque discipulis deberi; neque effectum illum singularem, qui nobis, olim Gentibus, contigit, alii quam Jesu Christo, quem Messiam agnoscimus, adscribi posse ipsimet Adversarii nostri fateri coguntur. 5. Jesus ergo Nazarenus solus caussa illa est, ut tantus hominum numerus brevi temporis spatio (quod antea nunquam accidit) Librorum V. T. divinam originem agnoscerent, ut ipsum Israëlis Deum colerent, ut sanctiorem, quam hactenus factum erat, disciplinam profiterentur. Quod ante ipsum nemo unquam vel fecit vel potuit facere, id Jesus Nazarenus in tot hominum millibus perfecit; nihil simile omnibus retro sæculis ante Messiam nostrum, aut in Israële, aut in reliquo terrarum orbe, auditum fuit.

"Rem melius exprimere non possum quam Chrysostomus [. . .]: 'Etenim, inquit, non est puri hominis, in tantis rebus, orbem terra marique tam brevi tempore comprehendere, et tam absurdis moribus præventum, tantisque malis irretitum liberare humanum genus. Et non Romanos tantum, sed et Persas, et omne (ut [sic] dicam) barbarorum genus. Insuper quod hæc confecit, nullis usus armis, nullos faciens sumtus, nullos movens Exercitus, nulla prælia committens; sed per undecim viros, principio ignobiles, viles, rudes, idiotas, pauperes, nudos, persuasit tot hominum tribubus: idque non præsentibus solum, sed et futuris. Quid? quot subvertit Leges patrias, abolevit consuetudines inveteratas, evellit stirpes tanto tempore radicatas, et pro illis suas alias implantavit?

4. MS: "&."
5. MS: "&."

abduxit ab his in quæ propensi eramus, et in ardua et difficilia induxit. Considera et cogita tecum, quid sit in tam brevi tempore omnem sub sole terram tantis Ecclesiis impleri, tantas gentes ad fidem transferri, populos persuaderi, ut patrias leges abrogent, consuetudinem stabilitam et radicatam revellant: altaria et templa, et statuas et sacrificia, et prophana festa et immundum odorem, sicut fumum aliquem aboleant.'"

Stapferus, *Theol. Polem.*, Tom. III, pp. 68–71.[6]

6. "In him [however long ago] that great Prophet showed himself, because not only of one particular people, but of all, even Gentiles, he stood out as a teacher. It was predicted so often and so reverently in the oracles of the prophets that he was for the purpose of the conversion of the nations to himself, that it is impossible that such diverse sayings, repeated so many times, can be explained by the Jews other than as about the conversion of the Gentiles to God and the Messiah. . . .

"Thence it is not only evident that Jesus of Nazareth is the teacher of the nations, but also that this criterion agrees with the Messiah himself, the fact that he ordered his disciples should go to teach all the nations [Matt. 28:19]. But the accomplishment itself attests the matter. If we compare the undoubtedly earlier state of the Gentiles with that which followed the times of Jesus of Nazareth and his apostles, there is none who would not know or would be able to deny that an immense change had been made in the rationale of the doctrine and religion of the Gentiles. Now they worship undoubtedly the same God, Jehovah, whom Abraham, Isaac, and Jacob once professed. Nor was it so much one or two led to the knowledge of the true God and faith in the Messiah—whom we confess is Jesus of Nazareth—but whole peoples and entire nations; so that clearly another theology, another religion had been introduced by Jesus of Nazareth to his disciples, standing apart in all heaven from that which once held sway among the Gentiles.

"We add to these the following observations, which all depend on very sure experience and on faithful histories. 1. Nothing of this kind ever happened before the times of Jesus of Nazareth and his disciples; for very few proselytes had embraced the teaching of the Jews; but now, it hardly can be said how great a number of Gentiles in a very brief space of time have been persuaded to profess the doctrine contained in the books of the Old and New Testaments. 2. That was not done by force or by arms, but by the simplicity of that doctrine, through men instructed in no external privileges, by preaching and by recommendation. 3. This doctrine was by no means favorable to the depraved emotions and twisted interests of men or commended itself to fleshly allurements. But it was diametrically turned away from the lusts of the flesh. 4. The Jews themselves do not deny that that whole doctrine contained in the books of the New Testament is owed to Jesus of Nazareth and his disciples; those enemies of ours are compelled to admit that that solitary occurrence which touched us, once Gentiles, is not able to be attributed to any other than to Jesus Christ, whom we did not recognize as Messiah. 5. Therefore Jesus the Nazarene is that sole reason that so great a number of people in a short space of time [which never earlier happened] should know the divine source of the Old Testament, that they should worship the very God of Israel, that they should profess a holier teaching than had happened hitherto. Jesus of Nazareth accomplished in so many thousands of people that which before him no one ever either did or was able to do. Nothing like it has been heard in all the ages back before our Messiah, either in Israel or in the rest of the world.

"I cannot express the situation better than Chrysostom [. . .]: 'It is not,' he says, 'even in the power of pure man, in such great things, to take in the earth in land and sea in so short a time and to free the human race, hindered by such foolish customs and entangled in such great evils—not only the Romans, but the Persians and, as I say, the race of the Gentiles. Moreover,

That one great event of the conversion of the Gentile world from idols to the acknowledgment and worship of the God of Israel, together with the acknowledgment of himself, the Messiah, and subjection to him, so often foretold as what should be the great work and distinguishing honor of the Messiah, is a great and glorious seal and evidence of the divine mission of Jesus of Nazareth, and of his true Messiahship.

To set this in its proper light, the following things may be considered:

1. How often this is foretold, and how greatly and abundantly it is insisted on as a great, remarkable and wonderful event which the Messiah should accomplish. See "Fulfillment of Prophecies of [Messiah]," §§ 123–39.[7]

2. It is plainly foretold as a great, glorious and most distinguishing work of the Messiah, and his peculiar honor, thus to turn the heathen world from idolatry to the acknowledgment and worship of the God of Israel, and to bring them to submit to him and trust in him as their teacher, lawgiver and Savior. See in what a pompous manner is this great honor promised to the Messiah in Is. 42:1–9. 'Tis promised as the Messiah's great reward and peculiar manifestation of the great and distinguishing love of God to him (Ps. 2:8; Is. 53, latter end; and Ps. 110). 'Tis prophesied of as a mighty and peculiar work of God—to which that of Abraham's victory over the kings and their armies was but an image— was a challenging of the gods of the heathen and all their abettors to try their strength with him (Isaiah, chs. 40–42).

3. Though according to the modern Jews, some of the doctrines that Christ has taught the Gentiles are very erroneous, as that he was the Mes-

---

the fact that he accomplished these things using no weapons, making no expenses, using no army, trusting no warriors. Instead, through twelve men, in the beginning obscure, lowly, ignorant, unlearned, poor, naked, he persuaded so many human tribes, and that not only present, but future. Why? How many ancestral laws did he subvert, how many long-standing customs did he abolish, how many entrenched roots did he upturn, how many of his own did he plant for those? He led us away from those things into which we had been disposed and led us into hard and difficult matters. Consider and think within yourself why it is that in such a short time all the earth under the sun is filled with such great churches, so many nations transferred to the faith, peoples persuaded to abrogate their ancestral laws and banish their stabile and rooted customs; they abolish altars and temples, statues and sacrifices, profane feasts and foul odors, like so much smoke.'"

7. This group of sections, originally numbered 121–37 in "Fulfillment of the Prophecies of the Messiah," begins with proof texts showing that the number of God's people would increase early and swiftly beyond Canaan to include the entire world (§§ 123–29); that the Jews would reject the Messiah and be rejected by him, leading to the destruction of Jerusalem (§§ 130–35); and that the heathen and Gentiles would be brought under the Messiah's dominion by peaceable means in order to enlighten and cleanse them and convert them to the true religion (§§ 136–39).

siah, etc., yet 'tis indisputable that he has introduced and established among them those same great and important things that it was foretold should be introduced and established by the Messiah. He has brought 'em to forsake all their ancient idols, to destroy all their images of silver, gold, brass and iron, wood and stone, and utterly abandon all things of that nature. He has brought ['em] to forsake the worship of the sun, moon and stars, and all the host of heaven, and to forsake the worship of devils, and of all creatures in heaven above and in the earth beneath and in the waters under the earth; to destroy the altars, statues, temples and oracles of these false gods, with all their idolatrous rites; has overthrown all those kinds of idolatry that were spoken in the Old Testament as practiced by the heathen nations round about the land of Canaan, and in all countries, far and near, that were known in those times; has abolished all those heathenish practices that were condemned in the Old Testament, in Israel and in other nations; has brought ['em] to profess and worship only one God, that in six days made heaven earth and the sea and all that in them is, to worship Jehovah, the God of Abraham, Isaac and Jacob, the same God that brought the children of Israel out [of] Egypt, led 'em through the wilderness, and brought 'em into Canaan, and dwelt in their tabernacle and temple, and spake to them of old by their prophets; and to profess subjection to his commands, particularly those Ten Commands delivered by Moses and written in two tables of stone; and to receive the whole of his written word delivered to them by Moses and the prophets; to receive all those commands in these writings which God always insisted upon as of greatest weight and importance; to use their book of Psalms in their public worship.

And, as to those things that the Jews call errors that Jesus taught the nations, the main of them was that he taught the nations that he was the Messiah.[8] And the supposing this to be an error is a perfect, plain, bald begging of the question. For 'tis implied in the prophecies that, when the Messiah did indeed come, this is one thing that he should teach the nations and bring 'em to acknowledge, that they might submit to him as the great Messiah. And if Jesus had not brought the nations to acknowledge this with respect to himself, it would have [been] an evidence against him.

Another error which they suppose he taught was that he was God. But this is certainly agreeable to the prophecies of their own Scriptures, which often teach that the Messiah should be God.

8. MS: "the main of them is that he taught the nations, the main of them was that he was the Messiah."

Another is the doctrine of the Trinity. But this also is plainly agreeable to their own Scriptures.

Another is the abolishing of the ceremonial law. But this was foretold as what should be done by the Messiah, and therefore is rather a confirmation of Christ as the Messiah, and is one plain instance of his fulfilling the prophecies.

4. The idolatry that Christ delivered the nations from is that same kind of idolatry that it was foretold the Messiah should abolish. This is exceeding plain in the fortieth, forty-first, and following chapters of Isaiah. It was that kind of idolatry by images, etc., which had been practiced by the nations round about Canaan, and by the heathen nations that were famed in the history of the Old Testament.

5. It may be considered how great and important a work such a change and conversion of the world is in its nature and kind. 'Tis represented as a great work of God to heal the diseases of the body. But 'tis much greater to heal the diseases of the mind. Opening the eyes of the blind is spoken of in the Old Testament as a great work of God; but much greater to deliver the heathen world from their exceeding spiritual blindness. Sin is the most pernicious fatal disease, as is manifest abundantly in the Old Testament as well as New. And the heathenism and idolatry of the world is often spoken of as the greatest disease of the world. Idolatry is spoken of as a sin peculiarly abominable and fatal. 'Tis called especially that abominable thing which God hates. 'Tis represented as a great work of God, to cause light to shine out of darkness. But the heathenish darkness that overspread the world is often represented as the most dreadful darkness. Delivering the heathen world from this disease and calamity is spoken of as a thing far beyond their own power. Is. 44:19–20, "And none considereth in his heart, neither is there any knowledge nor understanding to say, I have burnt part of it in the fire," etc. "He feedeth on ashes: a deceived heart hath turned him aside, that he cannot deliver his soul, nor say, Is there not a lie in my right hand?"

God's appearing above the idols of the nations, and getting the victory over them in instances, as it were, infinitely less than this, is spoken of as a great work of God, a glorious display of his power, majesty and greatness, as his appearing above the idols of Egypt in the thing wherein they dealt proudly. How much greater was the victory of Christ over the gods of the nations! How much greater the overthrow! How much greater that dominion and empire of theirs, in which Christ overthrew a dominion wherein their pride was most remarkably manifested and in a vastly greater opposition, even that which they made for three hundred years successively, first by the Jews and afterwards by the heathen world, in ten successive, general persecutions, and otherwise—and the degree in which they were destroyed much greater. They were brought vastly lower; their images all burnt; temples forsaken; oracles silenced; altars forsaken, etc., and their worship and dominion utterly abolished.

God honored him as above the heathen gods in causing the image of Dagon to fall before him, and breaking off his head and hands [I Sam. 5].

So God is represented in the prophecies of Isaiah as gloriously manifesting himself as above the gods of the heathen, in appearing above Bel and Nebo, the idols of Babylon, when Babylon was destroyed and the Jews delivered from their captivity there.

6. The vast extent to which Christ accomplished this great effect is to be considered. It was done through all the heathen countries that were known in the times of the Old Testament, through all the nations there mentioned, far and near, east, west, north and south, and not only so, but vastly beyond the utmost limits of the then-known world, or of all those parts of the habitable world that are anywhere mentioned in any of those ancient writings. Nebuchadnezzar overrun the greater part of the nations that were then known. But the Babylonish Empire was but a small thing in comparison of the Roman Empire, which Christ converted from heathenism. And 'tis to be considered that the Mahometans have all the nations they have of the true God, originally from Jesus Christ.

'Tis to be considered that America is now, in effect, in the possession of them that own the name of Jesus, and taken from the heathen by this vast extent of Christ's influence. Not only all the heathen gods, all those kinds of idolatry which are mentioned in any part of the Old Testament were abolished, but innumerable other kinds of idols and idolatry.

7. Jesus overthrew heathenism not only in so vast an extent, but at that time wherein it was in its greatest strength that it ever had arrived at from the foundation of the world to that time; yea, or ever since that time. He overthrew it in its strongest empire, when it had the greatest earthly powers, authority, riches and wisdom on its side that ever it had. He overthrew it in that kingdom that the Scripture says was strong as iron, and that broke in pieces and subdued all things, as iron is made use of to cut and break and subdue all things. He conquered the god of this world in his greatest glory and magnificence, when he was most secure, most ready to say, "I sit a king forever."

And as heathenism at that time had its greatest strength and advantage to maintain itself, so it exerted all that power and strength that it had obtained in opposition to Jesus, to endeavor to hinder this great effect we are speaking of. But all in vain. Jesus overcame heathenism in all this its strongest opposition.

8. Our Jesus not only wrought this work to so great a degree and extent, and against the greatest strength to oppose it that ever had been, but he wrought the work effectually and durably. Though, indeed, other bad things have arisen since, yet that ancient idolatry remains abolished even to this day. As long a time has now passed since Constantine the Great as passed from the time of Moses to Christ.

9. This effect wrought by our Jesus is vastly the greatest and best revolution that ever was brought to pass in the world. 'Tis vastly the greatest revolution that ever was, the most like creating the world anew. And it was the best, the most happy, consisting in abolishing things that were worst, most absurd, most debasing to mankind and most pernicious and most hateful to God, and introducing instead thereof that light and knowledge and those laws and constitutions and regulations and means that were most noble, excellent, worthy and tending to the dignity, perfection and happiness of men and the honor of God.

10. This was a work wherein God put peculiar honor upon our Jesus, vastly distinguishing him from, and exalting him above, all the rest of mankind, even the greatest and best, and those that in other respects had been most favored and honored of God. None of the greatest wise men among the heathen that had some notion of the true God and the vanity of idols, though there had been a succession of great philosophers who came to great attainments in knowledge of the nature of things in many respects, and philosophic knowledge had been increasing in the world for five or six hundred years, yet all availed nothing for the producing any such effect—but, after all, the world grew worse and worse in their idolatries.

God in this put an infinitely greater honor upon Jesus than ever he had done on any of his own people, than upon any of the most eminent saints that ever had been, from the foundation of the world. He did that which none of the prophets could do. Daniel was a great prophet, and remarkably and openly honored of God as his most peculiar favorite, and seemed to be under advantages for the accomplishing an effect of this kind in many respects beyond any other of the prophets. He dwelt for about seventy years in Babylon, in the head and heart of the heathen world, and there was a person very publicly known, had acquaintance with the greatest men in the world, was exceedingly famed among them for his wisdom, and was openly honored of God in their view by a most miraculous intercourse with heaven; and not only so, but set in a place of high authority and power in two of the monarchies of the world successively, that of the Chaldeans and that of the Medes and Persians, and exhibited many clear demonstrations of the vanity of their idols, and of the glory of the true God as infinitely above them. But no such effect followed, nor anything like it.

David was a man highly favored of God, often declared a man after God's own heart, was a zealous hater and opposer of the idolatry of the heathen, had his heart much on the setting up the kingdom of the true God through the world and his being worshipped and praised by all nations, as appears abundantly by his psalms, and had the advantage of great earthly power and authority. He was both a prophet and king. And God made him the greatest prince that was in his day in the world, subdued most of the heathen nations in that part of the world to him, and brought them under his dominion. But yet he was made the instrument of no such revolution as this.

Solomon, his son, was yet a much greater prince in wisdom, magnificence, great authority, great fame and extensive influence in the world, in wisdom and wealth exceeding all princes that ever were on earth. And all nations used to come to him for instruction. And he did great things for the honor of the true God, that all the nations of the earth might hear his fame and might be induced to worship, as appears by his prayer, I Kgs. 8. But God never honored him by making him the instrument of any such great revolution as that which we are speaking of accomplished by Jesus Christ. He was not so much as made the instrument of the conversion of those nations that were under his own dominion, or within his empire, or so much as one heathen nation, whereas Jesus produced this through more than twenty times the extent of Solomon's empire.

It was a great work of the ancient judges, prophets and kings of Israel, that God raised up and most distinguishingly favored, to bring to pass the reformation of that one nation of Israel when they had corrupted themselves with idolatry for forty or fifty years. This was the highest honor of the ancient judges. This was the glory of those excellent princes so highly favored of God, Hezekiah and Josiah. This was a great work of Moses, to recover the people Israel after corrupted with Egyptian idolatry, and what he could not thoroughly accomplish. Elijah and Elisha and all other prophets sent to the Ten Tribes never could thoroughly reclaim them from their idolatrous corruption. Those great prophets, Isaiah, Jeremiah and Ezekiel, could not thoroughly purge the Jews from their idolatry.

And as to converting the heathen world from their idolatry, it was what the whole nation of the Jews could not do, though they were, after the captivity, for four or five hundred years together, dispersed abroad over great part of the heathen world, not only the vulgar and illiterate, but multitudes of their scribes and doctors and heads of their synagogues. Yet they never were successful so as to convert so much as the greater part of one country or city in all that time (excepting the Edomites that came and dwelt in the land of Israel); and that, although there was a great disposition appeared in them to endeavor to make proselytes, they compassed sea and land to make one proselyte.

'Tis spoken of as a great honor that God in his providence put upon Joseph, that he was advanced to be an instructor of the Egyptians, and to teach the senators of Egypt wisdom. But how small was the effect! As to the knowledge of God, which the Scripture of the Old Testament often speaks of as the highest part of wisdom, there was no great abiding alteration. But the Egyptians, in the generations immediately following, were sunk into vastly greater degrees of heathenish darkness than ever—and not only so, but drew the Israelites, Joseph's own people, into corruption with them.

Abraham, Isaac and Jacob were separated from the rest of the world because of their idolatry, that the knowledge and worship of the true God might be kept up in the world. But they were not made the instruments of reclaiming any people from idolatry, or of preventing the inhabitants of the land where they dwelt from sinking apace into the grossest and most impious idolatrous principles and practices.

11. Jesus converted those parts of the world that it was foretold the Messiah should convert, as that he should convert the chief nations of the world for power, arts, wealth, merchandise and seafaring (see "Fulfillment of Prophecies of the Messiah," § 158),[9] and those parts of the world that had belonged to the four monarchies, and especially the last of them, viz. the Roman monarchy (ibid., § 159),[1] and particularly the inhabitants of the lesser Asia and Europe (ibid., §§ 161–62),[2] and Egypt,[3] many parts of Arabia, Philistia, Tyre, Babylonia, Tubal, Tarshish,

---

9. "Fulfillment," § 154, renumbered 158, on MS p. 123, begins, "It was foretold that the chief nations of the world for power, arts, wealth, merchandise and seafaring should be brought into the kingdom of the Messiah."

1. "Fulfillment," § 155, renumbered 159, on MS p. 124, begins, "It was foretold that the Messiah in his kingdom should be possessed of those parts of [the world] that had belonged to the four monarchies, and especially the last of them, viz. the Roman monarchy."

2. "Fulfillment," §§ 157–58, renumbered 161–62, on MS p. 125, respectively treat the propagation of the Messiah's kingdom "especially towards the north and west" and in "Lesser Asia and Europe in particular."

3. MS: "that Egypt."

Javan, the ends of the earth and the isles in the sea, those that are far off upon the sea, as is remarkably fulfilled in the conversion of the utmost parts of Europe and those great islands, Great Britain and Ireland, and America, and many other circumstances which are exactly fulfilled in what Jesus has done (observed in "Fulfillment of Prophecies of the Messiah").[4]

12. Let it be considered how unreasonable it is to suppose that, after this great effect had been so abundantly insisted as the peculiar and most distinguishing honor of the Messiah, God should suffer it to be anticipated by another, a grand impostor, one most wickedly pretending himself to be the Messiah (such as the Jews most blasphemously suppose our Jesus to be), that he would so favor him in his imposture as to give him this honor of conquering the heathen world, in his greatest monarchy, in his highest advancement, strength and authority, etc., producing this effect, foretold as the prerogative of the Messiah, in such vast extent, to so great a degree, and in so durable a manner, and in so many respects, in such places, and with respect to such subjects, and in such a manner as is foretold of the true Messiah—and all not only agreeable to God's frequent and abundant predictions in the Old Testament, but also agreeable to his own predictions declaring that he was the Messiah, and that as such he would accomplish this effect.

13. It may further be considered that this effect has been so accomplished already that it can't now be accomplished by another messiah, according to the prophecies. The prophecies are already fulfilled, and don't remain to be fulfilled by another. Jesus has abolished heathenish idolatry in all the nations round about Canaan, and in every heathen nation at any time mentioned in the Old Testament. And it don't now remain to be accomplished in any one of them. It don't remain to be accomplished in those isles mentioned in the prophecies. It don't remain to be accomplished in the countries that had been subject to the four monarchies. It don't now remain to be accomplished in that fourth and greatest monarchy, the Roman Empire.

14. If this revolution, which is vastly the greatest that ever was accomplished in the world of mankind, be not that which it is so often foretold as what the Messiah should accomplish, then it is not foretold at all, which would be very strange—strange indeed that there should nowhere

---

4. These nations are all individually treated in "Fulfillment," § 163, MS p. 126, which asserts that "very wild and barbarous nations have by Jesus Christ been instructed and civilized and brought to the profession and practice of the true religion."

be any hint of an event more considerable than any others that ever were predicted, in any prophecy concerning any change or revolution in any nation or nations, a revolution that was of such a nature as would have been most likely to be foretold, being of a religious nature, and so most nearly concerning the kingdom and city of God.

1328. CHRISTIAN RELIGION. THE MESSIAH IS ALREADY COME. "Contra elapsum adventus Messiæ tempus Judæi nihil habent quod objiciant, sed ipsimet convicti sunt, dudum præterlapsum esse tempus illud quo venire debuit. Si autem ex temporum signis clarissimisque vaticiniis contra illos argumentamur: 'Dudum Messiæ tempus præteriit, E[rgo] jam venit Messias'; illi excipiunt, propter Populi peccata dilatum esse ejus adventum. . . .

"Vulgaris veterum Judæorum sententia erat, quater mille post mundi creationem annis Messiam venturum. . . . Judæai etiam olim fuisse persuasissimos tempus Messiæ advenisse, inde quoque patet, quod tantus illorum numerus à variis Pseudo-Messiis decipi se passus est, dum omnes temporis circumstantiæ ipsis indicabant ea nunc impleri debere, quæ à Prophetis fuere promissa. . . . Ante nimirum Jesu Nazareni tempora nemo se Messiam esse professus est, post eum vero à multis hoc factum fuit; unde consequitur Jesum Nazarenum primum fuisse, qui Messiam se esse dixit. . . . Concludere licet Judaeos et olim primo jam sæculo vel ab initio secundi, et nostris temporibus esse persuasissimos, tempus manifestationis Messiæ [. . .] à Deo definitum jam esse præterlapsum, et tamen Messiam jam advenisse agnosere nolint? Dicunt, peccata sua in culpa esse propter quæ Messiæ adventus differatur . . .

"Ut Judæis [etiam] hoc adimatur effugium observanda sunt sequentia. 1. Deum, concedentibus ipsis Judæis, certum definivisse tempus, quo Messias venire debeat. 2. Deum per omniscientiam suam omnia præscivisse impedimenta, quæ adventui Messiæ obicem objicere potuissent, adeo ut Deus conditionate locutus fuisset, si Messiæ Adventum ab hac vel illa conditione, quam prævidit, pendere voluisset. 3. Tempus illud, quod Deus definite fixit, non negantibus id Judæis, in eam incidit ætatem, qua Christiani Messiam venisse contendunt, et quam ipsimet Judæorum antiquissimi probatissimique definiverunt. 4. Concedimus autem Messiæ adventum adeo exacte definiri minime debuisse, ut vel ipsemet annus sciri ab Hominibus potuisset; at saltem jam septendecim saecula praeterlapsa sunt, ex quo Tempus illud exspiravit quod sacri prædixere vates. 5. Cum sub nulla conditione Deus aureum illud sæculum præfixit, veritas illa non potuit non esse firma et immutabilis, et

Deus veracissimus non potuit non esse verax, ut præstet ea, quæ sæpis-
simi promiserat [. . .]. 'Deus Abrahami non derelinquit benignitatem
suam et fidem suam.' Gen. 24:27. 'Non excidit quidquam ex ullis rebus
bonis, quas elocutus fuerat Jehovah domui Israëlis, cuncta evenerunt.'
Jos. 21:44–45. 'Cognovistis toto corde vestro, et toto animo vestro, non
excidisse rem ullam ex omnibus rebus bonis, quam promiserat Jehovah
Deus vester vobis, [. . .] non excidisse ex iis rem ullam' [Jos. 23:14]. 6.
Perpendendum porro Messiæ missionem rem maximi momenti esse, ut
cogitari minime possit promissum Domini hic labascere, ubi Gloriæ illius quammaxime interest. Neque ullum in quacunque re produci potest
exemplum, quod Deus in promissis suis retardaverit implementum,
quare ergo id in re maxima faceret nulla reddi potest ratio. Judicent ex
his omnibus ipsimet Judæi, judicet quivis præjudiciis non imbutus index,
annon argumenta nostra Judæorum longe potiora sint.[5] [. . .]

"Precipuum adventus [Messiæ] finem satisfactionem liberationemque
à peccatis esse, à nobis demonstratum est; quod ipse etiam Propheta
Daniel innuit, dicens: 'Septimanas septuaginta decisas esse super Populum Israëlem, et super sanctam civitatem, ad cohibendum defectionem,
ad obsignandum peccata, ad expiandum iniquitatem, et adducendum
justitiam perpetuam . . .' Dici propterea minime potest propter id re-
tardari Messiæ adventum propter quod venire debet. Ipsi denique Judæi
in Talmude confitentur improba futura isse illa tempora in quibus Davidis filius venturus sit, dicit enim R. Joannes in Sanhedrin Cap. XI. 'Non
veniet filius Davidis, nisi aut sæculo, quod omni vitio careat, vel quod universum vitio succumbat. Quoniam scriptum Jes. 59:16. Et vidit non esse
virum, et obstupuit, non esse intercessorem.' R. Jehuda autem, uti eodem loco traditur, dixit: 'Quo sæculo filius Davidis venturus sit, domum
conventus in lupanar conversum iri.' R. Nehorai: 'Quo sæculo filius Davidis veniet, adolescentes viros provectæ ætatis pudefacient; seniores
adolescentulis assurgent; filia insurget[6] contra genitricem, et nurus contra socrum; frons sæculi canina erit, neque filius Patrem reverebitur.' R.
Nechemias ait: 'Omne Regnum superstitioni et perversis dogmatibus
erit debitum: neque erit qui redarguat.' R. Johannes idem asserit, scilicet: 'Non veniet filius Davidis, donec omne Regnum prava de Deo et divinis opinione occupetur.' Quæ omnia tempore adventus Messiæ nostri
ita sese habuerunt, dum omnia scelerum genera ante Urbis et templi
desolationem Hierosolymis nefando modo grassabantur. Testis est Jose-

5. MS: "esse."
6. MS: "assurget."

phus Lib. 6 de Bello Judaico Cap. 16. 'Non equidem,' inquit, 'recusabo dicere, quæ dolor, jubet. Puto si Romani contra noxios venire tardassent, aut hiatu terræ devorandam fuisse civitatem, aut diluvio perituram, aut fulmina, aut Sodomæ incendia passuram, multo enim magis impiam progeniem tulit, quam illa protulerat.'"[7] Stapferus, *Theol. Polem.*, Tom. III, pp. 155–63.

7. "Against the time elapsed for the coming of the Messiah, the Jews have nothing to object, but are themselves convinced that a long time ago the time in which he ought to have come had elapsed. But if we argue against them from the signs of the times and from clearest prophecies, 'The time of the Messiah has long passed, therefore the Messiah already came' they counter that his coming has been delayed because of the sins of the people. The common opinion of the ancient Jews was that the Messiah would come 4000 years after the creation of the world. . . .

"The Jews also thought that once they were very persuaded that the time of the Messiah had arrived. . . . From this it is also apparent that so great a number of them allowed themselves to be deceived by various false messiahs, while all the circumstances of the time were indicating to them that those things ought at that time to be fulfilled which had been promised by the prophets. . . . Certainly before the times of Jesus of Nazareth no one professed himself to be the Messiah, but after him this was done by many. Whence it follows that Jesus of Nazareth was the first to say he was the Messiah. . . . Is it right for the Jews—both in the past, in the first or from the beginning of second century, and in our times—to have been persuaded that the time of the Messiah, determined by God, has already passed by and nevertheless not wish to know that the Messiah has already come? They say that their sins are at fault for the coming of the Messiah being delayed . . .

"In order that this escape be taken away from the Jews, the following should be observed: 1. That God had determined a certain time, conceded by the Jews, in which the Messiah ought to come. 2. That God foreknew through his omniscience all hindrances which were able to throw an obstacle to the Messiah's coming, so that God would have spoken conditionally if he wished that coming to depend on this or that condition which he foresaw. 3. That time which God fixed definitely—which the Jews do not deny—fell in the age in which Christians assert that the Messiah came and which the most ancient and approved themselves of the Jews marked out. 4. Now we concede that the Messiah's coming by no means ought to be defined so exactly that either the year itself could be know by men, but at least seventeen ages have already elapsed since that time expired which the sacred prophets had predicted. 5. Since God fixed that golden age under no condition, that truth was unable not to be firm and unchanging, and the most true God was unable not to be truthful, so that what he had most often promised stands out. [. . .] 'God did not forsake his goodness and faithfulness to Abraham,' Gen. 24:27. 'Nothing failed from any good things which Jehovah had spoken to the house of Israel; all things happened,' Josh. 21:44–45. 'You have known with all your heart and with all your mind, that no thing from all the good things which the Lord your God had promised to you failed; . . . nothing from them had failed' [Josh. 23:14]. 6. Furthermore, that the sending of the Messiah should be weighed as the thing of greatest importance, where his glory is most concerned. No other example can be produced in whatever thing, which God will have slowed down the implementation of his promises. On this account, then, no reason can be given that he does it in the greatest thing. From these things let the Jews themselves judge, let whatever indication is not steeped in prejudices determine whether our arguments are far preferable of the Jews. [. . .]

"It has been shown by us that the superiority of the coming of the Messiah is the end, the satisfaction and liberation from sins; this fact even the prophet Daniel himself affirmed, saying:

1329. CONFIRMATION OF THE ANGELS. 'Tis an argument that the angels were not confirmed till Christ ascended into heaven, that Jesus Christ, God-man, risen and ascended, is appointed as the head of the new creation, which only is that which cannot be shaken. As to the old creation, 'tis all that which is liable to pass away. Christ himself, while in the flesh, did in some respect belong to the old creation that passed away. But in his rising again to glorious immortal life, and so being the first born from the dead, he is the beginning of the creation of God, the first born of every creature, the beginning and head of the new creation.

1330. CHRISTIAN RELIGION. CHRIST'S RESURRECTION, concerning that supposition that the disciples stole away the body of Jesus. "At quinnam fuere audaces illi homines, [. . .] quales eos Adversarii describunt, simplices, rudes, superstitiosi, Reqni mundani spe, cum Christus ad huc in vivis esset, lactati. Sequentia autem ut Adversarii nobis ostendant petimus. 1. Qui factum fuerit, ut homines illo modo rudes et simplices, nunc una vice fiant callidissimi, maximæ fraudi committendæ, moliminique magistri sui exsequendo, et quidem in circumstantiis periculosissimis, aptissimi? 2. Cur Discipuli non potius cum Josepho ab Arimathæa de Corpore Christi in alium locum transferando convenerint, ubi fraus facilius potuisset committi, cur ipsum hoc in ilo loco sepeliri permis-

---

'Seventy weeks were determined upon the people of Israel, and upon the holy city, for the finishing of transgression, for the sealing of sins, for the expiation of iniquity and the bringing in of eternal righteousness . . .' [Dan. 9:24]. Furthermore, it can by no means be said because of this that the coming of the Messiah was delayed because of how he ought to come. Finally, the Jews themselves confess in the Talmud that those times would be bad in which the Son of David would come, for Rabbi Joannes says in *Sanhedrin,* ch. XI: 'The Son of David will not come except either in the age which lacks all vice or which surrenders wholly to vice. Since it is written, Is. 59:16, "And he saw that there was not man, and he was astounded that there was no intercessor."' But Rabbi Jehuda, as it is given in the same place, said: 'In which age the Son of David would come, the house of meeting is going to be turned into a brothel.' Rabbi Nehorai: 'The Son of David will come in that age when young men shame men of advanced age, elders rise up to young men, a daughter rises against her mother and a daughter-in-law against her mother-in-law; the face of the age will be dog-like, nor will a son reverence his father.' Rabbi Nechemias says: 'Every kingdom will be a debtor to superstition and twisted teachings, nor will there be one who refutes.' Rabbi Johannes likewise asserts, of course: 'The Son of David will not come, until every kingdom is occupied by a perverse opinion about God and divine matters.' All which things held themselves thus in the time of the coming of our Messiah, while all kinds of crimes were proceeding before the desolation of the city and temple of Jerusalem in an abominable manner. Josephus, Bk. 6 of the *Jewish War,* is witness to this: 'Certainly,' he says, 'I will not refuse to say those things which grief bids. I think if the Romans had delayed in coming against those criminal men, that either the city should have been swallowed up by a gaping hole in the earth, or would be destroyed by flood, or would suffer the lightning and fires of Sodom, for it bore a much more impious offspring than Sodom had produced.'"

serint, ubi nulla illum surripiendi spes superfuit? 3. Quomodo meticu-
losi illi homines, qui Christo capto omnes diffugerant, ausi fuerint ob-
niti Romano Præfecto senatuique Judaico, et non obstante militum Cus-
todia sigillum frangere, lapidem devolvere, Corpus Magistri sui alio
transferre, et ita quidem ut nunquam quo illud transtulerint detectum
fuerit? 4. Quomodo hæc omnia efficere potuerint Apostoli, quomodo
lapidem amovere, corpusque ex sepulchro efferre, ut nullus tamen evig-
ilaverit miles, quomodo accedere ad sepulchrum fuerint ausi, cum scire
nequaguam potuerint, an milites ad unum omnes dormiant hec ne; tempore præcipue plenilunii, quale tunc erat, res difficilior adhuc fuisset,
cum detegi conspicique facile potuissent? [5.] An discipuli illi numero
undecim, omnibus noti, facinus ejusmodi committere potuissent, ita ut
magistratus, in re maxime momenti, ne minimum quidem commissi criminis vestigium deprehendere et deinceps ab uno vel altero Discipulorum confessionem facinoris hujus extorquere potuerit? Qui deinceps
ausi fuerint Discipuli præsente senatu publice protestari, et ceu ad rem
notissimam provocare, Jesum Christum à Judæis crucifixum à mortuis
resurrexisse. Act. III, IV et V. Stephanus Chap. 7:6. Cur non plane à
Christo alienatus fuerit Apostolorum animus, cum ab ipso fuerunt decepti, ut pudefacti plane à proposito illo, de Regno erigendo, suscepto
destiterint, metuerintque ne et ipsi ceu imposturæ seditionisque con-
sortes ultimis afficiantur suppliciis; adeoque misere à magistro suo se-
ducti, majus potius periculum effugere, quam pœnæ gravissimæ sese ex-
ponere quæsiverint?

"Causam, cur Apostoli crimen hoc commiserint, Increduli hanc fuisse
dicunt; quod vivente adhuc Magistro suo spem conceperint, quod
Monarcha mundanus atque potens futurus sit, quam spem etiam post
ipsius mortem non plane amiserint, uti contendit Autor *Du Discours sur
les Fondemens & les Raisons du Christianisme.*[8] At hoc si fuerit, concipere
non possumus, cui bono corpus mortuum hoc ipsis inservire debuerit
. . . Contendunt vero Adversarii, eum in finem Apostolos corpus Christi
abstulisse, ut hominibus persuaderent è mortuis ipsum resurrexisse, et
hac ratione Regnum illud mundamum facilius erigerent. . . . Observandum adhuc:[9] Apostolos simplices illos atque rudes, quales ab Adversariis
describuntur, sperare nullo modo potuisse, id se effecturos, quod ipsorum Magister non potuit, et quod nunc magis adhuc impossibile erat
postquam factionis Antesignanus ceu seditiosus atque rebellis ultimo af-

---

8. Stapfer cites "pag. 33."
9. MS: "est."

fectus erat supplicio; cujus miserabilis exitus meticulosos illos Asseclas ab instituto suo deterrere debuisset. Et cum Apostoli ex communi Judæorum opinione Principem speraverint mundanum, qualem Prophetarum descripserint Oracula, propriæ adversi fuissent hypothesi, si hominibus persuadere voluissent Jesus Christum illum ultimis nuper affectum suppliciis, nunc redivivum, in cœlum sublatum, adeoque invisibilem, Principem illum mundanum esse, inter Judæos Regnum erecturum, Judæosque à Romanorum jugo liberaturum."[1] Stapferus, *Theolog. Polem.*, Tom. III, pp. 240–43.

1. "But rather there were those bold men, [. . .] such as their enemies will describe, simple, unlearned, superstitious, childish, with hope of a worldly kingdom when Christ was here among the living. However, we ask our enemies to show us the following. 1. What will have happened that men simple and unlearned in this way, now are made at once the most clever by following the greatest fraud to be committed and the undertaking of their Master and indeed are made the most fit in the most dangerous circumstances? 2. Why would the disciples not rather agree with Joseph of Arimathea about the body of Christ being moved to another place where deception could be easier to commit; why would they permit him to be buried in that place where there would be no hope left of him being spirited away? 3. How would those timid men, who scattered when Christ was seized, have dared to stand against the Roman Prefect and the Jewish senate and to break the seal with the guards not opposing them, to roll away the stone, and to transfer the body of their teacher to another place in such a way that it would never be detected where they transported it? 4. How would the apostles have been able to accomplish all this, how move the stone and bear the body out of the tomb in a way that no soldier would wake up, how would they have dared to approach the tomb when they were completely unaware whether every soldier was sleeping or not? And especially at the time of a full moon, such as then was, it would have been a rather difficult task besides, when they could have been uncovered and easily spotted. [5.] Or could those disciples numbering eleven, known to all, have committed an action of this sort, so that the magistrate, in a matter of greatest import, would be absolutely unable to detect the trail of the crime committed and then extract from one or another of the disciples a confession of this action? Next, what disciples would have dared to affirm publicly before the senate as if to proclaim to a well-known matter, that Jesus Christ, crucified by the Jews, had risen from the dead. Acts 3, 4, and 5, Stephen, ch. 7:6. Why would the mind of the apostles not clearly be estranged from Christ when they had been deceived by him, that they, made ashamed, were deserted by that accepted proposition about ruling a kingdom? Why not clearly fear lest they themselves, as if companions of the impostor and sedition, should suffer the ultimate punishment? And thus wretchedly seduced by their teacher, would they seek more to flee danger than to expose themselves to the most severe punishment?

"The unbelievers say that this was the reason why the apostles committed this crime: they conceived a hope while their Master was still living that he would be a powerful earthly monarch. Evidently they did not lose this hope even after his death, as contends the author of *Du Discours sur les Fondemens et les Raisons du Christianisme*. But if this were so, we cannot understand what good a dead body ought to serve them. . . . Indeed, our adversaries contend that in the end the apostles bore away the body of Christ in order to persuade men that he had risen from the dead and in this way to direct that earthly kingdom more easily. . . . At this point it should be observed: those simple and unlearned apostles (as they are described by our adversaries) could in no way hope to effect that which their Master could not, and which now was even more impossible after the leader of the faction had suffered the ultimate punishment as a insurgent and rebel. His wretched end ought to frighten off those timid followers from his way of life.

"Nonnulla adhuc restant quæ omnem furti commissi suspicionem plane removent, [et ad] quæ Adversarii nostri respondere nunquam poterunt. Cur scilicet, 1. Apostoli postquam fraus illa, in Corporis mortui ablatione commissa, fuit detecta, Hierosolymam nihilominus intrare ausi fuerint, publiceque se ibi in Templo ostendere conati sint, cum tamen nonnisi mortem ignominiosissimam propter commissa illa crimina expectare potuerint? Cur 2. Pontifices Senatusque Judaicus minis, verberibus, carcere Apostolos ab Evangelii inter Judæos prædictione cohibere voluerint, nunquam tamen furti hujus patrati illos accusaverint publiceque convicerint, cum tamen solum hoc suffecisset omni Evangelii progressui coercendo, et sat caussæ fuisset ad supplicium Apostolis sumendum. 3. Cum senatui nota fuerit fraus illa, neque hoc Apostolos latere potuit, qui fit ut simplices illi ac rudes homines ipsimet à Magistro suo decepti, spe erigendi regni plane frustrati, integro senatu præsente Judæorum proceres accusare ausi sint, quod principem Gloriæ crucifixerint? 'Deus,' inquiunt, 'majorum nostrorum Jesum suscitavit, quem vos in patibulo suspensum interfecistis.' Act 5:30. Si senatores illi certi fuere totum illud Christi Apostolorumque negotium nonnnisi meram esse Imposturam, qui fit ut Apostolos ad enormem illam accusationem dimiserint, Gamalielique Aures præbuerint dicenti, 'Nunc quoque vobis suadeo, ut vobis ab his hominibus temperetis, eosque missos faciatis. Si enim ab hominibus est hoc consilium atque opus, abolebitur; sin à Deo est, id abolere non potestis, ne forte cum deo pugnare comperiamini. Huic illi obtemperarunt.' Act 5:38–39. [. . .]

"Objiciunt porro Increduli, [. . .] cur [nimirum] Jesus à mortuis resuscitatus Magistratui Judæorum se nunquam monstraverit?[2] Hoc enim si factum fuisset, omnes statim dissipatæ essent difficultates, certitudo facti hujus in clarissima luce posita, sufficiensque fuisset Testium fide dignissimorum numerus. Quam difficultatem ut denuo difflemus ad sequentia attendi debet. Ad certitudinem rei alicujus [probandam] nonnisi certo fide dignorum Testium numero opus est; in Foris enim humanis nullibi consuetum est, ut aliquot Testium millia ad rem aliquam probandam producantur; nonnulli enim omnia Testium requisita habentes sifficiunt; supponamus ergo nonnisi duodecim Apostolos, Paulum

---

And although the apostles, in the common opinion of the Jews, hoped for an earthly prince such as the oracles of the prophets described, they would be adverse to their own hypothesis if they wished to persuade men that Jesus Christ—the one who had recently suffered the ultimate punishment, now revived, carried up to heaven, now invisible—was that earthly prince about to set up the kingdom among the Jews and liberate them from the Roman yoke."

2. MS: "monstravent."

enim hic illorum numero comprehendimus, Testes Christi resuscitati oc-
ulatos esse; jure major numerus requiri non posset, cum hi optimorum
Testium Characteres omnes habeant. Si autem duodecim Testes oculati
fide digni non sufficiunt, nec major etiam sufficit numerus, dum certitudo rei gestæ hac ratione nequaquam augeatur. Si vero Christus redi-
vivus apparuisset Judæorum senatui, requiri posset, ut Præfectum etiam
adivisset Romanum, dum major adhuc [resurrectionis] certitudo fuisset.
Si etiam hac fuisset factum, Increduli poscerent, ut omnibus et singulis
Hierosolymorum Incolis sese monstraverit; et cum non iis solum qui
in Urbe illa habitabant, Evangelium prædicari debuit, sed et reliquis
[Terræ] Cananææ habitatoribus, necessum fuisset ut iis omnibus con-
spiciendum sese præbuisset. Nec Judæorum solum, sed et Gentilium debuit esse servator, quare ergo non Romanis etiam et Græcis eo tempore
viventibus apparuit, omnibus Asiæ, Africæ et Europæ Incolis? At non iis
solum prædicatur Christus, qui ea vixerunt ætate sed seris etiam posteris;
si ergo et his, ipsum à mortuis resurrexisse, certum esse debet, et iis sese
ut monstret requiri posset; imo si magnus testium numerus rei certitudinem efficere debet, necessum omnino esset, ut inde ab ejus Resurrectione ad finem usque sæculorum omnibus hominibus conspicien-
dum se dare et in illorum oculis miracula, ut et ipsi fidem habeant Jesum
redivivum esse, patrare debuisset, quod non absurdum moda sed impossibile plane esset. Ex quibus apparet Incredulorum Animo sceptico
satisfieri nunquam posse. [. . .] Christus eos Resurrectionis suæ testes
elegit, quos ad veritatem hanc in universa terra prædicandam adhibere
voluit, quibus, infallibilitatis suæ certissima edentibus documenta, si
Gentiles fidem non habuissent, etiam nec Magistratui credidissent Judaico; sed potius magis suspecta Ethnicis veritas hæc visura fuisset, si in-
teger Judæorum Magistratus, imo universa illa gens testimonium huic
rei præbuisset; putassent enim hæc nonnisi ad Religionum Judæorum
pertinere, à qua aversus erat Ethnicorum animus. [. . .] Omne veritati
robur accedere putant Adversarii nostri, si Principes hujus sæculi ei cal-
culum suum addidissent, illique testimonium dedissent. At quid inde sequeretur? Deus testimonium ab hominibus acciperet, et non amplius
proprio suo fundamento staret divina veritas."³ Stapferus, *Theolog. Polem.*, Tom. III, pp. 245–48, 250.

3. "Some things remain at this point which clearly remove all suspicion of a theft committed and to which our adversaries have never been able to respond. Why 1. after that fraud committed in the carrying off of the dead body had been detected, did the Apostles dare to enter
Jerusalem no less and publicly try to show themselves in the temple there, when they could expect the most disgraceful death because committing that crime? Why 2. did the priests and Jew-

1331. FITNESS, NATURAL. Faith is appointed the condition of an interest in Christ because there is a PROPRIETY in it, that such only should

---

ish Sanhedrin wish to restrain the Apostles by means of threats, whips, and prison from preaching the Gospel among the Jews, yet never accused them of perpetrating this theft and convicted them publicly, when this alone would have sufficed to hinder all progress of the Gospel et would have been enough cause to execute the Apostles. 3. when this fraud became known to the Sanhedrin and it was not possible for the Apostles to hide it, how did it happen that those simple and unlearned men, themselves deceived by their Master and clearly frustrated in the hope of directing a kingdom, dared to accuse the leaders of the Jews with the whole Sanhedrin present that they crucified the Prince of Glory? 'The God of our fathers,' they said, 'raised Jesus, whom you yourselves killed, hanging him on the cross,' Acts 5:30. If those elders were sure that all that business of Christ and the apostles was only pure deceit, how is it that they let slip the apostles for that enormous accusation and offered their ears to Gamaliel, who said, 'Now I urge you to restrain yourselves from these men and let them be dismissed. For if this plan and work are from men, it will fail; but if it is from God, you are not able to abolish it, lest you be found fighting with God.' They complied with this,' Acts 5:38–39. [. . .]

"Unbelievers object further: Why did Jesus never show himself risen from the dead to the magistrate of the Jews? For if this had been done, immediately all difficulties would vanish, the certainty of this fact would be placed in the clearest light, and the number of witnesses most worthy of trust would be sufficient. The following ought to be attended to so that we blow apart once again this difficulty. To prove the certainty of any matter it is necessary only for a certain number of witnesses worthy of trust. Indeed, it is customary nowhere in human marketplaces that so many thousands of witnesses be produced to prove any matter. The fact that some have all the things required of witnesses is sufficient. Therefore, let us suppose none except the twelve apostles (for we included here Paul in their number) were eye-witnesses of Christ's resurrection; by law a greater numbers could not be required, since these all have the characters of the best witnesses. But if twelve eye-witnesses worthy of trust do not suffice, neither does an even greater number so long as the certainty of the thing attested to does not increase at all in this reckoning. If indeed a resurrected Christ had appeared to the senate of the Jews, he could be required to go also to the Roman prefect until there was a greater certainty of the resurrection. If even this had been done, the incredulous would ask that he would have shown himself to every inhabitant of Jerusalem one by one. And since the gospel should be preached not only to them who lived in that city, but also the the rest living in the land of Canaan, it would be necessary that he show himself to be seen by all. Since he ought to have been the Savior not of Jews alone but also of the Gentiles, why then did he not appear to the Romans also and to the Greeks who were living at that time, to all the inhabitants of Asia, Africa, and Europe? But Christ is not preached to these alone who lived in that age but also to later generations. If, then, the fact that he rose from the dead ought to be made sure to these people, it would be possible to require that he show himself to them. Or rather, if a great number of witnesses should effect the certainty of a matter, it would be wholly necessary that he ought to allow himself to be seen by all people from the time of his resurrection until the end of the ages and to produce miracles before their eyes. All this in order that they may have faith that Jesus is alive. But this would be not only absurd but clearly impossible. From the above it is apparent that it is never possible to satisfy the skeptical mind of unbelievers. [. . .] Christ chose those witnesses of his resurrection, those whom he wished to apply to the preaching of this truth in all the world. If the Gentiles would not have had faith in those who gave out most sure documents of Christ's infallibility, neither would they have believed the Jewish magistracy. On the contrary, this truth would have seemed more suspicious to the Gentiles, if the whole magistracy of the Jews, indeed, that entire race should have offered testimony to this matter. For they would think that these things only pertain to the religion of the Jews, from which the mind of the Gentiles be interested in him as do believe in him, or that such only should be looked upon as in him, or one with him, whose hearts are united to him as their Savior.

1332a. CHRISTIAN RELIGION. CHRIST NO IMPOSTOR. "Impostoris Characteres ipsi tribui minime posse, patet ex ipsius Doctrina, quam Factis et Vita, moribusque.

"Illius Doctrina quod spectat, erat illa sublimis, ad pietatem tamen, quantaquanta est, composita. Ad sublimitatem quod spectat, Christus quidem non minus ac illius discipuli ex infima plebe natus erat, cui studiis vacare non licuit, unde nullis Disciplinarum præsidiis instructus, à Judæis nonnisi abjectus aliquis Faber lignarius habebatur, qui in Patris sui hominis rudis et illiterati domo educatus, eruditum ex hominibus Magistrum non habuit, à quo doctrinam hanc accipere potuisset, imo nec habere potuit, dum et Gentilium Plactis, et Judæorum Opinionibus e diametro fuerit opposita.

"Doctrina illius, inquam, ita est composita, ut 1. longe excellentiora omnibus Philosophis qui hucusque extiterunt de Deo docuerit; ut quæcunque locutus est divinæ sapientiæ reliquisque illius Attributis sint convenientissima, quod ipsimet nostri Adversarii fateri coguntur, Deum omnia spirant quæcunque loquutus[4] est, nobilissimas supremi numinis tradidit Ideas. Sed undenam quæsumus hæc hausit; a sapientioribus ex Gentilibus [ea] habere non potuit, cum ipsimet hac in re cœcuiverint; nec à Judæorum Magistris, omnia enim quæ de perfectissimi spiritus spirituali cultu protulit, Judæorum principiis, vel potius opinionibus, plane fuere contraria.

"Ab aliis ergo Christus dogmata sua habere non potuit: unde aut ipsemet illorum Autor censendus, aut à Deo ea habuisse necessum est. Ipse homo rudis et illiteratus fuit, si ad externas illius circumstantias adtendimus, et tamen doctrinam protulit à Gentilium Judæorumque sapientia plane diversam, pereximias de Deo notiones tradens, et ad hominum veram felicitatem et salutem tendentes; unde probabilius fit, doctrinam hanc divinam potius, quam figmentum sapientiæ humanæ et meram fraudem esse. [. . .]

---

had been turned. [. . .] Our adversaries think that great firmness comes to the truth, if the princes of this age would add their vote to it and given their testimony to it. But what would follow from this? God would receive testimony from human beings and divine truth would stand no more on its own foundation."

4. MS: "locutus."

"'Si forte' (inquit Acutiss. Theologus Sam. Werenfelsius)[5] 'adolescentulus ea dicit aut scribit, quæ captum ejus longe superant, statim suspicamur, eum, quæ dicit, ab alio se doctiore accepisse: quod si fatetur, se id hausisse à Præceptore suo, eujus genio ea quæ audivimus plane conveniunt, quin verum dicat non dubitamus; non alia scriptorum sacrorum (Christi et Apostolorum suorum) ratio est. Scribunt ea quæ sunt supra captum hominum; . . . aut si hoc alicui dubium videtur, saltem scribunt ea, quæ sunt supra captum talium hominum, quales ipsi fuerunt, supra captum hominem rudium, opificum, Piscatorum: scribunt ea de Deo et rebus divinis, de summo hominis bono, de vita recte instituenda, quæ tot homines docti et sapientes, denique totus fere mundus non dubitant omnibus aliis, quæ de hac materia à summis Ingeniis edita sunt, longe anteponere. Quis non hic merito quærat, unde tanta venerit, tam abjectis in speciem hominibus, sapientia? Num igitur cum dicunt à Deo se præclara hæc accepisse, nemo de eorum fide dubitabit, qui et hæc, quæ dicunt Deo dignissima cernit, et alioquin videt, nullum his hominibus fuisse cum doctis et sapientibus commercium.'"[6] Stapferus, *Theolog. Polem.,* Tom. II, pp. 1120e–23.

5. Stapfer cites Werenfels, "Opp. Sect. II. Dissert. VIII. De Triplici teste de Verbo Dei testante p. 175."
6. "That the characteristics of an impostor can in no way be attributed to him is [as] clear from his doctrine as from his deeds, life and customs.

"In that we see that, however great that sublime doctrine of his was, it was arranged for piety. For sublimity, in that we see that . . . Christ indeed had been born, no less than his disciples, from the lowest common people. It was not permitted him to have the leisure for studies, from where he was instructed by no help of teachers. He was considered by the Jews only some lowly carpenter who was educated in the home of his unlearned and ignorant father; he had no learned teacher among men from whom he could accept this teaching, nor was he able to have so long as his teaching was diametrically opposed to both the intricacies of the Gentiles and the opinions of the Jews.

"His doctrine, I say, was so arranged that 1. it taught far more excellent things about God than all the philosophers who have thus far been in existence; that whatever he spoke is most fitting to divine wisdom and his other attributes. Our adversaries themselves are compelled to say as much. But whence, we ask, did he draw these things. He was not able to have [these things] from the wisest of the Gentiles (although they themselves in this matter concur), nor from the teachers of the Jews, for everything he proposed about the spiritual worship of a most perfected spirit was clearly contrary to the principles of the Jews, or rather, to their opinions.

"From others, then, Christ could not have his teachings. Whence, either he himself should be thought the author of those, or it is necessary that he had them from God. He was an unlearned and unschooled man—if we look at his external circumstances—and yet he brought forth a teaching clearly different from the wisdom of the Gentiles and the Jews, passing on extraordinary ideas about God and attending to the true happiness and salvation of human beings. From this fact, it is more probable that his teaching was divine rather than a deception and a creation of human wisdom. [. . .]

1332[b]. CHRIST HAD THE SPIRIT OF PROPHECY. Add this at the end of No. 972.[7] "Unicum ergo Adversariis remanet subterfugium, nempe aut integros hos Libros evangelicos post harum rerum implementum demum litteris fuisse consignatos. [...] At 1. probatissimi, qui extant, et antiquissimi scriptores, tres saltem priores Evangelistas ante Excidium Hierosolymitanum sua litteris consignasse memorant. [...]

"2. Acta Apostolorum autem ante Hierosolymitanum Excidium exarata fuisse, non unum est quod suadet. ... Tempore Captivitatis Paulinæ exaratam fuisse hanc Historiam inde patet, quod cum omnia Pauli gesta exactissime narrentur, nulla tamen ejus e vinculis liberationis fiat mentio; sed Historiographus in medio illius Historiæ desinit. Lucas vero antequam Acta Apostolorum scripsit, jam Evangelium suum litteris consignaverat, ad id enim statim ab Actorum initio provocat, antiquius vero adhuc Matthaei Evangelium est, unde hæc omnia jam ante urbis Eversionem scripta fuerint[8] oportet.

"3. Nec omittendum, ipsa hæc Christi vaticinia ita comparata esse, ut ea neutiquam post Politiæ illius sacræ abrogationem litteris consignata esse ex illorum modo quam clarissime appareat; in illis enim stylo Prophetico, mundi finis immediate cum veteris mundi typici abrogatione conjungitur, ac si unum alterum statim exciperet, quod factum non fuisset, si post Urbis demum vastationem Vaticinia hæc ab hominibus impostoribus fuissent edita, hoc enim in casu stylum[9] Prophetis maxime consuetum evitassent."[1] Stapferus, *Theolog. Polem.*, Tom. II, pp. 1126–28.

"'If perhaps' (said the most astute theologian Samuel Werenfels) 'a young man either speaks or writes these things, which far surpass his capacity, we would immediately suspect that he had received them from another, more learned than him. But if he says that he had taken it from his teacher, the things we hear are clearly fitting to his genius, [and] we should not doubt but that he speaks the truth. The reckoning of the sacred writers (Christ and the apostles) is not otherwise. They write things which are beyond the capacity of humans; or, if this seems doubtful to someone, alternately they write the things which are beyond the capacity of the men such as they were: unschooled, workers, fishermen. They write the things about God and divine matters, about the highest good of man, and about a life to be lived correctly. So many learned and wise men, indeed almost the whole world, do not hesitate to place these things far ahead of all others which have been said about these matters by the highest intellects. Who would not rightly ask here whence such great wisdom came to men so lowly in appearance? Therefore there is no one, is there—discerning that the things they [i.e. the Apostles] speak are most worthy of God and otherwise seeing that these men had no communictation with the learned and wise—who will doubt their trustworthiness when they say that they received these things from God?'"

7. *Works*, 20, 274.
8. MS: "fuere."
9. MS: "stylo."
1. "Therefore there remains one subterfuge for our opponents: [that] truly all these evangelical books have been sealed with the letters of these things after completion. But 1. the most

1333. CONCERNING OBJECTIONS AGAINST THE REALITY OF CHRIST'S RESURRECTION, that he was not immediately known, that his body was not always visible, often vanished out of sight, etc. Christ's body rose to be as much like the body which it was before, as was consistent with that state which it was requisite his risen body should be in.

It was no wonder the form of it was considerably changed when it rose not in its former infirmity, but was raised in power, and to immortality and to impassability; no wonder it was not always visible and the constant object of men's external senses, for, if so, it would have remained still in some connection with this wicked world of mankind, still connected with the society of the polluted, depraved inhabitants of the earth, and so still within their reach in many respects, within the reach of their malignity and reproach, and the exercise of their enmity in other respects.

It was necessary that his risen body should not be connected universally with this earthly, changeable, corruptible world by the laws of the bodies which belong to this world, as it was in the days of his flesh. For, if so, his body must still remain liable to suffering and decay, would waste by perspiration, would need the constant repairs of food and sleep, would be liable to suffer injury by the weather, heat and cold, rains and dews, would be incommoded by darkness, etc. But this was not proper. For his body did not now belong to this world as it did before, but was an heavenly body, though the change of his body was not perfected to fit it for its heavenly state till his ascension.

1334. In what respects the PROPAGATION OF MAHOMETANISM is far from being worthy to be looked upon as parallel with the PROPAGATION OF CHRISTIANITY.

---

approved, which still exist, and the most ancient writers mention that the three earlier at least had recorded their ideas to writing before the fall of Jerusalem. [. . .]

"2. But that the Acts of the Apostles had been written before Jerusalem's fall, there is not one thing which is persuasive. . . . It is clear that this history was written at the time of Paul's imprisonment from the fact that when all of Paul's deeds are told in great detail, still no mention is made of his freedom from chains, but the writer stops in the middle of his history. Certainly before Luke wrote the Acts, he had already written his own Gospel, for at the beginning of Acts he immediately appeals to that fact. Certainly the Gospel of Matthew is more ancient whence it is right that all these things had already been written before the destruction of the city.

"3. Nor should it be forgotten that this prophecy of Christ is arranged in such a way that it appears most clearly from the manner of those things to have been committed to writing by no means after the abrogation of that holy city. For in the writings, by a prophetic style, the end of the world is immediately joined with the abrogation of the type of the old world. Moreover, if he were immediately expecting another world, which had not been made, if at length after the wasting of the city this prophecy had been edited by false men, they would avoid in this case this style most accustomed to the prophets."

1. The revolution that was brought to pass in the world by the propagation of Mahometanism was not so great a revolution as that which was by the propagation of Christianity—yea, in this respect was by no means worthy to be compared to it—if we consider the state the world was in before Christianity was propagated, how dark, ignorant, barbarous and wicked, how strongly these things were established by long, universal, immemorial custom, how fixed in men's hearts, how established by all human power and authority and inclination, and how vast the alteration when Christianity was introduced and established; how vast the overthrow of that which had been built up before and had stood from age to age, how great and how strong the building, how absolute the destruction, and also how great the building that was erected in its room, and of how different and opposite a nature from that which had stood on the same ground before.

But as to [the] revolution brought to pass in the world by the propagation of Mahometanism, it consisted either in the change made among the heathen, barbarous nations, which had their original from Arabia or Scythia, or that made among professing Christians. But with respect to neither of these was the revolution comparably so great as the other. As to the change made among those heathens, they long had had some obscure notices of the true God, and many of the great truths of what is called natural religion they had obtained by those glimmerings of the light of the gospel which had diffused over great part of the world, even that part of it that had not fully embraced Christianity. And Mahometanism carried them very little further in these things, was an occasion of but a small advance of light and knowledge.

And as to the change made among Christians, there was no advance at all made in knowledge or anything that was good. And as to the change made among Christians as to religious custom, the Christians had so degenerated before, were become so superstitious, that the alteration was not vastly great.

2. The difference of the two revolutions was, as it were, infinitely great with respect to goodness.

The change made in the world by the propagation of Christianity was a great change indeed with regard to light and knowledge. It was a change from great darkness to glorious and marvelous light. By the preaching of the gospel in the world, the dayspring from on high visited the earth, and the sun arose after a long night of the most gross darkness. But as to the change made in Christendom by the propagation of

Mahometanism,[2] there was no increase of light by it, but, on the contrary, it was evidently a change from light to darkness. It was a propagation of ignorance and not of knowledge.

And as to the change made among the heathen, as was observed before, there was but a small degree of increase of light. And all the light that was added, was borrowed from Christianity. The increase of knowledge that there was, was only by Mahomet, and his followers communicated what had before be[en] communicated to them by Christian teaching. There can be no pretense of the least degree of addition of anything beyond what they had before received from the gospel.

And as to rules and precepts, examples, promises, or inducements to virtue of any kind, no addition at all was made. What alteration there was, was only for the worse; the examples, histories, representations and promises of the new Mahometan religion only tending exceedingly to debase, debauch and corrupt the minds of such as received it.

3. The revolution that was made by the propagation of Christianity was an infinitely greater and more wonderful effect, if we consider the opposition that was overcome in bringing it to pass. Christianity was propagated against all the opposition that could be made by men's carnal dispositions, strengthened by inveterate general customs, principles, habits and practice, prevailing like a mighty flood.

Mahometanism was propagated, not in opposition to these inclinations, but by complying with them and gratifying 'em in examples, precepts and promises, as Stapferus observes, *Theolog. Polem.*, Tom. III, [p.] 292. Speaking of Mahomet's laws, [he] says, "Lex, quam ille tulit, non hominum modo opinionibus, sed populorum illorum etiam corruptæ naturæ ac moribus et innatis vitiis præprimis accommodata erat; nec fere nisi in exercitiis externis, homini carnali, spiritualibus illis quæ sacræ præscribunt paginæ, præstitu longe facilioribus, consistebat."

"Muhamet injuriæ allatæ ultionem, ab uxoribus levissimam ob caussam discedendi licentiam, alias super alias mulieres, nova semper libidinis irritamenta permittit, sibique primas in promiscua & turpissima lascivia explenda concessit partes; cæterum in cærimoniis externis, ad pietatem neutiquam proficuis, verum Dei cultum constituit: tota denique religio illa nonnisi ad fundendum sanguinem facta."[3] Ibid., pp. 337–

---

2. MS: "Xtianity."

3. "The law, which he brought, was fitted not only to the opinions of humankind, but of those people also of a nature corrupted in customs and especially in inborn faults; indeed it

38. This religion, in particular, [can be likened] to the luxurious, sensual, beastly disposition of the Pharisees.

Christianity was extremely contrary to the most established and darling opinions of the world, whereas Mahomet accommodated his doctrine to all such notions as were most pleasing at that day among the heathens, Arabians, Jews, and the several most prevailing sects of Christians, as Stapferus observes in the place last referred to.[4] "Multa ex veterum Arabum placitis retinuit Muhammedes, uti constat ex Historia Arabum, quam edidit Abrahamus Eschellensis; quod etiam patet ex ipsa Peregrinatione Meccana et Visitatione Saphæ & Marvæ, ex Jejunio Ramadhan, aliisque. Tum quod Judæorum Fabulis suam commiscuit doctrinam; tum quod ex reliquarum tunc temporis dominantium religionum disciplinis multa retinuit.

"'Est enim,' inquit Celeb. Reineccius [Cap. I], in Hist. Alcorani [sec. v], 'hæc rapsodia ex sacris ethnicorum, Judæorum et Christianorum veris & falsis commixta & propriis hujus impostoris & cooperariorum Gnosticorum, Nestorianorum et id genus hominum somniis aucta.'[5]

Ibid., p. 340. "Religio [. . .] Mahumedana ita comparata est, ut præjudiciis tam Judaicis quam ethnicis faveret, ut carnis cupiditatibus atque mundi illecebris accommodata esset.

"Religio quam Christus docebat ita erat comparata, ut pravis hominum affectibus, carnisque voluptatibus ne in re minima quidem faveret, sed e diametro iis opposita esset, neque in ulla re præjudiciis vel Judæorum vel ethnicorum accommodata erat, sed præconceptis hominum

---

consisted only in those external exercises, far easier for the fleshly person than those spiritual exercises which the holy Scriptures prescribe.

"Muhamet permits revenge for injuries, the right of divorcing wives for the slightest reason, multiple wives, and ever new incitements of desire. For himself he allowed the first part in satisfying promiscuity and the most base desires. Also, he set up the true worship of God in external ceremonies not at all beneficial for piety. Finally, all that religion was done only for shedding blood."

4. JE copied the following series of quotations not from "the place last referred to," but from Stapfer, *Institutiones Theologiæ Polemicæ*, 3, 292, 340, as in the third paragraph above. The disjuncture arises from JE's insertion of the quote from ibid., pp. 337–38, by means of cue signs.

5. "Muhamet kept many things pleasing to ancient Arabs, just as it says in the *History of the Arabs*, which Abraham Eschellensis edited. And this also appears in the journey to Mecca, the visitation of Sapha and Marva, in the fast of Ramadan, and others. Then there is the fact that he mixed his own teaching to the stories of the Jews, the fact that he kept in his teaching many things from the rest of the religions dominant at the time.

"'For,' says the celebrated [Christian] Reineccius [ch. 1], in *Histo. Alcorani* [sec. v], 'this taking from the sacred things of the Gentiles, has been mixed with the true and false ideas of both the Jews and Christians and has been increased by the dreams belonging to that impostor and of cooperating Gnostics and Nestorians and that kind of people.'"

opinionibus plane contraria; unde apostoli religionem hanc annuntiantes statim religionem tam Judaicam quam ethnicam impugnabant. Act. 3:12–13, 14:15, 17:22–31, etc."[6]

Christianity was propagated against the most violent, universal and cruel persecution of all the powers of the world. Mahometanism was not so; never made its way anywhere, in any remarkable instance, against persecution.

4. The difference will appear great if we consider the time when each of these were propagated. Christianity was propagated at a time when human learning and science was at its greatest height in the world. But Mahometanism was broached and propagated in ages of great darkness, after learning had exceedingly decayed and was almost extinguished in the world.

5. The difference will further appear if we consider the places from whence these religions were[7] propagated. Christianity was first begun in a place of great light, the greatest light with regard to religious knowledge in the world, and a very public part of the world where resorted innumerable multitudes of people three times every year, from almost all parts of the known world. And besides the vast resort of Jews and proselytes thither, it was a country that was at that time under the inspection and government of the Romans, where they had a governor and other public officers constantly residing. It was propagated especially from Jerusalem, the chief city in that country and one of the greatest and most public cities in the world; and indeed, all things considered, was, next to Rome itself, above all others as a city set on an hill, and in some respects far beyond that.

And the nations among whom it was first propagated after the Jews were not the more ignorant and barbarous nations, but the most knowing and learned in the world, as particularly the Greeks and Romans. And the cities where it was very early received, and from whence it was sounded out to other parts, were the greatest, most public and polite,

---

6. "The Mohammedan religion was so arranged that it favored the prejudices of the Jews as well as the Gentiles, and that it was fitted to the desires of the flesh and the attractions of the world.

"The religion which Christ taught was arranged thus that it was not agreeable to the depraved affections of humans, nor indeed to the desires of the flesh in the smallest of matters, but was set diametrically opposed to these. Neither was it fitted in any way to the prejudices of the Jews or the Gentiles, but was clearly contrary to preconceived human views. This is why the apostles, as they proclaim this religion, immediately fought against both the Jewish and the pagan religion. Acts 3:12–13, 14:15, 17:22–31, etc."

7. MS: "these religion was."

such as Antioch, Ephesus, Alexandria, Corinth, Athens and Rome. And some of these were the greatest seats of learning and philosophy of any on earth.

Whereas Mahometanism was broached in a dark corner of the earth, in Arabia. And the people among whom it first gained strength, who sent out armies to propagate it to the rest of the world, were an ignorant and barbarous sort of people, such as the Saracens and Turks, who originated from Scythia.

6. The difference appears in the means and method of propagation. Christianity was propagated by light, instruction and knowledge, reasoning and inquiry. These things were encouraged by the gospel. And by these means the gospel prevailed.

But Mahometanism was not propagated by light and instruction, but by darkness, not by encouraging reasoning and search but by discouraging knowledge and learning, shutting out these things and forbidding inquiry; and so, in short, by hoodwinking mankind and blinding their eyes.

"Ita comparata est Jesu Christi doctrina, ut rigidissimum etiam sustinere possit examen; unde omnibus & singulis sedula ejus lectio commendatur, quippe 'quæ homines ad salutem sapientes reddere possit, dum omne scriptum divinitus inspiratum est, & utile ad doctrinam, ad reprehensionem, ad correctionem, ad justitiæ disciplinam, ut compositus sit divinus homo, ad omne recte factum bene comparatus.' II Tim. 3:15–17, & 'Berrhoenses Thessalonicensibus generosiores prædicantur, quippe qui summa cum aviditate doctrinam admiserint, quotidie litteras examinantes, an ea sic se haberent.' Actor. 17:11. 'Felix,' prædicatur, 'qui legit, & qui oraculi dicta audiunt.' Apoc. 1:3.

"Religio autem Mahumedana credi sibi vult absque ulla credendi libertate; unde librorum etiam, qui sacri habentur, lectio prohibita est plebi, quod manifestum iniquitatis indicium est, Ita legitur Sura V, 110. 'O qui crediderunt, ne interrogetis de rebus, quæ si manifestantur, vobis molestiam allaturæ sunt vobis; & si interrogetis de rebus; quando revelatur Alcoranus, manifestabuntur vobis, condonat Deus vobis culpam ob interrogationem de illis.'"[8] Stapfer, *Theolog. Polem.*, Tom. III, [pp.] 338–39.

8. "Thus the doctrine of Jesus Christ was arranged to be able to sustain even the most rigorous examination. Whence a diligent reading of it is commended to everyone, one by one, indeed, 'which is able to make wise men unto salvation, since all scripture is divinely inspired and useful for teaching, for reproof, for correction, for training in righteousness, that the godly person may be settled, well prepared for every good deed,' II Tim. 3:15–17, and 'the Bereans were said to be more magnanimous than the Thessalonians, because they gave access to the teaching with highest eagerness, daily pouring over the scriptures about whether these things

Mahometanism was propagated by the power of the sword, by potent sultans, absolute tyrants and mighty armies. Christianity was propagated by the weakest of men, unarmed with anything but meekness, humility, love, miracles, clear evidence, a most virtuous, holy and amiable example, and the power and fervor of eminent virtue, joined with assured belief of the truth, with self-denial and suffering for truth and holiness. And by such weapons as these it was propagated against the power, authority, wealth and armor of the world. It was against the greatest potentates, most absolute and cruel tyrants, their most crafty counsels and greatest strength, utmost rage and cruelty, and determined resolutions to put a stop to it and extirpate [it]. It was propagated against all the strength of the strongest empire that ever was in the world.

"Muhamedismi [. . .] doctores nulla plane ediderunt miracula, nulla gravissima ac durissima propter confessionem illam perpessi sunt supplicia, nullas perpessi persecutiones & varii generis ærumnas; sed quocunque arma eunt religio illa sequitur. Omnes enim infideles, qui religionem illam non amplecterentur, interficere jubet Mahumet. Sur. 4:88. 'Desideraverunt, ut infideles essetis, sicut ipsi infideles sunt: & essetis pares ipsis in impietate, ne ergo adsumetis ex eis amicos, donec emigrent e patria pro via Dei quod si tergiversati fuerint, capite eos, & occidite eos, ubicunque inveneritis eos, & ne accipiatis ex eis amicum, neque adjutorem' [. . . .] Adde plura alia loca Sur. 8, passim. Nec aliud ipsi Mahumedani argumentum proferunt, quam felicem bellorum successum, imperiique magnitudinem."[9] Stapferus, *Theolog. Polem.*, Tom. III, [pp.] 340–41.

Mahometanism was propagated very much by means of the con-

---

were so,' Acts 17:11. 'Happy,' it is said, 'is the one who reads and those who hear the words of the oracle,' Rev. 1:3.

"But the Mohammedan religion wants itself to be believed without any freedom of believing; whence also the reading of the books, which are considered holy, is prohibited to the people, because it is clear evidence of wickedness. Thus says Sura V, 110: 'O you who have believed, do not ask about things which if they are revealed will bring trouble to you; and if you ask about things, when Alcoranus [the Koran] is revealed, they will be revealed to you, God gives blame to you on account of your asking about them.'"

9. "The teachers of Mohammedism clearly gave no miracles, they endured no serious and difficult entreaties because of their confession, they endured no persecutions and hardships of various kinds; but wherever their weapons go, that religion follows. For Mohammed's orders are to kill all unbelievers who do not embrace that religion. Sura 4:88, 'They desired that you be unbelievers just as they themselves are unbelievers and that you be equal to them in impiety; therefore, don't take up friends from among them until they leave their fatherland for the way of God; but if they will have turned back, take them and kill them wherever you find them, and do not take a friend from among them nor a helper.' [. . .] Add more such places here and there, Sura 8. Nor do the Mohammedans themselves offer any argument than their happy success in war and the greatness of their empire."

tentions which [arose] among Christians about their religion. So Stapferus, speaking of Mahometanism, says, "Maxime ad sectæ hujus planta-
tionem contulerunt acerbissima Christianorum dissidia, per quæ eccle-
siam orientalem non in varias modo dividebant partes, sed disciplinam
etiam Christianam continuæ illæ contentiones apud infideles maxime
exosam reddebant."[1] Stapfer, ibid. ut supra, p. 292.

The propagation was extremely diverse as to the instruments.

"Primi Christi discipuli fuerunt viri in Deum pientissimi, vitæ simpli-
cis, nulla quidem humana sapientia ac scientia instructi, quales ad tantum opus perficiendum adhibere Deo conveniebat, ut appareret illud
non hominum sed Dei opus esse.

"Ii vero, qui primi Mahumedismum amplexi sunt, erant prædones,
homines ab omni pietate & humanitate alienissimi; ipsa enim vox Sara-
ceni id ostendit, quæ ληστρικος denotat."[2] Ibid. ut supra, p. 339.

7. One principal way wherein the propagation of Christianity is a proof
of the truth of [it], is as an evidence of the facts that are the foundation
[of] it. Christianity is built on certain great and wonderful, visible facts,
such as Christ's resurrection from the dead, and the great and innumerable miracles wrought by him and his apostles and other followers
in Judea and in many parts of the world. These facts were always referred
to as the foundation of the whole, and Christianity always pretended to
be built on them.

That Christianity, which in effect is no other than the belief of these
facts, should be extensively propagated in and near the place and time
wherein the facts were said to be wrought, when and where there was so
much opportunity and advantage to know the truth of the matter, is a
great, standing, everlasting evidence of the truth of the facts.

But as to Mahometanism, it pretends to no facts for the proof and
foundation, but only Mahomet's[3] pretenses to intercourse with heaven,
and his success in his rapine, murder and violence. The religion in no
part consists in any belief of sensible miracles as public attestations of

1. "The very bitter disagreements of the Christians added greatly to the growth of that sect.
Those disagreements not only divided the eastern church into various parties, but also those
continual strifes made the Christian doctrine most exceedingly hateful to unbelievers."

2. "The first disciples of Christ were men most pious towards God, of simple life, indeed, educated in no human wisdom or knowledge, men such as were fit to adhere to God for so great
a work to be done, so that that work would appear to be not that of men but of God.

"But those who first embraced Mahometanism were thieves, strangers to all piety and humanity; for the voice itself of Saracen shows that, which *lesrikos* denotes."

3. MS: "Mahometans."

heaven to Mahomet's authority and doctrine, so that no such belief was propagated in propagating Mahometanism.

8. If we consider the propagation of Christianity in the view last mentioned, viz. as a doctrine or belief of wonderful divine facts, so Mahometanism is not set up in opposition to it or competition with it, because the Mahometan religion itself owns the principal facts of Christianity, though it has no facts of its own to pretend to. And so Mahometanism rather confirms Christianity than weakens it. And the propagation of Mahometanism itself may be considered as one thing belonging to the propagation of Christianity, and as a part of that propagation, so far as that consists in a propagation of a professed belief of those facts. 'Tis an instance of the propagation of that which is the foundation of Christianity so far that it proves all the rest.

The Alcoran owns Jesus to be a great prophet, the messenger of God (Sura V, 84); that he wrought miracles, [healing] a man blind from his birth, and the leprous (Sura V, 119); also raising the dead; and that Jesus, as born of Mary, himself was a miracle (Sura XXIII, 52; Stapfer, Tom. III, p. 296). It often speaks of Jesus as the servant and messenger of God, as Sura IV, 158; III, 152; IV, 169–70; V, 84 (ibid., p. 306). Now owning this is, in effect, owning the whole, for 'tis the foundation of the whole, and proves all the rest. It owns Jesus to be miraculously conceived and born (Sura III, 47; XIX, 20–21), and without sin (Sura III, 36; XIX, 9 (ibid., p. 306). Mahomet owns Jesus, ascribes the conception of Christ alone to the power of God and inflation of his Spirit (ibid., p. 321a). In Sura XXI, 19, are these words as the words of God: "'Et Maria fuit virgo intacta et insufflavimus in eam de Spiritu nostro, et posuimus eam, et filium ejus in miraculum omnibus sæculis'"[4] (ibid., p. 335). He owned Jesus to be the Messiah foretold in the Law and the Prophets: "Jesus ipso Muhammede confitente est Messias ille in lege et prophetis promissus (Sura III, 45). 'Cum dixerunt angeli, O Maria certe Deus annuntiat tibi verbum ex se; nomen ejus erit Christus Jesus filius Mariæ' (Sura XIX, 29; Sura IV). 'Certe Christus Jesus filius Mariæ est legatus Dei, et verbum ejus'"[5] (ibid., p. 335).

---

4. "In Sura XXI, 19, are these words as the words of God: 'And Mary was an untouched virgin and we breathed into her from our Spirit, and we placed her and her son in a miracle to all the ages.'"

5. "Jesus is that Messiah promised in the Law and the Prophets, as Muhamet himself confessed (Sura III, 45). When the angels said, 'O Mary, surely God announces to you a word from himself; his name will be Christ Jesus, the son of Mary' (Sura XIX, 29; Sura IV). Surely, Christ Jesus, the son of Mary, is the ambassador of God and his word."

He owned Christ's ascension into heaven. "Sur. 4, 157. 'Elevavit eum (Christum) Deus ad se'"[6] (ibid., p. 336). Concerning Christ's miracles, Mahomet says, "Sura 3, 48; 5, 119. [. . .] 'dicet Deus O Jesus fili Mariæ— corroboravi te Spiritu Sanctitatis—et sanabas cœcum a nativitate rt leprosum ex concessione mea, et cum educeres e sepulchris mortuos ex concessione mea'"[7] (ibid., p. 337).

9. In this respect the great propagation of the Mahometan religion is a confirmation of revealed religion, and so of the Christian in particular, which alone can have any pretext to be a religion revealed by God, viz. as this is a great demonstration of the extreme darkness, blindness, weakness, childishness, folly and madness of mankind in matters of religion, and how greatly they stand in need of a divine guide and divine grace and strength for their help, such as the gospel reveals. And that this gross delusion has continued so long, in such great extent, it shows how helpless mankind are, under ignorance and delusions in matters of religion, and what absolute need they have of extraordinary divine interposition for their relief. And besides, such a miserable, blind, helpless state of mankind, is also exactly agreeable to the representation made in the Christian revelation.

1335. CHRISTIAN RELIGION. THE JEWISH NATION have, from their very beginning, been a remarkable STANDING EVIDENCE to the truth of REVEALED RELIGION. They have been so in two respects:

1. In being so distinguished from all the world in their religion, and preserved in so great a distinction. When every other nation under heaven had forsaken the true God and [been] overwhelmed in heathenish darkness, they had among them the knowledge and worship of the true God, and rational and true notions of his being, attributes and works, and his relation to mankind, and our dependence upon him, the worship and regards due to him, etc.; which was upheld among them, and them alone, for so many ages, to the coming of Christ, when they were so surrounded everywhere, on every side, with nations so vastly differing from 'em, being some of the grossest pagans and worst of idolaters.

The following things render this remarkable:

(1) That the whole world besides themselves had forgotten the true

6. "Sur. 4, 157, 'God lifted him (Christ) to himself.'"
7. "God will say, 'O Jesus, son of Mary, I have strengthened you with the Holy Spirit and you healed the blind from birth.'"

God, and forsaken his worship, and were all that while involved in gross heathenism.

(2) That they lived in the midst of the thickest and most populous parts of the world.

(3) They did not live separated from the rest of the world by the sea, being an island or a peninsula, nor yet divided from others by vast deserts or impassable mountains, but on the continent, in the midst of the habitable world, with populous countries adjoining to them almost on every side.

(4) That those nations who were their next neighbors on every side were steadfastly gross pagans and some of the worst of idolaters.

(5) They were not a nation that studied philosophy, had no schools among them under the care of such who[8] instructed their pupils in humane science, yet had most apparently far better, more sublime and purer notions of God, and religion, and man's duty, and divine things in general, than the best of the heathen philosophers.

(6) They seem to be a people no way remarkably distinguished from other nations by their genius and natural abilities.

(7) They were a comparatively small people, not a great empire, a vast and potent monarchy or commonwealth.

(8) Such changes and revolutions frequently came to pass in their nation, and such was their peculiar state from time to time, that[9] they were often extremely [liable] to be corrupted and overrun with the heathenish notions and customs of idolatrous nations, and to grow into a conformity to the rest of the world in that respect.

They were above two hundred years in Egypt, which may be looked upon as the second, if not the first, for being the fountain of idolatry. And they were there under circumstances tending to their being corrupted with idolatry, and brought to a conformity with the Egyptians in that respect, of any that can be conceived of, especially on these three accounts:

They were there in the beginning and rise of their nation. There the nation had, as it were, its birth. It arose from one family of about seventy persons, with the father of the whole family at the head of it, to be more than a million of people, yea, probably (reckoning male and female) about two millions.

They were there not kept separate and distinct, having little or noth-

8. MS: "and."
9. MS: "they."

ing to do with the Egyptians, but had continual intercourse and daily concern with the Egyptians.

And they were there as inferiors, in subjection to the Egyptians, their slaves. And the Egyptians that had daily concern with them were their masters.

And after they came into the land of Canaan, they for several ages dwelt there with the remains of the ancient heathen inhabitants, that were so numerous and strong as sometimes to overcome the children of Israel and keep 'em long in subjection to 'em. And they were from time to time subdued by their heathen neighbors, and kept in servitude by them for many years together.

And after they had lived long in the land, ten of their tribes were carried away into a final captivity, and heathen inhabitants planted in their stead, by which the remaining two tribes were the more exposed. And, at last, these remaining two tribes, with the Levites and all that were left of the Ten Tribes that were mixed with them, were carried away into Babylon, the chief city of Chaldea, the country that, above all in the world (at least excepting Egypt), was the fountain of idolatry. And there they dwelt during the time of one generation. So that, before any of them returned, the body of the people were a new generation, born and brought [up] in that land of darkness, amongst idolaters that were their superiors and masters, and many of them the most honorable men that were then in the world. And a great part, perhaps the greater part, of the nation never returned, but continued dispersed in heathen countries till Christ's coming.

And as to the nation in general, those in Canaan and out of it, they were in the subjection to the three successive heathen monarchies that arose: the Persian, Grecian and Roman. And heathen people belonging to each of these empires often swarmed in their country.

(9) The people seemed to be, from their very beginning till the Babylonish captivity, exceedingly prone to idolatry, fond in that respect of the customs of their heathen neighbors, were apt to think it honorable to be like the rest of the nations and a disgrace to be so singular. And this appeared in that,

(10) They actually often apostatized to idolatry, embraced the worship of the heathen gods and neglected the worship of the true [God], and continued sometimes for a long time in their conformity to their heathen neighbors. And yet they were wonderfully reclaimed from time [to time], so that they were never suffered finally to apostatize, as all other

nations in the world had done, and were left in their apostasy for so vast a space of time.

(11) All is the more remarkable, in that not only the true God and his spiritual worship, so infinitely diverse from the gods and religion of the heathen, but the external institution and rites of worship observed among the Jews, and the law of their worship and religion, was remarkably opposite and repugnant to the religious rites of their heathen neighbors. Thus they were exceeding opposite to the rites of the Egyptians among whom they lived so long in their first beginnings, and among whom they first became a nation. So they were also to the rites of the ancient inhabitants of Canaan, of the Philistines, Moabites, Ammonites, etc.

2. In being preserved for so long a time a distinct nation, and in so clear and perfect a distinction from all other nations, as from their father Jacob's time to this day, being neither destroyed and abolished nor lost by mixing with other nations.

Jacob himself was exposed to be destroyed by his brother Esau before he was married. His family were greatly exposed to be destroyed, at least as to any permanent distinction from other people, when Laban pursued after him with a design probably to kill him, and [to have] brought back his wives and children into Padan-Aram and have kept them there, at least by some means to have carried back his family, and to have prevented their ever going to Canaan. He and his family were in eminent danger of being destroyed when Esau came out against him with 400 men. His family were greatly exposed to be destroyed by the inhabitants of Canaan, after provoked by his sons' destroying the Shechemites.

A series of wonderful and miraculous providences respecting Joseph were the means of preserving the family, without which they would probably either have perished by the famine or, in the time of that famine, have wandered away from Canaan in such obscurity, and under such disadvantages, that [they] would have been likely to have proved [the occasion of their] never returning any more to Canaan—and so of the final breaking up of the family.

In Egypt they were greatly exposed to be destroyed when Pharaoh set himself to effect it by destroying all the males. When they had continued so long in Egypt, in such underling, abject circumstances, it could be owing to nothing but a course of the greatest miracles that ever they were separated from that people and land, so as to return again to dwell by themselves, to be kept a distinct nation.

They were in eminent danger of being swallowed up by Pharaoh and his host at the Red Sea, or receiving such a blow as wholly to have broken up the design of their proceeding to Canaan to live there. They were exposed to suffer that which would have prevented this when the Amalekites met them and fought with them. Nothing but a course of most astonishing miracles for forty years could have prevented their perishing in the wilderness, or being obliged to go back [to Egypt, or their being]¹ captivated and dispersed by the nations that dwelt around that wilderness. They were greatly exposed to have been ruined as a people by the opposition of the Moabites, Midianites, Amorites, and Og the King of Bashan.

That ever they got the possession of Canaan, which was prepossessed by many nations greater and stronger than they, was owing to a course of great miracles, and without that they must have perished as a people. After they had got the possession of the land, they were often greatly exposed to be utterly ruined in the time of the judges, when their enemies in those parts, which seemed to have had exceeding hatred of them, prevailed against them and had the mastery of them. It could be owing to nothing but the special providence of God that those enemies did not improve these advantages they had in their hands utterly to destroy them, or at least to drive them, or carry them captive, out of that land, particularly the provoked Canaanites before the deliverance by Deborah and Barak, and the Midianites, and the people of the east before the deliverance by Gideon, and afterwards the Philistines.

And afterwards, in the time of the kings, there were many efforts of the enemies of Israel utterly to destroy the whole nation, that they might be cut off from being a nation [and their] very name blotted out from under heaven, agreeable to Ps. 83:3–8, "They have taken crafty counsel against thy people, and consulted against thy hidden ones. They have said, Come, let us cut them off from being a nation; that the name of Israel may be no more in remembrance. For they have consulted together with one consent: they are confederate against thee: the tabernacles of Edom and the Ishmaelites; of Moab, and the Hagarenes; Gebal, and Ammon, and Amalek; the Philistines with the inhabitants of Tyre; Assur also is joined with them: they have holpen the children of Lot."

In David's time there was such a mighty combination of enemies against [them], and so great a force raised, that one would think should have been sufficient to have swallowed up the nation.

1. JE, Jr.'s interpolation in the MS.

After Solomon's time the nation was greatly weakened and much the more exposed to ruin by their division into two kingdoms, often contending and seldom in amity one with another.

The nation was greatly exposed in Rehoboam's time to be swallowed up by Shishak, king of Egypt.

And in Asa's time by the vast army of the Ethiopians.

And again by the mighty army of the Moabites, Ammonites and Edomites in Jehoshaphet's time (II Chron. 20). And when the kings of Assyria overrun and utterly destroyed the Ten Tribes, it was a wonder that the two tribes were spared. The people were greatly exposed to be finally ruined by Sennacherib's army, who intended nothing else.

And when the people were carried captive into Babylon by Nebuchadnezzar, and the whole land laid utterly waste, it was a wonder that this did not prove a final end to them as a people; that they were kept distinct in their captivity; that then they were delivered; and that after they had been in captivity so long, till those that had formerly lived in Canaan were generally dead and a new generation born in Chaldea risen up, that they should be brought back, and again settled in their own land, and established as a people there. It was a wonder that the land was kept vacant for them, and a wonder that they were not hindered in their design of resettling there by the mighty opposition to it made by the Samaritans.

The people was marvelously preserved from being blotted out from under heaven by Haman in the time of Esther and Mordecai.

They were wonderfully preserved in Antiochus' time, who was earnestly set on their utter destruction as a people.

And it may be observed in general concerning them, during the times of the Old Testament, that there was no nation whatsoever that the nations in general were at such enmity with as the nation of the Jews. And they were on this account more likely to be destroyed than any other nation.

And they lived in a part of the world where they were more exposed to be overrun by other nations, and so to be by them either trodden down or torn away and scattered abroad in the earth, than any other part of the world, being in the midst of the earth, in the middle between the three great continents, Asia, Africa and Europe. Their land was in the very road or thoroughfare between Asia and Africa, between Egypt and the great eastern and northern kingdoms, which for many ages were the greatest, most potent and active kingdoms in the world. It seems that the other nations thereabouts were all destroyed from being a people before

Christ's time, as the Midianites, the Moabites, Ammonites, Amalekites, the seven nations of Canaan, and the Philistines.

And these things are remarkable concerning great part of the time of the Old Testament, that, viz. from the Babylonish captivity to[2] Christ, a great part of the nation lived dispersed amongst other nations. And as to both those that were thus dispersed and those that lived in their own land, they were, as it were, all that time in the power of the heathen nations of the four monarchies.

And with respect to the time since Christ, their preservation as a distinct nation has been in many respects yet much more wonderful. It was wonderful that what happened to them in Titus' time, when the greater part of the nation [was] destroyed and the rest dispersed all over the world in such abject, wretched circumstances, did not prove their utter destruction as a people. And[3] the calamities that happened to the remnant soon afterwards make their continuance as a distinct people yet more wonderful. For within half a century after their destruction by Titus, in the reigns of Trajan and Hadrian, the nation in general everywhere rose in rebellion against the Romans, and finally were everywhere beaten, so that in these wars the Jews had a thousand cities and fortresses destroyed, with the slaughter of above five hundred and eighty thousand men. (See my Observations on Revelation, no. 93.)[4]

And though this people, what is left of them, have ever since remained in a total dispersion over all the world, mixed everywhere with other peoples, without anything like any government or civil community of their own, and often extremely harassed by other nations, yet they remain in a clear and perfect distinction still from all other people.

1336. There are these things that seem to show that there was No Creation before the Mosaic Creation.

1. Those that suppose that there was a creation before the Mosaic creation, generally suppose the Mosaic creation to respect only this globe of the earth, and that the heavenly bodies in general were created before, concerning which I would observe:

(1) That this don't well agree with the account Moses gives of the fourth day's work of the creation he gives an account of. The accounts we have of the creation of the heavenly bodies, here and elsewhere from time to time in the Old Testament, with reference to Moses' account, are

2. MS: "of."
3. MS: "and that they should."
4. MS: "p. 86. 87." "Notes on the Apocalypse," no. 93, in *Works,* 5, 219–20.

so expressed that it would be most unreasonable to understand their mention they make of the creation of sun, moon and stars of any other than a proper making, creation and formation, and not merely a scattering away of fogs and mists that were over the face of the earth, so that they might have been seen here on the face of the earth, if there had been any inhabitants here to see them.

(2) Nor does it well agree with his account of the creation of the light on the first day. For if the Mosaic creation was only of this earth, then we must suppose the sun was created before, and so the light would have existed before.

(3) If any should suppose that the Mosaic creation, though it extended beyond this earth, yet it respected only the solar system, I think there is no manner of reason to suppose any other than that, as the whole visible universe, the many suns or fixed stars that belong to it, are all one frame, so that they were created together, not first one and then two, or first ten and then ten more, so gradually increasing the number till they came gradually to be so many millions. As if we find a stately building erected, it would be unreasonable to suppose any other than that it was built together, and not first one stick of timber hewed and then, after a long time, another.

2. They that suppose there was any creation before the Mosaic creation, suppose the angels to have been created before, in opposition to which I would observe:

(1) That place in Neh. 9:6, "Thou, even thou, art Lord alone; thou hast made heaven, the heaven of heavens, with all their host, the earth, and all things that are therein, the seas, and all that is therein, and thou preservest them all; and the host of heaven worshippeth thee." Here I think it most reasonable to suppose that Nehemiah has reference to the very same creation that God speaks of in Ex. 20:11, "For in six days the Lord made heaven and earth, the sea, and all that in them is." The descriptions are the same. The things spoken of as created are plainly the same. The creation Nehemiah speaks of includes the angels. They are included in the host of heaven that he mentions, as part of the creation he speaks of, as is plain by what he says further of the host of heaven at the end of the verse, "and the host of heaven worshippeth thee." The angels are evidently that host of heaven that worships God.

(2) Christ's eternity is largely set forth by his existing before the creation of this lower world, and all the parts of it, Prov. 8:22–30, which would [not] be proper and significant if many created beings had existed long before these things, as well as he.

(3) God expresses his own eternity by that, that he was before the day, and that he then existed alone, existing before any other being that men erroneously worship as God. From whence we may conclude that no created ANGELS, who of old and most ages of the world have been worshipped as gods, had any existence before the day. And from Is. 43:13, with the three foregoing verses: from this place it is probable that the angels were created the first day with the light. See Pfaffius, *Theologiæ Dogmaticæ et Moralis,* pp. 190–91.[5]

1337. NECESSITY OF REVELATION. TINDAL'S main argument against the need of any revelation is that the LAW OF NATURE IS ABSOLUTELY PERFECT.[6] But how weak and impertinent is this arguing, that because the *law of nature* (which is no other than natural rectitude and obligation) is perfect, that therefore the *light of nature* is sufficient. To say that the law of nature is perfect, yea, absolutely perfect, is no more than to say that what is naturally fit or right in itself is indeed right, and that what is in itself or in its own nature perfectly and absolutely right is absolutely right. But this is empty, insipid kind of doctrine. It is an idle way of spending time and ink and paper, to spend them in proving that what is in its own nature perfectly true is perfectly true, and what is in its nature perfectly good is perfectly good; or that what is, is, and is as it is. But this is all that can be meant by the law of nature's being perfect.

And how far is this from having any reference to that question, Whether we have by mere nature, without instruction, all that light and advantage that we need clearly and fully to know what is right, and all that is needful for us to be and to do in our circumstances as sinners, etc., in order to the forgiveness of sin, the favor of God and our own happiness? What, according to the nature of things, is fittest and best may be most perfect, and yet our natural discerning and knowledge of this may be most imperfect.

If Tindal or any other Deist would assert, and urge it upon mankind as an assertion, that they ought to believe that the light of nature is so sufficient to teach all mankind what they ought, or in any respect need to believe and practice for their good, that any additional instruction is needless and useless, then all instruction in families and schools is needless and useless, all instruction of parents, tutors and philosophers, all that has been said to promote any such knowledge as tends to make men

5. Christoph Matthew Pfaff, *Institutiones theologiæ dogmaticæ et moralis* (Tubingen, 1720).
6. See Matthew Tindal, *Christianity as Old as the Creation* (London, 1730).

good and happy by word of mouth, or by writing and books, all that is written by ancient and modern philosophers and learned men. And then also all the pains the Deists take in talking and writing to enlighten mankind is wholly needless and vain, and all Tindal's own instructions, and particularly all the pains he takes to make men believe that 'tis not best to give heed to pretended revelations and traditionary religion, as what tends to make mankind miserable in society, as if the light of nature was not perfectly and absolutely sufficient to teach 'em what is needful to avoid misery without its being revealed to them by him.

If the perfection of the light [of nature] don't prove anything against the great need and usefulness of the further instruction of fellow creatures, so neither does it prove anything against as great usefulness and necessity of the further instruction of their Creator. If it is no evidence that mankind don't need to have something further revealed to them than the light of nature brings 'em to the knowledge of in order to the welfare of mankind, and human societies being delivered from foolish and destructive notions that have generally prevailed, so no more is it any evidence that they don't need to have something further revealed to them by God, that is wiser and more fit to be a teacher of mankind than Mr. Tindal.

When it is asserted that the light of nature, or the means and advantages which all mankind have by pure nature to know the way of their duty and happiness, are absolutely sufficient, without any additional means and advantages, one of these two things must be meant by it, if it is has any meaning: either that they are sufficient in order to a mere possibility of obtaining all needful and useful knowledge in these important concerns; or that these natural means have a sufficient tendency actually to reach the effect, either universally, or at least generally, or at least in a prevailing degree, as the state of mankind is.

If the former of these be meant, viz. that the means of knowledge and understanding of those things which all mankind have by mere nature is sufficient in order to a bare possibility of obtaining this knowledge: that, if it should be allowed, will not at all prove that further light is not extremely needed by mankind. A bare possibility, as here distinguished from all tendency to the actual attaining the effect or[7] end, may be, and yet there be no tendency or probability that ever the effect (however necessary, and however dreadful the consequence will be of its failing) will be reached in one single instance, in the whole world of mankind, from

7. MS: "of."

the beginning of the world to the end of it, though it should stand millions of ages.

But if by the sufficiency of these natural means be meant a sufficiency of tendency actually to reach the effect, either universally or in a prevailing degree, considering all things belonging to the state and circumstances of mankind—I say, if this be meant, asserting the light of nature to be sufficient to obtain the effect, it is the very same thing as to say that it actually does obtain the effect. For if the tendency, all things considered, be sufficient actually to obtain the effect, doubtless it does actually obtain the effect. For what should hinder a cause from actually obtaining the effect that it has a sufficient tendency to obtain, all things considered? So that here what we have to inquire is whether that effect be actually obtained in the world, whether the world of mankind be actually brought to all necessary or very important knowledge of these things merely by the means they have by nature. History, observation and experience are the things which must determine the question.

In order the more clearly to judge of this matter of the sufficiency of the light of nature, to know what is necessary to be known of religion in order to their happiness, we must consider what are the things that must be known in order to this, which are these two things: 1. the religion of nature, or the religion proper and needful considering the state and relations we stand in as creatures; 2. the religion of a sinner, or the religion and duties proper and necessary for us considering our state as depraved and guilty creatures, having incurred the displeasure of our Creator.

As to the former, 'tis manifest from fact that nature alone is not sufficient for the discovery of the religion of nature, in the latter sense of sufficiency. That is, no means we have by mere nature, without instruction, have any tendency to bring men to the nature of God, and our natural relation to and dependence on him, and the duties becoming these relations, sufficiently actually to reach the effect, either universally or generally, or in any prevailing degree. No, nor does it appear to have proved sufficient so much as in a single instance. A sufficiency to see the reasonableness of these things, when pointed out, is not the same thing as a sufficiency to find them out. None but either perfect dunces, or [those who are] perfectly willful, will deny that there is a vast difference.

And as to the latter, viz. the religion of a sinner, or the duties proper and necessary for us as depraved, guilty and offending creatures, 'tis most evident the light of nature cannot be sufficient for our information by any means, or in any sense whatsoever. No, nor [is] the law of nature sufficient to prescribe nor establish this religion. The light of nature is in no sense whatsoever sufficient to discover this religion. It has no sufficient tendency to it, nor indeed any tendency at all to discover it to any one single person in any age. And it not only has no tendency to the obtaining of this knowledge by mere natural means, but it affords no possibility of it. And not only is the light of nature insufficient to discover this religion, but the law of nature, as distinguished from the light of it, is not sufficient to establish it, or to give any occasion or room for it.

1338. NECESSITY OF REVELATION.[8]

Definition. By CONVERSATION I mean intelligent beings expressing their minds one to another in words or other significations equivalent, being signs intentionally directed to us for our notice, whose immediate and main design is to be significations to or expressions of the mind of him or them who causes or gives them to the knowledge or notice of him or them to whom they are directed; wherein those signs are evidences distinguished from works done by them, from which we may argue their minds, though the first and most immediate design of the work be something else besides a mere signification to us of the mind of the efficient. Thus I distinguish God's communicating his mind to us by word or conversation from giving us opportunity to learn it by philosophical reasoning. By the latter I mean arguing the nature and will of God by God's works, which we observe in the natural world.

There is a great difference between God's moral government of his creatures, that have understanding and will, and his general government of providential disposal. The nature, design and ends of the latter by no means require that it should be declared and made visible by a revelation of the method, rule, particular views, designs and ends of it. These are secret things that belong to God. So far as the distinction takes place or holds between this government and God's moral government, man's understanding and will are no way concerned. There is no application to these faculties in it. Nor are these faculties any otherwise concerned than the qualities or properties of inanimate and senseless things.

But it is quite otherwise with respect to God's moral government of a kingdom or society of intelligent and willing creatures, to which society he is united as its head, ruling for its good. The nature of that requires that it should be declared and open and visible, as is most apparent. How

---

8. After the title, JE wrote: "Remember in the beginning of this discourse to define what I mean by conversation, as distinct from making the mind known by philosophy." He did indeed remember to do this on the following MS page, marking his definition of conversation for insertion as the first paragraph of the entry.

can any moral government be properly and sufficiently established and maintained in a kingdom or commonwealth of intelligent agents, consisting in exhibiting, prescribing, and enforcing methods, rules and ends of their own intelligent, voluntary actions, without declaring and particularly promulgating to their understandings those methods, rules and enforcements? Moral government of a society, in the very nature of it, implies and consists in an application to their understandings, in directing of the intelligent will, and in enforcing of it the direction by the declaration made.

'Tis needful, in order to a proper moral government, that the head, or heads, or rulers of the society should enforce the rules of the society by threatening the just punishments and promising the most suitable and wise rewards. But without word or voluntary declaration, there is no threatening or promising in the case, in a proper sense. To leave the subject to find out what reward would be wise, if there appear in the state of things [room] for every subject to guess at it in some degree, would be a different thing from promising of it. And to leave men to their own reason to find out what would be a just, deserved and, all things considered, a wise punishment, though we should suppose some sufficiency in everyone's reason for this, would be a different thing from threatening of it.

'Tis needful in order to a proper maintaining of moral government in a moral kingdom, not in a ruined, deserted state, the union between the head and members remaining, that there should be conversation between the governor and governed. As it is requisite that the former should have intercourse with the latter in a way agreeable to their nature, that is, by way of voluntary signification of their mind to the governed, as the governed signify their minds voluntarily one to another; that there should be something equivalent to conversation between the rulers and ruled, and that thus the rulers should make themselves visible; that the designs and ends of government should be made known; that it should be visible what is aimed it, and what grand ends or events are in view in the ruler's disposals of the society; that the mind of the ruler should be declared as to the rules, measures and methods to be observed by the society. If the rulers are sovereign, absolute disposers, 'tis necessary their will should be particularly declared as [to] the good and evil consequence of obedience or disobedience which they intend as moral enforcements of the rule and laws, to persuade and, as it were, constrain the will to a compliance. For they can reach the will, or affect at all, no further than made known.

It is requisite something should be known particularly of the nature and weight and degree of the rewards and punishments, and of their time and place and duration.

It is requisite it should be declared what is the end for which God has made us, and made the world, supports it and provides for it, orders its events; for what end mankind are made in particular; what is intended to be their main employment; what they should chiefly aim at in what they do in the world; how far God the Creator is man's end; how far he is to have respect to him in what he does, in the great business he is made for, and what man is to aim at with respect to God, who stands in no need of us and can't be in the least dependent on us; how far and in what respect we are to make God our highest end, and how we are to make ourselves or our fellow creatures our end; what benefits he will have by complying with his end; what evils he shall be the subject of by refusing, and if we fail in a greater or lesser degree.

If we have offended and deserved punishment, it must be known on what terms we may be forgiven and restored to favor, and how far we may be restored to favor, and what benefits of favor we shall receive if we are reconciled.

'Tis apparent that there would be no hopes that these things would[9] ever be satisfyingly determined among mankind, in the present darkness and disadvantages which their understandings are under, without a revelation. Without a revelation now extant, or once extant, having some remaining influence by tradition, men would undoubtedly forever be at a loss what God expects from us and what we may expect from him; what we are to depend upon as to our concern with God, and what ground we are to go upon in our conduct and proceedings that relate to him; what end we are to aim at, and what rule we are to be directed by, and what good and what harm is to be expected from a right or wrong conduct. Yea, without a revelation, men would be greatly at a loss concerning God, what he is, what manner of being, whether properly intelligent and willing, a being that has will and design, maintaining a proper, intelligent, voluntary dominion over the world. Notions of the First Being like those of Hobbes and Spinoza would prevail. Especially would they be at a loss [as to] those perfections of God which he exercises as a moral governor. For we find that some of the Deists, though they from revelation have been taught these, yet having cast off revelation, they apparently doubt of them all. Lord Bolingbroke in particular insists that we have no evidence of them.

9. MS: "would not."

And if with regard to many—when they have a revelation fully setting forth the perfections of God, giving a consistent rational account of them, and pointing forth their consistence, and leading us to the reason of them—reason may rest in some measure satisfied in them, this is no evidence that it is not exceeding needful that God should tell us of them. 'Tis very needful that God should declare to mankind what manner of being he is. For though reason may be sufficient to confirm such a declaration after it is given, and see its consistence, harmony and rationality in many respects, yet reason may be utterly insufficient first to discover these things.

Yea, notwithstanding the clear and infinitely abundant evidences of the being of a God, we need that God should tell us that he is, that there is a great, intelligent and willing Being that has made and governs the world. 'Tis of most unspeakable advantage, as to the knowledge of this, that God has told us of it. And there is much reason to think that the notions that mankind in general have had in all ages of a Deity has been very much originally owing to revelation.

On the supposition that God has a moral kingdom in the world, that he is the head of a moral society consisting either of some part of mankind or of the whole, in what darkness and great obscurity must the affairs of this moral kingdom be carried on, without any manner of communication between the head and the body, the ruler never making himself known to the society he is the head of, and has the moral direction, government, and whole care of, by any sort of converse, either immediate or mediate, never exhibiting himself by any word or other equivalent expressions whatsoever, either by himself or by any mediators or messengers?

So far as we see or have any notice, all moral agents are conversible agents. It seems to be so agreeable to the nature of moral agents and their state in the universal system, that we see none without, and no beings that have so much as a shadow of intelligence and will, but that, so far as they have any image of this, they have also conversation or an image of it, as in all kinds of birds, beasts and even insects, so far as there is any appearance of having a mind, or something like a mind, so far they have their significations of their minds one to another, in something like conversation among rational creatures. And as we rise higher in the scale of beings, we don't see that an increase of perfection diminishes the need or propriety of communication and intercourse of this kind, but increases it. And, accordingly, we see most of it among the most perfect beings. So we see conversation more by voluntary, immediate significations of each other's minds, as it were, infinitely more fully, properly and variously between mankind than any other animals here below. And if there are creatures superior to mankind united in society, doubtless still voluntary converse is more full and perfect.

Especially do we find conversation proper and requisite between intelligent creatures concerning moral affairs, which are their most important affairs, and affairs wherein especially moral agents are concerned, as joined in society and having union and communion one with another. As to other concerns that are merely personal and natural, wherein we are concerned more separately and by ourselves, and not as members of society, in them is not equal need of conversation. Moral agents are social agents; affairs of morality are affairs of society. 'Tis concerning moral agents, as united in society, in a commonwealth or kingdom, that we have been speaking. Particular moral agents, so united, need conversation. The affairs of their social union can't well be maintained without conversation.

And, if so, what reason can be given why there should be no need of conversation with the head of the society? The head of the society, so far as it is united with it as a moral society, is a social head. The head belongs to the society as the natural head belongs to the body. And the union of the members with the head is greater, stricter, and more important than one with another. And if their union with other members of the society requires conversation, much more their greater union with the head.

By all that we see and experience, the moral and intelligent world and the conversible world are the same thing, and that it never was intended that the affairs of society, in any that are united in society among intelligent creatures, should be upheld and carried on without conversation.

There is no more reason to deny God any conversation with his moral kingdom, in giving laws and enforcing them with promises and threatenings, than to deny him any conversation with them in another world, in judging them. But [will] any that believe a future state rationally imagine, that when men go into another world to be judged by their supreme governor, that nothing will pass or be effected through the immediate interposition of the judge, but all things be left wholly to go on according to laws of nature established from the beginning of the world? the soul to pass into another state by a law of nature—as a stone, when shaken off from a building, falls down by gravity—and [with] no miraculous signification from God or disposal of his hand at all? But there is as much reason to suppose this as to deny any miraculous interposition in giving and establishing the laws of the moral society. If judgment, execution of the law, [is] by immediate interposition and declaration, why not legislation?

The ground of moral behavior and all moral government and regulation is society, or mutual intercourse and social regards. The special medium of union and communication of the members of the society, and the being of society as such, is conversation. And the well-being and happiness of society is friendship. 'Tis the highest happiness of all moral agents. But friendship, above all other things that belong to society, requires conversation. 'Tis what friendship most naturally and directly desires. 'Tis maintained and nourished by that, and the felicity of friendship is tasted and enjoyed by that. The happiness of God's moral kingdom consists, in an inferior degree, in the members' enjoyment of each others' friendship, but infinitely more in the enjoyment of the friendship of their head. Therefore, here especially, and above all, is conversation requisite.

Conversation between God and mankind in this world is maintained by God's word on his part, and prayer on ours. By the former he speaks to us and expresses his mind to us; by the latter we speak to him and express our minds to him. Sincere and a suitable high friendship towards God, in all that believe God to be properly an intelligent, willing being, does most apparently, directly and strongly incline to pray. And it no less disposes the heart strongly to desire to have our infinitely glorious and gracious friend expressing his mind to us by his word, that we may hear it. The same light has directed the nations of the world in general to prayer to some deity or deities, and to suppose that God, or the gods, have revealed themselves to men. And we see that the same infidelity that disposes men to deny any divine revelation disposes 'em to reject as absurd the duty of prayer.

If God's moral kingdom, or the society of his friends and willing subjects, shall be in a most happy state in another world, in the most perfect social state, united in the most complete friendship and in a most perfect and happy union with God their head (as some of the Deists pretend to believe), is it reasonable to suppose any other than that they will fully enjoy the sweets of their friendship one with another in the most perfect conversation, either by words or some more perfect medium of expressing their minds? And shall they have at the same time no conversation at all with their glorious head, the fountain [of] all the perfection and felicity of the society, in friendship with whom their happiness chiefly consists? That friendship and the happiness they have in it is begun in this world, and this is the state wherein they are trained up for that more perfect state. And shall they nevertheless live here wholly without any intercourse with God of this sort, though their union with God as their moral head and their great friend begins here, and their happiness, as consisting in friendship to him, is begun here, and the enjoyment of that subordinate happiness of enjoying a virtuous and holy conversation one with another be begun here?

The need of conversation in order properly to support and carry on the concerns of society may well appear by well considering the need of it in order to the answering the purposes of friendship, which is one of the main concerns of society, in some respects the main social concern, and the end of all the rest.

Let us suppose some friend, above all others dear to a person, in whose friendship consisted the main comfort of his life and the happiness which he depended on for all future time, should leave with us some piece of his workmanship, [some] work of his, or something that he had contrived and accomplished, some manifold, complicated effect that he had produced, which we might have always in our view—which work should be a very great, sure and manifold evidence of the excellencies of the mind of his friend, of his great and fixed and firm benevolence to him—and then should withdraw forever and never have any conversation with him; no word ever should pass, or anything of that nature, and no word left behind in writing, nor any word ever spoken left in the memory: would this sufficiently and completely answer the purposes of this great friendship, and satisfy its ends and desires, or be a proper support of this great end of society?

I can't but think every sober, considerate person will at once determine that it would be very far from [answering these purposes], for such reasons as these: that it would not give us those views of things pertaining to the support and enjoyment of friendship, suitable to the nature of intelligent, volitive and conversitile beings; not giving the direct and immediate view, nor at all tending in so great a degree and so agreeable a manner to affect and impress the mind. And as for these reasons, this alone would not answer the ends and purposes of society in this respect. So, for the same reasons, it would not answer other purposes of society.

As we may suppose that God will govern mankind in that moral kingdom, which he hath mercifully set up among them, in a manner agreeable to their nature, so it is reasonable to suppose that he would make his moral government with respect to 'em visible, not only in declaring the general ends and methods and rules of government, but also by making known many of the chief of his more particular aims and designs. As in human kingdoms, in order to the wisdom, righteousness and goodness of their administration's being properly visible, so far as is requisite for the encouraging and animating of the subject, and in order to the suitable concurrence, satisfaction and benefit of the whole society of intelligent agents, 'tis needful not only that the general end, viz. the public good, should be known, but also the particular design of many of the principal parts of the administration, the main negotiations, treaties and changes of affairs, the cause and end of wars that are engaged, the ground of treaties of peace and commerce, the design of general revolutions in the state of the kingdom, etc. Otherwise the society is not governed in a manner becoming their rational and active nature, but affairs are carried on all in the blind, and [the members] have no opportunity to consent or concur, to approve or disapprove, to rejoice in the goodness and wisdom and benefit of the administrations, and to pay proper regards to those in whose hands the government is, etc., etc. These things are necessary for the establishment and confirmation of the government.

God's moral government over his moral kingdom on earth can't in such like respects be carried on in a visible manner, and a way suitable to our nature, without divine history and prophecy. Without divine history we can't properly see the grounds and foundation of divine administrations in God's moral kingdom, the first formation or erection of God's moral kingdom, the nature and manner of the main revolutions that it has been the subject of, which are the ground of future designs, and to which future events and intended revolutions [they] have a relation and connection. 'Tis also necessary that these past events should be known in order to the reason, wisdom and benefit of the present state of the kingdom, and God's present dispensations towards it. And prophecy is needful to reveal the future designs and aims of government, what good things are to be expected.

These things are necessary in order to a proper establishment, health and prosperity of God's moral, intelligent kingdom. Without 'em, divine government, or [government] of an infinitely wise and good head, is not sensible. There is no opportunity to see the effects and success of the wisdom of the administration. There is no opportunity to find it by experience. Neither the designs of government nor the accomplishment of these designs are sensible. And the government itself, with respect to fact, is not made visible. We might guess this and the other fact and event,[1] on such a design and for such an end, but could not know the whole scheme. And wise connection of disposals would be hid by a veil and lie concealed in darkness, which is not a way of administering suitable for a society of intelligent creatures, made intelligent and volitive and active to that end, that they might be capable of seeing God's perfections as manifested in his[2] doings, and capable of concurring with God's ends and designs, and rejoicing in and praising his wisdom, holiness and goodness, and serving God, and being his active instruments in accomplishing his designs, and made to be happy in the view of the glory and favor of God manifested in his administrations, and thus enjoying the glorious ruler and head of the society.

If it be said that reason and the light of nature, without revelation, is sufficient to show us that the end of God's government in his moral kingdom must be to promote these two things among mankind, viz. their virtue and their happiness, in reply I would ask: What satisfaction can man, without revelation, have with respect to the design, wisdom and success of God's government, as to the end, when wickedness so generally prevails and reigns through all ages and nations hitherto in the far greater part of the world, and the world at all times is so full of calamities, miseries and death, having no prophecies of a better state of things in which all is to issue at last in the latter ages of this world, assuring us that all these miserable changes and great confusion is guided by infinite wisdom to that great final issue, and without any revelation of a future state of happiness of the city of God in another world?

Obj. God does maintain a moral government over all mankind, but we see, in fact, that many are not governed in way of conversation, or by revelation, in the[3] greater part of the world. For the most part have been destitute of divine revelation, which shows that God does not look upon conversation as necessary in order to his moral government of mankind, as God judges for himself and acts according to his own judgment.

Ans. 1. What I have been speaking of is God's moral government over a society of moral agents, which are his kingdom, or a society that have God for their king, united to them as the head of the society; as 'tis with earthly kings with respect to their own kingdoms, where the union between king and subjects is not broken and dissolved, and not of a society or country of rebels who have forsaken their lawful sovereign, with-

---

1. MS: "event to."
2. MS: "this."
3. MS: "that the."

drawn themselves from subjection to him and cast off his government. Though they may still be under the king's power and moral dominion in some sense—as he may have it in his power and design to conquer, subdue, judge and punish them for their rebellion—but yet the sense in which such a nation is under the moral government of this king, and may be said to [be] his kingdom or people, is surely extremely diverse from that of a kingdom remaining in union with their king. In that case of a people broken off from their king, the maintaining of intercourse by conversation is in no wise in like manner requisite. The reasons for such intercourse, which take place in the other case, don't take place in this.

In that case, society ceases, i.e. that union ceases between God and man by which they should be of one society. And where society ceases, there the argument for conversation ceases. If a particular member of the society were wholly cut off, it ceasing to be of the society, the union being entirely broken, the argument for conversation, the great medium of social concerns, ceases; so if the body be cut off from the head and entirely disunited from that. Moral government in a society is a social affair. 'Tis the main and most important thing, wherein consists the intercourse between superior and inferior constituents of a society of moral agents, between what which is original and dependent, directing and directed, in the society.

'Tis proper in this case that the rebel people should have sufficient means of knowing the evil of their rebellion, and that 'tis their duty to be subject to their king, to seek reconciliation with him, and to inquire after his will. But while they remain obstinate in their rebellion, and the king has not received 'em to favor, the state of things does not require that he should particularly declare his intentions with respect [to them], and open to them the designs and methods of his administration, and particularly to publish among them ways and terms of reconciliation, to make revelations of his goodness and wisdom and the great benefits of his government, and to converse with them as their friend, and so to open the way for their being happy in so great a friend, and that he should so particularly and immediately publish among them particular statutes and rules for their good as a society of moral agents, etc., etc. Conversation, in this case of an utter breach of the union, is not to be expected, nor is requisite, unless it be in judging and condemning.

Ans. 2. So far as the union between God and the heathen world has not been utterly broken, so far they have not been left utterly destitute of all benefit of divine revelation. They are not so entirely and absolutely cast off but that there is a possibility of their being reconciled. And God has so ordered the case that there is an equal possibility of their receiving the benefit of divine revelation.

If the heathen world, or any parts of it, have not only enjoyed a mere possibility of being restored to favor, but have had some advantages for it, so a great part, yea, mostly the greater part of the heathen world, have not been left merely to the light of nature. They have had many things, especially in times of the old testament, that were delivered to mankind in the primitive ages of the world by revelation, handed down from ancestors by tradition, and many things borrowed from the Jews—and, during those ages, by many wonderful dispensations and displays towards the Jews—wherein God did in a most public and striking manner display himself and show his hand: [so] that the world had, from time to time, notices sufficient to convince them that there was a divine revelation extant, sufficient to induce 'em to seek after it. And things to make revelation public and spread it abroad, to extend the fame of it and its effects to the utmost ends of the earth, and to draw men's attention to it, have been vastly more and greater than before.

Ans. 3. The nations that are separated from the true God and live in open and obstinate, full rejection of him as their supreme moral governor, they reject any friendly intercourse while their state is such. They are open enemies and, so far as God treats 'em as such, he don't exercise any friendly moral government over them. And they have light sufficient, without revelation, for any other exercise of moral government and intercourse besides those that are friendly, viz. in judging and condemning them. They have light sufficient for that judgment and condemnation which they shall be the subjects of. For their condemnation shall proceed no further than so far as to be proportioned to their light. They shall be condemned for the violation of the law of nations. And the degree of their condemnation shall be only answerable to the degree of the means and advantages they have had for information of the duties of this law, and of their obligations to perform them.

Ans. 4. What has appeared in those parts of the world which have been destitute of revelation, is so far from being any evidence that revelation is not necessary, that it has ever been so that, in those nations and ages that have been most destitute of revelation, the necessity of revelation has most evidently and remarkably appeared, by the extreme blindness and delusion which has prevailed and reigned, without any remedy, or any ability in those nations to help themselves for want of it.

1339. Glorious Times. Those passages wherein the Scripture speaks of there being few saved, and that we must through much tribula-tion enter into the kingdom of God, and that all that will live godly in Christ Jesus shall suffer persecution, are not to be understood as ex-tending to the promised glorious day of the church's rest and triumph on earth.

There are innumerable sayings and representations of Scripture that must be taken in this sense, as when Christ says that he came not to send peace on earth but a sword, etc. [Matt. 10:34]. This cannot be under-stood of that day when, according to abundant representations of Scrip-ture, there shall be abundance of peace, the mountains shall bring forth peace to God's people, the wolf shall dwell with the lamb, and nation shall no more lift up sword against nation, nor learn war any more.

So when the church of Christ is represented as a lily among thorns, as sheep amidst wolves, as being not of the world and therefore hated of the world.

There are many descriptions of the future glorious days of the church that do most manifestly signify and declare that the church's persecu-tions shall come to an end at that day, that her troubles shall be as the waters of Noah, that comforts shall be proclaimed to it, that all her ene-mies shall be subdued, that God will give her beauty for ashes, the oil of joy for mourning and the garments of praise for the spirit of heaviness, etc., etc.

So when it is represented as if the church's enemies should have the dominion: the desire of God's people should be to them, and they should rule over them; and that not many wise, not many mighty, not many no-ble are called, but God hath chosen the poor of the world, the base things of the world, etc.

There is nothing more apparent by abundant descriptions of the Word of God than that, in the church's glorious day, it shall be otherwise: when the kingdom and dominion, and the greatness of the kingdom under the whole heaven, shall be given into the hands of the saints of the most high God; when the saints shall possess the kingdom; when, according to the oath of the angel, Dan. 12, the long time will be ended for the scattering the power of the holy people, and there should be an end to those wonders of the great tribulation of God's people; that, in the days of the voice of the seventh angel, the mystery of God should be finished and the kingdoms of this world should become the kingdoms of our Lord and of his Christ; when, though the nations were angry, God's wrath shall come, and a reward given to the martyrs of Jesus Christ; when kings should be nursing fathers and queens nursing mothers, and the kings of the earth should bring their honor and glory into the church.

In the same discourse wherein Christ tells his church that, in the world, they shall have tribulation and shall be hated and persecuted, yet he intimates as if a time would come wherein their sorrow should be turned into joy. John 15:18–21 and 16:20–22, 33.

Here the following things may be observed:

1. The glorious time of the church is represented in Scripture as the time when the salvation of the church should be actually accomplished, though not in the highest degree, yet in a very high degree. That will be, remarkably, the day of salvation, a day wherein the end of the means of salvation of the church should be obtained; the end of the great, successive dispensations of God, from the beginning of the world, in order to the bringing about the salvation of his people; and the end of the great revolutions that have gone before, from age to age, wherein all nature has been, as it were, travailing in pain for the salvation of the children of God; and the end of the church's own, long-continued militant state, and His many and mighty struggles and conflicts with her enemies, whereby God's people have groaned within themselves while they have waited for God's salvation, and have been travailing in birth to bring forth God's event.

This is the day of redemption, the year of Christ's redeemed, wherein he shall see of the travail of his soul and be satisfied, the proper time of the kingdom of God, the time wherein the church shall have got the victory, the jubilee of the church, the day of her triumph and of her possessing that kingdom which she has been violent in her struggles for. That will be a day wherein the travails of the church shall be over, and she shall enter into her rest, and shall put on her crown, sit in her throne, and wear her garments of triumph in a very important sense and great degree.

And when God's people are told that through much tribulation they must enter into the kingdom, it is not meant of that time when the church has actually received the kingdom of God. And therefore they shall not suffer much tribulation and persecution, at least not at all in that manner and in that sense as in preceding times. The church shall not continue in travail after she has brought forth the Man-Child. She shall not continue in His conflict after victory is obtained and the day of triumph is come.

Nor will that then be true that few shall be saved, when the church's salvation shall come and the time of conflict and agonizing for salvation shall in so important a sense be over.

2. That glorious state of the church is represented as another world, a future world, or the world to come, as the gospel state introduced by Christ is spoken of as another world with respect to the old testament state.

The great dispensation of God's introducing, both the Christian dispensation and also that glorious state of the Christian church, are represented as a general judgment, God's coming to judgment, etc. Satan is called the "god of this world," "prince of the power of the air" [II Cor. 4:4, Eph. 2:2]. But he will not reign as god over the inhabitants of the earth at that day: for that will be the day wherein he shall be conquered and subdued under the feet of his people, and his kingdom be overthrown, and Christ and his people shall take the kingdom, and he shall be shut up in the bottomless pit and bound there, that he may not maintain his kingdom of darkness over the nations anymore.

The things forementioned, viz. that few shall be saved, and all that will live godly in Christ Jesus shall suffer persecution, are meant only of this present, evil world, this world of which Satan is the god, this dark world, this time of night, and not of that good and happy world, that world of light and state of salvation, peace and joy, when the earth shall be full of the knowledge of God as the waters cover the seas.

Many things said of Israel in the Old Testament without any express limitations are to be understood only of the times of their state under the old testament. For the end of that state was, as it were, the end of that world. And the new testament state was regarded as a new world.

3. The age of the kingdom of Christ and of the rest and glory of God's church is an exempt, distinguished age, as the sabbath day was an exempt day and the sabbatical year and the year of jubilee exempt years. Some things are said as things that should be every year that yet were not to be understood of the sabbatical year, such as the offering the sheaf of the first fruits of barley harvest at the Passover, and the two loaves of the first fruits of the wheat harvest at the feast of Pentecost, or feast of harvest or first fruits, and the feast of ingathering, when they had gathered in all the fruits of their land (Ex. 23:14–16 and 34:22, Lev. 23, Num. 28:26, Deut. 16:9). But these things have no reference to the sabbatical year. For on that year they should have no harvest, no first fruits, should not at all put the sickle into the corn; neither should there be any ingathering at the end of the year. So some things are spoken without ex-

press limitation or exception that were not to take place on the year of jubilee.

The age of Solomon was an exempt age in Israel. And therefore that is spoken of as being perpetual and at all times in Israel which should be at all other times but in that day of Israel's rest, peace and glory. As in Deut. 15:11 'tis said, "the poor should never cease out of the land." And yet it is intimated in vv. 4–5 that, in some exempt season of the extraordinary blessing of heaven upon them, it might be otherwise: "Save when there shall be no poor among you; for the Lord shall greatly bless thee in the land which the Lord thy God giveth thee for an inheritance to possess: only if thou carefully hearken to the voice of the Lord," etc. This probably was fulfilled in Solomon's days.

1340. REASON AND REVELATION.

Definition. By REASON I mean that power or faculty an intelligent being has to judge of the truth of propositions, either immediately, by only looking on the propositions, which is judging by intuition and self-evidence; or by putting together several propositions which are already evident by intuition, or at least whose evidence is originally derived from intuition.

Great part of Tindal's arguing, in his *Christianity as Old as the Creation,* proceeds on this ground: that seeing that reason is the judge whether there be any revelation, or whether any pretended revelation be really such, therefore reason without revelation, or undirected by revelation, must be the judge concerning each doctrine and proposition contained in that pretended revelation; which is an unreasonable way of arguing. (Here see book on "Controversies," p. 190e ff.)[4]

'Tis as much as to say that, seeing reason is to judge of the truth of any general proposition, therefore in all cases reason alone, without regard to that particular proposition, is to judge separately and independently of each particular proposition implied in, or depending and consequent upon, that general proposition. For whether any supposed or

4. JE is citing a lengthy passage, which begins with a cross-reference to "Miscellanies," No. 1340, in a section entitled "Importance of Doctrines and of Mysteries in Religion" in the "Controversies" notebook, MS pp. 190–97. Here JE criticizes "free thinkers" who, wishing to establish reason as the means to test the veracity of revelation, confuse the meaning of "faculty of reason" and "opinion," "reason" and "rule of reason," "reason" and "argument," and "reason" and "experience." JE concludes: "In the argument these men use to prove that reason is a better test of truth than revelation, they wretchedly deceive themselves, in sliding off from the meaning with which they use the word reason in the premise into another meaning of it, exceeding diverse, in the conclusion."

pretended divine revelation be indeed such, is a general proposition, and the particular truths delivered in and by it are particular propositions implied in and consequent on that general. Tindal supposes each of these truths must be judged of by themselves, independently of our judging of that general truth that the revelation that declares them is the Word of God, evidently supposing that if each of those propositions thus judged of particularly can't be found to be agreeable to reason, or if reason alone will not show the truth of them, then that general proposition that they depend on, viz. that the Word that declares 'em is a divine revelation, is to be rejected: which is most unreasonable and contrary to all the rules of common sense, and all rules of the proceeding of all mankind in their reasoning and judging of things in all affairs whatsoever.

For this is true, that a proposition may be evidently true, or we may have good reason to receive it as true, though the particular propositions that depend upon it and follow from it may be such that our reason, independent on it, can't see the truth, or can see it to be true by no other means than by first establishing that other truth that it depends upon. For, otherwise, there is an end of all use of our reasoning powers, an end of all arguing one proposition from another, and nothing is to be judged true but what appears true by looking on it directly and immediate, without the help of another proposition first established, on which the evidence of it depends.

For therein consists all reasoning or argumentation whatsoever, viz. in discovering the truth of a proposition whose truth don't appear to our reason immediately or when we consider it alone, but by the help of some other proposition on which it depends. If this ben't allowed, we must believe nothing at all, but only self-evident propositions. Then we must have done with all such things as arguments—all argumentation whatsoever, and all Tindal's argumentations in particular, are absurd. He, throughout his whole book, proceeds in that very method which this explodes. He argues and attempts to prove or make evident one proposition by another first established.

There are some general propositions the truth of which can be known only by reason, from whence an infinite multitude of other propositions are inferred, and reasonably and justly determined to be true, and rested in as such on the ground of the truth of that general proposition, from which they are inferred by the common consent of all mankind, being led thereto by the common and universal sense of the human mind. And yet not one of those propositions can be known to be true by reason if reason considers them by themselves, independent on that general proposition.

Thus, for instance, what numberless truths are known only by consequence from that general proposition that the testimony of our senses may be depended on. (Tindal says, p. 157, reason is to judge whether our senses are deceived.)[5] The reality of most sensible things whatsoever, or the truth of all those numberless millions of particular propositions which we have only by the testimony of our senses, cannot be known to be true by reason considered independent of that testimony, and without an implicit faith in that testimony.

So that general truth, that the testimony of our memories is worthy of credit, can be proved only by reason. And yet what numberless truths are there which we have no other way, and cannot be known to be true by reason considering the truths in themselves, or any otherwise than by the testimony of our memory, and an implicit faith in this testimony. So that the agreed testimony of all we see and converse with continually is to be credited, is a general proposition, the truth of which can be known only by reason. And yet how infinitely numerous are the propositions do men receive as truth that can't be known to be true by reason viewing them separate from such testimony, even all occurrences, and matters of fact, persons, things, actions, works, events, and circumstances, and all existence that we are told of in our neighborhood, in our country, or any part of the world that others tell us of, that we han't seen ourselves.

So that the testimony of history and tradition is to be depended [on] when attended with such and such credible circumstances, is a general proposition whose truth can be known only by reason. And yet how numberless are the particular truths concerning what has been before the present age that can't be known by reason considered in themselves and separate from this testimony, which yet are truths of that sort, and so circumstanced, that all mankind do, ever did, and ever will rely on the truth of.

That the experience of mankind is to [be] depended on, or that those things which the world finds to be true by experience are worthy to be judged true, is a general proposition which none doubts. And all that is meant by what the world finds true by experience can be meant nothing else than what is known to be true by one or the other of those fore-

---

5. Tindal, *Christianity as Old as the Creation.*

mentioned kinds of testimony, viz. either the testimony of history and tradition, the testimony of those we see and converse with, the testimony of our memories, and the testimony of our senses. I say, all that is known by the experience of mankind is known only by one or more of these [kinds of] testimony, excepting only the existence of that idea, or those few ideas, which are this moment present in our minds, or the immediate objects of present consciousness. And yet how unreasonable would it be to say that we must first know those things to be true by reason before we give credit to our experience of [the] truth of 'em.

Not only are there innumerable truths that are reasonably received, as following from such general propositions as have been mentioned, which can't be known by reason if they are considered by themselves, or otherwise than as inferred from these general propositions; but also many truths are reasonably received, and are received by the common consent of the reason of all rational persons, as undoubted truths, whose truth not only would not otherwise be discoverable by reason, but when they are discovered by their consequence from that general proposition, appear in themselves not easy and reconcilable to reason, but difficult, incomprehensible, and their agreement with reason not understood. So that men, at least most men, are not able to explain or conceive of the manner in which they are agreeable to reason.

Thus, for instance, it is a truth which depends on that general proposition that credit is to be given to the testimony of our senses, that our souls and bodies are so united that they act on each other. But it is a truth that reason otherwise can't discover. And now it is revealed by the testimony of our senses. Reason can't comprehend, or explain, or show or conceive of any way that that which is immaterial and not solid nor extended can act upon matter, which it cannot touch, and matter act upon that. Or, if any choose to say that the soul is material, then other difficulties arise as great. For reason can't imagine any way that a solid mass of matter, whether at rest or in motion, should have perception, and understand, and should exert thought and volition, love, hatred, etc. And if it be said that spirit acts on matter, and matter on spirit, by an established law of the Creator, which is no other than a fixed method of his own producing, still the manner how 'tis possible to be will be inconceivable. We can have no conception of any way or manner in which God, who is a pure Spirit, can act upon matter and impel it.

There are several things in mechanics and hydrostatics that, by the testimony of our senses, are true in fact, not only that reason never first discovered before the testimony of sense declared them, but now [that] they are declared, they are very great paradoxes, and if proposed would seem contrary to reason—at least to the reason of the generality of mankind and such as are not either mathematicians or of more than common penetration—and what they cannot reconcile to their reason. But God has given reason to the common to be as much their guide and rule as he has to mathematicians and philosophers.

Even the very existence of a sensible world, which we receive for certain from the testimony of our senses, is attended with difficulties and seeming inconsistencies with reason, which are insuperable by the reason at least of most men. For if there be a sensible world, that world either exists in the mind only or out of the mind, and independent on its imagination or perception.

If the latter, then that sensible world is some material substance altogether diverse from all the ideas we have by any of our senses: color, or visible extension and figure (which is nothing but the quantity of color and its various limitation), which are sensible qualities which we have by sight; and also diverse from any of the sensible qualities we have by other senses, as that solidity which is an idea we have by feeling, and that extension and figure which is only the quantity and limitation of those, and so of all other qualities. But that there should be any substance entirely distinct from any or all of these is utterly inconceivable. For if we exclude all color, solidity, or conceivable extension, dimensions and figure, what is there left[6] that we conceive of? Is there not a removal in our minds of all existence, and a perfect emptiness of everything?

But if it be said that the sensible world has no existence but only in the mind, then the sensories themselves, or the organs of sense by which sensible ideas are let into the mind, have no existence but only in the mind. And those organs of sense have no existence but what is conveyed into the mind by themselves, for they are a part of the sensible world. And then it will follow that the organs of sense owe their existence to the organs of sense, and so are prior to themselves, being the causes or occasions of their own existence, which is a seeming inconsistence with reason, which I imagine[7] the reason of all men cannot explain and remove.

There are innumerable propositions that we reasonably receive from the testimony of experience, all depending on the truth of that general proposition that experience is to be relied [on] (what is meant by ex-

6. MS: "life."
7. MS: "image."

perience has been already explained), that yet are altogether above reason, and are paradoxes attended with such seeming inconsistencies with reason that reason can't clearly remove nor fully explain the mystery.

By experience we know there is such a thing as thought, love, hatred, etc. But yet this is attended with inexplicable difficulties. If there be such a thing as thought and affection, where be they? If they exist, they exist in some place or no place. That they should exist, and exist in no place, is above our comprehension. It seems a contradiction to say they exist and yet exist nowhere. And if they exist in some place, then they are not in other places, or in all places, and therefore must be confined at one time to one place, and that place must have certain limits. From whence it will follow that thought and love, etc., have some figure, either round, or square, or triangular, which seems quite disagreeable to reason and utterly inconsonant to the nature of such things as thought and affection of mind.

'Tis evident by experience that something now is. But this proposition is attended with things that reason [cannot] comprehend, and which are paradoxes that seem contrary to reason, knots that reason cannot clearly untie. For if something now is, then either something was from all eternity, or something began to be without any cause or reason of its existence. The last seems wholly inconsistent with natural sense. And the other, viz. that something has been from all eternity, implies that there has been a duration that is past, is without any beginning, which is an infinite duration, which is perfectly inconceivable and is attended with difficulties that seem contrary to reason. For we can't conceive how an infinite duration can be made greater, any more than how a line of infinite length can be made longer. But yet we see that past duration is continually added to. If there were a duration past without beginning a thousand years ago, then that past infinite duration has now a thousand years added to [it]. And, if so, it is greater than it was before by a thousand years, because the whole is greater than a part. Now the past duration consists of two parts, viz. that which was before the last thousand years, and that which is since. Thus here are seeming contradictions involved in this supposition of an infinite duration past.

And moreover, if something has been from eternity, 'tis either an endless succession of causes and effects—as, for instance, an endless succession of fathers and sons—or something equivalent. But this supposition is attended with manifold apparent contradictions (see my sermons on the existence of God).[8] Or there must have been some eternal, self-

8. JE probably means his sermon series on Rom. 1:20, dated June 1743, with the doctrine, "The being and attributes of God are clearly to be seen by the works of creation."

existent Being having the reasons of his existence within himself, or he must [have] existed from eternity without any reason of his existence, both which are inconceivable. That a being should exist from eternity without any manner why it should be so, rather than otherwise, is altogether inconceivable, and seems quite repugnant to reason. And why a being should be self-existent, or have the reason of his existence within himself, seems also inconceivable, and never, as I apprehend, has yet been explained.

If there has [been] anything from eternity, then that past eternity is either an endless duration of successive parts—as successive hours, minutes, etc.—or it is an eternal duration without succession. The latter seems repugnant to reason and incompatible with any faculty of understanding that we have. And the other, an infinite number of successive parts, involves the very same contradictions, with the supposition of an eternal succession of fathers and sons.

If ever the world has existed from eternity without a cause—but this seems wholly inconsistent with reason. In the first place, 'tis inconsistent with reason that it should exist without a cause. For 'tis evident that there is not a thing the nature and manner of which is necessary in itself, and therefore it requires a cause or reason why it is so, and not otherwise, out of itself. And in the next place, if it exists from eternity, then succession has been from eternity, which involves the forementioned contradiction. But if it ben't without a cause and don't exist from eternity, then it has been created out of nothing, which is altogether inconceivable, and what reason cannot show to be possible; and many of the greatest philosophers have supposed it plainly inconsistent with reason.

Many other difficulties might be mentioned as following from the proposition that something now is, that are insuperable by reason.

'Tis evident by experience that great evil, both moral and natural evil, abound in the world. 'Tis manifest that great injustice, violence, treachery, perfidiousness and extreme cruelty to the innocent abound in the world; as well as innumerable, extreme sufferings, issuing finally in destruction and death, are general all over the world in all ages. But this could not otherwise [have] been known by reason, and now is attended with difficulties which the reason of many, yea, most of the learned men and greatest philosophers that have been in the world, have not been able to surmount. That it should be so ordered or permitted in a world absolutely and perfectly under the care and government of an infinitely holy and good God, has a seeming repugnancy to reason that few, if any, have been able fully to remove.

That men are to be blamed or commended for their good or evil voluntary actions is a general proposition received with good reason by the dictate of the natural, common and universal moral sense of mankind, in all nations and ages, which moral sense is commonly plainly included in what Tindal means by reason and the law of nature. And yet many things attend this truth that are difficulties and seeming repugnances to reason, that have proved altogether insuperable to the reason of most of the greatest and most learned men in the world.

I observe further, that when the difficulties which attend any general proposition which is recommended to us [as] true by any testimony or evidence that, considered by itself, seems sufficient, without contrary testimony or evidence[9] to countervail it, and difficulties attend that proposition: if these difficulties are no greater and of no other sort from what might reasonably be expected to attend true propositions of that kind, then these difficulties are not only no valid or sufficient objection against that proposition, but they are no objection at all.

Thus there are many things that I am told concerning the effects of electricity, magnetism, etc., and many things that are recorded in the *Philosophical Transactions of the Royal Society,* which I have never seen and are very mysterious. But being well attested, their mysteriousness is no manner of objection against my belief of the accounts, because from what I have observed and do know, such a mysteriousness is no other than is to be expected in a particular and exact observation of nature, and a critical tracing of its operations. 'Tis to be expected that the further it is traced, the more and more mysteries will appear.

To apply this to the case in hand: if the difficulties that attend that which is recommended by good proof or testimony to our reception as a divine revelation, and this revelation is attended with difficulties, but yet with difficulties no greater nor of any other nature than such as (all things considered) might reasonably be expected to attend a revelation of such a sort, of things of such a nature, and given for such ends and purposes, and under such circumstances; these difficulties not only are not of weight sufficient to balance the testimony or proof that recommends it, but they are of no weight at all as objections against [it]. They are not reasonably to be looked upon as of the nature of arguments against it. But, on the contrary, they may with good reason be looked upon as confirmations, and of the nature of arguments in its favor.

This is very evident, and the reason of it very plain. For certainly whatever is reasonably expected to be found in truth when we are seeking it,

9. MS: "evident."

cannot be an objection against its being truth when we have found it. If it be reasonably expected in truth beforehand, then reason unites it with truth, as one property of that sort of truth. And if so, then reason unites it afterwards, after it is found. Whatever reason determines to [be] a property of any kind of truth, that is properly looked upon in some degree as a mark of truth, or of truths of that sort, or as belonging to the marks and evidences of it. For things are known by their properties. Reason determines truth by things which reason determines to be the properties of truth. And if we don't find such things belonging to supposed truth that were before reasonably expected in truth of that kind, this is an objection against it, rather than the finding of it. The disappointment of reason is rather an objection with reason than something to induce its acceptance and acquiescence. If the expectation be reasonable, then the not answering of it must so far appear unreasonable, or against reason, and so an objection in the way of reason.

Thus, if anyone that is in search for persons or things of a certain kind, reasonably expects beforehand that if he be successful in finding the person or thing of the kind and quality that he is in search of, [it will be possessed of certain properties and circumstances], when[1] he hath actually found something with all these properties and circumstances that he expected, he receives it and rests in it so much the more entirely as the very thing that he was in quest of. And surely it is no argument with him that his invention is not right, that some things that he reasonably expected are wanting. But on the contrary, this would rather be an objection with his reason.

In order to judge what sort of difficulties are to be expected in a revelation made to mankind by God, such as Christians suppose the Scriptures to be, [we should remember that it is] a revelation of what God knows to be the very truth concerning his own nature; the acts and operations of his mind with respect to his creatures; the grand scheme of infinite wisdom in his works, especially with respect to the intelligent and moral world; a revelation of the spiritual and invisible world; a revelation of that invisible world which men shall belong to after this life; a revelation of the greatest works of God, the manner of his creating the world and of his governing of it, especially with regard to the higher and more important parts of it; a revelation delivered in ancient languages.

Difficulties and incomprehensible mysteries are reasonably to be expected in a declaration from God of the precise truth, as he knows it, in

---

1. MS: "and when."

matters of a spiritual nature; as we see things that are invisible, and not the objects of any of the external senses, are very mysterious, involved much more in darkness, attended with more mystery and difficulty to the understanding than others; as many things concerning even the nature of our own souls themselves, though the nearest to us and the most intimately present with us, and so most in our view of any spiritual thing whatsoever.

The further things are from the nature of those things that language is chiefly formed to express—viz. things appertaining to the common business and vulgar affairs of life, things obvious to sense and men's direct view and most vulgar observation, without speculation, reflection and abstraction—the more difficult. Our expressions concerning them, when words and language are applied to them, will be attended with greater abstruseness, difficulty and seeming inconsistence; language not being well fitted to express these things, words and phrases not being prepared for that end. Such a reference to sensible and vulgar things from the original use and design of words and phrases is unavoidably introduced, that naturally confounds and loses the mind, and involves it in darkness.

If God gives a revelation of things of religion, it must be mainly concerning those things that are spiritual, or the affairs of the moral and intelligent universe, which is the grand system of spirits, about himself and intelligent creatures.

It may well be supposed that a revelation concerning another and an invisible world, a future state that we are to be in after separated from the body, should be attended with much mystery. It may well be supposed that things of such a world are of an exceeding different nature from the things of this world, the things of sense, and all the objects and affairs which earthly language was made to express; and not agreeable to such notions, imaginations and ways of thinking that grow up with us and are connatural to us, being from our infancy formed to an agreeableness to the things which we are conversant with in this world. We could not conceive of the things of sense if we had never had these external senses. And if we had had only some of these senses and not others—as, for instance, if we had only a sense of feeling, without the senses of seeing and hearing—how mysterious would a declaration of things of these last senses be! Or if we had feeling and hearing but had been born without eyes or optic nerves, the things of light, being declared to us, would many of them be involved in mystery that would appear exceeding strange to us.

(Marginal note: I say, if we were born without eyes or optic nerves for, as to such as are born blind but yet born with optic nerves, I imagine they have some ideas by the state of the optic nerves other than they could otherwise have, as an idea of darkness or blackness, and without that confused intermixture of specks or streaks of light with blackness such as is in prints in mezzotint, which I suppose all have when they shut their eyes or when they are in darkness, and possibly such a kind of light-someness on some occasion as we have by pressing our eyes with our fingers when they [are] shut, which confused light is perhaps from some motion of the animal spirits in the optic nerves, though not excited by rays, yet in some degree like that which is excited by a few weak rays.)

Thus, one that was in this manner without the sense of seeing, but had the other senses, might be informed by all about them that they can perceive things at a distance, and perceive as plainly, and in some respects much more plainly, than by touching them—yea, that they could perceive things at so great a distance that it would take up many millions of ages to travel to them.

They might be informed many things concerning colors that would all be perfectly incomprehensible that yet might be believed. And it could not be said that nothing at all is proposed to their belief because they have no idea of color. They might be told that they perceive an extension, a length and breadth of color, and termination and limits, and so a figure of this kind of extension, and yet that it is nothing that can be felt; which would be perfectly mysterious to them, and would seem an inconsistence, as they have no ideas of any such things as length, breadth and limits and figure of extension, but only certain ideas they have by touch.

They might be informed by them that they can perceive at once the extent and shape of a thing so great and multiform as a tree, which is a thing that it would take them many days to perceive the extent and shape of by touch, which would seem very strange and impossible.

They might be told that, to them that see, some things appear a thousand times as great as some others that yet are made up of more visible points, or [at] least visible parts, than they, which would be very mysterious and seem quite inconsistent with reason.

These and many other things would be attended with unsearchable mystery to 'em concerning objects of sight, and what they could never fully see how they can be reconciled with reason, at least with[out] very long, particular, gradual and elaborate instruction. And, after all, they would not be fully comprehensible so as clearly to see how the ideas connected in these propositions do agree. And yet I suppose, in such a case, the most rational persons would give full credit to things that they knew not by reason, but only by the revelation of the word of them that see. I suppose a person born blind in the manner described would nevertheless give full credit to the united testimony of the seeing world in things which they said about light and colors, and would entirely rest in their testimony.

If God gives us a revelation of the very truth, not only about spiritual beings, and concerning them in an unexperienced and unseen state, but also concerning a spiritual being or beings of a superior kind, and so of an unexperienced nature, entirely diverse [not only] from anything we do now experience in our present state, but from anything that we can be conscious or immediately sensible of in any state whatsoever that our nature can be in, then especially may mysteries be expected in such a revelation.

The truth concerning any kind of perceiving being of a different nature from ours, though of a kind inferior, might well be supposed to be attended with difficulty by reason of the diversity from what we are conscious of in ourselves. But much more so when the nature and kind is superior. For a superior perceptive nature may well be supposed, in some respects, to include and comprehend what belongs to an inferior, as the greater comprehends the less and as the whole includes a part, and therefore what the superior experiences may give him advantages to conceive of what belongs to the nature of the inferior. But on the contrary, an inferior nature don't include what belongs to a superior. When one of an inferior nature considers what belongs to a kind of beings of a nature entirely above his own, there is something belonging to it that is over and above all that the inferior nature is conscious of.

A very great superiority, even in beings of the same nature with ourselves, sets them so much above our reach, that many of their affairs become incomprehensible and attended with inexplicable intricacies. Thus many of the affairs of adult persons are incomprehensible, and appear inexplicably strange, to the understandings of little children; and many of the affairs of learned men and great philosophers and mathematicians, things which they are conversant in and well acquainted with, are far above the reach of the vulgar, and appear to them not only unintelligible but absurd and impossible and full of inconsistencies. But much more may this be expected when the superiority is not only in degree of improvement of the faculties and properties of the same, but also is a superiority of nature itself as to its kind.

So that if there be a kind of created, perceptive beings, in their nature vastly superior to the human nature—which none will deny to be impossible—and a revelation should be given us concerning the nature, acts and operations of this kind of creatures, it would be no wonder if such a revelation should contain some things very much out of our reach, attended with great difficulty to our reason, being things of such a kind that no improvement of our minds that we are capable of will bring us to an experience of anything like them.

But above all, if a revelation be made [to] us concerning that Being that is uncreated and self-existent, who is infinitely diverse from and above all others in his nature, and so infinitely above all that any improvement or advancement of our nature can give us any consciousness of, in such a revelation it would be very strange indeed if there should not be some great mysteries quite beyond our comprehension and attended with difficulties which it [is] impossible for us fully to solve and explain.

It may well be expected that a revelation of truth concerning an infinite Being should be attended with mystery. We find that the reasonings and conclusions of the best metaphysicians and mathematicians concerning infinites are attended with paradoxes and seeming inconsistencies. Thus it is concerning infinite lines, surfaces and solids, which are things external. But much more may this be expected in spiritual things, such as infinite thought and idea, infinite apprehension, infinite reason, infinite will, love, and joy, infinite spiritual power, agency, etc.

Nothing is more certain [than] that there must be unmade and unlimited Being. And yet the very notion of such a Being is all mystery, involving nothing but incomprehensible paradoxes and seeming inconsistencies.

It involves the notion of a Being self-existent and without any cause, which is utterly inconceivable and seems repugnant to all our ways of conception.

An infinite spiritual Being, or infinite understanding and will and spiritual power, must be omnipresent, without extension, which is nothing but mystery and seeming inconsistence.

The notion of an infinite Eternal implies absolute immutability. That which is in all respects infinite, and so absolutely perfect, and to the utmost degree and at all times, can't be in any respect variable. And this immutability, being constant from eternity, implies duration without succession, is wholly mystery and seeming inconsistence. It seems as much as to say an infinitely great or long duration all at once, or all in a moment, which seems to be saying an infinitely great in an infinitely little, or an infinitely long line in a point without any length.

Infinite understanding, which implies an understanding of all things, of all existence, past, present and future, and of all truth, and all reason and argument—this implies infinite thought and reason. But how this can be absolutely without mutation or succession of acts seems mysterious and absurd. We can conceive of no such thing as thinking without successive acting of the mind about ideas. Perfect knowledge of all things, even of all the things of external sense, without any sensation or any reception of ideas from without, is inconceivable mystery. Infinite knowledge implies a perfect, comprehensive view of a whole future eternity, which seems utterly impossible: for how can there be any reaching of the whole of this to comprehend it, without reaching to the utmost limits of it? But this can't be where there is no such thing as utmost limits.

And again, if God perfectly views an eternal succession or chain of events, then he perfectly sees every individual part of that chain, and there is no one link of it hid from his sight. And yet there is no one link that he sees but that there is a link, yea, innumerable links, beyond it; from which it would seem to follow that there is a link beyond all the links that he sees, and consequently that there is one link, yea, unnumerable links, that he sees not, inasmuch as there are innumerable beyond every one that he sees. And many other like seeming contradictions might be mentioned which attend the supposition of God's omniscience.

If there be an absolute immutability in God, then there never arises any new act in God or new exertion of himself—and yet there arise new effects, which seems an utter inconsistence.

And so innumerable other such like mysteries and paradoxes are involved in the notion of an infinite and eternal intelligent Being, insomuch that, if there never had been any REVELATION by which God had made known himself by his word to mankind, the most speculative persons would, without doubt, have forever been exceedingly at a loss concerning the nature of the Supreme Being and First Cause of the universe. And that the ancient philosophers and wiser heathen had so good notions of God as they had, seems to [be] much more owing to tradition, which originated from divine revelation, than from their own invention, though human reason served to keep these traditions alive in the world, and led the more considerate to embrace and retain the imperfect traditions which were to be found in any parts remaining; they appearing, after once suggested and delivered, agreeable to reason.

If a revelation be made of the principal scheme of the wisdom of the supreme and infinitely wise ruler respecting his moral kingdom, wherein his all-sufficient wisdom is displayed in the case of its greatest trial, ordering and regulating the said moral kingdom to its great ends, when in the most difficult circumstances; extricating it out of the most extreme calamities in which it had been involved by the malice and subtlety of the chief and most crafty of all God's enemies; it being the principal of all the effects of the wisdom of him, the depth of whose wisdom [is] unsearchable and absolutely infinite; his deepest scheme, by which mainly the grand design of the universal, incomprehensibly complicated system of all his operations, and the infinite series of his administrations, is most happily, completely and gloriously attained; the scheme in which God's wisdom is mainly exercised and displayed: it may reasonably be expected that such a revelation will contain many mysteries.

We see that to be the case even as to many works of human wisdom and art. They appear strange, paradoxical and incomprehensible by those that are vastly inferior in sagacity, or entirely destitute of that skill or art. How are many of the effects of human artifice attended with many things that appear strange and altogether incomprehensible by children and many others, seeming to be beyond and against nature. And, in many cases, the effect produced not only seems to be beyond the power of any visible means, but inconsistent with being an effect, contrary to what would be expected. The means seem inconsistent with the end.

If God reveals the exact truth in those things which, in the language of the heathen sages, are matters of philosophy—i.e. not the things of sense and of common life, but matters of reflection and speculation, as especially things of morality and theology, things concerning the nature of the Deity, and the nature of man so far as related to the Deity, etc.— I say, if God reveals the real, precise truth concerning these things, it may most reasonably be expected that such a revelation should contain many mysteries and paradoxes, considering how many mysteries the doctrines of the greatest and best philosophers in all ages concerning these things have contained, or at least how very mysterious and seemingly repugnant they are to the reasons of the vulgar and persons of less understanding, and how mysterious the principles of philosophers, even concerning matters inferior far to those which are received for the most undoubted truth now, would have appeared in any former age, if they then had been revealed to be true, undoubted truths.

If God gives mankind his word in a large book, consisting of a vast variety of parts, many books, histories, prophecies, prayers, songs, parables, proverbs, doctrines, promises, sermons, epistles and discourses of very many kinds, all connected together, all united in one grand drift and design, and one part having a various and manifold respect to others, so as to become one great work of God and, as it were, one grand system, as it is with the system of the universe with its vast variety of parts connected in one grand work of God; it may well be expected that there should be mysteries, things incomprehensible and exceeding difficult to our understanding, analogous to the mysteries that are found in all other works of God, as the works of creation and providence, and particularly such as are analogous to the mysteries that are observable in the system of the natural world and the frame of man's own nature.

For such a system (or Bible) of the word of God is as much the work of God as any other of his works, the effect of the power, wisdom and contrivance of a God whose wisdom is unsearchable and whose nature and ways are past finding out. And as the system of nature and the system of revelation are both divine works, so both are in different senses a divine word. Both are the voice of God to intelligent creatures, a manifestation and declaration of himself to mankind. Man's reason was given him that he might know God and might be capable of discerning the manifestations he makes of himself in the effects and external expressions and emanations of the divine perfections.

If it be still objected that 'tis peculiarly unreasonable that mysteries should be supposed in a revelation given to mankind, because if there be such a revelation, the direct and principal design of it must be to teach and instruct mankind, and so to enlighten and inform their understandings, which is inconsistent with its delivering things to man which he can't understand, and so don't inform and enlighten, but only puzzle and confound his understanding, I answer:

1. Men are capable of understanding as much as is revealed, and as much as is pretended to be revealed, though they can't understand everything that belongs to the things that are revealed, or although there are secret things pertaining to the things revealed which God has not revealed. As, for instance, God may reveal that there are three that have the same nature of the Deity, that 'tis most proper for us to look upon as three persons, though the particular manner of their distinction, or how they differ, may not be revealed. And we may therefore understand so much as is revealed concerning it. So he may reveal that the Godhead was united to man so as to be properly looked upon [as] the same person, but not reveal how it was effected.

2. No allowance is made in the objection for what may hereafter be understood of the word of God in future ages, which is not now understood. And it is to be considered that divine revelation is not given only for the present or past ages.

3. The seeming force of this objection lies wholly in this, that we must suppose whatever God does tends to answer the end for which he does it. But those parts of a revelation that we can't understand don't answer the end, inasmuch as informing our understandings is the very end of a revelation, if there be any such thing.

But this objection is no other than just equivalent to objections which may be made against many parts of the creation, particularly of this lower world. 'Tis apparent the most direct and principal end of this lower world was to be for the habitation, use and benefit of mankind, the head of this lower world. But here are some parts of it that seem to be of no use to him, but rather for his inconvenience and prejudice, as the innumerable stones and rocks that overspread so great a part of the land, which, as to anything known, are altogether useless and of ten times greater inconvenience than benefit.

Thus it is reasonable to expect that in such a revelation there should be many things plain and easy to be understood, and that the revelation should be most intelligible wherein it is most necessary for us to understand it in order to our guidance and direction in the way to our happiness; but that there should also be many incomprehensible mysteries in it, yea, many things very difficult to our reason, in that degree which we have attained of the use of it: many things understood in part, but yet that room should be left for vast improvement in the knowledge of them; that the revelation should be of such a nature, containing such depths and hidden treasures of knowledge, that there should be room for improvement in understanding, and to find out more and more, to all the wisest and best of men to the end of the world; and that the case in this respect should actually be the same as concerning the works of nature: that there should actually be a gradual improvement in the understanding of it; that many things that were formerly great and insuperable difficulties, unintelligible mysteries, should now, by further study and improvement, be well cleared up and cease to remain any difficulty; and that other difficulties should be considerably[2] diminished, though not yet fully cleared up.

It may be expected that, as in the system of nature, so in this system of

2. MS: "considerable."

revelation, there should be many parts whose use is but little understood, and many that should seem wholly useless, yea, and some that should seem rather to do hurt than good.

So I might further observe, that if we have a revelation given in ancient languages, used among a people whose customs and phraseology is but very imperfectly understood, then many difficulties should arise from hence; and that in a very short, concise history, where only some particular facts and circumstances that concern the special purpose and design of that revelation are mentioned, and innumerable others are omitted that would be proper to be mentioned if the main design were to give a clear, full account and clear idea [of the] connected, continued history of such a people or such affairs as the history mentions—I say, in such a case, 'tis no wonder that many doubts and difficulties arise.

1341. OF THE COMPETITION OF MANY PRETENDED REVELATIONS. This that follows from Dr. Sherlock, the present Bishop of London, in his *Discourses Preached at Temple Church*,[3] [vol. 1], pp. 184–87: "the question is asked, how shall we distinguish between the pretenses to revelation, which are so many and various, all of which have an equal right to be heard, that it is endless to look for religion in such a crowd of pretenders to it, and difficult to determine the merit of the several claims? So that the only sure way is to take up with natural religion, which is everywhere uniformly the same, and in which there is no danger of being deluded and misled by imposture; for natural religion admits of no counterfeit.

"Now, to form a true judgment upon this case, it will be necessary first to state the question right upon the foot of this objection, and then to examine what weight of reason there is in it.

"First then, the question must relate to revelation considered only as a rule and measure of religion: for the dispute between nature and revelation is confined to this one point, which is the best and safest guide in religion? It is absurd therefore to bring instances of any revelations in this case, which do not pretend to this property, that were never given, or pretended to be given, as a rule of religion: for, when men talk of the various revelations that have been in the world, and the difficulty of determining which they ought to obey, they cannot take into their consideration the answer of the oracle to Crœsus, or the several answers on particular occasions recorded in the Greek and Roman histories . . . these

---

3. Thomas Sherlock, *Several Discourses Preached at the Temple Church* (2 vols. London, 1756, 1759).

are out of the present question, and have no relation to the inquiry concerning a rule or measure of religion. [. . .] On this view there are not many revelations that come into competition: in the heathen world I know of none; for, though there were sundry pretenses to revelation, yet none was set up as a common standard for the religion of mankind. The religion of Rome was chiefly introduced by Numa, who pretended a revelation for the foundation of his authority: but it is plain he aimed at nothing farther than modeling the religion of his city, and had no thought of the rest of the world in what he did; nor had the Romans any sense that their religion concerned any but themselves: and therefore, when they extended their conquests, religion was their least concern; they left the world in that respect as they found it, and men were not so much as invited to take their religion. Now it is evident, that no law, either human or divine, extends farther than the lawgiver intends. Suppose then, if you please, Numa's religion to be a revelation; yet, since it was given and declared only to the people of Rome, the rest of the world can have no concern in it. That no system of religion in the heathen world claimed [regard] as a general law, is evident from the answer returned by the oracle, when the inquiry was, which religion was the best? The answer was, that every man should worship according to the custom of the country where he was. So that all religions were esteemed equally good, and the most any religion pretended to was a local authority, which reached no farther than the laws of the country did: and, unless men are for giving more to the pretended heathen revelations, than ever they claimed for themselves, or was claimed for them by those that introduced them and lived under them, they cannot be brought into this question, since they have no relation to us, any more than the many civil laws and constitutions of the same countries had: and men may as reasonably complain of the great variety of civil and municipal laws that distract their obedience, and then instance in the laws of the Medes and Persians, as they now complain of the variety of revelations, instancing in such as, if they were true, concern them as little as the laws of Persia do.

"But perhaps it will be said, that, though these religions do not oblige us, yet nevertheless, if any of 'em were true, they effectually overthrow all others; for God cannot contradict himself, whether he speaks to one nation, or to all the world: and upon this foot these several pretenses come within our inquiry. This reasoning may be good . . . . But then not one of all these pretended revelations in the heathen world, within the period mentioned, pretends to the essentials necessary to constitute a law, either human or divine. Where was it published and declared? by whom, and how qualified? Can you name the persons, or produce the gospel of such a religion? Take the instance of Rome: What was Numa? a King, and therefore submitted to in the innovations of religion: but what one mark of a divine commission can you produce? and yet without such marks even a true revelation could be of no authority. Try all other instances, and you will see how weakly the objection against revelation is supported by any pretenses of the heathen world." Thus far Dr. Sherlock.

1342. OF THE COMPETITION OF PRETENDED MIRACLES IN THE HEATHEN WORLD WITH THOSE THAT CONFIRM THE CHRISTIAN REVELATION. Also from the same book of Dr. Sherlock cited in the last number:[4] "The miracles reported to have been done in the heathen world are unworthy of God, considered either in themselves, or the end proposed by them: for let it be observed, that God never works miracles merely to astonish and surprise people, but always to serve some great ends of providence: and though he has in favor of his people, and sometimes even of particular persons, wrought a miracle; yet, when he published the law and the gospel, he did not rest the authority upon one or more single miracles, but upon a long series of miracles exhibited from day to day for years together. And if miracles are properly applied as a proof of the purposes and will of God, miracles wrought without being attended with any declaration of God's will in which we have any concern, are very improper instances to be set up in opposition to those of Moses and Christ, upon which the happiness of mankind depends in this life, and that which is to come. This consideration gives weight and authority to the miracles of the gospel: for it was a design worthy of God to restore mankind to that happiness which they had forfeited; and it was a work in every view of equal dignity and benevolence with the creation.

"With what color of reason can the pretended miracles of the heathen world be brought into this question, which were done upon trifling occasions, unworthy of the interposition of God? Look into all the ancient oracles; see to what mean purposes they are applied, and how often they prove destructive to those who relied on them; and then tell me what marks you see of divine wisdom or goodness in them, that should set them upon an equal foot with the miracles of Christ Jesus. . . . Shall I undertake to prove, that it exceeds the power of man to raise the dead [. . .], and give sight to the blind, and to cure all diseases by the word of his mouth? No: never was any such attempt set up.

4. JE took the following material from ibid., vol. 1, pp. 210–17.

"But must they, you will say, of necessity proceed from God, because they could not be wrought by men? . . . especially considering that no effects, neither the miracles of the gospel, nor the works of nature, can prove directly an infinite power or wisdom? For who will be bold to say, that the wisdom and power of God were exhausted in the visible works of the creation, so that there is nothing either wiser or greater that infinite wisdom and power can contrive or execute?

"Let this matter be rightly stated. . . . The first and most natural notion of God is, that he is the maker of the world, and all things in it. This is the notion the Jews had of God; and, when they distinguished the true God from the heathen gods, they defined him to be the maker of the world and of mankind. Look then into the miracles of the gospel, and you will see this attribute of God as clearly demonstrated by them as by the works of nature: for there you will find, that the author of the Christian miracles is the maker of mankind; for by him men were made; that is, dead bodies were made into living men: for to raise a dead man, and to make a new man, are much the same thing. . . . If we believe that we received our senses, our reason, our natural strength and vigor, from the true God at first; look into the gospel, and you will find the miracles of Christ are from the same hand: for to the blind he gave sight, to the deaf hearing, to the lame and sick strength and soundness, to demoniacs and lunatics he gave reason and a right mind. Or, if you choose rather to look into the material world for a proof of a God; if you think the beauty, order, and regularity of the world speak God to be both the author and governor of nature; search the gospel, and you will find the miracles of Christ derive themselves from the governor of the world, and speak the same language with the works of nature: for at his word the stormy winds were laid; the sea obeyed his voice: when he suffered, all nature trembled; the earth shook, the veil of the temple was rent, the sun and the moon were darkened.

"If you appeal to the natural sense and notions of mankind for the idea of the true God, and thence collect his essential attributes, justice, righteousness, holiness, and goodness; let the voice of nature be still; and the gospel shall speak more plainly, how just, how righteous, how holy and good God is, who is author of the salvation and redemption which is by Christ Jesus. Take what way you will to prove the being or the attributes of God, and in the same way with equal advantage we will prove the God of the world [. . .] to be the author of Christianity; which all who believe the being of a God are bound to admit for a proof of the truth of Christianity. . . . And, when our Savior styled the wonders that he performed, 'the works that the Father had given him to finish,' he plainly appealed to the power of the creator, as manifested in the works that bore witness to him.

"There is a question commonly asked upon this occasion, to which it may be proper to give an answer: that is, How shall we know that these miracles did not proceed from an evil power, since we have instances, as some think, of miracles so wrought?

"The answer is, We know this the same way that any man knows the works of nature to proceed from a good being: for how do you know that the creator of the world was a good being? If you answer, that the maker of mankind, the author of nature, must of necessity be a good and holy being, because he has woven into the nature of man the love of virtue and hatred of vice" (it might more properly have been said, a conscience approving virtue and disapproving vice), "and given him distinct notions of good and evil, by which reason unerringly concludes the author of this nature and these principles to be himself good and holy; I answer the same for the gospel of Christ: the love of virtue, and hatred of vice, is as inseparable from the gospel of Christ, as from the reason of man; and the gospel of Christ more distinctly teaches to know and acknowledge the holiness and goodness of God, than reason, or the works of nature, can do: and therefore those who acknowledge the author of nature to be a good being, have much more reason to acknowledge the author of the Christian miracles to be a good being.

"But then we are told this is arguing in a circle; proving the doctrines first by miracles, and then the miracles again by doctrines. But this is a great mistake, and it lies in this, [that] men don't distinguish between the doctrines we prove by miracles, and the doctrines by which we try miracles; for they are not the same doctrines.

"The doctrines which are to be proved by miracles are the new revealed doctrines of Christianity, which were neither known nor knowable to the reason of man: such are the doctrines of salvation and redemption by Jesus Christ, of sanctification and regeneration by the Spirit of God: and whoever brought these doctrines to prove the truth or divine original of the miracles?"

1343. UNITY OF THE GODHEAD FROM THE UNITY AND CONNECTION OF THE WORLD. (See No. 976.)[5] Cudworth's *Intellectual System*, p. 225. Aristotle's *Metaphysics*, Bk. 14, ch. 10:[6] "They who say that mathematical num-

---

5. *Works, 20,* 280–86.
6. In the following two paragraphs, JE quotes Ralph Cudworth's translations of passages from

ber is the first, and suppose one principle of one thing, and another of another, would make the whole world to be like an incoherent and disagreeing poem, where things do not all mutually contribute to one another, nor conspire together to make up one sense and harmony; but the contrary is most evident in the world; and therefore there cannot be many principles, but only one."

P. 404. Cudworth cites Plato in *Timaeus* saying thus: "'Whether we have rightly affirmed, that there is only one heaven, or is it more agreeable to reason to hold many or infinite? We say there is but one, if it be made agreeable to its intellectual paradigm, containing the ideas of all animals and other things in it; for there can be but one archetypal animal, which is the paradigm of all created beings; wherefore that the world may agree with its paradigms in this respect of solitude or oneliness, therefore it is not two nor infinite, but one only begotten.' His meaning is, that there is but one archetypal mind, the Demiurgus or maker of all things, [. . .] and therefore but one world."

1344. LORD's DAY, with respect to these words, Ps. 118:24, "This is the day which Thou hast made." The words might have been translated, "This is the day which Thou hast sanctified," or "consecrated." The Hebrew word is so used, as in I Sam. 12:6, "It is the Lord that advanced Moses and Aaron"; *Gnasha* ("made," "sanctified," or "consecrated" Moses and Aaron), the same word that is used here.

1345. CHRIST's RIGHTEOUSNESS that expiates our sins and recommends us to God consists not only in his virtue and his holy behavior here in this world, as that expressed obedience and faithfulness to God his Father, but also as a most transcendent exercise and expression of mercy to men. Thus are these texts of Scripture true in their highest and most important sense: Prov. 16:6, "By mercy and truth iniquity is purged," or "expiated," as the word signifies; Jas. 2:13, "mercy rejoiceth against judgment."

1346. NATURAL FITNESS. If God had not regarded fitness and propriety in the affair of man's salvation, the whole mediatorial scheme might

Aristotle's *Metaphysics*, IV, 10, and Plato's *Timæus*. See Cudworth, *The True Intellectual System of the Universe: The First Part; wherein, All the Reason and Philosophy of Atheism is Confuted; and Its Impossibility Demonstrated* (London, 1678), pp. 225, 404, in both of which places Cudworth uses these ancient authorities to defend the unity of the Godhead and the integrity of the world, and to refute classical polytheism.

have been set aside, or never have taken place. If free grace exercised in a way of mere sovereignty, without regard to propriety, was all that was requisite, there would have been no need of the means and methods provided for man's salvation in the admirable scheme which infinite wisdom hath contrived. Therein appears the wisdom of this method of salvation, viz. in the perfect propriety that is observed throughout the whole of the complicated scheme and the fit connection of one part with another, or of one thing with another, in everything belonging to this great salvation.

God saw it necessary that a Mediator should be provided in order to man's salvation, because it was not proper that a sinner should be united to God without a Mediator. It was necessary that the Mediator should die for sinners. And if the sinner was saved on his account, it was not possible that that cup should pass from him, because propriety required it. So God will not bestow the benefits of the Mediator on them that are not united to him, because there is no propriety in it. It is not proper that they should have communion with Christ who have no union with him. And God's insisting on this propriety is not in the least inconsistent with the highest possible freedom of his grace. And furthermore, God will not look on those as in a state of union with the Mediator, and treat 'em as persons united to him, who don't cordially receive him and cleave to him, but reject him, because it is not proper that he should so do. There can be no propriety in looking on intelligent beings, capable of act and choice, as united to Christ that don't consent to it, and while their hearts are disunited. Therefore, active, voluntary union is insisted on. But neither does this in the least infringe on any possible freedom of grace in the method of salvation.[7]

[1347.] PROPHECIES OF THE OLD TESTAMENT which have been FULFILLED besides the prophecies of the Messiah and his salvation and kingdom, and the prophecies of Daniel.

First, the prophecies of the Pentateuch:

The prophecy of Eve concerning Seth and his posterity, that God had appointed her another seed instead of Abel, whom Cain slew (Gen. 4:25), implying that the church of God should be continued in the world

7. Halfway down the second column of MS p. 182, JE wrote "1347," but the rest of the column as well as the entirety of the following leaf (pp. 183–84) are blank. Pagination resumes at MS p. 687, which, along with pp. 688–99, is blank. References in other MSS such as the Table to the "Miscellanies" and the "Blank Bible" indicate that JE did fill in at least some of the now missing pages, but their contents are unknown. No. 1346 is the last entry numbered by JE; all subsequent entry numbers were supplied by JE, Jr.

in his posterity, and that the Messiah should be from him; and so the great promise made in the foregoing chapter, v. 15 (see note in loc.).[8]

Lamech's prophecy concerning Noah, that he should comfort the people of God concerning their work and the toil of their hands because of the ground which the Lord had cursed, Gen. 5:29 (see note in loc. in "Blank Bible," and also "Notes on Scripture," no. 323).[9]

The prophecies of the flood delivered to Noah.

The promises given to Noah after the flood that the world should never anymore be destroyed by a flood of water, etc.

Noah's prophecy concerning his three sons and Canaan (Gen. 9:25–29).

God's promises to Abraham that he would make of him a great nation (Gen. 12:2, ch. 15:5, etc.).

That Sarah's and Isaac's posterity should be greatly multiplied (Gen. 17:16).

That a nation and a company of nations should be of Jacob (Gen. 35:11).

The prophecies concerning Ishmael (Gen. 16:12 and 17:20 and 21:13).

It was told to Rebekah that two nations were in her womb, and two manner of people should be separated from her bowels, and the one people should be stronger than the other people, and the elder should serve the younger (Gen. 25:23).

In Isaac's blessing of Jacob it was foretold that people should serve him, and nations should bow down unto him, and that he should be lord over his brethren, and that his mother's sons should bow down unto him (Gen. 27:29).

Jacob foretold concerning Esau that he should live by his sword, and should serve his brother, but that at last he should break his yoke from off his neck (Gen. 27:40).

The promises of the land of Canaan to the posterity of Abraham and Jacob in the books of Moses are so many, so interspersed and interwoven everywhere with the rest of the Pentateuch (or the Book of the Law) as we now have it, that if the law itself was written before they became possessed of Canaan, we must suppose those promises were written also before. These promises are connected and blended with the whole history of Abraham (Gen. 11:27–32; 12:1–7; 13:14–18; 15:7, 18–21; 17:8;

---

8. *Works*, 15, 537.

9. "Blank Bible" note on Gen. 5:29, in which JE writes, "How Noah would comfort the church of God we may be led to understand by the manner in which the like expression is used in Ezek. 14:22." For "Scripture" no. 323, see *Works*, 15, 306–307.

the whole twenty-fourth chapter, especially v. 7; ch. 22:20–24); and so with the history of Isaac and Jacob (Gen. 26:3–4; the whole twenty-eighth chapter, especially vv. 4 and 13; ch. 29:5, 10–15, with the whole story in that and the following chapters of Jacob's sojourning in Padan-Aram; ch. 31:53; 35:12; 37:1; 46:3–4; 47:9; 48:3–6, 21–22).

See also Joseph's prediction, Gen. 50:24–26, compared with Ex. 13:19, and Josh. 24:32.

See the promises in Ex. 3:8, 17; ch. 6:3–4, 8. These promises in the beginning of Exodus are so connected with all the history of Moses' call and of his bringing the people out of Egypt that the whole history is built on the promises and can't [be] separated. They were plainly written together, or were originally parts of the same writing. And the whole story of their march from thence through the wilderness is, as it were, a comment on these promises, strictly connected. And all the transactions of the history have a manifold reference to the promises, and imply the promises in them. See Ex. 15:14–17; ch. 16:23, 27–36; 32:13; 33:1–3, 12–17; 34:10–16, 23–24; Num. 10:29–32; the whole thirteenth and fourteenth chapters of Numbers; ch. 20:5, 12, 24; 22:9, 11, 16–41; 24:8; 27:12–13; 33:50–56; the whole thirty-fourth, thirty-fifth, and thirty-sixth chapters; Deut. 1:6–8, 19–46; 2:29; 3:18–29; 4:1, 5, 14, 21–22, 26, 37–38, 40; 5:16, 31, 33; 6:1, 3, 10–11, 18–19, 23; 7:1–5, 16–26; 8:1, 7–20; 9:1–6, 27–28; 10:11; 11:8–17, 21, 23–25, 29–31; ch. 12, throughout; 13:12–16; 14:21–29; [ch.] 15, throughout; 16:2, 6, 9, 11, 13–18; 17:2, 8, 14; 18:1–9, 14; 19:1–14; 20:15–18; 21:1–8; 23:20; 24:19–22; 25:19; 26:1–15; 27:1–14; [ch.] 28, throughout; 29:22–29; 30:1–10, 18, 20; 31:1–8, 10–13, 20–21, 23; 32:13–14, 47–52; 33:13–16, 28; 34:1–3.

In like manner are those promises interwoven with, and supposed and implied in, the laws and precepts of the Pentateuch. Ex. 12:25, 48; 13:5, 11; so the Ten Commandments; Ex. 20:12; 23:10–11, 16–18; ch. 16:33–34; 34:10–16, 23–24; Lev. 14:34–35 ff.; 18:3, 27–28; 19:9–10, 23–25, 33–34; 20:23–24; 23:10–11 ff., vv. 22, 39; 24:22; 25:2–34, 39–55; 26:1, 4–6, 20, 22, 31–34, 43; 27:14–25, 30; Num. 9:14; 10:9; 15:2; 18:13, 20–32; and many other laws contained in passages referred to in the preceding paragraph concerning the history of the Pentateuch.

These predictions and promises are so blended with the whole of the history and the laws in general that, not only is there an express respect to them in very many places, but an evident regard to them runs through the whole. All manifestly supposes them and is built on a supposition of them, so that all together may be looked upon as one great and vastly complicated and variegated prediction of this event.

Many circumstances of the children of Israel's possessing the land of Canaan were foretold.

Preceding circumstances were foretold, as that first the people should be in a great affliction and distress in a strange land, where they should be slaves and should suffer very cruel bondage till, four hundred years from the time of the prediction, [the prediction] should be fulfilled, and that God would then wonderfully appear to plead the cause of his people, and to judge and punish the nation that should thus afflict them, and that by this means they should come out of that land with great substance, and that in the fourth generation they should return to the land of Canaan again (Gen. 15:7–17).

The circumstances of their introduction into the land were foretold.

That the inhabitants of the land should be exceeding wicked at that time (Gen. 15:16), agreeable to which was the event about 400 years after the prediction (by Deut 9:4, and 12:31, and 20:18, and other places).

That it should be by the expulsion and destruction of the former inhabitants (Gen. 15:16; Ex. 23:23, and 33:2, and 34:11; Lev. 18:28, and 20:23; Num. 33:50–53; Deut. 7:1–2, and 16–26, and 8:20, and 9:3–4, and 12:29).

That the expulsion and destruction of those old inhabitants should be by war, a war in which Israel must fight with them, and that it should be by their conquering them in their war with them (Ex. 13:17 and 23:22–23, 27; Num. chs. 13 and 14, throughout, and 23:24, and 24:8–9, and 32:6–32, and 33:50–53, 55; Deut. 7:1–2, 16–26, and 9:1–4, and 20:1 with vv. 16–17, and 31:3–8).

That the inhabitants of Canaan should be greatly afraid before they came (Ex. 15:14–16, and 23:27).

That they should not molest the people in their passing over Jordan, nor make any opposition or any attempt to hinder them in their entering the land (Ex. 15:16).

That Joshua should be the captain under whom they should fight, and that he should be their successful and victorious leader in this war (Num. 27:18–23; Deut. 3:28, and 31:3–4).

That God should very wonderfully fight for them (Ex. 23:20–23; Deut. 7:17–23, and 9:3, and 31:3, 8); and that it should be by such works of wonder as never had been in the world before (Ex. 34:10–11, compared with Num. 23:23).

That the old inhabitants should not be all driven out at once, but should be exterminated by little and little (Ex. 23:29–30, Deut. 7:22). And therefore, this prediction was long a-fulfilling, and was many ages after the prediction before it was completely fulfilled, it not being till David's time.

The bounds to which the settlements and possessions of the people should extend were foretold. Twofold bounds were set in the promise, more narrow and more extensive. The more narrow limits are set in Num. 34:1–12. The land was given them unto these limits in Joshua's time. And the more extensive limits, from the river of Egypt to the River Euphrates (Gen. 15:18–21; Ex. 23:31; Deut. 1:7–8, and 11:24; compare Josh. 1:4), this also was fulfilled at last in David's time, near 900 years after the promise was first made.

It was foretold that God [would] not extend their territories to these large limits at their first settlement in the land, but afterwards, in process of time (Deut. 12:20, and 19:8–9).

That kings should be of Abraham's and Isaac's and Jacob's posterity (Gen. 17:6, 16, and 35:11; Num. 24:7, 17–20). The fulfillment of this was not till Samuel's time.

The place which God should choose and appoint for the offering their sacrifices was signified to Abraham (Gen. 22:2–14) about 850 years before it was fulfilled and about 450 after Moses wrote this.

Jacob foretold concerning the tribe of Reuben that it should not excel (Gen. 49:4), which was remarkably fulfilled. It was a tribe of no distinction in famous men or renowned deeds, but on the contrary, in these respects of little note and greatly distinguished from the generality of the Israelites by meanness of spirit and behavior in the time of the war with Jabin and Sisera (Judg. 5:15–16).

Of the tribes of Simeon and Levi, Jacob foretold that they should be divided in Jacob and scattered in Israel (Gen. 49:7), which was remarkably fulfilled. See the fulfillment, as to Simeon, in note on I Chron. 4:24–43.[1]

Jacob foretold concerning the tribe of Judah that it was the tribe that [would] be chief, and above all the rest, in renown, authority and warlike deeds; and the state, order and authority of that tribe should last longer than of any other tribes (Gen. 49:8–10).

The precise part of the land in which Zebulun should dwell is foretold. Gen. 49:13, "Zebulun shall dwell at the haven of the sea; and he shall be for an haven of ships; and his border shall be unto Zidon."

1. In the "Blank Bible" note on this passage, JE, quoting Matthew Henry's gloss, asserts that when the Ten Tribes revolted from the House of David, the Simeonites left their cities in Judah and went elsewhere. God "owned" and "prospered" them, so that they escaped many of the "calamities of the captivity," and reside, scattered, in distant countries to this day.

Jacob's prophecy concerning Dan, his being as an adder in the path, etc., Gen. 49:17, was fulfilled in Samson and in the Danites that took Laish (Judg. 18:27).

That in Gen. 49:19, "a troop shall overcome him: but he shall overcome at the last," was fulfilled in what we have an account of in I Chron. 5:18 and 12:8, 15.

The great fruitfulness, large possessions, dignity and military prowess of the tribe of Joseph was foretold by Jacob (Gen. 49:22–26).

That prophecy concerning the tribe of Benjamin—Gen. 49:27, "Benjamin shall ravin as a wolf: in the morning he shall devour the prey, at night he shall divide the spoils"—if it be to be understood of temporal things only, doubtless denotes great exploits in war which were to be performed by that tribe, and in this sense the prophecy was verified. See my notes in loc., and also *Synopsis Criticorum*.[2] Or if it has some respect to spiritual things, spiritual spoils divided after ravening God's flock as a greedy, merciless wolf, and persecuting with great rage the Lamb of God, this was remarkably fulfilled in the apostle Paul, who, by his own account, thus persecuted Christ (in his members) in his youth, but afterwards was the greatest instrument of distributing[3] the benefits of Christ, which may be represented as Christ's spoils, the fleece, yea, the flesh and blood of the Lamb, and Christ's own infinite riches, glorious and eternal possessions, which are obtained for mankind by his being slain, as much as a kingdom with its riches are obtained[4] by destroying the king in war, and so is his spoils. If this be meant, the figure is no more violent than many others used concerning the manner of our obtaining the blessings of the kingdom of heaven, such as eating the flesh of the Son of man, and drinking his blood, taking the kingdom of heaven by violence as soldiers conquering in way, etc.

Moses foretold concerning the tribe of Judah that it should be [a] tribe eminent for prevalence with God by prayer (Deut. 33:7), which was remarkably fulfilled in David, Jehoshaphat and others, and also that it should be eminent for power and victory over his enemies (ibid.).

He also foretold of the tribe of Joseph that it should be eminent for warlike achievements (Deut. 33:17).

2. In the "Blank Bible" note on Gen. 49:27, JE, citing Arthur Bedford's *Scripture Chronology Demonstrated by Astronomical Calculations* (London, 1730), recounts the victories of the Benjamites over the other tribes of Israel, the Philistines, Haman, and other enemies of the Jews. On JE's use of Bedford and other writers in responding to modern criticism, see *Works*, *15*, 12–21. For Poole on this verse, see *Synopsis Criticorum*, *I*, Pt. I, col. 312.

3. MS: "distributed."

4. MS: "obtaining."

Moses foretold of Zebulun that he should live by the sea, and that the tribe should go forth by sea. Deut. 33:18, "Rejoice, Zebulun, in thy going out."

Jacob foretold of Ephraim that he should far exceed Manasseh (Gen. 48:19). And his having all the Ten Tribes under him, and so called by his name, is agreeable to what is said in the end of that verse, "and his seed shall become a multitude of nations."

It was often foretold concerning Caleb and Joshua that they only, of all the men of war that came out of Egypt, should enter into Canaan (Num. 14:24, 30, 38, and 26:65, and 32:12). And they not only outlived all the rest of that generation so as to enter into Canaan, though Caleb was forty years old when he went to spy out the land, yet he had lived six years after they entered into Canaan before he had his inheritance given him in Hebron, and when he was 85 years old, and then he says of himself, Josh. 14:11, "As yet I am as strong this day as I was in the day that Moses sent me: as my strength was then, even so is my strength now, for war, both to go out, and to come in." And Joshua lived twenty-four years after he entered Canaan.

As God promised concerning Caleb (Num. 14:24) that God would bring Caleb "into the land whereinto he went; and his seed should possess it," so punctually was this fulfilled that God gave for a possession to him and his seed that very part of the land which his feet had trod on when a spy, and where the giants lived, which chiefly terrified the other spies, and disheartened them and the congregation in general, and was the occasion of that unbelief, discouragement, murmuring and rebellion for which they were never allowed to enter into Canaan (see Josh. 14:9–15).

It was foretold in Moses' time that Israel's king should be higher than Agog (Num. 24:7)—fulfilled in Saul.

That a great and illustrious prince should rise out of Jacob that should smite the four corners of Moab and should conquer Edom (Num. 24:17–18), remarkably fulfilled in David.

It was foretold that the nation of the Amalekites should be utterly destroyed from under heaven, and that this should be gradually fulfilled by God's fighting against them in successive ages in his providence (Ex. 17:14, and Num. 24:20), fulfilled in what we have an account of in I Sam. ch. 14, and ch. 27:8, and ch. 30; I Chron. 4:43; and Esther 9:5–10.

It was foretold by Moses that the people, after his death, should show themselves very prone to idolatry (Deut. 31:16, 27–29, and 32:15–18); and, by greatly corrupting themselves in this and other respects, they should bring terrible judgments and extreme calamities on themselves (Deut. 31:16–18); that the greater part should be destroyed (Deut. 4:26, and 28:52, and 32:25–26), which seems to have [been] fulfilled in both their destructions, that by the Babylonians and that by the Romans.

It was foretold that their cities should be destroyed, and their land laid waste, and the whole be made desolate (Lev. 26:31–33; Deut. 32:20 ff.); that the temple should be destroyed (Lev. 26:31); that they should be carried captive out of their land (Lev. 26:34, 38–39, 44, and Deut. 28:41, 63, and 29:28, with 30:3), that they should be scattered among the heathen (Lev. 26:33; Deut. 4:27, and 28:64, and 32:26).

That God would thus destroy them by a nation which neither they nor their fathers had known (Deut. 28:36); and also a nation from a great distance, from the ends of the earth, whose language they could not understand—all these things were true concerning the Assyrians and the Chaldeans, and also the Romans; that their destruction should be attended with a great variety and multitude of unspeakable and unparalleled calamities and testimonies of God's wrath (Deut. 32:21–26), remarkably fulfilled in their destruction by the Babylonians, as appears by the history, and especially the Lamentations, of Jeremiah, but more remarkably fulfilled in their destruction by the Romans.

Yea, 'tis in that place foretold that a vast multiplicity of extreme, unequaled distresses should come upon them, attended with the sword without and terrible destruction within, and particularly famine, and great cruelty, without regard of any sort of persons, destroying the greater part of the nation, and ending in a great dispersion at that time when another nation that had been heathen should be taken in their room, which was all fulfilled with the last very remarkable circumstance, viz. their being rejected from being God's people and an heathen people taken in their room in the destruction by the Romans and, with most other circumstances, in the former destruction by the Chaldeans.

That they should eat their own children when distressed and besieged by their enemies, and that it should be thus with some of their finest and most delicate ladies (Lev. 26:29–30 ff., Deut. 28:53–57), fulfilled, II Kgs. 6:28 ff., Lam. 2:20 and 4:10, and in the time of the siege by the Romans.

That they should be brought into Egypt again (Deut. 28:68), fulfilled literally in the going of some into Egypt in Jeremiah's time, and in the many that dwelt in Egypt in the times of the Grecian and Roman monarchies, and fulfilled in both captivities in that bondage the nation in general were carried into, equivalent to the Egyptian bondage.

That in the land of their captivity they should serve other gods, fulfilled in the obstinacy and impenitence of those carried into Chaldea, as appears by Ezekiel ch. 2 and other places, and especially by the resolute idolatry of them that went down into Egypt (Jer. 44:25–26). And there is all reason to think that great part of them worshipped Nebuchadnezzar's golden image. See also Ezek. 14:3–7, and ch. 20:30–32, 39. Of the idolatry of those that were left in the land, see Ezek. 33:25 ff. And this was fulfilled in the Jews following false messiahs after their captivity and dispersion by the Romans.

It was foretold that, when they should be carried captive, the land should lie desolate until it had enjoyed its sabbaths (Lev. 26:34–35, 43); fulfilled, II Chron. 36:20–21 and other, parallel places, compared with the history in the two books of Kings and Chronicles.

That yet, on their repentance, they should be restored again to their own land (Deut. 30:1–10, and 32:36, 43).

That the restoration to their own land should be on the destruction of the nation that destroyed them, which should be with great manifestations of God's power, etc., and mercy to his people (Deut. 32:35–42).

That, in the end of all, Jews and Gentiles should together be the people of God, in the enjoyment of the same privileges (Deut. 32:43).

The conquests of the Assyrians were foretold (Num. 24:22).

The great and extensive conquests of the Macedonians and Romans over all the eastern parts of the world, and the dreadful destruction they should make, particularly of the Hebrews, was foretold (Num. 24:24), which destruction of the Hebrews was fulfilled in Antiochus and Titus and other Roman emperors after him.

That they that should be left in the land, should be in fear and terror, and flee when none pursued (Lev. 26:36), which was remarkably fulfilled by the account we have in Jer. 41:17–18, and 42:10–16, and 43:2–7.

That they should fall when none pursued, and should fall one upon another, as it were before a sword, when none pursued (Lev. 26:36–37). For the fulfillment, see Jer. 41:2, 7, 10, 12, 15.

That, after they were dispersed, God would draw out a sword after them (Lev. 26:33; compare Ezek. 5:7, 12, and 24:23, and 15:7), in part fulfilled in Jeremiah's time (Jer. 44:7, 11–14, 27, 29–30), but more remarkably fulfilled in the sword that pursued the Jews after their dispersion by the Romans. See "Miscellanies," No. 972.[5]

---

5. MS: "p. 9. b. c," located in part (3), subpoint 1 of No. 972 (*Works, 20,* 264), the paragraph beginning, "And after this the temple was burnt and made desolate . . ."

That they should find no rest among the nations (Deut. 28:66), remarkably fulfilled, especially since their dispersion by the Romans.[6]

[1348.] OBJECTIONS OF MODERN LIBERTINES AGAINST THE SCRIPTURES.

[1.] Evidences of future punishment, taken from a pamphlet on that subject lent me by Mr. Bellamy, printed 1720:[7]

"The word *Gehenna* signifies only the Valley of Hinnom. That fire was said to be everlasting, because it was kept burning night and day. [...]

"The word *ever* and *everlasting* the Greeks understand for 'an age.'

"The word *everlasting* is commonly used in the Law of Moses for a 'limited time.' [...]

"That fire is said to be durable, or everlasting, that goes not out till the fuel is consumed. [...]

"The fire that consumed Sodom and Gomorrah is called 'eternal fire.' [...]

"If the fire be everlasting, it will not follow that that which is cast into it is everlasting. The wicked are compared to chaff and stubble, which is quickly burnt up. [...]

"The Scripture often uses very hyperbolical expressions."

[2.] THE OBJECTIONS OF MR. WHISTON, as mentioned in Dodwell's sermons in answer to him.[8] Several of them are the same with those mentioned above.

That the words in the New Testament translated "everlasting" and "eternal" are sometimes used concerning things of a temporary duration.

That the use of the same word in both cases, viz. both the future reward of the saints and punishment of the wicked, does not imply the equal duration of the punishment and reward: because some of the pre-

6. At the end of the entry, JE left the remainder of MS p. 708 and the following four leaves blank, no doubt to provide space for continuing the entry. As it stands, JE never got beyond the first section dealing with the Pentateuch.

7. This pamphlet could not be identified. The placement of quotation marks and ellipses within the excerpts are conjectural, based on JE's use of horizontal lines to separate them.

8. JE gleaned the following information from William Dodwell, *The Eternity of Future Punishment Asserted and Vindicated. In Answer to Mr. Whiston's Late Treatise on That Subject. In Two Sermons Preached before the University of Oxford, on Sunday, March 21, 1741* (Oxford, 1743). See William Whiston, *The eternity of hell-torments considered, or, A collection of texts of Scripture, and testimonies of the three first centuries relating to them* (London, 1742).

cepts of the law of Moses are called everlasting that are moral and shall continue to the end of the world; others are so called, using the same word, that were only to last till the Christian church should be set up.

That if the words "eternal" and "everlasting" do signify a proper eternity when applied to the punishment of the wicked, it may mean only an everlasting privation of being.

That the "fire" and "smoke" and "worm," etc. [Mark 9:44, 46, 48; Rev. 14:11], may be eternal, and yet the pain not be eternal, because the wicked may be consumed and so their pain be at an end.

That Christ speaks of them that blaspheme the Holy Ghost as those that shall not be forgiven in this world nor the world to come [Matt. 12:32], implying that others shall be forgiven in the world to come.

That Christ went and "preached to the spirits in prison" [I Pet. 3:19], i.e. preached the gospel to departed souls of the wicked in order to their salvation.

That αιων in the New Testament signifies an age; that αιανες των αιϖνων signifies ages of ages.

That ἀιδιος is used for a limited time when, in Jude 6, the devils are said to be "reserved in everlasting chains," where the chains spoken of last no longer than till the day of judgment.

That "some shall be beaten with many stripes," others "with few" [Luke 12:47–48], which most naturally signifies that some shall suffer longer than others.

The eternity of punishment is inconsistent with the divine attributes, and that, therefore, can't be proved by any pretended revelation.

That eternal misery of sinners can be no advantage to God, to themselves or to others.

That it is inconsistent with God's mercy.

That it is inconsistent with justice to punish men eternally for their sinning during this short life.

That the threatening such a punishment will do no good, because if men won't be deterred from sin by the expectation of a great temporary punishment, neither would they by the expectation of eternal misery.

[3.] EVIDENCES OF THE DOCTRINE.

The word "everlasting" is used in the very sentence of the Judge at the last day [Matt. 25:41, 46], whom we can't suppose to use rhetorical tropes and figures.

The punishment of the devil doubtless will be eternal. But the wicked shall be sentenced to the same everlasting fire.

See argument from Matt. 12:31–32, pp. 36–37.

The wicked that are finally impenitent are represented as wholly cast away, lost, made no account of, etc., which is quite inconsistent with their punishment being medicinal, and for their good and purification, and to fit them for final and eternal happiness.

Eternal punishment is not eternal annihilation. Surely they will not be raised at the last day only to be annihilated.

The words used to signify "the duration of the punishment of the wicked [. . .] do in their etymology, truly signify a proper eternity, and [. . .] if they are sometimes used in a less strict sense, when the nature of the thing requires it, yet that can never pass as any reason, why they are not to be understood absolutely, when the subject is capable of it. They are terms the most expressive of an endless duration, of any that can be used or imagined; and they always signify so far positively endless, as to be express against any other period or conclusion, than what arises from the nature of the thing. They are never used in Scripture in any other limited sense, than to exclude all positive abolition, annihilation or conclusion, other than what the natural intent and constitution of the subject spoken of must necessarily admit. . . . The word Αἰώνιος, which is the word generally used by the sacred writers, is, we know, derived from the adverb ἀεί, which signifies forever, and cannot without force be used in any lower sense, and particularly this is the word, by which the eternal and immutable attributes of the Deity are several times expressed." Dodwell, Sermons in Answer to Whiston, pp. 15–17.[9]

Those words of Christ concerning Judas are a demonstration of the eternity of the misery of hell: "good had it been for that man that he had not been born" (Matt. 26:44).

On the supposition that God intends finally to deliver all mankind from misery and make all intelligent creatures at last eternally happy, and that to suppose the contrary (viz. the everlasting continuance of the torments of hell) be so extremely derogatory to God's moral character, and represents him in such black and odious colors, and as so cruel a Being: why have not Christ and his apostles, who have revealed a future and eternal world so clearly and brought life and immortality to light— I say, why have not they declared this doctrine when speaking of future punishment, and clearly revealed this glorious doctrine of such an uni-

---

9. JE has quoted this passage rather directly from Dodwell, *The Eternity of Future Punishment Asserted and Vindicated*, pp. 15–17.

versal eternal salvation, so much more evangelical and agreeable to the office of Christ as a Savior and the design of his coming into the world?[1]

If the wicked in hell are in a state of trial, under severe chastisements as a means in order to their repentance and obtaining the benefits of God's favor in eternal rewards, then these things will follow:

(1) That they are in a state of that freedom that makes 'em moral agents and the proper subjects of judgment and retribution; and,

(2) It will also follow, seeing that the torments of hell which they suffer, being the last means God uses, or such as will be effectual after all other means have failed and proved utterly ineffectual, so that it appeared in vain to use 'em any longer, so that there was no other way left than to have recourse to these severe means, which will finally be effectual with everyone, will bow all their hearts and thoroughly purge their minds and bring 'em to repentance—I say, if this be the case, then it is evident that these terrible chastisements are made use of as the most powerful means of all, more efficacious than all the means used in this life, which prove ineffectual, and which, proving insufficient to overcome sinners' obstinacy and prevail with their hard hearts, God is as it were compelled to relinquish 'em all, and have recourse to these as the last means, the most effectual and powerful. And again,

(3) If the torments of hell are to last a very long time, ages of ages, the torments of the sinners of [the] old world till the end of the world and after that, so long that the time is often and almost constantly represented figuratively as everlasting, lasting forever and ever, then it must be because sinners in hell all this while are obstinate and, though they [are] free agents as to this matter, yet willfully and perversely refuse even under such great means to repent, forsake their sins and turn to God. If the end of their torments is to bring 'em to repentance, 'tis unreasonable to suppose that will be continued under their torments after they are brought to repentance. They frowardly go on in their rebellion, enmity and opposition to the great God, whose power they feel in their misery, who continues not only with the greatest peremptoriness to command 'em to forsake their sins and submit to him immediately, without delay, and withal adding severe chastisements and terrible torments to bow their wills and bring 'em to compliance, yet they willfully and obstinately refuse and choose to go on in their rebellion. Though they feel

---

1. The following passage, beginning at this point and ending at point 4, "*Axiom*," were originally subpoints 7 and 8 under the list of considerations of whether "the damned are in a state of trial." JE indicated the insertion here.

the dreadful effects of it and know that they must be continued many ages under them if they refuse, yet they resolutely go on in their strong and desperate enmity and opposition. And,

(4) It must be further supposed that all this is while they not only suffer these dreadful chastisements for their obstinacy, and know they must suffer till they comply, though it be never so many millions of ages, but also have the offers of immediate mercy [and] deliverance made to 'em if they will comply.

Now if this be the case, and they shall go on in such wickedness and continue in such extreme and desperate obstinacy and pertinaciousness for so many ages (as is supposed by its being supposed their torments shall be for so long continued), how desperately will their guilt be increased, how many thousand times more guilty at the end of the term than at the beginning, and therefore so much the more proper objects of divine severity, deserving of his wrath, and still a thousand times more severe or longer continued chastisements than the past. And therefore, 'tis not reasonable to suppose that all the damned should all be delivered from misery, and received to God's favor, and made the subjects of eternal salvation and glory at that time, when they are many thousand times more unworthy of it, more deserving of continuance in misery than when they were first cast into hell. 'Tis not likely that the infinitely wise God should so order the matter. And if their misery should be added to and still lengthened out much longer to atone for their new contracted guilt, so they must be supposed to continue impenitent till that second additional time of torment is ended, at the end of which their guilt will still be risen higher and vastly increased beyond what it was before. And, at this rate, where can there be any place for an end of their misery?

It further appears, from what was observed above, that the sinner, continuing obstinate in wickedness under such powerful means to reclaim him for so long a time, will be so far from being more and more purged, or brought nearer to repentance, that he will be, as it were, infinitely further from it. Wickedness in his heart will be vastly established and increased. For it may be laid down as an AXIOM that the longer men continue willfully in wickedness, the more is the habit of sin established, and the more and more will the heart be hardened in it. And again, it may be laid down as another AXIOM that the greater and more powerful the means are that are used to bring men to reform and repent, which they resist and are obstinate under, the more desperately are men hardened in sin, and the principle of it in the heart confirmed. And it may be laid down as another AXIOM that especially does long continuance in perverse and obstinate rebellion against any particular kind of means tend to render those particular means vain, ineffectual and hopeless.

After the damned in hell have stood it out with such prodigious and devilish perverseness and stoutness for ages of ages in their rebellion and enmity against God, refusing to bow to his will under such constant, severe, mighty chastisements, attended all the while with offers of mercy, what desperate degree of hardness of heart and fixed and strength of habitual wickedness will they have contracted at last, and inconceivably[2] further from a penitent, humble and pure heart than when first cast into hell! And if the torments should be lengthened out still longer and their impenitence continued, as by the supposition[3] one will not end before the other does, still the further will the heart be from being purified. And so, at this rate, the torments will never at all answer their end, and must be lengthened out to all eternity.

4. *Axiom.* If the torments of hell are purifying pains that purge the damned from their sins, it must be by bringing them to repentance, convincing them of the evil of sin, and inducing them to forsake it, and with a sincere heart to turn from sin to God and heartily to choose and walk in the ways of virtue and holiness. There is no other way of sinners being purged as moral agents but this. And if hellfire is the means of any other purification, it can't be a moral purification. These flames don't purge from and bring to virtue of heart and life merely as a hot fire purges metals from dross and senseless, dead lumps of matter from material filth. But the defilement which they purge from is defilement of will. And the purity which they bring to must be purity of will, intention, choice and the active faculties and principles.

Axiom. If the wicked in hell are the subjects of torments there in order to their purification, and so being fitted for and finally brought to eternal happiness, then they are the subjects of a dispensation that is truly a dispensation of love and divine and infinite goodness and benevolence towards them.

Axiom. If the design of the pains of hell be that of kind and benevolent chastisements, to bring sinners to repentance and a yielding to God's authority and compliance with the divine will, then we can't suppose that they will be continued after the sin[ner] has repented and is actually brought to yield and comply. For that would be to continue 'em

2. MS: "inconceive."
3. MS: "suppose."

for nothing, to go on using means and endeavors to obtain the end when the end is accomplished and the thing aimed at is fully obtained already.

5. *Arg.* If the damned, after many ages suffering extreme torment in hell, are to be delivered and made perfectly and eternally happy, then they must be in a state of probation during this long season of their confinement to such extreme misery.

If they are not in a state of probation, or on any trial how they will behave themselves under these severe and terrible inflictions of wrath, but are to be delivered and made eternally happy at the end of a certain period, then what restraints are they under from giving an unbounded loose[ness] and license to their wickedness in expressions of enmity against God, in cursing and blasphemy and whatever their hearts are inclined to?

And if they are in such a state as[4] this, wherein they are thus left to unrestrained wickedness, and every curb to their most wicked inclinations is taken off, being nevertheless sure of deliverance and everlasting happiness, how far is this state fit to be a state of purgation of rational creatures and moral agents from sin, being a state wherein they are so far from means of repentance, reformation and entirely reclaiming and purging them from sin that all manner of means are rather removed, and even so much [that] every restraint [is] taken off and they are given up wholly [to] sin; which, instead of purifying them, will tend above all things that can be conceived to harden them in sin and desperately establish the habits of it.

A state of purgation of moral agents, that is, a state to bring sinners to repentance and reformation and not a state of trial, is a gross absurdity. If any shall say, that though we should maintain that the pains of hell are purifying pains to bring sinners to repentance in order to their deliverance and eternal happiness, yet there will be no necessity of supposing either that they may sin with impunity, and so without restraint, or that they are properly in a state of probation—for they have no probation whether they shall finally have eternally happiness, because that is absolutely determined by the benevolent Creator concerning *all* his intelligent creatures, that they shall finally be brought to a state of happiness—yet their circumstances may be such as may tend greatly to restrain their wickedness, because the case with them may be thus, that the time of their torment shall be longer or shorter according as they behave themselves under their chastisements more or less perversely, or that

4. MS: "of."

their torment shall be raised to a greater height, and additions be made, in proportion to the wickedness they commit in their purgatory flames:

Ans. Even on this supposition they are in a state of probation for a more speedy possession of eternal life and happiness and deliverance from further misery and punishment, which makes their state as much a[5] state of probation as their state in the present life. For here 'tis supposed by these men that sinners are not in a state of trial whether ever they shall obtain eternal happiness or no, because that is absolutely determined, and the determination known or knowable concerning all without any trial; but only [is] it a state of trial whether they shall obtain eternal life so soon as at the end of their lives, or at the day of judgment. Neither have they any trial, during this life, whether they shall escape any affliction and chastisement for sin or no, but whether they shall be delivered from a state of suffering so soon, and shall escape those severer and longer chastisements that, with respect to many, are to come afterwards.

And on the supposition of the objection, there must be the proper circumstances of a state of probation in hell as well as on earth. There they must, in like manner, be continued in that state of free agency that renders 'em properly the subjects of judgment and retribution. For on the supposition of the objection, they shall be punished for their wickedness in hell by an addition to their misery proportioned to their sin. And they shall be the subjects of God's merciful strivings and endeavors and means to bring to repentance as well as here. And there must be a divine judgment after the trial to determine their retribution as much as after this life. And the same or like things must be determined by the supreme Judge as will be determined at the day of judgment.

At that great day, on the supposition of such as I oppose, what will be determined concerning the impenitent will not be what their eternal state shall be, but only whether they must have eternal happiness immediately, whether they have repented and are qualified for immediate admission to heavenly glory, or whether the bestowment of it shall be delayed and further chastisements be made use of. And so it must be again after their castigatory, purifying pains. At the end of all there must be a judgment whether now they truly repent and so have performed the condition of deliverance and immediate admission to the state of the blessed, or whether there shall be a further season of misery: which brings it to be in all respects a proper judgment as much as that at the

5. MS: "as a."

general resurrection, and the preceding time of the use of means and God's striving with them to bring 'em to repentance as much a proper time of trial in order to judgment as the time of this life.

But if it be so that the damned are in a state of trial, let it be considered how unreasonable this is:

(1) If they are in a state of trial, then they must be in a state of liberty and moral agency (as these men will doubtless own), and so, according to their notion of liberty, must be under no necessity of continuing in their rebellion and wickedness, but may cast away their abominations and turn to God and their duty in a thorough subjection to his will very speedily. And then, seeing the end of their probation, and the severe means God uses with them to bring 'em to repentance, is obtained, how unreasonable will it be to suppose that God, after this, would continue 'em still under hell torments for a long succession of ages. But if [this is] not so, but God should speedily deliver 'em on their speedy repentance, how are the threatenings and predictions of their everlasting punishment fulfilled in any sense? According to the sense even of those who deny the absolute eternity of the misery of hell, and hold that the words everlasting and forever, etc., when applied to this misery, are not to be taken in the strictest sense, they yet allow that they signify a very long time, a great many ages.

(2) If the devils and damned spirits are in a state of probation, and have liberty of will, and are under the last and most extreme means to bring 'em to repentance, and consequently the greatest means, having the highest tendency of all to be effectual—I say, if thus, then it is possible that the greatest part, if not all of them, may be reclaimed by these extreme means, and may be brought to thorough repentance before the day of judgment. Yea, 'tis possible that it might be very soon. And if so, how could it certainly [be] predicted concerning the devil that he would do such and such great things in opposition to Christ and his church from age [to age], and that at last he should be judged and punished, and have God's wrath more terribly executed upon him? Rev. 20:10, "And the devil that deceived them was cast into the lake of fire and brimstone, where the beast and false prophet are, and shall be tormented day and night forever and ever."

And how is it said in Scripture that, when he fell, he was cast down from heaven and reserved in chains of darkness unto judgment? The expression seems naturally to signify strong and irrefragable bonds, which admit of no comfort or hope of escape. And besides, a being reserved in chains unto judgment is not consistent with the appointment of another time of trial and opportunity to escape the judgment or condemnation. 'Tis said, Jude 6, they are "reserved in everlasting chains under darkness unto the judgment of the great day."

And if any of the separated souls of [the] wicked that are in the case that the soul of the rich man was in, when he died and lifted up his eyes in hell, being in torments, should repent and be delivered before the day of judgment, and so should appear at the right hand among the righteous at that day; then how could that be verified, II Cor. 5:10, "For we must all stand before the judgment seat of Christ; that EVERY ONE may receive the things done in his body, [. . .] whether good or bad"? And we have reason to think that this time of standing before the judgment seat of Christ, which the Apostle has a special respect to, is the day of judgment, if we compare this with other scriptures; as that of the same Apostle, Acts 17:31, "he hath appointed a day, in which he will judge the world in righteousness by that man whom he hath ordained"; and many other places.

And how does their being in a state of trial, many of them for so many ages after death before the day of judgment, during all which time they have opportunity to repent, consist with those words of Christ, Mark 8:38, "Whosoever therefore shall be ashamed of me and my words in this adulterous and sinful generation; of him also shall the Son of man be ashamed, when he cometh in the glory of his Father with the holy angels"? How is their continuing in a state of trial from the time of that generation, and from the end of their lives to the day of judgment, consistent with its being declared to 'em from God beforehand that they shall certainly be condemned at the day of judgment, or Christ certifying them beforehand that, whatever trial they shall have, whatever opportunity God should give 'em for repentance and pardon, for so many ages, all would be in vain, which in effect is passing the sentence?

We may argue in like manner from these words, Matt. 10:14–15, "And whosoever shall not receive you, nor hear your words, ... Verily I say unto you, It shall be more tolerable for the land of Sodom and Gomorrah in the day of judgment, than for that city." So Matt. 11:21–24, "Wo unto thee, Chorazin! wo unto thee, Bethsaida! . . . I say unto you, It shall be more tolerable for Tyre and Sidon in the day of judgment, than for you. And thou, Capernaum, which art exalted up to heaven, shall be brought down to hell. . . . I say unto you, it shall be more tolerable for the land of Sodom in the day of judgment, than for thee."

Two things may be noted in these sayings of Christ:

1. 'Tis here declared what the state of those obstinate unbelievers should be at the day of judgment, for their wickedness here in the body, with an asseveration, "I say unto you." And sentence indeed is passed beforehand upon them by their Judge concerning the punishment that shall be executed upon them at the day of judgment. The declaration is made in the form of a solemn denunciation or sentence, "Wo unto thee, Chorazin," "Wo unto thee, Bethsaida," etc. And is it reasonable to suppose that the very Judge that is to judge 'em at the end of the world would peremptorily declare that they should not escape punishment at the day of judgment, yea, solemnly denounce sentence upon them, dooming them to the distinguished punishment they should then suffer for their obstinacy in their lifetime, and yet appoint another time of trial of a great many hundred years, between their death and the day of judgment, wherein they should have opportunity to escape that punishment?

2. 'Tis here also to [be] observed that the wicked inhabitants of Sodom and Gomorrah should be condemned to misery at the day of judgment, though they had already been in their purifying flames and in a state of probation, under the most powerful means to bring 'em to repentance already for 1900 years, and should be after that for more than 1700 years.

So we may argue from Rom. 2:3–12, 16, where the Apostle speaks of men's treasuring up "wrath against the day of wrath and revelation of the righteous judgment of God" by their abusing the day wherein God exercises towards them the riches of his goodness, forbearance and long-suffering, which should lead 'em to repentance, plainly intimating, v. 6, that the Judge in that day would "render every one according to his deeds: to them who by patient continuance in well doing," etc., "eternal life. But to them who are contentious," etc., "tribulation and wrath," etc. And that "as many as sinned without law" should "perish without law," and that "as many as have sinned in the law" should "be judged by the law," which plainly shows that they are to be judged according to their deeds during this life, wherein alone there is this distinction of some sinning without the law and some sinning in the law.

And then in v. 16 the Apostle repeatedly tells us when these things shall be, that men shall thus receive[6] their retribution according to their deeds and circumstances in their state wherein there are these distinctions: "In the day," says he, "when God shall judge the secrets of men according to my gospel," which shows that this life is the only state of trial, and that all men shall be judged at the end of this world according to their behavior in this life, and not according to their behavior in another

6. MS: "receiving."

state of trial between this life and that day; which, with respect to most, will be so vastly longer than this life, and when they (as is supposed) will be under more powerful means to bring 'em to repentance.

So 'tis apparent by II Thess. 1:5–9: "Which is a manifest token of the righteous judgment of God. . . . Seeing 'tis a righteous thing with God to recompense tribulation to them that trouble you; . . . when the Lord Jesus shall be revealed from heaven with his mighty angels, in flaming fire taking vengeance on them that know not God, and obey not the gospel of Jesus Christ: who shall be punished with everlasting destruction," etc. Here 'tis manifest that all that are obstinate unbelievers, rejecters of the gospel and persecutors of believers shall at the day of judgment [be punished] with everlasting destruction, so that no room is left for a state of trial, and a space to repent before that time for many ages in hell.

So 'tis apparent in Matt. 25 that none will be found at the right hand but they that have done such good works as can be done only in this world, which would not be declared beforehand if there was an opportunity given for millions of others to obtain that privilege.

(3) If that should be supposed (however unreasonably) that it were already declared, as it were by a peremptory sentence of the Judge, that [the notion of] all sinners continuing obstinate during this life should be condemned at the day of judgment is consistent with their being in a state of probation in order to escaping condemnation during the space between death and the general judgment; yet the account the Scripture gives of that day, in several of those forementioned texts, is inconsistent with men's being in a state of trial during that space. For if they are in a state of trial during that space, then they are accountable for their ill improvement of that space, and [are] the proper subjects of judgment and condemnation for their wickedness during that space, and so those works would come into the account when they appear at the great judgment as well as those committed in the body, which were no more committed in a state of probation than these. This is not consistent with everyone's receiving of things according to things done in the body, or in proportion to the guilt that everyone contracted then. 'Tis inconsistent with the description Christ gives of the day of judgment in Matt. 25, where Christ not only says to them at the right hand, "I was an hungered, and ye gave me meat" [v. 35], etc., and the good works are all such as are done only in this world, but all the wickedness which those are condemned for who are at the left hand is such as is committed in this life only.

(4) It may be proved that the day of man's trial, and the time of God's

striving in the use of means to bring him to repentance, and waiting for his repentance under the use of means, will not be continued after this life, from those words, Gen. 6[:3], "My Spirit shall not always strive with man, for that he also is flesh: yet his days shall be 120 years." 'Tis as much as to say: "'Tis not fit that the day of trial and opportunity should last always to obstinate, perverse sinners. 'Tis fit some bounds should be set to my striving and waiting on such as abuse the day of my patience. And those merciful means and gracious calls and knocks should not be continued without limits to them that trample all means and mercies under foot, and turn a deaf ear to all calls and knocks and invitations, and treat 'em with constant contempt. Therefore I will fix a certain limit. I will set his bounds to 120 years, when, if they repent not, I will put an end to all their lives, and with their lives shall be an end of my striving and waiting."

This which in Genesis is called God's Spirit's striving is by the apostle Peter expressed by "the long-suffering of God," its waiting (I Pet. 3:20). But according to the doctrine we are opposing, instead of God's striving and using means to bring those wicked men to repentance, and waiting in the use of strivings and endeavors 120 years, or to the end of their lives and no longer, he has gone on still since that for above 4000 years, striving with them in the use of more powerful means to bring 'em to repentance, and waiting on them, and will continue so afterwards for so long a time that the time is often called everlasting and represented as enduring forever and ever.

(5) Those words of Christ, "I must work the works of him that sent me, while it is day: the night cometh, wherein no man can work" (John 9:4), do prove that there is no other day of trial after this life. Christ, having undertaken for us and taken on him our nature, and appearing in the form of a servant, and standing as our surety and representative, he had a great work appointed him of God to do in this life for eternity. He could obtain[7] eternal life and happiness for himself no other way than by doing that work in this life, which was the time of his probation for eternity as well as ours. And therefore his words imply as much as if he had said, "I must do that work which God has appointed me to do for eternity, that great service which must be done as I would be eternally happy, now while the day of life lasts, which is the only day appointed for the trial of man's faithfulness in the service of God, in order to his being accepted to eternal rewards. Death is coming, which will be the setting of the sun,

7. MS: "not obtain."

and the end of this day, after which no work will remain, nothing to be done that will be of any significance in order to the obtaining the recompense of eternal felicity."

(6) And doubtless to the same purpose is that in Eccles. 9[:10], "Whatsoever thy hand findeth to do, do it with thy might; for there is no work" (or "no man can work"), "nor device, nor knowledge, nor wisdom, in the grave, whither thou goest." As much as to say, "After this life nothing can be done, nothing invented or devised in order to your happiness, no wisdom or art will serve you to any such purpose, if you neglect the time of the present life." 'Tis unreasonable to suppose the wise [man] means only that we should do all that we can in temporal concerns and to promote our temporal interests, and that nothing can be done towards this after this life, not only because this would be an observation of very little importance, as flat and impertinent, as if he had said, "Whatever your hand finds to do this year, do it with your might, for nothing that you do or devise the next year will signify anything to promote your interest and happiness this"; but also because the wise man himself, in the conclusion of this book, informs us that his drift through the whole book is to induce us to do a spiritual work, to fear God and keep his commandments, in order not to happiness in this life (which he tells us through the book is never to be expected), but in order to a future happiness and retribution in consequence of a judgment to come. Ch. 12:13–14, "Let us hear the conclusion of the whole matter: Fear God, and keep his commandments: for this is the whole" (i.e. the whole business, the whole concern) "of man. For God will bring every work into judgment, [. . .] whether it be good, or whether it be evil."

(7)[8] Matt. 5:25–26, "Agree with thine adversary quickly, while thou art in the way with him; lest at any time the adversary deliver thee to the judge, and the judge deliver thee to the officer, and thou be cast into prison. Verily I say unto thee, Thou shalt not come out thence, till thou hast paid the uttermost farthing." These words imply that sinners are in the way with their adversary, having opportunity to be reconciled to him but for a short season, inasmuch as it is intimated that they must agree with him quickly or they will cease to be in the way with him, or to have opportunity to obtain his favor any more. But if they will be continued in a state of probation after death to the end of the world, and after that for, as it were, endless ages, how far, how very far, are these words of Christ from representing the matter as it is.

8. MS: "9." See above, p. 394, n. 1.

(8)[9] If sinners after the day of judgment are to have another state of time of trial, then it will follow that after their trial there must be another judgment, and so that the judgment of that great and last day is not the last judgment. The sentence that will then [be] pronounced will not be the final sentence. Which seems to disagree with many things in Scripture, particularly with Heb. 9:27–28, "And as it is appointed to men once to die, and after this the judgment: so Christ was once offered to bear the sins of many; and to them that look for him shall he appear the second time without sin to salvation"; which plainly implies that as it is appointed to men once to die in consequence of their sin, and after death is but one judgment, but one sentence of condemnation, so Christ died but once, and by once dying removed that one, final condemnation and procured that, instead of that, he should come at the last day to pronounce a final, blessed sentence on them that look for him. These things imply that there is but one judgment after death, and that the great day of judgment that shall be at the end of the world shall be decisive and final, both with respect to sinners and saints, and not to be succeeded by another trial and another judgment.

Arg.[1] That some, even in this world, are utterly forsaken of God and given up to their own hearts' lusts proves that these men will never be purified from their sins. That God should use great means to purify 'em and fit 'em for eternal happiness and glory in the enjoyment of himself is not consistent with his having, after the use of great means and endeavors, given 'em up to sin because of their incorrigibleness and perverse, obstinate continuance in rebellion under the use of great means, and so leaving them to be desperately hardened in sin, and to go on and increase their guilt, and multiply transgressions to their utter ruin—which is agreeable to manifold Scripture representations. This is not agreeable to the scheme of such as suppose that God is all the while, both before and after death, prosecuting the design of purifying, and preparing them for and bringing them to eternal glory. (Consider Prov. 16:4. Also here observe Ps. 92:7. These places show that God has no merciful design with [those] whom he gives up to sin.)

Arg. The Apostle, in Heb. 6:4–6, says, "it is impossible for those who were once enlightened, and have tasted of the heavenly gift," etc., "If they

9. MS: "10." See above, p. 394, n. 1. A vertical use line runs through this entire paragraph in the MS.

1. JE stopped numbering his subheads here (in the MS, JE, Jr., has numbered the subsequent subheads). What follows is an unnumbered series of arguments and other notes against the notion of the future probation, purgation, and salvation of the impenitent after death.

fall away, to renew them again to repentance; seeing they crucify to themselves the Son of God afresh, and put him to an open shame," etc. The
Apostle speaks of their renovation to repentance as (at least) never likely
to be, on that account, that they have proved irreclaimable under such
great means to bring 'em to repentance, and have thereby so desperately
hardened their hearts, and contracted such great guilt by sinning against
such great light and trampling on such great privileges. But if so, how
much more unlikely still will it be that they should ever be renewed to
repentance after they have gone on still more and more to harden their
hearts by an obstinate, willful continuance in sin many thousand years
longer, under much greater means, and have therefore done immensely
more to establish the habit of sin and increase the hardness of their
hearts, and after their guilt is so vastly increased, instead of being diminished.

If it be impossible to bring 'em to repentance after they rebelled
against such great light and knowledge of Christ and the things of another world, as they had in this life, how much more impossible when,
added to this, they have had that infinitely greater and clearer knowledge of [and] view of these things which they will have at the day of judgment, when they shall see Christ in [the] glory of his Father, with all his
holy angels; shall see his great majesty, shall see the truth of the things
of the word of God and know the truth of its promises and threatenings
by sight and experience, and shall see all those ineffable manifestations
of the glory of Christ, of his power, omniscience, strict, inflexible justice,
infinite holiness and purity, truth and faith and infinite mercy to penitents; and the evidences of the dreadful consequences of rebellion and
wickedness, and the infinitely happy and glorious consequences of the
contrary withal, even at that time having the offers of mercy, of deliverance from that dreadful misery and the enjoyment of the favor of that
great Judge, and a participation of all the happiness and glory of the
righteous, which they shall see at his right hand, if then they will throw
down the weapons of their rebellion and repent and comply with his will;
and they still, from the greatness of their enmity and perverseness, obstinately and willfully refuse, yea, and continue still thus refusing even
after they have actually felt the terrible wrath of God and are cast into
the lake of fire, yea, after they have continued there many ages, all the
while under offers of mercy on repentance—I say, if it be impossible to
renew 'em to repentance after their rebelling against and trampling on
the light and knowledge and means used with them in this world, so that
[it] is not to be expected because of the degree of hardness and guilt

contracted by it, how much less is it to be expected after all this, and all the obstinacy manifested and hardness and guilt contracted at the end of all.

If guilt be contracted by despising such means and advantages as the Apostle has respect to in this life, that it may be compared to guilt that would be contracted by crucifying Christ afresh, how much more when, added to this, they shall so openly have despised Christ, when appearing to them in all the terrors and glories and love that shall be manifested at the day of judgment, in their immediate and most clear view, and all is offered to them if they will but yield subjection to him; and their enmity shall have appeared so desperate as rather to choose that dreadful lake of fire, and shall have continued in their choice even after they have felt the severity of that torment without rest, day or night, for many ages?

Arg. That all shall not be finally purified and saved is manifest from that, Matt. 12:31–32, with Mark 3:28–29 and Luke 12:10, I John 5:16. From each of these places it is manifest that he that is guilty of blasphemy against the Holy Ghost shall surely be damned, without any deliverance from his punishment or end to it. But the various expressions that are used serve much to certify and fix the import of others. In Matt. 12:31 it is said, "I say unto you, All manner of sin and blasphemy shall be forgiven unto men: but the blasphemy against the Holy Ghost shall not be forgiven unto men." The negative is general and equally respects all times. If this sin should be forgiven at a remote time, it would be as contrary to such a negative as this as if it were forgiven immediately.

But to determine us that Christ has respect to all times, even the remotest, and that he means to deny that he shall be forgiven at any time whatsoever, in Mark [3:29] it is said he shall NEVER be forgiven, or "hath NEVER FORGIVENESS." And lest this "never" should be interpreted "never as long as he lives," or "never in this world," 'tis said in Matt. 12:32, "it shall not be forgiven him, neither in this world, nor in the world to come." And lest it should be said, that although he never is forgiven, yet that don't hinder but that there may be an end to his punishment, because he may suffer all that he deserves in suffering a temporal punishment, or punishment of a limited, long duration, and he that is acquitted on paying all his debt is not said to be forgiven his debt; another expression is used in Mark [3:29], which shows that the thing that will show that he shall never be forgiven is that he shall ever suffer damnation and never have deliverance from his misery: "hath never forgiveness, but is in danger of eternal damnation." And the forementioned expressions of "he shall [never] be forgiven," "he hath never forgiveness," "shall not be forgiven in this world and the world to come," show the meaning of the word "eternal" here to be such as absolutely excludes any period, any time of favor, or wherein wrath, condemnation and punishment shall have ceased.

And what the apostle John says of such as commit the unpardonable sin confirms the whole, and proves that he that has committed this sin remains under no dispensation of mercy, and that no favor is ever to be hoped for from God for him; and therefore 'tis not our duty to pray for favor for such. I John 5:16, "If any man see his brother sin a sin which is not unto death, he shall ask, and he shall give him life for them that sin not unto death. There is a sin unto death: I do not say he shall pray for it"; or, "I give you no direction to pray for life for them that sin that sin unto death."

Thus it is evident that all wicked men will [not] have an end to their damnation, but when it is said they are in danger of eternal or everlasting damnation the word eternal is to be understood in the strictest sense. The same terms are used concerning all impenitent, all that die in sin, that they shall be sentenced to eternal punishment and shall "go into everlasting punishment," etc., that "their worm dieth not," and "their fire is not quenched," and that "they shall be tormented forever and ever," and such terms used, after this world comes to an end; and also when they that have committed the unpardonable sin and others shall be sentenced all together to an everlasting fire, in the same terms. 'Tis unreasonable to suppose that the punishment of some will be everlasting in an infinitely different sense from others jointly sentenced, that the duration of the punishment of one shall be perfectly as nothing compared with the duration of the punishment of the other, infinitely less than a second to a million ages. And 'tis unreasonable to suppose such a difference also on this account, that there cannot be such a difference in the demerit of them that commit the unpardonable sin and the demerit of the sins of all other wicked men, some of which are exceedingly and almost unconceivably wicked. There can't be a truly infinite difference in their guilt, as there must be a properly infinite difference between the dreadfulness of those torments that have an end, however long continued and however great, and the torments of a truly and strictly everlasting fire.

Arg. If the damned in hell shall all finally be saved, they shall be saved [without Christ]. 'Tis in itself unreasonable to suppose, that since God has done such great things for the salvation of mankind, things that are celebrated in such a manner in Scripture, in both Old Testament and

New, expressed everywhere in such exalted terms; things that the Prophet, and Apostle from him, says—"Eye had not seen, nor ear heard, nor had it entered into the heart, to conceive from the beginning of the world."[2]—I say, since God has done things so transcendently great for the salvation of sinners, to open a door for their escape from misery, 'tis unreasonable to imagine, that when this joyful tiding is proclaimed to sinners and this glorious Savior and great salvation are offered to 'em, and they fail of being saved by Christ only through their willful obstinacy and contempt, that after all God would put 'em into such a state that they shall have salvation offered to 'em at any time, whenever they (being left to the freedom of their own wills) see cause to repent and subject themselves to God without Christ, or any concern in that sacrifice he has offered for sin.

The Scripture teaches us that there is no remission of sin without sacrifice to atone for sin, that without the shedding of blood there is no remission. But since God has provided so great a sacrifice for sin as that of his only begotten Son, the Creator and Ruler and great Judge of the universe, surely 'tis unreasonable to expect that any other will be appointed in the room of this for sinners' salvation because they obstinately reject this. Besides, [the Scripture teaches] that there is salvation in no other, and no other name given under heaven by which men must be saved, and he is the true light that lighteth every man that ever is enlightened; that life and happiness for men is in him and him only; that he only is the way to the Father, and that his one sacrifice is the only sacrifice for sin, as is abundantly declared in the epistle to the Hebrews.

The Levitical priesthood lasted long, but finally gave place to that of Christ. But Christ gives place to no other, is not to be succeeded by another sacrifice by which the damned that have rejected this shall at last be saved. For by the oath of God he is a priest forever. He hath an everlasting priesthood. 'Tis plainly implied in Heb. 8 that God, finding fault with the ancient priesthood and sacrifices, removed 'em, as not making anything perfect, not completing the designs of God's holiness, wisdom and grace, to make way for the priesthood and sacrifice of Christ, which he finds no fault with, and by which perfection is arrived at, and which therefore God establishes with a design never to remove it or introduce any other, but that this should continue forever as an unchangeable priesthood. And therefore Christ, by the word of the oath, is consecrated forevermore.

2. A loose paraphrase and combination of I Cor. 2:9 and Is. 64:4.

In Heb. 10:26–27, the Apostle says, "if we sin willfully after we have received the knowledge of the truth, there remaineth no more sacrifice for sin, but a certain fearful looking for of judgment and fiery indignation, which shall devour the adversaries." By which two things are manifest: 1. that without a sacrifice for sin there is no deliverance from punishment; and 2. that there is no other sacrifice for sin by which sinners can be delivered but that of Christ.

But now I come to observe that the damned in hell never will be saved by Christ, or through his sacrifice. This is implied in that, Heb. 9:27–28, "As it is appointed to men once to die, and after this the judgment: so Christ was once offered," intimating that if after death there was not to be a final and decisive judgment, but still there was to be a door opened for sinners' salvation by Christ, there might be more reason to suppose it needful that he should be offered again, because Christ tabernacled with men in this world, was united to them and conformed to them, only to save men in this world or in this present, mortal state. But the Apostle's drift plainly supposes that this will not be, but that final judgment will be passed after death, and no door opened for salvation anymore, and so no occasion for any further sacrifice, or this sacrifice being offered again.

And further, 'tis manifest that Christ's saving work will be at an end at the day of judgment in that, as Christ has a twofold office, that of the Savior of the world, the other the Judge of the world, so the business of the latter office properly succeeds the former. And 'tis not fit, in the nature of things, that he should come into the world and appear openly in the character and work of universal Judge, to decide men's state in consequence of the trial there has been for making their state better by his salvation, till that trial is over and all its effects completed, when no more is to be hoped as to altering men's state for the better by his salvation. Then is the proper season for him to clothe himself with his other character and appear in his other character, that of a Judge, to decide and fix men's final and everlasting state. Therefore Christ, at his first coming, appeared to save men from condemnation and a sentence of eternal misery, and not to judge 'em, as he tells, John 12:47, "if any man hear my words, and believe not, I judge him not: for I came not to judge the world, but to save the world" (see also ch. 3:17, and 8:15). But the great business he will come upon at his second coming, as is abundantly declared, is to judge the world.

And 'tis also exceeding plain that Christ's saving work will be at an end at the day of judgment, because we read that all power was given him in heaven and earth, that he might give eternal life to as many as God had given him. He was exalted at God's own right hand to be a prince and a Savior, had a commission given him of the Father to govern the kingdom and manage the affairs of it by an universal dominion over heaven and [earth], that he might order all in subservience to the great design of accomplishing the salvation of men. He was made [head] over all things to the church. But we read, II Cor. 15, that [at] the end of the world he will deliver up this kingdom. He will resign this commission, which proves that the work of salvation, which is the design of it, will be at an end, when all his enemies, all that rejected him and would not have him to rule over 'em, and so have failed of his salvation, shall be made his footstool, and condemned and destroyed, instead of the heirs of salvation. He shall come in flaming fire to take vengeance on them that know not God and obey not the gospel of Jesus Christ, who shall be punished with everlasting destruction, etc., when he shall come to be glorified in his saints, and admired in all them that believe (II Thess. 1:8–10).

Arg. If the damned, after they have suffered a while, are to be delivered and to have eternal life, then the present dispensation of grace and life to the fallen children of men, that was introduced by Christ and his apostles after the ceasing of the old Mosaic dispensation, is not the last. But another is to be introduced after this ceases, and with regard to them with whom, through the flesh or through their sin and corruption, it has proved unprofitable and ineffectual.

A new method must be entered upon of God's gracious dealings with sinners. And as we must suppose [. . .]³

[1349. THE DIVINITY OF CHRIST.]⁴ If the temptation to the children of Israel was so great to idolize the BRAZEN SERPENT, a lifeless piece of brass, for the temporal salvation some of their forefathers had by looking on it, how great would be the temptation to idolatry by worshipping Christ if he were a mere creature from [whom] mankind receive so great benefits. If that BRAZEN SERPENT must be broken in pieces to remove

3. In the MS, entry No. [1348] ends here with a note by JE reading "see further, p. 970." This is a reference to the beginning of the materials numbered by JE, Jr., as "Miscellanies" No. [1356], which is simply an extension of No. [1348], picking up in mid-sentence, right where JE left off. See below, p. 575.

4. MS evidence suggests that this entry, too, constituted a set of notes in preparation for a treatise on the subject. Its entry number was provided by JE, Jr.

temptation to idolatry (II Kgs. 18:4), shall so great a temptation be laid before the world to idolize a mere creature by setting him forth in the manner that he is set forth in Scripture?

Must MOSES' BODY be concealed lest the children of Israel should worship the remains of him whom God made the instrument of such great things? And shall another mere creature, whom men, on account of the works he has done, are under infinitely greater temptation to worship, instead of his being concealed to prevent this, be most openly and publicly exhibited as exalted to heaven, seated at God's own right hand, made head over all things, ruler of the universe, etc., in the manner that Christ is?

Was not this the temptation to all nations to idolatry, viz. that men had been distinguished as great conquerors, deliverers, and the instruments of great benefits? And shall God make a mere creature the instrument of so many infinitely great benefits, and in such a manner as Christ has been and is represented to be in the Scripture, without an infinitely great temptation to idolatry?

When the rich young man called Christ "Good Master" [Matt. 19:16, Mark 10:17, Luke 18:18], not supposing him to be God, did [not] Christ reject it and reprove him for calling himself [by that name], supposing him not to [be] God, saying "there is none GOOD BUT ONE, that is, God," meaning that none other was possessed of that goodness that was to be trusted (see note on the place in "Blank Bible")?[5] And yet shall this same Jesus, when indeed not God, not that God who only is to be called good or trusted in as such, be called in Scripture he that is holy, he that [is] true, the Amen, the faithful and true witness, the mighty God, the everlasting Father, the Prince of Peace, the blessed and the only potentate, the King of kings and Lord of lords, the Lord of life that has life in himself, that all men might honor the Son as they honor the Father, the wisdom of God, the power of God, the Alpha and Omega, the Beginning and the End, God, Jehovah, Elohim, the King of Glory (see Mastrict, p. 254)?[6]

---

5. In the "Blank Bible" note on Matt. 19:17, JE observes that Christ's reproof to the young man meant that "there is none else who has a goodness that is to be depended upon but God. For Christ don't find fault with any man being called good, for he, using the same words, calls some men good himself."

6. Peter van Mastricht, *Theoretico-Practica Theologicae* (Rhenum, 1715), Lib. II, cap. 26, "De Deo Filio," § ix: "Ubi igitur *Assumptio* fuerit demonstrata, confectum erit negotium, demonstramus autem singulatim. *Primò,* divina *nomine* ipsi competere, eo patet, quod (a) *Jehova* appelletur [. . .] quibus locis, *tentatus* ab Israelitis, & proptera immittens serpentes igneos, dicitur suisse *Jehova:* idem rursus dicitur suisse *Angelus faciei* Jes. lxiii. 10. ac disertè etiam *Christi* I.

Is. 42:8. See "Notes on Scripture," no. 479;[7] compare Ps. 83:18.

Is. 45:20–21 ff., "and pray unto a god that cannot save. Tell ye, and bring them near; let them take counsel together: . . . there is no God else beside me; a just God and a Savior; there is none beside me." And yet it is said of Christ that "he is able to save unto the uttermost" [Heb. 7:25]. Yea, the Messiah, in this very book, is spoken [of] as "mighty to save," saving by his "own arm," and by "the greatness of his strength," Is. 63:1–6, compared with Rev. 19:15. And 'tis evident that 'tis his character in the most eminent manner to be the Savior of God's people, and that with respect to that which is infinitely [the] highest and greatest work of salvation, the greatest deliverance from the most dreadful evil, from the greatest, worst and strongest enemies, and bringing them to the greatest happiness.

It follows there, v. 22, "Look to me, and be ye saved, all the ends of the earth: for I am God, and there is none else." Here it is spoken of as the great glory of God, and peculiar to him, that he is an universal Savior, not only of the Jews but of all nations. And this is the peculiar character of Jesus. He is the Savior of all nations. The glory of calling and saving the Gentiles is represented as peculiarly belonging to him, so that he has this divine prerogative which is spoken of here as belonging to the one, only God, and to none else. And, which is more than all this, these very things that are spoken here about God as the only Savior, and the honor and trust due to him on that account, are applied to Christ in the New Testament. Phil. 2:10–11, "Every knee shall bow," etc. And the things spoken of in the following verses as the peculiar prerogatives of God in distinction from all other beings as the only Savior, viz. having righteousness and being justified in him, are most eminently ascribed to Christ, as in a most special manner belonging to him, everywhere in the New Testament.

Being the SAVIOR of God's people is everywhere in the Old Testament mentioned as the peculiar work of the Deity. The heathen are reproached for worshipping gods that could not save. And God says to the idolatrous Israelites, "Go to the gods whom ye have served; let them de-

---

Cor. x. 9. Rursus Psal. cii. 17. 26. 27. proculdubio sermo est de *Jehova;* sed ibi sermo est de *Filio* Heb. i. 9. Item Ps. lxviii. 19 quod de *Filio* dici, Paulus docet Eph. iv. 8. 9. Hoc autem *nomen,* soli *summo* Deo competere, supra demonstravimus Cap. iv. Quod (b) *Elohim* dicetur Psalm. xlv. 7. 8. & lxviii. 8. 9. 10. 19. 20. [. . .] Quod (e) δεος, non tantum *attributue* Rom. ix. 5. Rom. i. 3. 4. Tit. ii. 13. Jud. vers. 4. I. Joh. v. 20 [. . .] Quod (f) κυριος [. . .] cui respondet nomen *Jehova.*"

7. *Works, 15,* 576–77.

liver you" [Judg. 10:14]. See Is. 43:3, 10–14, in which verses we have another clear demonstration of the divinity of Christ. See also Hos. 13:4. See also Is. 49:26, and 60:16; Deut. 33:29; Jer. 3:23; Jonah 2:8–9; Ps. 3:8; Is. 25:9.

And how often is a being the Redeemer of God's people spoken of as the peculiar character of the mighty God of Jacob, the first and last, the only God, the Lord of hosts, the holy one of Israel. Is. 41:14, 43:14, and 44:6, 24, and 47:4, and 48:17, and 49:7, 26, and 54:5, and ch. 60:16.

And it may be observed that, from time to time, when God has this title of the Redeemer of Israel ascribed in those places in this book, it is from time to time joined with some other of the peculiar and most exalted names and titles of the most high God: such as the Holy One of Israel (so Is. 41:14, and 43:14, and 47:4, and 48:17, and 49:7, and 44:5), the mighty One of Jacob (ch. 49:26, and ch. 60:16), the Lord of hosts (Is. 47:4, and 44:6), the God of the whole earth (ch. 54:5), the first and the last, besides whom there is no God (44:6), the Jehovah that maketh all things, that stretcheth forth the heavens alone and spreadeth abroad the earth by himself (v. 24). Yet the Messiah, in this very book, is spoken [of] as the Redeemer of God's people in the most eminent manner (ch. 63:1–6). And the name Jehovah is given to him, the King, the Lord of hosts, the Holy One (Is. 6:1–5), the mighty God (Is. 9:6).

God is careful that his people should understand that their honor and love and praise for the redemption out of Egypt belongs alone to him, and therefore is careful to inform 'em that he alone redeemed 'em out of Egypt, and that there was no other God with him, and to make use of that as a principal argument why they should have no other god before him (see Deut. 32:12, Ex. 20:3, Ps. 81:8–10, Hos. 13:4). The words in that place [Hos. 13:4] are remarkable: "Yet I am the Lord thy God from the land of Egypt, and thou shalt know [no] god but me: for there is no savior beside me." If God insisted on that as a good reason why his people [should] know no God besides him, and he alone was their Savior to save 'em out of Egypt, would he afterwards appoint another God to be their Savior in an infinitely greater salvation?

See my discourse of the "Fulfillment of Prophecies of the Messiah," § 5.[8]

II Pet. 1:1, "through the righteousness of God and our Savior Jesus

---

8. MS: "p. 11 &c," meaning "Fulfillment," § 5, MS pp. 11–20, a long entry that gathers a multitude of Old Testament texts to demonstrate the proposition, "It is evident, by the prophecies of the Messiah, that he was to be God."

Christ" (εν δικαιοσυνη του θεου ημων και σωτηρος Ιησου Χριστ). Tit.
2:13, "Looking for the blessed hope, and glorious appearing of the great
God and our Savior Jesus Christ" (του μεγαλου θεου και σωτηρος Ιησου
Χριστ). 'Tis agreeable to the manner of the Apostle's expressing himself
in both places to intend one and the same person, viz. Christ, under two
titles, as when speaking of God the Father in Eph. 1:3: "Blessed be the
God and Father of our Lord Jesus Christ" (ο θεος και πατηρ). See Dr.
Goodwin's *Works,* vol. 1, pp. 23–24.[9]

Compare the following texts one with another: Gen. 1:26, John 1:1–
4, Is. 40:13–14, Is. 9:6, I Cor. 2:10–11, John 5:17–19, Is. 6:8, Prov. 8:27–
31, John 17:21–22.

That in Is. 40:13–14, "Who hath directed the Spirit of the Lord,"
proves Christ's divinity, for Christ directs the Spirit of the Lord. See John
16:13–15, and many other places.

Trusting is abundantly represented as a principal thing in that peculiar respect due to God alone, as a peculiar part of the essence of divine adoration, due to no other than God. And yet how is Christ represented as the peculiar object of the faith and trust of all God's people,
of all nations, as having all-sufficiency for them. Trusting in any others
is greatly condemned, is a thing than which nothing more is represented
as dangerous, provoking to God and bringing his curse on men. Men are
abundantly called upon to trust in Christ, not only in the New Testament
but the Old, as in the end of the second Psalm and elsewhere.

The work of creation's being ascribed to Christ does most evidently
prove the proper divinity of Christ. For God declares that he is Jehovah,
that stretched forth the heavens alone and spread abroad the earth by
himself (Is. 44:24; see also the next chapter, 45:5–7, 12). And not only
is the creation of the world ascribed to Christ often in Scripture, but that
which in this book of Isaiah is called the [new] creation, which is here
represented as an immensely greater and more glorious work than the
old creation, viz. the work of redemption, as this Prophet himself explains it (Is. 65:17–19), is everywhere, in a most peculiar and distinguishing manner, ascribed to Christ.

The following things from Dr. Waterland's *Answer to Some Queries.*[1]
Compare the following texts set in opposite columns one against another:

9. The reference is to an exposition of Eph. 1:3 in Goodwin's *Exposition on Ephesians, Works,*
vol. 1, Pt. 1, pp. 23–24.

1. Daniel Waterland, *An answer to some queries printed at Exon, relating to the Arian controversy*
(London, 1721).

Is. 45:5 and   John 1:1
44:8 and   Heb. 1:8
46:9 against   Rom. 9:5
a created God.   Phil. 2:6
                        Heb. 3:1

Texts where Christ is called Jehovah. Compare:

Ps. 102:25 ff.   Heb. 1:10
Zech. 11:12   Matt. 27:9–10
Zech. 12:10   John 19:37
Is. 40:3   Mark 1:3
Hos. 1:7   Luke 2:11

Compare:

I Kgs. 8:39   John 2:24 and 16:30, and Acts 1:24
Jer. 17:10   Rev. 2:3
Is. 44:6   Rev. 1:17
Rev. 1:8   Rev. 22:13
I Tim. 6:15   Rev. 17:14, 19:16
Is. 10:21   Is. 9:6
Rom. 10:12   Acts 10:36, Rom. 9:5
Ps. 90:2   Prov. 8:22 ff.
Neh. 9:6   John 1:3, Col. 1:16–17
Gen. 1:1   Heb. 1:10
Ex. 20:3   Luke 24:25, Heb. 1:6
Matt. 4:10   John 5:23

See Col. 1:16–17, Heb. 1:3, Gal. 4:8.

If Christ in the beginning created the heavens and the earth, he must be from ETERNITY. For then he is before the beginning, by which must be meant the beginning of time, the beginning of that kind of duration which has beginning and following, before and after, belonging to it, the beginning of created existence, or "the beginning of the creation which God created," as the phrase is, Mark 13:19.

In Prov. 8:22, 'tis said "The Lord possessed me [. . .] before his works of old," and therefore before those works which in Gen. 1:1 are said to be made in the beginning.

God's eternity is expressed thus, Ps. 90:2, "Before the mountains were brought forth, or ever thou hadst created the earth and the world, even from everlasting." So it is said, Prov. 8:22–26, "The Lord possessed me in the beginning of his way, before his works of old. I was set up from everlasting, from the beginning, or ever the earth was. When there were no depths, I was brought forth; when there were no fountains abounding with water. Before the mountains were settled, before the hills was I brought forth; when as yet he had not made the earth, nor the fields, nor the highest part of the dust of the world."

In Heb. 7:3, Christ is spoken of as being without "beginning of days, or end of life." And in Mic. 5:2, his "goings forth" are said to be "of old, from everlasting." See notes on the place.[2]

Moses' building an altar and calling it *Jehovah Nissi* is an evidence that Christ is Jehovah. 'Tis he especially that is set up as the banner or ensign of the church, agreeable to Is. 11:10. See note on the place, "Notes on Scripture," no. 205.[3] And this rod of Moses, that was held up by Moses over Israel in that battle with Amalek, was manifestly typical of that rod out of the stem or root of Jesse there spoken of.

CHRIST'S ETERNITY. Heb. 7:3, "having neither beginning of days, nor end of life; but made like unto the Son of God."

How the divinity of Christ is proved from II Pet. 3:8. See Poole's *Synopsis* in loc.[4]

Particularly consider John 5:17–29. Show how this context abounds with evidence of Christ's divinity, comparing one passage with another. And compare this context with John 10:30–38.

That the kingdom of the Messiah is so commonly called "the KINGDOM OF HEAVEN" is an evidence that the Messiah is God. By the kingdom of heaven is plainly meant a kingdom wherein God doth reign, or is King. The phrase "the kingdom of heaven" seems to be principally taken from Dan. 2:44, "And in the days of these kings shall the God of heaven set up a kingdom," where the meaning plainly is: After the heads of those four great monarchies have each one had their turn, and erected kingdoms for themselves in their turn, and the last monarchy shall be divided among ten kings, finally the God of heaven shall take the dominion from

2. "Scripture" no. 501a, in *Works, 15,* 594–98. In the "Blank Bible" note on the verse, JE, quoting Matthew Henry's *Exposition of the Old Testament* (4 vols., London, 1708–12), writes that "'Dr. Pococke observes that the "going forth" is used for a word which proceedeth out of the mouth (Deut. 8:3), and is therefore very fitly used to signify the eternal generation of him who is called the Word of God, that was in the beginning with God.'" "Dr. Pococke" is Edward Pococke, who wrote *A commentary on the prophecy of Micah* (London, 1677).

3. MS: "B. 4, p. 6." *Works, 15,* 128–29. As JE discusses there, *Jehovah Nissi* means "the Lord my banner."

4. Poole, *Synopsis Criticorum, IV,* Pt. II, col. 1574.

'em all, and shall set up a kingdom for himself. He shall take the kingdom and shall rule forever. In this book, ch. 4:26, "that thou shalt have known that the heavens do rule," the words in the foregoing verse express what is meant: "till thou know that the Most High ruleth in the kingdom of men."

Therefore, by the kingdom of heaven which shall be set up is meant the kingdom wherein God himself shall be the King, not as reigning and administering by other kings or judges as he was king in the time of the Judges and in the time of David, Solomon, Hezekiah and Josiah, etc., and as he always doth in the time of good kings; but he shall set up a kingdom that shall be his kingdom, in a distinction from all kingdoms or states that ever were administered by created heads, and wherein he himself shall reign, wherein the heavens shall rule, or God himself shall be king. And therefore, the kingdom of heaven is often called the kingdom of God in the New Testament. And 'tis abundantly prophesied in the Old Testament that, in the days of the Messiah, God shall take to himself the kingdom, and shall reign as King in contradistinction to other reigning, subordinate beings. And that God himself shall reign on earth as King among his people is abundantly manifest from many prophecies, as Ps. 93:1, and 96:10, and 97 at the beginning, and 99:1; Is. 33:22 (see "Fulfillment of Prophecies of the Messiah," § 5);[5] Is. 40:9–11; Zeph. 3:14–15; Mal. 3:1–3.

But in this very prophecy of Daniel ch. 7, where this kingdom, which the Lord of heaven should at last set up (plainly this same kingdom), is more fully spoken [of], 'tis manifest that 'tis the Messiah that is to be the King in that kingdom, who shall reign as vested with full power and complete kingly authority. He is the anointed king (see Dan. 9:25). So he is abundantly spoken of as King of God's people in the principal prophecies, as in Jacob's prophecy; in the blessing of Judah (Gen. 49); and in Balaam's prophecy; and in God's promises to David; and in David's last words; and in the second Psalm, and [Psalms] 110 and 89 and 45; and in those great prophecies of the Messiah: Is. 9 and ch. 11; and Zech. 6; and Jer. 23:5, and 30:9, and 33:15; Ezek. 34:23, and 37:24; Hos. 3:5; Zech. 6:12 ff.; and many others.

God is several times called in Scripture the "GLORY" OF ISRAEL, or of God's people. And 'tis a title given him as peculiar to him, wherein he

---

5. MS: "p. 18. b." In this passage of "Fulfillment," § 5, JE cites Is. 32 and 33 as evidence that the Messiah shall be "the great King that should reign over" the church as well as the "Lawgiver, Judge, and Savior, light and defense and refreshment of his church."

appears as especially distinguished from false gods. Jer. 2:11, "Hath a nation changed their gods, which yet are no gods? but my people have changed their glory for that which doth not profit." Ps. 106:2, "Thus they changed their glory into the similitude of an ox that eateth grass." But we find that Christ, in the New Testament, is spoken of as "the glory of God's people Israel" (Luke 2:32).

What is said in Job 19:25–27, "For I know that my redeemer liveth," etc., is a proof of the divinity of Christ. For here: 1. He that Job calls his "redeemer," his *Goel*,[6] is God, for he calls him [God]. "Yet in my flesh shall I see God" [v. 26]. But 'tis very manifest that Christ is he that is most properly and eminently our Redeemer, or *Goel*. And then, 2. Here Job says that God "shall stand at the latter day," and at the general resurrection, "on the earth," when he shall see him in his flesh [vv. 25–26]. But the person that shall then stand on the earth, we know, is no other than Jesus Christ. And how often in other places, both in Old Testament and New, is Christ's coming to judgment spoken of as God's coming to judgment, Christ's appearing as God's appearing, and our standing before the judgment seat of Christ as our standing before God's judgment seat.

Luke 1:16–17, "And many of the children of Israel shall he turn to the Lord their God. And he shall go before him in the spirit and power of Elias, to turn the hearts of fathers to the children, and of the disobedient to the wisdom of the just; to make ready a people prepared for the Lord." Here John the Baptist is spoken of as going before the Lord, the God of the children of Israel, to prepare his ways, agreeable to the prophecies, particularly Mal. 3:1, and 4:5–6.

But who is this person that is called the Lord, the God of Israel, whose forerunner, John the Baptist, is to prepare his way? And nothing is more manifest than that it is Jesus Christ. See Mark 1:1–3, "The beginning of the gospel of Jesus Christ, the Son of God; as it is written in the prophets, Behold, I send my messenger before thy face, who shall prepare thy way before thee. The voice of one crying in the wilderness, Prepare ye the way of the Lord, make his paths straight" (alluding to two prophecies, viz. Mal. 3:1 and Is. 40:3). Here is a distinction of two persons, the one speaking in the first person singular, "Behold, I send my messenger," the other spoken to in the second person, "before thy face, which shall prepare thy way before thee," which makes it evident that the person whose forerunner he was, to prepare his way, was Jesus Christ. So Matt. 11:10, Luke 7:27. See also how manifest this is by John 1:19, "And this is the

---

6. In Hebrew: גאל, meaning "kinsman, redeemer."

record of John"; v. 23, "I am the voice of one crying in the wilderness, Make straight the way of the Lord, as said the prophet Esaias," with the following verses, especially v. 31, "And I knew him not: but that he should be made manifest to Israel, therefore am I come baptizing with water."

So that 'tis evident that Christ is he that in that first [chapter] of Luke is called the Lord, the God of Israel, or Jehovah, the God of Israel, as the phrase is in the original of the Old Testament in places from whence this phrase is taken and rendered here in the Greek, according as those places are rendered in the Septuagint. Therefore 'tis evident that Christ is one God with God the Father. For the Scripture is very express that that Jehovah which is the God of Israel is but one Jehovah, as Deut. 6:4, "Hear, O Israel: Jehovah our God is one Jehovah."[7]

And if we look into those prophecies of the Old Testament referred to in these places of the Evangelists, 'tis manifest that what they foretell is a forerunner to prepare the way for the only true and supreme God, as Is. 40:3: "The voice of him that crieth in the wilderness, Prepare ye the way of JEHOVAH, make strait in the desert a high way for OUR GOD."

This is evidently the same that is spoken of in the following parts of the chapter, as in vv. 9, 10 and following verses:

> say unto the cities of Judah, Behold YOUR GOD! Behold, JEHOVAH GOD will come . . . He shall feed his flock like a shepherd . . . Who hath measured the waters in the hollow of his hand, and meted out heaven with a span, and comprehended the dust of the earth in a measure, and weighed the mountains in scales, and the hills in a balance? Who hath directed the Spirit of the Lord, or being his counselor hath taught him? With whom took he counsel, and who instructed him, and taught him in the path of judgment [. . .] Behold, the nations are as a drop of a bucket, and are counted as the small dust of the balance: behold, he taketh up the isles as a very little thing. And Lebanon is not sufficient to burn, nor the beasts thereof sufficient for a burnt offering. All nations before him are as nothing; and they

---

7. Here and very frequently below, JE renders the Hebrew Tetragrammaton (יֱהֹוִה or יְהֹוָה) in a much more literal and modern form than that found in the Septuagint (Κύριος), the Vulgate (*Dominus*), and thus the KJV as well ("the Lord"). Jews view this word as the most sacred name for God and, since well before the time of Jesus, have usually refused to pronounce it. But when vowel points were added to the extant MSS of the Hebrew Scriptures, those of another name for God (*Adonai*) were used to fill out the Tetragrammaton, making "Jehovah" a standard (Christian) rendering since the time of the Renaissance. In the KJV, Deut. 6:4 is translated, "Hear, O Israel: The Lord our God is one Lord."

are counted to him less than nothing, and vanity. To whom will ye liken God? or what likeness will ye compare unto him?

V. 22, "It is he that sitteth on the circle of the earth, and all the inhabitants thereof are as grasshoppers; that stretcheth out the heavens as a curtain, and spreadeth them out as a tent to dwell in: that bringeth the princes to nothing; and maketh the judges of the earth as vanity." If the supreme God is not spoken of here, where shall we find the place where he is spoken of? If it be an infinitely inferior being that is here spoken [of], where is God's distinguishing greatness and infinitely superior magnificence spoken of?

It here follows, v. 25, "To whom then will ye liken me, or shall I be equal? saith the Holy One." This plainly shows that 'tis the supreme, unequaled, unparalleled God that is here spoken of. A created being would not use such language and make such a challenge. He that is created himself would not say, as it follows in the next verse, "Lift up your eyes on high, behold who hath created these things."

So it is evident that it is the one only God that is spoken of, whose forerunner John was to be. Mal. 3:1, "Behold, I will send my messenger, and he shall prepare the way before ME: and JEHOVAH, whom ye seek, shall suddenly come into his temple." That God, whose forerunner John the Baptist is, is spoken of, as was observed before, as the God of Israel. But he is spoken of as the supreme God, II Chron. 6:14, "O Lord GOD OF ISRAEL, there is no God like thee in the heaven, nor in the earth" (see also Ps. 77:13). And he is spoken of as the only God, Is. 45:3, "I, JEHOVAH, which call thee by thy name, am the God of Israel." V. 5, "I am JEHOVAH, and there is none else, there is no God besides me." V. 6, "That they may know from the rising of the sun, and from the west, that there is none beside me. I am JEHOVAH, and there is none else." Vv. 14–15, "Surely God is in thee; there is none else, there is no God. Verily thou art a God that hidest thyself, O God of Israel, the Savior."

And then that God,[8] whose forerunner John the Baptist was, to prepare his way, is very expressly declared in the New Testament, as in Luke 1:76, "And thou, child, shalt be called the prophet of the HIGHEST, υψιστου: for thou shalt go before the face of the Lord to prepare his ways."

'Tis a great evidence that Christ is one being with the supreme God, that the SPIRIT of the supreme God is spoken of as his Spirit, and a Spirit

---

8. MS: "the God."

proceeding from him and sent and directed by him. The Spirit that the prophets of old were inspired by is spoken of as being the Spirit of Christ, I Pet. 1:11, "Searching what, or what manner of time the Spirit of Christ which was in them did signify, when it testified beforehand the sufferings of Christ, and the glory that should follow."

But it is very manifest that the Spirit that the prophets of old were inspired by was the Spirit [of] the one, only, living and true God, by which it came to pass that their word was the word of this God, as the Scripture ever represents. So that we must needs understand it, that the word written by the prophets is the word of the supreme God. See II Pet. 1:21, II Tim. 3:16. And that they spake by inspiration of the Spirit of the supreme God is manifest from Luke 1:69–70, "And hath raised up an horn of salvation for us in the house of his servant David; as he spake by the mouth of his holy prophets, which have been since the world began." Now none will deny but that the God that has raised up Christ as an horn of salvation for us is the supreme God. But we see that this God spake by the mouth of the prophets.

Again, none will deny but that it is the supreme God [that] is spoken [of], Heb. 1:5–12, "For unto which of the angels said he at any time, Thou art my Son, this day have I begotten thee? And again, I will be to him a Father, and he shall be to me a Son? And again, when he bringeth in the first begotten into the world, he saith, And let all the angels of God worship him. And of the angels he saith, Who maketh his angels spirits, and his ministers a flame of fire. But unto the Son he saith, Thy throne, O God, is forever and ever," etc. V. 10, "And, Thou, Lord, in the beginning hast laid the foundation of the earth; and the heavens are the work of thine hands: they shall perish; but thou remainest," etc. But if it is the supreme God that is spoken of as saying these things, then the prophets and inspired penmen of the Old Testament spake by inspiration of [the] Spirit of the supreme God. For, as to most of these things, God said them no otherwise than as the inspired penmen of the Scriptures said them. So God said, Ps. 104:4, he "maketh his angels spirits; and his ministers a flame of fire," no otherwise than as the penman of that Psalm said so by inspiration of his Spirit. So it was no otherwise that God said in Ps. 45:6–7, "Thy throne, O God," etc. Neither was it any otherwise that God said in Ps. 102:25 ff., "Thou Lord in the beginning hast laid the foundation of the earth," etc.

The word "Spirit," in the original languages, signifies wind, and sometimes is used to signify breath. Therefore Christ breathed on his disciples when he would signify to 'em that he would give 'em the Holy Ghost.

John 20:22, "And when he said this, he breathed on them, saying, Receive ye the Holy Ghost." This plainly teaches us that the Holy Ghost was his Spirit as much as man's breath is his breath. But the Holy Ghost is the Spirit of the supreme God and the Spirit of God the Father. For it was partly on this account that the virgin Mary's child is called the Son of God, because it was conceived by the power of the Holy Ghost (Luke 1:35), which shows that the Holy Ghost, by whose power he was conceived, was the Spirit of the Father.

Again, 'tis evident that the Spirit of God is the Spirit of Christ as much as a person's eyes are his own eyes. Rev. 5:6, "And I beheld, and, lo, in the midst of the throne [. . .] stood a Lamb as it had been slain, having seven horns and seven eyes, which are the seven Spirits of God sent forth into all the earth," alluding to Zech. 3:9, "upon one stone shall be seven eyes." But those seven eyes, in the next chapter, are spoken of as representing the Spirit of God, and the eyes of Jehovah. Ch. 4:6, "Not by might, nor power, but by my spirit, saith the Lord." V. 10, "and shall see the plummet in the hand of Zerubbabel with those seven; they are the eyes of the Lord, which run to and fro through the whole earth."

Christ is spoken of as sending the Holy Ghost and directing him. John 16:7, "I will send him unto you." Vv. 13–15, "Howbeit when he, the Spirit of truth, is come, he will guide you into all truth: for he shall not speak of himself; but whatsoever he shall hear, that shall he speak: and he shall show you things to come. He shall glorify me: for he shall receive of mine, and shall show it unto you. All things that the Father hath are mine: therefore said I, that he shall take of mine, and shall show it unto you." But 'tis spoken of as the peculiar prerogative of God to direct his Spirit. Is. 40:13, "Who hath directed the Spirit of the Lord?"

"Not all the wit of man, I believe, can devise a medium between the Creator and the creature, [. . .] whatever excellency of nature, or dignity of station, he might be distinguished by; suppose him a super-angelic spirit, incarnate in [the] human nature; still he must be only ranked with the hosts of the Lord; and not be distinguished by the honorable ascription of this most elevated divine character, 'the Lord of hosts.'" Mr. Foxcroft's Sermon Occasioned by the Earthquake, on Is. 29:6.[9] Jesus Christ is called "the Lord of hosts" in Is. 6:3.

9. Thomas Foxcroft, *A Sermon Preached to the Old Church in Boston, January 8, 1756. Being a Day of Publick Humiliation and Prayer, throughout the Province of the Massachusetts-Bay in New-England: Upon Occasion of the Repeated Shock of an Earthquake on This Continent, and the Very Destructive Earthquakes and Inundations in Divers Parts of Europe, All in the Month of November Last* (Boston, 1756), p. 17.

'Tis true that creatures are sometimes called god. The kings and judges of God's Israel, the ancient church, are called gods; but no otherwise than as types of Christ. And the angels, the highest of all, [are] called gods. But 'tis very remarkable that, in that only place where they are so called by God, they are commanded to worship Christ. And in the same verse a curse is denounced on all such as are guilty of idolatry. Ps. 97:7, compared with Heb. 1:6.

See argument from Rom. 8:32, MacLaurin's sermon on *God's Chief Mercy*, pp. 105–108.[1]

See argument for the divinity of Christ from II Pet. 1:1, "{Simon Peter, a servant and an apostle of Jesus Christ, to them that have} obtained like precious faith [. . .] through the righteousness of God and our Savior Jesus Christ." See Mr. Foxcroft's sermon on that text, pp. 27 ff., in the short box at the left hand of the larger bookcase, a pamphlet with a blue cover.[2]

The name that God calls himself by, viz. "jealous," and so often speaks of himself as a jealous God, signifying that he will by no means endure any other husband of his church, affords a clear evidence that Jesus Christ is the same God with God the Father. For Christ is spoken of often as that person who is, in the most eminent and peculiar manner, the husband and bridegroom of his church. And 'tis very manifest that that God, who is the same God with God the Father, is the husband of the church. For 'tis that God who is the Holy One of Israel, that is the husband of the church, as appears by Is. 54:5: "thy Maker is thy husband; the Lord of hosts is his name; and thy Redeemer the Holy One of Israel," or as the words are, "thy *Goel* the Holy One of Israel." The *Goel* was the near kinsman that married the widow who had lost her husband, as appears by Ruth 3:9, 12.[3] And, [as] such a desolate widow, the church is represented here in this chapter, at the beginning. But this Holy One of Israel is the name of that God that is God the Father, as appears by Is. 49:7 and 55:5, and so is the Lord of hosts, as appears by Is. 44:6.

That strongly argues the divinity of Christ in II Cor. 4:6, "For God, who commanded the light to shine out of darkness, hath shined in our hearts,

---

1. See John MacLaurin, "God's Chief Mercy," on Rom. 8:32, in Gillies, ed., *Sermons and Essays by the Late Reverend Mr. John M'Laurin*, pp. 105–108.

2. Thomas Foxcroft, *Like Precious Faith Obtained, through the Righteousness of Our God and Savior, by All the True Servants of Christ. A Sermon, Preached (in Sum) at the Old-Church-Lecture in Boston, Thursday, March 25th, 1756* (Boston, 1756). JE describes here the location of the sermon in his study.

3. See above, p. 419, n. 6.

to give the light of the knowledge of the glory of God in the face of Jesus Christ," or in the "person" of Jesus Christ, as the same word sometimes signifies, as Luke 20:21, II Cor. 1:11 and 2:10, Gal. 2:6, Jude 3, 16. Whether the latter be the most proper translation, yet doubtless God's glory as exhibited in the person of Christ is meant. And what is intended is the highest manifestation of glory that ever is made, even that by the gospel, which the Apostle speaks of as the highest. This appears by v. 4 and by ch. 3:9–11, 18. But if the greatest glory of God that ever he manifests to men be in the beauty and excellency of the person of Christ, surely he is the supreme, most glorious God. It cannot be his will that we should show higher respect to the supreme God than to him, and adore him as infinitely more excellent and glorious than the Son, if, in using the utmost means that ever he has used to gain our respect and excite our adoration, [he] has made no greater manifestation of his glory than what is exhibited to view in exhibiting the excellencies and beauties of Christ's person.

Christ is the Lord mentioned in Rom. 10:13, "For whosoever shall call upon the name of the Lord shall be saved." That it is Christ is spoken of is evident from the two foregoing verses, and also from the next verse, even the fourteenth. But the words are taken from Joel 2:32, where the word translated "Lord" is "Jehovah." See also I Cor. 1:2.

That text is a clear proof of Christ's divinity, I Cor. 2:16, "For who hath known the mind of the Lord, that he may instruct him? But we have the mind of Christ."

And so is that in I Cor. 9:21, "{To them that are without law, as without law,} (being not without law to God, but under law to Christ)."

And I Cor. 10:9, "Neither let us tempt Christ, as some of them also tempted." By this it appears that Christ was that God, that Holy One of Israel, that they tempted in the wilderness.

I Cor. 10:22, "Do we provoke the Lord to jealousy? are we stronger than he?" 'Tis evident that by "the Lord" here is meant Jesus Christ by the preceding context, and that therefore he is that being who says, "I the Lord thy God am a jealous God" [Ex. 20:5, Deut. 5:9].

Rev. 2:23: Christ says, "I am he that trieth the reins and the heart: and will give to every one of you according to his works." This is said by the Son of God, as appears by the eighteenth verse, foregoing. Compare this with other passages of Scripture where these things are spoken of as the prerogative of the supreme God. Parallel with it is John 21:17, "O Lord, thou knowest all things; thou knowest that I love thee."

Raising of the dead is spoken of as an instance of the exceeding greatness of the mighty power of God the Father (Eph. 1:19[–20]). But this very power is often ascribed to Christ, as in Phil. 3:20–21, "we look for the Savior, the Lord Jesus Christ: who shall change our vile body, that it may be fashioned like unto his glorious body, according to the working whereby he is able to subdue all things to himself." See also John 5:21, 28, compared with vv. 17–19.

It would be unreasonable to suppose that there is one being infinitely greater than all other beings, so that all others are as nothing to him, and infinitely exceeding them in power, and yet that [there] are no kind of WORKS or effects of his power that are peculiar to him, by which he is greatly distinguished from others.

He that appeared sitting on the throne above the cherubims and wheels in Ezekiel's visions (Ezek. 1:27 and other places) was undoubtedly Christ, because he appeared in the shape of a man, which God the Father never did. "No man hath seen God at any time" [John 1:18, I John 4:12], but by Christ. He is the image of the invisible God. But yet the person that there appeared was undoubtedly God. He is represented as one that has heaven for his throne and sits as supreme ruler of the universe. This is undoubtedly the same that rides on the heavens in the help of his people, and in his excellency on the sky, that rides on the heavens of heavens by his name Jah, or Jehovah [Deut. 33:26, Ps. 68:4, 33]. And this is called "the appearance of the likeness [of the] glory of the Lord," or image of the glory of the Lord (Ezek. 1:28, and 3:23, and 8:4).

This shows him to be a person truly divine, and also shows him to be Christ. For what can this image of the glory of the Lord—with an appearance of brightness round about, vv. 27–28—[be] but the same which the Apostle speaks of, who he says is "the brightness of God's glory, and the express image of his person" [Heb. 1:3]? And this is evidently the same that sat on the throne in the temple, that was called the chariot of the cherubims. And this person is called "the God of Israel" (Ezek. 10:20). And the whole that this person says to Ezekiel, from time to time, shows that he is truly God.

See after what manner the work of CREATING THE WORLD is claimed as the peculiar work of God, and a thing wherein it appears that none can be like him, or to be compared unto him (Is. 40:18, and vv. 22 and 25 and 28; so Is. 44:24).

CHRIST'S EXISTING BEFORE THE CREATION OF THE WORLD proves that he is God. See Is. 43:13.

'Tis a great evidence of the divinity of Christ that the Holy Ghost is put so into subjection to him as to become his messenger—the putting the Spirit of God, as the Holy Ghost is often called, or the Spirit of the Father, as he is called, Matt. 10:20. The same that is there called the Spirit of the Father is in Mark 13:11 called the Holy Ghost. Now certainly 'tis unreasonable to suppose that the Spirit of the supreme God should be put under the direction and disposal of a mere creature, one infinitely below God, under the disposal of his will.

The only evasion here must be this, that the HOLY GHOST is also a created Spirit, inferior to the Son. For if Christ be a mere creature, it would be unreasonable to suppose that he should have the Spirit of God subjected to him on any other supposition, whether the Spirit of God be supposed to be only the power and energy of the Most High, or a superior created spirit. But how does the Holy Ghost's being a creature inferior to the Son consist with Christ's being conceived by the power of the Holy Ghost, and his being honored by having the Holy Ghost descending upon him, and being anointed with it, and working his greatest miracles by the power of the Holy Ghost, and its being a great honor done to Christ that the Spirit was given to him not by measure?

And besides, the Holy Ghost's being a creature not only infinitely inferior to God, but inferior to the Son, who is infinitely inferior to him, is exceeding inconsistent with almost everything said of the Holy Spirit or Spirit of God in Scripture: as his being called the POWER of the highest; his searching all things, even the deep things of God, and knowing the things of God in a most distinguishing manner, as the spirit of a man within him knows the things of a man; the Scripture's being the word of God as it is the word of the Holy Ghost; Christians being the temple of the living God as they are the temples of the Holy Ghost; lying unto the Holy Ghost being called lying unto God; the chief works of God being ascribed to the Holy Ghost, as the works of creation, the forming man in the womb (Eccles. [11:5], "thou knowest not what is the way of the spirit," etc.; Job 33:4, "The Spirit of God hath made me"); giving life, as in the latter part of that verse [Job 33:4]; giving Adam his life and spirit—God breathed into him the breath of life; giving understanding to the heart of men; giving wisdom ("there is a spirit in man: the inspiration of the Almighty giveth me understanding" [Job 32:8]); giving the highest sort of wisdom, viz. spiritual understanding; forming the human nature of Christ; being the author of regeneration, sanctification, creating a new heart, and so being the author of the new creation, which is spoken of as vastly greater than the old.

Blasphemy against the Father is pardonable, but not against the Holy Ghost.

'Tis unreasonable to suppose that the body of Christ only was made by the Holy Ghost. 'Tis evident that the whole human nature, the holy thing that was born of the Virgin, was by the Holy Ghost (Luke 1:35). But the Son of the Virgin was a holy thing especially with regard to his soul.

The Spirit of God infuses the souls of other men. The soul of Adam more especially was from the Spirit of God, from God's breathing into him the breath of life. But this breath of life signifies the Spirit of God, as appears by Christ's breathing on his disciples after his resurrection, saying, "Receive ye the Holy Ghost" [John 20:22]. The Spirit of God is called the breath of God, Job 33:4, "The Spirit of God hath made me, the breath of the Almighty hath given me life." If God's Spirit gives life to other men, or mankind in general, doubtless it gave life to Adam. And if that Spirit of God which gives life to mankind in general be—in doing that work—called the breath of God, we may well suppose that, when we find that which gave life and soul to Adam, called God's breath, that thereby was meant God's Spirit.

The Spirit of God is represented as giving life to the body and infusing the living soul into it in a resurrection, or restoration to life: Ezek. 37:9–10, there called "wind" and "breath." But the same word in the original which signifies "wind" and "breath" signifies "spirit." And the Spirit of God is often in Scripture expressly compared to wind, as in John 3:8, Acts 2:2, Cant. 4:16. If it be the work of the Spirit of God to give understanding to the soul of man, we may well argue from that that 'tis the work of the Spirit of God to give that rational, intelligent thing the soul, and that the faculty of understanding, as well as the habit, is from him. But giving understanding to the heart is spoken of as the work of the Spirit of God. Job 32:8, "there is a spirit in man: and the inspiration of the Almighty giveth him understanding." Compare ch. 35:11 and 38:36, Prov. 2:6, Dan. 2:21.

'Tis the work of the Spirit of God to renew the soul, which the Scripture represents as creating it anew, and a greater work than the first creation of it. And therefore, doubtless 'tis the work of the Spirit to create it at first.

Again, 'tis the work of the Spirit of God to form Christ in the souls of men in their regeneration, whereby a renewed person is represented as becoming, as it were, the mother of Christ, as resembling the formation of Christ in the womb of his mother. But this formation of Christ in the soul is more like the causing of *Christ* to be born of the Virgin, than the body.[4]

How unreasonable must our notions be of the creation of the world by Arian principles. For 'tis manifest by the Scripture that the world was made by the Holy Ghost, or Spirit of God, as well as by the Son of God. But the Son of God is, according to them, a created spirit. And the Spirit of God must, therefore, also be a created spirit, inferior to him. Therefore, we must suppose that the Father created the world by the Son, and the Son did not create the world by himself, but by the Spirit of God, as his minister or instrument. So that the Spirit of God herein must act as the instrument of an instrument. [. . .][5]

TABLE OF SCRIPTURES

Note: The letter "F" refers to discourse on "The Fulfillment of Prophecies of the Messiah."[6]

Gen.: 1:1, pp. 416, 415.

Ex.: 17:15, p. 417; 20:3, 414 and 416; 14:19 and 23:20–21, F, p. 13a and p. 16c, d.

Deut. 32:12, p. 414; 33:29, p. 414; 34:6, p. 412; 32:4, F, p. 16e.

II Sam.: 22:32, F, p. 16e.

I Kgs.: 8:11, F, p. 11e; 8:39, p. 416.

4. At the end of this vivid (though somewhat cryptic) analogy, JE appears to be alluding to his earlier claim that the Spirit formed not only Christ's body but, more importantly, his soul as well in the womb of the Virgin Mary. Thus Christians should not assume what JE deemed an excessively corporeal doctrine of the believers' union with Christ. The Spirit forms the risen Christ, not his earthly body, in the souls of the regenerate. The union is thus a spiritual one, as most Reformed theologians taught.

5. Following this paragraph in the MS, JE inserted a note that reads, "see p. 1024," followed by one of his standard cue marks. The reference is to an extensive collection of notes beginning on p. 1024 of "Miscellanies" Bk. 9, in which JE continues his work on the subject of Christ's divinity. JE, Jr., labeled this material as No. [1358]. See below, p. 607.

6. JE made a complete list of all the books of the Bible for the table, but those for which he provided no citations have been omitted. Unless otherwise noted, the references that JE makes to the "Fulfillment" discourse in this index fall within § 14, MS pp. 11–18, which treats the proposition, "It is evident by the prophecies of the Messiah that he was to be God." JE's mistaken citations in this table are silently corrected.

II Kgs.:   18:4, pp. 411–12.

Neh.:   9:6, p. 416.

Job: 19:24–27, p. 419 and F, pp. 15b and 16a.

Ps.:   2:12, p. 415 and F, p. 14c; 3:8, p. 414; 20:9, F, p. 17b; 45:2–
               7, F, p. 14b; 45:11, F, p. 17d; 50, F, p. 14a; 62:2, F, pp. 16e and
               p. 17a; 72:4, 7, 15, 17, F, pp. 16a and p. 17b; 81:8–10, p. 414;
               82:6, F, p. 81c;[7] 83:18, p. 413; 89:19, F, p. 15a; 90:2, p. 416;
               93:1 and 96:10, p. 418; 96, F, p. 14a; 97:1, etc., p. 418; 97:7,
               [pp.] 418, 424; 98, F, p. 14a; 99:1, p. 418; 99 and 100, F,
               p. 14a; 102:25 ff., p. 416; 110:1, F, p. 17b, d; 110:4, F, p. 16b;
               113, F, p. 14a; 118:8–9, F, p. 14e; 146:3–4, F, p. 15a.

Prov.:   8:22, pp. 416–17; 8:27–31, p. 415; 30:4, F, p. 22a.[8]

Is.:   2:3–5, F, p. 14b; 2:22, F, p. 14d; 6:1–5 and 9:6–7, pp. 414–
               15 and F, p. 16b and p. 22a;[9] 6:3, p. 423; 9:6, F, p. 11b, c;
               10:21, p. 416; 11:10, p. 417; 25:9, p. 414; 26:13–14, F, p. 17d;
               28:15–18, F, pp. 14c, e and 16e; 32:1–2, 16–18, F, p. 18b;
               33:22, F, pp. 13c and 18b; 40:3, p. 416; 40:3 ff., pp. 420–21;
               40:9–11, p. 418 and F, p. 14a; 40:13, p. 423; 40:13–14, p. 415;
               40:18, 22, 25, 28, p. 426; 41:14, p. 414; 41, F, 13d; 41:23–29,
               F, p. 17a, b and p. 18e; 42, F, p. 13d; 42:1–8, p. 413 and F,
               pp. 11b, c and 17a, b and 18e; 43, F, p. 13d; 43:10–15, p. 414
               and F, p. 13d; 43:13, p. 426; 44:6, p. 416; 44:8, p. 416; 44:6,
               24, pp. 414, 426; 45:3 ff., p. 421; 45:5, p. 416; 45:5–7, 12,
               p. 415; 45:20–21 ff., p. 413; 45:22, p. 413; 46:9, p. 416; 47:4,
               p. 414; 48:11, F, p. 11b, c; 48:17, p. 414; 49:7, 26, p. 414;
               49:26, p. 414; 54:5, p. 414 [and] 424; 60:16, p. 414; 62:11–
               63:6, F, p. 14a; 63:1–6, p. 414 and F, p. 15a; 64:1, F, p. 18c;
               65:17–19, p. 415.

7. JE's reference is confusing, because there is no reference to Ps. 82:6 on p. 81 of "Fulfillment" (nor, apparently, anywhere else in the discourse). The part of the page JE refers to contains § 109, "The prophecies do represent the weapons by which the Messiah should conquer
the nations and deliver his people not to be carnal but spiritual, and particularly the main
weapon to be the word of God."

8. "Fulfillment," § 20, "It was foretold that the Messiah should be a very wonderful, mysterious person."

9. "Fulfillment," § 20; see preceding note.

Jer.:   3:23, p. 414; 17:5, 7, F, p. 14d; 17:10, p. 416.

Ezek.:   37:25, F, p. 16b; 44 ff., F, p. 16e.

Dan.:   2:44, p. 417 and F, 13d; 7:13–14, 27, F, pp. 12c and 13d and 16c.

Hos.:   1:7, p. 416; 13:4, p. 414; 13:4, 9–11, F, p. 13c.

Joel: 2:32, p. 425.

Jonah: 2:8–9, p. 414.

Mic.:   4:2–5, F, p. 14b; 5:2, p. 417 and F, p. 15b; 5:4, F, p. 16c, d.

Zeph.:   3:14–15 ff., p. 418 and F, pp. 13d and 14a.

Hag.:   2:3, 7–9, F, p. 11d.

Zech.:   3:9, p. 423; 3:9 and 4:10, F, p. 17b; 6:12–13, F, p. 11b; 11:12, p. 416; 12:8, F, p. 17c; 12:10, p. 416; 13:7, F, p. 17c.

Mal.:   3:1–3, pp. 418 and 419 and 421 and F, pp. 12d and 17d.

Matt.:   3:2, p. 417; 4:10, p. 416; 19:17, p. 412; 26:63–65, F, p. 21d;[1] 27:9–10, p. 416; 11:10, p. 419.

Mark: 1:1–3, p. 419; 1:3, p. 416; 13:19, p. 416.

Luke: 1:16–17, p. 419; 1:76, p. 421; 2:11, p. 416; 2:32, p. 419; 24:25, p. 416; 7:27, p. 419.

John: 1:1, p. 416; 1:3, p. 416; 2:24, p. 416; 5:17–19, p. 416; 5:17–29, p. 417; 5:23, p. 416; 10:30–33, p. 417 and F, p. 21d;[2] 16:13–15, p. 415; 16:30, p. 416; 17:21–22, p. 415; 19:37, p. 416; 1:19 ff., pp. 419–20; 20:22, p. 423; 16:7, 13–15, p. 423; 21:17, p. 425.

Acts: 1:24, p. 416; 10:36, p. 416.

---

1. "Fulfillment," § 16, "It was the doctrine of the ancient prophets that the Messiah was the Son of God."

2. "Fulfillment," § 16; see preceding note.

Rom.:   9:5, p. 416; 10:12, p. 416; 8:32, p. 424; 10:13, p 425.

I Cor.:   1:2, p. 426; 2:16, p. 415; 2:16, p. 425; 9:2, p. 425; 10:9, p. 425;
          10:22, p. 425.

II Cor.: 4:6, pp. 424–25.

Gal.:   4:8, p. 416.

Eph.:   1:3, p. 415.

Phil.:   2:10–11, p. 413; 3:20–21, p. 426.

Col.:   1:16–17, p. 416; 2:9, see "Blank Bible."[3]

I Tim.:   6:15, p. 416.

Tit.:   2:13, p. 415.

Heb.:   1:3, see note in "Blank Bible;"[4] 1:3, 6, p. 416; 1:6, p. 424; 1:10,
          p. 416; 7:3, p. 417; 7:25, p. 413.

I Pet.:   1:11, p. 422.

II Pet.: 1:1, p. 414; 3:8, p. 417.

Rev.:   1:8, 17 and 2:3 and 17:14, p. 416; 2:23, p. 425; 5:6, p. 423;
          19:15, p. 414; 19:16 and 22:13, p. 416.

[1350.] THE NECESSITY OF REVELATION. EXTRACTS FROM *DEISM RE-
VEALED.* See the "Table" at the end, pp. 459–61.[5] The following things
are abridged from *Deism Revealed,* 2nd ed.[6]

3. JE's "Blank Bible" note on Col. 2:9 quotes Philip Doddridge's paraphrase of and note on
the verse in his *Family Expositor:* "'I assuredly believe that as it contains an evident allusion to
the *Schechinah* in which God dwelt, so it ultimately refers to the adorable mystery of the union
of the divine and human natures, in the person of the glorious Emmanuel, which makes him
such an object of our hope and confidence.'"

4. MS: "p. 798," which contains the "Blank Bible" note on Heb. 1:3. JE writes, "It was Christ,
the second person of the Trinity, that was wont to appear of old in that effulgence of glory that
was commonly called the glory of the Lord." In later additions to the entry, JE dwells on the
phrase, "express image of his person," pointing out that "whatsoever is the express or exact image of a thing is, in the Apostle's sense, equivalent or of equal value with that thing."

5. MS: "P. 862. 863."

6. "Abridged" is the key word in this sentence. JE transcribed the following series of extracts
rather loosely and inconsistently, sometimes quoting verbatim, at other times condensing large
sections in paraphrase. In cases where JE has quoted Skelton more literally, the text is edited
in accordance with Skelton's original. Elsewhere, JE's abridgements stand with a minimum of
editorial interruption. JE's footnoted references are incorporated into the text at the appropriate places.

"Mankind cannot subsist out of society," especially "if we comprehend families in the number of societies." And "families cannot subsist without the protection of greater societies; as children depend absolutely on families for subsistence, so do families on kingdoms and commonwealths for peace, security, property, life, and everything. [...] And societies cannot subsist without laws. Its members must know by what constitutions or customs they are to regulate their actions. [...] And magistrates are as necessary as laws, for let the laws be never so good [...], they can't execute themselves. [...] And that laws and magistracy may answer their end, there is need of a supreme magistrate that is almighty, and perfectly wise, and just, and all-knowing, perfectly acquainted with the conduct of inferior magistrates, and of all the subjects, otherwise the greatest irregularities and enormities may be committed by both with impunity. And it is necessary officers and subjects should know that they are under such a supreme magistrate thus perfectly wise and just, and who perfectly inspects and takes care of the society, and will judge all, reward and punish, and that all must give account of themselves to him, other[wise] the welfare of society will not be influenced by his government. That man, who does not believe that he is to account in the severest manner for the use and application of his power, ought never to be trusted with any power, because he will endeavor to draw all the advantages of society to himself, and his instruments, and turn all its weight and strength against those who thwart his usurpations. How can mankind be more unhappy, than under a fallible, or I should rather say, a corrupt administration, that stands in awe of no superior? As to the subjects, if they do not look upon themselves as accountable of one that is omniscient, omnipotent, and inflexibly just, they will follow their own private ends, in all cases wherein authority can be resisted or evaded, which may be done in most cases. Public societies cannot be maintained without trials and witnesses. And if witnesses are not firmly persuaded, that he who holds the supreme power over 'em, is omniscient, just and powerful, and will revenge falsehood, there will be no dependence on their oaths or most solemn declarations.

"God, therefore, must be the supreme magistrate. [...] Society depends absolutely on him, and all kingdoms and communities are but provinces of his universal kingdom, who is King of kings, Lord of lords, and Judge of judges.

"Thus as mankind cannot subsist out of society, nor society itself subsist without religion, I mean without faith in the infinite power, wisdom and justice of God, and a judgment to come, religion cannot be a falsehood. It is not credible, that all the happiness of mankind, the whole civil world, and peace, safety, justice, and truth itself, should have nothing to stand on, but a lie. It is not to [be] supposed, that God would give the world no other foundation; so that religion is absolutely necessary, and must have some sure foundation.

"But there can be no good, sure foundation of religion, without mankind's having a right idea of God, and some sure and clear knowledge of him and our dependence on him. Lord Shaftesbury himself owns, that wrong ideas of God will hurt society as much, if not more, than ignorance of him can do.

"Now the question is whether nature and reason alone can give us a right idea of God, and is sufficient to establish among mankind a clear and sure knowledge of his nature, and the relation we stand in to him, and his concern with us." See No. 1301.[7]

"It may well be questioned, whether any man hath this from the mere light of nature. Nothing can seem more strange, than that the wisest and most sagacious of all men, I mean the philosophers, should have searched with all imaginable candor and anxiety for this, and searched in vain, if the light of nature alone is sufficient to give it and establish it among mankind in general." Vol. 1, pp. 47–53.

"There never was a man known or heard of who had an idea of God without being taught it." Vol. 1, p. 57.

"Whole sects of philosophers denied the very being of God, and some have died martyrs to atheism, as Vaninus, Jordanus Bruno, Casimir Liszinski, and Mahomet Effendi." Vol. 1, p. 60.

"A man confined to a dungeon all his days, and deprived of all conversation with mankind, probably would not so much as once consider who made him, or whether he was made or not, nor entertain the least notion of God. [...] There are many instances of people born absolutely deaf and blind, who never showed the least sense of religion, or knowledge of God." Vol. 1, p. 61.

"It is one thing to work out a demonstration of a point when once it is proposed, and another to strike upon the point itself. I cannot tell whether any man would have considered the works of creation as effects, if he had never been told they had a cause." (See Clarke's *Evidences of Natural and Revealed Religion*, p. 139b, c.)[8] "We know very well, that even

7. MS: "this book, p. 66."

8. This is JE's annotation for Samuel Clarke's *A Discourse Concerning the Unchangeable Obligations of Natural Religion, and the Truth and Certainty of the Christian Revelation* (London, 1706; 6th ed., 1724). On p. 220 of the 1706 edition, Clarke, speaking of the wisest ancient philosophers,

after the being of such a cause was much talked of in the world, and believed by the generality of mankind; yet many, and great philosophers,
held the world to be eternal; and others ascribed what we call the works
of creation to an eternal series of causes. If the most sagacious of the
philosophers were capable of doing this, after hearing so much of a first
cause, and a creation, what would they have done, and what would the
gross of mankind, who are inattentive and ignorant, have thought of the
matter, if nothing had been taught concerning God, and the origin of
things, but every single man left solely to such intimation as his own
senses and reason could have given him? [. . .] we find the earlier ages
of the world [...] did not trouble themselves about the question,
whether the being of God could be proved by reason, but either never
inquired into the matter, or took their opinions upon that head merely
from tradition. But, allowing that every man is able to demonstrate to
himself, that the world, and all things contained therein, are effects, and
had a beginning, which I take to be a most absurd supposition, and look
upon it to be almost impossible for unassisted reason to go so far; yet if
effects are [. . .] to be ascribed to similar causes, and a good and wise
effect must suppose a good and wise cause; by the same way of reasoning, all the evil and irregularity in the world must be attributed to an evil
and unwise cause; so that either the first cause must be both good and
evil, wise and foolish, or else there must be two first causes, an evil and
irrational, as well as a good and wise principle. Thus man, left to himself, would be apt to reason. If the cause and the effects are similar and
conformable, matter must have a material cause, there being nothing
more impossible for us to conceive, than how matter should be produced
by spirit, or anything else but matter. The best reasoner in the world, endeavoring to find out the causes of things by the things themselves, [. . .
] might be led into the grossest errors and contradictions, and find himself, at the end, in extreme want of an instructor." Vol. 1, pp. 62–63.

"It is manifest there is such a thing as evil in the world, and good and
evil have their distinct empires in the world. And the principle from
whence the one is derived, is to be feared, as well as the author of the
other to be loved. And fear is a cause of adoration, as well as love. Are
two opposite and supreme principles, therefore, to be worshipped, according to the belief of almost all the pagans now in the world? If the
mere reason of every man could relieve itself from this difficulty, why

---

states that "The Manner, in which God might be acceptably worshipped, These men were entirely and unavoidably ignorant of."

should the worship of devils prevail in many nations, and keep its ground during so long a series of ages? This, I think, is evident, that although reason should be so strong in one man, or in a few, as to find out the being of some superior power; yet this would not, probably, happen, till after many ages spent in vain attempts to account for the origin and regularity of the world; and when some notion of this kind should once be struck out, it would be so imperfect, so uncertain, and blended with so much absurdity and error, that it would scarcely be worth the propagating, which would also be a matter of infinite difficulty. But supposing it to prevail in some nations, or all over the world, having once preoccupied the minds of men, the improvements made by others in after-times on the first imperfect discovery, instead of having the notions, derived from the discovery, as a basis to build on, would find them, and the prejudices accompanying them, an infinite obstacle to their propagation. What is said of the first improvement, is as true of all the subsequent ones. The old notions would be so many bars against the new; and, considering the great difficulty of the inquiry, and the vast room for conceit and imagination to graft their wild scions on the fruitful stock, it would [require] an almost infinite number of debates, refinements, and improvements, each of which must have a course through the world before it could be examined, in order to settle the right idea of God, and support it with demonstrations universally convincing. Reason labors under a yet greater difficulty in finding out the right notion of God. . . . As the office of reason is not to supply the mind with ideas, but to judge of the connection or disagreement between those already received; so it can only exercise itself on such materials, as those other faculties, that hold intelligence with objects, supply it with. This latter is the function of the senses alone, which, for that purpose, are turned outward towards their proper objects, and set open as so many avenues as inlets to the ingredients of all our knowledge. It is vain to say we have any proper or immediate idea of spirit, and its operations, or that we have any other source of notions than sensation. . . . When we look into ourselves [. . .], we plainly perceive spirit represented there by our idea of some subtle matter, its operations by those of body, and both, not only in our external, but internal speech, by terms and signs appropriated to sensible objects. If then all our ideas are derived from sensation, if reason can operate no farther than it has ideas to work on, and if the divine being is not the object of any one sense, how much at a loss must reason be to fix our way of thinking concerning that which it is furnished with no idea of?" Vol. 1, pp. 63–65.

"Nevertheless, we may be enabled to form a right idea of God by him who taught us to believe, that the soul of man is formed in the image of God [. . .]; which, till it was revealed to us, the force of human reason could not give us a right notion, not to say assurance, of. But now that this resemblance between God and ourselves is discovered to us, we can lay the foundations of our knowledge here on earth, and raise the superstructure above the highest heavens. When men talk of reason, [. . .] and represent it able easily to find out God, they deceive themselves for want of considering the vast difference between reason uninstructed, undisciplined, and unfurnished with spiritual ideas, and reason already refined by divine and human culture. [. . .] The bodies and minds of men are so contrived, as to stand in need of continual care and culture. [. . .] Men come into the world with their minds ignorant, and, what is worse, rude, and prone to wild passions, and fierce dispositions. We have not even the full use of our senses, till art and culture have taught us how to employ them. [. . .] Though the under-faculties of the mind should supply the faculty of reason never so plentifully [. . .] with materials on which it is to operate, yet reason will stand in extreme need of instruction and exercise, to know how to dispose and connect them. You may lay a sufficient quantity of stone and timber, etc., on the spot where you intend to build; yet, if your architect is wholly unexercised and uninstructed, he will give you but an indifferent house." Vol. 1, pp. 66–67.

"Men who live in times and places of ignorance, hardly reason at all, and are little better than brutes, in comparison of such as have been bred up in ages and countries well enlightened. Uneducated and illiterate men are able to reason on few points, and those such as relate to their daily occupations and affairs." Vol. 1, p. 68.

"It is manifest that reason stands in great need of instruction in order to the right performance of her office; and most of all, when she is to weigh propositions, and draw conclusions about objects, that are only to be analogically apprehended and considered. The mind of man imports its rules of reasoning, as well as notions, from abroad; and one generation teaches another, not only religion, but all other sciences. The art of reasoning rightly, follows instruction, and is progressive, and traditional. We can trace it from Syria to Egypt, from Egypt to Greece, from Greece to Italy, and from thence westward and northward, to the rest of Europe; while all the other nations of the earth, excepting the Chinese, who made but little advances in knowledge, lying without the verge of right religious instruction, remained profoundly ignorant. Reason in them, not meeting with opportunities of culture, the seeds of knowledge, lay fallow, and produced little or no inventions, and scarcely any improvement in arts and sciences. No country, that we know of, ever became ingenious and learned, from barbarous and ignorant, merely of themselves. In all countries, we are acquainted with, knowledge bears an exact proportion to instruction. Why does the learned, and well-educated, reason better than the mere citizen? Why the citizen better than the boor? Why the English boor better than the Spanish? Why the Spanish better than the Moorish? Why the Moorish better than the Negro? And why he better than the Hottentot? If then reason is found to go hand in hand, and step for step, with education, what would be the consequence, if there were no education? There is no fallacy more gross, than to imagine reason utterly untaught and undisciplined, capable of the same attainments in knowledge as reason well-refined and instructed; or to suppose, that reason can as easily find in itself principles to argue from, as draw the consequences, when once they are found; I mean especially in respect to objects not perceivable by our senses. In ordinary articles of knowledge, our senses and experience furnish reason with ideas and principles to work on; and continual conferences and debates give it exercise in such matters; and that improves its vigor and activity. But, in respect to God, it can have no right idea nor axiom to set out with, till he is pleased to reveal it to them." Vol. 1, pp. 74–75.

"If men of themselves should reason from effects to causes; and if one man should form an important idea of the cause or causes of all things, and another should improve on his discovery, a third on his, and so on, [. . .] how long might it be before reason could be sufficiently improved in many or most men for an inquiry after the first causes of things, and how many ages must pass, after this improvement [. . .], ere all doubts and uncertainties could be cleared up, and the right idea of God found out and fixed? And then what an immense space of time it would take to propagate the right idea over all the world, against the current of all its received errors, and rooted prejudices, without miracles, and without a ministry, let every candid person judge. What must mankind do all this time for want of a divine law and obligation, the absolute necessity of which we have already considered? Besides, [. . .] mankind are full as apt to degenerate, as to improve in religious knowledge. I am sure we have fewer instances of the latter than of the former, in such ages and countries as were not kept in sight of the true religion by a continual series of revelations. If we believe the Jewish and Christian history, we shall be convinced, that all the nations of the world at first knew and served the true God, and fell from his worship, in process of time, to that of idols and devils, except the Jews, who were with the greatest difficulty restrained from doing the same, by revelations, miracles, and national judgments; and the Christians, whom the clearest lights have not altogether preserved from the encroachments of idolatry.

"And what instance can be mentioned from any history, of any one nation under the sun, that emerged from atheism or idolatry, into the knowledge or adoration of the one true God, without the assistance of revelation? The Americans, the Africans, the Tartars, and the ingenious Chinese, have had time enough, one would think, to find out the true and right idea of God [. . .]; and yet, after above five thousand years improvement [. . .], and the full exercise of reason, [. . .] they have at this day got no farther in their progress towards the true religion, than to the worship of stocks, and stones, and devils. How many thousand years must be allowed to these nations, to reason themselves into the true religion [. . .]? The Christian religion, it seems, came too late into the world, to be true; but natural religion, though not yet arrived, is recommended sufficiently by its truth, antiquity, and universality, according to the deists of the present age. What the lights of nature and reason could do to investigate the knowledge of God, is best seen by what they have already done. We cannot argue more convincingly on any foundation, than that of known and incontestable facts.

"Give me leave therefore to be particular in exposing the theology of the pagans from the records of their own writers. All the nations of the earth, that were left to themselves, fell, some sooner, and others later, into gross idolatry. At first they worshipped the luminaries of heaven, and then their departed kings and benefactors, for gods. Then they made images for them, and in a little time terminated the greater part of their adoration in those wooden representatives of their dead deities. It was not long after these first-fruits of nature, till they added to the catalogue of their gods, the most barbarous oppressors, the vilest impostors, the lewdest prostitutes, and the most infamous [. . .] murderers, and parricides, the earth ever groaned under. Such deities were to be worshipped with suitable rites and sacrifices. The Salii and Corybantes, priests of Mars and Cybele, performed the ceremonies of those deities with frantic dances, and outrageous fits of madness. In the rites of Bacchus, not only the priests, but all the people, men, women, and children, having their faces smeared with the lees of wine, and being half-drunk, ran about the fields, and through the woods, in a most horrible fit of distraction, howling like wild beasts, and frisking from place to place with such ridiculous and immodest gesticulations, as nothing but the strong possession of some demon could have prompted them to. It was, no doubt, a most rational kind of religion, that could have put the ancient men, the discreet matrons, and the modest virgins, on such wild extravagancies. [. . .] Much the same sort of friskings and howlings were used in the ceremonies of many other heathen gods; and in those of Baal they were accompanied with a custom most shocking and unnatural. The priests, as they capered about the altar, gashed their flesh with knives and lancets, and ran into furious fits of distraction. The most solemn act of worship, performed to the Syrian Baal by his ordinary devotees, was to break wind, and ease themselves, at the foot of his image. The religious rites performed in honor of Venus in Cyprus, and at Aphac on Mount Libanus, consisted in lewdness of the grossest kinds. The young people of both sexes crowded from all parts to those sinks of pollution, and, filling the groves and temples with their shameless practices, committed whoredom by thousands, out of pure devotion. All the Babylonian women were obliged to prostitute themselves once in their lives, at the temple of Venus or Mylitta, to the first man that asked them; and the money earned by this extraordinary act of devotion, be it more or less, was always esteemed sacred. The nocturnal mysteries at Rome were not carried to such enormous excesses; but they were nevertheless very scandalous meetings, and gave occasion to all sorts of debaucheries. The devils, [. . .] whom nature had chosen for her gods, were not contented with drunkenness and lewdness; but they must be worshipped with murder too, and that of the most shocking sort. Human sacrifices were offered up almost in all heathen countries; and, to make them the more acceptable to their good-natured gods, the parents burnt their own children alive to Baal, Moloch, and many other of their deities. Here in Britain, and in Gaul, it was a common practice to surround a man with a kind of wicker-work, and burn him to death, in honor of their gods. The Scythians sacrificed to Mars one in every hundred of the captives taken in war. The Peruvians, in their sacrifices, had a custom of tying a living man to a stake, and pulling his flesh off his bones by small pieces, which they broiled and eat in his sight, believing they did him the greatest honor in treating him after this manner. The Carthaginians, in times of public calamity, not only burnt alive the children of the best families to Saturn, and that by hundreds, but sometimes sacrificed themselves in the same manner in great numbers. Oracles, astrology, soothsaying, superstition, magic, etc., overran the whole heathen world [. . .]. This might be made apparent[9] by a great variety of quotations from profane

---

9. MS: "appear."

writers, who often speak on that topic just as Amasis did in his famous letter to Polycrates. [...] A female divinity was always remarkable for her spleen [...]. What the Romans thought of their gods, may be seen by their behavior on the death of Germanicus. They battered the temples, says Suetonius, with stones, they overthrew the altars of the gods, and flung their household deities into the streets. LeCompte and Dubald assure us, the Chinese, after offering largely to their gods, and being disappointed of their assistance, sometimes sue them for damages, and obtain decrees against them from the Mandarins. This ingenious people, when their houses are on fire, to the imminent peril of their wooden gods, hold them to the flames, in hopes of extinguishing them by it. . . . The Tyrians were a wise people, and therefore, when Alexander laid siege to their city, they chained Apollo to Hercules, to prevent his giving them the slip." Vol. 1, pp. 75–80.

"The heathen did not think themselves obliged to be better than their gods; and accordingly did not only indulge their lusts [...] out of principle, but ran into general customs of the most horrid and abominable nature. [...] Fornication was esteemed no sin among them; nor did they commit sodomy with half the shame or remorse that attend wenching among Christians. They exposed such of their children, as they did not like, to be eaten by wild beasts; a cruelty practiced at this day by the Hottentots, and some other African nations. Several nations, inhabiting the banks of the Danube, were wont to fling their new-born children into the river, and those only that swam were taken out and suckled. The Caribes frequently castrated their children, that they might grow the fatter, and be the more delicate food. The politest of them were entertained at their public shows with men killing men. [...] Some nations of them eat human flesh, which is a kind of diet, if we may believe our travelers, much relished by several pagan nations at this day. Others, [...] killed their parents at a certain age, and feasted on their flesh, thinking it the greatest tenderness to relieve them from the miseries of old age; and the highest honor that could be done them, to entomb them in their own bowels. It was a custom in most of the heathen[1] nations, and, they say, it is sometimes practiced at this day, for her, who loved her husband more than the rest of his wives, to kill herself at his funeral. The Persians made no scruple of marrying their own mothers or daughters [...]; and it was lawful among the Egyptians for brother and sister to marry. . . . Some nations carried out their sick, as soon as they thought their case desper-

---

1. Skelton reads: "eastern."

ate, and threw 'em on the ground to perish by the injuries of the wind and the weather; some forced their wives to miscarry, to save the expense of maintaining their children; the women, in the fury of battle, flung their infants on the lances of their enemies, to terrify them with a dreadful idea of their resolution. . . . Revenge and self-murder were not only tolerated, but esteemed heroic, by the best of the heathen. I know not, in all profane history, six more illustrious characters, than those of Lycurgus, Timoleon, Cicero, Cato Uticensis, Brutus, and Germanicus. The first encouraged tricking and stealing by an express law. The second, upon principle, murdered his own brother. Cicero, with all his fine talk about religion and virtue, had very little of either; as may appear by what he says (I think it is in a letter to Atticus) on the death of his daughter Tullia, 'I hate the very gods, who hitherto been so profuse in their favors to me,' and by deserting his friends and his country, and turning a servile flatterer to Caesar. Brutus concludes all his mighty heroism with this exclamation, 'Virtue, I have pursued thee in vain, and found thee to be but an empty name,' and then kills himself. Cato's virtue was not strong enough to hinder his turning a public robber and oppressor, witness his Cyprian expedition; nor to bear up against the calamities of life, and so he cut his own throat, and ran away, like a coward, from his country and the world. Germanicus, who exceeded all men in his natural sweetness of temper, at the approach of death called his friends about him, and spent his last moments in pressing them to take revenge of Piso and Plancina, for poisoning or bewitching him, in directing them how this might be best done, and in receiving their oaths for the performance of his request. His sense of religion he thus expressed on that occasion, 'Had I died by the decree of fate, I should have had just cause of resentment against the gods, for hurrying me away from my parents, my wife, and my children, in the flower of my youth, by an untimely death.'" Vol. 1, pp. 81–82.

"Upon consulting the writing of the philosophers, together with their lives and tenets, as given us by their own pagan historians, I find they knew little of true religion, and practiced less. It was owing to the want of higher and better principles than the mere light of nature and reason can suggest, that the ancient philosophers, who carried virtue as high as it was possible without divine assistance, fell into the gross enormities practiced by the people they lived among. They made all the efforts human strength was capable of, to find out the true object of worship, and came nearer to the discovery, in proportion as they had opportunities, by traveling into the East, of drawing hints from the stream of true tradition. And, after all, none but Socrates and Plato talked of one God, and that but obscurely, speaking, at other times, in favor of a plurality of gods, and recommending it to their disciples to worship the deities of their country. However, it must be owned they lived, in the main, as if they had better principles of religion than their countrymen and contemporaries. They did enough to show, that if they had been well acquainted with the true religion, they would not have taken long journeys by land, and made dangerous voyages by sea, to visit the celebrated prostitutes of their time; they would never have let out their wives for hire, nor kept their misses, nor given the world the strongest reason to think them guilty of greater crimes, than it was possible to commit with the other sex. What a condition must the pagan world have been in, when the ancient philosophers were esteemed [. . .] the wisest and best of men! [. . .] Those philosophers, however, had, generally speaking, little sense of religion, and as little sense of moral virtue, or even decency. Many of them were atheists, as Diagoras, Theodorus, and Critias. Epicurus denied the spirituality and providence of God, and so did all his followers. Aristotle denied his providence, as to this lower world. In the opinion of Hippasus and Heraclitus, God was fire; in that of Parmenides, a mixture of fire and earth; in that of Xenophanes, a great impassable sphere of matter. Socrates and Plato were, at least in practice, polytheists; so were Cicero and Plutarch, the [latter] holding, among a multiplicity of inferior gods, two supreme deities, the one infinitely good, and the other infinitely evil. The Stoics believed God to be the soul of the world, and that soul to consist of subtle flame. [. . .] Among the philosophers there were three hundred different opinions concerning their supreme deity, or rather, as Varro testifies, three hundred Jupiters, or supreme deities. The followers of Democritus and Epicurus denied the immortality of the soul. Pherecydes and Pythagoras believed it to be immortal, but gave it in common to brutes, as well as men. The Academics were doubtful as to this important point. Socrates, Plato, and Cicero, who were more inclined to the belief of a future existence, than the other philosophers, plead for it with arguments of no force, speak of [it] with the utmost uncertainty, and therefore are afraid to found their system of duty and virtue on the expectation of it. Their notions of morality were of a piece with their religion, and had little else for a foundation than vain-glory. Tully, in his treatise of friendship, says, that virtue proposes glory as its end, and hath no other reward. Accordingly he maintains that wars, undertaken for glory, are not unlawful, provided they are carried on without the usual cruelty. Zeno maintained, that all crimes are equal;

that pardon is never to be granted to one, who offends or injures us; and that a man may as lawfully use the utmost familiarity with his mother, as stroke her arm. It was not only his, but, likewise, the opinion of Cleanthes and Chrysippus, that the horrible sin of using the male for the female is a thing indifferent. The two former taught, that sons and daughters may as lawfully roast and eat the flesh of their parents, as any other food. Diogenes, and the sect of the Cynics, held, that parents have a right to sacrifice and eat their children; and that there is nothing shameful in committing the grossest acts of lewdness publicly, and before the faces of mankind. Epicurus allows of cohabitation with mothers and daughters. Aristippus, though a man of fortune, refused to maintain his own children, regarding them only as the spittle or vermin produced by his body; and as he placed the happiness of a man in the pleasures of a brute, so, to indulge those pleasures, he said, a wise man might commit theft, sacrilege, or adultery, if he had an opportunity. The virtuous sentiments, discovered by the philosophers on some occasions, will neither palliate these execrable principles, nor suffer us to [think] those who could abet them fit instructors for mankind.

"And their practices were like their principles. Socrates and Plato, the very best of them, have not escaped the censure of antiquity for crimes of the deepest dye. [. . .] Plutarch also represents Aristotle as a fop, a debauchée, and a traitor to Alexander his master. Dion Cassius is as severe on Seneca the moralist. Lucian, as well as Minutius Felix, represents the sages of antiquity as corrupters of youth, as adulterers, and tyrants. Diogenes kept a filthy strumpet, with whom he lay openly in the streets. Speusippus was caught, and slain, in the act of adultery. Aristippus kept a feraglio of boys and whores, and yet took journeys, at the peril of his life, to see the reigning courtesans of his time; nor was lewdness his only vice; he actually forswore a sum of money deposited in his hands. Crates, and the female philosopher Hipparchia, made a practice of strolling from place to place, and lying together publicly before multitudes of people. Xenophon not only kept a boy, called Clinias, with whom he was guilty of unnatural pollutions, but practiced the same execrable enormity with persons of riper years. Herillus was a filthy pathic[2] in his youth. Cleanthes, Chrysippus, Zeno, Cleombrotus and Menippus, committed murder on themselves; the last, because he had lost a considerable sum of money, which, as he was an usurer, went a little too near his heart. That I do not charge the philosophers with worse principles and practices

2. I.e. a subject of sodomy.

than they themselves maintain, and their own pagan historians ascribe to them, anyone may satisfy himself, who will consult Diogenes Laertius, Sextus Empiricus, Lucian, Plutarch, and the works of Plato, Aristotle, and Cicero." Here see Clarke's *Evidences,* pp. 137–38.[3]

Moncrieff[4] against Campbell, pp. 56–57, says, "Those who pretend to know the retirements of the life of Socrates accused him of impure commune with Alcibiades. He betrayed the chastity of his wife by giving her to his friend. And Plato and Xenophon, his admirers, declare his compliance with common idolatry. . . . What a villanous part did Seneca act in exciting Nero to murder his mother; and after, in writing an apology for it, employing the colors of his rhetoric to cover one of the foulest blots which hath appeared in the succession of all ages, he in a special manner exalts magnanimity in the contempt of earthly things. Yet the historians of those times tax him for insatiable avarice, and Tacitus tells us his philosophy was not a powerful antidote against the contagion of the court. A late writer (the author[5] of *The Strength and Weakness of Human Reason*): 'Consider what sort of a man Cicero himself was, and whether you can think him, with all his boasted reason, fitted and prepared for the favor of God in a heavenly state. He was guilty of one huge and glaring vice, and that is a most exorbitant ambition. His writings and behavior are full of self, and discover one of the proudest and vainest mortals that ever trod upon the earth. At present I will point to no other proof of it than his own letter to Lucceius, who was about to write the history of his own times: there you see him sacrificing even truth and honesty to the great idol of his pride. Again, let us see what his religion and piety were: he cannot find whether there is one God or many; he complied entirely with the polytheism and idolatry of the nation, and worshipped the multitude of their gods, that is, the stars, the devils, the departed heroes, or the chimeras, which the city of Rome had adopted into the number of their deities.'"

3. Clarke, *A Discourse Concerning the Unchangeable Obligations of Natural Religion.* Pp. 218 ff., 1706 ed.: "Having no knowledge of the whole Scheme, Order, and State of Things, the Method of Gods governing the World, his Design in Creating Mankind, the original Dignity of Humane Nature . . . : Having no knowledge, I say, of all This; their whole Attempt to discover the Truth of Things, and to instruct others therein, was like wandring in the wide Sea, without knowing whither they were to go."

4. Following the reference to Clarke at the end of the last paragraph, JE wrote, "see also forward p. 878," referring to a paragraph at the end of No. 1351, which, in accordance with JE's direction, is inserted here. The quote is taken from Alexander Moncrieff, *An enquiry into the principle, rule, and end of moral actions, wherein the scheme of . . . Mr. Archibald Campbell . . . is examined,* which JE had previously quoted in No. 1244.

5. I.e. Isaac Watts.

"Thus[6] [...] it is plain, whether we consider what the human understanding could do, or what it actually did, that it could not have attained to a sufficient knowledge of God without revelation; so that the demonstration, brought in favor of some religion, ends in a demonstration of the revealed. When we attentively consider the nature of man, we find it necessary he should have some religion; when we consider the nature of God, we must conclude he never would have made a falsehood necessary to the happiness of his rational creatures; and that, therefore, there must be a true religion. And when we consider, that by our natural faculties it is extremely difficult to arrive at a right idea of God till he reveals it to us, that all the Gentile world hath run into the grossest theological errors, and, in consequence of those, into the most enormous customs and crimes; and that no legislator ever founded his scheme of civil government on any supposed religious dictates of nature, but always on some real or pretended revelation; we cannot help ascribing all the true religion in the world to divine instruction, and all the frightful variety of religious errors to human invention, and to that dark and degenerate nature, by the imaginary light of which deists suppose the right idea of God may be easily and universally discovered." Vol. 1, pp. 86–89.

"Socrates, who never traveled out of Greece, [...] had nothing to erect a scheme of religion or morality on but the scattered fragments of truth, handed down from time immemorial among his countrymen, or imported by Pythagoras, Thales, and others, who had been in Egypt and the East. These he picked out from an huge heap of absurdities and errors, under which they were buried; and, by the help of a most prodigious capacity, laying them together, comparing them with the nature of things, and drawing consequences from them, he found reason to question the soundness of the Grecian theology and morality. But this is all the length he seems to have gone. He reasoned extremely well against the prevailing errors of his time; but was able to form no system of religion or morality. This was a work above the strength of his nature, and the lights he enjoyed. . . . He taught his disciples to worship the gods, and ground the distinction between right and wrong on the laws of their country; in the latter of which he followed the saying of his master Archelaus, who taught, that what is just or dishonest, is defined by law, not by nature. The notions of Plato, concerning the divine nature, were infinitely more sublime, and nearer the truth, than those of his master Socrates. He did not content him[self] merely with removing errors; he

6. Quotation from *Deism Revealed* resumes.

ventured on a system, and maintained that virtue is a science, and that God is the object and source of duty; that there is but one God, the fountain of all being, and superior to all essence; that he hath a son, called the Word; that there is a judgment to come, by which the just, who have suffered in this life, shall be recompensed in the other, and the wicked punished eternally; that God is omnipresent, and, consequently, that the wicked, if he were to dive into the deepest caverns of the earth, or should get wings, and fly into the heavens, would not be able to escape from him; that man is formed in the image of God; and that, in order to establish laws and government, relations, made by true TRADITIONS, AND ANCIENT ORACLES, are to be consulted. These points, so much insisted on by Plato, are far from being the growth of Greece, or his own invention, but derived from Eastern traditions, which we know he traveled for, at least as far as Egypt. He was wiser than his teacher, who was a much greater man, because his lights were better; but as they were not sufficient, he ran into great errors, speaking plainly, as if he believed in a plurality of gods, making goods, women, and children, common, etc.

"How should it come to pass, that Mount Taurus in Asia, and Mount Atlas, and the deserts of Barca in Africa, make so great a difference between the knowledge and politeness of the nations dwelling on the one side of them, and those of the nations dwelling on the other? Is knowledge progressive? And may it be stopped by a mountain, a sea, or a desert? The natural faculties of men in all nations are alike; and did nature itself furnish all men with the means and materials of knowledge, philosophy need never turn traveler, either in order to her own improvement, or to the communication of her lights to the world. How came it to pass, [. . .] that Scythia did not produce so many, so great, philosophers as Greece? I think it very evident that the great difference between these countries, as to learning and instruction, arose from this: the latter had the benefit of commerce with the Phœnicians, from whence they came by the knowledge of letters, and, probably, of navigation, and with the Egyptians, from whom they learned the greater part of their theology, policy, arts, and sciences. Such advantages the Scythians wanted; and therefore, although their natural talents were as good as those of the Grecians, they were not able to make any improvements in philosophy. [. . .] Why are the Asiatic Scythians at this day as ignorant as ever, while the European Scythians are little inferior to the other nations of Europe in arts and politeness? . . . And how does it come to pass, [. . .] that we, at this day, take upon us to approve the philosophy of Socrates and Plato, rather than of Epicurus and Aristippus? The Grecians were divided in this matter, some following the notions of the former, and others those of the latter. [...] Why did not reason put the matter out of question in those times, or, at least, immediately after? The infinite contradictions and uncertainties among the ancient philosophers produced the sect of the Skeptics. [...] In respect to religion, Socrates and Plato either were, or pretended to be, Skeptics, beating down the absurd notions of others, but seldom building up anything of their own, or, when they did, building on mere conjectures, or arguments suspected by themselves.

"If it be said the finding out of truth by the light of nature is a work of time, time hath taught the Tartars, Africans, and Americans, little or nothing of true theology or morality, even yet. Time of itself can teach nothing; it was the Christian religion that opened the eyes of the polite nations of Europe, and even of the deists of this age, wherein their eyes are still open, and they have any true principles by which they are able to examine the philosophy of the ancients, and by comparing their several opinions one with another, and with the truths derived from the Christian revelation, to decide in favor of some against the rest. Men are very apt to take that for the spontaneous produce of their own minds, which they were early taught, and long habituated to; and to call that the effect of nature, which was instilled insensibly into them, before they began to consider how notices and informations came in, or to keep any registry in their memories of the times when this or that addition to their fund of knowledge was made. But any man, who considers the matter candidly, will find, that the principles of all he knows, concerning either the authority or nature of morality, were communicated to him by instruction." Vol. 1, pp. 99–103.

"Lord Shaftesbury himself says, 'Few men are thinkers, and of those that are, some are vastly less able to manage their thoughts than others.'[7] Although, in the original frame of human nature, reason was the governing power or faculty of the mind, and ought to be so still; yet, like a weak prince, she is in most men dethroned by her usurping subjects, and that on account of inability to enforce her dictates, insomuch that, for once she issues any orders of her own, she is an hundred times either coaxed or compelled to lend her name and authority, [...] to the grossest extravagancies, and vilest crimes; and not only that, but to exert all the little ability that is left her, to find out ways and means to execute, and false arguments to palliate, the excesses committed by the under-

---

7. Skelton cites Shaftesbury, "Miscell. 5. Chap. iii."

faculties, the instincts, the sentiments, the passions and appetites, to which she is enslaved. She is ever giving proofs of her inability to determine points of the greatest plainness, and yet presuming to examine and pronounce most peremptorily about mysteries, and other matters, which, in her highest power and perfection, she was utterly unable to form any competent judgment of. . . . Were she able rightly to direct the conscience, and affix its approbation to actions really good in themselves, and its dislike, even to the worst of crimes, she had never suffered, [. . .] whole nations to offer human sacrifices to their gods, to kill and eat their own parents, and the very wisest and politest of them to destroy their own children, and to feast their eyes, at their public diversions, with the blood and slaughter of their fellow creatures. If she be not capable of approving the most horrible enormities, why does she, in this late age of the world, when she hath had time enough, one would think, to open her eyes, and come to a right sense of religion and morality, suffer the Americans and Africans to worship the devil, and even Christians, contrary to the express and repeated dictates of their religion, to hate, and persecute, and burn one another for God's sake?" Vol. 1, 119–21.

"As to the doctrine of the IMMORTALITY OF THE SOUL: It is certain, nothing can be more agreeable to reason, when once the doctrine is proposed, and thoroughly canvassed. But it is certain on the other hand, that there is no one probable opinion in the world, which mankind, left entirely to themselves, would have been more unlikely to have started. Who, if he were not assured of it by good authority, would ever take it into his head to imagine, that man, who dies, and rots, and vanishes forever, like all other animals, [. . .] still exists? [. . .] It is well if this, when proposed, can be believed. But to strike out the thought itself, is somewhat, I am afraid, too high and difficult for the capacity of man. . . . the only natural argument of any weight for the immortality of the soul, takes its rise from this observation, that justice is not done to the good, nor executed upon the bad man, in this life; and that as the governor of the world is just, man must live hereafter to be judged. But as this only argument, that can be drawn from mere reason, in order either to lead us to a discovery of our own immortality, or to support the opinion of it, when once started, is founded entirely on the knowledge of God, and his attributes; and as we have already seen, that such knowledge is almost unattainable by the present light of nature; the argument itself, which before the fall could not possibly have been thought of, is since the fall clogged with all the difficulties mere reason labors under, in finding out a right idea of God. And besides, this argument in itself is utterly inconclusive on the principles of the deists of our age and nation. [...] Because they insist, that virtue fully rewards, and vice fully punishes, itself.

"'Tis no wonder that many heathen nations believed a future state. They received it by tradition from their ancestors. But yet there is this evidence that mankind had not this doctrine merely from the easy and plain dictates of reason and nature: that many did not believe it. Herodotus informs us, that of all the Scythian nations there was but one (if I remember, it was that of the Getae, who were taught by their countryman Zamolxis, the disciple of Pythagoras) that believed this doctrine. [...] The Sadducees among the Jews, and not only the Epicureans, but several other sects of philosophers among the Greeks and Romans, were firmly persuaded, there is no life after this: nay, and Socrates, in the *Phaedon* of Plato, says, 'Most men were of opinion, that the soul, upon its separation from the body, is dissipated, and reduced to nothing.' And Tully in his first *Tusculan Question* says, Pherecydes Syrus, preceptor to Pythagoras, 'was the first person, known to the learned world, who taught the immortality of the soul.' [...] The other arguments brought by Plato and Cicero for the immortality of the soul, beside that already mentioned, are very inconclusive. They themselves thought so. [...] the treatise of old age makes the elder Cato talk of it, as an opinion he was fond of, rather than as a doctrine he could demonstrate; and comfort himself, after enumerating all the arguments he could think of for it, with this reflection upon the whole, that if the soul dies with the body, the petty philosophers, who opposed themselves to the opinion of the soul's immortality, ceasing to be, as well as he, would not laugh at his credulity. The former, in his *Phaedon,* makes Socrates speak with some doubt concerning his own arguments, and introduces Simmias saying to Socrates, after having listened to his principal reasonings, 'We ought to lay hold of the strongest arguments for this doctrine, that either we ourselves, or others can suggest to us. If both ways prove ineffectual, we must, however, put up with the best proofs we can get, till some PROMISE, OR REVELATION, shall clear up the point to us.'" Vol. 1, pp. 135–38.

"One of Plato's arguments for the immortality of the soul is this: 'every cause produces an effect contrary to itself,' and 'that, therefore, as life produces death, so death shall produce life.' [...] Cicero, [...] to prove that the soul will exist after it is separated from the body, endeavors to prove it existed before it was joined to it. [...] And to that end he insists that what we call aptness in children to learn, is nothing more than memory. [...] Another argument of Plato is this: 'That alone which moves itself, inasmuch as it is never deserted by itself, never ceases

to move; but the mind moves itself, and borrows not its motion from anything else; and therefore must move, and consequently exist, forever.'

"The law of nature must be extremely defective, if it do not give us full
assurances of very great rewards and punishments in another life, for
what we do here." (See "Miscellanies," [No.] 1229.) "And the light of nature hath been so far from doing this, that it hath suffered whole nations
to remain for several ages in perfect ignorance of this important truth;
[. . .] and [. . .] hath suffered the greater part of its most unerring oracles, the philosophers, to deny it; and, to the reproach of self-sufficient
and over-weaning nature, hath put little into the mouths of those few,
that believed it, [. . .] to defend it with, but nonsense and sophistry, although nature had done her utmost, and human literature had lent her
assistance, to make them the greatest men in the world. The wisdom of
Socrates and Plato, united, produced such arguments for a most favorite
opinion, as they themselves are dissatisfied with, and therefore call for
more than human help. Cicero, being so fond of this opinion, that, as
he says, he 'would rather err with Plato in holding it, than think rightly
with those who deny it,' poorly echoes the arguments of Plato, adds little to them himself, and, at the conclusion, in a manner giving up the
point, with all the arguments brought to support it, endeavors to comfort himself, and others, against the approach of death, by proving death
to be no evil, even supposing the soul to perish with the body." Vol. 1,
pp. 141–42.

"And this great philosopher, with all his knowledge, gives but one lot
to the good and evil in another life. It was his opinion, 'if the soul is immortal, it must be happy; if it perishes with the body, it cannot be miserable.' This consolation he administers alike to all men, without making any distinction; [. . .] and consequently, leaves moral obligation on
a mere temporal footing, which, in effect, is not a whit better than down-
right atheism. But, in his dream of Scipio, when he does not reason, nor
seem to inculcate any particular doctrine, he indeed introduces the elder Scipio telling the younger, by way of dream, that 'those who served
their country, and cultivated justice and the other virtues, should go to
heaven after death,' but that 'the souls of those that had violated the laws
of the gods and men, should, after leaving their bodies, be tossed about
on the earth, and not return to heaven for many ages.' [. . .] Now if a
person of Cicero's abilities and learning could, from the light of nature,
work out no better scheme than this, which renders futurity almost useless to moral obligation; how much further from truth and reason must
we suppose the bulk of mankind to stray, if each ignorant person is to be

left entirely to his own thoughts and discoveries in respect to the future rewards of virtue, and punishments of vice?" Vol. 1, pp. 144–45.

"As to the expectations which the people had of future rewards and punishments, which appears by their historians and poets, those they could have borrowed from nothing else but tradition." Vol. 1, p. 145.

"Plato, who makes all religious knowledge to depend on revelation, either drew his theory of futurity from his travels into countries bordering on the light of revelation, and the hints of those who were not altogether unacquainted with the sacred writings, and religion of the Israelites; or else he refined it from the crude opinions of his countrymen; extracting and separating, by the force of amazing talents, what was original and true, from what was novel and superstitious." Vol. 1, p. 146.

"Thus, upon considering the extent and strength of human faculties, we have found them at present utterly incapable of attaining to any competent notion of a divine law, if left wholly to themselves. [. . .] This is vastly confirmed by experience; from which it appears, that mankind, instead of being able, through a long series of ages, by the mere light of nature, to find out a right idea of God and his laws, on the contrary, after having, without doubt, been well acquainted at first with both, gradually, and at length almost universally, lost sight of both, insomuch that idolatry, as bad as atheism, and wickedness, worse than brutality, were established for religion and law in all countries. The philosophers, who lived, in the most knowing countries, and sought for religious and moral truth, but sought in vain, as the wisest of 'em confess, render this argument still more cogent and conclusive. I need not be particular, in order to show this, by accounting to you their infinite absurdities, and eternal contradictions. Nor need I tell you, that Pliny says, man could know nothing without instruction; that Plutarch asserts, he would be the wildest of all animals, if wholly left to himself; that all the ancient heathen poets, historians, and philosophers, represent the first men as the most fierce, outrageous race of savages in all the woods; that Plato calls philosophy, by which they were civilized, 'the gift,' and Cicero, 'the invention, of the gods'; that Iamblichus, observing the ignorance of the human nature, 'confesses there is no remedy for all its errors, but some portion of divine instruction or light'; that, as to moral obligation, Plato asserts, that 'there are no such things by nature, as just things, inasmuch as men perpetually differ in opinion about them, and are forever contriving new standards to distinguish right from wrong, and that therefore there can be no law, except God gives it to us'; that Socrates, Aristippus, Diogenes, Pyrrho, refer the distinction between right and wrong to the laws of so-

ciety; and that all legislators founded the obligation and authority of social laws upon either real or pretended revelations. If you would have
further satisfaction on these heads, and desire to have it proved to you,
that all the little advances made among the Greeks, in theology or morality, were derived from Egyptian, Phœnician, and Syrian traditions, either
oral or written, and brought into Greece and Italy by Thales, Pherecydes, Pythagoras, Plato, and others, [. . .] you may, at your leisure, consult Gale's *Court of the Gentiles*.[8] [. . .] Thus I think it is evident, that
through mere unassisted nature, in its present [. . .] blindness and corruption, we can neither have a religion, nor a law, sufficient to answer
the ends of society, or to render individuals good and happy; and that
we may therefore say with Cicero, in his third book *De natura Deorum*, 'If
it is a thing agreed on by all the philosophers, that no man attains to true
wisdom, we are all in a most wretched condition, although it is said, that
God hath taken the utmost care to provide for our happiness; for as it is
the same thing, whether nobody is in health, or whether nobody hath it
in his power to be in health, so to me there is no difference, whether no
man is wise, or no man can be wise.'" Vol. 1, pp. 149–51.

"As the apostle Paul observes in the first chapter of his epistle to the
Romans, men 'did not like to retain God in their knowledge; and professing themselves to be wise, they become fools, and changed the glory
of the incorruptible God into an image like to corruptible man, and to
birds, and four-footed beasts, and creeping things. Thus were their foolish hearts darkened; upon which God gave 'em over to a reprobate mind,
and gave 'em up to uncleanness, to sins of all kinds, even such as were
utterly against nature.' [. . .] St. Chrysostom, in his descant on this passage, says, 'the Gentiles fell into a kind of madness; insomuch that, having deprived themselves of the light, and involved their minds in the
darkness of their own thoughts, their attempt to travel towards heaven
ended in a miserable shipwreck, as his must do, who, in a dark night, undertakes a voyage by sea.' This is a true representation of St. Paul's meaning, in which the Gentiles stand charged with departing from the light
and reason bestowed on them by God, and plunging themselves into
such a state of ignorance [. . .], as they were never afterwards able to
extricate themselves out of. [. . .] being guided by conceit, and too great
attachment to sensible things, entered upon a wrong way; so that still the

8. Theophilus Gale, *The Court of the Gentiles: Or A Discourse touching the Original of Human Literature, both Philologie and Philosophie, From the Scripture & Jewish Church* (2nd ed., Oxford, 1672),
a source that JE did indeed consult.

longer they traveled, the further they wandered from the knowledge of the true God, and right religion. The doctrine of St. Paul concerning the blindness into which the Gentiles fell, is so confirmed by the state of religion in Africa, America, and even China, where, to this day, no advances towards the true religion have been made, that we can no longer be at a loss to judge [. . .] of the insufficiency of unassisted reason to dissipate the prejudices of the heathen world, and open their eyes to religious truths.

"If our knowledge of God had come by observation and philosophy, it must have risen, by degrees, from a discovery of causes by their effects. [. . .] Thus must reason, in its inquiry after God, have proceeded; and its last deductions must have been more perfect than its first. If the works of creation can, in our present blind condition, easily discover to us the being and attributes of God, surely they must be still better qualified to support that discovery, after it is made, and to correct any mistakes that might have arisen in the making of it; which is an easier matter by far, than to make the discovery itself. But St. Paul gives us quite another history of the business: he says, that 'from the Creation, απο κτισεως, the invisible things of God are clearly seen' [Rom. 1:20]; and afterwards, through philosophy, and the boasted wisdom of man, almost wholly lost, or changed into idolatry, worse in itself than even total ignorance. This seems plainly to intimate, that our knowledge of God did not take its rise from mere reason, but from revelation, or, at least, from extraordinary power or faculty in the nature of our fist parents, which their posterity are destitute of, and which to suppose, in respect to our present debate, is the same thing as to suppose a revelation." Vol. 1, pp. 159–62.

"Nothing but revelation and faith can, with any certainty, teach us, that 'the things that are seen,' viz. matter, and all its various modifications, were made out of things that do not appear, i.e. out of nothing, and by a pure Spirit. Philosophy could hardly have beat out so inconceivable a mystery, but must have either concluded matter to have been eternal, or must have supposed its efficient cause to have been material.

"This we see verified by experience: the heathens, as Porphyry himself acknowledged, never ascribed the creation of the world to God; but maintained, either that the universe is God, or that its matter was coeval with God. 'If we look back,' says the learned Shuckford,[9] 'and make a fair inquiry, we shall find, that the ancient wise men did not fall into their

---

9. Samuel Shuckford, whose famous *Sacred and Prophane History of the World Connected* . . . (2nd ed., 4 vols. London, 1731), JE used himself.

errors by paying too great a deference to tradition, and pretended revelations, but by setting up what they thought a reasonable scheme of religion, in opposition to the traditional; and that the frame and course of
nature was not sufficiently understood, to make men masters of true philosophy.' The same author further observes, that 'there is nothing so extravagant and ridiculous, which men of the greatest parts, and eminency
for the natural strength of their understandings, have not defended; as
is evident, by what Plato and Plutarch have said in vindication of the
Egyptian superstitions.' As for the latter, he says, in his book concerning
Isis and Osiris, that 'there is nothing in the heathen mythology unreasonable, idle, or superstitious; and that a good moral, historical, or philosophical reason, may be given for every part of every fable therein.' [. . .]
Socrates and Plato indeed saw an infinite deal of absurdity, and even
wickedness, in the pagan worship: yet, having no thorough assurances of
a better, and seeing plainly the necessity of religion, they labored to correct that of their own country; but, as for Cicero and Plutarch, they both
of them had a warm zeal for the superstitions they were educated in, especially the latter, who, it must be confessed, was one of the wisest and
greatest men that ever enriched the commonwealth of letters. If such
men as these were capable of thinking so like the vulgar and illiterate,
how could the more ignorant, i.e. almost the whole race of mankind,
have beat out from their own observations a right notion of God, and
their duty to him?" Vol. 1, pp. 163–64.

"The starting a proposition is one thing, and the proof of it quite another. Every science has its proofs in the nature of things: yet all sciences
require to be taught; and those require it most, the first principles of
which lie a little out of the reach of ordinary capacities. The first principles of religion, being of an high and spiritual nature, are harder to be
found out, than those of any other science; because the minds of men
are gross and earthy, used to objects of sense; and all their depraved appetites, and corrupt dispositions, which are by nature opposite to the
true religion, help to increase the natural weakness of their reason, and
clip the wings of their contemplation, when they endeavor, by their own
strength, to soar towards God, and heavenly things. No man, in his, nor
hardly in any other time, knew better how to catch at the evidence of divine truths, discovered in the works of creation, nor had better opportunities, than Plato: yet, with all the helps he derived from foreign and
domestic instruction, he finds himself, on every occasion, at a loss, when
he speaks of God, and divine matters; relies on oracles, traditions, and
revelations; and, having got a little taste of this kind of instruction, is

every now and then confessing his want of more, and wishing for it with the greatest anxiety." Vol. 1, pp. 166–67.

"If a few persons of superior talents and application should discover the true religion, this could be of little use, because merely by their own efforts, and without the assistance of miracles and grace, they could never so propagate their discovery, as to convert the world thereunto." Vol. 1, p. 168.

"The wisest of the heathen sages [. . .] made our knowledge of God to depend, not on philosophical inquiries, but on tradition. Plato is full of reflections to this purpose; and, not thinking the traditions, which he was acquainted with, sufficient, he talks of a future instructor to be sent from God, to teach the world a more perfect knowledge of religious duties. 'The truth is,' says he, speaking, in his first book *De Legibus,* concerning future rewards and punishments, 'to determine or establish anything certain about these matters, in the midst of so many doubts and disputations, is the work of God only.' In his *Phaedon,* one of the speakers says to Socrates, concerning the IMMORTALITY OF THE SOUL, 'I am of the same opinion with you, that, in this life, it is either absolutely impossible, or extremely difficult, to arrive at a clear knowledge in this matter.' In the apology he wrote for Socrates, he puts these words into his mouth, on the subject of reformation of manners: 'You may pass the remainder of your days in sleep, or despair of finding out a sufficient expedient for this purpose, if God, in his providence, doth not send you some other instructor.'" (See "Miscellanies," No. 1229.)[1] "And in his *Epinomis* he says, 'Let no man take upon him to teach, if God do not lead the way.' In the book *De Mundo,* ascribed to Aristotle, we have a remarkable passage to this effect: 'It is an old tradition, almost universally received, that all things proceeded from God, and subsist through him; and that no nature is self-sufficient, or independent of God's protection and assistance.' In his metaphysics he ascribes the belief of the gods, and of this, that the deity compasses and comprehends all nature, to a traditionary habit of speaking, handed down from the first men to after-ages. Cicero, in his treatise concerning the nature of the gods, introduces Cotta blaming those who endeavored, by argumentation, to prove there are gods, and affirming that this only served to make the point doubtful, which, by the instructions and traditions of their forefathers, had

---

1. MS: "N. 1228. the 2d p of that N. b." JE obviously means No. 1229 (which he cites later in this entry), an earlier extract from *Deism Revealed.* In the second paragraph of the entry, Skelton discusses the necessity of revelation.

been sufficiently made known to them, and established. Plutarch, speaking of the worship paid to a certain ideal divinity, which his friend had called in question, says, 'It is enough to believe pursuant to the faith of our ancestors, and the instructions communicated to us in the country where we were born and bred; than which we can neither find out, nor apply, any argument more to be depended on.'" Vol. 1, pp. 169–70.

"It will be further useful to observe, that the thoughts of men, with regard to any internal law, will be always mainly influenced by their sentiments concerning the CHIEF GOOD. Whatsoever power or force may do, in respect to outward actions of a man, nothing can oblige him to think or act, as often as he is at liberty, against what he takes to be his chief good, or interest. No law, nor system of laws, can possibly answer the end and purpose of a law, till the grand question, what is the chief happiness and end of man, be determined, and so cleared up, that every man may be fully satisfied about it. Before our Savior's time, the world was infinitely divided on this important head: the philosophers were miserably bewildered in all their researches after the chief good. Each sect, each subdivision of a sect, had a chief good of its own, and rejected all the rest. They advanced, as Varro tells us, no fewer than two hundred and eighty-eight opinions, in relation to this matter; which shows, by a strong experiment, that the light of nature was altogether unable to settle the difficulty. Every man, if left to the particular bias of his own nature, chooses out a chief good for himself, and lays the stress of all his thoughts and actions on it. Now if the supposed chief good of any man should lead him, as it often does, to violate the laws of society, to hurt others, and act against the general good of mankind; he will be very unfit for society, and, consequently, as he cannot subsist out of it, an enemy to himself. Robbers, thieves, assassins, rebels, are all instances of this; and so are, also, those more cunning, but more dangerous persons, who know how to evade the laws, or even, by their assistance, to gain unjust advantages to themselves, and hurt society.

"After the corruption of nature, the light of nature is become too dim for the discovery of true religion. But, whatever informations it was qualified to give us, it must have made a most unequal distribution of them, in proportion to the great inequality of men's capacities. So imperfect was this light, so feeble and uncertain, that society and civil government could in no country rest upon it; and so unequally was it dispensed to different countries, and different individuals, that, if this is an objection of any weight, it lies more strongly against natural than against revealed religion, and therefore better fits the mouth of an atheist than a deist.

Can any instance be given in any country, in which some, either real or pretended, revelation was not the established religion, and the basis of civil society? Is there any historian or traveler that gives any information of any people, who believe in nothing concerning God, but what each man draws from within himself; or who do not follow the customs and traditions of their forefathers in matters of religion? If Christianity came too late into the world, what is called natural religion came full as late; and there are no footsteps of natural religion, in any sense of the words, to be found at this day, but where Christianity hath planted [it]. In every place else religion hath no conformity with reason or truth; so far is the light of nature from lending sufficient assistance. It is strange, that the natural light should be so clear, and yet the natural darkness so great, that in all unassisted countries the most monstrous forms of religion, derogatory to God, and prejudicial to man, should be contrived by some, and swallowed by the rest with a most voracious credulity. I could wish most heartily, that all nations were Christians; yet, since it is otherwise, we derive this advantage from it, that we have a standing and contemporary demonstration of that, which nature, left to herself, can do. Had all the world been Christians for some ages past, our present Libertines would insist, that Christianity had done no service to mankind; that nature could have sufficiently directed herself; and that all the stories told, either in sacred or profane history, of the idolatry and horrible forms of religion in ancient times, were forged by Christian priests, to make the world think revelation necessary, and natural reason incapable of dictating true and right notions of religion. But, as the case stands at present, we have such proofs of the insufficiency of unassisted reason in this behalf, as all the subtlety of Libertines is unable to evade." Vol. 2, pp. 151–52.

"All that the Grecians, Romans, and present Chinese know of true religion, they were taught traditionally. As to their corrupt notions, and idolatries, [. . .] they were of their own invention. [. . .] The Grecians, who were by far the most knowing people of the three [. . .], were as gross idolaters as the rest, till Plato's time. He traveled into the East, and came home with better notions of theology, which he derived from tradition, than the other philosophers of his time were masters of. He ran higher towards truth in his sentiments of religion, than others; but still worshipped the gods of his country, and durst not speak out all he knew. However, he formed a great school, and, both through his writings and scholars, instructed his countrymen in a kind of religious philosophy, that tended much more directly and strongly to reformation of manners, than either the dictates of their own reason, or of their other philosophers." Vol. 2, p. 154.

"Some true religion there must be, and there can be but one. This religion must be fitted to the wants of all men, and ought to be universal. Now amongst all the religions hitherto known or heard of, there never was one, which did not require to be taught and learned. The deists say their religion is that of nature, and universally known without teaching. Yet the world hath been always trusting to real or pretended revelations, and knew nothing of an untaught religion, till about a century ago, that some deists began to set up a new one, which, if we may believe themselves, needed not to have been taught, because everybody knew it before." Vol. 2, p. 191.

"All the philosophy of the Gentile nations, excepting that of Socrates and Plato, was derived from the source of self-sufficiency. They two acknowledged the blindness of human nature, and the necessity of a divine instructor. And not one, excepting these two, founded his morality on any sense of religion, or ever dreamt of an inability in man to render himself happy." Vol. 2, p. 209.

Here see a large citation from Dr. Winder in papers on the history of the work of redemption, pp. 48–53.[2]

A TABLE TO THE FOREGOING EXTRACTS FROM *DEISM REVEALED*

Revelation necessary to men's subsisting in SOCIETY: pp. 443–34.

The light of nature insufficient to discover the true knowledge of God, and of man's duty in man's corrupt state, evident from the REASON AND NATURE OF THINGS: pp. 434–38, 448, 454, 455–56.

The evidence of the insufficiency of natural light from the state of all nations that were without revelation: pp. 437, 439, 439–41, 449, 454–55. See Clarke's Evidences, pp. 124–25.[3]

2. In "History of Redemption," Bk. 1, discussing the growth of error and delusion before Christ's birth, JE quotes Winder, *A Critical and Chronological History of the Rise, Progress, Declension, and Revival of Knowledge, Chiefly Religious,* vol. 2, pp. 336 ff. In these pages, Winder asserts that, despite its "strengthened Faculties" and "growing Powers of Reason," "the Pagan Religion degenerated into greater Absurdity, the further it proceeded," citing some of the "grossest abominations" in Egypt, Greece, and Rome. Though "an extraordinary Genius" arose from time to time, yet those who propagated the true knowledge of divine revelation "were but plain Fishermen, not like a Socrates or a Newton."

3. Clarke, *A Discourse Concerning the Unchangeable Obligations of Natural Religion,* 1706 ed., pp. 193 ff.

A description of the THEOLOGY of the heathen world: pp. 439–41.

The barbarous, impious PRINCIPLES AND CUSTOMS of the heathen nations: pp. 441–42.

The ignorance and errors of the PHILOSOPHERS: pp. 434–35, 442–44, 447, 450–51, 454–55. See forward, pp. 604 ff. [No. 1357].

Here see also Clarke's Evidences, pp. 138e, 139–42, 145–46, 158d, e., 149.[4]

VICES of the best among the heathen: p. 442.

VICES OF THE PHILOSOPHERS: pp. 443–46, 449; Clarke's Evidences, pp. 137–38.[5]

The morality of all other philosophers but Socrates and Plato founded in SELF-SUFFICIENCE: p. 459. See also Warburton's Sermons, p. 314.[6] See forward, p. 604, etc. [No. 1357].

Mere nature insufficient to discover man's CHIEF GOOD: p. 457.

The need of a revelation to discover a FUTURE STATE: pp. 449, 450–52, 456.

LENGTH OF TIME will do nothing without revelation to discover truth to mankind in religious and moral matters: pp. 438–39, 448, 449, 452, 453–54.

If the truth could have been found by a few without revelation, it could not have been PROPAGATED and made manifest to the world: pp. 438, 456. Here see Clarke, Evidences, pp. 132, 135, 147–48, 150–52.[7] See also p. 445.[8]

What of true religious knowledge was found among the nations either came from the REVELATION GOD MADE TO THE JEWS or from TRADITION handed down from the first fathers of mankind: pp. 437–38, 442–43, 446–47, 452, 453, 454–55, 458–59. Here see also [pp.] 469–70.

The ESTABLISHED RELIGION in all countries founded on some real or pretended revelation: pp. 457–58.

---

4. Ibid., 1706 ed., pp. 218 ff., 225 ff., 236 ff..

5. Ibid., 1706 ed., pp. 221 ff.

6. William Warburton, *The Principles of Natural and Revealed Religion Occasionally Opened and Explained; in a Course of Sermons* (vols. 1–2, London, 1753–54; vol. 3, London, 1767), *1*, 314. See *Works, 13*, 133–34, n. 3, on important text-critical issues.

7. Clarke, *Discourse Concerning the Unchangeable Obligations of Natural Religion.* See above, n. 4.

8. MS: "this book. p. 878," i.e. "Miscellanies," Bk. 9. The reference is to the paragraph quoting "Moncrieff against Campbell," originally at the end of No. [1351], which JE directs to be inserted in No. [1350].

LEGISLATORS always founded their schemes of civil government on real or pretended revelations: pp. 446, 452, 457–58. See No. 954.

THE BASIS OF CIVIL SOCIETY IN ALL COUNTRIES some real or pretended revelation: pp. 457–58.

The opinion of philosophers concerning men's dependence on PAST REVELATIONS for the knowledge of truth in divine and moral things: [pp.] 447, 452, 452–53, 455–56, 456–57. See [No.] 1012, and [No.] 973.

Philosophers sensible of the need of a FUTURE REVELATION: pp. 450, 456. See Clarke, Evidences, pp. 156–59.[9]

The knowledge of truth in things supposed to belong to natural religion much further from being universal than that which is by revealed religion: p. 457.

The knowledge of the truth by the light of nature comes later than by the light of revelation: pp. 439, 458.

The knowledge that is at present to be found in the world in matters of religion is owing to the Christian revelation: [p.] 448.

No natural religion in any nation but where Christianity has planted it: p. 458.

No man ever had a right notion of God and religion but it was derived from revelation: [p.] 434.

No religion ever professed in the world by any person but from a pretended or real revelation till about a century ago: p. 459.

Traditions among the heathen concerning the TRINITY: [p.] 447; a FUTURE JUDGMENT: [p.] 447; ETERNITY OF PUNISHMENT: [p.] 447; Concerning man's being made in the IMAGE OF GOD: [p.] 447.

1351. EXTRACTS OF *THE TRAVELS OF CYRUS*.[1] THE FIRST RELIGION OF MANKIND AGREEABLE TO THE RELIGION OF THE HOLY SCRIPTURES. THE WISER HEATHEN TAUGHT A SPIRITUAL WORSHIP.

9. Clarke, *Discourse Concerning the Unchangeable Obligations of Natural Religion*. See preceding page, n. 4.

1. Chevalier (Andrew Michael) Ramsay, *The Travels of Cyrus. To Which Is Annexed, a Discourse upon the Theology and Mythology of the Pagans*. JE used the 8th ed., London, 1752. All of the material extracted in this entry comes from the annexed "Discourse upon the Theology and Mythology of the Pagans." This entry has been edited to preserve Ramsay's and JE's variant spellings of the names of some philosophers, sects, and mythological figures.

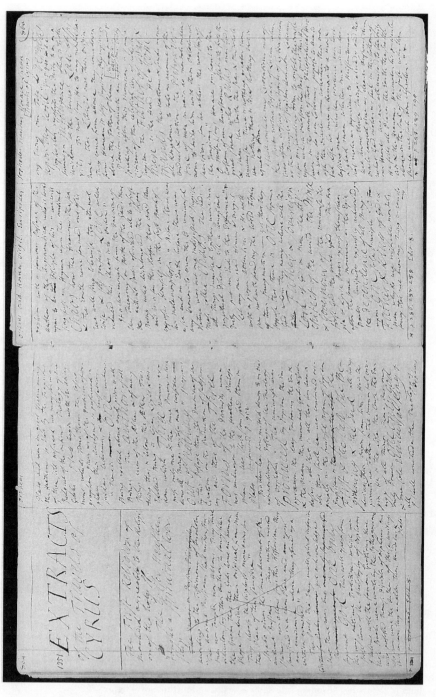

"Miscellanies," Bk. 9, showing the beginning of No. 1351, "Extracts of *The Travels of Cyrus*. . . ." Courtesy of Beinecke Rare Book and Manuscript Library, Yale University.

"According to the testimony of Herodotus, the ancient Persians had neither statues, nor temples, nor altars: 'They think [it] ridiculous,' says this author, 'to fancy, like the Greeks, that the gods have an human shape, or derive their original from men. They choose the highest mountains for the place of their sacrifice.'"

"Strabo gives the same account of the ancient Persians. 'They neither erected statues nor altars,' says this historian; 'they sacrificed in a clean place and upon an eminence, where they offered up a victim crowned.'" Pp. 275–76.[2]

"The poets, though they multiplied inferior gods, yet acknowledge that there was but ONE ONLY SUPREME GOD. This will appear from the very ancient traditions which we still have of the philosophy of Orpheus. [. . .] I believe with the famous Grotius, that those books were wrote by the Pythagoreans, who professed themselves disciples of Orpheus: but whoever were the authors of these writings, it is certain they are older than Heroditus and Plato, and were in great esteem among the heathens; so that by the fragments of them still preserved, we may form a judgment of the ancient theology of the Greeks. I shall begin with the abridgment which Timotheus the cosmographer gives us of the doctrine of Orpheus. This abridgment is preserved in Suidas, Cedrenus and Eusebius.

"'There is ONE unknown Being exalted above and prior to all beings, the AUTHOR of all things, even of the æther, and of everything that is below the æther: this exalted being is life, light and wisdom; which THREE names express only one and the same power, which drew all beings, visible and invisible, OUT OF NOTHING.' It appears by this passage that the doctrine of the creation (or the production of substances), and that of the THREE FORMS of the divinity were not unknown to the heathen philosophers. We shall soon find them in Plato." See forward, p. 560.[3]

"Proclus has transmitted down to us this extraordinary passage of the theology of Orpheus. 'The universe was PRODUCED by Jupiter, the empyræum, the deep Tartarus, the earth, and the ocean, the immortal gods and goddesses; all that is, all that has been, and all that shall be, was contained originally in the fruitful bosom of Jupiter. Jupiter is the FIRST AND THE LAST, THE BEGINNING AND THE END. All beings derive their origin from him. He is the primitive father and the immortal virgin. He is

2. JE put a large "X" through the preceding two paragraphs.

3. MS: "p. 952," in No. [1355]. The page cited contains a cross-reference to this point in No. [1351] with the heading, "Concerning the Greeks." The passage begins, "Justin Martyr, in his exhortation to the Greeks, has preserved to us this wonderful fragment of Orpheus . . ."

the life, the cause, the energy of all things. There is but one only power, ONE ONLY GOD, and one sole UNIVERSAL KING of all.'

"I shall conclude the theology of Orpheus with a famous passage of the author of the *Argonautica,* who is looked upon to be the disciple of his. 'We will sing first an hymn upon the ancient CHAOS; how the heavens, the sea, and the earth were formed out of it. We will sing likewise that eternal, wise, and self-perfect LOVE, which reduced this chaos into order.'

"It is clear enough from the doctrine of the theogony or birth of the gods, that the ancient poets ascribed all to a first being, who disentangled the chaos. And it is for this reason that Ovid thus expresses himself in the first book of his *Metamorphoses.* 'Before there was a sea and an earth, before there was any heaven to cover the world, universal nature was but one indigested sluggish mass, called CHAOS. The seeds [of] all things jumbled together were in a perpetual discord, till a beneficent diety put an end to the difference.'" Pp. 286–88.[4]

"Let anyone read Homer and Virgil with a proper attention, and he will see, notwithstanding the wild flights of their imagination [. . .] yet that they suppose that there is ONE supreme God, whom they everywhere call the FATHER, AND SOVEREIGN LORD of gods and men, the ARCHITECT of the world, the PRINCE AND GOVERNOR of the universe, the first god, the great God. [. . .] The tragic and lyric poets express themselves after the same manner as the epic poets. Euripedes expressly acknowledges the DEPENDENCE of all beings upon ONE sole principle. 'O FATHER, AND KING of gods and men! why do we miserable mortals fancy that we know anything, or can do anything? Our fate DEPENDS UPON THY WILL.'" P. 545.[5]

"Sophocles represents the deity to us as a sovereign INTELLIGENCE, which is truth, wisdom, and the eternal LAW OF SPIRITS. ''Tis not,' says he, 'to any mortal nature, that LAWS owe their origin; they come from above; they come down from heaven itself; Jupiter Olympius is alone the father of them.'" See forward, pp. 545–46.[6]

"Plautus introduceth an inferior deity speaking after this manner: 'I

4. JE's copy of Ovid's *Metamorphoses* is in the library of Jonathan Edwards College, Yale University.

5. MS: "p. 940. [col. 2,] e," a reference not to Ramsay but to a later page in "Miscellanies," Bk. 9, specifically a passage in No. [1355] beginning, "Euripides expressly acknowledges the dependence of all beings on one soul principle as author of life and knowledge . . ."

6. MS: "941 [col. 1,] c." See No. [1355], the passage beginning, "St. Justin Martyr quotes from Sophocles the following maxims . . ."

am a citizen of the celestial city, of which Jupiter, the FATHER OF GODS AND MEN, is the head. HE COMMANDS the nations, and sends us over all kingdoms, to take an account of the conduct and actions, the PIETY AND VIRTUE of men. In vain do mortals endeavor to bribe him with their oblations and sacrifices. [. . .] For he abhors the worship of the impious.'

"'O Muse,' says Horace, 'pursuant to the custom of our ancestors, celebrate first the great Jove, who RULES over gods and men, the earth, the seas, and the whole universe: there is nothing greater than he, nothing that is like, nothing that is equal to him.'

"I shall conclude my quotations out of the poets with a passage of Lucan. When Cato, after crossing the deserts of Lybia, arrives at the temple of Jupiter Ammon, Labienus is for persuading him to consult the oracle. Upon which occasion the poet puts this answer in the mouth of that philosophical hero, 'Why do you, Labienus, propose to me to ask the oracle . . . whether this mortal life be only a remora to a more lasting one? Whether violence can hurt a good man? Whether true virtue does not make us superior to misfortunes? [. . .] We know these things already, and the oracle cannot give us clearer answers than what God makes us feel in the bottom of our heart. We are all united to the deity. [. . .] He [. . .] fills all places, the earth, the sea, the air, and the heavens; he makes his particular abode in the soul of the just: why then should we seek him elsewhere?'" Pp. 289–90.

"Let us pass from the poets to the philosophers, and begin with Thales the Milesian, chief of the Ionic school, who lived above 600 years before the birth of Christ. We have none of his works now left; but we have some of his maxims, which have been transmitted down to us by the most venerable writers of antiquity. 'God is the most ancient of all beings; he is the AUTHOR of the universe, which is full of wonders; he is the mind which brought the CHAOS out of confusion into order; he is beginning and without ending, and nothing is hid from him; nothing can resist the force of fate; but this fate is nothing but the immutable reason and eternal power of PROVIDENCE.'

"Pythagoras is the second great philosopher after Thales, and chief of the Italic school. [. . .] Now these are the notions which he has left us of the deity. 'God is neither the object of sense, nor subject to passion; but invisible, purely intelligible, and supremely intelligent. In his body he is like the light, and in his soul he resembles truth. He is the universal spirit that pervades and diffuseth itself over all nature. All beings receive their life FROM HIM. There is but ONE ONLY GOD, who is not as some are apt to imagine, seated above the world, beyond the orb of the universe; but being all in himself, he sees all the beings that inhabit his immensity. He is the sole principle, the light of heaven, the FATHER OF ALL; he PRODUCES everything, he ORDERS and DISPOSES everything; he is the reason, the life, and the motion of all being.'" Pp. 291–92.

"I shall conclude the article of Pythagoras with a summary of his doctrine as it is given us by St. Cyril. 'We see plainly,' says this father, 'that Pythogoras maintained, that there is but ONE GOD, the original and CAUSE OF ALL THINGS, who enlightens everything, animates everything, and FROM WHOM everything PROCEEDS, who has GIVEN BEING to all things, and is the source of all motion.'

"After Pythagoras comes Anaxagoras of the Ionic sect [...]. This philosopher was the first after Thales in the Ionic school who perceived the necessity of introducing a supreme intelligence for the FORMATION of the universe. He rejected with contempt, and with great strength of reason refuted the doctrine of those who held, that blind necessity, and the casual motions of matter had produced the world. He endeavored to prove, that a pure uncompounded spirit PRESIDES OVER the universe.

"According to Aristotle's account, the reasoning of Anaxagoras was founded upon these two principles: 1. 'That the idea of matter not including that of active force, motion could not be one of its properties. We must therefore, said he, seek somewhere else to find out the CAUSE of its activity. Now this active principle, as it was the cause of motion, he called the soul, because it ANIMATES THE UNIVERSE. 2. He distinguished between this universal principle of motion, and the thinking principle, which last he called the understanding. He saw nothing in matter that had any resemblance to this property; and from thence he inferred, that there was in nature another substance besides matter. But he added, that the SOUL AND SPIRIT are one and the same substance distinguished by us only in regard of its different operations; and that of all essences it was the most simple, and most pure, and the most exempt from all mixture and composition.' This philosopher passed at Athens for an atheist, because he denied that the stars and planets are gods. He maintained, that the first were suns, and the latter habitable worlds." Pp. 295–96.

"Xenophon has left us an excellent abridgment of the theology of Socrates. [...] It contains the conversation of Socrates with Aristodemus, who doubted of the existence of a God. Socrates makes him at first take notice of all the characters of design, of art, of the wisdom that appears all over the universe, and particularly in the mechanism of the human body. [...] Aristodemus objecting that he did not see that wise architect of the universe; Socrates answers him. 'Neither do you see the soul which governs your own body, and regulates all its motions. You might as well conclude, that you do nothing yourself with design and reason, as maintain that everything is done by blind chance in the universe.' Aristodemus at length acknowledging a supreme being, is still in doubt as to providence; not being able to comprehend how the deity can see everything at once. Socrates replies, 'If the spirit that resides in your body moves and disposes it at its pleasure, why should not that sovereign wisdom which presides over the universe, be able likewise to regulate, and order everything as it pleases? If your eye can see objects at the distance of several furlongs; why should not the eye of God be able to see everything at once? If your soul can think at the same time upon what is at Athens, in Egypt, and in Sicily; why should not the divine mind be able to take care of everything, being everywhere present to his work?' Socrates perceiving at last that the infidelity of Aristodemus did not arise so much from his reason as from his heart, concludes with these words; 'O Aristodemus, apply yourself sincerely to worship God; he will enlighten you, and all your doubts will soon [be] removed!'

"Plato, a disciple of Socrates, follows the same principles. He lived [...] at a time when the doctrine of Democritus had made a great progress at Athens. The design of all his philosophy is to give us noble sentiments of the deity . . . and in fine, to teach that religion is the only way to restore us to our first glory and perfection. He despises all the tenets of the Athenian superstition, and endeavors to purge religion of them. The chief object of this philosopher is man in his immortal capacity: he speaks of him in his politic one, only to show that the shortest way to immortality is to discharge all the duties of civil and social life for the pure love of virtue.

"Plato in the beginning of his *Timaeus* distinguishes between the being which is eternally, and being which has been made. And in another of his dialogues he defines God the efficient cause that makes things exist which had no being before: a definition that shows that he had the idea of CREATION." See forward, p. 547.[7] "He first considers the deity in his eternal solitude before the production of finite beings. He says frequently like the Egyptians, 'That this first source of deity is surrounded with thick darkness, which no mortal can penetrate, and that this inaccessible God is to be adored only by silence.' 'Tis this first principle which he calls in several places THE BEING, the UNITY, and the supreme good;

7. MS: "p. 942 [col. 2]." See the passage on Plato in No. [1355] begining, "He calls God in his *Timæus*, 'The architect of the world, the father of the universe . . .'"

the same in the intelligent world, that the sun is in the visible world. He afterwards represents to us this first being as sallying out of his unity to consider all the various manners by which he might represent himself exteriorly; and that the IDEAL world, comprehending the ideas of all things, and the truths which result thence, was formed in the divine UN-DERSTANDING. Plato always distinguishes between the supreme good, and that WISDOM which is only an emanation from him. 'That which presents truth to the mind,' says he, 'and that which gives us REASON is the supreme good. He is the cause and source of truth. He hath BEGOTTEN it like himself. As the light is not the sun, but an emanation from it, so TRUTH is not the first principle, but his emanation.' And this is what he calls the WISDOM, or the *logos.* And lastly, he considers the first mover as displaying his power to form real beings, resembling those archetypal ideas. He styles him 'The energy, or sovereign ARCHITECT who CREATED the universe and the gods, and who does whatsoever he pleases in heaven, on earth, and in the shades below.' He calls him also 'Psyche, or the soul which presides over the world rather than the soul of the world.'

"Sometimes he considers the three divine attributes as three CAUSES, at other times as THREE BEINGS, and often as THREE GODS: but he affirms that they are but one sole divinity; that there is no essential difference between them; that the SECOND is the IMAGE of the first, and [. . .] that they are not three suns, but one: and that they differ only as the light, its rays, and the reflection of those rays . . . . The three forms of the divinity he calls *agathos, logos* and *psyche:* the sovereign good, which is the principle of deity, the intellect which drew the plan of the world, and the energy which executed it.

"Though we should suppose that Plato considered the *logos* and the *psyche,* the intellect and the energy, not only as two attributes, but as two hypostases, or emanations from the divine substance, yet it will not follow that the Christians took their doctrine of the Trinity from him. He might owe this idea to the ancient traditions transmitted from the infant world, whence the Orientals, Chaldeans, Egyptians and Greeks originally drew their soundest notions in divinity. The philosophers of all nations seem to have had some idea, more or less confused, of a certain triplicity in the supreme unity." Pp. 299–304. See "Miscellanies," No. 992.[8]

"Aristotle, Plato's disciple, and prince of the peripatetic philosophers, calls God 'The eternal and living being, the most noble of all beings, a substance entirely distinct from matter, without extension, without divi-

8. *Works,* 20, 321–23.

sion, without parts, and without succession; who understands everything by one single act, and continuing himself immovable, gives motion to all things, and enjoys in himself a perfect happiness, as knowing and contemplating himself with infinite pleasure.' In his metaphysics he lays it down for a principle, 'That God is a supreme intelligence which acts with order, proportion and design; and is the source of all that is good, excellent and just.' In his treatise of the soul, he says, 'That the supreme mind is by its nature prior to all beings, that he has a sovereign dominion over all.'

"And in other places he says, 'That that first principle is neither the fire, nor the earth, nor the water, nor anything that is the object of senses; but that a spiritual substance is the cause of the universe, and the source of all the order and all the beauties, as well as of all the motions and all the forms which we so much admire in it.' [. . .] 'There is,' says he, 'but one only mover, and several inferior deities. All that is added about the human shape of these deities, is nothing else but fiction, invented on purpose to instruct the common people, and engage them to an observance of good laws. All must be reduced to one only primitive substance, and to several inferior substances, which govern in subordination to the first. This is the genuine doctrine of the ANCIENTS, which has happily escaped from the wrecks of truth, amidst the rocks of vulgar errors and poetic fables.'

"Cicero, in his Book of Laws, describes the universe to us 'as a republic, of which Jupiter is the prince and common father. The great law imprinted in the hearts of all men is to love the public good, and the members of the common society AS THEMSELVES. This love of order is supreme justice, and this justice is amiable for its own sake. To love it only for the advantage it produces us, may be politic, but there is little of goodness in it. 'Tis the highest injustice to love justice only for the sake of recompense. In a word, the universal, immutable and eternal law of all intelligent beings, is to promote the happiness of one another like children of the same father.'

"He next represents God to us as a sovereign wisdom, from whose authority it is still more impracticable for intelligent nature to withdraw themselves than it is for corporeal ones. 'According to the opinion of the wisest and greatest men,' says this philosopher, 'the law is not an invention of human understanding, or the arbitrary constitution of men, but flows from the eternal reason that governs the universe. . . . Its origin is as ancient as the divine intellect: for the true, the primitive, and the supreme law is nothing else but the sovereign reason of the great

Jove. . . . The same immortal law is a rule to all nations, because it has no author but the ONE ONLY GOD who brought it forth and promulged it.'

"Seneca says, ''Tis of very little consequence by what name you call the first nature, and the divine reason that presides over the universe, and fills all the parts of it. He is still the SAME GOD. He is called Jupiter Stator, not as the historians say, because he stopped the Roman armies as they were flying, but because he is the constant support of all beings. They may call him fate, because he is the first cause on which all others depend. We Stoics call him sometimes Father Bacchus, because he is the universal life that animates nature; Hercules, because his power is invincible; Mercury, because he is the eternal reason, order and wisdom. You may give him as many names as you please, provided you allow but ONE SOUL[9] principle everywhere present. . . . Every workman,' says he, 'hath a model by which he forms his work. . . . So God produces within himself that perfect model, which is the proportion, the order and the beauty of all beings. The ANCIENTS,' says he in another place, 'did not think Jove such a being as we represent him in the capitol, and in our other buildings. But by Jove they meant the guardian and governor of the universe, the understanding and the mind, the master and the architect of this great machine. All names belong to him. You are not in the wrong if you call him fate, for he is the cause of causes, and everything depends on him. Would you call him PROVIDENCE; you fall into no mistake, it is by his wisdom that this world is governed. Would you call him nature: you will not offend in doing so, it is from him that all beings derive their origin, it is by him that they live and breathe.'" Pp. 306–10. See further, p. 553.[1]

"According to the testimony of Heroditus, the ancient Persians had neither statues, nor temples, nor altars: 'They think it is ridiculous,' says this author, 'to fancy, like the Greeks, that the gods have an human shape, or derive their original from men. They choose the highest mountains for the place of their sacrifice.' [. . .]

"Strabo gives us the same account of the ancient Persians. 'They neither erected statues nor altars,' says this historian; 'they sacrificed in a clean place and upon an eminence, where they offered up a victim crowned.'" Pp. 275–76.

9. In the MS, JE spelled this word "SOLE."

1. The first reference here is to Ramsay, the second to "Miscellanies," Bk. 9, which reads in the MS: "see further this Book. p. 947. [col. 1]." On MS p. 947 there is a cross-reference to this point in No. [1351]. The passage referred to begins, "Seneca says, 'God is the framer of the universe, the governor, disposer and keeper thereof . . .'"

"Plutarch has left us in his treatise of Isis and Osiris, a fragment of the theology of the Magi. This philosophical historian assures us, that they called the great god, Oromazes, or the principle of life,[2] that PRODUCED everything, and worketh ALL IN ALL.

"They admitted however another God, but of an inferior nature and order, whom they called Mythras or the Middle God. They speak of him sometimes as a being co-eternal with the Supreme Divinity, and at other times as the first production of his power.

"Eusebius in his *Præparatio Evangelica,* who is so far from being ever favorable to the pagans, that he makes it his business continually to expose and degrade their philosophy, and yet he says had read these express words in a book of Zoroaster, that was extant in his time, and known by the title of, *The Sacred Collection of Persian Monuments:* 'God is the first of all incorruptible beings, eternal and unbegotten: [...] there is nothing equal to him, or like him. He is the author of all good, and entirely disinterested; the most excellent of all excellent beings, and the wisest of all intelligent natures; the father of equity, the parent of good laws, self-instructed, self-sufficient, and the first FORMER of nature.'

"The modern writers among the Arabians and Persians, who have preserved to us what remains of the ancient doctrine of Zoroaster among the Guebri or worshippers of the fire, maintain that the first magi admitted only ONE eternal Principle of all things. Abulfeda, cited by the famous Dr. Pococke,[3] says, that according to the primitive doctrine of the Persians, 'God was prior to both light and darkness, and had existed from all eternity in an adorable solitude, without any companion or rival.' Saristhani, quoted by Dr. Hyde,[4] says 'that the first magi did not look upon the good and evil Principles as co-eternal; they thought that light was indeed eternal, but that darkness was produced in time by the disloyalty of Ahriman, chief of the genii.'" Pp. 275–78.

"The ancient Persians adored but ONE only supreme deity, but they considered the god Mythras and the goddess Mythra, sometimes as two emanations from his substance, and at other times as the first production of his power." P. 55.

"The ancient Persians had neither temples nor altars; they sacrificed upon high mountains and eminences.... Zoroaster had made no

2. Ramsay: "light."

3. Ramsay cites "Specim. Hist. Arab. p. 146" (Edward Pococke, *Specimen histori Arabum* [London, 1650]).

4. Ramsay cites "Relig. Ant. Persar. cap. 9. p. 161, & cap. 22, p. 290." The quotation may be found in Thomas Hyde (1636–1703), *Historia Religionis Veterum Persarum, Eorumque Magorum* (Oxford, 1700), p. 295.

change in the old rites, except by the introduction of music into divine worship.

"The author of *The Travels of Cyrus* represents the Persians under Zoroaster as using this hymn at their sacrifices: 'Oromazes is the first of incorruptible natures, eternal, unbegotten, self-sufficient, of all that is excellent most excellent, the wisest of all intelligences; he beheld himself in the mirror of his own substance, and by that view produced the goddess Mythra, Mythra the living image of his beauty, the original mother and the immortal virgin; she presented him the ideas of all things, and he gave them to the god Mythras to form a world resembling those ideas. Let us celebrate the wisdom of Mythra, let us do her homage by our purity and our virtues, rather than by our songs and praises.' [. . .]

"In the spaces of the empyreum a pure and divine fire expends itself; by means of which, not only bodies but spirits become visible. In the midst of this immensity is the great Oromazes, first principle of all things. He diffuses himself everywhere; but it is there he is manifested after a more glorious manner. Near him is seated the god Mythras, or the second spirit (Νος δευτερος; 'tis thus that Mythras is called in the oracles which pass under Zoroaster's name. Doubtless they are not genuine, but they contain the most ancient traditions, and the style of the Eastern theology, according to Psellus, Pletho, Plotinus and all the Platonists of the third century); and under him Psyche, or the goddess Mythra: around their throne in the first rank are the Jyngas, the most sublime intelligencies; in the lower spheres are an endless number of genii of all the different orders. Arimanius chief of the Jyngas aspired to an equality with the god Mythras, and by his eloquence persuaded all the spirits of his order to disturb the universal harmony and peace of the heavenly monarchy." Pp. 56–59. See forward, p. 557.[5]

There was this "inscription upon the temple of Isis, which is yet to be seen at Capua: 'TO THE GODDESS WHO IS ONE, AND WHO IS ALL.'" P. 104.

They sometimes called God "by the name of 'Incomprehensible Darkness,'" which "famous expression of the Egyptians is preserved by Dammascius." P. 105.

"The inhabitants of Thebes in Egypt adored but one sole deity, uncreated and eternal (see Plutarch in his *Isis and Osiris*)." P. 106.[6]

5. MS: "p. 949," in No. 1355, the section beginning, "Concerning the TRINITY, see what Mr. Ramsay observes concerning this from the ancient Chinese books . . ."

6. In the MS, a cross-reference by JE reads: "see this Book p. ~~339~~ 339. 340." However, there are no extant pp. 339–40 in Bk. 9.

The author of *The Travels of Cyrus* cites these passages from ancient heathen writers: "God 'gives being, life and motion to all creatures' (Epimen.[7]). 'No one can know God but he who seeks to resemble him' (Plut. Epinom.) 'The gods make themselves known to the heart, and conceal themselves from those who endeavor to comprehend them by the understanding alone' (Plut. Epinom.). [...] 'The gods take less delight to dwell in heaven than in the soul of the just, which is their true temple' (Hierocl. aur. carm.)." P. 165.

"The Orientals call the three forms of the deity Oromazes, Mythra and Mythras; the Egyptians Osiris, Isis and Orus; the Thracians Uranus, Urania and Love; the Tyrians Belus, Venus and Thammuz; the Greeks Jupiter, Minerva and Apollo." Pp. 170e–71a.

"It was the steadfast maxim of all nations, that men are not what they were in the golden age, that they are debased and degraded, and that religion is the only means to restore the soul to its original grandeur, to make her wings grow again, and to raise her to the ethereal regions from whence she is fallen." P. 172.

"When Cyrus entered the temple of Venus in Phoenicia, he found all the people, clad in mourning, in a cavern, where the image of a young man was lying upon a bed of flowers and odoriferous herbs; nine days were spent in fasting, prayer and lamentations, after which the public sorrow was changed into gladness; songs of joy succeeded to weeping, and the whole assembly began this sacred hymn: 'Adonis is returned to life, Urania weeps no more, he is reascended to heaven, he will soon come down again upon earth to banish thence both crimes and miseries forever.'" (Margin: "All these Tyrian rites are found in Lucian, St. Jerome, St. Cyril, Julius Firmicus Macrobius and Procopius. Adonis comes from the word *Adonai,* one of the ten names of God.") "The combats of Mythras, the murder of Osiris, the death of Adonis, the banishment of Apollo and the labors of Hercules represent to us the same truths; but different nations have painted them under different similitudes." [Pp. 214–15.]

"The doctrine of the Persians, Egyptians and Greeks, concerning the three states of the world," is the same. "Zoroaster being versed in the sciences of the Gymnosophists, spoke of the empire of Oromazes before the rebellion of Arimanius, as of a state in which all spirits were happy and perfect. In Egypt the religion of Hermes represents the reign of

7. Ramsay: "See Hammond on Acts of the Apostles. ch. xvii, v. 28." Henry Hammond (1605–1660), *A paraphrase, and annotations upon all the books of the New Testament* (London, 1653).

Osiris, before the monster Typhon broke through the egg of the world, as a state exempt from miseries and passions. Orpheus has sung the golden age as a state of simplicity and innocence. Each nation has formed an idea of this primitive world according to its genius: the magi, who are all astronomers, have placed it in the stars; the Egyptians, who are all philosophers, have fancied it a republic of sages; the Greeks, who delight in rural scenes, have described it as a country of shepherds. I farther observe that the traditions of all nations foretell the coming of a hero, who is to descend from heaven, to bring back Astrea to the earth: the Persians call him Mythras, the Egyptians Orus, the Tyrians Adonis, the Greeks Apollo, Hercules, Mars, Mercury, Jupiter [the] Conductor and Savior. It is true they differ in their descriptions, but they all agree in the same truths; they are all sensible that man is not now what he was, and believe that he will one day assume a more perfect form." Pp. 251–52.

"Iamblichus, who had studied the religion of the Egyptians, and understood it thoroughly, who lived in the beginning of the third century and was a disciple of the famous Porphyry, [. . .] gives this account of the theology which they taught: 'According to the Egyptians, Eicton, or the first God, existed in his solitary unity before all beings. He is the fountain and original of everything that either has understanding or is to be understood. He is the first principle of all things, self-sufficient, incomprehensible and the Father of all essences.' Hermes says likewise, 'that this supreme God has constituted another God, called Emeph, to be head over all spirits, whether ethereal, empyrean or celestial; and that this second God, whom he styles the Guide, is a WISDOM that transforms and converts into itself all spiritual beings. He makes nothing superior to this God-Guide, but only the first intelligent, and first intelligible, who ought to be adored in silence.'" Pp. 284–85.

All the poets, speaking of the golden age, or reign of Saturn, describe it to us as an happy state, in which there were neither calamities, nor crimes, nor labor, nor pains, nor diseases, nor death. They represent, on the contrary, the Iron Age as the time when physical and moral evil first appeared; then it was that sufferings, vices and all manner of evils came forth of Pandora's box, and overflowed the face of the earth. They speak to us of the golden age renewed, as of a time when Astrea was to return upon earth; when justice, peace and innocence were to flourish again with their original luster; and when everything was to be restored to their primitive perfection. In a word, they sing on all occasions the exploits of a son of Jupiter, who was to quit his heavenly abode and live among men. They give him different names, according to his different functions;

sometimes he is Apollo fighting against Python"[8] ("The letters of the Hebrew word פתן, which we translate *Asp*, are the very same with those of
the Greek word Πυθων, and the Latin *Python*, which was the great serpent that Apollo, the heathen god, *Light*, destroyed; under which fable
the heathens traditionally from revelation imitated Christ the Divine
Light destroying the old serpent, the devil, according to the original
promise of bruising the serpent's head." See Merrick's Sermon on *Christ
the True Vine*, p. 33.[9] Note the word *Orus* is the same with the Hebrew
word אור, which signifies light, and seems to be the name of the Messiah
that appeared in that light which they called the *Shechinah*.) "and the Titans; sometimes he is Hercules, destroying monsters and giants, and
purging the earth of their enormities and crimes; one while he is Mercury, or the messenger of Jove, flying about everywhere to execute his
decrees; and another while he is Perseus, delivering Andromeda, or human nature, from the monster that rose out of the great deep to devour
her. He is always some son of Jupiter giving battle and gaining victories."
Pp. 317–18.

Timaeus in Plato explains "the origin of things, and primitive state of
the world, to Socrates, thus: 'Whatever has been produced, has been produced by some cause. 'Tis no easy matter to know the nature of this
Maker, and Father of the universe; and though you should discover it, it
would be impossible for you to make the vulgar comprehend it. This Architect of the world,' continues he, 'had a model by which he produced
everything, and this model is himself. As he is good, and what is good
has not the least tincture of envy, he made all things as far as was possible like himself. He made the world perfect in the whole of its constitution, perfect too in all the various parts that compose it, which were subject neither to diseases, nor to decay of age. The Father of all things,
beholding this beautiful Image of himself, took a complacency in his
work, and this complacency raised in him a desire of improving it to a
nearer likeness to its model.'

"In the dialogue which bears the title of *Politicus Plato*, mentioning this
primitive state of the world, calls it the reign of Saturn, and describes it
in this manner: 'God was then the prince and common Father of all; he
governed the world by himself, as he governs it now by inferior deities:
rage and cruelty did not then prevail upon earth; war and sedition were

8. JE directs that the following passage in parentheses, originally located at the end of No.
1351, be inserted here.

9. Marshal Merrick, *The Parable of the Vineyard and Christ, the True Vine; A Sermon Preached in
the Parish Church of St. Ann's, Westminster . . .* (London, 1753).

not so much as known. God himself took care of the sustenance of mankind, and was their guardian and shepherd: there were no magistrates, no civil polity as there are now. . . . The fertile fields yielded fruits and corn without the labor of tillage. Mankind stood in no need of raiment to cover their bodies, being troubled with no inclemency of the seasons. [. . .] Under the reign of Jupiter, [. . .] the very foundations of the world were shaken by motions contrary to its principle and its end, and it lost its beauty and its luster. Then it was that good and evil were blended together. But in the end, lest the world should be plunged in an eternal abyss of confusion, God, the author of the primitive order, will appear again and resume the reins of empire. Then he will change, amend, embellish and restore the whole frame of nature, and put an end to decay of age, to diseases and death.'

"In the dialogue under the title of *Phædrus*, [. . .] he[1] says, 'The great Jupiter, animating his winged chariot, marches first, followed by all the inferior gods and genii; thus they traverse the heavens, admiring the infinite wonders thereof. But when they go to the great banquet, they raise themselves to the top of heaven, and mount above the spheres. None of our poets ever yet sung, or can sing that supercelestial place. It is there that souls contemplate with the eyes of the understanding the truly existing Essence, which has neither color nor figure, nor is the object of any sense, but is purely intelligible. There they see virtue, truth and justice not as they are here below, but as they exist in him who is Being it self. There they satiate themselves with that sight till they are no longer able to bear the glory of it, and then they return back to heaven,'" etc. Pp. 323–25.

"Hierocles, upon the Golden Verses ascribed to Pythagoras,[2] says, 'As our alienation from God, and the loss of the wings which used to raise us up to heavenly things, have thrown us down into this region of death, which is overrun with all manner of evils; so the stripping ourselves of earthly affections, and the revival of virtues in us, make our wings grow again, and raise us up to the mansions of life, where true good is to be found without mixture of evil. The essence of man being in the middle between beings that contemplate God without ceasing, and such as are not able to contemplate him at all, he has it in his power to raise himself up towards the one, or sink down towards the other.'" Pp. 326–27.

---

1. I.e. Plato.

2. *The life of Pythagoras, with his Symbols and Golden verses. Together with the life of Hierocles, and his commentaries upon the verses,* trans. N. Rowe (London, 1707).

There was "this inscription upon a statue of Pallas, or Isis, at Sais: 'I AM
ALL THAT IS, HAS BEEN AND SHALL BE, AND NO MORTAL HAS EVER YET RE-
MOVED THE VEIL THAT COVERS ME.'" P. 328.

"Zoroaster, says Plutarch, taught that there are two Gods, contrary to
each other in their operations; the one the author of all the good, the
other of all the evil in nature. The good principle he calls Oromazes, the
other the demon Arimanius. [. . .] There is likewise a middle God between these two, named Mythras, whom the Persians call the Intercessor
or Mediator.'" P. 333.

"The famous Dr. Hyde,[3] a divine of the Church of England who had
traveled into the East, and perfectly understood the language of the
country, has translated the following passages out of Sharisthani, an Arabian philosopher of the fifteenth century: 'The first magi did not look
upon the two principles as co-eternal, but believed that light was eternal
and that darkness was produced in time; and the origin of this evil principle they account for in this manner: light can produce nothing but
light, and never can be the origin of evil; how then was evil produced?
Light,' say they, 'produced several beings, all of them spiritual, luminous
and powerful; but their chief, whose name was Ahriman, or Arimanius,
had an evil thought contrary to the light: he doubted, and by that doubting became dark. From hence proceeded all evils, dissension, malice and
everything else of a contrary nature to light. These two principles made
war upon one another, till at last peace was concluded, upon condition
that the lower world should be in subjection to Arimanius for seven thousand years; after this space of time, he is to surrender back the world to
light.'" P. 334.

When Strabo "has described the life and manners of the Indian brachmans, he adds, 'These philosophers look upon the state of men in this
life to be like that of children in their mother's womb; death, according
[to] their notion, being a birth to a true and happy life. [. . .] They have
many notions in common with the Greeks; and like them believe that
the world had a beginning, and will have an end; and that God who made
it, and governs it, is everywhere present to his work.'

"The same author goes on in this manner: 'Onesecritus being sent by
Alexander the Great to inform himself of the life, manners and doctrine
of these philosophers, found a brachman named Calanus, who taught
him the following principles: Formerly, plenty reigned over all nature;
milk, wine, honey and oil flowed from fountains; but men, having made

3. I.e. Thomas Hyde (see above, p. 471, n. 4).

an ill use of this felicity, Jupiter deprived them of it, and condemned them to labor for the sustenance of their lives.'

"In order to form a better judgment of the doctrine of the ancient Gymnosophists, I have consulted what has been translated of the Vedam, which is the sacred book of the modern bramins. Though its antiquity be not perhaps so great as it is affirmed to be, yet there is no denying but it contains the ancient traditions of those people, and of their philosophers. 'Tis plain by this book, 'That the bramins acknowledge one sole and supreme God, whom they call Vistnou; that his first and most ancient production was a secondary God, named Brama, whom the supreme God formed out of a flower that floated upon the surface of the great deep before the formation of the world; and that Vistnou afterwards, on account of Brama's virtue, gratitude and fidelity, gave him power to form the universe.'" See forward, pp. 554–57.[4]

"Being desirous of carrying my researches as far as China, I applied myself to such as understand the language of that country, had spent several years in it, and were well versed in the original books of that nation. And in this point particularly I have made use of the informations I have received from a gentleman of a superior genius, who does not care to be mentioned till he has published a large work upon these matters, which will be of service to religion, and do honor to human understanding. In the meantime he has allowed me to publish the following passages, which he translated himself out of some ancient Chinese books that have been brought into Europe, and which may be seen both at Paris and Rome; so that all who understand the language may judge of the faithfulness of the translation.

"The ancient commentaries on the book *Yking*, i.e. the Book of Changes, continually speak of a double heaven, a primitive and a posterior. The first heaven is there described in the following manner: 'All things were then in a happy state, everything was beautiful, everything was good, all beings were perfect in their kind. . . . All things grew without labor; an universal fertility reigned everywhere.' [. . .]

"In the book which the Chinese call *King*, or Sacred, we read the following passage: 'Whilst the first state of Heaven lasted, a pure pleasure and perfect tranquillity reigned over all nature. There was neither Labor, nor Pains, nor sorrow, nor Crimes.' [. . .]

"The philosophers who stuck to these ancient traditions, and particu-

---

4. MS: "p. 947. 948," which falls in No. [1355], beginning at "The following things are from Ramsay's *Principles*, vol. 2, beginning p. 44 . . ."

larly Tchouangse, say, 'That in the state of the first heaven man was united inwardly to the supreme Reason, and that outwardly he practiced all the works of justice. The heart rejoiced in truth, and there was no mixture of falsehood. . . . There was nothing that did harm to man, or suffered any hurt from him. An universal amity and harmony reigned over all nature.'

"The philosopher Hoainontse, speaking of the latter heaven, says, 'The pillars of heaven were broken; the earth shaken to its very foundations; the heavens sunk lower towards the north; the sun, moon and stars changed their motions; the earth fell to pieces; the waters enclosed within its bosom burst forth with violence, and OVERFLOWED IT. Man rebelling against the system of the universe was quite disordered; the sun was 'clipsed; the planets altered their course, and the universal harmony was disturbed.' The philosophers Wentse and Lietse, who lived long before Hoainontse, express themselves almost in the same terms. 'The universal fertility of nature,' say these ancient authors, 'degenerated into an ugly barrenness, . . . miseries and crimes overflowed the face of the earth.' All these evils, says the book *Liki,* arose from man's despising the supreme Monarch of the universe: he would needs dispute about truth and falsehood, and these disputes banished the eternal Reason. He then fixed his looks on terrestrial objects, and loved them to excess; hence arose the passions; he became gradually transformed into the objects he loved, and the celestial Reason entirely abandoned him. Such was the original source of all crimes, which drew after them all manner of miseries sent by heaven for the punishment thereof.'

"The same books speak of a time when everything is to be restored to its first splendor, by the coming of a hero called Kiun-Tse, which signifies Shepherd and Prince, to whom they give likewise the names of the Most Holy, the Universal Teacher and the Supreme Truth. He answers exactly to the Mythras of the Persians, the Orus, or second Osiris of the Egyptians, the Apollo or Mercury of the Greeks, and the Brama of the Indians. The Chinese books speak likewise of the sufferings and conflicts of Kiun-Tse, just as the Persians do of the combats of Mythras, the Egyptians of the murder of Osiris, the Tyrians of the death of Adonis, and the Greeks of the labors and painful exploits of a son of Jupiter who came down upon earth to exterminate monsters. It looks as if the source of all these allegories was an ancient tradition common to all nations, that the Middle God was not to expiate and put an end to crimes but by his own great sufferings. [. . .]

"The Tyrians acknowledged one supreme God, named Bel, which is the same with the Jehovah of the Hebrews. They held likewise a subordinate God, whom they call Thammuz, Adon, Adonis, which signifies the Lord.[5] [. . .] The death of Adonis, killed by a boar, is the same with the murder of Osiris slain by Typhon, or the evil principle. Solemn days were instituted by the Phoenicians to bewail the death of Adonis, and to sing praises to him as risen from the dead. Some ancient and venerable Christians believed that the fable of Adonis was a corruption of an old tradition concerning the suffering Messiah, and apply all the Tyrian ceremonies to our mysteries.[6] Adonis loved Venus, espoused her, and she became mother of the gods. Urania, Assarte, Venus[7] and Proserpine are the same goddess. [. . .]

"We see then that the doctrines of the primitive perfection of nature, its fall and its restoration by a divine hero, are equally manifest in the mythologies of the Greeks, Egyptians, Persians, Indians and Chinese." Pp. 335–40.

A TABLE OF THE FOREGOING EXTRACTS OF *THE TRAVELS OF CYRUS*

Unity of the Godhead: pp. 463, 464, 465–66, 466–67, 470, 471, 478.

The Ancient Religion of Mankind Agreeable to the Religion of the Holy Scriptures: pp. 469, 470–71.

Right Notions of God: pp. 463, 464–65, 465–66, 466–67, 467–68, 469–70, 470, 472–73, 474, 475–76.

Trinity: pp. 463, 464, 466, 468, 471, 472, 473, 474, 478.

God is the Creator of All Things: pp. 463–64, 464, 465–66, 466–67, 468, 469–70, 470–71, 474–75, 476, 478–79.

God's Providence: pp. 464–65, 465–66, 466–67, 469–70, 470–71, 475–76.

God's Moral Government: pp. 464–65, 469–70, 471.

Chaos: pp. 464, 465.

The Spirit of God Being Love Brought Chaos to Order: p. 464.

5. JE notes: "Ramsay in his *Principles,* vol. 2, p. 199, says Hesychius says Adonis signifies Lord."
6. JE notes, copying Ramsay's own footnote: "Julius Firmius in particular."
7. JE mistakenly writes "Urania."

Spiritual Worship: pp. 463, 465, 467, 473. See Right Notions of Religion.

Spiritual Light: pp. 467, 473.

Spiritual Union with God: p. 473.

Dependence on Tradition: pp. 469, 470. Here also see pp. 460 and 461.

The Flood: p. 479.

Right Notions of Religion: pp. 469, 473.

Immortality of the Soul: pp. 465, 477.

Right Notions of the Happiness of Heaven: p. 476.

Original Righteousness: pp. 473–74, 474, 476, 478–79.

Fall of the Angels: pp. 471, 472, 477, 478–79.

Fall of Man: pp. 473–74, 474, 475–76, 477–78, 479.

The Redemption of the Messiah: pp. 474, 474–75, 479.

The Mediator: p. 476.

The Sufferings, Resurrection and Ascension of Christ: pp. 473, 479.

The Glorious Times; pp. 474, 476, 477.

1352. CHRIST'S SATISFACTION OR ATONEMENT, ETC.
Abigail, when she acts the part of a mediator between offending Nabal and offended David, she falls at David's feet and says, "Upon me, my lord, upon me let this iniquity be" (I Sam. 25:24).

The Apostle, when he would express his willingness to be made a sacrifice for his brethren the Jews, he says, "I could wish myself accursed from Christ for my brethren" (Rom. 9:3). See, concerning Moses, Ex. 32:32.

II Sam. 18:33, "O my son Absalom, my son, my son Absalom! would God I had died for thee."

Matt. 20:28, "to give his life a ransom for many." See, concerning this text and the force of the preposition αντι, Moncrieff's *Review and Examination of the Principles of Campbell,* pp. 113–14.[8]

See various parts of Owen's *Exposition on the Hebrews.* See his note on Heb. 9:27–28.[9]

Is. 53:4–6, 8, 10–12; Matt. 20:28; I Tim. 2:6; I Cor. 6:20; Rom. 3:25–26; Rom. 8:2–3; II Cor. 5:21; Gal. 3:10, 13.

See Poole's *Synopsis* on Lev. 1:4; also on Lev. 16:21 and 28.[1]

See Poole's *Synopsis* on Isaiah, ch. 53.[2]

The LAYING HANDS on the head of the sacrifice was a token of putting the guilt of sin upon [it], agreeable to the customary signification of the imputation of guilt among the Hebrews. Thus the phrase, "his blood shall be on his own head," or "on our heads," etc., was a phrase for the imputation of the guilt of blood lying on them. So Josh. 2:19. See I Kgs. 2:32–33, 37 (search the Concordance for other places). I Kgs. 2:44, "the Lord shall return thy wickedness upon thine own head" (look [in] the Concordance for other places).

Abigail, when mediating between David and Nabal, when he was provoked to wrath against him and had determined to destroy him (I Sam. 25:24), fell at David's feet and said, "upon me let this iniquity be: and let thine handmaid, I pray thee, speak in thine audience, and hear the voice of thine handmaid." And in v. 28 she calls Nabal's iniquity her iniquity (see *Synopsis Criticorum* on these verses).[3] By this it appears that a mediator's putting himself in the stead of the offender, so that the offended party should impute it to him, and look on the mediator as having taken it upon him, looking on him as the debtor of what satisfaction should be required and expected, was in those days no strange notion, as a thing in itself absurd and inconsistent with men's natural notions of things.

Heb. 12:24–26, "And to Jesus the mediator of the new covenant, and to the blood of sprinkling, that speaketh better things than that of Abel.

8. Alexander Moncrieff, *An enquiry into the principle, rule, and end of moral actions, wherein, the scheme of . . . Mr. Archibald Campbell . . . in his Enquiry into the original of moral virtue, is examined,* pp. 113–14.

9. The reference is to John Owen, *A Continuation of the Exposition of the Epistle of Paul the Apostle to the Hebrews. Viz. on the Sixth, Seventh, Eighth, Ninth, and Tenth Chapters* (London, 1680), where Owen treats Heb. 9:27–28 extensively on pp. 464–71. This volume is part of Owen's four-volume commentary, *Exercitations on the Epistle to the Hebrews.*

1. MS: "in places marked thus in the margin," followed by a cue mark. Poole, *Synopsis Criticorum, I,* Pt. I, cols. 511, 570–71

2. Poole treats Is. 53 in *Synopsis Criticorum, III,* Pt. I, cols. 500–29.

3. Ibid., *I,* Pt. II, cols. 226–28.

See that ye refuse not him that speaketh. For if they escaped not who refused him that spake on earth, much more shall not we escape, if we turn away from him that speaketh from heaven: whose voice then shook the earth: but now he hath promised, saying, Yet once more I shake not the earth only," etc. He that speaketh, which the Apostle warns us not to refuse, who spake once on earth and whose voice shook the earth, and who now speaketh from heaven and his voice shakes not only the earth but heaven, is he that is spoken of, v. 24, "Jesus the mediator," etc., whose blood speaketh.

The word χρηματίζω signifies to speak divine oracles, and in Scripture is applied to God alone. When it is said he spake on earth, respect is had to God's giving the Law at Mt. Sinai, when his voice shook the earth. 'Tis plain it was not the voice of Moses or any created angel that is intended, by the whole history of the affair in Exodus. The people made great preparation to meet with God. God descended on the mount. He was there in the midst of angels (Ps. 68:17). From his right hand went the fiery Law (Deut. 33:2). And, in giving the Law, he says "I am the Lord thy God" [Ex. 20:2], etc. He that in the book of Haggai, 2:6–7, [to] which the Apostle refers, says "Yet once more I shake the heavens and the earth" [Heb. 12:26], is God. See Owen in loc., pp. 273–74, 278.[4]

Christ is often represented as bearing our sins for us. Is. 53:4, "Surely he hath borne our griefs, and carried our sorrows." V. 11, "for he shall bear their iniquities." V. 12, "he bare the sin of many." And with an evident reference to this last place, the Apostle says, Heb. 9:28, "So Christ was once offered to bear [. . .] the second time without sin unto salvation." And with a plain reference to vv. 4–5 of this fifty-third chapter of Isaiah, the apostle Peter says, I Pet. 2:24, "Who his own self bare our sins in his own body on the tree."

The word translated "bear" in Is. 53:4 and 12 is נשא. The same word and the same phrase, of bearing sin and bearing iniquity, is often used concerning those things which are types of Christ's priesthood and sacrifice, viz. the Levitical priests and sacrifices. It was no unusual phrase, but common and well understood among the Jews. And we find it very often used in other cases, and applied to others besides either Christ or the types of him. And when it is so, 'tis plain that the general meaning

4. MS: "at places marked in the margin." Owen, *A Continuation of the exposition of the Epistle of Paul the Apostle to the Hebrews: (viz.) on the eleventh, twelfth, and thirteenth chapters . . .* (London, 1684), pp. 273–74, 278. JE's copy of Owen has not been located, so the places he marked in the margin cannot be ascertained.

of the phrase is, lying under the guilt of sin, having it imputed and charged upon the person as obnoxious to the punishment of it, or obliged to answer and make satisfaction for it, or liable to the calamities and miseries it exposes. In such a manner it seems always to be used, unless, in some few places, it signifies to take away sin by forgiveness. See Dr. Owen on Heb. 9:28, p. 468.[5] See also Poole's *Synopsis* on Is. 53.[6]

See, concerning their laying their hands on the head of the sacrifice, *Synopsis Criticorum* on Lev. 1:4.[7]

That God, in the instituted ceremonies concerning the scapegoat and the other goat that was sacrificed for a sin offering, intended that there should [be] a representation of laying the guilt of sin on those goats, see *Synopsis Criticorum* on Lev. 16:21–22, 28.[8] It was an evidence that the two goats were to appear as if they were made sinful with the sins of the people, or unclean with their uncleanness, or guilty with their guilt, because he that burnt the one and he that let go the other were both unclean, and were therefore to be washed themselves in water, etc. (Lev. 16:26, 28).

The translation of guilt or obligation to punishment was not a thing alien from men's conceptions and notions of old in Scripture times, neither the times of the old testament or new, as appears by what the woman of Tekoah says, II Sam. 14:9, "My lord, O king, the iniquity be on me, and on my father's house: and the king and his throne be guiltless." And by what the Jews said when Pilate said of Christ, "I am innocent of the blood of this just person: see ye to it" (Matt. 27:24–25): "His blood be on us, and on our children." And the words of Rebekah, when Jacob objected against doing as she proposed, that he should bring a curse on himself and not a blessing, Gen. 27:13, "On me be thy curse, my son: only obey my voice."

See MacLaurin's sermon on *God's Chief Mercy,* p. 104.[9]

I Cor. 15:17, "And if Christ be not raised, your faith is vain; ye are yet in your sins." "This plainly shows, how necessary it was, that there should be something more than reformation, which was plainly in fact wrought, in order to their being delivered from their sins; even that atonement,

5. MS: "the place marked in the margin." Owen, *A Continuation of the Exposition of the Epistle . . . to the Hebrews. Viz. On the Sixth, Seventh, Eighth, Ninth, and Tenth Chapters,* p. 468.

6. MS: "at places marked thus in the margin," with a cue mark. *Synopsis Criticorum, III,* Pt. I, cols. 500–529.

7. Poole, *Synopsis Criticorum, I,* Pt. I, col. 511.

8. Ibid., *I,* Pt. I, cols. 570–71.

9. MacLaurin, "God's Chief Mercy," p. 104, which includes a discussion of what MacLaurin refers to as the "necessity of the sacrifice."

the sufficiency of which God attested by raising our great Surety from the grave." Doddridge in loc.[1]

Socinus "excipit [...] quod, licet statuatur Christum infinitam subiisse pœnam, inde minime sequatur eam pro tanto hominum numero sufficere, quorum quilibet æternam meruit pœnam. ... 'Si quidem, ut dictum est, quilibet ex nobis per se eam pretii infinitatem debeat. Quare totidem pretii pœnarum infinitates existere opus fuisset, quot nos omnes sumus, non unicam tantum. ... '"

" ... cum vero redimendi, qui a Deo ceu unica massa considerantur, [...] (uti etiam post redemptionem ceu unicum corpus mysticum habentur,) infinitam meruerunt pœnam, pœna illa ceu aliud quiddam infinitum consideranda est; cum vero mors et passio Filii Dei sit aliquid infinitum, et mors totius massæ redimendorum infinitum quid, [...] ambo infinita sibi sunt æqualia .... Ad quid [...] necesse est, plures infinitates in infinita pœna, quam tota redimendorum massa meruit, distinguere, dum nonnisi unum infinitum efficiat; si hoc modo vellemus distinguere in eodem individuo iterum plurimas inveriremus infinitates, nempe anima meruit pœnam infinitam, corpus meruit pœnam infinitam, et in corpore iterum varia membra, et sic magnum iterum in unici hominis pœna infinitorum numerum inveriremus." Stapferus, *Theolog. Polem.*, Tom. 3, [pp.] 553–55.[2]

"Valerius Maximus Lib. VI, Cap. 3, hoc narrat: de Zaleuco Locrensium Judice, [...] qui iudex et mediator fuit, dum Filius legum a se latam transgrederetur. [...] 'Urbe Locrensium a se saluberrimis atque utilis-

---

1. Philip Doddridge, *The Family Expositor: or, a Paraphrase and Version of the New Testament: with Critical Notes; and a Practical Improvement of Each Section*, vol. 4, *Containing the Epistle of Paul the Apostle to the Romans, and His First, and Second, Epistles to the Corinthians* (London, 1753), p. 384n.

2. Socinus "later says that, although it is established that Christ had undergone infinite punishment, it would by no means then follow that that punishment is sufficient for so great a number of humans, any of whom deserved eternal punishment ... 'If indeed, as it has been said, anyone of us owes that infinity of payment through ourselves. For which reason it would have been necessary to judge ...'

" ... Indeed, when the ones to be redeemed, who are considered by God as one mass, [...] (just as also after redemption they are held as one mystical body), merit infinite punishment, that punishment should be considered as another infinite thing; indeed, when the death and passion of the Son of God should be something infinite, and the death of the whole mass of those to be redeemed something infinite, [...] both infinite things are equal to Him. ... To which it is necessary to distinguish more infinities in the infinite punishment which the whole mass of those to be redeemed merit, while only one infinite thing should effect; if in this way we would want to distinguish in the same individual again we would find more infinities, namely, the soul merits infinite punishment, the body merits infinite punishment, and in the body again the various members, and so we would find a great number again in the punishment of one human." Stapfer, *Institutiones*, 3, 553–55.

simis legibus munita, cum filius ejus adulterii crimine damnatus, secundum jus ab ipso constitutum utroque oculo carere deberet, ac tota
civitas in honorem patris pœnæ necessitatem adolescentulo remitteret,
aliquandiu repugnavit. Ad ultimum populi precibus evictus, suo prius,
deinde filii oculo eruto usum vivendi utrique reliquit. Ita debitum supplicii modum legi reddidit, æquitatis admirabili temperamento se
inter misericordem patrem et justum legislatorem partibus.'" Ibid.,
p. 557.[3]

CONCERNING THE REASONABLENESS OF THE DOCTRINE OF THE IMPU-
TATION OF MERIT.

Definition 1. By "merit" in this discourse I mean anything whatsoever
in any person or being, or about him or belonging to him, which, appearing in the view of another, is a recommendation of him to that
other's regard, esteem or affection. I don't at present take into consideration whether that which thus recommends be real merit, or something that truly, according to the nature of things, is worthy to induce esteem, etc., but only what actually recommends and appears worthy in the
eyes of him to whom it recommends the other; which is the case of everything that is actually the ground of respect or affection in one towards
another, whether the ground be real worth or only agreement in temper, benefits received, near relation, long acquaintance, etc., etc. Whatever it be that is by the respecting person viewed in the person respected
that actually has influence and is effectual to recommend to respect, is
merit, or worthiness of respect, or fitness for it, in his eyes.

Def. 2. By "patron" I mean a person of superior dignity or merit that
stands for and espouses the interest of another, interposes between him
and a third person or party in that capacity, to secure, maintain, or promote the interest of that other by his influence with him, improving his
merit with him, or interest in his esteem and regard for that end. And

---

3. "Valerius Maximus, Bk. VI, ch. 3, says this concerning Zaleucus the judge of the Locrenses, who was judge and mediator, until his son transgressed a law he himself had proposed:
[. . .] 'Since the city of the Locrenses had been strengthened by himself with the most wholesome and useful laws, when his son, condemned for the charge of adultery, ought to have lost
both eyes according to the law set up by him, and the whole state remitted the necessity of punishment for the youth in honor of the father, for some time Zalceus refused. At last, conquered
by the pleas of the people, he first had his own eye, then that of his son dug out, and he left
the use of one living eye to each. Thus the debt of punishment was given to law, between the
compassionate father and the just legislator." JE has skipped around a bit in quoting this excerpt, but has copied all of the material in this paragraph from Stapfer, *Institutiones Theologicæ
Polemicæ, 3,* 557.

by "client" I mean that other person, whose interest the patron thus espouses, and in this manner endeavors to maintain and promote.

Having explained how I use these terms, I would now observe the following things:

1. 'Tis not unreasonable, or against nature, or without foundation in the reason and nature of things, that respect should be shown to one on account of his relation to or union and connection with another; or, which is the same thing, that a person should be thought the proper object of respect or regard, viewed in that relation or connection, which he is not the proper object of, viewed as by himself, singly and separately; or, which still is the same thing, that a person should be thought worthy of respect, or meriting respect, on the account of the merit of the other person, whom he stands related to, which he would not merit viewed by himself, taking the word here as it has been explained.

2. Whenever one is thus viewed, as having a merit of respect on the account of the merit of another that he stands related to, which has not that merit considered by himself, the merit of the person he is related to is imputed to him, and these persons so far are substituted the one in the place of the other. This is plain. For the person now accepted as having merit of respect has not that merit in himself, considered alone, but only as related to another that has merit in himself, and so is respected for the sake of the merit of that other; which is the very same thing as, in our view or considering, transferring that merit from that other person to him, and viewing it as in him, as his merit, or merit that he is interested in, so that its recommending influence becomes his in some degree. So that, in all such cases, there is an imputation and substitution in some degree.

The merit of one becomes the merit of the other in some degree. Or, in other words, the recommending property, virtue, or influence of the one becomes the recommending influence of the other, or influence that prevails to recommend the other; which is the same thing.

Thus it is, when anyone respects a near relative, or a child, or spouse of a friend that is very dear and greatly esteemed for such a friend's sake, or shows the relative greater regard, seeks its welfare, and shows it more kindness than it would do if they were viewed out of such a relation or connection, and entirely by itself.

Thus it is reasonable and natural that one should be respected for the merit of another, and so his merit be in some degree imputed to another, and one person be substituted for another, according to the natural sense of all mankind.

3. As 'tis the relation of one to another, or his union with him, that is the ground of the respect that is exercised towards him for the other's sake, and so the ground of substitution of the other in his stead, and the imputation of the other's merit in some degree, as has been observed; so it is manifest, that the greater or nearer that relation is, and the stricter the union, so much the more does it prevail for the acceptance of the person as the object of respect, for the sake of him to whom he is united. Or, in other words, the union, by how much the greater and closer it is, by so much is it a ground of his [being] accepted as if he were one with the other, or of the other's being substituted for him, and his merits being imputed in a greater degree, and more, as if he were the same.

4.[4] If there be any such thing as an union of a person to another, as for instance a patron to a client, in such a certain degree, or in such a manner, as that on the account of the degree and manner it be peculiarly fit to look upon them as completely one and as it were the same, as to all that concerns the interest of the client with relation to the regard of the friend of the patron, then especially may the patron be taken by his friend as the substitute of the client, and his merit be imputed to him.

If it be inquired what degree or manner of union may be looked upon thus complete, I answer, When the patron's heart is so united to the client that, when the client is destroyed, he from love is willing to take his destruction on himself—or, what is equivalent thereto, so that the client may escape[5]—then he may properly be accepted as perfectly one with regard to the interest of the client, for this reason, that his love to the client is such as thoroughly puts into the place of the client in all that concerns his interest, even so as to absorb or swallow up his whole interest. Because his love naturally puts him in the room of the beloved, in that suffering or calamity, which being his total destruction, does swallow up and consume all his interest without leaving the least part of it.

Therefore, love that will take that destruction evidently takes in his whole interest. It appears to be an equal balance for it. His love puts him thoroughly in the client's stead. If his love were such as made him willing to put himself in the other's stead in many cases where his interest was concerned, but yet not in a case where all is concerned, the union is not complete; he is partially and not thoroughly united. But when the love of the patron is such as to go through with the matter, and make

4. MS: "5."
5. MS: "be escape."

him willing to put himself in the other's stead even in the case of the last extremity, and where the beloved is to be utterly and perfectly destroyed, then he is, as to his love, sufficiently united, so as to [be] accepted as completely one by his friend in all that concerns the client's welfare. See No. 398.[6]

5. If a friend that is very dear to any person, and of great merit in the eyes of any person, not only stands in a strict union with another, but also does particularly express a great desire of that other's welfare and appears much to seek it; it is agreeable to nature that the welfare of the person united to him should be regarded, for his sake and on his account, as if it were his own welfare. For by means of this desire of the other's welfare, his welfare becomes his own. For that good which anyone desires, sets his heart upon and seeks, thereby becomes his own good. It becomes a good that is grateful to him, or which tends to gratify and delight him. For 'tis grateful to all to have their desires gratified. In such a case, the dear and worthy person makes the other's interest his own by his explicit choice. By his own act he places his interest in the interest of the other, and so substitutes himself in the other's stead as to the affair of interest or welfare.

And the greater that desire appears, the more earnestly he seeks the other's welfare and the greater things he does to obtain it; so much the more does his interest become his own, and so much the more does he, as it were, substitute himself in the room of the other.

6. Especially is the client's welfare properly and naturally regarded for the sake of the patron that is very dear and worthy in the eyes of any person, when the way in which the patron expresses his desire of the client's welfare that he is closely united to, and in which he seeks it, is by suffering and being at expense of his own personal and private welfare, in any degree, for the welfare of the client. Expending one good or interest for another is properly transferring the interest in the good expended into the good sought. The expended good, which is the means, is properly set aside and removed in the regard of him that is at the expense, and is placed in that good which is the end. The good of the price is parted with for the good of the thing purchased. And, therefore, here is a proper substitution of one in the place of the other.

In such a case, therefore, in a more special manner will it be proper and natural for one in whose eyes the patron is very worthy, and to whom he is very dear, to have regard to the welfare of the client for the patron's

6. *Works, 13*, 463–64.

sake, or for the sake of the patron's merit. As suppose the client of the excellent and dear patron be a child or spouse in captivity, and the patron lays out himself exceedingly for the client's redemption, and goes through many and very great hardships, and is at vast expense, for the obtaining of it.

7. If the patron who seeks the welfare of the client, in his seeking of it, does particularly and directly apply himself to the person who has so high an esteem and affection for him, expressing his desires of the client's welfare be given to him, expended for him, for his sake, for the promoting his ends, or for anything that his friend regards as his own interest; then especially is it natural that the person of whom his client's welfare is sought should be ready to grant it for his sake.

8. 'Tis still more highly proper and natural to regard the client's welfare on account of the patron's merit, or to reckon the merit of the patron to the client's account, if the merit of the patron consists or especially appears in what he does for the client's welfare, or if the virtues and worthy qualities have their chief exercise and do chiefly exhibit their amiableness in those excellent and amiable acts which he performs in seeking the good of the client, in the deeds he performs on the account of the interest of the client, and in his applying to his friend for it, in the acts he performs as an intercessor with his friend for it, and the service he does him on this account.

In this case, it is peculiarly natural to accept the client on the account of the merit of the patron.[7] For the merit is on his account, has its existence for the sake of the client.

9. More especially is [it] natural when his merit above all consists and appears in the very expense the patron is at of his own welfare for the welfare of the client, or in the act of expending or exchanging the one for the other. For as was observed before, such expense is properly regarded as a price of the client's welfare. But when such merit is added to the price, this merit becomes the worth, value or preciousness of the price—preciousness of another kind besides merely the value of the natural good parted with. It adds a moral good to the price, equal to the natural good expended. So that the worthiness of the patron and the value expended are offered, both together in one, as the price of the welfare of the client.

10. The thus accepting the patron's merit as being placed to the account of the client will be more natural still if the patron puts himself in

7. MS: "client."

the place of the client, undertaking to appear for him, to represent him and act in his stead, and by an exceeding great change in his circumstances clothes himself with the form of his client, goes where he is, takes his place in the universe, puts himself into his circumstances and is in all things made like unto him, wherein this may be consistent with maintaining his merit inviolable.

11. If the client be unworthy, and an offender, and has deserved ill of the person whose favor he needs, then the abating and dismissing resentment, or lessening or withholding the evil deserved, for the sake of the merit of the patron, is equivalent to a positive favor for his sake in case of no offense, and demerit of punishment.

12. If the person that needs favor be an offender and unworthy, then in order to a proper influence and effect of union and merit of a patron, to induce his friend to receive him to favor on his account, the union of the patron with his client, and his undertaking and appearing as his patron to seek favor for him, should be in such a manner, and attended with such circumstances, as not to diminish his merit, i.e. so as that his union with and intercession for the client shall not in the least infringe on these two things: the patron's own union with his friend whose favor he seeks for the client; and his merit strictly so called, i.e. his own virtue. For if his own worthiness be diminished by his union with one that is unworthy, then his influence to recommend the client one way is destroyed one way at the same time that it is established another. For that recommending influence consists in these two things, viz. his merit, and his union with the client. Therefore, if one of these is diminished or destroyed as the other is established or advanced, nothing on the whole is done towards recommending the client.

Therefore, though on the whole the client be effectually recommended, 'tis necessary that the patron's union to an offending, unworthy client should be attended with such circumstances that it shall not be at all inconsistent with these two things: his regard to his friend, and his regard to virtue or holiness. For in these two things consists his merit in the eyes of his friend.

And, therefore, 'tis necessary that his appearing united to his unworthy and offending client should be with such circumstances as most plainly to demonstrate that he perfectly disapproves of his offense and unworthiness, and to show a perfect regard to virtue and to the honor and dignity of his offended, injured friend. And there is no way that this can be so thoroughly and fully done as by undertaking himself to pay the debt to the honor and rights of his injured friend, and to honor the rule of virtue and righteousness the client has violated by putting himself in the stead of the offender, into subjection to the injured rights and violated authority of his offended friend, and under the violated law and rule of righteousness belonging to one in the client's state; and so, for the sake of the honor of his friend's authority and the honor of the rule of righteousness, suffering the whole penalty due to the offender which would have been requisite to be suffered by him for the maintaining the honor and dignity of these things, and himself, by such great condescension and under such self-denial, honoring these rights and rules by his obedience and perfect conformity to them; hereby giving the most evident testimony to all beholders, that although he loves his client and seeks his welfare, yet he had rather be humbled so low, deny himself so greatly, and suffer so much, than that his welfare should be in the least [a] diminution of the honor of,[8] and weakening the authority and dignity of, these things.

13. If the patron be, in the eyes of him whose favor is sought, of very great dignity, 'tis agreeable to reason and nature that this should have influence to procure greater favor to the client than if he were of lesser dignity. And when it is inquired whether there be a sufficiency in the patron and his relation to his client to answer to such a degree of favor as is proposed to be obtained for him, the dignity of the patron is one thing that is to be estimated and, as it were, put into the scales [. . .][9]

[1353.] THE TWO DISPENSATIONS COMPARED, THAT UNDER MOSES AND THAT UNDER CHRIST.

First, wherein these two dispensations agree. See "Miscellanies," [No.] 874.[1]

1. The same salvation, in substance, was given under both. Sinners under the old testament were by nature children of wrath, came into the world in the same miserable condition as now. They were exposed to the same eternal damnation. And the saints were made partakers of the same benefits, the same effectual calling by the Spirit of God, the same justification, adoption and sanctification, and obtained the same eternal glory in heaven.

2. The grand medium of salvation was the same. They were saved, and

---

8. MS: "or."

9. At this point in the MS, JE inserted, "see further p. 1130," a reference to the materials further on in Bk. 9 that JE, Jr., labeled "Miscellanies" No. [1360]. See p. 713.

1. *Works*, 20, 115–18.

obtained the benefits mentioned above, by the same Mediator, by his incarnation, his suffering, his satisfaction, righteousness and intercession, and not at all by their own righteousness or by the mediation, sacrifice or righteousness of any other mediation.

3. The divine person applying Christ's redemption was the same, viz. the Holy Spirit, by enlightening the mind, renewing the heart, etc., acting herein especially as the Spirit of Christ.

4. The method of bestowing eternal salvation was, in substance, the same. There were the same grand conditions and qualifications of justification and salvation. The grand qualification for justification was faith, the active unition of the heart to Christ, attended with repentance, conviction of sin, etc. And the same way of coming to the actual possession of eternal life, by universal and persevering holiness of heart and life. Justifying faith was the same for substance. It was the same spirit of faith. The exercises differed only as opportunity and occasion differed[2] by different degrees of revelation.

That the saints under the old testament were justified the same way with those under the new, appears by the instances the apostle James mentions in the second chapter of his epistle, and the manner of his arguing from 'em. See also other evidences of this in "Miscellanies." See "Table" under the words "Covenants," "Testaments" and "Dispensations."[3]

5. The external means of the application of the benefits of redemption were, in general, the same. The main means then was the word of God, as now. God made use of ordinances then as well as now. The duties of divine worship agreed in many generals. The main duties of worship were then prayer and praise and reading and hearing the word of God, as now. There were sabbaths and sacraments then as well as now. Men were saved by revealed religion under the old testament as well as now.

6. The grand benefits of the covenant of grace, with the grand means, Jesus Christ and his mediation, with the qualifications or condition of an interest in the Savior, and the way to the full possession of the benefits, were in some sort exhibited under both covenants. And where the exhibitions were not so plain as properly to be of the nature of a REVELATION of these things, as their many typical observances, yet they were of

---

2. MS: "difference."

3. I.e. the "Table" to the "Miscellanies." For the topics JE mentions, see *Works*, *13*, 129, 131, 147.

such a nature, and so contrived, as naturally tended to lead those to whom they were exhibited to a gospel temper of mind, such a habit and frame of heart, as on an exhibition of greater light would naturally appear in a more explicit faith in Christ and his satisfaction, righteousness and redemption.

7. Not only were these things, mentioned under the last head, in some sort exhibited and represented under both dispensations, but also were in some degree made known and revealed under both. The great spiritual benefits of the covenant of grace were generally revealed in the wilderness and at Mt. Sinai: as that God would be the God of true saints, they should be his peculiar favorites, their sins should be forgiven, they should have God's Spirit given 'em, and their hearts sanctified on their repenting and turning to God, etc. See Ex. 34:5–7; Lev. 26:12, 42–46; Deut. 30:1–6, 15, 19. And these blessings were to be obtained by God's mere mercy, in a manner consistent with perfect holiness and the strict justice and the rights of his law, and that favor was to be obtained by a divine person, the angel of the Lord, dwelling with the people, as having espoused them and become their Mediator.

But these things were gradually more revealed and insisted on afterwards by the prophets, with much more plain intimations given of a future state and eternal life, and more revealed concerning the Mediator and the spiritual blessings of the covenant and the condition of justification.

8. The future blessings of the covenant of grace, the life and happiness of a future state, were not only in some degree revealed, but also in some sort promised, i.e. the revelation was such as did convey a right to these blessings and brought God under obligation to bestow them. The general promises of the covenant, which were express—the promises of God's being their God and their being his people, his portion, his special favorites, his peculiar treasure; of God's being their exceeding great reward; of God's making them happy in a vast distinction from the wicked—implied happiness, and could not be fulfilled without. The things of this world, which are in their own nature so mean, worthless and vain, and which are abundantly set forth to be so in the Old Testament, could not answer these promises.

And especially did these promises, taken with God's providence, imply an obligation to bestow future happiness. For it was manifest that all things came alike to all, and that many of those that were the most eminent saints, and with whom in a special manner God's covenant was established—as Abraham, Isaac, and Jacob, and David—met with abundance of affliction in the world. The promises of life so often made to the righteous in the Old Testament, as a blessing by which they should be distinguished, plainly implied future life. The promises of satisfying the desires and answering the prayers of God's people, by just construction, imply a promise of eternal life. For they imply at least that God will gratify their holy desires, the desires occasioned by the love of God, and which must be increased and be more strong as that principle of love to God is increased. Such is a desire of eternal life in the glorifying and enjoying God, as we find this principle especially made Hezekiah to dread death, and to desire life, and rejoice at the news of the lengthening out his life. Is. 38:11, "I said, I shall not see the Lord, even the Lord, in the land of the living." Vv. 18–19, "the grave cannot praise thee, death cannot celebrate thee: they that go down the pit cannot hope for thy truth. The living, the living, he shall praise thee, as I do this day: the father to the children shall make known thy truth." V. 22, "What shall be the signs that I shall go up to the house of the Lord?"

Secondly, wherein the two dispensations differ. See "Miscellanies," [No.] 439.[4]

It appears by the things which have been observed that the two testaments don't differ as to the essence and substance of the covenant itself. It therefore follows that they differ only in manner and circumstances, and that in three respects: 1. In that the method that was principally taken in that constitution, as it was first published in the wilderness for the introducing and establishing the great things of the gospel, is so indirect, viz. under a cover, and not only so, but a cover so diverse in its nature from the great things which God aimed to establish. 2. That the revelation of the things of the gospel, wherein it is direct, is so important, i.e. that those things are spoken so seldom, and that [when] they are directly spoken of, they are revealed no more plainly and fully. 3. In various things which are the result of these.

1. The exhibition of things pertaining to men's duty and happiness that was made, or revelation that was given, in order to the introducing and establishing the covenant of grace and its benefits: these things were made use of as means of this, that were very diverse from the thing aimed at, so that [God] did, as it were, make use of contraries to obtain his end. There were other, subordinate constitutions made use [of] that were, with respect to the covenant of grace, as a cover or cortex. There was a

4. JE cites No. 438, "Fall of Angels," but obviously means No. 439, "Covenant. Testaments." See *Works, 13,* 487–89.

cortex and medulla, a putamen and a nucleus, the letter and the spirit, the one very diverse from the other. Therein the exhibition which God made of man's happiness and the way to it under the old testament, differed from that which is made under the new. In the present, evangelical dispensation, the nucleus or medulla is delivered more simply and directly, not covered and enveloped in a cortex or putamen, and the revelation not attended with anything of so heterogeneous a nature. All is uncovered. The thing itself, on which we must depend, the things wherein the essence of our true happiness consists, and the true way to it, are exhibited in their simplicity, and in their own natures. All is simple and homogeneous.

This cortex consisted of two covenants that were revealed, diverse from the covenant of grace, viz. (1) *the covenant of works;* and (2) *the covenant God made and established with Israel according to the flesh:* the former entirely diverse and opposite to the covenant of grace, and not at all appertaining to it, and in itself independent of it, though delivered to Israel in subordination to it; the other diverse, in some respect appertaining to it, or appointed only to be subservient to it.

But here must be observed: There is a great difference in the manner of exhibiting these two covenants, which constitute what I call the cortex of the old testament. The latter, viz. the covenant God made with Israel according to the flesh, was not only exhibited, but established. It was a covenant God truly entered into with that people as the way to their safety and happiness. But the former, viz. the covenant of works, was exhibited and proposed, but not established as the method in which God intended to bestow on them the blessed fruits of his favor. The covenant of works was particularly revealed and expressly and formally made known to the children of Israel in the wilderness, which it had not been before since the fall. Nor was it only explicitly revealed, but proposed. It is revealed to us in these days of the gospel. But it was proposed to them as a way of life for their trial, set before them that they might make use of [it] as a method in which they might seek life and happiness, as Christ proposed keeping the commandments to the rich young man. Indeed, the same is now proposed in the course of a sinner's convictions in these days, but 'tis not properly by that new revelation that Christ introduced, which is of another nature, not by any formal exhibition and proposal of the covenant of works in the new testament.

Indeed, the covenant of works was not merely proposed as an antiquated thing, which the people were fond of, for their trial and conviction, but as a thing still in force and of the greatest importance, in several respects. It was, indeed, wherein was the supreme and everlasting, unalterable rule of righteousness between God and man that must some way or other be fulfilled; in some sense the rule of God's proceeding with them all, the rule of his proceeding with the righteous and faithful among them mediately and through a Mediator, but immediate with all such of them as should continue in sin. And in these respects it was not only proposed but established, or re-established, with the children of Israel at Mt. Sinai in the Ten Commandments. Therein the covenant of grace was established as the immediate rule of God's bestowment of favor and salvation, but the covenant of works as the mediate rule of this [and] as the immediate rule of his punishing sinners.

But in the old testament, the covenant of works was no covenant that God established or entered into with his people as the designed, immediate method of his favor. 'Twas not proposed with a command to men that they should seek and hope for life in this way, not proposed as anything that they were necessitated personally to fulfill as the only method of justification. Both the law and the gospel were proposed, but the gospel only was established.

(1) The law, or covenant of works, which God revealed and proposed to the children of Israel, I call a cortex or shell, enveloping the gospel as the medulla or kernel, though it be of a very diverse nature from the gospel, for the following reasons:

1. Because it was revealed not for itself, or to that end, that men might fulfill it and obtain justification in that way, for that was impossible: but wholly and entirely in subserviency to the gospel, and in subordination to the grand design of bringing men to life in a new and living way. It was revealed that men might understand the other way that God would establish, and that they might be prepared for it and brought into it. The law was a schoolmaster to bring us to Christ.

2. The revelation of the law was, as it were, a shell containing the gospel, or covenant of grace, as its kernel, because it was not only a revelation given wholly in subordination to the gospel, but it was exhibited together with it in the very same revelation and under the same words, having a different aspect and application; the words with regard to one being called "the letter," and the sense conveyed by the words in the other aspect being called "the spirit." Such words are used as in their proper signification may be applied to signify that perfect obedience which is the condition of the covenant of works, and that sincere obedience of faith which is the great qualification of the covenant of grace. The thing revealed and applied is holiness and obedience, and in such words that they may be understood either of holiness, or our offering to God as it is considered in the covenant of works, or as it [is] the compliance and acceptance of God offering his fullness to us, as it is to be considered in the covenant of grace. (See my discourse of the agreement and difference between the covenant of works and covenant of grace, "Controversies" papers under the head of "Justification").[5]

Thus those words, "Thou shalt love the Lord thy God with all thine heart, and with all thy soul, with all thy mind, and with all thy strength" [Mark 12:30], may be taken both these ways: either for a perfect love to God as our offering unto God, as the price of his favor; or the sincere and entire acceptance of our hearts of God and Christ, graciously offering themselves and their fullness to [us] for our relief and supply, who are in ourselves poor, empty, unworthy, miserable creatures. So the Ten Commandments—or the words spoken out of the midst of the fire at Mt. Sinai and afterwards engraven on tables of stone, called the tables of the covenant—in one sense were the covenant of works, and in another the covenant of grace. [See] what is written on this subject, pp. 504–6.[6]

3. This revelation of the covenant of works, or exhibition of the law, may properly [be] represented as the shell with respect to the revelation of the gospel, which was the kernel, on this account, because this is, as it were, outermost, being first objected to view. The legal sense was most obvious, and that which would occur first to a cursory view, and would be most easily and plainly seen by such as were not spiritually enlightened, and by all such as were chiefly under the influence of a carnal and legal, self-righteous disposition. The gospel, or covenant of grace,[7] was really and sufficiently implied, and signified, and properly established by the words, yet was not so obvious, but more hidden; though when the words with their circumstances were duly considered, it was evident the real intent and design of them was to establish the covenant of grace, and that only. Yet in order to discern that, there was need of diligently attending to the words and thoroughly considering them, and there was also need of a truly humble, penitent and pious mind well to discern this secret design and grand aim of the revelation. It being thus, that the

5. This refers to two essays in the section on "Justification" in the "Controversies" notebook: "Question: Wherein Do the Two Covenants Agree as to the Method of Justification, and the Appointed Qualification For It?" and "The Things Wherein the Way of Justification by Mere Law and that by Grace Through Christ Differ as to the Qualification of the Subject that Primarily Entitles Him to Justification." See *Works*, 21, 354–371.

6. MS: "p. 900. col. 2 &c.," referring to the portion of this entry entitled, "The Ten Commandments Contained Not Only in the Covenant of Works, but the Covenant of Grace."

7. MS: "grace, that."

gospel was a covenant of grace, being the true design of the Spirit of God in them, and the design and meaning which men were enabled rightly to discern and apply to themselves only by the gracious influences of that Spirit, and so to taste and be nourished by the kernel: hence this nucleus is called "the spirit" and the other is called "the letter," because the words in their more obvious meaning, and to them who viewed only the letter with a carnal eye, saw no more contained in them than the law. These are the letter that "kills," and the spirit that "gives life" (II Cor. 3:6).

(2) There was another covenant also which God delivered to the children of Israel, which was, as it were, a calyx that contained, or cortex that enveloped, the gospel, [which] is the covenant that God made with Israel according to the flesh, or the covenant which he made with the external Israel, or the seed of Abraham, as one of the peoples or nations of this world.

'Tis evident there was such a covenant, which was diverse from the covenant that is established between God and the mystical church. The people with whom this covenant was made was an external, temporal society. In the very nature of it, it was properly a national covenant. The promises of the covenant were external and carnal, of outward safety and prosperity, and that in the enjoyment of the inheritance and blessings of an external, earthly country, the land of Canaan. They had a worldly sanctuary, an external, carnal priesthood, carnal sacrifices, an external altar, an external holy of holies, and an external mercy seat.

In the requisite conditions of an interest in the blessings of this covenant, chiefly those things were regarded that are external: external conformity to the law of God, an outward conformity to the moral law, and a conformity to an external and carnal law, viz. the precepts of the ceremonial and judicial law, an external, carnal worship. The pardon and sanctification that belonged to that covenant was external: a freedom from guilt as it excluded from external privileges; and a sanctification that consisted in the purifying of the flesh, delivering from carnal pollutions, and qualifying for carnal privileges.

It is not absolutely necessary to my present purpose to dispute and determine, whether it be the most proper way of expressing things, to speak of this covenant as a distinct covenant from the covenant of grace, or rather as an appurtenance of the different administration of the covenant of grace. 'Tis evident that it was in some respects a different covenant. 'Tis evident that the covenant by which God promised to Abraham, and afterwards to the nation of Israel, the land of Canaan and its temporal blessings, was of the nature of a promise, and that so far as there were mutual stipulations, it was of the nature of a covenant. And 'tis also evident that it was [not] the very same with that covenant of grace that extends universally to all God's people, of all nations and ages, nor included in it.

'Tis true that covenant of grace that extends to all ages and nations contains the promise of things of this life and that which is to come, i.e. therein God has promised such a portion of the things of this life as he sees to be best. But that don't hinder, but that if God is pleased to add to such a general promise, a promise of some one, particular, outward benefit, or a particular kind of outward blessings—I say, it don't [hinder] but that this is truly and properly a distinct promise, not included in the other, especially if the promise be made to qualifications that are also, in some respects, distinct from the condition of the other, and not included in it.

This covenant was a mixed covenant; that is, it partly partook of the nature of the covenant of works, and partly of the nature of the covenant of grace. In this it resembled the covenant of works, that it required a perfect, legal purity in every respect in order to being admitted into the congregation of the Lord, and that the qualification or condition consisted so much in men's own laborious and operose doings, and in their multiplied gifts to God; which savors more of the first covenant, in which men offer a price of their own to God to procure his favor, than of the covenant of grace, where all the condition is receiving and accepting, which don't so directly appear in our own works and gifts. And in many things it provided no means of reconciliation.

In this it resembled the covenant of grace, that it admitted of confession, sacrifice, and reconciliation in some things.

The true reason why this covenant was thus mixed may be thus given: it resembled the covenant of works in the respect that has been mentioned, because it was given as an additament and appendage to the covenant of works as it was delivered and proposed to them for the trial of their obedience. The positive precept of not eating the forbidden fruit was added to the covenant [of] works as delivered to our first parents. A main law or rule in the covenant of works is to [be] obedient to all God's positive commands. Therefore, when God proposed the covenant of works to the children of Israel, he [added] to the moral law a great number of positive precepts, which would render unclean and utterly exclude everyone from the congregation of the Lord, had not purifications been appointed. And it resembled the covenant of grace also in the respect mentioned, because it was given on purpose to be a type and representation of that covenant and things belonging to it. See further, as to the reasons why this national covenant was legal, pp. 529–30.[8]

Therefore, this covenant was like a shell enveloping the gospel two ways: first, as an appendage [to] the covenant of works delivered to the children of Israel (and how that was as a calyx or cortex to the gospel has already been explained); and secondly, as all things appertaining to it were typical of gospel things, shadows of good things to come, and so exhibited them under a veil.

Thus we see that under the old testament the kernel of the gospel was delivered under a twofold shell: viz. *1.* the law, or covenant of works, containing the moral with the ceremonial and judicial laws; *2.* the symbolical cortex, and which also in Scripture language may be called the carnal covenant, which is the thing the Scripture calls the "veil." This cortex, though blessed to be a means to bring God's elect to partake of the nucleus, yet it actually hid it from the careless, carnal, unhumbled, unconvinced sinners, and blinded their minds, and was an occasion of their self-righteousness.

Both these things may be signified by "the letter" and "the spirit." The symbols themselves, which are expressed by the letters of the institution, are well expressed by "the letter," as well as the covenant of works in the Ten Commandments. And the spiritual thing typified, which was the substance and end of the type aimed at by the Spirit of God in the institution, is "the spirit."

Both these are in some respects, considered absolutely and as in themselves, of a nature very heterogeneous and diverse from the gospel or covenant of grace that they were exhibited to subserve. The diversity of the first consists in its *legality,* and is opposite, as law is opposite to gospel, works to grace. The diversity of the latter consists in its *carnality,* and is opposite, as that [which] is external is opposite to that which is spiritual, and the things which are worldly or earthly are from the things which are heavenly. Both these covenants, or laws, are a schoolmaster to bring the church to Christ, in different ways.

N. B. The difference between the two dispensations, which has been spoken of under this first head, consisting in the gospel's being thus covered and enveloped in such a cortex, is the main difference, chiefly insisted on by the apostles in their writings.

---

8. MS: "p. 924. col. 2 &c.," in No. [1354], the fifth answer to the second objection, the paragraph beginning, "There was a temporal, national covenant between God and the nation of Israel . . ."

2. The second thing wherein the dispensation under the old testament differs from the new dispensation was, that under the old testament, that the revelation of the things of the gospel, wherein it was direct, was so imperfect, in that the things which are purely evangelical are spoken of so seldom, and that, when they are spoken, they are revealed no more plainly and fully.

Thus it is with respect to the promises of the covenant of grace. They are chiefly the things of another world. These sometimes are directly spoken in the Old Testament, but yet they are spoken very rarely in comparison of what they are in the New Testament, and in no measure with that plainness and fullness, and much less plainly, fully and directly in the law of Moses than in other parts of the Old Testament.

So it is with regard to the way of procuring those future and eternal blessings; the revelation of the Mediator, his person and states; the union of the divine and human nature; his suretyship; his obedience and sufferings, resurrection, ascension into heaven and intercession for us there; the method of applying and obtaining the benefits of redemption; the grand qualification and condition of the covenant of grace; the particular nature of the Redeemer's kingdom; the concern of the several persons of the Trinity in this affair, and our concern with them in it, etc.; the essence of the duty of the redeemed and the great foundations and enforcements thereof, etc.; the certainty of the perseverance of true saints, etc.

3. These two things, which have been already mentioned, are the things wherein the difference between the two dispensations does most fundamentally consist. But yet there are many other circumstantial differences which may be considered as the result of these things taken together with that circumstance of time—viz. that the Messiah, the Mediator, was then to come; now he is actually come, and has obeyed and died, is risen and ascended, and rules as God-man, etc.—particularly:

(1) The conditions of the covenant of grace, or those qualifications requisite to eternal life under the old testament, differed circumstantially from those which are required under the new testament.

So with regard to that qualification which is in a peculiar manner the condition of an interest in Christ, viz. faith. That faith which was justifying faith under the old testament differed circumstantially from that which is required in order to justification now. The spirit or principle of faith in the heart was the same; and the person who is the object of faith is the same, viz. the Son of God, as Mediator. The same spirit of repentance and humiliation belonged to it then as does now. But not exactly the same exercises of faith were then required as are now, but there was a difference, answerable to the difference of the revelation in which the Mediator and his salvation is exhibited. As the revelation now is much more plain, particular and full, so a more particular and explicit regard to the Mediator, with respect to the things revealed, is required.

So with regard to other duties which are the subordinate conditions of eternal life, being the expressions and fruits of faith and the way to the possession of the future inheritance. Those that are required now differ in degree and circumstances from what were absolutely necessary of old—the degree and manner of weanedness from the world, self-denial, spirituality of worship, heavenly-mindedness, love to men, the degree and manner of our loving them, forgiveness of injuries, love to enemies, love to the wicked, love to all mankind, etc. According to the more particular and full revelation of the grounds of these duties, and the new obligations laid upon us to them, evangelical duties, with their grounds, were not so fully revealed, so particularly prescribed, nor so much insisted on.

(2) There is a circumstantial difference between the spiritual and eternal blessings bestowed on true saints under the old testament and those bestowed in the new.

As to the spiritual blessings bestowed in this world, they were attended with a manifold greater imperfection. The saints were not admitted to that visible, revealed nearness to God as the children of God and the spouse. The nature and high degree of these privileges were not then made known. That exalted union and communion of the saints with God, which is brought to light by the gospel, was comparatively but little of it known under the old. And therefore their grace was less manifested in love and joy, and more in fear. The Spirit of God was not so much given as a Spirit of adoption as it is now, and not so much as an earnest of the future inheritance, giving foretastes of heavenly joy and glory.

And the heavenly happiness itself, to which the souls of saints ascended in the times of the old testament, proportionably differed from heaven as it is now since Christ's ascension, being probably made immensely more a world of light, of love, and joy, and glory, than it was before.

(3) The means of the application of the benefits of redemption are in many respects very different. The word is different, more legal, insisting more on the law, less on the gospel, more dark and enigmatical; and the ordinances very burdensome, very enigmatical and of obscure signification, etc.

(4) Though the saints were saved in like manner by Christ's righteousness and death and intercession, yet not in like manner by his resurrection and ascension into heaven. In like manner in the exercise of the priestly office, but not of his prophetical and priestly office, not actually dispensed by Jesus Christ, God-man, etc.

I might here go on to observe how the old testament differed from the new in its being a more imperfect, a more legal, carnal and enigmatical, terrible, childish, burdensome and servile dispensation in many respects, and more confined and limited in its effects, and was but a temporary dispensation. But these things are easy. And what has been observed already may be sufficient to lead our thoughts into a right way of conceiving of the difference between the two dispensations.

The TEN COMMANDMENTS contained not only the covenant of works, but the COVENANT OF GRACE, at least considered with the manner and circumstances with which it was delivered at Mt. Sinai: first with a great voice being joined with those laws of sacrifices which we have in the nineteenth chapter of Exodus, which Moses at that time rehearsed together with the Ten Commandments, and which they consented to with them, and were written in the book with them there under the Mount, then called the book of the covenant, and sealed with the blood of the sacrifices in a solemn manner with them, as together making up the covenant (see Ex. 24:1–8); considered also with the circumstances under which the Ten Commandments were afterwards delivered unto Moses in tables of stone, being given in the hand of a mediator, to be laid up in the ark, under the mercy seat, or the "propitiatory," as the word is called, before which the high priest alone was to appear once a year with blood and incense.

The following things make it manifest that in the Decalogue was exhibited not only the covenant of works, but the covenant of grace.

1. That the two tables of stone in which they were written are so often called the tables of the covenant; and the ark that contained them, and whose special use it was to be a sacred chest that should contain this precious treasure, a repository in which it might be laid up and kept safe— I say, that this is so often called the ark of the covenant. By these things it is manifest that the Decalogue was eminently, and above all other things, contained in the revelation God made to Moses, the covenant of God with his people Israel; not only a covenant revealed and proposed to 'em for their conviction, etc., but the covenant that [God] had entered into and established between him and that people, by which they were united one to another, and he became their God and they his people, and he was, as it were, married to that people. The tables of stone are called "the tables of the covenant which God made" with the people (Deut. 9:9).

2. It is an evidence of the same thing, that the Ten Commandments are called "the words of the covenant." Ex. 34:28, "And he wrote upon the tables the words of the covenant, the Ten Commandments." And Deut. 4:13, "And he declared unto you his covenant, which he commanded you to perform, even Ten Commandments; and he wrote them upon two tables of stone."

3. The preface to the Ten Commandments (which was a part of what was delivered with a great voice out of the midst of the fire, and a part of that which was written on the tables of stone) confirms that the Decalogue was a covenant of grace, the covenant which he entered into as the Lord their God and Redeemer. The words of that preface do not only declare that God is their God and Redeemer, or will as such treat all that observe that covenant; but they also imply that God now was about to declare how they should behave towards him as Jehovah their God and Redeemer, or as their living, all-sufficient, faithful Redeemer, and do argue that he gave those Ten Commandments as an instruction to them how to receive him and cleave to him and trust in him as such.

The preface with the first command was doubtless what was all together called the first commandment, or the first "word" (as it is in the original). This first word comprehended the whole. It was a general of which the following are particulars, or particular explications, or direction of the manner in which they should cleave to Jehovah and trust in him as their only and all-sufficient, living Redeemer. As the last commandment, against concupiscence, is also in some sense a general, explaining the spiritual design of the rest, showing how that God means not only to forbid those external, gross sins, or overt acts, that had been mentioned, but that internal lust whence they all proceed.

The preface of the Decalogue, taken in connection with the words of the first commandment immediately following, do much confirm this to be what is implied in God's meaning and design in them. "I am Jehovah thy God" and Redeemer. "Thou shalt have no other gods before me" [Ex. 20:2–3], i.e. thou shalt cleave to me, and me only, as thy God and Redeemer, as being a sufficient Savior, and full and everlasting, unchangeable fountain of all good to you, alone worthy to be trusted in. For to have any being for a God, according to the received notions of the nations of the world, and in the sense of the Holy Scripture, is not only to have such a being as an object of reverence and observance, but especially as [an] object of trust, as a defense and Savior, and author of blessing and happiness.

5. Those words annexed to the second commandment, "showing mercy to thousands of them that love me, and keep my commandments" [Ex. 20:6], do show the Decalogue to be of the nature of a covenant of mercy and grace.

6. It is an evidence that the Decalogue contained the covenant of grace, that the mercy seat was placed over it, where God dwelt among the people as their Savior by this covenant, or according to this rule.

7. 'Tis an evidence that the Decalogue was not delivered merely as a covenant of works, because these Ten Commandments, together with other words which God delivered at Mt. Sinai at the same time, which were annexed to them, were sealed with the blood of the sacrifice, which typified the blood of Christ. See Ex. 24:5–8, compared with Heb. 9:18–23.

See notes on Ex. 32:19 and 34:1; and on chs. 32–34, "Notes on Scripture," no. 441.[9]

[1354.] JUSTIFICATION. OBJECTION against the doctrine of JUSTIFICATION by faith alone from the conditions of God's favor chiefly insisted on in the OLD TESTAMENT.

THE OBJECTION STATED.

Whereas it is insisted that we are justified by faith alone in that sense, viz. that we are justified[1] (i.e. accepted of God as free from guilt, wrath and the punishment of sin, and as now righteous and so the objects of favor, and as properly entitled to the rewards of righteousness), not by any righteousness of ours, any virtue in us as recommending us to such a privilege by its moral beauty or value in the sight of God, considering us as we are in ourselves, but only by faith in Christ, or our cordial reception of Christ and active unition with him as our atoning and righteous Mediator; and that though faith be indeed an excellent virtue, yet in this affair it is not the virtuousness or value of its moral excellency that

---

9. In the "Blank Bible" note on Ex. 32:19, JE remarks that Moses' breaking the tablets signifies, first, that sin breaks the law as a covenant of works, and second, that God broke his covenant between himself and his people and so threatened to cast them off; and in the note on Ex. 34:1, Moses' being commanded to carve two new stone tables signifies that after humankind had broken the law, their hearts needed to be prepared "by being hewed, i.e. hewed by the Law of Moses, or by legal convictions." For "Scripture" no. 441, see *Works*, *15*, 522–24.

1. MS: "not justified."

is the thing considered, but only its relation to Christ, as making one with him and so interesting the believer in his satisfaction and righteousness; and that it was always thus with regard to the justification of fallen man, the main qualification and condition of justification being the same in substance under the old testament as under the new:

Now 'tis inquired how this consists with what is so much insisted on as the grand condition of God's favor in the Old Testament, viz. obedience to God, loving God, doing that which is good in his sight, etc.? As Ex. 19:5–6, "Now therefore, if ye will obey my voice indeed, and keep my covenant, then ye shall be a peculiar treasure unto me above all people: for all the earth is mine." See also Ex. 15:26. Ex. 23:22, "But if thou shalt indeed obey his voice, and do all that I speak; then I will be an enemy unto thine enemies." Deut. 4:40, "Thou shalt keep therefore his statutes, and his commandments, that I commanded thee this day, that it may go well with thee, and thy children after thee, and that thou mayest prolong thy days upon the earth, which the Lord thy God giveth thee, forever." So ch. 5:29 and ch. 6:1–5. And [ch. 6], vv. 17–18, "You shall diligently keep the commandments of the Lord your God, and his testimonies, and his statutes, which he hath commanded thee. And thou shalt do that which is RIGHT AND GOOD in the sight of the Lord: that it may be well with thee, and that thou mayest go in and possess the good land which the Lord sware unto thy fathers." Vv. 24–25, "And the Lord commanded us to do all these statutes, to fear the Lord our God, for our good always, that he might preserve us alive, as at this day. And it shall be OUR RIGHTEOUSNESS, if we observe to do all these commandments before the Lord our God, as he hath commanded us."

Ch. 7:12–13, "Wherefore it shall come to pass, if ye hearken to these judgments, and keep, and do them, that the Lord thy God shall KEEP unto thee the COVENANT and the mercy which he sware unto thy fathers: and he will LOVE THEE, AND BLESS THEE, and multiply thee," etc. Ch. 8:1, "All the commandments which I command thee this day shall ye observe to do, that YE MAY LIVE, and multiply, and go in and possess the land which the Lord sware unto your fathers." Ch. 11:26–28, "Behold, I set before you this day a blessing and a curse; A BLESSING, IF YE OBEY the commandments of the Lord your God, which I command you this day: and a CURSE, IF YE WILL NOT OBEY the commandments of the Lord your God, but turn aside out of the way which I command you this day." Ch. 13:17–18, "that the Lord thy God may TURN FROM THE FIERCENESS OF HIS ANGER, AND SHOW THEE MERCY, AND HAVE COMPASSION UPON THEE, AND MULTIPLY THEE, as he hath sworn unto thy fathers; when thou shalt hearken to the voice of the Lord thy God, to keep all his commandments which I command thee this day, to do that which [is] RIGHT IN THE EYES OF THE LORD THY GOD." Ch. 28:1–2, "And it shall come to pass, if thou shalt hearken diligently unto the voice of the Lord thy God, to observe and to do all his commandments which I command thee this day, that the Lord thy God will set thee on high above all nations of the earth: AND ALL THESE BLESSINGS SHALL COME UPON THEE, and overtake thee, if thou shalt hearken unto the voice of the Lord thy God."

Ch. 30:1–3, "when all these things are come upon thee, . . . and thou shalt call them to mind among all the nations, whether the Lord thy God hath driven thee, and thou shalt return unto the Lord thy God, and shalt OBEY HIS VOICE according to all that I command thee this day, thou and thy children, with all thy heart, and all thy soul; that then the Lord thy God will TURN thy captivity, and have COMPASSION upon thee, and WILL RETURN and gather thee." V. 6, "And the Lord they God will CIRCUMCISE THINE HEART," etc., "that thou mayst live." Vv. 15–16, "See, I have SET BEFORE THEE this day LIFE AND GOOD, AND DEATH AND EVIL; in that I command thee this day to love the Lord thy God, to walk in his ways, and to keep his commandments and his statutes and his judgments, that thou mayest live and multiply: and the Lord thy God shall bless thee in the land whether thou goest to possess it." Vv. 19–20, "I call heaven and earth to record this day against you, that I HAVE SET BEFORE YOU LIFE AND DEATH, BLESSING AND CURSING: therefore choose life, that thou and thy seed may live: that thou mayest love the Lord thy God, and that thou mayest obey his voice, and that thou mayest cleave unto him: for he is thy life, and the length of thy days: that thou mayst dwell in the land which the Lord sware unto thy fathers, to Abraham, to Isaac, and to Jacob, to give them."

Lev. 18:5, "Ye shall keep my statutes, and my judgments: which if a man do, he shall live in them." So Ezek. 20:11, 13, 21. Ex. 20:6, "SHOWING MERCY to thousands of them that love me, and keep my commandments." So Deut. 7:9. Deut. 10:12–13, "And now, O Israel, what doth the Lord thy God REQUIRE OF THEE, but to fear the Lord thy God, to walk in all his ways, and to love him, and TO SERVE the Lord thy God with all thine heart and all thy soul, To keep the commandments of the Lord, and his statutes, which I command thee this day for thy good?" Jer. 7:22–23, "For I spake not unto your fathers . . . concerning burnt offerings and sacrifices: BUT THIS THING commanded I them, saying, Obey my voice, AND I WILL BE YOUR GOD, AND YE SHALL BE MY PEOPLE: and walk ye in all the ways that I have commanded you, that it may be well unto you." Jer. 11:3–4, "Cursed be the man that obeyeth not the words of THIS COVENANT, which I commanded you fathers in the day that I brought them forth out of the land of Egypt, from the iron furnace, saying, Obey my voice, and do them, according to all which I command you: SO SHALL YE BE MY PEOPLE, AND I WILL BE YOUR GOD."

Mic. 6:7–8, "Will the Lord be pleased [with] thousands of rams, with ten thousands of rivers of oil? shall I give my firstborn for my transgression . . . ? He hath showed thee, O man, WHAT IS GOOD; and WHAT DOTH THE LORD REQUIRE OF THEE, but to do justly, and to love mercy, and to walk humbly with thy God?" Ezek. 33:14–16, "when I say unto the wicked, Thou shalt surely die; if he turn from his sin, and do that which is lawful and right; if the wicked restore the pledge, give again that which he had robbed, WALK IN THE STATUTES OF LIFE, without committing iniquity; HE SHALL SURELY LIVE, HE SHALL NOT DIE. NONE OF THE SINS THAT HE HATH COMMITTED SHALL BE MENTIONED UNTO HIM: HE HATH DONE THAT WHICH IS LAWFUL AND RIGHT; HE SHALL SURELY LIVE." See also Ezek. 3:21. Ezek. 18:9, "he is just, he shall surely live." V. 20, "the righteousness of the righteous shall be upon him," etc. Vv. 21–22, "But if the wicked will turn from his sins that [he] hath committed, and keep all my statutes, and do that which is lawful and right, he shall surely live, he shall not die. All his transgressions that he hath committed, they shall not be mentioned unto him: IN HIS RIGHTEOUSNESS THAT HE HATH DONE HE SHALL LIVE."

Ps. 15, throughout: "Lord, who shall abide in thy tabernacle?" etc. "He that walketh uprightly, and worketh righteousness, and speaketh the truth in his heart. He that backbiteth not with his tongue," etc. Ps. 24:3– 5, "Who shall ascend," etc. "He that hath clean hands, and a pure heart; who hath not lift up his soul to vanity, nor sworn deceitfully. He shall receive the blessing from the Lord, and RIGHTEOUSNESS from the God of his salvation." Is. 33:15–16, "He that walketh righteously, and speaketh uprightly; he that despiseth the gain of oppressions, that shaketh his hands from holding of bribes, that stoppeth his ears from hearing of blood, and shutteth his eyes from seeing evil; he shall dwell on high: his place of defense shall be the munitions of rocks: bread shall be given him; and his waters shall be sure."

Is. 1:16–20, "Wash ye, make you clean; put away the evil of your doings from before my eyes; cease to do evil; learn to do well; seek judgment, relieve the oppressed, judge the fatherless, plead for the widow. Come now, and let us reason together, saith the Lord: though your sins be as scarlet, they shall be as white as snow; though they be red like crimson, they shall be as wool. If ye be willing and obedient, ye shall eat the good of the land: but if ye refuse and rebel, ye shall be devoured with the sword: for the mouth of the Lord hath spoken it."

Added to these things, it is manifest that the Ten Commandments contained the terms of the covenant God established with Israel, or settled the terms on which they should be his people and he their God, as has been proved already (see pp. 504–6).[2] The condition of this covenant was obedience. For in the account we have of the solemn, federal transaction between God and the people at the time when the Ten Commandments were first delivered with a great voice, God proposes the covenant thus: Ex. 19:5, "Now therefore, if ye will obey my voice indeed, and keep my covenant, then ye shall be a peculiar treasure unto me above all the people of the earth," etc. And when the people reply on their part, this is what they agree to: v. 8, "All that the Lord hath spoken we will do." So when Moses came to write the covenant in a book and solemnly to renew and confirm it with the people, sealing it with the blood of the sacrifice, Ex. 24:7–8, Moses "took the book of the covenant, and read in the audience of the people: and they said, All that the Lord hath said will we do, and be OBEDIENT. And Moses took the blood, and sprinkled it on the people, and said, Behold the blood of the covenant, which the Lord hath made with you concerning all these words."

And it seems as though God showed favor to righteous men because he LOVED THEIR RIGHTEOUSNESS, by Ps. 11:7, "the righteous Lord loveth righteousness; his countenance doth behold the upright."

Now the OBJECTION from these and such like passages in the Old Testament is this: It appears from hence that obedience is not only insisted on as a thing consequentially necessary, and so a kind of secondary condition of the covenant, but as the main thing required, the grand condition of the covenant that was established between him and the people, the grand condition of God's mercy and favor and blessing, of escaping death and obtaining life, of being accepted as God's people and having him as our God; and the condition of the forgiveness of sin, or God's turning from the fierceness of his anger and having compassion on 'em (as in Deut. 13:17–18), and that this is the term of not having any past sins any more remembered or mentioned; and that because in obedience persons practice virtue, do justly, love mercy, and do what is lawful and right (as Ezek. 33:14–16 and Mic. 6:7–8), and do what is valuable

---

2. MS: "p. 900 col. 2 &c.," referring to the last section of No. [1353], titled "The Ten Commandments Contained Not Only the Covenant of Works, But the Covenant of Grace."

in God's eyes, or right in his sight, and what he loves (Deut. 13:17–18, Deut. 6:17–18, Ps. 11:7), as though the moral value of their obedience was the price of God's favor. Yea, it is said that if this obedience was performed by God's people, it should be their righteousness (Deut. 6:24–25), and that the repenting sinner, in turning to obedience to God's statutes, etc., should live in the righteousness he had done (Ezek. 18:21–22). At least these things, as expressed from time to time, must have a natural tendency to lead the people to such an apprehension that their obedience was the thing which recommended them by its moral value.

Now in ANSWER to this objection, I would say the following things:

1. Nothing is more apparent by the Scripture than that the terms of the covenant of works, or terms of that kind, were often proposed in the Old Testament to men as though God insisted on their being fulfilled, and as though God expected that they should fulfill 'em, and in that way obtain life, because the fulfillment of those terms was indeed their duty, and because God would put 'em on trial for their conviction and humiliation, to fit them for the proper exercises of faith in a Mediator.

It is out of all dispute that the Ten Commandments were delivered at Mt. Sinai as a covenant of works, in this manner and for these ends, by what the Apostle says, Gal. 3:17–25, Rom. 7:1–13, Rom. 3:19–21 with ch. 5:13–14, II Cor. 3:7–9.

The same is no less manifest concerning other passages in the Law of Moses, as particularly that in Lev. 18:5, "Ye shall therefore keep my statutes, and my judgments: which if a man do, he shall live in them," and other passages of the same tenor. This is manifest by Rom. 10:5. and Gal. 3:12. And the same is evident not only concerning some passages in the Pentateuch, but in other parts of the Old Testament which were, as it were, appendages to the Pentateuch, and additional revelation given under the same dispensation and, as it were, on the same foundation. 'Tis all called the law by the Apostle, and that when speaking of the affair of justification (Rom. 3:19).

If those words in Lev. 18:5 were legal according to the tenor of the covenant of works, as it is manifest they were, then undoubtedly the same words proposed in the same manner in other parts of the Old Testament may justly be taken in the same manner, as particularly in Ezek. 20:11, "And I gave them my statutes, and showed them my judgments, which if a man do, he shall even live in them" (and the same words again, vv. 13 and 21). Nor need it seem strange if we often meet with things of this nature in other parts of the Old Testament besides the Law of Moses (though it be confessed that many other parts are more evangelical than the Pentateuch), seeing we have something of the same nature even in the New Testament. Christ, after he appeared in the flesh, still went on to treat men after the same manner. He proposed legal terms to the rich young man for his conviction.

There are many things in the Old Testament that agree with the Apostle's interpretation of such like passages. It was signified to the people, at the same time that these legal terms were proposed to 'em, that they could not fulfill them. When the people appeared forward to promise a fulfillment, God says, Deut. 5:29, "O that there were such an heart in them," intimating that they did not know their own hearts. And when Joshua solemnly renewed the covenant with Israel a little before his death, and the people appeared very forward to promise obedience, he says to 'em, Josh. 24:19, "Ye cannot serve the Lord: for he is an holy God; he is a jealous God; he will not forgive your transgressions nor your sins." He intimates plainly to 'em that the holiness, strictness and perfection of God's law is such that they can never answer the demands of it, and that the forwardness of their profession and promises arose from ignorance of themselves. Nevertheless he leaves this law and covenant with them for their conviction. V. 22, "And Joshua said unto the people, Ye are witnesses against yourselves that ye have chosen you the Lord, to serve him." Vv. 26–27, "And Joshua wrote these words in the book of the law of God, and took a great stone, and set it up there under an oak, that was by the sanctuary of the Lord. And Joshua said unto all the people, Behold, this stone shall be witness unto us; for it hath heard all the words of the Lord which he spake unto us: it shall therefore be a witness unto you, lest you deny your God."

And when God gave the Law at Mt. Sinai, he expressly declared that it was for their trial, to see whether they would obey or no. Ex. 20:20, "And Moses said unto the people, Fear not: for God is come to prove you." The end of this word of God to the people was the same with that end of his providential dealings with them, which we have an account of in Ex. 16:4, "Then said the Lord unto Moses, Behold, I shall rain bread from heaven for you; and the people shall go out and gather a certain rate every day, that I may prove them, whether they will walk in my law, or no." See also ch. 15:24. Deut. 8:2, "the Lord thy God led thee these forty years in the wilderness, to humble thee, and to prove thee, to know what was in thine heart, whether thou wouldst keep his commandments, or no." Vv. 15–16, "Who led thee through that great and terrible wilderness, . . . who brought thee forth water out of the rock of flint; who fed thee in the wilderness with manna, . . . that he might humble thee, and that he might prove thee, to do thee good at thy latter end."

And, which is very express to the purpose, when God laid up the Law in the tabernacle, his declared end was that it might be a witness against the people, to testify and show the wickedness of their hearts (Deut. 31:24–30). Thus manifestly does the apostle Paul declare God's end in exhibiting and proposing the people's duty in a legal manner, according to what is clearly to be gathered from the Old Testament itself.

There is nothing in the Old Testament that I know of that affords so plausible an objection against the doctrine of justification by faith, as I have stated, as those places mentioned in Ezekiel, ch. 33:14–16 and 18:21–22.

In the sequel of this discourse I shall take notice of several things relating to those passages, which, jointly considered, may serve to remove all difficulty arising from them.

That which I would observe now, as proper to be taken notice of under this head which we are now upon, is that there is a great deal of reason to suppose that these are some of those passages of the Old Testament wherein the aim of the Holy Ghost is the same as in that passage of the Law of Moses cited by the Apostle, Lev. 18:5, viz. to propose terms of life in a legal manner for the people's conviction. And the reasonableness of supposing this may appear by the following considerations:

(1) 'Tis certain that this Prophet, in some parts of his prophecy, does take the same method, does propose legal terms of life in the very same manner as the Law of Moses in that place in Leviticus. For we have in some parts of this prophecy the very same words, viz. these words, "my statutes and judgments, which if a man do, he shall live in them," as Ezek. 20:11, 13, 21.

(2) That there is so much in these words in Ezekiel, in the places objected, that is parallel to that in Leviticus, that it confirms that they are delivered with the same aim, and are to be taken in the same manner and sense. These words in ch. 33[:16], "he hath DONE that which is lawful and right" (in the original, "justice and judgment"), "HE SHALL SURELY LIVE"; and those in ch. 18[:21], "and DO that which is lawful and right, HE SHALL SURELY LIVE"; and those [ch. 18:22], "in the righteousness that he hath done he shall live": these expressions are most undeniably exactly parallel with those, Lev. 18:5, "Ye shall keep my STATUTES, and my JUDGMENTS: which if a man do, he shall live in them," and so exactly parallel with those other places in this same prophecy (ch.

20:11, 13, 21). And the name that the prophet Ezekiel gives to the statutes he speaks of—[he] calls them "the statutes of life" [Ezek. 33:15]—further shows the places to be parallel, and argues that the Prophet, in calling them so, and in all he says in that place, had that place in the Law of Moses in his eye, which 'tis plain [he] had much in his eye by his citing it three times in ch. 20.

(3) Our taking these passages in Ezekiel in this manner agrees with [the] plain and express design and drift of the Prophet in these places, which is to convince 'em of their wickedness and God's justice in their punishment. This is his express design in Ezek. 33. See v. 17, in the very next words to the passage objected, "Yet the children of thy people say, The way of the Lord is not equal: but as for them, their way is not equal." So again, v. 20, still speaking of the same thing, "Yet ye say, The way of the Lord is not equal. O ye house of Israel, I will judge you every one after his ways." These are the very things that the law is proposed to fallen men for, to convince 'em of sin and of God's justice in their punishment.

And so we have the very same declared design annexed to the passage objected in the eighteenth chapter. See v. 25, "Yet ye say, The way of the Lord is not equal. Hear now, O house of Israel; Is not my way equal? are not your ways unequal?" And vv. 29–30, "Yet saith the house of Israel, The way of the Lord is not equal. O house of Israel, are not my ways equal? are not your ways unequal? Therefore I will judge you, O house of Israel, every one according to his ways, saith the Lord God."

And it may be further observed that the words in Ezekiel are plainly in the strain of the covenant of works, even [more] than those in Leviticus. For in Ezekiel [33:15], the terms of life are expressed by walking "in the statutes of life, without committing iniquity," which does as naturally and fully express the terms of the covenant of works as consisting in perfect obedience as those, Deut. 27:26, "confirming [. . .] all the words of the law to do them," yea, more fully.

The whole agrees with God's providential dealings with that people in Ezekiel's time, which was to convince and humble the people for their sin and fit [them] for the great mercy of God in their redemption from the Babylonish captivity, as God convinces men of sin and humbles 'em by the law to fit 'em for mercy and salvation. Thus God's word by his prophets and his providence agree and sweetly harmonize as to the aim and design of both.

The main OBJECTION against understanding the words of the Prophet as proposing legal terms for the conviction of the people, is that the Prophet, in the words objected, supposes the persons he speaks to [to] have been, in time past, sinners, and that he speaks of three things that the covenant of works is wholly ignorant of, and that are alien from the nature of it: *1*. He proposes future obedience as the term of life, supposing it has been wanting, and wickedness committed and lived in in times past; whereas this is not the term of the covenant of grace, for they are perfect obedience at all times, innocence and holiness of heart and life without any guilt at all. *2*. What the prophet Ezekiel speaks of as belonging to that condition of life, the terms of life which he proposes, is repentance, or turning from sin, whereas the covenant of works knows of no such thing as turning from sin—repentance is entirely alien from the covenant of works. *3*. One benefit which the Prophet promises in the passages cited is pardon of sin, or forgetting, passing by and not mentioning past sin. But pardon of sin is a benefit which don't belong to the covenant of works, but is indeed inconsistent with it, and is plainly peculiar to the covenant of grace.

To this I ANSWER: The objection is grounded on a mistake of the manner of God's proposing a covenant of works to fallen men for their trial and conviction. It must be considered that God never proposed the covenant of works in the whole of it, and in its true and complete nature, including both past and future fulfillment. Nor was this necessary to God's end, which was not the bringing men to eternal life and happiness in that way, but only a conviction of their sinfulness and impotence. When God is pleased to take this method with men for their conviction, viz. to put 'em on endeavors of their souls, that they may be convinced by experiment, it would not have been proper for him to put them on endeavors to alter what was past, to endeavor that their past lives might be perfectly innocent and holy. That would have [been] absurd. Therefore, God is pleased to put 'em on future trial, and to promise life to 'em if they will perfectly obey for the future, which implies a forgetting all that is past—though merely their future obedience would make no atonement for past disobedience, and so could not have at all answered the eternal rule or covenant of works. Nor would there have [been] any ground in the reason and nature of things for a connection between their future obedience and their being forgiven all that's past, and having eternal life without an atonement for what was past sin. But seeing the bringing them to life in this way being not at all God's end, it being known to be utterly impossible, but only men's conviction, the proposal of such impossible terms had a proper tendency to answer that which was truly God's end.

Thus if any vain man had supposed that he was strong enough to conflict with and conquer the Most High, and God, to convince him, should propose it to him to try his utmost, promising that if he prevailed, he would bestow heaven upon him: this would not have implied that there would have been any connection, in the reason of things, between his sins being forgiven and his being possessed of heavenly happiness, and such a conquest, if that were possible.

When God delivered the Ten Commandments from Mt. Sinai and proposed this Law as a covenant of works to that congregation, it was after many of them had committed great sin—many of them had long lived in idolatry in Egypt, the most direct breach of the two first of those commands—and also after they had been publicly reproved for their murmurings against the Lord and told that God took notice of their sin therein (Ex. 16:7–11), and then, after that, had been reproved as a very disobedient and rebellious people. In v. 28, "And the Lord said unto Moses, How long refuse ye to keep my commandments and my laws?"

And when God proposed legal terms of life to that congregation in those words which the Apostle takes notice of, Lev. 18:5, "Ye shall therefore keep my statutes, and my judgments: which if a man do, he shall live in them," it was after they had committed that great sin of making the golden calf, for which God had so greatly testified his displeasure against them. But God still, for the further conviction of the people, is pleased to put the affair of their obtaining life on the issue of the trial of their future strength and righteousness, proposing legal terms to them.

So when the self-confident rich young man came to Christ to know what he should do that he might have eternal life, Christ proposes to 'im a future keeping the commandments. Yea, he promises him life only on the condition of a fulfillment of the commands of the second table of the Law, though his only keeping them would not have been a fulfilling the covenant of works, which requires perfect obedience to the commands of both tables. And, therefore, there would have been no connection, in the reason and nature of things, between a fulfillment of that part of the Law only and his eternal happiness. And then, after that, for his conviction, he promises him treasure in heaven if he would go and sell all that he had, and give to the poor, and come and take up his cross and follow him—though if he had done these external things, it would have [been] no fulfillment of the conditions either of the covenant of works or covenant of grace. For if men do all this, if they give all their goods to feed the poor, and give their bodies to be burned, and have not love, it will profit them nothing. Yet Christ, who knew all things, knew that under the circumstance which he saw attended the young man's case, he would not, and could not, be willing to do this without love, and so that this direction under these circumstances would be a sufficient trial whether he had a heart to comply with the true terms of life.

2. It is nothing against the doctrine of justification by faith alone, as I have elsewhere explained that doctrine, to represent obedience as the most proper condition of the covenant of grace, or that qualification in us by which especially we come to be accepted and justified. For as I have observed in my discourse on the difference between the two covenants ("Controversies"),[3] obedience, as the word signifies in both testaments, implies a hearing and yielding to the voice of God. And this there is equally in complying with the precepts of pure law and in complying with the calls and offers of the gospel.

So with regard to that expression of "keeping the commandments of the Lord," this may signify indifferently either the yielding to the authority of a mere Lawgiver, demanding what is due to him from us for his pleasure and honor, or an adhering to and attending the directions of a Redeemer and spiritual head and husband, following a captain of salvation, obeying his word of command in order to our deliverance from our enemies, as a manifestation of trust in him. The word "trust" is often, in the Old Testament, put to signify that adherence and active subjection to a prince that was appointed as the people's protector and head of influence for their good. That in the first chapter of Isaiah that is translated "willing and obedient" [Is. 1:19] properly signifies "willing and hearkening," which truly does most naturally lead us to suppose that obedience is here spoken of with regard to that in its nature which was last taken notice of.

The exceeding fairness and reasonableness and mercy of God's methods of dealing with sinners which is suggested by that expression, "Come, let us reason together" [Is. 1:18], remarkably appears in this, that justification is offered on such terms that they shall be perfectly and freely forgiven if they will but hearken, are but willing to yield to their Redeemer and Author of their good, and won't rebelliously refuse their own happiness; as Christ sets forth the fairness and kindness of his terms by that, "how often would I have gathered thy children together, as a hen gathered her chickens under her wings, and ye would not!" [Matt. 23:37].

---

3. MS: "p. 207 &c.," a reference to the section on "Justification" in the "Controversies" notebook, within the essay entitled, "Question: Wherein Do the Two Covenants Agree as to the Method of Justification?" Pp. 207–08 contain pt. III. See *Works*, 21, 364.

The[4] obedience of a wife and the obedience of a mere servant are quite of a different nature. The obedience of the latter is a yielding and giving up himself to him that commands as an expression of subjection to mere authority, demanding that he should devote himself to him most directly for his sake, to be for his profit or pleasure. The obedience of the former is the proper expression [of] acceptance, of love, benevolence and trust in the superior wisdom and strength and the goodness and faithfulness of a protector and head of beneficent communication. The character under which Jehovah, that divine person that redeemed 'em out of Egypt, spake with 'em at Mt. Sinai, went before 'em, brought 'em into Canaan, and dwelt with them in the temple, was that of a Redeemer and spiritual husband and tutelar Deity. When God made [them] his people and became their God, it was the day of their redemption and of their espousals. He redeemed 'em out of Egypt. He went before them as the captain of their salvation. He espoused 'em to himself at Mt. Sinai. He led 'em and protected 'em by a pillar of cloud and fire, and upheld 'em by a series of miracles, and went before 'em as their captain and mighty Savior, to bring 'em into Canaan, fight their battles for them, and give them the victory over their enemies. (See my discourse in answer to that question, In what sense the saints under the old testament trusted in Christ to justification, "Controversies").[5]

And therefore, that hearkening and obeying and keeping the commandments of the Lord that was revealed by Moses as the terms of the covenant between God and the people (i.e. of that covenant that was not only proposed, but established) was a complying with his voice, yielding and adhering to him as a spiritual husband, Redeemer, protector and captain of salvation. What he everywhere insists upon is that they should with all their hearts receive, submit to him as their spiritual husband, and as such faithfully and constantly cleave to him. And therefore, the argument so often used to enforce the obedience required, was that God was a jealous God. And this is insisted on as the condition of his favor, and reconciliation, and enjoying the great blessings of being his people and having him for our God.

That obeying or hearing God's voice, which is so often mentioned as the condition of the covenant in the Law of Moses and other parts of the Old Testament, was thus proposed as the term of the covenant, as it was

4. MS: "There is the."
5. MS: "p. 213 &c," the essay "Question: In What Sense Did the Saints Under the Old Testament Believe in Christ to Justification," in the section on "Justification" in the "Controversies" notebook. See *Works*, 21, pp. 372–408.

the exercise and expression of faith, is evident by the Apostle's own interpretation (Heb. 3:6–19). Holding fast our confidence in v. 6 is expressed in the next verses in the words of [the] Old Testament (and as citing the Old Testament) by hearing God's voice: vv. 7–8, "Wherefore, as the Holy Ghost saith, Today if ye will hear his voice, harden not your hearts, as in the provocation, in the day of temptation in the wilderness." And in v. 12 the Jews' disobedience in erring and departing in their hearts, as not knowing God's ways, is spoken as the sin of unbelief. So again, holding fast our confidence, etc., is again expressed by that Old Testament phrase of hearing (or obeying) God's voice and not hardening our hearts, as in the provocation, which hardening of their hearts is represented to be that unbelief that destroyed them (vv. 18–19). That disobedience of the people, which in Num. 14:22, the place referred to by the Apostle, is called their not hearkening to (or not obeying) God's voice, was what ruined them and caused them to come short of God's rest, as it was their unbelief. Therefore, their hearkening to or obeying God's voice, that was the condition of life and of entering into God's rest, was so as it was the exercise and expression of faith.

Therefore, we are doubtless thus to understand that, Jer. 7:23–24, "But this thing commanded I them, saying, Obey my voice, and I will be your God, and ye shall be my people: and walk ye in all the commands which I have commanded you, that it may be well with you. But they hearkened not, nor inclined their ear." See also v. 26, "Yet they hearkened not unto me, nor inclined their ear, but hardened their neck." Let this be compared with the Heb. 3:7–10. All that is expressed here as the condition of the covenant which God made in the wilderness is called obeying God's voice. So there, walking in all God's ways; so there in Heb. [3:]10, "they have not known my ways." As in Hebrews the thing mentioned wherein they failed was not hearing God's voice, so here in Jer. [7:]24 it is their not hearkening. There they are said to harden their hearts. So here they are said to harden their necks ([Jer. 7:]26). See also Jer. 11:4–5, 7.

That the hearkening unto the voice of the Lord to keep his commandments and his statutes, which were written in the book of the Law, with all the heart and all the soul, which was the condition of the covenant which God made with his people in the wilderness, as the exercise and expression of that faith which is the condition of the gospel covenant, is[6] evident by Deut. 30:10–14 compared with Rom. 10:6. "Who

6. MS: "as is."

shall go over the sea for us, to bring it to us, that we may hear it, and do it?" [Deut. 30:13], and so have the benefit of it, that deliverance and salvation which is to be obtained by it, as is evident by the context. For this is the supposed interrogation of the people in captivity, seeking deliverance from that calamity. 'Tis deliverance or salvation they are inquiring after, as contained in the word, as in the gospel. Therefore the Apostle says, 'tis "the word of faith, that we preach" [Rom. 10:8], implying a supposition, that if they could obtain the word, or the "commandment" (as it is called, [Deut. 30:]11), and receive it, they therein received deliverance. They therein received God, whose law it was, as their Savior. In inquiring after the commandment, they inquire after a savior. And God tells 'em that the word is near 'em, so that if they would receive it in their heart, mouth and practice, they should therein have the benefit of salvation. The Lawgiver would become their Savior. In receiving it they would receive life, as is expressed in what follows: "I have set life and death before thee; the word and its salvation is nigh thee; God sends it to thine heart and thy mouth; if thou wilt but receive it, there thou shalt have it, and have life; thou shalt have it for accepting."[7] So that obedience is here spoken of under the notion of an acceptance or reception of a savior, a receiving the Author of the word as the Author of the gospel of life. Being in the mouth and heart means a being received. "The word is very nigh thee, in thy mouth, and in thy heart, that thou mayest do it" [Deut 30:14], i.e. so nigh thee that there is need of nothing but the consent of your heart, or your cordial reception, and you have it in your heart and practice and have the benefit of it.

So that 'tis plain that hearkening to the voice of the Lord and obeying his commandments, etc., is here spoken of as the condition of life and salvation, as an expression of hearty receiving the Savior whose word it is, heartily receiving God as the Author of life. The word is not here spoken of as being in the heart and mouth any other wise than as heartily received by faith, as appears by the Apostle's interpretation and also by the words themselves as compared with other scriptures. For men are here spoken of as being in such circumstances wherein the law had departed out of their heart and mouth, viz. when their hearts had turned away from the true God to idols, and their mouths professed their worship and a dependence on them.

The obeying God and keeping his commands so much insisted in the book of Proverbs as the way to favor, life and happiness is thus recom-

7. These phrases are condensed and paraphrased from Deut. 30:14–20.

mended there as an expression of trusting in God, as is manifest by Prov. 22:17–20. "Bow down thine ear, and hear the words of the wise, and apply thine heart unto my knowledge. For it is a pleasant thing if thou KEEP them within thee; they shall be withal fitted in thy lips. THAT THY TRUST MAY BE IN THE LORD, I have made known to thee this day, even to thee. Have I not written to thee excellent things in counsels and knowledge?"

From this place, by the way, I would observe that the phrase "KEEPING GOD'S COMMANDS," when spoken of as the condition of the covenant, don't necessarily imply anything alien from the covenant of grace, from what is said, v. 18, "if thou keep them within thee." In the original it is "keep in thy belly," or "in thy heart," which expression naturally implies no more than a perseverance in cordially receiving, embracing and adhering to.

To know or acknowledge God, worship and serve him, be subject to him and keep his words or rules in their hearts and practice, was the proper expression of receiving Jehovah as their God and Savior, or uniting themselves to him as his people, and receiving him as their spiritual husband, captain and Redeemer. This was a real and effectual doing of it, and is plainly and abundantly revealed to be the condition of God's covenant in this manner, it being no other than voluntarily and by their own act becoming his people and putting themselves under his care as their prince and Savior.

The commands of God were given to his people as the precepts and directions of a kind physician, a tender father and loving husband, and so many directions and rules for healing, deliverance, safety, and happiness. Deut 6:24, "And the Lord commanded us to do all these statutes, to fear the Lord our God, for our good always." And Deut. 10:12–13, "And now, Israel, what doth the Lord thy God require of thee, but to fear the Lord thy God, to walk in all his ways, and to love him, and to serve the Lord thy God with all thy heart and with all thy soul, to keep the commandments of the Lord, and his statutes, which I command thee this day for thy good?" So Deut. 30:19–20. Obedience to these commands, therefore, was the condition of life, not as the price of life and happiness, but as an accepting it, a closing with it and embracing it, as the gift of the love of a spiritual Father, Savior and husband, which is what seems to be implied in Deut. 30:19–20. "I call heaven and earth to witness this day against you, that I have set life and death before thee [. . .]: therefore choose life [. . .]: that thou mayest love the Lord thy God, and that thou mayest obey his voice, and that thou mayest cleave unto him: for HE IS THY LIFE, AND THE LENGTH OF THY DAYS." In this chapter we have the terms of the covenant of grace. The Apostle testifies, Rom. 10:6 ff., compared [with] vv. 11–15 of this chapter.

That the Ten Commandments were given as prescribed methods of cleaving to God as a Redeemer is confirmed from the preface to the Decalogue.

The condition of the covenant of God with his people of old is often expressed by "fearing God" (Ps. 15:12–14; Ps. 31:19, and 85:9, and 103:11–13, 17, and 115:13; Eccles. 8:12; Mal. 4:2). Fearing God is put for worshipping him, as worshipping other gods is called fearing those gods. And worshipping the true God, or other gods, is also often called trusting in them, because worshipping tutelar deities was especially an act of trust. Therefore, idols were called vanity, a lie, because they failed the trust of their votaries, could not profit or deliver (I Sam. 12:20–25).

So the worship and service of God, which was the condition of the covenant, is often called "knowing God," which phrase especially denotes a cleaving to him as our own in a near relation and special propriety. But the observing all prescribed moral duties is included in the notion of fearing, worshipping, knowing and trusting in God in the Old Testament, as all are included in the requisite and proper exercises and expressions of faith in the New Testament (see Ps. 34:11–14, Deut. 31:13). Jer. 22:16, "He judged the cause of the poor and needy; . . . was not this to know me? saith the Lord," which is agreeable to the language of the New Testament concerning faith, which does in effect say from time to time concerning such moral duties, Was not this to believe in Christ? We are there taught that God will own no other faith as true but that which works by love and shows itself in deeds of charity (Jas. 1:27 and 2:14–26).

That when serving and obeying God and keeping his commands is spoken of as the special terms of his covenant and favor, it is so spoken of as an expression of trust and hope in God and waiting on God, which signifies much the same, may be argued from the following places: Ps. 2:11–12, "Serve the Lord with fear, . . . Kiss the son . . . Blessed are all they that put their trust in him." Ruth 1:16, "thy people shall be my people, and thy God my God," with ch. 2:12, "under whose wings thou art come to trust." Job 13:15–16, "Though he slay me, yet will I trust in him: but I will maintain mine own ways before him. He also shall be my salvation: for an hypocrite shall not come before him." Ps 37:3–9, 27, 34, 37, 39–40, and Ps. 4:5; Jer. 39:16–18 compared with ch. 38:7, 12; II Kgs. 18:5–6; Ps. 4:3–5; Ps. 5:10–12, and 16:1 with the rest of the psalm, and 17:3–7, and 25:1–5, 10, 12, 20–21; Ps. 26:1–6; Ps. 31:6 with foregoing verses and vv. 23–24, and 32:10–11, and 33:18, and 34:7–22; Ps. 36:7–10, and 37, and 52:7–8 with the rest of the psalm, and 55:22–23, and 62 (mind especially the last verse); and Ps. 64:10, and 73:27–28, and 84:11–12; Ps. 112:7, and 119:41–49 and vv. 113–20, 145–48, and v. 166; Ps. 147:11; Is. 26:2–4; Is. 36:2–4; Is. 40:4, and 57:13, and 64:4 compared with I Cor. 2:9; Jer. 17:5–10; Jer. 38:7–12, and 39:18; Hos. 12:6; Zeph. 3:2, 11–13. The whole of the people's duty to God is often called trusting in God, this being the proper respect to be exercised towards God in [the] character God stood in to them.

"Seeking God" is a phrase used to express faith in the Old Testament, as I have observed elsewhere.[8] But obeying God and living a virtuous, holy life is spoken of as the terms of favor and happiness, as the exercise of seeking God. So Ps. 24:5–6 with the foregoing part of the Psalm; Ps. 22:25–26; Ps. 34:9–10 ff. See "Miscellanies," No. 861.[9]

What manner of obedience was the condition of God's favor, and with regard to what in the nature of this obedience it was that it was the condition of justification, may be seen by the book of Psalms in general, and especially by the 119th Psalm.

Fearing God, keeping God's commandments, and trusting in God are often used synonymously in the Old Testament. Compare Prov. 13:13 with Prov. 16:30. See notes on the latter place.[1]

In that noted prophecy of the Christ, Deut. 18:15, in which all are commanded to believe in him, the same word is used as is elsewhere in the Old Testament translated "obey." "The Lord thy God will raise up unto thee a Prophet from the midst of thee, of thy brethren, [. . .] unto him shall ye hearken," or "obey," which is agreeable to the voice from heaven in the time of Christ's transfiguration, "This is my beloved Son, in whom I am well pleased; hear ye him" [Matt. 17:5].

The reason why loving and obeying Christ, or hearkening to him, is the special condition of life and happiness: viz. that this is but accepting of and cleaving to the great Author, fountain and means of life and happiness. Deut. 30:19–20, "I have set before you life and death, blessing and cursing: [. . .] that both thou and thy seed may live: that thou mayest love the Lord thy God, and that thou mayest obey his voice, and that thou mayest cleave unto him: for he is thy life, and the length of thy days."

8. E.g. "Faith," nos. 24, 96, 110, in *Works, 21*, 421, 442–43, 449.
9. *Works, 20*, 85–86.
1. "Blank Bible" note on Prov. 16:30, in part: "these expressions intimate the secret, subtil, sly, deceitful way of his injuring his neighbor. He shuts his eyes, that is, he conceals his aim and design, as though he did not see or aim at the mischief that will follow . . ."

And those passages objected in Ezekiel may be interpreted in an evangelical sense, as the Ten Commandments are to be taken both in a legal and evangelical sense. So when it is said in Ezek. 33:14–15 that "if the wicked turn from his wickedness, and do justice and judgment" (as the words are in the original), and "walk in the statutes of life, [. . .] he shall live," there is no necessity of understanding it, that 'tis on account of the moral excellency and value of the righteousness or virtue there is in such a conversion and change of practice. Though in its being said he hath done "justice and judgment; [. . .] he shall surely [live]," it may seem as if such a manner of speaking implied that his doing that which [is] so good, so right and virtuous, was the proper reason why he should live, and that it was the value of his right doing that would recommend him to it, yet there is no necessity of taking it thus. Doing justice and judgment may be only a common expression among that people to signify that a man was a godly man and lived piously. And it may be as much as to say, "However wicked the man has been, and however wickedly he has lived heretofore, yet if it appears that now [he] is a true penitent, truly changed, and it is now sincerely otherwise, and really has left his old, wicked course, and has turned his feet into God's ways, his former wickedness shall not be mentioned." And his doing justice and judgment may here be mentioned, not as the procuring cause of favor by its moral value, but only as the evidence of the reality of the man's repentance, an evidence that he has accepted the way of life and embraced the methods of grace which bestows eternal life, because he walks "in the statutes of life" universally, "without committing iniquity," without living in any sin.

And though in Ezek. 18:21–22 there is added to the expressions like those in ch. 33 this other expression, "in the righteousness that he hath done he shall live," yet this is well capable of an evangelical sense. There is no necessity of understanding it, that he shall [have] life as the purchase of the moral value of his righteousness. But it may well be understood thus: seeing he has repented, has forsaken the ways of wickedness (which were ways that both by their natural tendency and by their merit lead to unavoidable death), and has[2] turned in the way of true piety, which is the way that leads to life, in that way he shall be saved.

3. Many of the texts which have been mentioned, and others of a like sort, may well be understood, not as declaring the grand qualification that has primary influence in persons' justification and acceptance in

---

2. MS: "have."

the sight of God, as being the thing in the person which makes it fit and suitable that he should be looked upon in distinction from others as a proper subject of divine acceptance and favor; but only as descriptions of the persons exhibiting their distinguishing character and sure marks, and so the qualification which will be required of them in his judicial proceedings with them, and what shall turn the scale in pronouncing sentence. So that in the fifteenth Psalm [vv. 1–2], "who shall dwell in thy holy hill? He that walketh uprightly, and worketh righteousness," etc. So to the like purpose in the twenty-fourth Psalm [vv. 3–4], "Who shall ascend into the hill of the Lord? who shall stand in his holy place? He that hath clean hands, and a pure heart."

This may well be understood as only giving the character of such as should be admitted to those privileges, as was proper and natural in answer to such a question as is there proposed; which is as much as to say, "How shall we know who those are that shall be thus highly favored? How are they distinguished?" In answer to such a question, 'tis proper to give their distinguishing characteristics and marks, by which they are most certainly known. And the mentioning these don't at all imply that this is that righteousness, that virtue, whose value it is that primarily recommends 'em to be received to a title to these privileges. And indeed, the words of the twenty-fourth Psalm do most naturally lead us to understand them as mentioned only as signs of that faith which is the more primary condition of acceptance, which faith in the Old Testament, and sometimes in the New, is sometimes called "seeking of God" (as I have observed in my papers on "Faith").[3] V. 6, "This is the generation of them that seek thee, that seek thy face, O Jacob." Very much like those places in the fifteenth and twenty-fourth Psalms is that in Is. 33:15–16, "He that walketh righteously," etc., "He shall dwell on high"; which may be understood as an answer to the hypocrite's exclamation, "Who among us shall dwell with the devouring fire?" [v. 14]. The answer shows, not who can bear to dwell with or in everlasting burnings, but who shall be safe from it, and set on high out of the reach of it, in the day of wrath, when God's fury shall come forth like fire and shall burn unquenchably.

'Tis as proper and natural to answer such inquiries by mentioning the distinguishing character of persons, as their names. If the answer had been given by mentioning the names of the persons, nobody would have taken it that the name was the thing that first recommended the person to a title to the benefit, but only that the persons who were accepted to

---

3. "Faith," nos. 24, 96, 110, in *Works, 21,* 421, 442–43, 449.

a title might be known by it. And no more can be argued, when the answer is made, by mentioning the distinguishing character instead of the name.

So when it is said in Ezek. 18:9, "he is just, he shall surely live," speaking of him that has walked in God's statutes and kept his judgments, 'tis not needful for us to understand that it is God's design to tell us on what account it is thought proper and fit that such an one should be accepted as the heir of life, or what that righteousness is the value of which primarily recommends him to such great favor; but that 'tis only his drift to tell us that 'tis [his] own state, and not the state of his father, which shall be regarded by the Judge of the world, and that 'tis his own, personal character only that shall be considered in the judgment and shall determine his state in the sentence of the Judge. If it appears in the judgment that his state is the state of a good man, and that his personal character is that of a truly righteous person, the sentence shall be, accordingly, "HE PERSONALLY IS JUST, whatever is the character of his father, and therefore he shall surely live." "IN HIS RIGHTEOUSNESS WHICH HE HATH DONE" (as 'tis said, v. 22), "he shall live." In his own, personally good estate and character he shall be sentenced to life. Every man's own, personal[4] state and character shall be reckoned to him and esteemed his, and not his father's; as 'tis said, v. 20, "The soul that sinneth, it shall die. The son shall not bear the iniquity of the father, neither shall the father bear the iniquity of the son: THE RIGHTEOUSNESS OF THE RIGHTEOUS SHALL BE UPON HIM, AND THE WICKEDNESS OF THE WICKED SHALL BE UPON HIM."

The design and argument of the chapter no way leads to declare ON WHAT ACCOUNT God has promised to save a man that is in such a [state] and has such a character, but only that his state and character is that which is distinguishing of such as have a title to the promise, and that his personal state and character, and not that of any of his relations, shall be reckoned to him, or "SHALL BE UPON HIM," or "TO HIM," as it might have been translated. So when it is said, v. 22, "IN THE RIGHTEOUSNESS WHICH HE HATH DONE HE SHALL LIVE," that is as much as to say, "he shall be judged according to his own, personal works, or what he has done, and not according to what his parents or children have done."

And as to the place before mentioned in the twenty-third chapter, vv. 14–16, which is in many respects parallel with that in the eighteenth

---

4. MS: "personally."

chapter, God, speaking of the wicked man who turns from his wicked-ness, and does justice and judgment, and walks in the statutes of life, he says: "None of his sins which he hath committed shall be mentioned unto him: he hath done justice and judgment; he shall surely live." The drift and argument of the place don't at all lead to enter into the considera-tion of any such question as why God's statutes are statutes of life, or how it becomes fit that such as heartily comply with the revelation which God has given have life promised to them, but only to declare what state of the man shall be regarded by God when he judges. The man has been in two states and of two opposite characters: the state and character of a wicked man, and that of a good man. The design of the discourse is only to show which of the two states shall be looked upon as his by the Judge, and to declare that it is the last, and the last only. Though it may be he has done more wickedness than justice and judgment, yet all that is past shall not be mentioned to him, shall not be looked upon as his, or that which he has now any relation to, as at all denominating or characteriz-ing the man in God's sight.

God, both in the eighteenth and also the twenty-third chapters, is de-claring how God will treat men when he comes to act towards 'em as a judge, and what ways or works men should live or die in in the judgment, when God proceeds in his judicial character to convict men, or to award to them their retribution; as ch. 33:20, "O ye house of Israel, I WILL JUDGE YOU EVERY ONE ACCORDING TO HIS WAYS," which is exactly agree-able to what is everywhere declared to be God's method of judgment, through Old Testament and New. So the design of the eighteenth chap-ter is to show the reason and method of the punishments which God brought, or had threatened to bring, on the people, [for] which they found fault with him as if they were punished for their father's sins. See the beginning of the chapter. And then [it] concludes, v. 30, "Therefore I will judge you, O house of Israel, every one according to his ways, saith the Lord. Repent, and turn yourselves from all your transgressions; so iniquity shall not be your ruin."

4. It is true that every virtue and grace of God's Spirit, and all true obe-dience and holy practice, if we consider it not as faith itself, or that very qualification on account of which God looks upon it proper and fit that a person should be looked upon as in Christ, and so interested in his benefits, but only as that sure, attendant fruit and distinguishing mark of it—I say, considered only thus, it may, by virtue of God's promise and covenant, give a title to life and all the blessed fruits of God's favor, and

be a proper ground of a claim of these blessings, as I have shown particularly in my discourse of the agreement and difference of the two covenants ("Controversies").[5]

And therefore, if the objected places in the Old Testament show that God has promised justification and the blessings dependent on it, and that other graces besides faith and holiness of heart and life in general give a title to these things by God's covenant, and so are good ground of a claim of them, this is nothing against the doctrine of justification by faith as I have laid it down. This consideration may fitly be applied to most of the places objected, as greatly tending to remove the difficulty arising from them.

Particularly, there is no necessity from such a manner of expression in the places objected in Ezekiel, "HE HATH DONE JUSTICE AND JUDGMENT; HE SHALL SURELY LIVE," to understand any more than this: "He appears to have those qualifications to which I have promised life, and that give a claim to life by virtue of my covenant; therefore, he shall surely have life, as I have promised," without meddling with the cause or ground of the connection of these things and life in the promise. God's promise, or declared and public constitution, is sufficient and proper ground for the Judge [to] proceed upon in his judicial dealings with men, which is the thing spoken of in these places, as has been already shown.

And here I would observe that it is a great confirmation that the design of the Prophet (or of God speaking by him) is not in these places to represent as though it was originally on the account of the value of a man's own righteousness or virtue, as the price or primary recommendation, that favor is showed and mercy bestowed on penitents. Because this Prophet, in this book, is in a special manner very full and express in the contrary doctrine, and in carefully guarding the people against any such apprehension, and thorough in his care to impress it on their minds, that it is not on account of any righteous beauty or moral value which God sees or will ever see in them, that he would hereafter pardon them and restore them to favor, when they should repent and return to him. Ezek. 36:22, "Therefore say unto the house of Israel, Thus saith the Lord God; I do not this for your sakes, O house of Israel, but for mine holy name's sake, which ye have profaned among the heathen, whither ye went." Vv. 31–33, "Then shall ye remember your own evil ways, and

---

5. MS: "p. 236," the essay "Question: Wherein Do the Two Covenants Agree as to the Method of Justification?" in the section on "Justification" in the "Controversies" notebook. P. 236 contains pt. VII. See *Works*, *21*, 367.

your doings that were not good, and shall loathe yourselves in your own sight for your iniquities and your abominations. Not for your sakes do I this, saith the Lord God, be it known unto you: be ashamed and confounded for your own ways, O house of Israel. Thus saith the Lord God; In the day that I shall have cleansed you from all your iniquities I will also cause you to dwell in the cities, and the wastes shall be builded," compared with Is. 43:25, "I, even I, am he that blotteth out thy transgressions for mine own sake, and will not remember thy sins."

5. There was a temporal, national covenant between God and the nation of Israel that is abundantly insisted on by Moses and the prophets, which they have reference to in very many things that we find written by them, that was in some respects a legal covenant, as I have observed in my discourse of the difference of the two dispensations. See back, pp. 498–99.[6] In this covenant, men's external religion, virtue and obedience was the qualification chiefly insisted on, not that it indeed was the righteousness that primarily recommended any sinners whatsoever to God's favor, but because it was what was especially to be regarded in the promises, rewards, punishments and the judicial proceedings which were founded upon it, which related to things external, visible and temporal, nations being temporal, external and visible societies. All that is properly national is external and temporal. And therefore, in dealing with such societies, it was proper that external and visible things should be chiefly insisted on.

There is this further reason why an external covenant, establishing visible conditions and visible benefits, should be more legal than the covenant of grace: that there is an external beauty, loveliness and value in men's righteousness to such as see only what is external, or if the heart ben't seen or had respect to. To the eye of man, who sees not the hearts of men and their secret abominations, that appears to have loveliness and great value, which it would not seem to have if we viewed all things visible and invisible alike, as God views them. "That which is highly esteemed among men is abomination in the sight of God" [Luke 16:15]. Thus Christ, as man, loved the external righteousness of the rich young man. As it is said, "Jesus beholding him loved him" [Mark 10:21]. And God, in an external, temporal, national covenant, treats men according to what is visible to men. There are just such rewards as there is a righ-

6. MS: "p. 895. &c.," meaning a passage in No. [1353], where JE is discussing "wherein the two dispensations differ," the entirety of the third subpoint under pt. I, beginning, "This revelation of the covenant of works, or exhibition of the law . . ."

teousness, value and loveliness. The virtue, value and beauty is only external to a human view. 'Tis no real price or amiableness. So the happiness that is the reward is no real, true happiness.

And though in many of the promises in Moses and the Prophets, wherein God speaks to Israel as a nation, there is truly respect to something further than God's dealings with them as a nation and in things temporal, yet those things which related to 'em as a nation were so much regarded, that it naturally occasioned the language and manner of speaking to appear more legal and more accommodated to the nature of that national covenant.

So in most, if not all, the places alleged out of the Pentateuch and the book of the prophet Ezekiel and the first chapter of Isaiah, 'tis evident that God, in these places (most of 'em), speaks to and of the nation as a nation.

6. That part of the objection which is made from those texts which seem to speak of obedience and holy practice as the condition of God's favor, because it was good and right in his sight, and because the righteous Lord loveth righteousness, etc., as though it was the amiableness and moral value of such obedience and virtuous conduct in his sight that recommended them to his acceptance and favor, particularly these three places: Deut. 6:17–18, and ch. 13:17–18; and Ps. 11:7—I say, this part of the objection may require a particular consideration, and therefore I would here observe the following things with relation to this part of the objection:

(1) As to those places in the Pentateuch, they may well be understood as belonging to the national covenant between God and the people, respecting national, temporal blessings, such as multiplying their nation, giving the possession of the good land promised to their fathers, etc., which will be confirmed by a particular view of the places with their contexts. Deut. 6:18, "And thou shalt do that which is right and good in the sight of the Lord: that it may be well with thee, and that thou mayest go in and possess the good land which the Lord sware unto thy fathers, to cast out all thine enemies from before thee, as the Lord hath spoken." And that in Deut. 13:17–18 is spoken especially[7] with respect to a public, national proceeding, concerning their meeting to destroy an idolatrous city and so to put away the cursed thing from among them. And 'tis a national blessing is promised, viz. multiplying their nation. "And there shall cleave naught of the cursed thing to thine hand: that the Lord

7. MS: "& especially."

may turn from the fierceness of his anger, and show thee mercy, and have compassion on thee, and multiply, as he hath sworn unto thy fathers; When thou shalt hearken to the voice of the Lord thy God, to keep all his commandments which I command thee this day, to do that which is right in the eyes of the Lord thy God." And, therefore, here is to be considered what was observed in Answer 5 concerning that national covenant.

(2) If we suppose these places truly to have respect to something beyond temporal, national benefit, even eternal life and the blessings of the heavenly Canaan—if we take them thus, as proposing the terms of eternal life, we may as well suppose that [God] here proposes legal terms for their conviction, as in the Decalogue and almost all places in the Law of Moses where terms of life and of God's favor are proposed.

(3) If it should be insisted that the true design of the words is something further still than either or both the things already mentioned, viz. to lead the people into the true way to God's favor, the way in which they may hope to obtain real acceptance with him, the pardon of their sins and the blessings of his children, still there is no unsurmountable difficulty if they will be well considered, and that upon three accounts:

1. The words "doing what is good and right in the sight of God" may imply no more than that they must yield to God, or as the phrase in the Old Testament commonly is, hearken to his voice; must comply with their protector, Savior and divine head, must be subject to him; their hearts must close with his methods and prescriptions: which signifies no more than [that] there must indeed be an active unition of their hearts to him in the way his infinite wisdom and goodness takes to accomplish their happiness. They must accept cordially—and with all their hearts receive—him who is their life and the length of their days, and receive his salvation and his measures and means in order to their blessedness. Receiving and accepting implies compliance as well as giving, as was observed in my discourse on the difference of the two covenants.[8]

2. That there is no need to suppose that the using such expressions to signify the terms of God's favor, as "doing what is right and good in the sight of the Lord," is to point to[9] the grounds of the acceptance of such terms as the thing wherein lies the propriety of fitness of their being appointed as the special terms of favor; but only to show particularly what

---

8. The essay, "The Things Wherein the Way of Justification by Mere Law, and that by Mere Grace Through Christ, Differ as to the Qualification of the Subject," in the "Controversies" notebook, MS pp. 202 ff. See *Works*, 21, 368–71.

9. MS: "for."

the terms are, to declare the nature of the thing required, and the qualification which must be found, as distinguished from the false appearances of it which men are ready to trust in. It must be doing that which
is good and right in the sight of the Lord, i.e. that which is really good,
sincere and universal piety and holiness, and not a mere appearance of
virtue; not that partial and hypocritical virtue and religion which is good
in the sight of men only. For that which is highly esteemed in the sight
of men is abomination in the sight of God.

3. If the people should go on to do what was not good and right in the
sight of the Lord, its being otherwise than good in his sight, or its being
odious in his sight, would be the proper primary ground of his displeasure and wrath against 'em, and the very reason why, instead of showing
them favor, he would destroy them. Their wickedness and the moral evil
of their wickedness would be a fatal obstacle in the way of his showing
mercy to them, as it [would] excite his hatred and vengeance. And therefore it was proper to mention a doing what was right in the sight of God
as one thing belonging to the conditions of God's favor, absolutely necessary in order to it, as having a negative influence in obtaining his favor, i.e. as implying the absence of that which [would] have a contrary
influence and effect. This is very applicable to the places mentioned in
the Pentateuch, as to that in Deut. 6:18, "thou shalt do that which [is]
good and right in the sight of the Lord: . . . thou mayest go in and possess the good land as the Lord sware," etc., which may be as much as to
say that "thou mayest lay no fatal block in the way of the promise which
God hath made being fulfilled to thee, which God is ready to fulfill if
thou layest no obstacle in the way." So that the design may not be to mention a condition or qualification required in order to move God to bestow the benefit, but the avoiding an hinderance. For God is represented
as already moved and engaged by oath to bestow it, if no fatal obstacle
be laid in the way by their wickedness, which by its demerit and heinousness would bring divine wrath. To the like purpose are the words in Deut.
13:17–18, and this salvation is in like manner applicable to them.

4. The agreeableness of the thing, which is the qualification and special condition of life in the covenant of grace to the holy nature and will
of God, is in some respects a positive ground of its being the appointed
term of justification. For though the holiness of faith and evangelical
compliance with the Savior is not [that] which recommends the person
to a justified state, and in itself considered is not sufficient to do anything
towards it; yet that God is an infinitely holy and wise God, is a reason why

he would contrive no way but[1] such an one as secured and promoted holiness, and therefore would appoint no terms of salvation but such as implied holiness, or an agreement with the infinitely holy heart of God. And we have reason from God's holy nature to determine that he would not appoint or accept any terms but what implied this. And more than this can't be argued from the manner of expression in the texts alleged. Here see my discourse on the agreement and difference of the two covenants ("Controversies").[2]

5. If more than what was last mentioned can be argued from these texts, yet it may be observed that this further is true: that the moral value there is in the obedience of believers, arising from their relation to Christ, is a secondary recommendation of them to all the blessings that the saints are entitled to that are consequent on their justification, as I have observed elsewhere (see "Controversies").[3]

N.B. These three things last observed may be applied for the solution of the seeming difficulty in that place, Ps. 11:7, and also from those words in Ezek. 18:20, "the righteousness of the righteous shall be upon him, and the wickedness of the wicked shall be upon him." But,

(4) As to that place in particular, Ps. 11:7, "the righteous Lord loveth righteousness; and his countenance doth behold the upright," the meaning of it seems to be mistaken. The main design is to declare the righteousness of God as a judge, that he will thoroughly and impartially try the cause of the righteous, wherein the wicked contends with him and persecutes him without cause; and that he will condemn him whose cause is bad, or who is [in] the wrong; and that he will favor and approve of him who is right (as the word translated "upright" signifies), or who has the right of the cause; and that because he is a righteous judge, one that delights in righteousness or in judging righteously, and abhors partiality and injustice. The rest of the Psalm shows this to be the main thing intended, as also other, parallel places, such as Ps. 37:28, and 99:4. So that the thing spoken of which God loves is not men's righteousness, but his own righteousness as the judge of men.

7. That part of the objection which is taken from Deut. 6:25, "And it shall be our righteousness, if we observe to do all these commandments

1. MS: "of."

2. MS: "p. 208," in Pt. V of the essay, "Question: Wherein Do the Two Covenants Agree as to the Method of Justification?" in the "Controversies" notebook. See *Works, 21,* 365–66.

3. MS: "p. 209," in Pt. VI of the essay, "Question: Wherein do the Two Covenants Agree as to the Method of Justification?" in the "Controversies" notebook. See *Works, 21,* 366–67.

before the Lord our God, as he hath commanded us," the seeming force of the objection depends on a mistake of the meaning of the words. See my note on the text.[4]

8. Whereas it is said in the objection that at least those things in the Old Testament, as expressed from time to time, must have a natural tendency to lead the people to such an apprehension that their obedience was the grand condition of their pardon and acceptance with God, as being that righteousness which recommended 'em thereto by its moral value, in answer to this I would say the following things:

(1) There is no proper and positive tendency in these things to lead the people to any such apprehension, and none but what is, as it were, negative, accidental, and by occasion of the people's inattentiveness, inconsideration and corruption. The things declared, or in any respect signified, in these places are nothing but the truth, and the truth signified in an intelligible manner to persons that were considerate, of a good and honest heart; the truth delivered in language that was more plain and intelligible to the Jews than to us, who better understood the language and phraseology in use among them than we do. And the truths that were declared were truths taught in the new testament (as well as the old) with the doctrine of justification by faith alone, and truths in themselves not at all inconsistent with the evangelical doctrine of justification as I have explained it.

'Tis true that under the old testament, the doctrines that are purely evangelical and above the light [of nature] were less clearly revealed, and the truths relating to what is necessary in order to the favor [of God] which are manifest by the light of nature, were insisted on [and] spoken with much greater plainness, agreeably to the nature of that more dark dispensation that went before the coming of the great Prophet of God and Light of the World, who was to bring the glorious doctrines of the gospel to light with great clearness.

But God was not to blame for insisting on these things in the revelation which he gave, which are the truth, and truths that the light of nature teaches. He was no more to blame for making them known by the light of revelation than by the light [of nature], for they are both his teaching. These truths of the light of nature, which God taught them,

---

4. In his "Blank Bible" note on Deut. 6:25, JE first observes that the Septuagint does not use the word "righteousness" but "mercy," which "seems to be the true meaning." Later he adds, "But upon further consideration, I think this is the true meaning: In the original it is, 'It shall be righteousness unto us.' It signifies as much as that God will remember it, and reward it, and give thee a blessing for it . . ."

were necessary for them to know, viz. that he was a holy God and hated sin, that he would never save men in a way of wickedness, that all that are admitted to his favor must be of a holy character, that he would judge of men's character according to their works, etc. And therefore God was not to blame for declaring and inculcating these things. Nor was he to blame that as yet he did not so clearly and fully reveal those evangelical, supernatural truths which the Messiah was afterwards to bring clearly to light.

'Tis very true that the less there is of gospel light, the greater will be the danger of men's falling into error. But this don't arise from God's teaching, as it don't arise from the light that God gives 'em, but is occasioned by the remaining darkness that God don't remove. And the depravity and blindness of men's own minds is the proper source of this error.

There are, and always have been, from Moses' time, many nations to whom God made no revelation at all of gospel truth; and he is not obliged to reveal it to 'em. And yet the ignorance they are left in has a negative tendency to their error and delusion—that is, means to prevent error are wanting. Nevertheless, it can't be said that God's dispensations towards these nations tend to lead 'em into error and delusion, because their corruption will take occasion, by the absence of clearer light, to mislead 'em.

There was not so much in that old dispensation to lead the people to the knowledge of the true way of salvation as there is [in] that more excellent and glorious dispensation that Christ introduced, as there was not so much that tended to men's salvation in other respects. If there had [been], wherein would the new dispensation have been so much more glorious, implying advantages so vastly superior?

(2) There were many things in the revelation which God made of himself under the old testament, to prevent any such improvement of those things which are supposed to have a tendency to lead the people to trust in their own moral righteousness for justification, and to convince 'em that their justification must be an act of sovereign grace, and not any moral value in them. God took care as to that matter, care sufficient to guard and direct serious, considerate and honest minds.

1. Those things which are supposed to have such a tendency, viz. God's proposing legal terms of his favor, considered in the manner and circumstances in which they were delivered, had a contrary tendency to convince 'em of their sinfulness, guilt and the utter impossibility of their being brought to favor and life by their own righteousness. The delivering of the law tended to make 'em dead to the law, and utterly to despair of life through the law; so the delivering of the Ten Commandments at Mt. Sinai in so awful a manner, with such manifestations of terrible wrath, ready to consume those that should violate that law. God's treating the people with such distance and terror under that dark dispensation, tended to convince 'em of their guilt, and to bring 'em to despair of commending themselves to his favor by their own righteousness. The curses of the law, so terribly denounced against those who continued not in all things written in the book of the law to do them, tended to this.

2. The institution of sacrifices, and there being such a vast number of sacrifices required to be offered continually, from year to year, from month to month, from week to week, and from day to day, naturally tended to lead 'em to suppose that their own moral value was not sufficient to commend 'em to God. Those sacrifices were offered as atonement for sin, which taught 'em that their own righteousness made no satisfaction, but [they] were put in mind that, notwithstanding all their righteousness, they deserved the most terrible punishment. They saw the image of what their guilt exposed 'em to. They saw the creature's blood shed, and its dying struggles, and its very vitals—its inward, vital parts, or the fat about them, and the blood—burnt, scorched and consumed in the fire. And by this also they were put in mind of the necessity of a satisfaction to be made, that death should be suffered and God's threatening of wrath some way fulfilled, and justice in some respect satisfied, that they might not think that for the sake of value in them God abated of his threatenings, relinquished the honor of his majesty and authority. For they must conceive of this terrible suffering of the creature as the effect of the wrath of God against their sin.

These sacrifices also were offered as a sweet savor to recommend 'em to God, which intimated to 'em that their own righteousness was not sufficient to recommend. 'Tis very evident from God's own word that he made use of personal types of Christ to that end, that they might not trust in their own righteousness, turning the people's eyes off from their own righteousness to those personal types. Deut. 9:5, "Not for thy righteousness, . . . but to perform the word which the Lord sware unto thy fathers." So there is all reason to think that the real types were made use [of] for the same end.

3. God so manifested himself to the people as tended to lead 'em to think that he pardoned and accepted them to favor, not as being induced to it by any worthiness or valuableness in them, but as disposed to do it already otherwise, as of his own sovereign good pleasure, and for the

sake of their fathers, etc.; and as only waiting for an opportunity to show them mercy in a manner that should be fit and decent and consistent with his own honor, by their forsaking sin and yielding to him, hearkening to him and obeying him, and so receiving him as their Savior from sin and misery, and as the God of their mercy. He represents himself as not waiting for a compensation or satisfaction for sin from them, but as having no pleasure in the death of sinners, waiting to be gracious, proclaiming his name to be the Lord God, gracious and merciful, forgiving iniquity, transgression and sin, being a God of great mercy, delighting in mercy, ready to forgive, and that will abundantly pardon, wishing that there were an heart in them to yield to him, that they might be happy. God says in the first [chapter] of Isaiah, "If ye be willing and obedient, ye shall eat the good of the land" [v. 19]. And elsewhere God represents himself as willing and waiting, and the only reason why the people failed of mercy, to be that they refused to yield to God and accept his mercy. They pulled away the shoulder and loved death, agreeable to those words of Christ, "how often would I have gathered thy children together, even as a hen gathereth her chickens under her wings, but ye would not" [Matt. 23:37]. The same thing is manifest by God's promising to pardon sin only on confessing and forsaking sin, though sins be never so numerous and heinous.

4. When God offers to pardon 'em on their repentance, brokenness of heart, etc., he does it in such a manner as not at all to lead sinners to suppose that it was on account of the valuableness of their repentance, or because it made any compensation so as in its own nature, as it were, to abolish and destroy the transgression. For God represents the removing or abolishing their guilt as his own and free act, of his mere motion and great grace. Is. 43:22–27, "But thou hast not called upon me, O Jacob; . . . thou hast not honored me with thy sacrifices [. . .] but thou hast made me serve with thy sins, thou hast wearied me with thine iniquities. I, even I, am he that blotteth out thy transgressions for mine own sake, and will not remember thy sins. Put me in remembrance . . . Thy first father sinned," etc.

Their sins remained as much after repentance as before, notwithstanding any supposed atonement their repentance made. But God, of his own great grace, as it were, covers them, doth not behold iniquity in them, don't impute it to 'em, turns away his eyes from seeing it in them, casts 'em behind his back, buries them in the depth of the sea that they mayn't be in sight—many such expressions are used. The Apostle argues the doctrine of justification by faith alone from such expressions, as particularly that of God's not imputing sin in the thirty-second Psalm. If repentance and obedience were a moral loveliness and value, and were viewed as such in the affair of justification of a sinner, then they must be taken as something to put in the balance against the unworthiness and guilt of sin, and so would in themselves do away the transgression in some degree at least. And so it would [not be] so absolutely God's own act to do away sin as is represented.

5. That dispensation was so contrived that when it encouraged the people to hope in God's mercy, yet not in such a manner as tended to excite presumption on mercy that should be at all inconsistent with the full manifestation of God's perfect and infinite holiness and justice, and perfect vindication of the honor of his authority and sacred majesty. Sacrifices were instituted partly for this end. And for this end, when God proclaimed his name "The Lord God, gracious and merciful, [. . .] forgiving iniquity," etc., it was added that God would "by no means clear the guilty" [Ex. 34:6–7]. And when God pardoned the nation of Israel after their murmuring at the report of the spies, he says to Moses, "I have pardoned according to thy word: but as I live," saith the Lord, "all the earth shall be filled with the glory of the Lord" [Num. 14:20–21]; meaning, as appears by the context, in what the [Israelites] shall see of the testimonies of his holy displeasure and vindications of his authority, agreeable to what is said, "thou [. . .] forgavest their iniquity, but tookest vengeance of their inventions" [Ps. 99:8]. The awful manner of delivering the Law at Mt. Sinai, and the many terrors of that dispensation, and the awful distance God kept them, tended to keep up in the people's mind a sense of the necessity of satisfaction to the justice and holiness of God, and vindication of his kingly majesty. Hence in part it was that the fear of God was so much insisted on as essential to true religion, and was revealed to be necessary to attend, hoping in his mercy and rejoicing in his favor (Ps. 33:18, and 147:11 and 2:11). These things naturally tended to keep 'em from trusting in their own righteousness.

6. More than all those things, it was often signified to the people, very expressly and abundantly inculcated upon them, that it was not for the sake of their righteousness, or any moral value in them, that God showed them favor. And they were carefully led to conceive that it was on other accounts. Deut. 9:4–7, "Speak not thou in thine heart, . . . saying, For my righteousness the Lord hath brought me in to possess the land: but for the wickedness of these nations the Lord doth drive them out before thee. Not for thy righteousness, or for the uprightness of thine heart, dost thou go to possess their land: but for the wickedness," etc., "and that

he may perform the word which the Lord sware unto thy fathers, Abraham, Isaac and Jacob. Understand therefore, that the Lord thy God giveth thee not this good land," etc., "for thy righteousness; for thou art a stiff-necked people. Remember, and forget not, how thou provokedst," etc. Ch. 7:7–8, "The Lord did not set his love upon you, nor choose you, because ye were more in number . . . : but because the Lord loved you, and because he would keep the oath which he had sworn unto your fathers," etc. So in that forementioned Is. 43:23[–27], "Thou hast brought me no small cattle of thy burnt offerings," etc., "neither hast thou filled me with the fat of thy sacrifices: but thou hast made me to serve with thy sins, thou hast wearied me with thine iniquities. I, even I, am he that blotteth out thy transgressions for mine own sake, and will not remember thy sins. Put me in remembrance: let us plead together: declare thou, that thou mayest be justified" (i.e. "declare thy righteousness, tell me of anything you have that is valuable and worthy to recommend you"). "Thy first father hath sinned," etc. Ch. 48[:9], "For my name's sake will I defer mine anger, and for my praise will I refrain for thee, that I cut thee not off." Gen. 26:24, "I am the God of Abraham thy father: . . . I am with thee, and I will bless thee," etc. "for my servant Abraham's sake." To Jacob God represents as though he showed mercy for Abraham's and Isaac's sake (Gen. 28:13). II Kgs. 13:23, "And the Lord was gracious unto them, and had compassion on them, and had respect to them, because of his covenant with Abraham, Isaac, and Jacob." So Ex. 2:24–25, and 3:14–15 and 6:3–4. Ezek. 36:25–26, "Then will I sprinkle clean water upon you, and ye shall be clean: from all your filthiness, and from all your idols, will I cleanse you. A new heart also will I give unto you," etc. And then v. 32, "Not for your sakes do I this, saith the Lord God, be it known unto you: be ashamed and confounded for your own ways, O house of Israel." So v. 22, "Therefore say unto the house of Israel, Thus saith the Lord God; I do not this for your sakes, but for mine holy name's sake, which ye have profaned among the heathen, whither ye went." See Ezek. 20:9–10, 13–14, 21–22, 43, 33; and I Sam. 12:20–22; Ps. 106:7–8. Ezek. 20:43–44, "And there shall ye remember your ways, and all your doings, wherein ye have been defiled; and ye shall loathe yourselves in your own sight for all your evils that ye have committed. And ye shall know that I am the Lord, when I have wrought with you for my name's sake, not according to your wicked ways, nor according to your corrupt doings, O ye house of Israel, saith the Lord God."

So from time to time, where God is represented as granting pardon on repentance, it is yet plainly implied that pardon and favor are not bestowed for any moral value in them, consisting in their repentance or anything else.

Is. 48:11, "For mine own sake, even for mine own sake, will I do it: for how should my name be polluted?" II Kgs. 19:34, "For I will defend this city, to save it, for mine own sake, and for my servant David's sake." So ch. 20:6, and Is. 37:35.

God often is spoken of as showing mercy to those that were in themselves very unworthy for his servant David's sake (I Kgs. 11:12, 32, 34, and 15:4; II Kgs. 8:19).

(3) The way of justification by faith was truly revealed. Sufficient instructions were given concerning it to lead convinced, penitent sinners to hope for justification in no other way. Thus trusting in God and hoping in his mercy, seeking God, waiting for or upon the Lord, calling on the name of the Lord, looking to God, looking towards God's holy temple, laying hold on God's strength—I say, these things are abundantly insisted on as the terms of acceptance and salvation. But these things, as I have elsewhere shown,[5] are expressions that signify the exercise of faith. As to trusting in God, waiting on him and hoping in him, 'tis needless to enumerate places, they are so many. With respect to seeking God, see I Chron. 28:9, Ps. 34:10, 15, Amos 5:4.

Calling on God, see Ps. 50:15, and 65:2, and 86:5–7 and 145:18–19; Jer. 10:25.

God proposed to the children of Israel their duty much more in a legal manner in the books of Moses, for their trial, than afterwards. And the way of faith was not so fully revealed till after the nation had had some ages' experience of their utter inability to obtain justification in the way of the law.

I have elsewhere shown particularly that God's people under the old testament were not only instructed in the way of faith in general, but that they were particularly led by the revelation they were under to faith in the second person in the Godhead as their Mediator and advocate, and in the Messiah as their great high priest and sacrifice. See this matter largely handled in my discourse on the faith of the Old Testament saints ("Controversies").[6]

5. See many entries in the "Faith" notebook (*Works, 21*): on trusting, hoping, and seeking, nos. 13, 28, 48–49, 71, 78, 81, 86–88, 103, 107, 110–20; on waiting, nos. 132, 140; on calling, no. 58; on looking to God, nos. 80, 121, 142; on looking towards God's temple, nos. 96, 115; and on laying hold of God's strength, no. 97.

6. MS: "p. 213," at which begins the essay "Question: In What Sense Did the Saints under the Old Testament Believe in Christ to Justification?" in the "Controversies" notebook. See *Works, 21*, 372–408.

In order to determine what way of justification is pointed out in the Old Testament revelation, we should observe more especially what things are chiefly proposed to men when they are treated with as sinners, what conditions of acceptance, pardon and life are proposed to them. And we shall find those things mainly insisted on that imply faith, such as repenting, confessing and turning to the Lord, trusting in God, hoping in his mercy, calling on his name, seeking him, laying hold on his mercy, calling on his name, seeking him, laying hold on his strength, looking to his holy temple and the like.

(4) Not only was care taken and provision made to prevent the people's trusting in their own righteousness, and to lead 'em off from all dependence on any moral value of their own, but the provision that was made proved sufficient in that it was actually effectual, so that the saints under the old testament were not wont to trust in their own righteousness for justification before God.

[In] the book of Psalms we have many of the Old Testament saints of different ages expressing the sentiments of their hearts, and breathing forth their souls in the language of Old Testament devotion and piety, by which, therefore, above all other parts of the Old Testament, we may learn the nature of the Old Testament devotion. But by things continually expressed in this book, to which many other parts of the Old Testament agree, we see that the saints did not trust in their own worthiness for justification and acceptance with God. Nor was that what they pleaded. But they sought God's favor for God's mercy's sake (Ps. 6:4, and 31:16, and 44:26, and 115:1), for his truth's sake (Ps. 115:1), his goodness' sake (Ps. 25:7), and his name's sake (in places very many). See this matter particularly and largely handled in my discourse on the faith of Old Testament saints ("Controversies").[7]

(5) It may be further considered, that although the way of justification by the satisfaction and righteousness of another, without any righteousness of ours, was not so fully revealed under that dark, imperfect and legal dispensation, so that truly honest and pious minds were not so much guarded from self-righteousness as now; so misapprehensions as to that matter were not so total then as under the clear light we now enjoy, as they were not so great evidences and so necessarily the fruits of a proud, self-exalting, self-sufficient temper. A more full and explicit re-

---

7. MS: "p. 213 &c especially p. 219 &c." "Question: In What Sense did the Saints under the Old Testament Believe in Christ to Justification?" in the "Controversies" notebook, which starts on MS p. 213. Pt. IV is on MS p. 219. See *Works, 21*, 383–84.

nunciation of our own righteousness, and dependence on the righteousness of Christ, is necessary now than was then, inasmuch as the want of it under such clear light will be a far greater evidence of [the want of] true humiliation of heart and an evangelical temper of mind.

A greater sense of our own unworthiness, and the worthlessness of all our own righteousness, may well be expected now in the days of the gospel. For we have unspeakably more to show us the infinite evil of sin. Such a manner and degree of renunciation of their own righteousness, and such a kind and degree of exercise of faith was necessary, as was a true expression of real humiliation of soul and a truly evangelical, believing heart, a heart of acknowledgment of the glory and sufficiency and faithfulness of the Mediator, according to the nature and manner of the revelation of these things that was given them.

A child may have these mistakes about its own strength and the like without betraying that pride of disposition that the same degree of error would discover in a grown person. So the church might be tolerated in a greater degree of ignorance and mistake about the vanity of our own righteousness, and our absolute, universal and infinite dependence on a mediator, under the old testament than now under the new, when the church is adult.

(6) If, after all that has been said, any shall suppose that these things are attended with obscurity and intricacy, it need not be wondered at that God's ways during that time, when there shone no other than a dim starlight or moonlight, are not so plainly to be seen, so easily traced, and so laid open to view with that clearness that they are when the sun shines on his paths. If we are not able perfectly to explain all things, and trace all the steps of divine wisdom in conducting the souls of his people to their eternal happiness, and reconcile all the dark passages of that obscure revelation, nor all the mysterious steps of his wisdom in that dark administration wherein law and gospel are mixed together; nevertheless, this is no reason why we should reject the most plain, positive doctrine of the glorious gospel as introduced in its clearness by the great Messiah, the light of the world, a doctrine in which the New Testament is so explicit, full and particular, and which the whole scheme of this new revelation does so evidently imply. We are to be determined by the evident doctrines, the voice of him who speaks to us from heaven in this gospel day, when the darkness is past and the true light shines. Would not he act like a madman, that had his choice whether he would be directed in his way through a great wilderness by the clear light of the day or dim light of the night, if he should choose the latter, and should refuse to be

determined by what is plainly manifest in the sunshine, because it differs from the imagination he had by viewing the way only by starlight?[8]

[1355.] EXTRACTS FROM RAMSAY'S *PHILOSOPHICAL PRINCIPLES OF RELIGION*.[9]

Vol. 2, pp. 54 ff. "Plutarch in his treatise of Isis and Osiris tells us 'that the end of all the Egyptian rites and mysteries was the knowledge of that first God,[1] who is the Lord of all things, and only intelligible by the mind; that the theology of the Egyptians had two meanings, the only holy and symbolical, the other vulgar and literal, and consequently that the figures of animals which they had in their temples, and which they seemed to adore, were only so many hieroglyphics to represent the divine attributes.' After which he declares 'that the first God of the Egyptians is[2] a hidden deity, and that the crocodile was one of his symbols because this animal hid in the water sees all things, and is itself unseen, which is a property of the supreme God.'

"Origen, who was contemporary with Plutarch, [...] expresses himself in this manner: 'The Egyptian philosophers have sublime ideas of the divine nature which they keep secret and never discover to the people but under a veil of fables and allegories. . . . All the eastern nations— the Persians, the Indians, the Syrians—conceal sacred mysteries under their religious fables. The wise men of all these religions see into the sense and true meaning of them, whilst the vulgar go no further than the exterior symbol and bark that covers them.' [...]

"St. Cyprian says 'that Hermes Trismegistus acknowledged one God whom he confessed to be ineffable and inestimable.' Lactantius maintains 'that Thoth, or Hermes, a most ancient philosopher instructed in all kinds of learning, and therefore called Trismegist, wrote many books concerning the knowledge of divine things, wherein he asserts the majesty of one supreme God, calling him, as we do, God and Father; and

---

8. Part of MS p. 937, on which this entry ends, and the entirety of the following page, are blank.

9. The entry comprises pp. 939–63 of Bk. 9 and includes running heads that are largely descriptive, giving either the subject under discussion ("Trinity," "The Messiah," etc.) or the name of individuals being considered ("Cicero," "East Indians," etc.). On pp. 957–63 (where JE starts quoting from "Ramsay's *Principles,* vol. 2, pp. 429 ff."), JE also wrote further descriptions in the left and right margins. These, too, are descriptive, though the marginalia of nearly every one of the concluding pages includes the phrases "Right Notions of God," "Right Notions of Religion," or "Right Notions of God and Religion," which may indicate JE's positive estimation of the excerpts.

1. Ramsay's and JE's capitalization of the names of the Deity is retained throughout entry.

2. Ramsay: "was."

lest anyone should ask his name, he said that he was without any name, that is, ineffable and incomprehensible.' Justin Martyr adds, 'Ammon, in his books called God THE MOST HIDDEN, and Hermes, plainly declares that 'tis hard to conceive God, but impossible to express him.'

"Let us now hear the testimony of the pagan writers who had studied the religion of the Egyptians, and understood it perfectly. Iamblichus one of the chief. He lived in the beginning of the third century and was a disciple of the former Porphyry This is the account he gives of the Egyptian theology: 'According to the Egyptians, Eicton, or the first God, existed in his solitary unity before all beings. He is the fountain and original of everything that either has understanding or is to be understood. He is the first principle of all things, self-sufficient, incomprehensible, and the Father of all essences.' The same Iamblichus, in his answer to an epistle of Porphyry's wrote to Anebo, an Egyptian priest, gives us a summary account of the Egyptian theology in these words: 'God, who is the cause of all nature and all its powers, is separated from, elevated above, and expanded over all the powers and elements of the world, and transcending the same, yet so as to be immaterial, incorporeal, supernatural, unmade, indivisible, ruling over all things and containing all in himself.' The same Iamblichus adds 'that as the Egyptian hieroglyphic for material things was muddy and floating water, so they pictured God sitting above the lote-tree and above the watery mud, which signifies the transcendent eminency of the divine nature above matter and its intellectual empire over the world, because the leaves and fruit of that tree are round, representing the motion of the intellect.' In the same book he answers thus to the Porphyrian queries: 'According to the Egyptians, before all entities and principles there is one God, who is in order of nature before him who is called the sovereign Lord. This first God is immovable and always remaining in the solitude of his own unity, there being nothing intelligent nor intelligible complicated with him.' [...]

"Proclus, another Platonic disciple of the Porphyrian and Plotinian school, [says] that 'according to the tradition of the Egyptians, matter was not unmade nor self-existent, but produced by the Deity'; for, adds he, 'The divine Iamblichus hath recorded that Hermes would have materiality to have been produced by essentiality or the Being to whom essence belongs. And it is very probable from hence that Plato was also of the same opinion concerning matter, because he is supposed to have followed Hermes and the Egyptian philosophers.'

"We shall conclude here with the testimony of Damascius in his book of principles, who speaks in this manner of the ancient Egyptians: 'The

Egyptian philosophers of our times have declared the hidden truth of their theology, and have found in the ancient writings of their sages that there was but one principle of all things, praised under the name of the Unknown Darkness, and that THRICE REPEATED.' [. . .]³

"Pindar calls the loud-sounding Jupiter 'the most powerful of the Gods, the Lord of all things, the first cause, the great artificer and framer of the universe.' 'It was this same God whom Chiron instructed Achilles to honor and worship transcendently above all other gods.' 'If any man is so foolish as to imagine any of his actions can be concealed from God, he is greatly deceived.' The same poet represents God as the author, source and cause of all good, and that 'men became wise and good only by the assistance of the Deity'; that 'the endowments both of body and mind, wisdom, natural strength and eloquence, are all the gifts of the gods.' 'God,' says he, 'overturns the proud, but gives immortal glory to the humble'; that 'we are beings of one day: today we are something, to-morrow nothing. Man is a dream of a shadow; but when God emits his splendors, a bright light and sweet life attends us.'

"Euripides expressly acknowledges the dependence of all beings on one sole principle as author of life and knowledge, existence and reason. 'O Father and King of gods, why do we miserable mortals fancy that we know anything, or can do anything? Our fate depends upon thy will.' The same Euripides speaks thus in another place, quoted by Dr. Cudworth: 'Thou self-sprung Being which contains all things and embraces the celestial spheres, though encompassed with light, yet thou art surrounded with a shady night.' [. . .] The same tragedian says in another place, 'I offer to thee, Lord of all, libations of wine and a salt cake. Whatever be thy name, whether that of Dis or Jupiter, thou alone holdest the supreme scepter among the gods, and thou governest the terrestrial kingdom. Infuse light into these souls of men, that they may know the root whence all evil springs, and by what sacrifice they may attain to a true rest from their labors.' [. . .]

"St. Justin Martyr quotes from Sophocles the following maxims: 'There is one sovereign power and one God who CREATED the heavens, the earth, the seas and the force of winds. The most part of men, deprived of all true understanding, consecrate to him statues of wood and stone, images of gold and ivory; they endeavor to appease him with sacrifices,

3. JE skips from p. 57 to p. 67; in the intervening pages, Ramsay shows how the ancient pagans recognized different divine attributes and divided them into separate deities. JE capitalized the final term.

to solemnize festivals in his honor, and foolishly fancy that by this they
are pious.'

"The same Justin Martyr mentions an ancient oracle of the Greeks
which runs thus: 'God is self-originated, THRICE great, indivisibly one,
omnipotent and invisible; he sees all things and can be perceived by
none.'

"Aratus, quoted by St. Paul, calls God 'he of whom all things are full,
who penetrates and pervades all beings everywhere, whose beneficence
we all constantly enjoy, for we are his offspring. Therefore he is always
propitiated and adored as the first and the last. Hail universal Father, the
great wonder of the universe and the great interest of mankind.' Many
such passages are quoted by the Greek fathers from Terpander, Aristophanes, Menander, Hermionax and others. We might multiply volumes
on this subject. We shall therefore sum up all we are to say of the Greek
poets by this assertion of Dion Chrysostom: 'All the poets universally,
without exception, call the first and greatest God [the] Father and King
of all the rational kind. Agreeably to this idea, men erect altars to Jupiter
King, and call him father in all their devotions.' [. . .][4]

"Xenophanes the Colophonian, the head of the Eleatic sect, says in a
verse preserved by St. Clemens Alexandrinus, 'There is one God, the
greatest both among gods and men, who moveth the whole world without any labor, merely by mind.' Simplicius, in his commentary upon Aristotle's *Physics,* says, 'Theophrastus affirms that Xenophanes the Colophonian, master to Parmenides, made one principle of all things, which
is neither finite nor infinitely extended, neither in local motion nor in
rest; a solitary Being, unmade, self-originated, the best and most powerful of all things, the supreme unity, which presides and rules over all degrees of entity.'

"Heraclitus, whom St. Justin Martyr looks upon as inspired as well as
Socrates by the Logos, lived in a continual retreat, contemplation and
penitence, mourning over the follies of mankind. As he frequented very
little the temples and lived like an ascetic, he was accused of impiety by
Euthycles and the superstitious priests of his country. To justify himself,
he writes thus to Hermodorus: 'O ye unwise and unlearned, teach us first
what God is, then tell us where God is, that so you may be believed in accusing me of impiety. Is he shut up in the walls of temples? Is this your
piety, to place God in the dark or to make him a stony God and a statue?
Know you not that God is not made with hands, and has no support to

---

4. JE skips from p. 70 to p. 77.

stand upon, nor can he be enclosed within walls. The whole world, varied with plants, animals and stars, is his temple. Am I impious, O Euthycles, who alone know what God is? Is there no God without altars, or are stones the only proofs of his existence? No, his own WORKS give testimony of him, and principally the sun. Night and day bear witness of him, the fruitful earth declares his might, and the orb of the moon is an echo of his power.'

"Parmenides, disciple of Xenophanes, called God ONE AND ALL. Some think, most falsely, that Parmenides confounded nature with God by this expression. But Simplicius, who was well acquainted with the opinions of the ancients, and who had by him a copy of Parmenides' works, says 'that this expression "one and all" must not be understood physically but metaphysically, because the supreme, intelligible source of all things, of mind and understanding, contains and comprehends in himself all things compendiously and by way of unity. This was the unity, monad or one being of Parmenides whom he called indivisible and immutable.' [...] Simplicius has preserved to us some verses of Parmenides which explain fully his sense: 'The supreme Deity,' says he, 'is one, singular, solitary and most simple Being, unmade, self-originated and necessarily existent, whose duration is immutable, remaining always in himself without flux or succession.'

"Dr. Cudworth, to whom we owe a great many of the foregoing remarks, has demonstrated that Empedocles, Melissus, Archytas, Ornatus, Ocellus, Timaeus Locrus, Archelaus, Antisthenes, Diogenes Syropensis and Euclides Megarensis were all true theists. But as the scraps and fragments of these authors, which have been preserved, are only repetitions of what has been already said, we proceed to Plato, the great light of Greece. [...]

"He calls God, in his *Timæus,* 'The architect of the world, the Father of the universe, the Creator of nature, the God over all, the sovereign mind which orders all things and penetrates all things, the sovereign beauty and the supreme good.' In his *Sophist* he defines God 'the self-originated, efficient cause which makes all things exist that had no being before.' In his *Republic,* 'He that made the heavens and the earth and the gods, and is the original life and force of all things in heaven, upon earth and under the earth.' [...]

"Proclus, in commenting upon the Platonic theology, says, 'The divine philosophy of Plato despises all corporeal things when compared with what is intellectual. He demonstrates that mind is more ancient than matter, and depends upon an intelligent hypostasis; that intellect was the cause of bodies and the father of spirits.' In another place the same Proclus adds, 'Plato, following the Pythagoreans, maintains that generated things are many and various, but there is one supreme cause that connects and joins all the subordinate causes, that there may be nothing in vain nor accessory in the universe. There is one King, one cause, one providence. There are besides many agents, different causes, a multiform providence and a various order; but in all, multiplicity must adhere to unity, variety to simplicity, what is multiform to what is uniform, and different particulars to one universal, that so there may be a golden series in the whole, and that all things may be regulated with order, harmony and proportion.' It was then with good reason that Numenius the Pythagorean said, 'What is Plato but Moses speaking in the Attic language?' Eusebius adds that Plato, 'agreeing with Moses, teaches in the *Timaeus* that as there is but one heaven, so there is but one God; for that which contains all intelligibles can never be second to anything.' [. . .]

"The stoics, Zeno, Cleanthes, Chrysippus and all their disciples, [. . .] acknowledged one only supreme God who produced all things by his power, and beatifies all beings by his goodness. They endeavored to prove the existence of this one God, whom they Called Zeus, Zen or Jupiter, by several arguments drawn from the orderly system of the world and the characters of wisdom and design therein remarked. Hence they concluded 'that it was no more likely that the world could have been made by chance than that Homer's *Iliad* could have proceeded from the fortuitous projection of innumerable letters thrown at random on the ground.' They proved also the existence of an all-perfect Being from the gradual ascent and scale of perfection we observe in nature. There must needs be therefore, said they, some most excellent and perfect Being at the head of all. In fine, they endeavored to prove the existence of a God from this, that the cause must be more perfect than the effect, and that the whole must contain all the perfections of the parts, in a most transcendent manner.

"The later philosophers among the Greeks, who lived after the times of Christianity, [. . .] whether Pythagoreans, Platonists, Peripatetics or Stoics, all acknowledge one supreme Deity.

"The first, the greatest and most moral of all these philosophers is Hierocles, who lived towards the end of the second century. [. . .] He says thus: 'We can only discover the true grandeur of God, the most excellent artificer and maker of the world, by believing him to be the cause of the indeviating intelligences whom the verses call the immortal gods, because they constantly and uniformly contemplate God the Creator, and have their thoughts constantly intent upon his goodness, and receive from him completely and invariably being and well-being as his living images void of passion and evil.' In another place he calls God 'the first source of all good, the fountain of eternal nature, [...] who diffuses his beneficence through the whole universe like a pure and intellectual light.' [...] He says 'that human souls have lost their wings and ARE FALLEN into a state of CORRUPTION.' [...]

"Plutarch, who lived much about the same time, says, 'The ancients gave the name of gods to the various productions of the Deity; care should be taken, however, not to transform, dissolve and scatter the divine nature into rivers, winds, vegetables or bodily forms and motions. This would be as ridiculous as to imagine that the sails, the cables, the rigging and anchor are the pilot, or that the thread, the shuttle and the woof are the weaver. Such senseless notions are unworthy of the heavenly powers, whom men blaspheme when they give the name of gods to beings of an insensible, inanimate and corruptible nature. Nothing that is without a soul, nothing that is material, nothing that can be perceived by our senses, can be God. Neither must we imagine that there are different gods according to the different countries of Greeks and barbarians, northern and southern nations. As the sun is common to all the world, though called by different names in different places, so there is but one sole, supreme mind or reason, and one and the same PROVIDENCE, that governs the world, though he is worshipped under different names and has appointed some inferior powers for his ministers.' [...]

"Dion Chrysostom, Plutarch's contemporary, though he acknowledged many inferior gods, yet he asserts that 'there is an opinion, common to all the humankind as well barbarians as Greeks, that it is naturally implanted in them as rational beings and not derived from any mortal teacher. This opinion is that the whole world is under the kingly power or monarchy of one supreme God who is the common Lord of gods and men, their governor and father, the universal president who orders and governs the heavens and the earth as a wise pilot doth a ship.'

"Alcinous, who is supposed to have lived towards the beginning of the second century, speaks thus: 'Since the first mind is the most beautiful, he must have before him the most beautiful object of contemplation. But there is nothing more beautiful than himself. He must then always contemplate himself, and this energy is called his IDEA. The first God is eternal, inexpressible, self-sufficient, perfect in all times and in all places. He is good because he does good to all and is the cause of all good. He is beautiful because by nature he is fullness and order. He is truth because he is the principle of all truth, as the sun is the source of all light. He is the universal Father as he is the cause of all things [. . .].'

"Galen, in his book *Of the Use of Human Members,* speaks thus: 'I compose this holy oration as a true hymn to the praise of him that made us. I conceive that true piety and religion towards God does not consist in sacrificing many hecatombs nor in burning much incense, but in this, that I should first acknowledge myself, and then declare to others, how great his power, his wisdom and his goodness are: for to adorn the world as he has done, envying to nothing that good which it is capable of, is a demonstration of the most absolute goodness; and that he was able to find out how all things ought to be adorned after the best manner, is a sign of the greatest wisdom; and lastly, to be able to effect and bring to pass all those things which he had thus decreed, argues an insuperable power.'

"Maximus Tyrius says, 'Imagine a great and powerful empire in which all conspire freely and with one consent to direct their actions agreeably to the will and command of one supreme king, the oldest and best. Then suppose that the bounds of this empire are neither the Halys nor the Hellespont, the Meotian Lake nor the shores of the great ocean, but the heavens above, the earth below, and the boundless expanse. Here let that great king sit immovable in himself, present everywhere though unextended, prescribing to all his subjects laws in which consist their security and felicity,' etc. Such a noble image of the divine monarchy he gives us in the end of his first dissertation.

"The same author says, 'Amidst so great a war, discord, and contention of opinions, there is through the whole earth an universal law and sentiment, agreeing that there is one God, the King and Father of all things, and many gods his children that reign with him. The Greeks and the barbarians agree in this doctrine, he that inhabits the continent, he that lives by the sea, the wise and the unwise. Now do you imagine that Plato would oppose these sentiments, and not agree with mankind in the most beautiful of all truths, and feel with them the truest of all sentiments. What is that? Mine eye says it is the sun, my ear says it is thunder; but what are all those things really? My soul says that they are the works of God; it desires the artist in discovering the art. Though there may have arisen since the beginning of the world two or three atheistical, low, or stupid men that wander with their eyes, are deceived by their ears, and maimed in their souls, irrational, barren and without fruit, like a lion without courage or a bird without wings; yet this does not destroy the universal sentiment of mankind concerning the Divinity. Though you deny his goodness, as Leucippus; though you ascribe human passion to him, as Democritus; though you change his nature, as Strabo; though you make him a god of pleasure, as Epicurus; though you deny his existence, as Diagoras; though you say you know not what he is, as Protagoras: yet you cannot destroy in yourself nor in them the natural ideas all have of a Deity, for they, even they, know and speak of God against their inclinations.' In another place he says, 'The Deity is invisible to the eyes, inexpressible by language, impalpable by sense; he cannot be heard of by the ear, but only by the most beautiful, most pure, most intellectual and most ancient powers of the soul: for the Diety, entirely collected into himself, enters into a recollected mind. . . . The Father and Creator of all being is more ancient than the sun, older than heaven, greater than time and every flowing nature, a lawgiver without name, inexpressible by words, invisible to the eye. Incapable to comprehend his essence, we assist our weakness by words, names, symbols, images, animals, plants, rivers, mountains, fountains, desiring to understand him.' [. . .]" (See further forward, p. 554.)[5]

"Aristides the Adrianean sophist and orator, in his first oration or hymn consecrated to Jupiter, speaks thus: 'Jupiter made all things, and all things that exist are the work of Jupiter, heavens and earth, sea and rivers, all that is above and all that is below, gods and men, everything that has life, whatsoever is perceivable either by sense or by mind. Jupiter was self-existent. He was not educated in the flowery, odoriferous caves of Crete, neither was Saturn ever about to devour him, nor instead of him did he swallow down a stone; for Jupiter was never in danger, nor will be ever so. Neither is there anything older than Jupiter, no more than there are sons older than their parents, or works than their artificers. He is the first, the oldest and the parent of all things, self-originated, nor can it be declared when he was made, for he was from the beginning. No man can tell the time, since there was not then any time, and nothing else besides him.' [. . .]

"The Emperor Marcus Antoninus calls God 'the oldest of all the gods, the nature which governs all things, [. . .] the supreme reason which orders and dispenses all according to appointed periods, and the intellectual principle which contains the whole.' The same emperor says 'that as our bodies breathe the common air, so should our souls suck and draw

---

5. JE's original reference is to MS p. 947 of Bk. 9, col. 2, which contains more material from Maximus Tyrius.

in vital breath from that great mind which comprehends the universe, becoming as it were one spirit with him.' In other places he calls God 'the mind and understanding of the whole world, the intellectual fountain of all beings, one God through all, one substance, and one law.'

"Epictetus and his true disciples, such as Arcianus, Simplicius, and many other Stoics, are full of such noble sentiments of God. They were so convinced of his existence and omnipresence, of his power, wisdom and goodness, that it never entered into their heads to give speculative proofs of such plain and universal truths. It is true indeed, they called him Nature and Universal Nature, but at the same time, 'Creator, self-existent, the law, the reason, and the light of all intelligent beings, the author of all good, the universal father of men and gods, to whom all submission, resignation, confidence, thanksgiving and internal adorations are due.' [...]

"Dr. Cudworth has further demonstrated that this belief of a supreme, self-existent Being was not only the sentiment of the wiser Greek philosophers, such as Pythagoras, Socrates, Plato, Antisthenes, Xenocrates, Zeno, Cleanthes Chrysippus, Scaevola the Roman high-priest, Varro, Cicero and Pliny, but also of the poets. To this purpose the learned Doctor quotes a passage of Hermesianax the Colophonian who declares that Jupiter, Pan, Apollo, Pluto, Neptune, Mercury, Cupid, Nereus and Triton, Proserpine, Ceres, Venus, Thetis, Juno and Diana were all but one and the same God under different names. [...]

"All the wise men and philosophers of the Romans had the same notions of one supreme Deity. Thus Numa, second king of the Romans, [...] says expressly, 'That first principle of all things is neither subject to sense nor suffering, but invisible, uncorruptible, and conceivable only by the mind.' Plutarch assures us that 'as the ancient Persians, so the Romans, during a hundred and sixty years, had no images nor statues of the Deity in their temples, believing that it was a crime to represent what is august by what is low, and that we could attain to the knowledge of the Deity by mind only.' [...]

"Cicero [...], in his book *Of Divination,* says 'that the beauty of the universe and the order of the heavenly bodies compel us to confess that there is some excellent and eternal nature to be looked to and admired by mankind.' . . . In another place he speaks thus: 'Who is so mad or stupid when he looks up to the heavens, and is not presently convinced that there are gods? or can persuade himself that those things, which are made with so much mind and wisdom that no human skill is able to comprehend the artifice and contrivance of them, did all happen by chance?

No, no' (says he), 'there is, there is certainly a divine force in the world; neither is it reasonable to think that in these gross and frail bodies of ours, there should be something that hath life, sense and understanding, and yet no such thing in the whole universe: if men will conclude that there is none because they do not see it, they must also deny the existence of their own mind, which they do not see, though it is by it that we understand, foresee and order all that we do.' In his *Tusculan Questions* he says 'that God cannot be understood by us otherwise than as a free mind, disengaged and separated from all mortal concretion, which both perceives and moves all Things. Without his government, neither any family, city, nation, nor mankind in general, nor the whole of nature, nor the universe, could subsist: for this also obeyeth God; the seas and the earth are subjected to him, and the life of man is disposed of by the commands of the supreme law. He rules over all mankind and FORBIDS THEM TO DEPART HENCE WITHOUT HIS LEAVE. He is the supreme God, Lord and governor, whose divine power all things obey, the chief and principal God who governs the whole world in the same manner as an human soul governs the body it is set over.'

"Terentius Varro, contemporary with Cicero, [. . .] says, 'According to the literal [sense], the poetical, mythical theology contains many things contrary to the dignity and nature of immortal beings. It derives the genealogy of one god from the head, another from the thigh, another from drops of blood. Some are represented as thieves, others as adulterers; in fine, the poets attribute to the gods all sorts of defects that are incident not only to men, but to the most contemptible men. These alone understand what God is, who believe him to be a soul governing the world with activity and wisdom.'"

Seneca (see No. [1351][6]) says, "'God is the framer of the universe, the governor, disposer and keeper thereof, the artificer and Lord of the whole mundane fabric. He is present everywhere, and sustaineth himself by his own force, and his power extends to all things [. . .] great and small with equal intention.' [. . .]

"Apuleius [. . .] represents God 'as the highest of the gods, who not only knows and sees all things by his wisdom, but who penetrates and comprehends within himself the beginning, the middle and the end, and intimately present to all beings, he governs them by the universal care of his providence.' [. . .]

6. JE's original reference was to MS p. 870, col. 1, of Bk. 9, which coincides with the paragraph in No. 1351 beginning, "Seneca says, 'Tis of very little consequence by what name you call the first nature'" and ending "it is by him that they live and breathe" (p. 470).

"The Latin poet Manilius extols Mercury as 'the first who taught men the knowledge of heaven and the stars, to display the beauty of the universe, and show how venerable the power who formed it, that the nations might feel how great that God must be who ranged heaven and its varying scenes in order, and gave nature all her force.' Elsewhere he describes the Deity as animating and over-ruling the whole world. 'This vast fabric of the world' (says he), 'and all the members of nature, so different in their figure—the air, the fire, the earth and the level sea—are ruled by the force of the divine mind. God breathes within them in a sacred way, and sways them by silent reason. To their numerous parts he gives different laws that, one part strengthening and supporting another, the whole universe may be allied by its different forms.' In another place he teaches the same truth: 'I will sing of God who presides over nature with a silent understanding, who is diffused through the heaven, the earth and sea, and who governs the vast universe by equal laws.' After this, he endeavors to prove that the beautiful and orderly appearances of nature, without the all-wise providence of the Deity, would soon be changed, and the universe immediately fall into the utmost confusion. [...]"

Maximus Tyrius (see back, p. 551):[7] "'If there were a meeting called of all the several trades and professions, a painter, a statuary, a poet and a philosopher: if all of them were required to declare their opinion about God, do you think that the painter would say one thing, the statuary another? [...] No, nor the Scythians neither, nor the Greeks, nor the Hyperboreans. In other things we find men speaking and thinking very discordantly to one another. Nevertheless, in this so great war, contention and discord, you may find everywhere throughout the whole world one uniform law and opinion that there is one God, the King and Father of all.'"

The following things are from Ramsay's *Principles,* vol. 2, beginning p. 44.

"Megasthenes, in his third book of the *Indian History,* writes thus, according to the testimony of Eusebius: 'All that was said of eternal nature by the ancient Greeks is also said by the philosophers or sages of other nations, as by the Brahmins of India and the people called the Jews in Syria.' The same Eusebius assures us from Numenius that 'the Brahmins, the Jews, the magi and the Egyptians had all the same notions of the

---

7. MS: "p. 945," referring back to the earlier passage on Maximus Tyrius.

supreme God.' Eusebius in the same place quotes this passage from Porphyry: 'The brazen way to the gods is steep and craggy. The barbarians found out many of its paths, but the Greeks wandered from them, and those who kept them spoiled them by their fictions. God discovered this brazen way to the Chaldeans, Assyrians and Hebrews, as also to the Egyptians, Phoenicans and Lydians.'

"In the *Vedam* we find the doctrine of one supreme God, superior to all, the author and governor of the universe. In the letters wrote by the Malabarians to the Danish missionaries, among many others we find the following passage: 'God alone rules the world and all that is therein; 'tis he alone that rules the 84,0000 kinds of living creatures, but because of his different and various appearances he has different names. Hence we say that Biruma creates, Wischtnu rules, Ischuren annihilates, all which different expressions denote but one supreme Being. And when we attribute the protection of towns and villages to tutelar gods, our meaning is that the great God does mediately protect towns and countries by his vicegerents and governors. For there is neither government nor the least motion in the world without the will of the first prime cause or supreme Being. Indeed there are many gods, but they of themselves cannot so much as move a straw out of its place without the assistance of the prime cause; therefore he is justly called the Lord of the world, for it is his power and excellent majesty that rules all things, and his power is infinite and incomprehensible.'

"In La Croze,[8] who had access to the original manuscripts of the same missionaries, we meet with this passage taken from one of the books of the Brahmins: 'The supreme Being is invisible, incomprehensible, immovable and without figure or outward form. No man hath seen him; time hath not comprehended him; his essence fills all things, and everything is derived from him. All power, all wisdom, all knowledge, all holiness and all truth dwell in him. He is infinitely good, just and merciful. He hath created all, he preserves all, and delights to dwell among men that he may conduct 'em to eternal happiness, a happiness which consists in loving and serving him.'

"In another treatise of the Brahmins entitled *Tchiva Vaikkium*,[9] the Deity is thus described: 'The Being of beings is the only God, eternal, immense, present in all places, who has neither end nor beginning, and

8. Ramsay cites "Histoire de Christianisme des Indes. Haye 1724. p. 452" (Maturin Veyssiïere La Croze [1661–1739], *Histoire du Christianisme des Indes* [La Haye, 1724]).

9. Ramsay cites "Idem. p. 457."

who comprehends all things. . . . There is no God but him. He alone is Lord of all things, and will be through all eternity. . . . O God! before I knew thee, I was in perpetual agitation; but since I knew thee, and have been recollected within myself, thou art all my desire.' La Croze assures us that these sublime ideas of the Deity are expressly contained in the Vedam, as appears from those passages of it communicated to Ziegenbalg[1] by the Brahmins themselves.

"The Jesuit missionaries give us pretty much the same account of the Indian religion with those of the Protestants. In an Indian book called *Panjangan,* the Divinity is thus addressed: 'I adore that Being that is subject to no change or disquiet; that Being whose nature is indivisible; that Being whose simplicity admits of no composition of qualities; that Being who is the origin and cause of all beings and who surpasses all in excellence; that Being who is the support of the universe and the source of triple power.'" (See p. 562.)[2]

"In Tabari, an ancient Persian historian, we meet with the following speech of Manugjahr, the King of Media, to his nobles: 'The most holy and high God gave me this kingdom to thank and praise him, to preserve the state, to study the happiness of my subjects and execute justice among my people. By these only shall God, the greatest and best of beings, aggrandize my throne. If I ungratefully neglect to thank and praise God, he will take my kingdom from me and punish me in the NEXT WORLD. Since, then, the high and holy God hath made me a king and given me a kingdom, I shall never destroy it.' The same king's second speech runs thus: 'O men, there is one Creator and governor of that numerous people you see. All the blessings of mankind flow from him; therefore we ought to serve him and thank him for his favors, and resign ourselves to his will. Whatever exists, must exist; and nothing is weaker than the creature, for when the creature seeks anything, it finds it not. Nothing is stronger than the Creator. I thank God who from his goodness gave me my kingdom, and implore he would guide me in the right way, and fortify my heart with truth. All things proceed from him, and must return to him again.'

"We find the same doctrine about the Deity in the speech of Lohrasp, King of Persia, to his people, as contained in Ahmed Ibn Jusuph, the Ara-

---

1. On Ziegenbalg, see below, p. 562, n. 4.
2. MS: "p. 875," a passage in No. 1351 at the paragraph beginning "In order to form a better judgment of the doctrine of the ancient Gymnosophists" and ending "Broma's virtue, gratitude, and fidelity gave him power to form the universe." See p. 478.

bian historian:[3] 'All you who are present, fear the almighty God, the most holy and glorious of all beings, who prepared channels for the sea, established the mountains, elevated the heavens and planted us on the spacious earth amidst the spheres.'

"We shall conclude with a passage taken from the introduction to a Persian book called *Sad-der*:[4] 'In the name of the Lord of divine essence and attributes, the Lord of abundance and the God of life: God who created the intellect and the mind, God who framed the body and the soul; the Lord of existence and the Lord of life, the only God of the whole world; God who of various elements made the revolving heaven and the fixed Earth. He hath beautified heaven with the embroidery of stars, and raised the orbs with nine stories. He planted the earth with the human race and illuminated it by the sun and moon. He made the world of substance and accidents, in which man was his chief care. Turn not away from rectitude and holiness, for there is nothing else in the RELIGION of the blessed.'"

Concerning what Mr. Ramsay observes from the Chinese, see No. 1181.

Concerning the TRINITY, see what Mr. Ramsay observes concerning this from the ancient Chinese books, No. 1181, and No. [1351], pp. 478–79.[5]

Concerning the Persians and other nations, he, in his *Principles of Religion*, [vol. 2,] observes as follows (p. 121).

"The Persian Mythras was commonly called threefold or triple, Τριπλασιος. Thus Dionysius the Pseudo-Areopagite says,[6] 'The Persian magi to this very day celebrate a festival solemnity in honor of the triplasian or threefold Mythras.' Plutarch adds[7] 'that Oromasdes thrice augmented or triplicated himself.' From whence it appears that Mythras or Oromazis were one and the same numen, or different names to express the two first hypostases of the divine essence. The third was called *Psyche* by the Greeks, who translated the Zoroastrian tradition. But Herodotus calls this hypostasis Mythra, and maintains it is the same with Urania. In a Chaldaic oracle quoted by Proclus, we read these words: '*Af-*

---

3. Ramsay cites "Idem. c. 8. p. 158."

4. Ramsay cites "Idem. c. 33. p. 396."

5. JE's original reference was to "this book, pp. 875–76," indicating the passage beginning "Being desirous of carrying on my researches as far as China" and ending "all manner of misery sent by heaven for the punishment thereof."

6. Ramsay: "See Cudworth intellect. system. ch. iv. pag. 288" (Cudworth, *The True Intellectual System of the Universe*).

7. "Plutarch. de Isid. et Osirid" (*De Iside et Osiride*).

ter the mind of the father, I psyche dwell. Now the mind of the Father, as Psellus informs us, "is the second God, the immediate artificer of the world."'

"In the same magical, Zoroastrian oracles we find these words: 'The Father or first Deity perfected all things, and delivered them to the second Mind, who is that whom the nations of men commonly take for the first.' Psellus glosses thus upon this oracle: 'The first Father of the triad, having produced the whole creation, delivered it to Mind or Intellect, which Mind the whole generation of mankind commonly call the first God, being ignorant of the paternal transcendency.' Psellus takes notice of the difference betwixt this Chaldaic theology and that of the Christians: 'The Christian doctrine,' says he, 'maintains that the first Mind or Intellect, being the Son of the great Father, made the whole creation; whereas, according to the Chaldaic theology, the first hypostasis of the divine triad was the immediate architect of the world.' He pretends that the Platonic doctrine was more conformed to that of the Christians when he says, 'The Father perfected, or produced freely in his divine understanding, the archetypal ideas, and then delivered them to the second God to create substances answerable to these models. Wherefore, whatsoever was produced by the second God, owes its original to the highest Father, according to its intelligible essence. Most of men take this second God for the first, looking up no higher than to the immediate architect of the world.'

"The same Proclus adds that 'the Chaldaic philosophy, divinely inspired, affirmeth the whole world to have been completed from these three: *Zeus,* or Jupiter, who is above the *Demiurgus* or Creator of the world, and *Psyche,* who is under this Mind or Intellect of the Father.' To those testimonies of Proclus may be superadded a Chaldean or Persian oracle quoted from Damascius by Patritius: 'In the whole world shineth forth a triad or trinity, which is a perfect monad or unity.'

"Thus what the Chinese called Hi, Yi and Ouei, the Persians named Oromazdes, Mythras and Mythra. The Chaldeans also had three names, which the Greeks translated by Zeus, or Life; Demiurgus, or Intellect; Psyche, or the animator of all things. [. . .]

"It is certain these Chaldaic oracles are not so modern as some would suspect, they being quoted by Synesius, Psellus, Pletho Porphyrius [. . .] and Suidas, which last says that 'Julianus a Chaldean, in the time of Marcus Antoninus the Emperor, compiled and wrote the Theurgic and Telestic oracles in Greek verse.' They are called Theurgic and Telestic because they contained a divine doctrine that[8] served to render the mind

8. JE: "and."

perfect. Now, that they were not forged by the Christians, as some of the Sibylline oracles were, seems probable from hence, that so many pagan philosophers make us of their testimony, and lay no small stress upon them. [. . .]

"In these accounts of the Zoroastrian and Chaldean theology, we find the following expression: 'The paternal monad, multiplying itself, engendered two. This duality sits by him and shines in all the intellectual tribes. This triad, of which unity is the principle, manifests itself through the whole universe. In this subsist force, wisdom and omniscient truth, which composed the link of the triad long before the existence of any measurable essence, whence multiplicity was produced. The Father perfected all things, and gave them to the second Mind, who unites them all by love, and by this Love all things subsist and persist forever.'

"These expressions don't resemble the style of the Christian fathers, neither before nor after the Council of Nicea. The ideas are the same, but the turn is quite different."

Concerning the Egyptians:

"In the Pamphylian obelisk, the Deity is represented by this symbol, a winged globe with a serpent coming out of it. In a Chaldaic fragment imputed to Sanchoniathon, we find this explanation of that hieroglyphic: 'The globe signifies the first, self-existent, incomprehensible Deity without beginning or end; the serpent, the divine wisdom and creative power; and the wings signify that active spirit that cherisheth and enliveneth all things.' The pyramidal obelisks of Egypt, with three different faces placed before the temples, was, according to the pagan philosophers, a symbol of the Deity, not only among the Egyptians but also among the Amazons and many other people of the east. A Brahmin of India, according to Father Bouchet, explained this symbol in the same sense as the ancients: 'We must, said that Brahmin, believe God and his three [different] names, which answer to his three principal attributes, to be represented in some sense by these triangular pyramids erected at the entry of our temples.'

"Whatever be in this, it is certain that Iamblichus gives us this account of the Egyptian theology: 'Hermes places the God *Emeph* as the prince and ruler over all the celestial gods, the *demiurgic Mind* and president of truth which produced all things with wisdom. Before Emeph, however, Hermes places one indivisible monad called Eicton, in whom exist the first intelligent and the first intelligible, and who can be adored only by silence. After which two, *Eicton* and *Emeph*, he places *Ptha*, which is a spirit that animates all things by his vivifying flame.'

"Eusebius informs us from Porphyry that the Egyptians acknowledged 'one intellectual demiurgus or maker of the world, . . . and that from this Emeph was said to be generated another god, whom the Egyptians called *Ptha*.' St. Cyril quotes several passages out of the Hermaic writings extant in his time to prove that there was a first and supreme God superior to the demiurgic Mind: 'The demiurgic Word or Logos is the first power after the supreme Lord. He looks out from him, is increated, infinite and the genuine Son of the first omnipresent Essence.' Conformed to this passage of St. Cyril's, Iamblichus, in speaking of the mysteries of the Egyptians, says, 'Before finite beings and universal causes there is one God who is ever prior to the universal[9] King. He remains immovable in the solitude of his own unity. No ideas of finite are mixed with him, nor anything else.' [. . .] Porphyry continues thus: 'He is seated as the exemplar of the second God, for there is something greater and first, the fountain of all and the root of all intelligible ideas. From this one the second God shone forth. This one is self-begotten, the God of gods, the superessential monad and first principle of all beings. These two are the most ancient principles of all, whom Hermes places before the ethereal, empyreal and celestial gods.'

"Here then is a full acknowledgment of the two first hypostases of the divine nature, and if we join this passage with those quoted above from Porphyry and the same Iamblichus, we have the Ptha, or the third hypostasis, and so a full declaration of the Hermaic trinity.

"Thus the Egyptians called Eicton, Emeph and Ptha what the Persians called Oromasdes, Mythras and Mythra; the Chaldeans Life, Intellect and Soul; the Chinese Hi, Yi, Ouei. [. . .][1] These three hypostases, Eicton, Emeph and Ptha, the Egyptians, according to the testimony of Damascius, 'looked upon as one essence, incomprehensible, above all knowledge, and praised him under the name of the 'unknown darkness thrice repeated.'" As it was the custom of the Jews to repeat thrice the great name of Jehovah in all their public worship, doxologies and thanksgivings.

Concerning the Greeks (see back, pp. 463–70):[2]

"Justin Martyr, in his exhortation to the Greeks, has preserved to us this wonderful fragment of Orpheus, where the poet speaks thus of the Logos: 'I swear by the Word of the Father, which went out of his mouth

---

9. Ramsay (p. 129) reads "first."

1. Ramsay (p. 130) adds: "the Hebrews Ab, El and Ruach."

2. MS: "p. 864. &c." JE refers to the opening pages of No. 1351, from the very beginning of the entry through the consideration of Seneca at the passage ending, "it is by him that they live and breath."

and became his counselor when he created the world.' Compare this with Prov. 8:22, 27, 29. [...]

"Timotheus says that 'Orpheus declared that all things were made by the same Godhead under three names, called Uranus, Chronus and Phanes.' Phanes, according to Father Kircher, is an Egyptian name that signifies *Love*, and accordingly Proclus, in commenting upon Plato's *Timæus*, calls *Phanes* 'αζρος Ερος, soft and tender Love,' which is the personal character of the third hypostasis. Conform to this, Proclus assures us that Amelius the Platonic, who was contemporary with Plotinus, makes a 'threefold demiurgus, or Creator of the world, three minds and three kings: him that *is*, him that *has* and him that *beholds;* which three minds differ thus: the first is essentially he that is; the second possesses in himself intelligence but receives all from the first, and so is the second; the third possesses also in himself intelligence but hath what is in the second and looks up to the first, for all these three are the same essence with their conjoined intelligibles.' Amelius therefore supposes 'those three minds and demiurgic principles to be the same with Plato's three kings and Orpheus' trinity.' Damascius also, in his book of *Principles,* assures us that Orpheus maintained *a triform Deity.* [...] Considering these things, no wonder if Timotheus, who was a Christian, affirmed that 'Orpheus long ago had declared that all things were made by a co-essential triad.' [...]

"It was a great maxim of the Pythagoric philosophy, 'God is a monad from whom proceeds an infinite duality.' [...] Moderatus, in a fragment preserved to us by Simplicius, says, 'According to the Pythagoreans, the first one, monad or unity, is above all essence; the second contains all ideas; and the third, which [is] Psyche or soul, partaketh of both, of the first unity and of the ideas.' Numenius, according to Proclus, says 'that the Pythagoreans, having praised the three Gods, called them the Grandfather, the Son and the Grandson, thereby intimating that as the second was the offspring of the first, so the third proceeds from the second.' Iamblichus adds, according to the testimony of Proclus, 'that there were three Gods also praised by the Pythagoreans.' [...]"

PLATO. "Though he speaks in the plural, as Moses and the Hebrews, of the divine essence, yet he restrains this plurality to three, which he calls AGATHON or EN, NOUS or LOGOS, PSYCHE or EROS; that is, the supreme Good or Unity, the Mind or Word, the Soul or Love. The substance of all his doctrine concerning this triad may be reduced to the three following heads or principles:

"1. Plato did not understand by those three distinctions in the God-

head, three simple attributes, names, modes or forms of the Diety, for
he calls them not only three principles, three causes, three agents, three
kings, but also three Gods, the first, the second and the third, which subsist and act in the divine essence as if they were three distinct substances,
though, as we shall see, he believed them to be one monad. Hence Plotinus, one of Plato's principal disciples, who lived in the third century of
the Christian era, calls this triplicity in the divine nature, 'three hypostases.'

"2. Though Plato and his disciples called these three divine hypostases
not only three natures but also three Gods, yet it is sure that they always
supposed these three to be only one Deity or essence, This appears evidently from Plato's second epistle to Dionysius, where he maintains that
these three hypostases in the divine nature are co-eternal, consubstantial and uncreated. [. . .]

"3. The three distinctions of the Platonic trinity are not only all co-
eternal but also necessarily existent, and no ways free productions of the
divine will; for the first of them, say the genuine Platonists, can no more
exist without the second than original light can exist without its splendor. Yea, there can neither be more of them, nor fewer. [. . .]³

"According to the Danish missionaries,⁴ the Gods of the Malabarian
trinity in INDIA are Biruma, Wischtnu, and Ruddiren or Isuren. Wischtnu
is described by those Brahmins as a protector and deliverer who came
nine times into this world to redeem men from destruction and restore
them again to purity. In the first of the thirty-four conferences between
the same missionaries and the Malabarian Brahmins, translated out of
high Dutch by Phillips, we find the same triad of divinities. There, the
second of them, Wischtnu, is said to have been born a man among the
Malabarians to save 'em, and has at different times undergone a vast variety of metamorphoses. Henry Lord, in his history of the sect of the Ban-
ians,⁵ gathered from their Brahmins as contained in the book of their
law called the Shaster, mentions their trinity under the names of Bremaw, Vystney and Ruddery; and speaks of several manifestations of the

3. JE leaves off copying at p. 137 in the chapter "Of the Sacred Trinity," and resumes at
p. 186, in "The Three Manifestations of the Middle God."
4. Ramsay cites "An account of the religion of the Malabarians, in several letters from the
most learned Indians to the Danish missionaries" (Bartholomaeus Ziegenbalg [1683–1719],
*Propagation of the gospel in the East: being an account of the success of two Danish missionaries, lately
sent to the East-Indies, for the conversion of the heathens in Malabar,* trans. Phillips [London, 1717]).
5. Henry Lord (b. 1563), *A display of two forraigne sects in the East Indies vizt: the sect of the Ba-
nians the ancient natiues of India and the sect of the Persees the ancient inhabitants of Persia together with
the religion and maners of each sect* (London, 1630).

Vystney to preserve, support and exalt souls to happiness. When we consult the missionaries of the Roman church,[6] we meet with the same truths: 'The Indians have a sacrifice called Ekiam (it is the most celebrated of all those in India); they sacrifice a sheep and repeat a kind of prayer with a loud voice, in these words: *"When shall the Savior be born? when shall the Redeemer appear?"'* At the same time that the Brahmins teach the doctrine of the trinity, they still maintain the existence of one supreme Being, as appears by other accounts in the same collection of accounts of the Jesuits: 'The three principal Gods of the Indians are Bruma, Vichnou and Routren. The greater part of the Gentiles say they are three different divinities, and in reality separated. But many of the Nianiguculs, or spiritual men, assure us that these three Gods, different in appearance, are really nothing but one God. When this God creates and exerts his omnipotence, he is called Bruma; when he preserves created beings and gives proofs of his goodness, he is called Vichnou; and lastly, when he destroy cities, chastises the guilty and makes them feel the effects of his just resentment, he takes the name of Routren.' They tell us that one of these Gods frequently made his appearance on the earth. 'All the Indians agree that God was incarnate many times, and most of them ascribe these incarnations to Vichnou, the second God of their trinity. According to them this God was never incarnate, but in quality of the Savior and preserver of men, [...] in different forms, and sometimes under the figure of a man.' This God is also represented by 'em as their teacher and instructor. [...] 'Elsewhere the same Vichnou is called God the preserver of all beings.' We find the following remarkable passage in an Indian book called Bartachastram: 'At the end of Caliougam, a Brahmin called Vichnou shall be born in the city Shambelam. He shall understand the divine writings and all the sciences without spending any more time to learn them than is sufficient to pronounce one single word. Therefore they shall give him the name of *Sarva Baoumoudou* ("he who excellently understands all things"). This Brahmin Vichnou, by conversing with those of his own race, shall purge the earth of sinners, a thing impossible to any other but himself. He shall make justice and truth to reign in it, offer sacrifice, and subject the universe to the Brahmins. When he arrives at old age, he shall retire into the desert to suffer penance. This is the order Vichnou shall establish among men. He shall confirm the Brahmins in virtue and truth, and keep the four tribes within

6. Ramsay cites *Lettres edifiantes et curieuses, ecrites des missions etrangeres, par quelques missionaires de la compagnie de Jesus* (Paris, 1730).

the bounds of their laws; and then we shall see the first age appear again. That supreme King shall render sacrifice so common among all nations, that the very deserts shall not be deprived of it. The Brahmins, confirmed in goodness, shall only employ themselves in the ceremonies of religion and sacrifices. Mortification shall flourish among them; all the other virtues shall march in the train of truth, and the light of the divine writings shall be diffused everywhere. The seasons shall succeed one another in invariable order, and the rains, in their proper time, deluge the plains. Autumn in its turn shall furnish great plenty. Milk shall flow down in abundance to those who receive it. The earth, as in the first age, shall be inebriated with gladness and prosperity, and all people shall enjoy ineffable delights.' The same doctrine is confirmed to us by Herbelot in his *Bibliotheque Orientale:*[7] 'Beschen,' says he, 'is the second of all beings, whom God created before the world, according to the doctrine of the Indian Brahmins. He is that Being whose name signifies "existing in all things," who preserves the world in its present state. He is the Being who was several times incarnate. In his first incarnation he assumed the body of a lion; in his second he entered into that of a man; and in the tenth, which must be the last, he shall appear like a warrior to destroy all religions contrary to that of the Brahmins. The Christians, and particularly the missionaries who have got some knowledge of the Indian religion, affirm that this Beschen is the second person of the adorable trinity, and that the Brahmins ascribe to him qualities in same measure applicable to our Savior Jesus Christ.' From all these accounts it appears evident that Wischtnu, Vystney, Vichnou and Beschen are all one and the same God manifested on different occasions for the interest of mankind. [. . .][8]

"The Egyptians represent [Osiris] as the Son of the supreme God, to whom he gave the government of the worlds long before the origin of Typhon, or the evil principle. During the happy reign of Osiris, all is said to be full of peace, joy, righteousness and felicity, exempt from all moral and physical evil. [. . .]

"During the reign of Osiris, the Egyptian tradition says that Typhon revolted against his empire, tore the body of the God in pieces, mangled his limbs, scattered them about the world, and filled the universe with

7. Barthóelemy d'Herbelot (1625–1695), *Bibliothèque orientale: ou Dictionnaire universel, contenant généralement tout ce qui regarde la connoissance des peuples de l'Orient. Leurs histoires et traditions . . . leurs religions, sectes et politique . . . les vies . . . de tous leurs saints, docteurs, philosophes . . .* (Paris, 1697).

8. JE skips from p. 190 to p. 195, leaving out an account of the Persians on the middle God.

rage and violence. The death of Osiris was annually mourned in Egypt for many days, and afterwards great festivals were celebrated with joy for his resurrection. [. . .] The God Osiris is very often represented with a cross in his hand. 'This sacred symbol' (says Father Lafittau in his *Manners of the American Savages*) 'was common in all pagan religions, but especially among the Egyptians. It was engraved upon all their monuments and obelisks; we see it in the hands of Osiris, Isis and Orus, hung about the necks of the god Apis and Jupiter Ammon. It is found also in the Thyrsus of Bacchus, about the neck of Vestals, upon the sacred vessels, and the cymbals of the Corybantes. It was also a sacred symbol among the Phoenicians, and the goddess of Syria is represented as holding it in her hand, or upon her shoulder. Among the Chinese and American hieroglyphics, this sign is a symbol of perfection, and also amongst the Tartars. Their Lama, or high priest, wears this sacred symbol; and his name, Lama, in the language of Tartary, signifies a cross.' These ancient customs of nations seem to come from the primitive traditions of the first men, that the cross was to be the means of salvation to mankind and of felicity without end. Hence Socrates, Sozomen, Suidas and Ruffinus, who understood the hieroglyphical language, maintain that the cross was a symbol of immortality. [. . .]

"Justin Martyr, in writing to the Emperor Antoninus Pius and the senate, expressly teaches 'that all the fables made of, and all the wonders attributed to, Mercury, Bacchus, Hercules, Perseus, Esculapius, [and] Bellerophon, were only disguises of ancient traditions concerning the Messiah.' Horace and Virgil speak of Apollo, the son of Jupiter, as he that was to restore the world to its primitive innocence. And Mars was but another name of the middle God humanized. . . .

"Apollo, according to Plutarch, was looked upon by all the Greeks as the same with the sun. [. . .] As the Messiah was called by the Hebrews, 'the Sun of righteousness, the light of the world.' . . . He is said to have been banished from heaven and to have lived for many years upon earth as a shepherd, where he kept the flocks of Admetus or Adametus, which may be derived from the Hebrew word *Adamah,* that signifies human nature; . . . during his exile he is said to fall in love with Daphne, which may be derived from Daphen—*opprobrium, infamia, degradatio, corruptio*— and so signify degraded intelligences, with whom he is enamored. . . . Horace seems to have had in view this ancient Tradition of a divine person that was to come down from heaven, when he says, 'Divine Apollo, to whom the great Jupiter has given the function of expiating the sins of the world, come at last, we beg of thee, surrounded with clouds. Alas!

wars and slaughter have too long desolated the earth.' Virgil had the same ideas of a divine Apollo, who was to come down from heaven to restore the world to its primitive perfection and happiness: 'The last age sung by the Cumean sybil is come; the great revolution or re-establishment is at hand. Justice is going to return upon the earth, and the happy reign of Saturn is to be restored. A divine child is to descend from heaven. So soon as he is born, the iron age will cease and the golden age will be renewed all over the earth. Be favorable to him, divine Urania, that so thy Apollo may reign everywhere. Under his empire, all remains of vice shall be destroyed, and the earth be delivered from all fear and remorses. He will partake of the divine life, see the heroes associated with the gods; and they shall see him governing the world in peace, by his Father's virtue. Then the earth shall produce all things of its own accord; all wars shall cease, and everything be restored to its primitive felicity. Beloved offspring of the gods, great son of Jupiter, see how the earth, the seas, the heavens and the whole universe rejoice at thy coming.'"

As to what Mr. Ramsay observes of the tradition of the Chinese concerning the Messiah, and also concerning the paradisaic state and the fall of man and angels, see "Miscellanies," No. 1181.[9]

"Strabo says that Onesicritus, being sent by Alexander the Great to inform himself of the life, manners and doctrine of the BRAHMINS or Gymnosophists, found a Brahmin named Calanus, who taught him that in the first origin of the world, plenty reigned over nature. Milk, wine, honey and oil flowed from fountains; but men having made an ill use of this felicity, Jupiter deprived them of it and condemned them to labor for the sustenance of their lives.[. . .][1]

"The Egyptians" (according to Plutarch, *De Iside et Osiride*) "talk of the pre-existent state, as the reign of the gods and demi-gods, when all were happy. Afterwards, Typhon revolted against Osiris, tore his body in pieces, mangled his limbs, scattered them about, [and] filled the universe with rage and violence. [. . .] The eternal and immortal soul of Osiris led his son Orus to the shades below, to the Hades, where he taught him how to fight and vanquish Typhon. Orus returned upon the earth, fought and defeated Typhon, but he did not kill him; he only bound him and took away his power of doing mischief. The wicked one made his escape afterwards, and was going to throw all again into disorder. [. . .]

9. JE skips from p. 204 to p. 279, in ch. IV, "Of the Three States of Human Nature Degraded."
1. JE skips from p. 280 to p. 358, in ch. V, "Of the Three States of Angelical Nature."

But Orus fought him in two bloody battles and destroyed him entirely. [. . .]²

"Strabo says the Gymnosophists 'imagine this present life the infancy as it were of our being, and that death is an entry into a truly happy life for those who philosophize.' [. . .]

"Porphyry says, concerning the same, 'that such are their views of death, that with reluctance they endure life as a piece of necessary bondage to nature, and haste to set the soul at liberty from the body. Nay often, when in good health and no evil to disturb 'em, they depart life, advertising it beforehand. No man hinders them, but all reckon them happy, and send commissions along with them to their dead friends. So strong and firm is their belief of a future life for the soul, where they shall enjoy one another. After receiving all their commands, they deliver themselves to the fire, that they may separate the soul as pure as possible from the body, and expire singing hymns. Their old friends attend them to death with more [ease] than other men their fellow citizens to a long journey. They deplore their own state for surviving them, and deem them happy in their immortality.' [. . .]

"Pletho, in his commentary, says, 'The magi, Zoroaster's followers, with many others believe the immortality of the human soul.' [. . .]"³

"Heraclitus, who lived near 500 years before the Christian era, speaks thus: [. . .] 'This body shall be fatally changed, but my soul shall not die nor perish; but being an immortal thing, shall fly away, mounting upwards to heaven. These ethereal houses shall receive me, and I shall no longer converse with men but gods.'"

Ramsay's *Principles,* [vol. 2,] pp. 429 ff.:

"We find the following account of the sentiments of the Egyptians in Iamblichus: 'Illumination by prayer discovers itself and operates of its own accord without any constraint; it manifests itself by a divine energy and perfection, and as far excels the voluntary motions of our will as the divine desire of the supreme good surpasses a life of choice. By this desire the gods plentifully dart forth their light, are benevolent and propitious to their votaries, recall their souls to themselves, [. . .] accustom them even while in the body to forsake the body, and lead them around their eternal and intelligible source. In the contemplation of blessed vi-

---

2. JE goes from p. 358 to p. 411, in ch. VI, "Of the Three Internal, Essential, and Universal Means of Re-Union, Known to Men of All Ages, Nations and Religions."

3. JE turns from p. 419 to p. 438, skipping over the Persians and Turks and going directly to the Greeks. With the following quote, he retraces his steps to include the Egyptians.

sions, the soul assumes another life, operates in another manner and justly esteems itself no longer man. It often exchanges its own life for the most blessed operation of the gods. For the gods are immediately present with and united to all those who make the least approaches to them. It is impossible to discourse of the gods without their aid; much less can we perform divine works without them. The human race is mean and weak, sees but a small way, [and] is naturally possessed of nothingness. There is but one remedy for its inherent error, confusion and inconstancy: to admit as much of the divine light as possible. He who shuts out this, acts the same part with those who produce a *soul* from *inanimate* objects or create *intellect* from things void of understanding: for without a cause he produces divine works from things not divine.[4] God is all, can do all, hath filled all with himself, and he is alone worthy of regard, dignity, praise and divine honor. Human nature is deformed, of no account, and a mere trifle when compared with the Divinity. Man contemplative and intelligent, when formerly united to the vision of the gods, became another soul fitted to the human shape, and thus fell under the chains of fate and necessity. We must consider what way we can set ourselves at liberty from these chains. There is none other but by the knowledge of the gods. The idea of happiness is the knowledge of what is good, as the idea of evil is the forgetfulness of good things. The one is the knowledge of the Father; [the other] is a departure from him and a forgetfulness of the super-essential, self-sufficient Father God. The one preserves true life, leading back to the Father of it; the other leads men downwards to instability and a perpetual flux. The sacred and divine gift of happiness is called the gate to the CREATOR of the universe, the court and residence of the supreme good. By its power it first gives a degree of sanctity to the soul much more perfect than that in the body; and then disposes the intellect for the participation and vision of the supreme good, and frees it from everything contrary to it, and unites us to the gods, the givers of all good. After it has united the soul to particular parts of the universe and to the universal divine powers diffused through it, then it introduceth her to and placeth her in the universal CREATOR, sets her free of all matter and unites her to the eternal LOGOS alone. It unites the soul to the self-begotten, self-moved, all-sustaining, intellectual, universally adorning, elevating to intelligible truth, self-perfect, the forming and other creating powers of God; so that the soul is perfectly fixed in their operations, contemplations and creating powers. At last, it places the soul in

4. JE's italics.

the universally CREATING GOD. This is the end of the sacred Egyptian re-ligion.'[5] [. . .]

"St. Justin has preserved to us this fragment of Orpheus: 'Respect the divine Word, adhere to him continually. Adore this God and sovereign of the world.' [. . .]

"Hierocles, who gives us an abridgment in his *Golden Verses* not only of the Pythagoric but of the Chaldaic and the oriental philosophy, speaks thus: 'Philosophy is the purification and perfection of the human life. It is purification from sensual folly and the mortal body. It is perfection, because it restores the soul to its primitive happiness by leading it back to the divine image. These are best accomplished by virtue and truth, the one banishing the excess of passions, the other procuring the divine image to those who are candidly disposed to receive it. We must first be-come men and then gods. The civil virtues render a man good, but the knowledge that leads up to the divine virtue divinizes him. The death of a rational being is its ignorance of and absence from God, which are at-tended with an unbounded insurrection of the passions. When we are ignorant of what is good, we become necessarily slaves to what is bad; and it is impossible to free ourselves from them otherwise than by con-verting ourselves to the pure spirit and to God by recollection. Here is continual necessity of divine grace and of spiritual, mental prayer. [. . .] Thou canst not honor God by giving anything to him, but by becoming worthy to receive from him; for, as the Pythagoreans say, thou wilt honor God best if thou resemble him in the mind. Whoever honors God as a Being that needs anything from him, forgets that by this he fancies him-self superior to the Deity. The expense of offerings is no honor to God, unless they are offered with divine sentiments. The gifts and sacrifices of the foolish are but fuel for the fire, and their consecrations an occasion of sacrilege; but the divine inspirations, when sufficiently attended to, unite us to God: for what is like must necessarily tend to its like. Hence, the wise man alone is called the priest and the beloved of God, who alone knows how to pray; for he alone knows how to honor, who first of all of-fers himself a sacrifice, forms his soul an image of the Deity and prepares his intellect for the reception of the divine light. . . . God has not upon earth a more proper habitation than a pure soul; and Apollo says, "I re-joice in pious mortals as much as in heaven." The same Apollo said of old to one that sacrificed hecatombs but not with a pious mind, and who asked the god how he had accepted his gifts, "The barley cake of the fa-

---

5. The capitals in this paragraph are JE's.

mous Hermion was more acceptable to me," to show that he preferred
the meanest offering to all this profusion, because it was not adorned
with a pious mind. With this, all things are acceptable to God, and without it nothing can please him. That man is truly pious who, with divine
science, offers his own perfection as the best worship to the cause of all
good.' [. . .] Hierocles says, 'To consider all things as they lie in God the
CREATOR leads us to the summit of divine science, which is always accompanied with a resemblance of God.' Hierocles afterwards shows that
all these virtues cannot be practiced nor produced by our own efforts
and activity, for he adds, 'Though the choice of virtue is in our own
power, yet since we have this very power of choosing from God, we absolutely need from him a cooperation and accomplishment of our desires. Our own endeavors resemble a hand stretched out for the reception of virtue. What is done by God in us resembles the action of him
that gives; it is our part to receive and search after what is beautiful, and
God's to discover to the right inquirer. Now, prayer is the medium between our receiving and God's giving; for thus we adhere to the cause
which gives both being and well-being. How can one receive happiness
unless God give it? And can a God, whose nature is bounty, give it to one
who has his desires in his own power and yet asks not? That we may not
make our prayer by the mouth only, but strengthen it by action, let us
not confide in our own activity alone; but by action pray for the cooperation of God, and adapt prayer to action, as the form to the substance.
The simple knowledge of what is beautiful is not capable to set us right
without the operation of God. We ought not to satisfy ourselves with the
bare words of prayer, without adding something to procure what we desire. Otherwise, we shall either pursue a virtue without God, or a prayer
without works. The one of these, as it is without God, DESTROYS THE
ESSENCE OF VIRTUE; the other, as it is indolent, takes off the activity of
prayer. For how can anything be beautiful that is not done according to
the DIVINE LAW? And how is it possible for that which is done according
to this law not to want God's ASSISTANCE? For virtue is the IMAGE OF GOD
IN THE RATIONAL SOUL. Now, every image wants the exemplar for its PRO-
DUCTION; and we cannot acquire this image unless we look to that object, by resembling of which we shall acquire the beautiful. Those that
aspire after virtue should pray, and when they pray be active to obtain
what they pray for. They should do this by looking to what is godlike and
shining, and vigorously pursue wisdom, at the same time adhering to the
first cause of all good. . . . The end of the Pythagorean discipline is to be
all over wings for the reception of the divine good, that when the time

of death comes we may leave behind us upon earth the mortal body, and, putting off its nature, become champions in the combats of wisdom, ready girt for our heavenly journey. Then we are restored to our primitive state and deified as far as it is possible for men to become gods. This, says Plato, is the great combat, the great hope, the most perfect fruit of philosophy. . . . Having at last become what these heroes always [were], who never fall into CORRUPTION.'"6

There is much more to the like purpose. To the like purpose says Heraclitus, who lived near 500 years before Christ (as Ramsay observes),7 concerning the future state, immortality of the soul and the nature of the blessed state in another world.

"Cleanthes, a philosophical poet, says thus: 'Hail! great king and father of gods, who hast many names but art one, sole, omnipotent virtue, Jupiter, AUTHOR of nature, who GOVERNEST all by thy wisdom. Allow all mortals to call upon thee [. . .] and exalt thy power without end. Thou DIRECTEST ALL by an unerring LAW, and so collectest into one all good, though now mixed with evil, that from thence will result at last an eternal and universal order. Ah! how miserable are we to be ignorant of this universal law, which, if we obeyed it, would make us live a good and happy life, and hinder us from being precipitated into all sorts of crimes and passions? O Jupiter, GIVE us wisdom and take away the foolish mind from unhappy mortals, that so they may sing thy praises; for no greater gift can be bestowed on mortals nor immortals than to sing thy immutable, universal law with eternal hymns.' [. . .]8

"Plato, in his *Eutiphron,* defines holiness: 'That continual commerce between God and the soul by which it asks and renders to God all it receives from him—life, reason, virtue and all hood things—retains nothing for itself, but restores all to the sovereign owner.' In his *Philebus,* he places the sovereign good in a resemblance to the divine nature, which can flow from God alone. 'As nothing is like the sun but by solar influences, so nothing can resemble God but by an emanation of the divine light into the soul.' In the *Hippias,* he shows 'that the supreme beauty [consists] in his resemblance to the divine sun, or light of all intelligences.' In his *Feast,* he maintains 'that the supreme beauty ought to be loved for itself, that is the source and center of all beauty, the CREATOR, the MASTER and CONSERVATOR of all things; that it has no perfect simil-

6. The capitals in this paragraph are JE's.
7. *Philosophical Principles,* 2, 438.
8. The capitals in this paragraph are JE's.

itude with anything we behold upon earth or in the heavens; that whatever else is beautiful is only so by participation of its beauty; that all other beauties may increase, decay, change or perish, but this is still the same in all times and in all places; that it is by carrying our thoughts beyond all inferior beauties that we at length reach to that supreme beauty, which is simple, pure, uniform, immutable, without color, figure or human qualities. And in fine, that this sovereign beauty is incorporeal, the splendor of the divine image, and God himself.'"

Many other such things are cited from Plato, particularly showing the disinterestedness of a truly virtuous and divine love, about p. 444 of vol. 2.[9] Many things are also in the following pages quoted from Epictetus that speak of God as the universal Creator, orderer and governor of the world, of his moral government, and dependence on his assistance in order to be virtuous.

"Antoninus Philosophus[1] says, 'I owe to the gods all those good examples and instructions, yea, all the good things I have received: a good father, a good mother, good preceptors, good friends, and good servants, and especially to have given me the grace never to offend nor disoblige them; though I have been sometimes in certain dispositions to have done so, if the occasion had presented itself, but by the particular bounty of the gods, such occasions never offered.' [. . .]

"In the second book[2] the same Emperor says, 'Everything that comes from the gods carries with it the works of a providence. What some impute to hazards and fortune proceeds from the order of eternal nature, or from the chain of causes that providence overrules.' [. . .]

"In the third book he says, [. . .] 'It is the propitious Deity that renders a man unvanquished by pleasure, invulnerable by grief, insensible to injuries and violence, inaccessible to vice and all irregular desires. It is this Deity that makes him a valiant hero in the greatest of all combats, so as never to be overcome by any of his passions, and that gives him true righteousness, by which he is entirely penetrated. It is that indwelling God that makes him receive with pleasure whatever happens to him by the orders of providence, that occupies him entirely, that leaves him no time to think of what others think, say or do, unless it be when public interest or pressing necessity require it.'"

9. On p. 444, for example, Ramsay writes: "Thus, according to Plato, what makes man a God, is to prefer others to himself, even to forget himself, sacrifice himself, and count himself as nothing."

1. I.e. Marcus Antoninus.

2. I.e. of the Emperor's *Meditations*.

Many other things are there cited from Marcus Antoninus, pp. 450–51, concerning providence, etc.

"In the fifth book he says, [. . .] 'Men are little snarling dogs one to another, sometimes laughing and sometimes weeping. Fidelity, modesty, justice and truth are gone from the wide-traveled earth to heaven. When then can detain thee longer here below . . . ? What do you wait for in tranquillity? for extinction or transplantation? What ought to suffice, till that time come, is to worship the gods, do good to men, bear and forbear them, and remember that whatever is without this little body and soul is not thy own.' In another place in the same book he says, 'So soon as the soul gets free from the body and this earthly abode, it passes as it were from a Cimmerian darkness to the clear ether, free from desires, free from diseases, free from misfortunes; [. . .] lives with the gods and the children of the gods above the highest summit of heaven and, ranked among the army of the gods, it traverses the universe under Jove, their leader and general.' [. . .]

"In his sixth book he says, 'Let all thy joy and peace consist in this alone: in passing from one good action to another, in remembering and thinking of God present everywhere. . . . If the world be a confused heap of parts that tend to disunion, why desire to stay in it? If all be governed by providence with order and union, I adore the AUTHOR of my being,[3] I wait upon him with a firm assurance, and I place all my confidence in him. Call upon God in all thy actions.' [. . .]

"In the tenth book: 'If a man despises me, it is his business to see why he does so; mine is to take care to do nothing that deserves contempt. If he hates me, it is his affair; for me, I will have the same goodness and benevolence for human nature in general, and for this man in particular: and I will always be ready to show to him his faults without any reproaches, nor showing any ostentation of patience, but with sincerity and charity, as Phocion. This virtue must come from God, who sees the inmost center of men and tries their hearts, and who knows that the truly good man is offended with nothing and complains of nothing.' [. . .]

"Proclus, a heathen philosopher who lived after the Christian era, says thus: 'Prayer properly belongs to good men because it is an union to the Divinity. Like loves to be united to like, and a good man must resemble the gods. Those who adhere to virtue are confined to the body. They should therefore continually beg the gods for transportation; as children

3. JE's capitals.

torn from the bosom of tender parents, they ought to pray for a return to their fathers, the gods. The wise men in all nations exercised themselves unto prayer—the Brahmins among the Indians, the magi among the Persians, and the greatest divines among the Greeks. As we are a part of the universe, we ought to pray to the CAUSE of the universe. A conversion to the whole is the safety of every particular being. If thou hast virtue, thou must invoke him that hath universal virtue. Prayer is the conversion of the mind to the eternal Logos. It joins the spirit of the gods to the soul of those that pray. First of all, a KNOWLEDGE of the divine powers must precede a true and perfect prayer; for we cannot truly approach them when we are ignorant of their perfections. Therefore the oracle ordered "that penetrating thought should have the first place in divine worship." The second next to this is a resemblance to the Divinity in all manner of purity, chastity and order. The third is UNION, by which we touch, so to speak, the divine essence with the summit of the soul. This union with the supreme unity fixes the soul in God and renders our operation the same as his. By this, we are no longer our own, but God's. We continue in the divine light and are surrounded by it. The end of true prayer is to join conversion with perseverance, replace everything in the supreme unity that is gone out from it, and join our light to the light of the gods. He that would study prayer in a genuine manner must awaken in himself just notions of the gods and practice the virtues that purify from corruption, such as faith, hope truth, love, the constant reception of divine light and a freedom from all other pursuits, that we may converse alone with God. Should one attempt to UNITE himself to the supreme unity by multiplicity, he would be frustrated in his design and separate himself from the gods. As it is impossible for that which is to converse with that which is not, so it is impossible for us to be UNITED to unity by multiplicity. Nothing imperfect can be UNITED to the all-perfect. . . . This is the true DISCOVERY of him, to be united to him, to CONVERSE with him alone, and abstract from all other considerations on his account. When the soul CONVERSES thus with God, it is feasted with the truth of what truly is. And this is the supreme REWARD of souls after their EGRESS, departure and detachment from all that is animal. The Mind, the LOGOS, the God-guide lands them in the FATHER and fixes them untainted in the CREATING principle, JOINS light to [light], not that of a science but a KNOWLEDGE far more beautiful, intellectual and uniform. It is impossible for souls that thus FIND OUT GOD to describe him to others, for he is not found out by reason but by a total conversion of the mind to the DIVINE LIGHT, not by our own proper activity but by preserving a profound silence.'"[4]

Many other things are there cited by Ramsay from many other philosophers that show that all the chief philosophers placed virtue primarily in devotion, spiritual knowledge, and union with God; and believed God to be the Creator, universal orderer and moral governor of the world; and [believed in] the immortality of the soul and spiritual happiness of heaven.

[1355a.][5] GLORY OF GOD THE END OF HIS WORKS. Endeavor to show how, that although God in those communications of his beauty and happiness may be said to act for the creature, and so that it is grace and goodness in God, yet he may be said to act for himself and to make himself his end, and that the creature in what he does should act for God and make God his end. To show how, in both the acts of God and the right acts of the creature, God's glory and the creature's true and infinite good are one, supreme end.

Def. Explain what is meant by an ultimate end, and how this differs from a chief end, and that supposing a thing to [be] one's chief end in what he does don't necessarily suppose it to be his ultimate end.

Def. An ultimate end is an end which alone is sought for its own sake. An end that is wholly a subordinate end, and not at all an ultimate end, is not at all sought for its own sake, or not in any wise beheld by the agent as desirable absolutely and in itself considered, but only for the sake of the ulterior end to which it is subordinated.[6]

[1356.][7] [. . .] that God will proceed with them in this great affair in a method agreeable to the intelligent, volitive and active nature he has given, and deal with them as moral agents, and creatures he has made to love him, be in subjection to him and serve him; and so that there must be made to them a new revelation of the designs of his wisdom, ho-

---

4. The capitals in this paragraph are JE's.

5. In the MS, this entry has been marked (or struck through) with a vertical line slightly to the left of the center of each column, probably to indicate JE's appropriation of it in *Dissertation Concerning the End for Which God Created the World.* See *Works, 8,* 406–7, n. 2, 691–92, n. 9. Neither JE nor JE, Jr., assigned it an entry number.

6. The remainder of MS p. 964, on which this entry ends, as well as the entirety of pp. 965–69, are blank.

7. No. [1356], whose entry number was provided by JE, Jr., is, by JE's direction ("join this with p. 820"), an extension of No. [1348] (pp. 391–411).

liness and grace with respect to their deliverance, and being received to favor and the eternal, happy fruits of it, concerning the way in which it is to be done, the qualifications or acts of theirs previously requisite; and so there must be some new treaty set afoot, either while they are under their punishment or afterwards, in some intermediate space between that and their being exalted to glory. Doubtless they themselves must have some active concern in the affair, in a way of repenting, seeking, obeying or yielding subjection to God, some acknowledgment of him, some yielding themselves to him. For God immediately to advance 'em from a state of great wickedness and misery in hell to a state of perfection and confirmed, eternal happiness, is neither agreeable to reason and the nature of things, nor to God's known methods of dealing with his intelligent creatures. It would be much further from it than it would have been for God immediately to have instated all angels and men in their confirmed state of life and eternal glory and blessedness[8] in the instant of their creation, without any terms, any previous concern or act of theirs in order to it.

But that a new dispensation of grace should thus be introduced because that which was brought in by Christ and his apostles proves weak and unprofitable through men's corruptions, and there appears to be need of one that shall be more effectual, is not agreeable to the Scripture. For this dispensation is spoken of as the last and most perfect, wherein perfection was reached. Heb. 7:19, "For the law made nothing perfect, but the bringing in of a better hope did." And ch. 11:40, "God having provided some better thing for us, that they without us should not be made perfect." The ancient dispensation is spoken of as that which God found fault with, it proving ineffectual through the corruption of men, and so introducing a new administration that should not be liable to exception, and therefore should not wax old or be ever liable to vanish away and give place to another (Heb. 8:6–13). So he speaks of the things of that ancient dispensation as things [that] were liable to be shaken and removed; but the things of the new dispensation that was then introduced as those that could not be shaken, but should remain forever (Heb. 12:25–29 and II Cor. 3:11). The dispensation of the New Testament is often spoken of in the prophecies of the Old Testament as an everlasting dispensation (Jer. 31:31–32, ch. 32:40; Is. 61:8; Ezek. 37:26).

Arg. To suppose that after all the means of grace that are used in this

8. MS: "blessed."

world—Moses and the prophets, Christ and the gospel, the warnings of God's word and the exhibitions of glorious gospel grace—that after these means have been despised and obstinately withstood, so as to make the case desperate as [to] their success, God has other means in reserve to be used afterwards to make men holy that will be more powerful and shall be effectual, is not agreeable to Scripture. That those are the best and last means that [God] will use with men seems to be a thing that it was Christ's design to teach us in the parable of the rich man and Lazarus. Luke 16:27–31, "Then he said, I pray thee therefore, father, that thou wouldst send him to my father's house: for I have five brethren; that he may testify to them, lest they also come into this place of torment. Abraham saith unto him, They have Moses and the prophets; let them hear them. And he said, Nay, father Abraham: but if one went unto them from the dead, they will repent. And he said unto him, If they hear not Moses and the prophets, neither will they be persuaded, though one rose from the dead."

But this is especially manifest from Rev. 22:10–12, "And he saith unto me, Seal not the sayings of the prophecy of this book: for the time is at hand. He that is unjust, let him be unjust still: and he which is filthy, let him be filthy still: and he that is righteous, let him be righteous still: and he that is holy, let him be holy still. And, behold, I come quickly; and my reward is with me, to give every man according as his work shall be."

I think the meaning must either be this: "The time is quickly coming, when every man's state will be fixed, inasmuch as I am quickly coming to judgment, to fix every man's state unalterably, according as his work shall be; and after, then there will be no alteration, nor any means or endeavors in order to it: but he that is unjust, let him be unjust still, and he that is filthy, let him be filthy still." And if this be the meaning, it makes it evident that Christ, instead of this, will not immediately proceed to the use of the more powerful and effectual means of all to change the state of the unjust and filthy, to purify 'em and make 'em holy and fit them for eternal glory with infallible success.

Or secondly, the meaning must be this, which seems to be much the most probable: Christ, having given this last Revelation to his church to be added to the books of Scripture, [with] which the canon was to be shut up and sealed by the instrumentality of the apostle John, who lived the longest of the apostles and wrote this book after all the rest were dead: Christ therefore orders John (v. 10) to publish this book, wherein such great, future judgments are revealed as coming on the wicked, and such an affecting declaration of the future glory of the saints, to enforce the rest of God's word and means of grace, and then intimates that no more revelations are to be expected, no more instructions and warnings to be added to the word of God, as the standing means of grace, any further to confirm and enforce the rest; that the next revelation that is to be expected Christ will make of himself to the world, is to be his immediate appearance to judgment, to fix unalterably every man's state according to his works, according to the improvement he shall have made of those past revelations, instructions and warnings. And therefore, those that will not be purified by those means, are to expect no better or other means will ever be used with them; but he that is unjust must remain so still, and he that is filthy must be filthy still, and he that is righteous shall be righteous still, and he that is holy shall be holy still. Thus Christ takes leave of his church, as it were, till his last coming, warning 'em to improve the means of grace they have, and informing them they never are to have any other: "They have Moses and the Prophets and the more glorious, powerful and efficacious revelations of me—who speaks from heaven and am greater than Moses—in the writings of the New Testament, which I now finish and seal. Let 'em hear these and make a good improvement of 'em, for these are the last means I shall ever use to change men's state." This is no less inconsistent with his reserving[9] his greatest and most powerful means with a determined, certain success, to be used after the day of judgment.

Arg. They that suppose the damned are made to suffer the torments of hell for their purification, suppose that God herein is prosecuting his grand design of benevolence to his creatures, yea, and benevolence to the sufferers, and that he don't use these severe means but from necessity for their good, because all gentler remedies prove ineffectual.

Now 'tis unreasonable to suppose that God is under any necessity of inflicting such extreme torments upon them, and holding them under them for so long a time, in order to their being brought to repentance; and that,

(1) If we consider the nature of things. Torments inflicted have no tendency to bring a wicked man to repentance directly and properly, if by "repentance" we mean an alteration of the disposition and appetites and taste of the mind. We know this by experience, that pains inflicted for gratifying an appetite may make men afraid to gratify the appetite, but they don't change the inclination or destroy the appetite. They may make men willing to comply with those exercises, etc., of which they have

9. MS: "reservest."

a distaste, and to which their heart in its relish and inclinations was averse; but not from love to the things complied, but from another cause and for another end, from hatred of pain and love of ease. So that the man complies in some sense, but his heart don't comply. He is only driven and, as it were, forced. And an increase of pain alters not the nature of things. It may make a man more earnestly to desire freedom from pain, but still there is no more to [be] expected from it than is in the tendency of pain, which is not to give a new nature, a new heart or new natural relish and disposition. (N.B. It alters not the argument whether long, continued pains and practice won't gradually raise a habitual love to virtue.)

The pains of the damned, being great and long continued, may more and more convince them of the folly of their negligence and fearlessness in sin, and may make 'em willing to take pains in religion, but not show 'em the beauty of holiness or the odiousness of sin, so as to cause them to hate sin on its own account. They have no tendency to beget love to God and virtue.

But to make 'em willing to take pains in religion and comply with the requisite outward self-denial, 'tis unreasonable to suppose but that far less torment would be sufficient. Can anyone that considers human nature, especially of those that deny an innate, desperate wickedness of heart (as the men that we have this controversy with generally do), doubt in the least whether, if a man should be in a furnace of fire for one day only, alive and full of quick sense, and should retain a full and lively remembrance of his misery, that it would not be sufficient to make him willing to comply with all the pains and outward self-denial requisite in order to an universal obedience to the precepts of the word of God, rather than have those torments renewed and continued for ages, and indeed rather than endure one more such day? What pains would not such a man held to these terms be willing to comply with? What labors could be too much? What would he [not] be willing to part with, foregoing of worldly wealth or pleasure? Would not the most covetous man that had felt such a rod as this be willing to part with all his treasures of silver and gold? And the most ambitious man to live in a cottage or wilderness? The most voluptuous man to part with his pleasures? Would he need first to endure many ages of such torment before he would be willing to comply?

'Tis against all principles of human nature. If he retains the remembrance of torment, in a lively idea of it, it must unspeakably outweigh the most lively and affecting and attractive ideas of the things of the world.

The supposition, therefore, of his not being brought to a compliance with less torment is as unreasonable as to suppose that a mite, or dust, would sink the scale, being put in a balance with a talent of lead, or ten thousand talents.

If the Most High compassionates these poor wretches, and has nothing but a kind and gracious design[1] of infinite mercy and bounty, what, should he take such dreadful measures with them? Will no other do? Can't infinite wisdom find out some gentler method to bring to pass the same design?

If it be said that no other can accomplish the effect consistent with the freedom of will, I answer, What means can be devised having a greater tendency to drive men and compel them to comply with the thing required (if there be any such thing) without acting freely, and as persons left to their own free choice, than such a rod, not only held over, but used upon them in such an amazing manner by an omnipotent hand?

(2) 'Tis apparent, from what has often come to pass, that God is [under] no necessity of making use of such dreadful and long-continued torments in order to bring such sinners (equally wicked and obstinate) as die impenitent to repentance. 'Tis most unreasonable to suppose that no sinners that ever were converted in this world were, before their conversion, as wicked and as hard-hearted as some of them that have died impenitent, as Saul the persecutor, afterwards the apostle Paul; and some of the converts in the second chapter of the Acts who had a hand in Christ's crucifixion, in whom Christ's prayer was answered, "Father, forgive them; for they know not what they do" [Luke 23:34]; and innumerable instances of persecutors and others who have been brought to repentance since those days. Such were converted by gentler means than those pains of hell in what the Scripture calls everlasting burnings, and that without any infringement of any liberty of the persons necessary to their being moral agents. It would be unreasonable to suppose that all those eighteen on whom the tower of Siloam fell were good men [Luke 13:4]. But Christ would not have his hearers imagine they were worse themselves, and yet intimates that there is a possibility of their escaping future misery by repentance.

(3) So far as pain and affliction is concerned or made use of to bring men to repentance, 'tis apparent God can make infinitely less severe chastisement effectual together with such influences and assistances of his Spirit as were not inconsistent with the persons' moral agency in their

---

1. MS: "a design."

repentance, or in their forsaking sin and turning to God. And if it should be said that it may be they were none of them so great sinners, and had not the habits of sin so confirmed as all such as die in sin, I would answer: *1.* that this is very unreasonably supposed; and *2.* if it should be allowed, yet it can't be pretended that the difference of guilt and hardheartedness is proportionable at all to the severity of the chastisement used for purgation. And unless this be supposed, the force of the argument is not hurt. If no more than ten degrees of pain, or an one year's chastisement, be requisite for the overcoming five degrees of strength of the habit of sin, one would think that less than 100,000 degrees, or 10,000 year's chastisement, should be sufficient to overcome ten degrees of strength of the same habit.

Arg. If the torments of hell are purifying pains, means used by a God of universal benevolence towards his creatures as necessary means for the purgation of the wicked from sin, and their being fitted for and finally brought to eternal happiness in the enjoyment of the love of God; then it will follow that the damned in hell are still the objects of God's mercy and kindness, and that in the torments they suffer, they are the subjects of a dispensation of grace and benevolence. All is for their good. All is the best kindness that can be done 'em, the most benevolent treatment they are capable of in their state of mind; and that, in all, God is but chastising them, as a wise and loving Father, with a grieved, compassionate heart, gives necessary chastisement to a son whom he loves and whose good he seeks to his utmost, that in all that he does he is only prosecuting a design of infinite kindness and favor. And indeed some of the chief of those who are in the scheme of hell torments being purifying pains do expressly maintain that,[2] instead of being the fruits of vindictive justice, they are really the effects of God's benevolence, not only to the system of intelligent creatures in general, but to the sufferers themselves.

Now how far are these things from being agreeable to the representation which is made of things in the holy Scriptures, which represent the damned as thrown away of God, as things that are good for nothing, and which God makes no account of (Matt. 13:48); as dross, and not gold and silver or any valuable metal (Ps. 119:119, "Thou puttest away all the wicked of the earth like dross"; so Ezek. 22:18, Jer. 6:28–30); as salt that has lost its savor, as good for nothing but to be cast out and trodden under foot of men; as stubble that is left, and as the chaff thrown

---

2. MS: "that they."

out to be scattered by the wind and go whither that shall happen to carry it, instead of being gathered and laid up as that which is of any value (Ps. 1:4, Job 21:18, and [Ps.] 35:5); as that which shall not only be thrown away as wholly worthless, but what shall be thrown into the fire to be burnt up as a mere nuisance, as chaff, and as stubble, and tares, all which are thrown away as not worthy [of] any care to save, yea, as thrown into the fire as fit for nothing but to be destroyed, and therefore cast into the fire to be destroyed and done with (Matt. 3:12 and 13:30, Job 21:18); as barren trees, trees that are good for nothing, and not only so, but cumberers of the ground, and as such shall be cut down and cast into the fire (Matt. 3:10 and 7:19, Luke 13:7); as barren branches in a vine that are cut off and cast away as good for nothing, and gathered, and burned (John 15:6), thrown out and purged away as the filth of the world.

Thus it is said, Job 20:7, that the wicked "shall perish forever as his own dung." [They] are spoken of as those that shall be spewed out of God's mouth, as thrown as it were into the lake of fire, as the great sink of all the filth of the creation—Rev. 21[:8], "But the fearful, and the unbelieving, and the abominable, and murderers, and whoremongers, [. . .] and idolaters, and all liars, shall have their part in the lake that burns with fire and brimstone"—as briars and thorns that are not only wholly worthless in a field, but hurtful and pernicious, and as such are "nigh unto cursing; whose end is to be burned" (Heb. 6[:8]). Their end is to be burnt, i.e. the husbandman throws 'em into the fire and so has done with them forever. He don't still take care of 'em in order to make 'em fruitful and flourishing plants in his garden of delights.

The wicked, it is said, "shall be driven from light into darkness, and chased out of the world" (Job 18:18). Instead of being treated by God with benevolence, chastening them with the compassion and kindness of a father for their great and everlasting good, that at that day when God gathers his children together to make 'em experience the blessed fruits of the love of an heavenly [Father], these be shut out as dogs (Rev. 21:7–8, with ch. 22:14–15). They are represented as vessels to dishonor, vessels of wrath, fitted for nothing else and designed for nothing but to contain wrath and misery. They are spoken as those that perish and lose their souls, that are lost (II Cor. 4:3), those that lose themselves and are cast away, those that are destroyed, consumed, etc.; which representations don't agree with such as are under a dispensation of kindness and the means of a physician in order to their eternal life, health and happiness, though the means are severe.

When God of old, by his prophets, denounced God's terrible judgments against Jerusalem and the people of Israel, against Moab, Tyre, Egypt, Assyria, etc.—which judgments, though long continued, were not designed to be perpetual—there were, mixed with those awful denunciations, or added to 'em, promises or intimations of future mercy. But when the Scripture speaks of God's dealings with ungodly men in another world, there are nothing but declarations and denunciations of wrath and misery, and no intimations of mercy, no gentle terms used, no significations of divine pity, no exhortations to humiliation under God's awful hand, or calls to seek his face and turn and repent.

The account the Scripture gives of the treatment that wicked men shall meet with after this life, is very inconsistent with this notion of their being from necessity subjected to harsh means of cure and severe chastisements, with a benevolent, gracious design of their everlasting good—particularly the manner in which Christ will treat them at the day of judgment. He will bid the wicked depart from him as cursed. We have no account of any invitations to accept of mercy, no counsels to repent that they may speedily be delivered from this misery. But then 'tis represented that they shall be made his footstool. He shall triumph over them. He will trample upon 'em as men are wont to tread grapes in a winepress, when they trample with all their might to that very end that they effectually crush them in pieces. He will tread 'em in his anger and trample 'em in his fury and, as he says, their blood shall be sprinkled on his garments, and he will stain all his raiment (Is. 63:3; Rev. 14:19–20, and ch. 19:15, in which last place it is said "he treadeth the winepress of the fierceness and wrath of Almighty God"). These things don't savor of chastising with compassion and benevolence, and as still prosecuting a design of love towards them, that he may in the end actually be their Savior and means of their eternal glory.

There is nothing in the accounts of the day of judgment that looks as though the saints had any love or pity for the wicked on account of the terrible, long-continued torments which they must suffer. Nor indeed will the accounts that are given admit of supposing any such thing. We have an account of their judging them, and being with Christ in condemning them, concurring in the sentence wherein he bids 'em be gone from him as cursed with devils into eternal fire; but no account of their praying for them, nor of their exhorting them to consider and repent.

They shall not be grieved, but rather rejoice at the glorious manifestations of God's justice, holiness and majesty in their dreadful perdition, and shall triumph with Christ (Rev. 18:20 and 19:1–3). They shall be made Christ's footstool, and so they shall be theirs. They shall dip their feet in their blood, at least the blood of some of them, the blood of their persecutors (Ps. 68:23).

If the damned were the objects of divine benevolence, and designed by God for the enjoyment of his eternal love, doubtless it would be required of all God's children to love 'em, and to pity 'em, and pray for 'em, and seek their good; as here in this world 'tis required of 'em to love their enemies, to be kind to the evil and unjust, and pity and pray for the wickedest and vilest of men, though their own persecutors, because they are the subjects of God's mercy in many respects, and are capable subjects of infinite, divine mercy and love.

If Christ, the head of all the church, pities the damned and seeks their good, doubtless his members ought to do so too. If the saints in heaven ought to pity the damned, as well as the saints on earth the wicked that dwell here, doubtless their pity ought to be in some proportion to the greatness of the calamity of the objects of it and the greatness of the number of those they see in misery. But if they had pity and sympathizing grief in such measure as this for so many ages, what an alloy would it be to their happiness.

God is represented as whetting his glittering sword, and bending his bow, and making ready his arrows on the string against wicked men, and lifting his hand to heaven and swearing that he'll render vengeance to his enemies and reward them that hate him, and make his arrows drunk with their blood, and that his sword shall devour their flesh (Deut. 32:40–42 and Ps. 7:11–13). Certainly this is the language and conduct of an enemy, and not of a friend and of a compassionate, chastening Father.

The degree of misery and torment that shall be inflicted is an evidence that God is not acting the part of benevolence and compassion, and only chastening from a kind and gracious principle and design. 'Tis evident that 'tis God's manner, when he thus afflicts men for their good and chastens them with compassion, he is wont to stay his rough wind in the day of his east wind, to correct in measure, not to stir up all his wrath, to consider the frame of those that are corrected, to remember their weakness and consider how little they can bear; he turns away his anger, and don't stir up all his wrath (Ps. 78:37–39, Is. 27:8, Jer. 30:11 and 46:28). And 'tis his manner in the midst even of the severest afflictions to order some mitigating circumstances and to mix some mercy.

But the misery of the damned is represented as unmixed. The wine of the wrath of God "is poured out without mixture into the cup of his indignation," that they may be "tormented with fire and brimstone in the presence of the holy angels, and in the presence of the Lamb: and the smoke of their torment shall ascend up forever and ever: and they have no rest day nor night" (Rev. 14:10–11). They are tormented in a flame that burns within them as well as round about them, and they shall be denied so much as a drop of water to cool their tongues. And God's wrath shall be inflicted in such a manner as [will] show his wrath and make his strength known, as on vessels of wrath fitted for no other use but to be destroyed, and shall be punished with everlasting destruction, answerable to that glory of Christ's power which he shall appear in at the day of judgment, when he shall come in the glory of his Father, with power and great glory, in flaming fire, to take vengeance on them that know not God and obey not the gospel. Can any imagine that, in all this, God is only correcting from love, and that the subjects of these inflictions are some of those happy ones whom God corrects in order to teach 'em out of his law, whom he makes sore and bindeth up (Job 5:17–18, Ps. 94:12)?

There is nothing in Scripture that looks as if the damned were under the use of means to bring 'em to repentance. 'Tis apparent God's manner is, when he afflicts men to bring to repentance with affliction, to join instructions, admonitions and arguments to persuade. But if we judge by Scripture representation of the state of the damned, they are left destitute of all these things. There are no prophets or ministers or good men to admonish them, reason and expostulate with them, or set 'em good examples. There is perfect separation made between all the righteous and the wicked, with a great gulf, so that there can be no passing from one to the other. They are left wholly to the company of devils and others like 'em. When the rich man in hell cries to his father Abraham, begging a drop of water, he denies his request and adds no exhortation to repentance.

Wisdom is abundantly represented in the book of Proverbs as counseling, warning, calling, inviting and expostulating with such as are under means for the obtaining wisdom, and that [God] is waiting upon in the use of means, that they may turn at his reproof. But as to such as are obstinate under these means of grace and calls of wisdom till the time of their punishment comes, 'tis represented their fear shall come as desolation and destruction as an whirlwind; that distress and anguish shall come upon them, and that then it will be in vain for 'em to seek wisdom; that if they seek her early they shall not find her, and if they call upon her she will not hear, but instead of this will laugh at their calamity and mock when their fear cometh. Which certainly don't consist with wisdom, or the God of wisdom, still striving with them and using means in a benevolent and compassionate manner to bring 'em to seek and embrace wisdom; still offering wisdom, with all her unspeakable, infinite benefits, if they will hearken to her voice and comply with her, and not only so, but actually using the most powerful and effectual means to bring them to this happiness, even such as shall surely be successful, though they have obstinately refused all others, and when wisdom called they heretofore refused, and when she stretched forth her hand they did not regard; and so still most effectually doing the part of a friend to deliver 'em from their distress and anguish instead of laughing at their calamity (Prov. 1:24–33). This declaration of wisdom, if ever it be fulfilled at all, will surely be fulfilled most completely and perfectly at the time appointed for obstinate sinners to receive their most perfect and complete punishment.

If all mankind, even such as live and die in their wickedness, are and ever will be the objects of Christ's good will and mercy, and those whose eternal happiness he desires and seeks, then surely he would pray for all. But Christ declares that there are some that he prays not for. John 17:9, "I pray for them: I pray not for the world, but for them which thou hast given me; for they are thine," compared with v. 14, "the world hath hated them, because they are not of the world, even as I am not of the world"; v. 25, "the world hath not known thee: but I have known thee, and these have known that thou hast sent me"; and v. 20, "Neither pray I for these alone, but for them also which shall believe on me through their word." By all which it appears that Christ prayed for all that should ever be true believers. But he prayed [not] for those who should not be brought by the word of the apostles, and such means of grace as are used in this world, to believe in him, and should continue notwithstanding not to know God. And [those] in enmity against true holiness, or Christianity, were such as Christ prayed not for.

Arg. If sin and misery and the second death are to continue and prevail for so long a time after the day of judgment, with respect to great multitudes that Christ finally will save and deliver from these things, having perfectly conquered and abolished them, then how can the Scriptures truly represent that all enemies shall be put under his feet at the end of the world, and that the last enemy that shall be destroyed is death, and that then, having perfectly subdued all his enemies, he shall resign up the kingdom to the Father, and he himself be subject to the Father, as in I Cor. 15:20–28? The time of Christ's victory over death will be then, at the general resurrection and day of judgment, as is evident by vv. 54–55 with the foregoing context.

The chief enemies that Christ came to destroy, with regard to such as should be saved and be of his church, were sin and misery, or death consisting in sin and death consisting in suffering, the second death, unspeakably the greatest enemy that came by sin, infinitely more terrible than temporal death. But if the notion I am opposing be true, these greatest and worst enemies, instead of be[ing] subdued, shall have their principal reign afterwards for many ages, at least the latter; and the former, viz. sin, in the sad effects and consequences of it, viz. men's misery. And God shall have[3] his greatest and strongest conflict with these enemies afterward, that is, shall strive against them in the use of the most powerful means.

Arg. There is great evidence that the devil is not the subject of any dispensation of divine mercy and kindness, and that God is prosecuting no design of infinite goodness towards him, and that his pains are not purifying pains. It is manifest, that instead of any influence of his torments to bring him nearer to repentance, that he has been, from the beginning [of] his damnation, constantly, with all his might, exerting himself in prosecuting[4] his wickedness, his violent, most haughty and malignant opposition to God and man, fighting especially with peculiar virulence against Christ and his church, opposing with all his might everything that is good, seeking the destruction and misery of all mankind with boundless and insatiable cruelty; on which account he is called Satan, the Adversary, and Abaddon, and Apollyon, the Destroyer, is represented as a roaring lion seeking whom he may devour, a viper, the old serpent, the great red dragon—red on account of his bloody, cruel nature. He is said to be a murderer from the beginning. He has murdered all mankind, has murdered their souls as well as their bodies. He was the murderer of Jesus Christ by his instigating Judas and his crucifiers. He has most cruelly shed the blood of an innumerable multitude of the children of God. He is called emphatically the evil one, the wicked one, that wicked one, etc. He is a liar and the father of lies, and the father of all the sin and wickedness that is or ever has been in the world. He is the spirit that worketh in the children of disobedience (II Cor. 4:3–4). 'Tis said that "he that committeth sin is of the devil, for the devil sinneth from the beginning" [I John 3:8]; and all wicked men are spoken of as his children. He has set up himself as god of this world in opposition to the true God, and has erected a vast kingdom over the nations, and is constantly carrying

3. MS: "having."
4. MS: "prosecute."

on a war with the utmost earnestness, subtlety, malice and venom against Jesus Christ and all his holy and gracious designs, maintaining a kingdom of darkness, wickedness and misery in opposition to Christ's kingdom of light, holiness and peace, and thus will continue to do to the end of the world, as appears by Scripture prophecies.

And God's dealings with him are infinitely far from being those of a friend kindly seeking his infinite good and designing nothing else but, in the end, to make him eternally happy in love and favor and a blessed union with him. God is represented everywhere as acting the part of an enemy to him that seeks and designs nothing in the final event but his destruction. The grand work of God's providence, which God is prosecuting from the beginning to the end of the world, viz. the work of redemption, it is against him: to bruise or break in pieces his head, to cast him [like] lightning from heaven, from that height of power and dominion to which he had exalted him, to tread him under foot and to cause his people to trample and bruise or crush him under foot and gloriously to triumph over him. Christ, when he conquered him and made a show of him, openly triumphed[5] over him.

Now concerning this two things may be observed: (1) that seeing the devils are not to have an end put to their misery, and their pains are not purifying pains in order to their being brought to eternal happiness at last, it appears that 'tis not God's design finally to make all his creatures happy, and that the torments of hell are not purifying pains inflicted with a merciful design with respect to all damned spirits; and (2) 'tis evident, that as it will be with the devil in this respect, so it will be with [the] wicked. This is reasonable to suppose from what the Scripture represents of the relation wicked men stand in to the devil: as his children, servants, subjects, instruments, his property and possession, are all ranked together as one kingdom, in one interest and one company, and many of them the great ministers of his kingdom that he has set up and committed authority to, such as the beast and false prophet that we read of in the Revelation. Now how reasonable and natural is it to suppose that those that have their lot and portion together as Christ's disciples, subjects, followers, soldiers, children, instruments and faithful ministers shall have their part with him and his eternal glory, so that the devil's disciples, followers, subjects, soldiers in his army, his children, instruments and ministers of his kingdom should have their part with him and be dealt with as he is, and not that such an infinite difference should be

5. MS: "triumphing."

made between them that the punishment of the one should be eternal and of the other but temporal and, therefore, infinitely less, infinitely disproportionate, so the proportion between the punishment of the latter to that of the former is as nothing, infinitely less, of an unit to a million million. This is unreasonable to suppose in itself, as the difference of guilt and wickedness cannot be so great, but must be infinitely far from it, especially considering the aggravations of the wickedness of a great part of damned men—as against Christ and gospel grace and love—which exceeding great aggravation the sin of the devils never had.

As the devil's ministers, servants and instruments of the angelic nature, those that are called the devil's angels, shall have their part with him, for the like reason we may well suppose his servants and instruments of the human nature will share with him. And not only is this reasonable in itself, but the Scripture plainly teaches us that it shall be so. In Rev. 19:20, it is said the beast and the false prophet were both "cast alive into the lake of fire burning with brimstone." So it is said, ch. 20:10, "the devil that deceived them was cast into the lake of fire and brimstone, where the beast and the false prophet are, and shall be tormented day and night forever and ever," so expressing both the kind of misery and the duration. Just in the same manner it is said concerning the followers of the beast. It is said, ch. 14:9–11, "saying with a loud voice, If any man worship the beast," etc., "The same shall drink of the wine of the wrath of God, which is poured out without mixture into the cup of his indignation; and he shall be tormented with fire and brimstone [. . .] And the smoke of their torment ascendeth up forever and ever: and they have no rest day nor night, who worship the beast and his image, and whosoever receiveth the mark of his name." And ch. 21:8, of wicked men in general 'tis said, they "shall have their part in the lake which burneth with fire and brimstone."

So we find in Christ's description of the day of judgment, the wicked are sentenced to everlasting fire prepared for the devil and his angels. By which it appears most plainly that they share with the devils in suffering misery of the same kind, and also share with him in suffering misery of the same, everlasting continuance.

And indeed, not only would the punishment infinitely differ as to quantity and duration if the punishment of the devils was to be eternal and of wicked men only temporal, but if this were known it would, as it were, infinitely differ in kind, the one suffering God's hatred and mere vengeance, inflictions that have no pity or kindness in them, the other the fruit of his mercy and love and infinitely kind intention; the one attended with absolute despair and a black and dismal sinking prospect of misery absolutely endless, the other with the light of hope and supporting prospect not only of an end to their misery, but of an eternal, unspeakable happiness to follow.

Arg. This notion we are opposing is repugnant to the representations which the Scripture makes, as though at the day of judgment would be the consummation of all, the finishing of God's design, an end to the revolutions and changes of a state of trial, preparation and proficience, and the bringing all the great mutations of the world to their fixed period, and the settling of all things in their final state. Thus the Apostle says, I Cor. 15:24, "Then cometh the end, [. . .] when he shall have put down all rule and all authority and power." And the things there spoken that shall then be done show that then will be the finishing of things and settling them in their final state, such as the end of Christ's kingdom, given him for the subduing of all enemies, and his resigning his commission for the conquering all enemies and subduing all evil, and the restitution of all things (as having completed his design), that God henceforth may be all in all according to the most natural state of things.

And therefore, when the general resurrection and day of judgment had been represented to the apostle John, God then proclaims, Rev. 21:6, "And he said unto me, It is done. I am Alpha and Omega, the beginning and the end." By which it is very manifest that God will have so far finished his design as to have brought the whole course of things, in all their mutations, to their proper and intended period, final issue and fixed state; whereby it shall appear at last how that, as God was the beginning, the first cause of all things, from whom the whole system and series of things originated at their beginning, so he, now [that they] are brought to their final issue, appears to be also their last end, so that as things took their first rise from him, so they shall have their last end in him. He shall appear to be the last end of all things when their last end is reached in the issue of all their changes, revolutions and labors. Agreeable to this, the day of judgment is from time to time called the last day (John 6:40, 44, 54) and the great day (Jude 6).

By these things it is most manifest that at that day the moral world shall be settled in its final state, and that the judgment of that day will be the last judgment. But if the multitude of the damned are yet to be kept in a state of preparation and under the use of means in order to their repentance and so vast a change as that from infernal misery to heavenly and eternal glory, how far are things from being all brought to their consummation, last issue, and settled in their final state. And if so, then the judgment of that day can't be the last judgment. For the design of the last judgment, whenever that is, must be to settle things in the moral world, or among such creatures in their last state as are the proper subjects of moral government and of a judicial proceeding. But the last judgment for this end can't be till the day of preparation and proficience and use of means in order to repentance—the day of God's striving and opportunity for the obtaining the favor and rewards of the great Judge— is over. According to the notion which I am opposing, the judgment that shall be at the end of the world will be so far from the last judgment, or any proper judgment to settle all things in their final state, that it will, with respect to the wicked, be no more than the judgment of a physician whether more sharp and powerful remedies must not be applied in order to the relief of sinners and the cure of their disease, which, if not cured, will make 'em eternally miserable.

Arg. 'Tis evident that the future misery of the wicked in hell is not to come to an end and to be succeeded by eternal happiness, and that their misery is not subservient to their happiness, because the Scripture plainly signifies concerning those that die in their sins that they have all the good and comfort in this life that ever is designed for 'em. Luke 6:24, "woe unto you that are rich! for ye have received your consolation." Luke 16:25, "Son, remember that thou in thy lifetime receivedst thy good things." Ps. 17:13–14, "deliver my soul from the wicked, . . . from the men of the world, which have their portion in this life, and whose belly thou fillest with thy hid treasure."

Arg. According to the opinion I am now opposing, God will surely at the last deliver all the damned from their misery and make them happy, so that God will see to it that the purifying torments shall certainly at last have their effect to turn them from sin.

Now how can this consist with God's treating them as moral agents, and their acting from the freedom of their own wills in the affair of their turning from sin and becoming morally pure and virtuous? According to the notions of freedom and moral agency which now prevail and are strenuously maintained by some of the chief assertors of this opinion concerning hell torments, which notion of freedom implies contingence and is wholly inconsistent with the necessity of the event: if, after all the torments of the damned used to bring sinners to repentance, the consequence aimed [at], viz. the sinners' turning from sin to virtue, be not necessary, but it still remains a contingent event, a thing contingent whether there ever will be any such consequence of those severe, long-continued chastisements or no, then how can it be determined that this will surely be the consequence? How can it be a thing infallible that such a consequence of means used will follow when, at the same time, it is not a necessary consequence, no way necessarily connected with the means used, and it is a thing contingent whether it will ever follow or no? If God has determined absolutely to make 'em all pure and happy, and yet their purity and happiness depends on the freedom of their will, then here is an absolute divine decree consistent with the freedom of men's wills, which is a doctrine utterly rejected by the generality of that sort of men who deny the eternity of hell torments.

If it be said that God has not absolutely determined the duration or measure of their torments, but to continue 'em till they do repent, or to try lesser torments first, and if they don't do, to increase 'em till they are effectual, determining that he will raise or continue them till the effect finally shall infallibly follow, that is the same thing as to necessitate the effect. And here is necessity in such a case, as much as when a founder puts a piece of metal in a furnace with a resolution to melt it, and if continuing it there a little while won't dissolve it, that he will keep it there till it does dissolve; and if by reason of its peculiar hardness an ordinary degree of heat of the furnace won't be effectual, that he will increase the vehemence of the heat till the effect shall certainly follow.

Method. N. B. Some of those things observed in opposition to the notion of hell torments being only purifying pains, may be used as arguments to prove the eternity of future misery in general, as what is said concerning the CONSUMMATION of all things, pp. 590–91;[6] concerning the rich man's having received his good things, p. 591;[7] the punishment of BLASPHEMY against the Holy Ghost, p. 407;[8] concerning the LAST DISPENSATION, p. 411;[9] Rev. 22:10–12, p. 577;[1] sinners being THROWN

6. MS: "p. 985 &c." No. [1356], the passage beginning, "*Arg.* This notion we are opposing is repugnant to the representations which the Scripture makes, as though as the day of judgment would be the consummation of all . . ."

7. MS: "p. 987." No. [1356], the paragraph beginning, "*Arg.* 'Tis evident that the future misery of the wicked in hell is not to come to an end and to be succeeded by eternal happiness . . ."

8. MS: "p. 816." No. 1348, the paragraph beginning, "*Arg.* That all shall not be finally purified and saved is manifest from that, Matt. 12:31–32 . . ."

9. MS: "p. 820." No. 1348, the paragraph beginning, "*Arg.* If the damned, after they have suffered a while, are to be delivered . . ."

1. MS: "p. 971." No. [1356], the paragraph beginning, "But this is especially manifest from Rev. 22:10–12 . . ."

AWAY, CAST, etc., pp. 581–86;[2] the last ENEMY subdued, pp. 586–87;[3] concerning the DEVIL, pp. 587–88.[4]

IF any should maintain this scheme of temporary future punishments, viz. that the torments in hell are not purifying pains, and that the damned are not in any state of trial with regard to any expected admission to eternal happiness, and that therefore they are not properly the objects of the divine benevolence; that the dispensation which they are under is not truly a dispensation of mercy, but that their torments are properly penal pains wherein God displays his vindictive justice; and that they shall suffer misery to such a degree and for so long a time as their obstinate wickedness in this world deserves, and that indeed they shall be miserable a very long time, so long that it is often figuratively spoken of in Scripture as being everlasting, and then be annihilated:

Ans. On this I would observe that there is nothing got by such a scheme, no relief from the arguments taken from Scripture for the proper eternity of future punishment. For if it be owned that Scripture expressions denote a punishment that is properly eternal, but said that they are properly eternal in no other sense than as their annihilation, or their state of non-existence that they shall return to, will be eternal; and this eternal annihilation is that death which is so often threatened for sin, and that *perishing forever,* that *everlasting destruction,* being lost, perishing, [being] utterly consumed, etc., so often denounced to wicked men; and the fire of hell be called eternal fire—as some suppose the external fire that consumed the cities of Sodom and Gomorrah is called eternal fire (Jude 7)—because it utterly consumed those cities, that they might never be built more; and the fire is called that which shall not be quenched, as it cannot be quenched till it has destroyed them that are cast into it: if this be all that these expressions denote, then they don't at all signify the length of their torments or long continuance of their misery. So that the supposition of the length of their torments is brought in without any necessity, the Scripture saying nothing of it, having no re-

2. MS: "p. 975 &c." No. [1356], the passage beginning, "*Arg.* If the torments of hell are purifying pains, means used by a God of universal benevolence towards his creatures . . ."

3. MS: "p. 982." No. [1356], the paragraph beginning, "*Arg.* If sin and misery and the second death are to continue for so long a time after the day of judgment . . ."

4. MS: "p. 982." No. [1356], paragraph beginning, "*Arg.* There is great evidence that the devil is not the subject of any dispensation of divine mercy . . ."

spect to it when it speaks of their punishments being everlasting. And it answers the Scripture expressions well to suppose they shall be annihilated immediately, without any long pains, provided the annihilation be everlasting.

IF any should suppose that the torments of the damned in hell are properly penal and in execution of penal justice, but yet that they are neither eternal nor shall end in annihilation, but they shall be continued till justice is satisfied and they have truly suffered as much as they deserve, whereby their punishment shall be so long as to be called everlasting, but that then they shall be delivered, and finally shall be the subjects of everlasting happiness; and that therefore in the mean time they shall not be in a state of trial, nor will they be waited upon in order to repentance, nor will their torments be used as means to bring 'em to it, for [the] term and measure of their punishment shall be fixed, from which they shall not be delivered on repentance or any terms or conditions whatsoever, till justice is satisfied:

Ans. One thing that I would observe in answer to this is that, if it be, the damned, while under their sufferings, are answerable for the wickedness that is acted by 'em while in their suffering state, and may properly be the subjects of a judicial proceeding for it, or not.

If the former be supposed—viz. that they are answerable and accountable for all the wickedness that is acted by them during their long state of suffering for the sins of this life, and must also be punished for all that wickedness, as much as it deserves, and so as fully to satisfy justice (as is supposed with respect to the sins of this life)—then it will follow that they must have another state of suffering and punishment, after the ages of their suffering for the sins of this life are ended. And it can't be supposed that this second period of suffering will be shorter than the first, for the first is only for the sins committed during a short life, often represented in Scripture for its shortness as[5] a dream, a tale that is told, a blast of wind, a vapor, a span, a moment, a flower, etc. But the time of punishment is always represented as exceeding long, called everlasting, represented as enduring forever and ever, as having no end, etc.

If the sins of a moment must be followed with such, as it were, endless ages of punishment, then doubtless the sins of those endless ages must

5. MS: "to."

be followed with another, second period of suffering, much longer. For it must be supposed that the damned continue sinning all the time of their punishment. For none can rationally imagine that God would hold 'em under such extreme torments and terrible manifestations and executions of his wrath after they have thoroughly repented and turned from sin, and are become pure and holy and conformed to God, and so have left off sinning. And if they continue in sin during this state of punishment with assurance that God still has a great benevolence for them, even so as to intend finally to make 'em everlastingly happy in the enjoyment of his love, their sin must be attended with great aggravations, as they will have the evil and ill desert of sin set before 'em in the most affecting manner in their dreadful sufferings for it, attended still with evidence of that, that God is infinitely benevolent towards 'em and intends to bestow infinite blessings upon them.

But if it be so that this first long period of punishment must be followed with a second as long or longer, for the same reason the second must be followed with a third as long or longer than that, and so the third must be followed with a fourth, and so *in infinitum*. And at this rate there can never be an end of their misery. So this scheme overthrows itself.

If the second thing mentioned be affirmed—viz. that the damned are not answerable for the wickedness they commit during their state of punishment—then we must suppose that, during the whole of their long and, as it were, eternal state of punishment, they are given up of God to the most unrestrained wickedness, having this to consider: that how far soever they go in the allowed exercises and manifestations of their malice and rage against God and Christ, saints and angels, and their fellow damned, they have nothing to fear from it; it will be never the worse. And surely, continuing in such unrestrained wickedness for such exceeding and, as it were, endless length of duration must most desperately confirm the habit of sin, must increase the root and fountain of it in the heart, as it were, infinitely.

Now how unreasonable is this, to suppose that God would thus deal with such as were objects of his infinite kindness, and the appointed subjects of the unspeakable and endless fruits of his love, in a state of perfect holiness and purity and conformity to and union with himself, thus to give 'em up beforehand to a kind of eternity of unrestrained malignity against himself, and every kind of hellish wickedness, as it were infinitely to increase the fountain of sin in the heart and the strength of the principle and habit?

If they are thus given up to unrestrained wickedness during the period of their punishment, and there be evidence of this, then this certain continuance in unbounded wickedness for so long a time must be part of the punishment they are sentenced to, and that is bound upon them by an irreversible doom; which certainly supposes such a necessity that they are laid under that is not consistent with freedom, as this sort of people must suppose. Now how incongruous is this to suppose, with regard to those that God has great benevolence to and designs eternal favor for, that he would go to lay 'em under a necessity of extreme, unbounded hatred of him, and blasphemy and rage against him for so many ages, such necessity as should exclude all liberty of their own in the case.

If God intends not only punishment but purification by their torments, on this supposition, instead of their being purified, they must be set at an infinitely greater distance from purification. And if God intends them for a second time of probation in order to their being brought to repentance and the love of God after their punishment is finished, then how can it be certain beforehand that they shall finally be happy, as is supposed? How can it be certain they will not fail in their second trial, or in their third, if there be a third? Yea, how much more likely that they will fail of truly turning in heart from sin to the love of God in this second trial, if there be any proper trial in the case after their hearts have been so much more brought under the power of a strong habit of sin and enmity to God. If the habit proved so strong in this life that the most powerful means and mighty inducements of the gospel would not prevail, so that God was, as it were, under a necessity of cutting down and dealing in this severity with them, how much less likely will it be that they will be prevailed upon to love God and the ways of virtue after their hearts are set at a so much greater distance from these things. Yea, unless we suppose a divine interposition of almighty, efficacious power to change the heart in the time of this second trial, we may be sure that under these circumstances the heart will not turn to love God. But such an interposition of efficacious power is not agreeable to the notions of freedom and moral agency which that sort of people maintain who deny the eternity of hell torments.

So it would be yet more plainly contrary to their notions of freedom and moral agency to suppose, that after their state of suffering is over, they would be immediately made perfectly holy from such a degree of confirmed wickedness without any time of trial at all. Such perfect holiness so immediately wrought from the greatest depths of wickedness and the most extremely confirmed malignity and depravity of heart, could not be the effect of free will in their notion of it, and therefore would be no virtue, no rewardable or praiseworthy holiness.

Besides, the supposition of God's thus setting his creatures at once in a state of confirmed, eternal holiness and happiness is not agreeable to God's way of dealing with his creatures. How much better and more fitly might the creature be thus confirmed the first instant of its creation, than to be thus confirmed in perfection of favor and glory after so many ages of actual enmity and most extreme wickedness, without any previous trial or space of repentance.

And besides, if it be so that they are laid under such a necessity of hating and blaspheming God for so many ages in the manner that has been spoken—a necessity utterly inconsistent with human liberty—then they will have no reason to condemn themselves at all for all this enmity and blasphemy of theirs, for so long a time, after they are made perfectly holy and happy and see that they had no reason at all for such malice and rage, but that all was infinitely against reason, and that at the same time there was infinite reason that they should love and honor God. But how extremely incongruous is such an imagination, that God would lay those he intended for the eternal beauty and blessedness of dear children under such circumstances that they must necessarily hate him, and with devilish fury curse and blaspheme him for innumerable ages in the most unreasonable manner; and yet never have cause, even when they are delivered and made happy in God's love, to condemn themselves for it, though they see the infinite hatefulness and unreasonableness of it, because God laid 'em under such a necessity of it that they could use no liberty of their own in the case. I leave it to all to judge whether God's thus ordering things with regard to such as he, from great benevolence, intended for eternal happiness, in a most blessed union with him, be credible.

METHOD. In a treatise of future punishment, to show when will be the season of it, and here prove particularly that it will begin at death. And consider the state of the wicked in their separation from their bodies. And then show how the day of judgment is the proper season of punishment, etc.

Arg. That which lasts as long as the world stands is sometimes said to be forever. Yet the space of man's life in comparison of the state that succeeds is often represented as a moment, the shortest space, yea, as nothing. And so the space of time to the end of the world is represented as very short (see Heb. 10:37). Here, in a particular manner, those words of Christ, Rev. 22:10–12; after Christ had shown John the end of the world, the day of judgment and consummation of all things, he says, "the time is at hand. He that is unjust, let him be unjust still," etc. "Behold, I come QUICKLY; and my reward is with me, to give every man according as his work shall be." Here Christ represents to his beloved disciple the space from that time to the end of the world to be very short, after he had from time to time represented to him (in the course of those visions of which this is the conclusion) the state of the punishment of the wicked to be everlasting, and forever and ever; as ch. 14:10–11, and 19:3, and 20:10. Even as in this twenty-second chapter, v. 7, when Christ says, "Behold, I come quickly," and so represents the time to the end of the world to be but short, we are naturally and justly led to compare this representation with the representations made of the duration of the future state, both of good and bad, after the judgment, and to draw inferences accordingly concerning the duration of that following state, upon many accounts, as:

(1) The same Jesus, in the same course or series of visions which John is directed in [in] the same book, makes both representations. And the future state of the righteous and wicked, especially of the latter, is set forth in a representation that is insisted on and repeated from time to time as being forever and ever.

(2) He, at this very time and in the same vision (as may be seen, v. 5 of this same twenty-second chapter), says of the blessedness of the righteous that it shall be "forever and ever," the very same phrase that is used before, from time to time, to set forth the duration of the misery of the wicked.

(3) After he had spoken of the glory of the righteous as being forever and ever, he, in the midst of those words wherein he represents the time to the end of the world as very short, joins both righteous and wicked together, representing their state as fixed, unalterable and everlasting in the same expressions: "the time is at hand. He that is unjust, let him be unjust still: and he that is filthy, let him be filthy still: and he that is righteous, let him be righteous still: and he that is holy, let him be holy still. Behold, I come quickly" [vv. 10–12]. The shortness of the time to the end of the world is expressed in the last words immediately preceding those that express the endlessness of the state of both righteous and wicked. And then again, the words immediately following express the same thing over again, "Behold I come quickly." And,

(4) The words immediately following these naturally lead us to the same comparison, even to compare the duration of the time before the coming of the Judge and the duration of those rewards and punishments which he will render to men according as their works shall be: "behold, I come quickly; and my reward is with me, to give every man according as his work shall be" [v. 12]. The shortness of the time before his coming to judge and recompense men, is declared for the comfort of the righteous and terror of the wicked. And the thing that justly renders the consideration of the measure of duration before Christ's coming comfortable to the saints, though it seems so long on some accounts, is that it is very short in comparison of the duration of the reward that shall follow. And so the thing that should justly make the measure of time before the judgment terrible to the wicked is that, though they may be ready to please themselves that time is so long, yet 'tis very short in comparison of the punishment that shall follow.

And in other places of Scripture, the time preceding the punishment of the wicked in particular is represented as very short. Thus 'tis threatened that God would bring on them swift destruction, and 'tis said the things that shall come upon them make haste, and that vengeance shall come speedily on the enemies of the elect, and the like. And the punishment of the wicked itself is always represented as everlasting and endless. Whence we may most reasonably suppose that these phrases, when applied to the future punishment, are used in their most proper sense, and not at all in the same manner as when applied to the space preceding, which is spoken as comparatively very short.

Hutcheson on the *Passions*, 3rd ed., p. 77,[6] says, "no misery is farther the occasion of joy" to a sedate temper "than as it is necessary to some prepollent happiness in the whole." Particularly to examine this matter and inquire whether there be not something in the natural sense of desert which God has implanted in creatures that are moral agents which tends to acquiescence in the pain or suffering of the ill-deserving, not merely from a natural desire of God to ourselves or others, or good to the universal system, but as what a sense of desert naturally tends to as a gratification of that sense.

When the fire of hell is represented as that which "NEVER SHALL BE

---

6. Hutcheson, *An Essay on the Nature and Conduct of the Passions and Affections*, 3rd ed. (1742), p. 77. On JE's engagement with Hutcheson and moral sense theory, see *Works, 8,* 689–705.

QUENCHED" [Mark 9:43, 45], thereby is not meant that it shall not be quenched till it has consumed its fuel and goes out itself: for by being "quenched," as the word is used in Scripture, is meant not only a being extinguished or put out, but going out, or ceasing, or ending in any respect. So the word is to be understood, Is. 43:17, "they are extinct, they are quenched as tow," i.e. their power and rage shall be like the fire of tow that lasts but a very little while and then goes out.

"VESSELS OF MERCY" and "VESSELS OF WRATH" are expressly distinguished [Rom. 9:22–23]. And the apostle James speaks of some that "shall have judgment without mercy" (Jas. 2:13), which proves that the punishment of hell is not the effect of mercy, and that mercy or pity never shall be exercised towards the damned.

"Ipsæ autem S. Litteræ pœnarum infernalium æternitatem clarissime docent; imo prolixius Scriptura S. dogma hoc inculcat, quam ipsam beatitudinis æternitatem [. . .]

"Argumenta ad stabiliendum hocce dogma, ex S. Litteris deprompta in varias dividi possunt classes; quarum celeb. Lampius in Dissertatione I. de hac materia, octo facit. Ad primam classem ea pertinent dicta, ubi ista damnatorum pœna expresse æterna vocatur. Ignis æternus Isai. 33:14, Matt. 18:8, 25:41. Opprobrium æternum Dan 12:2. Interitus æternus. II Thess. 1:9. Vincula æterna. Judæ 6. Caligo tenebrarum æterna. V. 13.

"Hæc testimonia ab omnibus exceptionibus vindicata vide apud celeb. Lampium Dissert. I. de pœnarum æternitate § IV. seqq.

"Classis II. Cum autem præcedentia hæc dicta, diversis ab adversariis premantur exceptionibus, omnem dubitationem tollere possunt loca illa, in quibus vox æternitatis multiplicatur; quando fumus tormentorum ascendere dicitur εἰζ τους αιωνας των αιωνων in sæcula sæculorum. Apoc. 14:11, 20:10. cruciandi dicuntur die & nocte, εις τους αιωνας των αιωνων. Phrasis autem hæc omnem excludit limitationem, quia duplicatio ejusmodi summum indicat gradum; quod abunde probavit Glassius Philol. S. Lib. III. Tract. I. Can. 16. Imo hac ratione ipsa Dei æternitas describi solet, unde phrasis hæc non de alia æternitate, quam quæ omni destituitur fine, intelligi potest.

"Classis III. Hæc etiam æternitas subinde maxima cum emphasi per formulas negantes exprimitur: 'Vermis eorum non moritur, & ignis eorum non extinguitur.' Quod ex Esajæ 66:24. aliquoties repetitur, Marci 9:44, 46, 48. Ita et Lucæ 3:17. 'Paleas comburet,' πυρι ασβεστω, 'igne inextinguibili.'

"Classis IV. Quarta argumentorum classis inde desumitur, quod æternitas beatitudinis ac damnationis inter se in eodem dicto comparantur & sibi invicem opponuntur, Dan 12:2. Matt. 25:46. Uti ergo beatitudinis æternitas finem habitura non est, ita talis etiam damnatorum æternitas intelligi debet [. . .]

"Et hoc unicum Scripturæ S. testimonium Ven Moshemius ad veritatem hancce probandam & ad omne dubium removendum sufficere putat [. . .]

"Classis argumentorum V. Ea porro ad rem probandam Scripturæ adducuntur dicta, quæ omnem plane ex Inferno liberationis spem excludunt; uti Matt. 5:26. Amen dico tibi, inde non exibis, usquedum ultimum solveris obolum. Idem dicitur Lucæ 12:59. Matt. 18:34–35. Omnem etiam remissionis peccatorum spem post hanc vitam evanescere, ex expressissimis Christi verbis apparet, quæ extant Matt. 12:32. 'Et si quis quid dixerit contra homine natum, ignoscetur ei: At si quis contra Sanctum Spiritum dixerit, non ignoscetur ei, nec in hoc sæculo, nec in futuro.' Marci 3:29. hoc modo exprimitur: 'Sed qui Sancto Spiritui maledixerit, nunquam adsequuuturus est veniam, sed obnoxius est supplicio sempiterno.' Imo pro iis, qui post semel agnitam veritatem petulanter peccant, nullum amplius pro peccato supereat sacrificium, neque aliud quidquam iis restat præter terribilem judicii expectationem, & iræ divinæ, quæ refractarios consumet. Heb. 10:26–27. nec prætermittendum hic, quod Christus diserte dicit: 'Iram Dei manere super hominem incredulum' Joh. 3:36. Manente itaque ira divina etiam damnatio manet. Et 'ingens' inter beatos & condemnatos[7] 'chasma confirmatum' dicitur, Lucæ 16:26. ut nemo ex uno loco in alterum, [adeoque ex uno statu in alterum][8] transire possit. si porro pœnarum infernalium daretur finis, illæque nonnisi divinæ bonitatis effectus essent, ut Deus nonnisi summam suam bonitatem erga omnes suas creaturas exercere vellet, omniaque quæcunque facit nonnisi huc tenderent, ut omnes tandem creaturæ in æternum felices reddentur, Christus de proditore Juda minime absque ulla restrictione ac limitatione dicere potuisset: 'Satius ipsi esset, si nunquam natus fuisset.' Matt. 26:24. Impossibilitas[9] etiam 'restitutionis' post hanc vitam inde apparet, quod diserte Apostolus testatur ad Heb.

---

7. Stapfer: "damnatos."

8. JE apparently skipped the bracketed phrase by mistake, possibly because his eye fell on "alterum" in the next line.

9. Stapfer: "Impossibiles."

6:4–6. 'Impossibile esse, ut qui semel collustrati sunt——[1] & tamen vo-
labuntur, ii iterum vitæ correctione renoventur: Qui sibi Filium Dei
iterum crucifigunt, eumque ludibrio habent. Terra enim quæ imbrem
sæpius in se venientem combibit, & herbam profert, ea Dei favore felic-
itatur. At quæ spinas effert & tribulos improba est, & adfinis exsecrationi,
ad extremumque exurenda.'

"Classis VI. Ea complectitur dicta, quæ diabolis etiam omnem ab æter-
nis supplicii liberationem abjudicant; hic referuntur dicta Genes. III:14
& Heb. 2:16.

"Ad VII. Classem ea pertinent Scripturæ loca quæ infinitum sacrificii
Christi valorem docent: ab una enim parte S. Litteræ testantur solu-
tionem lytri omnem creaturarum vim excedere, uti Psalmo 49:8–9. Jer.
30:21. Christi vero merito infinitus adscribitur valor, unde vocatur
'æterna Justitia.' Dan. 9:24. 'æternam adeptus est liberationem.' Heb.
9:12. 'Uno pro peccatis functus dicitur in perpetuum Sacrificio.' Heb.
10:12. Et tale ipsi adscribitur sacerdotium, vi cujus plane servare potest
eos, qui per ipsum Deum adeunt, quippe 'qui semper vivit ad suppli-
candum pro eis.' Heb. 7:25. [. . .]

"Ad Classem VIII. ea pertinent testimonia, quæ præter Christi meritum nullam aliam redemtionis caussam agnoscunt; ut adeo Christus
unica perfectissimaque salutis peccatoris caussa sit. Dantur nimirum S.
Scripturæ dicta, quæ omnem justitiam ac salutem, exclusis omnibus aliis
caussis soli merito Christi tribuant. I Cor. 1:30. Ephes. 1:3–8. Col. I. 9.
20. Ut post rejectum Christi meritum nullum amplius pro peccato sacrificium supersit. Hebr. 10:26. Imo nemo aluid fundamentum salutis[2]
ponere potest, præter id quod positum est Jesum Christum, I Cor. 3. Et
in nullo alio datur hominibus salus, Act. 4. Nec aliud quidquam est,
præter sanguinem ac spiritum Christi, quod nos purgare potest ab omnibus peccatis. I Joh. 1:7.

"Hoc omnino certissimum est, non obstantibus omnibus adversariorum effugiis, quod si ulla veritas in S. Litteris clare expressa reperitur,
certe hæc est; et si non satis firma sunt illa argumenta, quæ pro pœnarum
infernalium æternitate afferuntur, nullo etiam beatudinis æternitas nititur fundamento; siquidem prior multo clarioribus stabiliatur dictis
quam posterior; unde optimo ab adversariis petere possumus jure ut
probent, beatam æternitatem, multo clarioribus, fortioribus magisque
emphaticis phrasibus doceri, quæ solidiori modo infinitam æternitatem

---

1. The dash is in Stapfer.
2. In Stapfer, the preceding two words are reversed.

extra omne dubium ponant, quam pœnarum infernalium æternitas asseritur atque probatur."[3]

3. "However, the holy Scriptures themselves most clearly teach the eternity of infernal punishments. Indeed, holy Scripture impresses this doctrine more widely than the eternity of blessedness itself [. . .]

"The arguments to establish this dogma, drawn out of the holy Scriptures, can be divided into various classes. The celebrated Lampius, in Dissertation I about this material, says there are eight. To the first class pertains those sayings where the punishment of the damned are expressly called eternal. Eternal fire: Is. 33:14, Matt. 18:8, 25:41. Eternal disgrace: Dan. 12:2. Eternal ruin: II Thess. 1:9. Eternal chains: Jude 6. Eternal gloom of darkness: Jude 13.

"This testimony has been vindicated by all the exceptions. See in the celebrated Lampius, Dissertation I about the eternity of punishments.

"Class 2. However, although the preceding sayings are pressed by adversaries with different exceptions, those places in which the voice of eternity is multiplied can remove all doubt; where the smoke of their torments is said to ascend εἰζ τους αιωνας των αιωνων, to the ages of ages, Apoc. 14:11, 20:10. They are said to be tormented day and night, εις τους αιωνας των αιωνων. But this phrase excludes all limitation, because duplication of this sort indicates the highest degree. [Salomon] Glassius [1593–1656], in *Philol. S[acra]*, Bk. III, Tract. I, ch. 16, proves this abundantly. Indeed, the eternity of God itself is accustomed to be described in this manner. Whence this phrase cannot be understood as about any eternity than that which is set down without end.

"Class 3. Also, this eternity is repeatedly expressed with the greatest emphasis through negative formulas. 'Their worm does not die, and their fire is not extinguished.' That which is from Is. 66:24 is repeated several times, Mark 9:44, 46, 48. Also thus, Luke 3:17, 'The chaff he burns,' πυρι ασβεστω, 'with inextinguishable fire.'

"Class 4. The fourth class of arguments then is taken up, that the eternity of blessedness and of damnation are compared in the same saying and are opposed alternately to the other, Dan. 12:2, Matt. 25:46. Therefore, as the eternity of blessedness will not have an end, thus also the eternity of the damned ought to be understood [. . .]

"And [Johann Lorenz] Moshemius [1593–1755] thinks that this one testimony of holy Scripture is sufficient to prove this truth and remove all doubt [. . .]

"Class V arguments. Next, those sayings are brought forth to prove the matter of the scriptures, which clearly exclude all hope of freedom from the underworld; as Matt. 5:26, 'Truly I say to you, you will not go from there, until you have paid the last farthing.' It is said likewise in Luke 12:59, Matt. 18:34–35. Also, that all hope of forgiveness of sins vanishes after this life, is apparent from the very clear words of Christ which are in Matt. 12:32, 'And if anyone should say something against Son of Man, he will be forgiven: but if any should say something against the Holy Spirit, he will not be forgiven, not in this age or in the age to come.' Mark 3:29, it is expressed this way: 'But the one who speaks badly of the Holy Spirit, will never attain favor, but is subject to eternal punishment.' Indeed, for those who sin impudently after once the truth has been known, no longer does any sacrifice for sin remain, nor is there anything other existing for them except a fearful awaiting of judgment, and of divine anger which will consume the stubborn. Heb. 10:26–27. Nor should this, which Christ clearly says, be omitted: 'the anger of God remains on the unbeliever,' John 3:36. And so since divine anger remains, also damnation remains. And it is said that between the blessed and the damned 'an immense chasm' has been established, Luke 16:26, so that no one is able to cross over from one place to the other, [and thus from one state to the other]. Further, if an end of infernal punishments were given and there would be effects of that divine goodness only, so that God would want to exercise the height of his goodness toward all his creatures, and all things whatever he makes only would tend to this place, so that in the end all creatures would be returned happy into eternity, Christ

[1357.] DEFECTS OF THE MORALITY OF THE HEATHEN PHILOSOPHERS, FROM MR. JOHN BRINE. (See back, "Table," p. 460.)[4]

"1. Natural religion requires love to God, as the spring of obedience to his commands. . . . Love to any object, can't bear with a diminution of its glory, nor can be content, that another should rival him in that honor and dignity, which he alone hath a right to claim. Hence it is evident,

---

would by no means be able to say about Judas the betrayer without any restriction and limitation: 'It would have been better for him if he had never been born,' Matt. 26:24. The impossibility of 'restitution' after this life would then appear, which the Apostle clearly testifies in Heb. 6:4–6. 'It is impossible for those who were once enlightened . . . if they shall fall away, to renew them again to repentance: who crucify once again the Son of God for themselves and hold him in derision. For the earth which often drinks in the rain coming often upon it, and produces grass, is blessed with the favor of God. But that which produces thorns and weeds is perverse, and close to cursing, and at the end will be burned.'

"Class 6. It embraces those sayings, which for devils deny all freedom from eternal punishment. Here are brought the sayings, Gen. 3:14 and Heb. 2:16.

"To Class 7 pertains those places of the Scripture which teach the infinite value of the sacrifice of Christ: for by one part of the holy Scripture they testify that redemption exceeds all the power of creatures, as Ps. 49:8–9, Jer. 30:21. Truly, infinite value is attributed to the merit of Christ, whence it is called 'eternal justice,' Dan. 9:24. 'It has attained eternal liberation,' Heb. 9:12. He is said to have 'served as one sacrifice for sins in perpetuity,' Heb. 10:12. And such a priesthood is ascribed to him, by which power he can save those who approach God himself. Indeed, 'he lives for always to plead for them,' Heb. 7:25. [. . .]

"To Class 8 belong those testimonies which, except for the merit of Christ, recognize no other cause of redemption; that indeed Christ is the unique most complete cause of the salvation of the sinner. Truly, sayings of holy Scripture are given which attribute all righteousness and salvation solely to the merit of Christ, with all other causes excluded. I Cor. 1:30; Eph. 1:3, 8; Col. 1:9, 20. That after the merit of Christ has been rejected there remains no longer any sacrifice for sin, Heb. 10:26. Indeed, no one can lay another foundation for salvation, except that which was laid in Jesus Christ, I Cor. 3. And in none other is salvation given to men, Acts 4. Nor is there anything else except the blood and spirit of Christ, which can cleanse us from all sins, I John 1:7.

"This is entirely most certain—with none of our adversaries' objections standing in the way—the fact that if any truth is found to be clearly expressed in the holy Scriptures, certainly it is this one; and if those arguments which are brought forward for the eternality of infernal punishments are not firm enough, neither does the eternality of blessedness rest on any foundation; if indeed it would be established earlier by much clearer sayings than later, whence we are able to seek from our adversaries by the best law that they prove a blessed eternity, to be taught by much clearer, stronger and more emphatic phrases, which they place infinite eternity without any doubt, in a more solid manner than the eternity of infernal punishments is asserted and proved." Stapfer, *Institutiones Theologicæ Polemicæ*, 5, 397–403.

4. MS: "p 862. [col.] 2. d. e." The reference is to the Table to No. 1350, specifically, the entries on "Vices of the best among the heathen," "Vices of the philosophers," and "The morality of all other philosophers but Socrates and Plato founded in self-sufficiency." In No. [1357], JE is quoting from John Brine (1703–65), *A Treatise on Various Subjects: viz. . . . Defects which attended the doctrine of morality, as taught by philosophers and poets* (London, 1750), ch. III, "Of the Defects which attended the Doctrine of Morality, as taught by Philosophers and Poets," pp. 104–15.

that the philosophers were destitute of love to God, because they allowed
of religious honors being paid to demons and heroes, which they could
not have thought of without indignation, if they had been real lovers of
the Deity. No affection is more warm than love; it can't but resent any
detraction from the real honor of the object on which it is fixed. [. . .]

"2. Submission to the divine authority. Reason discerns, that he who
made us has a right to govern us. The will of God therefore, is the law
which we are obliged to observe. Wherein are two things observable: one
is, the matter of the law; the other is, the authority of God requiring those
actions of us, which are the matter of the law. With respect to the former,
[philosophy] recommends many branches of it [. . .]. But as to the latter, the authority which we ought to regard in the practice of virtuous actions, philosophy is defective. For it does not teach us to practice virtue,
as matter of duty, which we owe to our Maker; it indeed recommends the
beauty of virtue, and teaches the turpitude of vice, [. . .] in an abstracted
view from the will of God, requiring of us to practice the former, and
avoid the latter. Doing which is obedience to our reason; but obedience
to God it is not, because the mind is not influenced by his authority, in
what it acts. [. . .]

"3. The religion of nature requires us to have respect to the glory of
God in all our actions. It is not sufficient, that what we do is materially
good. If our end in doing it is not the honor of our Maker, we use not
our powers in a subservience to the great end for which they were given
us by God. . . . A regard to his glory ought to influence us in the whole
course of our behavior, as a determining principle. Nothing short of this
is living to him, by virtue of whose almighty will we exist, and are what
we be, in our nature, and all our powers, and from whose exuberant
goodness all our supplies spring. In vain you will search for the recommendation of this truly noble, this just, this reasonable service from the
philosophers. [. . .]

"4. [. . .] Humility is not among the number of the virtues" of the
philosophers. They were guilty of such arrogance as "to compare themselves with God, and in some sense allowed, of an excellency in themselves above what is found even in God himself. . . . They nourished
pride, where it least of all ought to have any place, viz. in the practice of
virtue. [. . .]

"5. It is a principle of natural religion, that all our virtue springs from
God. If we are dependent on God, for our existence, we can't be independent on him, as to our well-being and happiness. But philosophers
and poets ascribe our felicity to ourselves. They deny, that external things

are good, viz. riches, honors, pleasures, ease, health, liberty and life. These things not being in our power, they grant, that they are given us of God, and therefore they allow of thanks being given to him for them. But, as to virtue, wherein they place the happiness of man, they deny, that it is of God. He formed man capable of practicing virtue, but his so doing is of man himself, and, therefore, they deny that thanks are due to our Maker for virtue, wherein they make human happiness to consist. So that according to them, God made us, and we make ourselves happy; that we be is owing to him, but that we enjoy what is really and intrinsically good is from ourselves. Epictetus observes, that 'it is the note of the vulgar, to expect loss and gain from without; but that it is the condition and state of the philosopher to look for both from himself.' And Cicero allows of no thanks to God for virtue. [. . .]

"6. It is certainly a truth of natural religion, that God is our chiefest good. That he who is infinite good and glorious is the highest good, is most evident. In his favor we are, we must be, happy; in his displeasure, and in a state of alienation and distance from him, we must be miserable. The philosophers, therefore, were blind to true happiness and the *summum bonum* of the intelligent creature, who placed it in virtue." (Which by what was observed under the former heads was not derived from God, nor had God for its supreme object or end.)

"7. Natural religion requires perfect obedience to the will of God, in order to [. . .] God's approbation, and being entitled to his favor," and that "if once the creature fails of his duty to God, he forfeits all claim to his favorable regard, and becomes obnoxious to his righteous vengeance. Of this the philosophers seem to be wholly ignorant, and constantly express themselves, in such a manner, as leads one to conclude, that they thought God does not require of man perfect virtue in order to the enjoyment of happiness. [. . .]

"8. These authors where wholly ignorant of the necessity of other principles being produced in men, in order to the performance of duty in an acceptable manner, than those which are natural. . . . They were entirely ignorant of the necessity of the sanctification of our hearts. And, therefore, nothing of the nature of true holiness can ever be learned of them. It is only ignorance of the nature of real holiness, which causes men to think, that a mind under the influence of vicious habits, can perform holy acts. [. . .]

"9. Philosophers and poets did [not] teach every branch of virtue. Seneca represents prayer as needless. Cicero is an advocate for fornication, and thinks it cruel not to allow of it in young men. [. . .] And philosophers and poets agree in countenancing idolatry, and of performing religious worship, according to the custom of the country."[5]

[1358. DIVINITY OF CHRIST.][6] [. . .] The supreme God is doubtless distinguished by some works or other. As he must be infinitely distinguished from all other beings in his nature, so doubtless there are some manifestations or other of this vast superiority of his above all other beings. But we can have no other proper manifestations of the divine nature but by some effects of it: for we can't immediately look upon and behold God, and see what he is intuitively. The invisible things of God are seen by the things that are made. The word of God itself is no demonstration of the superior, distinguishing glory of the supreme God, any otherwise than by the works of God, and that two ways: 1. as we must have the perfections of God first proved by his works, in order to know that his word is to be depended on; 2. as the works of God, appealed [to] and declared in the word of God, declare and make evident that divine greatness and glory which the word of God declares. There is a difference between declaration and evidence. The word declares, but the works are the proper evidence of what is declared.

Undoubtedly, therefore, the vastly distinguished glory of the supreme God is manifested by some distinguishing, peculiar works of his or other. That the supreme God is distinguished very remarkably and most evidently from all other beings, by some works or other, is certain by the Scripture. So the matter is often represented that he most plainly and greatly shows his distinguishing majesty, power and wisdom, and vast superiority to other beings, by his works that are seen and set in the view of the children of men. So Ps. 86:8, "Among the gods there is none like unto thee, [. . .] neither are there any works like unto thy works." See also v. 10. Ex. 15:11, "Who is like unto thee, O Lord, among the gods? who is like unto thee, glorious in holiness, fearful in praises, doing wonders?" Ps. 89:5–6, 8–10, "the heavens shall praise thy wonders . . . For who in heaven can be compared to the Lord? who amongst the sons of the mighty can be likened unto the Lord? . . . O Lord of hosts, who is a strong Lord like unto thee? or to thy faithfulness round about thee? Thou rulest the raging of the sea: when the waves thereof arise, thou stillest them. Thou hast broken Rahab in pieces," etc. Ps. 136:2–4, "O give thanks unto the God of gods . . . O give thanks unto the Lord of

5. MS pp. 1013–23, following No. [1357], are blank.
6. "Miscellanies" No. [1358], whose entry number was supplied by JE, Jr., is the continuation of No. [1349]. See pp. 411–32.

Lords . . . To him who alone doth great wonders." Deut. 3:24, "what God
is there in heaven or in earth, that can do according to thy works, and
according to thy might?" Ps. 72:18, "Blessed be the Lord God, the God
of Israel, who only doth wondrous things." Ps. 77:13–14, "who is so great
a god as our God? Thou art the God that dost wonders: thou hast declared thy strength among the people." See Ps. 111:1–8. Ps. 145:3–6,
"Great is the Lord, and greatly to be praised; and his greatness is unsearchable. One generation shall praise thy works to another, and shall
declare thy mighty acts. I will speak of the glorious honor of thy majesty,
and of thy wondrous works. And men shall speak of the might of thy terrible acts: and I will declare thy greatness." Vv. 11–12, "They shall speak
of the glory of thy kingdom, and talk of thy power; to make known to the
sons of men thy mighty acts, and the glorious majesty of his kingdom."
Is. 28:29, "This also cometh forth from the Lord of hosts, which is wonderful in counsel, and excellent in working." Jer. 32:18–19, "the Great,
the Mighty God, the Lord of hosts, is his name, great in counsel, and
mighty in work." Ps. 92:5, "O Lord, how great are thy works!" This is often added to the declaration of God's works: "That ye may know that I
am the Lord," or "that I am Jehovah." And this: "That ye may know that
there is none like unto me," etc. (Ex. 8:10, 22, ch. 9:14, 16, and 10:2,
and innumerable other places).

'Tis[7] evident that the same WORD, the same Son of God, that made the
world or gave it being, also UPHOLDS it in being and governs it. This is
evident in part unto reason. For upholding the world in being and creating of it, are not properly distinct works. For 'tis manifest that upholding the world in being is the same with a continued creation, and
consequently that creating of the world is but the beginning of upholding of it, if I may so say, the beginning to give the world a supported and
dependent existence; and preservation is only continuing to give it such
a supported existence. So that truly the giving the world a being at first
no more differs from preserving it through all successive moments, than
the giving a being the last moment differs from the giving a supported
being this moment.

7. MS: "1.) Tis," a false start by JE at numbering his subheadings. There are several cue marks
in this part of the entry, signaling JE's intended rearrangement of the text. But while he must
have intended to move the following three paragraphs as well—to the section below on God's
preservation of the creation (he probably meant to insert them immediately above the paragraph beginning "Preserving the creation is spoken of as the work of the one, only Jehovah")—
he failed to mark them for rearrangement. Thus they are printed in the order in which they
appear in the MS.

And the Scripture is as express that the world is upheld by Christ as that it was created by him. Col. 1:16–17, "For by him were all things created, . . . and by him all things consist." Heb. 1:2–3, "by whom also he made the worlds; . . . and upholding all things by the word of his power." And 'tis he that shall bring the world to an end. Heb. 1:10–12, "Thou, Lord, in the beginning hast laid the foundations of the earth," etc. "They shall perish; but thou shalt endure; . . . as a vesture shalt thou change them, and they shall be changed: but thou art the same, and thy years shall not fail."

But if these things are so, what shall we think of the upholding and government of the world while Christ was in his humbled state? and while an infant, when he had less knowledge than afterwards, when it is said that he increased in wisdom and stature, and [had] far less strength than he had afterwards? when we are told that he was wearied with his journey, wearied and his strength in a measure spent only with governing the motions of his own body? Who upheld and governed the world at that time? Doubtless it will be said that God the Father took the world out of the hands of the Son for that time, to uphold and govern it, and returned it into his hands again at his exaltation. But is there any ground to suppose such a mighty change as this as to the Author of the universe, its having[8] such different authors of its being and of all its properties, natural principles and motions and alterations and events, both in bodies and all created minds, for one, three, or four and thirty years, from what it had ever before or since? Have we any hint of such a thing? or have we any revelation of anything analogous that ever has been? Has God ever taken the work of a creature out of its hand—that which is that creature's ordinary operation and care according to the ordinary course of things, out of that creature's hands—performing it precisely and exactly in the same manner that that creature did, as if the creature still went on in his own way, and then returned it into the hand of the creature again so that no interruption, not the least, should appear?

But now what are these distinguishing works of God,[9] or the works by which his distinguishing dignity and glory are clearly manifested and plainly to be seen? What works are they that can be named or thought of? Is it CREATING THE WORLD? Or is it the creating of the spiritual, intellectual world, which undoubtedly is an unspeakably greater work than

---

8. MS: "have."

9. JE is referring to the distinguishing works discussed at the beginning of No. [1358] (pp. 607–8) and the very end of No. [1349] (pp. 427–29).

creating the material world? PRESERVING and upholding the world? Or
is it GOVERNING THE WORLD? Or is it REDEMPTION and salvation, or at
least some particular great salvation? Was it the redemption out [of]
EGYPT, and carrying the people of Israel through the wilderness, and giving them the possession of Canaan? Or is it the greatest work of redemption of all, that which is infinitely greater than that from Egypt,
even salvation from spiritual, total and eternal destruction and bringing
to eternal holiness and glory?

Or is it some NEW spiritual CREATION that is vastly greater and more
noble than the old? Is it CONVERSION, regeneration, restoring a fallen,
sinful creature, and making men new creatures, giving them holiness
and the image of God in the heart, or giving wisdom to the heart, the
truest and greatest wisdom? Is it the conversion of the Gentile world and
renewing the whole world of mankind, as consisting of Jews and Gentiles? Or [is] it conquering Satan and all the powers of darkness, and
overcoming all evil, even the strongest holds of sin and Satan, all God's
enemies in their united strength? Is it searching the hearts of the children of men? Is it working miracles, or any particular kind of great miracles? Is it raising the dead to life, or raising all in general at the last day?
Is it judging the world, angels and men? Is it judging all in the last and
greatest judgment? Is it bestowing on the favorites of God their highest,
most consummate and eternal glory, even both men and angels? Is it destroying the visible creation and bringing all to their final period and
consummation, and to their most perfect and eternal state? Or are there
any other works greater than any of these that can be thought of, which
we can find appealed to from time to time as clearly manifesting the most
peculiar and distinguished glory of the supreme God, in comparison of
whom all other beings whatsoever are absolutely as nothing?

Concerning those particular works which have been mentioned, these
two things are evident in Scripture: 1. that they all are spoken of as the
peculiar works of the supreme [God], by which he manifests his divine,
supreme and most distinguished glory; 2. that they, every one of them,
are plainly ascribed to Christ in Scripture.

It[1] is thus with respect to the work both as to the creation of the world
in general and especially the creation of the intellectual, spiritual world.

Thus it is as to the creation of the world in general.

This is often spoken of as the peculiar work of the supreme God, a
work wherein he manifests his glory as supreme and distinguished from

1. MS: "I. It," another false start by JE at numbering his subheadings.

all other beings. Rom. 1:19–20, "Because that which may be known of God is manifest in them; for God hath showed it unto them. For the invisible things of him from the creation of the world are clearly seen, being understood by the things which are made, even his eternal power and Godhead." Doubtless it is the supreme God which is here spoken [of]. And what Godhead of the supreme God—that which is clearly to be seen by the creation of the world—but his supreme Godhead? And what can that invisible glory and power of this God here spoken of be but that by which he is distinguished from other beings and may be known to be what he is? 'Tis said, that which may be known of God is clearly manifest by this work. But doubtless one thing, and infinitely the most important thing, that may be known of God is his supreme dignity and glory, that glory of his which he has as supreme God. But if the creation of the world ben't a work peculiar to him, how are these things so clearly manifested by this work?

Again, the work of creation is spoken of as one of the great wonders done by him who is God of gods and Lord of lords, who alone doth great wonders, in Ps. 136:2–9. "O give thanks unto the God of gods . . . O give thanks to the Lord of lords . . . To him who alone doth great wonders . . . To him that by wisdom made the heavens . . . To him that stretched out the earth over the waters . . . To him that made great lights . . . The sun to rule by day," etc.

This work is spoken of as the work of the supreme God, which he wrought alone. Job 9:8, "Which alone spreadeth out the heavens"; and II Kgs. 19:15, "O Lord God of Israel, which dwellest between the cherubims, thou art the God, even thou alone, of all the kingdoms of the earth; thou hast made heaven and earth."

I Chron. 16:24–26, "Declare his glory among the heathen; his marvelous works among all nations. For great is the Lord, and greatly to be praised: he is also to be feared above all gods. For all the Gods of the people are idols: but the Lord made the heavens." Here how plain are these things, viz. that that glory of God is here spoken of which is his glory as the supreme God, and above all gods; and that this glory of his is clearly manifested by his marvelous works, and particularly by his making the heavens, that by this, that glory and supreme greatness is clearly manifested that shows him to be worthy of supreme worship, or to be feared and praised above all gods. We have the same again in almost the same words in Ps. 96:3–5.

In Neh. 9:5–6, the creation of heaven and earth is spoken of as a glorious work of God, manifesting the peculiar glory of him who is Jehovah alone. "Bless Jehovah your God forever and ever: and blessed be thy glorious name, which is exalted above all blessing and praise"; which implies at least that [he] is exalted above all that blessing and praise that any other being can claim. "Thou, even thou, art Jehovah alone; thou hast made heaven, the heaven of heavens, with all their host, the earth, and all things that are therein."

Is. 40:25–26, "To whom then will ye liken me, or shall I be equal? saith the Holy One. Lift up your eyes on high, and behold who hath created these things." How plain is it here that creating the world is spoken of as a work of the supreme God, most evidently showing that none is like him or to be compared to him. So v. 12, compared with v. 18.

God asserts the creation of the world to [be] his work only, so as to deny any associate or instrument, in Is. 44:24. "Thus saith Jehovah, thy redeemer, and he that formed thee from the womb, I am Jehovah that maketh all things; that stretcheth forth the heavens alone; that spreadeth abroad the earth by myself."

So this is claimed as the peculiar, distinguishing work of God, the only true God, in the forty-fifth chapter of Isaiah. In vv. 5–7, God says, "I am Jehovah, and there is none else, there is no God besides me: [. . .] that they may know from the rising of the sun, and from the west, that there is none besides me. I am the Lord, and there is none else. I form the light, and create darkness." V. 12, "I have made the earth, and created man upon it: I, even my hands, have stretched out the heavens." V. 18, "thus saith Jehovah that created the heavens; God himself that formed the earth and made it." V. 21, "I Jehovah? and there is no God else beside me; a just God and a Savior; there is none beside me."

God's creating the world is made use of as argument to show the nations of the world the reasonableness of forsaking all other gods and worshipping the one, true God only. Rev. 14:7, "Saying with a loud voice, Fear God, and give glory to him; . . . and worship him that made heaven, and earth, and the sea, and the fountains of waters." See also Acts 14:15 and Rev. 10:6.

The work of creation is spoken [of] as the distinguishing work of the supreme, only-living and true God, showing him to be alone worthy to be worshipped, in Jer. 10:6–7, 10–12. "Forasmuch as there is none like unto thee, O Lord; thou art great, and thy name is great in might. Who would not fear thee, O king of nations? for to thee doth it appertain . . . . Jehovah is the true God, he is the living God, and an everlasting king . . . . Thus shall ye say unto them, The gods that have not made the heavens and the earth, even they shall perish from the earth, and from under these heavens. He hath made the earth by his power, he hath established the world by his wisdom, and hath stretched out the heavens by his discretion."

The work of creation is spoken of as the work of the one, only, supreme God, the first and the last. Is. 48:12–13, "I am he; I am the first, and the last. Mine hand also hath laid the foundation of the earth, and my right hand hath spanned the heavens."

So creation is spoken of as the work of the only God in Ps. 100[:3]: "Know ye that Jehovah he is God: it is he that made us."

See also Job 38:5–10 and Ps. 104.

[That] 'tis represented that the works of creation do most manifestly show that they are the workmanship of the supreme [God], so that his power and his glory are manifest in this work in distinction from any other workman, is most plain and undeniable. Job 12:7–9, "But ask now the beasts, and they shall teach thee; and the fowls of the air, and they shall tell thee: or speak to the earth, and it shall teach thee: and the fishes of the sea shall declare unto thee. Who knoweth not in all these that the hand of Jehovah hath wrought this?" Ps. 19:1–4, "The heavens declare the glory of God; and the firmament showeth his handiwork. Day unto day uttereth speech, and night unto night showeth knowledge. There is no speech nor language, where their voice is not heard. Their line is gone out through all the earth, and their words to the end of the world. In them hath he set a tabernacle for the sun."

See Job 38:5–10 and Ps. 104.[2]

But the creating of the world is ascribed to JESUS CHRIST in John 1:3, Col. 1:16, Heb. 1:10. 'Tis ascribed to him as being done by his POWER, as the WORK OF HIS HANDS (Heb. 1:10). And in the same place 'tis spoken [of] as his work in such a manner as to be a proper manifestation of his greatness and glory; and 'tis mentioned as being his work in such a manner as to show him to be God (John 1:1–3).

Is the CREATION OF THE SPIRITUAL, INTELLIGENT WORLD, consisting of angels and the souls of men and the world of glory, a peculiar work of the supreme God? Doubtless it is so, and is so spoken of—God's creating the souls of men in particular. Zech. 12:1, "which [. . .] formeth the spirit of man within him." Num. 16:22, "the God of the spirits of all flesh." And in Num. 27:16, God has the same title; and in Heb. 12:9, God is called "the Father of spirits." Eccles. 12:7, "the spirit shall return to God that gave it." Is. 57:16, "and the souls which I have made." So the cre-

---

2. JE had cited these same texts before the previous paragraph.

ation of angels and that glorious, invisible world where they dwell; as in Neh. 9:6, "Thou, even thou, art Lord alone; thou hast made heaven, the heaven of heavens, with all their host, . . . and the host of heaven worshippeth thee." Ps. 104:4, "Who maketh his angels spirits; and his ministers a flame of fire."

But so is the creation of the spiritual and intelligent world, in every part of it, ascribed to Christ. For it is said, John 1:3, the world was "made by him; and without him was not anything made that was made"; and to him is expressly ascribed the creation of the invisible world, and of the angels in particular, even the very highest and most exalted of them; and all the most glorious things in the invisible heaven, the highest and most glorious part of the creation of God. Col. 1:16, "by him were all things created, that are in heaven, and that are in earth, visible and invisible" (these include the invisible things on earth as well as heaven, even the souls of men), "whether they be thrones, or dominions, or principalities, or powers: all things were created by him."

PRESERVING THE CREATION is spoken of as the work of the one, only Jehovah. Neh. 9:6, "Thou, even thou, art Jehovah alone; thou hast made heaven, the heaven of heavens, with all their host, the earth, and all things that are therein, [. . .] and thou PRESERVEST THEM ALL." Is. 40:26, "Lift up your eyes on high, and behold who hath created these things, that bringeth out their host by number: he calleth them all by names by the greatness of his might, for that he is strong in power; not one faileth." Job 12:7–10, "But ask now the beasts, and they shall teach thee . . . Who knoweth not in all these that the hand of Jehovah hath made this? In whose hand is the soul of every living thing, and the breath of all mankind." See also Ps. 36:6–7.

But the preservation of the creation is ascribed to Christ. Heb. 1:3, "Who being the brightness of his glory, and the express image of his person, and upholding all things by the word of his power." Col. 1:17, "by him all things consist."

GOVERNING THE CREATION is another thing often spoken of as the peculiar work of God, as in Is. 40:21–31: there governing the world is spoken of as the manifest and peculiar work of him to whom none is like, and none equal. And in Is. 45:5–13, there governing the world, making peace and creating evil, and doing all such things, bringing to pass revolutions in nations, etc., are spoken of as the peculiar works of him who is Jehovah alone, and God alone. See II Chron. 29:11–12 and Ps. 22:28, Ps. 47:2 ff.

Governing both the natural and moral world is spoken of as the peculiar work of the great Jehovah, to whom none is like, the Jehovah, the true God, the living God and the King of eternity, in Jer. 10:6–13. See also Jer. 14:22.

So it is spoken of as the peculiar work of the first and last, i.e. the only God, to govern the world which God hath made (Is. 48:12–13). The government of the natural world from day to day is spoken of as God's peculiar work most plainly and manifestly to the reason of all mankind (Ps. 19:1–6). But Christ is often, in the New Testament, spoken of as the governor of the world, is prayed to as such and spoken of as he whose will disposes all events.

Sitting as King in heaven, having his throne there, and governing the universe for the salvation of his people is spoken of as peculiar to the supreme God, that God whom none is like, in Deut. 33:26–27, "There is none like the God of Jeshurun," etc. See also Ps. 103:19, Ps. 135:4–6 ff., and Ps. 113:4–9; and Ps. 115, throughout; Ps. 11:4.

But how often and eminently are these things ascribed to Christ! his having his throne in heaven, being exalted far above all heavens, thrones, dominions, etc., being made subject to him, being made head over all things to the church, etc., etc.

JUDGING THE WORLD is another thing spoken of as peculiarly and distinguishingly belonging to the supreme God. I Sam. 2:3, 10; Job 21:22; Ps. 11:4–5; Ps. 75:6–7; Ps. 82:1, 8; Judg. 11:27; Ps. 94:2. Judging the world at a general, public judgment is spoken of as the peculiar work of God. Ps. 50:1–7, "The mighty God, even Jehovah" (This Fiftieth Psalm begins thus: *El Elohim Jehovah,* "The God of gods, Jehovah," or "The most mighty God, even Jehovah." Who can believe that these three most magnificent names of the Deity are thus united to signify any other than the supreme God? See *Synopsis Criticorum*[3]) "hath spoken, and called the earth from the rising of the sun unto the going down thereof. . . . Our God shall come, . . . a fire shall devour before him . . . . He shall call to the heavens from above, and to the earth, that he may judge his people. . . . And the heavens shall declare his righteousness: for God is judge HIMSELF. Hear, O my people, and I will speak; O Israel, I will testify against thee: I am God, even thy God." See also Ps. 9:7–8, I Chron. 16:25–33, Ps. 96:4–13; also Ps. 98.

But 'tis apparent that Christ is abundantly spoken of as eminently the judge of the world, the judge of the whole universe, all nations, all degrees, quick and dead, angels and men. We are particularly and fully in-

---

3. Poole, *Synopsis Criticorum,* II, Pt. I, cols. 871–72.

structed that 'tis his distinguishing office to judge the world, John 5:22, II Tim. 4:8, Rev. 19:11, and many other places.

DESTROYING THE WORLD at the consummation of all things is spoken of as a peculiar work of God, Ps. 102:25–27. This is there spoken of as the work of Jehovah (vv. 1, 12, 16, 18, 21–22), and of him who is the God of the people of God and the Creator of the world (vv. 24–25, 28). See also Ps. 97:1–6 and Nah. 1:4–6. Here see Jer. 10:6–7, 10; Ps. 46:6; Ps. 104:32; Ps. 144:5; Is. 64:1–3; Job 9:4–7. But this is spoken of as the work of the Son of God (Heb. 1, latter end).

The wonderful alterations made in the natural world at the coming out of Egypt, the giving of the Law, and entrance into Canaan, are often spoken of as the peculiar works of God, greatly manifesting the divine majesty, as vastly distinguished from all other gods; such as dividing the sea, drowning Pharaoh and his hosts there, causing the earth to tremble, the mountains to quake at him, the heavens to drop, the hills as it were to skip like rams and lambs, Jordan being driven back, the sun and moon's standing still, etc., etc. But those were, as it were, infinitely small things in comparison of what shall be accomplished at the end of the world, when the mountains and hills shall indeed skip like rams and lambs, and shall be thrown into the midst of the sea; and not only some particular mountains shall quake, but the whole earth, yea, the whole visible world, shall be terribly shaken, shook all to pieces. Not only shall Mount Sinai be on fire as if it would melt, but all the mountains and the whole earth and heavens shall melt with fervent heat. The earth shall be dissolved even to its center. And not only shall the Red Sea and Jordan be dried up for a few hours in a small part of their channels, but the whole ocean, all the seas and oceans and rivers through the world, shall be dried up forever. Not only shall the sun and moon be stopped for the space of one day, but they with all the innumerable mighty globes of the heavens shall have an everlasting arrest, an eternal stop and end put to their courses. Instead of drowning Pharaoh and his host in the Red Sea, the devil and all the wicked shall be plunged into the eternal lake of fire and brimstone, etc. The former kind of effects were but as little, faint shadows of the latter. And the former are spoken of as the peculiar, manifest, glorious works of the supreme, one, only God, evidently manifesting his peculiar majesty and glory. But the latter are the work of the Son of God, Jesus Christ, as is evident by Heb. 1:10–12.[4]

---

4. Here JE first wrote out the statement, which he repeated after the next paragraph, on "SALVATION, or the redeeming and saving men from misery and bringing them into an happy

This is here worthy to be remarked, that whereas the Scripture teaches that Christ's majesty shall at the last day appear to be so great in his coming in power and great glory, and those works which have been mentioned—his judging the world with such great solemnity, and then so terribly destroying this visible universe—and the terrible majesty of Christ's face shall be such that "the kings of the earth, and the great men, and the rich men, and the chief captains, [. . .] and every bondman, and every free man" shall hide "themselves in the dens and in the rocks of the mountains," and shall say "to the mountains and rocks, Fall on us, and hide us from the face of him that sitteth on the throne, and from the wrath of the Lamb" [Rev. 6:15–16]: I say, 'tis remarkable that 'tis said that when these things shall be, God alone should be exalted, in opposition to men and to other gods (Is. 2:10–22).

SALVATION, or the redeeming and saving men from misery and bringing them into an happy state in general, is often spoken of as the peculiar work of the supreme God.[5]

THE WORK OF SALVATION is often spoken of as peculiar to God. 'Tis said "the salvation of the righteous is of the Lord" (Ps. 37:39), and that "Salvation belongeth unto the Lord" (Ps. 3:8), that "Salvation is of the Lord" (Jonah 2:9). God's people acknowledge him to be the God of their salvation (Ps. 25:5 and 27:1, and Is. 12:2). Saving effectually is spoken of as his prerogative. Jer. 17:14, "Heal me [. . .] and I shall be healed; save me, and I shall be saved: for thou art my praise." Ps. 68:20, "He that is our God is the God of salvation; and to the Lord our God belong the issues from death."

Salvation is spoken of as being of God in opposition to man and to all creature helps. Jer. 3:23, "Truly in vain is salvation hoped for from the hills, and from the multitude of mountains: truly in the Lord our God is the salvation of Israel." Ps. 60:11, "Give us help from troubles: for vain is the help" (Hebrew: "salvation") "of man." [Is. 60], v. 16, "I Jehovah am thy Savior." Ps. 146:3, 5, "Put not your trust in princes, nor in the son of man, in whom is no help" (or "salvation"). "Happy is he that hath the God of Jacob for his help, whose hope is in the Lord his God." Salvation in or by any other is denied. Is. 59:16, "And he saw that there was no man, and wondered that there was no intercessor: therefore his

---

state in general, is often spoken of as the peculiar work of the supreme God." Apparently, he wanted to insert one more paragraph on Christ's majesty at the last day before starting his next point. The initial appearance of this statement, therefore, has been omitted.

5. JE, Jr., drew a vertical line through this paragraph because it repeated the statement made before the last paragraph (see preceding note).

arm brought salvation unto him; and his righteousness, it sustained him."

'Tis spoken of as his prerogative to be the rock of salvation, to be trusted in by men. Ps. 95:1, "let us make a joyful noise to the rock of our salvation." See Ps. 95:1. Ps. 62:2, "He only is my rock and my salvation; he is my defense." Vv. 5–9, "My soul, wait thou on God alone; for my expectation is from him. He only is my rock and my salvation: he is my defense; I shall not be moved. In God is my salvation and my glory: the rock of my strength, and my refuge, is in God. Trust in him at all times; [. . .] pour out your heart before him: God is a refuge for us. Surely men of low degree are vanity, and men of high degree are a lie: to be laid in the balance, they are altogether lighter than vanity." See Deut. 32:4; II Sam. 23:3; Ps. 18:2; II Sam. 22:1–2, 31–32; Ps. 18:2, 30–31, 46; Is. 26:4; Hab. 1:12.

'Tis said that there is no other Savior besides the one, only Jehovah. Is. 43:3, "I am Jehovah thy God, the Holy One of Israel, thy Savior." [Is.] 43:11, "I, even I, am Jehovah; and beside me there is no savior." Is. 60:16, "and thou shalt know that I Jehovah am thy Savior and thy Redeemer, the mighty One of Jacob." See Is. 47:4; ch. 54:5. Is. 45:15, "O God of Israel, the Savior." Vv. 21, 25, "I Jehovah? and there is no God else beside me; [. . . .] Look unto me, and be ye saved, all the ends of the earth; for I am God, and there is none else." Here observe, that is given as a reason why all nations in the world should look to him only for salvation—because he only was God—taking it for granted and as an universally established point that none but a god could be a savior. And here salvation is claimed as the prerogative of the one, only God, and therefore exclusive of a secondary and subordinate god. It follows, "I have sworn by myself, the word is gone out of my mouth in righteousness, and shall not return. That unto me every knee shall bow, and every tongue shall swear. Surely, shall one say, in Jehovah have I righteousness and strength: even to him shall men come; and all that are incensed against him shall be ashamed. In the Lord shall all the seed of Israel be justified, and shall glory." Hos. 13:4, "Yet I am Jehovah thy God from the land of Egypt, and thou shalt know no god but me: for there is no savior besides me."

God is so the only Savior of his people, that others are not admitted to partake of this honor as mediate and subordinate saviors. Hos. 1:7, I "will save them by Jehovah their God, and will not save them by bow, nor by sword, nor by battle, by horses, nor by horsemen." And therefore the heavenly hosts, in giving praise to God, ascribe salvation to him as his peculiar and distinguishing glory. Rev. 19:1, "I heard a great voice of much people in heaven, saying, Alleluia; Salvation, and glory, and honor, and power, unto the Lord our God."

But now nothing is more evident by the express and abundant doctrine of Scripture than that Jesus Christ is most eminently and peculiarly the Savior of God's people and the Savior of mankind, the Savior of the world (John 4:42). His very name is Jesus, "Savior." He is spoken of as the author of eternal salvation (Heb. 5:9), and the captain of the salvation of his people (Heb. 2:10), a prince and a savior. He is called Zion's salvation. Is. 62:11, "Behold, thy salvation cometh." He is spoken of saving by his own strength, and able to save to the uttermost, one mighty to save, and therein distinguished from all others. Is. 63:1, "I that speak in righteousness, mighty to save." V. 5, "I looked, and there was none to help; and I wondered that there was none to uphold: therefore mine own arm brought salvation unto me; and my fury, it upheld me." What is said in this place is meant of Christ, as is manifest by comparing v. 3 with Rev. 19:15. And the very same things that are said of Jehovah, the only God, as the only savior, in whom only men shall trust for salvation, in Is. 45:21–25, are from time to time applied to Christ in the New Testament. And 'tis expressly said, Acts 4:12, there is salvation in no other, neither is there any other name given under heaven amongst men, whereby we must be saved. And the heavenly hosts, in their praises, ascribe salvation to Christ in like manner as to God the Father. Rev. 7:10, "Salvation to our God which sitteth upon the throne, and to the Lamb." See also ch. 5. Christ is a rock sufficient, sure and perfectly to be trusted (Is. 28:16–17, I Cor. 10:4).

THE REDEMPTION FROM EGYPT, and bringing the children of Israel through the wilderness to the possession of Canaan, is often spoken of as a great salvation which was most evidently the peculiar work of the one, only Jehovah, greatly manifesting his distinguishing power and majesty. II Sam. 7:22–23, "Wherefore thou art great, O Lord God: for there is none like thee, [. . .] according to all that we have heard with our ears"; meaning what they had heard of his great fame, or name he had obtained by his wonderful works in bringing them out of Egypt, etc., as appears by what follows: "And what one nation in the earth is like thy people, even like Israel, whom God went to redeem for a people to himself, and to make him a name, and to do for you great things and terrible, for thy land, before thy people, which thou redeemedst to thee from Egypt, from the nations and their gods?" With Ex. 6:6–7, "Wherefore say unto the children of Israel, I am Jehovah, and I will bring you out from under the burdens of the Egyptians, and I will rid you out of their bondage, and I will redeem you with a stretched out arm, and with great judgments: . . . and ye shall know that I am Jehovah your God." The same work is mentioned as an evidence that the doer of it is Jehovah, and that there is none like unto him, and [as] that which makes known God's name through the earth, ch. 8:10, 22, and 9:14, 16, and 10:2. See also ch. 15:6–11, and 18:11, and 34:10.

Deut. 3:24, "O Lord God, thou hast begun to show thy servant thy greatness, and thy mighty hand: for what God is there in heaven or in earth, that can do according to thy works, and according to thy might?" Ch. 4:35, "Unto thee it was showed, that thou mightest know that Jehovah he is God; there is none else besides him." Ex. 20:2–3, "I am Jehovah thy God, which brought thee out of the land of Egypt, out of the house of bondage. Thou shalt have no other gods before me." Deut. 10:17, "For the Lord your God is God of gods, and Lord of lords, a great God, a mighty, and a terrible"; with v. 21, "He is thy praise, and he is thy God, that hath done for thee these great and terrible things, which thine eyes have seen." Josh. 3:10, "Hereby shall ye know that the living God is among you," i.e. by his dividing Jordan, etc. See Deut. 9:26 and 11:2–3.

Ps. 77:13–20, "who is so great a God as our God? Thou art the God that doest wonders: thou hast declared thy strength among the people. Thou hast with thine arm redeemed the people . . . . The waters saw thee, O Lord," etc. Deut. 32:12, "the Lord alone did lead him, and there was no strange God with him." Ps. 111:6, "He hath showed his people the power of his works, that he may give them the heritage of the heathen." Josh. 4:23–24, "Jehovah your God dried up the waters of Jordan [. . .], as Jehovah your God did to the Red Sea, . . . that all the people of the earth might know the hand of Jehovah, that it is mighty: that you might fear Jehovah your God forever." Ps. 135:5 ff., "For I know that Jehovah is great, and that our Jehovah is above all gods. Whatsoever the Lord pleased, that he did in heaven, and in earth, in the seas, and in all deep places. . . . Who smote the firstborn of Egypt," etc. Hos. 13:4, "I am Jehovah thy God from the land of Egypt, and thou shalt know no god but me: for there is no savior besides me."

But it was Jesus Christ that wrought that salvation. Is. 63:9–10, "the angel of his presence saved them: in his love and in his pity he redeemed them; and he bare them, and carried them all the days of old. But they rebelled, and vexed his holy Spirit." This rebelling and vexing his holy Spirit is evidently the same thing with that spoken of, Ps. 95:8–10, "as in the provocation, and as in the day of temptation in the wilderness: when your fathers tempted me, proved me, and saw my works. Forty years long was I grieved with that generation." But 'tis evident that he whom they tempted, provoked and grieved was that God whose great works they saw, and therefore that God who wrought those wonderful works in Egypt and the wilderness. And 'tis evident by that psalm, v. 3, that that was "Jehovah [. . .] a great God, and a great King above all gods." But 'tis evident by that in Is. 63 that it was the angel of God's presence, and by I Cor. 10:9, "Neither let us tempt Christ, as some of them also tempted." He whom they tempted is, in Ps. 95:1, called the rock of their salvation. And in Deut. 32[:4] 'tis said of Jehovah that "He is the Rock." And [in] II Sam. 23:3 he is called "the Rock of Israel." And the rock out of which water came to save the people from perishing, if it was a type of the[6] Rock of Israel's salvation, as it is evident it was, was doubtless a type of him who is called Israel's Rock, and the Rock of their salvation. But that Rock was a type of Christ (I Cor. 10:10).

And as 'tis said, Is. 63, that the angel of God's presence saved them, etc., so 'tis plain by Ex. 23:20–23 that God's angel, a different person from him, who acts as first in the affairs of the Deity, brought 'em into Canaan, etc. And 'tis plain that the person that appeared in the bush, that said his name was Jehovah, and I Am That I Am, was the angel of Jehovah (Ex. 3:2, 14, and 6:3; Acts 7:30). And nothing is more evident by the whole history [than] that the same person brought 'em out of Egypt. And it appears that it was the same angel which appeared and delivered the Ten Commandments at Mt. Sinai, and that conversed there with Moses, and manifested himself from time to time to the congregation in the wilderness. Acts 7:38, "This is he, that was in the church in the wilderness with the angel which spake to him in the Mount Sinai, and with our fathers: who received the lively oracles to give unto us." That angel that entered into covenant with the people at Mt. Sinai, that spake the words of the covenant there, and delivered to Moses the tables of the covenant, and appeared in the cloud of glory over the ark of the covenant, doubtless was the same that is called the angel of the covenant. Mal. 3:1, "Behold, I will send my messenger, and he shall prepare the way before me: and the Lord, whom ye seek, shall suddenly come into his temple, even the messenger of the covenant, whom ye delight in: behold, he shall come, saith the Lord of hosts." And that, without doubt, was Christ. 'Tis plain that he that spake at Mt. Sinai was Christ by Heb. 12:26–27.

Thus we see, that however the work of salvation be so often spoken of as peculiar to God, yet this salvation out of Egypt so much celebrated in

6. MS: "a."

Scripture is not peculiar to God the Father, but that the Son wrought this work as well as the Father. Therefore, let us consider what greater salvation there is celebrated in Scripture, and consider whether that be not a salvation peculiar to God the Father. And 'tis true that the Scriptures abundantly speak of an infinitely greater and more glorious salvation than that out of Egypt, viz. the salvation of men from sin, Satan and eternal death and ruin, and bringing them to the heavenly Canaan, to eternal life and happiness there. This is spoken of as a far greater work than the other, so that, in comparison of it, that is not worthy to be remembered or mentioned. Jer. 23:6–8, it shall no more be said, "The Lord liveth," etc. See also ch. 16:14–15. Is. 43:18–21, "Remember ye not the former things," etc. Is. 64:3–4, "When thou didst terrible things which we looked not for, thou camest down, and the mountains flowed down at thy presence. For since the beginning the world men have not heard," etc. But I need not stand to show the reader how this great salvation is in Scripture ascribed in a peculiar manner to Christ as the author.

We read in Scripture of two CREATIONS: the first, that which Moses gives an account of in the first chapter of Genesis; the other, a spiritual creation, consisting in restoring the moral world, and bringing it to its highest perfection, and establishing it in its eternal felicity and glory. And the latter [is] spoken [of] as most incomparably the greatest work (Is. 65:17–18, and 66:22).

Now as creation is so much spoken of as a most peculiar work of the supreme God, one may well determine that if the first creation be not so, yet the second is, which is so much greater and evidently the greatest of all God's works.

But this new creation, which is the same with the work of redemption, is in the most special manner spoken of as the work of Jesus: for he is ever spoken of as the great Redeemer and restorer. This work is committed to him; for this he has a full commission. It is left in his hands; all things are committed to him; all power in heaven and earth given him, that he might accomplish this work and bring it to its most absolute perfection. To this end are subjected to him thrones, dominions, principalities and powers, and he is made head over all things. And to this end the world to come, i.e. all the affairs of the new creation, are put in subjection unto him. And he, with regard to all the transactions belonging to this new creation that are written in the book of God, is the Alpha and Omega, the first and the last. Christ built the house; he built all things especially in this new creation; and he is God. These things are plainly asserted in Heb. 3:3–4.

Thus that work, the work of redemption, which is both the greatest work of salvation and the greatest work of creation (the two kinds of works chiefly spoken of in Scripture as divine), is accomplished by the Son of God. And if any, in order to find out something or other, some work or operation peculiar to God the Father, should suppose, that although this new creation and great salvation in general is wrought by Christ, yet some particular part or parts of it are appropriated to God the Father; I would say further that each particular part of it is ascribed to Christ. Let us consider each part:

Particularly that part of this work which consists in purchasing the redeemed. This indeed is ascribed to God. I Cor. 6:19–20, "which ye have of God, and ye are not your own? [...] therefore glorify God in your body, and in your spirit, which are God's." Ch. 7:23, "Ye are bought with a price; be ye not the servants of men." Acts 20:28, "feed the church of God, which he hath purchased with his own blood." But I need not go about to[7] show particularly that purchasing the redeemed is peculiarly ascribed to Christ.

The giving spiritual and saving light is one chief part of the new creation, as creating the light was a chief part of the old creation. The causing this spiritual light is spoken of as the peculiar work of God. II Cor. 4:6, "For God, who caused the light to shine out of darkness," etc. John 6:45, "It is written in the Prophets, And they shall be all taught of God. Every man therefore that hath heard, and learned of the Father." Matt. 11:25, "thou hast hid these things from the wise and prudent, and revealed them unto babes." And so in innumerable places. But the giving this light is especially ascribed to Christ as the author and fountain of it. He is called the light of the world, the light of life, the true light that lighteneth every man that cometh into the world. He is the Sun of righteousness. No man "knoweth the Father but the Son, and he to whom the Son will reveal him," etc., etc. [Matt 11:27].

So with respect to calling men into Christ's fellowship and kingdom, this also is ascribed to God. Rom. 8:30, "whom he did predestinate, them he also called." Acts 2:39, "as many as the Lord our God shall call." I Cor. 1:9, "God is faithful, by whom ye were called unto the fellowship of his Son Jesus Christ our Lord." I Thess. 2:12, "That ye would walk worthy of God, who hath called you unto his kingdom and glory." II Thess. 2:13–14, "God hath from the beginning chosen you to salvation . . . whereunto he called you by our gospel." II Tim. 1:[8–]9, "according to the

7. MS: "the."

power of God; who hath saved us, and called us with an holy calling, not according to our works, but according to his own purpose and grace." I Pet. 5:10, "the God of all grace, who hath called us unto his eternal glory." See Rom. 9:24, I Pet. 1:15.

This is ascribed to Jesus Christ. Rom. 1:6, "Among whom also ye are the called of Jesus Christ." I Cor. 7:17, "as the Lord hath called everyone." John 10:3, "and he calleth his own sheep by name, and leadeth them out." V. 16, "other sheep have I, which are not of this fold: them also I must bring in, and they shall hear my voice." Eph. 1:18, "that ye may know what is the hope of his calling."

Regeneration, or the changing and renewing of the heart, this is spoken of as the peculiar work of God. John 1:13, "Which were born, not of blood, nor of the will of the flesh, nor of the will of man, but of God." Jas. 1:18, "Of his own will begat he us with the word of truth, that we should be a kind of firstfruits of his creatures." I John 5:1, 4, 18, "born of God," . . . "begotten of him." So I John 3:9, and 4:7. I Pet. 1:3, "hath begotten us again." Eph. 2:1, 4, 5, "hath quickened." Ch. 1:19, according to "the exceeding greatness of his power," etc.

This also is ascribed to Christ. Saints are born of him in their spiritual generation and therefore are called his seed (Gal. 3:29). 'Tis Christ that baptizes men with the Holy Ghost, which is called the washing of regeneration and renewing of the Holy Ghost, and a being born of water and of the Spirit. So 'tis evident by Tit. 3:4–5 that "the kindness and love of God our Savior" appears in his saving us "by the washing of regeneration, and renewing of the Holy Ghost."[8] Christ sanctifies and cleanses the souls of men as "by the washing of water by the word" (Eph. 5:26).

Justification, washing from sin, delivering from guilt, forgiving sin, admitting to favor and to the glorious benefits of righteousness in the sight of God, are often spoken as belonging peculiarly to God. Rom. 3:26, "To declare, I say, at this time his righteousness: that he might be just, and the justifier," etc. V. 30, "Seeing it is one God" that justifieth, etc. Ch. 8:30, when he called he also justified. V. 33, "It is God that justifieth." Is. 43:25, "I [. . .] am he that blotteth out thy transgressions for mine own sake." Ps. 51:2, 4, "Wash me thoroughly from mine iniquity, and cleanse me from my sin. . . . Against thee, thee only, have I sinned." Therefore the Jews said, Luke 5:21, "Who can forgive sins, but God only?"

But Christ hath power to forgive sins, as it follows in the last mentioned place, v. 24, "But that ye may know that the Son of man hath power on

8. JE, Jr., crossed this sentence out of the MS.

earth to forgive sins," etc. He washes "us from our sins in his own blood" (Rev. 1:5). And he justifies those that know and believe in him. Is. 53:11, "He shall see of the travail of his soul, and shall be satisfied: by his knowledge shall my righteous servant justify many." The Father hath committed all judgment to the Son to justify his people and condemn his adversaries.

Overcoming SATAN, and delivering men from him, and giving his people victory over him is spoken of as the peculiar work of God's glorious power. Is. 27:1, "In that day Jehovah with his great and strong sword shall punish leviathan the piercing serpent, even leviathan that crooked serpent; he shall slay the dragon that is in the sea." Ps. 8:1–2, "O Jehovah our God, how excellent is thy name in all the earth! who hast set thy glory above the heavens. Out of the mouths of babes and sucklings hast thou ordained strength because of thine enemies, that thou mightest still the enemy and the avenger." Ps. 91:13, "Thou shalt tread on the lion," etc.

But 'tis the special work of Christ to bruise the serpent's head, to destroy the works of the devil, and that by his own strength. For he is represented as conquering him, because he is stronger than the "strong man armed" [Luke 11:21], and so overcoming him and taking from him all his armor wherein he trusted, and spoiling his goods. 'Tis he that has spoiled principalities and powers and made a show of them, openly triumphing over them. He is the spiritual Samson that has rent the roaring lion "as he would have rent a kid" [Judg. 14:6], and the spiritual David that has delivered the lamb out of his mouth and has slain that great Goliath. He is that Michael who fights with the dragon and casts him out, and at last will judge Satan, and cause his saints to judge him, and he will utterly destroy him and inflict those everlasting torments on him spoken of, Rev. 20:10; in the apprehension of which he now trembles, and trembled for fear that Christ would inflict these torments on him, when he cried out and fell down before him, saying "art thou come to torment me before the time?" [Matt. 8:29], and "I beseech thee, torment me not" [Luke 8:28].

If any should imagine that those parts of the work of redemption which are initial and are wrought in this world, being more imperfect, may be wrought by the Son of God, but that more glorious perfection of it which is brought to pass in heaven is peculiar to God the Father: in opposition to this it may be observed, it belongs to Christ to take care of the souls of his saints after death, and to receive them to the heavenly state, and give them possession of heaven. Therefore the Scriptures represent that he redeems his saints to God and makes 'em kings and priests. He has the key of David, the key of the palace, and the keys of Hades, or the separate state, and of death, and opens and no man shuts, and shuts and no man opens. He is gone to heaven as the forerunner of the saints. He has in their name taken possession of that inheritance which he has purchased for them, that he may put them in possession of it in due time. He is gone to prepare a place for them, that he may in his time come and take them to himself, that where he is, there they may be also, and make them sit with him in his throne, and give them the glory which God hath given him. And therefore Stephen, when dying, commended his spirit into Christ's hands.

Or if any shall say, that not only those parts of salvation that the saints are the subjects of in this world, but also what they receive in heaven before the resurrection is but initial and exceeding imperfect in comparison of what will be brought to pass at the day of judgment; and should imagine that, although Christ may accomplish these more imperfect parts of the new creation, yet that far more glorious salvation which shall be affected at the end of the world, when all things shall be brought to their highest consummation, shall be the peculiar work of God the Father: 'tis abundantly manifest from Scripture that that consummation of all things shall be by Christ. He shall raise the dead by his voice, as one that has power and life in himself. He shall raise up the bodies of his saints in their glorious resurrection, making their bodies like to his glorious body (John 5:25–29 and 6:39–40). He, as the universal and final Judge, shall fully purge the world of all filthiness, put an end to all confusion and disorder in it, put all things to rights, and bring everything to its last and most perfect state. He shall bestow that great gift of eternal life, in both soul and body, in the whole church, in every individual member, in a state of most consummate glory—the thing aimed at in all the preceding steps of the great affair of redemption—shall present his church to himself, and to his Father a glorious church, not having spot or wrinkle or any such thing, all in perfect purity, beauty and glory. And the glory which God hath given him, he will give them in the most perfect manner, that they may reign with him forever and ever. And thus he will cause the New Jerusalem to appear in its brightest glory, as a bride adorned for her husband, and will perfect the new creation, and cause the new heavens and new earth to shine forth in their consummate and eternal beauty and brightness, when God shall proclaim, "It is done. I am Alpha and Omega, the first and the last" [Rev. 21:6]. John 11:25 and 5:22–23, 27; Eph. 5:27; I Cor. 15:20–28; Matt. 25:34; II Tim. 4:8; Luke 22:29–30; Matt. 24:47; Rev. 2:7, 10 and 3:21; Rev. 22:11–17. Christ is represented as being himself the light and glory that enlightens the New Jerusalem, that fills with brightness and glory the church of God in its last, consummate and eternal glory (Rev. 21:23).

With regard to MIRACLES, how the miracles that Christ wrought were such as are spoken of as the peculiar works of God, see "Table" [to the] "Miscellanies" under the word "Miracles."[9]

Concerning the name JEHOVAH, take notice of Neh. 9:6, "thou, art Jehovah alone; thou hast made heaven, and earth, the heaven of heavens, with all their host, the earth," etc. Deut. 4:35, "that thou mightest know that Jehovah he is God; there is none else besides him." So v. 39. Deut. 6:4, "Hear, O Israel: Jehovah our God is one Jehovah." II Sam. 22:32, "Who is God, save Jehovah? who is a rock, save our God?" So Ps. 18:31. I Kgs. 18:39, "Jehovah, he is the God; Jehovah, he is the God." Ps. 118:27, "God is Jehovah." Jer. 16:21, "and they shall know that my name is Jehovah." So when [God] proclaimed his name in Mt. Sinai, Ex. 34:5–6, he "passed by [. . .] and proclaimed, Jehovah, Jehovah." Josh. 22:22, "Jehovah God of gods, Jehovah God of Gods." Hos. 12:5, "Even Jehovah God of hosts; Jehovah is his memorial." Deut. 28:58, "that thou mayst fear this glorious and fearful name, Jehovah thy God." Is. 43:3, "I am Jehovah thy God, the Holy One of Israel, thy Savior." Is. 47:4, "As for our Redeemer, Jehovah Zebaoth is his name, the Holy One of Israel." Is. 48:2, "the God of Israel; Jehovah Zebaoth is his name." Ch. 51:15, "I am the Jehovah thy God, that divided the sea, whose waves roared: Jehovah Zebaoth is his name." Ch. 54:5, "thy maker is thy husband; Jehovah Zebhaoth is his name; and thy Redeemer the Holy One of Israel; the God of the whole earth shall he be called." Jer. 10:16, "Jehovah Zebhaoth is his name." So ch. 31:35. Ch. 32:18, "the Great, the Mighty God, Jehovah Zebhaoth is his name." And 50:34, "Their Redeemer is strong; Jehovah Zebhaoth is his name." And 51:19. Is. 42:8, "I am Jehovah: that is my name." Ex. 18:11, "Jehovah is greater than all gods." Jer. 10:10, "Jehovah is the true God, he is the living God, and an everlasting king." Amos 5:8, "Jehovah is his name." Ch. 9:6, "Jehovah is his name." Ex. 15:11, "Who is like unto thee, O Jehovah." I Chron. 17:20, "O Jehovah, there is none like unto thee." Ps. 86:8, "there is none like to thee, O Jehovah." II Sam. 6:2, "whose name is called by the name of Jehovah Zebhaoth." Ps. 68:4, "extol him that rideth on the heavens by his name JAH." Ps. 83:18, "whose name alone is Jehovah."

It might well be expected, that in that abundant revelation which God

---

9. See *Works, 13,* 141.

has made of himself, that he would make himself known by some one name at least, which should be expressly delivered as the peculiar and distinguishing name of the Most High. And we find it to be. God has with great solemnity declared a certain name as his most peculiar name, that he has expressly and very often spoken of as a name that belongs to him in a most distinguishing manner, and belongs only to the Supreme Being, and asserted that it belongs to no other. But notwithstanding all this,[1] the Arians, to serve their particular purpose, reject this name as not the distinguishing name of the supreme God, and fix on some other name, nowhere in so express a manner appropriated to him.

KING OF KINGS and LORD OF LORDS are titles peculiar to the Supreme Being. Deut. 10:17, "For the Lord your God is God of gods, and Lord of lords." Ps. 136:3, "O give thanks to the Lord of lords: for his mercy endureth forever." Dan. 2:47, "Of a truth it is, that your God is a God of gods, and Lord of kings." I Tim. 6:14–16, "until the appearing of our Lord Jesus Christ: which in his times he shall show, who is the blessed and only Potentate, the King of kings, and Lord of lords; who only hath immortality, dwelling in light which no man can approach unto; whom no man hath seen, nor can see: to whom be honor and power everlasting. Amen."

CHRIST'S ETERNITY. Ps. 102:24–27, "Of old hast thou laid the foundations of the earth: and the heavens are the work of thy hands. They shall perish, but thou shalt endure." See v. 12, compared with Heb. 1:10–12, compared with Gen. 21:33, "and called on the name of the Lord, the everlasting God." Deut. 33:27, "The eternal God is thy refuge, and underneath are everlasting arms." Ps. 9:7, "the Lord shall endure forever." And 104:31, "The glory of the Lord shall endure forever." And 92:8, "But thou, O Lord, art most high for evermore." And 135:13, "Thy name, O Lord, shall endure forever; and thy memorial, [. . .] throughout all generations." Jer. 10:10, "the Lord is the true God, he is the living God, and an everlasting king." Dan. 4:2–3, "the signs and the wonders that the high God hath wrought towards me. How great are his signs! and how mighty are his wonders! his kingdom is an everlasting kingdom, and of his dominion there is no end." And Lam. 5:19, compared with Dan. 7:14. Rom. 1:23, "the incorruptible God." I Tim. 6:16, the King eternal, immortal. Rev. 4:9–10, and 5:14, and 10:5–6, and 15:7. Heb. 7:3, "having neither beginning of days, nor end of life."

Many things make it manifest that he that dwelt in the tabernacle and temple, between the cherubims, was Christ. But 'tis evident that the God

---

1. MS: "thing."

that dwelt there was the only true God. II Kgs. 19:15, "O Lord God of Israel, which dwellest between the cherubims, thou art the God, even thou alone." And v. 19, "that all the kingdoms of the earth may know that thou art the Lord God, even thou only." I Kgs. 8:6, with vv. 12–13, v. 23, vv. 27, 60.

All the ANGELS worship Christ. Heb. 1:6, "let all the angels of God worship him." But this is the prerogative of the supreme God. Neh. 9:6, "Thou, even thou, art Jehovah alone; thou hast made heaven, the heaven of heavens, with all their host . . . ; and the host of heaven worshippeth thee."

The supreme divinity of the Son of God is most manifest from Heb. 12:24–26, "And to Jesus the mediator of the new covenant, and to the blood of sprinkling, that SPEAKETH better things than the blood of Abel. See that ye refuse not him that SPEAKETH. For if they escaped not who refused him who spake on earth, much more shall not we escape, if we turn away from him that speaketh from heaven: whose voice then shook the earth: but now he hath promised, saying, Yet once more I shake not the earth only, but also heaven." Here I observe:

1. 'Tis plain that he who spake, whose voice "shook the earth," meaning him that spake at Mt. Sinai, was the supreme and only God (see this proved, back, p. 619).[2]

2. 'Tis manifest that he that speaks to us from heaven now, under the gospel, is the same whose voice then shook the earth. For this the words are express.

3. If any should say that he that speaks to us from heaven is not the same with him that spake on earth, whose voice then shook the earth, yet they must allow him to be either equal or superior. But he that speaks to us from heaven, in his so speaking, is mentioned as much the most to be regarded.

4. 'Tis manifest that, by "him that speaks" to us "from heaven," the Apostle means Christ, the Mediator of the new covenant. This appears two ways: first, by the connection of the twenty-fifth with the twenty-fourth verse, in the former of which he speaks of Christ, as of him that speaketh good things to us by his blood, and then immediately bids us beware that we don't refuse him that speaketh; and second, 'tis plain that he that speaks the gospel to us from heaven, whose voice is so much more to be regarded than the voice of the law at Mt. Sinai, is [Christ], by that

2. MS: "p. 1035." JE refers to the section beginning, "THE REDEMPTION FROM EGYPT, and bringing the children of Israel through the wilderness to the possession of Canaan . . ."

parallel place in the same epistle, ch. 2:2–3: "For if the word spoken by angels was steadfast, and every transgression and disobedience received a just recompense of reward; how shall we escape, if we neglect so great salvation; which at the first began to be SPOKEN TO US BY THE LORD, and was confirmed to us by [them] that heard him."

There must be a vast difference, not only in the degree but in the kind, of respect and WORSHIP due to the supreme God and other things, as there is so infinite a difference between this Being and all other beings. There is a great difference as to the kind of respect proper for a wife to her husband, and that which is proper for her exercise towards other men. So it is with respect to the respect due to God. Otherwise, there would not be a foundation for that jealousy which God exercises on occasion of his people's worshipping other beings.

With respect to what has been observed of the WORKS and WORSHIP OF GOD is worthy to be observed these sayings of Christ: John 5:17, "My Father worketh hitherto, and I work"; v. 19, "what things soever the Father doth, these also doth the Son likewise"; v. 23, "That all men should honor the Son, even as they honor the Father": together with what has been said of God's JEALOUSY arguing that it is not only a different degree of respect, but also a different kind of respect, that is due to the supreme God from what is due to any creature. 'Tis plain God is jealous in that respect, that no other being may share with him in honor, that he alone may be exalted. 'Tis expected that other beings should humble themselves, should be brought low, should deny themselves for God and esteem themselves as nothing before him. And as he requires that they should abase themselves, he would not set others to exalt them to a rivalship with him. Jealousy desires that others should be contemned in comparison with us. If men may pray to Christ, may adore him, may give themselves up to him and trust in him, and praise him, and serve him, what kind of worship is due to the Father entirely distinct in[3] nature and kind?

When Satan tempted Christ to fall down and worship him, as one that had power to dispose of the kingdoms of this world and the glory of them, Christ replies, "it is written, Thou shalt worship the Lord thy God, and him only shalt thou serve" [Matt. 4:10, Luke 4:8]. But the Arians must suppose we are required to worship and serve another than this Lord God which Christ speaks of, as the disposer not only of the kingdoms of this world but of the kingdom of heaven and the glory of that.

---

3. MS: "and."

On the supposition of Christ's being a creature, he would much more properly be ranked with creatures than with God (as he so generally is, being called by his names and titles, having ascribed to him his attributes, dominion, etc.). However great a creature he is, he is infinitely nearer to the rest of the creatures than to God.

Præcipua argumenta contra deitatem filii "continentur in epistola illa quam Andreas Wissowatius Socinianus celebris ad Baronem Boineburgium anno 1665 exaravit . . . . De qua epistola hoc illustris Leibnitii judicium est, quod in illa omne fere robur sophismatum contra mysterium hoc contineatur. Ita autem sonat hæc epistola:

"'. . . Unus Deus altissimus est Pater ille, ex quo omnia. Filius Dei Jesus Christus non est Pater ille ex quo omnia. E. Filius Dei Jesus Christus non est unus Deus altissimus.

"'Syllogismi hujus propositio [major] habetur I Cor. 8:6, in verbis Apostoli, qui docere volens, quis nobis Christianis habendus sit Deus ille unus, nempe non talis, quales sunt multi Dii, quos esse ibidem supra dixit, ait, eum esse Patrem illum, ex quo omnia, nempe primam Personam, ex qua ut fonte & causa, primoque principia, omnia proficiscuntur. Non dicit, ut nunc dici solet, unum illum Deum esse & Patrem & Filium & Spiritum Sanctum, cujus mysterii dicendi hic erat vel maxima occasio, si usquam.

"'Minor probatur præter alia inde, quod ibidem vox Jesus Christus distinguatur [. . .] alio modo: Unus Dominus per quem omnia. Nempe divinus non supremus, qui est solus Pater, ex quo omnia, sed is, quem Deus ille fecit Dominum & Christum seu unctum suum, ut ait S. Petrus Apostolus alter Act. 2:36, per quem ut secundam & mediam causam Deus ille supremus ex quo omnia, ut prima causa, facit ista omnia. De quo vide etiam Eph. 2:9. Ebr. 1:2, 13:24. Act. 2:22. Tit. 3:4–6. II Cor. 5:18. I Cor. 15:57. II Cor. 4:14. Rom. 2:16.

Qui nescivit diem judicii, is non est Deus altissimus.
Filius nescivit diem judicii.
E. Filius non est Deus altissimus.

"'Major probatur, quia esse omniscium, est Dei altissimi attributum proprium. Qui autem nescivit diem judicii, is non est Deus altissimus. Implicat hoc contradictionem. Minor patet ex verbis ipsius Christi primo Matt. 24:36, de illa hora nemo scit . . . nisi Pater meus solus. Deinde expressius Marci 13:32, de die & hora nemo scit, neque angeli, qui sunt de cœlo, neque Filius nisi Pater. Quantopere hæc verba Christi torserint, & torqueant homoousianos, & quomodo ipsi vicissim torquere soleant, patet ex Maldonato. . . . Vulgata responsio, præsertim Reformatorum: (nam alii eam rejicere solent) est ex distinctio[4] partium in Christo: nescivisse eum hunc diem quoad humanitatem; at scivisse quoad divinitatem. Sed distinctione ista vana est quando ponit unum suppositum Filii Dei esse Deum altissimum & hominem simul, atque Deum supremum esse hominem, quod est absurdum, & implicans contradictionem, etenim Deus & homo sunt disparata, at disparata non possunt & de alio tertio & de seinvicem prædicari proprie, quod omnes ratione sana utentes nec eam obnubilantes agnoscunt. Ut ferrum esse lignum, animam esse corpus, absurdum est. Si idem esset Deus & homo, sequeretur simul Deum esse simul non Deum summum, quod est contradictorium. Nec una pars de toto composito potest prædicari propria, univoce. Deinde quod composito cuidam inest secundum partem quandam & quidem majorem ac potiorem, atque affirmari de eo simpliciter potest ac debet, id de eo non licet negare simpliciter, quamvis ei non insit secundum partem minorem. Ut quamvis corpus hominis non ratiocinetur, nec sciat aliquid, tamen cum anima ejus ratiocinetur, atque sciat, quis dicat simpliciter, hominem non ratiocinari neque aliquid scire? An ipsi concedent ut dicere liceat, Filius Dei non creavit mundum, non est Patri coessentialis, quia ipsi non conveniunt secundum humanam naturam, nisi per idiomatum commenticiam communicationem.

"'2. Cum ista Christi natura humana dicatur conjuncta Deitati hypostaticæ in unitate personæ, nonne deitas humanitati suæ tam arcte conjunctæ scientiam hujus secreti cujus capax esset, communicavit?

"'3. Si persona Filii, quæ est divina, scivit istum diem, quomodo potuit vere dici, filium nescivisse eum, cum illa persona sit iste Filius?

"'4. Simpliciter hic dicitur filius nescivisse diem judicii, ergo hoc de Filio toto dicitur, non de parte Filii inferiore, quæ non solet vocari simpliciter & absolute Filius.

"'5. Patet hic per Filium Dei quatenus est Dei Filius, primo ob id ipsum, quia non dicitur Filius hominis, sed absolute Filius, per quem solet intelligi Filius Dei. Deinde quia huc Filio statim opponitur Pater ejus, qui est Deus; ergo istius Patris Filius intelligitur & dicitur solus Pater scire, & quidem opposite ad Filium, idque ita ut Filius nescire, Pater vero solus scire dicatur. Tale hinc emergit argumentum arcte stringens:

Quicunque scivit tunc diem judicii, is est Pater Jesus Christi.
At Filius etiam secundum divinitatem consideratus non est Pater Jesu Christi.

---

4. MS: "distinctione."

E. Filius etiam secundum deitatem consideratus non scivit diem
   judicii.

"'Major probatur ex verbis Christi, quibus dixit, solum Patrem suum
diem istum scivisse. Nam si solus Pater Christi scivit, ergo quicunque
scivit, is est Pater Jesu Christi, & quicunque non est Pater Jesu Christi, is
nescivit, seu exclusus ab ista scientia.

"'Minor negari non potest, quia est in concesso apud onmes. Ergo con-
clusio est firma. Simile argumentum potest peti ex eo, quod sicut hic
ominiscientiam ita alibi omnipotentiam talem, ut omnia a se ipso facere
posset, Filius Dei sibi denegavit. Joh. 5:19, 30; 8:28. Tum ex eo quod Filius omnia habeat non a se, sed a Deo Patre sibi data, Matt. 2:27; 28:18.
Joh. 3:35; 13:3; 17:2, 7.

"'Unicum numero & singulare ens non prædicatur de multis. Quia
hoc est de definitione singularis seu individui, alias non esset singulare,
sed contra universale.

"'Atqui Deus altissimus est unicum numero & singulare ens.

"'E. Deus altissimus non prædicatur de multis. Sed Trinitarii, qui negare non audent, eum esse Ens singularissimum, unicum numero, non
specie vel genere, tamen eum prædicant de tribus personis, quarum un-
aquæque cum sint distincta substantia, est illis distincte Deus altissimus.
At ut ter unum sunt tria, sic ter unus sunt tres. Ergo ubi est ter unus, ibi
sunt tres Dii.

"'Ex regula illa infallibili, quæ duo in uno singulari tertio conveniunt,
procedit tale argumentum ex singularibus:

"'Deus ille altissimus unicus individuus est Pater Filii Dei Domini Jesu
Christi.

"'Deus ille altissimus unicus individuus est Filius Dei Dominus Jesus
Christus. E. Filius Dei Dominus Jesus Christus est Pater Filii Dei Domini
Jesu Chrsiti. Atqui hoc implicat contradictionem & est palam falsum.[5] E.
aliqua præmissarum est falsa. Non major, quam onmes Christiani agnoscunt. E. minor.'" Stapferus, *Theolog. Polem.*, Tom. 3, 488–93.[6]

---

5. MS: "falsunt."
6. "The chief arguments against the deity of the Son 'are contained in that letter which the
celebrated Andreas Wissowatius Socinianus wrote to Baron Boineburgius in the year 1665. . . .
This is the judgment of the illustrious [Gottfried Wilhelm] Leibniz about this epistle, that in it
is contained almost all the strength of sophistries against that mystery. But thus this epistle
sounds:
"'. . . The one Most High God is that Father from whom are all things. The Son of God, Jesus Christ, is not that Father from whom are all things. Therefore, Jesus Christ, the Son of God,
is not the Most High God.
"'The major proposition of this syllogism is contained in the words of the Apostle in I Cor.

Concerning the grand OBJECTION FROM THAT TEXT, "of that day and hour knoweth no man, nor the angels in heaven, nor the Son, but the Father" [Matt. 24:36, Mark 13:32], I would observe that even the Arians

8:6. He wishes to teach who that one God to be held by us Christians is, that he is certainly not such as those many gods whom he mentioned earlier in the same place. So he says that the Father is he from whom are all things, indeed, the first person from which, as from the source and cause, all principles are derived. He does not say, as now it is accustomed to be said, that that one God is Father and Son and Holy Spirit. This, if anywhere, was the greatest occasion for speaking this mystery.

"'The lesser is proved in addition to others there, where in the same place the voice is distinguished as Jesus Christ [. . .] in another manner: One Lord through whom all things (exist). Indeed not the supreme divinity, who is the Father alone, from whom are all things, but he, whom that God made Lord and Christ, or his anointed one, as St. Peter, the other Apostle, says, Acts 2:36, through whom as the second and intermediary cause that supreme God, from whom are all things as the first cause, makes all those things. About which see also Eph. 2:9, Heb. 1:2, 13:24, Acts 2:22, Tit. 3:4 and 6, II Cor. 5:18, I Cor. 15:57, II Cor. 4:14, Rom. 2:16.

Who does not know the day of judgment, is not God Most High.

The Son does not know the day of judgment.

Therefore, the Son is not God Most High.

"'The greater is proved, because to be omniscient is a proper attribute of God Most High. But whoever does not know the day of judgment is not God Most High. This implies a contradiction. The lesser is revealed from the words of Christ himself, first in Matt. 24:36, 'concerning that day no one knows . . . except my Father alone.' Then, more expressly in Mark 13:32, 'concerning the day and hour no one knows except the Father, neither the angels who are from heaven, nor the Son.' How they have twisted these words of Christ, and they twist *homoousianos*, and how they themselves are accustomed to twist in turn the common response (especially of the Reformers, for others are accustomed to reject it), is revealed by [Juan de] Maldonado [1534–1583]. . . . That is, it is from a distinction of parts in Christ: he does not know this day with respect to his humanity, but he knows with respect to his divinity. But that distinction is futile when it places a supposition that the Son of God is God Most Migh and human at once, and that the supreme God is human. But that is absurd and implies a contradiction, for God and human are separate things, and separate things are not able properly to be predicated about a third thing and about themselves in turn, a fact which everyone using sound reason and not obscuring it recognizes. It is absurd (to say) that iron is wood, that mind is body. If indeed the same being were God and man, it would follow that he is at the same time God and not the highest God, which is a contradiction. Nor can one part from a whole composite be predicated as its own univocally. Next, what pertains to some composite according to a certain part (and indeed a greater and more powerful part), and can and ought to be affirmed about itself simply, cannot simply deny that about itself, although it does not pertain to it according to the lesser part. As the body of a human does not reason or know anything, nevertheless when its mind reasons and knows, who would say simply that the human does not reason or know something? Or do they concede that it is allowable to say, The Son of God did not create the universe, he is not co-essential to the Father, because they do not come together according to human nature, except through the fabricated communication of attributes?

"'2. Since that human nature of Christ has been joined to the deity in the union of the hypostatic person, doesn't the deity communicate to its humanity, so closely joined, the knowledge of this secret of which it is capable?

"'3. If the person of the Son, which is divine, knows that day, how can it be truly said that the Son does not know it, since that person is that Son?

"'4. This Son is simply said not to know the day of judgment, therefore this is said about the themselves, with regard to some things said of Christ, must make the distinction between his power or knowledge as to his inferior and superior nature. Or, if they don't allow two natures, then at least as to his humbled state, and his state both before and after his humiliation; as Mark 7:24, "and would have no man know it: but he COULD NOT BE HID." This can't mean that the person who created the whole world, visible and in-

---

entire Son, not about an inferior part of the Son, which is not accustomed to be called the Son simply and absolutely.

"'5. This lies open through the Son of God as far as he is the Son of God, first on account of the thing itself, because he is not said to be the son of a human, but absolutely the Son, through who it is accustomed to be understood as the Son of God. Secondly, because hither his Father, who is God, is immediately opposed to the Son; therefore, of that Father the Son is understood and the Father alone is said to know, and indeed oppositely to the Son, even thus that the Son does not know, the Father alone is truly said to know. From here, such an argument is closely binding:

Whoever knows the day of judgment is the Father of Jesus Christ.

But the Son, even though considered a second divinity, is not the Father of Jesus Christ.

Therefore the Son, even though considered a second divinity, does not know the day of judgment.

"'The greater is proved from the words of Christ. He said that that Father of his alone knew that day. For if only the Father of Christ knows this, therefore whoever knows is the Father of Jesus Christ, and whoever is not the Father of Jesus Christ does not know, or he has been excluded from that knowledge.

"'The lesser cannot be denied, because it is in agreement among all. Therefore, the conclusion is firm. A like argument can be sought from this, the fact that just as he denies for himself omniscience, likewise in other respects the Son of God denies for himself such omnipotence that he can do all things from himself. John 5:19, 30; 8:28. Also from this, the fact that the Son does not have all things from himself, but all things have been given to him by God the Father. Matt. 2:27, 28:18; John 3:35, 13:3, 17:2 and 7.

"'It is not declared about many that there is a unique being in number and individuality, because this is from the definition of a singularity or individual. Otherwise it would not be singular, but on the contrary, the whole.

"'Nevertheless, God Most High is a unique being in number and individuality.

"'God Most High is not declared about many. But the Trinitarians, who do not dare deny that he is one most singular being, one in number, not in species or kind, nevertheless say that he is three persons, of whom there are three distinct substances. And as three times one thing are three things, so three times one being are three beings. Therefore, where there is three times one being, there three Gods exist.

"'From that infallible rule, which brings together two in one third individual, such an argument proceeds from individuals.

"'God, that Most High, unique individual is the Father of the Son of God, the Lord Jesus Christ.

"'God, that Most High, unique individual is the Son of God, the Lord Jesus Christ. Therefore, the Son of God, the Lord Jesus Christ, is the Father of the Son of God, of the Lord Jesus Christ. Nevertheless, this involves a contradiction and clearly is false. Therefore, one of the premises is false. Not the greater, which all Christians recognize. Therefore, the lesser."'"
Stapfer, *Institutiones Theologicæ Polemicæ*, 3, 488–93.

visible, etc., and by whom all consist and are governed, had not power to order things so that he might be hid.

Concerning the ATTRIBUTE OF ETERNITY: this is ascribed to God as one thing distinguishing of the only true God. Gen. 21:33, "And Abraham planted a grove [. . .], and called on the name of Jehovah, the everlasting God." Ps. 90:2, "from everlasting to everlasting, thou art God." Is. 63:16, "thy name is from everlasting." [I Tim. 6:16], "Who only hath immortality."

Of Christ it is said, "Of old hast thou laid the foundation of the earth," etc. "Thou art the same, and thy years shall not fail" [Ps. 102:25, 27]. "Jesus Christ, the same yesterday, today, and forever" [Heb. 13:8]. Prov. 8:23, "I was set up from everlasting." Heb. 7:3, without "beginning of days, or end of life." Mic. 5:2, "whose goings forth have been from of old, from everlasting." Is. 9:6, "The mighty God, The everlasting Father."

That Christ is so frequently called God absolutely, θεος and ο θεος, by which the heathens themselves always understood the supreme God, see extracts from Cudworth, pp. 642–43.[7]

Dr. Cudworth, in his *Intellectual System,* abundantly shows that the heathens generally worshipped but one supreme, eternal, universal, uncreated Deity (though he shows that their best philosophers maintained that this Deity subsisted in three hypostases), but many created gods. And in p. 627, Dr. Cudworth says, "It now appears from what we have declared, that as to the ancient and genuine Platonists and Pythagoreans, none of their trinity of gods, or divine hypostases, were independent, so neither were they [. . .] creature gods, but uncreated; they being all of them not only eternal, and necessarily existent, and immutable, but also universal, i.e. infinite and omnipotent; causes, principles, and creators of the whole world. From whence it follows, that these Platonists could not justly be taxed with idolatry, in giving religious worship to each hypostasis of [. . .] their trinity. And as [. . .] one grand design of Christianity being to abolish the pagan idolatry, or creature worship, itself cannot justly be charged with the same from that religious worship given to our Savior Christ, and [. . .] the Holy Ghost, they being none of them, according to the true and orthodox Christianity, creatures; however the Arian hypothesis made them such. And this was indeed the grand rea-

---

7. MS: "P. 1070. [col. 2]. c. d. e. & 1071, [col. 1]. a. b. c," or the fourth and fifth paragraphs of No. [1359], where JE quotes from pp. 243 and 260–61 of Cudworth's *The True Intellectual System of the Universe.*

son, why the ancient fathers so zealously opposed Arianism. . . . we shall [. . .] cite a remarkable passage out of Athanasius' fourth oration against the Arians," to this purpose, as follows: "'Why therefore don't these Arians, holding this, reckon themselves amongst the pagans or Gentiles, since they do in like manner worship the creature, besides the creator?' [. . .] Τη κτισει λατρευγσι παρα του κτισαντα; Athanasius' meaning here could not well be, that they worshipped the creature more than the Creator; forasmuch as the Arians constantly declared, that they gave less worship to [. . .] the Son than [. . .] to the Father [. . .]. 'For though the pagans worship one uncreated and many created gods, but these Arians only one uncreated, and one created, to wit, the Son or Word of God; yet will not this make any real difference betwixt them; because the Arians' one created is one of those many pagan gods; and those many gods of the pagans or Gentiles, have the same nature with this one, they being alike creatures.'"

'Tis remarkable that, in so many places, both in the Old Testament and New, when Christ is spoken [of], his glory and prerogatives represented and the respect due to him urged, that vanity of idols in the same places should be represented and idolatry warned against. See Ps. 16:4. 'Tis manifest that it is the Messiah that there speaks. See also many prophecies of Isaiah and other prophets. I John 5:20–21, I Cor. 19–22.

Ps. 45:6, "Thy throne, O God," etc. See *Synopsis Criticorum.*[8]

Ps. 49. See note on vv. 6–10, 15, in "Harmony of the Old and New Testament."[9]

"There is not the least intimation where Christ is styled God, either in the texts themselves," or context, "that this is to be understood of his office, and not of his person. Where magistrates are styled gods, the very next words explain it, and tell us what is to be understood by it: and [. . .] where Moses and angels are called gods, no one, who attends to the whole discourse, could easily mistake the meaning, and not see that

8. Poole, *Synopsis Criticorum, II*, Pt. I, cols. 839–40.

9. MS notebook, "The Harmony of the Genius, Spirit, Doctrines and Rules of the Old Testament and the New," pp. 111–12, on Ps. 49: "[Vv.] 6–10: No mere man is sufficient to redeem any of mankind from death and to procure for him eternal life, no, not the best and holiest of men. The price that is given for this must be something far more precious than silver or gold, and all corruptible riches, or the holiness of mere men. . . . V. 15: Though no mere man is sufficient to redeem any of mankind from death and to procure eternal life for him, and though no earthly riches are sufficient for it, nor men's own righteousness, yea, not the holiness of the best of men (as in vv. 6–10); yet [Christ] is sufficient thus to redeem men, and doth actually thus redeem and save the saints."

the term god was there used in an inferior and metaphorical sense." *Letter to Dedicator of Mr. Emlyn's Inquiry*, etc., pp. 7–8.[1]

"Matt. 19:17, 'Why callest thou me good? there is no one good but one, that is, God.' Mr. Emlyn affirms it to be evident, that Christ here distinguishes himself from God, and denies of himself what he affirms of God. [. . .] But the truth of his interpretation entirely depends upon the opinion which the young man had of Christ, who received this answer from him." Ibid., pp. 17–18.

"Mark 13:32, 'of that day knows no man; . . . nor the Son; but the Father.' [. . .] i.e. [. . .] he did not then know it, considered as man, and as the prophet and teacher of mankind. . . . The disciples [. . .] inquire of him as their prophet and teacher . . . . He tells them, he [. . .] did not know . . . , 'but the Father.' The general term 'Father' here comprehends the whole Godhead." Ibid., pp. 22, 27, 30.

"Your author inquires, in what words Jesus Christ could [. . .] have denied himself to be God more plain," etc. "The question may be returned, at least with equal force . . . , In what words could he or his apostles have affirmed him to be truly God, more plain and full [. . .]? . . . And that which your author opposes has vastly the advantage; not only for reasons [. . .] already mentioned, but as having the whole current of Scripture in its favor. . . . And further, what I look upon [. . .] in favor of the interpretation I am pleading for is, that it's founded upon expressions which either Christ himself uttered when professedly and designedly discoursing of himself; or were uttered by his apostles, when designedly speaking of him and describing [. . .] him to mankind. Whereas this text" (Mark 13:32), "which your author lays the greatest stress upon (and indeed many of the others), may be termed accidental." Ibid., p. 34.

"John 16:30, 'Now we are sure, that thou knowest all things,'" etc. The

---

1. Aaron Burr, *The Supreme Deity of Our Lord Jesus Christ, Maintained. In a Letter to the Dedicator of Mr. Emlyn's Inquiry into the Scripture-Account of Jesus Christ: Inscribed to the Reverend the Clergy of All Denominations in New-England. Wherein Mr. Emlyn's Objections Are Fairly Answered, and Shown to Have No Validity* (Boston, 1757), pp. 7–8. Burr was responding to the dedicator of Thomas Emlyn's *An Humble Inquiry into the Scripture-Account of Jesus Christ: Or, A Short Argument Concerning His Deity and Glory, According to the Gospel. By the Late Reverend, Learned and Pious Mr. Thomas Emlyn of Dublin. . . . Now Re-Published, with a Dedication to the Reverend Ministers of All Denominations in New-England. By [G. S.] a Layman* (Dublin, 1702; 5th ed., Boston, 1756). Thomas Emlyn (1663–1741), a Presbyterian minister in Dublin, reputedly inaugurated the modern Arian controversy in Britain. Though jailed for his opinions, his form of Arianism became the predominant heresy in Britain in the latter years of Emlyn's life. Michael R. Watts, *The Dissenters* (2 vols. Oxford, Clarendon, 1978), *1*, 373.

following places are objected as parallel: II Sam. 14:20, "the woman of Tekoah to David [. . .], declaring that he was wise as an angel of God to know all things on earth"; and that, I John 2:20, "'Ye know all things,' which he expressly limits to [. . .] matters or truths concerning which he was writing. [. . .] But I challenge a single sentence in Scripture [to be produced],[2] where an expression of the like nature was uttered with that air of assurance, . . . or, where the expression itself, or what immediately precedes or follows, does not plainly confine it to certain bounds; or show that it's to be understood in a limited sense." Ibid., pp. 40–42.

"If our Savior had not infinite, divine omniscience," when St. Peter said, "Lord, thou knowest all things; thou knowest that I love thee' [John 21:17], "he must have argued very foolishly, [. . .] to have inferred, that Christ knew his heart; or [. . .] his love to him, merely because he knew many things." Ibid., p. 43.

"That Christ had [. . .] divine omniscience, [. . .] appears [. . .] from his own words, Rev. 2:23, [. . .] 'and all the churches shall know, that I am he which search the reins and the hearts.' Now Solomon declares, I Kgs. 8:39, 'Thou, [. . .] even thou ONLY, knowest the hearts of all the children of men'; and Jer. 17:10," God says, "'I the Lord search the heart; I try the reins.' [. . .] And Christ does not say, the churches shall know that I search the reins and the hearts; but, that 'I am HE,' etc. Which, if words have any force in them—yea, if the expression is not altogether unintelligible—implies, I am he who is distinguished by this character; or the churches shall know that I am the God, who searcheth," etc. Ibid. pp. 43–44.

"I add, that the expression 'I AM HE,' as it is here spoken of Christ, seems to be peculiarly appropriated to the supreme God in Scripture. Thus Is. 41:4, 'I the Lord, the first, and [. . .] the last, I AM HE'; ch. 46:4, 'I AM HE,' [. . .] and 51:12, 'I, even I, that comforteth you.' The great God here distinguishes himself from all others, by saying 'I AM HE'; this evidently denotes his great power, might and supremacy: and this expression, if I mistake not, is nowhere in the Scripture used in the same manner by any but God himself. . . . But what confirms it, that our Savior intends here to represent himself as the supreme, omniscient God, is his expressly claiming another distinguishing character of God almighty, in the preceding chapter, vv. 8 and 11. See Is. 44:6, 'Thus saith the Lord, the King of Israel, and his Redeemer, the Lord of Hosts, I am the first, and I am the last'; and, ch. 41:4, and 48:12. [. . .] And in the

2. Burr reads: "I challenge a single instance to be produced from."

same manner our Savior distinguishes and characterizes himself." Ibid., pp. 50–51.

That the eternal Logos should be subordinate to the Father, though not inferior in nature—yea, that Christ, in his office, should be subject to the Father and less than he, though in his higher nature not inferior—is not strange. 'Tis proper among mankind [that] a son should be subordinate to his Father, yea, subject in many respects, though of the same human nature, yea, though in no respect inferior in any natural qualification. It was proper that Solomon should be under David his father, and be appointed king by him, and receive charges and directions from him, though even then in his youth probably not inferior to this father.

The disciples of Christ, or those that trusted in him when here on earth, applied to him as trusting in his ability [not only] to heal all diseases of body and to raise the dead, but as having their souls in his hands and being able to heal the diseases of their minds, as being the author and fountain of virtue. So Luke 17:5, "the apostles said unto the Lord, Increase our faith." So the father of the demoniac, Mark 9:24, "Lord, I believe; help thou mine unbelief."[3]

1359. Extracts from Dr. Cudworth Concerning the Opinions and Traditions of Heathen Philosophers Agreeable to Truth Concerning Matters of Religion.[4]

Concerning the unity of the godhead.

P. 233. Thales in Laertius: "'God is the oldest of all things, because he is unmade and unproduced, and the only thing that is so.'"

Onatus the Pythagorean, in Stobæus: "'It seemeth to me that there is not only one God, but that there is one, the greatest and highest God, that governeth the whole world, and that there are many other gods besides him differing as to power, [. . .] greatness and virtue. This is that God, that contains and comprehends the whole world; but the other gods are those who, together with the revolution of the universe, orderly follow that first and intelligible God.'"

Anaxagoras seems to have acknowledged only one God, denying all

---

3. MS pp. 1052–69 are blank, suggesting that JE intended to add more to the entry.

4. Ralph Cudworth, *The True Intellectual System of the Universe* (London, 1678). In the following extracts, JE often quotes loosely from Cudworth, whose own quotations from ancient philosophers are sometimes imprecise or drawn from secondhand accounts. Significant deviations from Cudworth's original are provided in footnotes or indicated with bracketed ellipses, but slight paraphrases are not indicated.

"Miscellanies," Bk. 9, showing the beginning of No. 1359. "Extracts from Dr. Cudworth. . . ." Courtesy of Beinecke Rare Book and Manuscript Library, Yale University.

those other gods then commonly worshipped, asserting one perfect mind ruling over all. "He effectually degraded all those other pagan gods, the sun, moon and stars, from their godships, by making the sun nothing but a globe of fire, and the moon, earth and stones and the like of other stars and planets. And some such there were amongst the ancient Egyptians. . . . Moreover, Proclus upon Plato's *Timæus* tells us that there hath been always less doubt and controversy in the world concerning the one God, than concerning the many gods."

P. 234. "The more intelligent pagans did not only assert one God that was supreme and the most powerful of all the gods, but also who, being omnipotent, was the principle and cause of all the rest, and therefore the only unproduced and self-existent Deity. Maximus Tyrius affirms this to have been the general sense of all the pagans, that there was one God, the King and Father of all, and many gods, the sons of God, reigning together with God. Neither did the poets imply anything less, when Zeus was so often called by the Greeks, and Jupiter by the Latins, the Father of gods and men."

P. 243. In Plato's *Timæus* is this passage: "'When therefore all the gods, both those who move visibly about the heavens and those which appear to *us* as often as they please, [. . .] were generated or created, that God who made this whole universe bespoke these generated gods after this manner, "Ye gods of God (whom I myself am the Maker and Father of), attend."'"

Pp. 260–61. "The pagans did not only signify the supreme God by these proper names, but also frequently by the appellatives themselves, when used not for a god in general but for *the God*, or God, καταε[5] ἐξοχήν. And thus ὁ Θεὸς and Θεὸς are often taken by the Greeks not for Θεᾶν τις, a god, or one of the gods, but for God or the supreme Deity. So by Aristotle, in these words: 'What is there therefore that can be better than knowledge, than only God?' And also that other of his, that happiness consisteth principally in virtue. He says, 'It is a thing that ought to be acknowledged by us from the nature of God.' So likewise in that of Thales, 'God is the oldest of all things, because he is unmade'; and that of Maximus Tyrius, 'Many gods, the sons of God and co-reigners with God.' Besides which there have been many others," more timid, "which we shall not here repeat. And immeasurable more instances of this kind might be added, as that of Antiphanes: 'God is like nothing, for which cause he cannot be learned by any from an image.' This of Socrates: 'If

5. Cudworth: "κατ'."

God will have it so, let it be so.' And that of Epictetus: 'Do thou only re-member these catholic and universal principles . . . What would God have me now to do, and what would he have me not to do.' But we shall mention no more of these, because they occur so frequently in all man-ner of Greek writers, both metrical and prosaical."

"Furthermore, the pagan writers frequently understand the supreme God by the τὸ θεῖον, when the word is used substantively. As, for exam-ple, in these words of Epicharmus: οὐδὲν διαφεύγει τὸ θεῖον . . . αδυνατεῖ δαε ουδεν θεῷ, 'nothing is hid from God . . . nothing is impossible with God.' Likewise in this of Plato's: 'God (τὸ θεῖον) is far removed both from pleasure and from grief.' And Plotinus calls the supreme God the το ἐν τῷ παντὶ θεῖον, 'the divinity that is in the universe.' But because the in-stances hereof are also innumerable, we shall decline the mentioning of any more.

Pp. 336–37. Iamblichus says, "'According to the Egyptians, before all entities and principles there is one God, who is in order of nature before him that is commonly called the first God and King,[6] immovable, and al-ways remaining in the solitareity of his own unity, there being nothing intelligible, nor anything else complicated with him.' Again, 'Thus the Egyptian philosophy, from first to last, begins from unity and thence de-scends to multitude; the many being always generated by the One, and the infinite or undetermined nature everywhere mastered and con-quered by some finite and determined measure, and all ultimately by that highest unity that is the first cause of all things.'"

P. 366. "We have these verses of Valerius Soramus, an ancient and em-inent poet, recorded by Varro:

Jupiter Omnipotens, Regum Rex ipse deumque,
Progenitor Genitrixque Deum, Deus UNUS et OMNIS."[7]

P. 377. Xenophanes, the head of the Eleatic sect, says "'There is one God, the greatest both among gods and men.'"

Theophrastus affirmeth that Xenophanes the Colophonian made "one principle of all things, calling it One and All." Theophrastus de-clares that Xenophanes' One and All "'was nothing else but God, whom

---

6. Cudworth: "who is in order of nature before (him that is commonly called) the first God and King," i.e. the Supreme Being who is above all other divine beings and thus is the source of all things. See Iamblichus of Chalcis, *On the Mysteries*, trans. Thomas Taylor and Alexander Wilder, ed. Stephen Ronan (Hastings, England, Chthonios, 1989), § 262.

7. Cudworth translates "Omnipotent Jupiter, the King of Kings and Gods, and the Progeni-tor and Genitrix, the both Father and Mother of those Gods; One God and all Gods."

he proved to be one solitary being from hence, because God is the best and most powerful of all things; and there being many degrees of entity, there must needs be something supreme to rule over all, which best and most powerful being can be but one.'"

P. 398. Antisthenes, the founder of the Cynic sect, is said to have affirmed "'Esse populares Deos multos, sed naturalem unum,'" or as it is expressed in Lactantius, "'Unum esse naturalem deum, quamvis Gentes et urbes, suos habeant populares.'"[8]

P. 402. Eusebius cites this passage out of Plato's thirteenth epistle to Dionysius, thus: "'When I begin my epistles with God, then may you conclude I write seriously, but not so when I begin with gods.'"

Pp. 423–34. Dr. Cudworth shows largely that the Stoics acknowledged one only supreme, eternal and immortal God.

Innumerable other things are quoted by Cudworth which show that the learned men in general among the heathen, the Greeks, Romans, Chaldeans, Persians, Indians, the philosophers and poets, own one only supreme, independent, eternal God.

See many more of those produces in what follows under the heads of The Names of God, his Nature, Attributes, Works and Worship, and Hypostases.[9]

NAMES OF GOD: THE NAME JEHOVAH.

P. 260. "The word Jupiter or Jovis, though Cicero etymologize it 'à Juvando,' or from 'Juvans Pater,' as not knowing how to do it otherwise, yet we may rather conclude it to have been of Hebraical extraction, and derived from the Tetragrammaton, [. . .] the abbreviation of which was *Jah*."

Pp. 375–76. "Pythagoras did not only call the supreme Deity a monad but also a tetrad or tetractys. . . . which tetractys in *The Golden Verses* is called 'the fountain of the eternal nature.'"

So Hierocles says "'There is nothing in the whole world which doth not depend upon the tetractys as its root and principle.' Now the later Pythagoreans and Platonists endeavor to give reasons why God should be called tetras or tetractys, from certain mysteries in the number *four* . . . which being all trifling, slight, and fantastical [. . .] the late conjec-

---

8. Cudworth translates: "Though there were many Popular Gods, yet there was but One Natural God," and Lactantius, "That there was but One Natural God, though Nations and Cities had their Several Popular Ones."

9. JE frequently departs from these headings, derived from topics covered in Cudworth, in the excerpts to follow.

ture of some learned men among us, seems much more probable that Pythagoras' tetractys was really nothing else but the Tetragrammaton.[1] . . . Neither ought it to be wondered at that Pythagoras (who besides his traveling into Egypt, Persia, and Chaldea, and his sojourning at Sidon, is affirmed by Josephus, Porphyrius,[2] and others to have conversed with the Hebrews also) should be so well acquainted with the Hebrew Tetragrammaton since it was not unknown to the Hetrureans and Latins, their *Jove* being certainly nothing else. . . . It is the received doctrine of the Hebrews that God and his name are all one."

Pp. 337–39. Cudworth supposes that ZEUS, the Greek name for the supreme God, is from the Egyptian Ammon and the Hebrew[3] which signifies heat, as ζέω in the Greek is "to be hot." He observes that Hesychius says that Ammous (the same with Ammon) according to Aristotle is the same with Zeus. See "Notes on Scripture," no. 400.[4]

Agreeable to that name which God makes himself known by, I AM, and, I AM THAT I AM [Ex. 3:14], and his saying, "there is none else beside me" [Is. 45], [and,] "he that is, and that was, and is to come," "the first and the last" [Rev. 1:8], "in whom, through whom, and to whom are all things" [Rom. 11:36, Heb. 2:10], are the following things observed from the heathen writers by Cudworth:

P. 383. "Parmenides, as well as Xenophanes, called the supreme Being ἓν τὸ πᾶν, '*One that was all.*'"

P. 384. "Simplicius, a man well acquainted with the opinions of the ancient philosophers, says that Parmenides, when he speaks of ἓν τὸ πᾶν, wrote '*not concerning a physical element or principle, but concerning the true Ens, or divine transcendency.*'"

P. 385. "Simplicius concludes that Parmenides' ἓν ὄν, his one ENS, was a certain divine principle superior to mind or intellect. [. . .] In the next place, Parmenides with others of those ancients, called also his ἓν ὄν τὸ πᾶν [. . .] because, [. . .] as Simplicius writes, '*all things are from this one distinctly displayed.*'"

P. 386. "Plotinus seems to think that Parmenides in his writings, by his to; ὄν or ENS, did frequently mean a perfect mind or intellect."

P. 389. "It is well known that Melissus held forth the same doctrine with Parmenides, that One immovable was *all,* which he plainly affirmed to be incorporeal likewise. Simplicius says thus of Melissus, 'Melissus also

---

1. The sacred name in Hebrew Scripture for the Deity, יהוה.
2. I.e. Porphyry.
3. MS: "the Hebrew ~~Cham~~."
4. See *Works, 15,* 399.

declared that his one ENS must needs be devoid of body because if it had any crassities in it, it would have parts.'"

P. 341. "There is an excellent monument of Egyptian antiquity preserved by Plutarch and others; ... it is that inscription upon the temple at Sais: 'I am he[5] that hath been, is, and shall be, and my peplum, or veil, no mortal hath ever yet uncovered.'" (Which is like that of the Scripture, "invisible" [I Tim. 1:17], "who dwelleth in light that no man can approach unto; whom no man hath seen, or can see," and that, "no man shall see my face, and live" (Ex. 34:20), and other such like things in Scripture.) "The God here described [...] is some *one thing* which was *all:* according to that other inscription upon an altar dedicated to the goddess Isis, [...] 'Tibi una quæ es omnia.'"[6]

[P. 343.] "Plutarch cites this passage out of Hecatæus concerning the Egyptians, τὸν πρῶτον θεὸν τῷ παντὶ τὸν αὐτὸν νομίζουσιν, that 'they take the first God and the universe for one and the same thing.' [According to the Egyptians, the first God, and] τὸ πᾶν [or the universe,][7] can't mean the senseless and corporeal world, Plutarch himself in the very next words declaring him to be invisible and hidden ... as he elsewhere affirmeth '*that the Egyptians' first God or supreme Deity did see all things, himself not being seen.*'"

"And this doctrine was from the Egyptians derived to the Greeks, Orpheus declaring that ἕν τι τὰ πάντα, that 'all things were one,' and after him Parmenides and other philosophers ἓν εἶναι τὸ πᾶν, that 'one was the universe or all,' and that τὸ πᾶν was ἀκίνητον, 'immovable.'"

P. 344. "The Arcadic Pan was not the corporeal world alone but chiefly the intellectual ruler and governor of the same, [as] appears from this testimony of Macrobius: 'Hunc Deum Arcades colunt appellantes [...] non sylvarum Dominum, sed universæ substantiæ materialis dominatorem ...'"[8]

"Agreeably to which, Diodorus Siculus determines that Πάν and Ζεὺς were but two several names for one and the same deity (as it is well known that the whole universe was frequently called by the pagans Jupiter also, as well as Pan). And Socrates himself in Plato directs his prayer in the most devout and serious manner to this Pan that is not the corporeal

5. Cudworth: "all."
6. "To You Who are One Goddess in All."
7. Bracketed passages (from Cudworth) inserted for clarity.
8. Cudworth translates the full quotation as: "The Arcadians worship this God Pan (as their most ancient and honorable God) calling him the Lord of Hyle, that is, not the Lord of the Woods, but the Lord or Dominator over all Material Substance."

world or senseless matter, but an intellectual principle ruling over all, or the supreme Deity diffusing himself through all. He therefore distinguishes him from the inferior gods: 'O Good (or gracious Pan), and ye other gods that rule over this place, grant that I may be beautiful and fair within,'" etc.

P. 345. "And here we cannot but by the way take notice of that famous and remarkable story of Plutarch's in his *Defect of Oracles* concerning the dæmons lamenting the death of the great Pan. In the time of Tiberius (saith he) certain persons embarking from Asia for Italy, towards the evening sailed by the Echinades, where being becalmed, they heard from thence a loud voice calling one Thamous an Egyptian mariner amongst them, and after the third time commanding him, when he came to the Palodes to declare that the great Pan was dead. He with the advice of his company resolved that if they had a quick gale when they came to the Palodes he would pass by silently, but if they should find themselves there becalmed, he would then perform what the voice had commanded. But when the ship arrived thither, there was neither any gale of wind nor agitation of water. Whereupon Thamous looking out of the hinder deck, towards the Palodes, pronounced those words with a loud voice: *the Great Pan is dead*. Which he had no sooner done, but he was answered with a choir of many voices, making a great howling and lamentation, not without a certain mixture of admiration. Plutarch, who gives much credit [to this relation,] adds how solicitous Tiberius the Emperor was, first concerning the truth thereof, and afterwards when he had satisfied himself therein concerning the interpretation, he making great inquiry amongst his learned men, who this Pan should be. . . . It is probably concluded by Christian writers that this thing coming to pass in the reign of Tiberius, when our savior Christ was crucified, was no other than a lamentation of evil dæmons . . . sadly presaging evil to themselves from thence."

P. 346. "This point of the old Egyptian theology, viz. God's being *all things,* is everywhere insisted upon throughout the Hermaic and Trismegistic writings. We shall begin with the Asclepian Dialogue, translated into Latin by Apuleius, in the entrance of which, the writer having declared '*omnia unius esse*' and '*unum [esse] omnia,*' afterwards adds this explication thereof: 'Have we not already declared that *all things are one and one all things?* For as much as all things existed in the Creator, before they were made; neither is he improperly said to be all things, whose members all things are. Be thou therefore mindful in this whole disputation of him who is one and all things, or was the Creator of all.'"

There are very many things there produced from the same writer in that and the three next pages of the same part.

P. 349. "Plutarch affirms that Isis and Neith were really one and the same god among the Egyptians. . . . And this is confirmed from that ancient inscription and dedication to the goddess Isis, still extant at Capua:

TIBI.

UNA. QUÆ.

ES. OMNI.

DEA. ISIS."9

Pp. 393–94. Iamblichus cites a passage of Archytas as follows: "'Whosoever is able to reduce all kinds of things under one and the same principle, this man seems to me to have found out an excellent *specula*, or high station, from whence he may be able to take a long view and prospect of God, and of all other things; and he shall clearly perceive that God is the beginning and end and middle of all things.'"

P. 304. In the writer *De Mundo*[1] are found those Orphic verses which in plain prose is this: "'The high-thundering Jove is both the first and the last; Jove is both the head and middle of all things; all things were made out of Jupiter; Jove is both a man and an immortal maid; Jove is the profundity of the earth and starry heaven; Jove is the breath of all things; Jove is the force of the untameable fire; Jove is the bottom of the sea; Jove is sun, moon, and stars; Jove is both the original, and king of all things: there is one power, and one God, and one great ruler over all.'" Here God's PROVIDENCE is asserted.

Pp. 506–7. "The Orphic theology is thus epitomized by Timotheus the Chronographer, that 'all things were MADE by God and that himself is all things.'" To which purpose is that of Æschylus, turned into Latin thus: 'Et terra, et æther, et poli arx est Jupiter. Et cuncta solus, et aliquid sublimius.' And also this of Lucan among the Latins: ' . . . Superos quid quærimus ultra? Jupiter est quodcunque vides, quocunque moveris.' Whereunto agree also these passages of Seneca the philosopher: 'Quid est Deus? Quod vides totum, et quod non vides, totum.' And, 'Sic solus est omnia, opus suum et extra et intra tenet.'"[2]

9. "To You Who are One Goddess in All."

1. Cudworth's references throughout to "the writer *de Mundo*" actually denote the pseudo-Aristotelian treatise, *De Mundo*, of unknown origin.

2. The quote from Aeschylus translates, "Both earth and the air and citadel of the heavens is Jupiter. And he alone made all things and anything sublime"; that from Lucan, "Why do we seek gods further? Jupiter is whatever you see, by whatever you are moved"; and those from

"With which agrees the author of the Asclepian Dialogue, when he maketh 'unus omnia' and 'CREATOR omnium' to be but equivalent expressions, and when he affirmeth that before things were made, 'In eo jam tunc erant, unde nasci habuerunt.'[3] So likewise the other Trismegistic books, when they give this account of '*God's being all things that are and all things that are not, because those things that are he hath manifested from himself and those things that are not he still containeth within himself,*' or as it is elsewhere expressed, '*he doth hide them and conceal them in himself.*' And the Orphic verses likewise gave this same account of God's '*being all things because he first concealed and hid them all within himself, before they were* MADE *and thence afterwards, from himself displayed them, and brought them forth into light.*'"

P. 336. Iamblichus, giving a summary of the Egyptian theology, among other things mentions *His*[4] "'*virtually comprehending all things and imparting and displaying the same from himself.*'"

P. 441. L[ucius] Apuleius says, "'The highest of the gods comprehends within himself the beginning, middle, and end of all things.'"

CONCERNING THE NATURE and ATTRIBUTES OF GOD.

P. 291. Zoroaster as cited by Eusebius says, "'God is the First Incorruptible, eternal, unmade, indivisible, most unlike to everything.'"

P. 335. Iamblichus gives a summary account of the Egyptian theology thus: "'God, who is the CAUSE of generation and the whole nature, and of all the powers in the elements themselves, is separate, exempt, elevated above, and expanded over, all the powers and elements in the world. For being above the world and transcending the same, immaterial, and incorporeal, supernatural, unmade, indivisible, manifested wholly from himself, and in himself, he ruleth over all things,'" etc.

P. 312. D. Porphyry, in Eusebius, cites an oracle of Apollo in which "the Chaldeans are joined with the Hebrews as worshipping likewise in a holy manner one self-existent Deity."

P. 341. Philo, glossing an Egyptian inscription, says: "'It is sufficient for a wise man to know God a posteriori, or from his effects, but whosoever will needs behold the naked essence of the Deity, will be blinded by the transcendent radiancy and splendor of his beams.'"

[P. 364.] In Euripides we have these verses, which in English are thus:

Seneca, "What is God? All you see and all you do not see." . . . "Thus he alone is all things, his own necessity both without and within."

3. Cudworth translates: "They then Existed in him, from whom afterwards they proceeded."
4. I.e. God's.

"Thou self-sprung Being, that dost all enfold,
And in thine arms heavens whirling fabric hold!
Who art encircled with resplendent light,
And yet liest mantled o'er in shady night!
About whom the exultant starry fires,
Dance nimbly round, in everlasting gyres."

[P. 367.] In Virgil we have this verse, "'O Pater, O hominum divumque, æterna potestas.'"[5]

Pp. 341–42. Cudworth there shows that Athena or Minerva was the same with the Egyptian *Neith,* which he shows as a name of the supreme God, and he observes that Athenagoras tells us that the pagan theologers interpreted the την Αθηνᾶν or Minerva to be "wisdom [or mind] passing and diffusing itself through all things."

P. 377. Xenophanes is cited as saying concerning the one God "'that he MOVETH the whole world without any labor or toil, merely by mind.'"

P. 389. "Melissus declared that his one Ens must needs be devoid of body, because if it had any crassities in it, it must have parts."

Simplicius says that "'Melissus, considering the immutability of the Deity, yet attending to the inexhaustible perfection of its essence, the unlimitedness and unboundedness of its power, declareth it to be infinite as well as ingenit[6] and unmade.'" (And says,) "'Moreover, Xenophanes, looking upon the Deity as the CAUSE of all things and above all things, placed it above motion and rest and all those antitheses of inferiour beings, as Plato likewise doth in the first hypothesis of his *Parmenides.*'"

P. 388. Simplicius cites some Greek verses from Parmenides "in which the supreme Deity is plainly described as one single, solitary, and most simple being, unmade or self-existent, and necessarily existing, incorporeal and devoid of magnitude, altogether immutable and unchangeable, whose duration therefore was very different from that of ours, and not in a way of flux or temporary recession,[7] but a constant eternity without either past or future."

P. 417. Aristotle says that "'in God, intellect is really the same thing with the intelligibles'. . . . And that 'God, being an immovable substance, his essence and act or operation are the same, and that there must needs be some such principle as this whose essence is act or energy.'"

P. 504. "Sextus Empiricus thus represents the sense of Pythagoras,

---

5. "O Father of gods and men, eternal power."
6. Archaic: "not born," "not begotten."
7. Cudworth: "Succession."

Empedocles, and all the Italic philosophers 'that there is one spirit which, like a soul, pervades the whole world and unites all the parts thereof together.'"

"Clemens Alexandrinus thus writeth of the Stoics, 'They affirm that God doth pervade all the matter of the universe and even the most vile parts thereof.' [. . .] And Tertullian, that 'the Stoics will have God so to run through matter, as the honey doth the combs.'"

Seneca declares in his opinion that God is "'a divine Spirit, diffused through all things, whether smallest or greatest, with equal intention.'"

"God in Quintilian's theology is 'a spirit which insinuates itself into, and is mingled with, all the parts of the world; and that spirit which is diffused through all parts of nature.'"

"Apuleius likewise affirmeth that 'God doth permeate all things . . . and that God is not only present to our cogitation but to our eyes and ears in all these sensible things.'"

"Servius, agreeably with this doctrine, determineth that 'there is no part of the elements devoid of God.' And that the poets also fully closed with the same theology is evident from those known passages of theirs.'"

"Jovis: μεσταὶ δε Διὸς πᾶσαι μὲν ἀγυιαὶ, etc., i.e. 'all things of nature and parts of the world are full of God,' as also from this of Virgil . . . 'deum namque ire per omnes, terrasque, tractusque maris, cœlumque profundum.'"[8]

P. 505. "Lastly we shall observe that both Plato and Anaxagoras, who neither of them confounded God with the world, but kept 'em both distinct, and affirmed God to be *unmingled with* anything, nevertheless concluded that he did order and GOVERN all things, passing through and pervading all things."

P. 200, etc. "The pagan theists vulgarly acknowledge omnipotence as an attribute of the Deity. [. . .] Homer says, Ζεὺς δύναται γὰρ ἅπαντα once and again.

[P. 201.] "And before Homer, Linus, and after him Callimachus say that 'all things are possible for God to do and that nothing transcends his power.' So Virgil calls Jupiter '*omnipotens*' and '*pater omnipotens*' and '*Jupiter omnipotens.*' Ovid calls him *pater omnipotens.*"[9]

"Agatho, an ancient Greek poet, is commended by Aristotle for af-

---

8. "For God goes through all people and lands and stretches of the sea and the highest heaven."

9. "So Virgil calls Jupiter 'omnipotent' and 'all powerful father' and 'all powerful Jupiter.' Ovid calls him '*father all-powerful.*'

firming nothing to be exempted from the power of God, but only this, that he cannot make that [not] to have been which hath been."

[Pp. 201–2.] Because omnipotence was looked upon by the pagans as an attribute of the Deity, Lucretius tells us that Epicurus set himself to confute infinite power.

P. 365. "D. Plautus [. . .] acknowledgeth one OMNISCIENT Deity: 'Est profecto Deus, qui quæ nos gerimus, auditque and videt.'"[1]

Pp. 399–400. Socrates says to Aristodemus, "'Do you think that you only have wisdom in your self, and that there is none anywhere else in the world without you? Though you know that you have but a small part in your body, of that vast quantity of earth that is without you, and but a little of that water and fire and so of every other thing that your body is compounded of, in respect of that great mass and magazine of them which is in the world. Is mind and understanding therefore the only thing, which you fancy you have some way or other luckily got and snatched unto your self, whilst there is no such thing anywhere in the world without you; all those infinite things thereof being thus orderly disposed by chance.'"

And again, "'If your eye can discern things several miles distant from it, why should it be thought impossible for the eye of God to behold all things at once? And if your soul can mind things both here and in Egypt, and in Sicily, why [may] not the great mind or wisdom of God be able to take care of all things in all places?' Again, 'God is such and so great a being, as that he can at once see all things, [. . .] and be PRESENT EVERY-WHERE, and take care of all affairs.'"

CONCERNING GOD'S INFINITY AND ETERNITY.

P. 771, etc. "Plato in his *Timæus* condemns this for a vulgar error, that whatsoever is, must of necessity be in some place or other, and that what is in no place, is nothing. 'The third kind is space, which gives room to all things that are generated. And when we look upon this, we dreamingly affirm that everything that is, must of necessity be in some place, and possess a certain room and space, and that whatsoever is not somewhere, either in earth or in heaven, is nothing, which drowsy or dreaming imagination continually haunts us [and] like a ghost possesseth man, and even then, when they think of that true and awakened nature of the Deity.'"

"And this philosopher elsewhere discoursing of God describeth him

1. "Indeed, God is the one who both sees and hears what we bear."

after this manner: 'that which is not any where, either in earth or in heaven, but itself alone is by itself, and with itself, all other beautiful things partaking of it.'"

[Pp. 771–72.] "Aristotle's sense in this particular [. . .] appears from that whole chapter or section at the end of his *Physics* spent upon this very subject to prove that his 'first immovable mover (which is God Almighty) must of necessity be devoid of parts, or indivisible, and have no magnitude at all.'"

[P. 772.] And in his *Metaphysics,* he says: "'From what has been declared, it is manifest that there is an external and immovable substance, separate from sensibles; as also that this substance cannot possibly have any magnitude, but is devoid of parts, and indivisible. Because no finite thing can have infinite power, and there is no such thing as infinite magnitude.'"

[Pp. 772–73. Aristotle] asserts the same of all spirits, particularly of the human mind. He says, "'Everything that is devoid of matter, is indivisible, as the human mind.'" Again he says, "'Wherefore the intellect is not so continuous, but either devoid of all parts, or not continuous, as magnitude. For how, being magnitude, could it understand with all its parts, whether conceived as points, or as lesser magnitudes; since either way, there would be an innumerable company of intellections?'" Simplicius says, "'See how Aristotle doth everywhere remove or exclude from the soul corporeal motions.'" Philoponus observes the same of Aristotle.

[Pp. 772–73.] "But none hath more industriously pursued this business than Plotinus . . . who abundantly asserts that there is an incorporeal substance, which is devoid of quantity, of magnitude, and of parts, locally distant one from another; 'it having in its nature transcended the imperfection of quantity.' And who hath written two whole books on this very subject, that 'one and the self same numerical thing may all of it be everywhere,' wherein his principal design was to prove that the Deity is not a part of it here, and a part of it there; and so much of it in one place, and so much in another, as if the very substance of it were measurable by yards and poles, but the whole undivided Deity everywhere, saith he, 'God is before all things that are in place.' And, 'It is not at all to be wondered at, that God being not in a place should be present to everything that is in a place, wholly and entirely: reason pronouncing that he, having no place, must therefore of necessity be all of him indivisibly present to whatsoever he is present.'"

[Pp. 774–75.] "Simplicius, proving that the body is not the first principle, because there must of necessity be something self-moving, and what is so must needs be incorporeal, writeth thus: 'Because what is such, must of necessity be indivisible and indistant, for were it divisible and distant, it could not all of it be conjoined with its whole self; so that the whole should both actually move, and be moved.' [. . .] And again, 'Since the soul is not in a place, it is not capable of any local motion.'"

[Pp. 775–76.] "Porphyrius is full and express herein; [. . .] He says, 'Though every body be in a place, yet nothing that is properly incorporeal, is in a place.' And afterwards thus, 'Neither does that which is incorporeal move locally by will, place being relative only to magnitude and bulk. But that which is devoid of bulk and magnitude is likewise devoid of local motion. Wherefore it is only present by a certain disposition and inclination of it, to one thing more than to another, nor is its presence there discernible otherwise than by its operations and effects.' Again, 'The supreme God is therefore everywhere, because he is no where.' [. . .] And afterwards, 'If there were conceived to be such an incorporeal space or vacuum (as Democritus and Epicurus supposed) could mind or God possibly exist in this empty space, for this world only be receptive of bodies, but could not receive the energy of mind or intellect, nor give any place nor room to that, being no bulky thing.' And again, 'The corporeal world is distantly present, to the Intelligible, [or the Deity,] and that is indivisibly and indistantly present with the world. But when that which is indistant and unextended is present with that which is distant and extended, then is the whole of the former one and the same numerically, in every part of the latter. That is, it is indivisibly and unmultipliedly and illocally there, according to its own nature, present with that which is naturally divisible and multipliable and in a place.' Lastly, he affirmeth the human soul to be a substance devoid of magnitude."

P. 777, etc. Plotinus says, "'God and all other incorporeal substances are not so indivisible, as if they were parvitudes, or little things, as physical points, for so they would still be mathematically divisible; nor yet as if they were mathematical points neither, which indeed are no bodies nor substances, but only the *termini* of a line. And neither of these ways, could the Deity *congruere,* with the world; nor souls with their respective bodies, so as to be all present with the whole of them.' Again he writeth particularly concerning the Deity thus, 'God is not so indivisible as if he were the smallest or least of things, for he is the greatest of all, not in respect of magnitude but of power. Moreover, as he is indivisible, so is he also to be acknowledged infinite, not as if he were either a magnitude or a number, which could never be passed through, but because his power is incomprehensible.' [. . .] Again he says, 'We commonly looking upon this sensible world as great, wonder how that nature of the Deity, can everywhere comply and be present with it. Whereas that which is vulgarly called great, is indeed little, and that which is thus imagined to be little is indeed great. For as much as the whole of this diffuseth itself through every part of the other; or rather this whole corporeal universe, in every one of its parts, findeth that whole and entire, and therefore greater than itself.'"

[Pp. 777–78.] "To the same purpose Porphyrius, 'The Deity which is THE ONLY TRUE BEING, is neither great nor little (for as much as great and little properly belong to corporeal bulk or magnitude) but it exceedeth both the greatness of everything that is great, and the littleness of whatsoever is little (it being more indivisible, and more one with itself than anything that is little, and more powerful than anything that is great). So that it is above all both the greatest and the least; it being found, all one and the same, by every greatest and every smallest thing participating thereof. Wherefore you must neither look upon God as the greatest thing, for then you may well doubt how, being the greatest, he can all of him be present with every least thing, neither diminished nor contracted; nor yet must you look upon him as the least thing neither; for if you do so, then you will be at a loss again how, being the least thing, he can be present with all the greatest bulks, neither multiplied nor augmented.'"

P. 779. Plotinus says, "'Sense indeed, which we attending to, disbelieve those things, tells us of here and there; but Reason dictates that here and there is so to be understood of the Deity, not as if it were extendedly here and there; but because every extended thing, and the several parts of the world, partake everywhere of that, being indistant and unextended.'

"To the same purpose Porphyrius: "We ought therefore, in our disquisitions concerning corporeal and incorporeal beings, to conserve the property of each, and not to confound their natures, but especially to take heed that our fancy and imagination, do not so far impose upon our Judgments, as to make us attribute to incorporeals, what properly belongeth to bodies only. For we are all accustomed to bodies, but as for incorporeals, scarcely any one reaches to the knowledge of them, men always fluctuating about them and diffiding[2] them, so long as they are held under the power of the imagination.'" And again he says that "'the

---

2. Archaic: "distrusting."

indistant and unextended Deity, is the whole of it present in infinite parts of the distant world, neither divided or applying part to part, nor yet multiplied into many wholes, according to the multiplicity of those things that partake thereof, but the whole of it, one and the same in number, is present to all the parts of the bulky world, and to every one of those many things in it, undividedly and unmultipiedly; that in the meantime partaking thereof dividedly.'"

P. 780. Simplicius says, "'All corporeal substance is simply divisible, some parts of it being here and some there, but intellectual substance is indivisible and without dimensions, though it hath much of depth or profundity in it in another sense.'"

[P. 781.] The ancients also supposed a duration without past, present, and future; a permanent duration and therefore without beginning; ἄχρονος αἰών, a timeless eternity, differing from that successive flux of time which is one of Plato's γεννητὰ, things generated. Plotinus says, "'For the same reason that we deny local extension to the Deity must we also deny temporal distance to the same; and affirm that God is not in time, but above time in eternity. For as much as time is always scattered, and stretched out in length and distance, one moment following after another; but eternity remaineth in the same, without any flux, and yet nevertheless outgoeth time, and transcendeth the flux thereof, though seeming to be stretched and spun out more into length.'"

P. 783. Plotinus says, "'If God be everywhere it cannot possibly be that he should be so dividedly, because then himself would not be everywhere, but only a part of him here and a part there, throughout the whole world; himself being not one undivided thing. Moreover, this would be all one, as if a magnitude were out and divided into many parts, every one of which part could not be that whole Magnitude. Lastly, this would be the very same, as to make God a body.'"

(In all these things concerning God's not being extended, these philosophers speak of God as incorporeal and spiritual. But Cudworth mentions many other things in which they spoke of God as a spirit or mind.)

P. 380. Themistius speaking of Anaxagoras says, "'He was the first (i.e. among the Ionic philosophers) who brought in mind and god into the Cosmopœia, and did not derive all things from senseless bodies.'" So Plutarch says, "'Thereafter Ionic philosophers before Anaxagoras made fortune and blind necessity, that is the fortuitous and necessary motion of the matter, to be the only original of the world, but Anaxagoras was the first who affirmed a pure and sincere mind to preside over all.'"

P. 399. Xenophon, in his first *Book of Memoirs,* giving an account of Socrates' discourse with Aristodemus, speaks of the latter's objecting against what Socrates had said of a wise ARTIFICER OF THE WORLD, that he could not see any artificer that made the world as he could those artificers that made all human things. Socrates replied, "'Neither do you see your own soul which rules over your body; so that you might for the same reason conclude yourself to do nothing by mind and understanding neither, but all by chance, as well as all things in the world are done by chance.'"

P. 414. Aristotle says, "'Mind is the CAUSE not only of all order but also of the whole world . . . and that from such a principle as this depends the heaven and all nature.'" Again, "'Though some affirm the elements to have been the first beings; yet it is the most reasonable thing of all to conclude that mind is the oldest of all things, and senior to the world and elements; and that according to nature it had a princely and sovereign dominion over all.'"

P. 440. M. Fabius Quintilianus says, "'Deum esse spiritum omnibus partibus immistum.'"[3]

P. 503. "We observed before out of Horus Apollo that the Egyptian theologers conceived of God as 'a spirit pervading the whole world.'"

P. 504. Sextus Empiricus speaks of it in the sense of Pythagoras, Empedocles, and all the Italic philosophers, "'there is one spirit which like a soul pervades the whole world and unites all the parts thereof together.'"

P. 389. "Melissus declared that his one Ens must needs be devoid of body, because if it had any crassities in it, it would have parts."

(From these things are collected this notion of the nature and attributes of God, viz. that he is the first being; from eternity; unmade; incorruptible; infinite; incomprehensible; self-existent; necessary existing; self-sufficient; invisible; dwelling in light which no man can approach unto, whom no man hath seen or can see; a spirit or mind altogether incorporeal; a pure act whose essence is energy; without all extension [or] bulk; indivisible; unmultipliable; one most simple; everywhere present yet not properly in place; perfectly immutable. [God's] whole external duration is a permanent, unsuccessive duration without past, present, and future, or any successive flux, pervading and diffused through all things, without local motion or rest. [God is] intelligent; infinitely wise; yea, infinite intellect and wisdom itself; an omnipotent being who can

---

3. Cudworth translates: "God is a Spirit mingled with and diffused through all parts of the World."

do everything that don't involve a contradiction; that being who only truly has being.)

CONCERNING THE MORAL PERFECTIONS OF GOD.

P. 390[–91]. "Aristotle informs us that Zeno endeavored to demonstrate that there was but one God, from that idea which all men have of him, as that which is the best [. . .], saying, 'If God be the best of all things, he must needs be one.' Which argument was thus pursued by him, 'this is God and the power of God to prevail, conquer, and rule over all. Wherefore how much anything falls short of the best, by so much does it fall short of being God. Now if there be supposed more such beings, whereof some are better, some worse, those could not be all gods, because it is essential to God not to be transcended by any; but if they are conceived to be so many equal Gods, then would it not be the nature of God to be the best, one equal being neither better nor worse than another; wherefore if there be a God, and this be the nature of him, then there can be BUT ONE. And indeed otherwise he could not be older to do whatever he would.'"

Pp. 394–395, 397. Timæus Locrus, a Pythagorean senior to Plato, sometimes calls God τ' ἀγαθὸν, "the very good"; sometimes ἀρχὰ τῶν ἀρίστων, "the principle of the best things"; sometimes δαμιουργὸς τοῦ βελτίονος, "the maker of the better"; sometimes κράτιστον αἴτιον, "the best[4] cause."

[P. 397.] "Euclides Megarensis, the head of the Megaric sect [. . .] his doctrine is thus set down by Laertius, that he 'made the first principle of all things, to be one the very good, called sometimes wisdom, sometimes God, sometimes mind, and sometimes by other names, but that he took away all that is opposite to good, DENYING IT TO HAVE ANY REAL ENTITY.'

"And thus do we understand that of Cicero when he represents the doctrine of the Megarics after this manner, 'Id bonum solum esse, quod esset unum, et simile, et idem et semper.'[5] [. . .] Which doctrine Plato seems to have derived from him, he calling the supreme Deity by those two names τὸ ἓν and τ' ἀγαθὸν."[6]

P. 203[–4]. "Plato, in his dialogues *De Republica*, discoursing about moral virtue, occasionally falls upon the dispute about the summum bonum [. . .] Wherein he says, 'You know that to the vulgar, pleasure

4. Cudworth: "Best and most Powerful Cause."
5. Cudworth translates: "Good or Goodness it self . . . is also One, and Like, and the Same, and Alwayes."
6. Cudworth translates: "the One," and "the Good."

seems the highest good, but to those who are more elegant and ingenious, knowledge. But they who entertain this latter opinion, can none of them declare what kind of knowledge it is, which is that highest and chiefest good,' . . . and afterwards says, 'Though knowledge and truth be both of them excellent things, yet he that shall conclude the chief good to be something which transcends them both, will not be mistaken. For as light and sight, or the seeing faculty, may both of them rightly be said to be soliform things, or akin to the sun, but neither of them to be the sun itself, so knowledge and truth may likewise both of them, be said to be boniform things, and of kin to the chief good but neither of them to be that chief good itself; but this is still to be looked upon as something more august and honorable.'"

[P. 204.] "Now whatever this chiefest good be, which is a perfection superior to knowledge and understanding, that philosopher resolves that it must needs be first and principally God who is therefore called by him 'the very idea or essence of Good.' Wherein he trod in the steps of the Pythagoreans, and particularly of Timæus Locrus, who, making two principles of the universe 'mind' and 'necessity' adds concerning the former, 'The first of these two is of the nature of good and is called God, the principle of the best things.'"

P. 771. "Plato, discoursing elsewhere of God under that title *The Vast Sea of Pulchritude,* describeth him after this manner, 'as that which is not anywhere, either in earth or in heaven, but itself alone by itself, and with itself, all other beautiful things partaking of it.'"

P. 416. Aristotle discoursing of those "things that are more than praiseworthy says, 'Such are God and good, for to these all other things are referred.'"

Pp. 202–3. "Plutarch, in the *Life of Aristides,* says, 'God seems to excel in three things: incorruptibility, power, and virtue, of all which the most divine and venerable is virtue; for vacuum and the senseless elements have incorruptibility; earthquakes and thunders, blustering winds and overflowing torrents, much of power and force. Wherefore the vulgar being affected three manner of ways towards the Deity, so as to admire its HAPPINESS, to fear it, and to honor it; they esteem the Deity happy for its incorruptibility; they fear it and stand in awe of it for its power; but they worship it, that is, love and honor it, for its justice.'"

Pp. 291–92. "Zoroaster [. . .] in his description of God extant in Eusebius says, 'God is the first incorruptible, eternal, unmade, indivisible, most unlike to everything, the head or leader of all good, unbribable, the best of the good, the wisest of the wise; he is the father of love and

justice, self-taught, perfect and the only inventor of the natural holy.'"
Cyprian says thus: "'Hermes quoque triloquitur, eumque ineffabilem
and inestimabilem confitetur.'"[7]

P. 401. The thing which Socrates was condemned and suffered for was
"his free and open condemning [of] those traditions concerning the
gods, wherein wicked, dishonest, and unjust actions were imputed to
them, as he himself, in his *Euthyphro*[8] informs us." For when Euthyphro
justified his father, when guilty of murder, from the example of the gods,
Socrates thus bespeaks him: "'Is not this the very thing, O Euthyphro,
for which I am accused? Viz. because when I hear anyone affirming such
matters as these concerning the gods, I am very loath to believe them,
and stick not publicly to declare my dislike of them? And can you, O Euthyphro, in good earnest think that there are indeed wars and con-
tentions amongst the gods, and that those other things were also done
by them which poets and painters commonly impute to them?'"

P. 438. "The mythical and poetical theology is censured after this manner by Varro, 'That according to the literal sense, it contained many
things contrary to the dignity and nature of immortal beings, the genealogy of one God being derived from the head, of another from the
thigh, of another from drop of blood: some being represented as thieves,
others as adulterers, etc., and all things attributed to the Gods therein
that are not only incident to men, but even to the most contemptible
and flagitious of them.'"

P. 350. Apuleius invoking Isis says, "'Thou holy and perpetual savior
of mankind, that art always bountiful in cherishing mortals, and dost
manifest the dear affections of a mother to them in their calamities, thou
extricatest the involved threads of fate, mitigatest the tempests of fortune, and restrainest the noxious influences of the stars.'"

P. 399. Aristodemus, in his dialogue with Socrates in Xenophon's first
book *Memoirs*, says: "'I am now convinced from what you say that the
things of this world were the WORKMANSHIP of some wise artificer who
also was a lover of animals.'"

P. 444. Galen, [in] *De Usu Partium*, says: "'Should I any longer insist
on such brutish persons as those, the wise and sober might justly condemn me, as defiling this oration, which I compose as a true hymn to
the praise of him that MADE US; I conceiving true piety and RELIGION to-

---

7. "Also Hermes, the thrice-blessed, confesses him ineffable and inestimable." This sentence
is an interlineation by JE; its location in Cudworth is unknown.
8. JE: "Euthiprio."

wards God to consist in this, not that I should sacrifice many hecatombs, or burn much incense to him, but that I should myself first acknowledge, and then declare to others, how great his wisdom is, how great his power, and how great his goodness. For that he would adorn the whole world after this manner, envying to nothing that good which it is capable of, I conclude to be a demonstration of most absolute goodness; and thus let him be praised by us as good. And that he was able to find out how all things might be adorned after the best manner is a sign of the greatest wisdom in him. And lastly, that he was able to effect and bring to pass all those things which he had thus decreed, argues an insuperable power.'"

THE HAPPINESS OF GOD. See back, p. 659.[9]

P. 203. Aristotle says, "'That every man hath so much happiness as he hath of virtue and wisdom, and of acting according to these, ought to be confessed and acknowledged by us, it being a thing that may be proved from the nature of God, who is happy, but not from any external goods, but because he is himself, or that which he is, and in such a manner affected according to his nature.'"

Pp. 408–9. Aristotle says, "'That perfect happiness is a speculative or contemplative energy may be made manifest from hence, because we account the gods most of all happy.'" And again, "'Because other animals, who are deprived of contemplation, partake not of happiness. For to the gods all their life is happy; to men so far forth, as it approacheth to contemplation; but the brute animals that do not at all contemplate, partake not at all of happiness.'"

Pp. 415–16. Aristotle says again, "'God possesseth all good things and is self-sufficient.'"

THE TRINITY

"Preface," pp. [xi–xii].[1] "It is certain that the Platonics and Pythagoreans at least, if not other pagans also, had their trinity, as well as Christians . . . There was a double Platonic trinity: the one spurious and adulterated of some latter Platonists; the other true and genuine of Plato himself, Parmenides, and the ancients [. . .] betwixt which and the Christian trinity there is a wonderful correspondence . . . We shall find that the freest wits amongst the pagans and best philosophers [. . .] were

---

9. MS: "p. 1084 [col. 2] e," a reference to the quotation of Plutarch on God's happiness (Cudworth, pp. 202–3).

1. JE: "p. 10–11." Cudworth's "Preface to the Reader" is unpaginated.

so far of being shy of such an hypothesis as that they were very[2] fond thereof. And that the pagans had indeed such a Cabbala amongst them might be further convinced from that memorable relation of Plutarch of Thespesius Solensis, who after he had been looked upon as dead for three days, reviving, affirmed among other things which he thought he saw or heard in the meantime in his ecstasy, this, of three gods in the form of a triangle, pouring in streams into one another; Orpheus' soul, being said to have arrived so far; accordingly as from the testimonies of other pagan writers, we have proved that a trinity of divine hypostases was a part of the Orphic Cabbala. . . . these things are reasonably noted by us to this end; that they should not be made a prejudice against Christianity and revealed religion nor looked upon as such an affrightful bugbear or *mormo*[3] in it; which even pagan philosophers themselves, and those of the most accomplished intellectuals, and uncaptivated minds, though having neither councils nor creeds nor scriptures, had so great a propensity and readiness to entertain, and such a veneration for."

Pp. 546–47. "The Pythagoreans and Platonists [. . .] distinguished between the *supermundane* and *mundane* gods; the *eternal* and *generated* gods; and lastly the *intelligible* and the *sensible* gods. And the supermundane, eternal, and intelligible gods of these Pythagoreans and Platonists, were first of all and principally those three divine hypostases, as Plotinus calls them, that have the nature of principles in the universe, viz. τ' ἀγαθὸν,[4] or ἕν, νοῦς, and ψυχή: monad, mind, and soul. That this trinity was not first of all a mere invention of Plato's but much ancienter than him, is plainly affirmed by Plotinus in these words: 'That these doctrines are not new, nor of yesterday, but have been very anciently delivered, though obscurely (the discourses now extant being but explications of them) appears from Plato's own writings, Parmenides before him having insisted on them.'

"Now it is well known that Parmenides was addicted to the Pythagoric sect, and therefore probable that this doctrine of a divine triad was one of the arcanums of that school also, which is further confirmed from hence that Numenius, a famous Pythagorean, entertained it as such. And Moderatus, as Simplicius informs us, plainly affirmeth this trinity of principles to have been a Pythagoric Cabbala. Simplicius says of him thus, 'He declareth that according to the Pythagoreans the first one or unity

2. Cudworth: "even."
3. Archaic: "hobgoblin."
4. I.e. the good. Cudworth transliterates this and the following three Greek terms; JE restores the original Greek letters.

is above all essence; that the second one, which is that which truly is, and intelligible, according to them, is ideas; and that the third which is psychical or soul, partaketh both of the first unity and of ideas.' And lastly we have Iamlichus' testimony, also in Proclus, to the same purpose, that 'there were three gods also praised by the Pythagoreans.'"

[P. 547.] "And that a trinity was part of the Orphic Cabbala we have already proved out of Amelius, [he affirming] in Proclus that Plato's three kings were the same with Orpheus' trinity of Phanes, Uranus, and Cronus."

(Here Cudworth refers to what had been cited before in p. 306, etc., where he cite Proclus' words thus:)

[P. 306.] "Amelius makes a threefold Demiurgus or OPIFEX of the world, three minds and three kings: him that is, him that hath, and him that beholds, which three minds differ thus, in that the first is essentially that which is.[5] The second is its own intelligible, but hath the first [. . .] and indeed partakes [thereof, and] therefore is the second. The third is also that intelligible of its own, [. . .] but hath that which is in the second and beholds the first. For how much soever every being departs from the first so much the obscurer it is. After which Proclus immediately subjoins, 'Amelius therefore supposeth these three minds and demiurgic principles of his to be both the same with Plato's three kings, and with Orpheus' trinity of Phanes, Uranus, and Chronus; but Phanes is supposed by him to be principally the DEMIURGUS.' But Proclus [. . .] contends against Amelius that it was not the first hypostasis, neither in the Platonic nor Orphic trinity, that was chiefly and properly the Demiurgus and OPIFEX of the world, but the second. And thus Proclus' his master Syrianus had before determined that in the Orphic theology, the title of Opifex did properly belong to Orpheus' πρωτόγονος θεός, or first begotten God, which was the same with Plato's Νοῦς or divine intellect. Agreeably whereto Proclus' conclusion is, 'Thus much may suffice to have declared who is the DEMIURGUS of the world, viz. that it is the divine intellect which is the proper and immediate CAUSE of the whole CREATION and that it is one and the same demiurgical Jupiter, who is praised both by Orpheus and Plato.'

"Now besides this, it is observable that Damascius, in his book *Concerning the Principles*, tells us that Orpheus introduced τρίμορθον θεὸν, a triform deity. [To all] which[6] may be added what was before cited out of

---

5. Cudworth: "that which he is."
6. JE crosses out from here to the end of the paragraph.

Timotheus the Chronographer, that God had three names, *Light, Counsel,* and *Life.* [. . .] Where Cedrenus concludes in this manner: 'These things Timotheus the Chronographer wrote, affirming Orpheus so long ago to have declared that all things were MADE by a coessential, consubstantial trinity,' Τριάδα ὁμοούσιον."

Pp. 547–48. "Moreover, since all these three, Orpheus, Pythagoras, and Plato, traveling into Egypt, were there initiated in that Arcane Theology of the Egyptians (called Hermaical), it seemeth probable that this doctrine of a divine triad was also part of the Arcane Theology of the Egyptians. It hath also been noted that there were some footsteps of such a trinity in the Mithraic Mysteries among the Persians, derived from Zoroaster; as likewise that it was expressly contained in the Magic or Chalday oracles [. . .] Moreover, it hath been signified that the Samothracians had very anciently a certain trinity of Gods. . . . Lastly the ternary or triad was not only accounted a sacred number among the Pythagoreans, but also as containing some mystery in nature, was therefore made use of by other Greeks and Pagans in their religious rites; as Aristotle informeth us, in these words: 'Wherefore from nature, and as it were observing her laws, have we taken this number of three making use of the same in the sacrifices of the gods, and other purifications.'

"Now since it cannot be conceived how such a trinity of divine hypostases should be first discovered merely by human wit and reason, . . . we may reasonably conclude that which Proclus asserteth of this trinity, [. . .] that it was at first θεοπαράδοτος θεολογία, 'a theology of divine revelation,' viz. amongst the Hebrews at first and from them afterwards communicated to the Egyptians and other nations."

(In these things mention being made of a trinity maintained by Parmenides, the Egyptians, Persians, etc., I would therefore here mention some things which Cudworth had observed before concerning these.)

Pp. 386–87. Plotinus says, "'Parmenides' whole philosophy was better digested and more exactly and distinctly set down in Plato's *Parmenides.*'" These are his words: "Parmenides, in Plato, speaking more exactly, 'distinguishes three divine unities subordinate; the first of that which is perfectly and most properly *one;* the second of that which is called by him *one-many;* the third of that which is thus expressed *one and many.* So that Parmenides did also agree in this acknowledgment of divine or Archical hypostases.'"

P. 330[–31]. St. Cyril cites this passage out of the Hermaic writings among the Egyptians: "'The world hath a governor set over it, that word of the lord of all, which was the maker of it; this is the first power after himself, uncreated, infinite, looking out from him, and ruling over all things that were made by him; this is the perfect and genuine son of the first omniperfect being.'"

P. 336. Iamblichus says, "'The Egyptians acknowledge before the heaven, and in the heaven, a living power, and again they place a pure mind or intellect above the world.'"

P. 337. Damascius "writes after this manner concerning the Egyptians, 'Eudemus hath given us no exact account of the Egyptians, but the Egyptian philosophers that have been in our times, have declared the hidden truth of their theology, having found in certain Egyptian writings, that there was according to them, one principle of all things, praised under the name of the UNKNOWN DARKNESS, and that thrice repeated.'"

P. 353[-54]. "But the clearest footsteps that we can find anywhere of an Egyptian trinity are in Iamblichus' book written concerning the Egyptian Mysteries," where he says as follows: "'According to another order or method, Hermes places the God *Emeph* as the prince and ruler over all the celestial gods, whom he affirmeth to be a mind understanding himself, and converting his cogitations or intellections into himself. Before which *Emeph* he placeth one indivisible, which he calleth *Eicton,* in which is the first intelligible and which is worshipped by silence. After which two, Eicton and Emeph, the demiurgic mind and president of truth, as with wisdom it proceedeth to generations, and bringeth forth the hidden powers of the occult reasons into light, is called in the Egyptian language *Ammon;* as it artificially effects all things with truth, *Phtha*[7] [. . .] as it is productive of good, Osiris, besides other names that it hath according to its other powers and energies.'"

P. 288. "It is observable that the Persian Mithras was commonly called Τριπλάσιος, threefold or treble. Thus Dionysius the Pseudo-Areopagite, 'The Persian Magi to this very day celebrate a festival solemnity in honor of the threefold Mithras.' And something very like this is recorded in Plutarch concerning Oromasdes: 'Oromasdes thrice augmented himself.'"

The magical or Zoroastrian oracles thus represent this Persian trinity: "'The Father perfected all things, and delivered them to the second mind, who is that whom the nations of men commonly take for the first.'"

[P. 289.] "Besides these two hypostases, there is also a third mentioned in a certain other magic or Chaldaic oracle, cited by Proclus under the name of Psyche: 'After the paternal mind, I Psyche dwell,' [. . .] as Psel-

7. Cudworth: "which Phtha the Greeks . . . call Hephestus or Vulcan."

lus informs us, [. . .] 'the paternal mind is the second god, and the immediate Demiurgus or Opifex of the soul.'"

[Pp. 289–90.] "Though both these names, Oromasdes and Mithras, were frequently used by the Magi for the deity in general, yet this being threefold, according to their theology, as containing three hypostases; the first of those three seems to have been that which was most properly called Oromasdes, and the second Mithras. And this is not only confirmed by Pletho, but also with this further addition to it, that the third hypostasis of that Persian trinity was called *Arimanius;* he gathering as much even from Plutarch himself: 'They say that Zoroaster made a threefold distribution of things, and that he assigned the first and highest rank of them to Oromasdes, who in the Oracles is called the father; the lowest to Arimane; and the middle to *Mithras* who in the same Oracles is likewise called the second mind.' Whereupon he observes the great agreement there was betwixt the Zoroastrian and Platonic trinity, they differing only in words."

P. 290. "Plutarch affirms that the Persians called any mediator or middle betwixt two *Mithras.*"

P. 294. Proclus, speaking of the Magic or Chalday oracles, says, "'Thus the divinely delivered theology affirmeth the whole world to have been completed from these three.' [. . .] To which Testimony of Proclus we might add that oracle cited out of Damascius by Patritius: 'In the whole world shineth forth a triad, the bead whereof is a monad.'"

Pp. 450–51. "The great Capitoline Temple had three Sacella or lesser Chapels in it [. . .] Jupiter's in the middle, Minerva's on the right hand, and Juno's on the left, according to that of the Poet:

  Trina in tarpeio fulgent consortia templo."[8]

[P. 451.] Vossius supposes that here was aimed at a trinity of divine hypostases. "For these three Roman gods were said to have been first brought into Italy out of Phrygia by the Trojans, but before that [into] Phrygia [by] Dardanus, out of the Samothracian Island . . . And as these were called by the Latins 'Dii Penates';[9] [but] Varro in Arnobius interprets this, 'Dii qui sunt intrinsecus, atque in intimis penetralibus cœli';[1] so were they called by the Samothracians Κάβειροι or Cabiri, that is, as

8. "The three partners shine in the Tarpeian temple."
9. Cudworth: "which Macrobius thus interprets, 'Dii Per quos Penitus spiramus, per quos habemus Corpus, per quos rationem animi possidemus,' that is, 'The Gods by whom we live, and move, and have our being.'"
1. Cudworth translates: "the Gods, who are in the most Inward Recesses of Heaven."

Varro rightly interprets the word, 'the powerful and mighty gods.' Which Cabiri being plainly the Hebrew כבירים, gives just occasion to suspect that this ancient tradition of three divine hypostases (unquestionably maintained by Orpheus, Pythagoras, and Plato among the Greeks, and probably by the Egyptians) sprung originally from the Hebrews. The first of these divine hypostases, called Jove, being the fountain of the godhead; and the second of them called by the Latins, Minerva (which, as Varro interprets it, was that wherein *ideæ et exempla rerum* were contained) [. . .]; and the third Juno, called 'amor ac delicium Jovis.'"[2]

(This Minerva, as Cudworth elsewhere observes, is a name of the supreme deity, as pp. 341–42, where speaking of that inscription upon the temple of Sais in Egypt, "*I am all that hath been, is, or shall be, and my peplum* (or veil) *no mortal hath yet uncovered.*" He observes that this temple was dedicated to the god in the Egyptian language which was called *Neith,* the same with *Athena* among the Greeks and *Minerva* among the Latins, and cites Proclus saying, "'Sais and Athens had one and the same tutelar God.'" And Theompompus affirmeth the Athenians to have been a colony of the Saites. And that the Athena of the Greeks was famous for her peplum or veil too as well as the Egyptian goddess, and observes as follows: "'Peplum (saith Servius) est proprie palla picta fæminea, Minervæ consecrata,'[3] which rite was performed at Athens, in the great Panathenaics, with much solemnity, when the statue of this goddess, was also by those noble virgins of the city, who embroidered this veil, clothed all over therewith. [. . .] Proclus hath recorded that there was something more belonging to this Egyptian inscription than is mentioned by Plutarch; namely these words: '*and the sun was the fruit or offspring which I produced.*' Athenagoras tells us that the pagan theologers interpreted Τὴν Ἀθηνᾶν or Minerva to be '*wisdom or mind passing and diffusing itself through all things.*' [. . .] Iamblicus in his Mysteries interprets the meaning of the forementioned Egyptian inscription: [. . .] that it declared the name of that God that diffuses himself through the whole world.")

P. 487. Aristides, in his Oration upon Minerva, says, "'All the most excellent things are in Minerva, and from her: but to speak briefly of her, this is the only immediate offspring of the only MAKER and KING of all things; for he had none of equal honor with himself, upon whom he should beget her, and therefore retiring into himself he begat her and

---

2. Cudworth renders the first phrase: "the Ideas and first Exemplars or Patterns of things." The second translates, "the love and delight of Jupiter."

3. Cudworth translates: "Peplum is properly a womanish Pall or Veil, embroidered all over, and consecrated to Minerva."

brought her forth from himself: so that this is the only genuine offspring of the first father of all.' And he concludes his Oration thus: 'He that from what we have said will conclude that Minerva is as it were the power and virtue of Jupiter himself will not err. Wherefore we conclude thus concerning her, that all the works of Jupiter are common with Jupiter and Minerva.'

"Pindar also affirmeth concerning Minerva, that 'sitting at the right hand of her father, she there receiveth commands from him, to be delivered to the Gods. For she is greater than the ANGELS, and commandeth them some one thing and some another, according as she had first received of her father: she performing the office of an interpreter and introducer to the Gods when it is needful.' Where we may observe by the way, that this word *Angel* came to be in use among the pagans from Jews and Christians, about this very age that Aristides lived in; after which we meet with it frequently in the writings of their philosophers."

(As to the third person in the Capitoline Trinity, viz. Juno, called as was observed before, "amor ac delicium Jovis," there is much reason to think it the same with the third person in the Platonic trinity, called Love, which was called the heavenly Venus, which as Cudworth shows, was one name of the supreme Deity, as I shall have occasion particularly to observe afterwards.)

P. 551. "When the Pagans spake of the first, second, and third gods, and no more, though having innumerable other gods besides, they did by this language plainly imply that these three gods of theirs were of a very different kind from all the rest of their gods, i.e. not θεοὶ γεννητοὶ but ἀΐδιοι, not created, but eternal and uncreated ones. And many of them did really take this whole trinity of gods for the τὸ Θεῖον in general, and sometimes called it the first god too, in way of distinction from their generated gods; [. . .] or the gods that were made in time together with the world," as will be showed afterwards.

(In p. 570 Cudworth, after having in many preceding pages taken notice of vari[ous] depravations of the divine Cabbala of the trinity by later Platonists observes that Plato himself and some of the Platonists retained much of the ancient genuine Cabbala, and made a very near approach to the true Christian Trinity.)

P. 572. "Plato, speaking of the ἀΐδιος οὐσία or φύσις, the eternal nature, which always is and never was made, Plato speaks of it not singularly only as we Christians now do but often in the paganic way plurally also; as when in his *Timæus* he calls the world 'a made or created image of the eternal gods.' By which eternal gods he doubtless meant that τὸ πρῶτον, and τὸ δεύτεπον, and τὸ πρῶτον,[4] which in his second epistle to Dionysius, he makes to be the principles of all things; [. . .] agreeable to these words of Plotinus, 'This world is an image always iconized or PERPETUALLY RENEWED (as the image in a glass is) of that first, second, and third principle, which are always STANDING.'"

Pp. 573–74. "That the second hypostasis in Plato's trinity, viz. mind or intellect, though said to have been generated, or to have proceeded by way of emanation from the first called τ' ἀγαθὸν,[5] was notwithstanding unquestionably acknowledged to have been eternal or without beginning, might be proved by many express testimonies of the most genuine Platonists; but we shall here content ourselves with two, one of Plotinus writing thus concerning it, 'Let all temporal generation here be quite banished from our thoughts, whilst we treat of things eternal, or such as always are, we attributing generation to them only with respect to causality and order, but not of time.' And though Plotinus there speaks particularly of the second hypostasis or *Nous*, yet does he afterwards extend the same also to the third hypostasis of that trinity, called Psyche.

"The other testimony is of Porphyrius, cited by St. Cyril, where he sets down the doctrine of Plato after this manner: 'Plato thus declareth concerning the FIRST GOOD, that from it was generated a certain mind incomprehensible by mortals, in which subsisting by itself, are contained all the things that truly are, and the essences of all beings. This is the first FAIR and PULCHRITUDE itself, which proceeded or sprung out of God from all eternity as its cause, but notwithstanding after a peculiar manner, as self-begotten, and as its own parent. For it was not begotten from that as any way moved towards its generation; but it proceeded from God as it were self-begottenly. And that not from any temporal beginning, there being as yet no such thing as time. Nor when time was afterwards made, did it any way affect him; for mind (Νοῦς) is always timeless, and alone eternal.' [. . .] Neither is Porphyrius singular in this language; we find the same expression of αὐτοπάτωρ and αὐτογονος[6] in Iamblichus' Mysteries, as follows, 'From this one, the self-sufficient god, made himself to shine forth into light, and therefore he is called αὐτοπάτωρ καὶ αὐτογονος.'"[7]

Pp. 576–77. Plotinus and others suppose that Plato held a double Psyche, the one mundane and the other supramundane, the first of which

4. Cudworth translates: "First, and Second, and Third."
5. Cudworth translates: "the Good."
6. Cudworth translates: "Self-Parent and Self-Begotten."
7. Cudworth translates: "his own Father, and Self-begotten."

Plotinus, calling it the heavenly Venus, thus describeth it, "'This heavenly Venus, which they affirm to have been begotten from Saturn, that is from a perfect mind or intellect, must needs be that most divine ψυχὴν,[8] which being immediately begotten, pure from that which is pure, always remains above, so that it neither can nor will ever descend down to these lower things, so as to be immersed in them.' [. . .] After which he speaks of another soul of the world, which is not separate from it but closely conjoined with it, calling it a lower Venus and Love."

Plato, in his second epistle to Dionysius says, speaking of these three hypostases, "'The mind of man has always a great desire to know what these things are, and to that end does it look upon things cognate to it, which are all insufficient, imperfect, and heterogeneous. But in that KING of all things, and in the other, second, and third, which I spake of, there is nothing of this kind.'

"The three hypostases in Plato's trinity [. . .] are necessarily existent . . . Plotinus says, (Cudworth, p. 578): 'Wherefore we ought not to entertain any other principles, but having placed first, the SIMPLE GOOD; to set mind or the supreme intellect next after it, and then universal soul in the third place. For this is the right order according to nature, neither to make more intelligibles [. . .] nor fewer than these three. For he that will contract the number, and make fewer of them, must of necessity either suppose soul and mind to be the same, or else mind and the first good. But that all these three are diverse one from another, hath been often demonstrated by us. It remains now to consider that if there be more than these three principles, what natures they should be.'"

Pp. 578–79. "And as these three hypostases were supposed to be eternal and necessarily existent, so they were supposed not to be particular but universal beings; that is, such as contain and comprehend the whole world under them, and preside over all things. . . . For which reason they are called by Platonic writers ἀπχαὶ, and αἴτια, and δημιοθργοὶ: principles, and causes, and opificers of the whole world." So concerning Νοῦς or mind. [. . .] Plato, in his Philebus, says, "'Mind rules over the whole universe.'

"And as to the third hypostasis, called ψυχή, Plato in his Cratylus, bestowing the name of Ζεὺς, that is, of the supreme God upon it, [. . .] in these words: 'There is nothing which is more the cause of life to us and all other animals, than this prince and king of all things; and therefore God was called by the Greeks Ζεὺς; because it is by him that all animals

---

8. Cudworth translates: "Soul."

live.' That he means the third hypostasis is manifest from those words that follow: 'It is agreeable to reason, that Zeus should be the progeny of a certain great mind.'" (By mind Plato meant the second hypostasis.)

[P. 579.] "It is true that by the δημίουργος, or opificer in Plato, is commonly meant Νοῦς or intellect, his second Hypostasis; (Plotinus says, 'The Demiurgus to Plato is intellect.') Nevertheless, both Amelius and Plotinus and other Platonists called this third hypostasis also δημίουρ-γον, [. . .] Atticus and Amelius also called the first good, Demiurgus. Wherefore as was before suggested, according to the genuine and most ancient Platonic doctrine, all these three hypostases were the joint Creators of the whole world, and all things besides themselves; as Ficinus more than once declares, the tenor thereof, '*Hi tres uno quodam Consensu omnia PRODUCUNT*,'[9] and before him Proclus, 'All things depend upon the first one by *mind* and *soul*'; and therefore we shall conclude in the words of Porphyrius, that 'the true and real deity, according to Plato, extends to three divine hypostases, the last of which is Psyche or soul.'"

P. 583. Numenius says, "'It is not fit to attribute the ARCHITECTURE of the world to the first [god], but rather to account him the father of that god, who is the ARTIFICER.'"

P. 584. Plotinus says, "'To understand is not the first; neither in essence nor in dignity, but the second; a thing in order of nature after the FIRST GOOD, and springing up from thence, as that which is moved with desire towards it.'"

P. 585. Plotinus says, "'That which was generated from the first principle was Logos manifold; but the first principle itself was not Logos: if you demand therefore, how word or reason should proceed from that which is not word or reason, we answer as that which is boniform, from GOODNESS ITSELF.'"

P. 588. "The second thing which we shall observe concerning the most genuine Platonical and Parmenidian trinity is this; that though these philosophers sometimes called their three divine hypostases not only three natures, and three principles, and three causes, and three opificers, but also three gods; [. . .] yet they did often for all that, suppose all these three to be really one Θεῖον, one divinity or numen."

P. 589. "Thus it is expressly affirmed by Porphyrius in St. Cyril, that 'the essence of the divinity proceeds or propagates itself (by way of descent downwards) unto three hypostases. The highest God is the τ' ἀγαθὸν or SUPREME GOOD; the second next after him is the DEMIUR-

---

9. Cudworth translates: "These Three with one common consent produce all things."

GUS; and the soul of the world is the third: for the Divinity extends itself so far as to this soul.'"

P. 590. "The Platonists therefore first of all suppose such a close and near conjunction between the three hypostases of the Trinity, as is nowhere else to be found in the whole world. To which purpose Plotinus: 'Intellect is said to behold the first good; not as if it were separated from it, but only because it is after it, but so as that there is nothing between them: as neither is there betwixt νοῦς and ψυχή.'[1]

"Again the Platonists [further declare] that these three hypostases of their trinity are ἀδιαίρετοι, absolutely indivisible and inseparable, as the ajpauvgasma is indivisible from the φῶς, the splendor indivisibly conjoined with the sun.

"Thirdly, the Platonists seem likewise to attribute to their three divine hypostases such an Εμπεριχώρησις, circuminsession, or mutual in-being, as Christians do."

P. 591. "According to the principles of Plato and Plotinus and others, the Deity does not properly understand anywhere but in the second hypostasis, which is the mind and wisdom of it. And the Emperichoresis of the second and third hypostases, was thus intimated by Plato also, in these words, 'But Σοφία[2] and Νοῦς can never be without ψυχή. Wherefore in the nature of Jupiter is at once contained both a kingly mind (Νοῦς) and a kingly soul (ψυχή).' Here he makes Jupiter to be both the second and third hypostases of his trinity, Νοῦς and ψυχή; and consequently these two to be but one god. Which Νοῦς is also said to be γενούστης, i.e. of the same kind, and co-essential with the first CAUSE of all things. To conclude, as that first Platonic hypostasis, which is itself said to be above mind and wisdom, is properly wise and understanding in the second; so do both the first and second, move and act in the third. Lastly, all these three hypostases τ'ἀγαθὸν, Νοῦς, and ψυχή, are said by the Platonists to be one Θεῖον or divinity; just in the same manner as the center, immovable distance, and movable circumference of a sphere or globe. Thus Plotinus, 'This Psyche is a venerable and adorable thing also; it being the circle fitted to the center, an indistant distance. For these things are just so as if one should make the τ'ἀγαθὸν to be the center of the universe; in the next place *mind* to be the immovable circle or distance; and lastly soul to be that which turns round, or the whole movable circumference; acted by love or desire.'"

---

1. Cudworth translates: "Intellect and Soul."
2. Cudworth translates: "Wisdom."

P. 259. "The word Ζεύς is by Plato attributed severally to each of the Hypostases, which Proclus observed on the *Timæus* thus, 'We say therefore that there are several orders, ranks, or degrees of Zeus or Jupiter in Plato; for sometimes he is taken for the DEMIURGUS, as in *Cratylus;* sometimes for the first of the saturnian triad, as in *Gorgias;* sometimes for the superior soul of the world, as in *Phædrus;* and lastly, sometimes for the lower soul of heaven.' Though by Proclus' leave[3] that Zeus or Jupiter is mentioned in Plato's *Cratylus* (being plainly the superior Psyche or soul of the world) is not properly the *Demiurgus* or opificer, according to him."

Pp. 407–8. "The first of the divine hypostases is that which is properly called by the Platonists πηγή τῆς θεότητος, the fountain of the godhead. The first divine bypostasis is by Plato called, 'the father of the prince [and cause] of all things.' Wherein we cannot but take notice of an admirable correspondence between the Platonic philosophy and Christianity."

Pp. 456–57. Macrobius says, "'This starry sphere, being but a part of the heaven, was made or produced by *soul*. Which soul also proceeded from a perfect *mind or intellect;* and again mind was begotten from that God, who is truly supreme.'"

OF THE SECOND HYPOSTASIS.

P. 275. Julian the Emperor says, "'This uniform cause of all things, [. . .] produced from himself a certain intelligible sun, every way like himself, of which the sensible sun is but an image.' Thus Dionysius Petavius rightly declares the sense of Julian in this oration: '[. . .] that from the first and chief deity was produced a certain intelligible and archetypal sun, which hath the same place or order, in the rank of intelligible things, that the sensible sun hath in the rank of sensibles.'"

Pp. 487–88. Though Apollo was "often taken for the sensible sun animated, and so an inferior deity, yet was not always understood in this sense . . . And that he was sometimes taken for the supreme universal numen, the maker of the sun and of the whole world, is plainly testified by Plutarch (who is a competent witness in this case, he being a priest of this Apollo)."

OF THE THIRD HYPOSTASIS.

Pp. 488–89. "Moreover Urania Aphrodite, the heavenly Venus or Urania, was a universal numen also, or another name of God according to

---

3. Cudworth: "lieve."

Plutarch's more general notion, *as comprehending* the whole world, it being the same with that Ερως, or Love, which Orpheus and others in Aristotle made to be the first original of all things. For it is certain that the ancients distinguished concerning a double Venus and Love. Thus Pausanias in Plato's *Symposium* [. . .], 'There are two Venuses and therefore two loves: one the older without a mother, the daughter of Uranus or heaven, which we call the heavenly Venus; another younger, begotten from Jupiter and Dione, which we call the vulgar Venus.' [. . .] The elder of these two Venuses is in Plato said to be senior to Japhet and Saturn, and by Orpheus the oldest of all things, and the first begetter of all things. [. . .] This was also the same with Plato's *First Fair,* the cause of all pulchritude, order and harmony in the world. And Pausanias the writer tells us that there were temples severally erected to each of these Venuses or Loves, [. . .] and that Urania or the heavenly Venus was so called, [. . .] because the love belonging to it was pure and free from all corporeal affection; which as it is [in] men, is but a participation of that first Urania, or heavenly Venus and Love, God himself. And thus Venus is described by Euripides in Stobæus as the supreme Numen, thus: 'Do you not see how great a god this Venus is? But you are never able to declare her greatness, nor to measure the vast extent thereof. For this is she that nourisheth both thee and me and all mortals, and which makes heaven and earth friendlily to conspire together.' But by Ovid this is more fully expressed in his *Fastorum:*

> Illa quidem totum dignissima temperat orbem,
> Illa tenet Nullo regna minora deo:
> Jura[que] dat Cœlo, Terræ natalibus Undis;
> Perque suos Initus, continet omne Genus.
> Illa Deos omnes (longum enumerare) creavit;
> Illa satis Causas, Arboribusque dedit."[4]

Pp. 591–92. From the account we have given "of the true and genuine Platonic and Parmenidian or Pythagorean trinity," it appears that this trinity did "approach so near to the doctrine of Christianity as in a manner to correspond therewith, in those three fundamentals:

---

4. "She, indeed most worthy, rules all the earth, / She holds her power no less than any god, / She gives laws to heaven, earth and the waves which birthed her, / And through her entrance, she contains every birth. / She created all the gods (it is long to enumerate); / She gave existence to crops and trees."

"First, in not making a mere trinity of names and words, or of logical notions and inadequate conceptions, of one and the same thing; but a trinity of hypostases, subsistences, or persons.

"Secondly, in making none of their three hypostases to be creatures, but all eternal, necessarily existent, and universal; infinite, omnipotent; and CREATORS of the whole world; which is all one in the sense of the ancients, as if they should have affirmed them to be *homoousian.*

"Lastly, in supposing these three divine hypostases, however sometimes paganically called three gods, to be essentially one *divinity.*"

P. 595. It may well "be wondered at, that living so long before Christianity as some of them did, they should in so abstruse a point, and dark a mystery, make so near an approach to the Christian truth afterwards revealed. . . . They not only extending the true and real deity to three hypostases, but also calling the second of them Λόγος, reason or word (as well as Νοῦς, mind or intellect) and likewise the son of the first hypostasis the father; and affirming him to be the δημιουργὸς and αἴτιον, the artificer and cause of the whole world; and lastly describing him as the Scriptures do, to be the image, the figure, or character, and the splendor or brightness of the first."

P. 597[-98]. "The Platonists distinguished between οὐσία and ὑπόστασις, the essence of the godhead and the distinct hypostases or personalities thereof.

The Platonists as pagans, being not so scrupulous in their Language as we Christians are, do often call them three Gods . . . ; yet notwithstanding as philosophers, did they declare 'em to be one Θεῖον or Divinity; and that as it seems on these several accounts following:

"First, because they are indivisibly conjoined together as the splendor is indivisible from the sun.

"And then, because they are mutually inexistent in each other, the first being in the second, and both first and second being in the third. And,

"Lastly, because the entireness of the whole divinity is made up of all these three together, which all have one and the same action or energy *ad extra.* And therefore as the center, radius distance, and movable circumference may all be said to be coessential to a sphere, and the root, stock, and Branches coessential to an entire tree; so, but in a much more perfect sense, are the Platonic Tagathon, Nous, and Psyche coessential to that ἐν τῷ παντὶ θεῖον, that divinity in the whole universe."

P. 621[-23]. "As the Platonic pagans after Christianity did approve of the Christian doctrine concerning the Logos, as that which was exactly agreeable with their own; so did the generality of the Christian fathers, before and after the Nicene council, represent the genuine Platonic trinity, as really the same thing with the Christian. The former of these is evident from that famous passage of Amelius, contemporary with Plotinus, recorded by Eusebius, St. Cyril, and Theodoret: [. . .] 'And this was the *Logos* or Word, by whom existing from eternity according to Heraclitus, all things were made; and whom that barbarian also placeth in the rank and dignity of a principle, affirming him to have been with God, and to be God; and that all things were made by him, and that whatsoever was made, was life and being in him. As also that he descended into a body, and being clothed in flesh, appeared as a man, though not without a demonstration of the divinity of his nature. But that afterwards being loosed or separated from the same, he was deified, and became God again, such as he was before he came down into a mortal body.' In which words Amelius also speaks favorably of the incarnation of the eternal logos. And the same is further manifest from what St. Austin writeth concerning a Platonist in his time: [. . .] 'We have often heard from that holy man Simplicianus, afterward Bishop of Milan, that a certain Platonist affirmed, the beginning of St. John's Gospel deserved to be writ in letters of gold, and to be set up in all the most eminent places throughout the Christian churches.' And the latter will sufficiently appear from these following testimonies. Justin Martyr in his Apology affirmeth of Plato, [. . .] 'That he gave the second place to the Word of God, and the third to that Spirit which is said to have moved upon the waters.' Clemens Alexandrinus, speaking of that passage in Plato's second epistle to Dionysius, says, 'I understand this no otherwise, than that the holy Trinity is signified thereby, the third being the Holy Ghost, and the second the Son by whom all things were made, according to the will of the Father.' Origen also affirmeth the Son of God to have been plainly spoken of by Plato in his epistle to Hermias and Coriscus. [. . .] Morever St. Cyprian, or whoever were the author of that book inscribed *De Spiritu Sancto*, affirmeth the Platonists' first and universal Psyche to be the same with the Holy Ghost in the Christian theology . . . In the next place Eusebius gives a full and clear testimony of the concordance and agreement of the Platonic, at least as to the main, with the Christian Trinity, which he will have to have been the Cabbala of the ancient Hebrews. [. . .] But it is most observable what Athanasius himself affirmeth of the Platonists; that though they derived the second hypostasis of their trinity from the first, and the third from the second, yet they supposed both their second and third hypostases to be uncreated, and therefore doth he send the Arians to school thither." See back, pp. 674–75.[5]

P. 601. "There is another Platonic hypothesis (which St. Austin hinteth from Porphyrius, though he professed he did not well understand it) wherein the third hypostasis is made to be a certain middle betwixt the first and second. And this does Proclus also sometimes follow, calling the third in like manner *a middle power,* and *the relation of both the first and second to one another.* Which exactly agreeth with that apprehension of some Christians, that the third hypostasis is as it were the nexus, betwixt the first and second, and the love whereby the father and son love each other." (See further concerning the third hypostasis under the head of "Traditions Concerning the Mosaic Creation," p. 687.)[6]

GOD'S WORKS OF CREATION and PROVIDENCE.

See passages in the preceding extracts where are found written in larger letters the words CREATOR, CAUSE, DEMIURGUS, ARTIFICER, ARCHITECTURE, MADE, PROVIDENCE, GOVERN, WORKMANSHIP, OPIFEX, CREATION, KING.

Pp. 264–65. "The Pagans do often characterize the supreme God by such titles, epithets, and descriptions . . . as *Demiurgus;* the Opifex; architect or maker of the world; the prince and chief ruler of the universe; . . . the principle of principles; the first cause; he that generated or created this whole universe; he that ruleth over the whole world; the supreme governor and lord of all; the God over all . . . ; and lastly, to name no more, provnoia, or providence."

P. 335. Horus Apollo, in his Hieroglyphics, gives this as one reason "why the serpent was made to be the hieroglyphic of the deity [. . .], 'Because the serpent feeding as it were on its own body, doth aptly signify that all things generated in the world by divine Providence are again resolved into him.'"

Ibid. Plutarch tells us "that in the porch of an Egyptian temple at Sais, were engraven these three hieroglyphics: a young man, an old man, and an hawk; to make up this sentence, 'That both the beginning and end of human life depend on God, or providence.' But we have two more remarkable sentences in Horus Apollo concerning the Egyptian theology;

5. MS: "p. 1098 [col. 1] b," a reference to the notes on pp. 591–92 of Cudworth.
6. MS: "p. 1108."

the first is that according to them, 'there is a spirit passing through the whole world, to wit, God.' And again, 'It seemeth to the Egyptians that nothing at all consists without God.' Iamblichus, who made it his business to inform himself thoroughly of the Egyptian theology, [. . .] gives a summary of their theology after this manner: 'That God, who is the cause of generation and the whole nature, and of all the powers in the elements themselves, is separate, exempt, elevated above, and expanded over all the powers and elements in the world. For being above the world and transcending the same, immaterial and incorporeal, supernatural, unmade, indivisible, manifested wholly from himself, and in himself, he ruleth over all things and in himself containeth all things. And because he virtually comprehends [all things], therefore does he impart and display the same from himself.'"

P. 427. "Epictetus makes reason in men a gift of the gods," in the following sentence: "'Is reason therefore given us by the gods, merely to make us miserable and unhappy?' [. . .] One and the same celebrated speech of Socrates is sometimes expressed singularly, 'If God will have it be so let it be so,' and sometimes plurally, 'If the gods will have it so.' We have this religious passage of the Stoic philosophers, 'To be instructed is to will things to be as they are made: and how are they made? As that great disposer of all things hath appointed.'"

[P. 428.] These philosophers call him "'the one intellectual fountain of all things,'" and also "'one God, through all, one substance, one law.'"

P. 419. "'There is one divine principle of all things, by or from which all things subsist and remain.'" Theophrastus.

P. 442. "'There is one harmonious system made out of all things, and all things are derived from one.'" Heraclitus.

"'It is an ancient opinion or tradition, that hath been conveyed down from all men by their progenitors, that all things are from God, and consist by him, and that no nature is sufficient to preserve itself, if left alone, and devoid of the divine assistance and influence.'" [The writer of *De Mundo*.]

P. 26. Plato says, "there was besides atoms 'an ordering, disposing Mind that was the cause of all things.' Which Mind (as Aristotle tells us) he made to be 'the only simple, unmixed, and pure thing in the world,' and this to be that which brought the confused chaos of omnifarious atoms into that orderly compages of the world that now is."

God is "'only a holy and ineffable mind, that by swift thoughts agitates the whole world.'" Empedocles.

Stobæus says, "'Ecphantus held the corporeal world to consist of

atoms, but yet to be ordered and governed by a divine providence.'
[. . .] The same is observed of Arcesilaus by Sidonius Apollinaris:

> Post hæc[7] Arcesilaus divina mente paratam
> Conjicit hanc molem, confectam partibus illis
> Quas atomos vocat ipse leves.[8]

"Plato, in his *Timæus,* introduces the supreme Deity, bespeaking those
inferior gods, the sun, moon, and stars after this manner: 'Those things
which are made by me are indissolvable by my will, and though everything that is compacted be in its own nature dissolvable,'" etc.

GOD THE CREATOR.

P. 227. Aristotle tells us that it was the generally received opinion before his time that the whole world was generated or had a beginning.

P. 239. "Aristotle affirmeth that before his time, this genesis or temporary production of the world was universally entertained by all, and
particularly that Plato was an assertor of the same."

P. 240. Plato in his *Timæus* states the question, "'Whether the world always were, having no beginning or generation, or whether it was made
or generated, having commenced from a certain epocha?' To which the
answer is, 'that it was made or had a beginning.'" Where he also says,
"'Time was made together with the heaven, that being both generated
together, they might be dissolved together likewise, if at least there
should ever be any dissolution of them.'"

P. 243. "'When therefore all the gods, both those which move visibly
about the heavens, and those which appear to us as often as they please,
were generated or created, that God which made this whole universe,
bespake these generated gods, after this manner: Ye gods of gods, whom
I myself am the maker and father of, attend.'" Plato, *Timæus.*

P. 247. Strabo says concerning providence or the deity, after this manner, "'That having a multiform fecundity in it, and delighting in variety
of works, it designed principally to make animals, as the most excellent
things, and amongst them chiefly those two noblest kinds of animals,
gods and men; for whose sakes the other things were made.' [. . .] Thus
also Seneca in Lactantius, speaking concerning God, 'Hic cum prima
fundamenta molis pulcherrimæ jaceret, et hoc ordiretur, quo neque ma-

---

7. Cudworth: "hos."
8. "After these things Arcesilaus contends that this Mass was prepared by the divine mind,
put together from those parts which he himself calls 'light atoms.'"

jus quicquam novit natura nec melius; ut omnia sub ducibus irent, quamvis ipse per totum se corpus intenderat, tamen ministros regni sui Deos genuit.'"9

P. 258. Porphyrius in Eusebius thus declares "the mind of the more intelligent of the Greekish pagans [. . .], 'By Zeus, the Greeks understand that mind of the world which framed all things in it, and containeth the whole world.'"

P. 259. Proclus observes thus: "'We say therefore that there are several [orders,] ranks, or degrees of Zeus [or Jupiter] in Plato; sometimes he is taken for the Demiurgus, as in *Cratylus;* sometimes for the first of the saturnian triad, as in *Gorgias;* sometimes for the superior soul of the world, as in *Phædrus;* and lastly, sometimes for the lower soul of heaven.'"1

P. 264. The supreme God is sometimes called "ὁ Δημιουργὸς, [the Opifex, architect, or maker of the world, . . .] sometimes the *principle of principles; the first cause; he that generated this whole universe.*"

P. 286. Porphyrius says thus, "'Zoroaster first of all, as Eusebius testifieth, in the mountains adjoining to Persis, consecrated a native orbicular cave, adorned with flowers and watered with fountains, to the honor of Mithras, the maker and father of all things; this cave being an image or symbol to him, of the whole world, which was made by Mithras.'"

P. 292. "Proclus upon the *Timæus* says, 'The maker of the universe is celebrated both by Plato and Orpheus, and the oracles, as the father of gods and men.'"

P. 293[–94]. "Psellus thus glosseth upon that oracle, '*All things were the offspring of one fire.* [. . .] All things whether intelligible or sensible receive their essence from God alone, and return back again only to him.' [. . .] Proclus upon Plato's *Timæus*, when he had asserted that there is '*one thing the cause of all things; and that the supreme God, being the cause of all things, is also the cause of matter*'; he confirms this assertion of his from the authority of the oracles: 'From this order also do the oracles deduce the generation of matter in these words, "*From thence*" (that is, from one supreme Deity) "*altogether proceeds the genesis of multifarious matter.*"' Which undoubtedly are one of the Magic or Chalday oracles; and it may be fur-

---

9. Cudworth translates: "God when he laid the Foundations of this most beautiful Fabrick, and began to erect that Structure, than which Nature knows nothing greater or more excellent; to the end that all things might be carried on under their respective Governours orderly, though he intended Himself through the whole, as to preside in chief over all, yet did he Generate Gods also; as subordinate Ministers of his Kingdom under him."

1. See above, p. 673, where JE quotes the same passage.

ther proved from hence, because it was by Porphyrius set down amongst them, as appears from Æneas Gazeus in his *Theophrastus,* 'Neither was matter void of generation, or beginning, which the Chaldeans and Porphyrius teach thee; he making this the title of a whole book published by him, *The Oracles of the Chaldeans,* in which it is confirmed that matter was made.'"

P. 303[–04]. Proclus upon the *Timæus* cites some Orphic verses in English to this sense: "'Wherefore, together with the universe, were made within Jupiter, the height of the ethereal heaven, the breadth of the earth and sea, the great ocean, the profound Tartara, the rivers and fountains, and all other things; all the immortal gods and goddesses, whatsoever hath been, or shall be, was at once contained in the womb of Jupiter.' [. . .] Again Proclus in the same place ushers in another copy of Orphic verses (which are also found in the writer *De Mundo*) after this manner: 'The *Demiurgus,* being full of ideas, did by these comprehend all things within himself, as that theologer also declareth in these following verses: Ζεὺς πρῶτος γένετο, etc.'"[2]

P. 312. "It cannot be denied that this tradition of the world's beginning was at first in a manner universal among all nations. For concerning the Greeks and Persians we have already manifested the same, and as Sanconiathon testified the like concerning the Phoenicians, so does Strabo of the Indian Brachmans, affirming that they did agree with the Greeks in many things and particularly in this, 'That the world was both made, and should be destroyed.'" . . . The Egyptians "had the clearest and strongest persuasion of the Cosmogonia [. . .]. And though Diodorus affirm the contrary of the Chaldeans, yet we ought in reason to assent rather to Berosus, in respect of his greater antiquity, who represents the sense of the ancient Chaldeans to be otherwise."

P. 319. Porphyrius: "'Nor do the Egyptians resolve all things into (senseless) nature, but they distinguish both the life of the soul, and the intellectual life, from that of nature, and that not only in ourselves, but also in the universe; they determining mind and reason, first to have existed of themselves, and so this whole world to have been made where-

---

2. Eight lines of Greek follow that JE did not copy out but which Cudworth translates as: "The high-thundering Jove is both the First and the Last; Jove is both the Head and Middle of all things; All things were made out of Jupiter; Jove is both a Man and an Immortal Maid; Jove is the Profundity of the Earth and Starry Heaven; Jove is the Breath of all things; Jove is the Force of the untameable Fire; Jove the Bottom of the Sea; Jove is Sun, Moon and Stars; Jove is both the Original, and King of all things: There is one Power, and One God, and one great Ruler over all."

fore they acknowledge before the heaven and in the heaven a living power, and place pure mind above the world, as the *Demiurgus* or architect thereof.'"

P. 337. Iamblichus says, "'The Egyptian philosophy, from first to last, begins from unity and thence descends to multitude; the many being always governed by the one; and the infinite, undetermined nature, everywhere mastered and conquered by some finite and determined measure; and all ultimately, by that highest unity that is the first cause of all things.' . . . In answer to that question, whether the Egyptians thought matter to be unmade and self-existent, or made, [Iamblichus] thus replies: 'That according to Hermes and the Egyptians, matter was also made or produced by God' [. . .]. Which passage of Iamblichus, Proclus upon *Timæus* (where he asserts that God '*was the ineffable cause of matter*') takes notice of in this manner: 'And the tradition of the Egyptians agreeth herewith, that matter was not unmade or self-existent, but produced by the Deity: for the divine Iamblichus hath recorded that Hermes would have materiality produced from essentiality [. . .] And it is very probable from hence that Plato also was of the same opinion concerning matter.' Proclus also affirms 'that Orpheus did also in the same manner deduce or derive matter from the first hypostasis of intelligibles.'"

P. 352. "Eusebius from Porphyrius informs us that the Egyptians acknowledge one intellectual *Demiurgus* under the name of Cneph whom they worshipped in a statue of human form, and a blackish sky-colored complexion, holding in his hand a girdle and a scepter, and wearing upon his head a princely plume and thrusting forth an egg out of his mouth. The reason of which hieroglyphic is thus given, 'Because that wisdom and reason, by which the world was made, is not easy to be found out but hidden and obscure. And because this is the fountain of life and king of all things; and because it is intellectually moved, signified by the feathers upon his head. Moreover by the egg thrust out of his mouth is meant the world, created by the eternal Logos.' [. . .] The scholiast upon Ptolemy says, 'The Egyptians were wont to talk perpetually of the genesis of the world.' Asclepius, an ancient Egyptian writer, affirms that according to the Egyptian tradition, the sun was made in Libra."

P. 362. Pindar calls the supreme Deity "'the most powerful of the gods,' 'the Lord of all things,' and 'the cause of everything,' and says 'that God is the best artificer,' and was 'the framer of the whole world.'"

P. 363. Sophocles, cited by Justin Martyr, says, "'there is in truth one only God, who made heaven and earth, the sea, air and winds,'" etc.

P. 391. "The writer *De Mundo,* [. . .] a pagan of good antiquity, says

'All the things that are upon the earth and in the air and water, may truly be called the works of God, who ruleth over the world. Out of whom, according to the physical Empedocles, proceed all things that were, are, and shall be, viz. plants, men, beasts, and gods.'"

P. 394. "Stobæus cites this out of Archytas' Book of Principles: [. . .] 'There is another more necessary cause, which moving, brings the form to the matter, and that this is the first and most powerful cause, which is fitly called God. So that there are three principles, God, matter, and form; God the artificer and mover, and matter that which is moved, and form the art introduced into the matter.' In which Stobean exerption it follows afterwards, 'that there must be something better than mind, and that this thing better than mind, is that which we (properly) call God.'

"Ocellus also in the same Stobæus thus writeth, 'Life contains the bodies of animals, the cause of which life is the soul; concord contains houses and cities, the cause of which concord is law; and harmony contains the whole world, the cause of which mundane harmony is God.' And to the same purpose Aristæus, 'As the artificer is to art, so is God to the harmony of the world.'

"Timæus Locrus, a Pythagorean senior to Plato, in his book concerning nature, or the soul of the world (upon which Plato's *Timæus* was but a kind of commentary)," says, "'The world, made up of God, men, and other animals,' is 'all created according to the best pattern'" of the divine ideas.[3]

P. 395. "In this book of Timæus Locrus, the supreme God is often called ὁ θεὸς; and sometimes ὁ Δαίμων, [God in way of eminency]; sometimes νοῦς, [mind]; sometimes τ' ἀγαθὸν, the very good; sometimes '*the principle of the best things*'; sometimes '*the best and most powerful cause*'; sometimes '*the prince and parent of all things*'; which God, according to him, is not the soul of the world, but the creator thereof." He says, "'God willing to make the world the best, that it was capable of, made it a generated God, such as should never be destroyed by any other cause but only by God himself who framed it, if he should ever will to dissolve it.'" He says further, "'Before the heavens was made, existed the idea, matter, and God, the Opifex of the best.' [. . .] Aristotle pronounces of the first Pythagoreans without exception, '*that they generated the world*.'" Clemens Alexandrinus cites this passage of Timæus Locrus, "'Would you hear of one only principle of all things amongst the Greeks? Timæus Locrus, in his Book of Nature, will bear me witness thereof; he there in express

3. Cudworth: "the Eternal and Unmade Idea."

words writing thus, *"There is one principle of all things unmade; for if it were made it would not be a principle, but that would be the principle from whence it was made.'"*

P. 396. Timæus Locrus, speaking of the world as a made[4] god, writes thus: "'That eternal God, who is the prince, original, and parent of all these things, is seen only by the mind, but the other generated god is visible to our eyes, viz. the world and those parts thereof that are heavenly.'" Parmenides says, "'Time is but an image of that unmade duration, which we call eternity; wherefore as this sensible world was made according to that eternal exemplar or pattern of the intelligible world, so was time made together with the world, as an imitation of eternity.'"

P. 399. "Socrates, in his discourse with Aristodemus in Xenophon's first Book of Memoirs," says, "'I am now convinced from what you say that the things of this world were the workmanship of some wise artificer, who also was a lover of animals.'"

P. 400. "Socrates in his discourse with Euthydemus [in Xenophon's Fourth Book . . .]: 'And that God who framed and containeth the whole world.'"

P. 404[–05]. Plato in *Timæus:* "'We say there is but one only heaven, if it be made agreeable to its intellectual paradigm, containing the ideas of all animals and other things in it; for there can be but one archetypal animal, which is the paradigm of all created being; wherefore that the world may agree with its paradigms in this respect of solitude or oneliness, therefore it is not two nor infinite, but one only begotten.'" Plato, in *Timæus* and elsewhere, sometimes calls God the *Demiurgus,* "sometimes *'the maker and father of this universe'*; [. . .] sometimes *'the sole principle of this universe,'* [. . .] sometimes *'he that generated the sun,'* sometimes *'he that makes earth, and heaven, and the gods'*; again, *'he by whose efficiency the things of the world were afterwards made when they were not before.'"* He somewhere says, "It was as easy for God to produce 'those real things, the sun, moon, stars, and the earth, etc., from himself, as it is for us to produce the images of ourselves and whatsoever else we please, only by interposing a looking glass.' Lastly he is called 'he that causeth or produceth all other things, and even himself,' the meaning whereof is this (as the same Plato also calls him), 'αὐτοφυὴς, a self-originated being, and from no other cause besides himself, but the cause of all other things.'"

Pp. 421–22. "The Stoics disputed after this manner: 'Whence did man

---

4. I.e. generated.

snatch life, reason, and understanding? Or from what was it kindled in him? For is it not plain that we derive the moisture and fluidity of our bodies from the water that is in the universe, their consistency and solidity from the earth, their heat and activity from the fire, and their spirituosity from the air? But that which far transcendeth all these things, our reason, mind and understanding, where did we find it? Or from whence did we derive it? Hath the universe all those other things of ours in it, and in far greater proportion? And hath it nothing at all of that which is the most excellent thing in us? Nothing that is devoid of mind and reason can generate things animant and rational, but the world generateth such, and therefore itself (or that which contains it and presides over it) must needs be animant, and rational or intellectual.' Which argumentation is further set home by such similitudes as these: 'If from the olive tree should be produced pipes sounding harmoniously, or from the plain tree fiddles, playing of their own accord musically, it would not at all be doubted, but that there was some musical either skill or nature, in those trees themselves; why therefore should not the world be concluded to be both animant and wise (or to have something in it which is so) since it produceth such beings from itself?'"

P. 429. "'Hoc animal providum, etc., quem vocamus hominem, præclara quadam conditione generatum esse, a summo deo.'"[5] Cicero, *De Legibus.*

"'God made all things in the world, and the whole world itself, perfect and unhinderable; but the parts thereof, for the use of the whole . . . Who made the sun? Who the fruits of the Earth? Who the seasons of the year? Who the agreeable fitness of things? Wherefore thou having received all from another, even thy very self, dost thou murmur and complain against the donor of them, if he take away any one thing from thee? Did he not bring thee into the world? show thee the light? bestow sense and reason upon thee?'" Epictetus.

"'If any one could be thoroughly sensible of this, that we are all made by God, and that as principal parts of the world, and that God is the father both of men and gods, he would never think meanly of himself knowing that he is the son of Jupiter also.'" Epictetus.

P. 430. "'God made all men to this end, that they might be happy.'" Epicet[us].

Pp. 432–34. Cleanthes, in an hymn of praise to God, calls him "the

---

5. "That this foreseen animal, etc., which we call a human being, was generated in some very clear condition by the highest god."

great father of gods; the omnipotent power; the author of nature; of whom we who creep on the ground are the offspring and as it were the image and echo of his eternal voice."[6]

P. 434. "'Esse præstantem aliquam, eternamque naturam, et eam suspiciendam admirandamque hominum generi, pulchritudo mundi, ordoque rerum cœlestium cogit confiteri.'"[7] Cicero, *De Natura Deorum.*

"'Quis est tam vecors, qui cum suspexerit in cœlum, Deos esse non sentiat, et ea quæ tanta mente fiunt, ut vix quisquam arte ulla, ordinem rerum ac vicissitudinem persequi, possit, casu fieri putet?'"[8] Cicero, *De Haruspicum Responsis.*

P. 440. Seneca calls God "'Formatorem universi; . . . mundani hujus operis dominum et artificem . . . ex quo nata sunt omnia.'"[9]

P. 444. "'Should I any longer insist on such brutish persons as those, the wise and sober must justly condemn me, as defiling this holy oration, which I compose as a true hymn to the praise of him that made us; I conceiving true piety and religion towards God to consist in this, not that I should sacrifice many hecatombs, or burn much incense to him, but that I should myself acknowledge, and then declare to others, how great his wisdom is, how great his power, and how great his goodness. For that he would adorn the whole world after this manner, envying to nothing that good which it was capable of, I conclude to be a demonstration of most absolute goodness, and thus let him be praised by us as good. And that he was able to find out, how all things might be adorned after the best manner, is a sign of the greatest wisdom in him. And lastly to be able to effect and bring to pass all those things which he had thus decreed, argues an insuperable power.'"[1] Galen.

P. 445–46. "'Jupiter made all things, and all things whatsoever that exist are the works of Jupiter, rivers and earth, and sea and heaven, and what are between these, both gods and men, and all animals, whatsoever is perceivable either by the sense or by the mind.'" Aristides.

6. JE's own translation of the first lines of the poem, which Cudworth quotes in both the original Greek and in a Latin translation.

7. Cudworth translates: "That there is some Most Excellent and Eternal Nature, which is to be admired and honoured by mankind, the Pulchritude of the World, and the order of the Heavenly Bodies compell us to confess."

8. Cudworth translates: "Who is so mad or stupid, as when he looks up to Heaven, is not presently convinced that there are Gods? Or can perswade himself, that those things which are made with so much Mind and Wisdom, as that no humane skill is able to reach and comprehend the artifice and contrivance of them, did all happen by chance?"

9. Cudworth translates: "The Framer and Former of the Universe . . . The Artificer and Lord of this whole Mundane Fabrick . . . From whom all things spring."

1. JE quotes the same passage above, pp. 660–61.

P. 478. "The generality of the more civilized and intelligent pagans, and even of the poets themselves, did constantly retain thus much of natural and true theology amongst them, *that Jupiter was the father both of gods and men,* that is, *the maker of the whole world.*" [See forward,] p. 703.[2]

TRADITIONS OF THE MOSAIC CREATION.

P. 120. Aristotle tells us "'there are some who conceive that even the most ancient of all, and the most remote from the present generation, and they also who first theologized, did physiologize after this manner; forasmuch as they made the ocean and tethys to have been the original of generation; and for this cause the oath of the gods is said to be by water (called by the poets Styx), as being that from which they all derived their original.'"

Homer says,

"The father of all gods, the ocean is,
Tethys their mother."

P. 120–21. Aristophanes gives us description in his *Aves,* which may be Englished thus:

"First of all chaos, one confused heap,
Darkness enwrapped the disagreeing deep,
In a mixt crowd, the jumbled elements were,
Nor earth, nor air, nor heaven did appear;
Till on this horrid vast abyss of things,
Teeming night spreading o'er her coal-black wings,
Laid the first egg; whence after times due course,
Issued forth Love (the world's prolific source)
Glistering with golden wings; which fluttering o'er
Dark chaos, gendered all the numerous store
Of animals and gods . . .

"The poet makes the birds to have been begotten between love and chaos before all the gods . . ."

Parmenides and Hesiod "did make love the supreme deity, and derived all things from love and chaos."

P. 122. "Simmias Rhodius in his *Wings,* an hymn made in honor of this love, that is senior to all the gods, and a principle in the universe, tells us plainly that it is not Cupid, Venus' soft and effeminate son, but another kind of love:

---

2. MS: "P. 1118 [col. 2] *," a reference to the quotation of Plato in Cudworth, pp. 750–51.

I am not that wanton boy,
The sea-frothed goddess' only joy.
Pure heavenly love I hight, and my
Soft magic charms, not iron bands, fast tie
Heaven, earth, and seas. The gods themselves do readily
Stoop to my laws. The whole world dances to my harmony."

P. 124. "Cicero tells us that Thales, besides water, which he made to be the original of all corporeal things, asserted also mind for another principle, which formed all things out of the water."

P. 212. The ancient scholiast upon Hesiod writes thus, that Hesiod's love was "'the heavenly love, which is also God, that other love which was born of Venus, being junior.'"

Joannes Diaconus says, "'By love here we must not understand Venus' son, whose mother was yet unborn, but another more ancient love, which I take to be the active cause or principle of motion naturally inserted into things.'"

P. 238. Hesiod, in the beginning of his *Theogonia,* invokes the Muses after this manner (translated into Latin thus):

"Salvete natæ Jovis, date vero amabilem cantilenam:
Celebrate quoque immortalium divinum genus semper existentium
Qui tellure prognati sunt, cœlo stellato,
Nocteque; caliginosa, quos item salsus nutrivit pontus.
Dicite insuper, ut primum dii et terra facti fuerint,
Et flumina, et pontus immensus æstu fervens,
Astraque; fulgentia,and cælum latum superne,
Et qui [ex] his nati sunt dii datores bonorum."[3]

P. 239. "This was the general tradition amongst the pagans, that the world was made out of an antecedent chaos."

P. 240. "'God taking all the matter which was (not then resisting but moving confusedly and disorderly), he brought it into order, out of confusion.'" Plato.

---

3. "Hail, children of Jupiter! Sing now a lovely song: / Celebrate also the divine birth of the ever-existing immortals, / Who are the offspring from the Earth, from the starry Sky, / And from gloomy Night, whom thus the salted Sea nourished. / Tell, moreover, how at first the gods and the Earth had been made / And the rivers, and the immense sea roiling with surging tide, / And the gleaming stars, and the wide heaven above, / And who out of these were born as gods, the givers of good things."

Pp. 244–46.

"Ante mare et terras, et quod tegit omnia, cœlum,
Unus erat toto naturæ vultus in orbe,
Quem dixere chaos; rudis indigestaque moles,
Nec quicquam nisi Pondus iners, congestaque eodem
Non bene junctarum discordia semina rerum.
Nullus adhuc mundo præbebat lumina Titan,
Nec nova crescendo reparabat cornua Phœbe,
Nec circumfuso pendebat in ære Tellus,
Ponderibus librata suis; nec brachia longo
Margine Terrarum porrexerat Amphitrite.
Quaque erat et Tellus, etc.[4] [. . .]
Hanc Deus et melior litem natura diremit,
Nam cœlo terras, et terris abscidit undas:
Et liquidum spisso secrevit ab ære cœlum, etc.[5] [. . .]
Sanctius his animal, mentisque capacius altæ
Deerat adhuc, et quod dominari in cætera posset:
Natus homo est: sive hunc divino semine fecit,
Ille Opifex rerum, mundi melioris origo:
Sive recens tellus, seductaque nuper ab alto
Æthere, cognati retinebat semina cœli.
Quam satus Iapeto, mistam fluvialibus undis,
Finxit in effigiem Moderantum cuncta Deorum."[6]
Ovidius.

P. 248–49. Orpheus, in Latin thus: "'Noctem concelebro genetricem
Hominumque deumque.'"[7]

"It was a most ancient and in a manner universally received tradition
among the pagans, as hath been often intimated that the cosmogonia or

4. Cudworth quotes "Mr. [George] Sandys [1578–1644] his English, with some little alter-ation": "Before that Sea and Earth and Heaven was fram'd, / One face had Nature which they Chaos nam'd. / No Titan yet the World with Light adorns, / Nor waxing Phebe fills her wained Horns; / Nor hung the self-poiz'd Earth in thin Air plac'd, / Nor Amphitrite the vast shore em-brac'd; / Earth, Air and Sea Confounded, &c."
5. Cudworth translates: "This Strife (with Better Nature) God decides, / He Earth from Heaven, the Sea from Earth divides: He Ether pure extracts from Grosser Air."
6. Cudworth translates: "The Nobler Being, with a Mind possest, / Was wanting yet, that should command the rest. / That Maker, the best Worlds Original, / Either him fram'd of seed Celestial; / Or Earth which late he did from Heaven divide, / Some sacred seeds retain'd to Heaven allied: / Which with the living stream Prometheus mixt, / And in that Artificial Struc-ture fixt, / The Form of all the All-ruling Deities."
7. "I celebrate Night, the Mother of gods and men."

generation of the world took its first beginning from a chaos (the divine cosmogonists agreeing herein with the atheistic ones), this tradition having been delivered down from Orpheus and Linus, by Hesiod and Homer and others; acknowledged by Epicharmus; and embraced by Thales, Anaxagoras, Plato, and other philosophers who were theists: the antiquity whereof is declared by Euripides," in Latin thus:

> "Non hic meus, sed matris est sermo meæ,
> Figura ut una fuerit et cœli et soli,
> Secreta quæ mox ut receperunt statum,
> Cuncta ediderunt hæc in oras luminis;
> Feras, volucres, arbores, ponti gregem,
> Homines quoque ipsos."[8]

"Neither can it reasonably be doubted but that it was originally Mosaical, and indeed at first a divine revelation; since no man could otherwise pretend to know what was done before mankind had any being. 'Thus *Mus Araneus*,' (saith Plutarch) 'being blind is said to be deified by the Egyptians because they thought that darkness was older than light.' [. . .]

"The ancient Cabbala, which derived the Cosmogonia from chaos and love, was at first religious and not atheistical, and that the love understood in it was not the offspring of chaos may be concluded from hence, because this love as well as chaos was of a Mosaical extraction also, and plainly derived from that spirit of God which is said in the Scripture, 'to have moved upon the face of the waters'; . . . From whence also it came that as Porphyrius testifieth the ancient Pagans thought the water to be divinely inspired," in the words following (translated into English): "'They thought that souls attended upon the water, or resorted thereunto, as being divinely inspired, as Numenius writeth, adding the Prophet also, therefore [to have] said, the spirit of God moved upon the water.'

"And that this Cabbala was thus understood by some of the ancient pagan cosmogonists themselves, appears plainly, not only from Simmias Rhodius and Parmenides, but also from these following verses of Orpheus, or whoever was the writer of those Argonautics, undoubtedly ancient where chaos and love are thus brought in together," thus Englished:

---

8. "Nor is this mine, but the word of my mother, / The figure when it will have been one of both sky and earth, / The secrets which soon when they have received their position, / Gave all these things into the shores of light; / Beasts, birds, trees, the herd of the sea, / And even men themselves."

"'We will first sing a pleasant and delightful song, concerning the ancient chaos, how heaven, earth, and seas, were framed out of it; as also concerning that much wise and sagacious love, the oldest of all, and self-perfect which actively produced all these things, separating one thing from another.'"

P. 250. Aristotle says thus in his Metaphysics: "'Others, besides the material cause of the world, assign an efficient or cause of motion, viz. whosoever make either mind or love a principle.' Wherefore we conclude that that other atheistic Cabbala or Aristophanic tradition [. . .] generating all things whatsoever, [. . .] out of night and chaos, making love itself likewise to have been produced from an egg of the night, [. . .] was nothing else but a mere depravation of the Mosaic Cabbala."

Pp. 299–300. The following, an epitome of the Orphic doctrine, made long since by Timotheus the Chronographer, in his *Cosmopœia*, still extant in Cedrenus and Eusebii *Chronica*, and imperfectly set down by Suidas (upon the word Orpheus) as his own without mentioning the author's name: 'First of all the æther was made by God, and after æther a chaos; a dark and dreadful night then covering all under the whole æther.' Orpheus hereby signifying, (saith Timotheus) 'that night was senior to day.' . . . 'He having declared also in his Explication, that there was a certain incomprehensible being, which was the highest and oldest of all things, and the maker of everything, even of the æther itself, and all things under the æther. But the earth being then invisible by reason of the darkness, a light breaking out through the æther, illuminated the whole creation: this light being said by him to be that highest of all beings (before mentioned) which is called also counsel and life. These three names in Orpheus (light, counsel, and life) declaring one and the same force and power of that God, who is the maker of all, and who produceth all out of nothing into being whether visible or invisible.' . . . And the same Orpheus declared in his book, 'that all things were made by one godhead in three names, and that this God is all things.'"

P. 312. Borosus "represents the sense of the ancient Chaldeans after this manner, 'There was a time when all was darkness and water, but Bel, cutting the darkness in the middle, separated the earth and heaven from one another and so framed the world; this Bel also producing the stars, the sun and the moon, and the five planets.'"

P. 313. "Simplicius, a zealous contender for the world's eternity, affirms the Mosaic history of its creation by God to be nothing else but Egyptian fables." His words in English are as follows: "'If Grammaticus here means the lawgiver of the Jews writing thus, "In the beginning God made heaven and earth, and the earth was invisible and unadorned, and darkness was upon the deep, and the spirit of God moved upon the waters," and then afterwards when he had made light and separated the light from the darkness adding "*and God called the Light day*"; I say, if Grammaticus thinks this to have been the first generation and beginning of time, I would have him to know that all this is but a fabulous tradition, and wholly drawn from Egyptian fables.'"

P. 336. "Iamblichus tells us that as the Egyptian hieroglyphic for material and corporeal things was mud or floating water, so they pictured God '*sitting upon the Lote-tree over the watery mud.*' Which signifies the transcendent eminency of the Deity above matter and its intellectual empire over the world, because both the leaves and fruit of that tree are round, representing the motion of intellect."

P. 358. "'The ocean from whence the gods are generated.'" Homer. Eustathius observes that the gods are here principally "'put for the stars.'" Homer elsewhere speaking of the ocean calls it "'*the original of all things.*'"

P. 365 Among the Latin poets Ennius "first appears deriving the gods in general from Erebus and night, as supposing them all to [...] be generated out of chaos, nevertheless acknowledging one who is 'divumque hominumque pater, rex.'"

P. 429. "Zeno in Laertius thus describes the Cosmopœia: 'That God at first, being alone by himself, converted the fiery substance of the world by degrees into water, [...] out of which water, himself afterwards as the spermatic reason of the world, formed the elements and whole mundane system.'"

GOD'S WORKS OF PROVIDENCE.

Pp. 207–08. Epicurus takes notice of and opposes the notion of one God's being present everywhere to animadvert order and dispose all things, in these words:

> "Quis regere immensi summam, quis habere profundi
> Indu manu validas potis est moderanter habenas?
> Quis pariter cœlos omnes convertere, et omnes
> Ignibus ætheriis terras suffire feraces?"[9]

---

9. "Who is able to rule the height of the vastness, / Who is able to hold with control the strong reins of the sea in hand, / Who is able equally to reverse all the heavens, and / To suffuse all fruit-bearing lands with ethereal fires?"

In like manner he further pursues the same argument in these words: "'Sive ipse mundus Deus est, quid potest esse minus quietum, quam, nullo puncto temporis intermisso, versari circum axem cœli, admirabili celeritate? Sive in ipso mundo Deus inest aliquis qui regat, qui gubernet, qui cursus astrorum, mutationes temporum, hominumque commodo vitasque tueatur; næ ille est implicatus molestis negotiis et operosis.'"[1]

P. 350. In Apuleius we have an oration of the Egyptian goddess Isis in the following words: "'Behold here am I, moved by thy prayers, Lucius, that nature which was the parent of things; the mistress of all the elements; the beginning and original of ages; the sum of all the divine powers; the queen of the seas; the first of the celestial inhabitants; the uniform face of gods and goddesses; which with my becks dispense the luminous heights of the heavens, the wholesome blasts of the sea, and the deplorable silences of hell.'

"And thus was Isis worshipped and invoked, as the 'unicum numen,' [or only divine power,] by Apuleius himself in these following words:[2] 'Thou holy and perpetual savior of mankind, that art always bountiful in cherishing mortals, and dost manifest the dear affections of a mother to them in their calamities, thou extricatest the involved threads of fate, mitigatest the tempests of fortune, and restrainest the noxious influences of the stars; the celestial gods worship thee; the infernal powers obey thee; thou rollest round the heavens, enlightenest the sun, governest the world, treadest upon Tartarus; the stars obey thee, the elements serve thee, at thy beck the winds blow,' etc."

P. 26. Empedocles affirms that God is "'only a holy and ineffable mind that by swift thoughts agitates the whole world.'"

Anaxagoras affirmed "that there was besides atoms, 'an ordering and disposing mind that was the cause of all things.'" Stobæus says concerning Ecphantus the Pythagorean that he "'held the corporeal world to consist of atoms, but yet to be ordered and governed by a divine providence.'"

P. 503. "Aristotle or the writer *De Plantis*" says, "'What is the principle in the life or soul of animals? Certainly no other than that noble animal,

---

1. Cudworth translates: "Whether you will suppose the World itself to be a God, what can be more unquiet, than without intermission perpetually to whirle round upon the Axis of the Heaven, with such admirable celerity? Or whether you will imagine a God in the World distinct from it, who does govern and dispose all things, keep up the Courses of the Stars, the Successive Changes of the Seasons, and Orderly Vicissitudes of things, and contemplating Lands and Seas, conserve the Utilities and Lives of men; certainly He must needs be involved in much solicitous trouble and Employment."

2. JE quotes a portion of this same paragraph above, p. 660.

that encompasses and surrounds the whole heaven, the sun, the stars and the planets.'"

P. 251. Diodorus Siculus affirms of the Chaldeans that "'they believe that the order and disposition of the world is by a certain divine providence, and that every one of those things, which comes to pass in the heavens, happens not by chance, but by a certain determinate and firmly ratified judgment of the gods.'"

Pp. 255–56. Cicero, *De Legibus:* "'Deorum immortalium vi, ratione, potestate, mente, numine, natura omnis regitur.'[3] And again in his second book: 'Deos esse dominos ac moderatores omnium rerum, eaque quæ geruntur, eorum geri judicio atque numine, eosdemque optime de genere hominum mereri, et qualis quisque sit, quid agat, quid in se admittat, qua mente, qua pietate religiones colat, intueri, piorumque and impiorum habere rationem; a principio civibus suasum esse debet.'"[4]

P. 258. "'By Jupiter you are to understand that most ancient and princely mind, which all things follow and obey.'" Porphyrius in Eusebius.

"Phornutus by Jupiter understands the 'soul of the world,' he writing thus concerning it: 'As we ourselves are governed by a soul, so hath the world in like manner a soul that containeth it; and this is called Zeus, being the cause of life to all things that live; and therefore Zeus or Jupiter is said to reign over all things.'

"Plato, in his *Cratylus,* taking those two words, Ζῆνα and Δία, both together, etimologizeth them as one, after this manner: 'These two words compounded together declare the nature of god; for there is nothing that is more the cause of life both to ourselves and all other animals, than he who is the prince and king of all things; so that God is rightly thus called; he being that by whom all things live.'"

P. 260–61. "'If God will have it so, let it be so.'" Socrates.

P. 264. e. "The pagans sometimes thus characterize the supreme God [. . .] Κρατέων τοῦ παντος, 'he that ruleth over the whole world, summus rector and dominus'; [. . .] ὁ ἐπι πᾶσι θεὸς, ['the God over all']."

---

3. Cudworth translates: "The Whole Nature, or Universe, is governed by the Force, Reason, Power, Mind, and Divinity of the Immortal Gods."

4. Cudworth translates: "The Minds of Citizens, ought to be first of all embued with a firm perswasion, that the Gods are the Lords and Moderators of all things, and that the Conduct and Management of the whole World is directed and over-ruled by their Judgement and Divine Power; that they deserve the best of mankind, that they behold and consider what every man is, what he doth and takes upon himself, with what Mind, Piety, and Sincerety he observes the Duties of Religion; and Lastly, that these Gods have a very diffeent regard to the Pious and the Impious."

P. 366.

Jupiter, qui genus colis alisque hominum, per quem vivimus
Vitale ævum, quem penes spes, vitæque sunt Homimum omnium,
Da diem hunc sospitem, quæso, rebus meis agundis.[5]

Plautus.

[P. 394.] "'All these things hath Nemesis decreed to be executed in the second circuit by the ministry of vindictive terrestrial demons.'" ["Timæus Locrus, in his book concerning nature."]

Pp. 399–400. "'Consider, friend, I pray you, if that mind which is in your body does order and dispose it every way as it pleases; why should not that wisdom which is in the universe, be able to order all things therein also, as seemeth best to it? And if your eye can discern things several miles distant from it, why should it be thought impossible for the eye of God to behold all things at once? Lastly, if your soul can mind things both here and in Egypt and in Sicily, why may not the great mind or wisdom of God be able to take care of all things in all places?'[6] Socrates to Aristodemus in Xenophon. And then Socrates concludes, that if Aristodemus would diligently apply himself to the worship of God, he should be convinced 'that God is such and so great a being, as that he can at once see all things and hear all things, and be present everywhere and take care of all affairs.'

"Socrates to Euthydemus, in Xenophon's fourth book, speaks thus concerning that invisible Deity which governs the whole world: 'The other gods giving us good things, do it without visibly appearing to us; and that God who framed and containeth the whole world (in which are all good and excellent things) and who continually supplieth us with them, he, though be seen to do the greatest things of all, yet is himself invisible and unseen.'"

Pp. 426–27. "'Pray to the Gods.'" Epictetus.

"'Revere the gods. . . . In everything implore the aid and assistance of the gods. . . . I owe to the gods that I had good progenitors and parents. . . . For all these things need the assistance of the gods and fortune. . . . That reason which passes through the substance of the universe, and through all eternity, orders and dispenses all according to appointed periods.'" M. Antoninus.

---

5. "Jupiter, you who tend and nourish the race of men, through whom we live, / Give this saving day, I ask, a sustaining life (in which are the hopes and the lives of all men) / for the things I must do."

6. JE quotes the same passage above, p. 652.

"'A good man submits his mind to the governor of the whole universe as good citizens do theirs to the law of the city. . . . To be instructed is to will all things to be as they are made: and how are they made? As that great disposer and orderer of all hath appointed.'" Epictetus.

P. 428. M. Antoninus calls God "'one God through all, one substance, one law.'"

Epictetus says, "'Will nothing but what God willeth, and then who can be able to hinder thee?' [. . .] Also where he speaketh of the regular course of things in nature: 'That it proceedeth orderly, everything as it were obeying the command of God; when he bids the plants to blossom, they blossom; and when to bring forth fruit, they bring forth fruit.' To which innumerable other instances might be added. . . . The government of the whole world was called the '*government or economy of Jupiter.*'" Epictetus.

"'I have, whom I ought to be subject to, whom to obey, God and those who are next after him. . . . Let Jupiter alone with these things, and the other gods; deliver them up to be ordered and governed by them.'" Ibid.

P. 429. "'Wherefore, thou having received all from another, even thy very self, dost thou murmur and complain against the donor of them, if he take away any one thing from thee? Did he not bring thee into the world? show thee the light? bestow sense and reason upon thee?'"[7] Idem. [Epictetus.]

Pp. 430–32. "'Things would not be well governed if Jupiter took no care of his own citizens, that they also might be happy like himself. . . . Did I ever complain of thy government? I was sick when thou wouldst have me to be, and so are others, but I was so willingly. I was poor also at thine appointment, but rejoicing; I never bore any magistracy or had any dignity, because thou wouldst not have me, and I never desired it. Didst thou ever see me the more dejected or melancholy for this? Have I appeared before thee at any time with a discontented countenance? Was I not always prepared and ready for whatsoever thou requiredst? Wilt thou now have me depart out of this festival solemnity? I am ready to go; and I render thee all thanks for that thou hast honored me so far, as to let me keep the feast with thee, and behold thy works and observe thy economy of the world. Let death seize upon me no otherwise employed, than thus thinking and writing of such things.'" Idem. [Epictetus.]

"'Dare to lift up thine eyes to God and say, Use me hereafter to whatsoever thou pleasest. I agree and am of the same mind with thee, indif-

---

7. JE quotes a portion of the same passage above, p. 685.

ferent to all things. I refuse nothing that shall seem good to thee. Lead me whither thou pleasest. Let me act what part thou wilt, either of a public or private person, of a rich man or beggar.'" Idem. [Epictetus.]

"M. Antoninus speaketh of a double relation that we all have, one '*to those that live with us,*' and another '*to that divine cause from which all things happen to all.*' As likewise, '*that no human thing is well done without a reference to God.*'"

"'Now remember the supreme God; call upon him as thy helper and assistant, as the mariners do upon Castor and Pollux in a tempest.'" Epictetus.

"'Lead me, O Jupiter, and thou Fate, whithersoever I am by you destined: and I will readily and cheerfully follow; who though I were never so reluctant, yet must needs follow.'" [Epictetus.]

Pp. 433, etc.

"Magne pater divum, cui nomina multa, sed una
Omnipotens semper virtus, tu Jupiter autor
Naturæ, certa qui singula lege gubernas!
Rex salve. . . .
Quippe tuo hic totus, terram qui circuit orbis
Paret (quoquo agis) imperio [. . .]
Tantus tu rerum dominus, rectorque supremus.
Nec sine te factum in terris, Deus, aut opus ullum,
Æthere nec dio fit, nec per cærula ponti,
Errore acta suo, nisi quæ gens impia patrat.
Confusa in sese tu dirigis ordine certo;
Auspice te ingratis and inest sua gratia rebus;
Fœlice harmonia, tu scilicet, omnia in unum
Sic bona mixta malis compingis, ut una resurgat
Cunctorum ratio communis et usque perennans:
Quam refugit, spernitque hominum mens læva malorum.
Heu miseri! bona qui quærunt sibi semper et optant,
Divinam tamen hanc communem et denique legem
Nec spectare oculis, nec fando attendere curant:
Cui si parerent poterant traducere vitam
Cum ratione and mente bonam . . ."[8]

Cleanthes' Hymn, translated into Latin.

8. "Great father of gods, to whom are many names, but one / Always omnipotent power, Jupiter, author / Of nature, who govern each single thing by your law! / Hail, King. . . . / In-

Pp. 435, etc.

[P. 436.] "'Nec vero Deus ipse alio modo intelligi potest, nisi mens so-
luta quædam, et libera, segregata ab omni concretione mortali, omnia
sentiens and movens.'"⁹ Cicero.

"'Hæc igitur et alia innumerabilia [cum cerniumus,] possumusne du-
bitare, quin his præsit aliquis vel effector, si hæc nata sunt ut Platoni videtur; vel si semper fuerint ut Aristoteli placet, moderator tanti operis et
muneris?'"¹ Idem. [Cicero.]

"'Sine imperio nec domus ulla, nec civitas, nec gens, nec hominum
universum genus stare, nec rerum natura omnis, nec ipse mundus potest. Nam et hic deo paret, et huic obediunt maria terræque, et hominum
vita jussis supremæ legis obtemperat.'"² Cicero.

[Pp. 436–37.] "Elsewhere Cicero speaks of 'dominans ille nobis Deus,
qui nos vetat hinc injussu suo demigrare'; . . . of 'Deus cujus numini parent omnia'; . . . of 'the divine power of the supreme Lord and governor'; [. . .] of 'princeps ille Deus, qui omnem hunc mundum regit, sicut animus humanus id corpus cui præpositus est.'"³

P. 437 "When Balbus in Cicero, to excuse some seeming defects in
Providence, . . . pretended, 'Non animadvertere omnia Deos,' [. . .] Cotta

---

deed all this which circles the land of the earth / Obeys your rule, by whatever you do. [. . .]
/ You, such a great master of all and the supreme ruler. / There is no work done without you,
god, on the earth / Or in the divine sky or through the blue seas / Driven by your wandering,
except what an impious race brings to pass. / You direct those confused things into yourself in
sure order. / With you as the founder, your grace is even in ungracious things; / You, indeed,
unite all things into one in blessed harmony, / The good thus mixed with the bad, in order
that one common system / Of all things might rise perpetually. / This system the foolish mind
of bad people flees and spurns. / Alas, wretches! Who always seek and choose good things for
themselves, / Nevertheless do not take care to look at this divine, common law with their eyes,
/ Nor to attend to it by speaking. / If they were to obey it, they would be able to lead a good
life."

    9. Cudworth translates: "Neither can God himself be understood by us otherwise, than as a
certain Loose and Free Mind, segregated from all mortal Concretion, which both perceives and
moves all things."

    1. Cudworth translates: "When we behold these and other wonderful works of Nature, can
we at all doubt, but that there presideth over them, either One Maker of all, if they had a beginning as Plato conceiveth; or else if they always were as Aristotle supposeth, One Moderator
and Governor?"

    2. Cudworth translates: "Without Government, neither any House, nor City, nor Nation, nor
Mankind in general, nor the whole Nature of things, nor the World it self could subsist. For
this also obeyeth God, and the Seas and Earth are subject to him, and the Life of man is disposed of, by the Commands of the Supreme Law."

    3. Cudworth translates: "that God who rules over all Mankind and forbids them to depart
hence without his lieve . . . of that God, whose Divine Power all things obey, . . . of that Chief
or Principal God, who governs the whole world in the same manner as a Humane Soul governeth that Body which it is set over."

amongst other things replied thus, 'Fac divinam mentem esse distentam, cœlum versantem, terram tuentem, maria moderantem, cur tam multos Deos nihil agere, and cessare patitur? Cur non rebus humanis aliquos otiosos Deos præfecit, qui a te Balbe innumerabiles explicati sunt?'"[4]

P. 335. "Horus Apollo in his Hieroglyphics tells us that the Egyptians acknowledging a παντοκράτωρ and a κοσμοκράτωρ, an 'omnipotent being that was governor of the whole world,' did symbolically represent him by a serpent, 'they picturing also a great house or palace within its circumference because the world is the royal palace of the Deity.'" He "also gives another reason why the serpent was made to be the hieroglyphic of the Deity: 'Because the serpent feeding as it were upon its own body, doth aptly signify that all things generated in the world by divine Providence are again resolved into him.'"[5]

Pp. 367–68.

"... O qui res hominumque deumque
Eternis regis imperiis..."[6]

Virgil.

"... Qui res hominum et deorum,
Qui mare et terras, variisque mundum temperat horis."[7]

[Horace.] Again,

"Qui terram inertem, qui mare temperat
Ventosum et urbis, regnaque tristia,
Divosque, mortalesque turmas
Imperio regit UNUS æquo."[8]

Horace.

P. 423[–24]. Plutarch, pleading "for a plurality of worlds, says 'Neither is it all considerable, what the Stoics object against a plurality of worlds,

---

4. Cudworth translates: "That the Gods did not attend to all things, [...] Should it be granted, that the Divine Mind (or Supreme Deity) were distracted with turning round the Heavens, observing the Earth, and Governing the Seas, yet why does he let so many other Gods to do nothing at all? Or why does he not appoint some of those Idle Gods over Humane affairs, which according to Balbus and the Stoicks are innumerable?"

5. JE quotes the same passage above, p. 677.

6. "O you who rule the affairs of men and gods / By your eternal power ..."

7. "Who regulates the affairs of men and gods, / Who regulates the sea and lands, and regulates the world with different seasons."

8. "The one who directs the unmoved earth and the windy sea and cities, and sad kingdoms, / And divine and mortal crowds, / The ONE who rules with equal power."

they demanding how there could be but one fate and one providence, and one Jove, were there many worlds? For what necessity [is there,] that there must be more Zens or Joves than one, if there were more worlds? and why might not that one and the same God of this universe, called by us the Lord and Father of all, be the first prince, and highest governor of all those worlds? Or what hinders but that a multitude of worlds might be all subject to the fate and providence of one Jupiter or supreme God, himself inspecting and ordering them every one; and imparting principles and spermatic reasons to them according to which all things in them might be governed and disposed. For can many distinct persons in an army or chorus, be reduced into one body or polity? and could not ten, or fifty, or an hundred worlds in the universe, be all governed by one reason, and be ordered together in reference to one principle?'"

P. 440. Annæus Seneca asserted one supreme God whom he calls: "'Formatorem universi; rectorem et arbitrum et custodem mundi; ex quo suspensa sunt omnia; animum ac spiritum universi; mundani hujus operis Dominum et artificem; cui nomen omne convenit; ex quo nata sunt omnia; cujus spiritu vivimus; totum suis partibus inditum, et se sustinentem sua vi; cujus consilio huic mundo providetur, ut inconcussus eat, et actus suos explicet; cujus decreto omnia fiunt; divinum spiritum per omnia maxima and minima equali intentione diffusum; Deum potentem omnium; Deum illum maximum potentissimumque, qui ipse vehit omnia; qui ubique and omnibus presto est; cœli et Deorum omnium Deum, a quo ista numina quæ singula adoramus et colimus, suspensa sunt.'"[9]

Pp. 442–45. "The writer *De Mundo* elegantly illustrates by similitudes how God by one simple motion and energy of his own, without any labor or toil, doth produce and govern all the variety of motions in the universe; and how much he doth *'contain the harmony and safety of the whole.'*" And lastly he concludes with saying, "'that what a pilot is to a

---

9. Cudworth translates: "The Framer and Former of the Universe; the Governour, Disposer and keeper thereof; Him upon whom all things depend; The Mind and Spirit of the World; the Artificer and Lord of this whole Mundane Fabrick; To whom every name belongeth; From whom all things spring; By whose Spirit we live; Who is in all his parts and susteineth himself by his own force; By whose Counsel the World is provided for, and carried on in its Course constantly and uninterruptedly; By whose Decree all things are done; The Divine Spirit that is diffused through all things both great and small with equal Intention; The God whose power extends to all things; The Greatest and most Powerful God who doth himself support and uphold all things; Who is present every where to all things; The God of Heaven and of all the Gods, upon whom are suspended all those other Divine Powers, which we singly worship and adore." JE quotes a portion of the same passage above, p. 686.

ship, a charioteer to a chariot, the coryphæus to a choir, law to a city, and a general to an army, the same is God to the world.'" And the same writer adds, "'God being himself immovable, moveth all things, in the same manner as law, in itself immovable, by moving the minds of the citizens, orders and disposes all things.'"

Dio Chrysostomus, Plutarch's equal, asserteth: "'That the whole world is under a kingly power or monarchy,' he calling the supreme God, 'the common king of gods and men, their governor and father, . . . the God that rules over all, . . . the chief president over all things, who orders and governs[1] the whole heaven and world as a wise pilot doth a ship, . . . the ruler of the whole heaven, and lord of the whole essence'"; and says, "'Concerning the nature of the gods in general, but especially of that supreme ruler over all, there is an opinion in all humankind, as well barbarians as Greeks, that is naturally implanted in them as rational beings, and not derived from any moral teacher.'"

Maximus Tyrius represents his own theology thus: "'I will now more plainly declare my sense by this similitude. Imagine in your mind a great and powerful kingdom or principality, in which all the rest freely and with one consent conspire to direct their actions, agreeably to the will and command of one supreme king, the oldest and best. And then suppose the bounds and limits of this empire, not to be the River Halys, nor the Hellespont, nor the Meotian Lake, nor the shores of the ocean; but heaven above and the earth beneath. Here then let that great king sit immovable, prescribing laws to all his subjects, in which consists their safety and security: the consorts of his empire, being many both visible and invisible gods; some of which that are nearest to him and immediately attending on him, are in the highest royal dignity, feasting as it were at the same table with him; others again are their ministers and attendants; and a third sort, inferior to them both. And thus you see how the order and chain of this government descends down by steps and degrees, from the supreme God to the earth and men.'"

DIVINE CONCURRENCE.

P. 504. "Apuleius affirmeth 'deum omnia permeare,' and that 'nulla res est tam præstantibus viribus, quæ viduata Dei auxilio, sui natura contenta sit.'"[2]

---

1. Cudworth: "guides."

2. Cudworth translates: "God doth permeate all things," and that "There is nothing so excellent or powerful, as that it could be content with its own Nature alone, void of the Divine Aid or Influence."

P. 482. "The several names of God which the writer *De Mundo* instanceth in, [...] are such as these: ... '*the giver of rain* ... *the bestower of fruits* ... *the keeper of cities* ... and the *savior and assertor of liberty.*'"

Jupiter was called "'Victor, Invictus, Opitulus, Stator'; the true meaning of which [last] (according to Seneca) was [...] 'because all things by means of him stand firm and are established.' [...] He was styled also by the Latins '*Almus*' and '*Ruminus,*' i.e. 'He that nourisheth all things as it were with his breasts.'

"Again the writer *De Mundo* adds another sort of names by which God was called, as Ἀνάγκη, '*necessity,*'" concerning which Cicero says, "'Interdum deum necessitatem appelant, quia nihil aliter esse possit, atque ab eo constitutum sit.'³ Likewise, Εἱμαρμένη, because all things are by him connected together and proceed unhinderably; Πεπρωμένη, because all things in the world are determined, and nothing left [...] undetermined; [...] Ἀδράστεια, because his power is such that none can possibly avoid or escape him.' Lastly, that ingenious fable of the three fatal sisters, Clotho, Lachesis, and Atropos, according to him meant nothing but God neither." He says, "'All this is nothing but God as the noble and generous Plato also intimates, when he affirmeth, God to contain the beginning, and middle, and end of all things.'

"And both Cicero and Seneca tell us that amongst the Latins God was not only called '*Fatum,*' but also '*Natura,*' and '*Fortuna.* Quid aliud est Natura,' saith Seneca, 'quam Deus and divina ratio, toti mundo et partibus ejus inserta?'⁴ Adding 'that God and nature were no more two different things than Annæus and Seneca.' And 'Nonnunquam Deus,' saith Cicero, 'Fortunam appellant, quod efficiat multa improvisa, et nec opinata nobis, propter obscuritatem ignorationemque causarum.'"⁵

PRESERVATION a CONTINUED CREATION.

P. 572.⁶ "'This world is an image always iconized, or perpetually renewed, [...] of that first, second, and third principle.'" Plotinus.

---

3. Cudworth translates: "they sometimes call God Necessity, because nothing can be otherwise than as it is by Him appointed."

4. Cudworth translates: "What is Nature else, but God and the Divine Reason, inserted into the Whole World and all its Several Parts?"

5. Cudworth translates: "They sometimes call God also by the name of Forture, because he surprizeth us in many Events, and bringeth to pass things unexpected to us, by reason of the Obscurity of Causes and our Ignorance."

6. JE incorrectly cites p. 752; he quotes the same passage above, p. 668.

See back, p. 687.[7] Pp. 750–51. Plato, in his *Sophist,* says, "'Shall we not then say that all animals and other things were made by the divine efficiency alone, after they had not been made to be?'" And in "his *Timæus* he declareth concerning the soul, 'that God did not make it after the body, and junior to it, since it was not fit that the elder should be governed and ruled by the younger; but he made soul before body, older than it and superior to it, as well with respect to time as dignity.'" Which notion he pursues further, and says, "'Wherefore it was rightly, properly, and most truly affirmed by us, that soul was made first, as that which ruleth, but body afterwards as that which is to be ruled and governed thereby.'"

THE WORLD WAS MADE and IS ORDERED IN THE BEST MANNER POSSIBLE.

P. 382. Socrates, in Plato's *Phædo,* says, "'Hearing one sometime read out of a book of Anaxagoras, that mind was the orderer and cause of all things, I was exceedingly pleased herewith, concluding that it must needs follow from thence that all things were ordered and disposed of after the best manner possible; and therefore the causes even of things in nature (or at least the grand strokes of them) ought to be fetched from the Τοῦ Βελτίστου.'"[8]

[Pp. 382–83.] Again, there are some "'who devise many odd physical reasons for the firm settlement of the earth, without any regard to that power which orders all things for the best (as having a divine force in it); but thinking to find out an Atlas far more strong and immortal, and which can better hold all things together; good and fit, being not able, in their opinions to hold or bind anything.'"

P. 247. "Seneca in Lactantius, speaking concerning God: 'Hic cum prima fundamenta molis pulcherrimæ jaceret, et hoc ordiretur quo neque majus quicquam novit natura nec melius [. . .]'"[9]

P. 394–95. Timæus Locrus: "'Which world is completed and made up of gods, men, and other animals, all created according to the best pattern of the eternal and unmade idea.'"[1]

Again, "'God, willing to make the world the best that it was capable of,

7. MS: "p. 1108 [col. 2] b," a reference to the paragraph beginning, "The generality . . ."

8. Cudworth translates: "That which is Absolutely the Best."

9. Cudworth translates: "God when he laid the Foundations of this most beautiful Fabrick, and began to erect that Structure, than which Nature knows nothing greater or more excellent . . ."

1. JE quotes the same passage above, p. 683.

made it a generated god, such as should never be destroyed by any other cause, but only by that god himself who framed it, if he should ever will to dissolve it. But since it is not the part of that which is good to destroy the best of works, the world will doubtless ever remain incorruptible and happy; the best of all generated things, made by the best cause, looking not at patterns artificially framed without him, but the idea and intelligible essence, as the paradigms, which whatsoever is made conformable to, must needs be the best, and such as shall never need to be mended.'"

Again, "'Before the heaven was made existed the idea, matter, and God, the opifex of the best.'"

P. 415. "Theophrastus, Aristotle's scholar and successor, describeth God after this manner: 'That first and divinest being of all, which willeth all the best things.'"

Aristotle commended the doctrine of Anaxagoras, "'That mind was together with well and fit, the cause and principle of things themselves.'"

Copernical system.

P. 378. Xenophanes maintained "'that there were infinite suns and moons,' by which moons he understood planets, affirming them to be all habitable earths, as Cicero tells us."

Pp. 402–3. Plato affirmed the Earth to be "'the oldest of all the gods within the heavens, made or created to distinguish day and night, by its diurnal circumgyration upon its own axis, in the middle or center of the world.' For Plato, when he wrote his *Timæus,* acknowledged only the diurnal motion of the earth, though afterwards he is said to have admitted its annual too."

P. 235. These words from the "ancient copies of Plato's *Timæus,* used both by Cicero and Proclus: 'God fabricated the earth also, which is our nurse, turning round upon the axis of the world, and thereby causing and maintaining the succession of day and night, the first and oldest of all the gods, generated within the heavens.' [. . .] We may conclude that afterwards, when in his old age, as Plutarch records from Theophrastus, he gave entertainment also to that other part of the Pythagoric hypothesis, and attributed to the earth a planetary annual motion likewise about the sun (from whence it would follow, that, as Plotinus expresseth it, the earth was ἐν τῶν ἀστρων, 'one of the stars')."

[Principle of contention.]

Pp. 391–92. This from Empedocles' poems: "'Things are divided and segregated by contention, but joined together by friendship; from which

two all that was, is and shall be proceeds; as trees, men, and women, beasts, birds and fishes, and last of all the long-lived and honorable gods.'"

Aristotle's *Metaphysics:* "'Empedocles makes contention to be a certain principle of corruption [and generation]; nevertheless he seems to generate this contention itself also from the very One. For all things according to him are from this contention, God only excepted; he writing after this manner, [From which] (i.e. contention and friendship) all things that have been, are or shall be derived their original.'"

Aristotle thus objects against this opinion of Empedocles: "'This therefore happens to Empedocles, that, according to his principles, the most happy God is the least wise of all other things; for he cannot know the elements, because he hath no contention in him, all knowledge being by that which is like; himself writing thus: We know earth by earth, water by water, air by air, and fire by fire, friendship by friendship, and contention by contention.'"

ANGELS.

P. 487. "Pindar also affirmeth concerning Minerva, 'That sitting at the right hand of her father, she there receiveth commands from him to be delivered to the gods. For she is greater than the ANGELS, and commandeth them some one thing and some another, according as she had first received of her father.' [. . .] Where we may observe, by the way, that this word *angel* came to be in use amongst the pagans from Jews and Christians, about this very age that Aristides lived in; after which we meet with it frequently in the writings of their philosophers."

GOD'S MORAL GOVERNMENT OF THE WORLD.

P. 255[–56]. Cicero, De Legibus, [Second Book], "'Deos esse Dominos ac moderatores omnium rerum, eaque quæ geruntur, eorum geri judicio atque numine, eosdemque optime de genera hominum mereri, et qualis quisque sit, quid agat, quid in se admittat, qua mente, qua pietate religiones colat, intueri; piorumque et impiorum habere rationem, a Principio Civibus suasum esse debet.'"[2]

---

2. Cudworth translates: "The Minds of Citizens, ought to be first of all embued with a firm perswasion, that the Gods are the Lords and Moderators of all things, and that the Conduct and Management of the wole World is directed and over-ruled by their Judgement and Divine Power; that they deserve the best of mankind, that they behold and consider what every man is, what he doth and takes upon himself, with what Mind, Piety and Sincerity he observes the Duties of Religion; and Lastly, that these Gods have a very different regard to the Pious and the Impious."

P. 261. Epictetus: "'Do thou only remember these catholic and universal principles: What is mine and what is not mine? What God would have me now to do? And what would he have me not to do?'"

P. 264. Demosthenes: "'The gods and the Deity will know or take notice of him that gives not a righteous sentence.'"

P. 365. Plautus: "'Est protecto deus, qui quæ nos gerimus, auditque et videt.'"[3]

Pp. 365–66. Plautus:

"Qui gentes omnes mariaque et terras movet,
Ejus sum civis civitate cœlitum;
Qui est imperator divum atque hominum Jupiter,
Is nos per gentes alium alia disparat,
Hominum qui facta, mores, pietatem et fidem
Noscamus . . .
Qui falsas lites falsas testimoniis
Petunt, quique in jure abjurant pecuniam,
Eorum referimus nomina exscripta ad jovem.
Cotidie ille scit, quis hic quærat malum.
Iterum ille eam rem judicatam judicat.
Bonos in aliis tabulis exscriptos habet.
Atque hoc scelesti illi in animum inducunt suum
Jovem se placare posse donis, hostiis;
sed operam and sumptum perdunt, quia
Nihil ei acceptum est a perjuris supplicii."[4]

Again,

"Facilius, siqui pius est, a diis supplicans,
Quam qui scelestus est, inveniet Veniam sibi."[5]

P. 394. Timæus Locrus: "'All these things hath Nemesis decreed to be executed in the second circuit by the ministry of vindictive terrestrial

---

3. "God is as a covering, who both hears and sees whatever we do."

4. Cudworth translates: "Where Jupiter the Supreme Monarch of Gods and Men, is said to appoint other Inferiour Gods under him, over all the parts of the Earth, to observe the Actions, Manners and Behaviours of men every where; and to return the names both of bad and good to him. Which Jupiter judges over again all unjust Judgments, rendring a righteous retribution to all. And though wicked men conceit that he may be bribed with sacrifices, yet no worship is acceptable to him from the Perjurious."

5. "It is easier that one finds grace for oneself, if one is pious and beseeching the gods, than if one is wicked."

demons[6] that are overseers of human affairs; to which demons that supreme God, the ruler over all, hath committed the government and administration of the world.'"

P. 428. [M.] Antoninus. "'One God through all, one substance, one law.'" Again, "'Affect to seem fair to God, desire to be pure with thy pure self, and with God.'"

Epictetus: "'I have, whom I ought to be subject to, whom to obey, God and those who are next after him.'"

Pp. 334–35. "Plutarch, giving a reason why the Egyptians made the crocodile, an "'animal without a tongue,'" the "symbol of the deity": "'The divine reason, standing not in need of speech, and going on through a silent path of justice in the world, does without noise righteously govern and dispense all human affairs.'"

P. 430. "'No man hath power over me. I am made free by God. I know his commandments, and no man can bring me under bondage to himself.' . . . 'Those things would I be found employing myself about, that I may be able to say to God, Have I transgressed any of thy commandments? Have I used my faculties and anticipations (or common notions) otherwise than thou requirest?'" Epictetus.

[P. 431.] "A man will never be able otherwise to expel grief, fear, desire, envy, etc., than by looking to God alone, [. . .] and the observance of his commandments.'" Epictetus.

GOD THE GIVER OF DIVINE WISDOM AND AUTHOR OF VIRTUE.

Pp. 363–64. We have an "excellent [prayer] of Euripedes to the supreme governor of the world," the sum of which is this: "'That God would infuse light into the souls of men, whereby they might be enabled to know what is the root from whence all evils spring, and by what means they may avoid them.'"

P. 344. Socrates in Plato prays thus: "'O gracious Pan, and ye other gods, who preside over this place, grant that I may be beautiful within,[7] and that those external things which I have may be such as may best agree with a right internal disposition of mind, and that I may account him to be rich that is wise and just.'"

P. 407. Plato calls the first hypostasis "'the king of all things, about whom are all things, and for whose sake are all things, and the cause of all good and excellent things.'"

6. JE quotes the same passage above, p. 695.
7. JE quotes the same passage above, p. 647.

P. 427.[8] Epictetus imputes virtue to the gods in these words: "'Hast thou overcome thy lust, thine intemperance, thine anger? How much greater cause hast thou of offering sacrifice, than if thou hadst got a consulship or a prætorship? For those things come only from thyself, and from the gods.'"

P. 434.

> "At tu, Jupiter alme, tonans in nubibus atris,
> Da sapere, et mentem miseris mortalibus aufer
> Insanam, hanc tu pelle pater; da apprendere posse
> Consilium, fretus quo tu omnia rite gubernas;
> Nos ut honorati pariter, tibi demus honorem,
> Perpetuis tua facta hymnis præclara canentes,
> Ut fas est homini; nec enim mortalibus ullum,
> Nec superis, majus poterit contingere donum,
> Quam canere eterno communem carmine legem."[9]

Cleanthes' Hymn.

TRUE RELIGION and WORSHIP.

P. 365. Terpander, cited by Clemens Alexandrinus, thus translated into Latin:

> "Rerum universarum imperatorem et patrem,
> Solum perpetuo colere suppliciter decet,
> Artificem tantæ et largitorem copiæ."[1]

P. 381. "It may be made a question whether Anaxagoras, besides the supreme Deity, acknowledged any of those other inferior gods, then worshipped by the pagans? Because it is certain that though he asserted infinite Mind to be the maker and governor of the whole world, yet he was accused by the Athenians for atheism, and banished from the same; the

---

8. JE incorrectly cites p. 437.

9. "But you, kind Jupiter, thundering in the dark clouds, / Give us to be wise and bear away the unsound mind from wretched mortals, / You, Father, drive this out; / Make us able to apprehend / Your counsel, relying on which you govern all things rightly. / Let us, as those honored as well, give honor to you, / Singing your illustrious deeds in unending hymns, / As is right for man; for no greater gift can touch mortals nor their works, / Than to sing the common law in eternal song."

1. The Latin quotation is actually from Menander; JE skips two lines in which Cudworth quotes Terpander: "Thou Jupiter who art the Original of all things, Thou Jupiter who art the Governour of all." The quote from Menander translates, "The ruler and father of all things, / Alone in perpetuity it is fitting to worship with supplications, / The maker and bestower of such a great bounty."

true ground whereof was no other than this, because he affirmed the sun to be nothing but a mass of fire, and the moon an earth having mountains and valleys, cities and houses in it." And "his ungodding the sun, moon, and stars was then looked upon by the vulgar as atheism." Plato speaks also of some new philosophers who said the stars were "'nothing but earth and stones.'"

P. 379. "'O you unwise and unlearned! teach us first what God is, that so you may be believed in accusing me of impiety. Tell us where God is. Is he shut up within the walls of temples? Is this your piety, to place God in the dark, or to make him a stony God? O you unskillful! know ye not that God is not made with hands, and hath no basis or fulcrum to stand upon, nor can be enclosed within the walls of any temple; the whole world variegated with plants, animals and stars being his temple.'" And again, "'Am I impious, O Euthycles, who alone know what God is? Is there no God without altars? Or are stones the only witnesses of him? No, his own works give testimony to him, and principally the sun; night and day bear witness of him; the Earth bringing forth fruits declares him; the circle of the moon, that was made by him, is a heavenly testimony of him.'" Heraclitus.

P. 396. "It hath been already observed that Onatus, a Pythagorean, took notice of an opinion of some in his time that there was one only God, who comprehended the whole world, and no other gods besides, or at least none such as was to be religiously worshipped."

P. 398. Antisthenes, founder of the Cynic sect, in a certain physiological treatise, is said to have affirmed: 'Esse populares Deos multos, sed naturalem unum.'"[2]

To Antisthenes might be added Diogenes Sinopensis, of whom it is recorded by Laertius, that observing a woman too superstitiously worshipping the statue or image of a god, endeavoring to abate her superstition, he thus bespake her: 'Don't you take care, O woman, of not behaving yourself unseemly, in the sight of that God, who stands behind you? for all things are full of him.'"

P. 417. Aristotle gives us this short summary of his own creed, "agreeable to the tradition of his pagan ancestors: 'It hath been delivered down to us from very ancient times, that the stars are gods also, besides that supreme Deity that contains the whole of nature. But all the other things were fabulously added hereto, for the better persuasion of the multitude,

---

2. Cudworth translates: "Though there were many Popular Gods, yet there was but One Natural God"; JE quotes the same passage above, p. 644.

and for utility of human Life and political ends, to keep men in obedience to civil laws. As for example that these gods are of human form, or like other animals; with such other things as are consequent hereupon.'"

P. 439. Varro, according to St. Austin, says the gods would be worshipped more purely and chastely, without images, as they were by the first Romans for 170 years; he concluding, 'Qui primi simulacra Deorum populi posuerunt, eos civitatibus suis, et metum dempsisse et errorem addidisse.'"³

P. 444. "'I conceive true piety and religion towards God to consist in this, not that I should sacrifice many hecatombs, or burn much incense to him, but that I should myself first acknowledge, and then declare to others, how great his wisdom is, how great his power, and how great his goodness.'"⁴ [Galen.]

P. 431. Epictetus: "'Had we understanding, what should we do else, but both publicly and privately praise God, bless him, and return thanks to him? Ought not they who dig, plow, and eat, continually sing such an hymn to God as this: Great is that God who gave us these organs to cultivate the earth withal; great is that God who gave us hands, etc., who enabled us to grow undiscernibly, to breathe in our sleep. But the greatest and divinest hymn of all is this, to praise God for the faculty of understanding all these things. What then if for the most part men be blinded, ought there not to be some one who should perform this office, and sing an hymn to God for all? If I were a nightingale I would perform the office of a nightingale, or a swan, that of a swan; but now being a reasonable creature, I ought to celebrate and sing aloud the praises of God.'"

P. 397. Plato concludes that "true humane FELICITY CONSISTS IN A PARTICIPATION OF THE FIRST GOOD, OR OF THE DIVINE NATURE."

P. 24. Empedocles, according to Clemens Alexandrinus, maintained that "'if we live holily and justly, we shall be happy here, and more happy after our departure hence; having our happiness not necessarily confined to time but being able to rest and fix in it to all eternity, feasting with other immortal beings.'"

P. 314. "Chalcidius reports that Hermes Trismegist, when he was about to die, made an oration to this purpose: 'That he had here lived in this earthly body, but an exile and stranger, and was now returning home to

---

3. Cudworth translates: "That those Nations who first set up Images of the Gods, did both take away Fear from their Cities and add Errour to them."

4. JE quotes the same passage twice above, pp. 660 and 686.

his own country, so that his death ought not to be lamented, this [life] being rather to be accounted death.' Which persuasion the Indian Brachmans also were imbued withal, whether they received it from the Egyptians (as they did some other things) or no; 'That this life is but the life of embryo's, and that death is a generation or birth into true life.' And this may the better believed to be the Egyptian doctrine, because Diodorus himself, hath some passages sounding that way; as that the Egyptians lamented not the death of good men, but applauded their happiness, 'as being to live ever in the other world with the pious.'"

P. 378[-79]. Heraclitus in his Epistles: "'My soul seemeth to vaticinate and presage its approaching dismission and freedom from this its prison; and looking out as it were through the cracks and cranies of this body, to remember those its native regions.'" Again, "'This body shall be fatally changed to something else, but my soul shall not die or perish, but being an immortal thing, shall fly away mounting upwards to heaven; those ethereal houses shall receive me, and I shall no longer converse with men but gods.'"

FALL OF ANGELS.

P. 24. Empedocles, "besides the immortal souls of men, acknowledged dæmons or angels, declaring that some of these fell from heaven, and were since prosecuted by a divine Nemesis. As these in Plutarch are called those Empedoclean dæmons 'lapsed from heaven and pursued with divine vengeance'; whose restless torment is there described in several verses of his."

OF THE DEVIL and HIS DESTRUCTION AT THE END OF THE WORLD.

Pp. 222-23. "Theodorus in Photius calls the Persian Arimanius by that very name, Satanas." And Plutarch thus records the traditions of the Persian Magi: "'There is a fatal time at hand, in which Arimanius, the introducer of plagues and famines, must of necessity be utterly destroyed.'"

DELUGE and CONFLAGRATION.

P. 328. "'When the world becomes thus degenerate, then the Lord and Father, the supreme God, and the only governor of the world, beholding the manners and deeds of men, by his will (which is his benignity) always resisting vice and restoring things from their degeneracy, will either wash away the malignity of the world by water or else consume it by fire, and restore it to its ancient form again.'" The Asclepian Dialogue concerning the opinions of the Egyptians.

We find in Julius Firmicus that there was a tradition among the Egyptians concerning the apocatastasis[5] of the world, 'partly by inundation, and partly by conflagration.'"

INCARNATION OF THE LOGOS.

P. 621[–22]. The following famous passage of Amelius, "contemporary with Plotinus, is recorded by Eusebius, St. Cyril, and Theodoret: 'And this was the Logos, by whom, existing from eternity, according to Heraclitus, all things were made: and whom that barbarian also (meaning the Apostle John) placeth in the rank and dignity of a principle, affirming him to have been with God, and to be God; and that all things were made by him, and that whatsoever was made was life and being in him. And also that he descended into a body, and being clothed in flesh, appeared as a man, though not without demonstration of the divinity of his nature. But that afterwards being loosed or separated from the same, he was deified and became God again, such as he was before he came down into a mortal body.' In which words Amelius speaks favorably of the incarnation of that eternal Logos." . . . And "St. Austin writeth concerning a Platonist in his time, 'We have often heard from that holy man Simplicianus, afterwards Bp. of Milan, that a certain Platonist affirmed the beginning of St. John's Gospel deserved to be writ in letters of gold, and to be set up in all the most eminent places throughout the Christian churches.'"[6]

SPIRITUAL KNOWLEDGE.

P. 23. Empiricus, speaking of Aristotle's judgment of Empedocles, says, "'Others say that, according to Empedocles, the criterion of truth is not sense but right reason; and also that right reason is of two sorts, the one Θεῖος, or divine, the other ἀνθρώπινος, or human; of which the divine is inexpressible, but the human declarable.'"

FUTURE GLORIOUS TIMES, GENERAL RESURRECTION, and PERFECT STATE OF THINGS AFTER THE END OF THE WORLD.

Pp. 222–23. Plutarch gives the following account of the opinion of the Magi: "'That there is a fatal time at hand, in which Arimanius, the introducer of plagues and famines, must of necessity be utterly destroyed,[7]

5. I.e. restoration, renovation.
6. JE quotes the same passage above, p. 676.
7. JE quotes the same passage above, p. 711.

and when the earth being made plain and equal, there shall be but one life, and one polity of man, all happy and speaking the same language.'"

Theopompus represents their sense thus: "'That in conclusion, hades shall be utterly abolished and then men shall be perfectly happy, their bodies neither needing food, nor casting any shadow. That God, which contrived this whole scene of things, resting only for the present a certain season, which is not long to him, but like the intermission of sleep to men.'"

P. 291. "Abulfeda represents the Zoroastrian doctrine after this manner: 'That God was older than darkness and light, and the creator of them, so that he was a solitary being, without companion or corrival; and that good and evil, virtue and vice, did arise from a certain commixture of light and darkness together, without which this lower world could never have been produced; which mixture was still to continue in it, till at length light should overcome darkness: and then light and darkness shall each of them have their separate and distinct worlds, apart from one another.'" (N.B. These things seems to have been derived from what God says to Cyrus the Persian by the prophet Isaiah, in Is. 45:1, 5–9, 21–25.)

[1360. OF SUBSTITUTION AND IMPUTATION OF MERIT.][8] [. . .] with the degree of favor sought, in order to know whether it be sufficient to countervail it. By dignity I here intend not only the degree of virtue and relation to his friend of whom he seeks favor, but the greatness of the person of the patron.

If in adjusting this matter, the dignity that is viewed in the patron and his friend's regard to him, be so great, that considered with the degree of the patron's union with his client, there is a sufficiency to countervail all the favor that the client needs, or the utmost that he is capable of receiving, then there is a perfect sufficiency in the patron for the client, or a sufficiency completely to answer and support the whole interest of the client, or a sufficiency in his friend's regard to the patron wholly to receive, take in and comprehend the client with regard to his whole interest, or all that pertains to his welfare; or, which is the same thing, a sufficiency fully to answer for him as his representative and substitute in all that pertains to his welfare.

14. If the patron and client are equals as to greatness of being or de-

---

8. The material that JE, Jr., labeled No. [1360] is a continuation, by JE's own directions at this point ("add this at p. 888 [col. 2] e"), of the material that JE, Jr., numbered No. [1352].

gree of existence, and the degree of the patron's union with his client should be such (and that were possible) that he regarded the interest of the client equally with his own personal interest, then it would be natural for the patron's friend to regard the client's welfare, for the sake of the client, as much as he regards the patron's own personal welfare. Because when the case is so, the patron is as strictly united to the client as he is to himself, and his client's welfare becomes perfectly, and to all intents and purposes, his own interest, as much as his personal welfare; and therefore as the love of his friend to him disposes him to regard whatever is his interest, to such a degree as it is his interest, so it must dispose him to regard the client's welfare in equal degree with his own personal interest, because by the supposition 'tis his interest in equal degree.

But this must be here provided or supposed, viz. not only that so strict an union of the patron with the client be possible, but also that it be proper, or that there be no impropriety or unfitness [in] it. Because if it be unfit, then the patron's being so strictly united to him diminishes his merit, because merit, at least in part, consists in a regard to what is proper and fit. And if the degree of union be unfit, it diminishes the influence of the union to recommend the client one way as much as it increases [it] another.

15. If the patron and client are not equals, but the patron be greater and vastly superior as to rank and degree of existence, it gives greater weight to his union, as to its influence with the friend of the patron, to recommend the client; so that a less degree of union of the patron with his client may be equivalent to a greater union in case of equality. And therefore in this case, though the union be not so great as that his regard to the client's interest should be equal with his own personal interest, but may be much less, yet his regard to it may be such that its recommending influence may be equivalent to that which is fully equal in the case of equality of persons, and therefore may be sufficient to answer the same purposes towards the client, and consequently to be perfectly sufficient for the client with regard to the client's whole interest.

16. From these things we may gather this as a rule whereby to judge whether there be a sufficiency in the patron's union with his client to answer for the whole interest of the client with the patron's friend, with respect to the degree of union of the patron, and the degree of greatness, where there is no defect of merit in other respects: viz. that the patron's union with the client shall be such that, considering jointly both the degree of greatness and degree of union, the patron's union with his client shall be as considerable and weighty, and have as much recommending

influence, as if in case of equality of the patron with his client the union between them was so great that the patron's regard to the welfare of the client were equal with his regard to his own.

17. Then the union of the patron has its measure and proportion according to the rule now mentioned, and so is sufficient to answer his whole interest, when the degree of his regard to the client's interest stands in the same proportion to his regard to his own personal interest, as the degree of the capacity of the client stands in to the degree[9] of his own capacities. For the degrees of capacity are as the greatness or the degrees of existence of the persons.

18. When the patron's regard to his client is thus proportioned—that is, when he regards the client's interest as his own, according to the client's capacity—such an union may most fitly and aptly be represented by the client's being taken by the patron to be as a part or member of himself, as though he were a member of his body. For men love each part of themselves as themselves, but yet not each part equally with themselves, but each part as themselves according to the measure of the capacity of the part. A man loves his little finger as himself, but not equally with the head, but yet with the same love he bears to himself, according to the place, measure and capacity of the little finger.

19. The most proper and plain trial and demonstration of this sufficiency of union of the patron with the client, consisting in such a proportion of regard to his welfare as has been mentioned, is the patron's being willing to bear sufferings for the client, or in his stead, that are equivalent to sufferings which properly belong to the latter; which equivalence of suffering must be determined by a joint estimation of these two things, viz. the degree of suffering, and the greatness of the sufferer. When the effect of the patron's love to the client is a suffering for the client that is equal in value or weight to the client's suffering, considering the difference of the degree of persons, it shows that the love to the client that is the cause of this suffering is also equal or equivalent to his love to himself, according to the different degree of persons.

The most proper and clear trial of the measure of love or regard to the interest of another is the measure of suffering or expense of personal interest for the interest of the beloved. For so much as the lover regards the welfare of the beloved, so much in value or weight of his own welfare will he be willing to part with for it. If the value of the welfare obtained be, in the regard of the sufferer, fully equal to the value of welfare parted

9. MS: "degree of the degree."

with, then being on an equal balance, no preponderance of self-love will hinder parting with one for the other. The love, therefore, is sufficient and equal to self-love, allowing only for the difference of capacity or greatness of the persons, as the sufferings are equal, allowing for the same difference of the degree of persons.

20. There can be but one thing more requisite, according to the nature of things, in order to its being, to all intents and purposes, proper and suitable that the patron should be accepted as one with the client in what pertains to the client's interests, and his merits being imputed to the client, and his having favor on the account of it, which is this: that seeing the client is an intelligent being, capable of act and choice, he should therefore actively and cordially concur in the affair, that the union between the patron and him should be mutual; that as the patron's heart is united to the client, so the client's heart should be united to the patron; that as there is that disposition and those acts appearing in the patron that are proper to the character and relation of a patron in undertaking for the client to appear for him before his friend as his representative, guardian, deliverer and savior, and condescending to him to do and suffer all for him needful for his help and advancement, so there also mutually appear in the client those dispositions and acts that are proper to the character and relation of a client—cleaving to him, committing his cause to him, and trusting in him, in an entire approbation of the patron's friendship, kind undertaking, and patronage of his patron—and not only an approbation of the patron's union to him, which[1] avails for his being looked upon as one with him, but also of the patron's union to his friend, whose favor he seeks: which union with his friend avails to the acceptance of the patron, and also an entire approbation of the benefits which the patron seeks of his friend for the client; or, in one word, a cordial and entire faith of the client in his patron. When there is thus a mutual union between patron and client, and an union throughout between them both and the friend whose favor is sought, together with those things before mentioned, there is everything requisite in order to the fitness of the acceptance of the client on the account of the patron, and his receiving such favor from the patron's friend as is requisite to all that pertains to the client's welfare. So that such acceptance and such favor shall be in all respects proper, according to the nature of things and common sense of intelligent beings, and of no evil or improper consequence.

1. MS: "by which."

GENERAL INDEX

The abbreviation JE has been used in this index for Jonathan Edwards. All works are by Edwards unless otherwise indicated.

Aaron, 110, 173, 231, 281, 381
Abel, 173, 382, 482, 629
Aben Ezra, 299
Abigail, 481, 482
Abraham: victory of, in battle, 111, 112, 305; as type of Christ, 112; posterity of, 183, 301, 383, 386, 499; God's promise to, 210, 226–27, 228, 383, 494, 508, 539; God of, 302, 304n6, 311; and sacrifices by Israelites, 386; suffering of, 494–95; and parable of rich man in hell, 577, 585
Absalom, 481
Abulfeda, 471, 713
Academics, 443
"Account Book," 10
Achilles, 545
Adam: and *prisca theologia*, 26; covenant with, 93–94, 147, 170; sin of, 94, 155, 170, 300–301; soul of, 205, 428; God's communication with, 208, 221; Christ as second, 219
Adamah, 565
Adon, 480
Adonai, 473
Adonis, 473, 479, 480
Adultery, 129, 244, 444, 486n3
Aeneas Gazeus, 681
Aeschylus, 648
Africa, 441, 447, 448, 449, 454
Agatho, 651–52
Agathon, 561
Agog, 388
Ahab, 234–35
Ahasuerus, 222
Ahlstrom, Sydney, 22
Ahmed Ibn Jusuph, 556–57
Ahriman, 471, 477
Alcibiades, 445
Alcinous, 549–50
Alexander the Great, 70, 169, 271, 441, 444, 477, 566
Alexandria, 330
Alix, Dr., 191
Amalek, 338, 417

Amalekites, 340, 388
Amasis, 441
Amelius, 561, 663, 676, 712
America, 308, 312, 448, 449, 454, 565
Ammon, 338, 544, 645
Ammonites, 25, 123n9, 337, 339, 340
Amos, 280
Ananias, 86, 87, 271
Anaxagoras, 466, 640, 642, 651, 656, 690, 693, 703, 704, 708–9
Andromeda, 475
Anebo, 544
Angels: God's relationship with, 63; virtue of, 70; Chinese on fall of, 102–3; fall of, 102–3, 118, 173, 198–200, 213–14, 711; judgment of fallen angels, 118; compared with saints, 181–82; honor and dignity of, 182; in scale of existence, 207; creation of, 208, 341, 613–14; as stars, 212; ignorance of, concerning mystery of gospel until Christ's coming, 224; confirmation of, 316; and Christ, 422, 629; as gods, 424, 637; and last judgment, 615; and exodus of Israelites from Egypt, 621; philosophers and heathens on, 668, 705
Animals. *See* Beasts
Annaeus, 702
Answer to a Late Book Intituled Christianity as Old as the Creation (Leland), 240n1
Answer to Some Queries (Waterland), 415–16
Antichrist, 156, 217
Antinomianism, 31
Antioch, 330
Antiochus Epiphanes, 269, 271nn7–8, 272, 339, 390
Antiphanes, 642
Antisthenes, 547, 552, 644, 709
Antoninus. *See* Marcus Antoninus, Emperor
Antoninus Pius, Emperor, 565
Aphrodite, 673–74
Apis, 565
Apollo, 441, 473–75, 479, 552, 565–66, 569–70, 649, 657, 673, 677, 699
Apollonius of Tyre, 272–73

Apology (Socrates), 251, 252*n*9
Apostles, 156, 230, 231, 285–86, 289–91, 318, 319, 320–21*n*3, 332, 393–94. *See also specific apostles*
Apuleius, 553, 647, 649, 651, 660, 693, 701
Arabia and Arabians, 311, 326, 330, 471, 477, 556–57
Aratus, 546
Arcesilaus, 679
Archelaus, 446, 547
Archytas, 547, 648, 683
Arcianus, 552
Argonautica, 464
Arianism, 24, 29, 174, 429, 630, 634–35, 637, 638*n*1, 677
Arimane, 666
Arimanius, 471, 472, 473, 477, 666, 711, 712
Aristides, 551, 667–68, 686, 705
Aristippus, 444, 445, 447, 452–53
Aristodemus, 466–67, 652, 657, 660, 684, 695
Aristophanes, 546, 687, 691
Aristotle: on unity and connection of world, 380–81; on God, 443, 456, 466, 468–69, 642, 645, 650–53, 657–59, 661, 674, 678; Plutarch on, 444; Simplicius on *Physics* by, 546; on virtue, 642; on happiness, 661; on number three, 664; on creation of world, 679, 704; on Pythagoreans, 683; on Mosaic creation, 687, 691; on animals, 693–94; on principle of contention, 705; creed of, 709–10; on Empedocles, 712
Arminianism, 11
Asa, 124, 339
Asclepian Dialogue, 647, 649, 711
Asclepius, 682
Assarte, 480
Assur, 338
Assyria and Assyrians, 265*n*9, 389, 390, 555, 583
Astrea, 474
Athanasius, 637
Atheism, 171, 434, 439, 443, 457, 466, 708–9
Athena, 650, 667
Athenagoras, 650
Atonement, 126–31, 161–65, 481–86, 536, 537–38. *See also* Satisfaction of Christ
Atropos, 702
Atticus, 442
Austin, Saint, 676, 677, 710, 712
Aves (Aristophanes), 687
Awakening. *See* Great Awakening
Azarius, 271

Baal, 440
Babylon and Babylonians, 68, 114, 265*n*9, 280, 308, 311, 336, 339, 340, 389, 440
Bacchus, 470, 565
Balaam, 78, 84
Baptism, 74, 420
Barak, 338
Bartachastram, 563
Baxter, Andrew, 169*n*6
Baxter, Richard, 31, 35, 228
Beasts: nature of, compared with human nature, 80–83, 207; satisfaction of appetites of, 126; in scale of existence, 206; as images of Satan, 300, 587, 625; philosophers on, 684, 693–94, 703
Bedford, Arthur, 387*n*2
Beebe, Keith, 93*n*5
Bel, 479–80
Bellamy, Joseph, 391
Bellerophon, 565
Belus, 473
Benevolence. *See* Goodness
Benjamin, 125, 387
Benjamites, 387*n*2
Berkeley, George, 22
Berosus, 681
Beschen, 564
Bethel, 125, 173
Bible: higher criticism of, 29; JE's defense of generally, 29; and revelation, 62; and Gospels, 72, 108–12, 115–17, 224, 279; double senses of, 88; divine authority of book of Daniel, 268–72; Pentateuch of, 270, 383–84, 512, 530; history of New Testament, 292–93; as word of God, 373–74; objections to of modern libertines, 391–411. *See also* New Testament; Old Testament
Biruma, 562
"Blank Bible," 119*n*3, 123*n*9, 125*n*2, 156*nn*4–5, 182*n*6, 210*n*5, 382*n*7, 383, 386*n*1, 387*n*2, 412, 417*n*2, 432*nn*3–4, 506*n*9, 534*n*4
Blasphemy, 129, 131, 171, 244, 312, 397, 407, 428, 592, 596, 601, 603*n*3
Blindness, 62, 112, 115, 369, 454
Boineburgius, Baron, 631, 633*n*6
Bolingbroke, Lord, 243–44, 347–48
Bond, Lee, 93*n*5
Book of Memoirs (Xenophon), 657
Borosus, 691
Bouchet, Father, 559
Brahmins, 477–78, 554–56, 562–64, 566, 574, 681, 711. *See also* India
Brainerd, John, 9
Brama, 478, 479

Bremaw, 562
Bridegroom. *See* Marriage
Brine, John, 12 *n* 6, 604–7
Britain and Britons, 190, 215, 312, 440
Bruma, 563
Brutus, 442
Burr, Aaron, 5 *n* 2, 29–30 *n* 9, 36, 637–38
Burr, Esther Edwards, 5 *n* 2

Cabbala, 192, 662–63, 668, 676, 690–91
Cain, 173, 382
Calanus, 477, 566
Caleb, 388
Callimachus, 651
Calvinism, 22–23
Cambridge Platonists, 15, 22
Cameron, Archibald, 195
Campbell, Archibald, 176, 445, 482
Canaan, 109, 227, 281, 305 *n* 7, 306, 307,
    336, 337, 339, 340, 383, 385–86, 388,
    499, 518, 616, 621
Canaanites, 338
Cannibalism, 441, 444
Caribes, 441
Carnal covenant, 496, 499–501
Carthaginians, 440
Castration, 441
"Catalogue," 10
Catholicism. *See* Roman Catholicism
Cato, 450, 465
Cato Uticensis, 442
Causality, 56–60, 243, 364, 438, 454. *See also*
    Reason
Cedrenus, 664
Ceremonial law, 123–24, 125
Ceres, 552
Cestius Gallus, 282
Chai, Leon, 28 *n* 6
Chalcidius, 710–11
Chaldea and Chaldeans, 280, 310, 336, 339,
    389, 390, 468, 555, 558–60, 569, 644,
    645, 649, 681, 691, 694
Chaldee Paraphrasts, 191–92
Chamberlain, Ava, 1
Chan-Hai-King, 101
Chan-kai-king, 102–3
Chi-King, 95, 99, 100, 101–2, 103
Children: hatred against father by, 49, 50–
    52; love and honor for parents by, 49, 51;
    virtues of, 70; education of, 143–44; of
    heathens, 440, 441, 444; as human sacri-
    fices, 440, 444; mistakes of, 542
China and Chinese, 95–104, 123, 171, 190,
    225, 253, 437, 439, 441, 454, 458, 478–
    79, 480, 557, 560, 565, 566
Chiron, 545

Choueuen, 98
Christ. *See* Jesus Christ
Christianity as Old as the Creation (Tindal), 27,
    342 *n* 6, 359–61
Christianity Not Founded on Argument (Dod-
    well), 242
Christian religion: agreeableness of, to rea-
    son, 61–71; and Jews' knowledge of true
    God, 72; and conversion of Gentiles, 73,
    115, 122, 302–13; authority of councils
    and power of civil magistrate regarding,
    85–86; and necessity of revelation, 88,
    157–59, 161–65, 240–46, 251–64, 275,
    275–76 *n* 6; and satisfaction of Christ, 88–
    89, 126–41, 145–50, 157–59, 166, 236,
    481–86; and success of Gospel in over-
    throw of heathenism, 108–12, 115–17;
    and Jesus Christ as Messiah, 112–15, 281,
    302–15; and Lord's Day, 131, 143–44,
    170, 197, 225, 234, 235, 288–89, 381; na-
    ture of true religion, 139–40; and mira-
    cles, 159–60, 165–66, 265–66, 287–93,
    291–92 *n* 3; and Constantine, 217, 309;
    and Old Testament, 233; and God's provi-
    dence, 246–48; and Jewish religion, 264–
    65; and unreasonableness of infidelity,
    274; compared with heathen morality,
    276–77, 277–78 *n* 7; and Christ's prophe-
    cies, 278–82; and Christ as no impostor,
    282–84, 322–23; and apostles, 285–86,
    289–91; enemies of, 291, 292 *n* 3, 293;
    and history of New Testament, 292–93;
    and resurrection of Christ, 294–97; prop-
    agation of, 298, 325–34; and teachings of
    Christ, 322–23; compared with Mahomet-
    anism, 325–34; Jewish nation and truth
    of revealed religion, 334–40; persecution
    of Christians, 356, 387, 580. *See also*
    Church; Jesus Christ; New Testament;
    Redemption
*Christ the Righteousness of His People; or, The
    Doctrine of Justification by Faith in Him*
    (Rawlin), 145, 147–48, 149, 153–55
Chronological Antiquities (Jackson), 35, 123
Chronus, 561, 663
Chrysippus, 444, 548, 552
Chrysostom, 303–4, 453
Chubb, Thomas, 44, 145–46, 242–43
Chu-King, 95, 99, 103
Church: reasonableness of, 62–63; Christ's
    relationship with, 73, 194; and apostles,
    156; foundation of, 209–10; and saints,
    228; persecution of Christians, 356, 387,
    580; glorious times of, 356–59; and last
    judgment, 626–27. *See also* Christian reli-
    gion

Cicero: on conscience, 214; on God, 251, 252n9, 456–57, 469–70, 552–53, 644, 658, 685, 686, 702; and vices of heathens, 442, 445, 606; as polytheist, 443, 455; on immortality of soul, 450–53; on God's works of providence, 498–99, 694; on creation, 686, 688, 704; on Copernican system, 704; on God's moral government of world, 705

Clarke, Samuel, 60n1, 167–68, 434, 445, 460

Cleanthes, 444, 548, 552, 571, 685–86, 697, 708

Clemens Alexandrinus, 546, 651, 676, 708, 710

Cleombrotus, 444

Clinias, 444

Clotho, 702

Collection of Tracts (Chubb), 44n, 145–46

College of New Jersey (Princeton), 2, 5n2, 7, 8–9, 36

Collins, Anthony, 88n2

Colophonian, 546

Commandments. *See* Ten Commandments

Commentary on the Whole Bible (Henry), 124n1

Concerning the Nature of the Gods (Cicero), 251, 252n9

Concerning the Principle (Damascius), 663–64

Confirmation of angels, 316

Conflagration, 117–18, 200–201, 391, 711–12

Confucius, 95, 97, 99, 100, 104, 123, 171

Conscience, 105, 129, 140–41, 158, 160, 164, 214

Constantine, 217, 309

Contention, principle of, 704–5

Contingency. *See* Causality

Continuation of the Exposition of the Epistle of Paul the Apostle to the Hebrews (Owen), 229nn6–7, 482–84

"Controversies" notebook, 5, 7, 25n2, 31n3, 112n3, 192n7, 359, 498n5, 517, 518, 528, 531n8, 533, 540, 541

Conversation, 345, 348–51

Conversion: and self-determining power, 60; and law of God, 72; and Holy Spirit, 72–74; of Jews, 73; of Gentiles, 73, 115, 122, 302–13; and baptism, 74; of Paul, 86–87; mustard-seed parable on, 196; and progress of work of redemption, 196–98; of Roman Empire, 217, 308, 309, 311, 312; as God's work, 610

Copernical system, 704

Corinthians, 182

Corruption of human nature, 61, 62, 69. *See also* Redemption; Sin and sinners

Corybantes, 439–40, 565

Cosmopoeia (Timotheus), 691

Cotton, John, 18

Council of Nicea, 559, 676

Court of the Gentiles (Gale), 176n9, 453

Covenant: of redemption, 90–91; with Jacob, 92; with Adam, 93–94, 147, 170; and Ten Commandments, 143–44, 497, 498, 501, 504–8, 510, 511, 516, 522, 524, 531, 621; of grace, 493–95, 499–500, 502–3, 504, 508–9, 515, 521–22; with Moses, 494; of Moses and God, 494, 510; carnal, 496, 499–501; of works, 496–501, 511–12, 515–16, 529–30

Covetousness, 53

Crates, 444

Cratylus (Plato), 670–71, 673, 680, 694

Creation: of world, 28–29, 32, 64–65, 89–92, 379, 467, 468, 545, 552, 561, 609–14, 622; of humans, 64–65, 154, 163, 207, 208, 256; and Christ, 89–92, 415, 416, 426, 609, 613, 614, 622–23; end of, 104–6, 131–41, 150–53, 157, 178–79, 213, 222–24, 575; of new heavens and new earth, 196–98, 236–40; of angels, 208, 341, 613–14; of soul, 208, 209; Mosaic, 340–42, 687–92; Plato on, 467, 468; heathens' views on, 467, 468, 475, 545, 552, 561, 568–69, 571, 677–87; of spiritual, intelligent world, 609–10, 613–14; as God's distinguishing work, 609–14, 622; God's preservation of, 610, 614, 702–3

Credibility of the Gospel History (Lardner), 87

Criminals, pardon of, 128, 172, 259

Critias, 443

Croesus, 376

Cromwell, Oliver, 19

Cross as symbol, 565

Cudworth, Ralph, 12, 15, 16, 27, 35, 380, 545, 547, 552, 636–37, 640–713

Cupid, 552, 687–88

Cybele, 439–40

Cynics, 444, 644, 709

Cyprian, Saint, 543, 660, 676

Cyril, Saint, 466, 473, 560, 664–65, 669, 671–72, 676, 712

Cyrus the Great, 14, 70, 114, 473, 713

Damascius, 472, 544–45, 558, 561, 663–65, 666

Dan, 124, 173, 387

Daniel, 111, 169, 268–72, 281, 309–10, 314, 315n7

Danites, 387

Daphne, 565

Dardanus, 666

Darkness. *See* Light and darkness

David: and Ammonites and Moabites, 15,

123 n9; importance of, 70; and Ten Tribes, 124; posterity of, 173, 422; as king, 210, 310, 338, 386, 388, 418; on wickedness, 298–99, 300 n1; as prophet, 310; and tribe of Judah, 387; and Abigail, 481, 482; suffering of, 494; and God's mercy, 540; as type of Christ, 625; wisdom of, 639; as father of Solomon, 640

Davies, Samuel, 35, 94, 159

Dawes, William, 27, 214–16

Deafness, 115

Death: of humans, 61, 66, 77–83, 157, 209, 230, 477; of Christ, 73, 90, 146, 170, 199, 230, 282, 387, 405, 580, 587; and godly humans, 77–82; of wicked, 78–80, 82, 183–84; of beasts, 80–83; as punishment of sin, 83; Reynolds on, 127; fear of, 157; raising of the dead, 425–26. *See also* Resurrection

Deborah, 338

Decalogue. *See* Ten Commandments

Defect of Oracles (Plutarch), 647

Defence of the Catholick Faith Concerning the Satisfaction of Christ (Grotius), 148

De Haruspicum Responsis (Cicero), 686

De Iside et Osiride (Plutarch), 566

Deism, 11, 13, 17, 24, 27–29, 88 n2, 159–75, 185–87, 240, 242–46, 275, 276 n6, 342–45, 347, 350, 448, 457

Deism Revealed (Skelton), 17, 35, 159–75, 432–61

De Legibus (Cicero), 469, 685, 694, 705

De Legibus (Plato), 456

Delphos, oracle of, 84

Deluge, 200–201, 210, 383, 711–12

Demiurgus, 381, 558, 559–60, 663, 666, 671–73, 677, 680–83

Democritus, 176, 443, 467, 551, 654

Demonstration of Messias (Kidder), 108, 192 n7

Demonstration of the Being and Attributes of God (Clarke), 60 n1, 167–68

Demosthenes, 706

De Mundo (anonymous), 456, 648, 678, 681, 682–83, 700–702

De Natura Deorum (Cicero), 453, 686

De Plantis (anonymous), 693–94

De Rerum Natura (Lucretius), 162 n2

Derrida, Jacques, 26 n3

De Spiritu Sancto (anonymous), 676

De Usu Partium (Galen), 660–61

Devils: Christ and possession of Gadarene by, 52; and inspiration of Holy Spirit, 84; gods of heathens as, 109; punishment and misery of, in hell, 116–17, 588, 589, 602, 604 n3; and last judgment, 118; sin of, 173, 198–200, 213–14; worship of, as gods, 217; possession by, 232–33; in state

of probation in hell, 399; misery of, 588. *See also* Satan

Diagoras, 443, 551

Diana, 552

Diodorus Siculus, 214–15, 646, 681, 694

Diogenes, 444, 452–53

Diogenes Laertius, 445

Diogenes Sinopensis, 709

Diogenes Syropensis, 547

Dion Cassius, 444

Dion Chrysostom, 546, 549, 701

Dionysius, 562, 644

Dionysius Petavius, 673

Dionysius the Pseudo-Areopagite, 557, 665

Directory for Public Worship (Assembly in Westminster), 18

Discourse Concerning the Unchangeable Obligations of Natural Religion (Clarke), 434 n8, 445, 459 n3, 460 n7

Discourse of Grounds and Reasons of the Christian Religion (Collins), 88 n2

Discourse Proving That the Christian Religion Is the Only True Religion (I. Mather), 24 n9

Discourses on Several Important Subjects (Williams), 106 n8, 107 nn2,9

Discourses on Various Important Subjects, Nearly Concerning the Great Affair of the Soul's Salvation, 83

Dissertation Concerning the End for Which God Created the World, 7, 104 n4, 131 n6, 150 n1, 157 n7, 575 n5

Divine Government over All Considered (Tennent), 35, 106 n7

Divine Legation of Moses (Warburton), 25 n3, 88

Divinity of Christ, 29, 411–32, 607–40

"Doctrines [of] the Word of God, Especially [the . . .] Justice [and] Grace of God" notebook, 45 n3

Doddridge, Philip, 35, 89 n4, 228, 432 n3, 484–85

Dodwell, Henry, 242

Dodwell, William, 391, 393

Dreams, 85

Drowning, 53

Drunkenness, 47–48

Dubald, 441

Dwight, Sereno, 48 n1, 226 nn3–4

Dwight, Timothy, 24 n8

Earthquake, 423

Ecphantus, 678–79, 693

Edom, 338, 388

Edomites, 311, 339

Education, 143–44

Edwards, Jonathan: writings by, in 1750s, 1, 2, 4, 5, 7, 8, 35–36; and Great Awakening,

Edwards, Jonathan (*continued*)
  2; dismissal of, from Northampton
  church, 2, 3, 25; and presidency of College of New Jersey (Princeton), 2, 7, 8–9,
  36; at Stockbridge mission, 2–9, 30; travels by, to New York City and New Jersey,
  4–5n2; illness and injuries of, 5–9; and
  French and Indian War, 6; death of, 9;
  reading by, 10–19; *reductio* method used
  by, 28n6; at Yale College, 31. *See also specific works*
Edwards, Jonathan, Jr., 382n7, 405n1, 411n4,
  429n5, 617n5
"Efficacious Grace," 5, 39n1, 56n1
Egypt: and salvation of Messiah, 68, 146; exodus of Israelites from, 69n6, 73, 74, 116,
  131, 265, 338, 384, 414, 610, 616, 619–
  22; miracles in, 70, 109; Pharaoh of, 84–
  85, 109, 111, 337–38, 616; religious beliefs and symbols of, 109, 190, 307, 455,
  468, 472–74, 479, 480, 543–45, 555,
  559–60, 564–65, 566–69, 643, 646,
  647–49, 657, 664–65, 667, 677–78, 681–
  82, 690, 693, 699, 707, 711–12; Roman
  conquest of, 170; and future judgment,
  214–15; Israelite captivity in, 265n9,
  335–38, 389–90, 516; and Joseph, 311;
  Shishak as king of, 339; reasoning in,
  437; marriage in, 441; influence of, on
  philosophers, 446, 447, 453; arts and sciences of, 447; God's judgment against,
  583; Pythagoras's travels in, 645, 664;
  temple in, 646
Eicton, 474, 544, 559, 560, 665
Ekiam, 563
Eleatic sect, 546, 643
Eleazar, 214
Election, 177–81
Electricity, 366
Elias, 419
Elijah, 110, 124, 183, 234–35
Elisha, 110–11, 112
Elohim, 119, 175–76, 412, 615. *See also* God
Emeph, 474, 559–60, 665
Emlyn, Thomas, 638
Empedocles, 547, 651, 657, 678, 683, 693,
  704–5, 710, 711, 712
Empiricus, 712
End of creation, 104–6, 131–41, 150–53,
  157, 178–79, 213, 222–24, 575
End of the world, 65, 120–21, 208, 597–98,
  616, 711–12. *See also* Judgment
Enlightenment, 10–19, 22–29
Ennius, 692
Enquiry Concerning the Principles of Morals
  (Hume), 10n1

Enquiry into the Nature of the Human Soul
  (Baxter), 168, 169n6
Ephraim, 125, 388
Epicharmus, 690
Epictetus, 552, 572, 643, 678, 685, 695–97,
  706–8, 710
Epicureans, 233, 444, 447, 450
Epicurus, 443, 551, 652, 654, 692–93
Epinomis (Plato), 456
Epistulae Morales (Seneca), 214
Eros, 561, 674. *See also* Love
Erskine, Rev. John, 4, 5–6, 10
Esaias, 420
Esau, 337, 383
Eschellensis, Abraham, 328
Esculapius, 565
Essay Concerning Understanding (Locke), 53n8
*Essay on the Nature and Conduct of the Passions
  and Affections* (Hutcheson), 233n2, 599–
  600
Esther, 339
Eternal nature: of future state, 61, 66; of
  hell, 94–95, 107, 391–411, 575–603; of
  God, 168, 342, 364–65, 371–72, 652–58;
  of Christ, 341, 416–17, 426, 628–29, 636.
  See also Immortality
*Eternity of Future Punishment Asserted and Vin-
  dicated* (Dodwell), 391n8
Eternity of hell-torments considered (Whiston),
  391n8
Ethiopians, 339
Euclides Megarensis, 547, 658
Euripides, 464, 545, 649–50, 674, 690,
  707
Eusebius, 215, 471, 548, 554–55, 559–60,
  644, 649, 676, 680, 682, 691, 694, 712
Eustathius, 692
Euthycles, 546–47
Euthydemus, 695
Euthypro (Plato), 660
Eutiphron (Plato), 571
Eve, 173, 205, 208, 221, 299, 300, 301n1,
  382
Evil. *See* Devils; Good and evil; Satan; Sin and
  sinners
Excellency of God, 137, 157, 213, 222–24.
  See also Glory
Exodus of Israelites from Egypt, 69n6, 73,
  74, 116, 131, 265, 338, 384, 414, 610,
  616, 619–22
Experience, 363–64
Exposition of the Old Testament (Henry), 417n2
Exposition on the Epistle to the Ephesians (Good-
  win), 19, 216–21, 222n9, 224n6, 415n9
Ezekiel, 172, 272, 280, 310, 426, 514–15,
  528–29, 530

Faith: justification by, 31, 83–84, 93–94, 107–8, 183, 225–26, 502, 506–43; perseverance in, 31, 107–8; living by, 67; reasonableness of, as condition for salvation, 70–71; Christ's purchase of saving, 72–74; and Holy Spirit, 72–74; fruits of, 503; as "seeking God," 523, 525. *See also* Justification

Faithful Narrative, 2

"Faith" notebook, 540*n*5

Fall: Lucifer before, 90, 212; of humans, 101–2, 126, 173; Chinese beliefs about, 101–3, 566; of angels, 102–3, 118, 173, 198–200, 213–14, 711; Hierocles on, 549

Family Expositor (Doddridge), 35, 228, 432*n*3, 485*n*1

Fastorum (Ovid), 674

Fasts, 87

Fathers. *See* Parents

Fear: of hell, 52; of God, 75–76, 80, 404, 522, 523, 612; of death, 157

Feast (Plato), 571–72

Federal theology, 31

Fénelon, Archbishop, 13

Fifth Volume of Sermons (Manton), 72

Fire. *See* Conflagration; Hell

First Fair (Plato), 674

Fitness. *See* Natural fitness

Flood, 200–201, 210, 383, 711–12

Forgiveness: of sins, 126–31, 157–59, 161–65, 230, 257–64, 536–40, 580, 624–25; pardon of criminals, 128, 172, 259; denial of, 407–8; Christ's work of, 580, 624–25; God's work of, 624. *See also* Redemption; Repentance

Fornication, 441, 443–45, 606

Fourth Commandment, 143–44

Foxcroft, Thomas, 6*n*5, 25, 29*n*9, 423, 424

Freedom of the Will, 4, 5, 28, 30, 39*n*1, 44*n*9, 51*n*4

"Freedom of the Will" notebook, 44, 57, 59–60

Free will: and commands of God, 39–43, 46; and self-determining power, 39–60; and sovereignty of the will, 43–44; and drunkenness, 47–48; and marriage, 48–49; and child's hatred against father, 49, 50–52; and willingness for virtue, 50–52; and sincerity, 51, 52–56; and contingency, 56–60; and omniscience of God, 59, 60*n*1

French and Indian War, 6

Friendship, 350–51

"Fulfillment of the Prophecies of the Messiah," 110, 113, 305, 311, 312, 414, 418, 429–32

Future state: eternal nature of, 61, 66; Old Testament evidence for, 74–83; and immortality of soul, 87, 194, 234; and satisfaction of appetites and desires of all living things, 126; necessity of, 141–42; and promotion of virtue, 144–45; Skelton on, 160–61; philosophers' and heathens' views on, 214–15, 233, 443, 452, 456, 461, 556, 571, 573, 712–13; heathens on future judgment, 214–15, 556; Chubb on, 243; and glorious times of church, 358; arguments against temporary nature of future punishments, 391–411, 575–603. *See also* Heaven; Hell; Immortality; Judgment

Gad, 124

Gale, Theophilus, 27, 176–77, 453

Galen, 550, 660–61, 686, 710

Garden, George, 13

Gaul and Gauls, 190, 215, 440

Gay, Peter, 11*n*4

"Gazeteer Notebook," 45*n*3

Gebal, 338

General History and State of Europe (Voltaire), 35, 225

Gentiles: conversion of, 73, 115, 122, 302–13; idolatry of, 115, 173; Paul on, 453–54

Germanicus, 441, 442

Germans, 190

Gersom, Rabbi Levi ben, 299

Getae, 450

Gideon, 112, 124, 125, 338

Gillespie, Thomas, 25

Glassius, Salomon, 600, 603*n*3

Glory: of God, 94, 104–6, 109, 131, 131–41, 150–53, 157, 202–3, 213, 216, 222–25, 230, 418–19, 426, 575, 605, 607–14; of Messiah, 117; of saints, 181–82, 217–21, 237–38, 598; of Christ, 211, 217–21, 225, 426, 432*n*4, 617, 626–27, 637; of heaven, 229; church's glorious times, 356–59

Glory of Christ as God-Man Display'd (Watts), 89*nn*3–4

Gnostics, 174, 328

God: intelligence of, 16, 184–86, 371–72, 464, 469; union of soul with, 19, 94, 103–4; immediate and arbitrary operation of, 20–21, 29, 201–12; Word of, 23, 71, 72, 373–74; works of, 23, 609–30; as Creator, 28–29, 32, 64–65, 131–34, 154, 163, 255–56, 257, 258, 264, 379, 426, 609–14, 622, 679–87; and natural law, 28–29, 202–9; commands of, 39–43, 46, 62; obedience to, 43, 510–11, 515, 518–23, 530–34, 537, 604–5; omniscience of, 59, 60*n*1, 372, 631–32, 634*n*6, 639–40,

God (*continued*)
652; moral government of world by, 63–
65, 105–6, 118, 254–64, 345–55, 433–
34, 610, 614–15, 651, 705–7; and end of
the world, 65; anger of, 65, 87, 141, 157,
356–57, 507, 510, 525, 536, 582–84,
601, 603*n*3; power and majesty of, 65,
109–10, 116–17, 134–35, 211, 230, 412,
651–52, 657–58; righteousness of, 71–
72, 94, 108, 149, 157–58, 216, 414–15,
533, 624; as Father, 74, 106, 475–76, 521,
547, 551, 554, 558, 559, 568, 574, 638,
642, 673; as Judge, 74–80, 135–36, 141,
145–47, 149, 157–58, 162, 175, 401–2,
526, 527, 528, 533, 582–83, 615; fear of,
75–76, 80, 404, 522, 523, 612; Christ as
Son of, 90–92, 178–81, 191–92, 199,
207, 213, 217, 417, 423, 429, 608–9, 616,
631–33; Israelites' relationship with, 92,
149, 175, 494–516, 518, 529–43; and hatred of sin, 92–93, 145, 158, 536; glory
of, 94, 104–6, 109, 131, 131–41, 150–
53, 157, 202–3, 213, 216, 222–25, 230,
418–19, 426, 575, 605, 607–14; philosophers' and heathens' views of, 97–98,
103–4, 123, 165–66, 171, 173–74, 381,
443, 446–47, 454–57, 463–81, 543–75,
604–7, 636–37, 640–713; happiness of,
104–5, 137–38, 138–39, 152*n*2, 213,
222–24, 661; goodness of, 104–5, 150–
52, 167, 186–87, 252, 549, 606; providence of, 105–6, 242–43, 246–48, 465,
470, 588, 648, 677–79, 692–701; as Jehovah, 106, 111, 119, 175, 302, 304*n*6, 412,
414, 415, 420–21, 423, 426, 480, 505,
518, 521, 560, 611–16, 618–21, 625,
627–28, 636, 644–49; love of, 108, 178–
80, 187–88, 255, 559; as Elohim, 119,
175–76, 412, 615; excellency of, 137,
157, 213, 222–24; humans' love for, 139–
40, 188–90, 498, 604–5; communication
of, 152–53, 213, 222–24, 345, 348–51; as
Lawgiver, 154, 164, 483, 520; mercy of,
162, 507, 508, 510, 517, 534*n*4, 537–41;
eternal nature of, 168, 342, 364–65, 371–
72, 416–17, 652–58; and election, 177–
81; unity of Godhead, 184, 380–81, 467–
68, 640–44; as infinite agent and mind,
184–86, 371–72, 652–58; Christ's resigning up the kingdom to, 194–95, 220–21;
existence of, 254; immutability of, 371–
72; as King, 417–18, 628; and Tetragrammaton, 420*n*7, 644–45; jealousy of, 424,
425, 518, 630; holiness of, 532–33, 538;
preservation of creation by, 610, 614,
702–3; and salvation, 610, 617–24; and
destruction of world, 616; worship of,
630; moral perfection of, 658–61. *See also*
Covenant; Trinity

Gods. *See specific countries and gods*

God's Chief Mercy (MacLaurin), 424, 484

Golden Verses (Hierocles), 569, 644

Goldgar, Anne, 10*n*3

Goliath, 625

Good and evil, 435–36, 457, 471, 476, 477,
479, 564, 658–59. *See also* Light and darkness; Sin and sinners; Virtue

Goodness: of God, 104–5, 150–52, 167,
186–87, 252, 549, 606; philosophers on,
658–59, 670, 671

Goodwin, Thomas: percentage of extracts
from, in "Miscellanies," 12; biographical
information on, 18–19; writings by, 19; on
election, 177; on Christ's resigning up the
kingdom to God, 194–95; on progress of
work of redemption, 196–98; on fall of
angels, 198–200, 213–14; on devils, 216–
17; on saints in heaven, 217–21; on glory
of God, 222–24; on angels' ignorance of
mystery until Christ's coming, 224; on incarnation of Christ, 225; on justification,
225; on Christ's divinity, 415

Gorgias (Plato), 673, 680

Gorionides, Josephus, 300, 301*n*1

Gospels, 72, 108–12, 115–17, 156, 224,
279, 324, 325*nn*2–3. *See also* New Testament

Government: God's moral, of world, 63–65,
105–6, 118, 254–64, 345–55, 433–34,
610, 614–15, 651, 705–7; authority of
councils and power of civil magistrate regarding religion, 85–86; by Christ, 90;
pardon of criminals by temporal governors, 128, 259

Grace: and justification, 32; reasonableness
of, 61–62; means of, 71–72; Christ's purchase of saving faith and converting, 72–
74; and Holy Spirit, 86; and salvation,
382; covenant of, 493–95, 499–500,
502–3, 504, 508–9, 515, 521–22; new
dispensation of, 575–78

Grammaticus, 691–92

Great Awakening, 2

Greece: sciences in, 72; philosophers of, 84,
173–74, 443–58, 547–49, 552, 561–62;
religious beliefs and symbols of, 190, 215,
463, 468, 470, 473–74, 480, 546, 552,
555, 560–62, 574, 642, 644, 667; propagation of Christianity in, 329, 330; and
Jews, 336; revelations from, 376; monarchy in, 389; reasoning in, 437. *See also*
Philosophers; *and specific philosophers*

Grotius, Hugo, 148, 149, 463

Grundlegung zur wahren Religion (Stapfer), 18

Guebri, 471
Gymnosophists, 473, 478, 566, 567

Habakkuk, 280
Hadrian, 340
Hagarenes, 338
Haman, 339, 387n2
Hanmingti, Emperor, 99
Hannah, 117
Happiness: eternal future state of, 61, 62; of
humans, 82, 104–5, 140, 142, 151–52,
160–61, 213, 685; of Christ, 93, 217–21;
of God, 104–5, 138–39, 152n2, 213,
222–24, 661; and virtue, 142, 160–61,
213; of elect, 181; and humiliation, 192–
94; of saints, 217–21, 226, 228, 503; of
heaven, 503; Egyptian beliefs about, 568
Harmon, Matthew S., 2n4, 232
"Harmony of the Old and New Testament,"
7, 8
Haroutunian, Joseph, 22
Hawley, Gideon, 6, 9
Healing miracles, 108, 116, 230, 232–33,
287, 333, 379–80
Heathens: and *prisca theologia*, 26–27; Jews'
impact on traditions of, 27; salvation of,
56; philosophers and inspiration of Spirit
of God, 84–85; and Messiah, 85, 100,
123, 171, 190–91, 565; theology of, 95–
104, 123, 165–66, 171, 173–74, 176–77,
214–15, 381, 439–41, 443, 446–47,
454–57, 460, 463–81, 543–75, 604–7,
636–37, 640–713; Ramsay on, 95–104,
192–94, 461–81, 534–75; on fall of man,
101–2; on fall of angels, 102–3, 711; on
prayer, 103, 573–75, 606; success of
Gospel in overthrow of heathenism, 108–
12, 115–17; and original sin, 176–77;
symbols of, 190–91, 707; and necessity of
humiliation, 192–94; and conscience,
214; on future state, 214–15, 233, 443,
452, 456, 461, 556, 571, 573, 712–13;
and hell, 214–16; compared with Deists,
245; vices of, 272, 273n2, 441–46, 606–
7; Christian religion compared with
morality of, 276–77; conversion of Gentiles from heathenism, 302–13; union between God and, 354–55; and competition
of pretended revelations, 376–80; and
miracles, 378–80; Skelton on, 434, 438–
61; ignorance and errors of philosophers,
435, 442–47, 460, 604–7; sacrifices of,
440, 472, 536, 545, 563, 569–70; on immortality of soul, 443, 449–51, 456, 468,
571, 573; on virtue, 443–44, 447, 569–
71, 573–74, 605–7, 642, 707–8; first religion of mankind as agreeable to religion

of Holy Scriptures, 461–81; and Trinity,
461, 468, 561–62, 636–37, 661–77; on
creation, 467, 468, 475, 545, 552, 561,
568–69, 571; defects of morality of heathen philosophers, 604–7; on unity of
Godhead, 640–44; on names of God,
644–49; on providence, 648, 677–79,
692–701; on nature and attributes of
God, 649–52; on God's moral government of world, 651, 705–7; on God's infinity and eternity, 652–58; on moral perfection of God, 658–61; on happiness of
God, 661; on Mosaic creation, 687–92;
on divine concurrence, 701–2; on preservation of creation, 702–3; on world as
made and ordered in best manner possible, 703–4; on Copernican system, 704;
on principle of contention, 704–5; on angels, 705; on God as giver of divine wisdom and author of virtue, 707–8; on true
religion and worship, 708–11; on devil,
711; on deluge and conflagration, 711–
12; on incarnation of Logos, 712; on spiritual knowledge, 712. *See also* Idolatry;
Philosophers; *and specific countries*
Heaven: as garden of universe, 33; as palace
of glorious king, 33; and Trinity, 33; ascension of Christ to, 33, 73, 90, 210, 229,
240, 316, 334; Christ in, 33, 615, 625–26;
reasonableness of, 61, 65–66; eternal
state of, 66; and saints, 66, 120–21, 216,
217–21, 227–28, 503, 625–26; evidences
of future state in Old Testament, 74–83;
location of, 155–56; in Old Testament,
155–56; angels in, 182; kingdom of, 194–
95, 220–21, 417–18; glory of, 229; happiness of, 503. *See also* Future state
Hebron, 124
Hecataeus, 646
Heereboord, Adrian, 31n6
Hell: fear of, 52; torments of, 94–95, 107,
121, 200, 215–16, 235, 391–98, 575–
603; eternal nature of, 94–95, 107, 391–
411; devils in, 116–17, 589; fires of, 121,
200, 391–92, 589, 600, 603n3; heathens
on, 214–16; as Hades, 227; arguments
against temporary nature of punishments
of, 391–411, 575–603; damned in state
of trial in, 399–400; parable of rich man,
577, 585. *See also* Devils; Satan
Henry, Matthew, 124, 386n1, 417n2
Henry, Prince of Wales, 15
Heraclitus, 443, 546–47, 571, 676, 678,
709, 711, 712
Herbelot, Barthelemy d', 194, 564
Herbert, Lord, 162
Hercules, 441, 470, 473, 474, 475, 565

Herillus, 444
Hermes, 473–74, 543–44, 560, 660, 682
Hermesianax, 552
Hermes Trismegistus, 543–44, 647, 710–11
Hermionax, 546
Hermodorus, 546
Herodotus, 450, 463, 470, 557
Hesiod, 687, 688, 690
Hesychius, 645
Hezekiah, 70, 124, 125, 310, 418, 495
Hierarchy of existence, 206–8
Hierocles, 272, 273*n*2, 476, 548–49, 569–71, 644
Hieroglyphics, 190–91, 543, 544, 559, 565, 677, 682, 699
Hipassus, 443
Hipparchia, 444
Hippias (Plato), 571
History of Europe (Voltaire). See *General History and State of Europe*
History of Knowledge (Winder), 68
"History of the Work of Redemption," 7, 8, 32, 69
Hoainantsee, 101, 479
Hobbes, Thomas, 242, 347
Hoi-ai-nang-wang, 101
Hoian-nantsee, 97, 98, 103
Holifield, E. Brooks, 23*n*7
Holiness: of elect, 181; of God, 532–33, 538; heathen philosophers on, 571, 606. *See also* Virtue
Hollis, Isaac, 4
Holy Spirit: and conversion, 72–74; and faith, 72–74; and Pentecost, 73; and heathen philosophers, 84–85, 673–77; and grace, 86; and salvation, 86, 493; operations of, 88–89; and Christ, 93, 422–23, 427–29, 493; Ramsay on, 95; in Trinity, 153, 188, 189, 191–92, 213; influences and fruits of, 182; and saints, 220; blasphemy against, 407, 428, 592, 601, 603*n*3; and obedience to God, 519; regeneration and renewal by, 624. *See also* Trinity
Homer, 464, 548, 651, 687, 690, 692
Hopkins, Samuel, 1*n*2, 9*nn*6,8
Horace, 465, 565, 699
Horus Apollo, 677–78, 699
Hosea, 280
Hottentots, 441
Howe, John, 149*n*9
Huldah, 280
Human nature: and mystical union with God, 19, 94, 103–4; God's lack of absolute promise to natural men, 56; corruption of, 61, 62, 69; and original sin, 61, 94, 155, 170, 173, 176–77; stupidity of mankind, 62; and God's creation of hu-

mans, 64–65; mortality of humans, 80–82; compared with that of beasts, 80–83; and shortness of life, 82, 83; and happiness, 82, 104–5, 140, 142, 151–52, 160–61, 213, 685; and fall of man, 101–2, 126; and conscience, 105, 158, 214; mind of humans, 207, 437–38; Hobbes on body versus soul, 242; Egyptian beliefs on, 568; Marcus Antoninus on, 573. *See also* Reason
Human sacrifices, 440, 444
Humble Inquiry, 4
Hume, David, 10, 17, 243
Humility and humiliation, 86–87, 92–93, 103–4, 173–75, 192–94, 542, 605, 635
Husbands. *See* Marriage
Hutcheson, Francis, 233, 235, 599–600
Hyde, Thomas, 471, 477
Hydrostatics, 362–63
Hypocrites, 67

Iamblichus, 474, 544, 560, 643, 648, 649, 665, 667, 678, 682, 692
Idolatry: and Israelites, 72, 173, 250, 310–11, 336–37, 388–90, 411–12, 439, 516, 522; of heathens, 84, 156, 190–91, 272, 273*n*2, 307–12, 334–37, 438–39, 445, 458, 607, 636, 637; of Gentiles, 115, 173; God's forgiveness of, 131; God's curse on, 424. *See also* Heathens
Iliad (Homer), 548
Immortality: of soul, 87, 161, 194, 234, 443, 449–51, 456, 571, 573; Chinese on, 101; philosophers' and heathens' views on soul's immortality, 443, 449–51, 456, 468, 571, 573; rich young man's question on, 516–17, 529; cross as symbol of, 565. *See also* Eternal nature; Future state
Imputation: Stapfer on, 18; of Adam's sin, 94; of Christ's righteousness, 106; of sin and righteousness, 171–72; of merit, 486–92, 713–16
India, 215, 253, 477–78, 479, 480, 543, 554–56, 559, 562–64, 574, 644, 681, 711
Indian mission. *See* Stockbridge mission
Infidelity, 24*n*8, 25, 274
Inheritance, 171–72
Inquiry into the Original of Our Ideas of Beauty and Virtue (Hutcheson), 235
Inspiration, 156
Institutiones theologiæ dogmaticæ et moralis (Pfaff), 342
Institutiones Theologicæ Polemicæ Universæ (Stapfer), 17, 69, 251–52, 264–68, 271*n*8, 272–79, 282–304, 322–23, 327–29, 331–34, 486*n*3, 600–603, 631–33
Intelligence: of God, 16, 184–86, 371–72,

464, 469; of humans, 207, 437–38. *See also* Omniscience; Reason

Ionic school, 465, 466

Ireland, 312

Isaac, 302, 304n6, 311, 383–84, 386, 494, 508, 539

Isaiah, 159, 280, 308, 310, 637, 713

Isemakouang, 100

Ishbosheth, 124

Ishmael, 383

Ishmaelites, 338

Isis, 455, 471, 472, 473, 477, 543, 565, 648, 660, 693

Islam, 174, 250, 325–34

Israel, Jonathan I., 11n4

Israelites: exodus of, out of Egypt, 69n6, 73, 74, 116, 131, 265, 338, 384, 414, 610, 616, 619–22; and knowledge of true God, 72; and idolatry, 72, 173, 250, 310–11, 336–37, 388–90, 411–12, 439, 516, 522; drink for, in desert, 74; and covenant with Jacob, 92; God's relationship with, 92, 149, 175, 494–516, 518, 529–43; and miracles of Moses, 108–9; and ceremonial law, 123–24, 125; Ten Tribes of, 124–25, 310, 336, 339, 386n1, 388; and Ten Commandments, 143–44, 497, 498, 501, 504–8, 510, 511, 516, 522, 524, 531, 621; in China, 171; punishment of, 172; and Assyrian and Babylonian captivity, 265n9, 280, 336, 339, 340, 389; and Egyptian captivity, 265n9, 335–38, 389–90, 516; and revealed religion, 334–40. *See also* Jews; *and specific leaders and prophets*

Isuren, 562

Italy. *See* Roman Empire

Jabin, 386

Jackson, John, 35, 123

Jacob: and inheritance, 73; covenant between God and, 92, 494–95, 508, 539; prophecies of, 169, 386–88, 418; God of, 302, 304n6, 311; and Esau, 337; in Padan-Aram, 337, 384; posterity of, 383; and Rebekah, 484; suffering of, 494–95

Jaddua, 271

Jahias, Rabbi Joseph, 299, 300n1

James I, king of England, 15

James III, Pretender to British throne, 14

Jansenius, 177

Japhet, 674

Jarchi, Solomon, 300, 301n1

Javan, 312

Jehoshaphat, 339, 387

Jehovah, 106, 111, 119, 175, 302, 304n6, 412, 414–17, 420–21, 423, 425, 426, 480, 505, 518, 521, 560, 611–16, 618–

21, 625, 627–28, 636, 644–49. *See also* God

Jehuda, Rabbi, 314, 316n7

Jeremiah, 280, 310, 389, 390

Jericho, 125

Jeroboam, 124, 173

Jerome, Saint, 473

Jerusalem: destruction of, 114–15, 120, 121–22, 159, 278–82, 289, 305n7; Jews in, after return from captivity, 125; temple in, 125; Roman conquest of, 170; New, 239–40, 626–27

Jesus Christ: divine and human natures of, 19, 29, 69, 89–92, 153–54, 411–32, 607–40; ascension of, 33, 73, 90, 210, 229, 240, 316, 334; in heaven, 33, 615, 625–26; and devils possessing Gadarene, 52; as judge at last judgment, 67–68, 90, 93, 117–18, 120, 208–9, 400–402, 410–11, 577–78, 583–86, 589–91, 598–99, 615–17, 626–27; as Messiah, 68–69, 112–15, 199, 281, 302–15; as Savior and Redeemer, 69, 71, 72–74, 146, 154, 177, 194–95, 229–30, 257–59, 410–11, 413–14, 492–506, 619–26; suffering and death of, 73, 74, 90, 146, 166, 170, 172, 199, 230, 282, 387, 405, 580, 587; bridegroom imagery for, 73, 119; as Logos, 87, 180, 189, 210, 640; righteousness of, 88–89, 93–94, 106, 147–48, 154, 155, 172, 381, 414–15, 542; satisfaction of, 88–89, 126–31, 145–50, 157–59, 166, 236, 481–86; and creation, 89–92, 415, 416, 426, 609, 613, 614, 622–23; governing of world by, 90; as Son of Man, 90, 120, 197; as Son of God, 90–92, 178–81, 191–92, 199, 207, 213, 217, 417, 423, 429, 608–9, 616, 631–33; happiness of, 93, 217–21; and Holy Spirit, 93, 422–23, 427–29, 493; on eternity of hell torments, 94–95; healing by, 108, 116; obedience of, 108, 155; God's love for, 108, 178–80, 217–18; types of, 108–12, 114, 146, 231, 424, 506, 621, 625; miracles of, 108–12, 116, 159–60, 165–66, 230–33, 265, 287–93, 333, 379–80, 426, 627; resurrection of, 110, 159–60, 165–66, 210, 211, 294–97, 316–20, 325, 484–85; prophecies of, 114–15, 116, 119–23, 159, 231, 278–82, 324, 325n3; parables of, 119, 122, 196, 577, 585, 626; second coming of, 119–23; and saints, 126, 624; incarnation of, 147–48, 162, 166–67, 210, 225, 429, 712; in Trinity, 153, 188, 189, 191–92, 213, 432n4; as Mediator, 154, 194–95, 382, 482–83, 493, 502, 506, 540, 629–30; fullness of time for coming of, 169–

Jesus Christ (*continued*)
  71; and election, 177–81; and resigning
  up the kingdom to God, 194–95, 220–
  21; and progress of work of redemption,
  196–98; glory of, 211, 217–21, 225, 426,
  432n4, 617, 626–27, 637; disciples, 230,
  231, 332; as no impostor, 282–84, 322–
  23; and conversion of Gentiles, 302–13;
  teachings of, 322–23; Muslim views of,
  333–34; eternal nature of, 341, 416–17,
  426, 628–29, 636; as Lamb, 387, 423,
  585, 617, 619, 625; works of, 403–4; trust
  in, 415; as Jehovah, 416, 417, 425; mercy
  of, 517, 537; and preservation of creation,
  614; Satan's temptation of, 630; and omniscience, 631–36, 638–40. *See also* Messiah; Redemption; Trinity
Jews: and *prisca theologia*, 26; impact of, on
  heathen traditions, 27; and knowledge of
  true God, 72; conversion of, to Christianity, 73; and destruction of Jerusalem,
  114–15, 121–22, 289, 305n7; and Roman Empire, 169–70, 315, 316n7, 336,
  340, 389–91; and Sibylline Oracles, 170;
  and rabbis, 173; cabbalistical, 192; sin and
  punishment of, 199, 282; religion of,
  264–65; lack of miracles by in first century, 265–66; and Christ's miracles, 287–
  88; sabbath of, 288–89, 358; and Christ's
  resurrection, 297; and original sin, 298–
  302; rejection of Messiah by, 301–2, 305–
  6, 312, 313–15; and Trinity, 307. *See also*
  Israelites
Joannes, Rabbi, 314–15, 316n7
Joannes Diaconus, 688
Job, 419
John (apostle), 577–78, 598, 676, 712
Johnson, Thomas H., 10n2
John the Baptist, 197, 419–20, 421
Jordanus Bruno, 434
Joseph, 69, 311, 337, 384, 387
Joseph of Arimathea, 316, 318n1
Josephus, 270, 271, 645
Josephus of Voisin, 300, 301n1
Joshua, 88, 92, 175–76, 210, 220, 385, 386,
  388, 512
Josiah, 70, 124, 310, 418
Jove, 465, 470, 475, 573, 645, 648, 667, 681
  n2, 700
Jovis, 644, 651, 668
Judah, 124, 125, 386, 387, 418
Judas, 95, 393, 601, 603n3
Judea, 121, 266
Judgment: last, 67–68, 90, 93, 117–18, 120,
  208–9, 400–402, 410–11, 577–78, 583–
  86, 589–91, 598–99, 615–17, 626–27; of
  God, 74–80, 135–36, 141, 145–47, 149,

  157–58, 162, 175, 401–2, 526, 527, 528,
  533, 582–83, 614; heathens on future,
  214–15
Julia, Empress, 272, 273n2
Julian, Emperor, 673
Julianus, 558–59
Julius Caesar, 190, 442
Julius Firmicus, 473, 712
Juno, 552, 666, 667, 668
Jupiter, 166, 463–65, 470, 473–76, 478,
  479, 545, 546, 548, 551, 552, 558, 565–
  66, 571, 642–44, 646, 648, 651, 666, 668,
  672, 673, 680, 681, 685–87, 694–97,
  700, 702
Justification: Lee's analysis of, 30–31; JE's
  language of federal theology on, 31; JE's
  master's thesis on, 31; JE's sermon on, 31;
  by faith, 31, 83–84, 93–94, 107–8, 183,
  225–26, 502, 506–43; and natural fitness,
  31–32, 196, 225; and grace, 32; reasonableness of, 62; and covenant with Adam,
  94–95; and God's righteousness, 216,
  624; objection against, 506–43. *See also*
  Faith
Justification by Faith Alone, 31n3
"Justification by Imputed Righteousness"
  (Williams), 106n8
Justin Martyr, 215, 544, 545–46, 560–61,
  565, 569, 676, 682
Juvenal, 214
Jyngas, 472

Kidder, Richard, 108, 112, 192n7
King (Chinese books), 95–104, 478–79
Kircher, Father, 561
Kiun-Tse, 479
Korah, 110, 173
Kouan-y-antsee, 97
Kouci-rout-see, 99

Laban, 337
Labienus, 465
Lachesis, 702
La Croze, Maturin Veyssiǀere, 555, 556
Lactantius, 87, 277, 278n7, 703
Laertius, 658, 692, 709
Lafittau, Father, 565
Laish, 387
Lama, 565
Lamb image, 387, 423, 585, 617, 619, 625
Lamech, 383
Laokun, 171
Laotsee, 98, 99, 100
Lardner, Nathaniel, 87
Last judgment. *See* Judgment
Law: natural, 27–29, 160–61, 164, 202–9,
  244, 342–45; ceremonial, 123–24, 125;

Ten Commandments, 143–44, 497, 498, 501, 504–8, 510, 511, 516, 522, 524, 531, 621; God as Lawgiver, 154, 164, 483, 520; of Moses, 249–51, 265n9, 483, 494, 502, 510–14, 518, 529–30, 538, 540, 616, 629; covenant of works as, 496–501; "letter" versus "spirit" of, 497–98, 501; ceremonial and judicial, 499–501. *See also* Covenant; Government

Lazarus, 577

Leaven hidden in measures of meal parable, 122

LeCompte, 441

Lee, Sang Hyun, 21n3, 30–31

Leibniz, Gottfried Wilhelm, 631, 633n6

Leland, John, 240, 242–45

Leprosy, 108, 111, 230

Leucippus, 551

Levi, 124, 281, 386

Levites, 123n9, 125, 336

Lietse, 479

Life of Aristides (Plutarch), 659

Light and darkness, 62, 80, 144, 212, 213, 216, 286, 287n7, 326–27, 369, 424–25, 471, 475, 477, 575, 582, 612, 623, 665, 690, 692, 713. *See also* Sun

Like Precious Faith Obtained (Foxcroft), 424n2

Liki, 95, 479

Lillback, Peter A., 31n6

Linus, 651, 690

Liou-pouci, 97

Liszinski, Casimir, 434

Li-yong, 98

Locke, John, 22, 53, 143, 149

Locrenses, 485–86

Logos: Christ as, 87, 180, 189, 210, 640; philosophers on, 468, 546, 560–61, 671, 675–76, 682, 712; incarnation of, 712

Lohrasp, king of Persia, 556–57

Lopi, 102

Lord, Henry, 562

Lord's Day, 131, 143–44, 170, 197, 225, 234, 235, 288–89, 381; Sabbath of Jews, 288–89, 358

Lord's Supper, 230, 231

Lot, 338

Love: and Trinity, 95; of God, 108, 178–80, 187–88, 217–18, 255, 559; humans', of God, 139–40, 188–90, 498, 604–5; Eros as, 561, 674; philosophers on, 561, 674, 687–88, 691

Love (Thracian deity), 473

Lucan, 465, 648

Lucceius, 445

Lucian, 445, 473

Lucifer, 90, 173, 212. *See also* Satan

Lucretius, 162, 652

Ludolf of Saxony, 286, 287n7

Luke, 278, 279n8, 324, 325n2

Lunghong, 99

Lycurgus, 442

Lydians, 555

Maccabees, 214

Macedonians, 390

MacLaurin, John, 201, 236, 424, 484

Macrobius, 646, 673

Magi, 84, 471, 474, 554–55, 557, 567, 574, 665, 666, 711, 712–13. *See also* Persia and Persians

Magnetism, 366

Mahomet and Mahometanism, 174, 250, 325–34

Mahomet Effendi, 434

Malabarians, 555, 562–64

Malachi, 268

Maldonado, Juan de, 632, 634n6

Malebranche, Nicolas de, 235

Manasseh, 124, 125, 388

Manillus, 554

Mankind. *See* Human nature

Manners of the American Savages (Lafittau), 565

Manton, Thomas, 72

Manugjahr, king of Media, 556

Marcus Antoninus, Emperor, 176, 551–52, 558, 572–73, 695–97, 707

Marriage: of humans, 48–49, 70; bridegroom imagery of Christ, 73, 119; Christ's parables on, 119, 122, 626; and polygamy, 234; in Egypt, 441; obedience and respect of wife toward husband, 518, 630

Mars, 439–40, 474, 565

Mary (mother of Jesus), 333, 423, 429

Mastricht, Peter van, 412

Mathematics, 371, 380–81

Mather, Cotton, 24

Mather, Increase, 24n9

Matthew, 278–79, 324, 325n2

Maximus Tyrius, 550–51, 554, 642, 701

McClymond, Michael, 21

McDermott, Gerald, 13

Mechanics, 362–63

Medes, 310, 377

Mediator: Christ as, 154, 194–95, 382, 482–83, 493, 502, 506, 540, 629–30; in Persian beliefs, 477; Moses as, 481; Abigail as, 481, 482; Zaleucus as, 486n3; and covenant of grace, 494; time of coming of, 502; revelation of, 502, 503

Megasthenes, 554–55

Melchizedek, 111

Meletemata philosophica (Heerebord), 31n6

Melissus, 547, 645–46, 650, 657

Memnon: Histoire Orientale (Voltaire), 225

Memoirs (Xenophon), 660

Menander, 546

Menasse ben Israel, 298–300, 301*n*1

Mengtsee, 100, 103

Menippus, 444

Mercury, 470, 474, 475, 479, 552, 554, 565

Mercy: of God, 162, 507, 508, 510, 517, 534 *n*4, 537–41; of Christ, 517, 537

Merit: definition of, 486; imputation of, 486–92, 713–16

Merrick, Marshal, 475

Messiah: Christ as, 68–69, 112–15, 199, 281, 302–15; heathens on, 85, 100, 123, 171, 190–91, 565; Chinese beliefs on, 100, 123, 171, 566; in Old Testament, 112–15, 417–18, 540, 542–43; corruption of ancient traditions on, 190–91; Jews' rejection of Jesus as, 301–2, 305–6, 312, 313, 313–15; time of coming of, 313–15, 502; kingdom of, 417–18; and Adonis, 480; in New Testament, 542–43. *See also* Jesus Christ

Metamorphoses (Ovid), 464

Metaphysics, 371

Metaphysics (Aristotle), 380–81, 653, 691, 705

Micah, 280

Michael (angel), 625

Midianites, 112, 338, 340

Milbank, John, 26*n*3

Millennium, 156

Miller, Perry, 9–10*n*9, 22

Miller, Peter N., 10–11*n*3

Mimti, 171

Mind. *See* Intelligence; Reason

Minerva, 473, 650, 666, 667–68, 705

Miracles: of Elijah, 10; of Elisha, 12, 110–11; in Egypt, 70; of Moses, 108–11, 231; of Christ, 108–12, 116, 159–60, 165–66, 230–33, 265, 287–93, 333, 379–80, 426, 627; in Old Testament, 108–12, 230–31, 232, 337–38, 616; and Christianity, 265–66; of Apollonius of Tyre, 272–73; Stapfer on, 272–74; and heathens, 378–80

Miriam, 230*n*9

Miscellaneorum Sacrorum Libri Quatuor (Witsius), 269, 271, 272

"Miscellanies": Hopkins on, 1; significance of, 1; dates for composition of, 1, 2*n*4, 4, 5, 7, 35–36; differences between volumes of, 2; extracts from other authors copied by JE in, 12–19, 35; themes of later "Miscellanies," 19–33; covers, paper, and inks used for, 33–34; textual note on, 33–36; running heads in, 35; tables of indexes for, 35; sample pages from, 96, 241, 462, 641

"Miscellanies" No. gg, 234

"Miscellanies" No. tt, 203

"Miscellanies" No. *398*, 489

"Miscellanies" No. 438 (Fall of Angels), 495 *n*4

"Miscellanies" No. 439 (Covenant. Testaments), 495

"Miscellanies" No. 729 (Perseverance), 107

"Miscellanies" No. *769*, 177

"Miscellanies" No. *836*, 156

"Miscellanies" No. *842*, 119

"Miscellanies" No. *856*, 107*n*9

"Miscellanies" No. *861*, 523

"Miscellanies" No. *864*, 105

"Miscellanies" No. *874*, 492

"Miscellanies" No. 891 (Prophecies of the Messiah), 1*n*1

"Miscellanies" No. 922 (Prophecies of the Messiah), 1*n*1

"Miscellanies" No. 972 (Christian Religion. That Jesus Truly Had the Spirit of Prophecy), 280, 281, 282, 289, 324, 390

"Miscellanies" No. *973*, 461

"Miscellanies" No. *976*, 380

"Miscellanies" No. *992*, 468

"Miscellanies" No. *1012*, 461

"Miscellanies" No. *1044*, 114, 281

"Miscellanies" No. 1067 (Prophecies of the Messiah), 1*n*1

"Miscellanies" No. 1068 (Fulfillment of the Prophecies of the Messiah), 1*n*1, 113*nn*5–6

"Miscellanies" No. 1069 (Types of the Messiah), 1*n*1, 33

"Miscellanies" No. *1074*, 147

"Miscellanies" No. *1075b*, 60

"Miscellanies" No. *1152*, 39*n*1

"Miscellanies" No. 1153 (Moral Inability. Free Will. Self Determining Power), 33, 39–56, 60

"Miscellanies" No. 1154 (Free Will Contingency. Self-Determining Power), 33–34, 56–60

"Miscellanies" No. 1155 (Free Will. Self-Determining Power), 34, 41, 60

"Miscellanies" No. 1156 (Observation on the Agreeableness of the Christian Religion to Reason), 34, 61–71, 112

"Miscellanies" No. 1157 (Means of Grace), 71–72

"Miscellanies" No. 1158 (Christian Religion), 72

"Miscellanies" No. 1159 (Christ Purchased Saving Faith and Converting Grace), 72–74

"Miscellanies" No. 1160 (Evidence of a Future State from the Old Testament), 74–83

"Miscellanies" No. 1161 (Justification), 31, 83–84

"Miscellanies" No. 1162 (Heathen Philosophers), 26–27 n4, 84–85

"Miscellanies" No. 1163 (Authority of Councils. Power of the Civil Magistrate), 85–86

"Miscellanies" No. 1164 (Trusting in Our Own Righteousness), 86

"Miscellanies" No. 1165 (Conviction, Humiliation, Conversion), 86–87

"Miscellanies" No. 1166 (Trinity. Christ the Logos), 87

"Miscellanies" No. 1167 (Future State. Immortality of the Soul), 87

"Miscellanies" No. 1168 (Title to a Treatise), 7 n2, 87

"Miscellanies" No. 1169 (Mysteries), 87–88

"Miscellanies" No. 1170 (Christian Religion. Necessity of a Revelation), 88

"Miscellanies" No. 1171 (Mysteries), 88

"Miscellanies" No. 1172 (Double Senses of Scripture), 7 n2, 88

"Miscellanies" No. 1173 (Christ's Satisfaction and Righteousness, and the Operations of the Spirit), 88–89

"Miscellanies" No. 1174 (Pre-existence of Christ's Human Soul), 89–92

"Miscellanies" No. 1175 (Humiliation), 92–93

"Miscellanies" No. 1176 (Progress of the Work of Redemption. Day of Judgment), 7 n2, 93

"Miscellanies" No. 1177 (Christ's Righteousness. Obedience), 31 n4, 93–94

"Miscellanies" No. 1178 (Imputation of Adam's Sin), 94

"Miscellanies" No. 1179 (Eternity of Hell Torments), 94–95

"Miscellanies" No. 1180 (Trinity), 5, 35, 95

"Miscellanies" No. 1181 (Traditions of the Heathen), 5, 35, 95–104, 123, 557, 566

"Miscellanies" No. 1182 (End of Creation. Glory of God), 7 n2, 104–5, 138 n3

"Miscellanies" No. 1183 (Conscience in Natural Men, Spiritual Sense), 105

"Miscellanies" No. 1184 (Providence. God's Moral Government of the World. Glory of God the End of the Creation), 5, 7 n2, 35, 105–6

"Miscellanies" No. 1185 (Imputation of Christ's Righteousness), 106

"Miscellanies" No. 1186 (Perseverance in Faith. Justification), 31, 107

"Miscellanies" No. 1187 (Eternity of Hell Torments), 107

"Miscellanies" No. 1188 (Perseverance. Justification), 107–8

"Miscellanies" No. 1189 (Invitations of the Gospels), 108

"Miscellanies" No. 1190 (Christian Religion. Success of the Gospel in the Overthrow of Heathenism. Christ's Miracles), 70, 108–12, 115

"Miscellanies" No. 1191 (Trinity), 112

"Miscellanies" No. 1192 (Christian Religion), 7 n2, 112–14

"Miscellanies" No. 1193 (Christian Religion. Jesus the True Messiah. His Spirit of Prophecy), 7 n2, 114–15, 116

"Miscellanies" No. 1194 (Christian Religion. Success of the Gospel), 7 n2, 34, 110, 115–17

"Miscellanies" No. 1195 (Conflagration), 117–18

"Miscellanies" No. 1196 (God's Moral Government), 118

"Miscellanies" No. 1197 (Trinity), 118–19, 175

"Miscellanies" No. 1198 (Christ's Coming Being Spoken of as Nigh at Hand), 119

"Miscellanies" No. 1199 (Christ's Coming), 119–23

"Miscellanies" No. 1200 (Traditions of the Chinese), 5, 35, 101, 123

"Miscellanies" No. 1201 (Ceremonial Law), 123–24, 125

"Miscellanies" No. 1202 (Ten Tribes), 124–25

"Miscellanies" No. 1203 (Ceremonial Law), 125

"Miscellanies" No. 1204 (Knowing God and Jesus Christ), 126

"Miscellanies" No. 1205 (Future State), 126

"Miscellanies" No. 1206 (Christian Religion), 126–31, 157, 161

"Miscellanies" No. 1207 (Lord's Day), 131

"Miscellanies" No. 1208 (End of Creation. Glory of God. Redemption. Satisfaction of Christ. True Virtue and Religion), 7 n2, 131–41

"Miscellanies" No. 1209 (Future State), 141–42

"Miscellanies" No. 1210 (Lord's Day. Perpetuity of Fourth Commandment), 143–44

"Miscellanies" No. 1211 (Future State), 142, 144–45

"Miscellanies" No. 1212 (Satisfaction of Christ), 145

"Miscellanies" No. 1213 (Satisfaction of Christ), 145–46

"Miscellanies" No. 1214 (Satisfaction of Christ), 146–47

"Miscellanies" No. 1215 (Covenant), 31 n4, 47

"Miscellanies" No. 1216 (Incarnation, Satisfaction and Righteousness of Christ), 147–48

"Miscellanies" No. 1217 (Satisfaction of Christ), 148–50

"Miscellanies" No. 1218 (End of the Creation. Glory of God), 7n2, 150–53, 157

"Miscellanies" No. 1219 (Communication of Properties), 153–54

"Miscellanies" No. 1220 (Christ's Righteousness), 31n4, 154

"Miscellanies" No. 1221 (Christ's Righteousness), 155

"Miscellanies" No. 1222 (Heaven), 155–56

"Miscellanies" No. 1223 (Inspiration and Miracles), 156

"Miscellanies" No. 1224 (Millennium), 156

"Miscellanies" No. 1225 (End of the Creation, Glory of God), 7n2, 153, 157

"Miscellanies" No. 1226 (Revelation to Reveal Pardon. Satisfaction. Christian Religion), 157–59, 161

"Miscellanies" No. 1227 (Of Prophecies), 5, 35, 159

"Miscellanies" No. 1228 (Christian Religion. Credibility of Christ's Miracles), 159–60, 165

"Miscellanies" No. 1229 (Future State. Revealed Religion), 60–61, 451, 456

"Miscellanies" No. 1230 (Christian Religion. Necessity of Revelation to Reveal Pardon and Atonement), 156, 161–65

"Miscellanies" No. 1231 (Christian Religion. Credibility of Christ's Miracles), 160, 165–66

"Miscellanies" No. 1232 (Infinite Evil of Sin. Satisfaction of Christ. Equivalence of His Sufferings), 166

"Miscellanies" No. 1233 (Incarnation), 166–67

"Miscellanies" No. 1234 (Mysteries. Mystery of the Trinity), 167–68

"Miscellanies" No. 1235 (Fullness of Time), 169–71

"Miscellanies" No. 1236 (Traditions of the Chinese. Messiah. Trinity), 171

"Miscellanies" No. 1237 (Imputation of Sin and Righteousness), 171–72

"Miscellanies" No. 1238 (Humiliation), 173–75

"Miscellanies" No. 1239 (Necessity of Revelation), 175

"Miscellanies" No. 1240 (Certainty and Sensibility of Damnation), 175

"Miscellanies" No. 1241 (Trinity), 34, 119, 175

"Miscellanies" No. 1242 (Threatenings, Absolute), 175

"Miscellanies" No. 1243 (Trinity), 34, 175–76, 182, 191

"Miscellanies" No. 1244 (Traditions of Heathens on Original Sin), 176–77, 445n4

"Miscellanies" No. 1245 (Election), 177–81

"Miscellanies" No. 1246 (Saints Higher in Glory Than the Angels), 181–82

"Miscellanies" No. 1247 (Angels), 182

"Miscellanies" No. 1248 (Influences and Fruits of the Spirit), 182

"Miscellanies" No. 1249 (Trinity), 34, 176, 182–83, 191

"Miscellanies" No. 1250 (Justification by Faith), 183

"Miscellanies" No. 1251 (Eternal Death of Wicked Not Annihilation), 183–84

"Miscellanies" No. 1252 (Unity of the Godhead), 184

"Miscellanies" No. 1253 (Trinity), 184–88

"Miscellanies" No. 1254 (Supernatural Principles), 7n2, 188–90

"Miscellanies" No. 1255 (Original of Idolatry. Corruption of Ancient Traditions Concerning the Messiah), 190–91

"Miscellanies" No. 1256 (Trinity), 183, 191–92

"Miscellanies" No. 1257 (Opinions and Traditions of the Persians on Humiliation), 192–94

"Miscellanies" No. 1258 (Immortality of the Soul. Future State), 194

"Miscellanies" No. 1259 (Christ's Resigning Up the Kingdom to the Father), 194–95

"Miscellanies" No. 1260a (Justification, Natural Fitness), 31n5, 196

"Miscellanies" No. 1260b (Progress of the Work of Redemption. Creation of New Heavens and New Earth), 7n2, 196–98

"Miscellanies" No. 1261 (Occasion of the Fall of the Angels), 198–200, 213

"Miscellanies" No. 1262 (Conflagration), 200–201

"Miscellanies" No. 1263 (God's Immediate and Arbitrary Operation), 20–21, 29, 201–12

"Miscellanies" No. 1264 (Devil Before the Fall the Highest of All Creatures), 212

"Miscellanies" No. 1265 (Trinity), 212

"Miscellanies" No. 1266a (Glory of God, the End of the Creation), 7n2, 213

"Miscellanies" No. 1266b (Occasion of the Fall of the Angels), 200, 213–14

"Miscellanies" No. 1267 (Opinions of the Ancient Jews Concerning a Future Punishment), 214

"Miscellanies" No. 1268 (Natural Conscience, Its Forebodings of Punishment. Traditions of the Heathen Concerning This), 214

"Miscellanies" No. 1269 (Traditions and Opinions of the Heathen Concerning a Future Judgment), 214–15

"Miscellanies" No. 1270 (Greatness of Hell Torments), 215–16

"Miscellanies" No. 1271 (Righteousness. God's Righteousness), 26

"Miscellanies" No. 1272 (Devils), 216–17

"Miscellanies" No. 1273 (How the Pope Is Antichrist), 217

"Miscellanies" No. 1274 (The Saints in Heaven Shall Partake of Christ's Own Happiness and Glory), 19, 217–21

"Miscellanies" No. 1275 (Glory of God. End of God's Works), 7n2, 222–24

"Miscellanies" No. 1276 (Angels Ignorant of the Mystery of the Gospel Till Christ's Coming), 224

"Miscellanies" No. 1277a (Glory of God the End of His Works), 7n2, 24, 224

"Miscellanies" No. 1277b (Lord's Day), 5, 35, 225

"Miscellanies" No. 1278 (Incarnation. The Advantage with the Glory of God Appears to Us in the Person of Christ, God-Man), 225

"Miscellanies" No. 1279 (Justification. Natural Fitness of Faith), 31n5, 225

"Miscellanies" No. 1280 (Justification), 226

"Miscellanies" No. 1281 (Hades. Souls of Saints before Resurrection), 5, 35, 226–28

"Miscellanies" No. 1282 (Christ's Ascension), 229

"Miscellanies" No. 1283 (Old Testament Saints Saved by Christ), 7n2, 229–30

"Miscellanies" No. 1284 (Death Eternal, Not Eternal Annihilation), 230

"Miscellanies" No. 1285 (Christ's Miracles), 230

"Miscellanies" No. 1286 (Christ's Miracles), 230–31

"Miscellanies" No. 1287 (Prophecies), 231–32

"Miscellanies" No. 1288 (Christ's Miracles), 232–33

"Miscellanies" No. 1289 (Future State), 233

"Miscellanies" No. 1290 (Christian Religion), 7n2, 233

"Miscellanies" No. 1291 (Lord's Day, Scripture Consequences), 234

"Miscellanies" No. 1292 (Immortality of the Soul), 234

"Miscellanies" No. 1293a (Prophecy), 234–35

"Miscellanies" No. 1293b (Lord's Day), 235

"Miscellanies" No. 1294 (Hell Torments, Their Extremity: The Justice of It), 235

"Miscellanies" No. 1295 (Satisfaction of Christ), 236

"Miscellanies" No. 1296 (New Heavens and New Earth), 33, 236–40

"Miscellanies" No. 1297 (Revealed Religion), 28, 240–45, 246

"Miscellanies" No. 1298 (Necessity of Revelation), 245–46

"Miscellanies" No. 1299 (Christian Religion), 246–48

"Miscellanies" No. 1300 (Christian Religion. The Divine Legation of Moses), 249–51, 264

"Miscellanies" No. 1301 (Christian Religion. Necessity of Revelation), 251, 434

"Miscellanies" No. 1302 (Christian Religion. Necessity of Revelation), 252

"Miscellanies" No. 1303 (Planets), 253

"Miscellanies" No. 1304 (Necessity of Revelation. Christian Religion), 253–64

"Miscellanies" No. 1305 (Christian Religion), 251, 264–65

"Miscellanies" No. 1306 (Christian Religion), 265–66

"Miscellanies" No. 1307 (Of Prophecies Respecting Different Events), 266–67

"Miscellanies" No. 1308 (Prophecies of Scripture), 267–68

"Miscellanies" No. 1309 (Christian Religion. Divine Authority of the Book of Daniel), 268–72

"Miscellanies" No. 1310 (Christ's Miracles), 272–73

"Miscellanies" No. 1311 (Miracles), 273–74

"Miscellanies" No. 1312 (Christian Religion. The Unreasonableness of Infidelity), 24, 274n8

"Miscellanies" No. 1313 (Christian Religion. Necessity of Revelation. The Knowledge of Deists from Revelation), 275

"Miscellanies" No. 1314 (Christian Religion), 276–77

"Miscellanies" No. 1315 (Christian Religion. The History of the New Testament Early Written. Christ's Prophecies of the Destruction of Jerusalem), 278–79

"Miscellanies" No. 1316 (Christian Religion. Christ Had the Spirit of Prophecy. The Destruction of Jerusalem), 279–82

"Miscellanies" No. 1317 Christian Religion. Christ No Impostor), 282–84

"Miscellanies" No. 1318 (Christian Religion. The Apostles Not Enthusiasts), 285–86

"Miscellanies" No. 1319 (Christ's Miracles), 287–88

"Miscellanies" No. 1320 (Lord's Day), 288–89

"Miscellanies" No. 1321 (Christian Religion), 289–91

"Miscellanies" No. 1322 (Christian Religion. The Truth of the History of the New Testament), 292–93

"Miscellanies" No. 1323 (Christian Religion. Evidences of Christ's Resurrection), 294–97

"Miscellanies" No. 1324 (Christian Religion), 298

"Miscellanies" No. 1325 (Original Sin), 7n2, 298–302

"Miscellanies" No. 1326 (Christian Religion), 302

"Miscellanies" No. 1327 (Christian Religion. Fulfillment of the Prophecies of the Messiah), 7n2, 302–13

"Miscellanies" No. 1328 (Christian Religion. The Messiah Is Already Come), 313–15

"Miscellanies" No. 1329 (Confirmation of the Angels), 316

"Miscellanies" No. 1330 (Christian Religion. Christ's Resurrection), 316–20

"Miscellanies" No. 1331 (Fitness, Natural), 321–22

"Miscellanies" No. 1332a (Christian Religion. Christ No Impostor), 322–23

"Miscellanies" No. 1332b (Christ Had the Spirit of Prophecy), 324

"Miscellanies" No. 1333 (Concerning Objections Against the Reality of Christ's Resurrection), 325

"Miscellanies" No. 1334 (Propagation of Mahometanism. Propagation of Christianity), 325–34

"Miscellanies" No. 1335 (Christian Religion. The Jewish Nation. Revealed Religion), 334–40

"Miscellanies" No. 1336 (No Creation before the Mosaic Creation), 340–42

"Miscellanies" No. 1337 (Necessity of Revelation), 27–28, 342–45

"Miscellanies" No. 1338 (Necessity of Revelation), 27, 345–55

"Miscellanies" No. 1339 (Glorious Times), 356–59

"Miscellanies" No. 1340 (Reason and Revelation), 359–76

"Miscellanies" No. 1341 (Of the Competition of Many Pretended Revelations), 376–78

"Miscellanies" No. 1342 (Of the Competition of Pretended Miracles in the Heathen World with Those That Confirm the Christian Revelation), 378–80

"Miscellanies" No. 1343 (Unity of the Godhead from the Unity and Connection of the World), 16, 380–81

"Miscellanies" No. 1344 (Lord's Day), 381

"Miscellanies" No. 1345 (Christ's Righteousness), 381

"Miscellanies" No. 1346 (Natural Fitness), 31n5, 32, 34, 381–82

"Miscellanies" No. 1347 (Prophecies of the Old Testament), 7n2, 382–91

"Miscellanies" No. 1348 (Objections of Modern Libertines against the Scriptures), 29, 391–411, 575n7, 592nn8–9

"Miscellanies" No. 1349 (Divinity of Christ), 29, 411–32, 607n6, 609n9

"Miscellanies" No. 1350 (The Necessity of Revelation. Extracts from *Deism Revealed*), 17, 35, 166, 432–61, 604n4

"Miscellanies" No. 1351 (Extracts of *The Travels of Cyrus*. The First Religion of Mankind Agreeable to the Religion of the Holy Scriptures. The Wiser Heathen Taught a Spiritual Worship), 15n3, 35, 445n4, 460n8, 461–81, 553, 556n2, 557, 560n2

"Miscellanies" No. 1352 (Christ's Satisfaction or Atonement), 481–92, 713n8

"Miscellanies" No. 1353 (The Two Dispensations Compared, That under Moses and That under Christ), 7n2, 31n4, 492–506, 510n2, 529n6

"Miscellanies" No. 1354 (Justification), 501 n8, 506–43

"Miscellanies" No. 1355 (Extracts from Ramsay's *Philosophical Principles of Religion*), 35, 98, 463n3, 464nn5–6, 467n7, 472n5, 478n4, 543–75

"Miscellanies" No. 1355a (Glory of God the End of His Works), 7n2, 575

"Miscellanies" No. *1356*, 29, 411n3, 575–603

"Miscellanies" No. 1357 (Defects of the Morality of the Heathen Philosophers, from Mr. John Brine), 604–7

"Miscellanies" No. 1358 (Divinity of Christ), 5, 16, 23, 29, 30n9, 36, 429n5, 607–40

"Miscellanies" No. 1359 (Extracts from Dr. Cudworth Concerning the Opinions and Traditions of Heathen Philosophers Agreeable to Truth Concerning Matters of Religion), 16, 35, 636n7, 640–713

"Miscellanies" No. 1360 (Of Substitution and Imputation of Merit), 492, 713–16

Mishael, 271

Misrepresentations Corrected, 4

Mithras. *See* Mythras

Mixed modes, 53

Moab and Moabites, 123n9, 125, 337–40, 388, 583

Moderatus, 561, 662–63

Moloch, 440

Moncrieff, Alexander, 176–77, 445, 482
Money, 86
Monotheism, 16, 63. *See also* God
Monthly Review, 35, 123, 225
"Moral Agency" notebooks, 5, 53*n*7
Moral government of world, 63–65, 105–6, 118, 254–64, 345–55, 433–34, 610, 614–15, 651, 705–7
Moral inability, 39–52
Moral living, 28
Mordecai, 70, 339
More, Henry, 15
Mortality. *See* Death
Mosaic creation, 340–42, 687–92
Moses: importance of generally, 69, 637; miracles of, 108–12, 231; and self-sufficiency, 173; death of, 183, 412; and foundation of Jewish church, 210; leprosy of, 230*n*9; Law of, 249–51, 265*n*9, 483, 494, 502, 510–14, 518, 529–30, 538, 540, 616, 629; and Pentateuch, 270, 383; time between Christ and, 309; and Mosaic creation, 340–42, 687–92; sanctification of, 381; and exodus of Israelites from Egypt, 384; prophecies of, 387–89; altar built by, 417; rod of, 417; as mediator between Israelites and God, 481; comparison of salvation under Christ and, 492–506; covenant between God and, 494, 510, 518; and Ten Commandments, 504, 506*n*9, 516, 621; and grace, 577, 578
Moshemius, Johann Lorenz, 601, 603*n*3
Mothers. *See* Parents
Muhammad. *See* Mahomet
Munster, 300, 301*n*1
Murder, 53, 129, 163, 173, 382, 442–43, 445, 660
Muslims, 174, 250, 325–34
Mustard-seed parable, 122, 196
Mysteries, 37, 87–88, 167–68, 224, 372–73
Mythra, 471, 472, 473, 557, 558, 560
Mythras, 471, 472, 473, 474, 479, 557, 558, 560, 665, 666, 680

Naaman, 111, 230*n*9
Nabal, 481, 482
Naboth, 234–35
"Narrative of the Communion Controversy," 4
Natural fitness, 31–32, 196, 225, 321–22, 381–82
Natural law, 27–29, 160–61, 164, 202–9, 244, 342–45
Natural men. *See* Human nature; Reason
Natural religion. *See* Heathens
Nature of True Virtue, 5, 7, 87, 131*n*6
Nebuchadnezzar, 85, 125, 232, 308, 339, 390

Necessity of Gratitude for Benefits Conferred (Tennent), 106*n*7
Necessity of revelation, 27, 28, 88, 126–31, 157–59, 161–65, 175, 240–46, 251–64, 275, 342–55, 432–61
Nechemias, Rabbi, 314, 316*n*7
Nehemiah, 341
Nehorai, Rabbi, 314, 316*n*7
Neith, 648, 650, 667
Nemesis, 695, 706–7
Neo-Platonists, 26
Neptune, 552
Nereus, 552
Nero, 445
Nestorians, 328
New heavens and new earth, 196–98, 236–40
New Jerusalem, 239–40, 626–27
New Testament: Gospels in, 72, 108–12, 115–17, 156, 224, 279, 324, 325*nn*2–3; Paul's conversion in, 86–87; salvation in, 87, 492–506, 619–25; on perseverance in faith and justification, 107–8; miracles in, 108–12, 116, 159–60, 165–66, 230–33, 379–80, 426, 627; Christ's prophecies in, 114–15, 116, 119–23, 159, 231, 278–82, 324; parables in, 119, 122, 196, 577, 585, 626; influences and gifts of Spirit in, 182; justification by faith in, 183; Christ's happiness and glory in, 217–21; and glory of God, 222–25; history of, 292–93; and eternal nature of hell, 391–411, 575–603; objections of modern libertines against, 391–411; and divinity of Christ, 411–32, 607–40; and Christ's satisfaction, 481–84; Book of Revelation in, 577–78; misery of damned in, 581–86. *See also* Apostles; Bible; Jesus Christ; Redemption
Nianiguculs, 563
Nicene Council, 559, 676
Niebuhr, H. Richard, 22
Niebuhr, Reinhold, 22
Noah, 26, 69, 190, 200, 210, 383
"Notes on Scriptures," 119*n*3, 383, 413, 506, 645
"Notes on the Apocalypse," 340*n*4
Nous, 561, 663, 669, 671–72, 675
Numa, 377, 378, 552
Numenius, 548, 554–55, 561, 662, 671, 690

Obedience, 43, 108, 155, 510–11, 515, 518–23, 530–34, 537, 604–5
Ocellus, 547, 683
Of Divination (Cicero), 552–53
Offerings. *See* Sacrifices
Of the Knowledge of God the Father, and His Son Jesus Christ (Goodwin), 213–14

Of the Use of Human Members (Galen), 550

Old Testament: exodus of Israelites out of Egypt, 69*n*6, 73, 74, 116, 131, 265, 338, 384, 414, 610, 616, 619–22; saints of, 69–70, 226, 229–30, 493, 503–4, 540, 541; God as Judge in, 74–80; and future state, 74–83; righteous versus wicked in, 74–83, 509–10, 524, 526–27, 530–34, 538–39, 581–86; Son of God in, 89; covenant with Jacob in, 92; God's relationship with Israelites in, 92, 149, 175, 494–516, 518, 529–43; covenant with Adam in, 93–94, 147, 170; Jehovah in, 106, 111, 119, 175, 302, 304*n*6, 412, 414–17, 420–21, 423, 425, 426, 480, 505, 518, 521, 560, 611–16, 618–21, 625, 627–28, 636; types of Christ in, 108–12, 114, 146, 424, 506, 621, 625; miracles in, 108–12, 230–31, 232, 337–38, 616; prophets of, 110–11, 112, 159, 169, 172, 197, 231, 232, 234–35, 272, 280, 308–10, 382–91, 418, 422; Trinity in, 112, 118–19, 175–76, 182–83, 191–92, 212; Messiah in, 112–15, 417–18, 540, 542–43; ceremonial law in, 123–24, 125; sacrifices in, 124, 125, 130, 170, 173, 229, 482, 484, 504, 506, 508–9, 536; Ten Tribes in, 124–25, 310, 336, 339, 386 *n*1, 388; heaven in, 155–56; sin of self-sufficiency in, 173; and foundation of church, 209–10; and Christian religion, 233; divine legation of Moses, 249–50; and divinity of Christ, 411–32, 607–40; Redeemer of Israel in, 413–14, 424; and Christ's satisfaction, 481–84; salvation in, 492–506, 617–618; objection against justification by faith in, 506–43; revelation through, 534–40; and eternal nature of hell, 575–603; and glory of God, 607–14; God's work of creation in, 609–14, 622; and preservation of creation, 614; and governing creation, 614–15; and destruction of world, 616. *See also* Bible; Israelites; *and specific persons*

Omniscience: of God, 59, 60*n*1, 372, 631–32, 634*n*6, 639–40, 652; and Christ, 631–36, 638–40. *See also* Intelligence

Onatus, 640, 709

Onesecritus, 477, 566

Ophiomaches, or Deism Revealed (Skelton), 17, 35

Oracle of Delphos, 84

Oracles, 84, 170, 447, 465, 483, 546, 557–59, 649, 666, 681

Oracles of the Chaldeans (Porphyry), 681

Origen, 543, 676

Original sin, 61, 94, 155, 170, 173, 176–77, 298–302. *See also* Sin and sinners

Original Sin, 7, 18, 28–29, 30

Ornatus, 547

Oromasdes, 471, 472, 473, 557, 558, 560, 665, 666

Orpheus, 463–64, 474, 560–61, 569, 646, 662–64, 667, 674, 680, 682, 689, 690, 691

Orphic Cabbala, 662–63

"Orthodoxy and Charity" (Watts), 89

Orus, 473, 475, 479, 565–67

Osiris, 455, 471, 473, 474, 479, 480, 543, 564–66, 665

Ovid, 464, 651, 674, 689

Owen, John, 19, 48–49, 229, 482–84

Pagans. *See* Heathens

Palestine, 265*n*9

Pallas, 477

Pan, 552, 646–47, 707

Pandora, 474

Panjangan, 556

Papists. *See* Roman Catholicism

Parable of the Vineyard and Christ, the True Vine (Merrick), 475

Parables, 119, 122, 196, 577, 585, 626

Paradise, 101. *See also* Future state; Heaven

Paraphrase and Notes on the Epistle of St. Paul to the Romans (Locke), 149*n*8

Parents: child's hatred against father, 49, 50–52; children's love and honor for, 49, 51; heathen parents, 440, 441, 444. *See also* Children

Parmenides, 443, 546, 547, 645, 650, 661, 662, 664, 671, 674, 687, 690

Parmenides (Plato), 650, 664

Passover, 125, 358

Patience, reasonableness of, 61

Patritius, 558, 666

Paul, 86–87, 182, 197, 271, 278, 279, 319–20, 321*n*3, 387, 453–54, 513, 546, 580

Pausanias, 674

Pauw, Amy Plantinga, 1

Peace, 356

Peiresc, Nicolas-Claude Fabri de, 10–11*n*3

Pelagius, 177

Pentateuch, 270, 383–84, 512, 530. *See also* Bible; Old Testament

Pentecost, 73, 197, 358

Peripatetics, 548

Persecutions, 356, 387, 449, 580

Perseus, 475, 565

Perseverance in faith, 31, 107–8

Persia and Persians: Magi of, 84, 471, 474, 554–55, 557, 567, 574, 665, 666, 711, 712–13; and Israelites, 125, 336; and humiliation, 192–94; and Daniel, 310; laws of, 377; marriage in, 441; religious prac-

tices of, 463, 470–72, 543, 552; and unity
of Godhead, 463–64, 471, 556–57, 644;
and Orpheus, 463–64, 474, 560–61, 569,
646, 662, 663–64, 667, 680, 682, 689,
690, 691; and Trinity, 471, 477, 557–59,
664–66; and Zoroaster, 471–73, 477,
557–58, 567, 649, 659–60, 664, 666,
680, 713; compared with religious beliefs
of other cultures, 479, 480; travels by
Pythagoras in, 645
Peruvians, 440
Peter, 63, 86, 110, 154, 231, 289, 291n3,
403, 424, 483, 634n6, 639
Peter the Great, 70
Pfaff, Christoph Matthew, 342
Phaedo (Plato), 450, 456, 703
Phaedrus (Plato), 476, 673, 680
Phanes, 561, 663
Pharaoh, 84–85, 109, 111, 337–38, 616. *See
also* Egypt
Pharisees, 87, 270, 287, 288n9, 328
Pherecydes, 443, 453
Pherecydes Syrus, 450
Philebus (Plato), 571, 670
Philistia, 311
Philistines, 337, 338, 340, 387n2
Phillips, 562
Philo, 191, 649
Philoponus, 653
Philosophers, 84–85, 173–74, 233, 442–47,
449–61, 464–71, 543–75, 604–7, 640–
713. *See also* Heathens; Plato; *and other spe-
cific philosophers*
Philosophical Essays Concerning Human Nature
(Hume), 10n1
*Philosophical Principles of Natural and Revealed
Religion* (Ramsay), 4, 35, 95, 184–92,
543–75
Philosophical Transactions of the Royal Society,
366
Philostratos, 273
Phoenicia and Phoenicians, 447, 453, 473,
480, 555, 565, 681
Phornutus, 694
Photinians, 174
Photius, 711
Phtha (Ptha), 559–60, 665
Physics (Aristotle), 546, 653
Pilate, 294, 295n6, 484
Pindar, 545, 668, 682, 705
Piscator, Johannes, 31n6
Piso, 442
"Places of the Old Testament Which Inti-
mate a Future State," 74n3
Plancina, 442
Planets, 253, 466, 479
Plato: and *prisca theologia*, 26; and inspiration

of Holy Spirit, 84; on God, 165–66, 173–
74, 381, 443, 446–47, 455–56, 467–68,
475–76, 547–48, 552, 561–62, 571–72,
642–44, 646–47, 650–53, 658–59, 663,
678, 679, 680, 684, 688, 690, 694, 702,
707; on human nature, 173–74, 176, 710;
on hell, 215–16; on morality, 443, 446–
47, 458–59; immoral practices of, 444,
445; as Skeptic, 448; on immortality of
soul, 450–51, 456; on philosophy, 452;
on future state, 452, 456, 571; influences
on, 453, 455, 458, 463, 544, 664; on pagan beliefs, 455; on reason, 468; on soul,
468, 703; on Trinity, 468, 661, 662, 663,
666, 667, 668–74, 676; on holiness, 571;
on Parmenides, 650, 664; on flux of time,
656; on *summum bonum*, 658–59; on
Venus, 674; on creation of world, 679,
688, 703; on matter, 682; on paradigm,
684; on Copernical system, 704; on atheism, 709
Platonists, 472, 548, 562, 636, 644, 661–62,
671–77, 712
Plautus, 464–65, 652, 695, 706
Pletho, 472, 558, 567, 666
Pliny, 298, 452, 552
Plotinus, 472, 544, 561, 562, 643, 645,
654–56, 662, 664, 669–72, 676, 702, 704
Plutarch: on conscience, 214; on God, 443,
457, 549, 659, 661n9, 673–74, 699–700;
on Aristotle, 444; on vices of heathens,
444, 445; on human nature, 452; on
Egyptians, 455, 543, 566, 646, 648, 667,
677–78, 690, 707; on Persians, 471, 477,
552, 557, 665, 666; on Apollo, 565, 673;
on death of Pan, 647; on Thespesius
Solensis, 662; on Cicero, 704; on devil,
711; on Magi, 712–13
Pococke, Edward, 417n2, 471
Poiret, Pierre, 13
Polycrates, 441
Polygamy, 234
Polytheism. *See specific countries and gods*
Pompey, 170
Pontius Pilate, 294, 295n6, 484
Poole, Matthew, 112n1, 119n4, 176, 230n9,
271, 387n2, 417, 482, 484, 615n3, 637n8
Popes, 174, 217. *See also* Roman Catholicism
Porphyry: on divine authority of Book of
Daniel, 268–72; on miracles, 272, 273n2;
on creation, 454; disciple of, 474, 544; on
God, 555, 649, 654, 655–56, 680–82,
690, 694; and Chaldean oracles, 558; on
Egyptians, 559–60; on Gymnosophists,
567; on Pythagoras, 645; on Trinity, 669,
671–72, 677
Præparatio Evangelica (Eusebius), 471

Prayer, 87, 103, 573–75, 606
Predestination, 180, 623
Preservation of creation, 610, 614, 702–3
Prideaux, Humphrey, 271
Princeton. *See* College of New Jersey
Principles of Moral and Christian Philoso-
    phy (Turnbull), 12n6, 142, 143–45
*Principles of Natural and Revealed Religion Oc-
    casionally Opened and Explained* (Warbur-
    ton), 460n6
Prisca theologia, 26–27
Proclus, 463–64, 544, 547–48, 557–58,
    561, 573–74, 642, 663, 666, 667, 671,
    673, 677, 680, 681, 682, 704
Procopius, 473
Progress of work of redemption, 93, 196–98
Pro Milone (Cicero), 214
Prophecy: in Old Testament, 110–11, 112,
    159, 169, 197, 232, 234–35, 272, 280,
    308–10, 382–91, 418, 422; of Christ,
    114–15, 116, 119–23, 159, 231, 278–82,
    324, 325n3; as fruits of the Spirit, 182;
    fulfillment of, 266–67; clarity of, 267–68;
    in Book of Revelation, 577–78. *See also spe-
    cific prophets*
Proserpine, 480, 552
Protagoras, 551
Providence, 105–6, 242–43, 246–48, 465,
    470, 572, 588, 648, 677–79, 692–701. *See
    also* God
Psellus, 472, 558, 665–66, 680
Psyche, 468, 472, 557, 558, 561, 665, 669–
    73, 675, 676
Ptha (Phtha), 559–60, 665
Ptolemy, 682
Pythagoras, 443, 446, 450, 453, 463–64,
    476, 552, 644–45, 650, 657, 664, 667
Pythagoreans, 463, 548, 561, 569–71, 636,
    640, 644–45, 658, 661–64, 674, 683,
    693, 704, 709. *See also specific philosophers*
Python, 475

Quæstio, 31n3
Quintilian, 651, 657

Ramsay, Andrew Michael: percentage of ex-
    tracts from, in "Miscellanies," 12; bio-
    graphical information on, 13–14; writings
    by, 14–15, 27, 35; on Trinity, 95, 184–92,
    557; on Chinese, 95–104, 557; on unity
    of Godhead, 184; on supernatural princi-
    ples, 188–90; on Persians and necessity of
    humiliation, 192–94; on heathen reli-
    gions and philosophers, 461–81, 534–75
Ramsey, Paul, 131n6
Rawlin, Richard, 145, 147–48, 149, 153–55
Reason: and natural law, 28; and eternal na-

ture of future state, 61; and heaven, 61,
    65–66; agreeableness of Christian reli-
    gion to, 61–71; and virtue, 62, 68, 70–71;
    and church, 62–63; and revelation, 62–
    63, 66–67, 71, 359–76, 433–38, 448–49,
    454–55; and monotheism, 63; and God's
    moral government of world, 63–65; and
    resurrection of saints' bodies, 66, 68; and
    salvation, 68–69, 71; and Christ's lowly
    condition in world, 69; and faith, 70–71;
    humans' ill use of, 86; and Christ's righ-
    teousness, 106; and forgiveness of sinners,
    259–60, 262; definition of, 359; Skelton
    on, 433–38, 459; philosophers on, 468,
    655, 678; and imputation of merit, 487;
    and obedience to God, 605. *See also* Hu-
    man nature
Reasonable Religion (C. Mather), 24
Reason Satisfied and Faith Established (C.
    Mather), 24n9
Rebekah, 383, 484
Redemption: faith as condition of, 30–32,
    70; of heathens, 56; reasonableness of,
    68–69, 71; Christ as Savior and Re-
    deemer, 69, 71, 72–74, 146, 154, 177,
    194–95, 229–30, 257–59, 410–11, 413–
    14, 492–506, 619–26; and means of
    grace, 71–72; and Holy Spirit, 86, 493;
    and satisfaction of Christ, 88–89, 126–41,
    145–50, 157–59, 166, 236, 481–86; cove-
    nant of, 90–91; progress of work of, 93,
    196–98; nature of, 131–41, 146; and glo-
    rious times of church, 357–58; compari-
    son of, under Moses and Christ, 492–506;
    benefits of, 503; of Israelites from Egypt,
    610, 616, 619–22; as God's work, 610,
    617–24
Reductio method, 28n6
Regeneration, reasonableness of, 61–62
Rehoboam, 124, 339
Reineccius, 328
Religion. *See* Christian religion; God; Hea-
    thens; *specific gods and goddesses; and specific
    countries, such as Egypt*
Religion of Jesus Delineated (Reynolds), 12n6,
    67, 68, 126–31, 157–59
Renaissance, 26
Repentance, 126–31, 162–64, 175, 197,
    262–64, 395–99, 402, 403, 406, 515,
    527, 537–40, 578, 580–81. *See also* For-
    giveness
Reprobation, 29
"Republic of letters," 10–11
Republic (Plato), 547, 658–59
Resurrection: of saints' bodies, 66, 68, 226;
    of Christ, 110, 159–60, 165–66, 210,
    211, 294–97, 316–20, 325, 484–85; of

dead at end of world, 120, 198, 586, 626; heathens on, 712–13
Reuben, 386
Revelation: necessity of, 27, 28, 88, 126–31, 157–59, 161–65, 175, 240–46, 251–64, 275, 342–55, 432–61; reasonableness of, 62–63, 66–67, 71; and reason, 62–63, 66–67, 71, 359–76, 433–38, 448–49, 454–55; and heathen philosophers, 84–85; and Jewish nation, 334–40; Tindal's argument against need for, 342–45, 359–61; competition of many pretended revelations, 376–80; and covenant of grace, 493–94; of Mediator, 502; in Old Testament, 534–40
Reynolds, John, 12*n*6, 67*n*1, 68, 126–31, 157–59
Righteousness: compared with wickedness in Old Testament, 74–83, 509–10, 524, 526–27, 530–34, 538–39, 581–86; death of righteous people, 77–82; trust in own, 86, 541–42; of Christ, 88–89, 93–94, 106, 147–48, 154, 155, 172, 381, 414–15, 542; of God, 94, 107, 149, 157–58, 171–72, 216, 414–15, 533, 624; of rich young man, 516–17, 529; and mercy, 534*n*4; Book of Revelation on, 577–78; glory of righteous, 598. *See also* Saints; Virtue
Robe, James, 93
Roell, Herman Alexander, 252, 274
Roman Catholicism, 13, 29, 174, 197, 217, 563
Roman Empire: significance of, 70; sciences of, 72; heathen theology in, 109, 440, 441, 445; destruction of Jerusalem by, 159, 280; and Jews, 169–70, 315, 316*n*7, 336, 340, 389–91; prophecies on, 170, 272; religious beliefs and symbols of, 190, 377, 378, 552–54, 644, 666–67, 702; beginning of Roman monarchy, 197; and beliefs on future judgment, 215; conversion of, to Christianity, 217, 308, 309, 311, 312; and propagation of Christianity, 329–30; revelations from, 376–78. *See also* Philosophers; *and specific philosophers*
Routren, 563
Ruddery, 562
Ruddiren, 562
Ruffinus, 565
Ruth, 123*n*9, 125

Sabbatical year, 358–59
Sabellians, 174, 188
Sacred and Prophane History of the World Connected . . . (Shuckford), 454*n*9
Sacred Collection of Persian Monuments (Zoroaster), 471

Sacrifices: of Israelites, 124, 125, 130, 170, 173, 229, 482, 484, 504, 506, 508–9, 536; human, 440, 444; of heathens, 440, 472, 536, 545, 563, 569–70
Sad-der, 557
Saducees, 270, 287, 288*n*9, 450
Sage, 103–4
Saints: resurrection of bodies of, 66, 68, 226; and heaven, 66, 120–21, 216, 227–28, 503, 625–26; Old Testament, 69–70, 226, 229–30, 493, 503–4, 540, 541; death of, 81; and knowledge of God and Christ, 126; and Christ, 126, 624, 625–26; compared with angels, 181–82; glory of, 181–82, 217–21, 237–38, 598; happiness of, 217–21, 226, 228, 503; and Holy Spirit, 220; and God's glory, 223–24; blessings for, 503; and misery of damned, 583–84; and last judgment, 583–84, 626
Salii, 439–40
Salvation. *See* Redemption
Samaritans, 270, 339
Samosatenians, 174
Samson, 387, 625
Samuel, 386
Sanconiathon, 681
Sarah, 383
Satan: redemption from bondage of, 73; as Lucifer before his fall, 90, 173, 212; and Eve's sin, 173, 300; defeat of, 197, 358, 588, 625, 711; hatred of, for Christ, 199; images of, 300, 587, 625; as "god of this world," 358; wickedness of, 587–90; relationship of wicked to, 588–89; torments of, in hell, 589, 625; temptation of Christ, 630; heathen beliefs on, 711. *See also* Devils
Satire (Juvenal), 214
Satisfaction of Christ, 88–89, 126–41, 145–50, 157–59, 166, 236, 481–86
Saturn, 474, 551, 670, 674
Saul, King, 173, 388
Savoy Declaration, 19
Scaevola, 552
Scale of existence, 206–8
Scapegoat, 482, 484, 536
Schafer, Thomas A., 1–2
Schechinah, 475
Sciences, 72, 169, 362–63, 366, 455
Scripture Chronology Demonstrated by Astronomical Calculations (Bedford), 387*n*2
Scriptures. *See* Bible
Scythia and Scythians, 36, 144, 326, 330, 440, 447, 450
Second coming of Christ, 119–23
Second Commandment, 506
Second Volume of Sermons (Robe), 93

Self-determining power: and commands of God, 39–43, 46; and free will, 39–60; and obedience, 43; and willingness for virtue, 50–52; and sincerity, 51, 52–56; and contingency, 56–60

Self-sufficiency, 173–75, 459, 460, 541–42

Seneca, 176, 214, 251, 252 n 9, 444, 445, 470, 553, 606, 648, 651, 679–80, 686, 700, 702, 703

Sennacherib, 339

Septimius Severus, 272–73

Sergeant, Rev. John, 3, 4

Sermon, Preached before the Reverend Presbytery of New-Castle, October 11, 1752 (Davies), 35, 159

Sermon on Man's Primitive State: and the First Covenant (Davies), 94

Sermons and Essays (MacLaurin), 201, 236, 424 n 1

Serpents, 102, 300, 301 n 1, 411–12, 475, 587, 625, 699

Servius, 651, 667

Seth, 382

Several Discourses Preached at the Temple Church (Sherlock), 12 n 6, 376–80

Sextus Empiricus, 445, 650–51, 657

Shaftesbury, earl of, 242, 434, 448–49

Sharisthani, 477

Shaster, 562–63

Shechemites, 337

Sherlock, Thomas, 12 n 6, 129, 376–80

Shishak, king of Egypt, 339

Shuckford, Samuel, 454–55

Siang-Sangasko, 99

Sibylline Oracles, 170

Sidon, 400

Sidonius Apollinaris, 679

Simeon, 124, 386

Simeonites, 386 n 1

Simmias Rhodius, 687–88, 690

Simon Magus, 86

Simplicianus, 676

Simplicius, 547, 552, 561, 645–46, 650, 653–56, 691–92

Sin and sinners: original sin, 61, 94, 155, 170, 173, 176–77, 298–302; reconciliation of sinners to God, 62; God's anger against, 65, 87, 92–93, 141, 145, 157, 158, 356–57, 507, 510, 525, 536, 582–84, 601, 603 n 3; righteous versus wicked in Old Testament, 74–83, 509–10, 524, 526–27, 530–34, 538–39; and death, 78–80, 82, 83, 183–84; and humiliation, 86–87, 92–93, 103–4, 173–75, 192–94; Adam and Eve's sin, 94, 155, 170, 173, 300–301; and fall of humans, 101–2, 126; invitations of the Gospels to, 108;

and last judgment, 117–18, 208–9, 400–402, 410–11, 577–78, 583–86, 589–91, 598–99, 615–16; forgiveness of sin, 126–31, 157–59, 161–65, 230, 257–64, 536–40, 624–25; and repentance, 126–31, 162–64, 175, 197, 262–64, 395–99, 402, 403, 406, 515, 527, 537–40, 578, 580–81; punishment of, 145–46, 162–65, 172, 175, 183–84, 214, 235, 391–403, 527; remorse of sinners, 160; evil of sin, 166; imputation of sin, 171–72; Lucifer's sin, 173; of fallen angels, 173, 198–200, 213–14; Cain's sin, 173, 382; and self-sufficiency, 173–75, 459, 460, 541–42; heathens on original sin, 176–77; Jews' sin, 199; heathens' vices, 272, 273 n 2, 441–46, 606–7; forsaken sinners, 405–7; guilt of sinners and hardness of heart, 406–7; philosophers on, 443–44; Book of Revelation on, 577–78; Christ's enmity against, 584, 586. *See also* Hell

Sincerity, 51, 52–56

Sirach, 214

Sisera, 386

Sittenlehre (Stapfer), 18

Skelton, Arabella (Cathcart), 17

Skelton, Philip: percentage of extracts from, in "Miscellanies," 12; biographical information on, 16–17; writings by, 17, 35; on Christ's miracles, 159–60; on future state and revealed religion, 160–61; on pardon and atonement, 161–65; on necessity of revelation, 161–65, 432–61; on resurrection of Christ, 165–66; on satisfaction of Christ, 166; on incarnation of Christ, 166–67; on Trinity, 167–68; on fullness of time for Christ's coming, 169–71; on Chinese beliefs, 171; on imputation of sin and righteousness, 171–72; on humiliation, 173–75; on society, 433–34, 459; on reason, 433–38, 459; on heathens, 434, 438–61; on philosophers, 435, 442–47, 449–61; on immortality of soul, 449–51

Skelton, Richard, 16

Skeptics, 448

Slaves, 144

Sleeki, 98, 101

Smith, Caleb, 9

Smith, John, 15

Society, 433–34, 459, 461

Society for Propagating Christian Knowledge, 4–5 n 2

Socinians, 74, 185–87

Socinianus, Andreas Wissowatius, 631–32, 633–34 n 6

Socinus, 485

Socrates: and inspiration of Holy Spirit, 84; on human nature, 173–74, 459, 652; death of, 251, 252*n*9; theology of, 443, 446–48, 450, 452–53, 455, 456, 466–67, 475, 552, 642–43, 646–47, 652; vices of, 444; on soul, 450, 456, 657; and Logos, 546; on cross as symbol of immortality, 565; on God, 657, 684, 694, 695, 707; reason for condemnation of, 660; on creation of world, 684, 703; and prayer, 707

Sodom and Gomorrah, 391, 400, 401

Sodomy, 441

Solomon: importance of, 70; on duty of humans, 75; on just versus wicked, 77–79; on humans compared with beasts, 81; as king, 124, 159, 310, 339, 359, 418; sacrifice of, 125; on vanity of things under the sun, 155; on foolishness of children, 298, 299*n*1; on God's omniscience, 639; David as father of, 640

Sophist (Plato), 547, 703

Sophocles, 464, 545–46, 682

Soteriology, 30

Soul: union of, to God, 19, 94, 103–4; and commands of God, 39–43, 46; and self-determining power, 39–52, 60; conversion of, 60, 72–74; and means of grace, 71–72; immortality of, 87, 161, 194, 234, 443, 449–51, 456, 571, 573; and Christ, 89–92, 428–29; of Adam, 205, 428; creation of, 208, 209; Hobbes on body versus, 242; philosophers' and heathens' views on, 443, 449–51, 456, 468, 571, 573, 657, 673, 703; Egyptian beliefs on, 567–69

Sozomen, 565

Speusippus, 444

Spinoza, Baruch, 242, 347

Stapfer, Johann Friedrich: percentage of extracts from, in "Miscellanies," 12; writings by, 17, 18; biographical information on, 17–18; on Christ's lowly condition in world, 69; on divine legation of Moses, 249–51; on necessity of revelation, 251–52, 275; on Jewish religion, 264–65; on prophecies, 266–68, 324; on Book of Daniel, 271; on miracles, 272–74, 287–88; on Christian religion compared with heathen morality, 276–77; on Christ as no impostor, 282–84, 322–23; on apostles, 285–86, 289–91; on history of New Testament, 292–93; on propagation of Christian religion, 298; on Mahometanism, 327–29, 331–34; on Zaleucus, 486*n*3; on eternal nature of hell, 600–603; on arguments against divinity of Christ, 631–33

Star imagery, 212

Stebbing, Henry, 60

Sterne, Laurence, 26*n*3

Stobaeus, 678–79, 683

Stockbridge mission, 2–9, 30

Stockton, Richard, 7

Stoics, 176, 443, 470, 548, 552, 644, 651, 678, 684–85, 699–700. *See also specific philosophers*

Strabo, 463, 470, 477–78, 566–67, 679, 681

Strength and Weakness of Human Reason (Watts), 176*n*8, 445

Suarez, Francis, 198

Substitution and imputation of merit, 713–16

Suetonius, 170

Sufferings: patience under, 61; of Christ, 73, 74, 90, 146, 166, 172; of sinners, 171–72

Suicide, 442, 444

Suidas, 558, 565, 691

Sun, 92, 213, 239, 246, 379, 403, 468, 479, 542–43, 550, 565, 571, 616, 642, 648, 667, 673, 682, 694, 709. *See also* Light and darkness

Supreme Deity of Our Lord Jesus Christ (Burr), 30*n*9, 36, 637–38

Symposium (Plato), 674

Synesius, 558

Synopsis Criticorum aliorumque Sacræ Scripturæ Interpretum (Poole), 112*n*1, 119, 176, 230, 271, 387, 417, 482, 484, 615, 637

Syria and Syrians, 112, 437, 440, 453, 543, 554, 565

Syrianus, 663

Tabari, 556

Tacitus, 170, 445

Targumists, 191–92

Tarshish, 311

Tartars, 565

Tching-ming-hian, 99

Tchiva Vaikkium, 555–56

Tchon-yong, 99

Tchou-angtre, 101

Tchouantsee, 99, 100

Tchuchi, 103–4

Tchunsion, 95

Telestic oracle, 558–59

Telluchi, 103

Ten Commandments, 143–44, 497, 498, 501, 504–8, 510, 511, 516, 522, 524, 531, 621

Tennent, Gilbert, 35, 106

Ten Tribes, 124–25, 310, 336, 339, 386*n*1, 388

Terpander, 546, 708

Tertullian, 215, 651

Tetragrammaton, 420*n*7, 644–45

Thales, 446, 453, 465, 640, 642, 688, 690

Thammuz, 473, 480
Thamous, 647
Themistius, 656
Theodoret, 215, 676, 712
Theodorus, 443, 711
Theogonia (Hesiod), 688
Theophrastus, 546, 643–44, 678, 704
Theophrastus (Aeneas Gazeus), 681
Theopompus, 667, 713
Theoretico-Practica Theologicae (Mastricht), 412n6
Thespesius Solensis, 662
Thetis, 552
Theurgic oracle, 558–59
Thoth, 543
Thracians, 473
Thuesen, Peter J., 10n2
Tiberius, 647
Tillotson, John, 280n9
Timaeus (Plato), 381, 467, 475, 547, 548, 561, 642, 652, 668–69, 673, 679, 681, 682, 683, 703, 704
Timaeus Locrus, 547, 658, 683–84, 695, 703–4, 706–7
Timoleon, 442
Timotheus, 463, 561, 648, 664, 691
Tindal, Matthew, 27–28, 342–45, 359–61
Titans, 475
Titus, 340, 390
Toland, John, 242
Tonchu, 98
Trajan, 298, 340
Travels of Cyrus (Ramsay), 14–15, 35, 461–81
Treatise Concerning the Operations of the Holy Spirit (Stebbing), 60n1
Treatise of Human Nature (Hume), 10n1
Treatise on Various Subjects (Brine), 12n6, 604 n4
Tree of life, 77, 147, 156
Trevor-Roper, Hugh, 11n4
Trinity: in Old Testament, 22, 112, 118–19, 175–76, 182–83, 191–92; and creation of world, 32; and Heaven, 33; Lardner on, 87; disputes on, 88; and love, 95; Ramsay on, 95, 184–92, 557; Chinese on, 97–101, 171; Kidder on, 112; nature of, 153, 187–88; Skelton on mystery of, 167–68; rejection of doctrine of, 174; cabbalistical Jews on, 192; and Jews, 307; philosophers' and heathens' views on, 461, 468, 561–62, 636–37, 661–77; Persians on, 463, 557
Tristram Shandy (Sterne), 26n3
Triton, 552
Triumph of Infidelity (Dwight), 24n8
True Grace, Distinguished from the Experience of Devils, 5n2

True Intellectual System of the Universe (Cudworth), 16, 35, 380–81, 636–37, 640–713
Trust and trusting, 86, 415, 517, 521, 522–23, 540, 541
Tsengt-see, 104
Tubal, 311
Tu-his, 104
Tullia, 442
Tully. *See* Cicero
Turnbull, George, 12n6, 142, 143–45
Turretin, Francis, 31n6, 265
Turretinus, Alphonsus, 69, 251, 268, 290–91, 292n3, 293
Tusculan Question (Tully [Cicero]), 450
Two Dissertations, 7, 32, 131n6
Two Sermons Preach'd June the 7th, 1752, in the Presbyterian Church . . . Philadelphia (Tennent), 106n7
Types: of Christ, 108–12, 114, 146, 231, 424, 506, 621, 625; of hell fires, 200, 525; and antitypes, 231, 267
Typhon, 474, 480, 564–67
Tyre and Tyrians, 311, 338, 400, 441, 473, 479–80, 583

Unitarians, 185–87
Unity: of Godhead, 184, 380–81, 467–68, 640–44; of world, 380–81
Urania, 473, 480, 557, 673–74
Uranus, 473, 561, 663, 674
Use and Intent of Prophecy (Sherlock), 129
Uzziah, 230n9

Valerius Maximus, 485–86
Valerius Soramus, 643
Vaninus, 434
Varro, 443, 552, 553, 643, 660, 666–67, 710
Vedam, 478, 555, 556
Venus, 440, 473, 480, 552, 668, 670, 673–74, 687, 688
Vestals, 565
Vices. *See* Sin and sinners
Vichnou, 563–64
View of Deistical Writers (Leland), 244–45
Vindiciæ Evangelicæ: or The Mystery of the Gospell Vindicated (Owen), 149n7
Vineyard imagery, 119, 122
Virgil, 464, 565–66, 650, 651, 699
Virtue: willingness for, 50–52; fear of hell as, 52; and sincerity, 52–56; reasonableness of, 62, 68, 70–71; of angels compared with humans, 70; of children, 70; of men compared with women, 70; righteousness versus wickedness in Old Testament, 74–83, 509–10, 524, 526–27, 530–34, 538–

39, 581–86; Chinese on, 103–4; nature of true, 139–40; and happiness, 142, 160–61, 213; future state and God's promotion of, 144–45; philosophers' and heathens' views on, 443–44, 447, 569–71, 573–74, 605–7, 642, 658–59, 707–8. *See also* Holiness

Vistnou, 478

Voltaire, 35, 225

Vossius, 666

Vystney, 562–63, 564

Warburton, Bishop William, 25, 88, 460

Waterland, Daniel, 25, 415–16

Watts, Isaac, 89–92, 176, 445n5

Wealth, 516–17, 529, 577, 585

Wedding. *See* Marriage

Wentse, 479

Werenfelsius, Samuel, 275, 276n6, 323, 324n6

Whichcote, Benjamin, 15

Whiston, William, 391, 393

Wickedness. *See* Hell; Sin and sinners

Wigglesworth, Edward, 29n9

Wilderness, 115–16

Will. *See* Free will

Williams, Daniel, 31, 106, 107

Willingness for virtue, 50–52

Winder, Henry, 68

Wings (Simmias Rhodius), 687–88

Wischtnu, 562, 564

Wisdom, 76–79, 585–86, 707–8

Witsius, Hermann, 147–48, 269, 271, 272

Wives. *See* Marriage

Woodbridge, Timothy, 3n8

Word of God, 23, 71, 72, 373–74

Works: of God, 23, 609–30; of Christ, 403–4; covenant of, 496–501, 511–12, 515–16, 529–30

Works (Dawes), 214–16

Works (Goodwin), 19, 195–200, 213–14, 222–25

Xenocrates, 552

Xenophanes, 443, 546, 547, 643–44, 645, 650, 704

Xenophon, 444, 445, 466, 657, 660, 684, 695

Yale College, 31

Yarbrough, Robert, 93n5

Year of jubilee, 358–59

Y-King, 95, 99–100, 102, 478

Yntchin, 97

Young, B. W., 11n4

Zakai, Avihu, 21n3

Zaleucus, 485–86

Zamolxis, 450

Zanchi, Girolamo, 198

Zanchius, Hieronymus, 31n6

Zebulon, 386, 388

Zechary, 220

Zen, 548

Zeno, 443–44, 548, 552, 658, 692

Zephaniah, 280

Zerubbabel, 423

Zeus, 273, 548, 558, 642, 645, 670–71, 680, 681, 694

Ziegenbalg, 556

Ziklag, 124

Zoroaster, 471–73, 477, 557–58, 567, 649, 659–60, 664, 666, 680, 713

OLD TESTAMENT

Genesis		29:10–15	384
1	622	31:53	384
1:1	416, 429	35:11	383, 386
1:26	191, 415, 429	35:12	384
2:26–27	221	37:1	384
3:11	155	43:3	200 n 3
3:14	602, 604 n 3	46:3–4	384
3:15	383	47:9	384
4:25	382	48:3–6	384
5:29	383	48:19	388
6:3	403	48:21–22	384
8:20	298, 299 n 1	49	418
9:25–29	383	49:4	386
11:27–32	383	49:7	386
12:1–7	383	49:8–10	386
12:2	383	49:13	386
13:14–18	383	49:17	387
15:5	383	49:19	387
15:6	108	49:22–26	387
15:7	383	49:27	387
15:7–17	385	50:24–26	384
15:16	385		
15:18–21	383, 386	Exodus	
16:12	383	2:24–25	539
17:6	386	3:2	621
17:8	383	3:8	384
17:16	383, 386	3:14	621, 645
17:20	383	3:14–15	539
21:13	383	3:17	384
21:33	628, 636	4	108
22:2–14	386	4:6–8	230 n 9
22:20–24	384	4:8	108
24	384	4:9	109
24:7	384	6:3	621
24:27	314, 315 n 7	6:3–4	384, 539
24:58	200 n 3	6:6–7	619–20
25:23	383	6:8	384
26:3–4	384	7:3–5	70
26:24	539	7:12	112
27:13	484	7:17	109
27:29	383	7:19	109
27:40	383	8:10	70, 109, 608, 620
28	384	8:19	70
28:4	384	8:22	70, 608, 620
28:13	384, 539	9:14	70, 608, 620
29:5	384	9:14–17	230

Exodus (continued)

9:16	608, 620	32:13	384
9:29	70, 111	32:19	506
10:2	70, 608, 620	32:32	481
11:7	70	33:1–3	384
12:12	70	33:2	385
12:25	384	33:12–17	384
12:48	384	34:1	506
13:5	384	34:5–6	627
13:11	384	34:5–7	494
13:17	385	34:6–7	538
13:19	384	34:7	145
14:18	70	34:10	620
14:19	429	34:10–11	385
15:6–11	620	34:10–16	384
15:11	607, 627	34:11	385
15:14–16	385	34:20	646
15:14–17	384	34:22	358
15:16	385	34:23–24	384
15:24	512	34:28	505
15:26	507	*Leviticus*	
16:4	512	1:4	482, 484
16:7–11	516	1:5–6	123 *n* 9
16:23	384	10:3	145
16:27–36	384	14:34–35 ff.	384
16:28	516	16:21	482
16:33–34	384	16:21–22	484
17:14	388	16:26	484
17:15	429	16:28	482, 484
18:11	620, 627	17:7	109
19	504	18:3	384
19:5–6	507	18:5	508, 511, 513, 516
19:5	510	18:27–28	384
19:8	510	18:28	385
20:2	483	19:9–10	384
20:2–3	118–19, 505, 620	19:23–25	384
20:3	414, 416, 429	19:33–34	384
20:5	425	20:23	385
20:6	506, 508	20:23–24	384
20:11	341	23	358
20:12	384	23:10–11 ff.	384
20:20	512	23:15–16	197
23:10–11	384	23:22	384
23:14–16	358	23:39	384
23:16–18	384	24:22	384
23:20–21	429	25:2–34	384
23:20–23	385, 621	25:39–55	384
23:22	507	26:1	384
23:22–23	385	26:4–6	384
23:23	385	26:12	494
23:27	385	26:20	384
23:29–30	385	26:22	384
23:31	386	26:29–30 ff.	389
24:1–8	504	26:31–33	389
24:5–8	506	26:31–34	384
24:7–8	510	26:33	389, 390
32–34	506	26:34	389

26:34–35	390	33:50–56	384
26:36	390	34–36	384
26:36–37	390	34:1–12	386
26:38–39	389	35:50–53	385
26:40–42	92	35:55	385
26:42–46	494		
26:43	384	*Deuteronomy*	
26:44	389	1:6–8	384
27:14–25	384	1:7–8	386
27:30	384	1:9–46	384
		2:29	384
Numbers		3:18–29	384
9:14	384	3:24	608, 620
10:9	384	3:28	385
10:29–32	384	4:1	384
11:15	183	4:5	384
12:10–15	230 n 9	4:7	176
13–14	384, 385	4:13	505
14:9–15	388	4:14	384
14:20–21	538	4:21–22	384
14:22	519	4:26	384, 389
14:24	388	4:27	389
14:30	388	4:35	620, 627
14:38	388	4:37–38	384
15:2	384	4:39	627
16:5	110	4:40	384, 507
16:22	613	5:9	425
16:28–30	110	5:16	384
18:13	384	5:29	507, 512
18:20–32	384	5:31	384
20:5	384	5:33	384
20:11–12	231	6:1	384
20:12	384	6:1–5	507
20:24	384	6:3	384
22:9	384	6:4	420, 627
22:11	384	6:10–11	384
22:16–41	384	6:17–18	507, 511, 530
23:10	78	6:18	530, 532
23:23	385	6:18–19	384
23:24	385	6:23	384
24:7	386, 388	6:24	521
24:8	384	6:24–25	507, 511
24:8–9	385	6:25	533–34
24:17	212	7:1–2	385
24:17–18	388	7:1–5	384
24:17–20	386	7:7–8	539
24:20	388	7:9	508
24:22	390	7:12–13	507
24:24	390	7:16–26	384, 385
26:65	388	7:17–23	385
27:12–13	384	7:22	385
27:16	613	8:1	384, 507
27:18–23	385	8:2	512
28:26	358	8:3	417 n 2
32:6–32	385	8:7–20	384
32:12	388	8:15–16	512–13
33:50–53	385	8:20	385

Deuteronomy (continued)

9:1–4	385	28	384
9:1–6	384	28:1–2	508
9:3	385	28:36	389
9:3–4	385	28:41	389
9:4	385	28:52	389
9:4–7	538–39	28:53–57	389
9:5	536	28:58	627
9:9	505	28:63	389
9:26	620	28:64	389
9:27–28	384	28:66	391
10:11	384	28:68	389
10:12–13	508, 521	29:2–29	384
10:17	620, 628	29:28	389
10:21	620	30:1–3	508
11:2–3	620	30:1–6	494
11:8–17	384	30:1–10	384, 390
11:21	384	30:3	389
11:23–25	384	30:6	508
11:24	386	30:10–14	519
11:26–28	507	30:11	520
11:29–31	384	30:11–15	522
12	384	30:13	520
12:20	386	30:14	520
12:29	385	30:14–20	520 n 7
12:31	385	30:15	494
13:12–16	384	30:15–16	508
13:17–18	507–8, 510, 511, 530, 532	30:18	384
14:21–29	384	30:19	494
15	384	30:19–20	508, 521, 523
15:4–5	359	30:20	384
15:11	359	31:1–8	384
16:2	384	31:3	385
16:6	384	31:3–4	385
16:9	358, 384	31:3–8	385
16:11	384	31:8	385
16:13–18	384	31:10–13	384
17:2	384	31:13	522
17:8	384	31:16	388
17:14	384	31:16–18	389
18:1–9	384	31:20–21	384
18:14	384	31:23	384
18:15	523	31:24–30	513
19:1–14	384	31:27–29	388
19:8–9	386	32:4	429, 618, 621
20:1	385	32:12	414, 429, 620
20:15–18	384	32:13–14	384
20:16–17	385	32:15–18	388
20:18	385	32:17	109
21:1–8	384	32:20 ff.	389
23:3	123 n 9	32:21–26	389
23:20	384	32:25–26	389
24:19–22	384	32:26	389
25:19	384	32:35–42	390
26:1–15	384	32:36	390
27:1–14	384	32:40–42	584
27:26	514	32:43	390
		32:47–52	384

33:2	483	12:20-22	539
33:7	387	12:20-25	522
33:9	126	14	388
33:13-16	384	25:24	481, 482
33:17	387	25:28	482
33:18	388	27:8	388
33:26	426	27:30	388
33:26-27	615		
33:27	628	*II Samuel*	
33:28	384	6:2	627
33:29	414, 429	7:22-23	619
34:1-3	384	14:9	484
34:6	429	14:20	639
		18:33	481
Joshua		22:1-2	618
1:4	386	22:31-32	618
2:19	482	22:32	429, 627
3:10	620	23:3	618, 621
3:14-16	175		
4:23-24	620	*I Kings*	
10:12	92	2:32-33	482
14:11	388	2:37	482
19:1-9	124	2:44	482
21:44-45	314, 315n7	8	310
22:22	627	8:6	629
23:14	314, 315n7	8:11	429
24:15	176	8:12-13	629
24:19	145, 175, 512	8:23	629
24:22	512	8:27	629
24:26-27	512	8:39	416, 639
24:32	384	8:60	629
		11:12	540
Judges		11:32	540
5:15-16	386	11:34	540
6:14	112	15:4	540
6:24 ff.	125	17:24	110
6:26	124	18:31-32	124
7:2	112	18:39	627
7:7	112	21:19	234
10:14	414	21:28-29	234
11:27	615	21:37-38	234
14:6	625		
18:27	387	*II Kings*	
		4:1-7	110
Ruth		4:42-44	110
1:16	522	5	230n9
2:12	522	5:7	111
3:9	424	6:18 ff.	112
3:12	424	6:28 ff.	389
		8:19	540
I Samuel		8:39	429
2	117, 232	9:25-26	235
2:3	615	13:23	539
2:10	615	18:4	412, 429
4:8	176	18:5-6	522
5	308	19:15	611, 629
12:6	381	19:19	629

II Kings (continued)
19:34 — 540
20:6 — 540

I Maccabees
2:59–60 — 271

I Chronicles
4:24–43 — 124, 386
4:31 — 124
4:43 — 388
5:18 — 387
9:3 — 125
11:39 — 123, 125
11:46 — 125
12:8 — 387
12:8–15 — 124
12:15 — 387
12:19–22 — 124
16:24–26 — 611
16:25–33 — 615
17:20 — 627
28:9 — 540

II Chronicles
6:14 — 421
7:7 — 125
11:13–14 — 124
11:16 — 124
15:9 — 124
20 — 339
26:16–21 — 230 n 9
29:11–12 — 614
29:34 — 123, 125
30:11 — 124
30:17–20 — 125
34:6 — 124
34:9 — 124
36:20–21 — 390

Ezra
2:28 — 125
2:34 — 125
6:17 — 125
8:35 — 125

Nehemiah
9:5–6 — 611–12
9:6 — 341, 416, 429, 614, 627

Esther
9:5–10 — 388

Job
3:20–21 — 183
5:11–16 — 117
5:17–18 — 585

7:20 — 145
9:4–7 — 616
9:8 — 611
9:21 — 126
10:14 — 145
12:7–9 — 613
12:7–10 — 614
12:17–19 — 117
13:15–16 — 522
14:4 — 299, 300 n 300
14:21 — 82
18:18 — 582
19:24–27 — 429
19:25–27 — 419
20:6–8 — 234
20:7 — 582
21:18 — 582
21:22 — 615
22:12 — 156
32:8 — 427, 428
33:4 — 427, 428
34:10–11 — 145
35:11 — 428
38:5–10 — 613
38:12–14 — 239
38:14 — 236
38:31–33 — 212
38:36 — 428
39:14–16 — 106

Psalms
1:3–6 — 82
1:4 — 582
2 — 415, 418
2:8 — 305
2:11 — 538
2:11–12 — 522
2:12 — 430
3:8 — 414, 430, 617
4:3–5 — 522
4:5 — 522
5:10–12 — 522
6:4 — 541
7:11–13 — 584
8:1–2 — 625
9:7 — 628
9:7–8 — 615
10:25 ff. — 416
11:4 — 615
11:4–5 — 615
11:6–7 — 145
11:7 — 510, 511, 530, 533
15 — 509
15:1–2 — 525
15:12–14 — 522
16:1 — 522
16:4 — 637

17:3-7	522	45:6	637
17:13-14	591	45:6-7	422
18:2	618	45:7-8	413n6
18:30-31	618	45:11	430
18:31	627	46	117
18:46	618	46:6	616
19:1-4	613	47:2 ff.	614
19:1-6	615	49	637
19:7	72	49:6-10	637
20:9	430	49:6-20	82
22:25-26	523	49:8-9	602
22:28	614	49:10	78
24:3-4	525	49:10-12	80
24:3-5	509	49:15	637
24:5-6	523	49:19-20	80
24:6	525	50	430
25:1-15	522	50:1-7	615
25:5	617	50:15	540
25:7	541	50:21	230
25:10	522	51:2	624
25:12	522	51:4	624
25:20-21	522	51:7	298, 299-300n1
26:1-6	522	52:7-8	523
26:9	78	55:22-23	523
27:1	617	58:11	175
31:6	522	60:11	617
31:7	126	62	523
31:16	541	62:2	430, 618
31:19	522	62:5-9	618
31:23-24	523	64:10	523
32	538	65:2	540
32:10-11	523	68	117
33:10-22	117	68:4	426, 627
33:18	523, 538	68:8-10	413n6
34:7-22	523	68:17	483
34:9-10 ff.	523	68:19-20	413n6
34:10	540	68:19	413n6
34:11-14	522	68:20	617
34:15	540	68:23	584
35:5	582	68:33	426
36:6-7	614	72	159
36:7-10	523	72:4	117, 430
36:8	216	72:18	608
36:9	216	73:27-28	523
36:37	523	75:6-7	615
37:3-9	522	77:13	421
37:27	522	77:13-14	608
37:28	533	77:13-20	620
37:34	522	78:34-36	87
37:37	522	78:37-39	584
37:37-38	78	81:1-7	131
37:39	617	81:8-10	414, 430
37:39-40	522	82:1	615
44:26	541	82:6	430
45	220, 418	82:8	615
45:2-7	430	83:3-8	338
45:3-5	117	83:18	413, 426, 430, 627

Psalms (*continued*)
84:11–12	523
85:9	522
86:5–7	540
86:8	607, 627
86:10	607
89	418
89:5–6	607
89:8–10	607
89:19	430
90:2	416, 430, 636
90:6–10	256
91:13	625
92:5	608
92:7	405
92:8	628
93:1	418, 430
94:2	615
94:6–10	67
94:12	585
95:1	618, 621
95:3	621
95:8–10	620–21
96:3–5	611
96:4–13	615
96:10	418, 430
96:12–13	239
97	418
97:1	430
97:1–6	616
97:7	424, 430
98	430, 615
98:8–9	239
99	430
99:1	418, 430
99:4	533
99:8	538
100	430
100:3	613
102	81
102:1	616
102:12	616, 628
102:16	616
102:18	616
102:21–22	616
102:24–25	616
102:24–27	628
102:25	636
102:25–27	616
102:25 ff.	422, 430
102:27	636
102:28	616
103:11–13	522
103:17	522
103:19	615
104	613
104:4	422, 614

104:31	628
104:32	616
106:2	419
106:7–8	539
106:37	109
110	73, 305, 418
110:1	430
110:4	430
111:1–8	608
111:4	235
111:6	620
112:7	523
113	430
113:4–9	615
115	615
115:1	541
115:13	522
118:5–23	117
118:8–9	430
118:24	381
118:27	627
119	523
119:41–49	523
119:113–20	523
119:119	581
119:145–48	523
119:166	523
135:4–6 ff.	615
135:5 ff.	620
135:13	628
136:2–4	607–8
136:2–9	611
136:3	628
144:5	616
145:3–6	608
145:11–12	608
145:18–19	540
146:3	617
146:3–4	430
146:5	617
147:11	538
149:2	212

Proverbs
1:24–33	586
1:31–32	75
2:6	428
2:11	75
2:21–22	75
3:2	75
3:4	75
3:8	75, 77
3:13–18	75
3:16	82
3:21–26	75
3:22	77
3:32	75

3:35	75	21:18	75
4:4	77	21:21	75, 77
4:5–13	75	22:4	75, 77
4:22	75, 77	22:8	75
4:24 ff.	108	22:15	298, 299 n 1
7:2	77	22:17–20	521
8	108	23:4–5	82
8:17–21	75	23:17–18	75
8:18	82	24:1–5	75
8:22	416, 430, 561	24:12	75
8:22–26	416–17	24:15–16	75
8:22–30	341	24:19–22	75
8:22 ff.	416	28:3–14	75
8:23	91, 636	28:10	75
8:27	561	28:18	75
8:27–31	415, 430	29:6	75
8:29	561	30:4	430
8:35–36	75		
9	108	*Ecclesiastes*	
9:2	77	1:3	155
9:5–6	75	1:9	155
9:11–12	75	1:11	82
10:7	77	1:14	155
10:16–17	75	2:11	79, 155
10:17	77	2:14–16	76–77, 79
10:25	78, 82	2:15–17	82
10:27	82	2:16	75, 78, 82
10:27–29	75	2:17	79
11:7	78, 78–79, 82	2:17–20	79, 155
11:7–8	75	2:20–22	79
11:18–19	75	2:22	79, 155
11:21	75	2:26	75
11:30	77	3:1–10	82
11:30–31	75	3:2	78
12:2–3	75	3:14	78, 80
12:14	75	3:16	155
12:21	75	3:16–17	77
12:28	75, 77	3:16–22	83
13:9	75	3:17	75
13:13	523	3:18–20	81
13:13–15	75	3:19	82
13:14	77	3:22	82
13:21	75	4:1	155
14:19	75	4:1–2	77
14:26–27	75	4:2–3	79
14:27	77	4:3	155
14:32	78, 79	4:7	155
15:3	75	5:5–6	77
15:6	75	5:8	75, 77
15:24	75	5:13	155
16:3–7	75	5:14–16	82
16:4	405	5:18	155
16:6	381	6:3–4	78
16:22	77	6:6–8	80
16:30	523	6:8	75
19:23	75	6:12	78, 80, 155
21:15–16	75	7:1	77–78

Ecclesiastes (continued)

7:12	76	19:1		109
7:15	76	19:12		115
7:18	76	25:1–8		117
8:5	76	25:9		414, 430
8:9	155	26:2–4		523
8:11	76	26:4		618
8:12	80, 522	26:13–14		430
8:12–13	75–76	27:1		625
8:14	75	27:8		584
8:15	155	28:15–18		430
8:17	155	28:16–17		619
9:1–2	76	28:29		608
9:2	75, 77	29:6		423
9:3	79, 155	32		418 n5
9:3–5	82	32:1		430
9:5–6	78, 83	32:16–18		430
9:6	155	33		418 n5
9:9	155	33:14		525, 600, 603 n3
9:10	404	33:15–16		509, 525
9:11	155	33:22		418, 430
9:13	155	35:1–2		239
10:5	155	36:2–4		523
11:5	427	37:35		540
11:8	80	38:11		495
11:9–10	80	38:18–19		495
12:1	191	38:22		495
12:7	613	40–42		305
12:13	80	40:3		416, 419, 420, 430
12:13–14	75, 80, 404	40:3 ff.		430
		40:4		523
Canticles		40:8		639
4:16	428	40:9–10		420–21
8:5	156	40:9–11		418, 430
		40:11		639
Isaiah		40:12		612
1	530	40:13		423, 430
1:16–20	509–10	40:13–14		415, 430
1:18	517	40:18		426, 430, 612
1:19	517, 537	40:21–31		614
2:3–5	430	40:22		421, 426, 430
2:10–22	617	40:22–24		117
2:22	430	40:25–26		612
6	176, 182	40:25		421, 426, 430
6:1–5	414, 430	40:26		614
6:3	423, 430	40:27–31		117
6:8	415	40:28		426, 430
9	418	41		111–12, 430
9:4	112	41:1–7		111
9:6	91, 414, 415, 416, 430, 636	41:4		639
9:6–7	430	41:11–12 ff.		117
10:21	416	41:14		414, 430
11	418	41:16		182
11:4	117	41:18–20		115–16
11:6	200	41:21		114
11:10	417, 430	41:21–27		114
12:2	617	41:23–29		430
		41:27		115

41:28	115	48:9	539
42	117	48:11	430, 540
42:1–8	430	48:12	639
42:1–9	305	48:12–13	613, 615
42:4	115	48:17	414, 430
42:8	413, 627	49:7	414, 424, 430
42:8–9	115	49:13	239
42:10–17	115	49:24–26	117
42:21	114	49:26	414, 430
43	430	51:6	81
43:3	146, 414, 618, 627	51:12	639
43:6–13	115	51:15	627
43:10–14	414	53	305, 482, 484
43:10–15	430	53:4	483
43:11	618	53:4–5	483
43:13	342, 426, 430	53:4–6	482
43:14	414	53:8	482
43:15–21	116	53:10–12	482
43:17	600	53:11	483, 625
43:18–21	622	53:12	483
43:22–27	537	54:5	212, 414, 424, 430, 618, 627
43:23–27	539	54:10	81
43:25	529, 624	54:15–17	117
44:2	212	55:3	82
44:3–8	115	55:5	414, 424
44:5	414	55:12	239
44:6	414, 416, 424, 430, 639	56:6–7	183
44:8	416, 430	57:13	523
44:19–20	307	57:16	613
44:23	239	59:16	314, 316 *n* 7, 617
44:24	414, 415, 426, 430, 612	60:14	182
44:25–26	115	60:16	414, 430, 617, 618
44:25–28	114	61:8	576
45	645	62:11	619
45:1	713	62:11–63:6	431
45:3	421, 430	63	621
45:5	416, 421, 430	63:1	619
45:5–7	415, 430, 612	63:1–6	413, 414, 431
45:5–9	713	63:3	583, 619
45:5–13	614	63:5	619
45:6	421	63:9–10	620
45:12	415, 612	63:16	636
45:14–15	421	64:1–3	616
45:15	618	64:3–4	622
45:18	612	64:4	409 *n* 2, 523
45:20–21 ff.	413, 430	65:17–18	622
45:21	115, 612, 618	65:17–19	415, 431
45:21–25	619, 713	66:22	622
45:22	430	66:24	600, 603 *n* 3
45:25	618		
46:4	639	*Jeremiah*	
46:9	416, 430	2:11	419
46:10	114	3:23	414, 431, 617
47:1–13	115	6:28–30	581
47:4	414, 430, 618, 627	7:22–23	508–9
48	115	7:23–24	519
48:2	627	7:24	519

Jeremiah (continued)

7:26	519
10:6–7	612, 616
10:6–13	615
10:10	616, 627, 628
10:10–12	612–13
10:16	627
10:25	540
11:3–4	509
11:4–5	519
11:7	519
14:22	615
16:14–15	622
16:21	627
17:5	431
17:5–10	523
17:7–8	82
17:10	416, 431, 639
17:14	617
22:16	522
23:5	418
23:6–8	622
28:5	183 n 7
30:9	418
30:11	584
30:21	602
31:31–32	576
31:35	627
32:18	627
32:18–19	608
32:40	576
33:15	418
38:7	522
38:7–12	523
38:12	522
39:16–18	522
39:18	523
41:2	390
41:7	390
41:10	390
41:12	390
41:15	390
41:17–18	390
42:10–16	390
43:2–7	390
43:12	109
44:7	390
44:11–14	390
44:25–26	390
44:27	390
44:29–30	390
46:28	584
50:34	627
51:5	183
51:19	627

Lamentations

2:20	389
4:10	389
5:19	628

Ezekiel

1:27	426
1:27–28	426
1:28	426
2	390
2:6	301 n 2
3:21	509
3:23	426
5:7	390
5:12	390
6:10	175
8:4	426
10:20	426
14:3–7	390
14:14	272
14:20	272
14:22	383 n 9
15:7	390
18:9	509, 526–27
18:20	509, 526, 533
18:21	513
18:21–22	509, 511, 513, 524
18:22	513, 526
20	514
20:9–10	539
20:11	508, 511, 513, 514
20:13	508, 511, 513, 514
20:13–14	539
20:21	508, 511, 513, 514
20:21–22	539
20:30–32	390
20:33	539
20:39	390
20:43	539
20:43–44	539
22:18	581
23:14–16	526–27
24:23	390
28:3	272
33	524
33:14–15	524
33:14–16	509, 510, 513
33:15	514
33:16	513
33:17	514
33:20	514, 527
33:25	514
33:25 ff.	390
33:29–30	514
33:30	527
34:23	418
36:22	528, 539
36:25–26	539
36:31–32	528
36:32	539

37:9–10	428	5:8	627
37:24	418	9:6	627
37:25	431		
37:26	576	*Jonah*	
		2:8–9	414, 431
Daniel		2:9	617
2:2	115		
2:21	428	*Micah*	
2:44	197, 417, 431	4:2–5	431
2:47	628	5:2	91, 417, 431, 636
4:2–3	232, 628	5:4	431
4:8	176	6:7–8	509, 510
4:9	176		
4:17	232	*Nahum*	
4:18	176	1:4–6	616
4:25–26	232		
4:26	418	*Habakkuk*	
4:34–35	232	1:12	618
4:37	232		
5:11	176	*Zephaniah*	
7	418	3:2	523
7:12	269	3:11–13	523
7:13–14	431	3:14–15	418, 431
7:14	628		
8:1 ff.	269	*Haggai*	
9:2	269	2:3	431
9:24	316 n 7, 602	2:6–7	483
9:25	418	2:7–9	431
10:11–12	269		
12	356	*Zechariah*	
12:1	123	2:8	212
12:2	270, 600, 601, 603 n 3	2:8–9	175
12:4	269	2:11	175
12:6–7	123	3:8	220
		3:9	423, 431
Hosea		4:6	423
1:7	416, 431, 618	4:9	175
3:5	418	4:10	423
7:14	87	6	418
10:8	184	6:12–13	431
11:7	108	6:12 ff.	418
12:5	627	11:12	416, 431
12:6	523	12:1	613
13:4	414, 431, 618, 620	12:8	431
13:9–11	431	12:10	416, 431
		13:7	431
Joel			
2:32	425, 431	*Malachi*	
		3:1	419, 421, 621
Amos		3:1–3	418, 431
5:4	540	4:2	522
		4:5–6	419

NEW TESTAMENT

Matthew		3:2	197, 431
2:2	212	3:10	582
2:27	633, 635 n 6	3:12	582

Matthew (continued)

3:15	148
4:10	416, 431, 630
4:30	93n5
5:25–26	404
5:26	601, 603n3
7:12	283
7:19	582
8:28	232
8:29	625
9:2	230
9:13	108
10	283, 285n5
10:14–15	400
10:20	427
10:34	356
11:10	419, 431
11:21–24	400
11:25	623
11:27	623
12:31–32	393, 407, 592n8
12:32	392, 407, 601, 603n3
13:30	121, 582
13:31–33	122
13:39	121
13:39–42	121
13:43	121
13:48	581
16:28	119, 197
17:5	523
18:3	283
18:8	600, 603n3
18:10	182
18:34–35	601, 603n3
19:16	412
19:17	412n5, 431, 638
20:16	108
20:28	482
21:19	281
21:41	122
21:43	122
22:1–5 ff.	108
22:7	121
22:7–10	122
22:14	108
22:30	120
23:34–39	281
23:37	517, 537
24:2	120
24:3 ff.	281
24:4–5	120
24:6–16	120
24:15–17	121
24:15–21	120
24:19–20	121
24:20	288
24:21–22	123
24:28	120, 121
24:36	631, 634, 634n6
24:47	626
24:48	119
25	118, 402
25:5	119
25:12	126
25:19	119
25:21	216
25:23	216
25:31–46	120
25:34	121, 626
25:35	402
25:40	121
25:41	392, 600, 603n3
25:46	121, 392, 601, 603n3
26:24	95, 601, 604n3
26:28	230
26:29	220, 231
26:44	393
26:63–65	431
27:9–10	416, 431
27:24–25	484
28:18	633, 635n6
28:19	302, 304n6

Mark

1:1–3	419
1:3	416
1:14	197
1:16–17	431
1:76	431
2:11	431
2:32	431
3:28–29	407
3:29	407, 601, 603n3
4:26–32	122
5:3–5	232
5:8	233
7:24	635
8:38	400
9:24	640
9:43	600
9:44	392, 600, 603n3
9:45	600
9:46	392, 600, 603n3
9:48	392, 600, 603n3
10:17	412
10:21	529
11:13–14	281
12:30	498
13:3–4	120
13:11	427
13:14–15	121
13:17–18	121
13:19	416
13:32	631, 634, 634n6, 638

14:21	95	21:24	121, 122
14:25	231	22:18	231
		22:19–20	230
Luke		22:29	220
1	420	22:29–30	626
1:16–17	419	22:30	221
1:35	423, 428	23:30	184
1:69–70	422	23:34	580
1:76	421	24:25	416, 431
2:11	416		
2:32	419	*John*	
3:17	600, 603 n 3	1:1	416, 431
4:8	630	1:1–3	613
5:21	624	1:1–4	415
5:24	624–25	1:3	91, 416, 431, 613, 614
6:24	94, 591	1:13	624
7:27	419, 431	1:18	426
8:27	233	1:19	419–20
8:28	52, 625	1:19 ff.	431
8:29	233	1:23	420
8:35	233	1:31	420
11:21	625	2:19 ff.	231
12:10	407	2:24	416, 431
12:47–48	392	3:8	428
12:59	601	3:17	410
13:4	580	3:18	230
13:7	582	3:35	633, 635 n 6
13:19–21	122	3:36	601, 603 n 3
13:34–35	281	4:14	74
14:16 ff.	108	4:42	619
16	217	5:17	92, 630
16:15	529	5:17–19	415, 426, 431
16:25	591	5:17–23	231
16:26	601, 603 n 3	5:17–29	417, 431
16:27–31	577	5:19	92, 630, 633, 635 n 6
17:5	640	5:21	426
17:20–37	119	5:21–22	120
17:22	119	5:22	616
17:26–37	119, 120	5:22–23	626
17:30	281	5:23	416, 431, 630
17:37	120, 121	5:24	230
18:1	119	5:24–25	218
18:1–8	120	5:25–29	626
18:7–8	119	5:25–30	120
18:18	412	5:26	218
19:13–15	120	5:27	626
19:27	281	5:28	426
19:43–44	121	5:29	118
20:9	119	5:30	633, 635 n 6
20:15–16	122	6:4–71	230
20:21	425	6:29	108
20:34–36	20	6:39	74 n 2
21:7	120	6:39–40	626
21:20–22	121	6:40	590
21:20–24	120	6:44	590
21:23	121	6:45	623
21:23–24	121	6:54	590

John (continued)

6:57	218
7:38–39	74
8:15	410
8:25	199
8:28	633, 635 n 6
8:36	199
8:44	199, 216
8:45	199
9:4	403
10:3	624
10:10	219
10:14–15	126
10:16	624
10:30–33	431
10:30–38	417
11:25	626
12:47	410
13:3	633, 635 n 6
13:8	230, 231
13:10–11	230
14:1–3	121
15:4–10	108
15:6	582
15:18–21	357
15:26	92
16:2	283
16:7	92, 423, 431
16:13–14	92
16:13–15	415, 423, 431
16:20–22	357
16:30	416, 431, 638
16:33	357
17:2	633, 635 n 6
17:3	126, 224
17:7	633, 635 n 6
17:9	586
17:14	586
17:20	586
17:21	217
17:21–22	415, 431
17:22	21
17:23	217, 219, 221
17:24	121, 217, 224
17:25	586
17:26	217
17:27	219
18:36	69
19:37	416, 431
20:22	423, 428, 431
21:17	425, 431, 639

Acts

1:24	416, 432
2	580
2:2	428
2:22	631, 634 n 6
2:33	92
2:36	631, 634 n 6
2:39	623
3–5	317, 318 n 1
3:12–13	329
4	602, 604 n 3
4:12	619
5:30	319, 321 n 3
5:38–39	319, 321 n 3
7:30	621
7:38	621
8:20	86
9:11	87
10:36	416, 432
13:38	108
14:15	329, 612
17:11	330, 331 n 8
17:22–31	329
17:31	400
20:28	623
26:16–18	86

Romans

1	453
1:3–4	413 n 6
1:6	624
1:16	72
1:16–18	216 n 7
1:17	107
1:19–20	611
1:20	364 n 8, 454
1:23	628
2:3–12	401
2:16	401, 631, 634 n 6
3:5	149
3:19	511
3:19–21	511
3:21	149
3:23	149, 216
3:25–26	148, 482
3:26	624
3:28	25
3:30	624
4:3	108
4:11	228
4:13	228
4:16–17	228
5:13–14	511
7:1–13	511
7:10	147
8:2–3	482
8:4	147, 148 n 5
8:7	219
8:10	218
8:30	219, 623, 624

8:32 — 424, 432
8:33 — 624
8:34 — 195
8:39 — 218
9:3 — 481
9:5 — 413n6, 416, 432
9:22 — 224
9:22-23 — 600
9:23 — 224
9:24 — 624
9:30-31 — 149
10:3 — 149
10:4 — 149
10:5 — 147, 511
10:6 — 519-20
10:6 ff. — 522
10:8 — 520
10:11-12 — 425
10:12 — 416, 432
10:13 — 425, 432
10:14 — 425
11:22 — 108
11:36 — 645

I Corinthians
1:2 — 425, 432
1:5-7 — 182
1:9 — 623
1:30 — 602, 604n3
2:9 — 409n2, 523
2:10-11 — 415, 432
2:16 — 425, 432
3 — 602, 604n3
3:1-4 — 182
3:22-23 — 219
3:23 — 221
4 — 218
5:17 — 197
5:20-28 — 66
6:19-20 — 623
6:20 — 482
7:17 — 624
7:23 — 623
8:6 — 631, 633-34n6
9:2 — 432
9:21 — 425
10:4 — 619
10:9 — 412-13n6, 425, 432, 621
10:10 — 621
10:22 — 425, 432
12:13 — 74
15 — 195, 238
15:17 — 484
15:20-28 — 586
15:24 — 590
15:54-55 — 586

15:57 — 631, 634n6
19-22 — 637

II Corinthians
1:11 — 425
2:10 — 425
3:6 — 499
3:7-9 — 511
3:9-11 — 425
3:11 — 576
3:18 — 33n9, 425
4:2 — 286, 287n7
4:3 — 582
4:3-4 — 587
4:4 — 358, 425
4:6 — 225, 424-25, 432, 623
4:14 — 631, 634n6
5:10 — 400
5:18 — 631, 634n6
5:21 — 482
8:9 — 219
15 — 411

Galatians
1:4 — 73
2:6 — 425
2:17 — 183
3:10 — 482
3:11-14 — 183
3:12 — 511
3:13 — 482
3:17-25 — 511
3:29 — 624
4 — 196
4:4 — 148
4:8 — 416, 432

Ephesians
1:1 — 19
1:3 — 415, 432
1:3-8 — 602, 604n3
1:4 — 177
1:9-10 — 179
1:18 — 216, 624
1:19 — 624
1:19-20 — 210-11, 219, 426
1:19-22 — 210n5
2:1 — 624
2:2 — 358
2:4 — 217, 624
2:5 — 19, 218, 624
2:6 — 219
2:7 — 222
2:9 — 631, 634n6
3:9 — 224
3:10 — 224

Ephesians (continued)
3:11	177, 178
3:16	224
3:20–21	432
4:8–9	413 n6
4:32	183
5:26	624
5:27	626

Philippians
1:11	216
2:6	416
2:7	219
2:10–11	413, 432
3:20–21	426

Colossians
1:9	602, 604 n3
1:15–19	178
1:16	613, 614
1:16–17	91, 416, 432, 609
1:17	614
1:20	602, 604 n3
1:21–23	108
1:26–27	223 n3, 224
2:9	432
3:11	200

I Thessalonians
2:12	623
5:21–22	286, 287 n7

II Thessalonians
1:5–6	148
1:5–9	402
1:8–9	117
1:8–10	411
1:9	600, 603 n3
2:13–14	623

I Timothy
1:17	646
2:6	482
2:15	108
6:14–16	628
6:15	416, 432
6:16	628, 636

II Timothy
1:8–9	623–24
1:9	177 n4
3:15–17	330
3:16	422
4:7–8	108
4:8	148, 616, 626

Titus
2:11	432
2:13	413 n6, 415
2:14	146
3:4–5	624
3:4–6	631, 634 n6

Hebrews
1:2	631, 634 n6
1:2–3	609
1:3	416, 426, 432, 614
1:5–12	422
1:6	416, 424, 432, 629
1:8	416
1:9	413 n6
1:10	416, 422, 432, 613
1:10–12	609, 616, 628
1:26–27	621
2	197
2:2–3	630
2:8	91
2:10	619, 645
2:14	148
2:16	602, 604 n3
3:1	416
3:3–4	622
3:6	108
3:6–19	519
3:7–10	519
3:11	216, 228
3:14	108, 216, 228
3:18	108
3:19	108
4	197
4:1	108, 228
4:3	228
4:5	216
4:9–10	216
4:9–11	228
4:11	108
5:9	619
6:4	108
6:4–6	405–6, 601–2, 604 n3
6:8	582
6:9	226
6:11	108
6:12	108, 226
6:13–14	228
6:20	229
7:3	417, 432, 628, 636
7:10	576
7:25	413, 432, 602, 604 n3
8	409
8:6	228
8:6–13	576
9:8	229, 484

9:12	602, 604 n 3
9:15	149, 228
9:18–23	506
9:22	230
9:26	69, 229
9:27–28	405, 410, 482
9:28	229, 483
10:1–4	229
10:10–11	229
10:12	602, 604 n 3
10:26	602, 604 n 3
10:26–27	410, 601, 603 n 3
10:34	228
10:35–39	107–8
10:36	227
10:37	598
11	271
11:12	228
11:13	226
11:13–16	227
11:39–40	228
11:40	576
12:1–2	228
12:9	613
12:16–29	228
12:24–26	482–83, 629
12:25–29	576
12:26	197, 483
13:8	636
13:24	631, 634 n 6

James

1:17	25
1:18	624
1:27	522
2	493
2:13	381, 600
2:14–26	522

I Peter

1:3	624
1:5	107
1:11	422, 432
1:15	624
1:18	146
2:24	483
3:19	392
3:20	403
5:10	624

II Peter

1:1	414–15, 424, 432
1:21	422
2:4	118, 199
2:9	118
3	117

3:5–7	200–201
3:7	118
3:8	417, 432

I John

1:1	218
1:7	602, 604 n 3
2:20	639
2:24–28	108
3:8	587
3:9	624
4:1	286, 287 n 7
4:7	624
4:12	426
5:1	624
5:4	624
5:11	218
5:16	407, 408
5:18	624
5:20–21	637
20	413 n 6

Jude

3	425
4	413 n 6
6	198, 392, 400, 590, 600, 603 n 3
7	593
13	600, 603 n 3
16	425

Revelation

1:3	330, 331 n 8
1:5	625
1:8	416, 432, 645
1:17	416, 432
2:3	416, 432
2:7	626
2:10	626
2:23	425, 432, 639
3:18	108
3:20	108
3:21	220, 221, 626
4	176
4:4	181
4:9–10	628
5	619
5:6	181, 423, 432
5:9–10	181
5:11	181–82
5:14	628
6:15–16	617
6:16	184
7:10	619
7:11	182
8:10–11	212
9:6	183

Revelation (continued)

		19:16	416, 432
10:5–6	628	19:20	589
10:6	612	19:22	413
12:9	217	20	156
14:2	217	20:10	399, 589, 598, 600, 603 *n* 3, 625
14:7	612	21	239
14:9–11	589	21:6	590, 626
14:10–11	585, 598	21:7	219
14:11	392, 600, 603 *n* 3	21:7–8	582
14:13	35, 228	21:8	582
14:19–20	583	21:11–17	626
15:5–7	148	21:18	589
15:7	628	21:23	627
17:14	416, 432	22:2	156
18:20	583	22:5	598
19:1	618–19	22:7	598
19:1–3	583	22:10–12	577, 592, 598–99
19:2	148	22:13	416, 432
19:3	598	22:14	147
19:5	583	22:14–15	582
19:11	616	22:16	212
19:15	413, 432, 619		

APOCRYPHA

Stephen

7:6	318 *n* 1